Contemporary Authors®

NEW REVISION SERIES

ISSN 0275-7176

REF
Z
1224
'C6
NRS
v.127

Contemporary

Authors®

A Bio-Bibliographical Guide to
Current Writers in Fiction, General Nonfiction,
Poetry, Journalism, Drama, Motion Pictures,
Television, and Other Fields

NEW REVISION SERIES *volume* 127

GALE®

THOMSON
—★—™
GALE

Detroit • New York • San Diego • San Francisco • Cleveland • New Haven, Conn. • Waterville, Maine • London • Munich

THOMSON
GALE

Contemporary Authors, New Revision Series, Vol. 127

Project Editor
Tracey Watson

Editorial
Katy Balcer, Shavon Burden, Sara Constantakis, Natalie Fulkerson, Michelle Kazensky, Julie Keppen, Joshua Kondek, Jenai A. Mynatt, Lisa Kumar, Mary Ruby, Lemma Shomali, Susan Strickland, Maikue Vang

Research
Michelle Campbell, Tracie A. Richardson, Robert Whaley

Permissions
Margaret Chamberlain, Jacqueline Key, Sue Rudolph

Imaging and Multimedia
Randy Bassett, Dean Dauphinais, Leitha Etheridge-Sims, Lezlie Light, Michael Logusz, Dan Newell, Christine O'Bryan, Kelly A. Quin

Composition and Electronic Capture
Kathy Sauer

Manufacturing
Lori Kessler

LIBRARY OF CONGRESS CATALOG CARD NUMBER 81-640179

ISBN 0-7876-6719-6
ISSN 0275-7176

Printed in the United States of America
10 9 8 7 6 5 4 3 2 1

Contents

Indexing note: All *Contemporary Authors* entries are indexed in the *Contemporary Authors* cumulative index, which is published separately and distributed twice a year.

As always, the most recent Contemporary Authors cumulative index continues to be the user's guide to the location of an individual author's listing.

Preface

Contemporary Authors (*CA*) provides information on approximately 115,000 writers in a wide range of media, including:

- Current writers of fiction, nonfiction, poetry, and drama whose works have been issued by commercial publishers, risk publishers, or university presses (authors whose books have been published only by known vanity or author-subsidized firms are ordinarily not included)

- Prominent print and broadcast journalists, editors, photojournalists, syndicated cartoonists, graphic novelists, screenwriters, television scriptwriters, and other media people

- Notable international authors

- Literary greats of the early twentieth century whose works are popular in today's high school and college curriculums and continue to elicit critical attention

A *CA* listing entails no charge or obligation. Authors are included on the basis of the above criteria and their interest to *CA* users. Sources of potential listees include trade periodicals, publishers' catalogs, librarians, and other users.

How to Get the Most out of *CA*: Use the Index

The key to locating an author's most recent entry is the *CA* cumulative index, which is published separately and distributed twice a year. It provides access to *all* entries in *CA* and *Contemporary Authors New Revision Series* (*CANR*). Always consult the latest index to find an author's most recent entry.

For the convenience of users, the *CA* cumulative index also includes references to all entries in these Gale literary series: *Authors and Artists for Young Adults, Authors in the News, Bestsellers, Black Literature Criticism, Black Literature Criticism Supplement, Black Writers, Children's Literature Review, Concise Dictionary of American Literary Biography, Concise Dictionary of British Literary Biography, Contemporary Authors Autobiography Series, Contemporary Authors Bibliographical Series, Contemporary Dramatists, Contemporary Literary Criticism, Contemporary Novelists, Contemporary Poets, Contemporary Popular Writers, Contemporary Southern Writers, Contemporary Women Poets, Dictionary of Literary Biography, Dictionary of Literary Biography Documentary Series, Dictionary of Literary Biography Yearbook, DISCovering Authors, DISCovering Authors: British, DISCovering Authors: Canadian, DISCovering Authors: Modules* (including modules for Dramatists, Most-Studied Authors, Multicultural Authors, Novelists, Poets, and Popular/ Genre Authors), *DISCovering Authors 3.0, Drama Criticism, Drama for Students, Feminist Writers, Hispanic Literature Criticism, Hispanic Writers, Junior DISCovering Authors, Major Authors and Illustrators for Children and Young Adults, Major 20th-Century Writers, Native North American Literature, Novels for Students, Poetry Criticism, Poetry for Students, Short Stories for Students, Short Story Criticism, Something about the Author, Something about the Author Autobiography Series, St. James Guide to Children's Writers, St. James Guide to Crime & Mystery Writers, St. James Guide to Fantasy Writers, St. James Guide to Horror, Ghost & Gothic Writers, St. James Guide to Science Fiction Writers, St. James Guide to Young Adult Writers, Twentieth-Century Literary Criticism, 20th Century Romance and Historical Writers, World Literature Criticism,* and *Yesterday's Authors of Books for Children.*

A Sample Index Entry:

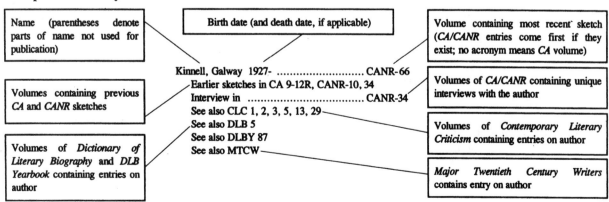

How Are Entries Compiled?

The editors make every effort to secure new information directly from the authors; listees' responses to our questionnaires and query letters provide most of the information featured in *CA*. For deceased writers, or those who fail to reply to requests for data, we consult other reliable biographical sources, such as those indexed in Gale's *Biography and Genealogy Master Index,* and bibliographical sources, including *National Union Catalog, LC MARC,* and *British National Bibliography.* Further details come from published interviews, feature stories, and book reviews, as well as information supplied by the authors' publishers and agents.

An asterisk (*) at the end of a sketch indicates that the listing has been compiled from secondary sources believed to be reliable but has not been personally verified for this edition by the author sketched.

What Kinds of Information Does An Entry Provide?

Sketches in *CA* contain the following biographical and bibliographical information:

- **Entry heading:** the most complete form of author's name, plus any pseudonyms or name variations used for writing

- **Personal information:** author's date and place of birth, family data, ethnicity, educational background, political and religious affiliations, and hobbies and leisure interests

- **Addresses:** author's home, office, or agent's addresses, plus e-mail and fax numbers, as available

- **Career summary:** name of employer, position, and dates held for each career post; resume of other vocational achievements; military service

- **Membership information:** professional, civic, and other association memberships and any official posts held

- **Awards and honors:** military and civic citations, major prizes and nominations, fellowships, grants, and honorary degrees

- **Writings:** a comprehensive, chronological list of titles, publishers, dates of original publication and revised editions, and production information for plays, television scripts, and screenplays

- **Adaptations:** a list of films, plays, and other media which have been adapted from the author's work

- **Work in progress:** current or planned projects, with dates of completion and/or publication, and expected publisher, when known

- **Sidelights:** a biographical portrait of the author's development; information about the critical reception of the author's works; revealing comments, often by the author, on personal interests, aspirations, motivations, and thoughts on writing

- **Interview:** a one-on-one discussion with authors conducted especially for *CA*, offering insight into authors' thoughts about their craft

- **Autobiographical essay:** an original essay written by noted authors for *CA*, a forum in which writers may present themselves, on their own terms, to their audience

- **Photographs:** portraits and personal photographs of notable authors

- **Biographical and critical sources:** a list of books and periodicals in which additional information on an author's life and/or writings appears

- **Obituary Notices** in *CA* provide date and place of birth as well as death information about authors whose full-length sketches appeared in the series before their deaths. The entries also summarize the authors' careers and writings and list other sources of biographical and death information.

Related Titles in the *CA* Series

Contemporary Authors Autobiography Series complements *CA* original and revised volumes with specially commissioned autobiographical essays by important current authors, illustrated with personal photographs they provide. Common topics include their motivations for writing, the people and experiences that shaped their careers, the rewards they derive from their work, and their impressions of the current literary scene.

Contemporary Authors Bibliographical Series surveys writings by and about important American authors since World War II. Each volume concentrates on a specific genre and features approximately ten writers; entries list works written by and about the author and contain a bibliographical essay discussing the merits and deficiencies of major critical and scholarly studies in detail.

Available in Electronic Formats

GaleNet. *CA* is available on a subscription basis through GaleNet, an online information resource that features an easy-to-use end-user interface, powerful search capabilities, and ease of access through the World-Wide Web. For more information, call 1-800-877-GALE.

Licensing. *CA* is available for licensing. The complete database is provided in a fielded format and is deliverable on such media as disk, CD-ROM, or tape. For more information, contact Gale's Business Development Group at 1-800-877-GALE, or visit us on our website at www.galegroup.com/bizdev.

Suggestions Are Welcome

The editors welcome comments and suggestions from users on any aspect of the *CA* series. If readers would like to recommend authors for inclusion in future volumes of the series, they are cordially invited to write the Editors at *Contemporary Authors*, Gale Group, 27500 Drake Rd., Farmington Hills, MI 48331-3535; or call at 1-248-699-4253; or fax at 1-248-699-8054.

Contemporary Authors Product Advisory Board

The editors of *Contemporary Authors* are dedicated to maintaining a high standard of excellence by publishing comprehensive, accurate, and highly readable entries on a wide array of writers. In addition to the quality of the content, the editors take pride in the graphic design of the series, which is intended to be orderly yet inviting, allowing readers to utilize the pages of *CA* easily and with efficiency. Despite the longevity of the *CA* print series, and the success of its format, we are mindful that the vitality of a literary reference product is dependent on its ability to serve its users over time. As literature, and attitudes about literature, constantly evolve, so do the reference needs of students, teachers, scholars, journalists, researchers, and book club members. To be certain that we continue to keep pace with the expectations of our customers, the editors of *CA* listen carefully to their comments regarding the value, utility, and quality of the series. Librarians, who have firsthand knowledge of the needs of library users, are a valuable resource for us. The *Contemporary Authors* Product Advisory Board, made up of school, public, and academic librarians, is a forum to promote focused feedback about *CA* on a regular basis. The seven-member advisory board includes the following individuals, whom the editors wish to thank for sharing their expertise:

- **Anne M. Christensen,** Librarian II, Phoenix Public Library, Phoenix, Arizona.

- **Barbara C. Chumard,** Reference/Adult Services Librarian, Middletown Thrall Library, Middletown, New York.

- **Eva M. Davis,** Youth Department Manager, Ann Arbor District Library, Ann Arbor, Michigan.

- **Adam Janowski, Jr.,** Library Media Specialist, Naples High School Library Media Center, Naples, Florida.

- **Robert Reginald,** Head of Technical Services and Collection Development, California State University, San Bernadino, California.

- **Stephen Weiner,** Director, Maynard Public Library, Maynard, Massachusetts.

International Advisory Board

Well-represented among the 115,000 author entries published in *Contemporary Authors* are sketches on notable writers from many non-English-speaking countries. The primary criteria for inclusion of such authors has traditionally been the publication of at least one title in English, either as an original work or as a translation. However, the editors of *Contemporary Authors* came to observe that many important international writers were being overlooked due to a strict adherence to our inclusion criteria. In addition, writers who were publishing in languages other than English were not being covered in the traditional sources we used for identifying new listees. Intent on increasing our coverage of international authors, including those who write only in their native language and have not been translated into English, the editors enlisted the aid of a board of advisors, each of whom is an expert on the literature of a particular country or region. Among the countries we focused attention on are Mexico, Puerto Rico, Spain, Italy, France, Germany, Luxembourg, Belgium, the Netherlands, Norway, Sweden, Denmark, Finland, Taiwan, Singapore, Malaysia, Thailand, South Africa, Israel, and Japan, as well as England, Scotland, Wales, Ireland, Australia, and New Zealand. The sixteen-member advisory board includes the following individuals, whom the editors wish to thank for sharing their expertise:

- **Lowell A. Bangerter,** Professor of German, University of Wyoming, Laramie, Wyoming.

- **Nancy E. Berg,** Associate Professor of Hebrew and Comparative Literature, Washington University, St. Louis, Missouri.

- **Frances Devlin-Glass,** Associate Professor, School of Literary and Communication Studies, Deakin University, Burwood, Victoria, Australia.

- **David William Foster,** Regent's Professor of Spanish, Interdisciplinary Humanities, and Women's Studies, Arizona State University, Tempe, Arizona.

- **Hosea Hirata,** Director of the Japanese Program, Associate Professor of Japanese, Tufts University, Medford, Massachusetts.

- **Jack Kolbert,** Professor Emeritus of French Literature, Susquehanna University, Selinsgrove, Pennsylvania.

- **Mark Libin,** Professor, University of Manitoba, Winnipeg, Manitoba, Canada.

- **C. S. Lim,** Professor, University of Malaya, Kuala Lumpur, Malaysia.

- **Eloy E. Merino,** Assistant Professor of Spanish, Northern Illinois University, DeKalb, Illinois.

- **Linda M. Rodríguez Guglielmoni,** Associate Professor, University of Puerto Rico—Mayagüez, Puerto Rico.

- **Sven Hakon Rossel,** Professor and Chair of Scandinavian Studies, University of Vienna, Vienna, Austria.

- **Steven R. Serafin,** Director, Writing Center, Hunter College of the City University of New York, New York City.

- **David Smyth,** Lecturer in Thai, School of Oriental and African Studies, University of London, England.

- **Ismail S. Talib,** Senior Lecturer, Department of English Language and Literature, National University of Singapore, Singapore.

- **Dionisio Viscarri,** Assistant Professor, Ohio State University, Columbus, Ohio.

- **Mark Williams,** Associate Professor, English Department, University of Canterbury, Christchurch, New Zealand.

CA Numbering System and Volume Update Chart

Occasionally questions arise about the *CA* numbering system and which volumes, if any, can be discarded. Despite numbers like "29-32R," "97-100" and "219," the entire *CA* print series consists of only 274 physical volumes with the publication of *CA* Volume 220. The following charts note changes in the numbering system and cover design, and indicate which volumes are essential for the most complete, up-to-date coverage.

CA First Revision

- 1-4R through 41-44R (11 books)
  Cover: Brown with black and gold trim.
  There will be no further First Revision volumes because revised entries are now being handled exclusively through the more efficient *New Revision Series* mentioned below.

CA Original Volumes

- 45-48 through 97-100 (14 books)
  Cover: Brown with black and gold trim.
  101 through 220 (120 books)
  Cover: Blue and black with orange bands.
  The same as previous *CA* original volumes but with a new, simplified numbering system and new cover design.

CA Permanent Series

- *CAP*-1 and *CAP*-2 (2 books)
  Cover: Brown with red and gold trim.
  There will be no further Permanent Series volumes because revised entries are now being handled exclusively through the more efficient *New Revision Series* mentioned below.

CA New Revision Series

- CANR-1 through CANR-127 (127 books)
  Cover: Blue and black with green bands.
  Includes only sketches requiring significant changes; **sketches are taken from any previously published CA, CAP, or CANR volume.**

If You Have:	You May Discard:
CA First Revision Volumes 1-4R through 41-44R and *CA Permanent Series* Volumes 1 and 2	*CA* Original Volumes 1, 2, 3, 4 and Volumes 5-6 through 41-44
CA Original Volumes 45-48 through 97-100 and 101 through 220	**NONE:** These volumes will not be superseded by corresponding revised volumes. Individual entries from these and all other volumes appearing in the left column of this chart may be revised and included in the various volumes of the *New Revision Series*.
CA New Revision Series Volumes *CANR*-1 through *CANR*-127	**NONE:** The *New Revision Series* does not replace any single volume of *CA*. Instead, volumes of *CANR* include entries from many previous *CA* series volumes. All *New Revision Series* volumes must be retained for full coverage.

A Sampling of Authors and Media People Featured in This Volume

Daniel Callahan

Callahan is a bioethicist and founder of the Hastings Center, a think tank that focuses on ethical issues of medicine, biology, and the environment. He has devoted his career to exploring many of the controversial issues that make news headlines today—rationing health care, cloning, stem cell research, abortion, aging, dying, and alternative medicine, to name a few. The author or editor of some thirty-seven books, Callahan published *What Price Better Health:? Hazards of the Research Imperative* and edited *The Role of Complementary and Alternative Medicine: Accommodating Pluralism,* both in 2003.

Michael Crichton

Crichton—a successful physician, teacher, film director, and screenwriter—may be best known for his unique blend of science and suspense in "techno-thriller" novels like *The Andromeda Strain, The Terminal Man,* and *Jurassic Park,* and the popular motion pictures they became. Acknowledged by critics for stories that are both entertaining and thought-provoking, Crichton has been honored with two Edgar Awards from the Mystery Writers of America as well as an Emmy Award for his TV hit *ER,* which he created and produced. His latest novel, *Prey,* was published in 2002. Paramount Pictures released the film version of his novel *Timeline* in 2003.

Helen Fielding

Fielding rose to international fame with her second novel *Bridget Jones's Diary*, which sold more than four million copies and was published in thirty countries. The book, which centers around the humorous trials of a single British woman over thirty, is based on the manifestation of a persona Fielding created for a column in the London *Independent. Bridget Jones's Diary* garnered Fielding a British Book Award in 1997, and was later released as a film of the same name by Miramax in 2001. Two sequels were generated as a result of the book's and movie's success–*Bridget Jones: The Edge of Reason* and *Bridget Jones's Guide to Life.* The former was filmed for release in 2004.

John Gardner

Gardner, once an Anglican priest, became a successful writer of suspense novels noted for their style and wit. Critics applauded his series of novels featuring Herbie Kruger, a German-born British Intelligence agent, and another series built around the cowardly, inept Boysie

Oakes, a clever parody of James Bond. Gardner later accepted an invitation to take on James Bond himself, continuing the series begun by the late Ian Fleming, with novels like *License Renewed, License to Kill,* and *Death Is Forever.* The latest installments in Gardner's non-Bond canon include *Day of Absolution,* 2000, *Bottled Spider,* 2002, and *The Streets of Town,* 2003.

Kaye Gibbons

Gibbons was born and raised in North Carolina, and she has never strayed far from her roots in her award-winning novels. Set in the rural South, her books feature strong women whose traditional values give them the wisdom and courage to bear the heavy burdens of their lives. Praised for her compassion and finely drawn characters, Gibbons became an instant celebrity and best-selling author when her novels *Ellen Foster* and *A Virtuous Woman* were chosen by Oprah Winfrey for her TV book club. Gibbons's latest offering is *Divining Women,* published in 2004.

Berry Gordy, Jr.

Gordy, a member of the Rock and Roll Hall of Fame with a star on the Hollywood Walk of Fame, has been credited with changing the course of twentieth-century pop music. As the founder of Hitsville U.S.A., which would become later known as Motown Records—and the guiding light of performers like Smokey Robinson, Marvin Gaye, the Temptations, Diana Ross, and the Jackson Five—Gordy developed the enterprise into the largest black-owned business in America by 1988. An accomplished songwriter, Gordy has a list of hit songs, including *I'll Be There, You've Made Me So Very Happy,* and *Shop Around,* which he augmented with *Do You Love Me?* in 2000.

Ruth Rendell

Rendell, who writes under her own name and the pseudonym Barbara Vine, has won numerous awards, including a British National Book Award, for her compelling suspense novels that feature an intimate relation between the physical and the psychological. Readers and critics have taken kindly to the protagonist of many of her books, Chief Inspector Reginald Wexford, who is shown to age and develop, from his 1964 debut in her first novel through his return engagements into the 1990s. As Barbara Vine, Rendell has written *Grasshopper,* published in 2000, and *The Blood Doctor,* published in 2002.

Robert J. Sternberg

Sternberg, an award-winning Yale professor of psychology and education, pioneered the study of human intelligence with the book *Beyond IQ,* proposing a broader view in assessing intellectual abilities. A sampling of his later works reflects the wide range of his theory: *Intelligence Applied: Understanding and Increasing Your Intellectual Skills, Love the Way You Want It: Using Your Head in Matters of the Heart,* and *Successful Intelligence: How Practical and Creative Intelligence Determine Success in Life.* Sternberg continues his study with 2003's *Wisdom, Intelligence, and Creativity Synthesized* and 2004's *Psychology 101 1/2 : The Unspoken Rules for Success in Academia.*

Acknowledgments

Grateful acknowledgment is made to those publishers, photographers, and artists whose work appear with these authors' essays. Following is a list of the copyright holders who have granted us permission to reproduce material in this volume of *CA*. Every effort has been made to trace copyright, but if omissions have been made, please let us know.

Photographs/Art

Ken Alder: Alder, photograph. © Jerry Bauer. Reproduced by permission.

Maude Barlow: Barlow, photograph by Andrew Balfour. Reproduced by permission of Maude Barlow.

Karleen Bradford: Bradford, photograph by Michael McLuhan, MPA. Reproduced by permission of Karleen Bradford.

David Brin: Brin, photograph by Jerry Bauer. © by Jerry Bauer. Reproduced by permission.

Daniel Callahan: Callahan, photograph. The Library of Congress.

Michael Chabon: Chabon, photograph. © Jerry Bauer. Reproduced by permission.

Warren I. Cohen: Cohen, photograph by Mark Samuel Lee. Reproduced by permission of Warren I. Cohen.

Catherine Fisher Collins: Collins, photograph. Reproduced by permission.

Ilene Cooper: Cooper, photograph by Smith/Wright Photography. Reproduced by permission of Ilene Cooper.

Michael Crichton: Crichton, photograph by Jerry Bauer. © Jerry Bauer. Reproduced by permission.

Rachel Cusk: Cusk, photograph. Rune Hellestad/Corbis. Reproduced by permission.

Walter de las Casas: de las Casas, photograph by Angela Lee. Reproduced by permission of Walter de las Casas.

Fred Ebb: Ebb, photograph. AP/Wide World Photos. Reproduced by permission.

Stephen C. Evans: Evans, photograph. Reproduced by permission.

Helen Fielding: Fielding, photograph. Getty Images. Reproduced by permission.

Richard J. Foster: Foster, photograph. Ted Spring Photography, Castle Rock, Colorado, USA. Reproduced by permission of Richard J. Foster.

Zev Garber: Garber, photograph by Joyce Glantz. Reproduced by permission of Zev Garber.

John Gardner: Gardner, 1973, photograph. AP/Wide World Photos. Reproduced by permission.

Kaye Gibbons: Gibbons, photograph by Jerry Bauer. © Jerry Bauer. Reproduced by permission.

Mel Glenn: Glenn, photograph. Reproduced by permission.

A

ABERCROMBIE, Barbara (Mattes) 1939-

PERSONAL: Born April 6, 1939, in Evanston, IL; daughter of William F. (a businessman and writer) and Grace (a pianist; maiden name, Mann) Mattes; married Gordon E. Abercrombie (a stockbroker), March 8, 1964; children: Brooke Louise, Gillan Grace. *Education:* Attended Briarcliff College and Los Angeles Harbor College.

ADDRESSES: Home—Santa Monica, CA. *Agent*—Aaron M. Priest Literary Agency, 150 East 35th St., New York, NY 10016. *E-mail*—Barbara@Barbara Abercrombie.com.

CAREER: Actress, educator, and author. Actress in stage and television productions, including appearances on television series *Ironside* and *Route 66;* freelance writer. University of California, Los Angeles, teacher in extension writer's program; teacher of creative writing to children. Conductor of workshops for Wellness Community.

WRITINGS:

FOR YOUNG PEOPLE

(Editor) *The Other Side of a Poem,* Harper (New York, NY), 1977.
Amanda and Heather, and Company, illustrated by Mimi St. John, Dandelion (New York, NY), 1979.
Cat-Man's Daughter, Harper (New York, NY), 1981.

Charlie Anderson, illustrated by Mark Graham, McElderry (New York, NY), 1990.
Michael and the Cats, illustrated by Mark Graham, Macmillan (New York, NY), 1993.
Bad Dog, Dodger!, illustrated by Adam Gustavson, McElderry (New York, NY), 2002.

OTHER

(With Norma Almquist and Jeanne Nichols) *Traveling without a Camera* (poems), Peck Street Press, 1978.
Connections (novel), Harper (New York, NY), 1979.
Good Riddance (novel), Harper (New York, NY), 1979.
Run for Your Life (novel), Morrow (New York, NY), 1984.
Writing out the Storm: Reading and Writing Your Way through Serious Illness or Injury, St. Martin's Press (New York, NY), 2002.

Contributor of articles, essays, and poems to newspapers and magazines, including *Los Angeles Times, Christian Science Monitor,* and *United Airlines Hemisphere Magazine.*

SIDELIGHTS: Barbara Abercrombie is the author of several books for children, as well as of *Writing out the Storm: Reading and Writing Your Way through Serious Illness or Injury,* which is based on her own struggle with breast cancer.

In *Michael and the Cats,* a young boy visiting his aunt tries to befriend her two cats. "He tries things that would make him happy if he were a cat," as Ellen

Fader explained in *Horn Book*. But nothing he tries seems to work, until he decides to learn what it is that cats actually like. Emily Melton in *Booklist* noted that, thanks to Abercrombie's story, "children will learn, just as Michael does, that imposing their own ideas of friendship may not work, but putting themselves in another's place usually produces the desired response." Fader concluded: "Abercrombie perfectly captures the tenuous nature of friendship between pets and small children; she never preaches, yet manages to convey the necessity of accepting animals on their own terms."

Another boy befriends an animal in Abercrombie's *Bad Dog, Dodger!* In this story, Sam wants to have a dog but his parents insist he must prove to them that he is responsible enough. When he shows them that he is responsible, a new problem begins. The rambunctious Dodger is full of energy and needs to be trained. He knocks over the garbage, chews things, and even follows Sam to school. Sam must get up early each morning and put Dodger through a training program. A critic for *Kirkus Reviews* called *Bad Dog, Dodger!* "a perfect cautionary tale for a youngster about to get a first dog." According to Dorian Chong, writing in *School Library Journal*, the book is "a well-written, charmingly illustrated story with a satisfying, happy ending."

Speaking of her books for children, Abercrombie once told *CA:* "I write to make things clear to myself. This is especially true of the stories I write for children. I write about the things that happen in my own family from my own viewpoint, which, at age thirty-eight, I find not very different from the way I was in terms of thoughts and feelings at age ten."

In *Writing out the Storm* Abercrombie draws on her own experience of having breast cancer to show others how writing can be a faith-building activity for those going through a serious illness. A critic for *Publishers Weekly* called *Writing out the Storm* "a moving, unsentimental portrait of the author with breast cancer." In an article for the *Baltimore Sun*, Abercrombie spoke of her bout with cancer. She does not call herself a "survivor," noting that for her, the word is "overly dramatic, implying courage that hadn't been earned." She explained: "The majority of women I know who are diagnosed with breast cancer get treatment and go on with their lives, and many of these women don't want to be identified for all time as a breast cancer survivor."

BIOGRAPHICAL AND CRITICAL SOURCES:

PERIODICALS

Baltimore Sun, October 30, 2002, Barbara Abercrombie, "A Brighter Outlook on Breast Cancer," p. 11A.
Booklist, December 15, 1993, Emily Melton, review of *Michael and the Cats*, p. 762.
Horn Book, January-February, 1994, Ellen Fader, review of *Michael and the Cats*, p. 58.
Kirkus Reviews, April 15, 2002, review of *Bad Dog, Dodger!*, p. 560.
Publishers Weekly, June 24, 2002, review of *Writing out the Storm: Reading and Writing Your Way through Serious Illness or Injury*, p. 52.
School Library Journal, November, 2002, Dorian Chong, review of *Bad Dog, Dodger!*, p. 110.

ONLINE

Barbara Abercrombie Web site, http://www.barbara abercrombie.com/ (November 4, 2003).*

         *   *   *

ALDER, Ken(neth L.)

PERSONAL: Male. *Education:* Harvard University, Ph.D., 1991.

ADDRESSES: Office—Department of History, Northwestern University, Evanston, IL 60201. *E-mail*—k-alder@northwestern.edu.

CAREER: Educator, novelist, and author of nonfiction. Northwestern University, Evanston, IL, assistant professor, 1991, associate professor, beginning 1997, currently Anderson associate professor of history and director of Science in Human Culture program.

AWARDS, HONORS: Senior fellow, Northwestern University Center for Humanities, 1994-95; Dexter Prize, Society for the History of Technology, 1998, for *Engineering the Revolution: Arms and Enlightenment in France, 1763-1815;* Scholar's Award for Science,

Ken Alder

National Science Foundation; National Endowment for the Humanities fellow, Newberry Library; Alice Berline Kaplan Center for the Humanities fellow; Henry R. Phillips research grant in jurisprudence, American Philosophical Society.

WRITINGS:

The White Bus (novel), St. Martin's Press (New York, NY), 1987.
Engineering the Revolution: Arms and Enlightenment in France, 1763-1815, Princeton University Press (Princeton, NJ), 1997.
The Measure of All Things: The Seven-Year Odyssey and Hidden Error That Transformed the World, Free Press (New York, NY), 2002.

Contributor to periodicals, including the *Journal of American History, Robotics and Automation,* and *Science.*

SIDELIGHTS: Historian Ken Alder is the author of both fiction and nonfiction. Stemming from his interest in the changing face of technology in the eighteenth

century, he has written *Engineering the Revolution: Arms and Enlightenment in France, 1763-1815,* and he explores the creation of the metric system of measurement in *The Measure of All Things: The Seven-Year Odyssey and Hidden Error That Transformed the World.* He also wrote *The White Bus,* a 1987 novel about a teenager's attempts to deal with the issue of racism.

The predominantly black student body of San Francisco's Martin Luther King High School calls Caucasian Ira Allen's mode of transportation "the white bus," thus explaining the title of Alder's 1987 novel. Ira defies his parents' plans to send him to an elite private school because he wants to attend the same school as his black friend Marc. At King High School, Ira tries to identify with the school's African-American majority as he learns to talk jive and dates a black girl named Jessica. He eventually views Jessica and other African-American students "as individuals, not representatives of the group," wrote Hazel Rochman in *Booklist,* who noted that the novel could be "too didactic" but praised its "sharp, often humorous candor." Betty Lukas, reviewing *The White Bus* in the *Los Angeles Times Book Review,* noted that while Alder's characters are not fully realized, "some of Ira's internal musings are wry and touching." A *Publishers Weekly* contributor judged *The White Bus* to be "promising" and concluded that "the narrative displays a lively intensity that helps to compensate for its flaws."

In *Engineering the Revolution: Arms and Enlightenment in France, 1763-1815,* Alder argues that Marxist philosophy misinterprets the French Revolution. He contends that from the dismantling of the French monarchy through the violent and bloody revolutionary government to the militaristic empire of Napoleon Bonaparte, little actually changed in France, especially with regard to industry and technology. Alder maintains that, despite political change, French social structure and practice remained relatively stable. He illustrates this thesis largely by examining the country's production of arms and ammunition as well as the governmental bodies that controlled technology. According to R. W. Mackey, reviewing *Engineering the Revolution* for *Choice,* the author ably includes material from "extensive primary and secondary sources," and Mackey recommended the volume for "upper-division undergraduates and above."

The Measure of All Things: The Seven-Year Odyssey and Hidden Error That Transformed the World tells the story of how the metric system of measurement was created in the 1790s by two French astronomers. Scientists of the time hoped to create a standard, accurate measurement system that could be used throughout the world. They determined that one meter was to be exactly one-ten-millionth of the distance between the North Pole and the Equator. Jean-Baptiste-Joseph Delambre and Pierre-François-Andre Mechain were charged with finding out precisely what this distance was. Their seven-year effort to measure one meridian arc, and the mistake made and covered up by Mechain in his calculations, is the subject of Alder's book. The result, Douglas Johnson wrote in the *Spectator,* is "a straightforward and clear narrative of what happened. But an enormous amount of research has gone into this book." A critic for *Science News* found the book to be "an enchanting portrait" and "a marvelous tale." "Alder's writing sparkles with wit and life. The book melds historical documentary, riveting biography, scientific discourse (on error analysis and measurement), and personal essay," Andrew S. Fazekas wrote in *Astronomy.*

BIOGRAPHICAL AND CRITICAL SOURCES:

PERIODICALS

Astronomy, January, 2003, Andrew S. Fazekas, review of *The Measure of All Things: The Seven-Year Odyssey and Hidden Error That Transformed the World,* p. 95.
Booklist, September 15, 1987, Hazel Rochman, review of *The White Bus,* p. 107; September 1, 2002, Gavin Quinn, review of *The Measure of All Things,* p. 32.
Canadian Journal of History, August, 1999, Howard G. Brown, review of *Engineering the Revolution: Arms and Enlightenment in France, 1763-1815,* p. 280.
Choice, October, 1997, R. W. Mackey, review of *Engineering the Revolution,* p. 362.
Historian, summer, 1999, Carol E. Harrison, review of *Engineering the Revolution,* p. 941.
History: Review of New Books, winter, 1998, Eric A. Arnold, Jr., review of *Engineering the Revolution,* p. 82.
Kirkus Reviews, August 15, 1987, p. 1174; July 1, 2002, review of *The Measure of All Things,* p. 925.

Library Journal, August, 2002, review of *The Measure of All Things,* p. 135.
Los Angeles Times Book Review, December 27, 1987, Betty Lukas, review of *The White Bus,* p. 4.
New Statesman, September 23, 2002, review of *The Measure of All Things,* p. 53.
Publishers Weekly, September 11, 1987, Sybil S. Steinberg, review of *The White Bus,* p. 79; July 1, 2002, review of *The Measure of All Things,* p. 48.
Science News, November 9, 2002, review of *The Measure of All Things,* p. 303.
Spectator, October 19, 2002, Douglas Johnson, review of *The Measure of All Things,* p. 57.
Tribune Books (Chicago, IL), November 15, 1987, p. 7.
Village Voice, November 24, 1987, p. 62.

ONLINE

CNN Online, http://www.cnn.com/ (December 12, 2002), Todd Leopold, "Why the Metric System Is Wrong: Author Takes 'The Measure of All Things.'"
Northwestern University Web site, http://www2.mmlc. nwu.edu/ (March 5, 1999), "Ken Alder."
Princeton University Press Web site, http://pup. princeton.edu/ (March 5, 1999).*

*   *   *

ANDERSEN, Christopher P(eter) 1949-

PERSONAL: Born May 26, 1949, in Pensacola, FL; son of Edward Francis (a commander in the U.S. Navy) and Jeanette (Peterson) Andersen; married Valerie Jean Hess (a banker), February 3, 1972; children: Katharine, Kelly. *Education:* University of California, Berkeley, B.A. (political science), 1971.

ADDRESSES: Home—171 Blackville Rd., Washington, CT, 06794. *Agent*—Trident Media Group, 41 Madison Ave., Fl. 36, New York, NY 10010 .

CAREER: Time, New York, NY, correspondent in San Francisco, CA, 1969-71, staff writer in New York, NY, 1971-72, and in Montreal, Quebec, Canada, 1972-74; *People,* New York, NY, assistant editor, 1974-75, associate editor, 1975-80, senior editor, 1980-86; writer.

MEMBER: Authors Guild, Players Club.

WRITINGS:

The Name Game, Simon & Schuster (New York, NY), 1977.

A Star Is a Star Is a Star!: The Life and Loves of Susan Hayward, Doubleday (Garden City, NY), 1980.

The Book of People: Photographs, Capsule Biographics, and Vital Statistics of Over 500 Celebrities, Putnam (New York, NY), 1981.

Father: The Figure and the Force, Warner (New York, NY), 1983.

(With Albert M. Myers) *Success over Sixty,* Summit (New York, NY), 1984.

The New Book of People: Photographs, Capsule Biographies, and Vital Statistics of Over 500 Celebrities, Putnam (New York, NY), 1986.

The Po-Po Principle, Pan Productions (Victoria, British Columbia, Canada), 1986.

The Baby Boomer's Name Game, Putnam (New York, NY), 1987.

The Serpent's Tooth, Harper (New York, NY), 1987.

Young Kate, Holt (New York, NY), 1988.

(With John Marion) *The Best of Everything: The Definitive Insider's Guide to Collecting—For Every Taste and Every Budget,* Simon & Schuster (New York, NY), 1989.

Citizen Jane: The Turbulent Life of Jane Fonda, Holt (New York, NY), 1990.

Madonna: Unauthorized, Simon & Schuster (New York, NY), 1991.

Jagger: Unauthorized, Delacorte (New York, NY), 1993.

Michael Jackson: Unauthorized, Simon & Schuster (New York, NY), 1994.

Jack and Jackie: Portrait of an American Marriage, Morrow (New York, NY), 1996.

An Affair to Remember: The Remarkable Love Story of Katharine Hepburn and Spencer Tracy, Morrow (New York, NY), 1997.

Jackie after Jack: Portrait of the Lady, Morrow (New York, NY), 1998.

The Day Diana Died, Morrow (New York, NY), 1998.

Bill and Hillary: The Marriage, Morrow (New York, NY), 1999.

The Day John Died, Morrow (New York, NY), 2000.

Diana's Boys: William and Harry and the Mother They Loved, Morrow (New York, NY), 2001.

George and Laura: Portrait of an American Marriage, Morrow (New York, NY), 2002.

Sweet Caroline: Last Child of Camelot, Morrow (New York, NY), 2003.

Contributor of articles to periodicals, including *New York Times, Reader's Digest, Ladies' Home Journal, People, Life,* and *Vanity Fair.*

SIDELIGHTS: Christopher P. Andersen once told *CA:* "As a professional journalist since the age of seventeen, I have done stories on thousands of personalities, from presidents to axe murderers to movie stars. Hence my books have all dealt with people—some famous, most not—and what motivates them. In short, how and why we all do what we do. It is a daunting pursuit, but it is hard to think of a more rewarding one."

Since the mid-1980s Andersen has emerged in the front tier of celebrity biographers. A former senior editor at *People* magazine, Andersen has penned a series of bestsellers on the private lives of such notables as Princess Diana, Jacqueline Kennedy Onassis and her children Caroline and John Kennedy, Jr., Bill and Hillary Clinton, and George and Laura Bush. Andersen's list of biographies also includes movie stars, including Katharine Hepburn, Spencer Tracy, and Jane Fonda, as well as entertainers Madonna, Mick Jagger, and Michael Jackson. The author uses his skills as a reporter to uncover telling details in the lives of his subjects, generally relying on interviews with close friends, family members, and published documents. Although they are occasionally excoriated by reviewers, the books sell quite well indeed and have been translated into more than twenty foreign languages.

Some critics have written about Andersen's attribution of sources and his tendency to highlight salacious anecdotes. *San Francisco Chronicle* reporter Patricia Holt called *Jackie after Jack: Portrait of the Lady* "one of those reprehensible pseudo-biographies with more unidentified 'sources close to the subject' than even Kenneth Starr could dredge up." In *Entertainment Weekly,* Lisa Schwarzbaum described *Bill and Hillary: The Marriage* as "a cold, damning book, jammed with tattle . . . a prime example of a kind of opportunistic celebrity muckraking—sometimes known as selling people out—that has become junky big business." On the other hand, in his *Newsweek* review of *The Day Diana Died,* Daniel Pedersen wrote: "Remarkably, after all the rehashings and inaccuracies in the oft-told saga of Charles and Diana, Andersen's book actually makes some fresh contributions. . . . The worthiness of Andersen's efforts comes partly from solid reporting." *People* correspondent Alex Tresniowski found that in *Jackie after Jack* "Andersen's scavenged clues to the reality behind the Jackie myth make for compelling reading." In *Library Journal,* Susan McCaffrey felt that Andersen created "an entirely sympathetic portrait of the most beloved royal."

Andersen's books are sometimes timed to be released upon anniversaries of their subjects' deaths. At other times they seek to understand the generational legacy of those in politics, royalty, or entertainment. To quote Francine Prose in *People,* his work reminds readers "how much damage grown-up romance can sustain—and how a life-changing passion can outlive the lovers themselves."

BIOGRAPHICAL AND CRITICAL SOURCES:

PERIODICALS

Booklist, November 15, 1994, Ilene Cooper, review of *Michael Jackson: Unauthorized,* p. 554; August, 1996, Ilene Cooper, review of *Jack and Jackie: Portrait of an American Marriage,* p. 1850; April 15, 2001, Mary Frances Wilkens, review of *The Day John Died,* p. 1574; January 1, 2003, Brad Hooper, review of *George and Laura: Portrait of an American Marriage,* p. 809.

Buffalo News (Buffalo, NY), November 6, 2002, Mary Kunz, "An Insider's View of the First Couple," p. C1.

Chicago Tribune, July 14, 1985; July 15, 1985; July 16, 1985.

Daily News (Los Angeles, CA), August 12, 1998, "Queen of Heartlessness?," review of *The Day Diana Died,* p. L5.

Entertainment Weekly, August 20, 1999, Lisa Schwarzbaum, "Public Lives," p. 117.

Houston Chronicle, March 29, 1998, Clifford Pugh, "Oh, No! Jackie O?," review of *Jackie after Jack: Portrait of the Lady,* p. 26; August 23, 1998, Clifford Pugh, "A Year Later, Diana's Story Still Surprises," review of *The Day Diana Died,* p. 20.

Library Journal, March 1, 1999, Susan McCaffrey, review of *The Day Diana Died,* p. 126.

Newsweek, February 23, 1998, Barbara Kantrowitz, review of *Jackie after Jack,* p. 65; August 24, 1998, Daniel Pedersen, "The Never-Ending Story," p. 56; July 24, 2000, "JFK Jr., One Year Later," p. 64.

New York Times, October 6, 1986.

New York Times Book Review, September 13, 1987; August 7, 1988; September 1, 1996, Larissa MacFarquhar, review of *Jack and Jackie,* p. 5; December 1, 2002, Elisabeth Bumiller, "Dubya in Love," review of *George and Laura,* p. 4.

People, August 17, 1987; June 2, 1997, Francine Prose, review of *An Affair to Remember: The Remarkable Love Story of Katharine Hepburn and Spencer Tracy,* p. 37; February 23, 1998, Alex Tresniowski, review of *Jackie after Jack,* p. 33.

Publishers Weekly, April 27, 1990, Genevieve Stuttaford, review of *Citizen Jane: The Turbulent Life of Jane Fonda,* p. 48; July 24, 2000, Daisy Maryles, "A Compelling Chronicler," p. 19; September 3, 2001, Daisy Maryles, review of *Diana's Boys: William and Harry and the Mother They Loved,* p. 20.

Record (Bergen County, NJ), August 26, 2001, Bill Ervolino, "On a Princely Course," review of *Diana's Boys,* p. E3.

Rocky Mountain News (Denver, CO), March 8, 1998, "Jackie O—And Her Evil Twin," review of *Jackie after Jack,* p. 3E; August 30, 1998, "Queen of Contempt Rules Di Book," review of *Diana's Boys,* p. 3E.

San Francisco Chronicle, February 25, 1998, Patricia Holt, review of *Jackie after Jack,* p. E3; August 20, 1998, Leah Garchik, "The Ways in Which We Remember," review of *The Day Diana Died,* p. C16.

Star-Ledger (Newark, NJ), September 19, 1999, "Did You Hear the Latest about the Clintons?," review of *Bill and Hillary: The Marriage,* p. 5.

Time, August 19, 1996, Elizabeth Gleick, review of *Jack and Jackie,* p. 67.

Washington Post Book World, October 30, 1977; July 19, 1987; August 7, 1988.

*   *   *

**ANDREWS, John (Malcolm) 1936-
(John Malcolm)**

PERSONAL: Born August 21, 1936, in Manchester, England; son of Ernest (an engineer) and May (Whiteley) Andrews; married Geraldine Lacey (a picture restorer), March 25, 1961; children: Simon Charles. *Education:* St. John's College, Cambridge, M.A., 1958.

ADDRESSES: Home—Carriers Oast, Northiam, Sussex TN31 6NH, England. *Agent*—Teresa Chris, 43 Musard Rd., London W6 8NR, England. *E-mail*—jma 2274@aol.com.

CAREER: Design engineer, 1958-63; export manager, 1963-70; management consultant, 1970-76; international marketing manager, 1976-90; machinery broker, 1990—.

MEMBER: Crime Writers Association, Society of Authors.

WRITINGS:

NOVELS; UNDER NAME JOHN MALCOLM

A Back Room in Somers Town, Collins (London, England), 1984, Scribner (New York, NY), 1985.
The Godwin Sideboard, Collins (London, England), 1984, Scribner (New York, NY), 1985.
The Gwen John Sculpture, Collins (London, England), 1985, Scribner (New York, NY), 1986.
Whistler in the Dark, Scribner (New York, NY), 1986.
Gothic Pursuit, Scribner (New York, NY), 1987.
Mortal Ruin, Scribner (New York, NY), 1988.
The Wrong Impression, Scribner (New York, NY), 1990.
Sheep, Goats and Soap, Scribner (New York, NY), 1991.
A Deceptive Appearance, Scribner (New York, NY), 1992.
The Burning Ground, HarperCollins (London, England), 1993.
Hung Over, HarperCollins (London, England), 1994, St. Martin's Press (New York, NY), 1995.
Into the Vortex, HarperCollins (London, England), 1996, St. Martin's Press (New York, NY), 1997.
Simpson's Homer, Allison & Busby (New York, NY), 2002.
Circles & Squares, Allison & Busby (New York, NY), 2003.
Mortal Instruments, Allison & Busby (New York, NY), 2003.

OTHER; UNDER NAME JOHN ANDREWS

The Price Guide to Antique Furniture, Antique Collectors Club (Woodbridge, Suffolk, England), 1969, new edition published as *British Antique Furniture,* 1989.
The Price Guide to Victorian Furniture, Antique Collectors Club (Woodbridge, Suffolk, England), 1970.
The Price Guide to Victorian, Edwardian, and 1920s Furniture, Antique Collectors Club (Woodbridge, Suffolk, England), 1980, new edition published as *Victorian and Edwardian Furniture,* 1992.
The ACC Guide to the Antique Furniture of the Western World, Antique Collectors Club (Woodbridge, Suffolk, England), 1996.

Contributor of short stories, under name John Malcolm, to anthologies, including *A Suit of Diamonds,* Collins (London, England), 1990; *Midwinter Mysteries,* Scribner (New York, NY), 1991; and *Winters Crimes 24,* Macmillan, 1992.

WORK IN PROGRESS: Rogues Gallery.

SIDELIGHTS: John Andrews applies his expert knowledge of antiques and art to his sophisticated mystery novels, which involve the theft of valuable collectibles. His detective character is Tim Simpson, a "tough young art expert with an easily kindled temper," as Newgate Callendar described him in the *New York Times Book Review.* Simpson repeatedly finds himself involved in cases of theft, forgery, and fraud.

The fictional Simpson works for a British bank as a specialist in art investment. In the first book to feature him, *A Back Room in Somers Town,* Tim travels all the way to Brazil in order to track down the perpetrators of a web of fraud and murder. Along the way, he encounters "more physical punishment from altercations with criminals than the average boxer would expect to encounter in a lifelong career," Judith Rhodes stated in *St. James Guide to Crime and Mystery Writers.*

Tim's frequent run-ins with violence are a source of concern to his girlfriend, Sue Westerman, and his employer, Jeremy White. Sue, who eventually marries

Tim, frequently works with him in her position as an administrative assistant at London's Tate Gallery. Another foil is provided for the detective in the form of his friend Nobby Roberts, a professional policeman who is constantly irritated by Tim's amateur snooping. "But violence, although endemic in these books, is in fact a lesser feature than the wealth of information on antiques and fine art. Malcolm's obvious love of, and expertise in, the art and artifacts of his chosen period permeate the stories," commented Rhodes, who credited the author with creating "genuine atmosphere" and illustrating the close relationships between various artistic movements of the late nineteenth and early twentieth centuries.

In *Hung Over,* Tim is angered to find that his bank has purchased a mediocre collection of paintings, apparently to help out one of its best customers, who is struggling with financial difficulties. The murder of an art dealer friend of Tim's seems to be unrelated, but as time progresses he realizes there is a sinister link between the two events. His investigation makes for "a delightful tale, full of wit and charm," that will appeal to any mystery lover, but most especially to "Anglophiles and art lovers," recommended a *Booklist* reviewer. A *Publishers Weekly* reviewer added: "The novel's taut ending is a thing of beauty."

Into the Vortex is marked by "dry wit, subtle wordplay, and literate references," all woven into a tale of a murder connected to a Wyndam Lewis painting, according to Rcx E. Klett in *Library Journal. Simpson's Homer* is another "intelligent, well-plotted story," in the estimation of a *Publishers Weekly* reviewer, as Tim and Sue investigate reports that an old friend of Tim's has become mentally unbalanced. That friend soon turns up dead, as do two of his associates. The adventures continue in *Circles & Squares,* a book that "proves that this series ages as profitably as the works of art it features," reported Jenny McLarin in *Booklist.* This time the art that figures prominently in the narrative is that of William and Ben Nicholson, whose styles were very unalike. "Malcolm manipulates plot twists as deftly as a skilled artist wields a paintbrush. His graceful prose and obvious but unobtrusive knowledge of fine art and the finishing touches to an outstanding mystery," concluded McLarin.

BIOGRAPHICAL AND CRITICAL SOURCES:

BOOKS

St. James Guide to Crime and Mystery Writers, St. James Press (Detroit, MI), 1996.

PERIODICALS

Booklist, August, 1995, Emily Melton, review of *Hung Over,* p. 1932; May 1, 2003, Jenny McLarin, review of *Circles & Squares,* p. 1550.
Library Journal, September 1, 1995, Rex E. Klett, review of *Hung Over,* p. 212; June 1, 1997, p. 154; May 1, 1985, Lynette Friesen, review of *A Back Room in Somers Town,* p. 82; January, 1987, Jo Ann Vicarel, review of *Whistler in the Dark,* p. 111; November 1, 1992, Rex E. Klett, review of *A Deceptive Appearance,* p. 121; Regan Robinson, review of *Sheep, Goats, and Soap,* p. 144.
Listener, July 19, 1984.
New York Times Book Review, June 8, 1986, p. 34; March 15, 1987, Newgate Callendar, review of *Whistler in the Dark,* p. 24; November 1, 1987, Newgate Callendar, review of *Gothic Pursuit,* p. 34.
Observer (London, England), August 26, 1984.
Publishers Weekly, September 6, 1985, Sybil Steinberg, review of *The Godwin Sideboard,* p. 58; February 28, 1986, Sybil Steinberg, review of *The Gwen John Sculpture,* p. 118; November 28, 1986, Sybil Steinberg, review of *Whistler in the Dark,* August 7, 1987, Sybil Steinberg, review of *Gothic Pursuit,* p. 437; June 24, 1998, Sybil Steinberg, review of *Mortal Run,* p. 97; July 6, 1990, Sybil Steinberg, review of *The Wrong Impression,* p. 61; November 22, 1991, review of *Sheep, Goats and Soap,* p. 40; October 12, 1992, review of *A Deceptive Appearance,* p. 67; August 7, 1995, p. 445; March 4, 2002, review of *Simpson's Homer,* p. 59.
Punch, May 30, 1984.

*   *   *

ANDREWS, Sarah 1949(?)-

PERSONAL: Born c. 1949; daughter of an art teacher and an English teacher; married Damon Brown (a geologist), c. 1986; children: Duncan. *Education:* Colorado College, B.A., Colorado State University, M.S. (geology), 1981.

ADDRESSES: Home—Sebastopol, CA. *Office*—Department of Geology, 1801 Sonoma State University, East Cotati Ave., Rohnert Park, CA 94928. *E-mail*—canyonwren@aol.com.

CAREER: Writer. U.S. Geological Survey, WY, field geologist, c. 1976-80; Amoco Oil Company, Denver, CO, geologist, 1980-83; Angus Petroleum, Golden, CO, geologist, 1983-86; consultant geologist, c. 1990—; Sonoma State University, Rohnert Park, CA, instructor in geology.

MEMBER: American Association of Petroleum Geologists.

AWARDS, HONORS: Journalists Award, American Association of Petroleum Geologists, 1999.

WRITINGS:

NOVELS

Tensleep, Penzler Books (New York, NY), 1994.
A Fall in Denver, Scribner (New York, NY), 1995.
Mother Nature, St. Martin's Press (New York, NY), 1997.
Only Flesh and Bones, St. Martin's Press (New York, NY), 1998.
Bone Hunter, St. Martin's Minotaur (New York, NY), 1999.
An Eye for Gold, St. Martin's Press (New York, NY), 2000.
Fault Line, St. Martin's Press (New York, NY), 2002.
Killer Dust, St. Martin's Press (New York, NY), 2003.

Contributor of short stories and articles to *Armchair Detective, Journal of Sedimentary Petrology,* and *Colorado College Bulletin.*

SIDELIGHTS: Sarah Andrews, a former field geologist for the U.S. Geological Survey, has put her scientific knowledge to an unusual use—writing mystery novels featuring Emily "Em" Hansen, a forensic geologist who utilizes the earth sciences to help solve crimes. "Science and detective work," noted a writer for *Publishers Weekly,* "should go together naturally. . . . But aside from medical thrillers, not many writers nowadays embark upon the scientific mystery. Of those who do, Andrews . . . has become a leading light." David Pitt of *Booklist* admitted, "It's arguable if there really is such a thing as a 'forensic geologist,' but the resourceful and intelligent Hansen makes a terrific series heroine either way." David

Templeton, writing in the *Sonoma County Independent,* called the "Em Hansen" books "a unique and increasingly popular mystery series."

In 1994's *Tensleep,* Em is working as a mudlogger, or roustabout, on an oil rig in Meeteese, Wyoming, when two suspicious deaths take place. After visiting the scene of the crime, Em is convinced that the deaths were not accidental, leading her to use all her skill as a geologist and sleuth to find the real answer behind the tragedy. Commentators responded to Andrews's first novel with qualified praise. *Booklist* reviewer Elise Kinney lauded the novel's realistic portrayal of an oil rig's "rough work and its rougher workers," and a *Library Journal* critic praised Andrews for her "steady, thoughtful prose." Allen J. Hubin of *Armchair Detective* declared that "*Tensleep* offers a fresh setting, boldly captured, and a good mystery."

Hansen's next adventure, *A Fall in Denver,* takes place in Colorado, where she has taken a new job as a geologist for the well-known Blackfeet Oil Company. Her job there is evaluating the likelihood of finding oil in Lost Coyote Field, but after two "suicides" jump from the company's high-rise office building, she takes on the additional task of finding out the truth behind the deaths. "The author's scientific explanations make geology come to life," declared a reviewer for *Publishers Weekly.* The critic continued: "Em's first-person narrative gives the prose added punch." *New York Times Book Review* contributor Marilyn Stasio, who declared that Hansen's "unabashed naivete is endearing," also lauded Andrews's second novel for "a direct style that takes the humbug out of her scientific explanations for what's been going on at Lost Coyote." Emily Melton, in a review of *A Fall in Denver* for *Booklist,* found the novel "a gripping, original mystery" and applauded its "intelligent, appealing heroine."

The third novel in the "Em Hansen" series, 1997's *Mother Nature,* takes the amateur detective to California. Grieving the recent death of her father, the unemployed geologist reluctantly accepts an assignment from a U.S. senator from California. The senator's daughter Janet, a geologist working to remove leaking underground gasoline tanks which had been polluting local aquifers, has been found dead in a ditch, and Em sets out to solve the crime. A *Publishers Weekly* critic described *Mother Nature* as "a complex and engaging" mystery that features "snappy dialogue and fully realized characters."

In *Only Flesh and Bones* Hansen is called upon by a millionaire oilman to look into the murder of his wife and soon finds herself in the middle of a family's tangled problems. GraceAnne A. DeCandido, writing in *Booklist,* called the novel a "fine mystery with an edgy and vulnerable heroine." A critic for *Publishers Weekly* believed that, "thoughtful and uncertain, Em is especially appealing as she makes the quiet point that murder involves more than flesh and bones."

Bone Hunter finds Hansen invited to give a lecture at a paleontology conference, only to find that the scientist who invited her has been murdered. To the investigating police, Hansen seems to be the most likely suspect. "The novel is," wrote David Pitt in *Booklist,* "in addition to a fine mystery, a lively exploration of the high-stakes world of dinosaur research and a perceptive rumination on the debate between science and creationism." Templeton believed that the novel "makes you think, while remaining a grade A mystery [and] a kick-in-the-pants page-turner."

In *An Eye for Gold,* Hansen investigates the murders of witnesses in a case involving environmental issues and mining rights in Nevada. She also tries to keep her relationship with Mormon boyfriend, Ray, on track. DeCandido believed that "the mystery is complicated and absorbing, and the reader does learn a great deal about geology." Dawn Goldsmith in *Crescent Blues* online praised the novel, concluding that "Andrews tells a tense story that boasts tight writing, good pacing and an eye for detail."

The plot of *Fault Line* revolves around an earthquake in Salt Lake City, the murder of a state geologist, and behind-the-scenes machinations between developers and building inspectors. A *Kirkus Reviews* contributor maintained that Andrews "offers excellent tutelage on debris flow, fault scarps, seismic retrofits, crust slippage, and geologic hazards." "Andrews gets honors for her graphic, frightening and entertaining use of earthquake science and lore," a critic for *Publishers Weekly* added.

Andrews draws on current headlines for the plot of *Killer Dust,* in which a terrorist threat involving anthrax takes Hansen from the rural West to the Bahamas. She also has a new boyfriend, an FBI agent who suddenly leaves without an explanation. A *Publishers Weekly* critic noted that, "Ably combining science and suspense, Andrews once again entertains and educates."

BIOGRAPHICAL AND CRITICAL SOURCES:

PERIODICALS

Armchair Detective, summer, 1995, Emily Melton, review of *A Fall in Denver,* p. 245.
Booklist, April 15, 1994, p. 15; December 1, 1995, p. 611; April 15, 1998, GraceAnne A. DeCandido, review of *Only Flesh and Bones,* p. 1374; August, 1999, review of *Bone Hunter,* p. 2031; May 1, 2000, review of *A Fall in Denver,* p. 1593; August, 2000, GraceAnne A. DeCandido, review of *An Eye for Gold,* p. 2118; December 15, 2001, David Pitt, review of *Fault Line,* p. 706.
Kirkus Reviews, April 1, 1994, p. 435; October 15, 1995, p. 1457; November 1, 2001, review of *Fault Line,* p. 1516; December 15, 2002, review of *Killer Dust,* p. 1804.
Library Journal, May 1, 1994, p. 142; November 1, 1995, p. 110; April 15, 1996, p. 152; September 1, 1999, review of *Bone Hunter,* p. 237; September 1, 2000, review of *An Eye for Gold,* p. 255; January, 2002, Rex Klett, review of *Fault Line,* p. 158.
New York Times Book Review, January 7, 1996, Marilyn Stasio, review of *A Fall in Denver,* p. 24.
Publishers Weekly, May 9, 1994, p. 66; October 2, 1995, review of *A Fall in Denver,* p. 58; April 14, 1997, review of *Mother Nature,* p. 59; May 4, 1998, review of *Only Flesh and Bones,* p. 206; August 2, 1999, review of *Bone Hunter,* p. 77; August 28, 2000, review of *An Eye for Gold,* p. 60; December 10, 2001, review of *Fault Line,* p. 54; January 13, 2003, review of *Killer Dust,* p. 45.
Sonoma County Independent, September 16-23, 1999, David Templeton, "Sarah Andrews Turns up Old Bones, New Controversies."

ONLINE

Crescent Blues, http://www.crescentblues.com/ (February 10, 2003), Dawn Goldsmith, "Sarah Andrews: An Eye for Gold."
Sonoma State University Web site, http://www.sonoma.edu/ (November 10, 2003), "Sarah Andrews."*

* * *

ANDREWS, V. C.
See Andrew Neiderman

APPEL, Alfred, Jr. 1934-

PERSONAL: Born January 31, 1934, in New York, NY; son of Alfred and Beatrice (Hoffman) Appel; married Nina Schick, September 1, 1957; children: Karen Appel Oshman, Richard James. *Education:* Attended Cornell University, 1952-54; Columbia University, B.A., 1959, M.A., 1960, Ph.D., 1963.

ADDRESSES: Home—717 Greenleaf Ave., Wilmette, IL 60091. *Office*—Department of English, Northwestern University, Evanston, IL 60201.

CAREER: Columbia University, New York, NY, instructor in English, 1961-62; Stanford University, Stanford, CA, assistant professor of English, 1963-68; Northwestern University, Evanston, IL, assistant professor, 1968-69, associate professor, 1969-74, professor of English, 1974, currently emeritus professor of English. *Military service:* U.S. Army, 1955-57.

MEMBER: Modern Language Association of America, Philological Association of the Pacific Coast.

AWARDS, HONORS: Guggenheim fellow, 1972; Best Creative Essay Award, Arts Council of Illinois, 1974; Rockefeller Foundation fellow, 1976.

WRITINGS:

A Season of Dreams: The Fiction of Eudora Welty, Louisiana State University Press (Baton Rouge, LA), 1965.
(Editor) John DeForest, *Witching Times,* College and University Press (New Haven, CT), 1967.
(Editor) *Vladimir Nabokov: A Collection of Critical Essays,* Prentice-Hall (New York, NY), 1969.
(Editor and contributor) *The Annotated Lolita,* McGraw (New York, NY), 1970, revised and updated, Vintage Books (New York, NY), 1991.
(Editor with Charles Newman) *Nabokov: Criticism, Reminiscences, Translations, Tributes,* Northwestern University Press (Evanston, IL), 1970.
Nabokov's Dark Cinema, Oxford University Press (New York, NY), 1974.
(Editor, with Simon Karlinsky) *The Bitter Air of Exile: Russian Writers in the West, 1922-1972,* revised edition, University of California Press (Berkeley, CA), 1977.

Signs of Life, Knopf (New York, NY), 1983.
The Art of Celebration: Twentieth-Century Painting, Literature, Sculpture, Photography, and Jazz, Knopf (New York, NY), 1992.
Jazz Modernism: From Ellington and Armstrong to Matisse and Joyce, Knopf (New York, NY), 2002.

Contributor to books, including *Nabokov: The Man and His Work,* University of Wisconsin Press (Madison, WI), 1967; *The Single Voice,* 1969; *A Book of Things about Vladimir Nabokov,* 1974; *Vladimir Nabokov: A Tribute,* 1979; and *Nabokov's Fifth Arc,* 1982. Contributor to periodicals, including *Denver Quarterly.*

SIDELIGHTS: Alfred Appel, Jr., emeritus professor of English at Northwestern University, is the author of books on literature and music. Perhaps his best-known work is *Jazz Modernism: From Ellington and Armstrong to Matisse and Joyce,* which discusses the influence of jazz greats such as Louis Armstrong, Duke Ellington, Charlie Parker, and Billie Holiday on American culture. As David Yaffe wrote in the *Nation,* jazz artists "changed the way Americans think about language, race, style and gender." Appel links jazz to other artistic fields, finding its influence on visual art, literature, and philosophy. Yaffe wrote, "Appel is an entertaining and learned reader, and it is a treat to walk through his record collection bookshelves and art prints and get his witty and beguiling asides on them."

In *Commentary,* Terry Teachout explains Appel's thesis that "classic jazz (1920-1950) . . . is indeed part of 'the great modernist tradition in the arts.'" Teachout continued, "Hitherto known mainly for his writings on Vladimir Nabokov, Appel is a highly knowledgeable connoisseur of jazz and the visual arts. *Jazz Modernism* is a somewhat idiosyncratic work, both in its richly allusive style and in some of its terminology. Still, it is to the best of my knowledge the first sustained attempt by any critic, musical or otherwise, to locate jazz in the larger context of modernism."

BIOGRAPHICAL AND CRITICAL SOURCES:

PERIODICALS

Antioch Review, summer, 1993, review of *The Art of Celebration: Twentieth-Century Painting, Literature, Sculpture, Photography, and Jazz,* p. 472.

Booklist, September 1, 2002, Donna Seaman, review of *Jazz Modernism: From Ellington and Armstrong to Matisse and Joyce,* p. 36.

Chronicle of Higher Education, November 4, 1992, review of *The Art of Celebration,* p. A12.

Commentary, Terry Teachout, review of *Jazz Modernism,* p. 49.

Kirkus Reviews, September 1, 1992, review of *The Art of Celebration,* p. 1095.

Library Journal, October 15, 1992, Joan Levin, review of *The Art of Celebration,* p. 66; August, 2002, James Perone, review of *Jazz Modernism,* p. 96.

Nation, October 21, 2002, David Yaffe, review of *Jazz Modernism,* p. 31.

New Statesman, August 29, 1975.

New York Times Book Review, December 20, 1992, Nicholas Fox Weber, review of *The Art of Celebration,* p. 10; December 5, 1993, review of *The Art of Celebration,* p. 42; June 6, 1993, review of *The Art of Celebration,* p. 34.

Publishers Weekly, August 24, 1992, review of *The Art of Celebration,* p. 68; July 8, 2002, review of *Jazz Modernism,* p. 40.

Saturday Review, December 18, 1965; June 13, 1970.

Times Literary Supplement, May 16, 1975.

Tribune Books (Chicago, IL), October 11, 1992, review of *The Art of Celebration,* p. 6.

Washington Post Book World, June 14, 1970.*

* * *

APPLEBOME, Peter

PERSONAL: Born in New York, NY; married Mary Catherine Bounds; children: Ben, Emma. *Education:* Duke University, graduated, 1971; Northwestern University, M.A. (journalism), 1974.

ADDRESSES: Agent—c/o Author Mail, Harcourt, 15 East 26th St., New York, NY 10003-4793. *E-mail*—peappl@nytimes.com.

CAREER: Journalist. Staff member for periodicals in Texas, including *Corpus Christi Caller, Dallas Morning News,* and *Texas Monthly Magazine,* 1976-86; *New York Times,* New York, NY, from national correspondent to bureau chief, 1986-89, bureau chief in Atlanta, GA, 1989-94, national education correspondent in Atlanta, beginning 1994, currently in New York, NY, office.

AWARDS, HONORS: Winner, Bad Hemingway Competition, 1987.

WRITINGS:

Dixie Rising: How the South Is Shaping American Values, Politics, and Culture, Time Books (New York, NY), 1996.

(With Georg R. Sheets, L. Douglas Wilder, and Charles Reagan Wilson) *The Grand Review: The Civil War Continues to Shape America,* Bold Print (York, PA), 2000.

Scout's Honor: A Father's Unlikely Foray into the Woods, Harcourt (New York, NY), 2003.

Contributor to periodicals, including *Wall Street Journal, Washington Monthly, New Republic,* and *Texas Observer.*

SIDELIGHTS: A transplanted Northerner, journalist Peter Applebome has spent several decades living in and writing about the South. His *Dixie Rising: How the South Is Shaping American Values, Politics, and Culture* is the offshoot of a series of newspaper articles that Applebome wrote for the *New York Times* in 1994. Here Applebome posits that many of the South's ideas are behind U.S. thought in the 1990s. "Only the blind could look at America at the century's end and not see the fingerprint of the South on almost every aspect of the nation's soul," Applebome declares in his book. Among the topics he discusses in *Dixie Rising* are the appeal of former columnist Lewis Grizzard, national conservatism, racial preoccupations, country music, the gun ownership debate, and the spread of states' rights groups and Southern Baptist congregations.

In the words of David Greising, the Atlanta bureau chief of *Business Week,* Applebome "delivers a nuanced, insightful, and sometimes even affectionate appreciation of the South." Greising also remarked on the work's weaknesses, maintaining that "Applebome sometimes confuses coincidence with cause and effect." Karal Ann Marling in the *New York Times* noted that "Mr. Applebome has marshaled impressive firsthand evidence to prove his point, but beneath the slick political surface of his argument lurks a corrosive cultural crisis that has not been so much analyzed as viewed in passing, from the front seat of a speeding pickup truck." In the *New York Times Book*

Review, historian William H. Chafe described *Dixie Rising* as a "thoughtful and provocative book," one that "offers a striking thesis and a searching question."

Applebome completed a much more personal book, *Scout's Honor: A Father's Unlikely Foray into the Woods,* which is about his changing relationship with his son, Ben. Unlike his father, who was into sports as a youth and was not a fan of nature hikes and camping, Ben fell in love with the Boy Scouts at an early age. Applebome had always thought that the Scouts were rather "dorky," and he objected to the uniforms the boys were forced to wear, which he considered emblematic of a kind of "faux fascism." Nevertheless, he did not want to be seen as a bad father, so when Ben became involved in the Scouts, Applebome dutifully joined in on the activities and was a Scoutmaster for three years. To his own surprise, he came to appreciate what the Boy Scouts could do for young boys, although he never got used to the lack of indoor plumbing when his troop went camping. Writing about his experiences with his son in *Scout's Honor,* Applebome not only tells some humorous and touching anecdotes about the father-son bonding experience, but also provides some history about scouting and insights about the recent controversy involving the organization's refusal to allow homosexuals into its membership.

Although a *Publishers Weekly* reviewer felt that Applebome "too easily dismisses" the homosexual issue involving the Scouts, the critic praised *Scout's Honor* as an "engaging book" that is a "loving and often amusing description of his son's scouting adventures." *Christian Science Monitor* writer David Conrads, meanwhile, found Applebome's history of scouting to be "fascinating," especially the fact that the Boy Scouts were founded not in America, but in England, by the rather eccentric—and, Applebome implies, homosexually suppressed—Robert Baden-Powell. The author also talks about two early American Boy Scout leaders, naturalist Daniel Carter Beard and writer/artist Ernest Thompson Seton, both of whom were almost as quirky as Baden-Powell. But the highlight of the book is Applebome's conversion from someone who believed in competitive sports to a father who comes to realize the benefits of a less macho viewpoint. As Applebome described his changing attitude, "I liked being in a group that . . . wasn't about whose kid was going to be treated like royalty because he had the best fastball and whose was just tolerated because he

wasn't a star." In the end, becoming involved in Scouting proved to be just as important in easing Applebome's journey through a mid-life crisis as it was for his bond with his son.

BIOGRAPHICAL AND CRITICAL SOURCES:

PERIODICALS

Atlanta Journal-Constitution, May 18, 2003, Don O'Briant, "Scouting As a Bridge between Father and Son."

Booklist, October 15, 1996, p. 401.

Business Week, December 2, 1996, p. 22.

Chicago Tribune, June 8, 2003, "Scout's Honor."

Christian Science Monitor, May 22, 2003, David Conrads, "On My Honor, I Will Do My Best; Peter Applebome Thought He Was Prepared for Fatherhood, till His Son Wanted to Be a Boy Scout," p. 20.

Dallas Morning News, July 23, 2003, David Tarrant, "For Author's Son, Scouting Wasn't Just a Phase After All."

Economist, February 15, 1997, review of *Dixie Rising: How the South Is Shaping American Values, Politics, and Culture,* p. S11.

Kirkus Reviews, September 1, 1996, p. 1284.

Library Journal, September 15, 1996, p. 82.

New York Times, December 20, 1996, p. C37.

New York Times Book Review, December 1, 1996, p. 26; June 15, 2003, Diane Scharper, review of *Scout's Honor: A Father's Unlikely Foray into the Woods,* p. 14.

Publishers Weekly, September 23, 1996, p. 62; April 7, 2003, review of *Scout's Honor,* p. 58.

Washington Monthly, November, 1996, Jon Meacham, review of *Dixie Rising,* p. 51.

ONLINE

Peter Applebome Web site, http://www.peterapplebome.com/ (July 19, 2003).*

*   *   *

ATKINS, (Arthur) Harold (Foweraker) 1910-
(J. P. Jackson)

PERSONAL: Born March 27, 1910, in Nottingham, England; son of Horace George and Grace Adeline (Foweraker) Atkins; married Lily Buxton (in social services), September 17, 1938 (died, November 1998). *Education:* Balliol College, Oxford, B.A., 1938, M.A., 1942; further graduate study at London School of Economics and Political Science. *Politics:* Social Democrat. *Religion:* Church of England. *Hobbies and other interests:* Archaeology, history, English literature, music, theatre, ballet, World War II espionage and resistance movements, science.

ADDRESSES: Home—2 Hallgate, Blackheath Park, London SE3, England.

CAREER: Nottingham Journal, Nottingham, England, reporter, 1928, scientific and radio correspondent, 1929-35, assistant drama critic, 1931; Reuters, London, England, subeditor at general news desk, 1938-39; *Daily Dispatch,* Manchester, England, subeditor, 1940-41; *Manchester Guardian,* Manchester, foreign subeditor, 1941-44; *Evening News,* London, special writer, 1944-49, political correspondent, 1944-45; *Star,* London, news and diary writer, 1949-51; Ministry of National Insurance, London, headquarters press and public relations officer, 1951-53; *Daily Telegraph,* London, foreign subeditor, 1954-55, features subeditor, 1955-56, arts and leader page subeditor and contributor to and subeditor of "London Day by Day," 1956-76, book reviewer, 1956-81, and assistant theatre critic, 1962-81; freelance writer, 1976—. Press officer for National Assistance Board, 1951-53; deputy director of Visual Education Research Group, 1956-59.

MEMBER: National Union of Journalists (life member), National Liberal Club, Oxford Union Club (life member).

WRITINGS:

Sinister Smith (novel), Duckworth (London, England), 1938.
(With Archie Newman) *Beecham Stories,* Robson Books (London, England), 1978.
(With Peter Cotes) *The Barbirollis: A Musical Marriage,* Robson Books (London, England), 1983.

Contributor of articles and reviews to magazines, including *Socialist Commentary, Contemporary Review,* and *British Weekly,* and to newspapers (sometimes under pseudonym J. P. Jackson).

WORK IN PROGRESS: With Peter Cotes, a short life of John Barbirolli, former conductor of Le Halle Orchestra and the New York Philharmonic Orchestra.

SIDELIGHTS: In addition to having a distinguished career in British journalism and public relations, Harold Atkins has also published in book form. His first work, *Sinister Smith,* appeared during the late 1930s. More recently, however, he is better known for his 1983 collaboration with Peter Cotes on a biography of famous British orchestra conductor Sir John Barbirolli and his oboist wife, the former Evelyn Rothwell: *The Barbirollis: A Musical Marriage. Publishers Weekly* reviewer Genevieve Stuttaford described *The Barbirollis* as an "affectionate, intimate biography," while a writer for *Choice* appreciated the "masterful juggling of details of the two musicians' lives."

BIOGRAPHICAL AND CRITICAL SOURCES:

PERIODICALS

Choice, December, 1984, review of *The Barbirollis: A Musical Marriage,* p. 566.
Library Journal, September 15, 1984, review of *The Barbirollis,* p. 1760.
Publishers Weekly, July 27, 1984, Genevieve Stuttaford, review of *The Barbirollis,* p. 131.*

* * *

AYERS, Edward L(ynn) 1953-

PERSONAL: Born January 22, 1953, in Asheville, NC; son of Tom (an automobile salesman) and Billie L. (a teacher; maiden name, Buckner) Ayers; married Abby Brown, August 24, 1974; children: Nathaniel. *Education:* University of Tennessee, Knoxville, B.A., 1974; Yale University, M.A., 1977, Ph.D., 1980.

ADDRESSES: Home—1770 Dudley Mountain Road, Charlottesville, VA 22901. *Office*—Department of History, 201 Randall Hall, University of Virginia, Charlottesville, VA 22903. *E-mail*—ela@virginia.edu.

CAREER: University of Virginia, Charlottesville, assistant professor of history, 1980-86, associate professor of history, 1986-90, professor of history, 1990-92, Hugh P. Kelly professor of history, 1993—, dean of the college and Graduate School of Arts and Sciences, 2001—.

MEMBER: Organization of American Historians, American Historical Association, Southern Historical Association, Phi Beta Kappa.

AWARDS, HONORS: Grant from American Philosophical Society, 1984; fellow of National Endowment for the Humanities, 1985; finalist for Pulitzer Prize and National Book Award, 1993; member of the Academy of Arts and Sciences, 2000; winner of the E-Lincoln Prize of the Gilder-Lehrman/Gettysburg College Center on the Civil War; winner of the J. Franklin Jameson Prize of the American Historical Association; National Professor of the Year, 2003, Carnegie Foundation.

WRITINGS:

Vengeance and Justice: Crime and Punishment in the Nineteenth-Century American South, Oxford University Press (New York, NY), 1984.
(Editor, with John C. Willis) *The Edge of the South: Life in Nineteenth-Century Virginia,* University Press of Virginia (Charlottesville, VA), 1991.
The Promise of the New South: Life after Reconstruction, Oxford University Press (New York, NY), 1992.
Southern Crossing: A History of the American South, 1877-1906, Oxford University Press (New York, NY), 1995.
(With others) *All Over the Map: Rethinking American Regions,* John Hopkins University Press (Baltimore, MD), 1996.
(Editor, with Bradley C. Mittendorf) *The Oxford Book of the American South: Testimony, Memory, and Fiction,* Oxford University Press (New York, NY), 1997.
(Editor) *A House Divided: A Century of Great Civil War Quotations,* Wiley (New York, NY), 1997.
Momentous Events in Small Places: The Coming of the Civil War in Two American Communities, Marquette University Press (Milwaukee, WI), 1997.
(With others) *American Passages: A History of the United States,* Harcourt (New York, NY), 2000, 2nd edition, Thomson/Wadsworth (Belmont, CA), 2004.
(With Robert Weise) *U.S. History Documents Collection to Accompany American Passages: A History of the United States,* Harcourt (New York, NY), 2000.

(With Anne S. Rubin) *Valley of the Shadow: Two Communities in the American Civil War,* Norton (New York, NY), 2000.
In the Presence of Mine Enemies: War in the Heart of America, 1859-1863 (Volume 1 of "The Valley of the Shadow" series), Norton (New York, NY), 2003.

WORK IN PROGRESS: What Caused the Civil War and Other Essays, publication by Norton expected in 2005; Volume 2 of "The Valley of the Shadow" series.

SIDELIGHTS: Edward L. Ayers is a historian whose area of expertise is the American South. His books on this subject include *Vengeance and Justice: Crime and Punishment in the Nineteenth-Century American South, The Promise of the New South: Life after Reconstruction,* and *In the Presence of Mine Enemies: War in the Heart of America, 1859-1863.* Ayers once told *CA:* "History appeals to me because it tries, at its best, to understand the totality of a society—something no other social science or humanistic study even attempts. I am drawn to American Southern history in particular because the South is so complex and enigmatic, and because the Southern past has been filled with so much suffering and triumph over suffering. Both of those conditions have a great deal to teach us."

To demonstrate the very different effect that the Civil War had on the North and South, Ayers examined the history of two communities that stand fairly close geographically, but which experienced the war and its aftermath very differently. Augusta County, Virginia, and Franklin County, Pennsylvania, are only about two hundred miles apart, lying at either end of the Shenandoah Valley, separated by the Mason-Dixon line. The two localities shared many similarities before the war. During and after the conflict, however, great differences developed between them. In his book *In the Presence of Mine Enemies,* Ayers focuses on the public events of the time and the ways they affected the everyday life of these two areas. An *Atlantic Monthly* reviewer, Benjamin Schwarz, found the book's juxtaposition of large and small events "sometimes engrossing," yet he found that at times the author's "narrative ambitions exceed his writerly abilities." This view was not shared by Gilbert Taylor of *Booklist,* who wrote that "Ayers unfolds this historical process with penetrating analysis and relevant quotations, emphasizing the anxiety, excitement, and misery that the war provoked." *In the Presence of Mine Enemies* was also highly recommended by Carver Edwards, who in a *Library Journal* review called it an "original and gracefully written work, based on exhaustive primary research," and added that it "should be required reading for Civil War enthusiasts and scholars alike."

BIOGRAPHICAL AND CRITICAL SOURCES:

PERIODICALS

American Historical Review, February, 1985, D. Bruce Dickson, Jr., review of *Vengeance and Justice: Crime and Punishment in the Nineteenth-Century American South,* p. 217; June, 1993, Steven M. Stowe, review of *The Promise of the New South: Life after Reconstruction,* p. 951; October, 2001, Stephen V. Ash, review of *Valley of the Shadow: Two Communities in the American Civil War,* p. 1319.

Atlantic Monthly, December, 1997, review of *Oxford Book of the American South: Testimony, Memory, and Fiction,* pp. 117-126; July-August, 2003, Benjamin Schwarz, review of *In the Presence of Mine Enemies: War in the Heart of America, 1859-1863,* p. 128.

Booklist, May 1, 1997, Brad Hooper, review of *Oxford Book of the American South,* p. 1475; July, 2003, Gilbert Taylor, review of *In the Presence of Mine Enemies,* p. 1859.

Journal of American History, March, 1985, David J. Bodenhamer, review of *Vengeance and Justice,* p. 882; March, 1993, Richard Lowe, review of *The Edge of the South: Life in Nineteenth-Century Virginia,* p. 1599; September, 1993, Earl Lewis, review of *The Promise of the New South,* p. 697; December, 1996, John L. Thomas, review of *All Over the Map: Rethinking American Regions,* p. 985.

Journal of Southern History, February, 1993, Mitchell Snay, review of *The Edge of the South,* p. 126; August, 1993, Howard N. Rabinowitz, review of *The Promise of the New South,* p. 505; February, 1997, Carl Abbott, review of *All Over the Map,* p. 217; May, 2003, Richard Lowe, review of *Valley of the Shadow,* p. 428.

Library Journal, July, 1992, Charles K. Piehl, review of *The Promise of the New South,* p. 98; April 15, 1997, Charles C. Hay III, review of *Oxford Book of the American South,* p. 82; June 15, 2003, John Carver Edwards, review of *In the Presence of Mine Enemies,* p. 84.

New York Review of Books, March 25, 1993, George M. Frederickson, review of *The Promise of the New South,* p. 40.

New York Times Book Review, August 30, 1992, Pete Daniel, review of *The Promise of the New South,* p. 18.

Publishers Weekly, December 23, 1983, review of *Vengeance and Justice,* p. 48; May 26, 2003, review of *In the Presence of Mine Enemies,* p. 57.

Social Science Quarterly, Randall K. Wilson, review of *All Over the Map,* p. 1023.

Washington Post, November 17, 1992, Ken Ringle, "Historian of the Unsung South," p. D1.

B

BAKER, Jean H(ogarth Harvey) 1933-

PERSONAL: Born February 9, 1933, in Baltimore, MD; daughter of F. Barton (an insurance agent) and Rose Lindsay (Hopkins) Harvey; married Ralph Robinson Baker (a physician), September 12, 1953; children: Susan Dixon, Robinson Scott, Robert Walker, Jean Harvey. *Education:* Goucher College, A.B., 1961; Johns Hopkins University, M.A., 1965, Ph.D., 1971. *Politics:* Democrat. *Religion:* Episcopalian. *Hobbies and other interests:* Tennis, swimming, and reading mystery stories.

ADDRESSES: Home—8717 McDonogh Rd., Baltimore, MD 21208-1021. *Office*—Department of History, Goucher College, Towson, MD 21204. *E-mail*—jbaker@goucher.edu.

CAREER: Notre Dame College, Baltimore, MD, instructor of history, 1967-69; Goucher College, Towson, MD, instructor, 1969, assistant professor, 1969-75, associate professor of history, 1975-78, professor of history, 1979-82, Elizabeth Todd professor of history, 1981—. *Maryland Historical Magazine*, editor, 1979.

MEMBER: Organization of American Historians, American Historical Association, Berkshire Conference of Women Historians, Phi Beta Kappa.

AWARDS, HONORS: American Council of Learned Societies fellow, 1976; Goucher College Faculty Teaching prize recipient, 1979; National Endowment for the Humanities fellow, 1982; Berkshire Prize in History, 1983, for *Affairs of Party: The Political Culture of Northern Democrats in the Mid-Nineteenth Century;* Willie Lee Rose prize in Southern history, 1989; Newberry Library fellow, 1991.

WRITINGS:

The Politics of Continuity, Johns Hopkins University Press (Baltimore, MD), 1973.

Ambivalent Americans: The Know-Nothing Party in Maryland, Johns Hopkins University Press (Baltimore, MD), 1976.

Affairs of Party: The Political Culture of Northern Democrats in the Mid-Nineteenth Century, Cornell University Press (Ithaca, NY), 1983, new edition, with new preface, Fordham University Press (New York, NY), 1998.

Mary Todd Lincoln: A Biography, Norton (New York, NY), 1987.

The Stevensons: A Biography of an American Family, Norton (New York, NY), 1996.

The Lincoln Marriage: Beyond the Battle of Quotations, Civil War Institute (Gettysburg, PA), 1999.

(Editor, with David Herbert Donald and Michael F. Holt) *The Civil War and Reconstruction*, Norton (New York, NY), 2001.

(Editor) *Votes for Women: The Struggle for Suffrage Revisited*, Oxford University Press (New York, NY), 2002.

Feminist Sisters: Profiles of the American Suffragists, Norton (New York, NY), 2003.

James Buchanan, Times Books (New York, NY), 2004.

Also author of *Maryland: A History;* author of lecture "Not Much of Me: Abraham Lincoln As a Typical American," Louis A. Warren Lincoln Library and Museum (Fort Wayne, IN), 1988, part of the Alfred Whital Stern Collection of Lincolniana, Library of Congress, delivered at the 11th Annual R. Gerard Mc-Murtry Lecture, Fort Wayne Museum of Art, 1988.

SIDELIGHTS: A respected feminist historian and history professor at Goucher College in Maryland, Jean H. Baker is an acclaimed writer of historical biographies. Her in-depth approach displays comprehensive research as she discerns cultural and sociological influences to support feminist interpretations of the consequences of a male-dominated order in history. Although critics sometimes discount her feminist interpretations as limited in deciphering the complexities of historical personalities, many commend her accomplished prose which recounts the sights and sounds of each era gracefully.

One of Baker's earlier works focuses on the social dynamics of the Democratic Party in the Northern states before, during, and after the Civil War. Published in 1983, and then reissued in 1998, *Affairs of Party: The Political Culture of Northern Democrats in the Mid-Nineteenth Century* examines "the education, political thought, and behavior" of Northern party members, in the words of Heather Cox Richardson in the *Historian.* Explaining that Northern Democrats of that period endorsed "personal liberty, small government, [and] states' rights," but that their sense of nationalism allowed them to support the Union side in the Civil War, the critic noted that the volume "shines brightest when it explores the relationship of education, minstrel shows, and party rituals to the Democratic mindset."

Mary Todd Lincoln: A Biography, published in 1987, investigates the work of Baker's predecessors in assessing the life of this puzzling woman. Baker includes meticulously collected letters by scholars to further understanding of the First Lady as a gifted woman whose life was constricted by her times and whose personage was damaged by male-dominated historical interpretation.

Her telling story of the life of Mary Todd Lincoln is considered a comprehensive, but not wholly definitive, work by critics. In her analysis of Baker's book,

American Historical Review writer Anne Firor Scott stated that "Feminist historians can find many better cases than this to illuminate the real (as opposed to the self-imposed) consequences of a male-dominated social order." She nonetheless wrote that *Mary Todd Lincoln* will "undoubtedly become the accepted interpretation of Mary Todd Lincoln's troubled life," and praised Baker's prose and comprehensive research.

The Stevensons: A Biography of an American Family, Baker's 1996 chronicle of the Stevenson family, spans two centuries in relating the lineage of a clan who exemplified American liberalism in Illinois. The eldest, Adlai Stevenson, was Grover Cleveland's second vice president and Adlai Stevenson III was a senator. The lives of the Stevenson women mirror emerging societal patterns. Commendatory but unbiased in her tone, Baker focuses especially on the figure of Adlai Stevenson II. Baker's presentation of the one-time governor and failed presidential candidate who confronted McCarthyism in the Red scare era and the Soviets during the Cuban Missile crisis heightens her familial theme.

Richard Norton Smith reflected in the *Chicago Tribune,* "Baker's sweeping narrative, beautifully written and scrupulously evenhanded, does full justice to Stevenson and his people." *New York Times Book Review* critic Richard Norton Smith noted Baker's "sharp eye for theme and irony," while Charles H. Zwicker in *Presidential Studies Quarterly* praised "Baker's thorough study of the Stevensons."

Baker has also edited volumes of history. With David Herbert Donald and Michael F. Holt, she helped compile the 2001 revision of *The Civil War and Reconstruction.* Their version includes more material on the lives of women during the period, as well as other updates. In 2002, Baker edited *Votes for Women: The Struggle for Suffrage Revisited,* presenting essays covering the years between 1850 and 1920, when women were granted the vote in the United States. Baker provides an introductory essay which explains how the American women's suffrage movement interacted with other concurrent events in U.S. history.

BIOGRAPHICAL AND CRITICAL SOURCES:

PERIODICALS

American Heritage, spring, 1987, review of *Mary Todd Lincoln: A Biography,* p. 34.

American Historical Review, February, 1989, review of *Mary Todd Lincoln,* p. 221.

Booklist, August, 1987, review of *Mary Todd Lincoln,* p. 1713.

Book World, October 4, 1987, review of *Mary Todd Lincoln,* p. 4; July 23, 1989, review of *Mary Todd Lincoln,* p. 12; February 25, 1996, review of *The Stevensons: A Biography of an American Family,* p. 3.

Chicago Tribune, February 25, 1996, p. 47.

Choice, February, 1988, review of *Mary Todd Lincoln,* p. 959; July, 1996, review of *The Stevensons,* p. 1856; December, 1998, review of *Affairs of Party: The Political Culture of Northern Democrats in the Mid-Nineteenth Century,* p. 740.

Christian Science Monitor, September 3, 1987, review of *Mary Todd Lincoln,* p. 20; April 8, 1996, review of *The Stevensons,* p. 13.

Contemporary Review, October, 1996, review of *The Stevensons,* p. 220.

Historian, fall, 2000, Heather Cox Richardson, review of *Affairs of Party,* p. 135.

History: Reviews of New Books, September, 1983, review of *Affairs of Party,* p. 228; summer, 1996, review of *The Stevensons,* p. 189.

Journal of American History, December, 1983, review of *Affairs of Party,* p. 668; December, 1998, review of *Mary Todd Lincoln,* p. 953.

Journal of American Studies, August, 1984, review of *Affairs of Party,* p. 291; December, 1990, review of *Mary Todd Lincoln,* p. 415.

Journal of Interdisciplinary History, winter, 1985, review of *Affairs of Party,* p. 544.

Journal of Southern History, May, 1986, review of *Affairs of Party,* p. 307; February, 1989, review of *Mary Todd Lincoln,* p. 128.

Kirkus Reviews, June 15, 1987, review of *Mary Todd Lincoln,* p. 899; December 15, 1995, review of *The Stevensons,* p. 1740.

Library Journal, February 15, 1983, review of *Affairs of Party,* p. 394; August, 1987, review of *Mary Todd Lincoln,* p. 118; February 1, 1996, review of *The Stevensons,* p. 82.

Los Angeles Times, August 7, 1987.

National Review, July 31, 1987, review of *Mary Todd Lincoln,* p. 48.

New Yorker, November 9, 1987, review of *Mary Todd Lincoln,* p. 156.

New York Times, August 25, 1987, review of *Mary Todd Lincoln,* p. 23.

New York Times Book Review, September 13, 1987, review of *Mary Todd Lincoln,* p. 38; April 14, 1996, review of *The Stevensons,* p. 20.

Presidential Studies Quarterly, Charles H. Zwicker, review of *The Stevensons.* pp. 460-462.

Publishers Weekly, June 19, 1987, review of *Mary Todd Lincoln,* p. 109; January 1, 1996, review of *The Stevensons,* p. 62.

Reference & Research Book News, review of *Affairs of Party,* p. 141.

Tribune Books (Chicago, IL), August 9, 1987, review of *Mary Todd Lincoln,* p. 3; February 25, 1996, review of *The Stevensons,* p. 1.

Virginia Quarterly Review, spring, 1998, review of *Mary Todd Lincoln,* p. 50.

Washington Post, February 25, 1996.

Wilson Library Bulletin, January, 1998, review of *Mary Todd Lincoln,* p. 91.

*   *   *

BARLOW, Maude (Victoria) 1947-

PERSONAL: Born May 24, 1947, in Toronto, Ontario, Canada; daughter of William Thomas (a criminologist) and Flora (a homemaker; maiden name, Wilkie) McGrath; married Andrew Davis (a lawyer), July 29, 1983; children: Charles Barlow, William Barlow. *Education:* Carleton University, B.A., 1972.

ADDRESSES: Home—525 C Bay St., Ottawa, Ontario K1R 6B4, Canada. *Office*—Council of Canadians, 251 Laurier Ave. W, Ottawa, Ontario K1P 5J6, Canada. *E-mail*—mbarlow@canadians.org.

CAREER: Women Associates Consulting Inc., vice president, 1975-80; City of Ottawa, Ontario, director of equal opportunities, 1980-83; senior adviser to Prime Minister Pierre Trudeau, Ottawa, 1983-84; Council of Canadians, Ottawa, chairperson, 1988—. Visiting scholar, University of Ottawa, 1991. Member of council of advisers, Canadian Centre for Arms Control and Disarmament; consultant on equality and social justice issues; Canadian Action Network, co-founder.

AWARDS, HONORS: Ontario Teachers' Federation fellow; honorary Doctorate of Laws, Memorial University; awards from British Columbia Teachers' Federation, Ontario Teachers' Federation, Women Teachers'

Maude Barlow

Association of Ontario, and Ontario Public Teachers' Association.

WRITINGS:

Parcel of Rogues: How Free Trade Is Failing Canada, Key Porter (Toronto, Ontario, Canada), 1990.

(With Bruce Campbell) *Take Back the Nation,* Key Porter (Toronto, Ontario, Canada), 1991.

(With others) *Meeting the Global Challenge: Competitive Position and Strategic Response,* Captus Press (North York, Ontario, Canada), 1992.

(With Bruce Campbell) *Take Back the Nation 2: Meeting the Threat of NAFTA,* Key Porter (Toronto, Ontario, Canada), 1993.

(With Heather Jane-Robertson) *Class Warfare: The Assault on Canada's Schools,* Key Porter (Toronto, Ontario, Canada), 1994.

(With Bruce Campbell) *Straight through the Heart: How the Liberals Abandoned the Just Society,* HarperCollins (Toronto, Ontario, Canada), 1995.

(With James Winter) *The Big, Black Book: The Essential Views of Conrad and Barbara Amiel Black,* General Distribution Services (Buffalo, NY), 1997.

(With Tony Clarke) *MAI: The Multilateral Agreement on Investment and the Threat to Canadian Sovereignty,* Stoddart (Toronto, Ontario, Canada), 1997, Stoddart (New York, NY), 1998.

The Fight of My Life: Confessions of an Unrepentant Canadian (autobiography), Harper Collins (Toronto, Ontario, Canada), 1998.

(With Elizabeth May) *Frederick Street: Life and Death on Canada's Love Canal,* HarperCollins (Toronto, Ontario, Canada), 2000.

(With Tony Clarke) *Global Showdown: How the New Activists Are Fighting Global Corporate Rule,* Stoddart (Toronto, Ontario, Canada), 2001.

(With Tony Clarke) *Blue Gold: The Fight to Stop the Corporate Theft of the World's Water,* Norton (New York, NY), 2002.

Profit Is Not the Cure. A Citizen's Guide to Saving Medicare, McClelland & Stewart (Toronto, Ontario, Canada), 2002.

SIDELIGHTS: Maude Barlow is a Canadian writer, political activist, and policy critic. She has written or coauthored a number of books that reflect her advocacy of issues involving the environment, social programs, and public education. In 1995's *Straight through the Heart: How the Liberals Abandoned the Just Society,* Barlow and coauthor Bruce Campbell create a picture of a poverty-stricken Canada which has been bulldozed by the federal liberal party and the business elite. The authors contend that present-day liberals have compromised their ideals to please the business sector. A contributor to *Maclean's* noted that the authors put forth a convincing and "stridently" presented case against Canadian liberals.

Barlow takes up an environmental cause in her 2000 book *Frederick Street: Life and Death on Canada's Love Canal.* Together with coauthor Elizabeth May, the author tells the story of a steel-making plant in Sydney, Nova Scotia, that has devastated the local environment and wreaked havoc on the health of area residents. Barlow argues that the toxic plant has been in operation for a century and that the Canadian government has looked the other way. Parker Barss Donham in *Canadian Geographic* commented that "Barlow and May delineate the intricacies of steel-making and the insidious impact of polycyclic aromatic hydrocarbons with admirable clarity."

However, he also noted that the efforts of officials to attempt to clean up the plant are largely ignored in this book.

Another environmental book by Barlow is 2002's *Blue Gold: The Fight to Stop the Corporate Theft of the World's Water.* "This well-researched book provides a sobering, in-depth look at the growing scarcity of fresh water and the increasing privatization and corporate control of this nonrenewable resource," explained Margaret Aycock in her review for *Library Journal.* Barlow and coauthor Tony Clarke argue that since water is a basic human necessity, it is unlike other commodities and should not be given over to private parties. A critic in *Publishers Weekly* noted that "the authors marshal an impressive amount of evidence that corporate profits are increasingly drinking up precious water resources."

Barlow once told *CA:* "I do not view myself as a professional writer. I am an activist for social justice issues who became very involved against the free trade agreement and the corporate agenda it represents. The books I wrote were a response to the need to preserve my country, its heritage and distinct values."

BIOGRAPHICAL AND CRITICAL SOURCES:

PERIODICALS

Canadian Dimension, July-August, 1996, Kathleen O'Hara, "Building for the Long Term: Maude Barlow and the Council of Canadians," p. 17; September, 2001, David Orton, "Globalization from Below; or, Ending Industrial Civilization," p. 42.
Canadian Geographic, May, 2000, Parker Barss Donham, "Grappling with Sydney's Tarred Legacy," p. 89.
Library Journal, April 15, 2002, Margaret Aycock, review of *Blue Gold: The Fight to Stop the Corporate Theft of the World's Water,* p. 121.
Maclean's, December 4, 1995, Anthony Wilson-Smith, review of *Straight through the Heart: How the Liberals Abandoned the Just Society,* p. 82.
Multinational Monitor, April, 1999, interview with Maude Barlow, p. 19.
Northern Ontario Business, January, 2001, Graham Clayton, "Economic Literacy," p. 6.
Publishers Weekly, April 1, 2002, review of *Blue Gold,* p. 72.

ONLINE

Canspeak, http://www.canspeak.com/ (July 9, 2002), "Maude Barlow."
Writer's Union of Canada, http://www.writersunion.ca/ (July 9, 2002), "Maude Barlow."*

*   *   *

BAYM, Nina 1936-

PERSONAL: Born June 14, 1936, in Princeton, NJ; daughter of Leo and Frances (Levinson) Zippin; married Gordon Baym, June, 1958 (marriage ended); married Jack Stillinger, May 21, 1971; children: Nancy, Geoffrey. *Ethnicity:* "Caucasian of eastern European descent." *Education:* Cornell University, B.A., 1957; Radcliffe College, M.A., 1958; Harvard University, Ph.D., 1963. *Politics:* "Independent."

ADDRESSES: Office—Department of English, University of Illinois, Urbana—Champaign, 608 South Wright St., Urbana, IL 61801; fax 217-333-4321. *E-mail*—baymnina@uiuc.edu.

CAREER: University of Illinois, Urbana—Champaign, IL, instructor, 1963-67, assistant professor, 1967-69, associate professor, 1969-72, professor of English, 1972—, Liberal Arts and Sciences Jubilee Professor, 1989—, Swanlund Endowed Professor and Center for Advanced Study Professor of English, both 1997—; director of School of Humanities, 1976-87, associate at the Center for Advanced Studies, 1989-90.

MEMBER: Modern Language Association of America (executive committee, Nineteenth- Century American Literature division; chair, 1984; chair of American literature section, 1984), American Studies Association (executive committee, 1982-84; nominating committee, 1991-1993), American Association of University Women (fellow), Organization of American Historians, American Literature Association, American Antiquarian Society, Nathaniel Hawthorne Association, Phi Beta Kappa, Phi Kappa Phi, Mortarboard.

AWARDS, HONORS: Guggenheim fellowship, 1975-76; National Endowment for the Humanities fellowship, 1982-83; named University of Illinois Senior University Scholar, 1985; Jay Hubbel Medal for lifetime achievement in American literary studies from the American literature section of the Modern Language Association, 2000.

WRITINGS:

The Shape of Hawthorne's Career, Cornell University Press (Ithaca, NY), 1976.

Women's Fiction: A Guide to Novels by and about Women in America, 1820-1870, Cornell University Press (Ithaca, NY), 1978, 2nd revised edition including a new introduction and supplementary bibliography, University of Illinois Press (Urbana, IL), 1993.

(Editor) Kate Chopin, *The Awakening and Other Stories,* Random House (New York, NY), 1981, reprinted, Modern Library (New York, NY), 2000.

(Editor) Nathaniel Hawthorne, *The Scarlet Letter,* Penguin (New York, NY), 1982.

Novels, Readers, and Reviewers: Responses to Fiction in Antebellum America, Cornell University Press (Ithaca, NY), 1984.

The Scarlet Letter: A Reading, Twayne (Boston, MA), 1986.

(Editor) Maria Susanna Cummins, *The Lamplighter,* Rutgers University Press (New Brunswick, NJ), 1988.

(Coeditor) *Columbia Literary History of the United States,* Columbia University Press (New York, NY), 1988.

(Coeditor) *Norton Anthology of American Literature,* 3rd edition, Norton (New York, NY), 1989, 4th edition, 1994, 5th edition (general editor), 1998, 6th edition (general editor), 2003.

Feminism and American Literary History: Essays, Rutgers University Press (New Brunswick, NJ), 1992.

(Editor) Judith Sargent Murray, *The Gleaner,* Union College Press (Schenectady, NY), 1992.

(Editor) Juliette Magill Kinzie, *Wau-Bun, the "Early Day" in the North-West,* University of Illinois Press (Carbondale, IL), 1992.

American Women Writers and the Work of History, 1790-1860, Rutgers University Press (New Brunswick, NJ), 1995.

(Editor) E. D. E. N. Southworth, *The Hidden Hand,* Oxford University Press (Oxford, England), 1997.

American Women of Letters and the Nineteenth-Century Sciences: Styles of Affiliation, Rutgers University Press (New Brunswick, NJ), 2002.

(Editor and author of introduction) Hannah Gardner Creamer, *Delia's Doctors; or, A Glance behind the Scenes,* University of Illinois Press (Urbana, IL), 2002.

Contributor of over sixty articles and over 130 reviews to various literature journals and literary magazines, including *American Literary History, American Quarterly, American Literature, New England Quarterly, Studies in Modern Fiction, Studies in Short Fiction, Nineteenth-Century Fiction, Publications of the Modern Language Association (PMLA),* and *Journal of English and Germanic Philology;* contributor to *New York Times Book Review* and *New York Newsday.* Member of editorial board,*American Quarterly, American Literature, New England Quarterly, Tulsa Studies in Women's Literature, Legacy: A Newsletter of Nineteenth-Century American Women Authors, American Periodicals, American Studies, Hemingway Review, Nathaniel Hawthorne Review, Resources for American Literary Studies, Studies in American Literature and Culture,* and *Studies in American Fiction.*

SIDELIGHTS: Nina Baym once told *CA:* "I became interested in Hawthorne because of the disparity between the clear functional centrality of the heroine of *The Scarlet Letter* and the negative criticism of her character in scholarship at the time; I felt Hawthorne viewed her as a heroine, not a sinner. Interested in women in literature, I found it reasonable to extend my interest from major (male) authors to minor (female) authors. From there, it became reasonable to consider the matter of major and/versus minor authors, the contexts of authorship, the constitution of the canon, and other matters concerning the way in which we make our literary choices and, having made them, justify them. I find this subject particularly germane to fiction, where storytelling is the essence of the form but where literary choices are seldom validated by discussions of the writer's skill at telling a story or the interest of the story he or she tells."

Baym's *American Women Writers and the Work of History, 1790-1860* examines how women read and wrote history, and how their role in society affected their view of history. Dale M. Bauer wrote in *Signs,*

"Baym knows women novelists, reviewers, critics, and, now, nineteenth-century historians—with a compelling mastery."

In *American Women of Letters and the Nineteenth-Century Sciences: Styles of Affiliation,* Baym discusses the flowering of the sciences during the nineteenth century, and the role of women in that growth. Women were largely left out of scientific endeavor, but a few managed to enter that world. Baym explores the writing of several of these, and analyzes how they interpreted, used, or changed scientific beliefs and practices of their day. *Women's Review of Books* writer Valerie Jablow stated, "Baym is an astute reader and scholar."

BIOGRAPHICAL AND CRITICAL SOURCES:

PERIODICALS

Choice, June, 2002, J. S. Gabin, review of *American Women of Letters and the Nineteenth-Century Sciences: Styles of Affiliation,* p. 1766.

Review of English Studies, November, 1995, Lionel Kelly, review of *The Norton Anthology of American Literature,* 4th edition, p. 617.

Signs, autumn, 1998, Dale M. Bauer, review of *American Women Writers and the Work of History, 1790-1860,* p. 262.

South Atlantic Quarterly, winter, 1968.

Times Higher Education Supplement, May 28, 1999, Stephen Wade, review of *The Norton Anthology of American Literature,* 5th edition, p. S17.

Women's Review of Books, July, 2002, Valerie Jablow, p. 41.

*   *   *

BEELER, Janet
  See SHAW, Janet

*   *   *

BISHOP, Pike
  See OBSTFELD, Raymond

Karleen Bradford

*   *   *

BRADFORD, Karleen 1936-

PERSONAL: Born December 16, 1936, in Toronto, Ontario, Canada; daughter of Karl H. (an accountant) and Eileen (a homemaker; maiden name, Ney) Scott; married James C. Bradford (a foreign service officer), August 22, 1959; children: Donald, Kathleen, Christopher. *Education:* University of Toronto, B.A., 1959. *Hobbies and other interests:* Flying, scuba diving, reading.

ADDRESSES: Office—c/o Writers' Union of Canada, 40 Wellington St. E, 3rd Floor, Toronto, Ontario M5E 1C7, Canada; fax: 519-376-9847. *E-mail*—karleen. bradford@sympatico.ca.

CAREER: T. Eaton Co., Toronto, Ontario, Canada, advertising copywriter, 1959; West Toronto Young Women's Christian Association, Toronto, social worker, 1959-63; writer, 1963—.

MEMBER: International Board on Books for Young People, Writers Union of Canada (curriculum chair, 1984-85; first vice chair, 1997-98), Canadian Authors Association, Canadian Society of Children's Authors, Illustrators, and Performers, PEN.

AWARDS, HONORS: Grant from Ontario Arts Council, 1977; first prize in juvenile writing, Canadian Authors Association, 1978, for short story "A Wish about Freckles"; CommCept Canadian KiddLit Contest, best children's novel of the year, 1979, for *The Other Elizabeth;* grants from Canada Council, 1983, 1985, 1996; "Our Choice" Awards, Canadian Children's Book Centre, 1987-88, for *The Haunting at Cliff House, The Nine Days Queen,* and *The Stone in the Meadow,* 1990, for *Windward Island* and *Write Now!,* 1995-96, for *There Will Be Wolves,* 1995-96 and 1997-98, for *Animal Heroes, More Animal Heroes,* and *The Thirteenth Child,* 1998-99, for *Dragonfire,* 2000, for *Lionheart's Scribe,* and 2002, for *Whisperings of Magic,* and selection as an outstanding book of 1996, for *Shadows on a Sword;* Max and Greta Ebel Award, 1990, for *Windward Island;* Young Adult Canadian Book Award, Canadian Library Association, 1992, for *There Will Be Wolves;* cited among children's books of the year, Child Study Children's Book Committee, 1996, for *There Will Be Wolves;* Moose Jaw Young Readers' Choice Award, 2001, for *Dragonfire;* selection as one of 100 best Canadian Books for Today's Children and Teens, Toronto Public Library, for *There Will Be Wolves.*

WRITINGS:

FOR YOUNG PEOPLE

A Year for Growing, illustrated by Charles Hilder, Scholastic (New York, NY), 1977, revised edition published as *Wrong Again, Robbie,* 1983.
The Other Elizabeth, illustrated by Deborah Drew-Brook, Gage (Scarborough, Ontario, Canada), 1982.
I Wish There Were Unicorns, illustrated by Greg Ruhl, Gage (Scarborough, Ontario, Canada), 1983.
The Stone in the Meadow, illustrated by Greg Ruhl, Gage (Scarborough, Ontario, Canada), 1984.
The Haunting at Cliff House, Scholastic (New York, NY), 1985.
(Editor) *Our Books in the Curriculum,* three volumes, Writers' Union of Canada (Toronto, Ontario, Canada), 1985.

The Nine Days Queen, Scholastic (New York, NY), 1986.
Write Now!, Scholastic (New York, NY), 1988.
Windward Island, Kids Can Press (Toronto, Ontario, Canada), 1989.
There Will Be Wolves, HarperCollins (Toronto, Ontario, Canada), 1992, Dutton (New York, NY), 1996.
The Thirteenth Child, HarperCollins (Toronto, Ontario, Canada), 1994.
Shadows on a Sword, HarperCollins (Toronto, Ontario, Canada), 1996.
Dragonfire, HarperCollins (Toronto, Ontario, Canada), 1997.
A Different Kind of Champion, Scholastic Canada (Montreal, Quebec, Canada), 1998.
Lionheart's Scribe, HarperCollins (Toronto, Ontario, Canada), 1999.
Animal Heroes (originally published in mid-1990s), Scholastic Canada (Montreal, Quebec, Canada), 2001.
With Nothing but Our Courage: The Loyalist Diary of Mary MacDonald, Scholastic Canada (Montreal, Quebec, Canada), 2002.
You Can't Rush a Cat, Orca Publishers (Victoria, British Columbia, Canada), 2003.

Also author of the book *More Animal Heroes.* Work represented in anthologies, including *Beyond Belief,* Clarke, Irwin (Toronto, Ontario, Canada), 1980. Contributor to newspapers and magazines, including *Cricket, Canadian Children's Literature, Jabberwocky,* and *Instructor.* Editor of newsletters.

WORK IN PROGRESS: Angeline, a novel dealing with two survivors of the Children's Crusade.

SIDELIGHTS: Canadian children's author Karleen Bradford has combined her experiences living around the world with her interests in both young people and the past to produce a series of award-winning historical novels that profile teens from various times and places in difficult situations. Perhaps her most ambitious historical novels, *There Will Be Wolves* and its sequels, *Shadows on a Sword* and *Lionheart's Scribe,* depict life in the eleventh century, specifically the religious crusades in which Europeans journeyed to the holy lands of the Middle East with the intention of wresting the territory from non-Christians.

Bradford has spent many years "traveling from country to country," which, she once told *CA,* is "an experience that has proven to be wonderfully stimulating for me both as a person and as a writer." She has lived in Argentina, Southeast Asia, South America, Germany, and England. "During the time we lived [in England] we found that two of our favorite places were Cornwall and Wales, and two of my books take place in those locales: *The Stone in the Meadow* (Cornwall) and *The Haunting at Cliff House* (Wales)." Both these books, along with *The Other Elizabeth,* have what Bradford calls a "back to the past" theme. "In *The Stone in the Meadow* a young Canadian girl visiting her uncle is magically transported back to 300 BC, a time when Britain was occupied by warring tribes of Celts and their Druid priests," the author noted. "In *The Other Elizabeth,* a modern-day girl enters an old building in Upper Canada Village—a pioneer village [museum] in Ontario—and suddenly finds herself back in the year 1813, during the war between the United States of America and Canada. *The Haunting at Cliff House* concerns a Canadian girl who has accompanied her father, a novelist and university professor, on his sabbatical to a small town in Wales. They move into an old house on the coast which he has inherited, and the heroine finds that it is haunted by the ghost of another girl who lived there over a hundred years before." Describing the general theme of the novels, Bradford commented that they are "concerned with events that happened in the past, and the possibility of altering those events in such a way that the future, as well, is altered. It's a theme that has fascinated me for a long time."

In 1983 she traveled to England to research *Nine Days Queen,* a fictional portrait of Lady Jane Grey. The novel recalls the brief life of fifteen-year-old Queen Jane, from her privileged childhood through her love affair with young King Edward VI, her arranged marriage with Guilford Dudley, the political turmoil that led to her short-lived reign as queen, and the execution of both herself and her husband by order of Queen Mary in 1554. Praising Bradford's ability to present the political facets of Lady Jane's situation clearly, Sara Ellis noted in *Canadian Materials* that "Karleen Bradford will be a writer to watch as she expands her writing horizons."

Bradford presents her extensive research of the People's Crusade of the eleventh century in a number of her works. Beginning with her novel *There Will Be Wolves,* she tackled a compelling chapter in European and religious history—the Christian pilgrimage from Cologne, Germany, to the holy city of Jerusalem during which Christian zealots slaughtered many Jews and pillaged their homes under the guise of liberating the holy city from Turkish infidels. The book's protagonist, Ursula, is a young healer living with her ailing father in Cologne when the religious figure Peter the Hermit calls upon Christians to march to Jerusalem. Ursula, who has been harassed by the church for her supposed practice of witchcraft, is allowed to join Peter's followers to cleanse herself of sin in lieu of being burned at the stake. Accompanied by her father, who dies along the way, she is befriended by a young stonecutter named Bruno. Bradford continued the story of Ursula and Bruno in *Shadows on a Sword* and *Lionheart's Scribe,* the second and third of four projected novels on the period.

Other novels by Bradford, including *A Year for Growing* and *I Wish There Were Unicorns,* take place in present-day Canada and focus on such issues as learning to get along with others and coping with new and trying circumstances. *I Wish There Were Unicorns* concerns thirteen-year-old Rachel's move from the bustle of urban Toronto to a rural farm in Canada after her parents' divorce. Rachel is at first angry and resentful, but her feelings about her family change after her younger sister runs away in order to protect an abused dog that she has befriended. Although noting that some of the novel's characters are too upbeat to be believable, Frieda Wishinsky observed in *Quill and Quire* that Bradford is successful "in portraying a young girl's confused feelings without sounding pedantic, which, in itself, is an accomplishment."

Windward Island takes place on the southern coast of Nova Scotia, a world of lighthouse keepers and Atlantic shoreline fishermen. Research began for Bradford four years before the release of the book, in the spring of 1985; she was able to spend several weeks living on a small lighthouse island in the area. "There I found a peace and a strength that I have not found anywhere else, and I want[ed] very much to write about it," she admitted to *CA.* The novel that resulted is the story of teens Caleb and Loren and their feelings about leaving their island home and moving to the Nova Scotia mainland. Roger Burford Mason, writing in *Quill and Quire,* appreciated the way that *Windward Island* presents "the timeless aspirations, fears, jealousies, and problems of young people growing up."

Another of Bradford's stories set in modern times is *The Thirteenth Child,* a novel for young readers about a girl who lives in a fantasy world in order to avoid the harsh realities of her own life. Kate has watched as her father's alcoholism has destroyed her once-stable family. Writing romantic fantasies is Kate's way of coping with her problems, but fantasy becomes reality when she becomes drawn to Mike, a loner in town who strikes her as both "dangerous" and fascinating. *Canadian Materials* contributor Margaret Mackey praised the novel's "tight" plot and maintained that "the reactions of the characters are believable for the most part."

With Nothing but Our Courage: A Loyalist Diary of Mary MacDonald follows the fate of the MacDonald family after the American War of Independence. Forced to leave their home in Albany, New York, they make their way north to find a new home in Canada. This story brings to life the hardships the pioneers endured when faced with surviving and cutting a home for themselves out of the dense and inhospitable Canadian bush.

Bradford told *CA:* "I've often been asked why I write for young people and whether I might one day write a 'real' book. My answer is that books for young people are as real as books can get. It's important that our children and teenagers read about others their own ages who are facing problems, coping with those problems, and growing—moving on in their lives, no matter what happens to them. It is important for them to know that they are not alone, that others have gone through what they are going through, that there is a way out. It doesn't matter whether my books are set in contemporary times, in the past, or in a world of fantasy that I have created. When I write about teenagers who get caught up in the wars of the Middle Ages, I am writing about teenagers who are caught up in the wars that ravage our planet today. When I write in my fantasy novels *Dragonfire* and *Whisperings of Magic* about a young man who must fight to regain his birthright, a young girl who must learn to trust, the struggles that I write about are no different from the conflicts young people face today. If I cannot always offer solutions, I try my best to offer hope and, whenever possible, humor."

BIOGRAPHICAL AND CRITICAL SOURCES:

BOOKS

Baker, Deirdre and Ken Setterington, *A Guide to Canadian Children's Books,* McClelland & Stewart (Toronto, Ontario, Canada), 2003.

Buzzeo, Toni and Jane Kurtz, editors, *Terrific Connections,* Libraries Unlimited (Littleton, CO), 1999.
Meet Canadian Authors and Illustrators, Scholastic Canada (Montreal, Quebec, Canada), 2002.
The Storymakers: Writing Children's Books, Canadian Children's Book Centre (Toronto, Ontario, Canada), 2000.
Writing Stories, Making Pictures, Canadian Children's Book Centre (Toronto, Ontario, Canada), 1994.

PERIODICALS

Books in Canada, November, 1992, p. 38.
Bulletin of the Center for Children's Literature, October, 1996, p. 50.
Canadian Author, winter, 1995.
Canadian Children's Literature, Volume 48, 1987, pp. 85-86; Volume 62, 1991, Hilary Turner, review of *There Will Be Wolves,* p. 110; Volume 73, 1994, p. 71; Volume 77, 1995, pp. 88-89; Volume 83, 1996, pp. 75-77.
Canadian Materials, January, 1988, Sara Ellis, review of *Nine Days Queen,* p. 5; March, 1990, p. 70; November, 1992, p. 304; September, 1993; November-December, 1994, Margaret Mackey, review of *The Thirteenth Child,* p. 229.
CANSCAIP Newsletter, summer, 1998.
Kirkus Reviews, July 1, 1996, p. 964.
Ottawa Citizen, December 18, 1994.
Publishers Weekly, June 24, 1996, p. 62.
Quill and Quire, July, 1983, Frieda Wishinsky, review of *I Wish There Were Unicorns,* p. 60; August, 1985; October, 1989, Roger Burford Mason, review of *Windward Island,* pp. 14, 16; December, 1992, p. 27; September, 1994, Celia Barker Lottridge, review of *The Thirteenth Child,* pp. 73-74.
Resource Links, April, 1996.
Voice of Youth Advocates, April, 1997, p. 27.

*   *   *

BRIN, David 1950-

PERSONAL: Born October 6, 1950, in Glendale, CA; son of Herbert (an editor) and Selma (a teacher) Brin; married Cheryl Ann Bringham (a doctor of cosmochemistry), March, 1991; children: two sons, one daughter. *Education:* California Institute of Technology, B.S. (astronomy), 1973; University of California,

David Brin

San Diego, M.S. (applied physics), 1979, Ph.D. (space science), 1981. *Hobbies and other interests:* Backpacking, music, science, and "general eclecticism."

ADDRESSES: Home—11625 Montana, Number 9, Los Angeles, CA 90049-4676. *Office*—Heritage Press, 2130 South Vermont Ave., Los Angeles, CA 90007. *Agent*—(literary) Richard Curtis Associates, Inc., 164 East 64th St., New York, NY 10021; (film) Vince Gerardis, Created-By Agency, Formosa Bldg., 1041 North Formosa Ave., Hollywood, CA 90046.

CAREER: Hughes Aircraft Research Laboratories, electrical engineer in semiconductor device development in Newport Beach, CA, 1973-75, and Carlsbad, CA, 1975-77; managing editor, *Journal of the Laboratory of Comparative Human Cognition,* 1979-80; Heritage Press, Los Angeles, CA, book reviewer and science editor, 1980—. San Diego State University, instructor in physics and writing, 1982-83, also taught at San Diego community colleges, 1984-85; postdoctoral research fellow, California Space Institute, La Jolla, CA, 1983-86; Westfield College, University of London, visiting artist, 1986-87. Has also worked as a visiting scholar at the Center for Study of Evolution of

Life at the University of California, Los Angeles, and NASA's Jet Propulsion Laboratory and NSCORT for Exobiology. Member of board of advisors for corporations and nonprofit institutions.

MEMBER: Science Fiction Writers of America (secretary, 1982-84), Planetary Society, British Interplanetary Society.

AWARDS, HONORS: John W. Campbell Award nominations, 1982, for best new author, 2003, for *Kiln People;* Brazil SF Award, 1983, for novella *The Postman;* Hugo Award nominations, World Science Fiction Convention, 1983, for novella version of *The Postman,* 1985, for short story "Cyclops," 1986, for novel *The Postman,* 1987, for short story "Thor Meets Captain America," 1989, for short story "The Giving Plague," 1991, for *Earth,* 1994, for *Glory Season,* 1995, for *Brightness Reef,* and 2003, for *Kiln People;* Balrog Award, 1984, for *The Practice Effect;* Locus Award, Locus Publications, 1984, for *Startide Rising,* 1986, for *The Postman,* 1988, for *The Uplift War,* and 1995, for *Otherness: Collected Stories by a Modern Master of Science Fiction;* Nebula Award, Science Fiction Writers of America, 1984, for *Startide Rising;* Hugo Award, World Science Fiction Convention, 1984, for *Startide Rising,* 1985, for short story "The Crystal Spheres," and 1988, for *The Uplift War;* John W. Campbell Memorial Award, 1986, for *The Postman;* American Library Association Best Books for Young Adults citation, 1986, for *The Postman;* Nebula Award nomination, Science Fiction Writers of America, 1986, for *The Postman,* and 1988, for *The Uplift War;* Obeler Freedom of Speech Award, American Library Association, and McGannon Communication Policy Research Award, both 1999, both for *The Transparent Society: Will Technology Force Us to Choose between Privacy and Freedom?;* Analog Award for best novella, c. 1999, for *Stones of Significance;* Arthur C. Clarke Award shortlist, 2003, for *Kiln People.*

WRITINGS:

FICTION

The Practice Effect (science fiction novel), Bantam (New York, NY), 1984.
The Postman (science fiction novel), Bantam (New York, NY), 1985.

(With Gregory Benford) *Heart of the Comet* (science fiction novel), Bantam (New York, NY), 1986.

Earthclan, Doubleday (Garden City, NY), 1986.

The River of Time (short stories; includes "The Crystal Spheres"), Dark Harvest (Arlington Heights, IL), 1986.

Dr. Pak's Preschool (novella), illustrated by Alan Giana, Cheap Street (New Castle, VA), 1989.

Earth, Bantam (New York, NY), 1990.

Piecework (short stories), Pulphouse (Eugene, OR), 1991.

(With Poul Anderson, Greg Bear, and Gregory Benford) *Murasaki* (includes Brin's novella *Genji*), Bantam (New York, NY), 1993.

Glory Season, Bantam (New York, NY), 1993.

Otherness: Collected Stories by a Modern Master of Science Fiction, Bantam (New York, NY), 1994.

Foundation's Triumph (novel; based on Isaac Asimov's "Foundation" series), HarperPrism (New York, NY), 1999.

Forgiveness (graphic novel; part of the "Star Trek: The Next Generation" series), edited by Jeff Mariotte, WildStorm Productions (La Jolla, CA), 2001.

Kiln People, Tor (New York, NY), 2002.

Tomorrow Happens (short stories), limited edition, NESFA Press (Cambridge, MA), 2003.

"UPLIFT" SERIES; SCIENCE FICTION

Sundiver, Bantam (New York, NY), 1980.

Startide Rising (first printed in a shorter version in *Analog* magazine as the novella *The Tides of Kithrup*), Bantam (New York, NY), 1983, revised hardcover edition, Phantasia Press (West Bloomfield, MI), 1985.

The Uplift War (sequel to *Startide Rising*), Phantasia Press (West Bloomfield, MI), 1987.

Brightness Reef: Book One of the New Uplift Trilogy, Bantam (New York, NY), 1995.

Infinity's Shore: Book Two of the New Uplift Trilogy, Bantam (New York, NY), 1996.

Heaven's Reach: The Final Book of the New Uplift Trilogy, Bantam (New York, NY), 1998.

OTHER

(With Thomas Kuiper) *Extraterrestrial Civilization* (nonfiction science), American Association of Physics Teachers (College Park, MD), 1989.

The Transparent Society: Will Technology Force Us to Choose between Privacy and Freedom? (nonfiction), Addison-Wesley (Reading, MA), 1998.

(With Kevin Lenagh) *Contacting Aliens: An Illustrated Guide to David Brin's "Uplift" Universe,* Bantam (New York, NY), 2002.

Also author of novellas *The Loom of Thessaly* and *Stones of Significance,* published in *Lamps on the Brow,* 1998, and of graphic novel *The Life Eaters.* Contributor to *Far Frontiers,* Baen, 1985; *Thinking Robots, an Aware Internet, and Cyberpunk Librarians: The 1992 LITA President's Program: Presentations by Hans Moravec, Bruce Sterling, and David Brin,* Library of Information Technology (Chicago, IL), 1992; and anthology *War of the Worlds: Global Dispatches,* 1996. Creator of computer games, including *Tribes,* with Steve Jackson, Steve Jackson Games, 1998; *Ecco the Dolphin,* 1998; and *GURPS Uplift,* Steve Jackson Games.

Contributor of articles to professional journals, including *Astrophysical Journal, Information Technology & Libraries, Internet Life, iPlanet, ABA Journal on Dispute Resolution,* and *Liberty Magazine;* and of stories and articles to popular magazines, including *Analog, Fantasy & Science Fiction, Interzone, Popular Science, Amazing Stories, S.F. Age, Liberty Magazine, Omni, Nature,* and *Isaac Asimov's Science Fiction Magazine.* Contributor of articles to newspapers, including *Los Angeles Times Book Review* and the London *Times.* Contributor to online publications *Salon.com* and *Caltech Hyperforum on Sustainability.* Brin's manuscript collection is maintained at the J. Lloyd Eaton Collection of Science Fiction and Fantasy Literature, University of California, Riverside.

ADAPTATIONS: A film adaptation of *The Postman,* directed by and starring Kevin Costner, was released by Warner Bros. in 1997. *The Postman, Sundiver,* and *The Uplift War* have been adapted as audio recordings; the novella *The Loom of Thessaly* has been recorded on audio cassette by Off-Centaur Press. *Startide Rising* has been optioned for a film production.

SIDELIGHTS: Astrophysicist and author David Brin is an award-winning science fiction writer who is best known for his "Uplift" series, which begins with the novel *Sundiver.* By the time the second book, *Startide Rising,* was released, Brin had become famous as one of the genre's most promising new writers. Sweeping the field's major awards, this 1983 novel won the Hugo for its popularity among readers and the Nebula for impressing the critics. Brin has also won numerous other awards, including the John W. Campbell Memorial Award for Best Novel for *The Postman.*

Though Brin's first two novels were most commended by the science-fiction community, the ideas and ethical concerns they explore have earned them recognition from outside the genre, said reviewers Debra Rae Cohen of *Voice Literary Supplement* and Donald M. Hassler of *Science Fiction and Fantasy Book Review.* At home on both sides of that boundary, the novels also provide "space opera characteristics," noted Hassler. Both *Sundiver* and *Startide Rising* are set in the Progenitors universe, which teems with inhabited galaxies and their numerous races and is complicated by conflicts and technological problems on an epic scale. The most intelligent races in its five galaxies believe they were "uplifted" to sapience through the efforts of an elder but now-missing species, and that it is their duty to use genetic engineering to raise other species to the status of participants in their culture. "Some of these 'Galactics' are moderates; other races appear fanatical to a beleaguered humanity," Brin explained to *CA.* Without the presumably necessary aid of patrons, humans have achieved the ability to travel in space and have "uplifted" dolphins and chimpanzees. Such audacity must be checked, believe the "fanatics" who fight each other for the right to "adopt" the humans into a remedial retraining program.

Brin further explained to *CA* his thoughts behind creating his Progenitor universe: "I wanted to explore [genetic engineering, specifically] the ethical problems involved in changing more sophisticated creatures such as dolphins or apes, to give them the capabilities to become fellow-citizens in our culture. Do we have the right to meddle with species that have their own dignity? There are serious ethical questions about this whole matter of uplift, of being patrons of a client species. We'll face these questions in the real world in just a few years. . . . I [also] wanted to come up with a scenario in which a civilization would be possible in the galaxy which would have conservation of so-called 'nursery worlds' like the earth as a paramount objective. . . . It's basically a 'gedanken-experiment' or thought experiment. One role of SF is to explore the limits of an idea."

Sundiver introduces this universe; *Startide Rising,* taking place two centuries later, shows the Earth ship *Streaker* pursued by aliens and grounded on the water-world planet of Kithrup for repairs. The few humans aboard are observers of the ship's crew, a team of uplifted dolphins who speak in a poetic language akin to haiku, which Brin indicated to *CA* was derived primarily from his imagination—"it comes straight from the back of [my] skull." "Each of Brin's dolphins is a distinct and unique individual, without ever losing an essential dolphinity," wrote Stephen B. Brown in a *Washington Post Book World* review. In Brown's opinion, "the care and empathy with which Brin describes the relationships between his aquatic characters elevates this book into a substantial achievement." Brown commended the author for skillfully weaving "the byzantine intrigues of . . . various dolphin factions," while consistently developing "the idea that a viable human/dolphin collaboration can be something greater than each race on its own."

"Brin's toying with the vision of evolution is probably the strongest feature in both books," Hassler remarked. The author's "notion of managed development" as opposed to natural selection, "which by contrast seems blind, [and] inefficient," said Hassler, allows the author to examine ethical problems that result from the subordination of uplifted species to their patrons, and the universal search for the Progenitors, the supposed first species, as well. Hassler commented, "Such tales of origins and the running debate between [Charles] Darwin and [Erich] Von Daniken are truly sublime." Whereas most reviewers praised *Startide Rising*'s fast-paced action and complex plot, *Minneapolis Tribune* contributor D. R. Martin expressed his wish that "someone—Brin or his editor—had tightened things up along the way." Brin revised the book extensively for its hardcover printing in 1985, a reissue a *Publishers Weekly* critic dubbed "an SF event."

Because he feels that the creation of fictional worlds can foster egotistic and "self-indulgent" writing, Brin once explained to *CA* interviewer Jean W. Ross that he limits himself to write no more than two books in a row about any given universe. Consequently, he interrupted the telling of the story of the search for the Progenitors with a third novel in a lighter vein. In *The Practice Effect,* he gives indulgence full play, venting "all the bad puns" that do not belong, as he told Ross, in his "more serious work." "*The Practice Effect* [is] a light adventure-fantasy and romance which is accessible to bright children," Brin explained to *CA:* "I decided to have some fun with a strict formula piece that was completely self-indulgent. . . . It's a romp, it's fun."

Accordingly, reviewers have found *The Practice Effect* an enjoyable time-travel romance in the tradition of Mark Twain's *A Connecticut Yankee in King Arthur's Court.* Not surprisingly, in an interview with *CA,* Brin named Twain one of the "many . . . old masters" who greatly influence him. Like Twain's "Yankee," Brin's Dennis Nuel enters a strange world, rescues a princess, defeats a formidable enemy, and contributes to progress by virtue of skills that would be considered quite ordinary at home. This formula has been used often since Twain wrote the prototype, observed some reviewers, but Brin gives it a new twist: Nuel finds himself in a world where repeated use improves objects instead of wearing them out. Sequences showing what many simple objects become as the result of "practice" (flint knives become super-sabers; a zipper becomes a saw) are interlaced with Nuel's adventures "which can only be called rollicking," wrote Baird Searles in *Isaac Asimov's Science Fiction Magazine.* Adding to the fun are sometimes oblique references to "the great moments of SF history," noted the reviewer, who believed that "the high spirits and inventiveness" of the practice "more than compensate" for the plot's occasional "repetitiveness" and the author's somewhat "collegiate" humor.

Brin gives a new treatment to another branch of fiction with *The Postman,* his portrayal of life in North America after a nuclear world war. Unlike other post-apocalypse novels that bemoan total destruction, *The Postman* depicts what Brin told Ross is "the real horror of such a war"—the prospect of surviving in a holocaust-ravaged environment. As Brin explained to *CA:* "The real horror, to me, is not death and destruction. We've had that all our lives, and for thousands of years. If the curtain is all coming down, à la *On the Beach,* then it's all over; nobody suffers anymore. But it strikes me as more likely that some of our descendants would survive even the worst nuclear war, and they would probably go back to living like Michael Landon in *Little House on the Prairie.* But they would not be as happy as our pioneer forebears. They would be fundamentally scarred forever because of one fact: they would know how close we came to a sane, decent, better world, and that might-have-been would haunt them."

"The world Brin draws [in *The Postman*] is terrifying," said *Los Angeles Times Book Review* contributor Ronald Florence, referring to the power-hungry paramilitary bands that tyrannize people who live in small, unprotected settlements. Stripped by the bandits, protagonist Gordon Krantz finds a mail carrier's remains and borrows the dead postman's uniform. Thereafter, the villagers see him "as a symbol of civilization," related *Washington Post Book World* contributor Gregory Frost. Maintaining ever-larger lies about his identity, Krantz accepts the role of public servant and civil authority they ascribe to him. The story develops "Brin's premise that people need something bigger than survival to believe in," noted a *New York Times Book Review* contributor. *Analog* critic Tom Easton found it a recommendable demonstration of "the value of myths." Like other reviewers, Frost noted several "weaknesses" that he later deemed "minor," and praised the "mythic dimension" Brin brings to almost every element of the novel.

When discussing the benefits of writing fiction of different lengths, Brin described why *The Postman* has "a mythical tone": "I feel I get different things from the three different lengths. The short stories are attempts at epiphanies, at making a ringing note that will hang in the reader's ear, like the effect Joyce achieved in his smaller works. It's like a painting; you take it all in. My large novels, on the other hand, tend to be very complicated. They're explorations of many ideas, woven together trying to make a complex tapestry. In between is the length known as the novella, which happens to be my favorite. This length allows one to explore a mythic theme that one can't afford to muddy up with all sorts of complexities. This is the length that I believe is right for legend. And I think this helps explain why *The Postman,* of all of my novels, has more of a mythic feel to it; it actually is made up of three separate novellas." *The Postman* was later adapted into a 1997 motion picture, directed by and starring actor Kevin Costner.

Brin's next book, *The Heart of the Comet,* according to *Chicago Tribune Book World* reviewers James and Eugene Sloan, confirms his place among those writers "who are busy putting the hard science back into science fiction." Works in the genre drifted toward "softer" speculation and fantasy during the past decade, John R. Cramer reported in the *Los Angeles Times.* However, he noted with pleasure that then-NASA scientist Brin and coauthor Gregory Benford present "accurate physics and biology" when narrating the conditions that threaten a crew of scientists as they ride Halley's Comet to the farthest point of its range and try to move it into an orbit closer to earth.

Recounting his long distance collaboration with Gregory Benford, Brin described to *CA* how the book was organized: "We carefully outlined the book, divided it up among three points of view represented by three characters whose scenes alternated through the book. Benford took one character and wrote all of that person's scenes; I took another character and all of his scenes. We took turns with the third. It resulted in a very different voice for each character. It was a most intriguing, interesting experiment, and, I feel, a successful one." Applause from the critics included the Sloans remark that *Heart of the Comet* "may well be the masterpiece of [the hard science revival]. . . . Light years ahead of [Carl] Sagan's rival effort, this book is what science fiction is."

In *The Uplift War,* Brin goes back to the universe of his first two novels for a closer look at uplifted chimpanzees as they relate to humans in the struggle to rebuild an ecologically damaged planet while trying to resist alien invaders. "It's a very large book—220,000 words—and not so much a sequel as a parallel volume [to *Startide*]," Brin explained to *CA:* "I had a good time with the book. It's more fun than *Startide,* less ethereal. The apes get a little gritty at times. There's a scene in which a riot breaks out in a blue-collar, working chimps' bar. I think readers might like that." Brin's message, observed Easton, is the positive value of a sense of humor. "Humans and neochimps and Tymbrimi [a race of alien pranksters] together defeat [their attackers] and score massive points in the Uplift culture with the aid of one of the grandest jokes in galactic history," related Easton, who found Brin's handling of the Uplift concept enjoyable, his plots satisfying, and his ideas "beautifully" developed.

With 1993's *Glory Season,* "Brin begins by sticking his neck out a country mile," stated Tom Easton in an *Analog* review. The novel is heavily influenced by feminist theory: In an outlying colony called Stratos, which has become a woman-centered world, the female inhabitants have been engineered according to their original creators' ideal genetic standards and provided with the ability to clone themselves as a means of reproduction. However, men are still needed in order to create the biological diversity necessary to help the species adapt to change: to eliminate total reliance on cloning, mating continues on a limited basis, its frequency determined by the seasons. This continued reliance on males becomes one of the frictions in Stratos society, as an element of radical women wish to eliminate their presence altogether. Others want things to remain as they are; still others want men to have a more equal role in society. When Renna, a male representative from the colonizing planet, arrives to inform the Stratonians that they will soon be visited by their creators and that their society must become more egalitarian, these social tensions erupt.

"There is violence and death, pursuit and discovery, betrayal and maturation, immense enjoyment and final satisfaction, all in the service of a thoughtful approach to the question of intergender relations," commented Easton, comparing *Glory Season* favorably with Ursula LeGuin's classic *The Left Hand of Darkness.* While noting that the novel, which weighs in at 557 pages, is overly lengthy, *Washington Post Book World* critic Marin Morse Wooster praised *Glory Season* as a "cool and confident reexamination of a perennial science-fiction theme," and he called it "one of the most important sf novels of the year."

In 1995 Brin returned to his Uplift universe with a new trilogy including the novels *Brightness Reef: Book One of the New Uplift Trilogy, Infinity's Shore: Book Two of the New Uplift Trilogy,* and *Heaven's Reach: The Final Book of the New Uplift Trilogy.* All three books involve the planet Jijo, a world where six species coexist. The Buyur civilization has thus far protected Jijo from those that would continue their uplifting efforts because the planet possesses a fragile ecology that could be destroyed by such manipulations. In *Brightness Reef* the arrival of humans who want to uplift the species on Jijo wreaks havoc on the careful balance once maintained there. While a *Publishers Weekly* contributor complained that the first book ends too abruptly, the reviewer maintained that Brin "describes a universe that's immensely appealing, leaving readers hungry for more of this exciting, epic adventure." Furthermore, David Easton, writing in *Analog,* complimented the author for creating "a future both with immense potential for fiction and with such sheer biological and historical *likeliness* that it is easy to believe."

Infinity's Shore sees the return of the intelligent dolphin crew from the starship *Streaker,* which lands on Jijo, where the crisis is continuing and threatens the humans on the planet particularly. By the end of the book, the protected way of life the people of Jijo have enjoyed is gone as the planet experiences profound changes.

The complex tale that evolves here is "demanding SF," as one *Publishers Weekly* reviewer put it; "but just as undeniably, it is superior SF as well." Brin ends the trilogy with *Heaven's Reach,* in which the author pulls out all the stops to tell a story that involves aliens invading Earth, the *Streaker* fleeing the planet Jijo with valuable information that could preserve peace in the universe, a meeting with godlike beings, a sentient chimp who works as an intergalactic crime investigator, and the threat to the stability of space itself. A *Publishers Weekly* critic, however, felt that the conclusion to the trilogy was a "letdown," though the reviewer thought many Brin fans would be happy with it. And *Booklist* critic Roland Green similarly considered the quality of the novel to be uneven, but added that Brin "manages enough [to be] . . . at the top of his form to please all Uplift followers and many others as well."

After concluding his sixth Uplift book, Brin decided he wanted to write an installment of another series, though this one was begun by another author: the late Isaac Asimov. *Foundation's Triumph* is the latest book to feature Hari Seldon and his epic efforts to save a crumbling galactic civilization through the establishment of the Foundation. Other authors, including Gregory Benford and Greg Bear, have similarly continued the series after the grand master of sci-fi's death in 1992. Brin's contribution to the Foundation books finds Seldon near the end of his life during a time when a mental illness is spreading throughout humanity and threatens to destroy everything Seldon has tried to preserve. At the same time, a civil war appears to be looming between two groups of robots: one that abides by the old code never to harm human beings, and another group called the Giskardian robots that has come to believe it is justifiable to hurt some humans if necessary in order to help them in the long run. Brin's effort to continue Asimov's storyline, attested one *Publishers Weekly* reviewer, does not do it justice. The critic complained of drab characterization, a "preachy" style, and "laborious sociological theorizing." On the other hand, *Library Journal* contributor Jackie Cassada praised the book and asserted that it "deserves a wide readership," while Roland Green, writing in *Booklist,* found the novel to be a "literature coda to a grand vision of human evolution."

With 2002's *Kiln People* Brin created a stand-alone science fiction novel involving an original twist on the idea of cloning. It is set in the near future, when technology has made it possible in America for people to create "dittos" or "golems" of themselves by imprinting their personalities on clay bodies that last only a couple dozen hours before they are disposed of like empty food containers. Brin combines science fiction with a murder mystery format when his main character, private investigator Albert Morris, sets out to solve a murder of a scientist who specialized in this imprinting technique. His continuing investigations reveal something even more sinister than murder, however; something that could turn the very structure of human civilization upside down. Although a *Publishers Weekly* critic felt that tension in the story was weakened by Brin's use of expendable dittos, including dittos of the main character who can be killed without major consequences to the plot, the reviewer complimented the author's deft exploration of "the issues of identity, privacy and work."

Kiln People treats the themes of technology's effects on society in a fiction format, but Brin has also written about this subject in his nonfiction, especially in his book *The Transparent Society: Will Technology Force Us to Choose between Privacy and Freedom?* Here, the author explores the ways in which advances in computers, the "owning" of information, and surveillance technology—such as in the proliferation of cameras in public buildings and even on our streets—are making privacy a hot issue. But whereas many people would argue that the importance of personal freedoms and the right to privacy should lead to pressures that will change current laws, Brin feels that the solution to this issue lies not in restricting surveillance of people's activities but, as Christine Peterson explained in *Reason,* in "protecting freedoms through openness and accountability instead of secrecy. Openness—letting data flow where it may—promotes personal responsibility in both economic and social arenas. This in turn decreases the temptation to have the state intervene. By aligning the individuals' incentives with the results of their actions, accountability gives us more robust freedom than privacy alone can ever guarantee."

While Peterson felt that this half of Brin's argument was "brilliant," though, as the author admits, "not a new insight," she could not say the same about Brin's complaints against cyberpunks—those people who have been trying to protect private online communications through advances in encryption. Here, said Peterson, Brin relies more on "name calling and straw-man attacks" than on reason to argue against cyberpunk practices, which she considered sensible in light of the fact that it is easier to change one's own practices to protect privacy than it is to wait for politicians to change laws involving technologies they do not comprehend. In the end, however, Peterson asserted that *The Transparent Society* "is both convincing and relatively nonpolitical." Other critics felt that the book suffers from being superficial and from too many digressions that are not related to the author's main thesis. For example, a *Publishers Weekly* critic said that "despite a strong beginning, Brin's book ultimately lacks clarity and originality." Nevertheless, the same reviewer noted the book was useful for providing historical background to the issue and for offering information on encryption and other technology issues.

Besides writing on this subject, Brin has become more involved in advancing computer communications directly in his recent efforts to establish a company that will produce new realtime communication software that will represent a leap in human-to-human online interactions. He has also become involved in creating several new computer games. But despite these ventures, Brin will likely remain best known for his fiction writing, which has continued to be notable for its speculations into how technology and biological manipulations may one day affect human society.

BIOGRAPHICAL AND CRITICAL SOURCES:

BOOKS

Contemporary Literary Criticism, Volume 34, Gale (Detroit, MI), 1985.
St. James Guide to Science Fiction Writers, 4th edition, St. James Press (Detroit, MI), 1996.

PERIODICALS

Amazing, January, 1984.
Analog: Science Fiction/Science Fact, November, 1983; July, 1984; March, 1986; November, 1987; November, 1990; November, 1993; January, 1995; February, 1996, Tom Easton, review of *Brightness Reef: Book One of the New Uplift Trilogy,* pp. 159-161; March, 1997; October, 1998, Tom Easton, review of *Heaven's Reach,* p. 133; June, 2002,

Tom Easton, review of *Kiln People,* p. 132; February, 2003, Tom Easton, review of *Contacting Aliens: An Illustrated Guide to David Brin's "Uplift" Universe,* p. 138.
Booklist, September, 1, 1987; August, 1994; September 1, 1995; April, 1998, Roland Green, review of *Heaven's Reach,* p. 1277; May 15, 1998, Mary Carroll, review of *The Transparent Society: Will Technology Force Us to Choose between Privacy and Freedom?,* p. 1569; May 1, 1999, Roland Green, review of *Foundation's Triumph,* p. 1582; April 15, 2003, Regina Schroeder, review of *Tomorrow Happens,* p. 1454.
Book World, October, 19, 1986.
Chicago Tribune Book World, March, 23, 1986.
Fantasy Review, September, 1985; July, 1987.
Information Technology and Libraries, March, 1994.
Isaac Asimov's Science Fiction Magazine, December, 1983; July, 1984.
Library Journal, May 15, 1999, Jackie Cassada, review of *Foundation's Triumph,* p. 131; January, 2002, Jackie Cassada, review of *Kiln People,* p. 159.
Locus, June, 1990; July, 1990; August, 1990; February, 1991; March, 1991; July, 1991; April, 1993; May, 1993; October, 1993; February, 1994; July, 1994; October, 1994; February, 1995.
Los Angeles Times, December 16, 1985; April 1, 1986.
Los Angeles Times Book Review, December 15, 1985; January 12, 1986; May 20, 1990.
Magazine of Fantasy and Science Fiction, March, 1986; March, 1996.
Minneapolis Tribune, December 25, 1983.
New York Times Book Review, November 24, 1985; July 8, 1990; July 14, 1991; June 13, 1993.
Publishers Weekly, August 12, 1983; September 6, 1985; October 11, 1985; January 10, 1986; June 13, 1986; March 27, 1987; May 11, 1990, Sybil Steinberg, review of *Earth,* p. 252; April 2, 1993, review of *Glory Season,* p. 50; September 4, 1995, review of *Brightness Reef,* p. 54; November 18, 1996, review of *Infinity's Shore,* p. 65; April 13, 1998, review of *Heaven's Reach,* p. 56, review of *The Transparent Society,* p. 64; April 26, 1999, review of *Foundation's Triumph,* p. 60; December 17, 2001, review of *Kiln People,* p. 69; June 17, 2002, "July Publications," p. 48.
Reason, October, 1998, Christine Peterson, review of *The Transparent Society,* p. 69.
San Jose Mercury News, March 11, 1984.
School Library Journal, January, 1992; December, 1990.

Science Fiction and Fantasy Book Review, September, 1983; November, 1983.

Science Fiction Chronicle, December, 1985; March, 1987; June, 1987; September, 1987; February, 1996.

Science Fiction Review, August, 1984.

Voice Literary Supplement, December, 1983.

Washington Post Book World, April 22, 1984; December 22, 1985; July 25, 1993.

ONLINE

David Brin's Official Web site, http://www.davidbrin.com/ (October 7, 2003).*

*   *   *

BURLEIGH, Robert 1936-

PERSONAL: Born January 4, 1936, in Chicago, IL; married; children: three. *Education:* Attended DePauw University, 1953-57; University of Chicago, 1958-62.

ADDRESSES: Home—415 West North Ave., Chicago, IL 60610. *E-mail*—roburleigh@aol.com.

CAREER: Author and artist. Worked for Society of Visual Education as a writer and artist.

AWARDS, HONORS: Orbis Pictus Award, National Council of Teachers of English, 1992, for *Flight: The Journey of Charles Lindbergh.*

WRITINGS:

FOR CHILDREN

A Man Named Thoreau (picture book biography), illustrated by Lloyd Bloom, Atheneum (New York, NY), 1985.

Flight: The Journey of Charles Lindbergh (picture book biography), illustrated by Mike Wimmer, Philomel (New York, NY), 1991.

Who Said That? Famous Americans Speak (picture book biography), illustrated by David Catrow, Holt (New York, NY), 1997.

Hoops (picture book), illustrated by Stephen T. Johnson, Silver Whistle (San Diego, CA), 1997.

Home Run: The Story of Babe Ruth (picture book biography), illustrated by Mike Wimmer, Silver Whistle (San Diego, CA), 1998.

Black Whiteness: Admiral Byrd Alone in the Antarctic (picture book biography), illustrated by Walter Lyon Krudop, Atheneum (New York, NY), 1998.

It's Funny Where Ben's Train Takes Him, illustrated by Joanna Yardley, Orchard (New York, NY), 1999.

Hercules, illustrated by Raul Colon, Silver Whistle (San Diego, CA), 1999.

Edna, illustrated by Joanna Yardley, Orchard (New York, NY), 2000.

Messenger, Messenger, illustrated by Barry Root, Atheneum (New York, NY), 2000.

Lookin' for Bird in the Big City, illustrated by Marek Los, Harcourt (San Diego, CA), 2001.

I Love Going through This Book, illustrated by Dan Yaccarino, HarperCollins (New York, NY), 2001.

Goal (picture book), illustrated by Stephen T. Johnson, Harcourt (San Diego, CA), 2001.

Chocolate: Riches from the Rainforest, Abrams (New York, NY), 2002.

Pandora, illustrated by Raul Colon, Harcourt (San Diego, CA), 2002.

The Secret of the Great Houdini, illustrated by Leonid Gore, Simon & Schuster (New York, NY), 2002.

Into the Air: The Story of the Wright Brothers' First Flight (picture book biography), illustrated by Bill Wylie, Silver Whistle (San Diego, CA), 2002.

Into the Woods: John James Audubon Lives His Dream, illustrated by Wendell Minor, Atheneum (New York, NY), 2003.

(Editor) *Earth from Above for Young Readers,* photographs by Yann Arthus Bertrand, illustrated by David Giraudon, Abrams (New York, NY), 2003.

(Editor) *Volcanoes: Journey to the Crater's Edge,* photographs by Philippe Bourseiller, illustrated by David Giraudon, Abrams (New York, NY), 2003.

(Editor) *The Sea: Exploring Life on an Ocean Planet,* photographs by Philip Plisson, illustrated by Emmanuel Cerisier, Abrams (New York, NY), 2003.

Amelia Earhart: Free in the Skies, illustrated by Bill Wylie, Silver Whistle (San Diego, CA), 2003.

Langston's Train Ride, illustrated by Leonard Jenkins, Orchard (New York, NY), 2004.

Martin Luther King, Jr.: Until Justice Runs Down Like Water, illustrated by Bill Wylie, Silver Whistle (San Diego, CA), 2004.

American Moments: Scenes from American History, illustrated by Bruce Strachan, Holt (New York, NY), 2004.

Seurat and "La Grande Jatte": Connecting the Dots, Abrams (New York, NY), 2004.

(With Tiki and Ronde Barber) *By My Brother's Side,* Simon & Schuster (New York, NY), 2004.

OTHER

(With Mary Jane Gray) *Basic Writing Skills,* Society for Visual Education (Chicago, IL), 1976.

The Triumph of Mittens: Poems, Boardwell-Kloner (Chicago, IL), 1980.

Colonial America, illustrated by James Seward, Doubleday (Garden City, NY), 1992.

Also writer and producer of over one hundred filmstrips and cassettes on educational subjects.

SIDELIGHTS: A writer of informational books of biography and history as well as a poet, Robert Burleigh is noted for introducing difficult historical topics to young readers in an accessible and effective manner. Characteristically using a picture book format, the author presents facts about his subjects—most often notable Americans such as Henry David Thoreau, Charles Lindbergh, Babe Ruth, Harry Houdini, and Admiral Richard Perry—in simple language and present-tense narration. Burleigh favors clipped, staccato texts in both his prose and his poetry, a style credited with expressing the ideas, drama, and importance of each of his topics in an evocative fashion. Reviewers also note the successful marriage of the author's texts with the illustrations of such artists as Lloyd Bloom, Mike Wimmer, and Stephen T. Johnson.

Nineteenth-century writer and philosopher Henry David Thoreau is the subject of Burleigh's first biography, *A Man Named Thoreau.* Considered a balanced overview of Thoreau's life and influence, the book addresses its subject's time at Walden Pond, his love for nature, his literary works, and his civil disobedience, among other topics. Burleigh presents Thoreau and his ideas by combining biographical facts with quotes from the philosopher's popular work *Walden.* Writing in *School Library Journal,* Ruth Semrau called *A Man Named Thoreau* a book that "unfolds new pleasures on every page" and deemed it an "exquisitely simple introduction to a difficult subject." David E. White observed in *Horn Book* that the quota-

tions "interspersed throughout the text . . . are beneficial in capturing the essence of this noted figure." A reviewer for the *Bulletin of the Center for Children's Books* declared that to "have simplified concepts so much without distortion is a gift to the younger reader or listener."

In his picture book *Flight: The Journey of Charles Lindbergh,* Burleigh describes Lindbergh's famous nonstop flight from New York to Paris in 1927. Basing his text on Lindbergh's memoir *The Spirit of St. Louis,* Burleigh focuses on the pilot's journey at the age of twenty-five. Once again, the author is credited with successfully conveying a sophisticated concept, in this case the difficulty of, in the words of *New York Times Book Review* contributor Signe Wilkinson, "staying awake, alert and in charge of a plane and one's life for two days and a very long, lonely night before sleep" to an audience "too young to appreciate what pulling an all-nighter feels like." *Horn Book* reviewer Ann A. Flowers remarked that the text conveys Lindbergh's bravery, the drain on him personally, and the primitive state of his plane in "completely convincing detail" and noted that Burleigh's use of the present tense "keeps the reader in suspense from the moment the plane takes off until [its arrival in] Paris." Flowers concluded that the book is a "pioneer example of the 'right stuff,' splendidly and excitingly presented." Burleigh's use of sentence fragments and single-sentence paragraphs "conveys the excitement of Lindbergh's historic flight," noted a critic in *Kirkus Reviews,* who called *Flight* a book "that brings new life to one of the stories of the century." Burleigh received the Orbis Pictus Award in 1992 for this work.

Shifting to sports, Burleigh wrote a picture book biography of baseball's most widely known hero in *Home Run: The Story of Babe Ruth,* as well as two picture books of poetry, *Hoops* and *Goal,* that describe basketball and soccer in verses that simulate the action of the players and the excitement of the game. Filled with tactile imagery, *Hoops* and *Goal* outline the way the game feels to its players. "An ode to the game for older children, veteran players, and NBA fans," declared a *Publishers Weekly* reviewer of *Hoops,* "this book will give language to teenagers' experience both on and off the court." A *Kirkus Reviews* critic noted that *Goal* uses soccer as a frame "to demonstrate the power of teamwork to achieve success." The critic concluded that the book is "a real winner."

In his picture book *Black Whiteness: Admiral Byrd Alone in the Antarctic,* Burleigh retells the explorer's incredible six-month stay alone in the Antarctic. Based on Byrd's daily journal, *Black Whiteness* includes detailed descriptions of Byrd's enduring hardships—subzero temperatures, continuous darkness with limited lighting equipment, and loneliness. "Burleigh's spare prose eloquently captures the spartan surroundings in which Byrd conducted daily meteorological studies," observed a critic in *Kirkus Reviews,* who concluded that the explorer's story is "severe, often depressing, and always riveting." A similar adventurous hero can be found in *Into the Woods: John James Audubon Lives His Dream.* Burleigh uses rhyming couplets to communicate Audubon's decision to give up business in order to wander through the wilderness, painting and drawing the sights he sees during his adventures. A *Publishers Weekly* reviewer wrote of *Into the Woods* that Audubon's "philosophy wafts through the volume like a summer breeze." A *Kirkus Reviews* critic called the book a "tribute" to Audubon and a "feast for bird lovers."

Burleigh is as comfortable writing about big cities as he is about wilderness explorers. *Messenger, Messenger* follows a bike messenger through his busy day, from waking up in his book-filled apartment to making deliveries throughout the city. At the book's end, the tired worker returns to his flat to be warmly greeted by his cat. Writing in *Booklist,* Gillian Engberg felt that the picture book "beautifully captures the energizing pulse of urban life and satisfying work." In *Lookin' for Bird in the Big City,* a teenaged Miles Davis, trumpet in hand, makes music in the city streets as he goes in search of his hero, Charlie Parker. Once again, Burleigh employs poetic language and rhythms to convey the flavor of jazz music and the enthusiasm Davis feels for it. "Words and art harmonize in this creatively imagined account," observed a *Publishers Weekly* reviewer. *School Library Journal* contributor Mary Elam concluded that the work offers "a lovely and lyrical look at this all-American art form."

Ancient Greece abounds with mythical tales about super-human exploits and misadventures. Burleigh has brought two of these to younger readers with his *Hercules* and *Pandora.* In *Hercules,* the hero tests his mettle against supernatural challenges, culminating in his descent to the underworld to battle the three-headed dog, Cerberus. *Booklist*'s Ilene Cooper liked the fact that *Hercules* uses "language that draws on the strength of its subject yet speaks in the lilt of poetry." In her *Booklist* review, Stephanie Zvirin felt that *Hercules*

would inspire young readers to search for other ancient myths about Hercules and other Greek gods, calling the book a "beautiful retelling." *Pandora* puts a human face to the curious woman who, according to Greek myth, unleashed all the world's ills by opening a container. In his version of the story, Burleigh uses verse to illuminate how Pandora's curiosity becomes an obsession, despite her understanding of the danger she faces opening the jar. In a *School Library Journal* review of the work, Patricia Lothrop-Green praised "the graceful drama that unfolds" in the story, concluding: "This Pandora is tempting." Gillian Engberg of *Booklist* found *Pandora* to be "another fine retelling of a Greek myth."

Burleigh offers middle-grade readers a detailed look at a favorite confection in *Chocolate: Riches from the Rainforest.* The illustrated book covers many aspects of chocolate, from its history as a food of the Maya and Aztecs to its journey from cacao pod to candy bar. The author writes about the slave labor once used in the cacao and sugar industries, and about how Milton Hershey revolutionized the sale of milk chocolate from his factory in Pennsylvania. In a *School Library Journal* review, Augusta R. Malvagno praised the "delightful" book for its "kaleidoscope of fascinating information," while a contributor to *Kirkus Reviews* concluded that the title is "a well-conceived and executed work on a subject of great interest."

Some critics have particularly praised Burleigh's *The Secret of the Great Houdini.* Burleigh explores Houdini's escape from a trunk hurled into deep water from the point of view of a youngster named Sam and his Uncle Ezra, who have joined a crowd to watch the feat. While Sam and Uncle Ezra anxiously await Houdini's escape, Uncle Ezra tells Sam about Houdini's childhood and hardscrabble youth. Sam can hardly concentrate on what his uncle is saying, so terrified is he of the possibility that Houdini will drown. "Burleigh achieves immediacy by writing his poetic text in the present tense," observed Marianne Saccardi in *School Library Journal.* "Houdini is a fascinating figure for all ages," maintained a *Kirkus Reviews* critic. "This snapshot of one incredible feat . . . may spur further exploration, and inspiration." In her *Booklist* review, Gillian Engberg declared that the work "captures the mystique of its famous subject."

Burleigh lives and works in Chicago. In addition to his writing, he enjoys making presentations to schools on the subjects he writes about and the uses of poetry in literature. He has also served as the writer and producer of a variety of educational filmstrips and cassettes and has worked as a writer and artist for the Society of Visual Education.

BIOGRAPHICAL AND CRITICAL SOURCES:

PERIODICALS

Booklist, February 1, 1999, Stephanie Zvirin, review of *It's Funny Where Ben's Train Takes Him,* p. 979; August, 1999, Ilene Cooper, review of *Hercules,* p. 2050; March 15, 2000, Carolyn Phelan, review of *Edna,* p. 1377; May 15, 2000, Gillian Engberg, review of *Messenger, Messenger,* p. 1742, and Stephanie Zvirin, review of *Hercules,* p. 1758; February 15, 2001, Bill Ott, review of *Lookin' for Bird in the Big City,* p. 1152; June 1, 2001, Marta Segal, review of *I Love Going through This Book,* p. 1888; June 1, 2002, Gillian Engberg, review of *Pandora,* p. 1711; July, 2002, Gillian Engberg, review of *The Secret of the Great Houdini,* p. 1854; January 1, 2003, Julie Cummins, review of *Into the Woods: John James Audubon Lives His Dream,* p. 874.

Bulletin of the Center for Children's Books, December, 1985, review of *A Man Named Thoreau,* p. 63.

Horn Book, March, 1986, David E. White, review of *A Man Named Thoreau,* pp. 215-216; November, 1991, Ann A. Flowers, review of *Flight: The Journey of Charles Lindbergh,* p. 752.

Kirkus Reviews, August 15, 1991, review of *Flight,* p. 1086; December 1, 1997, review of *Black Whiteness: Admiral Byrd Alone in the Antarctic,* p. 1773;

February 1, 2001, review of *Goal,* p. 180; March 1, 2002, review of *Chocolate: Riches from the Rainforest,* p. 330; May 1, 2002, review of *Pandora,* p. 650; June 15, 2002, review of *The Secret of the Great Houdini,* p. 876; January 1, 2003, review of *Into the Woods,* p. 58.

New York Times Book Review, January 26, 1992, Signe Wilkinson, review of *Flight,* p. 21.

Publishers Weekly, October 6, 1997, review of *Hoops,* p. 83; August 9, 1999, review of *Hercules,* p. 352; May 14, 2001, review of *Lookin' for Bird in the Big City,* p. 82; June 19, 2000, review of *Messenger, Messenger,* p. 54; June 4, 2001, review of *I Love Going through This Book,* p. 79; April 1, 2002, review of *Pandora,* p. 83; June 3, 2002, review of *The Secret of the Great Houdini,* p. 88; December 2, 2002, review of *Into the Woods,* p. 52.

School Library Journal, January, 1986, Ruth Semrau, review of *A Man Named Thoreau,* p. 64; October, 1999, Nina Lindsay, review of *Hercules,* p. 135; April, 2000, Kate McClelland, review of *Edna,* p. 92; April, 2001, Lee Bock, review of *Goal,* p. 129; June, 2001, Marianne Saccardi, review of *I Love Going through This Book,* p. 104, and Mary Elam, review of *Lookin' for Bird in the Big City,* p. 104; April, 2002, Augusta R. Malvagno, review of *Chocolate,* p. 129; May, 2002, Patricia Lothrop-Green, review of *Pandora,* p. 134; July, 2002, Marianne Saccardi, review of *The Secret of the Great Houdini,* p. 85; September, 2002, Dona Ratterree, review of *Into the Air,* p. 241; January, 2003, Laurie von Mehren, review of *Earth from Above for Young Readers,* p. 150; February, 2003, Robyn Walker, review of *Into the Woods,* p. 128.

Teacher Librarian, June, 2000, Jessica Higgs, review of *Hercules,* p. 54.*

C

CALLAHAN, Daniel 1930-

PERSONAL: Born July 19, 1930, in Washington, DC; son of Vincent F. (an editor) and Florence Anita (Hawkins) Callahan; married Sidney Cornelia deShazo (a social psychologist), June 5, 1954; children: Mark, Stephen, John, Peter, Sarah, David. *Education:* Yale University, B.A., 1948; Georgetown University, M.A., 1957; Harvard University, Ph.D., 1965. *Politics:* Democrat. *Hobbies and other interests:* Tennis, gardening.

ADDRESSES: Home—P.O. Box 260 Ardsley-on-Hudson, NY 10503. *Office*—The Hastings Center, 21 Malcolm Gordon Rd., Garrison, NY 10524-5555. *E-mail*—callahan@thehastingscenter.org.

CAREER: Harvard Divinity School, Cambridge, MA, teaching fellow in Roman Catholic studies, 1959-61; *Commonweal,* New York, NY, 1961-68, became executive editor, 1967; The Population Council, staff associate, 1969-70; Hastings Center, Garrison, NY, co-founder and president, 1969-96; became director of International Programs, 1997; Harvard Medical School, Divison of Medical Ethics, senior fellow, 1998—. Visiting assistant professor at Temple University, 1963, Brown University, 1965, Harvard Center for Population and Development Studies, 1996. Lectures widely at American and Canadian universities and before professional and academic associations. Council for International Organizations of Medical Sciences, Geneva, Switzerland, consultant, 1992; Centers for Disease Control and Prevention, U.S. Department of Health and Human Services, member,

Daniel Callahan

Advisory Committee to the Director, 1995, Ethics Subcommittee, chair, 1997; Instituto De Bioetica, Madrid, Spain, committee member, 1996; Task Force on Corporate-Association Relationship, American Medical Association, member, 1997-98; Friends of Ethics, Harvard Medical School, chair, 1997; Kaiser Permanente, National Advisory Council on Professional and Organizational Ethics, member, 1998; Pan American Health Organization, Regional Program on Bioethics, International Adivsory Board, member, 1998; Public Agenda, Policy Review Board, member, 1998; Gene Therapy President's Committee, University of Pennsylvania, member, 2000. *Military service:* U.S. Army, Counterintelligence Corps. 1952-55; became sergeant.

MEMBER: National Academy of Sciences, Institute of Medicine, New York Council for the Humanities.

AWARDS, HONORS: National Catholic Book Award, 1964, for *The Mind of the Catholic Layman;* Thomas More Medal, 1970, for *Abortion: Law, Choice, and Morality.*

WRITINGS:

The Mind of the Catholic Layman, Scribner (New York, NY), 1963.
Honesty in the Church, Scribner (New York, NY), 1965.
The New Church, Scribner (New York, NY), 1966.
Abortion: Law, Choice, and Morality, Macmillan (New York, NY), 1970.
Ethics and Population Limitation, Population Council (New York, NY), 1971.
The American Population Debate, Doubleday (New York, NY), 1972.
The Tyranny of Survival: And Other Pathologies of Civilized Life, Macmillan (New York, NY), 1973.
Setting Limits: Medical Goals in an Aging Society, Simon & Schuster (New York, NY), 1987.
What Kind of Life?: The Limits of Medical Progress, Simon & Schuster (New York, NY), 1990.
The Troubled Dream of Life: Living with Mortality, Simon & Schuster (New York, NY), 1993, also published as *In Search of Peaceful Death,* Simon & Schuster (New York, NY), 1994.
False Hopes: Why America's Quest for Perfect Health Is a Recipe for Failure, Simon & Schuster (New York, NY), 1998, also published as *False Hopes: Overcoming the Obstacles to an Affordable, Sustainable Medicine,* Rutgers University Press (Newark, NJ), 1999.
What Price Better Health?: Hazards of the Research Imperative, University of California Press (Berkeley, CA), 2003.

EDITOR

(With D. O'Hanlon and H. Oberman) *Christianity Divided,* Sheed & Ward (New York, NY), 1961.
Federal Aid and Catholic Schools, Helicon (Baltimore, MD), 1964.
Generation of the Third Eye, Sheed & Ward (New York, NY), 1965.
The Secular City Debate, Macmillan (New York, NY), 1966.
(With others) *The Role of Theology in the University,* Bruce Publishing (Milwaukee, WI), 1967.
God, Jesus, Spirit, Herder & Herder (New York, NY), 1969.
The Catholic Case for Contraception, Macmillan (New York, NY), 1969.
The American Population Debate, Doubleday (New York, NY), 1971.
(With others) *The Ethical Issues in Genetic Counseling and the Use of Genetic Knowledge,* Plenum (New York, NY), 1973.
(With Sissela Bok) *Ethics Teaching in Higher Education,* Plenum Press (New York, NY), 1980.
(With Phillip G. Clark) *Ethical Issues of Population Aid: Culture, Economics, and International Assistance,* Irvington Publishers (New York, NY), 1981.
(With Arthur L. Caplan) *Ethics in Hard Times,* Plenum Press (New York), 1981.
(With H. Tristram Engelhardt, Jr.) *The Roots of Ethics: Science, Religion, and Values,* Plenum Press (New York, NY), 1981.
(With others) *The Teaching of Ethics in the Military,* Hastings Center (Hastings-on-Hudson, NY), 1982.
(With Bruce Jennings) *Ethics, the Social Sciences, and Policy Analysis,* Plenum Press (New York, NY), 1983.
(With wife, Sidney Callahan) *Abortion: Understanding Differences,* Plenum Press (New York, NY), 1984.
(With Arthur L. Caplan and Bruce Jennings) *Applying the Humanities,* Plenum Press (New York, NY), 1985.
(With others) *Congress and the Media: The Ethical Connection,* Hastings Center (Hastings-on-Hudson), NY), 1985.
(With Bruce Jennings) *Representation and Responsibility: Exploring Legislative Ethics,* Plenum Press (New York, NY), 1985.
(With G. R. Dunstan) *Biomedical Ethics: An Anglo-American Dialogue,* New York Academy of Sciences (New York, NY), 1988.

(With Philip J. Boyle) *What Price Mental Health?: The Ethics and Politics of Setting Priorities,* Georgetown University Press (Washington, DC), 1995.

(With others) *A World Growing Old: The Coming Health Care Challenges,* Georgetown University Press (Washington, DC), 1995.

(With Mark J. Hanson) *The Goals of Medicine: The Forgotten Issue in Health Care Reform,* Georgetown University Press (Washington, DC), 1999.

Promoting Healthy Behavior: How Much Freedom? Whose Responsibility?, Georgetown University Press (Washington, DC), 2000.

The Role of Complementary and Alternative Medicine: Accommodating Pluralism, Georgetown University Press (Washington, DC), 2002.

EDITOR, WITH H. TRISTRAM ENGELHARDT, JR.; "THE FOUNDATIONS OF ETHICS AND ITS RELATIONSHIP TO SCIENCE" SERIES

Science, Ethics, and Medicine, Hastings Center (Hastings-on-Hudson, NY), 1976.

Knowledge, Value, and Belief, Hastings Center (Hastings-on-Hudson, NY), 1977.

Morals, Science, and Sociality, Hastings Center (Hastings-on-Hudson, NY), 1978.

Knowing and Valuing: The Search for Common Roots, Hastings Center (Hastings-on-Hudson, NY), 1980.

Contributor to books, including *Theology and the University,* edited by John Coulson, Darton, Longmans & Todd (London, England), 1964; *Religion in America,* edited by William G. McLaughlin and Robert N. Bellah, Houghton Mifflin (Boston, MA), 1968; *American Catholic Thought on Social Questions,* edited by Aaron I. Abell, Bobbs-Merrill (Indianapolis, IN), 1968; *American Philosophy and the Future,* edited by Michael Novak, Scribner (New York, NY), 1968; *Ethical Issues in Genetic Counseling and the Use of Genetic Knowledge,* Plenum Press (New York, NY), 1972; *The Population Crisis and Moral Responsibility,* edited by Walbert and Butler, Public Affairs Press (Washington, DC), 1973; *The Population Crisis and Moral Responsibility,* edited by J. Philip Wogaman, Public Affairs Press (Washington, DC), 1973; *Ethical Issues in Health Care Management,* Center for Health Administration Studies, University of Chicago (Chicago, IL), 1975.

Also contributor to *Interdisciplinary Workshop on the Interrelationships between Science and Technology, and Ethics and Values,* edited by William A. Blanpied

and Wendy Weisman-Dermer, American Association for the Advancement of Science (Washington, DC), 1975; *The Nature of Scientific Discovery,* edited by Owen Gingerich, Smithsonian Institution (Washington, DC), 1975; *Small Comforts for Hard Times: Humanists in the Public Forum,* edited by F. Stuber and M. Mooney, Columbia University Press (New York, NY), 1976; *Genetics and the Law,* edited by Aubrey Milunsky, Plenum Press (New York, NY), 1976; *Ethics and Health Policy,* edited by R. M. Veatch and R. Branson, Ballinger Publishing (Cambridge, MA), 1976; *Modifying Man: Implications and Ethics,* edited by Craig Ellison, University Press of America (Washington, DC), 1977; *Population Policy and Ethics,* edited by Robert M. Veatch, Irvington Publishers (New York, NY), 1977; *Patterns for Progress: From the Sciences to Medicine,* edited by John A. Hogg and Jacob C. Stucki, Upjohn Company (Kalamazoo, MI), 1977; *Research with Recombinant DNA,* National Academy of Sciences (Washington, DC), 1977; *Philosophical Medical Ethics: Its Nature and Significance,* edited by Stuart F. Spicker and H. Tristam Engelhardt, Jr., D. Reidel Publishing (Boston, MA), 1977; *Risk/Benefit Decisions and the Public Health,* edited by J. A. Staffa, Office of Health Affairs, Food and Drug Administration (Washington, DC), 1978; *Life-Span,* edited by Robert M. Veatch, Harper & Row (New York, NY), 1979; *Genetics and the Law II,* edited by A. Milunsky, Plenum Press (New York, NY), 1980; *Who Decides? Conflicts of Rights in Health Care,* edited by Nora K. Bell, Humana Press (Clifton, NJ), 1982; *The Professions and Ethics,* edited by Louis H.Orzack and Annell L.Simcoe, Rutgers University (Newark, NJ), 1982; *By No Extraordinary Means: The Choice to Forgo Life-Sustaining Food and Water,* edited by Joanne Lynn, University of Indiana Press (Bloomington, IN), 1986; *The Medicare System of Prospective Payment,* edited by Mohan L. Garg and Barbara Barzansky, Praeger (New York, NY), 1986; *Medical Education: Making the Grade in Cost Containment,* edited by Russel D. Cunningham, W. K. Kellogg Foundation (Battle Creek, MI), 1986; *What Is a Person,* Humana Press (Clifton, NJ), 1988; *Casebook on the Termination of Life-Sustaining Treatment and the Care of the Dying,* edited by Cynthia B. Cohen, Indiana University Press (Bloomington, IN), 1988; *Health Policy, Ethics, and Human Values: European and North American Perspectives,* edited by Z. Bankowski and J. H. Bryant, Council for International Organizations (Geneva, Switzerland), 1988.

Also contributor to *Ethics in Medicine,* edited by Peter Allebeck and Bengt Jansson, Raven Press (New York,

NY), 1990; *A Good Old Age?: The Paradox of Setting Limits,* edited by Paul Homer and Martha Holstein, Simon & Schuster (New York, NY), 1990; *A Time to Be Born and a Time to Die,* edited by Barry S. Kogan, Aldine de Gruyter (New York, NY), 1991; *Emerging Issues in Biomedical Policy,* edited by Robert H. Blank and Andrea Bonnicksen, Columbia University Press (New York, NY), 1992; *Basic Benefits and Clinical Guidelines,* edited by David C. Hadorn, Westview Press (Boulder, CO), 1992; *Ending Human Life: Ethical Issues Surrounding Death and Dying,* Center for Ethics Development (Newberry, SC), 1992; *Heath Care for an Aging Population,* edited by Chris Hackler, SUNY Press (Albany, NY), 1994; *A World Growing Old: The Coming Health Care Challenge,* edited by Callahan, ter Meulen, and Topinkova, Georgetown University Press (Washington DC), 1995; *Controversies in Ethics in Long-Term Care,* edited by Ellen Olson, Springer (New York, NY), 1995; *Encyclopeida of Bioethics,* edited by Warren Reich, Macmillan (New York, NY), 1995; *Birth to Death: Science and Bioethics,* edited by David C. Thomasma and Thomasine Kushner, Cambridge University Press (Oxford, England), 1996; *Philosophical Perspectives in Bioethics,* edited by L.W.Summer and Joseph Boyle, University of Toronto Press (Toronto, Canada), 1996; *Physician-Assisted Suicide,* edited by Robert F. Weir, Indiana University Press (Bloomington, IN), 1997; *Getting Doctors to Listen: Ethics and Outcomes Data in Contest,* edited by Philip Boyle, Georgetown University Press (Washington, DC), 1998; *End of Life Decisions: A Psychosocial Perspective,* American Psychiatric Press (Washington, DC), 1998; *Mother Time: Women, Aging and Ethics,* edited by Margaret Walker, Rowman & Littlefield (Lanham, MD), 1999; *Is There a Duty to Die?,* edited by John Hardwig, Routledge & Kegan Paul (New York, NY), 1999; *Building Bioethics: Conversations with Clouser and Friends on Medical Ethics,* edited by Loretta M. Kopelman, Kluwer Publishers (Boston, MA), 1999; *Managing Health Behavior: Ethical Dilemmas in Health Promotion,* edited by Mark Hanson and Daniel Callahan, Georgetown Press (Washington, DC), 2000; *Health Care Reforms and Central and Eastern Europe,* edited by Jiri Simek, Institute of Postgraduate Medical Education (Prague, Czechoslovakia), 2000; *Ethics and the Kidney,* edited by Norman Levinsky, Oxford University Press (New York, NY), 2000

Associate editor of *IRB: A Review of Human Subjects Research* (1979). Member of the board of numerous journals, including *Ethics in Science and Medicine, Science, Technology and Human Values, Social Theory and Practice, Social Theory and Practice, Business and Professional Ethics, Technology in Society, Criminal Justice Ethics, Environmental Ethics, Advanced Studies in Professional Ethics, Medical Humanities Review, Journal of Medicine, Ethics and Law* (Canada), *Cambridge Quarterly for Healthcare Ethics,* and *American Journal of Bioethics.*

Contributor to numerous periodicals, including *American Journal of Ethics and Medicine, American Journal of Geriatric Cardiology, American Journal of Physical Medicine and Rehabilitation, Bioethics and Biolaw II, Bioethics Forum, Cambridge Quarterly, Business and Health, Commonweal, Daedalus, Harper's, Atlantic Monthly, Center Magazine, Hastings Center Report, Health Care Analysis, Health Progress, International Journal of Bioethics, Journal of the American Medical Association, Journal of Applied Gerontology, Journal of Evaluation in Clinical Practice, Journal of Health Politics, Policy and Law, Journal of Medicine and Philosophy, New England Journal of Medicine, New York Times, Progress in Palliative Care, Psychology, Public Policy and Law, Society,* and *Washington Post.*

SIDELIGHTS: When Daniel Callahan speaks and writes, people listen and read. Callahan, a bioethicist and founder of the Hastings Center, a think tank, has pondered much and written widely on such issues as rationing health care, cloning, stem cell research, abortion, aging, dying, alternative medicine, among other topics. He has written several dozen books, and numerous chapters and articles, and because of the controversial nature of his subject matter, Callahan's books often spark debate among scholars, health care professionals, and people interested in health-care issues. To quote Norman B. Levy, of the *New England Journal of Medicine,* Callahan "is well informed about the status of medical advances, is a well-known philosopher and ethicist, and is clearly a thoughtful and considerate person who writes simply and well."

In his award-winning *What Kind of Life?: The Limits of Medical Progress,* Callahan returns to a discussion that he had begun in 1987 with *Setting Limits: Medical Goals in an Aging Society,* expanding it to include all ages. Callahan probes the nature of the "healthcare problem," pondering, "Perhaps the healthcare problem is not what appears on the surface, just a matter of improved financing, equity and efficiency. Perhaps it is a crisis about the meaning and nature of health and about the place that the pursuit of health should have in our lives." Thus Callahan points to values as the crux of the problem, specifically Americans' obsession with medical progress which distorts the common view of what makes up good health. While we allot large sums to certain research and prolonging life beyond reasonable expectations, Callahan argues, we neglect other societal needs. He says that much new medical technology extends lives but offers poor quality of life. Callahan proposes having a central government agency determine societal needs for health care and the agency would pay for the allotted services, with employer-based insurance and individuals paying any costs beyond the stipulated amounts.

What Kind of Life? brought about much discussion among scholars and health care professionals, who offered varied assessments of his arguments' validity. Calling the work a "landmark analysis" in his *Hospital & Health Services Administration* review, Dean M. Crowder stated: "Often profound, the book provides a thoughtful examination of the values and desires that Americans have and on which our health-care decisions are based." Stanley J. Reiser, writing in the *Journal of the American Medical Association,* also praised *What Kind of Life?,* dubbing it a "challenging book, which makes a splendid effort to unite moral and policy analysis and succeeds at many levels. Callahan has many good thoughts on rationing and political strategies to achieve them." Yet the work did not go unchallenged. In the *New Leader,* Amitai Etzioni commented on the morality of Callahan's plan and remarked that "skeptics who consider Callahan's position morally dubious and politically naive will point out other ways to deal with health-care costs." Although *BioScience*'s Clyde J. Behney praised the work for providing a "needed diagnosis," he found Callahan's remedy "seriously flawed," because his "proposal falls short of being the needed vision and, even for those who might agree with his proposal, never really succeeds in being a practical blueprint for turning the vision into reality." This topic continued to be a focus of Callahan's research. In 1996 he published the results of a two-year joint research project by the Hastings Center and the Institute of Bioethics in Maastricht, The Netherlands, in *A World Growing Old: The Coming Healthcare Challenges.*

In 1993 Callahan served up *The Troubled Dream of Life: Living with Mortality,* in which he focuses on society's treatment of the dying. First he provides a

historical overview of death in the centuries prior to the twentieth, when people died rapidly of infectious diseases rather than lingering because of medical advances. Such improvements in medicine have promoted the perception that death is an enemy to be resisted rather than an integral part of the circle of life. Callahan wonders: "What should [death] mean to us, and what kind of persons should we try to become as we approach our end? How ought we to bear pain, suffering and fear? They are questions of meaning, purpose and character." Callahan proposes that each person must find meaning in his/her own death and that the dying need others to help them do this. We, Callahan says, must try "to see if we can be prodded as a people to begin the work of creating a common view of death . . . sufficient to allow us some shared language and public behavior." Although Callahan does not subscribe to religion or transcendence after death, he states, "I can envy those who have such hope, even if I cannot share it." He concludes, "Can death, and the life in which it is embedded, be transcended? I do not see this for myself, but I hope to live the remainder of my days in a way that at least puts me in a position to be (as Wordsworth put it) 'surprised by joy.' It is unlikely but perhaps not impossible. I wait and watch."

As Michael J. Farrell explained in *National Catholic Reporter, The Troubled Dream of Life* is a "fascinating" work because compared with other events, death is "a major event . . . and what we conclude about our deaths will determine much about our lives." The study elicited much attention. In *Christian Century,* Hugh McElwain declared that "only a person of Daniel Callahan's stature as a medical ethicist, with his many years of experience in the field and his capacity for penetrating analysis, could have written such a challenging work." Writing in the *Journal of the American Medical Association,* Norman B. Levy, noting that "it certainly was difficult to read, but once started it flowed easily," called it an "essential book for all physicians, nonphysicians, medical educators, and medical policymakers." McElwain shared this opinion when he stated that the work "should become regular reading if not required reading for all medical professionals, caregivers and indeed all who confront the task of integrating understandings of life and death."

Callahan returned to what he considers the debacle of the health-care system in his 1998 publication *False Hopes: Why America's Quest for Perfect Health Is a*

Recipe for Failure. Believing that medical advances have come nearly to their limits and subscribing to medical utilitarianism, Callahan espouses a system of health-care rationing to contain rising costs. In a Callahan-designed system, which would be global, measures intended to improve the health of a population would prevail over those geared to specific individuals. Promoting a healthful environment (such as keeping toxins out of the food supply, immunizing children, educating people about healthy behavior) would take precedence over medical research. According to Callahan appropriate goals for this new medical world view would include a normal lifespan, treatment of pain and trauma when a good prognosis exists, and alleviation of chronic pain, while other currently held goals (increased lifespan, cosmetic surgery, infertility treatment, and saving premature babies) would be cast aside.

Booklist's Mary Carroll described *False Hopes* as "cogently argued; likely to generate debate," which it did, some discussion over practicalities, some over the morality of Callahan's proposal. According to Wesley J. Smith, writing in *National Right to Life News,* "Callahan's antipathy toward medical progress—and his firm belief that some of us must be pushed out of the lifeboat to benefit others—can be said to reflect fairly the predominant view in the bioethical community." "Whether or not one agrees with Callahan's world view," wrote Robert H. Brook in *Lancet,* "this book must be read. Its arguments touch the core of current debates about the future relation between medicine and society." Brook tried to put Callahan's effort in perspective, stating, "To appreciate the book's relevance, one must understand something about the author's heart. *False Hopes* is not written by a person who hates the elderly, or who is anti-technology. It is written by a person who has a good soul, who is struggling with the inequality in health between the developing and developed worlds, and between classes within the developed world, and who firmly believes in the concept of solidarity as expressed in the social movements in Europe." Calling the work "required reading, important, indeed imperative to think about," *Washington Monthly* contributor Margaret P. Battin nevertheless decided that "we shouldn't swallow the medicine even after we've seen the prescription" because although "much of what he has to say is indeed the right medicine for what ails our health care system . . . 'good enough' isn't really good enough, when it means giving up on patients just as their needs become great. For the vast majority who will need only basic care throughout their lives to write off a minority who need more help is indecent."

Callahan told *CA:* "I seem to be one of those comparatively rare people who actually enjoys writing. I look forward to it, and when I am too tired to do other things turn to writing as a relief and a rest. I have often joked that one can write books or read them, but that it is hard to do both with equal energy. I am too restless to sit still for long periods of reading, but for me writing is not only a mental activity but a physical activity as well. I am also stimulated to write because my topics are now the daily fare of the media and public debate: the future of American health care, the debates over cloning and stem cell research and, in general, all of the ethical problems of contemporary medicine and biology. Simply by virtue of those topics there will be an interest in what I write; and that is a great help when the going gets tough in writing well about them.

"My writing process is to first read widely on my chosen topics, outline carefully, and work to write as clean a first draft as possible. I do not usually do any broadscale editing and rewriting, but do a good deal of tinkering with the language. While most of my writing these days is aimed at academics and intellectuals rather than the general public, I work hard to make my writing accessible to everyone. My time spent as an editor and editorial writer in my early career was a great help in that respect. I had to learn how to write fast, clearly, and to space what I had to meet hard deadlines, right to the minute."

BIOGRAPHICAL AND CRITICAL SOURCES:

PERIODICALS

Ageing and Society, January, 1997, Malvin Schechter, review of *A World Growing Old: The Coming Health Care Challenges,* pp. 75-76, review of *A World Growing Old,* pp. 77-78, Alan Maynard, review of *A World Growing Old,* pp. 78-80.
America, June 25, 1988, review of *Setting Limits: Medical Goals in an Aging Society,* p. 21; June 30, 1990, Edmund D. Pellegrino, review of *What Kind of Life?: The Limits of Medical Progress,* pp. 20-21.

Bioethics, January, 1998, Giles Yates, review of *What Price Mental Health?: The Ethics and Politics of Setting Priorities,* pp. 88-89.

BioScience, February, 1981, Van R. Potter, review of *Ethics Teaching in Higher Education,* p. 172; April, 1991, Clyde J. Behney, review of *What Kind of Life?,* p. 265.

Booklist, November 15, 1987, review of *Setting Limits,* p. 517; December 1, 1989, review of *What Kind of Life?,* p. 706; August, 1993, William Beatty, review of *The Troubled Dream of Life: Living with Mortality,* p. 2014; April, 1998, Mary Carroll, review of *False Hopes: Why America's Quest for Perfect Health Is a Recipe for Failure,* p. 1284.

Change, November, 1980, review of *Ethics Teaching in Higher Education,* p. 60; April, 1982, Robert L. Spaeth, review of *Ethics Teaching in Higher Education,* pp. 55-56.

Choice, June, 1981, review of *Ethics Teaching in Higher Education,* p. 1428; May, 1982, review of *The Roots of Ethics: Science, Religion, and Values,* p. 1262; January, 1988, review of *Setting Limits,* p. 844.

Christian Century, April 13, 1988, Bonnie Miller-McLemore, review of *Setting Limits,* pp. 372-373; May 1, 1991, Carole Bailey Stoneking, review of *What Kind of Life?,* pp. 493-494; November 17, 1993, Hugh McElwain, review of *The Troubled Dream of Life,* pp. 1156-1159; September 22, 1999, review of *False Hopes,* p. 913.

Commentary, December, 1980, review of *Ethics Teaching in Higher Education,* p. 62; April, 1988, review of *Setting Limits,* p. 23.

Commonweal, December 4, 1987, review of *Setting Limits,* p. 706; April 22, 1988, Drew Christiansen, review of *Setting Limits,* pp. 247-249; March 10, 1989, Margaret Farley, review of *Setting Limits,* pp. 153-154; May 18, 1990, review of *What Kind of Life?,* p. 328; October 22, 1993, William F. May, review of *The Troubled Dream of Life,* pp. 25-26; September 25, 1998, review of *False Hopes,* p. 24.

Conscience, fall, 1996, review of *Abortion: Law, Choice, and Morality,* p. 35.

Contemporary Sociology, July, 1987, Caroline Whitbeck, review of *Applying the Humanities,* pp. 549-550.

Ethics, April, 1982, James M. Giarelli, review of *Ethics Teaching in Higher Education,* pp. 549-552; October, 1983, Brian Barry, reviews of *The Roots of Ethics,* and *Ethics in Hard Times,* pp. 138-140; July, 1984, Susan Sherwin, review of *Ethics, the Social Sciences, and Policy Analysis,* p. 737; January, 1987, Norman E. Bowie, review of *Representation and Responsibility: Exploring Legislative Ethics,* pp. 485-486; April, 1987, Thomas D. Eisele, review of *Applying the Humanities,* p. 700; October, 1989, Larry R. Churchill, review of *Setting Limits,* pp. 169-176; January, 1991, David C. Thomasma, review of *What Kind of Life?,* pp. 419-420; July, 1997, review of *A World Growing Old,* p. 779; October, 2001, review of *Promoting Healthy Behavior: How Much Freedom? Whose Responsibility?,* p. 191.

Gerontologist, June, 1988, Robert H. Binstock and Jeff Kahana, review of *Setting Limits,* pp. 424-426; February, 1992, Edward F. Lawlor, review of *What Kind of Life?,* pp. 131-133.

Guardian Weekly (London, England), November 8, 1987, review of *Setting Limits,* p. 20; April 1, 1990, review of *What Kind of Life?,* p. 20.

Harvard Women's Law Journal, spring, 1986, Sarah Jane Reynolds, review of *Abortion: Understanding Differences,* pp. 245-251.

Hastings Center Report, March, 1996, review of *A World Growing Old,* p. 48; May, 1998, review of *False Hopes,* p. 42; January, 1999, review of *False Hopes,* p. 45.

Healthcare Financial Management, November, 1988, Carol Howe Hamblen, review of *Setting Limits,* p. 82.

Healthline, April, 1991, Bettina Wood, review of *What Kind of Life?,* pp. 15-16.

Hospital & Health Services Administration, fall, 1991, Dean M. Crowder, review of *What Kind of Life?,* p. 468.

Humanist, March-April, 1988, Ralph C. Greene, review of *Setting Limits,* p. 39.

Hypatia, summer, 1989, Nora K. Bell, "What Setting Limits May Mean: A Feminist Critique of Daniel Callahan's *Setting Limits,*" pp. 169-178.

Journal of Contemporary Health Law and Policy, spring, 1989, Giovanna M. Cinelli, review of *Setting Limits,* pp. 355-359; spring, 1992, Francis J. Hearn, Jr., review of *What Kind of Life?,* pp. 495-498.

Journal of Health Politics, Policy and Law, fall, 1989, Michael Reagan, review of *Setting Limits,* pp. 627-633.

Journal of Higher Education, May, 1982, review of *Ethics Teaching in Higher Education,* p. 360.

Journal of Law, Medicine & Ethics, fall, 1996, Kimberly Strom-Gottfried, review of *What Price Mental Health?,* pp. 267-269.

Journal of Legal Medicine, March, 1988, Marshall B. Kapp, review of *Setting Limits,* pp. 161-178; December, 1990, Dorothy Rasinski Gregory, review of *What Kind of Life?,* pp. 519-525.

Journal of Medical Ethics, June, 1995, Donna Dickenson, review of *The Troubled Dream of Life,* pp. 188-189; February, 1997, Hugh Series, review of *A World Growing Old,* pp. 56-57; February, 1997, Christopher Howard, review of *What Price Mental Health?,* pp. 57-58.

Journal of Policy Analysis & Management, fall, 1996, Steven M. Teles, review of *What Price Mental Health?,* pp. 658-670.

Journal of the American Medical Association, May 13, 1988, Steven Miles, review of *Setting Limits,* p. 2765; May 15, 1991, Stanley J. Reiser, review of *What Kind of Life?,* pp. 2591-2592; February 22, 1995, Norman B. Levy, review of *The Troubled Dream of Life,* pp. 677-678.

Jurimetrics Journal of Law, Science and Technology, spring, 1991, Wendy K. Mariner, review of *What Kind of Life?,* pp. 349-355.

Kirkus Reviews, August 1, 1987, review of *Setting Limits,* p. 1124; November 15, 1989, review of *What Kind of Life?,* p. 1643; June 1, 1993, review of *The Troubled Dream of Life,* p. 692; March 1, 1998, review of *False Hopes,* p. 311.

Kliatt Young Adult Paperback Book Guide, April, 1991, review of *What Kind of Life?,* p. 32.

Lancet, August, 1993, review of *The Troubled Dream of Life,* p. 132; June 15, 1996, C. Roffe, review of *A World Growing Old,* p. 1679; June 13, 1998, Robert H. Brook, review of "False Hopes or No Hopes?," review of *False Hopes,* pp. 1822-1823.

Library Journal, January, 1990, Mark L. Shelton, review of *What Kind of Life?,* p. 139; August, 1993, KellyJo Houtz Parish, review of *The Troubled Dream of Life,* p. 132; April 1, 1998, Mark L. Shelton, review of *False Hopes,* p. 116; March 1, 1999, review of *False Hopes,* p. 47;

Medical Humanities Review, January, 1991, review of *What Kind of Life?,* p. 35; spring, 1994, review of *The Troubled Dream of Life,* p. 68; spring, 2001, review of *Promoting Healthy Behavior,* p. 28.

National Catholic Reporter, February 4, 1994, Michael J. Farrell, review of *The Troubled Dream of Life,* p. 28.

National Right to Life News, August 12, 1998, Wesley J. Smith, review of *False Hopes,* pp. 11-12.

New England Journal of Medicine, August 18, 1988, Terrie Wetle and Richard W. Besdine, review of *Setting Limits,* pp. 452-453; August 9, 1990, Her-bert P. Gleason, review of *What Kind of Life?,* p. 424; December 30, 1993, Diane Meier, review of *The Troubled Dream of Life,* pp. 2042-2043; September 5, 1996, Richard M. Ratzan, review of *A World Growing Old,* pp. 756-757; September 12, 2002, Barrie R. Cassileth, review of *The Role of Complementary and Alternative Medicine: Accommodating Pluralism.*

New Leader, November 16, 1987, Barry Gewen, review of *Setting Limits,* p. 17; March 5, 1990, Amitai Etzioni, review of *What Kind of Life?,* p. 20.

Newsweek, June 8, 1970.

New Yorker, March 5, 1990, review of *What Kind of Life?,* p. 106.

New York Review of Books, April 28, 1988, Sidney Hook, review of *Setting Limits,* pp. 22-25; March 5, 1992, David J. Rothman, review of *What Kind of Life?,* pp. 32-37.

New York Times Book Review, September 27, 1987, review of *Setting Limits,* p. 7; December 24, 1989, review of *What Kind of Life?,* p. 1; February 3, 1991, review of *What Kind of Life?,* p. 32; April 5, 1998, review of *False Hopes,* p. 12.

People, August 12, 1985, "Pro-choice vs. Pro-life Is a Moral Dilemma, Says Daniel Callahan" (interview), pp. 89-92.

Public Administration Review, September-October, 1991, Barbara J. Holt, review of *What Kind of Life?,* pp. 453-454; January-February, 1993, Barbara H. Lord, review of *What Kind of Life?,* p. 87.

Publishers Weekly, July 17, 1987, review of *Setting Limits,* p. 44; June 7, 1993, review of *The Troubled Dream of Life,* p. 62; February 2, 1998, review of *False Hopes,* p. 72.

Reason, November, 1998, review of *False Hopes,* p. 66.

Reference & Research Book News, February, 1991, review of *What Kind of Life?,* p. 29.

Religious Studies Review, April, 1983, review of *Ethics Teaching in Higher Education,* p. 126; April, 1984, review of *Ethics Teaching in Higher Education,* p. 163; October, 1990, review of *Biomedical Ethics: An Anglo-American Dialogue,* p. 337; October, 1998, review of *A World Growing Old,* p. 398; April, 1991, review of *What Kind of Life?,* p. 151.

Science, May 23, 1986, Sheldon Rothblatt, review of *Applying the Humanities,* pp. 1013-1015.

Science Books & Films, November, 1981, review of *Ethics Teaching in Higher Education,* p. 64; November, 1999, review of *False Hopes,* p. 271.

Sciences, January-February, 1991, Louis Lasagna, review of *What Kind of Life?,* pp. 42-47.

SciTech Book News, November, 1988, review of *Biomedical Ethics,* p. 19; September, 1995, reviews of *What Kind of Life?* and *Setting Limits,* p. 33; March, 1996, review of *A World Growing Old,* p. 27; December, 1999, review of *False Hopes,* p. 69; June, 2001, review of *The Troubled Dream of Life,* p. 88.

Social Science & Medicine, August 15, 1996, Constance E. Putnam, review of *The Troubled Dream of Life,* pp. 566-567.

Social Service Review, March, 1984, review of *Ethics, the Social Sciences, and Policy Analysis,* p. 160.

Social Work, May, 1984, review of *Ethics, the Social Sciences, and Policy Analysis,* p. 309.

Teachers College Record, spring, 1982, review of *Ethics Teaching in Higher Education,* p. 474.

Tricycle: The Buddhist Review, fall, 1997, review of *The Troubled Dream of Life,* p. 93.

Virginia Quarterly Review, winter, 1994, review of *The Troubled Dream of Life,* p. 32.

Wall Street Journal, January 7, 1988, review of *Setting Limits,* p. 17.

Washington Monthly, June, 1998, Margaret P. Battin, review of *False Hopes,* pp. 48-50.

Washington Post Book World, January 19, 1974; October 11, 1987, review of *Setting Limits,* p. 1; January 7, 1990, review of *What Kind of Life?,* p. 11; August 22, 1993, review of *The Troubled Dream of Life,* p. 7.

West Coast Review of Books, Volume 15, number 4, 1999, review of *What Kind of Life?,* p. 37.

Wilson Quarterly, February, 1990, review of *What Kind of Life?,* p. 108.*

*   *   *

CEADEL, Martin (Eric) 1948-

PERSONAL: Born January 28, 1948, in Cambridge, England; son of Eric Bertrand (a university librarian) and Pamela Mary (a homemaker; maiden name, Perkins) Ceadel; married Deborah Jane Stockton (a solicitor), July 27, 1974; children: Jack, Jemima, Dickon. *Education:* Oxford University, B.A. (with first class honors), 1969, M.A. and D.Phil., 1977.

ADDRESSES: Home—47 Bainton Rd., Oxford OX2 7AG, England. *Office*—New College, Oxford University, Oxford OX1 3BN, England. *E-mail*—martin.ceadel@new.ox.ac.uk.

CAREER: University of Sussex, Brighton, England, lecturer in history, 1973-74; University of London, Imperial College of Science and Technology, London, England, lecturer in history and politics, 1974-79; Oxford University, Oxford, England, Fellow of New College and tutor in politics, 1979—.

WRITINGS:

Pacifism in Britain, 1914-1945: The Defining of a Faith, Oxford University Press (New York, NY), 1980.

Thinking about Peace and War, Oxford University Press (New York, NY), 1987.

The Origins of War Prevention: The British Peace Movement and International Relations, 1730-1854, Oxford University Press (New York, NY), 1996.

Semi-Detached Idealists: The British Peace Movement and International Relations, 1854-1945, Oxford University Press (New York, NY), 2000.

Also author of *Why People Disagree about War Prevention,* Oxford Project for Peace Studies, 1989.

SIDELIGHTS: English historian Martin Ceadel once told *CA:* "I am not a pacifist of any kind, but I feel that the political debate about war prevention has received less attention than debate about domestic issues and that this should be remedied." Indeed, Ceadel has brought attention to the various movements for peace in Great Britain through his carefully researched books. He began with *Pacifism in Britain, 1914-1945: The Defining of a Faith,* published in 1980, which covers the period from the beginning of World War I through the end of World War II. In *Thinking about Peace and War,* Ceadel develops a typology of peace movements, distinguishing between "pacific-ism," which refers to a desire to create a peaceful international order through reform but accepts the use of military force for defense, and "pacifism," which rejects all forms of military force.

Ceadel's *The Origins of War Prevention* begins following British peace movements from 1730 and continues to the Crimean War in 1854. He makes thorough use of the records of the Peace Society, founded in 1816. In part one, Ceadel discusses how the idea was developed that peace can be achieved between nations. In part two, he traces the course of Britain's peace movement from the 1790s, discussing the contribution of such groups as the Quakers and such individuals as politicians Richard Cobden and John Bright, who, says Ceadel, were not as involved in the movement as once believed. Donald Read, writing in the *English Historical Review,* observed: "In Britain more than anywhere else public opinion had accepted that discussion of peace-or-war was a legitimate part of the political debate." Ceadel's book, he said, "based upon a comprehensive range of archive and printed material, explains with commendable care how and why this breakthrough had been achieved by the mid-nineteenth century."

Ceadel's *Semi-Detached Idealists* picks up where *The Origins of War Prevention* leaves off and continues through the end of World War II. The book is a comprehensive and authoritative study of British efforts to abolish war. In an article for the *Times Literary Supplement,* T. G. Otte explained the book's title: "As Ceadel demonstrates persuasively in this cogently argued work, the country's geography, the absence of major domestic upheavals, the strength of religious dissent as well as of free-trade liberalism helped to foster an intellectual and political climate in which the advocates of an 'idealist[ic]' approach to international politics could establish their organizational presence."

Ceadel assumes that peace movements are more an expression of the activists' ideology than they are a vehicle for social change. Otte praised Ceadel's "painstaking and meticulous archival research," especially into the pamphlet literature of the periods he discusses. This research helped the author to pull apart the strands of ideology and detail their interaction. Ceadel follows the individuals and organizations that made their movements work, especially during the interwar years, when peace movements were at their height. He also explains how Adolf Hitler's Nazi regime and World War II discredited much of the ideology behind the peace movement. Ceadel calls the real achievement of Britain's early-twentieth-century peace movement the ongoing "intellectual conversation" it created about war and its causes. Otte concluded, "The peace movement was the grit in the machinery; and perhaps all machinery ought to have some grit in it, even if only to ensure its regular inspection."

BIOGRAPHICAL AND CRITICAL SOURCES:

PERIODICALS

Albion, summer, 1997, review of *The Origins of War Prevention: The British Peace Movement and International Relations, 1730-1854,* p. 315.

American Academy of Political and Social Science, Annals, July, 1981, review of *Pacifism in Britain, 1914-1945: The Defining of a Faith,* p. 179.

American Political Science Review, December, 2001, review of *Semi-Detached Idealists: The British Peace Movement and International Relations, 1854-1945,* p. 1030.

British Book News, August, 1987, review of *Thinking about Peace and War,* p. 504; September, 1987, review of *Thinking about Peace and War,* p. 587.

Choice, April, 1981, review of *Pacifism in Britain, 1914-1945,* p. 1151; April, 1988, review of *Thinking about Peace and War,* p. 1308; May, 1995, review of *Pacifism in Britain, 1914-1945,* p. 1408; January, 1997, review of *The Origins of War Prevention,* p. 766.

Economist, October 11, 1980, review of *Pacifism in Britain, 1914-1945,* p. 115.

English Historical Review, July, 1982, review of *Pacifism in Britain, 1914- 1945,* p. 672; April, 1998, Donald Read, review of *The Origins of War Prevention,* p. 488.

Guardian Weekly, September 28, 1980, review of *Pacifism in Britain, 1914- 1945,* p. 21.

Historian, February, 1982, review of *Pacifism in Britain, 1914-1945,* p. 253.

History: Reviews of New Books, March, 1981, review of *Pacifism in Britain, 1914-1945,* p. 120.

International History Review, June, 2002, Peter Brock, review of *Semi-Detached Idealists,* p. 425.

Journal of Modern History, June, 1982, review of *Pacifism in Britain, 1914- 1945,* p. 362.

London Review of Books, August 20, 1998, review of *The Origins of War Prevention,* p. 20.

Spectator (London, England), October 4, 1980, review of *Pacifism in Britain, 1914-1945,* p. 22.

Times Educational Supplement, September 12, 1980, review of *Pacifism in Britain, 1914-1945,* p. 20.

Times Literary Supplement, August 8, 1980, review of *Pacifism in Britain, 1914- 1945,* p. 887; January 29, 1988, review of *Thinking about Peace and War,* p. 105; April 5, 2002, T. G. Otte, "An English Affliction," review of *Semi-Detached Idealists,* p. 21.

ONLINE

Oxford University Press-USA Web site, http://www. oup-usa.org/ (September 23, 2002), review of *Semi-Detached Idealists.*

*   *   *

CHABON, Michael 1963-

PERSONAL: Surname is pronounced "shay-bahn"; born 1963, in Washington, DC; son of Robert (a physician, lawyer, and hospital manager) and Sharon (a lawyer) Chabon; married Lollie Groth (a poet; divorced, 1991); married Ayelet Waldman (a writer), 1993; children: (second marriage) Sophie, Ezekiel, Rosie. *Education:* University of Pittsburgh, B.A., 1984; University of California—Irvine, M.F.A.

ADDRESSES: Home—Berkeley, CA. *Agent*—Mary Evans, Inc., 242 East 5th Street, New York, NY 10003.

CAREER: Writer and screenwriter.

AWARDS, HONORS: Publishers Weekly best books, *New York Times* Notable Book, both 1995, and Scripter Award, Friends of the University of Southern California Libraries, 2000, all for *Wonder Boys;* O. Henry Award, Third Prize, 1999, for story "Son of the Wolfman"; National Book Critics Circle Award nomination, 2000, short-listed for PEN/Faulkner Award for Fiction, 2001, New York Society Library Award, 2001, Gold Medal, Commonwealth Club of California, 2001, and Pulitzer Prize for fiction, 2001, all for *The Amazing Adventures of Kavalier and Clay.*

WRITINGS:

The Mysteries of Pittsburgh (novel), Morrow (New York, NY), 1988.
A Model World, and Other Stories (includes "The Lost World," "The Little Knife," "More Than Human," and "Blumenthal on the Air"), Morrow (New York, NY), 1991.
Wonder Boys (novel), Villard (New York, NY), 1995.

Michael Chabon

Werewolves in Their Youth (stories), Random House (New York, NY), 1999.
The Amazing Adventures of Kavalier and Clay (novel), Random House (New York, NY), 2000.
Summerland (juvenile novel), Hyperion/Miramax (New York, NY), 2002.

Also author of screenplays, including *The Gentleman Host, The Martian Agent,* and *The Amazing Spider-Man,* a 2004 sequel to the original movie. Author of introduction to Ben Katchor's *Julius Knipl, Real-Estate Photographer,* Little, Brown (Boston, MA), 1996. Contributor to periodicals, including *Gentlemen's Quarterly, Mademoiselle, New Yorker, New York Times Magazine, Esquire, Playboy, Forward, Paris Review, Civilization,* and *Vogue.* Guest editor of *McSweeney's Mammoth Treasury of Thrilling Tales,* McSweeney's Books (San Francisco, CA), 2002. Contributor to *Fault Lines: Stories of Divorce,* edited by Caitlin Shetterly, Berkley (New York, NY), 2003. Contributor to *Michael Chabon Presents: The Amazing Adventures of the Escapist,* a quarterly comic book based on the character from Chabon's novel *The Amazing Adventures of Kavalier and Clay,* Dark Horse Comics (Milwaukie, OR), 2003.

ADAPTATIONS: Wonder Boys was adapted for film and released by Paramount Studios; *The Amazing Adventures of Kavalier and Clay* has been optioned for a film by Paramount.

WORK IN PROGRESS: A novel, *Hotzeplotz.*

SIDELIGHTS: Michael Chabon is considered by many critics one of the major literary authors of his generation, and with his 2002 novel, *Summerland,* he turned his hand to juvenile fiction, serving up a five-hundred page children's fantasy novel intended to give J. K. Rowling and her "Harry Potter" series a bit of American competition. As Patrick Meanor noted in *Dictionary of Literary Biography,* Chabon "consciously set out to create his own kind of American magical world, combining elements of Native American and Norse myth and folklore." Such a turn to juvenile fiction was all the more surprising, considering that Chabon won the Pulitzer Prize in 2001 for his novel *The Amazing Adventures of Kavalier and Clay,* a book that confirmed the early critical response to his first novel, *The Mysteries of Pittsburgh,* and of his second, the wryly humorous *Wonder Boys.*

Dubbed a "virtuoso" by *Booklist*'s Donna Seaman, and a "master stylist" by *Book*'s James Sullivan, Chabon has achieved "buzz most writers only dream about," according to Rex Roberts, writing in *Insight on the News.* Such "buzz" has made life easier at the Chabon household, where he and his wife, also a writer, of mysteries, share parenting duties of their children. The versatile Chabon has, in addition to his novels, penned two short story collections, *A Model World* and *Werewolves in Their Youth,* as well as television pilots, screenplays, and articles

Chabon was born in Washington, D.C., in 1963, the son of Robert and Sharon Chabon. His father was a physician, lawyer, and hospital manager; his mother later became a lawyer. At the age of six, Chabon and his family moved to the city-in-construction of Columbia, Maryland. They were, as Chabon wrote in "Maps and Legends" on his Web site, "colonists of a dream, immigrants to a new land that as yet existed mostly on paper. More than four-fifths of Columbia's projected houses, office buildings, parks, pools, bike paths, elementary schools and shopping centers had yet to be built; and the millennium of racial and economic harmony that Columbia promised to birth in

its theoretical streets and cul-de-sacs was as far from parturition as ever." It was in this never-never land of a city-in-the-making that Chabon came of age. "My earliest memories of Columbia are of the Plan," Chabon wrote, indicating the blueprint for the structure and shape of the city. Hanging a copy of this plan, or map of the projected town, on his wall, Chabon took to studying it as closely as he did the map of Walt Disney's new Magic Kingdom, also thumbtacked nearby. "I glanced up at the map at night as I lay in bed, reading *The Hobbit* or *The Book of Three* or a novel set in Oz. And sometimes I would give it a once over before I set out with my black and white friends for a foray into the hinterlands, to the borders of our town and our imaginations. . . . How fortunate I was to be handed, at such an early age, a map to steer by, however provisional."

A second guidance system for young Chabon was the world of comic books. "I was introduced to them pretty early," Chabon told Scott Tobias in an *Onion* interview, "right around the age of six or so, by my father, who had himself been a devoted reader of comics when he was a child." Chabon's paternal grandfather, a typographer in New York, worked in a plant where they printed comic books and would thus bring home loads of the comics to his son, Chabon's father. Repeating this favor, Robert Chabon introduced his own son to the wonders of DC Comics. Chabon remembered, in his interview with Tobias, the "naive, innocent, primary-colored" nature of these comics, "set in a world with very clear distinctions between good and evil." This was the world of Superman, primarily; as he grew older he sought out the "murkier and more ambiguous" world of the heroes found in Marvel comics. However, by the time he was fourteen or fifteen, he had given up the world of comics, science fiction, and fantasy for more adult, literary fiction, "the stuff my parents would recommend to me that they were enjoying," he told Tobias.

Graduating from high school, Chabon attended the University of Pittsburgh where he earned his undergraduate degree, and then attended the University of California—Irvine, ultimately earning a master's degree in creative writing. During his college years, Chabon expanded on his literally encyclopedic reading. The author has noted that as a child he read the dictionary and encyclopedia for fun; later, he adopted a disparate collection of favorite authors, from Thomas Pynchon to Herman Melville. Writing on his

Web site, Chabon lists the writers and works that changed his life, including Jorge Luis Borges and his *Labyrinths,* Gabriel Garcia Marquez and his *Love in the Time of Cholera,* John Cheever's collected stories, Edith Wharton's *The Age of Innocence,* Vladimir Nabokov's *Lolita* and *Pale Fire,* Robert Stone's *Children of the Light,* and F. Scott Fitzgerald's *The Great Gatsby,* among fiction works, and nonfiction works such as Robert Graves's *The White Goddess* and Jan Morris's *Among the Cities.* All of these writers have influenced Chabon in a style of writing that avoids popular minimalism. With more similarity to Marcel Proust than Ernest Hemingway, Chabon has developed a writing style at once expansive and lyric. As he explained to Goodman, "I'll start writing a sentence with a general idea. I want to say x about this character, and before I know it, it's 135 words long, and I've broken it up with a few parentheticals and something between dashes, and it just happens that way."

Chabon's first book, *The Mysteries of Pittsburgh,* was actually his master's thesis at the University of California—Irvine. Not only did the novel earn him his degree, but also his instructor thought highly enough of it to send the manuscript to his own agent, who quickly found a publisher for it. Upon the publication of the coming-of-age novel *The Mysteries of Pittsburgh* in 1988, Chabon earned recognition as a promising young fiction writer. The story centers on Art Bechstein, who has recently graduated from college and is about to experience what he perceives as the last summer of his youth.

Chabon followed *The Mysteries of Pittsburgh* with *A Model World, and Other Stories,* which includes tales previously published in the *New Yorker.* Many of the stories in this collection involve unrequited love, and five of the tales—collectively termed "The Lost World"—chart the angst of adolescent Nathan Shapiro as he grows from age ten to sixteen. Among these chronicles is "The Little Knife," showing Nathan agonizing over both his parents' antagonistic relationship and the Washington Senators' imminent demise from major-league baseball. In "More Than Human," another tale focusing on Shapiro, the boy must come to terms with his shattered family after his father leaves home. Another story in *A Model World,* "Blumenthal on the Air," centers on an American narrator who marries an Iranian woman simply to provide her with United States citizenship, then finds himself falling in love with her.

In her *New York Times Book Review* appraisal of *A Model World,* Elizabeth Benedict noted that Chabon sometimes uses his polished style as a means of remaining emotionally aloof from his material. "All too often he keeps his distance," she alleged, but she added that even in tales where Chabon remains reserved, he nonetheless manages to produce "fluent, astonishingly vivid prose." Benedict was particularly impressed with "The Lost World" stories, which she lauded for their "breathtaking" descriptive passages. Other tales in the volume, Benedict noted, recalled *The Mysteries of Pittsburgh.* Such stories, the critic affirmed, "have a kaleidoscopic beauty."

Chabon experienced considerable difficulty in following up the success of *The Mysteries of Pittsburgh* and *A Model World.* While living on a large advance from his publisher, he wrote 1,500 pages of what he intended to be his second novel, *Fountain City.* It was, Chabon told *Los Angeles Times* contributor Erik Himmelsbach, "sort of a map of my brain," and in it, he attempted to express his love for Paris, architecture, baseball, Florida, and more. After four-and-a-half years and four drafts, however, Chabon admitted to himself that he was never going to be able to craft *Fountain City* into a readable book. He explained to Himmelsbach, "Because I had taken that [advance] money, I felt like I couldn't dump the project, even when it was fairly clear to me that it wasn't working."

The *Fountain City* experience was demoralizing, but Chabon eventually turned it to his advantage. In early 1993, he began work on *Wonder Boys* and in less than a year had finished his second novel. *Wonder Boys* is a fast-paced, comic romp that chronicles one long, disastrous weekend in the life of Grady Tripp, a once-lauded writer now burdened with a 2,000-page manuscript he cannot finish. Joseph P. Kahn of the *Boston Globe* called Tripp "an instant classic . . . part Ginger Man, part Garp and altogether brilliantly original." Chabon confided to Lisa See in *Publishers Weekly* that until his wife read the manuscript of *Wonder Boys* and he heard her laughing as she turned the pages, he had no idea that he was writing a comic novel. "To me, Grady has a wry tone, but I felt sad writing about him. In a lot of ways, he is a projection of my worst fears of what I was going to become if I kept working on *Fountain City.*" He continued: "To me, the book is about the disappointment of getting older and growing up and not measuring up to what you thought, and the world and the people in it not being what you expected. It's about disillusionment and acceptance." *Wonder Boys* was adapted for a movie starring Michael Douglas as the burnt-out writer.

Library Journal reviewer Joanna M. Burkhardt called the stories in Chabon's 1999 collection *Werewolves in Their Youth* "remarkably crafted." "Brief synopses can't begin to convey the rich texture of Chabon's involved tales," added Donna Seaman in *Booklist.* Failed relationships serve as the recurring theme in the collection's nine stories, all set in the Pacific Northwest. The title story is of two eleven-year-old boys whose games turn extreme. In "The Harris Fetko Story," Harris is a football player in a failing football venture. His father, Norm, a coach who groomed his son to be an athlete, is now selling cars, but dreams of a new sport called "Powerball" that will revive his career. Although father and son have not spoken for years, Norm calls on Harris to be his main attraction. "When faced with difficult family relations, the protagonists in Michael Chabon's new stories, man and boy alike, harden their hearts and draw into their shells," noted Randall Holdridge in the *Tucson Weekly.* "But vulnerability in these male carapaces, a softness in their hearts, yields compassion at moments of crisis. Usually they pay a high cost in self-sacrifice, but they're rewarded by transfiguring new esteem."

Chabon's next tale, *The Amazing Adventures of Kavalier and Clay,* takes readers into the pulp world of the 1930s and 1940s through the experiences of two Jewish cousins. American Sammy Klayman is an opportunistic young fellow with a real knack for plotting pulp fiction, while Josef Kavalier, a Czech who has fled the Nazis, complements this storytelling talent with his own rare, bold drawing style. Together they create a Harry Houdini-like comic character in a series called *The Escapist,* a superhero who battles World War II enemies on the pages of the comic. Quickly, the cartooning duo become a phenomenal success, but Joe continues to be plagued by guilt and grief over the loss of his family. Finally, he leaves Sammy and his lover to join the Navy. Exploring themes from escapist literature to Golems and beyond, Chabon created, during four years of writing, a huge manuscript that he pared down by two hundred pages before publication. The book became the publishing sensation of the 2000 season.

Reviewing the novel in *Commentary,* John Podhoretz noted that it "combines fable, magical realism, boy's adventure storytelling, Horatio Alger, and mordant humor in an exhilarating stew that also attempts something entirely new in the depiction of the European Jewish catastrophe and the guilt suffered by those who succeeded in escaping it." Podhoretz ultimately felt, however, that while *The Amazing Adventures of Kavalier and Clay* was a "wonderful book," it was still, "despite its scope, a small one." Most other critics offered different opinions. *Booklist's* Seaman thought that Chabon was "equally adept at atmosphere, action, dialogue, and cultural commentary," plumbing the "depths of the human heart" and celebrating "the healing properties of escapism . . . with exuberance and wisdom." Writing in the *World and I,* Tom Deignan called *The Amazing Adventures* a "slam-bang accomplishment, dazzling and profound, cerebral yet wonderfully touching," and went on to proclaim, "Chabon has produced a great and very American novel, which feels both intimate and worldly."

Troy Patterson of *Entertainment Weekly* added to the chorus of praise, noting that Chabon's novel is "a long, lyrical one that's exquisitely patterned rather than grandly plotted, composed with detailed scenes, and spotted with some rapturous passages of analysis." Patterson concluded, "It's like a graphic novel inked in words and starring the author himself in the lead role: Wonder Boy." "Chabon has pulled off another great feat," wrote Susanna Meadows in *Newsweek,* while *Time* critic R. Z. Sheppard characterized the novel as one written with "much imagination, verve and affection." Roberts concluded his review in *Insight on the News* by commenting, "With *Amazing Adventures,* Chabon lives up to his early accolades, and takes a soaring leap into the literary stratosphere." Awards committees offered similar response, as *The Amazing Adventures of Kavalier and Clay* was nominated for both the National Book Award and the PEN/Faulkner Award for fiction before it took the Pulitzer Prize for fiction in 2001.

With his 2002 novel, *Summerland,* Chabon extended his literary ambitions to the world of young-adult literature. The inspiration for this book came from a couple of sources. "It originated in part," Chabon explained to a contributor for *Library Journal,* "with the experience of reading to my kids. . . . A big turning point for me was rereading *Charlotte's Web* and just being blown away again by how beautiful that book is." Combined with this was a youthful ambition he had had to write about American folklore in the same manner as C. S. Lewis and J. R. R. Tolkien had used British folklore as "the backdrops for their works."

Chabon was one of several well-known adult writers to turn his hand to children's books in 2002, and for this "complex, wildly ambitious novel," as *Booklist*'s Brian Wilson described the book, Chabon uses baseball as a symbol or metaphor for life. Eleven-year-old Ethan Feld is perhaps the world's worst baseball player, at least the worst in Clam Island, Washington, where he makes his home. But he and best friends tomboy Jennifer T. Rideout, a Native-American pitcher, and Thor Wignutt, are pressed into service one summer by the sports-loving faeries, the ferishers, to save the world. Coyote, the Native-American trickster, is out to create "Ragged Rock," or the destruction of the world. To this end, he kidnaps Ethan's father, who has invented a mysterious substance that is a universal solvent; Coyote plans to dissolve the world away. Ethan—whose mother has died of cancer—along with Jennifer, Thor, and the ferishers, set off on a mission to rescue Ethan's father and secure the fate of the universe. The family Saab—held aloft by a blimp—becomes their ship as they sail through various worlds on their rescue mission. These worlds include Winterland, Summerland, the Middling, and the Gleaming. They play baseball in Summerland and are joined by an unlikely cast of characters, including a talking rat, a former ball player from the Negro leagues, and a Sasquatch named Taffy whom they also rescue. In the end, the fate of the world depends on a baseball game between the villains and this bizarre cast of good guys and girls.

Chabon's first venture into children's books was widely reviewed. A contributor for *Publishers Weekly* felt that Chabon "hits a high-flying home run, creating a vivid fantasy where baseball is king." The same critic further commented that the author "unspools an elaborate yarn in a style that frequently crackles with color and surprise." Similarly, Kimberly L. Paone, writing in *School Library Journal,* thought that Chabon's debut foray into juvenile literature "will enchant its audience." Troy Patterson, writing in *Entertainment Weekly,* noted that Chabon's book "is a baseball novel that gives new meaning to the words fantasy league." Yet Patterson also wondered if *Summerland* were really a children's book. "By calling it such," Patterson observed, "Chabon gives himself prosaic license to indulge in open-hearted hokeyness and reflexive nostalgic revelry."

Laura Miller, writing for *Salon.com,* noted that while *Summerland* "is meant for kids, . . . it's just as rangy, eccentric, dreamy, and funky as [Chabon's] books for adults." However, some other reviewers also noted that the contents of the book might go over the heads of young readers. *Booklist*'s Bill Ott felt that even "committed fantasy buffs . . . will have to bring their A-games if they expect to digest this ingredient-rich plot." Robert Lipsyte, writing in the *New York Times Book Review,* felt that "Chabon drops the ball by giving us a nerdy hero who wins a baseball game in a derivative fantasy world." *Horn Book*'s Peter D. Sieruta also mentioned the "diffuse, somewhat baroque plot," but also went on to observe that "much of the prose is beautifully descriptive as Chabon navigates vividly imagined other worlds and offers up some timeless themes." James Sullivan, reviewing the novel in *Book,* likewise wrote, "Certainly young readers will delight in the author's masterful use of imagery, whatever they make of the story." A critic for *Kirkus Reviews* had less guarded praise for the book, however, declaring that "this raucous, exhilarating, joyful, and above all, fun offering displays an enormous respect for the tradition of great fantasies that come before it."

The versatile Chabon might have a sequel to *Summerland* up his creative sleeve, and most definitely intends to expand his award-winning writing into new directions. As Richard Lacayo noted in *Time* magazine, Chabon wants "literary fiction to enjoy the liberties of fantasy genres like science fiction and horror." Chabon told Lacayo, "I'm not going to become a fantasy writer or a writer of science fiction. But I'm going to ignore the conventions of literary fiction as much as I can. And whatever kind of fiction comes out of that, I'm just going to hope I can bring readers along with me."

BIOGRAPHICAL AND CRITICAL SOURCES:

BOOKS

Contemporary Literary Criticism, Vol. 55, Gale (Detroit, MI), 1989.
Dictionary of Literary Biography, Volume 278: *American Novelists since World War II, Seventh Series,* Gale (Detroit, MI), 2003, pp. 81-90.
Newsmakers, Issue 1, Gale (Detroit, MI), 2003.

PERIODICALS

Advocate, December 19, 2000, p. 62.
Atlanta Journal-Constitution, April 2, 1995, p. M12.

Book, November, 2000, James Sullivan, review of *The Amazing Adventures of Kavalier and Clay,* p. 66; September-October, 2002, James Sullivan, review of *Summerland,* p. 73; November-December, 2002, "Best Children's Book," p. 58.

Booklist, December 15, 1998, Donna Seaman, review of *Werewolves in Their Youth,* p. 726; August, 2000, Donna Seaman, review of *The Amazing Adventures of Kavalier and Clay,* p. 2074; August, 2002, Bill Ott, review of *Summerland,* p. 1884; February 1, 2003, Brian Wilson, review of *Summerland* (audiobook), p. 1006.

Boston Globe, May 14, 1995, Joseph P. Kahn, review of *Wonder Boys,* p. 50; May 22, 1995, p. 30.

Chicago Tribune, April 2, 1995, sec. 14, p. 5.

Commentary, June, 2001, John Podhoretz, review of *The Amazing Adventures of Kavalier and Clay,* p. 68; June, 2003, Sam Munson, "Slices of Life," review of *McSweeney's Mammoth Treasury of Thrilling Tales,* p. 67.

Entertainment Weekly, April 14, 1995, p. 61; September 29, 2000, Troy Patterson, "Comic Genius," p. 123; October 4, 2002, Troy Patterson, "The Natural," p. 146; April 11, 2003, Carina Chocano, "Monster's Ball: Michael Chabon Guest-Edits Dave Eggers' McSweeney's, Producing a Mixed-Bag of Genre Tales," review of *McSweeney's Mammoth Treasury of Thrilling Tales,* p. 80.

Gentlemen's Quarterly, March, 1995, p. 118.

Horn Book, November-December, 2002, Peter D. Sieruta, review of *Summerland,* p. 751.

Insight on the News, February 12, 2001, Rex Roberts, review of *The Amazing Adventures of Kavalier and Clay,* p. 26.

Interview, March, 1988, p. 48.

Kirkus Reviews, November 1, 1998, review of *Werewolves in Their Youth;* September 1, 2002, review of *Summerland,* p. 1305.

Library Journal, January, 1999, Joanna M. Burkhardt, review of *Werewolves in Their Youth,* p. 161; October 15, 2000, p. 100; September 1, 2002, "Ten Books for Fall," pp. 48-52.

Los Angeles Times, June 28, 1988; April 27, 1995, Erik Himmelsbach, "A Life of Wonder and Awe," p. E1; April 17, 2001, p. A16.

Los Angeles Times Book Review, April 17, 1988, Brett Lott, review of *The Mysteries of Pittsburgh,* pp. 1, 11; March 26, 1995, p. 3.

New Republic, June 26, 1995, p. 40.

New Statesman, May 13, 1988, M. George Stevenson, review of *The Mysteries of Pittsburgh,* pp. 34-35.

New Statesman and Society, June 9, 1995, Roz Kaveney, review of *Wonder Boys,* p. 38.

Newsweek, April 10, 1995, pp. 76-77; September 25, 2000, Susannah Meadows, "Golems and Superheroes," p. 69.

New York, April 3, 1988, p. 7; May 2, 1988, p. 30; April 1, 1991, p. 63.

New York Times, March 17, 1995, p. C28; September 21, 2000, p. B10.

New York Times Book Review, April 3, 1988, Alice McDermott, review of *The Mysteries of Pittsburgh,* p. 7; May 26, 1991, Elizabeth Benedict, review of *A Model World, and Other Stories,* p. 7; April 9, 1995, Robert Ward, review of *Wonder Boys,* p. 7; January 31, 1999, p. 10; September 24, 2000, pp. 8, 9; November 17, 2002, Robert Lipsyte, review of *Summerland,* p. 24.

People Weekly, May 1, 1995, p. 32; June 26, 1995, pp. 63-64; October 14, 2002, Francine Prose, review of *Summerland,* p. 53; December 16, 2002, Galina Espinoza, "Author, Author: She Writes. He Writes. And Both Ayelet Waldman and Michael Chabon Raise the Kids," p. 151.

Publishers Weekly, April 10, 1995, Lisa See, "Michael Chabon: Wonder Boy in Transition," pp. 44-45; November 6, 1995, p. 58; November 23, 1998, review of *Werewolves in Their Youth,* p. 57; August 21, 2000, review of *The Amazing Adventures of Kavalier and Clay,* pp. 44, 45; October 9, 2000, p. 22; June 24, 2002, review of *Summerland,* p. 57; February 24, 2003, review of *McSweeney's Mammoth Treasury of Thrilling Tales,* p. 51.

School Library Journal, Kimberly L. Paone, review of *Summerland,* p. 159.

Time, May 16, 1988, p. 95; April 8, 1991, p. 77; April 10, 1995, John Skow, review of *Wonder Boys,* p. 87; September 25, 2000, R. Z. Sheppard, "Biff! Boom! A Super Novel about the Golden Age of Comics," p. 103; September 23, 2002, Richard Lacayo, "Kids Are Us!," p. 68.

Times Literary Supplement, June 17, 1988, p. 680.

U. S. News and World Report, September 25, 2000, Holly J. Morris, "Smells Like Teen Comics," p. 74.

Village Voice, April 19, 1988, p. 60.

Wall Street Journal, September 22, 2000, p. W13.

Washington Post, June 9, 1995, p. B1.

Washington Post Book World, April 24, 1988, p. 5; April 26, 1991, p. 20; March 19, 1995, p. 3; September 17, 2000, p. X15.

World and I, February, 2001, Tom Deignan, "Playing with Kiddie Dynamite," p. 220.

Writer, August, 2001, p. 15; April, 2002, Kelly Nickell, "The WD Interview: Michael Chabon," pp. 20-21.

ONLINE

Michael Chabon Home Page, http://www.michael chabon.com/ (August 31, 2003).

Onion, http://avclub.theonion.com/ (November 22, 2000), Scott Tobias, interview with Chabon.

Oregon Live, http://www.oregonlive.com/ (February 8, 1999).

Powell's City of Books, http://www.powells.com/ (September 17, 2001), Dave Welch, "Michael Chabon's Amazing Adventures," author interview.

Salon.com, http://www.salon.com/ (February 22, 1999); (October 22, 2002), Laura Miller, "The Lost Adventure of Childhood."

Tucson Weekly, http://www.tucsonweekly.com/ (March 4-10, 1999), Randall Holdridge, review of *Werewolves in Their Youth.**

*   *   *

CHIGNON, Niles
   See LINGEMAN, Richard R(oberts)

*   *   *

COHEN, Warren I. 1934-

PERSONAL: Born June 20, 1934, in Brooklyn, NY; son of Murray and Fay (Phillips) Cohen; married Janice Prichard, June 22, 1957; children: Geoffrey Scott, Anne Leslie. *Education:* Columbia University, A.B., 1955; Fletcher School of Law and Diplomacy, A.M., 1956; University of Washington, Seattle, Ph.D., 1962.

ADDRESSES: Office—Department of History, University of Maryland, Baltimore, MD 21250. *E-mail*—wcohen@.umbc.edu.

CAREER: University of California, Riverside, lecturer in history, 1962-63; Michigan State University, East Lansing, assistant professor, 1963-67, associate professor, 1967-71, professor of history, beginning 1971; director of Asian Studies Center, beginning 1979; currently University of Maryland, Baltimore County,

Warren I. Cohen

distinguished university professor of history. Visiting professor, National Taiwan University, Taipei, 1964-66; Fulbright lecturer, Tokyo, Japan, 1969-70. Foreign policy consultant. *Military service:* U.S. Navy, 1956-59; became lieutenant.

WRITINGS:

(Editor) *Intervention, 1917: Why America Fought,* Heath (London, England), 1966.

The American Revisionists, University of Chicago Press (Chicago, IL), 1967.

America's Response to China, Wiley (Indianapolis, IN), 1971, 4th edition, Columbia University Press (New York, NY), 2000.

The Chinese Connection, Columbia University Press (New York, NY), 1978.

Dean Rusk, Cooper Square (Lanham, MD), 1980.

(Editor) *New Frontiers in American-East Asian Relations,* Columbia University Press (New York, NY), 1983.

(Editor) *Reflections on Orientalism,* Asian Studies Center, Michigan State University (East Lansing, MI), 1983.

Empire without Tears: America's Foreign Relations, 1921-1933, Temple University Press (Philadelphia, PA), 1987.

(Editor, with Akira Iriye) *The United States and Japan in the Postwar World,* University Press of Kentucky (Lexington, KY), 1989.

(Editor, with Akira Iriye) *American, Chinese, and Japanese Perspectives on Wartime Asia, 1931-1949,* SR Books (Wilmington, DE), 1990.

(Editor, with Akira Iriye) *The Great Powers in East Asia, 1953-1960,* Columbia University Press (New York, NY), 1990.

East Asian Art and American Culture: A Study in International Relations, Columbia University Press (New York, NY), 1992.

(Editor) *The Cambridge History of American Foreign Relations,* Cambridge University Press (Cambridge, England), 1993.

(Editor, with Nancy Bernkopf Tucker) *Lyndon Johnson Confronts the World: American Foreign Policy, 1963-1968,* Cambridge University Press (Cambridge, England), 1994.

(Editor and author of introduction) *Pacific Passage: The Study of American-East Asian Relations on the Eve of the Twenty-first Century,* Columbia University Press (New York, NY), 1996.

(Editor, with Li Zhao) *Hong Kong under Chinese Rule: The Economic and Political Implications of Reversion,* Cambridge University Press (Cambridge, England), 1997.

East Asia at the Center: Four Thousand Years of Engagement with the World, Columbia University Press (New York, NY), 2000.

The Asian American Century, Harvard University Press (Cambridge, MA), 2002.

Contributor of articles and reviews to *Journal of Asian Studies, Orbis, Journal of American History,* and other history and political science journals. Editor, *Diplomatic History,* 1979-82.

Author's works have been translated into Chinese.

SIDELIGHTS: Warren I. Cohen is a history professor and an expert in relations between America and Asia. He is also a prolific author, having written or edited over twenty books.

Cohen's expert knowledge of Asia and political relations is evident in his books such as *East Asia at the Center: Four Thousand Years of Engagement with the*

World. Here the author examines Asia's political system and traces modern practices to ancient times. Charles W. Hayford of *Library Journal* found the book "stimulating and informative."

In addition to his various academic texts, Cohen has also written for a more mainstream audience. *East Asian Art and American Culture* is a look at how Asian art has come to reside in so many American museums and art collections and the influence it has had on American culture. The author also discusses Asian art as a way to consider political relations between the two countries. *Journal of the American Oriental Society* reviewer Robert L. Thorp wrote that "Cohen's book has the virtue of taking a longer and wider view," but he also felt that Cohen should have focused more on the art itself and its impact on culture, rather than stories of art collection. Thorp also noted, "The focus on [art collections in] America suggests that the writings and collecting of Europeans had no appreciable impact on American ideas and tastes, surely a misleading interpretation."

In 2002 Cohen took another close look at Asian and American culture with *The Asian American Century,* based on a series of Cohen's lectures. He examines the American influence on eastern cultures, such as fast food and Disney-type icons, as well as the "Asianization of America." This term refers to Americans' love and fascination with Asian food, art, and religions. Kitty Chen Dean of *Library Journal* found this book "engrossing" and also noted that she wished it were longer.

BIOGRAPHICAL AND CRITICAL SOURCES:

PERIODICALS

American Historical Review, December, 1993, Frank Ninkovich, review of *East Asian Art and American Culture: A Study in International Relations,* p. 1705; February, 1994, Jerald A. Combs, review of *The Cambridge History of American Foreign Relations,* p. 178.

Canadian Journal of History, August, 1994, Francis M. Carroll, review of *The Cambridge History of American Foreign Relations,* p. 353.

English Historical Review, April, 1994, Bernd Martin, review of *American, Chinese, and Japanese Perspectives on Wartime Asia: 1931-1949,* p. 529;

June, 1995, Callum MacDonald, review of *The Cambridge History of American Foreign Relations,* p. 672.

Foreign Affairs, January-February, 1995, David Fromkin, review of *Lyndon Johnson Confronts the World,* p. 161; September-October, 1996, Donald Zagoria, review of *Pacific Passage,* p. 158.

Historian, summer, 1995, Lloyd E. Ambrosius, review of *The Cambridge History of American Foreign Relations,* p. 789.

History Today, June, 1995, Esmond Wright, review of *The Cambridge History of American Foreign Relations,* p. 51.

Journal of American-East Asian Relations, spring, 1994, Robert L. Beisner, review of *The Cambridge History of American Foreign Relations,* p. 77.

Journal of American History, June, 1993, Thomas A. Tweed, review of *East Asian Art and American Culture: A Study in International Relations,* p. 256; December, 1994, Emily S. Rosenberg, review of *The Cambridge History of American Foreign Relations,* p. 1260.

Journal of Commonwealth and Comparative Politics, March, 1998, N. J. Miners, review of *Hong Kong under Chinese Rule,* p. 137.

Journal of Contemporary Asia, January, 1998, Geoffrey C. Gunn, review of *Pacific Passage,* p. 122; March, 1998, Geoffrey C. Dunn, review of *Pacific Passage,* p. 122

Journal of Interdisciplinary History, winter, 1995, Anna Kasten Nelson, review of *The Cambridge History of American Foreign Relations,* p. 445.

Journal of the American Oriental Society, April-June, 1994, Robert L. Thorp, review of *East Asian Art and American Culture,* p. 329.

Library Journal, June 15, 1993, Ed Goedeken, review of *The Cambridge History of American Foreign Relations,* p. 82; February 1, 2001, Charles W. Hayford, review of *East Asia at the Center,* p. 107; March 1, 2002, Kitty Chen Dean, review of *The Asian American Century,* p. 124.

Pacific Affairs, fall, 1993, Hsio-Yen Shih, review of *East Asian Art and American Culture,* p. 469; summer, 1998, Maurice D. Copithorne, review of *Hong Kong under Chinese Rule,* p. 248.

Pacific Historical Review, August, 1994, Noel H. Pugach, review of *East Asian Art and American Culture,* p. 455; May, 1997, Norman A. Graebner, review of *Lyndon Johnson Confronts the World,* p. 293; November, 1997, Michael Schaller, review of *Pacific Passage,* p. 623.

Reviews in American History, December, 1994, H. W. Brands, review of *The Cambridge History of American Foreign Relations,* p. 717.

ONLINE

Asian American Books Web site, http://www.asian americanbooks.com/ (June 17, 2002), review of *The Asian American Century.**

*   *   *

COLEMAN, Jane Candia 1939-

PERSONAL: Born January 9, 1939, in Pittsburgh, PA; daughter of Joseph Riccardo (a physical therapist) and Sophia (a schoolteacher; maiden name, Weyman) Candia; married Bernard D. Coleman, 1965 (divorced, 1989); married Glenn G. Boyer (a military officer and writer), 1991; children: (first marriage) David A., Daniel N. *Education:* University of Pittsburgh, B.A., 1960.

ADDRESSES: Home—P.O. Box 40, Rodeo, NM 88056. *Agent*—Crawford Literary Agency, Box 198, Evans Rd., Barnstead, NH 03218. *E-mail*—elcisco@ candiasystems.com.

CAREER: University of Pittsburgh, Pittsburgh, PA, technical writer for medical school, 1960-65; Carlow College, Pittsburgh, PA, cofounder and director of women's creative writing center, 1980-85; writer, 1985—.

MEMBER: WWA International Poetry Forum (board of directors, 1983—), Associated Writing Programs, Western Writers of America.

AWARDS, HONORS: Sewickley magazine, first prize for fiction; grant from Pennsylvania Council on the Arts, 1986; Western Heritage Award, National Cowboy Hall of Fame for *No Roof but Sky* and *Stories from Mesa Country;* Western Writers of America Spur Award for *I, Pearl Hart* and *Doc Holliday's Woman.*

WRITINGS:

POETRY COLLECTIONS

No Roof but Sky: Poetry of the American West, High Plains Press (Glendo, WY), 1990.

Deep in His Heart J.R. Is Laughing at Us, Adastra Press (Easthampton, MA), 1991.

The Red Drum, High Plains Press (Glendo, WY), 1995.

SHORT STORY COLLECTIONS

Stories from Mesa Country, Ohio University Press/Swallow Press (Athens, OH), 1991.

Discovering Eve, Ohio University Press/Swallow Press (Athens, OH), 1993.

Moving On: Stories of the West, Five Star (Unity, ME), 1997.

Borderlands: Western Stories, Five Star (Unity, ME), 2000.

Wives and Lovers, Five Star (Waterville, ME), 2002.

Country Music: Western Stories, Five Star (Waterville, ME), 2002.

NOVELS; EXCEPT AS NOTED

Shadows in My Hands: A Southwestern Odyssey (nonfiction), Ohio University Press/Swallow Press (Athens, OH), 1993.

Doc Holliday's Woman, Warner Books (New York, NY), 1995.

I, Pearl Hart: A Western Story, Five Star (Unity, ME), 1998.

Doc Holliday's Gone: A Western Duo, Five Star (Unity, ME), 1999.

The O'Keefe Empire: A Western Story, Five Star (Unity, ME), 1999.

The Italian Quartet, Five Star (Unity, ME), 2001.

Desperate Acts, Five Star (Unity, ME), 2001.

Mountain Time: A Western Memoir (nonfiction), Five Star (Waterville, ME), 2001.

Lost River: A Western Story, Five Star (Waterville, ME), 2003.

Matchless: A Western Story, Five Star (Waterville, ME), 2003.

Contributor of stories to periodicals, including *Pennsylvania Review, Agassiz Review,* and *South Dakota Review.*

SIDELIGHTS: Jane Candia Coleman writes in many different genres. Her poetry and her short stories have won awards, and her novels are praised by a wide as-sortment of critics. Her writing is often set in the West, but she has told *CA* that she prefers to not be termed a "western" writer. "I also write about the East Coast, Europe, the arts, music, and so on," she added. She does, however, live on a ranch, trains and rides horses, and is "constantly learning about the West," about which she most often writes.

Although Coleman expresses her thoughts through a variety of forms, there is a theme that recurs throughout her writing. It is the lives and challenges of women, recreated through Coleman's creative genius but based on bits and pieces of truth that Coleman carefully researches. Coleman is, as Emil Franzi wrote in a review of *Country Music* for the *Tucson Weekly,* "one of the few people who writes about the West who actually went out and found those folks, and tells us what the women were doing when the boys were all down at the OK Corral." Therefore many of her books are referred to as biographical novels.

One such work is her *Doc Holliday's Woman,* which, like many of her other books, critics refer to as a story that the history books left out. This novel portrays the tale of Kate Elder, the orphan of European aristocratic parents and the mistress of legendary gunslinger Doc Holliday. In order to fully recreate the story, not only did Coleman carefully research Kate's life, she also rode her own horse over the long trail that Kate followed in her westward pursuit of independence. As part of Coleman's research she read Kate's diaries, which depict details of her long and often wild relationship with Holliday. The result, as reported by a reviewer for *Publishers Weekly* is a "fast moving yarn" that is "enlivened by crisp dialogue and an abundance of historical cameos and detail."

Another diary-based biographical novel is Coleman's *The O'Keefe Empire.* The story is set right before the turn of the twentieth century and covers the fine points of a cattle drive that started in New Mexico and ended in San Diego. The drive was a critically required enterprise of survival for protagonist Joanne O'Keefe, a twenty-four-year-old widow and recent recipient of a large cattle ranch in New Mexico. Franzi, for another review in the *Tucson Weekly,* wrote, "Coleman's writing makes you feel the gritty scut work of moving a herd of cattle 1,000 miles over bleak terrain." There was little fun to be had in a cattle drive, and Coleman makes that very clear.

I, Pearl Hart: A Western Story is yet another fictionalized biography. Hart was about as wild as the wild women of the West could be. She was a notorious thief and spent five years in the Yuma State Prison in the latter part of the nineteenth century, the first woman to do time there. It is through Pearl's story that Coleman attempts to revise the image of the women who helped shape the West. After reading this Western tale, *Booklist* reviewer Wes Lukowsky concluded that Coleman "carefully" recreated the life of Pearl Hart and found the result to be a "compelling first-person narrative." Lukowsky praised Coleman for exposing Hart, "not as a ruthless outlaw" but as a woman who did the best she could to survive.

Coleman has also published collections of short stories. One of these collections is *Borderlands,* in which Coleman continues to focus on the lives of women who lived in the newly developing West. The story "Wild Flower," for instance, is based on the letters of Louisa Earp, the wife of Western hero Wyatt Earp's brother. Louisa wrote the letters as she traveled from Deadwood, South Dakota, to Tombstone, Arizona, detailing the hardships along the way. "*Borderlands* makes it easy to see why Coleman's so respected by fans of Western writing," wrote Jim Carvalho for the *Tucson Weekly. Library Journal* contributor Jack Hafer found that this collection "is a solid and rewarding effort."

Wives and Lovers provides the reader with another collection of Coleman's short fiction. A *Kirkus Reviews* critic wrote that the characters in these stories are somewhat interchangeable, as they all are "symbols of women of extraordinary sensibility," who are either limited by the men they choose or find their escape through them. There are fourteen stories included in this collection that both celebrates and condemns the female-male relationship.

Coleman also writes poetry, and for an even more personal account of her world, Coleman has written the memoir *Mountain Time* in which she praises the natural environment that surrounds her New Mexico home.

BIOGRAPHICAL AND CRITICAL SOURCES:

PERIODICALS

Booklist, February 1, 1997, Wes Lukowsky, review of *Moving On: Stories of the West,* p. 925; February 1, 1998, Wes Lukowsky, review of *I, Pearl Hart:* *A Western Story,* p. 898; December 1, 1998, Budd Arthur, review of *The O'Keefe Empire,* p. 650; April 1, 1999, Melanie Duncan, review of *Doc Holliday's Woman,* p. 1391; November 1, 1999, Budd Arthur, review of *Doc Holliday's Gone: A Western Duo,* p. 507; February 15, 2001, Patty Engelmann, review of *Desperate Acts,* p. 1120.

Kirkus Reviews, May 15, 2002, review of *Wives and Lovers,* p. 680.

Library Journal, September 15, 2000, Jack Hafer, review of *Borderlands,* p. 116.

Publishers Weekly, May 3, 1993, review of *Discovering Eve,* p. 295; August 30, 1993, review of *Shadows in My Hands,* p. 86; November 28, 1994, review of *The Red Drum: Poetry of the American West,* p. 55; April 3, 1995, review of *Doc Holliday's Woman,* p. 47; October 11, 1999, review of *Doc Holliday's Gone,* p. 53.

Women's Review of Books, July, 1993, Judith Grossman, review of *Discovering Eve,* pp. 38-39.

ONLINE

Tucson Weekly Online, http://www.weeklywire.com/ (August 17, 1998), Emil Franzi, review of *I, Pearl Heart;* (June 7, 1999), Emil Franzi, "Jane Candia Coleman Turns an Old-Fashioned Cattle Drive into High Adventure," review of *The O'Keefe Empire;* (August 9, 2001), Jim Carvalho, "Villa and Varmints," review of *Borderlands;* (July 25, 2002), Emil Franzi, "Jane Candia Coleman Introduces Us to Some Real Western Women," review of *Country Music;* (February 22, 2003), Emil Franzi, review of *The Italian Quartet.**

*   *   *

COLLINS, Catherine Fisher

PERSONAL: Born in Buffalo, NY; daughter of Herman and Catherine (Lynch) Fisher; married Clyde A. Collins, December 31, 1973 (deceased); children: Laura Harris, Clyde II. *Ethnicity:* "African American." *Education:* Trocaire College, A.A.S., 1970; State University of New York—College at Buffalo, B.S., 1975, M.S., 1979, Ed.D., 1990. *Religion:* Methodist.

ADDRESSES: Office—Department of Community Health and Human Services, State University of New

Catherine Fisher Collins

York—Empire State College, 617 Main St., Buffalo, NY 14203; fax: 716-831-1136. *E-mail*—catherine.ccollins@esc.edu.

CAREER: Model City Agency and Human Resource Department, Buffalo, NY, component manager, 1971-73; Comprehensive Health Planning Council of Western New York, Inc., Tonawanda, NY, coordinator of federal funds, 1973-76; Health Systems Agency, Tonawanda, NY, director of quality assurance, 1976-86; Erie County Medical Center, Buffalo, NY, director of ambulatory care, 1986-89; worked as an assistant academic dean, 1989-90; Erie Community College, Buffalo, NY, professor and department head, 1990-92; State University of New York—Empire State College, Buffalo, NY, associate professor of community health and human services, 1992—. Medaille College, professor, 1980-82; State University of New York—Buffalo, assistant professor, 1984-90; Erie Community College, adjunct assistant professor, 1988-90; State University of New York—Buffalo State College, adjunct assistant professor, 1998—. New York State Commission of

Corrections, past member of medical review board; Community Health and Human Services Committee, chair, 1974-75; Buffalo Black Media Coalition, member, 1984—; Health Committee of Western New York, member, 1984—; Jack and Jill of America, Inc., member, 1985—, eastern regional director, 1993-95, national editor, 1998-2000, national vice president, 2000-02; Hopevale, member of board of directors, 1989—.

AWARDS, HONORS: Certificate of Merit, Buffalo Urban League, 1976; outstanding service certificate, National Association for the Advancement of Colored People, 1980; citation, Citizens Commission on Criminal Justice, 1985; citation of appreciation, Jesse Nash Health Center, 1985; leadership in health award, Health Systems Agency of Western New York, Inc., 1986; award from Coalition of 100 Black Women, 1989; service award, State of Connecticut, 1994; Heritage Award, State of New Jersey, 1995; Outstanding Academic Book citation, *Choice,* 1997, for *The Imprisonment of African American Women: Causes, Conditions, and Future Implications;* elected Kentucky Colonel, 2001; special citation for outstanding contribution to health education, governor of New York; recognition awards for work at correctional facilities, including Attica.

WRITINGS:

(Editor) *African American Women's Health and Social Issues,* Greenwood Press (Westport, CT), 1996.
The Imprisonment of African American Women: Causes, Conditions, and Future Implications, McFarland (Jefferson, NC), 1997.
Sources of Stress and Relief for African American Women, Greenwood Press (Westport, CT), 2000.
Handbook for African American Women's Health and Social Issues, Greenwood Press (Westport, CT), 2003.
Imprisonment of African American Women, Book II, McFarland (Jefferson, NC), 2003.
Imprisonment of South African Women, McFarland (Jefferson, NC), 2003.

SIDELIGHTS: Catherine Fisher Collins once told *CA:* "I will continue to write books for college students and professionals in criminal justice and health care. These are areas where very few African-American writers are represented. I was inspired to write because of the lack of African-American textbooks for college courses. There is a need to help Americans understand how we feel about issues that affect us, rather than have others who are not culturally related shape public opinion through their writings."

*   *   *

COOPER, Ilene 1948-

PERSONAL: Born March 10, 1948, in Chicago, IL; daughter of Morris (a salesman) and Lillian Cooper (a homemaker; maiden name, Friedman). *Education:* University of Missouri, B.A.; Rosary College (River Forest, IL), M.L.S. *Religion:* Jewish.

ADDRESSES: Office—Booklist, American Library Association, 50 East Huron, Chicago, IL 60611. *E-mail—* icooper@ALA.org.

CAREER: Writer and editor. Winnetka Public Library, Winnetka, IL, children's librarian, 1976-80; *Booklist,* Chicago, IL, children's book editor, 1985—. Consultant to *ABC Afterschool Specials,* ABC-TV, 1976-82.

MEMBER: Society of Children's Book Writers and Illustrators.

AWARDS, HONORS: Children's Choice award, International Reading Association, for *Choosing Sides;* Best Books designation, *Chicago Tribune,* 1995, for *Buddy Love—Now on Video,* and 1997, for *The Dead Sea Scrolls.*

WRITINGS:

NOVELS

The Winning of Miss Lynn Ryan, illustrated by Susan Magurn, Morrow (New York, NY), 1987.
Buddy Love—Now on Video, HarperCollins (New York, NY), 1995.
I'll See You in My Dreams, Viking Penguin (New York, NY), 1997.

Ilene Cooper

"ROAD TO READING" SERIES

Absolutely Lucy, illustrated by Amanda Harvey, Golden Books (New York, NY), 1999.
Lucy on the Loose, illustrated by Amanda Harvey, Golden Books (New York, NY), 2000.
The Annoying Team, Golden Books (New York, NY), 2002.

"KIDS FROM KENNEDY MIDDLE SCHOOL" SERIES

Queen of the Sixth Grade, Morrow (New York, NY), 1988.
Choosing Sides, Morrow (New York, NY), 1990.
Mean Streak, Morrow (New York, NY), 1991.
The New, Improved Gretchen Hubbard, Morrow (New York, NY), 1992.

"FRANCES IN THE FOURTH GRADE" SERIES

Frances Takes a Chance, Bullseye Books (New York, NY), 1991.

Frances Dances, Bullseye Books (New York, NY), 1991.

Frances Four-Eyes, Bullseye Books (New York, NY), 1991.

Frances and Friends, illustrated by Vilma Ortiz, Bullseye Books (New York, NY), 1991.

"HOLLYWOOD WARS" SERIES

Lights, Camera, Attitude, Puffin (New York, NY), 1993.

My Co-Star, My Enemy, Puffin (New York, NY), 1993.

Seeing Red, Puffin (New York, NY), 1993.

Trouble in Paradise, Puffin (New York, NY), 1993.

"HOLIDAY FIVE" SERIES

Trick or Trouble, Viking (New York, NY), 1994.

The Worst Noel, Viking (New York, NY), 1994.

Stupid Cupid, Viking (New York, NY), 1995.

Star Spangled Summer, Viking (New York, NY), 1996.

No-Thanks Thanksgiving, Viking (New York, NY), 1996.

OTHER

Susan B. Anthony (biography), F. Watts (New York, NY), 1984.

(Editor, with Denise Wilms) *Guide to Non-Sexist Children's Books,* Volume II: *1976-1985,* Academy Chicago (Chicago, IL), 1987.

Jerry Pinkney: Achiever of Dreams, Harcourt (San Diego, CA), 1996.

The Dead Sea Scrolls, illustrated by John Thompson, Morrow (New York, NY), 1997.

Jewish Holidays All Year Round, illustrated by Elivia Savadier, Abrams (New York, NY), 2002.

Jack: The Early Years of John F. Kennedy, Dutton (New York, NY), 2003.

Has also written for television series, including *American Playhouse* and *The Jeffersons;* author of teleplay *Under the Biltmore Clock,* 1983.

WORK IN PROGRESS: *Jake's Best Thumb,* a picture book about a boy who cannot stop sucking his thumb.

SIDELIGHTS: Ilene Cooper has blended a career as a distinguished critic of children's books for the magazine *Booklist,* with that of a popular writer for teen and pre-teen audiences. The author of the humorous novel *Buddy Love—Now on Video* as well as the "Kids from Kennedy Middle School" and "Hollywood Wars" series, Cooper has also researched and written several works of nonfiction that follow her interest in women's history and her own religious roots, as well as a critically acclaimed biography of the early years of John F. Kennedy.

Born in Chicago, Illinois, and a graduate of the University of Missouri, Cooper was a children's librarian before beginning a career as a critic/author. Her first work, *Susan B. Anthony,* appeared in 1984 and profiled the life of that nineteenth-century pioneer of the women's suffrage movement and her unstinting efforts to win the vote for women. This book led to the writing of Cooper's first novel for young readers, *The Winning of Miss Lynn Ryan.* Revolving around a class of fifth-grade students' efforts to curry favor with a pretty and poised new teacher who demands perfection, Cooper's 1987 work illustrates how a teacher can "help her students see what is best in themselves or . . . stifle their better instincts," according to *Horn Book* contributor Nancy Vasilakis. Readers gain a sense of the schoolchildren's struggle through the perspectives of characters such as Carrie, whose messy work will never pass Miss Ryan's muster, and ultra-brainy but equally unpopular "Luke the Puke."

Cooper's most popular novel series—"Kids from Kennedy Middle School," first introduced to teen readers in 1988—delves into the inner politics of the "in-crowd." In *Queen of the Sixth Grade,* Veronica Volner, the self-proclaimed reigning queen of the "Awesome Kennedy Girls" (or AKG), commands that another girl, Robin, be cast out of the group when it becomes apparent that a boy Veronica likes favors Robin instead. Meanwhile, Robin manages to find activities to keep her busy until Veronica in turn is undone and the AKGs are no longer. "Sixth-grade meanness has rarely been better portrayed," commented Roger Sutton in the *Bulletin of the Center for Children's Books.* A reviewer for *Publishers Weekly* likewise praised the "snappy" dialog and "good" pacing, but felt that "the unique compassion and understanding" present in Cooper's first novel were "sorely missed here." However, critic Nancy Vasilakis, writing in *Horn Book,* declared that Cooper "probes with excellent understanding a specific problem of interpersonal relationships facing many schoolchildren."

The devilry continues in *Mean Streak,* as testy Veronica attempts to hide her discombobulated home-life by causing problems for her romantic rivals, especially for Gretchen Hubbard, an overweight girl in the sixth grade. Now that she has alienated her best friends, Veronica has no one to turn to when it appears that her divorced father is going to remarry. Writing in the *Bulletin of the Center for Children's Books,* Sutton remarked that while Veronica is an unsavory character, she is an engaging one that "captures our interest and sympathy, and . . . leaves us with some hope that she is capable of change."

In *Choosing Sides,* the focus shifts to Jonathan Rossi, another sixth grader who is not only a good student but also a fine basketball player. Jon's father wants his younger son to devote his free time to developing his game, just as Jon's older brother has with football, but Jon begins to find other directions and interests. His friends at middle school are interested in music and books, and he begins to find the demands of his father and of team sports too much for him. When a class assignment takes on real-life meaning for Jon, he learns that he has to stand up for himself. Reviewing the novel in *School Library Journal,* Katharine Bruner commented that it was "heartening to find a protagonist who does not have to be antisports in order to enjoy music and literature." Bruner also felt that Cooper's "view is keenly focused and convincing," and that the plot goes forward "at a sprightly pace."

The series continues with *The New, Improved Gretchen Hubbard,* which features the formerly overweight Gretchen, dubbed "Hippo Hubbard." But after a Christmas-time crash diet and a makeover including a new haircut and clothes, Gretchen returns to school a changed girl. With the attentions of a fifteen-year-old actor thrown her way, Gretchen positively blossoms. The actor, Tim, who is working on a movie filmed locally, finally asks her out, and Gretchen, on a dare from friends, accepts. Soon, however, she finds herself over her head not only in her social life, but with her parents' impending divorce as well as school work. "This latest series entry realistically explores the changes that come from weight loss," observed Jana R. Fine in a *School Library Journal* review of this fourth and final series title. Fine also commended the "convincing" characters and "well-structured story line" in Cooper's novel.

Cooper's next production for young readers was her four-volume "Frances in the Fourth Grade" series. Frances is a bright and plucky fourth grader, introduced in the lead-off title, *Frances Takes a Chance.* Here, she gets a new haircut as well as a new best friend. Frances's self-image continues to improve as her friendship with Polly Brock solidifies and as she begins to learn how to be her own person. The everyday adventures of Frances continue in *Frances Dances,* in which the young girl begins ballet and decides to test her self-confidence by dancing in the school pageant. *Frances Four Eyes* and *Frances and Friends* completes the quartet of novels. A reviewer for *Publishers Weekly* called the first two novels in the series "upbeat," and further noted that Cooper presents a "winning balance between Frances's home life and fourth grade year."

Cooper's "Hollywood Wars" series deals with the social pressures of teen life. In *My Co-Star, My Enemy,* fifteen-year-old Alison Blake suddenly finds herself with a role in a television show. Unfortunately, Alison's good luck results in the animosity of fellow cast-member Jamie, also fifteen, whose six-year acting career seems to be near an end. In addition to providing a look at how a television show is filmed, the series follows the changes that rising popularity makes in Alison's formerly quiet life. A contributor for *Publishers Weekly* felt that the "series gets off to a good start with this solid commercial offering." In the second offering in the series, *Lights, Camera, Attitude,* Alison prepares for her new television series, *Sticks and Stones,* but at the same time has to deal with not only a jealous boyfriend but also a manipulative friend. Jamie, meanwhile, has her own problems with a new diet and her father, who is as forceful and overbearing as ever. In *Seeing Red,* Alison must deal with her stage fright or else Jamie is sure to steal the limelight from her. In the final installment, *Trouble in Paradise,* an overly zealous fan could prove a danger to Alison.

Another fan-pleasing series from Cooper is "Holiday Five," which follows the lives of five friends who meet one summer at Camp Wildwood and agree to meet together throughout the year on certain holidays. Cooper plots story lines around these holidays, dealing with realistic crises in the lives of these pre-teens. In the premier volume, *Trick or Trouble,* Lia is visited by her camp friends and tells them of her recent troubles. When she returned from camp, she discovered that her next-door neighbor and good friend Scott grew up over the summer. Kids at school were soon talking about the two being more than friends, making the girls at her school jealous and eventually ending her long-time friendship with Scott. Lia's friends help her put the matter in perspective and teach her about friendship in this "entertaining" novel, as a critic for *Publishers Weekly* described the book. The same reviewer commended Cooper for her "keen understanding of upper-middle-class adolescent concerns." Similarly, a critic from *Kirkus Reviews* applauded the author's "skillful and sensitive treatment of pubescent angst."

The action continues in *The Worst Noel* in which Kathy, one of the five from Camp Wildwood, does not want to spend Christmas with her father and new family, and opts instead to stay with friend Erin from summer camp. *Stupid Cupid* finds Maddy, another of the camp kids, having to deal with her widowed mother and her own size. She finally decides to lose some weight when a new boy at school seems interested in her. Maddy also plans to solve the problem of her mother by setting her up with Lia's uncle. However, when the new boy at school is attracted to Lia, Maddy sees that she has lost weight for all the wrong reasons and understands that in the future she needs to do things for herself and not others. Christina Dorr, writing in *School Library Journal*, praised the "breezy, fast-paced style and high-interest plot [that] will keep readers anticipating the next installment in the series." In *Star Spangled Summer*, it seems that the girls' long-awaited return to Camp Wildwood may be ruined when three of them may not be able to attend. Erin's family is having financial problems, while Jill is thinking of going to an ice-skating camp instead, and Kathy may travel to Europe with her family. More lessons about individual responsibility and friendship are learned in this "typical coming-of-age story for today's youth," according to Carrie A. Guarria in *School Library Journal*. Guarria concluded that this installment was a "good read" and one that "imparts the importance of friendship, family, and honesty."

The "Holiday Five" series concludes with *No-Thanks Thanksgiving*. Here, Kathy looks forward to her birthday which she plans to spend in New York over Thanksgiving, taking in a show on Broadway and enjoying the traditional parade with her friends. Yet petty arguments between these friends suddenly threaten to ruin her fun.

Cooper has also turned her attention to chapter books in her "Road to Reading" series. In *Absolutely Lucy,* young Bobby is so timid and shy that he has problems making friends. Then he gets a beagle puppy for his eighth birthday and things begin to change in his life. He names the dog Lucy after a baby-sitter, and the pet helps Bobby meet new friends, including a young girl at a dog-training school, another boy who is as shy as Bobby, and also an older neighbor. Maura Bresnahan, writing in *School Library Journal,* found this story "entertaining and well plotted," and also felt that "Bobby is an endearing character." *Lucy on the Loose* is "a fresh, funny follow-up" to the first book in the series, according to Stephanie Zvirin in *Booklist.* In this tale, the rambunctious beagle gets lost when it is chasing a cat, and Bobby overcomes his shyness to ask strangers if they have seen his dog. A third installment in the series, *The Annoying Team*, deals with the theme of bullying, in a story of Tim, who has had enough of name calling from Big Jon Ferguson. To counter this bully, Tim initiates The Annoying Team, whose mission is to play pranks on the bullies for a change. Zvirin, writing in *Booklist,* noted that Cooper's chapter book would "keep . . . readers well entertained."

Cooper is also known for stand-alone novels. Published in 1995, *Buddy Love—Now on Video* features a thirteen-year-old protagonist who is desperate to find that one thing that will inspire him; so far, only girls and television have really caught his attention. Ultimately, Buddy finds a way to combine his two main interests after his father buys a video recorder and lets his son use it. Seeing his world through the viewfinder while mastering his filmmaking skills, Buddy eventually begins to view his life differently and find new appreciation for his family. "Cooper's sure touch paints the emotions of early adolescence accurately," noted *Voice of Youth Advocates* reviewer Faye H. Gottschall, who also praised the author's ability to imbue the story with humor. Critic Roger Sutton appreciated Cooper's use of comedy as well and called the author's sense of "middle-school reality . . . upbeat but sheared of didacticism" in his review in the *Bulletin of the Center for Children's Books.*

Older teens take center stage in Cooper's 1997 suspense novel, *I'll See You in My Dreams.* Years after suffering a spell of nightmares that occurred just before her father's tragic death in a car accident, sixteen-year-old Karen Genovese's dreams of a cute new boy at school begin to turn dark. Sensing that something bad is about to befall her new classmate, Mark Kennedy, and Mark's younger brother Brian, Karen sets about trying to avert another tragedy. While a *Publishers Weekly* reviewer claimed that "readers anticipating eerie renditions of psychic experiences may be disappointed" in the direction of the novel, a *Kirkus Reviews* contributor considered *I'll See You in My Dreams* a fun book for teen readers that has "a spooky atmosphere and a few surprising plot twists."

Cooper's *The Dead Sea Scrolls,* published in 1997, was only her second work of nonfiction in fifteen years. The book explores the history behind the collection of religious documents discovered by a shepherd in 1947 in a cave on the shore of the Dead Sea. Cooper recounts the efforts of scientists, translators, and scholars to authenticate and understand what many consider to be the most significant archaeological find of the twentieth century. The volume, which commemorates the fiftieth anniversary of the scrolls' discovery, contains a great deal of research that ranges from studying the techniques of archaeologists and computer scientists to learning the history of Judeo-Christianity and the Middle East. This wealth of factual information is presented in order to allow young readers to understand the many facets of a tale that encompasses two thousand years of human history.

In *The Dead Sea Scrolls,* "This fascinating story takes on new life," stated *Book Links* reviewer Judy O'Malley. "Despite the unavoidable jumping back and forth in time . . . [the text is] clear and accessible," noted Jennifer M. Brabander in her critique of the volume for *Horn Book.* The critic added that Cooper's work "dynamically proves that biblical history is anything but dead." Cooper commented on the writing of *The Dead Sea Scrolls* in a *Book Links* essay: "A special moment for me was my trip to Israel, when I finally got to the Dead Sea caves and Qumran, where excavations are still in progress. No matter how many books and articles I read, nothing could match actually climbing those limestone cliffs myself. There is a Hebrew word, *beshert,* that roughly translates as fate or something that is meant to be. The discovery of the scrolls in those desolate caves makes the word *beshert* come alive for me." Patricia Lothrop-Green, writing in *School Library Journal,* likewise felt that Cooper's book "honors . . . [the] vitality" of the scrolls, and that the author's "vivid descriptions . . . keep interest high."

More nonfiction from Cooper includes *Jewish Holidays All Year Round* and *Jack: The Early Years of John F. Kennedy.* With *Jewish Holidays,* Cooper provides "an excellent introduction to the special days on the Jewish calendar," according to Ron Kaplan of *BookPage.* The book, wrote a *Publishers Weekly* contributor, "strikes a tone both child-friendly and respectful." Cooper examines various holidays throughout the year, explains the significance of the rituals and traditions surrounding them, and provides activities for the whole family in celebrating them. Activities include making noisemakers for Purim and working out recipes for other holidays, such as potato pancakes for Hanukkah or a fruit dish for Sukkot, the celebration that inspired Thanksgiving. Cooper visited the Jewish Museum in New York in preparation for the work and was amazed at what she discovered. "I thought I knew something about Jewish holidays," Cooper told *Booklist*'s Zvirin in an interview. "But these special days are so rich. There is always more to learn." Martha Link, reviewing the same title in *School Library Journal,* concluded that it was "an informative and enjoyable survey."

With *Jack,* Cooper again turns her hand to biography, focusing on the childhood of John F. Kennedy, including his competition with his older brother, his trouble in school, and illnesses that plagued him early on. A critic for *Kirkus Reviews* found this to be "dependable nonfiction writing," while a contributor for *Publishers Weekly* called it "an engaging overview." The same critic further noted that the use of "primary resources and photographs help capture the high pressured and privileged Kennedy lifestyle." *Horn Book*'s Christine M. Heppermann praised Cooper's "revealing portrait" which works without "idealizing or sensationalizing." Heppermann went on to dub the work a "meticulously documented depiction." "I . . . wanted to write about what it was like to be a child in this remarkable, yet highly pressurized, family," Cooper told Zvirin in another *Booklist* interview. *School Library Journal*'s Carol Fazioli praised the "personal tone" and "lively style" of Cooper's biography of the future president.

"Kids always ask me where I get my ideas," Cooper once told *CA.* "Most of them come from my own childhood and teenage years. Although many things have changed since I was young, the hopes and fears and feelings seem to remain the same."

BIOGRAPHICAL AND CRITICAL SOURCES:

PERIODICALS

Book Links, May, 1997, Judy O'Malley, review of *The Dead Sea Scrolls,* p. 16, and Ilene Cooper, "The Dead Sea Scrolls," pp. 16-20.

Booklist, May 15, 1991, p. 1798; August, 1992, p. 2010; May 1, 1993, p. 1580; March 1, 1997, p. 1157; March 15, 2000, Stephanie Zvirin, review of *Absolutely Lucy,* p. 1376; October 1, 2000, Stephanie Zvirin, review of *Lucy on the Loose,* pp. 339, 350; May 1, 2001, Stephanie Zvirin, review of *I'll See You in My Dreams,* p. 1610; June 1, 2002, Stephanie Zvirin, review of *The Annoying Team,* pp. 1719, 1721; October 1, 2002, Stephanie Zvirin, "Ilene Cooper's *Jewish Holidays All Year Round,*" p. 345; January 1, 2003, Stephanie Zvirin, "Ilene Cooper's *Jack: The Early Years of John F. Kennedy,*" p. 868.

Bulletin of the Center for Children's Books, October, 1987, pp. 25-26; November, 1988, Roger Sutton, review of *Queen of the Sixth Grade,* p. 68; September, 1990, pp. 4-5; April, 1991, Roger Sutton, review of *Mean Streak,* p. 188; November, 1992, p. 70; December, 1995, Roger Sutton, review of *Buddy Love—Now on Video,* pp. 123-124; September, 1997, pp. 8-9.

Horn Book, January, 1988, Nancy Vasilakis, review of *The Winning of Miss Lynn Ryan,* p. 62; January, 1989, Nancy Vasilakis, review of *Queen of the Sixth Grade,* p. 68; September-October, 1997, Jennifer M. Brabander, review of *The Dead Sea Scrolls,* pp. 590-591; March-April, 2003, Christine M. Heppermann, review of *Jack,* pp. 222-223.

Horn Book Guide, spring, 1998, Christine Heppermann, review of *I'll See You in My Dreams,* p. 85; fall, 2001, Anita L. Burkam, review of *Lucy on the Loose,* p. 289.

Kirkus Reviews, May 15, 1991, p. 669; June 15, 1991, p. 787; August 15, 1994, review of *Trick or Trouble,* p. 1142; June 1, 1997, review of *I'll See You in My Dreams,* p. 870; December 15, 2002, review of *Jack,* p. 1847.

Publishers Weekly, October 14, 1988, review of *Queen of the Sixth Grade,* p. 77; June 14, 1991, review of *Frances Takes a Chance* and *Frances Dances,* p. 47; May 10, 1993, review of *My Co-Star, My Enemy,* p. 72; July 4, 1994, review of *Trick or Trouble,* p. 64; October 16, 1995, review of *Buddy Love—Now on Video,* p. 62; June 2, 1997, review of *I'll See You in My Dreams,* p. 72; September 30, 2002, review of *Jewish Holidays All Year Round,* pp. 68-69; December 16, 2002, review of *Jack,* p. 69.

School Library Journal, August, 1984, p. 82; May, 1990, Katharine Bruner, review of *Choosing Sides,* p. 103; October, 1992, Jana R. Fine, review of *The New, Improved Gretchen Hubbard,* p. 114; August, 1994, Bonnie L. Raasch, review of *Trick or Trouble,* p. 154; February, 1995, Christina Door, review of *Stupid Cupid,* p. 96; May, 1996, Carrie A. Guarria, review of *Star Spangled Summer,* p. 110; June, 1997, Patricia Lothrop-Green, review of *The Dead Sea Scrolls,* p. 133; March, 2001, Maura Bresnahan, review of *Absolutely Lucy,* p. 205; February, 2003, Carol Fazioli, review of *Jack,* p. 156; March, 2003, Martha Link, review of *Jewish Holidays All Rear Round,* p. 216.

Voice of Youth Advocates, April, 1996, Faye H. Gottschall, review of *Buddy Love—Now on Video,* p. 24.

ONLINE

BookPage, http://www.bookpage.com/ (December, 2002), Ron Kaplan, review of *Jewish Holidays All Year Round.*

Ilene Cooper Home Page, http://www.ilenecooper.com/ (March 6, 2003).*

*　　　*　　　*

CRICHTON, (John) Michael 1942-
(Pseudonyms: Jeffrey Hudson, John Lange; Michael Douglas, a joint pseudonym)

PERSONAL: Surname is pronounced "*cry*-ton"; born October 23, 1942, in Chicago, IL; son of John Henderson (a corporate president) and Zula (Miller) Crichton; married Joan Radam, January 1, 1965 (divorced, 1970); married Kathleen St. Johns, 1978 (divorced, 1980); married Suzanne Childs (marriage ended); married Anne-Marie Martin, 1987 (divorced); children: (fourth marriage) Taylor (daughter). *Education:* Harvard University, A.B. (summa cum laude), 1964, M.D., 1969.

Michael Crichton

ADDRESSES: Office—(West Coast) Jenkins Financial Services, 433 North Camden Dr., Suite 500, Beverly Hills, CA 90210-4443; (East Coast) Constant C Productions, 282 Katonah Ave., No. 246, Katonah, NY 10536-2110. *Agent*—International Creative Management, 40 West 57th Street, New York, NY, 10019.

CAREER: Author and physician, 1969—. Salk Institute for Biological Studies, La Jolla, CA, postdoctoral fellow, 1969-70; visiting writer, Massachusetts Institute of Technology, Cambridge, 1988.

Director of films and teleplays, including *Pursuit* (based on his novel *Binary*), American Broadcasting Companies, Inc., 1972, *Westworld,* Metro-Goldwyn-Mayer, 1973, *Coma,* United Artists (UA), 1978, *The Great Train Robbery,* UA, 1979, *Looker,* Warner Bros., 1981, *Runaway,* Tri-Star Pictures, 1984, *Physical Evidence,* Columbia, 1989, and *The Thirteenth Warrior* (also known as *Eaters of the Dead),* Buena Vista, 1999. Executive producer of film *Disclosure,* Warner Bros., 1994; producer of films, including *Twister,* Warner Bros., 1996, *Jurassic Park III,* 1997; *Sphere,*

Warner Bros., 1998, and *The Thirteenth Warrior,* Buena Vista, 1999. Creator and executive producer, *ER* (television series), National Broadcast Company, Inc., 1994—.

MEMBER: Academy of Motion Picture Arts and Sciences, Aesculaepian Society, Authors Guild, Authors League of America, Directors Guild of America, Mystery Writers Guild of America (West), PEN, Phi Beta Kappa.

AWARDS, HONORS: Edgar Award, Mystery Writers of America, 1968, for *A Case of Need,* and 1979, for *The Great Train Robbery;* writer of the year award, Association of American Medical Writers, 1970, for *Five Patients: The Hospital Explained;* George Foster Peabody Award, 1995, and Emmy Award for Best Dramatic Series, 1996, both for *ER;* Modern Library Association Best Fiction List, 2001, for *Timeline.*

WRITINGS:

NOVELS

The Andromeda Strain, Knopf (New York, NY), 1969.
(With brother, Douglas Crichton, under joint pseudonym Michael Douglas) *Dealing; or, The Berkeley-to-Boston Forty-Brick Lost-Bag Blues,* Knopf (New York, NY), 1971.
The Terminal Man, Knopf (New York, NY), 1972.
Westworld, Bantam (New York, NY), 1974.
The Great Train Robbery, Knopf (New York, NY), 1975.
Eaters of the Dead: The Manuscript of Ibn Fadlan, Relating His Experiences with the Northmen in A.D. 922, Knopf (New York, NY), 1976.
Congo, Knopf (New York, NY), 1980.
Sphere, Knopf (New York, NY), 1987.
Jurassic Park, Knopf, 1990, published as *Michael Crichton's Jurassic World,* Knopf (New York, NY), 1997.
Rising Sun, Knopf (New York, NY), 1992.
Disclosure, Knopf (New York, NY), 1994.
The Lost World, Knopf (New York, NY), 1995.
Airframe, Knopf (New York, NY), 1996.
The Lost World, Jurassic Park: The Movie Storybook, (based on the motion picture and the novel), Grosset & Dunlap (New York, NY), 1997.

Timeline, Knopf (New York, NY), 1999.
Prey, HarperCollins (New York, NY), 2002.

NONFICTION

Five Patients: The Hospital Explained, Knopf (New York, NY), 1970.
Jasper Johns, Abrams (New York, NY), 1977, revised and expanded edition, 1994.
Electronic Life: How to Think about Computers, Knopf (New York, NY), 1983.
Travels (autobiography), Knopf (New York, NY), 1988.

SCREENPLAYS

Extreme Close-up, National General, 1973.
Westworld (based on novel of same title), Metro-Goldwyn-Mayer, 1973.
Coma (based on novel of same title by Robin Cook), United Artists, 1977.
The Great Train Robbery (based on novel of same title), United Artists, 1978.
Looker, Warner Bros., 1981.
Runaway, Tri-Star Pictures, 1984.
(With John Koepp) *Jurassic Park,* 1993.
(With Philip Kaufman and Michael Backes) *Rising Sun,* 1993.
Twister, Warner Bros., 1996.

UNDER PSEUDONYM JOHN LANGE

Odds On, New American Library (New York, NY), 1966.
Scratch One, New American Library (New York, NY), 1967.
Easy Go, New American Library (New York, NY), 1968, published as *The Last Tomb,* Bantam (New York, NY), 1974.
Zero Cool, New American Library (New York, NY), 1969.
The Venom Business, New American Library (New York, NY), 1969.
Drug of Choice, New American Library (New York, NY), 1970.
Grave Descend, New American Library (New York, NY), 1970.
Binary, Knopf (New York, NY), 1971.

UNDER PSEUDONYM JEFFREY HUDSON

A Case of Need, New American Library (New York, NY), 1968.

Contributor to periodicals, including *Wired,* and *Washington Monthly.*

ADAPTATIONS: The Andromeda Strain was filmed by Universal, 1971; *A Case of Need* was adapted as the film *The Carey Treatment* (also known as *Emergency Ward*) and filmed by Metro-Goldwyn-Mayer, 1972; *Binary* was filmed as *Pursuit,* ABC-TV, 1972; *The Terminal Man* was filmed by Warner Brothers, 1974; *Jurassic Park* was filmed by Steven Spielberg and released in 1994; *Congo* was filmed by Frank Marshall and released by Paramount, 1995; *Disclosure* was filmed and released in 1995; *The Lost World: Jurassic Park* was released by Universal, 1997; *Sphere* was adapted for the screen and released by Warner Brothers, 1998; *The Thirteenth Warrior* was released by Buena Vista, 1999; *Timeline* was filmed by Paramount Pictures, 2003. *Timeline* was also adapted as a computer game.

WORK IN PROGRESS: Developing a video game with Sega.

SIDELIGHTS: Michael Crichton has had a number of successful careers—physician, teacher, film director, screenwriter—but he is perhaps best known for pioneering the "techno-thriller" with novels such as *Jurassic Park, Andromeda Strain,* and *Congo* and for creating and producing the hit television series, *ER.* Whether writing about a deadly microorganism, brain surgery gone awry, or adventures in the Congo, Crichton has the ability to blend the tight plot and suspense of the thriller with the technicalities of science fiction, making him a favorite with readers of all ages. Summing up Crichton's appeal in the *Dictionary of Literary Biography Yearbook,* Robert L. Sims wrote, "His importance lies in his capacity to tell stories related to that frontier where science and fiction meet. . . . Crichton's best novels demonstrate that, for the immediate future at least, technological innovations offer the same possibilities and limitations as their human creators."

Crichton's first brush with literary success occurred during medical school. To help pay for tuition and living expenses, he wrote paperback thrillers on the weekends and during vacations. One of these books, *A Case of Need*, became an unexpected hit. Written under a pseudonym, the novel revolves around a Chinese-American obstetrician who is unjustly accused of performing an illegal abortion on the daughter of a prominent Boston surgeon. Critical reaction to the book was very positive. "Read *A Case of Need* now," urged Fred Rotondaro in *Best Sellers,* "it will entertain you; get you angry—it will make you think." Allen J. Hubin, writing in the *New York Times Book Review,* similarly noted that the "breezy, fast-paced, up-to-date first novel . . . demonstrates again the ability of detective fiction to treat contemporary social problems in a meaningful fashion."

Also published while the author was still in medical school, *The Andromeda Strain* made Crichton a minor celebrity on campus (especially when the film rights were sold to Universal Studios). Part historical journal, the novel uses data such as computer printouts, bibliographic references, and fictional government documents to lend credence to the story of a deadly microorganism that arrives on Earth aboard a NASA space probe. The virus quickly kills most of the residents of Piedmont, Arizona. Two survivors, an old man and a baby, are taken to a secret government compound for study by Project Wildfire. The Wildfire team—Stone, a bacteriologist, Leavitt, a clinical microbiologist, Burton, a pathologist, and Hall, a practicing surgeon—must race against the clock to isolate the organism and find a cure before it spreads into the general population.

The mix of science and suspense in *The Andromeda Strain* brought varied reactions from reviewers. While admitting that he stayed up all night to finish the book, Christopher Lehmann-Haupt of the *New York Times* observed that he felt cheated by the conclusion. Richard Schickel, writing in *Harper's,* was more concerned with a shortage of character development: "The lack of interest in this matter is . . . amazing. Perhaps so much creative energy went into his basic situation that none was left for people." Not all critics were as harsh in their evaluation of the novel, however. "The pace is fast and absorbing," claimed Alexander Cook in *Commonweal.* He went on to say, "The writing is spare and its quality is generally high; and the characters, if not memorable, are at any rate sufficiently sketched in and have been given little personal touches of their own."

Crichton also used the world of science and medicine as a backdrop for *The Terminal Man*. The title refers to computer scientist Harry Benson who, as the result of an automobile accident, suffers severe epileptic seizures. As the seizures grow in intensity, Benson has blackouts during which he commits violent acts. At the urging of his doctors, Benson undergoes a radical procedure in which an electrode is inserted into his brain. Hooked up to a packet in the patient's shoulder, the electrode is wired to locate the source of the seizures and delivers a shock to the brain every time an episode is about to occur. Something goes wrong, and Benson's brain is overloaded. As the shocks increase, Benson becomes more irrational, dangerous, and eventually, murderous.

John R. Coyne in the *National Review* found *The Terminal Man* "one of the season's best." He added, "Crichton proves himself capable of making the most esoteric material completely comprehensible to the layman. . . . Even more important, he can create and sustain that sort of suspense that forces us to suspend disbelief." And, in an *Atlantic* review of the novel, Edward Weeks opined that Crichton has "now written a novel quite terrifying in its suspense and implication."

In *The Great Train Robbery,* Crichton moved out of the realm of science and into the world of Victorian England. Loosely based on an actual event, the book explores master criminal Edward Pierce's attempt to steal a trainload of army payroll on its way to the Crimea. "*The Great Train Robbery* combines the pleasures, guilt, and delight of a novel of gripping entertainment with healthy slices of instruction and information interlarded," observed Doris Grumbach in the *New Republic.* Lehmann-Haupt enthused that he found himself "not only captivated because it is Mr. Crichton's best thriller to date . . . but also charmed most of all by the story's Victorian style and content." And Weeks, writing in the *Atlantic Monthly,* called the novel "an exciting and very clever piece of fiction."

Congo marked Crichton's return to the field of science and technology. In the novel, three adventurers travel through the dense rain forests of the Congo in search of a cache of diamonds with the power to revolutionize computer technology. The trio is accompanied by an intelligent, linguistically-trained gorilla named Amy, the designated intermediary between the scientists and a band of killer apes who guard the gems. The small band's search is hampered by cannibals, volcanoes, and mutant primates; it is also marked by a sense of desperation, as the team fights to beat a Euro-Japanese rival company to the prize. In a review of *Congo* for *Best Sellers,* Justin Blewitt termed the novel "an exciting, fast-paced adventure. It rang very true and at the same time was a terrific page-turner. That's a rare combination. . . . [*Congo* is] really a lot of fun."

A scientific—and monetary—search is also the emphasis of *Sphere.* An American ship laying cable in the Pacific hits a snag; the snag turns out to be a huge spaceship, estimated to be at least three centuries old. An undersea research team investigates the strange craft from the relative safety of an underwater habitat. Among the civilian and military crew is psychologist Norman Johnson, whose apprehension about the entire project is validated by a number of increasingly bizarre and deadly events: a bad storm cuts the habitat off from the surface, strange messages appear on computer screens, and an unseen—but apparently huge—squid attacks the crew's quarters.

"Crichton's new novel . . . kept me happy for two hours sitting in a grounded plane," wrote Robin McKinley in the *New York Times Book Review,* adding that "no one can ask for more of a thriller. . . . Take this one along with you on your next plane ride." While noting that he had some problems with *Sphere*—including stilted dialogue and broad characterizations—James M. Kahn mused that Crichton "keeps us guessing at every turn. . . . [He is] a storyteller and a damned good one." And Michael Collins of the *Washington Post Book World* noted that "the pages turn quickly." He urged readers to "suspend your disbelief and put yourself 1,000 feet down."

Crichton also authored the blockbuster *Jurassic Park,* in which he brings the dinosaurs back from extinction. *Jurassic Park* chronicles the attempts of self-made billionaire John Hammond to build an amusement park on a remote island off the coast of Costa Rica. Instead of roller coasters and sideshows, the park features actual life-sized dinosaurs bred through the wonders of biotechnology and recombinant DNA. There are some problems before the park opens, however: workmen begin to die in mysterious accidents and local children are attacked by strange lizards. Fearful that the project's opening is in jeopardy, Hammond calls together a team of scientists and technicians to look things over. Led by a paleontologist named Grant, the group is initially amazed by Hammond's creation. Their amazement quickly turns to horror when the

park's electronic security system is put out of commission and the dinosaurs are freed to roam at will. What ensues is a deadly battle between the vastly under-armed human contingent and a group of smarter-than-anticipated tyrannosaurs, pterodactyls, stegosaurs, and velociraptors.

Time correspondent John Skow considered *Jurassic Park* the author's "best [techno-thriller] by far since *The Andromeda Strain.*" Skow added that Crichton's "sci-fi is convincingly detailed." In a piece for the *Los Angeles Times Book Review,* Andrew Ferguson remarked that, "having read Crichton's fat new novel . . . I have a word of advice for anyone owning real estate within ten miles of the La Brea tar pits: Sell." Ferguson criticized the novel, saying its "only real virtue" lies in "its genuinely interesting discussion of dinosaurs, DNA research, paleontology, and chaos theory." Gary Jennings of the *New York Times Book Review* was more appreciative, arguing that the book has "some good bits. . . . All in all, *Jurassic Park* is a great place to visit."

Crichton left the world of science in *Rising Sun,* a political thriller revolving around the murder of a young American woman during a party for a huge Japanese corporation. The case is given to detective Peter J. Smith, who finds himself up against an Oriental syndicate with great political and economic power. As Smith gets closer to the truth, the Japanese corporation uses all its influence to thwart his investigation—influence that includes corruption and violence. John Schwartz in *Newsweek* recognized that Crichton had "done his homework," but the critic still felt that *Rising Sun* is too full of "randy propaganda instead of a more balanced view" to be effective.

If *Rising Sun* was criticized as having a xenophobic view of the Far East, *Disclosure,* Crichton's 1994 best-seller, opened a whole new vista for debate and discussion. A techno-thriller with a twist, *Disclosure* opens as a computer company executive named Tom Sanders discovers that he has been passed over for a promotion in favor of a woman executive with whom he had once been romantically involved. When he arrives at his new boss's office, she makes a pass at him. Now happily married, Sanders dodges the boss's advances, only to find within days that he has been named as the aggressor in a sexual harassment suit. How Sanders digs his way from beneath the spurious charges—while simultaneously unearthing wider corruption in the computer company—forms the core of the novel.

While critics duly observed the theme of sexual harassment in *Disclosure,* they tended to dwell more upon the thriller aspect of the novel. In *New Statesman and Society,* Douglas Kennedy commended *Disclosure* as an "acidic glimpse into the nasty gamesmanship of U.S. corporate life," adding, "Sexual harassment becomes a minor consideration in a narrative more preoccupied by the wonders of virtual reality and the vicious corporate battlefield." *People* magazine reviewer Susan Toepfer found that by casting the woman as the wrongdoer, "Crichton offers a fresh and provocative story," but contended he did not sufficiently explore the situation's possibilities. *National Review* contributor Michael Coren likewise noted of the novel, "This is provocative stuff, for to question the racial or gender exclusivity of self-awarded victim status is to kick at the very foundations of modern liberalism."

Both *Disclosure* and *Jurassic Park* were produced as feature films, the latter proving to be one of the top-grossing movies of all time. Perhaps the vast success of *Jurassic Park* as a book and a film inspired Crichton to revisit his scheming raptors and vicious tyrannosaurs in *The Lost World.* Also set on an island off the coast of Costa Rica, *The Lost World* follows the adventures of another team of scientists—with a return appearance by mathematical theorist Ian Malcolm—as they try to escape the clutches of the dinosaurs *and* thwart the ambitions of some egg-stealing opportunists. Noted Susan Toepfer in *People,* "Characteristically clever, fast-paced and engaging, Michael Crichton's . . . work accomplishes what he set out to do: offer the still-harrowing thrills of a by-now-familiar ride."

In *Prey,* Crichton exposes the sinister in nanotechnology—tiny machines less than half the thickness of a human hair with the ability to reproduce, learn, and evolve. The story centers on Jack, a Mr. Mom-parent of three children and his workaholic wife's top-secret career which turns out to be developing dangerous nanotechnology for the military. In true Crichton form the book is a page-turning adventure, extrapolating pages of both current and speculative science and technology into a best-selling novel. Critics had mixed reviews for the book, especially in comparison to Crichton's earlier successes. A *Kirkus Reviews* contributor described *Prey* as "nanotechnology [gone] homicidal" and considered the book a "disappointing effort from an author who simply refuses to change an

old, tired template." Michael Hilzik of the *Los Angeles Times* agreed, calling *Prey* lean of drama, tension, and peril and "decidedly lesser Crichton." A *USA Today* reviewer considered the book "overly technical," while a *New York Times* reviewer described it as "irresistibly suspenseful" and said he "turned the pages feverishly."

Crichton's ability to mesh science, technology, and suspense is not limited to novels. Many of the films that the author has directed, such as *Westworld* and *Runaway,* feature a struggle between humans and technology. Despite the often grim outlook of both his films and novels, Crichton revealed in an interview with Ned Smith of *American Way* that his primary goal in making movies and writing books is to "entertain people." He continued, "It's fun to manipulate people's feelings and to be manipulated. To take a movie, or get a book and get very involved in it—don't look at my watch, forget about other things," he said. As for critical reaction to his work, Crichton told Smith: "Every critic assumes he's a code-breaker; the writer makes a code and the critic breaks it. And it doesn't work that way at all. As a mode of working, you need to become very uncritical."

BIOGRAPHICAL AND CRITICAL SOURCES:

BOOKS

Authors and Artists for Young Adults, Volume 10, Gale (Detroit, MI), 1993, pp. 63-70.
Contemporary Literary Criticism, Gale (Detroit, MI), Volume 2, 1974, Volume 6, 1976, Volume 54, 1989.
Contemporary Novelists, 7th edition, St. James Press (Detroit, MI), 2001.
Dictionary of Literary Biography Yearbook: 1981, Gale (Detroit, MI), 1982.
St. James Encyclopedia of Popular Culture, St. James Press (Detroit, MI), 2000.
Shay, Don, and Jody Shay, *The Making of Jurassic Park,* Ballantine (New York, NY), 1993.
Trembley, Elizabeth A., *Michael Crichton: A Critical Companion,* Greenwood Press (Westport, CT), 1996.

PERIODICALS

American Spectator, May, 1992, John Podhoretz, review of *Rising Sun,* p. 71.

Atlanta Journal-Constitution, September 30, 1999, Don O'Briant, "Medical Thrillers Pay Off for Former Doctor," p. C2.

Atlantic, May, 1972, pp. 108-110.

Best Sellers, August 15, 1968, pp. 207-208; February, 1981, p. 388.

Book, November, 1999, review of *Timeline,* p. 69.

Booklist, November 15, 1996, Ray Olson, review of *Airframe,* p. 548; January 1, 1997, review of *Timeline,* p. 763; January 1, 2000, review of *Timeline,* p. 819; February 15, 2001, Mary McCay, review of *Timeline,* p. 1166; May 1, 2001, Karen Harris, audio book review of *The Great Train Robbery,* p. 1616; December 1, 2002, Kristine Huntley, review of *Prey,* p. 628.

Boston Herald, November 28, 1999, review of *Timeline,* p. 59.

Business Week, December 6, 1999, review of *Timeline,* p. 12E10; December 2, 2002, review of *Prey,* p. 103.

Commonweal, August 9, 1969, pp. 493-494.

Daily Telegraph (London, England), December 14, 2002, Toby Clements, review of *Prey.*

Entertainment Weekly, December 3, 1990, p. 80; December 16, 1994, Cindy Pearlman, "Michael Crichton Gets Criticism from Doctors for His Television Show *ER,*" p. 16; December 30, 1994, Albert Kim, "The Entertainers"; 1994: Michael Crichton, p. 30; January 13, 1995, Lisa Schwarzbaum, review of *Disclosure,* pp. 52-53; September 22, 1995, Tom De Haven, review of *The Lost World,* pp. 72-73; November 26, 1999, "Joust for Kicks, review of *Timeline,*" p. 84; November 29, 2002, Benjamin Svetkey, "Michael Crichton Gets Small" (interview), p. 628.

Forbes, June 21, 1993, Steve Forbes, review of *Jurassic Park,* p. 24; September 13, 1993, Steve Forbes, review of *Congo,* p. 26; September 13, 1993, Steve Forbes, review of *Sphere,* p. 26; February 14, 1994, review of *Disclosure,* p. 26; February 21, 1994, p. 108.

Globe and Mail (Toronto, Ontario, Canada), December 4, 1999, review of *Timeline,* p. D16.

Guardian (London, England), December 4, 1999, Mark Lawson, "We Have Been Here Before: Mark Lawson Sees Michael Crichton Collide with the Talent of H.G. Wells," p. 10; March 9, 2002, Nicholas Lezard, "Pick of the Week: Nicholas Lezard Learns How to Review Books," p. 11; December 14, 2002, review of *Prey,* p. 29.

Harper's, August, 1969, p. 97.

Journal of the American Medical Association, September 8, 1993, Andrew A. Skolnick, review of *Jurassic Park,* p. 1252.

Kirkus Reviews, November 1, 1999, review of *Timeline,* p. 1673; November 15, 2002, review of *Prey,* p. 1639.

Kliatt Young Adult Paperback Book Guide, September, 1999, audio book review of *The Lost World,* p. 56.

Knight Ridder/Tribune News Service, November 27, 2002, Chris Cobbs, review of *Prey,* p. 56.

Library Journal, January, 1997, Mark Annichiarico, audio book review of *Airframe,* p. 172; October 15, 1999, Stephen L. Hupp, audio book review of *The Lost World,* p. 122; December, 1999, Jeff Ayers, review of *Timeline,* p. 184; April 1, 2000, Cliff Glaviano, audio book review of *Timeline,* p. 152.

Los Angeles Times, November 29, 2002, Bettijane Levine, "Tall Tech Tales; Michael Crichton's Macabre Vision Finds Another Perch in *Prey,*" p. E37; December 22, 2002, Michael Hiltzik, "It's a Small World after All," p. R10.

Los Angeles Times Book Review, July 12, 1987, pp. 1, 13; November 11, 1990, p. 4; October 29, 1995, p. 2; December 15, 1996, p. 3; November 14, 1999, review of *Timeline,* p. 3; December 22, 2002, "It's a Small World after All," p. R10.

Nation, May 11, 1992, Karl Taro Greenfeld, "The Outnation: A Search for the Soul of Japan," p. 637.

National Review, June 23, 1972, pp. 700-701; August 17, 1992, Anthony Lejeune, review of *Rising Sun,* p. 40; February 21, 1994, Michael Coren, review of *Disclosure,* p. 63; December 6, 1999, review of *Timeline,* p. 68.

New Republic, June 7, 1975, pp. 30-1.

New Statesman, February 4, 1994, Douglas Kennedy, review of *Disclosure,* p. 49; December 20, 1997, p. 121.

New Statesman and Society, March 1, 1991, Elizabeth J. Young, review of *Jurassic Park,* p. 34.

Newsweek, November 19, 1990, Peter S. Prescott, review of *Jurassic Park,* p. 69; February 17, 1992, John Schwartz, review of *Rising Sun,* p. 64; January 17, 1994, David Gates, review of *Disclosure,* p. 52; December 9, 1996, Jeff Giles and Ray Sawhill, "Hollywood's Dying for Novel Ideas," p. 80; November 22, 1999, "Moving across Mediums: Why It's Hard to Get a Handle on Michael Crichton" (interview), p. 94.

New Yorker, February 7, 1994, review of *Disclosure,* p. 99; June 27, 1994, Anthony Lane, review of *Disclosure,* p. 81; December 16, 1996, John Lanchester, review of *Airframe,* p. 103.

New York Review of Books, April 23, 1992, Ian Buruma, review of *Rising Sun,* p. 3; August 12, 1993,

Stephen Jay Gould, review of *Jurassic Park,* p. 51; February 29, 1996, pp. 20-24; January 9, 1997, Louis Menand, review of *Airframe,* p. 16.

New York Times, May 30, 1969, p. 25; June 10, 1975; December 5, 1996, p. 35; October 15, 1999, Stephen L. Hupp, audio book review of *The Lost World,* p. 122; November 18, 1999, Christopher Lehmann-Haupt, review of *Timeline,* p. E9; November 24, 2002, Jim Holt, "It's the Little Things."

New York Times Book Review, August 18, 1968, p. 20; July 12, 1987, Robin McKinley, review of *Sphere,* p. 18; June 26, 1988, Patricia Bosworth, review of *Travels,* p. 30; November 1, 1990, pp. 14-15; November 11, 1990, Gary Jennings, review of *Jurassic Park,* p. 14; February 9, 1992, Robert Nathan, review of *Rising Sun,* p. 1; January 23, 1994, Maureen Dowd, review of *Disclosure,* p. 7; October 1, 1995, Mim Udovitch, review of *The Lost World,* pp. 9-10; December 15, 1996, Tom Shone, review of *Airframe,* p. 12; November 21, 1999, Daniel Mendelsohn, "Knights-errant: Michael Crichton's New Novel Employs Quantum Theory to Transport Some Twenty-first-Century Yalies into Fourteenth-Century France," p. 6.

Observer (London, England), December 5, 1999, review of *Timeline,* p. 11.

PC Magazine, May 27, 1997, Sebastian Rupley and Bill Howard, "Can the Web Hurt Schools? Author Michael Crichton and FCC Chief Reed Hundt Spar at PC Forum," p. 30; June 5, 2001, Les Freed, "Computer Game Review of *Timeline,*" p. 210.

People, January 17, 1994, Susan Toepfer, "Talking with . . . Michael Crichton: America's Tallest, Richest Writer?" (interview), p. 24; September 18, 1995, Susan Toepfer, review of *The Lost World,* p. 37.

Publishers Weekly, September 28, 1990, Sybil Steinberg, review of *Jurassic Park,* p. 84; January 27, 1992, review of *Rising Sun,* p. 91; July 22, 1996, p. 142; November 11, 1996, review of *Airframe,* p. 58; December 2, 1996, audio book review of *Airframe,* p. 30; December 16, 1996, Daisy Maryles, "Behind the Bestsellers," p. 20; November 1, 1999, "The High Concept of Michael Crichton" (interview), p. S3; November 8, 1999, review of *Timeline,* p. 51; October 28, 2002, review of *Prey,* p. 49; December 9, 2002, Daisy Maryles, review of *Prey,* p. 15.

St. Louis Post-Dispatch, November 21, 1999, "Crichton's Latest Thriller Takes Readers to Fourteenth-Century France," p. F13.

School Library Journal, April, 2000, Molly Conally, review of *Timeline,* p. 158.

Science Fiction Chronicle, April, 2001, review of *Timeline,* p. 38.

Time, November 12, 1990, John Skow, review of *Jurassic Park,* p. CB6; February 24, 1992, John Skow, review of *Rising Sun,* p. 63; January 10, 1994, Gregory Jaynes, "Pop Fiction's Prime Provocateur: Michael Crichton" (interview), p. 52; September 25, 1995, Gregory Jaynes, "Meet Mr. Wizard: Author Michael Crichton," p. 60; September 25, 1995, Michael D. Lemonick, "How Good Is His Science?," p. 65; December 9, 1996, p. 90; November 22, 1999, James Poniewozik, review of *Timeline,* p. 107; December 2, 2002, Lev Grossman, "Death Swarmed Over: Crichton's Latest Is a Soulless, By-the-Numbers Techno-Thriller—And You Won't Be Able to Put It Down" p. 96.

U.S. News and World Report, March 9, 1992, p. 50.

Vanity Fair, January, 1994, Zoe Heller, "The Admirable Crichton," p. 32-49.

Wall Street Journal, December 9, 1996, Tom Nolan, review of *Airframe,* p. A12; December 11, 1996, p. B12; November 19, 1999, Thomas Bass, "Click Here for the Middle Ages, Review of *Timeline,*" p. W6.

Washington Post Book World, June 14, 1987, pp. 1, 14; September 5, 1999, review of *Timeline,* p. 3.

ONLINE

Official Michael Crichton Web site, http://www.crichton-official.com/ (November 9, 2003).

Random House Web site, http://www.randomhouse.com/ (November 9, 2003), "Michael Crichton."*

*   *   *

CUNNINGHAM, Bob
See MAY, Julian

*   *   *

CUSK, Rachel 1967-

PERSONAL: Born February 8, 1967, in Canada; daughter of Peter and Carolyn Cusk; married Josh Hillman (a photographer), 1995; children: Albertine, Jessye. *Education:* Attended St. Mary's Convent

Rachel Cusk

(Cambridge, England), and New College, Oxford. *Hobbies and other interests:* Walking, football, piano.

ADDRESSES: Home—57 Carleton Rd., London N7 0EY, England. *Agent*—c/o Author Mail, Picador USA, 175 Fifth Ave., New York, NY 10010.

CAREER: Novelist.

AWARDS, HONORS: Whitbread First Novel Award, 1993, for *Saving Agnes;* Somerset Maugham Prize, 1997, for *The Country Life;* named among best young novelists, *Granta,* 2003.

WRITINGS:

NOVELS

Saving Agnes, Picador (London, England), 1992, Picador USA (New York, NY), 2000.

The Temporary, Macmillan (London, England), 1995.
The Country Life, Picador (London, England), 1997, Picador USA (New York, NY), 1999.
The Lucky Ones, Fourth Estate (London, England), 2003.

OTHER

(With others) *Nadav Kander: Beauty's Nothing,* edited by Nadav Kander, photography by Gerard Malanga, Arena Editions, 2001.
A Life's Work: On Becoming a Mother, Fourth Estate (London, England), 2001, St. Martin's Press (New York, NY), 2002.

SIDELIGHTS: British novelist Rachel Cusk is highly regarded as a chronicler of the emotional turmoil experienced by many women of her generation. Her characters tend toward alienation, depression, unchallenging employment, and unwisely chosen lovers, and critics have particularly praised Cusk's style, voice, powers of observation, and sense of comedy. Her first novel, published in 1992 when she was twenty-five years old, won Cusk the prestigious Whitbread Award.

Saving Agnes, Cusk's literary debut, tells the story of a comfortably middle-class young woman freshly graduated from college and settling into what she hopes will be a special life in London; she has a magazine job, politically aware housemates, and, rather quickly, a lover. Almost as quickly, Agnes Day finds herself close to a nervous breakdown, anxious about her newfound feminism's conflict with her Catholicism. She is introspective, self-deprecating, and insecure—"a lost sheep," as *New Statesman* reviewer Agnes Fletcher put it. Because of her self-absorption, she fails to see that her new lover is a drug addict and that she is about to lose her job. But she learns, she grows, and ultimately she confronts the uncertainties of adulthood. Alex Clark pointed out in the *Times Literary Supplement* that Cusk keeps "firm control" of her characters and guarantees our continued sympathy with them because of "the quality of her prose and the delicacy of her narration." Fletcher observed that "style leaks out all over the place" in "Cusk's shimmering similes and delicious verbal confections."

On the surface, *The Temporary,* published in 1995, is about the hazards of contemporary urban existence and the tedium of office life. But underneath, in the words of *Times Literary Supplement* critic Katy Emck, "it is a bleak, ironic tale that . . . deals with a common female predicament that is largely taboo in contemporary fiction." Francine is a temporary office worker by choice, waiting for the moment when her fine looks and her belief that she is destined to rise to exceptional heights take hold. She is a victim of glossy magazines. On her way up, because—she thinks—it is helpful to have the right man in her life, she picks Ralph because of his—she thinks—superior birth. In reality, he is something less than superior, and he does not even like Francine. Too late: she is pregnant, and her dreams of glory dissolve into hospital waiting rooms, desperate measures, and suspiciously acquired ready cash.

Emck called Cusk's "satire of feminine vanity . . . knowing and sharp" and her sense of comedy "absolutely distinctive. She shows the sadness of existence with an edge of worldly-wise malice." Chris Savage King in the *New Statesman* commented that "Cusk's take on dullness and inertia is little short of spectacular," and that her style "perfectly illustrates her characters' slo-mo and waterlogged states." Kate Hubbard in the *Spectator* called *The Temporary* "a fine achievement."

Stella Benson is the emotionally damaged protagonist of Cusk's 1997 novel, *The Country Life.* While on her honeymoon, Stella decides her marriage was a mistake and flees from her husband, her parents, and London altogether, for a job as an au pair in a small, rural village. Her charge is Martin, the disabled teenaged son of a very well-off farming family. Almost immediately, Stella's life collapses in a series of calamities: she breaks out in hives, walks through a thorny hedge, gets badly sunburned, then throws up. All she wants is "to exist in a state of no complexity whatever," but the family is dysfunctional, she is pursued by inappropriate suitors, and she appears to perform no task with competence. Her anxiety, already acute due to the emotional baggage she has brought, only gets worse. Martin's mother, who dominates her husband and the farm, is in turn manipulated by all of her children, save Martin, who forms an unlikely alliance with Stella. Rural living turns out to be no less strenuous than city life and no less convoluted; but for all of that, as Lucy Atkins pointed out in the *Times Literary Supplement, The Country Life* "heralds the triumph of the ordinary." *Spectator* contributor Cressida Connolly noted that there are some "brilliant set pieces" in the

novel, and called the book "a comedy of manners." A reviewer for *Publishers Weekly* said that Stella's attempts to "face her own inner oppression" would win new readers for Cusk's two previous novels as well.

In *The Lucky Ones* Cusk tells five separate but related stories. On the edges of all the stories are the characters Victor, a lawyer dying of cancer, and his wife Serena, a newspaper columnist. The stories ultimately come together as the couple finally tells their own story. But, according to John Mullan in the *Guardian,* "what binds the whole together is something stronger: the business of having children." Mullan explained that each story involves the limitations that becoming a parent puts on one's life. Lloyd Evans in the London *Daily Telegraph* noted that "at the heart of the book lies a discussion about feminism conducted by two women who represent opposing strands of the maternal experience." Reviewing *The Lucky Ones* for the *Observer,* Stephanie Merritt found that "very little happens; the big, dramatic events take place elsewhere, off the page, and the narratives instead trace the ripples these events leave in the consciousness of the characters." "Cusk's restrained, elegant and fiercely observant novel is interesting right from the start," Jane Shilling maintained in the *Daily Telegraph.*

Cusk turns to nonfiction with her book *A Life's Work: On Becoming a Mother,* an account of her pregnancy and the first year of her daughter's life. Along the way, she seeks to shatter some of the romantic notions about the process. A reviewer for *Publishers Weekly* found that Cusk's "dry, honest style is a refreshing change for anyone seeking to understand the daily realities of undertaking such an enormous responsibility." "Ultimately," wrote Rachel Collins in *Library Journal,* "what Cusk offers is an expose of motherhood that extracts its myths and reworks them into personal truths." "Cusk has written something fine and beautiful," Caitlin Flanagan claimed in the *Atlantic Monthly.* Similarly, Suzanne Moore in the *New Statesman* concluded: "Cusk has crafted a work of beauty and wisdom."

BIOGRAPHICAL AND CRITICAL SOURCES:

PERIODICALS

Atlantic Monthly, September, 2002, Caitlin Flanagan, review of *A Life's Work,* p. 154.

Book, May-June, 2002, Steve Wilson, review of *A Life's Work,* p. 84.

Booklist, November 1, 1999, GraceAnne A. DeCandido, review of *Saving Agnes,* p. 508.

Daily Telegraph (London, England), April 13, 2003, Lloyd Evans, "A Writer's Life: Rachel Cusk," and Jane Shilling, review of *The Lucky Ones.*

Fit Pregnancy, August-September, 2002, Celeste Fremon, review of *A Life's Work,* p. 26.

Guardian, April 5, 2003, John Mullan, review of *The Lucky Ones.*

Library Journal, October 1, 1999, Nancy McNicol, review of *Saving Agnes,* p. 132; May 1, 2002, Rachel Collins, review of *A Life's Work,* p. 120.

New Statesman, June 4, 1993, Agnes Fletcher, review of *Saving Agnes,* p. 39; July 28, 1995, Chris Savage King, review of *The Temporary,* p. 41; September 3, 2001, Suzanne Moore, review of *A Life's Work,* p. 37; December 17, 2001, Jennie Bristow, "Playpen World: Jennie Bristow on the Cult of Mummy Lit," p. 114.

Observer (London, England), March 30, 2003, Stephanie Merritt, "Mum's the Word."

Publishers Weekly, October 12, 1998, review of *The Country Life,* p. 55; November 15, 1999, review of *Saving Agnes,* p. 54; March 25, 2002, review of *A Life's Work,* p. 52.

Spectator, July 15, 1995, Kate Hubbard, review of *The Temporary,* pp. 32-33; July 5, 1997, Cressida Connolly, review of *The Country Life,* p. 36; April 19, 2003, John de Falbe, review of *The Lucky Ones,* p. 40.

Times Literary Supplement, May 21, 1993, Alex Clark, review of *Saving Agnes,* p. 23; July 21, 1995, Katy Emck, review of *The Temporary,* p. 21; June 20, 1997, Lucy Atkins, review of *The Country Life,* p. 23.

Voice Literary Supplement, February, 1999, Stacey D'Erasmo, review of *The Country Life.*

ONLINE

Contemporary Writers.com, http://www.contemporarywriters.com/ (June 11, 2003).*

* * *

CUYLER, Margery S(tuyvesant) 1948-
(Daisy Wallace)

PERSONAL: Born December 31, 1948, in Princeton, NJ; daughter of Lewis Baker (a banker) and Margery Papperrell (Merrill) Cuyler; married John Newman Hewson Perkins (a psychoanalyst), August 23, 1979; children: Thomas, Timothy. *Education:* Sarah Lawrence College, B.A., 1970. *Politics:* Democrat. *Hobbies and other interests:* Jungian psychology, mythology.

ADDRESSES: Home—261 Fillow St., West Norwalk, CT 06850. *Office*—Holiday House, 18 East 53rd St., New York, NY 10022. *Agent*—McIntosh & Otis, Inc., 475 Fifth Ave., New York, NY 10017. *E-mail*—margery.cuyler@verizon.net.

CAREER: Editor, publishing executive, and children's book author. Atlantic Monthly Press, Boston, MA, assistant to editor of children's books, 1970-71; Walker and Co., New York, NY, editor of children's books, 1972-74; Holiday House, New York, NY, vice president and editor-in-chief of children's books, 1974-95. Lecturer at Rutgers University, 1974, New School for Social Research, 1975, and Vassar College, 1984. Member of board of trustees, Sarah Lawrence College Library.

MEMBER: Women's National Book Association (member, board of directors of Children's Book Council, 1980-82).

WRITINGS:

FOR CHILDREN

Jewish Holidays, illustrations by Lisa C. Wesson, Holt (New York, NY), 1978.

The All-Around Pumpkin Book, illustrations by Corbett Jones, Holt (New York, NY), 1980.

The All-Around Christmas Book, illustrations by Corbett Jones, Holt (New York, NY), 1982.

The Trouble with Soap, illustrations by Marcia Winborn, Dutton (New York, NY), 1984.

Sir William and the Pumpkin Monster, illustrations by Marcia Winbarn, Holt (New York, NY), 1984.

Rufus and Max: A Valentine Story, Holt (New York, NY), 1985.

Freckles and Willie, Holt (New York, NY), 1986.

Fat Santa, Holt (New York, NY), 1987.

Shadow's Baby, Clarion Books (New York, NY), 1989.

Weird Wolf, Holt (New York, NY), 1989.

Baby Dot, Clarion Books (New York, NY), 1990.

Daisy's Crazy Thanksgiving, Holt (New York, NY), 1990.

That's Good! That's Bad!, Holt (New York, NY), 1991.

The Christmas Snowman, Arcade (New York, NY), 1992.

Buddy Bear and the Bad Guys, Clarion Books (New York, NY), 1993.

Invisible in the Third Grade, Holt (New York, NY), 1995.

The Biggest, Best Snowman, Scholastic (New York, NY), 1998.

The Battlefield Ghost, Scholastic (New York, NY), 1999.

From Here to There, Holt (New York, NY), 1999.

100th Day Worries, Simon & Schuster (New York, NY), 2000.

Road Signs: A Harey Race with a Tortoise, Winslow Press, 2000.

Stop, Drop, and Roll: A Book about Fire Safety and Prevention, Simon & Schuster (New York, NY), 2001.

Ah-Choo!, Scholastic (New York, NY), 2002.

That's Good! That's Bad! in the Grand Canyon, Holt (New York, NY), 2002.

Skeleton Hiccups, Margaret K. McElderry (New York, NY), 2002.

Big Friends, illustrations by Ezra Tucker, Walker (New York, NY), 2004.

Please Say Please! Penguin's Guide to Manners, illustrations by Will Hilldenbrand, Scholastic (New York, NY), 2004.

EDITOR; UNDER PSEUDONYM DAISY WALLACE

Monster Poems, illustrations by Kay Chorao, Holiday House (New York, NY), 1976.

Witch Poems, illustrations by Trina Schart Hyman, Holiday House (New York, NY), 1976.

Giant Poems, illustrations by Margot Tomes, Holiday House (New York, NY), 1978.

Ghost Poems, illustrations by Tomie De Paola, Holiday House (New York, NY), 1979.

Fairy Poems, illustrations by Trina Schart Hyman, Holiday House (New York, NY), 1980.

SIDELIGHTS: Margery S. Cuyler has written many children's books. As she explained in an essay posted at her Web site, "I have always written stories, ever since I learned how to write. My creative and wacky family, most of whom are artists, actors, storytellers, and writers, helped me along. My childhood was never dull. I grew up in the oldest house in Princeton, New Jersey, with three brothers and one sister. There were also four cousins who lived with us after their mother died. Computers weren't invented yet and we didn't buy a television until I was eight years old. Most of my childhood was spent playing Charades, Hide-and-Go-Seek, Monopoly, and Chess with my siblings and cousins. We also wrote and performed plays. My parents read aloud to us every night."

Cuyler's books range from realistic depictions of children's lives to fantasy tales told for amusement. In the realistic story *100th Day Worries,* young Jessica and her classmates are asked to bring in a collection of one hundred items to celebrate one hundred days of school. While the other children bring in their collections, Jessica cannot imagine what she should do. Finally, her family gives her one hundred small items to help her out, something that her teacher explains as being one hundred "bits of love." A critic for *Publishers Weekly* found that Cuyler's "tight text keeps the story moving apace."

The traditional story of the race between the tortoise and the hare is rekindled in Cuyler's *Roadsigns: A Harey Race with a Tortoise.* In Cuyler's version, the signs along the road are the key to the plot. The confident hare disregards their warnings about road repairs, falling rocks, and other hazards. But the tortoise pays attention, avoids the time-wasting detours, and wins the race. Michael Cart in *Booklist* explained that most of the story is told "almost entirely in the words of the signs that appear throughout the course of the race." Louise L. Sherman in *School Library Journal* concluded that "*Roadsigns* will provide reading practice, sign recognition, and good fun for both one-on-one sharing and independent reading."

Cuyler's *Skeleton Hiccups* tells of a skeleton with such a bad case of annoying hiccups that he is driven from his grave in search of a cure. Helpful suggestions from a ghost friend are ineffectual; when the skeleton drinks water, for example, it simply splashes out of him. John Peters in *Booklist* noted that "Cuyler establishes a strong, infectious rhythm by sandwiching a 'hic hic hic' between each three- or four-word line." Piper L. Nyman in *School Library Journal* believed that "this book will be a treat for children who can laugh at the slightly macabre."

Cuyler once told *CA:* "I like to write about holiday themes because it's important for children in the United States to explore traditions and to learn about the roots of our polygenetic culture."

BIOGRAPHICAL AND CRITICAL SOURCES:

PERIODICALS

Booklist, December 1, 2000, Michael Cart, review of *Roadsigns: A Harey Race with a Tortoise,* p. 717; September 15, 2001, Annie Ayres, review of *Stop, Drop, and Roll,* p. 230; September 15, 2002, John Peters, review of *Skeleton Hiccups,* p. 245.
Horn Book, September-October, 2002, Joanna Rudge Long, review of *Skeleton Hiccups,* p. 549.
Kirkus Reviews, March 15, 2002, review of *That's Good! That's Bad! in the Grand Canyon,* p. 408.
Language Arts, November, 2002, review of *Stop, Drop, and Roll,* pp. 148-149.
Publishers Weekly, December 13, 1999, review of *100th Day Worries,* p. 81; July 10, 2000, review of *Roadsigns,* p. 62.
Rocky Mountain News (Denver, CO), February 13, 2000, review of *100th Day Worries,* p. 4E.
School Library Journal, December, 1999, Beth Wright, review of *The Battlefield Ghost,* p. 90; January, 2000, Lisa Gangemi Krapp, review of *100th Day Worries,* p. 93; September, 2000, Louise L. Sherman, review of *Roadsigns,* p. 193; October, 2001, Roxanne Burg, review of *Stop, Drop, and Roll,* p. 113; June, 2002, Marian Drabkin, review of *That's Good! That's Bad! in the Grand Canyon,* p. 92; October, 2002, Piper L. Nyman, review of *Skeleton Hiccups,* p. 100.

ONLINE

Margery Cuyler Web site, http://www.geocities.com/mcuyler02/ (November 7, 2003).*

D

DAUNTON, M(artin) J(ames) 1949-

PERSONAL: Born February 7, 1949, in Cardiff, Wales; son of Ronald J. (a bank official) and Dorothy (a homemaker; maiden name, Bellett) Daunton; married Claire Gobbi (a university administrator), January 7, 1984. *Education:* University of Nottingham, B.A., 1970; University of Kent at Canterbury, Ph.D., 1973. *Hobbies and other interests:* Architectural tourism, collecting modern ceramics, walking.

ADDRESSES: Office—Churchill College, Cambridge University, Cambridge CB3 0DS, England. *E-mail*—mjd42@cam.ac.uk.

CAREER: University of Durham, Durham, England, lecturer in economic history, 1973-79; University College London, London, England, lecturer, 1979-85, reader in history, 1985-89, professor, 1989-97; Churchill College–Cambridge, Cambridge, England, fellow and professor of economic history, 1997—. Visiting fellow, Australian National University, 1985 and 1994; visiting professor, Nikon University, 2000. Chair, Institute of Historical Research, 1994-98.

MEMBER: Royal Historical Society (treasurer, 1986-91, vice president, 1996-2000), British Academy (fellow), Economic History Society (member of council, 1985-88), Institute of Historical Research (chair, 1994—).

WRITINGS:

Coal Metropolis: Cardiff, 1870-1914, Leicester University Press (Leicester, England), 1977.

House and Home in the Victorian City: Working-Class Housing, 1850-1914, Edward Arnold (London, England), 1983.

(Editor) *Councillors and Tenants: Local Authority Housing in English Cities, 1919-1939,* Leicester University Press (Leicester, England), 1985.

Royal Mail: The Post Office since 1840, Athlone Press (Dover, NH), 1986.

A Property Owning Democracy?, Faber (London, England), 1987.

(Editor) *Housing the Workers, 1850-1914: A Comparative Perspective,* Leicester University Press (Leicester, England), 1990.

Progress and Poverty: An Economic and Social History of Britain, 1700-1850, Oxford University Press (New York, NY), 1995.

The Ransom of Riches: The Politics of Taxation in Britain since 1842, Longmans (London, England), 1996.

(Editor) *Charity, Self-Interest, and Welfare in the English Past,* St. Martin's Press (New York, NY), 1996.

(Editor, with Rick Halpern) *Empire and Others: British Encounters with Indigenous Peoples, 1600-1850,* University of Pennsylvania Press (Philadelphia, PA), 1999.

(Editor) *The Cambridge Urban History of Britain,* Volume 3: *1840-1950,* Cambridge University Press (New York, NY), 2000.

Trusting Leviathan: The Politics of Taxation in Britain, 1799-1914, Cambridge University Press (Cambridge, England), 2001.

Just Taxes: The Politics of Taxation in Britain, 1914-1979, Cambridge University Press (New York, NY), 2002.

Contributor to economic and history journals. *Studies in History,* chair of editors, 1995—.

SIDELIGHTS: M. J. Daunton is a professor of history whose publications deal with the social and economic changes wrought by the industrialization of countries in Europe and North America. His first book, *Coal Metropolis: Cardiff, 1870-1914,* was largely welcomed by critics as a much-needed and long overdue history of the Welsh city of Cardiff. The author considered the economic development of the city since 1870 and its social evolution as a city, extending his research into the areas of social culture and politics. Kenneth O. Morgan wrote in the *Times Literary Supplement:* "The result is impressive—a precise, fully documented, lucidly written and beautifully illustrated book which will be of great value and interest to historians . . . of the British urban experience." Although Daunton's work defies easy summarization, it does offer "a highly stimulating point of departure for the next generation of welfare historians," wrote David Vincent in the *English Historical Review.*

House and Home in the Victorian City: Working-Class Housing, 1850-1914 earned praises from some of its reviewers. In the *Times Literary Supplement,* P. J. Waller commented that Daunton's second book "combines very different perspectives to illuminate a complex topic: those of physical form, class culture, distinctive local habit, and particular personal preference." The author analyzes various approaches to planning and housing, and studies the nineteenth-century trends which resulted in sweeping changes in the relationships between public and private space. Daunton surveys the types of housing that characterized various localities, examines housing from the perspective of rents and investment values, and considers the political issues involved in the relationships of landlords to tenants and public officials. According to Waller, "Daunton integrates the subject better than any historian before him," providing "a more complete picture than we have yet had."

In *Progress and Poverty: An Economic and Social History of Britain, 1700-1850,* Daunton challenges any simplistic assessment of the social changes wrought by the Industrial Revolution. *Business History* reviewer John Armstrong wrote, "For the student or general reader who wants a good introduction to the issues, debates and current state of our knowledge on economic and social topics it acts as an excellent guide, combining general trends with relevant vivid examples which provide detailed flesh on the bone." *History Today* contributor Max Beloff summarized: "Professor Daunton's book is a remarkable achievement in combining an assessment of the present state of our knowledge of the period and the rise of the British economy to its apogee."

Daunton has also written an authorized history of the British postal service, described by Richard R. John, Jr. in *Business History Review* as being "of consistently high caliber" and "sure to be cited often in the years to come." Of greater scope is Daunton's two-volume study of taxation in the United Kingdom from 1799 through 1979, published as *Trusting Leviathan: The Politics of Taxation in Britain, 1799-1914* and *Just Taxes: The Politics of Taxation in Britain, 1914-1979.* In *Business History,* Anthony Howe described *Trusting Leviathan* as a "superb and masterly analysis. . . . Daunton's is a pioneering combination of a broad comparative understanding of the British state and a detailed grasp of its administrative mechanisms."

Daunton once told *CA:* "My work has now moved away from its earlier interest in the history of cities and architectural form to a concern for the nature of the modern British state, and the development of economic and social policy. The connection between the two sets of concerns is housing policy, which I analysed through international comparisons; my more recent publications have dealt with taxation and social policy. These themes have informed my general books on British economic and social history since 1700, as well as more specific studies. I hope in the future to move from Britain to a wider analysis of the British empire, considering issues such as taxation and land policy."

BIOGRAPHICAL AND CRITICAL SOURCES:

PERIODICALS

American Historical Review, April, 1987, Ian Inkster, review of *Royal Mail: The Post Office since 1840,* p. 417.
Business History, January, 1997, John Armstrong, review of *Progress and Poverty: An Economic and Social History of Britain, 1700-1850,* p. 91;

October, 2002, Anthony Howe, review of *Trusting Leviathan: The Politics of Taxation in Britain 1799-1914*, p. 146.

Business History Review, summer, 1988, Richard R. John Jr., review of *Royal Mail*, p. 352.

Contemporary Review, July, 2001, review of *The Cambridge Urban History of Britain,* Volume 3, *1840-1950*, p. 60.

English Historical Review, April, 1987, David Englander, review of *Councillors and Tenants: Local Authority Housing in English Cities, 1919-1939*, p. 403; July, 1988, Duncan Bythell, review of *Royal Mail,* p. 759; April, 1994, E. P. Hennock, review of *Housing the Workers, 1850-1914: A Comparative Perspective,* p. 507; June, 1997, Duncan Bythell, review of *Progress and Poverty,* p. 780; September, 1998, David Vincent, review of *Charity, Self-Interest and Welfare in the English Past,* p. 1047; June, 2000, Ged Martin, review of *Empire and Others: British Encounters with Indigenous Peoples, 1600-1850,* p. 724.

History Today, August, 1984, Anthony Sutcliffe, review of *House and Home in the Victorian City: Working-Class Housing, 1850-1914,* p. 52; March, 1996, Max Beloff, review of *Progress and Poverty,* p. 53.

Journal of American History, December, 2000, Eric Hinderaker, review of *Empire and Others,* p. 1005.

Journal of Modern History, September, 1999, Donald Woodward, review of *Charity, Self-Interest, and Welfare in the English Past,* p. 681.

Times Literary Supplement, March 4, 1977; January 20, 1984; November 29, 1985.*

*   *   *

DAWLEY, Alan (Charles) 1943-

PERSONAL: Born December 18, 1943, in Milwaukee, WI; son of Clarence F. and Thelma E. (Lee) Dawley; married Katherine Louise Wechsler, September 10, 1966; children: Aaron Michael, Evan Nicholas. *Education:* Attended University of Aix-en-Provence, 1962, and University of Wisconsin—Madison, 1964; Oberlin College, B.A. (cum laude), 1965; Harvard University, M.A., 1966, Ph.D., 1971. *Politics:* Democrat.

ADDRESSES: Home—235 Pelham Rd., Philadelphia, PA 19119. *Office*—College of New Jersey, Department of History, Ewing, NJ 08628-0718. *E-mail*—adawley@tcnj.edu.

CAREER: Mississippi Free Press, Jackson, MS, editor, 1963-64; Trenton State College, Trenton, NJ, director of Bicentennial Institute on the American Revolution, 1975; College of New Jersey, Ewing, NJ, assistant professor, 1970-78, associate professor, 1979-84, professor of history, 1984—. Worcester College of Higher Education, exchange professor, 1976-77; Princeton University, fellow of Davis Center, 1977-78, visiting professor, autumn, 1991, and autumn, 1992; University of Virginia, Jacobus Lecturer, 1979; University of Warwick, visiting senior lecturer at Centre for Social History, 1982-83; New York University, visiting member of graduate faculty, 1986; guest lecturer at Brown University, City University of New York, Columbia University, University of Pennsylvania, Rutgers University, State University of New York at Binghamton, McGill University, Concordia University, Oxford University, Cambridge University, University of Sussex, University of Birmingham, University of Manchester, and University of Bremen.

MEMBER: American Historical Association, Organization of American Historians, Historiale de la Grande Guerre, Pennsylvania Labor History Society, Phi Beta Kappa, Phi Kappa Phi.

AWARDS, HONORS: Woodrow Wilson fellowship, 1965-66; Harvard Prize fellowship, 1967-70; Bancroft Prize, 1977, for *Class and Community: The Industrial Revolution in Lynn;* National Endowment for the Humanities, summer stipend, 1980, fellowships, 1986-87, 1993-94; Beveridge grant, American Historical Association, 1982; Hagley Library grant in aid, 1984; grants from Mellon Foundation and Murray Research Center, 1985, 1986; Distinguished Research Award, Trenton State College, 1987-89; John Hope Franklin Prize in American Studies honorable mention, 1992, for *Struggles for Justice: Social Responsibility and the Liberal State.*

WRITINGS:

(Coeditor and contributor) *Working for Democracy: American Workers from the Revolution to the Present,* University of Illinois Press (Urbana, IL), 1985.

Struggles for Justice: Social Responsibility and the Liberal State, Harvard University Press (Cambridge, MA), 1991.

Class and Community: The Industrial Revolution in Lynn (originally published in *The Private Side of American History,* edited by G. Nash, [New York, NY], 1979), twenty-first anniversary edition, with new preface, Harvard University Press (Cambridge, MA), 2000.

Changing the World: American Progressives in War and Revolution, 1914-1924, Princeton University Press (Princeton, NJ), 2003.

Contributor to periodicals, including *Labor History, International Labor and Working Class History, Radical History Review,* and *Acoma.*

WORK IN PROGRESS: Writing *Global America: The United States in Twentieth-Century World History.*

SIDELIGHTS: Specializing in twentieth- and nineteenth-century American history, professor Alan Dawley has written several social histories, including the award-winning *Class and Community: The Industrial Revolution in Lynn,* in which he uses the example of a Massachusetts town to explore the vast social changes occurring in the United States during the early nineteenth century. Dawley's *Struggles for Justice: Social Responsibility and the Liberal State* and *Changing the World: American Progressives in War and Revolution, 1914-1924* focus on the progressive movement, synthesizing the works of numerous other historians into a more cohesive thesis concerning social changes in early twentieth-century America.

In *Struggles for Justice,* Dawley defines "progressives" and "liberals" and how these labels have changed over the decades, including how "managerial liberals" (those who emphasized that businesses can be self-policing) eventually won out over "progressive liberals" (those emphasizing a more leftist agenda of state-managed social reforms) to define the direction of "liberalism" today. To do this, Dawley ties together many social forces that were in play during the early twentieth-century Progressive Era, including the struggle for workers' rights and the increasing role of women in the workplace. "Thoroughly researched, beautifully written and ambitious in scope, this could almost be the book that finally sends Richard Hofstadter's 1955 classic *The Age of Reform: From Bryan to F.D.R.* out of print," commented Robin L. Einhorn in a *Nation* review. "Dawley here answers the many calls issued by Thomas Bender and other

historians over the past decade for a politically centered, synthetic narrative of a large chunk of U.S. history." Although Einhorn felt that Dawley's book becomes "less convincing" toward the end in which he discusses the New Deal years, because by this time the shift to the new liberalism has already been completed, the reviewer concluded that *Struggles for Justice* is "a stirring summary of the triumphs of progressivism."

Dawley returns to the subject of progressivism in his *Changing the World,* in which he covers the years of World War I, as well as the events preceding and following the Great War. Here, the author discusses the efforts of progressives and how their influence was felt during an era of war and political and social upheaval. A *Publishers Weekly* reviewer especially praised Dawley's coverage of the League of Nations and Woodrow Wilson's vision of the Fourteen Points, concluding that Dawley successfully uncovers the "philosophical roots" of the era's thinkers and leaders in what "is an especially timely book, given the tense state of world affairs."

BIOGRAPHICAL AND CRITICAL SOURCES:

PERIODICALS

Commonweal, February 14, 1992, Christopher Lasch, review of *Struggles for Justice: Social Responsibility and the Liberal State,* p. 25.

Journal of American History, September, 1992, Michael McGerr, review of *Struggles for Justice,* p. 687.

Nation, January 27, 1992, Robin L. Einhorn, review of *Struggles for Justice,* p. 99.

Publishers Weekly, March 17, 2003, review of *Changing the World: American Progressives in War and Revolution,* p. 65.*

*   *   *

de las CASAS, Walter 1947-

PERSONAL: Born February 3, 1947, in Havana, Cuba; naturalized U.S. citizen; son of Mario and Aracelia (Vivo) de las Casas. *Ethnicity:* "Hispanic." *Education:* Iona College, B.A. (cum laude), 1970; Hunter College of the City University of New York, M.A., 1977; doctoral study at City University of New York, 1987-94. *Politics:* Liberal Democrat.

Walter de las Casas

ADDRESSES: *Home*—323 Dahill Rd., Apt. 1A, Brooklyn, NY 11218-3848.

CAREER: Teacher of French and Spanish at middle schools in New Rochelle, NY, 1970-72, and Dobbs Ferry, NY, 1972-73; bilingual teacher at elementary schools in Roosevelt, NY, 1973-74; teacher of Spanish, bilingual Spanish, and other subjects at a high school in Brooklyn, NY, 1974-75, 1977-93; Science Skill Center High School, Brooklyn, NY, teacher of Spanish language and literature, 1994-96.

MEMBER: American Association of Teachers of Spanish and Portuguese.

AWARDS, HONORS: Medal from American Legion, 1965, for an essay on "Americanism."

WRITINGS:

La Ninez que dilata (poetry in Spanish), Editorial Catoblepas (Madrid, Spain), 1986.

Libido (poetry in Spanish), Linden Lane Press (Princeton, NJ), 1989.
Tributes (poetry in English), E. Press, 1993.
Discourse (poetry in English), Minerva Press (Toledo, OH), 1999.

Contributor to periodicals, including *Hispania.*

WORK IN PROGRESS: *Hojas Dispersas,* in Spanish.

SIDELIGHTS: Walter de las Casas once told *CA:* "Poetry is the lyrical expression of my intimate, interior, psychological life and of human relationships. It is also the lyrical expression of knowledge. Poetry should be transparent, a clean windowpane through which living feeling shines."

More recently he commented: "My main influence in writing comes from the work of the Cuban poet Heberto Padilla, in particular his poetry book *Fuera del juego.* Although my first poems were in English in 1968, I had a long hiatus from poetry because of my work as a teacher. In 1976, after rereading *Fuera del juego,* I began to write poetry again. Having almost finished my master's degree in Spanish, I wrote in Spanish, as my first two books attest. However, my subscription and readings from the *London Review of Books* influenced me to write also in English. My writing process up to this point is that I get an overwhelming feeling about something, and I just begin to write until the feeling is spent."

*   *   *

DESAI, Kiran 1971-

PERSONAL: Born 1971, in India; daughter of Anita Desai (a novelist). *Education:* Attended Columbia University; also educated in India and England.

ADDRESSES: *Agent*—c/o Author Mail, Atlantic Monthly Press, 841 Broadway, New York, NY 10019.

CAREER: Writer.

AWARDS, HONORS: Woolrich fellowship.

WRITINGS:

Hullabaloo in the Guava Orchard, Atlantic Monthly
   Press (New York, NY), 1998.

Contributor to *Mirrorwork: Fifty Years of Indian Writing,* edited by Salman Rushdie; contributor to the *New Yorker.*

SIDELIGHTS: Kiran Desai was still a student at
Columbia University when her first novel, *Hullabaloo
in the Guava Orchard,* was published in 1998. Hailed
as a promising new literary figure in the English-
language literature of contemporary India, Desai
enjoyed both the pedigree of her mother, acclaimed
novelist Anita Desai, and Salman Rushdie's conviction
in her talents; Rushdie, best remembered as the Indian
emigre writer who went into hiding for a time in the
1990s when Islamic fundamentalists called for his
death, included a story of Desai's in *Mirrorwork: Fifty
Years of Indian Writing.* Her work has also appeared
in the *New Yorker.*

Hullabaloo in the Guava Orchard centers around the
small Indian town of Shahkot and the Chawla family's
son, Sampath. Since he was born at the end of a
monsoon (their underdeveloped town's only claim to
fame has been, to date, its bad weather), his family
believes his destiny to be a great one. As he grows
into young adulthood, though, Sampath seems unlikely
to fulfill even modest hopes of success. In fact, Sampath is disinterested in going to school, establishing a
career, and even becoming an ordinary person who
leads an ordinary life. Instead, he prefers to daydream,
a tendency that confounds his father, a status-conscious
schemer; only his wise grandmother has faith in
Sampath's seeming lack of direction. His father obtains
a job for him in the local post office—a secure position for life—but Sampath drinks too much at his
boss's daughter's wedding and moons the guests. He
then flees, knowing his career is over, and finds a
peaceful guava orchard. He spots a tree, and climbs up
it in order to contemplate his future, or apparent lack
of it, and lives in the tree.

In a Random House interview, Desai explained that
the character Sampath stemmed from an article she
read in the London *Times* about "a man who was a
very famous hermit in India who really did climb up a

tree." The man lived in the tree "for many, many years
until he died," elaborated Desai. Desai explained that
the book "started really with that character, and then
the story built up around it."

While Sampath is in the tree, Desai's plot saves him
from actually having to decide upon anything. Villagers find him, and decide that anyone insane enough to
sit in a tree must be a prophet. Sampath begins to
fulfill this mission by offering advice that astounds the
villagers—he knows their secrets, and seems to foresee
the future. But Sampath has learned much of what he
knows at his post-office job, since he whiled away his
hours steaming open letters and reading them for fun.
Soon hundreds are flocking to hear his wisdom, his
father devises tie-ins that begin to enrich the family,
and a band of monkeys sets up camp at the bottom of
his tree.

Critics praised Desai's plot, which *IndiaStar* reviewer
Sonoo Singh described as "something of a roller-
coaster ride." Desai shifts from event to event using
what *Richmond Review* critic Holly Yates described as
"a series of gossipy asides and subplots almost
imperceptibly mimicking the diction of her characters."
Yates explained that Desai's writing switches "from
evocative lists compiled from the names of exotic
fruits and birds, sari silks and the ingredients of lavish
imaginary meals." Desai said that, when she was writing the novel, the plot "sort of gathered momentum
and drew me along." She admitted that her process of
writing was "very messy" and that she "had to throw
out many pages."

Desai has also been lauded for her characterization.
New York Times reviewer Zia Jaffrey observed that
Desai "drops her characters like juicy morsels." "These
bumbling characters may teeter on the edge of
caricature," observed Michiko Kakutani in the *New
York Times,* "but the author delineates them with such
wit and bemused affection that they insinuate them-
selves insidiously in our minds." Jaffrey noted that
Sampath is "indeed an idiot savant" who descended
from "a long line of eccentrics." Yates suggested that
"Desai's subtle exploration of the ambiguous nature of
Sampath's holiness is one of the novel's strengths."
"Equally engaging are other characters," concluded
Singh. Sampath's sister, Pinky, shows her affection to
a man by biting off his ear. Sampath's mother, Kulfi,
devotes her life to feeding her son exotic meals.
Sampath's grandmother prefers to wear her dentures

"a little loose." Jaffrey noted that even the alcoholic monkeys who invade Sampath's orchard "are beautifully evoked." "The only stereotypical character in the novel is the father, Mr. Chawla," reflected Singh. "Reminiscent of middle-class fathers, he is a government employee, who exercises regularly, shows his concern for his children's future, but remains aloof from the extraordinary oddities of life around him."

Critics expressed mixed reviews concerning the novel's ending. Yates described the conclusion as "abrupt" and declared that "in the midst of chaos" it is "disappointingly weak." In a review for *Rambles,* Elizabeth Badurina described the climax as "anticlimactic," but explained that "it sticks with you, making more sense as you mull it over."

Writing for the *Hindu,* Suchitra Behal used effusive words to describe the novel. "At one level this seems like a magical tale in a world gone awry," Behal wrote. "But at another, Desai through her imagination and apt words has conveyed the essence of Indian society at large." Singh declared that "leafing through *Hullabaloo in the Guava Orchard* is like sipping cool, tangy lemonade in the sweltering summer sun."

BIOGRAPHICAL AND CRITICAL SOURCES:

BOOKS

Contemporary Literary Criticism, Gale (Detroit, MI), 2003.

PERIODICALS

Booklist, May 15, 1998, Donna Seaman, review of *Hullabaloo in the Guava Orchard,* p. 1427.
Hindu, June 7, 1998.
Kirkus Reviews, March 15, 1998, review of *Hullabaloo in the Guava Orchard,* pp. 345-355.
Library Journal, May 1, 1998, Rebecca A. Stuhr, review of *Hullabaloo in the Guava Orchard,* p. 136.
New York Times, July 12, 1998, Zia Jaffrey, "The Prophet in the Tree," p.E45.
New York Times Book Review, July 18, 1999, review of *Hullabaloo in the Guava Orchard,* p. 28.

Observer, May 31, 1998, Christina Patterson, "He's Doing Quite Well. Then the Drunk Monkeys Arrive," p. 16; May 16, 1999, review of *Hullabaloo in the Guava Orchard,* p. 14.
Publishers Weekly, March 23, 1998, review of *Hullabaloo in the Guava Orchard,* p. 77.
Spectator, May 30, 1998, Simon Carnell, review of *Hullabaloo in the Guava Orchard,* p. 34.
Wall Street Journal, May 1, 1998, p. W4.
World Literature Today, review of *Hullabaloo in the Guava Orchard,* p. 213.

ONLINE

IndiaStar, http://www.indiastar.com/ (October 21, 2003), Sonoo Singh, review of *Hullabaloo in the Guava Orchard.*
Rambles, http://www.rambles.net/ (October 21, 2003), Elizabeth Badurina, review of *Hullabaloo in the Guava Orchard.*
Random House Web site, http://www.randomhouse.com/ (October 21, 2003), "An Interview with Kiran Desai."
Richmond Review, http://www.richmondreview.com.co.uk/ (October 21, 2003), Holly Yates, review of *Hullabaloo in the Guava Orchard.**

*   *   *

DeSALVO, Louise A(nita) 1942-

PERSONAL: Born September 27, 1942, in Jersey City, NJ; daughter of Louis B. (a machinist) and Mildred N. (Calabrese) Sciacchetano; married Ernest J. DeSalvo (a physician), December 22, 1963; children: Jason, Justin. *Ethnicity:* "Italian American." *Education:* Douglas College, B.A., 1963; New York University, M.A., 1972, Ph.D. (English education), 1977.

ADDRESSES: Home—1045 Oakland Ct., Teaneck, NJ 07666; Stoney Ridge, Sag Harbor, NY. *Office*—Department of English, Hunter College of the City University of New York, 695 Park Ave., New York, NY 10021-5024. *Agent*—Geri Thoma, Elaine Markson Agency, 44 Greenwich Ave., New York, NY 10011. *E-mail*—lad1942@aol.com.

CAREER: Wood-Ridge High School, Teaneck, NJ, English teacher, 1963-67; Fairleigh Dickinson University, Teaneck, coordinator of English education, 1977-

82; Hunter College of the City University of New York, New York, NY, professor of English and women's studies, 1982—.

MEMBER: Modern Language Association of America, National Council of Teachers of English, Bronte Society, Virginia Woolf Society (treasurer, 1979-82).

AWARDS, HONORS: National Endowment for the Humanities grant, 1980; seal from Committee on Scholarly Editions from Modern Language Association of America, 1980, for *Melymbrosia: Early Version of "The Voyage Out"*; distinguished achievement award from Educational Press Association of America, 1980, for "Writers at Work"; President's Award, Hunter College, 1986; Douglas Society award, 1990.

WRITINGS:

Virginia Woolf's First Voyage: A Novel in the Making, Rowman & Littlefield (Totowa, NJ), 1980.
(Editor) Virginia Woolf, *Melymbrosia: Early Version of "The Voyage Out,"* New York Public Library (New York, NY), 1980, revised edition, with new introduction, published as *Melymbrosia,* Cleis Press (San Francisco, CA), 2002.
(With Carol Ascher and Sara Ruddick) *Between Women,* Beacon Press (Boston, MA), 1984.
(Editor, with Mitchell A. Leaska) *The Letters of Vita Sackville-West to Virginia Woolf,* Morrow (New York, NY), 1984.
Nathaniel Hawthorne: A Feminist Reading, Humanities Press (Atlantic Highlands, NJ), 1987.
"Children Never Forget": Virginia Woolf on Childhood, Adolescence, and Young Adulthood, Beacon Press (Boston, MA), 1988.
Casting Off: A Novel, Harvester (New York, NY), 1988.
Virginia Woolf: The Impact of Childhood Sexual Abuse on Her Life and Work, Beacon Press (Boston, MA), 1989.
(Coeditor) *Territories of the Voice: Contemporary Stories by Irish Women Writers,* Beacon Press (Boston, MA), 1989.
Between Women: Biographers, Novelists, Critics, Teachers, and Artists Write about Their Work on Women, Routledge (New York, NY), 1993.
Conceived with Malice: Literature As Revenge in the Lives and Works of Leonard and Virginia Woolf, D. H. Lawrence, Djuna Barnes, and Henry Miller, Dutton (New York, NY), 1994.

Vertigo: A Memoir, Dutton (New York, NY), 1996.
Breathless: An Asthma Journal, Beacon Press (Boston, MA), 1997.
Writing As a Way of Healing: How Telling Our Stories Transforms Our Lives, HarperSanFrancisco (San Francisco, CA), 1999.
(Editor, with Kathleen Walsh D'Arcy and Katherine Hogan) *Short Fiction by Irish Women Writers,* Beacon Press (Boston, MA), 1999.
(Editor, with Kathleen Walsh D'Arcy and Katherine Hogan) *A Green and Mortal Sound: Short Fiction by Irish Women Writers,* Beacon Press (Boston, MA), 2001.
Adultery, Beacon Press (Boston, MA), 1999.
(Editor, with Edvige Giunta) *The Milk of Almonds: Italian-American Women Writers on Food and Culture,* Feminist Press at the City University of New York (New York, NY), 2002.
Crazy in the Kitchen: Food, Feuds, and Forgiveness in an Italian-American Family, Bloomsbury (New York, NY), 2004.

Contributing editor, *Media and Methods,* 1980-81. Contributor to literature journals.

ADAPTATIONS: The Letters of Vita Sackville-West to Virginia Woolf formed the basis for the play *Vita and Virginia.*

WORK IN PROGRESS: Moving On.

SIDELIGHTS: Louise A. DeSalvo has devoted much of her scholarly research and writing to the life and work of writer Virginia Woolf, but she has also written more personal books that in a way connect her to the famous author through their shared problems in childhood. It is widely known that Woolf was sexually molested by her half-brothers from the time she was six until she left the family home at the age of twenty-three, but DeSalvo was one of the first critics to examine the effect that this extended trauma had on the woman and her writings. She focused on this subject in *Virginia Woolf: The Impact of Childhood Sexual Abuse on Her Life and Work. Washington Post Book World* writer Julia Epstein noted: "DeSalvo attempts, not always successfully, to integrate readings on a variety of Woolf's works with recent research on child sexual abuse." Epstein found that DeSalvo failed to provide an adequate discussion of how Woolf's childhood experiences affected her adult love life, yet the critic concluded that despite some flaws, DeSalvo produced "an important book. She refutes standard notions about the idyllic, secure, affectionate household in which Virginia Woolf grew up, and questions the alleged sexual liberation of the Bloomsbury circle. Most important, she hears and believes Virginia Woolf's testimony to her childhood abuse, and in consequence offers a genuinely new account of her early life and work." *Women's Review of Books* writer Gillian Gill called the book "something of a milestone in women's studies." Woolf was also an important subject in *Conceived with Malice: Literature As Revenge in the Lives and Works of Leonard and Virginia Woolf, D. H. Lawrence, Djuna Barnes, and Henry Miller.* In this study, DeSalvo examines the various authors' works and the elements in them that probably sprang from a desire to take revenge on certain people in their lives.

DeSalvo has also written specifically on the fiction of Woolf in the study *Virginia Woolf's First Voyage: A Novel in the Making,* and more recently she spent seven years reediting the author's *Melymbrosia.* Originally published in a scholarly edition as *Melymbrosia: Early Version of "The Voyage Out,"* the new edition is simply titled *Melymbrosia* and has been marketed as a trade book with a new introduction by DeSalvo. The new version of the novel, which concerns the sexual awakening of an English woman, has been protested by Woolf's relatives, who have felt that the author would not have wanted this early work to see print. DeSalvo, however, believed it was an important project because the themes in the book tie in with Woolf's personal struggles with sexual abuse. *Library Journal* contributor Ron Ratliff agreed that although the novel does not represent Woolf at her best, it is still of interest to scholars and readers as a chance to see "the young artist working to find the voice and style that would later produce masterpieces like *Mrs. Dalloway* and *To the Lighthouse.*" *Bloomsbury Review* contributor Theresa Crater, however, found the book nothing less than "revolutionary," concluding that it "gives us a fresh look at an important modernist writer" and presents "a vision of Woolf's first novel as she would have preferred it."

DeSalvo took a look at her own life with *Vertigo: A Memoir,* in which she reveals a shared bond with her favorite subject, Virginia Woolf. Here she applies "a scholarly scalpel to the complex layers of her life," according to Carolyn Alessio in *Tribune Books.* The

author grew up in a working-class Italian neighborhood—Hoboken, New Jersey—during World War II. It was a woman's world, for most men were in the armed forces at that time. She recalls this as the happiest time in her life, however; when the men returned, "life became grim," as a contributor put it in a *Publishers Weekly* review. Her mother was institutionalized for depression, her sister took her own life, and DeSalvo herself was repeatedly molested by an aunt. She escaped the horrors of her life by burying herself in books and films, eventually becoming a respected professor of English. Still, depression haunted her as an adult, and part of *Vertigo* is the story of her struggle with this mental illness. In fact, the book was begun as a means of therapy.

"De Salvo clearly has a sense of humor, and although her success in life—she repeatedly stresses the problems of being Italian, working class and a 'girl'—may not be as unique as she seems to think, her clarity of insight and expression makes this an impressive achievement," wrote a *Publishers Weekly* critic. Carolyn See, writing in the *Los Angeles Times Book Review,* also endorsed *Vertigo,* declaring that "the writing here is terrific. DeSalvo constructs an inviting, unlikely heaven made up of women and children who have their tenement world to themselves. . . . The kids and their moms break all the old boundaries and rip around through each other's dwellings, laughing and talking. . . . Then the dads come home, reasserting their private territorial rights, slamming all the doors to all the apartments and yelling at their wives and kids until they shut up and stop having fun. Once again, the world is made safe for patriarchal 'democracy,' for brutish, humorless violence." See found the portions of the book covering the author's adult life less "riveting" than those describing her early years, but she concluded, "This is a highly subjective narrative of what it's like to grow up American, reject what's expected of you and then make your own fate."

DeSalvo has also written about infidelity in her marriage in 1999's *Adultery,* in which she admits that both she and her husband cheated on each other, and about her struggles with asthma in *Breathless: An Asthma Journal,* in which she links the disease to childhood trauma. In the former, personal accounts are complemented by examples of adultery from literature; she then explores the public's fascination with the subject of infidelity and why people like to read about both real-life and fictional stories. Her argument is simply that adultery makes for good storytelling in what a *Publishers Weekly* reviewer labeled a "tart and entertaining treatise on adultery" that "provides an intelligent and thought-provoking inquiry into why sexual infidelity will always fascinate us." In *Breathless,* DeSalvo argues that her long-undiagnosed illness has its roots in being touched inappropriately by an aunt and in the trauma of her sister's suicide. But *National Review* contributor Anthony Daniels did not find DeSalvo's claims convincing: "It must be admitted that her doctors took an unconscionable time in diagnosing her condition," noted Daniels, "but I can find no justification at all for her assertion that 'asthma is a breathing disorder that is caused by abuse and that it is probably a manifestation of post-traumatic stress.'"

In *Writing As a Way of Healing: How Telling Our Stories Transforms Our Lives,* DeSalvo expresses her belief that writing about one's personal traumas will speed up the healing process, which she divides into seven stages. Recommending that people keep a journal, she goes on to suggest that one's writing should then be shared with others as well. "DeSalvo's work is similar to Julia Cameron's *The Right to Write,*" observed Lisa S. Wise in *Library Journal,* "though [it is] more academic."

BIOGRAPHICAL AND CRITICAL SOURCES:

BOOKS

Giunta, Edvige, *Writing with an Accent: Contemporary Italian-American Women Writers,* Palgrave-Macmillan (New York, NY), 2002.

PERIODICALS

Bloomsbury Review, January-February, 2003, Theresa Crater, review of *Melymbrosia,* pp. 19-20.
Booklist, June 1, 1996, p. 1665.
Gay & Lesbian Review Worldwide, May, 2002, Alistair Williamson, "I Miss You Oh So Much," p. 35.
Globe and Mail (Toronto, Ontario, Canada), January 5, 1985.
Journal of American Studies, April, 1989.

Library Journal, July, 1996, p. 126; April 1, 1997, Anne C. Tomlin, review of *Breathless: An Asthma Journal,* p. 115; April 15, 1999, Lisa S. Wise, review of *Writing As a Way of Healing: How Telling Our Stories Transforms Our Lives,* p. 110; July, 2002, Ron Ratliff, review of *Melymbrosia,* pp. 81-82; November 1, 2002, Carolyn M. Craft, review of *The Milk of Almonds: Italian-American Women Writers on Food and Culture,* p. 89.
Literary Review, spring, 1990.
Los Angeles Times Book Review, December 23, 1984; February 26, 1995, p. 9; August 4, 1996, p. 4.
Modern Fiction Studies, summer, 1991.
National Review, October 27, 1997, Anthony Daniels, review of *Breathless,* p. 50.
New Statesman and Society, October 27, 1989.
New Yorker, November 6, 1989.
New York Review of Books, March 15, 1990.
New York Times, July 9, 1995, p. LI13.
Publishers Weekly, May 9, 1994, p. 27; September 19, 1994, p. 56; May 27, 1996, p. 57; July 26, 1999, review of *Adultery,* p. 75; June 24, 2002, review of *The Milk of Almonds,* p. 48.
Times (London, England), December 20, 1984.
Times Literary Supplement, December 21, 1984.
Tribune Books (Chicago, IL), August 18, 1996, p. 3.
Tulsa Studies in Women's Literature, fall, 1991.
Washington Post Book World, May 14, 1989, p. 4.
Women's Review of Books, March, 1995, p. 14.*

*   *   *

de VILLIERS, Marq 1940-

PERSONAL: Born 1940, in Bloemfontein, South Africa; son of Rene and Moira (Franklin) de Villiers; married Sheila Hirtle (a writer), March 20, 1965. *Education:* University of Cape Town, B.A., 1959; London School of Economics, diploma in international relations, 1961. *Politics:* "Changeable."

ADDRESSES: Home—Box 801, Lunenburg, Nova Scotia B0J 2C0, Canada. *Agent*—Westwood Creative Artists, 94 Harbord St., Toronto, Ontario M5S 1G6, Canada. *E-mail*—jacobus@fox.nstn.ca.

CAREER: Writer and journalist. Reporter and writer for South African newspapers, 1959-60; *Toronto Telegram,* reporter and editorial writer, 1962-65, became feature writer, 1967, went to Moscow Bureau, 1969-71; Reuters Wire Service, reporter in London and Spain; *Toronto Life,* executive editor, 1978-82, became editor, 1982, publisher, 1992-93; *WHERE* Magazines International, editorial director, 1993—.

AWARDS, HONORS: Alan Paton Award, 1987, for *White Tribe Dreaming;* Governor-General's Award nominee, 1993, for *The Heartbreak Grape: A California Winemaker's Search for the Perfect Pinot Noir;* Governor-General's Award, 1999, for *Water: The Fate of Our Most Precious Resource.*

WRITINGS:

White Tribe Dreaming: Apartheid's Bitter Roots As Witnessed by Eight Generations of an Afrikaner Family, Viking (New York, NY), 1987, also published as *White Tribe Dreaming: Apartheid's Bitter Roots: Notes of an Eighth-Generation Afrikaner,* Macmillan (Toronto, Ontario, Canada), 1987.
Down the Volga in a Time of Troubles: A Journey Revealing the People and Heartland of Post-Perestroika Russia, HarperCollins (Toronto, Ontario, Canada), 1991, also published as *Down the Volga: A Journey through Mother Russia in a Time of Troubles,* Viking (New York, NY), 1992.
The Heartbreak Grape: A California Winemaker's Search for the Perfect Pinot Noir, HarperCollins West (San Francisco, CA), 1994.
(With Garth Drabinsky) *Closer to the Sun: An Autobiography,* McClelland & Stewart (Toronto, Ontario, Canada), 1995.
(With wife, Sheila Hirtle) *Blood Traitors,* HarperCollins (Toronto, Ontario, Canada), 1997.
(With Sheila Hirtle) *Into Africa: A Journey through the Ancient Empires,* Key Porter (Toronto, Ontario, Canada), 1997.
Water: The Fate of Our Most Precious Resource, Stoddart (Toronto, Ontario, Canada), 1999, Houghton Mifflin (Boston, MA), 2001.
Guide to America's Outdoors: Eastern Canada, National Geographic (Washington, DC), 2001.
(With Sheila Hirtle) *Sahara: A National History,* Walker (New York, NY), 2002.

SIDELIGHTS: Journalist Marq de Villiers has distinguished himself with his ability to translate complex histories and scientific ideas into readable accounts.

Whether writing about his own family history in South Africa, Russia's heartland along the Volga River, a California vintner's thirty-year quest to make the perfect wine, the use and abuse of the earth's water resources, or the history of the Sahara region of Africa, de Villiers gives texture and meaning to these various settings. De Villiers has worked as an editor and publisher of *Toronto Life* and as editorial director of *WHERE* Magazines International.

In *Down the Volga,* de Villiers describes his 3,500-kilometer journey through Russia's heartland in the summer of 1990. Informed by an "air of melancholy," according to a *Publishers Weekly* reviewer, the book details the plight of the present-day people who live along the Volga River. De Villiers adds depth to his account by supplying historical details about the region, including references to the Huns and Tartars, the Cossacks, the Revolution, and World War II. A Russian speaker and former Moscow correspondent, de Villiers had access to parts of Russia rarely seen by tourists. Meeting with the local people, "he discerned widespread nostalgia for a noble dream corrupted, then abandoned," according to a *Publishers Weekly* reviewer. The reviewer considered the book "serious-minded, probing," and "knowledgeable." A *Kirkus Reviews* critic admired de Villiers's "smooth, well-written prose," concluding that *Down the Volga* is "a rich and deeply sympathetic look into parts of Mother Russia rarely visited by tourists."

Similarly, in *The Heartbreak Grape: A California Winemaker's Search for the Perfect Pinot Noir,* de Villiers encapsulates an entire culture in a detailed contemporary account. From vine to bottle, de Villiers traces the development of the Pinot Noir produced by California's Calera winery. Despite obstacles, which include "yearly droughts, suspicious neighbours, rapacious wildlife, contrary bureaucrats, [and] a dismissive wine-making establishment," according to *Quill & Quire* reviewer John Allemang, master vintner Josh Jensen of the Calera winery persists in his quest to develop fine wine from "heartbreak" grapes, which are named for their fickleness. Upon publication, the book met with critical praise and was nominated for the prestigious Governor's General Award in Canada. A *Kirkus Reviews* critic praised de Villiers's "great wit about the poetics of sensation." Drinking wine for de Villiers is an emotional experience. He wrote, "I closed my eyes and inhaled deeply, and the aroma went directly to the vaults in the brain where nostalgic memories are stored."

During 1998 de Villiers delved deeply into the important issues surrounding the earth's water supply, publishing his findings the following year in *Water: The Fate of Our Most Precious Resource.* A self-styled "water collector," de Villiers surveys global water use, presenting case histories from throughout the world. With over fifty percent of the world's rivers so polluted that they cannot be used for drinking or agriculture, the ensuing water shortages, contamination, and waste have caused many problems worldwide, including crop failures, epidemics, poverty, and the migration of some twenty-five million "water refugees." After noting that humans have not valued water as they should, de Villiers discusses the steps that must be taken to avert future disaster. He describes existing and potential water technologies and policies, in "science and engineering chapters [that] together support and inform excellent chapters on water politics," noted Tom Fyles on the *Natural Science Book Review* Web site. According to Fyles, the author "builds a persuasive case that water politics will dominate international and domestic agendas for at least the next decades." De Villiers's combination of "lyrical description" and "tough-minded analysis" of a crucial topic, to quote *Canadian Geographic*'s Stephen Hume, earned *Water* accolades and the Canadian Governor-General's award. Among the work's enthusiasts were Margaret Aycock of *Library Journal,* who praised the de Villiers's "entertaining yet thought-provoking narrative style," and a *Publishers Weekly* critic, who dubbed *Water* an "important, compelling, highly readable report." Moreover, in his *Business Economics* review, John J. Casson wrote, "Marq de Villiers is to be commended for providing an absorbing and informative account of issues that deserve a great deal of attention." Although the subject matter is serious and the future possibly dire, de Villiers ends the work optimistically by noting that world population growth is slowing, new technologies are coming on line, and people are learning water-conserving techniques. "Reading about water can be, paradoxically, dry, but de Villiers does an excellent job of rendering his oceans of data digestible," punned *Los Angeles Times* reviewer Tony Cohan. "Lucid and thorough, *Water* is a good place to tap into this subject, vast as the spreading Sahara yet intimate as your dripping kitchen faucet."

With his next book, written with his wife, Sheila Hirtle, de Villiers moved onto dry land, the Sahara desert of northern Africa. *Sahara: A Natural History* is a combination travel memoir, archaeological dig, and history written in an "evocative blend of reportage and concise historical overview," to quote a *Publishers Weekly* critic. The authors focus on the humans and places found in the three million square miles of desert, telling of the various peoples who have traveled this land throughout the ages and the tribes, such as Tauregs, Berbers, Moors, and Tubu, who continue to live there. *Library Journal*'s Tim Markus praised the work for its comprehensiveness and pointed out what he called the "fascinating account of a caravan crossing the desert." Indeed, a *Kirkus Reviews* commentator summed up the book as a "fully versed and admiring portrait" of a harsh land.

BIOGRAPHICAL AND CRITICAL SOURCES:

BOOKS

de Villiers, Marq, *The Heartbreak Grape: A California Winemaker's Search for the Perfect Pinot Noir,* HarperCollins West (San Francisco, CA), 1994.

PERIODICALS

Booklist, February 1, 1988, review of *White Tribe Dreaming: Apartheid's Bitter Roots As Witnessed by Eight Generations of an Afrikaner Family,* p. 902; December 15, 1993, review of *Down the Volga: A Journey through Mother Russia in a Time of Troubles,* p. 731.
Books in Canada, September, 1993, review of *Down the Volga in a Time of Troubles: A Journey Revealing the People and Heartland of Post-Perestroika Russia,* p. 52.
Business Economics, January, 2001, John J. Casson, review of *Water: The Fate of Our Most Precious Resource,* p. 71.
Canadian Geographic, May, 1999, Stephen Hume, review of *Water,* p. 89; May, 2000, review of *Water,* p. 83.
Economist (London, England), September 18, 1999, review of *Water Wars: The Looming Crisis in Global Fresh Water,* p. S9.
Geography, April, 2000, R. J. Knapp, review of *Water Wars,* p. 187.
Globe and Mail (Toronto, Ontario, Canada), May 1, 1999, review of *Water,* p. D16; July 3, 1999, review of *Into Africa,* p. D15.
Kirkus Reviews, November 1, 1991, p. 1383; December 15, 1993, review of *The Heartbreak Grape,* p. 1564; July 1, 2002, review of *Sahara: A Natural History,* pp. 928-929.

Kliatt Young Adult Paperback Book Guide, November, 2001, review of *Water,* p. 33.

Library Journal, November 15, 1991, review of *Down the Volga,* p. 45; July, 2000, Margaret Aycock, review of *Water,* p. 132; March 1, 2001, review of *Water,* p. 48; August, 2002, Tim Markus, review of *Sahara,* p. 136.

Los Angeles Times, October 5, 2000, Tony Cohan, review of *Water,* p. E-3.

Nature, September 16, 1999, Robert Gottlieb, review of *Water Wars,* pp. 212-213.

New Scientist, August 7, 1999, review of *Water Wars,* p. 50.

New York Times Book Review, April 17, 1988, review of *White Tribe Dreaming,* p. 18.

Publishers Weekly, January 8, 1988, review of *White Tribe Dreaming,* p. 70; November 8, 1991, review of *Down the Volga,* p. 58; January 10, 1994, review of *The Heartbreak Grape,* p. 54; June 12, 2000, review of *Water,* p. 63; July 8, 2002, review of *Sahara,* p. 42.

Quill & Quire, September, 1993, review of *Down the Volga,* pp. 57-58; May, 1999, review of *Water,* p. 29.

Time, August 14, 2000, Eugene Linden, review of *Water,* p. 78.

Times (London, England), July 29, 1999, Colin Tudge, "Low Tide in the Affairs of Men," review of *Water,* p. 45.

Times Literary Supplement, May 4, 1990, p. 482.

Tribune Books (Chicago, IL), October 28, 2001, review of *Water,* p. 6.

University of Denver Water Law Review, spring, 2002, Rachel M. Sobrero, review of *Water,* pp. 554-556.

Washington Post, July 23, 2000, Mark Hertsgaard, "Splish Splash," review of *Water,* p. X01.

Washington Post Book World, August 19, 2001, review of *Water,* p. 11.

ONLINE

Natural Science Book Review, http://naturalscience. com/ (September 24, 2002), Tom Fyles, review of *Water.**

*   *   *

DICKINSON, Mary-Anne
   See RODDA, Emily

DIVAKARUNI, Chitra Banerjee 1956-

PERSONAL: Born July 29, 1956, in Calcutta, India; daughter of R. K. and Tatini Banerjee; married S. Murthy Divakaruni, June 29, 1979; children: Abhay, Anand (sons). *Education:* Calcutta University, B.A., 1976; Wright State University, M.A., 1978; University of California—Berkeley, Ph.D., 1985.

ADDRESSES: Home—Sunnydale, CA. *Office*—Foothill College, English Department, 12345 El Monte Rd., Los Altos, CA 94022-4504.

CAREER: Diablo Valley College, professor of creative writing, 1987-89; Foothill College, Los Altos, CA, professor of creative writing, 1989—. Mid-Peninsula Support Network for Battered Women, 1990—; President, MAITRI (help-line for South Asian women), 1991—.

AWARDS, HONORS: Memorial Award, Barbara Deming Foundation, 1989; Writing Award, Santa Clara County Arts Council, 1990; Writing Award, Gerbode Foundation, 1993; Bay Area Book Reviewers Award for Fiction; PEN Oakland Josephine Miles Prize for Fiction; Allen Ginsberg Poetry Prize and Pushcart Prize, both for *Leaving Yuba City;* American Book Award, Before Columbus Foundation, 1996, for *Arranged Marriage: Stories;* California Arts Council Award, 1998; *The Mistress of Spices* was named a best book of 1997 by the *Los Angeles Times* and a best paperback of 1998 by the *Seattle Times.*

WRITINGS:

Dark Like the River (poems), Writers Workshop [India], 1987.

The Reason for Nasturtiums (poems), Berkeley Poets Press (Berkeley, CA), 1990.

Black Candle: Poems about Women from India, Pakistan, and Bangladesh, Calyx Books (Corvallis, OR), 1991.

(Editor) *Multitude: Cross-cultural Readings for Writers,* McGraw-Hill (New York, NY), 1993.

Arranged Marriage: Stories, Anchor Books (New York, NY), 1995.

The Mistress of Spices (novel), Anchor Books (New York, NY), 1997.

Leaving Yuba City: New and Selected Poems, Anchor Books (New York, NY), 1997.

(Editor) *We, Too, Sing America,* McGraw-Hill (New York, NY), 1998.

Sister of My Heart (novel), Doubleday (New York, NY), 1999.

The Unknown Errors of Our Lives: Stories, Doubleday (New York, NY), 2001.

The Vine of Desire: A Novel, Doubleday (New York, NY), 2002.

Neela, Victory Song (juvenile), illustrated by Troy Howell, American Girl (Middleton, WI), 2002.

The Conch Bearer: A Novel (juvenile), Roaring Brook Press (Brookfield, CT), 2003.

Queen of Dreams: A Novel, Doubleday (New York, NY), 2004.

Contributor to more than fifty periodicals, including *Ms., Beloit Poetry Journal, Chicago Review, Zyzzyva,* and *Chelsea.*

ADAPTATIONS: *The Mistress of Spices* was adapted as an audiobook.

SIDELIGHTS: Poet, novelist, and short-story writer Chitra Banerjee Divakaruni is known for her portrayals of immigrant Indian women. When Divakaruni, who was born in India, immigrated to the United States in 1976, she reevaluated the role of Indian women. She drew on her own experiences and those of other immigrant Indian women to write novels and verse. In *Black Candle,* she tells of women from India, Pakistan, and Bangladesh. *Arranged Marriage,* a collection of short stories, portrays immigrant Indian women who are caught between the two cultures. Her novel *The Mistress of Spices,* a blend of poetry and prose, revolves around a female character who must choose between her own culture and that of her non-Indian love.

The poems in *Black Candle,* which first appeared in various poetry magazines, are in free verse, "straightforward narrative poems," to quote Nina Mehta of *Bloomsbury Review.* They tell of women at various levels of desperation and despair, including women who are killed because their dowry was too small, who are driven into prostitution, or who commit suicide. "After reading these poems, it's clear that the collection's title is an apt metaphor for the scorched lives of the women Divakaruni portrays," commented Mehta, who wondered why Divakaruni did not tell these tales as short stories, but nevertheless gave "Sondra" and "All in My Head" special praise. *Booklist* reviewer Pat Monaghan remarked on the political nature of the work, yet considered it to be more than a tract because of Divakaruni's "sensuous" language and deep feeling. An "exemplary" collection, Monaghan asserted.

In the collection of short stories *Arranged Marriage,* Divakaruni depicts women living in India or in the United States for whom arranged marriages had been made, as is the custom in India. Each woman's struggles, according to Ginny Ryder in the *School Library Journal,* read like "tiny soap operas" with "appealing pathos." Reviewers praised the work highly. In the *New York Times Book Review,* Rose Kernochan described the stories as "appealing" and "irresistible;" and Donna Seaman, writing in *Booklist,* called Divakaruni a "virtuoso," lauding *Arranged Marriage* for its "ravishingly beautiful stories" in which the author gives glimpses of the soul in the everyday world.

Divakaruni's first novel, *The Mistress of Spices,* revolves around an Indian girl with magical powers. After Tilo survives a shipwreck and is trained by a mysterious figure, she is sent through transmigration to act as the Mistress of Spices in an Indian store in Oakland, California. There she serves the overt and hidden needs of her Indian immigrant clientele. When Tilo falls in love with an Indian American, she must choose between her magic and a more mundane life.

The novel garnered glowing reviews for the author's lyrical style, its combination of fantasy and realism, and its portrayal of the immigrant experience that goes beyond the stereotypical. "Divakaruni has written an unusual, clever and often exquisite first novel that stirs magical realism into the new conventions of culinary fiction and the still-simmering caldron of Indian immigrant life in America," praised Shashi Tharoor in the *Los Angeles Times Book Review.* In a review for *Chicago Tribune Books,* Tammie Bob noted Divakaruni's "distinct storytelling, setting, and subject," as well as the novel's "opulence of language, graceful narratives that weave intense, poetic images" and "fascinating characters." "If Tilo's choice is rather predictable, the way Ms. Divakaruni gets us there is anything but," enthused David Guy in the *New York Times Book Review.* According to Tharoor,

Divakaruni's style is "distinctive. Her penchant for sentence fragments, once you get used to her cadences, often works to good effect. . . . She has an allergy to question-marks that sometimes leads her interrogatories to fall flat. But her narrative is infused with poetry." Likewise, Bob maintained that "due to Divakaruni's lovely prose, the magic seems reliable and credible." On the topic of magic, Tharoor thought otherwise, however. "Although Divakaruni does the magic rather well, writing about the mystical spices in prose that raises light off the page like so many wisps of incense, she is best at the realism. She has a keen feel for immigrant life."

In her poetry collection *Leaving Yuba City,* for which she won a Pushcart Prize and an Allen Ginsberg Prize, Divakaruni joins "personal experience with cultural history in a soft but powerful voice," to quote *Library Journal* reviewer Ann van Buren. Her verse and prose poems treat such subjects as an abusive father, Indian men who immigrated to Yuba City, California, in 1910, Indian movies, and the dreamscapes of American painter Francesco Clemente. According to a *Publishers Weekly* critic, Divakaruni's treatment of women's experiences "often deepens as it is arrayed against varying cultural grounds." Likening the poems to meteors plunging into readers' hearts, Donna Seaman of *Booklist* described the poems as "lyrical and haunting" and "shimmeringly detailed and emotionally acute."

Divakaruni's second novel, *Sister of My Heart,* is a realistic treatment of the relationship between two cousins, Sudha and Anju, who narrate alternating chapters of this modern drama that develops over decades. While critics were less enthusiastic about this novel than *The Mistress of Spices,* they commended Divakaruni's efforts. *Library Journal* critic Wilda Williams faulted the author for a "contrived" plot and stereotypical characters; yet she found the novel to be an "engaging read" with many "tender, moving moments." So, too, a *Publishers Weekly* reviewer challenged her sometimes overwrought prose, but judged *Sister of My Heart* to be a "masterful allegory of unfulfilled desire and sacrificial love."

The author followed *Sister of My Heart* with another collection of short stories, *The Unknown Errors of Our Lives.* According to Grace Talusan for *AsianWeek,* in this volume "Divakaruni's characters discover [a] sense of belonging and safety through struggles faced negotiating relationships with family, friends, strangers and self. The protagonists must face the disparities between the lives they have and the realities of human existence. They face the limitations of love, the disappointment of dreams, and the consequences of errors that beg to be resolved." The critic went on to cite the title story and "Mrs. Dutta Writes a Letter" as particularly praiseworthy. Frederick Luis Aldama, reviewing *The Unknown Errors of Our Lives* in *World Literature Today,* championed the book as well. "Divakaruni's keen eye for detail and poetic turns of phrase make for a collection of stories that fill out the lives of those who experience the brunt of today's violence of racism and sexism. However," he concluded, "she does not leave her readers only with a sense of tragedy. Perhaps discovering one's creative possibilities will allow one to find happiness only to be experienced, as one character reflects, in 'the long effort of exploration.'"

Divakaruni returned to the lives of Sudha and Anju in 2002's *The Vine of Desire.* In this sequel, Sudha comes to live with Anju after leaving her abusive husband, and must fight the love she has always inspired in Anju's husband. After she loses this fight, Sudha takes her daughter and moves on to other adventures and experiences of her own. According to a *Publishers Weekly* critic, the author's "lyrical descriptions of the characters' inner and outer worlds bring a rich emotional chiaroscuro to an uplifting story about two women who learn to make peace with the difficult choices circumstances have forced upon them." As Robert E. Brown put it in the *Library Journal,* "the plot twists, the characters are engaging, and Divakaruni's vaunted style is evident." Chris Barsanti in *Book* concluded that *The Vine of Desire* "is a potent, emotional book delivered by a writer who knows how to step back and take in the poetry."

In the same year that *The Vine of Desire* appeared, Divakaruni also published a novel for middle readers. *Neela, Victory Song* is set during the struggle for Indian independence, and centers on the adventures of a twelve-year-old girl whose father becomes involved in that struggle. Sarah Stone reviewed the book for the *Voices from the Gaps: Women Writers of Color* Web site, saying that "*Victory Song* not only educates young readers about India's culture and past but also manages to entertain brilliantly with a likeable main character and a suspenseful plot that keep young readers interested." Divakaruni penned another book aimed at young audiences the following year. *The Conch Bearer* is a fantasy in which twelve-year-old Anand must return a magical conch shell to the far away Himalayas from which it came.

BIOGRAPHICAL AND CRITICAL SOURCES:

BOOKS

Contemporary Novelists, 7th edition, St. James Press (Detroit, MI), 2001.

PERIODICALS

Amerasia Journal, Volume 22, 1996, pp. 249-250.
Black Issues in Higher Education, September 18, 1997, p. 26.
Bloomsbury Review, September, 1992, p. 19.
Book, January-February, 2002, Chris Barsanti, review of *The Vine of Desire,* p. 76.
Booklist, December 15, 1991, p. 745; July, 1995, pp. 1860, 1869; December 15, 1996, p. 692; August, 1997, p. 1871; November 15, 2002, Gillian Engberg, review of *Neela, Victory Song,* p. 597; September 15, 2003, Ilene Cooper, review of *The Conch Bearer,* p. 236.
English Journal, September, 1997, pp. 99-100.
Horn Book Magazine, January-February, 2004, Susan P. Bloom, review of *The Conch Bearer,* p. 81.
Kirkus Reviews, July 1, 1995, p. 898; December 15, 1996, p. 1753; August 15, 2003, review of *The Conch Bearer,* p. 1071.
Kliatt, July, 1997, p. 49; September, 1997, p. 5.
Library Journal, June 15, 1995, p. 97; December, 1995, p. 192; February 1, 1997, p. 105; May 15, 1997, p. 118; July, 1997, p. 102; October 1, 1997, p. 86; January, 1999, p. 147; December, 2001, Robert E. Brown, review of *The Vine of Desire,* p. 170.
Los Angeles Times Book Review, March 9, 1997, p. 10; December 14, 1997, p. 5.
Ms., July, 1995, p. 77.
New York, June 23, 1997, p. 164.
New York Times Book Review, July 16, 1995, p. 53; April 13, 1997, p. 20; March 1, 1998, p. 32.
Publishers Weekly, June 5, 1995, p. 53; April 29, 1996, p. 69; January 13, 1997, pp. 51-52; August 25, 1997, p. 68; November 89, 1998, p. 55; May 14, 2001, Roxane Farmanfarmaian, "Writing from a

Different Place," p. 46; November 26, 2001, review of *The Vine of Desire,* p. 38; August 18, 2003, review of *The Conch Bearer,* p. 80.
School Library Journal, December, 1995, p. 142; December, 2002, Alison Follos, review of *Neela, Victory Song,* p. 136.
Times Literary Supplement, March 21, 1997, p. 24.
Tribune Books (Chicago, IL), May 25, 1997, pp. 1, 9.
Washington Post Book World, December 15, 1996, p. 4.
Woman's Journal, February, 1997, p. 16.
World Literature Today, winter, 1998, p. 207; winter, 2002, Frederick Luis Aldama, review of *The Unknown Errors of Our Lives,* pp. 112-113.

ONLINE

About Women Writers, http://womanwriters.about.com/ (April 29, 2003), review of *The Vine of Desire.*
AsianWeek, http://www.asianweek.com/ (April 27, 2001), Neela Banerjee, "Mistress of Self"; (April 27, 2001), Grace Talusan, "Wherever You Go, There You Are."
Chitra Banerjee Divakaruni Home Page, http://chitradivakaruni.com/ (February 18, 2004).
Time Online, http://www.time.com/ (April 29, 2003), "One Nation: America Remembers September 11, 2001: Chitra Banerjee Divakaruni."
Voices from the Gaps: Women Writers of Color, http://voices.cla.umn.edu/ (April 29, 2003), "Chitra Banerjee Divakaruni," Sarah Stone, review of *Neela, Victory Song.**

*   *   *

DOOLEY, Maura 1957-

PERSONAL: Born May 18, 1957, in Truro, Cornwall, England; daughter of Denis Joseph (a transport manager) and Mary Ellen (a civil servant; maiden name, Harrigan) Dooley. *Education:* University of York, B.A. (honors), 1978; attended University of Bristol, 1980-81.

ADDRESSES: Home—London, England. *Office*—Department of English, Goldsmiths College, University of London, New Cross, London SE14 6NW, England.

CAREER: Newport School, Essex, England, teacher of English, 1981-82; Arvon Foundation, Lumb Bank, Yorkshire, England, director of writing center, 1982-87, member of management committee council, 1989—; South Bank Board, London, England, director of literature program, 1987-93; Goldsmiths College, teacher of creative writing; has also worked as script developer for Jim Henson Films. Southern Arts literature panel, chair, 1988-90; London Arts Board literature panel, advisory member, 1992, board member, 1999—; Performing Arts Labs, advisory director.

MEMBER: Poetry Book Society (board member, 1986-89, chair, 2000).

AWARDS, HONORS: Major Eric Gregory Award for Poets under Thirty, 1987; Poetry Book Society Recommendation, 1991, for *Explaining Magnetism; Kissing a Bone* shortlisted for the T. S. Eliot Prize.

WRITINGS:

POETRY

Ivy Leaves and Arrows, Bloodaxe (Newcastle upon Tyne, England), 1986.
Turbulence, Giant Steps, 1988.
Explaining Magnetism, Bloodaxe (Newcastle upon Tyne, England), 1991.
Kissing a Bone, Dufour Editions (Chester Springs, PA), 1996.
Sound Barrier: Poems, 1982-2002, Bloodaxe (Newcastle upon Tyne, England), 2002.

EDITOR

(With David Hunter) *Singing Brink,* Arvon Press (Yorkshire, England), 1987.
(With David Morley and Philip Callow) *Northern Stories II,* Littlewood, 1990.
(With Jo Shapcott) *New Poetry International,* Harwood Academic Press, 1993.
Making for Planet Alice: New Women Poets, Dufour Editions (Chester Springs, PA), 1997.
How Novelists Work, Seren (Bridgend, Wales), 2000.
The Honey Gatherers: Love Poetry, Bloodaxe (Newcastle upon Tyne, England), 2002.

SIDELIGHTS: Maura Dooley's poetry ranges from pastoral reflections on life in the Yorkshire district of her native England to the concerns of modern urban life, sexuality, and nuclear war. Dooley has also edited several anthologies of poetry. Adam Thorpe, writing in the *Literary Review,* found that "The ability to enact and find images for complex feelings marks Dooley out as one of the most exciting new talents on the poetry scene."

Explaining Magnetism, Dooley's poetry collection published in 1991, contains a number of poems from her earlier short collections, 1986's *Ivy Leaves and Arrows* and *Turbulence,* published in 1988. The book was praised by *Poetry Review* contributor Helen Dunmore, who appreciated Dooley's "political consciousness" and "cinematic techniques." Overall, Dunmore found that "the intelligence behind this collection is a sharp and forceful one." Other reviewers noted that the poet captures the fragmentation and randomness of city life. "Many of Dooley's poems are free-verse lyrics," Mark Jarman noted in the *Southern Review,* "but she is at her best under the formal pressure of iambic pentameter."

In *Making for Planet Alice: New Women Poets,* Dooley gathers a selection of works from thirty women poets living in England, Scotland, and Ireland. Her goal is to provide a wide-ranging anthology, not one focusing on the domestic concerns found in so many women's poetry anthologies. According to a critic for *Publishers Weekly,* "The volume gives us one intense, personal and intelligent psychic landscape after another."

In an online interview with Lidia Vianu for the *Image of Contemporary Literature* Web site, Dooley explained: "As a reader I don't care if a poem rhymes or not. I look for a poem that offers a fresh perception in memorable language, where not a word is wasted. I look for a poem that will haunt me for a while: a poem that I'll have to come back to again and again."

BIOGRAPHICAL AND CRITICAL SOURCES:

PERIODICALS

Antioch Review, summer, 1997, Daniel McGuiness, review of *Kissing a Bone,* p. 380; spring, 1998, Diann Blakely, review of *Making for Planet Alice,* p. 245.

Booklist, April 15, 1992, Pat Monaghan, review of *Explaining Magnetism,* p. 1497.

Independent on Sunday, November 10, 1991.

Literary Review, August, 1988, Adam Thorpe, review of *Turbulence,* p. 30.

New Statesman, August 21, 1987, John Lucas, review of *Ivy Leaves and Arrows,* p. 24.

PN Review, spring, 1992.

Poetry Review, spring, 1992, Helen Dunmore, review of *Explaining Magnetism.*

Publishers Weekly, July 28, 1997, review of *Making for Planet Alice,* p. 70.

Southern Review, spring, 1994, Mark Jarman, review of *Explaining Magnetism,* p. 393.

Times Literary Supplement, June 9, 1989, Mark Wormald, review of *Turbulence,* p. 641; February 7, 1992, p. 19.

ONLINE

BBC Radio Web site, http://www.bbc.co.uk/ (March 10, 2003), "Biography of Maura Dooley."

Bloodaxe Books Web site, http://www.bloodaxebooks.com/ (March 10, 2003).

Image of Contemporary Literature Web site, http://lidiavianu.scriptmania.com/ (June 14, 2002), Lidia Vianu, "I Look for the Poem That Will Haunt Me for a While: An Interview with Maura Dooley."*

*   *   *

DOUGLAS, Michael
See CRICHTON, (John) Michael

*   *   *

DRYSDALE, Helena 1960-

PERSONAL: Born May 6, 1960, in London, England; daughter of Andrew (an insurance underwriter) and Merida (a conservationist; maiden name, Gascoigne) Drysdale; married Richard Pomeroy (a painter), May 21, 1987; children: Tallulah, Xanthe. *Education:* Cambridge University, B.A. (with honors); Trinity College, Cambridge, M.A., 1982.

ADDRESSES: Home—22 Stockwell Park Rd., London SW9 9TG, England. *Agent*—Derek Johns, A. P. Watt, 20 John St., London WC1N 2DR, England.

CAREER: Artscribe, London, England, editor, journalist, and art critic, 1982-84; writer, photographer, and lecturer, 1984—. Arts editor for *Richmond Times* and *Twickenham Times,* 1982-84.

MEMBER: PEN, Society of Authors, Royal Geographical Society, Globetrotters Club.

AWARDS, HONORS: Named an exhibitioner at Trinity College; *Looking for George* was shortlisted for Esquire/Apple/Waterstones nonfiction award and J. R. Ackerley award for autobiography.

WRITINGS:

Alone through China and Tibet, Constable (London, England), 1986.

Dancing with the Dead: A Journey through Zanzibar and Madagascar, Hamish Hamilton (London, England), 1991.

Looking for Gheorghe, Sinclair-Stevenson, 1995, published as *Looking for George: Love and Death in Romania,* foreword by Tobias Wolff, Picador (London, England), 1996.

Mother Tongues: Travels through Tribal Europe, Picador (London, England), 2001.

Contributor of articles and photographs to magazines and newspapers.

ADAPTATIONS: Dancing with the Dead: A Journey through Zanzibar and Madagascar, was filmed for Granada TV's "Compass" series and Thirteen/WNET's "Travels" series in 1991.

WORK IN PROGRESS: "A book set during the Maori Wars in nineteenth-century New Zealand, provisionally entitled *Weeping Water,* to be published by Picador."

SIDELIGHTS: Helena Drysdale told *CA:* "*Alone through China and Tibet* recounts a five-month journey starting in Canton during the new year festivities in February, 1985, continuing down to the remote hills of Hainan Island, across the wastelands of northwest China to Tibet, and thence to Nepal. The journey was undertaken purely in a spirit of adventure, and it is this that I have tried to capture in the book. My experiences along the way ranged from the hilarious to the macabre: I was hailed as a visiting VIP in Hainan, took part in a spectacular Lantern Festival, and witnessed the dawn Sky Burial in Tibet. Exploring back streets, markets, temples, on bicycles, buses, and trains, I traveled and lived with ordinary people—teachers, sailors, black marketeers, monks—made friends and visited their families, at a time when China was just beginning to open its doors to the West and when the lives of these peoples were changing dramatically.

"I discovered the exhilaration—and occasional anxiety—of traveling alone: the contradictory urge to go on, and yet also to turn and run back for home. This too I tried to capture, as honestly and straightforwardly as possible: the loneliness and discomfort, the thrill, the sadness. Reviewers have pointed out the candor of the book, and emphasized the personal nature of the account."

The title character of Drysdale's acclaimed memoir *Looking for George: Love and Death in Romania* (previously published as *Looking for Gheorghe*) is a young poet-priest who, "for one gloriously liberated week" in 1979, as Jason Cowley related in the *New Statesman,* defies authorities and accompanies the author and her friends on a journey through the Carpathian Mountains. The friendship between Drysdale and Gheorghe grew more intimate; they shared romantic moments in Romania and exchanged impassioned letters after the author returned home to England. Suddenly, Gheorghe's letters stopped. In 1991, after the fall of the dictator Ceaucescu, "Drysdale returned to Romania to find out what had become of her 'mad monk,'" Cowley wrote. She learned how her presence in Gheorghe's life had changed the young cleric, "filling him with impossible expectations, and how irresponsible she and her friends had been in allowing him to travel with them, monitored as they were by the secret police." The reviewer concluded that *Looking for George* "begins as a travel book . . . but slowly deepens into something stranger and more mysterious, an authentic metaphysical quest, in which truth shimmers brightly but elusively."

Drysdale undertook another journey, this time with husband and two small daughters in tow, for her 2001 volume *Mother Tongues: Travels through Tribal Europe.* The author's goal in this project was to seek out the origins and use of some of the lesser-known of

the world's 6,500 languages. Thirteen European regions were investigated in Drysdale's book, "from the Sami, in what we can no longer call Lapland, to the Basques in northern Spain and the Celts in Brittany," commented *Sunday Times* writer Anthony Sattin. But *Mother Tongues* is as much about the author's personal experience as her language study. Packed into a mobile home (called the Mob), Drysdale must deal with the demands of toddler Tallulah and ever-hungry infant Xanthe, as well as cope with the pressure when her husband, Richard, leaves the trip to tend to his dying father. While he was gone, "there immediately entered into his wife's life, on intimate terms, a Greek Lothario," wrote *Times Literary Supplement* contributor Philip Glazebrook, a man who took more than a casual liking to Drysdale and left her wondering what to do if he made a pass at her. "This is one of several beginnings to stories which do not have endings," Glazebrook commented.

"Though capable in her journalist role of handling interviews and making knowledgeable enquiries," Glazebrook added, "it is living on the road, with all its incident and diversion, which Drysdale really relishes." The *New Statesman*'s Cowley pointed out that in much modern travel writing, the authors present "truth-free zones, in which facts are never allowed to interrupt a good story," and "imaginative fancy is irresponsibly indulged." Drysdale, the writer continued, "is different. For a start, she can write; every page of [*Mother Tongues*] carries the imprint of her originality of thought and expression." As for her scholarly quest, the author "seems to have returned from her travels as uncertain as she was when she left as to the value of preserving minority language," noted Cowley. Drysdale does, however, advocate bilingual education for British children whose background may be Breton or Celt. To Cowley, the principle "is admirable, but it has always seemed pointless to me for a child to be taught [minority language] at the expense of a truly global second language such as Spanish." Cowley added that this criticism, however, "in no way [diminishes] Helena Drysdale or the achievements of this marvellous book."

BIOGRAPHICAL AND CRITICAL SOURCES:

PERIODICALS

Catholic Herald, October 31, 1986.
New Statesman, November 28, 1986; November 19, 2001, Jason Cowley, "Still Life in Mobile Homes," p. 49.

New Statesman & Society, July 26, 1991, review of *Dancing with the Dead: A Journey through Zanzibar and Madagascar,* p. 38.

Sunday Times, December 9, 2001, Anthony Sattin, "Speaking Up for Lost Voices," p. 39.

Times Literary Supplement, January 16, 1987; August 2, 1991, A. M. Daniels, review of *Dancing with the Dead,* p. 24; February 8, 2002, Philip Glazebrook, "Feeding Xanthe," p. 32.

World, July, 1991, Nicholas Crane, review of *Dancing with the Dead,* p. 75.

ONLINE

Helena Drysdale Home Page, http://www.helena drysdale.com/ (September 25, 2003).

E

EARLEY, Pete 1951-

PERSONAL: Born September 9, 1951, in Fowler, CO. *Education:* Phillips University, journalism degree, 1973.

ADDRESSES: Home—Herndon, VA. *Agent*—c/o Author Mail, Bantam Books/Random House, 1540 Broadway, New York, NY 10036.

CAREER: Writer. *Enid News & Eagle,* Enid, OK, intern, 1969-73, staff writer, 1973-75; *Emporia Gazette,* Emporia, KS, staff writer, 1975-70; *Tulsa Tribune,* Tulsa, OK, investigative reporter, 1980-86; *Washington Post,* Washington, DC, freelance author, 1986—.

AWARDS, HONORS: Robert F. Kennedy Book Award for Social Justice and Edgar Fact-Crime Award winner, 1995, for *Circumstantial Evidence: Death, Life, and Justice in a Southern Town.*

WRITINGS:

Family of Spies: Inside the John Walker Spy Ring, Bantam (New York, NY), 1988.
Prophet of Death: The Mormon Blood-Atonement Killings, Morrow (New York, NY), 1991.
The Hot House: Life inside Leavenworth Prison, Bantam Books (New York, NY), 1992.
Circumstantial Evidence: Death, Life, and Justice in a Southern Town, Bantam Books (New York, NY), 1995.

Confessions of a Spy: The Real Story of Aldrich Ames, Putnam (New York, NY), 1996.
Super Casino: Inside the "New" Las Vegas, Bantam Books (New York, NY), 2000.
(With Gerald Shur) *WITSEC: Inside the Federal Witness Protection Program,* Bantam Books (New York, NY), 2002.
Deep Cover, Tor Books (New York, NY), 2004.

ADAPTATIONS: Some of author's writings have been adapted for audiocassette.

WORK IN PROGRESS: The Apocalypse Stone.

SIDELIGHTS: Pete Earley is an investigative reporter who writes extensively on crime and espionage. He is widely respected as an "old school" reporter who covers tough stories and keeps his personal opinion to himself. Charles Bowden wrote in the *Los Angeles Times,* "Before we had schools of journalism, there was a straightforward task called reporting that took you where you had not been, and told you what you had not known. *The Hot House* is by this kind of reporter, and gives the readers reporting at its very finest."

"I want to take you places you normally wouldn't go and introduce you to people who you normally wouldn't meet," Earley said at his Web site. "So far, I've written books about the two most damaging spies in recent history—John Walker, Jr. and Aldrich Ames—and taken readers 'inside' a hard-core penitentiary, a sex-crazed religious cult, a racially-charged unsolved murder in the Deep South, a billion-dollar

Las Vegas casino and WITSEC: the Federal Witness Protection Program, which hides criminals who cooperate with prosecutors."

His first book, *Family of Spies: Inside the John Walker Spy Ring,* relates the various activities of naval officer John Walker and his relatives during a seventeen-year period in which the family relayed more than one million government secrets to Soviet authorities. During the course of his espionage work, Walker enlisted his brother and his best friend, and he even exploited his mother for delivery purposes. In addition, he assured his own security by luring his son into the spy ring, thus allowing for the maintenance of the operations—and substantial profits—after Walker personally withdrew from active spying.

New York Times Book Review writer Lucinda Franks described the Walker operation as "one of the most damaging spy networks in American history," and she praised Earley for using the comments of financially motivated ringleader Walker "to expose his superficially slick but profoundly distorted mind." Franks wrote that *Family of Spies* is "paced and organized as seamlessly as a novel," but she also noted that it is "a thoroughly researched and unblurred work of nonfiction."

The Hot House: Life inside Leavenworth Prison is an account of various individuals and activities at the maximum-security Federal prison in Leavenworth, Kansas. The book concentrates on several inmates and follows their day-to-day activities. Earley reports on the conditions of incarceration of Thomas Silverstein. "Of all the guards and convicts in my book," said Earley, "I'm asked the most questions about Thomas Silverstein, who stabbed a guard to death in 1983 and has been kept under 'no human contact' ever since. When I met him, he was locked in a basement cell buried so deeply under the prison that the only sounds were the buzzing of the fluorescent lights in the ceiling. Those lights were kept on twenty-four hours a day. Imagine being locked up in total isolation inside four walls since 1983—your only contact is with guards who detest you—and the entire time the lights are kept burning non-stop." Occasionally, Silverstein is allowed drawing and painting supplies and his remarkable drawings are part of Earley's book.

Wilbert Rideau and Ron Wikberg, Louisiana State Penitentiary inmates who jointly assessed *The Hot House* in the *San Francisco Review of Books,* noted

that these individuals "evoke no sympathy" and added, "they will make readers wonder why they should sustain these prisoners' lives." Rideau and Wikberg related that their own warden, John P. Whitley, characterized *The Hot House* as "a damn good book." Bowden wrote in the *Los Angeles Times Book Review* that *The Hot House* provides "reporting at its very finest," and he described it as "a very convincing piece of the truth." Bowden observed: "What we get in *The Hot House* is the life, and the life is brutal, dull and filled with the constant pursuit of power and the constant flight from fear."

Earley followed *The Hot House* with *Circumstantial Evidence: Death, Life, and Justice in a Southern Town,* a 1995 book that examines Walter McMillan's conviction and sentencing to death for murders committed in Monroeville, Alabama, in 1986. The police found McMillan, an African-American drug dealer, guilty on the basis of perjured testimony and withholding of evidence. But the intercession of lawyer Bryan Stevenson, together with a provocative report on CBS-TV's news show *Sixty Minutes,* finally prompted a new investigation that exposed questionable police practices and inconsistencies in previous testimony, whereupon McMillan was freed. *New York Times Book Review* contributor Glenna Whitley acknowledged that *Circumstantial Evidence* demonstrates "how subtle and overt racism conspired to condemn a man while giving lip service to the legal system's supposed objectivity."

Earley's next book, *Confessions of a Spy: The Real Story of Aldrich Ames,* concerns the Central Intelligence Agency (CIA) bureaucrat who spied for the Soviet Union and identified more than twenty U.S. agents. Ames's treasonous conduct is believed to have led to the executions of some of these American agents. Earley, who obtained access to the imprisoned Ames, quotes him as bragging about the money he made and even his perception of his accomplishments. *New York Times* reviewer Christopher Lehmann-Haupt, while writing that *Confessions of a Spy* lacks "much drama," concluded that it reveals Ames "as an example of a quintessential twentieth-century figure, the self-analytical man who doesn't understand himself at all."

In preparing his report on the new Las Vegas for *Super Casino,* Earley gained complete access to the billion-dollar Luxor casino. The owners of the Luxor, Circus Circus, gave Earley unprecedented carte blanche to attend any and all meetings, to interview any staff members he chose, and to freely observe life inside the Luxor and Circus Circus casinos. The first half of the book explains Las Vegas's transformation from the old Vegas of the Mob and the Rat Pack to the corporate, family-oriented Las Vegas of today. The second half is a series of interviews and anecdotes from the Luxor. He introduces Vegas executives, dealers, floor managers, and security personnel, hookers and dancers, all of whom talk with surprising candor about their job and the casino.

Written with Gerald Shur, *WITSEC: Inside the Federal Witness Protection Program* examines the controversial program. This book had its beginnings in Earley's research at the Leavenworth Federal Prison for *Hot House.* Several inmates with ties to organized crime told Earley how they had been convicted by testimony of co-conspirators who were given new identities. "Unfortunately," said Earley, "I kept running into dead ends until I met Gerald Shur, the government attorney who invented WITSEC. We joined forces and Shur took me behind the scenes. He knew every top mobster who had flipped over—beginning with Joe Valachi and ending with Sammy the Bull."

Shur was a career federal prosecutor who found his calling in Robert Kennedy's Organized Crime and Racketeering Section of the 1960s Justice Department. His years in the task force taught him only credible witnesses with important information could win convictions and that the government had to establish some way to get these witnesses to cooperate. Shur's creation, the WITSEC, is credited with gaining crucial convictions in the battle against organized crime and drug cartels in America.

It also has its detractors. Critics claim that some relocated criminals continued their criminal activities, and some non-criminal witnesses were treated like criminals themselves. Others criticize the use of government money to help criminals disappear into unsuspecting communities.

Shur began writing his memoirs about the same time Earley started researching the program for his own book. After several meetings they decided to collaborate. Eric Wargo commented in *Book,* "This book focuses much less on WITSEC'S achievements than on its mistakes, growing pains and critics.

Firsthand stories reveal the severe psychological toll that living a lie for the sake of justice inflicts on families (something Shur experienced when he and his wife had to use his own program's services after agents uncovered a plot against them in 1991)." After finishing the book, Earley said, "My favorite section of my book is about WITNESS X, the wife of a mobster whose entire world was turned upside down when her husband testified against his real-life Soprano's mob boss. She spent hours telling me her story. After hearing it, I came to believe that the most difficult challenge most criminals and their families ever faced was entering and surviving WITSEC."

BIOGRAPHICAL AND CRITICAL SOURCES:

PERIODICALS

Barron's February 7, 2000, Ann C. Logue, review of *Super Casino: Inside the "New" Las Vegas,* p. A36.

Book, March-April, 2002, Eric Wargo, review of *WITSEC: Inside the Federal Witness Protection Program,* p. 73.

Booklist, November 1, 1999, review of *Super Casino,* p. 482.

Corrections Today, May, 1992, Paul H. Hahn, review of *The Hot House: Life inside Leavenworth Prison,* p. 82.

Federal Bar News & Journal, July, 1992, review of *The Hot House,* p. 396.

Federal Probation, September, 1992, Stephen Loew, review of *The Hot House,* p. 85.

Kirkus Reviews, December 15, 2001, review of *WITSEC,* p. 1734.

Kliatt Young Adult Paperback Guide, March, 1999, review of *Confessions of a Spy,* p. 62.

Library Journal, January, 1992, Frances Sandiford, review of *The Hot House,* p. 154; July, 1995, Sandra K. Lindheimer, review of *Circumstantial Evidence: Death, Life, and Justice in a Southern Town,* p. 100; May 15, 1997, Daniel Blewett, review of *Confessions of a Spy: The Real Story of Aldrich Ames,* p. 87; August, 1999, James Dudley, review of *Confessions of a Spy,* p. 164; December 1999, review of *Super Casino,* p. 164; February 1, 2002, Diedre Root, review of *WITSEC,* p. 164.

Los Angeles Times Book Review, February 16, 1992, review of *The Hot House,* p. 3.

Moscow News, November 25, 1994, Nataliya Gev-orkyan, interview with Pete Earley, p. 14.

New Statesman, March 14, 1997, Brian Cathcart, review of *Confessions of a Spy,* p. 48.

New York Law Journal, October 31, 1995, Jennifer Kleiner, review of *Circumstantial Evidence,* p. 2.

New York Times, February 24, 1997, Christopher Lehmann-Haupt, review of *Confessions of a Spy,* p. C16.

New York Times Book Review, January 8, 1989, Lucinda Franks, review of *Confessions of a Spy,* p. 9; October 8, 1995, Glenna Whitely, review of *Circumstantial Evidence,* p. 26; March 29, 1992, Dennis J. Carroll, review of *The Hot House,* p. 16.

Pacific Historical Review, November, 2001, Hal K. Rothman, review of *WITSEC,* p. 627.

Publishers Weekly, December 20, 1991, review of *The Hot House,* p. 70; June 26, 1995, review of *Circumstantial Evidence,* p. 96; November 22, 1999, review of *Super Casino,* p. 47; November 26, 2001, review of *WITSEC,* p. 48.

San Francisco Review of Books, January, 1992, review of *Circumstantial Evidence,* p. 10.

Times Literary Supplement, July 11, 1997, L. Britt Snider, review of *Confessions of a Spy,* p. 28.

U.S. New and World Report, February 17, 1997, Harrison Rainie, review of *Confessions of a Spy,* p. 8.

Wall Street Journal, February 7, 2000, Allan T. Demaree, review of *Super Casino,* p. A36.

Washington Post, February 20, 2002, Anthan Theoharis, review of *WITSEC,* p. C03.

Washington Post Book World, March 14, 1993.

ONLINE

Pete Earley Home Page, http://www.peteearley.com/ (April 29, 2002).*

*   *   *

EBB, Fred 1933 (?)-

PERSONAL: Born April 8, 1933 (birth year also cited as 1932, 1935, and 1936), in New York, NY; son of Harry and Anna (Gritz) Ebb. *Education:* Attended New York University; Columbia University, M.A., 1957. *Hobbies and other interests:* Collecting musical show albums.

Fred Ebb

ADDRESSES: Agent—International Creative Management, 40 West 57th St., New York, N.Y. 10019.

CAREER: Lyricist and librettist. Worked previously as a trucker's helper for a hosiery company, worked in credit authorization, and as a baby-shoe bronzer.

AWARDS, HONORS: Emmy Awards from National Academy of Television Arts and Sciences, 1973, for *Liza with a Z,* and 1975, for *Gypsy in My Soul;* Academy Awards (Oscars) from American Academy of Motion Picture Arts and Sciences, 1974, for *Norman Rockwell,* and 1976, for "How Lucky Can You Get" from *Funny Lady; Chicago* received Antoinette Perry (Tony) Award from League of New York Theatres and Producers for book and lyrics, was a nominee for the Antoinette Perry Award for book of a musical, Grammy Award from National Academy of Recording Arts and Sciences for the album, and Golden Globe Award from Hollywood Foreign Press Association, all 1976; (with John Kander) Hammerstein Award from the York Theater Company, 2000; (with John Kander), Academy Award for best music, song, 2003, for "I Move On," from *Chicago.*

WRITINGS:

LYRICIST; MUSICALS

Flora, the Red Menace, first produced on Broadway at Alvin Theatre, May, 1965; revival with new songs produced in New York, NY, at Vineyard Theater, December, 1987.

Cabaret (also see below; score by John Kander; produced on Broadway at Broadhurst Theatre, November 20, 1966), Random House (New York, NY), 1967.

The Happy Time, produced on Broadway at Imperial Theatre, January 18, 1968.

Zorba (score by John Kander; produced on Broadway at Imperial Theatre, November 17, 1968), Random House (New York, NY), 1969.

(And author of book) *70, Girls, 70,* produced on Broadway at Broadhurst Theatre, April 15, 1971.

(And librettist, with Bob Fosse) *Chicago* (also see below), produced, 1975.

In Person, produced in Chicago, IL, July 4, 1977; produced as *The Act* in New York, NY, October, 1977.

Woman of the Year, score by John Kander, produced on Broadway at Palace Theatre, March 29, 1981.

The Rink, produced on Broadway at Martin Beck Theatre, February 9, 1983.

SCREENPLAYS

(Lyricist) *Cabaret,* Allied Artists, 1972.

Norman Rockwell, produced, 1974.

(Lyricist) *Funny Lady,* Columbia, 1975.

(Lyricist) *Lucky Lady,* Twentieth Century-Fox, 1975.

(Lyricist) *A Matter of Time,* American International Pictures, 1976.

(Lyricist) *New York, New York,* United Artists, 1977.

(Lyricist) *Diamonds* (score), Samuel French (New York, NY), 1986.

(Lyricist) *And the World Goes 'Round: The Songs of Kander and Ebb,* Fiddleback Music/Tommy Valando, 1991.

(Lyricist) *The Happy Time: Original Cast Recording* (sound recording), RCA Victor, 1992.

(Lyricist) *The Kiss of the Spider Woman* (libretto), Samuel French (New York, NY), 1997.

(Lyricist) *Steel Pier,* Samuel French (New York, NY), 1998.

(Lyricist) *The Complete Cabaret Collection: Vocal Selections* (vocal score, author's edition, revised), Carlin America/ Hal Leonard (Milwaukee, WI), 1999.

(Lyricist) *Chicago,* Miramax, 2002.

TELEVISION SPECIALS

Liza, produced June, 1970.

Liza with a Z, produced, 1972.

Ole Blue Eyes Is Back, produced, 1974.

Gypsy in My Soul, produced, 1976.

Baryshnikov on Broadway, produced, 1980.

OTHER

(With John Kander and Greg Lawrence) *Colored Lights: Forty Years of Words and Music, Show Biz, Collaboration, and All That Jazz,* Faber & Faber (New York, NY), 2003.

Writer for the television series *That Was the Week That Was;* lyricist for Off-Broadway musical *Morning Sun;* writer and director, *Liza in Concert at Carnegie Hall,* produced in New York, September, 1979.

SIDELIGHTS: For over three decades, lyricist Fred Ebb and composer John Kander have been creating some of Broadway's most famous musicals, including *Cabaret, Zorba,* and *Woman of the Year.* Ebb is particularly proud of *Chicago,* because he collaborated on the book of the popular play that became one of the most successful films of 2002 with the late Bob Fosse. Yet the team's success on stage, in movies and on television underscores the irony that their names are not as famous as those of such contemporaries as Stephen Sondheim or the late Michael Bennett. The relative anonymity, however, suits them fine. As Kander told Larry Kart in a *Chicago Tribune* interview with the partners, "Neither one of us lives what you might call a show business life. We work in the theater and we love that, but the things we find personally entertaining have nothing to do with that world."

"For me," Ebb said in the same interview, "a show consists of moments, and what you do is write those moments. You try to remain aware of the form of the piece, and then you just go. . . . I think that if you can walk away from a show and be proud of it, if you feel that you've satisfied your own intentions, then theoretically at least you have had a success. But I have to admit that's a very hard feeling to hang onto if they're taking the marquee down."

Ebb's childhood was an unlikely preparation for his later career, because there was little music played in the household. He fell in love with theater after he saw Al Jolson perform on Broadway in a musical. His inclinations in this direction were somewhat discouraged, however, when his family fell upon hard times. When Ebb was fourteen years old, his father, Harry, died. After his death, it was discovered that the senior Ebb's best friend had been embezzling from the family's dry goods business for years. Ebb and his mother were left practically penniless. He still managed to graduate as the valedictorian of his class at DeWitt Clinton High School, but when he informed his mother that he wanted to become a writer, she convinced him to enroll at New York University and study accounting.

While in college, however, Ebb changed his major to English and eventually obtained a master's degree in that subject from Columbia University. He worked his way through school with a string of odd jobs, including serving as a trucker's helper for a hosiery company, authorizing credit in a department store, and bronzing baby shoes. After finishing his degree, he traveled west, hoping to sell some short stories he had penned to Hollywood. He met with little success, and returned to New York with the burgeoning desire to become a songwriter.

A trumpet-playing friend of Ebb's introduced him to Phil Springer, with whom he subsequently created some popular tunes, including "Santa Baby." Over the next several years, Ebb wrote for nightclub acts, revues, and for the satirical television show *That Was the Week That Was.* In the early 1960s, music publisher Tommy Valando introduced him to pianist and choreographer Kander. Both had suffered recent failures—Ebb had provided lyrics for a soon-forgotten Off-Broadway musical called *Midnight Sun.* There was an instant rapport between the two men, and they composed their first song together, "Perfect Strangers," on the spot. Kander told *People* magazine: "A musician is supposed to improvise, but it's almost unheard-of for a lyricist. Yet Fred can improvise in rhyme and meter the way I can at the keyboard."

By 1965, the pair had come to the attention of famed Broadway director and producer Harold Prince. He asked them to write the songs for the Broadway musical *Flora the Red Menace. Flora,* a satire on bohemians, was set in 1930s Greenwich Village and marked the Broadway debut of seventeen-year-old Liza Minnelli, who would become Ebb's friend and frequent muse. The play opened to fairly tepid reviews and closed after eighty-seven performances, but it netted Minnelli a Tony award for outstanding actress. The day after *Flora* opened, Prince met with Kander and Ebb to make plans for their next project, *Cabaret,* a musical adaptation of John van Druten's play *I Am a Camera,* which in turn was based on Christopher Isherwood's *Berlin Stories.*

Cabaret, the work that made Kander and Ebb famous, opened in November, 1966, and was a major critical and box office success. *Cabaret* is the story of an American performer living in Berlin between the two world wars and reflects the anti-Semitism and growing political tumult of those times. *Cabaret* had a Broadway run of 1,166 performances and captured the Tony Award as the season's best musical. The original cast recording won a Grammy Award and the 1972 film adaptation won eight Academy Awards. From this triumph, Kander and Ebb went on to work steadily together in the years that followed, collaborating on the musicals *The Happy Time, Zorba, 70 Girls 70, The Act,* and *Woman of the Year.*

One of the duo's greatest successes, the hit musical *Chicago,* started out its performance history being overshadowed by 1975's other big hit musical, *A Chorus Line.* Since then, however, concert versions, revivals, and an immensely popular film version which took the Oscar for best song, among other honors, have increased *Chicago*'s fame. The story, which Ebb fine-tuned with Fosse, has its roots in history—a journalist's report on the murder trials of seven Chicago women in 1926. The material made its way to the big screen in earlier versions. As Edward Dorall, describing a Singapore production of the musical in *New Straits Times,* put it, "the action takes place mainly in prison and in the courthouse, and the cast [consists of] . . . two main and five minor murderesses, their crook lawyer Billy Flynn, Roxie's husband Amos, the prison matron Mama, softhearted reporter Mary Sunshine, and a mixed chorus of singing, dancing pimps, whores, and reporters, who also play small individual roles." "The show's joy," noted Jess Cagle in *Entertainment Weekly,* "its giddy, edgy personality—is rooted in its own gleeful mean streak, evident in the jazzy tunes and devilishly clever lyrics that never sound dated." Jon Burlingame, reviewing the 2002 film version in *Daily Variety,* maintained that "Any theater buff will tell you that no movie of a Broadway musical has been done right since *1776* thirty years ago," but that *Chicago* somehow "manage[s] to dodge the jinx."

Another of Ebb's notable musical collaborations with Kander is *Kiss of the Spider Woman.* Taking the pair's tradition of making musicals from non-traditional subject matter to new heights, *Kiss of the Spider Woman* centers on "a Latin American homosexual named Molina, in jail for seducing a minor," according to James S. Torrens in *America.* Molina "relieves his worst hours in prison by replaying in fantasy the roles of the movie actress Aurora," the Spider Woman of the title. These fantasies, Torrens continued, are "the counterpoint . . . to a prison-cell story, the tense interaction of Luis Molina . . . with a Marxist conspirator, Valentin Arregui, . . . whom they throw in with him." Dick Lochte in *Los Angeles Magazine,* praised *Spiderwoman*'s score as "constantly surprising and consistently satisfying." Calling *Spider Woman* "the most rousing and moving musical to reach the West End since *Miss Saigon,*" William A. Henry III in *Time* gleefully noted that "this musical must be among the first to feature torture, mutilation and threats of anal rape and is surely the first to portray one character washing another after a bout of diarrhea." Yet Henry also concluded that *Spider Woman* "is as much as anything a musical about the magic of musicals."

BIOGRAPHICAL AND CRITICAL SOURCES:

BOOKS

Encyclopedia of World Biography Supplement, Volume 21, Gale (Detroit, MI), 2001.

PERIODICALS

America, November 20, 1993, James S. Torrens, review of *Kiss of the Spider Woman,* p. 21.
American Theatre, February, 1997, Marilyn Stasio, "The Difference between Kander and Ebb," pp. 10-13.

Back Stage, April 5, 1991, Roy Sander, review of *And the World Goes 'Round,* p. 30; November 22, 1996, David Sheward, review of *Chicago,* p. 40; May 26, 2000, Mike Salinas, "York to Give Kander and Ebb Hammerstein Award," p. 2; November 17, 2000, Esther Tolkoff, "Composers and Lyricists," p. 34.
Chicago Tribune, February 12, 1984.
Daily Variety, January 6, 2003, Jon Burlingame, "*Chicago* Dodges Musical Jinx," p. A12.
Entertainment Weekly, June 20, 1997, Jess Cagle, review of *Chicago,* p. 32.
Los Angeles Magazine, July, 1993, Dick Lochte, review of *Kiss of the Spider Woman,* p. 93.
New Republic, January 6, 1997, Robert Brustein, review of *Chicago,* pp. 26-28.
New Straits Times, April 18, 2000, Edward Dorall, "An Exciting Trip to *Chicago.*"
Newsweek, May 5, 1997, Jack Kroll, Maggie Malone, review of *Steel Pier,* pp. 70-73.
New York Times, December 31, 1987.
Time, November 30, 1992, William A. Henry III, review of *Kiss of the Spider Woman,* p. 77; November 25, 1996, Richard Zoglin, review of *Chicago,* p. 102.
Variety, September 27, 1999, Robert Hofler, "*Chicago* Authors Win Judgment," p. 157; December 13, 1999, Charles Isherwood, review of *Minnelli on Minnelli,* p. 118.*

*   *   *

EIGE, (Elizabeth) Lillian 1915-

PERSONAL: Surname is pronounced "*Eye*-g"; born July 22, 1915, in Marshalltown, IA; daughter of Francis Joseph (a tailor) and Lillian (a homemaker; maiden name, McNary) Tuffree; married Gaylerd S. Eige (an engineer), October 17, 1937; children: Jonathan, Julia Eige Rula. *Education:* University of Iowa, correspondence courses, 1964-66; attended the Iowa Writers' Workshop, 1966-67. *Politics:* Independent. *Religion:* Methodist. *Hobbies and other interests:* "Theater, traveling, music, and of course, reading."

ADDRESSES: Home—401 Foote St. SW, Cedar Rapids, IA 52404.

CAREER: Iowa Training School for Boys, Eldora, IA, secretary, 1933-34; Northwestern Bell, Marshalltown, IA, office worker, 1935-37; writer, 1970—. United

Fund Drive, chairperson, 1969; UNICEF home drive, co-chairperson, 1973; Campfire Girls, board member, 1956-58; United Nations board, member, 1960-80.

MEMBER: National League of American PEN Women.

AWARDS, HONORS: Cady was included on the New York Public Library's 1987 list of "100 Books for Giving and Sharing" and received a Junior Literary Guild citation; Edgar Award for Best Juvenile Book, Mystery Writers of America, for *Dangling.*

WRITINGS:

The Kidnapping of Mister Huey (young adult novel), Harper (New York, NY), 1983.
Cady (young adult novel), illustrated by Janet Wentworth, Harper (New York, NY), 1987.
Dangling (young adult novel), Atheneum Books (New York, NY), 2001.

Contributor to periodicals, including *Jack and Jill.*

ADAPTATIONS: Cady was recorded by the Library of Congress National Library Service for the Blind and Physically Handicapped in 1988.

SIDELIGHTS: Lillian Eige is an author of young adult novels whose characters are often those who are rejected by others or exist on the fringes of society. For example, in her first novel, *The Kidnapping of Mister Huey,* she writes of a friendship between a teenage boy named Willy and the old man of the title. When his family plans to put Mr. Huey in an old folks' home, Willy decides it would be better for his friend to go back to the town of his childhood, so he takes the unconventional approach of "kidnapping" him. In *Cady,* the twelve-year-old of the title is abandoned by his father after his mother dies. Consequently, Cady finds himself being shuffled from house to house, finally ending up at the home of a woman named Thea McVey. To Cady, Thea seems rather mysterious because she refuses to tell him much about herself; nevertheless, after some time he begins to trust her. Along with the puzzle of Thea's identity, Eige throws in another mystery concerning an unidentified man appearing in the nearby woods. Although criticizing the novel for "plot developments [that] seem contrived,"

"careless attention to descriptive details," and poorly handled suspense, *School Library Journal* reviewer Allen Meyer found that the characters' problems "provoke sympathy" in the reader.

A *Publishers Weekly* contributor complained of "awkward shifts between present and past tense." However, the themes of the story are important ones, according to Shaun Johnson in a *Journal of Adolescent and Adult Literacy* review. *Dangling* is about two boys who form an unlikely friendship that helps them both to grow. Ring, like Cady, is without parents and has been shuttled from one foster home to the next; Ben is considered the "runt" of his small Midwestern town, and he is also different from other boys in that he is being raised by two women. Sharing a bond in that they both feel like outcasts, Ben and Ring become very close. The story opens, though, with Ring's sudden disappearance when he goes swimming in a river and no one sees him come out again. Eige then proceeds to tell the boys' story in flashbacks, coming back to the present to show Ben's continuing hopes that his friend is still alive. While Johnson found some issues with the narrative flow of the book, the critic asserted that "*Dangling* covers many issues related to alternative family groupings and adopted children," adding that "the book speaks to boys and young men alike, telling them it is all right to have intense feelings about a male friend."

Eige once commented: "During my early years until I reached high school I lived in Belmond, a typical, small Iowa town. For most of that time our home was in a flat above my father's shop. It meant the family was closely confined in work, play, and home. When you lived in a half block off Main Street, back of the hospital, across from the funeral home, and you could see the hotel from your front windows, you never lacked for excitement or entertainment. I learned, too, there were treasures to be found behind the stores in the alleys. I became a collector. I remember how rich I felt when I found a piece of foil and added it to the huge wad I already had. We lived near a Movie Palace (we didn't call it a theater), and I probably saw most of the movies that came to town. I haunted the library, too, that was only a half block down the street.

"But as in so many families there were good times and bad times. I was a Depression child, and like many we went from a happy, secure time to struggling for survival. That is when I grew up and learned to understand people's actions. And it was the time when we ate home-canned green beans and eggs until they came out our ears. I sometimes insist my characters eat green beans.

"I have been a dreamer, a pretender, and an actor all of my life. When I was a child I could entertain myself all afternoon by throwing myself about the room acting out everything from a sick child to being the most glamorous girl in the whole world. Most of us have to write from the child that we were, the child that we remember, and the child that we are. The part of us that refuses to grow up. We could not write for children otherwise. Some believe that children's books are for children only. That is not true. They are for everyone who hangs on to the magic and excitement of living.

"But sometimes writing for me has been like going to the grocery store for a dozen eggs and coming home with a sack of bananas. I usually start out with my characters and relationships, and I am not always sure what they are going to do. They surprise me. After years of raising children, dogs, orphan birds and rabbits, I decided to go back to school and to try to write. That is where I am today."

BIOGRAPHICAL AND CRITICAL SOURCES:

PERIODICALS

Gazette (Cedar Rapids, IA), April 24, 1983.
Horn Book, September-October, 1987, Ann A. Flowers, review of *Cady,* p. 610.
Journal of Adolescent and Adult Literacy, October, 2001, Shaun Johnson, review of *Dangling,* p. 171.
Junior Literary Guild, April, 1987; September, 1987.
Marshalltown Times Republican (Marshalltown, IA), October 21, 1983.
Publishers Weekly, May 27, 1983, review of *The Kidnapping of Mister Huey,* p. 67; May 8, 1987, Diane Roback, review of *Cady,* p. 71; January 15, 2001, review of *Dangling,* p. 76.
School Library Journal, May, 1983, review of *The Kidnapping of Mister Huey,* p. 81; May, 1987, Allen Meyer, review of *Cady,* p. 109; July, 2001, Faith Brautigan, review of *Dangling,* p. 106.*

EISENHOWER, John S(heldon) D(oud) 1922-

PERSONAL: Born August 3, 1922, in Denver, CO; son of Dwight David (General of the Army and thirty-fourth president of the United States) and Mamie Geneva (Doud) Eisenhower; married Barbara Jean Thompson, June 10, 1947 (divorced, 1986); married Joanne Thompson, April 9, 1990; children: (first marriage) Dwight David II, Barbara Anne, Susan Elaine, Mary Jean. *Ethnicity:* "Caucasian." *Education:* U.S. Military Academy, B.S., 1944; Columbia University, M.A., 1950; U.S. Army Command and General Staff College, graduate, 1955. *Politics:* Independent. *Hobbies and other interests:* Airplane piloting.

ADDRESSES: Home—27318 Morris Rd., Trappe, MD 21673.

CAREER: U.S. Army, cadet, 1941-44, regular officer, 1944-63 (resigned commission as lieutenant colonel, 1963), reserve officer, 1963—, brigadier general, 1974—; spent 1965-69 writing his book on World War II; U.S. Ambassador to Belgium, Brussels, 1969-71. Served with First U.S. Army, Europe, World War II, later with Army of Occupation in Europe, 1945-47; instructor in English at U.S. Military Academy, West Point, NY, 1948-51; battalion and division officer in Korea, 1952-53; member of War Plans Division, Army General Staff, Washington, DC, 1958-61; member of diplomatic council for board of governors, USO, 1983-85. Chair, Pennsylvania Citizens for Nixon, 1968, Interagency Classification Review Committee, 1972-73, and President's Advisory Committee on Refugees, 1975—. Academy Life Insurance Co., Atlanta, GA, chairman of the board. Member of advisory council, National Archives, 1974-77; trustee of Alumni Federation of Columbia University, 1976-80; Eisenhower College, Seneca Falls, NY; and of Eisenhower Exchange fellowships.

MEMBER: Diplomatic and Consular Officers Retired, Capitol Hill Club.

AWARDS, HONORS: Military—Legion of Merit; Bronze Star; Combat Infantryman's Badge; Belgium Order of the Crown Grand Cross; Chungmu Distinguished Service Medal (Korea). Civilian—L.H.D., Northwood Institute, 1970; Graduate Faculties Alumni Award for excellence, Columbia University, 1970.

WRITINGS:

The Bitter Woods: A Comprehensive Study of the War in Europe, Putnam (New York, NY), 1969, published with new introduction by Stephen E. Ambrose, Da Capo Press (New York, NY), 1995.

Strictly Personal (memoir), Doubleday (New York, NY), 1974.

(Editor) Dwight D. Eisenhower, *Letters to Mamie,* Doubleday (New York, NY), 1978.

Allies: Pearl Harbor to D-Day, Doubleday (New York, NY), 1982.

So Far from God: The U.S. War with Mexico, 1846-1848, Random House (New York, NY), 1989.

Intervention!: The United States and the Mexican Revolution, 1913-1917, W. W. Norton (New York, NY), 1993.

Agent of Destiny: The Life and Times of General Winfield Scott, University of Oklahoma Press (Norman, OK), 1999.

Yanks: The Epic Story of the American Army in World War I, Free Press (New York, NY), 2001.

General Ike: A Personal Reminiscence, Free Press (New York, NY), 2003.

SIDELIGHTS: The son of President and Army General Dwight D. Eisenhower, John S. D. Eisenhower also served his country with distinction during World War II and the Korean War; he later became a student of military history and an author. Reviewing Eisenhower's first book, *The Bitter Woods: A Comprehensive Study of the War in Europe* in *Saturday Review,* Robert Leckie declared the author a "top-flight military historian." Drawing on personal experience as well as German and American sources, Eisenhower chronicles the events leading up to and following the Battle of the Bulge, Adolf Hitler's last great attempt to turn the course of the war in Germany's favor. According to Leckie, "few writers on either side of the conflict are better qualified to tell this story. Himself a staff officer of that First Army against whose units the attack was launched, son of the Supreme Commander, who met in the Bulge the crisis of both his 'crusade' and his career, John Eisenhower reveals in this study not only his intimacy with the members of the Allied High Command but great diligence in consulting German archives and interviewing those German officers who are still living. [This work] may stand as the definitive account of the critical battle of the European Theater."

Gordon A. Craig, however, writing in *New York Times Book Review,* felt that the book "suffers in comparison with previous books on the subject. . . . It is too long; the author is slow in getting down to his subject; he is, particularly in the early pages, repetitive." Despite these criticisms, Craig credited Eisenhower with reconstructing "a complex series of events that involved simultaneous attacks by six German corps along a seventy-mile front with a clarity and attention to detail that are a tribute both to his hard and careful work in the sources and to his personal examination of the terrain. He has made the battle his own—and, particularly when he is dealing with small-unit actions, his account conveys an excitement that is hard to resist." "With an amazing . . . grasp of detail," said Charles Poore in *New York Times,* "[Eisenhower] tells us what was happening everywhere, at almost every level, within the German as well as the Allied lines. In short, he has bitten off an awful lot, and he chews it into the suburbs of infinity."

Eisenhower followed *The Bitter Woods* with *Allies: Pearl Harbor to D-Day,* which is based on a manuscript given the author by his father before the latter's death. The work examines, in the words of a critic for the *New York Times Book Review,* "the personalities who shaped the Allied cause during World War II," including such figures as Churchill, Stalin, Marshall, and de Gaulle. "John Eisenhower," the critic asserted, "has expanded [his father's] monograph into a lengthy, satisfying history that is at once colorful and clear."

Several of Eisenhower's other books have drawn in various ways on material from his father. In 1978, for example, he edited and published a collection of his father's correspondence, *Letters to Mamie;* more recently, he wrote about the former president from his unique point of view in 2003's *General Ike: A Personal Reminiscence.* As the title indicates, the biography focuses on Dwight Eisenhower's years in the military, and not on his presidency. The author, who occasionally served as a staff officer under his father when the senior Eisenhower was commanding troops in Europe, reveals the general's relationships with such historic figures as Winston Churchill, Charles de Gaulle, Field Marshal Bernard Montgomery, and General George Patton. Critics admired the fair-handed approach Eisenhower takes. As a *Publishers Weekly* writer noted, "The author paints no one in rosy hues, not even his father, and his research puts them all in their proper context." *New York Times Book Review* contributor Max Boot described *General Ike* as a "loving portrait" that deservedly paints its subject as, in John Eisenhower's words, "one of the most successful military commanders of all time."

Eisenhower has also written his own memoirs, published as *Strictly Personal* in 1974, but his military histories have generally received more attention. Among these are three books on the United States and Mexico. While reading nonfiction about General Winfield Scott's involvement in the Mexican War, Eisenhower was inspired to write *So Far from God: The U.S. War with Mexico, 1846-1848,* a major work about the war that "dismembered the huge if lightly populated Mexican Empire and increased the size of the United States by nearly 50 percent," according to Michael Kilian in the *Detroit Free Press.* The conflict "was as controversial in its day as the Vietnam War has been in ours," Kilian added. The title comes from Mexican President Porfirio Diaz's lament, "Alas, poor Mexico! So far from God and so close to the United States!"

Critics have remarked that *So Far From God* is an important book for a number of reasons. Robert W. Johannsen wrote in Chicago's *Tribune Books:* "Graphically and suspensefully, Eisenhower recounts the long and arduous marches, the tactical maneuvers, the epic engagements . . . and the desperate, hard-fought battles in the Valley of Mexico. It was, Eisenhower points out, a dirty war, costly to both sides. Using the letters and diaries of the soldiers themselves, he has captured the participants' suffering." Furthermore, "the story of this 'dirty little war' is splendidly narrated . . . Not only do his background and special expertise provide graphic and detailed descriptions of the battles themselves, but he offers insightful portraits of the many colorful personalities who crowd the pages of this book," observed Robert V. Remini in the *Washington Post Book World.* The author excels, according to Remini, "in explaining American success despite the interferences from Washington, the lack of resources, the danger of disease and the vast distances involved in transporting thousands of men to the war zone."

So Far from God puts the Mexican War into a new light. Often considered a scarcely justifiable act of military aggression, the conquering of the territory that now comprises the southwestern states was a key to the United States' survival, Eisenhower maintains. European powers were eyeing Mexico's northern regions and were aware of its military weakness. "For Americans the thought of a hostile, European-

controlled monarchy on the southern border of their democratic experiment was frightening indeed," Johannsen related. Therefore, Eisenhower reasons, Americans can be proud of the regulars and the volunteers who fought in it. *Los Angeles Times Book Review* contributor Ferol Egan concluded, "For those who want to grasp the military and political causes of this invasion of our neighbor south of the border, Eisenhower's history is an excellent source."

Eisenhower followed *So Far from God* with *Intervention!: The United States and the Mexican Revolution, 1913-1917.* The Mexican Revolution was a complicated time of political unrest in that country when the office of president was exchanged violently several times. After Francisco I. Madero overthrew the thirty-three-year-old regime of Porfirio Diaz, he was murdered after only a few months in office; Victoriano Huerta, his successor, was subsequently overthrown by Venustiano Carranza in 1917, and Carranza was assassinated in 1920 to be replaced by Alvaro Obregon, whose rise to the presidency marked the end of this long period of unrest. During the 1910s, several factions strove for power, and the United States became involved in two misguided forays into Mexican territory, including an occupation of Veracruz and an ill-fated hunt for the rebel Pancho Villa that gave rise to many ill feelings among Mexicans for the Americans, some of which still linger today. Eisenhower's book makes it clear, however, that the United States' role in the Mexican Revolution did nothing to influence the course of events, and that the eventual outcome was purely the result of Mexico working out its own political problems. While *Historian* reviewer Stephen G. Rabe found the book less than comprehensive in its scholarly research, and he was disappointed that Eisenhower did not put America's intervention in Mexico into context with its overall relationship with Latin America, the critic complimented the author for how he "expertly analyzes the key battles of the period" and felt that he was right to point out how "unfortunate" U.S. intervention was. Kenneth Maxwell furthermore attested in a *Foreign Affairs* article that *Intervention!* "provides a sympathetic and cogent account of events and personalities in this critical period."

The subject that originally inspired Eisenhower to write about Mexico, General Winfield Scott, is finally covered two books later in *Agent of Destiny: The Life and Times of General Winfield Scott.* Scott was involved in the Veracruz occupation in Mexico, but his military career spanned many more conflicts than that, as Eisenhower explains. The general, who served in wars ranging from the War of 1812 to the Mexican War and the Civil War, as well as being the officer in charge of relocating the Cherokees to Oklahoma, was a colorful and very humanly flawed figure. Eisenhower describes him in his glory moments, such as when he became a hero in 1812, and his less admirable moments, such as his contentious relationship with various politicians and his reputation for bluster that earned him the moniker "Old Fuss and Feathers." Critics generally applauded Eisenhower's thorough portrayal. For example, a *Publishers Weekly* contributor declared it "a first-rate biography," and Alan C. Aimone, writing in *Civil War History,* called it "a joy to read" and "a welcomed readable biography."

With 2001's *Yanks: The Epic Story of the American Army in World War I,* Eisenhower returned to war in Europe and how the Americans, instead of becoming integrated into European forces as was the original plan, managed to stay autonomous as the American Expeditionary Force to influence the course of history in remarkable ways. "This well-written work demonstrates how a small, ill-equipped force grew into an awesome fighting machine," according to *Library Journal* writer John Carver, who also praised the book for being "soundly researched."

Eisenhower once told *CA:* "I write principally for selfish reasons; I feel better when I have a continuing outlet for expressing ideas. Aside from the occasional book introduction and book review, I write generally on subjects unfamiliar to me. *The Bitter Woods* (1969) pertained to the Battle of the Bulge in the Ardennes, December, 1944, a battle I read about while back in the States. *Allies* (1982) dealt with the Mediterranean Theater of War, World War II; I was a cadet when those events were transpiring.

"I am not a scholar nor am I much of an original researcher. I use academic format only to verify facts. My objective is to put in simple, readable form those periods of history that are on the record but written in dull form. I try to popularize aspects of history that Americans should have some knowledge of but usually do not. The Mexican War fits handily in that category." He added, "Like many other writers, I would like to try something else, in my case, to branch out from the military. I am afraid, however, that I am confined to nonfiction."

BIOGRAPHICAL AND CRITICAL SOURCES:

PERIODICALS

Chicago Tribune, April 6, 1989.
Civil War History, June, 1999, Alan C. Aimone, review of *Agent of Destiny: The Life and Times of General Winfield Scott,* p. 161.
Detroit Free Press, April 19, 1989.
Foreign Affairs, July-August, 1994, Kenneth Maxwell, review of *Intervention!: The United States and the Mexican Revolution, 1913-1917,* p. 173.
Historian, spring, 1995, Stephen G. Rabe, review of *Intervention!,* p. 602.
Library Journal, April 1, 2001, John Carver, review of *Yanks: The Epic Story of the American Army in World War I,* p. 113; June 1, 2003, Mark Ellis, review of *General Ike: A Personal Reminiscence,* p. 138.
Los Angeles Times Book Review, June 25, 1989.
New Leader, April 3, 1989, Selden Rodman, review of *So Far from God: The U.S. War with Mexico, 1846-1848,* p. 20.
New York Times, January 23, 1969; April 5, 1989.
New York Times Book Review, February 9, 1969; October 24, 1982; April 2, 1989; September 7, 2003, Max Boot, "A Soldier First," p. 27.
Philadelphia Inquirer, April 6, 1975.
Presidential Studies Quarterly, spring, 1997, Travis Beal Jacobs, review of *Intervention!,* p. 373.
Publishers Weekly, October 4, 1993, review of *Intervention!,* p. 54; November 10, 1997, review of *Agent of Destiny,* p. 63; April 7, 2003, review of *General Ike,* p. 55.
Saturday Review, January 25, 1969.
Times Literary Supplement, January 15, 1970.
Tribune Books (Chicago, IL), April 9, 1989.
Washington Post Book World, March 26, 1989.

*   *   *

EMERSON, Steven A. 1954-

PERSONAL: Born June 6, 1954, in New York, NY; son of Michael and Elaine Emerson. *Education:* Brown University, B.A., 1976, M.A., 1977.

ADDRESSES: Home—3930 Connecticut Ave. NW, Suite 202, Washington, DC 20008. *Office*—Investigative Project, 5505 Connecticut Ave. NW, Washington, DC 20015. *Agent*—Morton Janklow, Janklow & Nesbit, 598 Madison Ave., New York, NY 10022.

CAREER: Journalist and author. U.S. Senate Foreign Relations Committee, Washington, DC, staff member, 1977-81; *U.S. News and World Report,* Washington, DC, senior editor, 1986-89; Cable News Network (CNN), contributing correspondent, 1990-94; Investigative Project, Washington, DC, executive director, 1995—.

AWARDS, HONORS: George Polk Award for television documentary, 1994; Albert J. Wood Public Affairs Award, Middle East Forum, 1997; has received three Investigative Reporters and Editors awards for best national investigative reporting.

WRITINGS:

The American House of Saud: The Secret Petrodollar Connection, F. Watts (New York, NY), 1985.
Secret Warriors: Inside the Covert Military Operations of the Reagan Era, Putnam (New York, NY), 1988.
(With Brian Duffy) *The Fall of Pan Am 103: Inside the Lockerbie Investigation,* Putnam (New York, NY), 1990.
(With Cristina Del Sesto) *Terrorist: The Inside Story of the Highest-Ranking Iraqi Terrorist Ever to Defect to the West,* Random House (New York, NY), 1991.
Worldwide Jihad Movement: Militant Islam Targets the West, Institute of the World Jewish Congress (Jerusalem, Israel), 1995.
American Jihad: The Terrorists Living among Us, Free Press (New York, NY), 2002.

Contributor to periodicals, including *American Journalism Review, Los Angeles Times, New Republic, New York Times, New York Times Magazine, Wall Street Journal,* and *Washington Post.* Also wrote and produced "Jihad in America," broadcast by PBS on November 21, 1994.

SIDELIGHTS: Steven A. Emerson is a freelance print and broadcast journalist who has gained considerable distinction with his probing, often controversial

investigations. In 1995 Emerson founded the Investigative Project, which has grown into the largest private intelligence organization focused on militant Islam. Since the terrorist attacks of September 11, 2001, he has been in great demand as an expert in Islamist terrorist organizations and the methods they use to recruit members and raise funds in the United States.

In his first book, *The American House of Saud: The Secret Petrodollar Connection,* Emerson reveals that many American companies and businesses in various dealings—including arms sales—with the Saudis became, in effect, unofficial lobbyists acting on behalf of the Saudis in Washington, D.C. According to *New York Times* reviewer Bernard Gwertzman, *The American House of Saud* constitutes "a full-length compendium which lists, in elaborate detail, the financial stake of many prominent American corporations, law firms, public-relations outfits and educational institutions in Saudi Arabia." Hoyt Purvis, writing in the *New York Times Book Review,* reported that with *The American House of Saud* Emerson has "unearthed some inside intelligence," and J. B. Kelly, in his assessment for the *Los Angeles Times Book Review,* noted that Emerson "has done his research with commendable assiduity." Kelly added that the book is written "in lively, at times even gripping, fashion."

Emerson followed *The American House of Saud* with *Secret Warriors: Inside the Covert Military Operations of the Reagan Era.* Here he reports that the U.S. Department of Defense established its own undercover operation, distinct from the Central Intelligence Agency (CIA), after the failed attempt to rescue hostages from Iran in 1980. One such military operation, Emerson continues, involved CIA director William Casey, National Security Council staff member Oliver North, and former army general Richard Secord, all of whom were eventually implicated in an alleged agreement to provide the hostile Iranian government with weapons in exchange for the release of hostages. Thomas Powers, writing in the *New York Times Book Review,* described *Secret Warriors* as "a reporter's book, full of stories and colorful characters," and he proclaimed it a "fine book."

With his next volume, *The Fall of Pan Am 103: Inside the Lockerbie Investigation,* Emerson teamed with Brian Duffy to provide an insightful probe into the explosion that killed 270 people aboard a jumbo jet over Lockerbie, Scotland, in 1988. The explosion was traced to a Syrian-supported Palestinian organization operating in West Germany. In uncovering the terrorism behind the explosion, according to Emerson and Duffy, various European and American teams revealed considerable shortcomings—including corruption and incompetence—in their efforts to uncover and defeat terrorists. "What arises from reading [*The Fall of Pan Am 103*]," contended *Los Angeles Times* contributor Robert H. Kupperman, "is the specter of negligence and arrogance by governments before the tragedy, and a trail of cover-up and interstate competition during the subsequent mammoth international investigation." He added that the book is "worthwhile reading." *Washington Post Book World* reviewer Steven Luxenberg was disturbed by the book's indication that terrorists possess the necessary resources and conviction to continue triumphing over present preventive measures. "The lesson that emerges from [*The Fall of Pan Am 103*] is not that good or well-intentioned people sometimes screw up," contended Luxenberg. "The lesson is that bad people—terrorists—are smart enough and obsessed enough to get around some of the best security systems in the world."

Emerson is also author—with Cristina Del Sesto—of *Terrorist: The Inside Story of the Highest-Ranking Iraqi Terrorist Ever to Defect to the West.* The book's subject is Adnan Awad, who surrendered to American authorities in 1982. According to Emerson and Del Sesto, Awad subsequently cooperated with Justice Department investigators who were tracking another suspected terrorist, Mohammed Rashid. The department's efforts, however, were reportedly undermined by CIA and National Security Council operatives eager to maintain their own covert ties with terrorist sympathizers in Iraq. Adrienne Edgar, writing in the *New York Times Book Review,* noted that *Terrorist* "offers new evidence of the bankruptcy of United States foreign policy under Ronald Reagan," and she deemed the volume "a chilling indictment of the cynicism and shortsightedness of the Reagan foreign policy team."

In 2002 Emerson published *American Jihad: The Terrorists Living among Us,* the culmination of a decade-long exploration of the ways terrorist organizations, such as Hamas and Islamic Jihad, and of course Al Qaeda, have operated in the United States, often with impunity, through undercover agents, front groups, and radical mosques. "Emerson paints a picture that, until recently, had been ignored or misunderstood by U.S. security and law enforcement officials, who in many cases were held back by inadequate funding, lack of linguistic skills, legal impediments, and a misunderstanding of the potential danger," explained *Security Management* contributor Mayer Nudell. Emerson recounts his initial encounter with radical Islam in 1992 when he wandered into a meeting of the Muslim Arab Youth Association in Oklahoma City. He was amazed to hear numerous speakers call for the killing of Jews and Christians and the annihilation of the West, and surprised to discover that the FBI knew nothing of this meeting and was not empowered to investigate even if it had known. Spurred on by this initial encounter, Emerson went on to discover numerous other organizations that have been set up or penetrated by Islamic militants and to call for greater scrutiny, and prosecution, of these terrorist recruitment methods. His efforts stirred considerable opposition, particularly after his documentary, "Jihad in America," was broadcast by PBS in 1994. Numerous Muslim leaders denounced him as an anti-Islamic extremist, and some commentators questioned his accuracy.

"Emerson may not be a scholar, and he may sometimes connect unrelated dots. He may also occasionally be quite wrong. But he is an investigator who has performed a genuine service by focusing on radical Islamic groups in this country. His information should be taken seriously—just not at face value," wrote *New York Times Book Review* critic Ethan Bronner in his review of *American Jihad.* Others were equally adamant in defending Emerson and denouncing his critics. Reviewing the book in *Commentary,* Terry Eastland, a former Justice Department official, wrote, "Groups that put incendiary speakers at their microphones or that permit themselves to be used by radicals bent on jihad, should be exempt neither from criticism nor from the scrutiny of the law. But the sad fact is that, for far too long, groups preaching hatred and violence have indeed escaped scrutiny. If Emerson's warnings had been heeded when he first issued them, our country might not be in the difficult straits in which it finds itself today."

BIOGRAPHICAL AND CRITICAL SOURCES:

PERIODICALS

Commentary, March, 2003, Terry Eastland, review of *American Jihad: The Terrorists Living among Us,* p. 77.

Los Angeles Times, August 7, 1990, Robert H. Kupperman, review of *The Fall of Pan Am 103: Inside the Lockerbie Investigation.*

Los Angeles Times Book Review, May 19, 1985, J. B. Kelly, review of *The American House of Saud: The Secret Petrodollar Connection,* p. 1.

New York Times, July 11, 1985, Bernard Gwertzman, review of *The American House of Saud,* p. 17.

New York Times Book Review, June 23, 1985, Hoyt Purvis, review of *The American House of Saud,* p. 14; June 26, 1988, Thomas Powers, review of *Secret Warriors: Inside the Covert Military Operations of the Reagan Era,* p. 12; May 19, 1991, Adrienne Edgar, review of *Terrorist: The Inside Story of the Highest-Ranking Iraqi Terrorist Ever to Defect to the West,* p. 14; May 17, 2002, Ethan Bronner, "Suspect Thy Neighbor," p. 10.

Security Management, June, 2002, Mayer Nudell, review of *American Jihad,* p. 128.

Washington Post Book World, May 6, 1990, Steven Luxenberg, review of *The Fall of Pan Am 103,* pp. 1, 4.*

*   *   *

ENGSTROM, Elizabeth 1951-

PERSONAL: Born Bette Lynn Gutzmer, May 11, 1951, in Elmhurst, IL; daughter of E. Robert and Dorothy Piper; married Evan Engstrom (marriage ended); married Alan Cratty; children: Nicole, Eron.

ADDRESSES: Home—598 Brookside Dr., Eugene, OR 97405. *Agent*—Howard Morhaim, 841 Broadway, New York, NY 10003. *E-mail*—Liz@ElizabethEngstrom. com.

CAREER: Horror writer, 1984—; writing instructor, 1990—; director of Maui Writers School Department of Continuing Education. Has also worked as an advertising copywriter and executive. *Military service:* United States Naval Reserve, 1990-98.

MEMBER: Horror Writers Association.

WRITINGS:

NOVELS

When Darkness Loves Us, Morrow (New York, NY), 1985.

Black Ambrosia, Tor (New York, NY), 1988.
Lizzie Borden, Tor (New York, NY), 1991.
Lizard Wine, Dell (New York, NY), 1995.
Black Leather, TripleTree (Eugene, OR), 2003.

SHORT STORIES

Nightmare Flower, Tor (New York, NY), 1992.
The Alchemy of Love: A Collaborative Endeavor, illustrated by Alan M. Clark, TripleTree (Eugene, OR), 1998.
(Editor) *Dead on Demand: The Best of Ghost Story Weekend,* TripleTree (Eugene, OR), 2001.
Suspicions, TripleTree (Eugene, OR), 2002.

OTHER

(Compiler, with John Tullius) *The Maui Writers Conference Presents Word by Word: An Inspirational Look at the Craft of Writing,* Writers House Books (Eugene, OR), 2000.
(Author of introduction) John Tullius, *Pronto! Writings from Rome,* TripleTree (Eugene, OR), 2002.

Contributor of numerous short stories and essays to magazines and anthologies.

WORK IN PROGRESS: The Tackle Shop, chronicles of a fictional Midwestern town; *Martini Moon,* an Outward Bound-type of adventure gone wrong.

SIDELIGHTS: Although Elizabeth Engstrom is often described as a horror writer, her fiction is not so easily classified. In works of horror, mystery, and fantasy, Engstrom chooses to focus on psychological nuances rather than supernatural forces. Beginning in 1985 with *When Darkness Loves Us,* Engstrom has created characters that usually perpetrate their crimes because they are mentally unsound or emotionally crushed. *When Darkness Loves Us* is actually two novellas condensed into one package. The first, from which the book takes it name, is the story of a woman who is trapped in a cave for twenty years, then escapes to the earth's surface to find that a series of distressing changes have taken place in the world. The second of the book's novellas, entitled "Beauty Is," is a tale about middle-aged Martha Mannes, a woman who is both physically deformed and mentally retarded. Having spent her entire life living on her parents' farmstead, Martha faces a whole set of new challenges when her parents suddenly pass away. The critical response to *When Darkness Loves Us* was somewhat mixed. Several reviewers nixed the title novella, while enjoying "Beauty Is." However, in the *St. James Guide to Horror, Ghost, and Gothic Writers,* Don D'Ammassa did call the first tale a "dark fable," which he felt "[read] like a modern fairy tale with a perverse twist." D'Ammassa also wrote that the story had an "effective blend of rural realism and the surreal." James B. Hemesath of *Library Journal,* on the other hand, called the first story "an embarrassment" and "totally unbelievable." Hemesath went on to laud "Beauty Is," declaring it "worth the price of the book." Feeling the first tale was "weird and bizarre," Pam Spencer went on to write that it suffered "from clichéd writing, although this is not a problem with 'Beauty Is.'" A contributor to *Publishers Weekly* dismissed both of the stories, feeling that they may "demand a more arduous suspension of disbelief than most people may be able to achieve."

In 1988 Engstrom published *Black Ambrosia,* the tale of a deluded young woman who thinks she is a vampire. *Black Ambrosia* was Engstrom's first real critical success. Labeling the book "effective," a contributor to *Science Fiction Chronicle* went on to write that Engstrom's "development of atmosphere and mood is superior." Barbara Jo McKee of *Voice of Youth Advocates* called it a "story that draws you in with every horrible detail." D'Ammassa felt the main character's "madness is one of the most convincing characterizations to occur in a horror novel."

Engstrom ventured into historical fiction with her 1991 novel *Lizzie Borden.* Using trial transcripts and old newspaper reports, Engstrom pieces together the tale of the 1892 axe murderess and possible victim of multiple personalities. *Lizzie Borden* earned a warm response from critics. Joan Hinkemeyer of *Library Journal* called it a "fast-paced book," in which Engstrom has "woven a fascinating, fresh tale." A *Kirkus Reviews* critic felt that Engstrom's "rather stiff-kneed and openfaced style states horror more than tingles with it." The same contributor wrote that the book contained "a complex concept that needs subtler treatment." While D'Ammassa felt the book was "of peripheral interest," a *Publishers Weekly* contributor praised the author for the way she "skillfully and subtly builds a psychological plot."

In 1995 Engstrom published the novel *Lizard Wine,* a tale of three women's harrowing experience when they decide to go to a cowboy bar to drink and party. On their way to the bar, their car breaks down during a rainstorm. When they decide to head off, looking for a phone, the girls, all students at the University of Oregon, run into three social outcasts, one of whom fixes the car. Two of the girls head to the bar as originally planned, but the third, Tulie, decides to stay and party with the three men, who she thinks are just regular guys. In different ways, all the girls encounter their share of trouble and violence during the rest of the night. *Lizard Wine* caught the notice of some critics. Calling it a "mesmerizing read," Emily Melton of *Booklist* felt the work was "dark" and "disturbing," as well as "powerful and deeply affecting."

In addition to her novels, Engstrom has published numerous short stories. Her first compilation was 1992's *Nightmare Flower,* which contains twenty horror and fantasy stories. A reviewer for *Publishers Weekly* called it a "genuinely imaginative and diverse collection," containing "subtle evocations of terror and evil." Calling the work "a horror collection in the classic vein," a *Kirkus Reviews* critic believed its stories were "inventive and fanciful, pat and pulpy, goose-bump yarns."

Engstrom is aware she is sometimes stereotyped as a "horror writer" because of her novels. "My work can be found, oddly enough, under horror, literature, biography, historical, mystery, and fiction," she said on the *Writers Review* Web site. "I would prefer that it was just found under 'fiction.'" In her 2002 collection *Suspicions,* the author demonstrates the versatility of her writing with stories that range from horror and fantasy to science fiction and even erotica. The author ties them together by examining themes of suspicion in each one. A *Kirkus Reviews* critic observed that the collection has "wide-ranging stories despite the theme that binds them, but unfortunately [they are] also wide-ranging in quality." *Booklist* contributor Regina Schroeder, however, praised the twists contained in *Suspicions* and concluded, "These stories make up a hefty, genre-crossing pie, spiced with images capable of snagging the imagination."

Engstrom returned to suspense in her 2003 novel *Black Leather.* The plot revolves around two very different sisters—Irene is an assertive, successful attorney, while her sister, Cynthia, is struggling with depression and a failing marriage. Cynthia follows her sister on a trip to Los Angeles, where she discovers Irene's secret life, haunting sleazy bars and indulging in sexual fetishes. When a Navajo man both Cynthia and Irene have slept with turns up dead, Cynthia is accused of his murder and Irene takes her case. Cynthia, however, believes Irene may have framed her and asks her estranged husband Joseph to investigate. As Joseph explores Irene's secret life, he becomes involved with his sister-in-law despite his growing suspicions. The erotic and psychological entanglements make for compelling reading, according to a *Midwest Book Review* critic, who called *Black Leather* "an artfully written and highly recommended erotic and psychological suspense from first page to last."

BIOGRAPHICAL AND CRITICAL SOURCES:

BOOKS

St. James Guide to Horror, Ghost, and Gothic Writers, St. James Press (Detroit, MI), 1998.

PERIODICALS

Booklist, January 1, 1996, Emily Melton, review of *Lizard Wine,* p. 786; January 1, 2002, Regina Schroeder, review of *Suspicions,* p. 824.

Kirkus Reviews, November 1, 1990, review of *Lizzie Borden* p. 1479; August 15, 1992, review of *Nightmare Flower,* pp. 1007-1008; February 1, 2002, review of *Suspicions,* p. 140.

Library Journal, February 1, 1985, James B. Hemesath, review of *When Darkness Loves Us,* p. 112; December, 1990, Joan Hinkemeyer, review of *Lizzie Borden,* p. 160; March 15, 2001, review of *Dead on Demand: The Best of Ghost Story Weekend,* p. 90.

Midwest Book Review, October, 2003, review of *Black Leather.*

Publishers Weekly, December 14, 1984, review of *When Darkness Loves Us,* pp. 39-40; December 7, 1990, review of *Lizzie Borden,* p. 70; August 10, 1992, review of *Nightmare Flower,* p. 55; February 11, 2002, review of *Suspicions,* p. 167.

Science Fiction Chronicle, June, 1988, review of *Black Ambrosia,* p. 52.

Voice of Youth Advocates, August, 1988, Barbara Jo McKee, review of *Black Ambrosia,* p. 130.

ONLINE

Elizabeth Engstrom Web site, http://www.elizabeth engstrom.com/ (October 24, 2003).

Writers Review, "An Interview with . . . Elizabeth Engstrom," http://jez.cc/writersreview/authors/ elizabeth_engstrom.htm/ (October 24, 2003).*

*   *   *

EVANS, C(harles) Stephen 1948-

PERSONAL: Born May 26, 1948, in Atlanta, GA; son of Charles Hinton (a bus driver) and Pearline (a teacher; maiden name, Prewett) Evans; married Jan Walter (a professor of Spanish), September 6, 1969; children: Kelley, Lise, Charles. *Ethnicity:* "White." *Education:* Wheaton College, Wheaton, IL, B.A. (with high honors), 1969; Yale University, M.Ph., 1971, Ph. D., 1974. *Politics:* Independent. *Religion:* Baptist. *Hobbies and other interests:* Running, golf.

ADDRESSES: Home—10000 Ridge Point Dr., Waco, TX 76712. *Office*—Department of Philosophy, Baylor University, P.O. Box 97273, Waco, TX 76798-7273; fax: 254-710-3838. *E-mail*—c_stephen_evans@baylor. edu.

CAREER: Trinity College, Deerfield, IL, assistant professor of philosophy, 1972-74; Wheaton College, Wheaton, IL, assistant professor, 1974-78, associate professor, 1978-83, professor of philosophy, 1983-84; St. Olaf College, Northfield, MN, professor of philosophy and curator of Hong Kierkegaard Library, beginning 1986-94, chair of Division of Philosophy, Religion, and History, 1991-93; Calvin College, Grand Rapids, MI, professor of philosophy, 1994-2001, William Spoelhof Teacher-Scholar, 1994-96, and dean for research and scholarship; Baylor University, Waco, TX, professor of philosophy and humanities, 2001—. Trinity Evangelical Divinity School, visiting lecturer, 1976; University of Rhode Island, William Oliver Martin Memorial Lecturer, 1980; Western Kentucky University, visiting associate professor, 1980-81; Northern Baptist Seminary, adjunct professor, 1982-84; Fuller Theological Seminary, John G. Finch Lecturer, 1988; Wheaton College, Scandrette Lecturer, 1988; Emory University, fellow at Center for Faith

C. Stephen Evans

Development, 1988-89; Regent College, Vancouver, British Columbia, Canada, visiting professor, 1990, 1992, 1995; University of Iowa, Geneva Lecturer, 1991; Northwestern College, Orange City, IA, Ronald Nelson Scholar in Residence, 1992; lecturer at other colleges and universities, including Knox College, Emory University, University of Georgia, and Gordon College; University of Copenhagen, member of international scholarly committee for Kierkegaard Research Centre, 1994-98.

MEMBER: American Philosophical Association, Kierkegaard Society (member of executive committee, 1989-91; president, 1991), Society of Christian Philosophers (member of executive committee, 1986-89, 1991-94; president, 1998-2001), American Academy of Religion, Institute for Advanced Christian Studies (member of executive committee).

AWARDS, HONORS: Danforth fellowship, 1969-74; George C. Marshall fellowship for Denmark, 1977-78; fellow of National Endowment for the Humanities, 1980, 1985, 1988-89, 2000-01; Pew Evangelical senior scholar, 1991-94.

WRITINGS:

Despair: A Moment or a Way of Life? An Existential Quest for Hope, Inter-Varsity Press (Downers Grove, IL), 1971, revised edition published as *Existentialism: The Philosophy of Despair and the Quest for Hope,* Zondervan (Grand Rapids, MI), 1984.

Preserving the Person: A Look at the Human Sciences, Inter-Varsity Press (Downers Grove, IL), 1977.

Subjectivity and Religious Belief: An Historical, Critical Study, Eerdmans (Grand Rapids, MI), 1978.

Kierkegaard's "Fragments" and "Postscript": The Religious Philosophy of Johannes Climacus, Humanities Press (Atlantic Highlands, NJ), 1983.

Contours of Christian Philosophy, Volume 4: *Philosophy of Religion: Thinking about Faith,* Inter-Varsity Press (Downers Grove, IL), 1984.

The Quest for Faith: Reason and Mystery As Pointers to God, Inter-Varsity Press (Downers Grove, IL), 1986, revised edition published as *Why Believe: Reason and Mystery As Pointers to God,* Eerdmans (Grand Rapids, MI), 1996.

Wisdom and Humanness in Psychology, Baker Book House (Grand Rapids, MI), 1989.

Søren Kierkegaard's Christian Psychology: Insight for Counseling and Pastoral Care, Zondervan (Grand Rapids, MI), 1990.

Passionate Reason: Making Sense of Kierkegaard's "Philosophical Fragments," Indiana University Press (Bloomington, IN), 1992.

(Editor, with George Connell) *Foundations of Kierkegaard's Vision of Community: Religion, Ethics, and Politics in Kierkegaard,* Humanities Press International (Atlantic Highlands, NJ), 1992.

(Editor, with Merold Westphal, and contributor) *Christian Perspectives on Religious Knowledge,* Eerdmans (Grand Rapids, MI), 1993.

(Translator, with wife, Jan E. Evans) Paul Müller, *Kierkegaard's "Works of Love": Christian Ethics and the Maieutic Ideal,* C. A. Reitzel (Copenhagen, Denmark), 1993.

The Historical Christ and the Jesus of Faith: The Incarnational Narrative As History, Oxford University Press (Oxford, England), 1996.

Faith beyond Reason: A Kiekegaardian Account, Edinburgh University Press (Edinburgh, Scotland), 1998.

Pocket Dictionary of Apologetics and Philosophy of Religion, Inter-Varsity Press (Downers Grove, IL), 2002.

Contributor to books, including *Kierkegaard's Fear and Trembling: Critical Appraisals,* edited by Robert Perkins, University of Alabama Press (Tuscaloosa, AL), 1981; *Readings in the Christian Faith and the Discipline of Psychology,* Baker Book House (Grand Rapids, MI), 1986; *Kierkegaard: Poet of Existence,* edited by Birgit Bertung, C. A. Reitzel (Copenhagen, Denmark), 1989; *Writing the Politics of Difference,* edited by Hugh J. Silverman, State University of New York Press (Albany, NY), 1991; and *God, Philosophy, and Academic Culture,* edited by William J. Wainwright, Scholars Press (Atlanta, GA), 1996. Editor of the series "Contours of Christian Philosophy," Inter-Varsity Press (Downers Grove, IL). Contributor of more than fifty articles and reviews to journals, including *Faith and Philosophy, International Journal for Philosophy of Religion, Philosophia Reformata, Journal of Mind and Behavior,* and *Christian Scholars Review.* Editor, *Søren Kierkegaard Newsletter,* 1989-95; contributing editor, *Journal of Psychology and Theology;* member of editorial board, *Religious Studies* and *Books and Culture.*

SIDELIGHTS: C. Stephen Evans once told *CA:* "My primary motivation for writing is to contribute to the development of Christian philosophy."

F

FAIRSTEIN, Linda A. 1947(?)-

PERSONAL: Born May 5, 1947 (one source says 1948), in Mt. Vernon, NY; daughter of Samuel Johnson (a physician) and Alice (a registered nurse; maiden name, Atwell) Fairstein; married Justin N. Feldman (a lawyer), May 2, 1987; children: three stepchildren. *Education:* Vassar College, A.B., 1969; University of Virginia School of Law, J.D., 1972. *Religion:* Jewish.

ADDRESSES: Office—P.O. Box 226, New York, NY 10021-0014. *Agent*—c/o Esther Newberg, International Creative Management, 40 West 57th St., New York, NY 10019.

CAREER: New York County District Attorney's Office, appointed to staff, 1972, chief of sex crimes prosecution unit, 1976-2002, deputy chief of trial division, 1981-2002; full-time writer and consultant to law enforcement agencies, 2002—. Member of the board of directors for several nonprofit organizations, including Mount Sinai Hospital Friends of the Rape Crisis Intervention Program, 1990—, New York Women's Agenda, 1993—, Phoenix House Foundation, 1994—, and Choice Cares (national advisory DNA project). Member of Governor Cuomo's Task Force on Rape, 1989-92; cochair of New York Women's Agenda Domestic Violence Committee, 1993—; member of President Clinton's Violence against Women Advisory Council, 1995; member of American Bar Association National Conference of Lawyers and Representatives of the Media, 1995—. National Lecturer on such topics as violence against women, domestic violence, and aspects of the criminal justice system to professional organizations, colleges and universities, health-care professionals, and women's groups.

MEMBER: Women's Bar Association, American College of Trial Lawyers, Federal Bar Council (member of Board of Trustees, 1993—), Mystery Writers of America, Sisters in Crime, New York Women's Forum, Association of the Bar of the City of New York (Judiciary committee member, 1985-88; Legal Issues affecting Crime Victims committee member, 1993—).

AWARDS, HONORS: Emory Buckner Award, Federal Bar Council, 1991, for distinguished public service; First Distinguished Alumna Award, University of Virginia Women's Center, 1991; "Life of the City Award," *New York Woman,* 1991; named one of twenty "Outstanding Young Lawyers" who make a difference, American Bar Association, 1991; "Woman of Achievement Award," American Association of University Women, 1992, for outstanding achievement in the legal profession; Proskauer Award, United Jewish Appeal-Federation of Jewish Philanthropies of New York, Lawyers Division, 1992, for distinguished public service; Woman of the Year Award, *Glamour,* 1993, for publication of *Sexual Violence: Our War against Rape;* Woman of the Year Award, *New Woman,* 1993; 1994 Achievement Award, National Women's Political Caucus; Woman of the Year Award, Women's Projects and Productions, 1994; Public Figure Leadership Award, Older Women's League, 1994; Distinguished Woman of the Year Award, Boy Scouts of America, 1994; Women's Focus Award, Central Synagogue, 1996; International Woman of Achievement Award, Soroptomists, 1996; *Sexual Violence* was named a *New York Times* notable book of the year; Humanitarian

Award, National Conference of Christians and Jews, 1996.

WRITINGS:

MYSTERY NOVELS; "ALEXANDRA COOPER" SERIES

Final Jeopardy, Scribner (New York, NY), 1996.
Likely to Die, Scribner (New York, NY), 1997.
Cold Hit, Scribner (New York, NY), 1999.
The Deadhouse, Scribner (New York, NY), 2001.
The Bone Vault, Scribner (New York, NY), 2003.
The Kills, Scribner (New York, NY), 2004.

NONFICTION

Sexual Violence: Our War against Rape, Morrow (New York, NY), 1993.

ADAPTATIONS: Final Jeopardy was made into a television film starring Dana Delaney and aired on ABC-TV in 2001. The Alex Cooper mysteries are available as abridged audio recordings.

SIDELIGHTS: With over twenty-five years as head of the New York City District Attorney's sex crimes unit, Linda A. Fairstein has used her wealth of experience about criminal activities, police procedure, and the impact of crime on victims to create the popular Alex Cooper mystery series. She was well known as a prosecutor before turning to fiction, however, using new scientific techniques and increased cooperation with police investigators to improve New York's conviction rate for sexual crimes. She led the teams that prosecuted many high profile criminal cases, including the "Preppie Murder" of Jennifer Levin and the shocking beating and rape of the Central Park Jogger. Working in the sex crimes unit "wasn't something I planned to do, or even particularly wanted to do," Fairstein told Benedicte Page in the *Bookseller.* "But I became thoroughly fascinated by and challenged by the work. It became a passion."

That passion informs Fairstein's first book, the nonfiction study *Sexual Violence: Our War against Rape.* Fairstein drew on her experience as head of the Sex Crimes Unit to write an account of actual crimes, combined with descriptions of the horrors of rape and the progress of the law. While presenting actual cases, Fairstein describes the response of her coworkers as they defend victims and pursue the criminals. In addition, Fairstein portrays rape for the violent crime that it is, whether it is committed by a total stranger or a known acquaintance of the victim. *Washington Post Book World* contributor Elizabeth Fox-Genovese observed that "the finest quality of this book lies in the author's ability to sustain a balance between her feelings as a woman and her professional loyalty to co-workers whom she obviously respects." Susan Estrich declared in the *Los Angeles Times Book Review* that Fairstein "has written a smart, serious, interesting book." One of the "remarkable" things about *Sexual Violence* is that "we're in the presence here of a genuinely unassuming and dedicated public servant who will not be discouraged," Ann Jones concluded in the *Women's Review of Books.* "In her spare time, Fairstein has written the kind of book that makes you want to shake her hand and then get to work."

Following the success of her first publication, Fairstein tried her hand at fiction. As she once told *CA:* "For me, the series of crime novels is an extraordinary opportunity to inform readers about the criminal justice system and to entertain them at the same time." In addition, as she revealed to Page, "I did think when I set out to do it that what I could bring to the genre was the authenticity of the work, both procedurally and, in a sense, emotionally. I wanted to put these crimes in fiction without tabloidizing, and I do explain how the system is meant to work and how the victim recovers and show she is treated in the criminal justice system."

Fairstein's debut novel, 1996's *Final Jeopardy,* presents New York Assistant District Attorney Alexandra Cooper; she, like her creator, is in charge of prosecuting sex crimes. When a friend staying at Alex's house on Martha's Vineyard is found dead, the young attorney finds herself questioning if she was really the target of the crime. Fairstein "brings to her exciting first novel the same passions and insights into the criminal and crime-busting minds that marked her memoir, *Sexual Violence,*" asserted a *Publishers Weekly* critic. *Library Journal* contributor Charles Michaud similarly observed, "This thriller, which will keep readers asking questions and turning pages, has the potential to be one of the summer's big hits."

Alex returned for a second outing in 1997's *Likely to Die.* The victim in this case is a prominent Manhattan neurosurgeon who is found dead in her own office. In working the case with detectives Mike Chapman and Mercer Wallace, Alex explores the underside of hospital life, with its records rooms, underground tunnels, and visitors from all walks of life. A *Publishers Weekly* critic faulted the novel's "minimal suspense" and "pedantic lecturing," but also observed that when Fairstein "sticks to the basics of these cases and the prosecutorial and police procedures used to handle them, she writes with an authority that crime buffs will relish." *Library Journal* contributor Molly Gorman also remarked on "a documentary feel that slows the narrative," but added that Fairstein's expertise creates "a world so real, its brittle police babble and mounting suspense make the pages crackle." "With its taut plot and classy setting," J. D. Reed concluded in *People, "Likely to Die* is an uptown act."

Fairstein's 1999 novel *Cold Hit* was also lauded by critics. "This fast-paced novel opens with a murder and rolls along from one plot twist to another: everything from the standard greed and revenge to unscrupulous art dealers trafficking in art treasures stolen by Nazis," as Vanessa Bush summarized it in *Booklist.* Though *Library Journal* contributor Gorman found the "frequent explanations of police procedures . . . jarring," she nonetheless called the novel "fascinating and fast paced."

One of New York City's most unusual landmarks was the inspiration for 2001's *The Deadhouse*: Roosevelt Island, which housed a smallpox sanitarium in the nineteenth century. When professor Lola Dakota is found murdered, the primary suspect is Lola's abusive husband. Alex's investigation, however, reveals Lola had other enemies and was also involved in an archeological dig on Roosevelt Island. Fairstein "once again treats readers to the companionable friendship between Alex and Mike," *Booklist*'s Bush observed, "as well as the intricacies of a murder investigation and the fascinating history of a long-forgotten part of New York history and geography." A *Kirkus Reviews* critic found Alex's "gooey love affair" with a news correspondent distracting, but also noted that when Alex is "going about her daily prosecutorial chores, the result is authoritative and interesting." As a *Publishers Weekly* writer similarly concluded, "Fairstein weaves present and past woes to good effect, while her focus on Roosevelt Island will intrigue New Yorkers who know little about its shameful former uses."

Alex Cooper's next outing drew on Fairstein's fondness for two of New York's great institutions: the

Metropolitan Museum of Art and the Museum of Natural History. "My earliest childhood recollections were of coming to visit these two museums," the author told Diana Pinckley in the New Orleans *Times-Picayune.* "I was curious to get behind the scenes." In 2003's *The Bone Vault,* Alex's attendance at a joint museum reception turns into another day at the office when a young woman is found dead in a sarcophagus. While investigating the case, Alex learns more about the unseen side of museum life, including the storage basements and attics that contain most of the museums' collections—including the Museum of Natural History's collection of fifty million human bones. The book also pays tribute to the heroes of September 11, 2001, as Alex witnesses the terrorist attacks on the World Trade Center from her office—which, like Fairstein's, was only ten blocks away from Ground Zero. In an emotional scene, Alex's friend and frequent collaborator, police investigator Mike Chapman, stops at her apartment after witnessing the loss of many of his fellow police officers. The resulting "romantic tension, the fast-paced plotting, and the New York setting will keep fans of Fairstein's series engrossed," Vanessa Bush observed in *Booklist.*

Other reviewers were similarly impressed with Fairstein's intriguing behind-the-scenes portrayal of New York landmarks. "The real stars are the museums themselves," Eugen Weber observed in the *Los Angeles Times Book Review,* adding that this "turbocharged mystery" supplies "a chilling puzzle." While *Library Journal* contributor Rebecca House Stankowski found Alex's character "fastidious and stilted," she noted that the "fast pacing, colorful suspects, and museum settings" made for "fun reading." A *Kirkus Reviews* critic noted that the author's museum settings help distinguish *The Bone Vault* from other mystery thrillers: "the fearless plunge into the dirty waters of museum politics suggests that Fairstein . . . may have found her own voice at last."

In her sixth Alex Cooper mystery, 2004's *The Kills,* Fairstein again shows Alex involved in several investigations—a hallmark of the series. "One of my pet peeves in mystery novels is when the big case falls on the prosecutor's or cop's desk, you can work on it 24/7," the author told Pinckley. "In my job, if a murder happens, I still have a 46-case caseload. That's why I love to have Alex and the cops working on many things at once." In *The Kills,* Alex finds that a man accused of rape and child abuse has a tangled history that ties him to a murdered former World War II spy and dancer. A *Publishers Weekly* critic noted that the complexity of Alex's caseload adds "texture and realism" to the novel and concluded that "Fairstein's style and skills have matured over the years, making this a consistently dependable series with a likable and intelligent heroine."

BIOGRAPHICAL AND CRITICAL SOURCES:

PERIODICALS

Booklist, May 1, 1997, Emily Melton, review of *Likely to Die,* p. 1460; August, 1999, Vanessa Bush, review of *Cold Hit,* p. 1985; August, 2001, Bush, review of *The Deadhouse,* p. 2050; November 15, 2002, Bush, review of *The Bone Vault,* p. 547.

Bookseller, September 20, 2002, Benedicte Page, "The Prosecutor's Case," p. 26.

Entertainment Weekly, July 19, 1996, Erica Cardozo, review of *Final Jeopardy,* p. 71.

Interview, June, 1989, Ed Hayes and Karen Kuehn, "Law Be a Lady," p. 48.

Kirkus Reviews, August 1, 2001, review of *The Deadhouse,* p. 1069; October 15, 2002, review of *The Bone Vault,* p. 1506.

Library Journal, April 15, 1996, Charles Michaud, review of *Final Jeopardy,* p. 121; May 1, 1997, Molly Gorman, review of *Likely to Die,* p. 138; August, 1999, Gorman, review of *Cold Hit,* p. 146; December, 2002, Rebecca House Stankowski, review of *The Bone Vault,* p. 177.

Los Angeles Times Book Review, December 19, 1993, Susan Estrich, review of *Sexual Violence: Our War against Rape,* pp. 1, 15; June 15, 2003, Eugen Weber, review of *The Bone Vault,* p. 13.

New York Times, September 16, 1993, Christopher Lehmann-Haupt, review of *Sexual Violence,* p. B2.

New York Times Book Review, September 19, 1993, Lynn Karpen, "Taking It Personally" (interview), p. 1.

New York Times Sunday Magazine, February 25, 1990, Katherine Bouton, "Linda Fairstein vs. Rape," p. 20.

People, July 8, 1996, Pam Lambert, "Double Trouble," p. 28; August 25, 1997, J. D. Reed, review of *Likely to Die,* p. 38.

Publishers Weekly, April 1, 1996, review of *Final Jeopardy,* p. 50; May 12, 1997, review of *Likely to Die,* p. 57; Sept 3, 2001, review of *The Dead-* *house,* p. 67; October 21, 2002, review of *The Bone Vault,* p. 53; October 13, 2003, review of *The Kills,* p. 54.

Time, October 14, 1991, Margaret Carlson, "The Trials of Convicting Rapists" (interview), p. 11.

Times-Picayune (New Orleans, LA), February 15, 2003, Diana Pinckley, "Murder at the Museum," p. E1.

Washington Post Book World, January 16, 1994, Elizabeth Fox-Genovese, "Fighting Back," p. 5.

Women's Review of Books, January, 1994, Ann Jones, review of *Sexual Violence,* p. 14.

ONLINE

Linda Fairstein Home Page, www.lindafairstein.com/ (October 24, 2003).*

*   *   *

FALCONER, Lee N.
See MAY, Julian

*   *   *

FARISH, Terry 1947-

PERSONAL: Born June 8, 1947, in Waterbury, CT; daughter of Clifford and Eleanor (Bronson) Dickerson; married Stephen Farish (a U.S. Air Force officer), 1970; children: Elizabeth. *Education:* Texas Woman's University, B.S., 1969; California State University—Fullerton, M.L.S., 1976; Antioch University, M.A. (literature and creative writing), 1985. *Politics:* Democrat.

ADDRESSES: Home—192 New Castle Ave., Portsmouth, NH 03801. *Agent*—Marilyn Marlow, Curtis Brown, Ltd., 10 Astor Pl., New York, NY 10003. *E-mail*—spring@terryfarish.com.

CAREER: Ralston Public Library, Ralston, NE, director, 1976-82; Leominster Public Library, Leominster, MA, head of children's services, 1986-90; Cambodian Mutual Assistance Association, Lowell, MA, director of Young Parent Program, 1990-91; Rivier College, Nashua, NH, writing instructor, beginning 1993; Salt

Institute for Documentary Studies, Portland, ME, instructor in nonfiction writing. Lecturer, workshop presenter, and literacy volunteer; involved in New Hampshire Theater Project, Arts Alliance of Northern New Hampshire, and Casey Family Services. Worked for American Red Cross in Cu Chi, Vietnam, 1969-70.

MEMBER: Society of Children's Book Writers and Illustrators, National Writers Union, American Library Association.

AWARDS, HONORS: New Hampshire individual artist fellow.

WRITINGS:

Why I'm Already Blue (young adult novel), Greenwillow (New York, NY), 1989.

Shelter for a Seabird (young adult novel), Greenwillow (New York, NY), 1990.

Flower Shadows (adult novel), Morrow (New York, NY), 1992.

If the Tiger (adult novel), Steerforth Press (South Royalton, VT), 1995.

Talking in Animal (young adult novel), Greenwillow (New York, NY), 1996.

A House in Earnest (adult novel), Steerforth Press (South Royalton, VT), 2000.

The Cat Who Liked Potato Soup (children's picture book), illustrated by Barry Root, Candlewick Press (Cambridge, MA), 2003.

WORK IN PROGRESS: Braids, and More True Stories about Sudanese Teenagers, a nonfiction book about a group of teens living in Portland, Maine.

SIDELIGHTS: In her novels for both adults and teen readers, Terry Farish focuses on issues such as divorce, teen pregnancy, illness, and loss. Drawing from the people and places she has encountered, the author uses these elements to help create her characters and settings. Her work in Vietnam for the American Red Cross after she graduated from college brought her face to face with the realities of war, and her more recent work with immigrant teens from Africa and Asia has allowed her to see typical adolescent concerns from a broader-than-usual perspective.

Working for many years as a children's librarian, Farish began her writing career penning fiction for young adults. Her first novel, *Why I'm Already Blue,* examines the complex feelings of an adolescent girl whose parents are on the verge of divorce. Feeling as if the burden of family stability lies on her shoulders, twelve-year-old Lucy Purcell begins to retreat into herself after her older sister, Jane, leaves for nursing school. She also distances herself from her closest childhood friend, Gus, who has muscular dystrophy. When Lucy's sister brings a baby from the hospital to the family cottage, Lucy reunites with Gus and begins to assume some responsibilities for the child's care. Thanksgiving dinner finally presents Lucy and her family with the opportunity to resolve differences, make plans, and adjust to new relationships in a novel that a *Publishers Weekly* reviewer described as "about the collision of emotions rather than a simple coming-of-age tale." *School Library Journal* contributor Bonnie L. Raasch noted the novel's serious tone, while a *Kirkus Reviews* critic called the story "atmospheric" and "moody," and maintained that Farish's "airy, elusive writing subtly conveys the full weight of each character's concerns."

With 1990's *Shelter for a Seabird,* Farish addresses a range of issues, including teen pregnancy, loss of community, and the desire for acknowledgment and understanding. Returning to her Shelter Island home after giving up her baby for adoption, sixteen-year-old Andrea is frustrated to find that her parents act as if nothing out of the ordinary has happened. For Andrea, her whole life and outlook has changed as a result of her summer fling and the consequential experiences of pregnancy and birth, and she soon realizes that this change has set her apart from her friends at school as well. Then Andrea meets Swede, an AWOL soldier who listens without judgment as Andrea talks about her life. Together, Andrea and Swede help each other deal with the erosion of stability in their lives and confront their problems responsibly in preparation for building a solid and mature relationship, in a novel a *Kirkus Reviews* contributor praised for its "ruggedly believable characters" and "pockets of tellingly placed details."

In *Talking in Animal,* pre-teen Siobhan realizes that her dog Tree, which has been a part of her family as long as she can remember, is quietly suffering great pain as he nears the end of his life. As if that imminent loss is not enough, her favorite person, wildlife rehabilitator Maddy Todd, is getting married, which means Maddy will not be able to spend as much time with Siobhan as she was once able. In frustration, she petulantly decides to make life miserable for Lester Grace, the girl who will soon be Maddy's stepdaughter. Ultimately, however, Siobhan comes to terms with her jealousy over Maddy's future and also summons the courage to take Tree to the vet to be euthanized. Calling Farish's protagonist "a really great kid" who makes the transition from her idealized world to reality "naturally and easily and believably," *Voice of Youth Advocates* critic Helen Turner dubbed the novel "a quiet, funny story," while in *Horn Book,* Jennifer Brabander noted that the author "writes with humor and precision about Siobhan's growing awareness of the many forms friendship can take."

Taking a break from more serious fare, Farish experimented with the picture-book genre in 2003's *The Cat Who Liked Potato Soup.* Illustrated by Barry Root, the book focuses on the close relationship between a curmudgeonly old man and a unique cat. Living together in their rural Texas home, the pair have things down to a routine, and despite the occasional cross word, they get along just fine. Instead of catching birds, the cat prefers to eat potato soup, which the old man enjoys sharing. And rather than exhibiting a usual cat's aversion to water, this cat likes nothing more than to sit in the bow of the old man's fishing dingy, feeling the spray in her face as they row to a likely fishing spot each morning. The two seem inseparable until one day when the cat exhibits normal cat behavior and disappears for several days in retaliation for a slight change in their daily routine. Noting that Farish "demonstrates herself an exciting new talent" as a picture-book author, *Bulletin of the Center for Children's Books* contributor Deborah Stevenson praised *The Cat Who Liked Potato Soup* as a "casually told yet tender tale about the prickly friendship between an old man and his cat." In *Kirkus Reviews,* a contributor had special praise for the restrained illustrations by Barry Root, noting that Farish's "evocative language" is enhanced by "the rich array of subtle verbal and visual nuances" created by the author-illustrator collaboration.

In addition to her picture book and her novels for teen readers, Farish has also penned several fictional works for adults, among them *Flower Shadows, If the Tiger,* and *A House in Earnest.* Based on the author's own experiences in Vietnam as a war-relief worker, *Flower*

Shadows describes the horrors faced by female Red Cross volunteers during the Vietnam War. The main character's "breathless innocence makes this story a particularly heartbreaking and memorable one," declared a *Kirkus Reviews* critic.

Also set against the backdrop of the war in Southeast Asia, Farish's *If the Tiger* describes the impact of war on two young, motherless women—one Cambodian, one American—whose fathers fought on opposite sides during the Cambodian conflict. Chanty Sun is the only member of her family to have survived the war. Now living in the United States with her Cambodian-born husband, Kob, and her infant son, Chanty realizes that Kob's abusive, controlling behavior is not love. Meanwhile, college student Laurel Sullivan is trying to come to terms with her dictatorial Air Force colonel father and her mixed feelings toward a hippie mother who abandoned her. The paths of the two women cross in a Massachusetts mill town, sparking a chain of events that include a tragic death, a trip to a Buddhist temple to chase away spirits from the past, and an emotional reconciliation in a novel that *New York Times Book Review* writer Laura van Wormer described as "fresh and lyrical." In *Publishers Weekly,* a reviewer praised *If the Tiger* as "quiet, sensuous, and intensely moving," remarking in particular on Farish's skill in weaving Eastern spirituality and the emotional vestiges of war into a "universal human story."

Published in 2000, the novel *A House in Earnest* also involves the emotional aftermath of war, this time through the lives of young married couple Cristy and Deborah Mahan. Through what a *Publishers Weekly* contributor described as a "languidly poetic story" covering the couple's twenty-five-year on-again, off-again relationship, Cristy remains haunted by violent memories of Vietnamese mine fields, while Deborah remains stuck in the hippie counterculture, where drugs, idealized fantasies of a better world, and a host of mundane worries fuel her disillusionment. While *Booklist* reviewer Michele Leber described Farish's protagonists as "alternately strikingly sensuous and exasperatingly introspective," Jim Dwyer wrote in his *Library Journal* review that through her writing skills, the novelist succeeds in portraying Cristy and Deborah as "multifaceted individuals with compelling stories."

BIOGRAPHICAL AND CRITICAL SOURCES:

PERIODICALS

Belles Lettres, fall, 1992, Bettina Berch, review of *Flower Shadows,* pp. 55-56.

Booklist, October 1, 1989, p. 347; November 15, 1990, p. 654; January 1, 1992, Cynthia Ogorek, review of *Flower Shadows,* p. 810; September 1, 1995, Joanne Wilkinson, review of *If the Tiger,* p. 38; May 1, 2000, Michele Leber, review of *A House in Earnest,* p. 1651.

Book Report, January-February, 1990, Rose M. Kent, review of *Why I'm Already Blue,* p. 46; March-April, 1991, Betty Jones, review of *Shelter for a Seabird,* p. 42; November-December, 1996, Holly Wadsworth, review of *Talking in Animal,* p. 39; May 1, 2000, Michele Leber, review of *A House in Earnest,* p. 1651; April 15, 2003, Carolyn Phelan, review of *The Cat Who Liked Potato Soup,* p. 1477.

Bulletin of the Center for Children's Books, June, 2003, Deborah Stevenson, review of *The Cat Who Liked Potato Soup.*

Choice, October, 1995, N. Tischler, review of *If the Tiger,* p. 291.

Horn Book, January-February, 1997, Jennifer Brabander, review of *Talking in Animal* p. 55.

Kirkus Reviews, November 1, 1989, review of *Why I'm Already Blue,* p. 1591; September 15, 1990, review of *Shelter for a Seabird;* October 15, 1991, review of *Flower Shadows,* pp. 1303-1304; June 15, 1996, review of *Talking in Animal,* p. 897; May 1, 2003, review of *The Cat Who Liked Potato Soup,* p. 676.

Library Journal, May 1, 1992, p. 144; April 15, 2000, Jim Dwyer, review of *A House in Earnest,* p. 122.

New York Times Book Review, January 14, 1996, Laura van Wormer, review of *If the Tiger,* p. 19; October 15, 2000, James Polk, review of *A House in Earnest,* p. 23.

Publishers Weekly, July 14, 1989, review of *Why I'm Already Blue,* p. 80; September 14, 1990, review of *Shelter for a Seabird,* p. 128; October 18, 1991, review of *Flower Shadow,* p. 54; May 8, 1995, review of *If the Tiger,* p. 289; October 7, 1996, review of *Talking in Animal,* p. 76; March 6, 2000, review of *A House in Earnest,* p. 80; May 5, 2003, review of *The Cat Who Liked Potato Soup,* p. 221.

School Library Journal, October, 1989, Bonnie L. Raasch, review of *Why I'm Already Blue,* p. 117; November, 1990, Judie Porter, review of *Shelter for a Seabird,* p. 138; November, 1996, Wendy D. Caldiero, review of *Talking in Animal,* p. 104; July, 2003, Steven Englefried, review of *The Cat Who Liked Potato Soup,* p. 95.

Times (London, England), April 14, 1990.

Times Educational Supplement, June 1, 1990, Mary Cadogan, review of *Why I'm Already Blue,* p. B8.

Voice of Youth Advocates, April, 1989, p. 29; October, 1989, p. 212; April, 1997, Helen Turner, review of *Talking in Animal,* p. 28.

Washington Post Book World, October 8, 1995, Hart Williams, review of *If the Tiger,* p. 8.

Women's Review of Books, July, 1995, Jeanne Schinto, review of *If the Tiger,* p. 31.

ONLINE

Terry Farish Home Page, http://www.terryfarish.com/ (January 3, 2004).*

*   *   *

FEILEN, John
See MAY, Julian

*   *   *

FIELD, Hartry H(amlin) 1946-

PERSONAL: Born November 30, 1946, in Boston, MA; son of Donald T. (a lawyer) and Adelaide (an editor; maiden name, Anderson) Field; children: Elizabeth. *Education:* University of Wisconsin, Madison, B.A., 1967; Harvard University, M.A., 1968, Ph.D., 1972.

ADDRESSES: Office—Department of Philosophy, New York University, 503 Silver Center, 100 Washington Square E, New York, NY 10003. *E-mail*—hf18@nyu.edu.

CAREER: Princeton University, Princeton, NJ, assistant professor of philosophy, 1970-76; University of Southern California, Los Angeles, associate professor, 1976-81, professor of philosophy, 1981-91; City University of New York, New York, NY, Graduate Center, distinguished professor of philosophy and Kornblith chair, 1991-97; New York University, New York, NY, professor of philosophy, 1997—.

MEMBER: American Philosophical Association, Philosophy of Science Association.

AWARDS, HONORS: Grants from National Endowment for the Humanities, 1972-73, and National Science Foundation, 1979-80 and 1982; Guggenheim fellowship, 1979-80; Lakatos Award, 1986, for *Science without Numbers: A Defence of Nominalism.*

WRITINGS:

Science without Numbers: A Defence of Nominalism, Basil Blackwell (Cambridge, MA), 1980.
Realism, Mathematics, and Modality, Basil Blackwell (Cambridge, MA), 1989.
Truth and the Absence of Fact, Oxford University Press (New York, NY), 2001.

Contributor to books, including *Philosophy of Mathematics Today,* edited by Matthias Schirn, Oxford University Press (New York, NY), 1998; *Truth in Mathematics,* edited by H. Garth Dales and Gianluigi Oliveri, Oxford University Press (New York, NY), 1998; *New Essays on the A Priori,* edited by P. Boghossian and C. Peacocke, Oxford University Press (New York, NY), 2000; *Liars and Heaps,* edited by Beall and Glanzberg, Oxford University Press (New York, NY), 2003; *Deflationism and Paradox,* edited by Beall and Armour-Garb, Oxford University Press (New York, NY), 2003; *One Hundred Years of Russell's Paradox: Logical Philosophy Then and Now,* edited by Godehard Link, Walter de Gruyter (New York, NY), 2003. Also contributor to *Oxford Handbook of Metaphysics.* Contributor of numerous articles to philosophy journals, including *Philosophical Review, Mind, Philosophy of Mathematics Today, Journal of Philosophical Logic,* and *Journal of Philosophy.*

SIDELIGHTS: Hartry H. Field once told *CA:* "A general theme throughout my work is the development of a scientific metaphysics and an account of the place of thought, reasoning, and values within such a metaphysics." Field is a professor of philosophy at New York University, where he teaches courses on logic and the philosophy of logic, metaphysics, causation, and mind and language issues.

Hartry's goal in *Science without Numbers: A Defence of Nominalism,* according to *Times Literary Supplement* critic Geoffrey Hunter, is to demolish the traditional argument that the existence of mathematical entities is necessary to an understanding of the physical world and to the science of physics. Field's view, Hunter wrote, is "that there is no need to postulate mathematical entities, or to regard mathematical claims about them as true, in order to pursue science." The author believes that, though mathematics provides convenient symbols for working with physical theories and concepts, the same scientific conclusions can be reached without the use of numbers. Even if numbers are used, he adds, it is not necessary to assume that the mathematical theories are true. They work equally well when mathematical entities are treated as fictions.

Truth and the Absence of Fact consists of thirteen essays on philosophical topics in language, epistemology, and mathematics. A *Directory of American Scholars* writer described this work as containing "outstanding insight" on these topics.

BIOGRAPHICAL AND CRITICAL SOURCES:

BOOKS

Directory of American Scholars, 10th edition, Gale (Detroit, MI), 2001.

PERIODICALS

Times Literary Supplement, February 20, 1981.*

*   *   *

FIELDING, Helen 1958-

PERSONAL: Born February 19, 1958, in England; daughter of a mill manager and a homemaker; companion of Kevin Curran (a television writer and producer); children: one son. *Education:* Oxford University, 1979.

ADDRESSES: Agent—c/o Author Mail, Penguin Putnam, 375 Hudson St., New York, NY 10014.

CAREER: BBC-TV, England, producer, 1979-89; freelance writer, c. 1989—; columnist for the London *Independent,* 1995—.

Helen Fielding

AWARDS, HONORS: British Book Award, 1997, for *Bridget Jones's Diary*.

WRITINGS:

(With Simon Bell and Richard Curtis) *Who's Had Who, in Association with Berk's Rogerage: An Historical Rogister Containing Official Lay Lines of History from the Beginning of Time to the Present Day,* Faber & Faber (Boston, MA), 1987, reissued as *Who's Had Who: An Historical Rogister Containing Official Lay Lines of History from the Beginning of Time to the Present Day,* Warner Books (New York, NY), 1990.

Cause Celeb (novel), Picador (London, England), 1994, Viking (New York, NY), 2001.

Bridget Jones's Diary (novel), Picador (London, England), 1996, Viking (New York, NY), 1998.

Bridget Jones: The Edge of Reason, Viking (New York, NY), 2000.

Bridget Jones's Guide to Life, Penguin (New York, NY), 2001.

Olivia Joules and the Overactive Imagination, Picador (London, England), 2003, Viking (New York, NY), 2004.

Contributor to the *Independent* (London, England) and *Newsweek.* Coauthor of screenplays for *Bridget Jones's Diary* and *Bridget Jones: The Edge of Reason.*

ADAPTATIONS: A film version of *Bridget Jones's Diary* was released in 2001 by Miramax. *Bridget Jones: The Edge of Reason* was filmed for release in 2004.

SIDELIGHTS: Helen Fielding achieved international fame with her humorous novel *Bridget Jones's Diary,* which sold more than four million copies worldwide, and was published in thirty countries. Fielding had already established herself as a producer for the British Broadcasting Corporation; in 1994, she had published her first novel, *Cause Celeb.* Its success led to an offer from the London *Independent* for Fielding to do a column in the persona of a character. The author responded by creating the beloved Bridget Jones, who discussed the often humorous trials of a single British woman over thirty in the column. Bridget and the column proved so popular that Fielding turned her adventures into a novel, *Bridget Jones's Diary,* which became a best-seller in 1996 in the author's native country, and then, two years later, in the United States. *Bridget Jones's Diary* also garnered Fielding the prestigious British Book Award, was made into a highly successful motion picture, and generated two sequels, *Bridget Jones: The Edge of Reason* and *Bridget Jones's Guide to Life.*

Even before *Cause Celeb,* Fielding collaborated with Simon Bell and Richard Curtis on the 1987 volume, *Who's Had Who, in Association with Berk's Rogerage: An Historical Rogister Containing Official Lay Lines of History from the Beginning of Time to the Present Day.* A spoof on the famous volume that outlines the ancestry of all of Great Britain's nobility, the "rogerage" and "rogister" of the subtitles play on the British slang verb "to roger," which means to have sex. One of Fielding's partners in this literary effort, Richard Curtis, was a classmate of hers at Oxford University, and went on to write the screenplay for the popular British film *Four Weddings and a Funeral.*

Cause Celeb features the adventures of Rosie Richardson, an administrator with an international food charity who attempts to escape the consequences of a bad love affair by traveling to Africa to aid famine relief. The book uses flashbacks to show readers Rosie's difficulties with television presenter Oliver Marchant, but in the novel's present timelines, she finds herself attracted to a young doctor also employed by her relief agency. The pair investigate the rumored possibility of a locust plague that threatens to send the region they explore into starvation; when their agency ignores the evidence, they return to England to enlist the aid of various celebrities, including Marchant, to publicize the coming disaster.

Reviewers of *Cause Celeb* frequently commented on Fielding's mingling humor with the serious subject of African famine relief. Nicola Walker in the *Times Literary Supplement* maintained that the novel was not completely successful. "*Cause Celeb* is neatly plotted and its attack on the iniquities of the Western media machine is topical and legitimate," Walker conceded. "However, Fielding is not a subtle or imaginative satirist, and the result is an uneasy combination of celebrity-bashing and African misery." In contrast, Kate Kellaway noted in the *Observer* that "*Cause Celeb* is amazingly poised. The plot is about as challenging as walking to Africa in stilettos but is managed without a wobble. What makes it such a pleasure to read," Kellaway continued, "is its variety of tone: flip, flirtatious, serious, mocking and moving." Another *Observer* reviewer praised the "bitter-sweet power" of Fielding's "comedy of manners."

It was Fielding's second novel that made her a literary celebrity. For *Bridget Jones's Diary,* the author knew that she could not just take the columns and put them into book form. According to Sarah Van Boven in *Newsweek,* Fielding based "the story on *Pride and Prejudice*" by Jane Austen. She quipped to Van Boven: "There's several hundred years of market testing on that plot." Hence the last name of the man that Bridget finally ends up with is Darcy. Bridget takes note of the irony before taking a liking to him: "It struck me as pretty ridiculous to be called Mr. Darcy and to stand on your own looking snooty at a party. It's like being called Heathcliff and insisting on spending the entire evening in the garden, shouting 'Cathy!' and banging your head against a tree." Before Bridget and Darcy come together, however, many pages are filled with Bridget's laments about bad dates, inappropriate relationships in the workplace, her parents' pressure on her to find a husband, and family friends who make ticking noises at her to suggest the running out of her biological clock. Bridget also struggles with her weight, or her perceptions of it; Fielding confided to Alexandra Jacobs in *Entertainment Weekly* that

"Bridget's height is kept deliberately vague, like her age, so people can fill in the rest as they choose to imagine and identify with their chosen level of paranoia." The heroine fights daily to quit drinking and smoking, and records the amount of alcohol consumed and the number of cigarettes she smoked in each day's diary entry along with her caloric intake.

Bridget Jones's Diary was met with predominantly favorable response, though some feminist critics lambasted the novel. Alex Kuczynski in the *New York Times* explained that she knew that "*Bridget Jones* is satire, a sassy spoof of urban manners. But Bridget is such a sorry spectacle, wallowing in her man-crazed helplessness, that her foolishness cannot be excused." Van Boven, however, asserted that "Bridget's post-feminist sorrows could be tedious in the hands of a less charming writer—they include such trivialities as the inability to find a pair of tights in her bureau without holes or bits of tissue stuck all over them." But, the critic countered, "Fielding has managed to create an unforgettably droll character." Similarly, Shane Watson hailed Bridget in *Harper's Bazaar* as "a wonderfully quirky comic creation," and elaborated: "To come up with a character who is loveable, ingenuous and a crack social commentator called for a mixture of kooky wit and razor-sharp professionalism." Schulman, in another review for the *Times Literary Supplement,* declared: "Quotation fails this novel. Its humour is not remotely aphoristic; and no quotation can convey the quality that constitutes Bridget's claim to be as durable a comic figure as Nigel Molesworth or the Provincial Lady." She went on to conclude that: "*Bridget Jones's Diary* rings with the unmistakable tone of something that is true to the marrow; it defines what it describes. I know for certain that if I were a young, single, urban woman, I would finish this book crying, 'Bridget Jones, c'est moi.'"

The success of *Bridget Jones's Diary* led to a sequel: *Bridget Jones: The Edge of Reason.* The fast-paced plot includes Bridget's disastrous interview with actor Colin Firth, her apparent happiness with Mr. Darcy, notes on her mother's trip to Africa, and even her imprisonment in a jail in Thailand. "Fans will adore this," advised Francine Fialkoff in *Library Journal,* who remarked that *The Edge of Reason* "actually has more of a plot than the original." Fialkoff found that "sidesplitting humor is still present" in Fielding's writing, and noted that if Jones seems "dumber and ditzier" here than in the original book, "it's not necessarily a drawback," as these qualities are part of Bridget's charm. Other reviewers found that another volume of Bridget was too much, especially since the character seemed to have learned nothing from any of her experiences. For example, Elizabeth Gleick wrote in *Time,* "Hapless can be endearing. But hapless with no sign of a learning curve, in a sequel that has none of the novelty of the original yet is much longer now that will try the patience of even a Bridget fan." The reviewer observed that Bridget seemed "unable to learn from her mistakes, move forward or pull herself together the tiniest bit," and concluded: "The fact that the reader is so much smarter and more observant than Bridget is, this time round, irritating rather than suspenseful." A reviewer for *Publishers Weekly* allowed that after a time, "Bridget's propensity to misunderstand and bungle everything becomes predictable," but still had praise for the book. The heroine's ups and downs with her Mr. Darcy, her attempts to deal with the impossible assignments handed out by her boss, and her trials in dealing with a carpenter who ruins her apartment are humorous, and Bridget's disastrous vacation in Thailand is "a genuinely suspenseful and hilarious episode." Fielding further capitalized on the popularity of her heroine by publishing a short parody of a self-help book, titled *Bridget Jones's Guide to Life.*

In her next book, Fielding created a heroine who is superficially worlds away from Bridget Jones. *Olivia Joules and the Overactive Imagination* is a fast-paced thriller featuring a young, female spy who must confront terrorists, bombs, and assorted other life-threatening scenarios. Reviewing the book for *Asia Africa Intelligence Wire,* Julian Satterthwaite called it "shamelessly of-the-minute," adding: "The novel aims to satisfy the airport blockbuster crowd with a litany of brand names and far-flung locations." While the title character may seem a far cry from Bridget Jones, however, Satterthwaite notes that like Fielding's earlier creation, Joules also struggles with male-female relationships and phones her girlfriends when things go wrong. The novel is really "firmly in Fielding territory," according to Satterthwaite; "indeed, it reads like the fantasies Bridget Jones might have had while not occupied pursuing Mr. Darcy. Get the guy and save the world, all while wearing the right accessories: This is Bridget Jones empowered." Amy Jenkins, reviewing the book for the London *Observer,* also noted that while Olivia is trim, effective, and superficially confident, "Bridget keeps bubbling back up to the surface, primarily because Fielding cannot resist those

klutzy BJ moments." Jenkins wrote, however, that "What was lovable in Bridget is mildly irritating in Olivia." Yet the reviewer concluded that "there is plenty of lively action and amusement to sweep you along, to say nothing of a marvellously cosy tone that is very addictive, even if it doesn't supply much dramatic tension."

Discussing her work with John Walsh in an interview for the London *Independent,* Fielding commented: "I'm interested in trying different kinds of writing. But I prefer being funny as a way of looking at things, because it's more enjoyable to read. I don't like books that are trying to impress rather than entertain. I like books that make you want to turn the page and see what happens."

BIOGRAPHICAL AND CRITICAL SOURCES:

BOOKS

Dictionary of Literary Biography, Volume 231: *British Novelists since 1960, Fourth Series,* Gale (Detroit, MI), 2000.
Newsmakers 2000, Issue 4, Gale (Detroit, MI), 2000.

PERIODICALS

Asia Africa Intelligence Wire, November 22, 2003, Boniface Linley, "From the Diary to the Dire"; December 14, 2003, Julian Satterthwaite, review of *Olivia Joules and the Overactive Imagination.*
Book, January, 2001, Mimi O'Connor, review of *Cause Celeb,* p. 70.
Booklist, December 1, 2000, Kristine Huntley, review of *Cause Celeb,* p. 675; July, 2000, Mary McCay, review of *Bridget Jones: The Edge of Reason,* p. 2054.
Daily Telegraph, June 6, 1998; April 13, 2000.
Dallas Morning News, April 16, 2000, p. 9J.
Entertainment Weekly, June 19, 1998, p. 68; July 31, 1998, p. 14; March 3, 2000, Lisa Schwarzbaum, review of *Bridget Jones: The Edge of Reason,* p. 65.
Harper's Bazaar, July, 1998, p. 62.
Independent (London, England), November 10, 2003, John Walsh, "From Singletons to Spies," p. 2.

Library Journal, December, 1999, Catherine Swenson, review of *Bridget Jones's Diary,* p. 205; February 1, 2000, Francine Fialkoff, review of *Bridget Jones: The Edge of Reason,* p. 116; June 15, 2000, Catherine Swenson, review of *Bridget Jones: The Edge of Reason* (audio version), p. 136; December, 2000, Francine Fialkoff, review of *Cause Celeb,* p. 187; September 15, 2001, Catherine Swenson, review of *Cause Celeb,* p. 127.

New Republic, September 7, 1998, p. 36.

New Statesman, July 26, 1999, review of *Bridget Jones's Diary,* p. 51; November 24, 2003, Zoe Williams, "Killer Joules," p. 54.

Newsweek, May 4, 1998, p. 82; June 29, 1998, pp. 64, 66; March 6, 2000, p. 69.

Newsweek International, November 29, 1999, p. 101.

New York, April 23, 2001, Peter Rainer, review of *Bridget Jones's Diary* (motion picture), p. 138.

New Yorker, April 16, 2001, Anthony Lane, review of *Bridget Jones's Diary* (motion picture), p. 90.

New York Times, June 14, 1998, section 9, p. 1; February 27, 2000.

New York Times Book Review, February 27, 2000, Anita Gates, review of *Bridget Jones: The Edge of Reason,* p. 12; February 25, 2001, Maggie Galehouse, review of *Cause Celeb,* p. 20.

New York Times Magazine, February 20, 2000, Susan Dominus, interview with Helen Fielding, p. 18.

Observer, July 17, 1994, p. 17; July 24, 1994, p. 14; November 9, 2003, Amy Jenkins, review of *Olivia Joules and the Overactive Imagination,* p. 15.

People, June 22, 1998, p. 199.

Publishers Weekly, January 24, 2000, review of *Bridget Jones: The Edge of Reason,* p. 293; April 3, 2000, review of *Bridget Jones: The Edge of Reason,* p. 36; December 11, 2000, review of *Cause Celeb,* p. 61; May 13, 2000, p. 22.

Rocky Mountain News, July 12, 1998, p. 1E.

Rolling Stone, April 26, 2001, Peter Travers, review of *Bridget Jones's Diary* (motion picture), p. 66.

Time, March 13, 2000, Elizabeth Gleick, review of *Bridget Jones: The Edge of Reason,* p. 88.

Time Canada, March 27, 2000, review of *Bridget Jones: The Edge of Reason,* p. 52A.

Time International, April 16, 2001, Richard Corliss, review of *Bridget Jones's Diary* (motion picture), p. 68.

Times Literary Supplement, August 19, 1994, p. 20; November 1, 1996, p. 26.

USA Today, May 28, 1998, p. 5D.

Vogue, February, 2001, Hilton Als, review of *Cause Celeb,* p. 196.

ONLINE

Internet Movie Database, http://www.imdb.com/ (November 7, 2003).*

*   *   *

FOREYT, John P(aul) 1943-

PERSONAL: Surname is pronounced For-et; born April 6, 1943, in Manitowoc, WI; son of John Otto and Ann Rose (Hynek) Foreyt. *Education:* University of Wisconsin—Madison, B.S., 1965; Florida State University, M.S., 1967, Ph.D., 1969.

ADDRESSES: Home—7708 Nairn, Houston, TX 77074. *Office*—Department of Psychiatry and Behavioral Sciences, Baylor College of Medicine, 6535 Fannin, MS F700, Houston, TX 77030. *E-mail*—jforeyt@ bcm.tmc.edu.

CAREER: University of Southern California Medical Center, Los Angeles, intern, 1968-69; Florida State University, Tallahassee, assistant professor of psychology, 1969-74; Baylor College of Medicine, Houston, TX, associate professor and director of Diet Modification Center, beginning 1974, currently professor of medicine and psychiatry and director of Nutrition Research Clinic. Private practice of clinical psychology, 1975—.

MEMBER: American Psychological Association, Academy for Behavioral Medicine Research, Association for the Advancement of Behavior Therapy, Behavior Therapy and Research (fellow), American Institute of Nutrition, American Dietetic Association (honorary member).

WRITINGS:

(Editor, with Julian C. Davis) *Medical Examiner's Source Book,* C. C. Thomas (Springfield, IL), 1975.

(Editor, with Ben J. Williams and Sander Martin) *Obesity: Behavioral Approaches to Dietary Management,* Brunner (New York, NY), 1976.

(Editor) *Behavioral Treatments of Obesity,* Pergamon (New York, NY), 1977.

(Editor, with Diana P. Rathjen) *Cognitive Behavior Therapy: Research and Application,* Plenum (New York, NY), 1978.

(Editor, with Diana P. Rathjen) *Social Competence: Interventions for Children and Adults,* Pergamon (New York, NY), 1982.

(Editor, with Ben J. Williams and G. Ken Goodrick) *Pediatric Behavioral Medicine,* Praeger (New York, NY), 1983.

(With Michael de Bakey, Antonio Gotto, Jr., and Lynne Scott) *The Living Heart Diet,* Simon & Schuster (New York, NY), 1984, revised edition, Fireside (St. Louis, MO), 1995.

(Editor, with Kelly Brownell) *Handbook of Eating Disorders,* Basic Books (New York, NY), 1986.

(With G. Terence Wilson, Cyril M. Franks, and Philip C. Kendall) *Review of Behavior Therapy,* Volume 11, Guilford (New York, NY), 1987.

(With G. Terence Wilson, Cyril M. Franks, and Philip C. Kendall) *Review of Behavior Therapy,* Volume 12, Guilford (New York, NY), 1990.

(With G. Ken Goodrick) *Living without Dieting,* Harrison, 1992, Warner Books (New York, NY), 1994.

(With Michael de Bakey, Antonio Gotto, Jr., and Lynne Scott) *The Living Heart Brand Name Shoppers Guide,* Mastermedia, 1992.

(With Kristine Napier) *The Xenical Advantage: How to Use the Remarkable New FDA-Approved Drug to Lose Weight Faster—and Keep It Off—Safely and Effectively,* Simon & Schuster (New York, NY), 1999.

(Editor, with others) *Lifestyle Obesity Management,* Blackwell (Malden, MA), 2003.

Member of scientific advisory board, *BioNutritional Encyclopedia.* Contributor of scientific articles to professional journals.

SIDELIGHTS: John P. Foreyt is a weight-loss scientist whose research and writing deals with many aspects of obesity-related illness and coping mechanisms for long-term dieters. Foreyt's books include the bestselling *The Living Heart Diet* and *Living without Dieting,* both of which address the permanent lifestyle changes necessary for cardiovascular health and the maintenance of a healthy body weight. A *Publishers Weekly* reviewer felt that the revised edition of *The Living Heart Diet* displays a "workmanlike approach" that "will help readers make changes for a more healthful diet."

Foreyt works at the Baylor College of Medicine in Houston, where he has embarked on a study of long-term health benefits to those who lose weight and keep it off. He once told *CA:* "*The Living Heart Diet* required seven years of research. Hopefully it will help readers reduce some of the cardiovascular risk factors associated with heart disease."

BIOGRAPHICAL AND CRITICAL SOURCES:

PERIODICALS

Environmental Nutrition, February, 1989, Laura Conway, "Coping with Diet Relapse, Preventing Diet Collapse," p. 6; August, 1992, review of *The Living Heart Brand Name Shoppers Guide,* p. 8.
Houston Chronicle, January 17, 1996, Leslie Sowers, "Two Baylor Doctors Want to Study Diet Drugs," p. 4; November 16, 1999, Claudia Feldman, "Dieting Dilemma," p. 1.
Publishers Weekly, December 18, 1995, review of *The Living Heart Diet,* p. 50.

ONLINE

Baylor College of Medicine Web site, http://www.bcm.tmc.edu/ (November 5, 2003), "John P. Foreyt."*

*   *   *

FOSTER, Don
    See FOSTER, Donald W(ayne)

*   *   *

FOSTER, Donald W(ayne) 1950-
(Don Foster)

PERSONAL: Born June 22, 1950, in Chicago, IL; son of David C. and Dorothy (Garasha) Foster; married Gwen Bell (an artist), 1974; children: Richard Blake, Eric W. *Education:* University of California, Santa Barbara, M.A., 1983, Ph.D., 1985. *Politics:* Independent.

ADDRESSES: Office—P.O. Box 388, Vassar College, 124 Raymond Ave., Poughkeepsie, NY 12601. *E-mail*—foster@vassser.edu.

CAREER: University of California, Santa Barbara, visiting lecturer, 1984-86; Vassar College, Poughkeepsie, NY, assistant professor, 1986-89, associate professor of English, 1990-91, Jean Webster chair of dramatic literature, 1992—. Visiting lecturer, College of Creative Studies, University of California, Santa Barbara.

MEMBER: American Association of University Professors, Modern Language Association of America, Shakespeare Association of America, Renaissance English Text Society, Folger Shakespeare Library, Society of Textual Scholars.

AWARDS, HONORS: William Riley Parker Prize, Modern Language Association of America, 1987, for article "Master W. H., RIP"; Delaware Shakespeare Prize, University of Delaware, 1987, for *Elegy by W. S.: A Study in Attribution.*

WRITINGS:

Elegy by W. S.: A Study in Attribution, University of Delaware Press (Newark, DE), 1989.
(As Don Foster) *Author Unknown: On the Trail of Anonymous,* Holt (New York, NY), 2000.

Contributor to *The Bible and Narrative Tradition,* edited by Frank McConnell, Oxford University Press, 1986. Also contributor of articles to literary journals.

SIDELIGHTS: "For Don Foster," wrote Brian Vickers in the *Times Literary Supplement,* "1996 was a pretty good year." Some years before, Donald W. Foster—a professor of English at Vassar College and a literary "detective" who specializes in tracing the identities of anonymous authors—revealed his evidence that a little-known 1612 poem called "A Funerall Elegye" ("A Funeral Elegy") was written, anonymously, by William Shakespeare. The news sent ripples through the scholarly community, with Foster attracting both detractors and defenders. He published his findings in the 1989 monograph *Elegy by W. S.: A Study in Attribution.* In 1996 the media picked up on Foster's research to assert their own evidence that the verse suggested Shakespeare's alleged homosexuality.

In the wake of the resulting media frenzy, Foster became a celebrity, invited to identify the secret author of the bestselling political *roman à clef, Primary Colors.* After researching the wording of the book, and comparing it with the literary stylings of numerous journalists, Foster correctly fingered the "Anonymous" author as *New York* and *Newsweek* columnist Joe Klein, who at first denied it, then eventually owned up to the authorship. The professor was called on again in 1997 to examine the so-named "Unabomber Manifesto," a lengthy tract written by the suspect in a series of mail-bomb attacks that killed and injured several victims. He participated in the investigation of a ransom note tied to the murder of child beauty-queen JonBenet Ramsey; Foster also assisted the FBI in finding the perpetrator of the bomb set off in Atlanta's Olympic Centennial Park. Foster then made headlines again when he unmasked the author of the classic verse *A Visit from St. Nicholas* (the poem that begins, "'Twas the night before Christmas . . .") not as Clement Moore, "but rather a bon vivant named Henry Livingston," as David Roberts remarked in a *Smithsonian* article.

Foster recounted his adventures in what he called "literary forensics" in his 2001 book *Author Unknown: On the Trail of Anonymous.* In his view, no two people use words exactly the same way. Thus through careful examination of word choices and syntax patterns—a process that involves intricate reading combined with modern technology—Foster can ascertain the identities of those who have written documents either anonymously or under a pseudonym. In the *Primary Colors* case, for example, Foster noticed that "Anonymous" shared with Klein some similar turns of phrase, such as "scruffy," "squishy," and "talky." As well, Klein's work and that of Anonymous used "mode" frequently, as in "listening mode," "explain mode," and "campaign mode."

Times Literary Supplement writer Brian Vickers commented on "Foster's egotistical self-presentation" in *Author Unknown,* saying that the volume "falls easily between a scholarly and a popularizing approach, too often giving anecdotal accounts of fairly trivial incidents instead of solid linguistic analysis." *London Review of Books* contributor John Lancaster commented, "*Author Unknown* tells a story a little different from the one it thinks it is telling. . . . The reader sees Foster as a much more bumptious, aggressive, disingenuous, insensitive, on-the-make figure than the country-mouse-cum-fearless-quester-after-truth he presents himself as being." But the same work was cited by *Spectator* critic Philip Hensher as "a deeply entertaining book on an original subject, which seems to me sound and convincing."

The dust had barely settled on *Author Unknown* when Foster made a stunning announcement. The poem *A Funeral Elegy,* which had launched him into the spotlight, the author said, was not in fact written by Shakespeare. In a message dated June 12, 2002, and posted on the Internet site www.shaksper.net, Foster wrote that "another poet and dramatist was more likely author of the poem," as *New York Times* reporter William Niederkorn stated. Foster and associate Richard Abrams went on to say that a Shakespeare contemporary named John Ford was the most likely author of "A Funeral Elegy." This theory had been put forward by Gilles Monsarrat, a professor of languages at the University of Burgundy in France. "I know good evidence when I see it," Foster posted on the Web site, "and I predict that Monsarrat will carry the day. No one who cannot rejoice in the discovery of his own mistakes deserves to be called a scholar."

In his *Smithsonian* profile of Foster, Roberts called the literary sleuth "a modest man, and celebrity has not come easily to him. He has tried hard to keep his public persona separate from his Vassar life. As I sat in on his Shakespeare class, one of his students . . . told me that in a weary moment, a week or two after his book had been published, the professor had said, 'I wish this were all over and I could go back to being a quaint old English professor.'"

BIOGRAPHICAL AND CRITICAL SOURCES:

PERIODICALS

Barron's, March 5, 2001, review of *Author Unknown: On the Trail of Anonymous,* p. 40.
London Review of Books, August 23, 2001, John Lanchester, "Lumpy, Semi-Dorky, Slouchy, Smarmy," review of *Author Unknown,* pp. 7-8.

New Statesman, May 28, 2001, Robert Macfarlane, "Reading Tony Blair," review of *Author Unknown,* pp. 55-56.
New York Times, June 20, 2002, William Niederkorn, "A Scholar Recants on His 'Shakespeare' Discovery," p. E1.
Publishers Weekly, November 6, 2000, review of *Author Unknown,* p. 84.
Smithsonian, September, 2001, David Roberts, "Dan Foster Has a Way with Words," p. 100.
Spectator (London, England), May 5, 2001, Philip Hensher, "Who Done It?," pp. 35-36.
Sunday Telegraph (London, England), June 23, 2002, Charles Laurence, "U.S. Literary Sleuth Admits Error over Discovery of 'Lost Shakespeare' Poem," p. 30.
Times Literary Supplement, June 8, 1990; July 6, 2001, Brian Vickers, "Retrieving It," p. 27.

ONLINE

Shaksper Web site, http://www.shaksper.net/ (November 1, 2003), material addressing author's research.*

*   *   *

FOSTER, Richard J(ames) 1942-

PERSONAL: Born May 3, 1942, in Albuquerque, NM; son of Lee Sherman and Marie (Temperance) Foster; married Alice Carolynn Kerr (a speech therapist), March 18, 1967; children: Joel Timothy, Nathan Lee. *Education:* George Fox College, B.A., 1964; Fuller Theological Seminary, D.Th.P., 1970. *Politics:* Democrat.

ADDRESSES: Office—Renovare, 8 Inverness Dr. E, Suite 102, Englewood, CA 80112-5624. *E-mail*—richard@renovare.org.

CAREER: Alamitos Friends Church, Garden Grove, CA, minister of youth, 1962-67; ordained clergyman of Society of Friends (Quakers), 1967; Family Counseling and Research Center, Garden Grove, counselor, 1967-68; Arcadia Friends Church, Arcadia, CA, associate pastor, 1968-70; Woodlake Avenue Friends Church, Canoga Park, CA, pastor, 1970-74;

Richard J. Foster

Newberg Friends Church, Newberg, OR, pastor, 1974-79; Friends University, Wichita, KS, professor of theology and writer-in-residence, beginning 1979; Renovare, Englewood, CA, founder and director. George Fox College, adjunct professor, 1974-79. Public lecturer. Member of publications board of California Yearly Meeting of Friends.

AWARDS, HONORS: Writer of the Year designation, Warner Pacific College, 1978, for *Celebration of Discipline;* Christy Award, Gold Medallion Award, and Logos Bookstores Religious Book Award for Inspirational Book, all 1982, all for *Freedom of Simplicity;* named Most Significant Author of the Year, Logos Bookstores, 1982; honorary doctor of letters, George Fox College, 1987.

WRITINGS:

Quaker Concern in Race Relations: Then and Now, Martin Keller Associates, 1970.

Celebration of Discipline: The Path to Spiritual Growth, Harper (New York, NY), 1978, twentieth-anniversary revised edition, HarperSanFrancisco (San Francisco, CA), 1998.

(Contributor) John L. Bond, editor, *Friends Search for Wholeness,* Friends United Press (Richmond, IN), 1978.

Freedom of Simplicity, Harper (San Francisco, CA), 1981.

Study Guide for Celebration of Discipline, Harper (San Francisco, CA), 1983.

Meditative Prayer (booklet), Inter-Varsity Press (Downer's Grove, IL), 1983.

Money, Sex, and Power: The Challenge of the Disciplined Life (with study guide), Harper (San Francisco, CA), 1985, published as *The Challenge of the Disciplined Life: Christian Reflections on Money, Sex, and Power,* 1989.

(With Kathryn A. Yanni) *Celebrating the Disciplines: A Journal Workbook to Accompany "Celebration of Discipline,"* HarperSanFrancisco (San Francisco, CA), 1992.

Prayer: Finding the Heart's True Home, HarperSanFrancisco (San Francisco, CA), 1992.

(Editor, with James Bryan Smith) *Devotional Classics: Selected Readings for Individuals and Groups,* HarperSanFrancisco (San Francisco, CA), 1993.

Coming Home: A Prayer Journal, HarperSanFrancisco (San Francisco, CA), 1994.

Prayers from the Heart, HarperSanFrancisco (San Francisco, CA), 1994.

Seeking the Kingdom: Devotions for the Daily Journey of Faith, HarperSanFrancisco (San Francisco, CA), 1995.

(With Janet Lindeblad Janzen) *Songs for Renewal: A Devotional Guide to the Riches of Our Best-Loved Songs and Hymns,* HarperSanFrancisco (San Francisco, CA), 1995.

(With Jana Rea) *A Spiritual Formation Journal: A Renovare Resource for Spiritual Renewal,* HarperSanFrancisco (San Francisco, CA), 1996.

Streams of Living Water: Celebrating the Great Traditions of Christian Faith, HarperSanFrancisco (San Francisco, CA), 1998.

(Editor, with Emilie Griffin) *Spiritual Classics: Selected Readings for Individuals and Groups on the Twelve Spiritual Disciplines,* HarperSanFrancisco (San Francisco, CA), 2000.

(Author of introduction) *Celtic Daily Prayer: Prayers and Readings from the Northumbria Community,* HarperSanFrancisco (San Francisco, CA), 2002.

Also author of audiotapes *The Liberty of Discipline* (based on his book *Celebration of Discipline*) and *Practicing Simplicity* (based on his book *Freedom of Simplicity*), both Word Publishing, 1983. Author of film series *Celebration of Discipline* (based on his book of the same title), Victory Films, 1984; also author of video *The Challenge to the Disciplined Life: A Christian View of Money, Sex, and Power*, David C. Cook, 1987. Contributor of column "Going Deeper" to *Faith and Work*; contributor of articles to periodicals in the United States and Europe.

Celebration of Discipline has been translated into Chinese, German, Dutch, Spanish, Portuguese, Swedish, Korean, and Japanese.

ADAPTATIONS: Money, Sex, Power: The Challenge of the Disciplined Life was recorded as an audiobook, Harper Audio, 1988.

SIDELIGHTS: The premise for Richard J. Foster's bestselling *Celebration of Discipline: The Path to Spiritual Growth* lies in its opening lines: "Superficiality is the curse of our age. . . . The desperate need today is not for a greater number of intelligent, or gifted people, but for deep people." Foster defines a theological solution to this "curse" of superficiality by introducing and examining twelve basic Christian principles: four "inward disciplines" (meditation, prayer, fasting, study), four "outward disciplines" (simplicity, solitude, submission, service), and four "corporate disciplines" (confession, worship, guidance, celebration). With its updated editions, study guides, and tape and video incarnations, *Celebration of Discipline* has become a contemporary Christian classic with wide appeal across sectarian and national lines. In its aftermath Foster has become a well-known author of books and articles that guide Christian believers to a deeper understanding of their faith. He is also the founder of Renovare, an ecumenical spiritual revival movement.

Foster's books vary in scope from wide treatments of the history of the Christian faith in *Streams of Living Water: The Great Traditions of the Christian Faith* to works intended for use as daily devotional or prayer guides. Into the latter category fall *Seeking the Kingdom: Devotions for the Daily Journey of Faith* and *Prayer: Finding the Heart's True Home*. A *Publishers Weekly* reviewer praised *Streams of Living Water*

for its "engaging writing and thoughtful presentation," noting that Foster is "adept at simplifying diffuse subjects." Another *Publishers Weekly* reviewer felt that the devotions in *Seeking the Kingdom* "are gentle yet speak directly to the heart." *Commonweal* correspondent Lawrence S. Cunningham concluded that *Prayer: Finding the Heart's True Home* is "an extremely readable and non-technical work of devotion in the best sense of the term."

BIOGRAPHICAL AND CRITICAL SOURCES:

BOOKS

Foster, Richard J., *Celebration of Discipline: The Path of Spiritual Growth*, Harper (New York, NY), 1978, revised edition, 1988.

PERIODICALS

America, December 9, 2000, Richard J. Hauser, "United under the Same Spirit: Ecumenical Reading," p. 24.
Christian Century, February 24, 1993, Malcolm Boyd, review of *Prayer: Finding the Heart's True Home*, p. 215; April 24, 2002, Richard A. Kauffman, review of *Celtic Daily Prayer: Prayers and Readings from the Northumbria Community*, p. 36.
Commonweal, March 26, 1993, Lawrence S. Cunningham, review of *Prayer: Finding the Heart's True Home*, p. 26.
Publishers Weekly, July 10, 1995, review of *Seeking the Kingdom: Devotions for the Daily Journey of Faith*, p. 28; September 28, 1998, review of *Streams of Living Water: The Great Traditions of the Christian Faith*, p. 93.

ONLINE

Renovare Web site, http://www.renovare.org/ (November 7, 2003).*

*   *   *

FOSTER, Steven 1957-

PERSONAL: Born February 27, 1957, in Portland, ME; son of Herbert (a builder) and Hope (a teacher; maiden name, Shain) Foster; married Jude Farar (a nurse), May, 1987; children: Colin, Abbey. *Hobbies and other interests:* Collecting books related to economic botany.

ADDRESSES: Home—P.O. Box 106, Eureka Springs, AR 72632. *Office*—Steven Foster Group, General Delivery, CR 158, Brixey, MO 65618.

CAREER: Shaker Community, Sabbathday Lake, ME, herbalist, 1974-78; Volunteers in Service to America (VISTA), Washington, DC, director of Herb Garden Project in Santa Cruz, CA, 1979; Ozark Resources Center, Brixey, MO, research director of Ozark Beneficial Plant Project, 1983-87; freelance writer, technical editor, photographer, and consultant in Eureka Springs, AR, 1987—; currently president, Steven Foster Group (stock photography provider), Brixey, MO. Izard Ozark Native Seeds (retail mail order company), proprietor, 1983-88. Organic Herb Growers and Producers Coop, member of founding board of directors, 1978-80; Santa Cruz County Community Gardens, member of board of directors, 1979; Arkansas Woodlands Heritage Resource Center and Museum, member of advisory committee. Clear Spring School, vice president of board of directors, 1988-91; American Botanical Council, special publications editor, 1989—.

MEMBER: International Herb Growers and Marketers Association (member of board of directors, 1989-92), American Herb Association, American Horticultural Society, American Institute of the History of Pharmacy, American Rock Garden Society, American Society of Pharmacognosy, Council of Biology Editors, Council for Botanical and Horticultural Libraries, National Audubon Society, Society for Economic Botany, Society of Ethnobiology, Canadian Wildflower Society, Eastern Native Plant Alliance, Arkansas Native Plant Society (charter member), Missouri Native Plant Society, Hunt Institute for Botanical Documentation, Josselyn Botanical Society, New England Botanical Club, Southern Appalachian Botanical Club.

WRITINGS:

(And photographer) *Herbal Bounty: The Gentle Art of Herb Culture,* Gibbs M. Smith (Salt Lake City, UT), 1984, revised edition published as *Herbal Renaissance: Growing, Using, and Understanding Herbs in the Modern World,* Gibbs-Smith (Salt Lake City, UT), 1993.

(Photographer) Bob Conrow and Arlene Hecksel, *Herbal Pathfinders,* Woodbridge Press, 1984.

(With James A. Duke, and photographer) *A Field Guide to Medicinal Plants: Eastern and Central North America,* Houghton Mifflin (Boston, MA), 1990, 2nd edition published as *A Field Guide to Medicinal Plants and Herbs of Eastern and Central North America,* 2000.

Echinacea: Nature's Immune Enhancer, Healing Arts Press (Rochester, VT), 1991.

(With Yue Chongxi) *Herbal Emissaries: Bringing Chinese Herbs to the West,* Healing Arts Press (Rochester, VT), 1992.

(With Roger Caras) *A Field Guide to Venomous Animals and Poisonous Plants of North America,* Houghton Mifflin (Boston, MA), 1994, expanded edition, 1998.

Forest Pharmacy: Medicinal Plants in American Forests, Forest History Society (Durham, NC), 1995.

Herbs for Your Health: A Handy Guide for Knowing and Using 50 Common Herbs, Interweave Press (Loveland, CO), 1996, expanded edition published as *One Hundred One Medicinal Herbs: An Illustrated Guide,* 1998.

(With Albert Y. Leung) *Encyclopedia of Common Natural Ingredients Used in Drugs and Cosmetics,* 2nd edition, Wiley (New York, NY), 1996.

Steven Foster's Guide to Herbal Dosages: How Much? How Often? What Not to Take, Interweave Press (Loveland, CO), 1999.

(With Varro E. Tyler) *Tyler's Honest Herbal: A Sensible Guide to the Use of Herbs and Related Remedies,* 4th edition, Haworth Herbal Press (New York), 1999.

(With Linda B. White) *The Herbal Drugstore: The Best Natural Over-the-Counter and Prescription Medicines,* Rodale (Emmaus, PA), 2000.

(Photographer) Ellen Evert Hopman, *Walking the World in Wonder: A Children's Herbal,* Healing Arts Press (Rochester, VT), 2000.

(With Christopher Hobbs) *A Field Guide to Western Medicinal Plants and Herbs,* Houghton Mifflin (Boston, MA), 2002.

Contributor to anthologies, including *Herbs, Spices, and Medicinal Plants: Recent Advances in Botany, Horticulture, and Pharmacology,* Volume IV, edited by L. E. Craker and J. E. Simon, Oryx, 1989. Contributor of articles, reviews, and photographs to professional journals and newspapers. Botanical editor, *Well-Being,* 1979-82; book review editor, *Herb News,* 1980-82; *Business of Herbs,* associate editor, 1985—, guest editor, 1986 and 1987; *HerbalGram,* contributing editor,

1985-89, associate editor, 1989—; editor, *Herb Business Bulletin,* 1986-88, and *Botanical and Herb Reviews,* 1989—; contributing editor, *Herb Quarterly* and *Bestways,* both 1989; associate editor and member of editorial board, *Journal of Herbs, Spices, and Medicinal Plants,* 1991—.

SIDELIGHTS: Steven Foster once told *CA:* "At the age of seventeen, I began my career at the Sabbathday Lake Shaker Community, America's oldest herb business, dating to 1799. There I established three acres of herb gardens, and there I came under the tutelage of the Maine botanist Les Eastman and Dr. Shiu Ying Hu of Harvard University's Arnold Arboretum. Both pushed my botanical interests forward, and Dr. Hu stimulated my interest in the botany of East Asia and the herbal traditions of China. This led me to study source plants of Chinese medicine with Professor Yue Chongxi in Beijing in 1987." This study resulted in the 1992 work *Herbal Emissaries: Bringing Chinese Herbs to the West,* which *Library Journal* contributor Katharine Galloway Garska called "an excellent resource for alternative medicine collections."

In the nearly thirty years since beginning his study of herbs and plants, Foster has become one of this country's most respected experts in the field, with over a dozen books to his credit. He is also a noted photographer of medicinal plants, with over 120,000 photos in his stock collection. "I know the plants that I photograph: their names, botany, history, and human connection (use)," Foster explained on his Web site. "I feel this gives me a special relationship to the plant as it reveals its beauty."

Foster's intimate knowledge of useful herbs is on display in several of his works, from his first book, 1984's *Herbal Bounty: The Gentle Art of Herb Culture,* to the various Peterson's Field Guides on medicinal and poisonous plants he has coauthored. His most popular work is *Herbs for Your Health: A Handy Guide for Knowing and Using 50 Common Herbs,* which he later expanded into *One Hundred One Medicinal Herbs: An Illustrated Guide.* This work contains straightforward information for the layperson on the use, preparation, and proper dosage of various medicinal plants, as well as the science behind their use. Science is also emphasized in *Tyler's Honest Herbal: A Sensible Guide to the Use of Herbs and Related Remedies,* a standard reference whose fourth edition Foster coauthored with Varro Tyler. This book explores the pharmaceutical science behind herbal remedies in a way general readers can understand. With the book's emphasis on science, "there is no hype and no special pleading," John Goodier noted in *Reference Review,* concluding that "those interested in the use and biochemistry of plants will find a lot of information in the *Honest Herbal.*"

BIOGRAPHICAL AND CRITICAL SOURCES:

PERIODICALS

Booklist, Sept 1, 1992, Jane Jurgens, review of *Herbal Emissaries: Bringing Chinese Herbs to the West,* p. 16.
Choice: Current Reviews for Academic Libraries, May, 2000, Joan M. Stachnik, review of *Tyler's Honest Herbal: A Sensible Guide to the Use of Herbs and Related Remedies,* p. HSS-26; July-August, 2000, C. T. Mason, Jr., review of *A Field Guide to Medicinal Plants and Herbs of Eastern and Central North America,* p. 2003.
Library Journal, July, 1992, Katharine Galloway Garstka, review of *Herbal Emissaries,* p. 112.
Los Angeles Times, Dec 23, 1984, Barbara Saltzman, review of *Herbal Bounty,* p. B8.
Quarterly Review of Biology, September, 1999, Hari M. Sharma, review of *Tyler's Honest Herbal,* p. 370.
Reference Reviews, 1999, John Goodier, review of *Tyler's Honest Herbal,* pp. 34-35.

ONLINE

Steven Foster Home Page, www.stevenfoster.com/ (October 24, 2003).*

*   *   *

FOWLER, Connie May 1959-

PERSONAL: Born 1959, in Raleigh, NC; daughter of Henry Jefferson (a country western musician and sometime traveling salesman) and Lenore (Looney) May; married Mika Fowler (a photographer), 1987 (divorced, 2003). *Ethnicity:* "Irish, French, German,

Native American." *Education:* University of Tampa, B.A., (English), 1985; University of Kansas, M.A., (English literature), 1990. *Politics:* "Liberal Democrat." *Religion:* "Fallen Catholic." *Hobbies and other interests:* Sumo wrestling, weaving, knitting, music, environmental issues, violence against women and children.

ADDRESSES: Home and office—Alligator Point, FL, and Winter Park, FL. *Agent*—Joy Harris, Joy Harris Literary Agency, New York, NY. *E-mail*—conniemayfowler@hotmail.com.

CAREER: Writer; Rollins College, Winter Park, FL, Bachellor Chair in Creative Writing, 2003—; Spalding University, professor of creative writing. Founder, Women with Wings Foundation for battered women and their children.

MEMBER: PEN, Writers Guild, Authors Guild, Society of American Poets, Florida Arts Council.

AWARDS, HONORS: Southern Book Critics Circle Award, 1996, for *Before Women Had Wings;* American Penwomen Prize, 1996, for *Before Women Had Wings;* Chautauqua South Literary Award, 1998, for *Remembering Blue;* grant from Florida Division of Cultural Affairs, 1992-93 and 1994-95, for *River of Hidden Dreams* and *Remembering Blue;* three-time Dublin International Literary Award nominee; 2002 Excellence Award from the Florida Coalition against Domestic Violence.

WRITINGS:

Sugar Cage, Putnam (New York, NY), 1992.
River of Hidden Dreams, Putnam (New York, NY), 1994.
Before Women Had Wings, Putnam (New York, NY), 1996.
Remembering Blue, Doubleday (New York, NY), 2000.
When Katie Wakes: A Memoir, Doubleday (New York, NY), 2002.

Contributor of poetry to literary journals; contributor to periodicals, including *New York Times Book Review.*

ADAPTATIONS: Before Women Had Wings was produced as a television movie by the American Broadcasting Company (ABC) in 1997. Fowler wrote the screenplay adaptation of the novel.

WORK IN PROGRESS: The Problem with Murmur Lee, for Doubleday.

SIDELIGHTS: Connie May Fowler is the author of four novels that, according to a *Publishers Weekly* reviewer, "reveal beauty and meaning beneath the obvious and discarded." The stories unraveled in each book are all told in the first person, take place in Fowler's native Florida, and are deeply connected with the author's own past. "I write to reaffirm the past," Fowler told Ellen Kanner in *Publishers Weekly.* "All I have left are the memories, the stories, and sometimes that's not enough."

In a *New York Times Book Review* essay titled "No Snapshots in the Attic: A Granddaughter's Search for a Cherokee Past," Fowler explained that storytelling is part of her heritage. She theorized that this familial tendency to tell stories rather than record thoughts or save items might explain why her family has so few tangible reminiscences about previous generations. "I believe that my relatives, Indians and Europeans alike, couldn't waste free time on preserving a baby's first bootee," she wrote. "There were simply too many tales to tell about each other, living and dead, for them to be bothered by objects that would only clutter our homes and our minds."

A family history of personal tragedy contributes to Fowler's poignant fiction. Her grandmother on her father's side was a Cherokee Indian from South Carolina. She married a white man who left her soon after the couple moved to the St. Augustine area of Florida with their three small children. Misfortune hit the family in the next generation when Fowler's father died while the author was still a child, leaving her and her sister to live with their alcoholic, abusive mother. Their home in Tampa was a dilapidated trailer parked in front of a motel.

Fowler recalls writing as a child, but her publishing career began during her undergraduate days at Florida's University of Tampa. At that time, she had already contributed poetry to literary journals. She would eventually gain recognition not as a poet, but as a novelist. Her first novel, *Sugar Cage,* came to life as a thesis for Fowler's graduate degree from the University of Kansas. At the urging of her writing instructor, she sent the manuscript to an agent who liked the novel and told an editor at Putnam about it. It was published in 1992.

Sugar Cage is described in a *Publishers Weekly* review as a "tale of domestic life, civil rights and the supernatural in 1960s Florida." In a series of interwoven first-person narratives, Fowler introduces a variety of characters to the reader: Inez Temple, a black housekeeper at a motel just south of St. Augustine; Rose Looney, a housewife neglected by her new husband, Charlie; and their neighbors, Junior and Eudora Jewel. The "sugar cage" of the title refers to the crystal remains of sugar Inez sees in the bottom of a drinking glass she retrieves from Rose while Rose and Charlie are staying at the motel where Inez works during their honeymoon. Using her innate psychic powers, Inez looks down at the crystals and foretells that Rose will in the future "let love eat her up"; she also predicts the future child the couple will have. Years pass and the Looneys' son, Emory—whose birth had correctly been predicted by Inez—becomes another narrator of the story. Emory tells of falling in love with a black half-Seminole, part-Haitian sugarcane cutter named Soleil Marie Beauvoir. Soleil, also one of the book's narrative voices, uses voodoo to win Emory's heart. Their biracial love affair and Inez's interest in the civil rights movement allows Fowler to comment on the racial tensions in the South during the 1960s.

Reviewers for both *Publishers Weekly* and the *New York Times Book Review* remarked on the oral quality of Fowler's prose. While the *Publishers Weekly* reviewer described *Sugar Cage* as "a lively, interwoven chorus of Southern voices," *New York Times Book Review* critic Roy Hoffman noted, "If *Sugar Cage* is a novel about the intertwining of people's lives—and their dammed-up dreams—it is also a novel about voices, for the characters take turns at the narration." Reviewers highlight Emory and Soleil as two superbly drawn characters. "Some of Fowler's most beautiful passages," wrote Joseph Olshan in Chicago *Tribune Books,* "can be found in the chapters that describe how Emory, sent to work in his uncle's cane fields after trying to defend his mother from his father's physical abuses, falls in love there with Soleil Marie." Hoffman called Soleil Marie "the most engaging talker" in the book. He continued: "She makes vivid both the backbreaking work of the cane fields and the erotic joy of her moments with Emory."

In "No Snapshots in the Attic," Fowler describes how she decided to make her "grandmother's life . . . a stepping-off point for a new novel." The book that would develop is *River of Hidden Dreams,* published in 1994. It is the story of Sadie Hunter—Fowler's grandmother's name was Oneida Hunter May—and her confrontation with her past in St. Augustine (where Fowler's grandmother lived). Scenes of Sadie and her Cuban refugee boyfriend, Carlos, alternate with those of Sadie's Plains Indian grandmother and mixed-raced mother, born of the grandmother's affair with a black man, Mr. Sammy. Fowler juxtaposes Sadie's attempt to heal her emotional wounds with the story of how the girl's grandmother lost and then found Mr. Sammy.

Both a *Publishers Weekly* reviewer and Judith Paterson in the *New York Times Book Review* detected similarities between Fowler's *Sugar Cage* and *River of Hidden Dreams.* "The power of stories and myths to shape our lives," remarked the *Publishers Weekly* critic, "is the leitmotif of Fowler's second novel, as it was in her well-received *Sugar Cage.*" Paterson found that *Sugar Cage* and *River of Hidden Dreams* have in common "much in theme, tone and territory." "Both stories unfold," the critic wrote, "around a group of narrators who are so different from one another in outlook and culture that the English they speak hardly seems to be one language." In summary, Paterson commented: "There is no denying the depth of Connie May Fowler's talent and the breadth of her imagination."

Like Fowler's other novels, *Before Women Had Wings,* published in 1996, is told in first-person narration, but this time there is only one narrator, a nine-year-old girl named Avocet "Bird" Jackson. After Bird's alcoholic father commits suicide, her mother—also an alcoholic—takes her daughters to Tampa where they live, as the author did as a child, in a trailer. "While *Sugar Cage* skirted some ugly family truths, *Before Women Had Wings* confronts them directly," noted Ellen Kanner in *Publishers Weekly.* "The book is a culmination of writerly skill and personal strength." In a *Publishers Weekly* critique of the novel the reviewer found a connection between this book and Fowler's first novel. "Fowler sweeps the narrative along with plangent, lyrical prose," the commentator observed. "Mixing the squalid details of Bird's life with the child's magical dreams of hope and healing, she has fulfilled the promise of her highly praised debut, *Sugar Cage,* and established herself as a writer of formidable talent." *Before Women Had Wings* was televised as an "Oprah Winfrey Presents" movie on ABC in 1997, and Fowler herself wrote the screenplay version of the story.

Remembering Blue is a tragic love story in which myth becomes overpowering. Narrated by a young widow named Mattie, the tale revolves around Mattie's marriage to a Greek-American fisherman named Nick Blue and her life with—and without—Nick on the Gulf Coast island of Lethe. Nick's family believes that they are the descendants of dolphins, and that eventually they must return to their ancestors in the sea. Nick fulfills that promise when his empty, drifting boat is discovered off Lethe. In memorial to Nick, Mattie writes the story about how she has come to feel at home among his gregarious and struggling family.

In the *New York Times Book Review,* Liza Featherstone found *Remembering Blue* "burdened by cliches," but she added nevertheless: "The novel is at its strongest in passages that refuse . . . sentimentality—like those describing Nick's dangerous but exhilarating work, and the stark accounts of parental negligence and abandonment." A *Publishers Weekly* reviewer noted, though the narrative is "awash in nostalgia . . . the love story carries strong appeal, and Fowler's tender portrayal of Nick and Mattie's idyllic relationship will please romantics everywhere." In *Library Journal,* Penny Stevens concluded: "Fowler endows her characters with a sense of humor and the ability to express joy. . . . This is a pleasure to read even though the reader knows that a tragedy is lurking."

When Katie Wakes: A Memoir is a personal account of Fowler's relationship after college with a charismatic older man who abused her both physically and emotionally. Fowler writes of her own life in much the same style as her fiction, to convey themes that are familiar to her readers. Fowler's abusive relationships seem a sadly preordained continuation of her past. A *Kirkus Reviews* critic commented, "She loved her parents, who had endured tough times and been beaten as children themselves: how could she blame her father for drinking too much and beating her mother? Then, when he suddenly died, Mama 'with not a clue how to manage . . . plunged deeper into the family tradition: mean bitterness fueled by alcohol.'"

In 1984, Fowler was a twenty-six-year-old college graduate who hoped to someday be a professional writer. She started living with a former local TV personality who promised to help her career. She soon found herself reliving the abuses of her childhood. Before long she was supporting him, being abused both physically and emotionally, while holding on for

the smallest scrap of praise. A *Publishers Weekly* reviewer noted, "Heartbreakingly honest about the naive wishfulness that keeps her with a monstrous boyfriend, she writes, 'When you tell me you'll turn me into a writer, that we'll pen movies together and live in Hollywood, my foolish hopefulness gushes like an opened vein.'"

The day Fowler adopted Katie, a Labrador puppy, marked the beginning of her personal transformation. Receiving unconditional love for the first time in her life, she found the courage to find a job writing for a magazine. Soon she made supportive friends and met her future husband. *Kirkus Reviews* called the book, "a searing and finely crafted memoir of youth and adulthood stunted by abuse."

Fowler once told *CA:* "When I was a small girl my parents fought every night. My sister and I would huddle together in our bedroom and I would beg her to read to me so that the sound of their voices might be drowned out. And so she would begin, reading to me from my children's books, night after night. Even then, before I had learned to read, I knew intimately the soul-saving power of literature."

BIOGRAPHICAL AND CRITICAL SOURCES:

BOOKS

Fowler, Connie May, *Sugar Cage,* Putnam (New York, NY), 1992.
Fowler, Connie May, *When Katie Wakes: A Memoir,* Doubleday (New York, NY), 2002.

PERIODICALS

Atlanta Journal-Constitution, January 23, 2000, Eileen M. Drennen, review of *Remembering Blue,* p. L11; March 10, 2002, Diane Roberts, review of *When Katie Wakes: A Memoir,* p. E5.
Booklist, April 1, 1994, Donna Seaman, review of *River of Hidden Dreams,* p. 1423; June 1, 1996, Donna Seaman, review of *Before Women Had Wings,* p. 1674; September 1, 1997, review of *Before Women Had Wings,* p. 65; November 15, 1999, Donna Seaman, review of *Remembering Blue,* p. 59; November 15, 2001, Carol Hoggas, review of *When Katie Wakes,* p. 442.

Cosmopolitan, April, 1994, Chris Chase, review of *River of Hidden Dreams,* p. 12.

Critique, spring, 2001, Elizabeth S. Bell, critical essay on *River of Hidden Dreams,* p. 327.

Entertainment Weekly, Ken Tucker, November 3, 1997, review of *Before Women Had Wings,* p. 82.

Kirkus Reviews, December 15, 1999, review of *Remembering Blue,* p. 1903; November 15, 2001, review of *When Katie Wakes,* p. 1594.

Kliatt Young Adult Paperback Book Guide, September, 1997, review of *Before Women Had Wings,* p. 10; March, 1998, review of audio version of *Before Women Had Wings,* p. 40.

Library Journal, January, 2000, Penny Stevens, review of *Remembering Blue,* p. 158; July, 2000, Catherine Swenson, review of audio version of *Remembering Blue,* p.164; February 15, 2001, review of audio version of *Remembering Blue,* p. 142; December, 2001, Lucille M. Boone, review of *When Katie Wakes,* p. 151.

New York Times Book Review, February 2, 1992, p. 16; May 22, 1994, Connie May Fowler, "No Snapshots in the Attic: A Granddaughter's Search for a Cherokee Past," pp. 49-50; July 3, 1994, Judith Paterson, review of *River of Hidden Dreams,* p. 22; July 21, 1996, p. 15; February 20, 2000, Liza Featherstone, review of *Remembering Blue;* April 21, 2002, Sara Ivry, review of *When Katie Wakes,* p. 29.

People, November 3, 1997, Terry Kelleher, interview with Connie May Fowler, p. 19.

Publishers Weekly, October 11, 1991, p. 49; February 14, 1994, review of *River of Hidden Dreams,* p.

78; March 11, 1996, review of *Before Women Had Wings,* p. 41; May 13, 1996, Ellen Kanner, "Connie May Fowler: Writing in Order to Reaffirm the Past," pp. 50-51; April 14, 1997, review of *Before Women Had Wings,* p. 72; November 15, 1999, review of *Remembering Blue,* p. 53; November 26, 2001, review of *When Katie Wakes,* p. 49.

Times (London, England), July 5, 1997, Elizabeth Buchan, review of *Before Women Had Wings,* p. 13; March 4, 2000, Mary Loudon, review of *Remembering Blue,* p. 21.

Tribune Books (Chicago, IL), December 29, 1991, p. 4; June 1, 1997, review of *Before Women Had Wings,* p. 8.

Variety, November 3, 1997, Ray Richmond, "Oprah Winfrey Presents: *Before Women Had Wings,*" p. 32.

Washington Post Book World, July 31, 1994, p. 6.

Women's Journal, June, 1997, review of *Before Women Had Wings,* p. 12.

ONLINE

BookPage Web site, http://www.bookpage.com/ (May 2, 2002), Ellen Kanner, author interview.

Connie May Fowler Home Page, http://www.conniemayfowler.com/ (May 2, 2002).

*   *   *

FROST, Jason
See OBSTFELD, Raymond

G

GALINSKY, Ellen 1942-

PERSONAL: Born April 24, 1942, in Pittsburgh, PA; daughter of Melvin H. (in business) and Leora (in business; maiden name, Osgood) May; married Norman Galinsky (an artist), August 15, 1965; children: Philip Andrew, Lara Elizabeth. *Education:* Vassar College, A.B., 1964; Bank Street College of Education, M.S.Ed., 1970.

ADDRESSES: Home—Lawrence Lane, Palisades, NY 10964. *Office*—Families and Work Institute, 267 Fifth Ave., Floor 2, New York, NY 10016. *Agent*—Virginia Barber, 353 West 21st St., New York, NY 10011.

CAREER: Bank Street College of Education, New York, NY, teacher, researcher, and project director, 1964-89; Families and Work Institute, New York, founder and director, 1989—. Speaker at national conferences, including 1997 White House Conference on Child Care and 2000 White House Conference on Teenagers; keynote speaker, *Working Mother* magazine Work-Life Conference, 2001. Commentator on parenting issues on television.

MEMBER: Authors Guild, Authors League of America, Work-Life Leadership Council, The Employer Group, National Association for the Education of Young Children.

AWARDS, HONORS: Wall Street Journal citation as one of the best work-life books of 1999, for *Ask the Children: What America's Children Really Think about Working Parents.*

WRITINGS:

(And photographer) *Catbird* (juvenile), Coward (New York, NY), 1971.
(And photographer) *The Baby Cardinal* (juvenile), Putnam (New York, NY), 1976.
Beginnings: A Young Mother's Personal Account of Two Premature Births, (nonfiction), Houghton Mifflin (Boston, MA), 1976.
(With William H. Hooks) *The New Extended Family: Day Care That Works,* Houghton (Boston, MA), 1977.
Between Generations: The Six Stages of Parenthood, Times Books (New York, NY), 1981, published as *The Six Stages of Parenthood,* Addison-Wesley (Reading, MA), 1987.
(With Judy David) *The Preschool Years: Family Strategies That Work—from Experts and Parents,* Times Books (New York, NY), 1988.
(With James T. Bond and Dana E. Friedman) *The Changing Workforce: Highlights of the National Study,* Families and Work Institute (New York, NY), 1993.
Ask the Children: What America's Children Really Think about Working Parents, William Morrow (New York, NY), 1999.
(Coauthor) *Feeling Overworked: When Work Becomes Too Much,* Families and Work Institute (New York, NY), 2002.

Coauthor of *The National Study of the Changing Workforce,* published every five years, and *The 1998 Business Work-Life Study.* Columnist, *Information Week.* Contributor of articles to magazines and scholarly journals, including *Parents* and *Redbook.*

WORK IN PROGRESS: A study of patterns of success and how to facilitate it based on interviews with high-level male and female executives.

SIDELIGHTS: Educator and researcher Ellen Galinsky once told *CA:* "I am interested in nature, in how natural forces wear away at and shape each other; I am interested in how the natural world relates to the human one; I am interested in people and how they change; I am interested in how institutions affect people; and I am interested in myths and realities. I write and photograph to probe the dualities that lie at the end of every search."

In *Between Generations: The Six Stages of Parenthood,* Galinsky, an early-childhood specialist, focuses on the relationship between parent and child. "The result," wrote Anthony Astrachan in the *New York Times Book Review,* "is a book that is useful and important but not truly innovative, a hybrid of Benjamin Spock/Jean Piaget/Berry Brazelton on the one hand and Daniel Levinson/Roger Gould/Gail Sheehy on the other." Nonetheless, *Between Generations,* which contains anecdotes and interviews, should be helpful to "both parents needing guidelines and the general reader interested in . . . human development," a *Library Journal* reviewer concluded.

In 1989 Galinsky founded the Manhattan-based Families and Work Institute, a nonprofit organization that researches work-life issues and the changing patterns of employment in America. From her base at the institute, Galinsky has become a nationally recognized expert on the relationship between working parents and their children. Her books, magazine articles, and scientific surveys all seek to bridge communication gaps between employers and their child-rearing employees, between parents and children, and between families and the community. One of Galinsky's most important studies was published as *Ask the Children: What America's Children Really Think about Working Parents,* a survey of more than 1,000 children and 650 adults on various aspects of working parenthood.

Galinsky's findings in *Ask the Children* were surprising to some. She found that children did not mind if their parents worked outside the home, but that children wanted their parents to be less stressed at the end of the working day. Galinsky also discovered that children worried about their parents' health and sometimes misunderstood or misinterpreted their parents' bad moods. The conclusions Galinsky drew from her data include the suggestions that parents talk frankly about their working challenges, that they find positive things to say about work, and that they find some down time to put aside work stresses and prepare for the challenges of the home environment. In an interview with *Fortune,* Galinsky said of children: "They're telling us that there is a problem, but its not that we work, its how we work."

Ask the Children was widely reviewed, and Galinsky was interviewed about the book when it was released in 1999. Many critics felt that the study answers important questions about work-life issues and could help quell parental guilt over working outside the home. *Library Journal* correspondent Paula Dempsey praised the book for its "succinct, vivid writing" as well as for its conclusions, which she found "original, compassionate, and realistic."

BIOGRAPHICAL AND CRITICAL SOURCES:

PERIODICALS

Better Homes and Gardens, September, 2001, Betsy Rubiner, "Work Lessons," p. 116.
Fortune, November 8, 1999, "The Child's View of Working Parents (It's Not So Bad)," p. 318.
Library Journal, December 15, 1980; October 15, 1999, Paula Depsey, review of *Ask the Children: What America's Children Really Think about Working Parents,* p. 90.
Los Angeles Times, February 12, 1981.
New York Times Book Review, February 12, 1978; June 28, 1981.
People, December 6, 1999, "Hey Mom, Its Okay to Work: Family Expert Ellen Galinsky Says Kids Don't Mind Their Parents Jobs, Just the Stress," p. 105.
Working Mother, November, 1999, Sarah Hutter, "Kids Speak Out," p. 12.

ONLINE

Families and Work Institute Web site, http://www.families andwork.org/ (November 5, 2003).*

GARBER, Zev (Warren) 1941-

PERSONAL: Born March 1, 1941, in New York, NY; son of Morris Benjamin (a pharmacist) and Pearl (a homemaker; maiden name, Borko) Garber; married Lois Koppelman, December 26, 1963 (divorced, November, 1975); married Susan Adriana Ehrlich (a writer), October 4, 1985; children: Asher, Dorit Garber. *Ethnicity:* Jewish. *Education:* Hunter College of the City University of New York, B.A., 1962; attended University of California, Los Angeles, 1962-65; University of Southern California, M.A., 1970. *Politics:* "Centralist-Right." *Religion:* Jewish. *Hobbies and other interests:* Films, plays.

ADDRESSES: Office—Los Angeles Valley College, 5800 Fulton, Van Nuys, CA 91401. *E-mail*—zevgarber@juno.com.

CAREER: Los Angeles Valley College, Van Nuys, CA, professor of Jewish studies, 1970—, currently chair of Jewish studies; writer. Visiting professor of religious studies at University of California, Riverside, 1983-1994. Educational consultant to the Philadelphia Center for the Holocaust. Member of the conference committee of Annual Scholars' Conference on the Holocaust. Editorial advisor of the *Western States Jewish History.* President, National Association of Professors of Hebrew (USA).

MEMBER: National Studies Review Journal, 1978-1980, American Oriental Society, American Schools of Oriental Research, American Academy of Religion, Society of Biblical Literature, Association of Jewish Studies, National Association of Professors of Hebrew, Society of Biblical Literature.

AWARDS, HONORS: Recognition Award, 1990, National Association of Professors of Hebrew.

WRITINGS:

Teaching Hebrew Language and Literature at the College Level, Educational Resources Information Center (Washington, D.C.), 1991.
Shoah: The Paradigmatic Genocide: Essays in Exegesis and Eisegesis, University Press of America (Lanham, MD), 1994.

Zev Garber

EDITOR

Methodology in the Academic Teaching of Judaism, University Press of America (Lanham, MD), 1986.
(With A. Berger and Richard Libowitz) *Methodology in the Academic Teaching of the Holocaust,* University Press of America (Lanham, MD), 1988.
(With Richard Libowitz) *Peace, in Deed: Essays in Honor of Harry James Cargas,* Scholars Press (Atlanta, GA), 1998.
Academic Approaches to Teaching Jewish Studies, University Press of America (Lanham, MD), 2000.

Editor-in-chief of "Studies in the Shoah" series, University Press of America. Contributor to books, including *What Kind of God?: Essays in Honor of Richard Rubenstein,* University Press of America, 1995.

Editor of *Iggeret;* editor of *Shofar* issues; contributing editor of *Israel Today* (became *Los Angeles Jewish News*). Member of editorial board of *Shofar.*

WORK IN PROGRESS: "Ongoing researching and writing on themes related to the Shoah."

SIDELIGHTS: Zev Garber is an educator specializing in the Holocaust, which he prefers to refer to as the Shoah. Garber explained to John Dart in the *Los Angeles Times* that the term *Holocaust* originally referred to religious sacrifices and thus bears a Biblical connotation that "makes the six million Jews an offering to God, and the priests are the Nazis." He told Dart that the Hebrew word *Shoah,* which means "destruction," is more appropriate. "Language determines how we think," Garber observed. "And because *Shoah* is a Hebrew term, we don't lose the Jewishness of the victims."

Garber wrote *Shoah: The Paradigmatic Genocide: Essays in Exegesis and Eisegesis,* and he has edited numerous academic volumes. In addition, he serves as editor-in-chief of the University Press of America's "Studies in the Shoah" series.

Garber once told *CA:* "My main research focuses on the central issues of human life, meaning, and consciousness in the post-Shoah (Holocaust) world. My writings and scholarly papers address historical, literary, pedagogical, philosophical, and theological concerns. What unites my approach to the Shoah is the quest for a meaningful agenda to learn and teach the Holocaust fifty years later, when the entire horrific enterprise is either forgotten, questioned, revised, or denied. For an age that ponders technologically administered mass death, global indifference, tribalism, and God forsakeness, my thinking is offered as a meditation in human responsibility and theological responsibility.

"The essence of Shoah thinking is 'dislike of the unlike.' It is the recognition of this force in our lives that must be at the core of any Holocaust presentation. I am concerned, therefore I am; I am appalled, therefore I write: Mankind is improvable. We must all be reminded of this, and writers and educators, above all, must believe it."

Garber coedited *Peace, in Deed: Essays in Honor of Harry James Cargas,* with fellow Hebrew scholar Richard Libowitz. The book is dedicated to the leading Catholic scholar in Holocaust studies, Harry James Cargas. In the foreword, Kurt Vonnegut identifies Harry Cargas as "a person of historical importance for having taken into his very bones, as a Christian, the horrifying mystery of how persons could profess love of Jesus Christ, as did most Nazis . . . yet commit a crime as merciless as the extermination of Europe's Jews."

Peace, in Deed consists of twenty essays exploring Holocaust issues, such as the Holocaust and higher education, the relationship between man and God after Auschwitz, and a call for philosophical examination of the question of evil. The title of the book is quoted from Cargas, "Converting the 'teaching of contempt' to the 'teaching of reconciliation' is the reality of *Peace, in Deed.*"

Academic Approaches to Teaching Jewish Studies, published in 2000, is a collection of essays by Jewish and non-Jewish scholars focused on the way that Jewish studies can be integrated into standard college and university curricula. The book is an extension of his 1986 book, *Methodology in the Academic Teaching of Judaism.* The essays cover diversified disciplines within the broad category of Jewish studies. Different scholars examine the teaching of Post-Resurrection Jewish history, gender studies, Hebrew literature, Biblical studies, and the Holocaust. David Patterson, in his included Holocaust essay, furthered Garber's editorial position, writing, "If non-Jews are to fathom the significance of the Shoah to the Jews . . . they must incorporate Jewish religious teachings into their study of the Shoah." Carol Harris-Shapiro wrote in the *Journal of Ecumenical Studies,* "Teachers will undoubtedly find at least one essay that provides helpful theoretical and curricular material, although it would be the rare individual who would profit from every essay."

BIOGRAPHICAL AND CRITICAL SOURCES:

BOOKS

Garber, Zev, *Academic Approaches to Teaching Jewish Studies,* University Press of America (Lanham, MD), 2000.

Garber, Zev, *Peace, in Deed: Essays in Honor of Harry James Cargas,* Scholars Press (Atlanta, GA), 1998.

PERIODICALS

Choice, November, 2000, A. J. Avery-Peck, review of *Academic Approaches to Teaching Jewish Studies,* p. 548.

Journal of Ecumenical Studies, winter, 2000, Carol Harris-Shapiro, review of *Academic Approaches to Teaching Jewish Studies,* p. 84.

Los Angeles Times, April 9, 1994, review of *Shoah: The Paradigmatic Genocide: Essays in Exegesis and Eisegesis,* p. B1.

Reference & Reference Book News, February, 1999, review of *Peace, in Deed,* p. 21.

Religious Education, spring, 1998, review of *Shoah,* p. 259.

Shofar, winter, 2002, Richard Libowitz, review of *Academic Approaches to Teaching Jewish Studies,* p. 129.

ONLINE

Humanities and the Social Sciences Online, http://www.2.h-net.msu.edu/ (May, 1999), review of *Peace, in Deed.*

John Gardner

*   *   *

GARDNER, John (Edmund) 1926-

PERSONAL: Born November 20, 1926, in Seaton Delaval, Northumberland, England; son of Cyril John (a priest of the Church of England) and Lena (Henderson) Gardner; married Margaret Mercer, September 15, 1952 (died, 1997); children: Alexis Mary, Simon Richard John, Miranda. *Education:* St. John's College, Cambridge, B.A., 1950, M.A., 1951; attended St. Stephen's House, Oxford, 1951-52.

ADDRESSES: Home—Hampshire, England. *Agent*—Lisa Moylett, Coombes Moylett Agency, 3 Askew Rd., London W12 9AA, England. *E-mail*—maestro@johngardner.com.

CAREER: Writer. Ordained priest of Church of England, 1953, legally released from obligations of the priesthood, 1958; magician with American Red Cross, Entertainments Department, 1943-44; curate in Evesham, England, 1952-58; *Herald,* Stratford-upon-Avon, England, theatre critic and arts editor, 1959-65. Lecturer in the United States and Soviet Union. *Military service:* Royal Navy, Fleet Air Arm, 1944-46; Royal Marines, Commandos, 1946; served in Hong Kong and Malta; became chaplain.

MEMBER: Crime Writers Association.

WRITINGS:

Spin the Bottle (autobiography), Muller (London, England), 1963.

Hideaway (stories), Corgi (London, England), 1968.

The Assassination File (stories), Corgi (London, England), 1972.

Ian Fleming's James Bond in John Gardner's Seafire, Chivers Press (Thorndike, ME), 1994.

NOVELS

A Complete State of Death (a Derek Torry novel), Viking (New York, NY), 1969.

The Censor, New English Library (London, England), 1970.

Every Night's a Festival, Morrow (New York, NY), 1971, published as *Every Night's a Bullfight,* M. Joseph (London, England), 1971.

The Corner Men (a Derek Torry novel), Doubleday (New York, NY), 1974.

The Return of Moriarty, Putnam (New York, NY), 1974, published as *Moriarty,* Pan Books (London, England), 1976.

The Revenge of Moriarty, Putnam (New York, NY), 1975.

To Run a Little Faster, M. Joseph (London, England), 1976.

The Werewolf Trace, Doubleday (New York, NY), 1977.

The Dancing Dodo, Doubleday (New York, NY), 1978.

The Last Trump, McGraw-Hill (New York, NY), 1980, published as *Golgotha,* W. H. Allen (London, England), 1980.

Flamingo, Hodder & Stoughton (London, England), 1983.

Day of Absolution: A Novel, Scribner (New York, NY), 2000.

Bottled Spider, Severn House (Surrey, England), 2002.

The Streets of Town, Severn House (Surrey, England), 2003.

BOYSIE OAKES NOVELS

The Liquidator, Viking (New York, NY), 1964.

Understrike, Viking (New York, NY), 1965.

Amber Nine, Viking (New York, NY), 1966.

Madrigal, Viking (New York, NY), 1968.

Founder Member, Muller (London, England), 1969.

Traitor's Exit, Muller (London, England), 1970.

Air Apparent, Putnam (New York, NY), 1970, published as *The Airline Pirates,* Hodder & Stoughton (London, England), 1970.

A Killer for a Song, Hodder & Stoughton (London, England), 1975.

JAMES BOND NOVELS

License Renewed, R. Marek (New York, NY), 1981.

For Special Services, Coward, McCann & Geoghegan (New York, NY), 1982.

Ice-breaker, Putnam (New York, NY), 1983.

Role of Honor, Putnam (New York, NY), 1984.

Nobody Lives Forever, Putnam (New York, NY), 1986.

No Deals, Mr. Bond, Putnam (New York, NY), 1987.

Scorpius, Putnam (New York, NY), 1988.

Win, Lose, or Die, Putnam (New York, NY), 1989.

License to Kill (based on the screenplay by Michael G. Wilson and Richard Maibaum), Diamond (New York, NY), 1989.

Brokenclaw, Putnam (New York, NY), 1990.

The Man from Barbarossa, Putnam (New York, NY), 1991.

Death Is Forever, Putnam (New York, NY), 1992.

Never Send Flowers, Putnam (New York, NY), 1993.

Seafire, Putnam (New York, NY), 1994.

Coldfall, Putnam (New York, NY), 1996.

HERBIE KRUGER NOVELS

The Nostradamus Traitor (first book of trilogy), Doubleday (New York, NY), 1979.

The Garden of Weapons (second book of trilogy), Hodder & Stoughton (New York, NY), 1980.

The Quiet Dogs (third book of trilogy), Hodder & Stoughton (New York, NY), 1981.

Maestro (first book of second trilogy), Otto Penzler (New York, NY), 1993.

Confessor (second book of second trilogy), Otto Penzler (New York, NY), 1995.

"GENERATIONS" TRILOGY; NOVELS

The Secret Generations, Putnam (New York, NY), 1985.

The Secret Houses, Putnam (New York, NY), 1988.

The Secret Families, Putnam (New York, NY), 1989.

Also author of *Goldeneye,* and "Smiley at the Circus: Cold War Espionage," in *Murder Ink: The Mystery Reader's Companion,* edited by Dilys Winn, Workman (New York, NY), 1977.

ADAPTATIONS: The Liquidator was released as a feature film by Metro-Goldwyn-Mayer in 1965; *A Complete State of Death* was released as *The Stone Killer* by Columbia, 1973.

SIDELIGHTS: John Gardner's suspense novels have enjoyed steady success since the early 1960s, but in 1981 he received international attention when his novel

License Renewed became a major bestseller. A reason for its immediate popularity: *License Renewed* was a new James Bond adventure, the first to appear in sixteen years. Bond, a fictional agent for England's Secret Service, was created by the late Ian Fleming in 1951, and quickly gained a loyal following. Fans are familiar with the most trivial details concerning Bond, or Agent 007, as he is also known; therefore, any flaws in a re-creation of Fleming's hero were certain to be noticed. The public's eager reception of *License Renewed* attests to Gardner's skill in performing his difficult task.

Gardner's interest in writing began early in life; he was an avid reader from the age of three. At eight, the author stated on his Web site, "I announced that I wanted to be a writer so my father gave me a notebook and some pencils that he'd probably liberated from the school where he was chaplain. I took them up to bed. The story goes that he came up an hour later and found me fast asleep while the notebook was still virgin white except for the first page on which I had written—The Complete Works of John Gardner." Before realizing that ambition, Gardner followed his father into the Anglican priesthood.

He had been in the ministry for five years when he realized that he had taken "the wrong turning." He explained to Fred Hauptfuhrer in *People:* "It came to me the way some others have a conversion . . . only mine was in reverse. I was preaching one Sunday and realized I didn't believe a word I was saying." Gardner left the priesthood in 1958. At that time, with the aid of hypnosis and aversion therapy, he was also able to overcome a heavy drinking habit. Gardner's first professional writing was done for the Stratford-upon-Avon *Herald,* where he acted as theatre critic and arts editor for six years. The experience was valuable, but, he later commented, "I realized I would not be happy forever acting as a critic of other people's work." Accordingly, in 1963, he published his first book, *Spin the Bottle,* an account of his struggle with alcohol. The next year he published *The Liquidator,* a book that established him in the suspense genre in which he was to become so successful.

Spy novels, including Ian Fleming's Bond series, were at the height of their popularity in the early-1960s. According to *New York Times Book Review* writer Anthony Boucher, Gardner had written "a deliberate (and skillful) parody of James Bond" in *The Liquidator.* That novel's protagonist was the cowardly, inept Boysie Oakes, who was faint-hearted enough to have to hire others to do his killing. Yet Boucher wrote that the book is more than a comedy: "Mr. Gardner succeeds in having it both ways; he has written a clever parody which is also a genuinely satisfactory thriller." Some years later Gardner created another spy quite unlike Bond. *The Nostradamus Traitor, The Garden of Weapons,* and *The Quiet Dogs* all featured Big Herbie Kruger, a German-born British intelligence agent who sees himself as a failure in both his life and work. The Kruger trilogy found an enthusiastic audience and drew praise from reviewers for Gardner's fine workmanship. T. J. Binyon described *The Garden of Weapons* in the *Times Literary Supplement* as "a solid, finely detailed and intricately constructed piece of work," and Henry McDonald, writing in the *Washington Post Book World,* called the same book "a skillfully crafted novel which sustains a high level of suspense from start to finish."

Gardner returned to the Big Herbie Kruger character in a second trilogy beginning with *Maestro,* published in 1993. In *Maestro,* Kruger is recalled from retirement to investigate the alleged Nazi collaboration of Louis Passau, a renowned German-born American conductor. Before Kruger can reach Passau, the conductor's sordid past is revealed, followed by several unsuccessful attempts on his life. Kruger abducts Passau and brings him to a safe location where the book assumes the character of biography as the distinguished conductor recounts his life and experiences for Kruger. In addition to his espionage work for the Nazis and Soviets, Passau recalls his upbringing as an Eastern European Jew, musical training in New York, and criminal involvement in Chicago during the days of Al Capone. *Armchair Detective* reviewer John F. Harvey concluded, "This story of a man who was at the same time a widely known symphony conductor and a spy for three different countries holds the reader's attention without release until he/she reaches the book's tragic ending." Gardner's incorporation of classical music is also praised. Commenting on the detail and effect of Gardner's musical references, Newgate Callendar wrote in the *New York Times Book Review,* "Here Mr. Gardner comes out in a triumphant fortissimo."

Following *Maestro* was *Confessor* in 1995. In this second installment of Gardner's second Kruger trilogy, the familiar protagonist is again brought out of retirement to investigate the car-bomb death of Gus Keene, a long-time friend and matchless interrogator for the British Secret Intelligence Service. As new terrorist attacks threaten Europe and America, Kruger learns of Keene's double-life as a skilled magician and discovers mysterious links between his friend and Middle Eastern operatives, the IRA, and the wars in both the Falkland Islands and the Persian Gulf. The suspense heightens when Kruger begins to suspect that Keene may still be alive. Chicago *Tribune Books* reviewer Chris Petrakos approved of Gardner's plot and character development: "Gardner pulls off his complex tale in high style."

When the owners of the copyright to the James Bond character, Gildrose Publications, decided to hire an author to continue the Bond series some fourteen years after Fleming's last novel was published, Gardner's background made him a natural candidate for the job. His facility in imitating the style of other writers was noted by Derrick Murdoch in the Toronto *Globe and Mail*: "John Gardner is technically a highly competent thriller novelist who never seems to be quite at ease unless he is writing in the same vein as another writer. . . . It's what makes him so well-qualified to continue the James Bond Saga." Gildrose's board of directors agreed, finally selecting Gardner from a list of twelve authors. Peter Janson-Smith, one of Gildrose's directors and formerly Ian Fleming's agent, told *People,* "We wanted someone with a respect for Fleming, not someone who'd start saying where Ian had gone wrong and threaten to walk out if we altered a word."

Gardner understood the difficulties inherent in the project. He explained to Hauptfuhrer, "[Bond is] a household name. Fans know how he cuts his fingernails, so the writer is a target for nitpickers. Mr. Fleming is a very difficult act to follow." Nevertheless, the author accepted the challenges of the assignment and began to write. He told Edwin McDowell in the *New York Times Book Review,* "I supplied [Gildrose] with four possible narrative outlines, and they picked one of them and asked me to do certain things. What they wanted was for me to think in terms of Bond having been on ice for a while, but being quite up to date about what's been going on in the world during the past two decades." He elaborated in *People,* "Then there's the matter of character. He's got to be the same man, but much more aware of women's position in society."

The result of these considerations was a Bond who drank less, drove a fuel-efficient Saab, and smoked low-tar cigarettes. Not unexpectedly, some critics reacted indignantly to this updating of the suave spy. Michael Malone's *New York Times Book Review* article stated, "Bond was so suited to his times, so right in [the 1950s,] that age of astronauts and Thunderbirds, perhaps he should have decided you only live once. . . . For Bond to be worrying about gas mileage is like shipping the Scarlet Pimpernel to Plymouth Colony."

And, although praising Gardner's skill, T. J. Binyon and Stanley Ellin, writing respectively in the *Times Literary Supplement* and *New York Times Book Review,* both expressed the opinion that because Bond originated as Fleming's alter ego, no other author could satisfactorily re-create him.

Gardner's third Bond book, *Ice-breaker,* is, according to Binyon, "full of good action; his torture scenes are splendidly painful; his villain is adequately megalomaniac, though perhaps not sufficiently *outré*; his girls are pretty, sexy, and available, and the courting routines as embarrassingly obvious as anything in the original. . . . But in the end Gardner's Bond doesn't really measure up to Fleming's. There isn't that maniacal snobbery about trivial and useless detail which the original so endearingly manifests. And, furthermore, Gardner simply hasn't grasped Bond's most important trait: he only takes assignments where his creator would like to take a holiday. And who? Certainly not the luxurious Bond." Ellin wrote that Gardner is somewhat overqualified for the job of following Fleming: "Ian Fleming was a dreadful writer, a creator of books for grown-up boys, a practitioner of tin-eared prose. As evidenced by his writing, he was also by nature a ferocious and humorless snob, a political primitive, a chauvinist in every possible area." Gardner, continued Ellin, is "a writer of style and wit and a sharp-eyed, acidulous and yet appreciative view of humanity and its foibles. Fleming's shoes are simply too tight and misshapen for Mr. Gardner to wear comfortably."

But *New York Times Book Review* critic Mel Watkins felt that Gardner's Bond is certainly equal to Fleming's original, and is perhaps superior, thanks to his more believable personality: "Although Mr. Gardner's Bond is less raffishly macho and arrogant than previously depicted," observed Watkins, "the spirit of the 007 series remains intact, and few Fleming admirers are likely to object. There is, in fact, something appealing about a James Bond who can react to women with some sympathy and confusion at a crucial moment." Bond fans, perhaps the sternest critics of all, made the final judgment: they bought and read the books eagerly. *License Renewed* sold more than 130,000 copies in hardcover alone, inspiring such confidence in its publishers that the sequel, *For Special Services,* enjoyed a first printing of 95,000 copies.

Gardner followed with additional Bond novels that proved popular but lacked critical affirmation. In *Scorpius* Bond infiltrates The Meek Ones, a mercenary terrorist group posing as a religious cult, to foil their plans to bomb British officials. *Win, Lose, or Die,* Gardner's eighth installment in the Bond canon, describes 007's effort to avert the terrorist seizure of a British aircraft carrier upon which George Bush, Mikhail Gorbachev, and Margaret Thatcher have gathered for arms reduction negotiations. As Frederick Busch wrote in a Chicago *Tribune Books* review, "the novel is literate, hard-working, sexless, somehow, and dull."

The archetypical Cold War spy continued his adventures at the center of crises fit for the post-Cold War era. In *Death Is Forever,* Bond investigates the murders of British and American secret agents in the newly reunified Germany and undermines the plot of a Stalinist East German security agent to wreak havoc in Western Europe. *Cold Fall,* published in 1996, follows Bond's mission to apprehend the perpetrators of an airline bomb, leading to the implication of Italian royalty, former mobsters, and American extremists in Idaho.

Outside of the Bond books, Gardner received favorable reviews for his "Generations" trilogy, the saga of a British and American family linked by marriage and connections to international espionage organizations. The first installment, *The Secret Generations,* published in 1985, traces the development of foreign intelligence agencies in the early decades of the twentieth-century. According to *Los Angeles Times Book Review* critic Nick Williams, with this book Gardner "emerges once more as a master of his craft." In *The Secret Houses,* the second volume in the series, the author describes cloak-and-dagger activity in occupied France during the Second World War, where a network of spies, including two family girls, operate under Nazi

oppression. *Books* reviewer Maureen Rissik wrote, "Faultless construction and a good deal of narrative pace combine to make this a thoroughly enjoyable read." Volume three, *The Secret Families,* is set in the 1960s and involves KGB infiltration, British and American counterspies, and attempts to restore both personal and family honor. Busch welcomed the book in Chicago *Tribune Books,* concluding that it is "as compelling an espionage novel as we've had in some time."

After producing books at a steady pace for decades, Gardner was forced into hiatus following a diagnosis of esophageal cancer in 1995. But all was not lost. "To my great surprise, and against the odds [I] recovered, following complex and very unpleasant surgery," as he remarked on his Web site. His health issues hadn't ended, however. Following successful surgery, the author told a *Wales on Sunday* interviewer, "after many dramas, including pneumonia, I fell and broke my right hip. There's always something." Sadly, the death of Gardner's wife, Margaret, in 1997 became yet another personal challenge to overcome. "When my life finally regained some equilibrium many people in publishing seemed to be astonished that I wanted to continue writing," he continued. "But what else to do? I have spent some forty years telling stories and delineating characters. I am not about to give it up now."

Thus Gardner's first book since 1996's *Coldfall* was the 2000 novel *Day of Absolution.* The latter work centers on the May-September marriage of young anti-terrorist officer Bex Olesker and her husband, the retired-but-still-investigating detective Charlie Gauntlet. The newlyweds have their honeymoon interrupted to find what Lisa Moylett of *Publishers Weekly* called "a world-class assassin called Alchemist" whose target is a high-ranking Russian official. Moylett welcomed Gardner back into publishing, saying the espionage veteran continued to show himself as "a smooth, polished master of the form."

Unsuspecting young women are the prey of deformed madman Golly Goldfinch, who heeds the voices in his head to kill them in the most savage ways imaginable. In Gardner's 2002 novel *Bottled Spider,* the author sets the action in World War II-era London and introduces new series detective Suzie Mountford. Her mission to track the killer is hampered by "seemingly insurmountable male opposition," according to a *Pub-*

lishers Weekly contributor. The reviewer called Gardner's depiction of London during the Blitz the best part of *Bottled Spider.* A *Kirkus Reviews* writer, while acknowledging the book as somewhat "overlong," was also taken with Gardner's characterization of Suzie Mountford and her "all out pursuit of a sociopathic villain, a meaningful career, and someone to take her virginity."

"In recent years," Gardner was quoted in the *St. James Guide to Crime and Mystery Writers:* "I have sought to combine the classic suspense story, together with espionage and detection of a different kind. The future? I think that, after one more attempt to recreate a classic suspense style from the past . . . it is probably ripe for the suspense story to take off into the future: not in terms of science fiction, but in political, military, and espionographical content."

BIOGRAPHICAL AND CRITICAL SOURCES:

BOOKS

Gardner, John, *Spin the Bottle,* Muller (London, England), 1963.
St. James Guide to Crime and Mystery Writers, St. James Press (Detroit, MI), 1996.

PERIODICALS

Armchair Detective, winter, 1989, p. 22; fall, 1993, John F. Harvey, review of *Maestro,* p. 102.
Booklist, April 15, 1992, p. 1483; September 1, 1993, p. 3; September 1, 1994, p. 26; June 1, 1996, pp. 1674, 1686; August, 2002, Candace Smith, review of *Day of Absolution: A Novel,* p. 1985; September 15, 2002, Emily Melton, review of *Bottled Spider,* p. 209.
Books, February, 1988, p. 21; April, 1988, p. 17; July-August, 1990, p. 14.
English Journal, March 24, 1994, p. 96.
Globe and Mail (Toronto, Ontario, Canada), December 24, 1983.
Kirkus Reviews, April 1, 1992, p. 414; April 15, 1996, p. 549; July 1, 2002, review of *Bottled Spider,* p. 919.
Library Journal, September 1, 2002, Rex Klett, review of *Bottled Spider,* p. 218.

Los Angeles Times Book Review, January 19, 1986, Nick Williams, review of *The Secret Generations,* p. 9; June 12, 1988, p. 8; July 16, 1989, p. 13.
New York Times, April 9, 1983.
New York Times Book Review, October 18, 1964, Anthony Boucher, review of *The Liquidator;* August 1, 1965; June 7, 1981; June 14, 1981; May 30, 1982; April 24, 1983, Stanley Ellin, review of *Ice-Breaker;* October 31, 1993, Newgate Callendar, review of *Maestro,* p. p. 27; March 27, 1994, p. 26.
Observer (London, England), July 3, 1988.
People, June 21, 1982.
Playboy, June, 1987, p. 27; July, 1988, p. 32.
Publishers Weekly, March 6, 1987, p. 102; October 23, 1987, pp. 45-46; May 4, 1992, p. 41; March 13, 1995, p. 60; April 29, 1996, p. 53; August 21, 2000, review of *Day of Absolution,* p. 46; July 29, 2002, review of *Bottled Spider,* p. 57; June 30, 2003, review of *The Streets of Town,* p. 61.
Punch, May 20, 1981; July 27, 1983.
Time, July 6, 1981; July 5, 1982.
Times Literary Supplement, December 26, 1980; June 5, 1981, T. J. Binyon, review of *The Garden of Weapons;* September 17, 1982; July 22, 1983, T. J. Binyon, review of *Ice-Breaker.*
Tribune Books (Chicago, IL), June 5, 1988, Frederick Busch, review of *The Secret Families,* p. 6; April 16, 1989, Busch, review of *Win, Lose, or Die,* p. 6; April 16, 1995, Chris Petrakos, review of *Confessor,* p. 7.
Virginia Quarterly Review, winter, 2001, review of *Day of Absolution,* p. 23.
Wales on Sunday (Cardiff, Wales), September 1, 2002, "Me and My Health," p. 8.
Washington Post Book World, April 5, 1981, Henry McDonald, review of *The Garden of Weapons;* January 5, 1996, p. 11.

ONLINE

John Gardner Web site, http://www.john-gardner.com/ (March 13, 2003).

*   *   *

GIBBONS, Kaye 1960-

PERSONAL: Born 1960, in Wilson, NC; daughter of Charles (a tobacco farmer) and Alice Butts; married Michael Gibbons (divorced); married Frank Ward (an attorney), 1995 (divorced); children: Mary, Leslie,

Kaye Gibbons

A Virtuous Woman, Algonquin Books (Chapel Hill, NC), 1989.

A Cure for Dreams, Algonquin Books (Chapel Hill, NC), 1991.

Charms for the Easy Life, Putnam (New York, NY), 1993.

Sights Unseen, Putnam (New York, NY), 1995.

On the Occasion of My Last Afternoon, Putnam (New York, NY), 1998.

Divining Women, Putnam (New York, NY), 2004.

Contributor to the *New York Times Book Review.* Her novels have been translated into French.

ADAPTATIONS: Ellen Foster was adapted for audiocassette by Simon & Schuster (New York, NY), 1996, and for the Hallmark Hall of Fame television movie, 1997; movie rights to *A Virtuous Woman* were bought by the Oprah Winfrey production company. *Charms for the Easy Life* was made into a television movie by Showtime Productions, 2001. *A Virtuous Woman* was recorded as an audiobook by Recorded Books, 1998, and *On the Occasion of My Last Afternoon* was recorded as an audiobook by Recorded Books, 1999. *Sights Unseen* was recorded as an audiobook by Chivers, 2001, and was developed into a movie script by the author.

WORK IN PROGRESS: Completing Jeanne Braselton's posthumous novel *The Other Side of Air;* a biography; a sequel to *Ellen Foster,* to be published in 2005.

SIDELIGHTS: Kaye Gibbons has won a number of literary awards and much praise for her body of fiction, a group of novels predominantly set in rural Southern communities not unlike Nash County, North Carolina, where Gibbons grew up. From the matriarchal folk healer to the uncompromising eleven-year-old, Gibbons's strong central characters—almost always female—possess a grounding and wisdom that transcends the often-difficult circumstances of lives. Writing in *Publishers Weekly,* critic Bob Summer termed them "Southern women who shoulder the burdens of their ordinary lives with extraordinary courage."

Gibbons was born and raised in North Carolina. The daughter of an alcoholic father and a mother who suffered from bipolar disorder and committed suicide

Louise (first marriage). *Education:* Attended North Carolina State University and the University of North Carolina at Chapel Hill.

ADDRESSES: Home—Raleigh, NC. *Agent*—Jane Pasanen, Chelsea Forum, Inc., 377 Rector Place, Suite 12-I, New York, NY 10280.

CAREER: Novelist.

AWARDS, HONORS: Sue Kaufman Prize for First Fiction, American Academy and Institute of Arts and Letters, and citation from Ernest Hemingway Foundation, both for *Ellen Foster;* National Endowment for the Arts fellowship, for *A Virtuous Woman;* Nelson Algren Heartland Award for Fiction, *Chicago Tribune,* 1991, and PEN/Revson Foundation Fellowship, both for *A Cure for Dreams;* Critics Choice Award, *Los Angeles Times,* 1995, for *Sights Unseen;* Chevalier de L'Ordre des Arts et des Lettres (French Knighthood), for contribution to French literature, 1996.

WRITINGS:

NOVELS

Ellen Foster, Algonquin Books (Chapel Hill, NC), 1987.

when Kaye was ten years old, Gibbons later drew on some of her experiences in her fiction. While she did not go to live with her grandmother, as Ellen Foster does in *Ellen Foster,* she did live with an older brother, and she did and does value books. "Books are the most important thing in my life," she told *Book* writer Liz Seymour in 2002. "I grew up walking three miles to a Bookmobile—books aren't property, they're a whole separate category." Like her mother, from the age of twenty Gibbons has suffered from bipolar disorder, once known as manic depression, in which a person veers dangerously from periods of depression to periods of mania (intense activity and sleeplessness). She wrote her first novel, *Ellen Foster,* during a six-week manic binge and her 1998 novel *On the Occasion of My Last Afternoon* during three months when she would write from forty to sixty hours at a time. And though this condition has become more treatable, Gibbons is careful, for she does not want to sacrifice the creativity that has allowed her to become an award-winning novelist.

The novel *Ellen Foster* began life as a poem Gibbons started while a student at the University of North Carolina at Chapel Hill, initially in the voice of the protagonist's young African-American friend, Starletta. The author admitted to being influenced by the work of early twentieth-century African-American poet James Weldon Johnson, and his use of common speech patterns and idioms in his prose. "I wanted to see if I could have a child use her voice to talk about life, death, art, eternity—big things from a little person," Gibbons told Summer. Ellen Foster's title character is a mere eleven years of age, and the story follows her travails in the rural southern states as she bounces from relative to relative. Speaking in the first person, Gibbons's heroine refers to herself as "old Ellen," and recounts her difficulties in flashback form. Deanna D'Errico described her in *Belles Lettres* as "the embodiment of tenacity, surviving with the tools of intelligence, sensitivity, a strong will, and a remarkable sense of humor." In the novel, Ellen's mother was the frail scion of a well-to-do family whom she alienated by marrying beneath her, and their offspring has it rough from the start. When her mother commits suicide, Ellen is left with a parent whom she describes as "a monster." His attempt at sexual abuse one drunken night leads Ellen to the jurisdiction of the court system, and a judge sends her to live with her wealthy, but extremely resentful, maternal grandmother.

Ellen's grandmother vents her grief at her daughter's suicide on her granddaughter, forcing her to work the family cotton fields and inflicting verbal and emotional abuse upon her. Over the course of Gibbons's novel, Ellen faces her problems with a good nature and determination: she learns to hoard money in a small box that contains all of her other vital belongings. She also befriends the aforementioned Starletta, who is mute. "Gibbons, unlike so many writers of the New South, doesn't evade the racism of Southern life," wrote Pearl K. Bell in a review of *Ellen Foster* for the *New Republic.* Growing up hearing the racial prejudices of her family, Ellen also feels such biases, and reminds herself that no matter how bad her own situation is, it would be worse to be "colored."

When Ellen's grandmother dies, she is sent to live with an aunt, and the aunt and Ellen's cousin also heap abuse upon her—at one point, ridiculing the picture she has drawn for them for a Christmas present as "cheap-looking." When the aunt sends her away, Ellen spends a night at Starletta's home, which eventually leads to the protagonist's realization that "now I know it is not the germs you cannot see . . . that will hurt you or turn you colored. What you had better worry about though is the people you knew and trusted they would be like you because you were all made in the same batch." In the end, Ellen discovers that her small town contains a "foster" family—a single woman who takes in children. She shows up on their doorstep and offers the $160 contents of her box in exchange for a home.

In the *New Republic* review, Bell praised Gibbons's evocation of Ellen's unique personality through her narrative, as did many other reviewers. "The voice of this resourceful child is mesmerizing because we are right inside her head," she noted. Alice Hoffman reviewed *Ellen Foster* for the *New York Times Book Review* and asserted that the first-time author "is so adept at drawing her characters that we know Ellen, and, yes, trust her from the start." Hoffman further noted that "in many ways this is an old-fashioned novel about traditional values and inherited prejudices. . . . What might have been grim, melodramatic material in the hands of a less talented author is instead filled with lively humor . . . , compassion and intimacy." *Sunday Times* critic Linda Taylor termed Gibbons's debut "fresh, instant and enchanting . . . a first novel that does not put a foot wrong in its sureness of style, tone and characterisation."

In her second novel, *A Virtuous Woman,* Gibbons again sets her characters in the rural South and allows them to speak in the idiomatic, direct language of her own upbringing. The 1989 work opens as Jack Stokes laments the loss of Ruby, his wife of many years, from lung cancer. "She hasn't been dead four months and I've already eaten to the bottom of the deep freeze," the farmer thinks to himself; despite her illness, Ruby had prepared months worth of meals ahead of time for Jack. Such details pointing to the ordinary, yet loving familiarities of the institution of marriage are what Gibbons attempts to call forth in the story. *A Virtuous Woman* is told in alternating first-person flashbacks for most of its course—Jack looking back after she is gone, alternating with Ruby's ruminations on their life together in the months before her death. The reader learns how Ruby's disastrous first marriage ultimately resulted in her inoperable tumors, and why her marriage to Jack was less vivid than her first, but over time, ultimately more satisfying.

As both characters in *A Virtuous Woman* come to grips with their impending tragedy, the interior monologues that Gibbons has Jack and Ruby voice in the novel propel it forward. Toward the end, Gibbons switches to a third-person perspective as the motivations and actions of other characters involved in Jack and Ruby's life come into play. "Too often, lacking a conflict of its own, the story wanders off to peek in at the neighbors," remarked *Los Angeles Times Book Review* critic Susan Heeger of this literary construction. "Pages are spent on the meanness of peripheral folk, whose main raison d'etre is to show up Jack's and Ruby's saintliness and to raise the question of why bad things happen to good people." The critic D'Errico, writing again for *Belles Lettres,* also found this switch disconcerting. "Technique suddenly looms over the tale," she lamented, "and it is difficult to view the scene without fretting over the strings that are showing."

In 1997 Oprah Winfrey chose *Ellen Foster* and *A Virtuous Woman* for her television book club, exposure that launched the books onto the best-seller lists and thrust their author into the limelight. Gibbons found the publicity both a blessing and a curse: blessing for the sale of books she believes in, but a curse in terms of the distractions of fan mail and telephone calls. *Ellen Foster* has come to be read in many high schools along with such classics as *To Kill a Mockingbird* and *The Adventures of Huckleberry Finn. Ellen Foster* was made into a Hallmark television movie that premiered in December, 1997.

Gibbons's third novel, *A Cure for Dreams,* won the *Chicago Tribune*'s Nelson Algren Heartland award for fiction that same year. In it, Gibbons recounts the multigenerational family saga of a trio of three women: Lottie, her daughter Betty, and granddaughter Marjorie. The novel begins as Marjorie introduces her recently deceased mother Betty to the reader, and relates how much her mother loved to talk. "Talking was my mother's life," she says, and the story is soon overtaken by Betty's own narrative voice. Betty describes her indomitable Irish immigrant grandmother—Lottie's mother—and the harsh life Lottie suffered in rural Kentucky during the early years of the twentieth century. Lottie escapes by marriage, but her workaholic husband isolates her emotionally until Betty arrives as a newborn in 1920.

As some reviewers noted, most of the male characters in *A Cure for Dreams* seem unsympathetic figures, absorbed in their own world of nonverbal communication, while the women ultimately triumph over adversity by virtue of their need to communicate with one another, resulting in strong bonds. In coming together, they manage to overcome both petty and grievous abuses inflicted upon them by the men of their families. Throughout the course of *A Cure for Dreams,* Gibbons lets Betty continue the decades-long tale of her family, recalling how her mother, Lottie, became the de facto community leader of the women around North Carolina's Milk Farm Road in the 1920s. She organized card parties, passed along useful gossip and wisdom, and at one point even protected a friend who may or may not have shot her abusive husband. Betty's own saga of coming of age in the South of the 1930s is also recounted, and the novel ends with the birth of her daughter Marjorie during World War II.

The overwhelming successes of Gibbons's literary career were also accompanied by periods of personal strife during the early 1990s. She went through a divorce, relocated to New York City but returned to North Carolina, and changed publishers. In 1993, her fourth novel, *Charms for the Easy Life,* was published. Like *A Cure for Dreams,* the story follows the exploits of a family of strong women, and develops through the recollections of its youngest member. Set over a forty-year span that ends during World War II, the novel begins with narrator Margaret recounting the courtship of her grandparents in Pasquotank County, North Carolina. Her grandmother, Charlie (Clarissa) Kate, becomes the central figure in the novel through her work as a local midwife and faith healer. Gibbons had originally modeled the character on an African-American midwife who served as the best friend of Lottie in her previous novel, but reconsidered doing a sequel after she began, and instead made Charlie into a completely separate entity.

Like Lottie in *A Cure for Dreams,* Charlie becomes a vital and important force in her rural community. When she saves an African-American man from a lynching, he gives her a rabbit's foot, her "easy-life charm." A folk healer who reads the *New England Journal of Medicine,* Charlie promotes sex education and manages to put a halt to the damaging medical treatment meted out by the charlatan local "trained" doctor. She is also the first person in the community to own a toilet. "She's an implacable force of nature, a pillar of intellect, with insight and powers of intuition so acute as to seem nearly supernatural," remarked Stephen McCauley of Gibbons's creation in the *New York Times Book Review.* As in previous works, the author allowed few compassionate male characters into the story of the three women. "The men in their lives are largely ineffectual," observed McCauley. "They can be relied upon only to disappoint, disappear and die." Charlie's husband simply does not return home one evening, an act which has little impact upon her young daughter, Sophie. Like her mother, Sophie later enters into a marriage with the wrong man, who passes away in the middle of the night; the two then move in with Charlie. Now all three women are free to pursue their ambitions and lend support to one another. They debate literature, Sophie and Margaret act as assistants to Charlie's unofficial doctor/dentist/midwife practice, and Charlie meddles in the affairs of her granddaughter, who in turn finds inspiration from the older woman.

Published in 1995, Gibbons's *Sights Unseen* tells the story, from the perspective of twelve-year-old daughter Hattie, of a mother's struggle with mental illness and its pervasive influence on her family's life. This novel was part of Gibbons's efforts to come to grips with the mental illness that had cost her mother her life and has plagued the author for decades. She struggled in its production, writing five drafts before she was satisfied. Her efforts paid off, for it garnered praised from critics. Comparing *Sights Unseen* to Gibbons's first novel, *Ellen Foster, New Yorker* critic James Wolcott noted that the narrator in each novel portrays "an avid need for normality and acceptance in a world of precarious

well-being." A *Publishers Weekly* reviewer cited Gibbons's "restrained prose of unflinching clarity" and praised the novel, declaring it "a haunting story that begs to be read in one sitting." As Donna Seaman noted in *Booklist,* "Gibbons writes seamless and resonant novels, the sort of fiction that wins hearts as well as awards." Indeed, *Sights Unseen* won the *Los Angeles Times* Critics Choice Award for that year.

For her next novel, Gibbons delved into the history of the twentieth-century South that had been the setting of her previous works. *On the Occasion of My Last Afternoon,* so titled because first-person narrator, Emma Lowell, is recalling her life as she prepares to die, follows the narrator's life as the daughter of a Southern slaveowner who follows her own path. In the *Winston-Salem Journal,* Anne Barnhill remarked how well Gibbons's research into the era served her: "It's evident that Gibbons has done a great deal of research for this book. The language has the authentic sound of yesteryear, and interesting details are peppered throughout the novel." *Library Journal's* Joanna M. Burkhardt likewise praised the novel for its "crystal clarity and brilliant realism." However, while *America* reviewer Jane Fisher found the novel "lively and readable," she questioned Gibbons's characterization of Emma, who, she complained, "seems almost too good to be true." Another reviewer found the novel to be too didactic at times: "Gibbons has wrought a balanced and highly accessible novel which, although well constructed and provocative, descends into cliched and tiresome tirades," wrote *London Times* critic Victoria Fletcher. Because of its fictional memoir structure, the reader knows that the narrator survives any perils, thus eliminating some of the possible suspense. Nevertheless, Dennis Love of the *San Francisco Chronicle* maintained that Gibbons overcomes any difficulties the structure might pose: "We see everything coming from miles away, yet it doesn't matter; this is a master storyteller who, like some arrogant, gifted athlete, telegraphs her every move but still scores at will." Despite any shortcomings, Fisher suggested that Gibbons's "major appeal as a novelist lies in her linking of unrelenting truth with the transformative power of unconditional love" and that she succeeds again in linking the two in *On the Occasion of My Last Afternoon.*

Despite the praise bestowed by critics and the numerous awards she has received, Gibbons admits that the writer's life is a strenuous one. "Nobody ever told me it was going to be easy," she noted in the interview with Bob Summer for *Publishers Weekly*. "If I weren't a writer, I'd probably be a lawyer or an architect. I wouldn't want to do anything easy, and I chose to be a writer." The author reflected that, "as a writer, it's my job to come up with three hundred pages or so every two years. Each time I begin, I know it's going to happen, but I'm scared it won't. It's working with that element of fear that keeps a book going," a process she also likened to "looking over an abyss and knowing I have to jump."

BIOGRAPHICAL AND CRITICAL SOURCES:

BOOKS

Authors and Artists for Young Adults, Volume 34, Gale (Detroit, MI), 2000.

DeMarr, Mary Jean, *Kaye Gibbons: A Critical Companion*, Greenwood Press (Westport, CT), 2003.

Lewis, Nancy, "Kaye Gibbons: Her Full-Time Women," in *Southern Writers at Century's End*, edited by Jeffrey J. Folks and James A. Perkins, University Press of Kentucky (Lexington, KY), 112-122.

Munafo, Giavanna, "'Colored Biscuits': Reconstructing Whiteness and the Boundaries of 'Home' in Kaye Gibbons's *Ellen Foster*," pp. 38-61.

Watkins, James, editor, *Southern Selves, from Mark Twain and Eudora Welty to Maya Angelou and Kaye Gibbons: A Collection of Autobiographical Writing*, Vintage (New York, NY), 1998.

PERIODICALS

America, January 2, 1999, Jane Fisher, review of *On the Occasion of My Last Afternoon*, p. 16.

Atlanta Journal-Constitution, June 2, 1998, "In Search of a Novel: Author Kay Gibbons Talks about Her New Civil War Book, the 'Oprah Hoopla' and Why She Tossed out 900 Pages," p. D1.

Belles Lettres, summer, 1987, Deanna D'Errico, review of *Ellen Foster*, p. 9; summer, 1989, Deanna D'Errico, "Two Timers," p. 7; winter 1993-94, Gale Harris, "Beyond the *Scarlett* Image: Women Writing about the South," pp. 16-18.

Book, November-December, 2002, Liz Seymour, "Oh, Kaye!," pp. 24-26.

Booklist, September 1, 1987, Brad Hooper, review of *Ellen Foster*, p. 27; June 1, 1999, reviews of *Ellen Foster* and *A Virtuous Woman*, pp. 1796-1797; August, 1999, review of *Charms for the Easy Life*, p. 2024; February 15, 2000, Donna Seaman, review of *On the Occasion of My Last Afternoon*, p. 1078; September 15, 2001, Karen Harris, review of *Sights Unseen* (audio version), p. 241.

Christian Century, September 23, Ralph C. Wood, "Gumption and Grace in the Novels of Kaye Gibbons," pp. 842-846.

Entertainment Weekly, April 4, 1995, Rebecca Ascher-Walsh, review of *Sights Unseen*, p. 53.

Globe and Mail (Toronto, Ontario, Canada), June 12, 1999, reviews of *A Virtuous Woman* and *Ellen Foster*, p. D4.

Grand Rapids Press (Grand Rapids, MI), April 14, 2002, Ann Byle, "Easter Story Inspires Gibbons' Latest Novel," p. 16.

Journal of American Studies, April, 1999, Sharon Monteith, "Between Girls: Kaye Gibbons's *Ellen Foster* and Friendship As a Monologic Formulation," pp. 45-46.

Kirkus Reviews, March 15, 1987, review of *Ellen Foster*, p. 404; January 15, 2004, review of *Divining Women*, p. 52.

Kliatt Young Adult Paperback Book Guide, September, 1997, p. 4; September, 1998, pp. 4, 61; July, 1999, review of *A Virtuous Woman* (audio version), p. 56.

Library Journal, June 1, 1998, p. 150; September, 1998, pp. 4, 61; February 15, 1999, review of *Ellen Foster* (audio version), p. 126; April 15, 1999, Joanna M. Burkhardt, review of *A Virtuous Woman* (audio version), p. 165; September 15, 1999, Joanna M. Burkhardt, review of *On the Occasion of My Last Afternoon* (audio version), p. 130.

Los Angeles Times Book Review, June 11, 1989, Susan Heeger, review of *A Virtuous Woman*, p. 15; May 19, 1991, Josephine Humphreys, review of *A Cure for Dreams*, p. 13.

New Republic, February 29, 1998, Pearl K. Bell, "Southern Discomfort," pp. 38-41.

New York, April 1, 1991, Rhoda Koenig, "Southern Comfort," p. 63.

New Yorker, June 21, 1993, p. 101; August 21 1995, James Wolcott, "Crazy for You," pp. 115-16.

New York Times Book Review, May 31, 1987, Alice Hoffman, "Shopping for a New Family," review of *Ellen Foster*, p. 13; April 12, 1989, pp. 12-13; April 30, 1989, Padgett Powell, "As Ruby Lay Dying," pp. 12-13; May 12, 1991, James Wilcox, review of *A Cure for Dreams,* pp. 13-14; April 11, 1993, Stephen McCauley, "He's Gone, Go Start the Coffee," pp. 9-10; September 24, 1995, Jacqueline Carey, "Mommy Direst," p. 30.

Observer (London, England), June 2, 1996, Kate Kellaway, review of *Sights Unseen,* p. 16.

People, June 15, 1998, review of *On the Occasion of My Last Afternoon,* p. 49.

Publishers Weekly, March 20, 1987, review of *Ellen Foster,* p. 70; February 8, 1993, Kaye Gibbons, with Bob Summer, "Kaye Gibbons," pp. 60-61; June 5, 1995, p. 48; April 20, 1998, review of *On the Occasion of My Last Afternoon,* p. 43.

San Francisco Chronicle, June 14, 1998, Dennis Love, "Home Is No Refuge for Southern Women in the Civil War," review of *On the Occasion of My Last Afternoon,* p. 3.

San Francisco Review of Books, spring, 1991, Benedict Cosgrove, review of *A Cure for Dreams,* pp. 31-32.

School Library Journal, September, 1993, p. 260; December, 1993, p. 29; September, 1998, Molly Connally, review of *On the Occasion of My Last Afternoon,* p. 229.

Southern Literary Journal, spring, 1994, Tonita Branan, "Women and 'The Gift for Gab': Revisionary Strategies in *A Cure for Dreams,*" pp. 91-101.

Southern Quarterly, winter, 1992, Veronica Makowsky, "'The Only Hard Part Was the Food:' Recipes for Self-Nurture in Kaye Gibbons's Novels," pp. 103-112; summer, 1997, Kathryn McKee, "Simply Talking: Women and Language in Kaye Gibbons's *A Cure for Dreams,*" pp. 97-106.

Southern Studies, summer, 1992, Stephen Souris, "Kaye Gibbons's *A Virtuous Woman,*" 99-115.

Time, April 12, 1993, Amelia Weiss, "Medicine Woman," pp. 77-78.

Times (London, England), May 22, 1999, Victoria Fletcher, "Slave to the Soapbox," review of *On the Occasion of My Last Afternoon,* p. 22.

Times Literary Supplement, November 25, 1988, Andrew Rosenheim, "Voices of the New South," p. 1306; September 15, 1989, Roz Kavaney, "Making Themselves Over," p. 998; July 2, 1999, review of *On the Occasion of My Last Afternoon,* p. 22.

Tribune Books (Chicago, IL), September 15, 1991, p. 7.

Washington Post Book World, July 12, 1998, Susan Dodd, "A Sentimental Education," *On the Occasion of My Last Afternoon,* p. 9.

Winston-Salen Journal (Winston-Salem, NC), July 12, 1998, Anne Barnhill, "Broken Promise: Gibbons' Memoir-Like Tale Lacks Drama," review of *On the Occasion of My Last Afternoon,* p. A22.

Women's Review of Books, July, 1989, Marilyn Chandler, review of *A Virtuous Woman,* p. 21; October, 1993, Judith Beth Cohen, "Daughters of the South," p. 24.

ONLINE

Chelsea Forum, http://www.chelseaforum.com/ (August 17, 2003), "Kaye Gibbons."

Kaye Gibbons Home Page, http://www.kayegibbons.com/ (February 19, 2004).

Syracuse Online, http://syracuse.com/ (August 17, 2003), Laura T. Ryan, "Gibbons Says Manic Depression Fuels Her Art."

Womankind Educational and Resource Center, http://www.womankindflp.org/ (1993), Steve Moore, "Conversation with Kay Gibbons."*

*   *   *

GLAISTER, Lesley (G.) 1956-

PERSONAL: Born October 4, 1956, in Wellingborough, Northamptonshire, England; daughter of Leonard Oliver Richard (a civil servant) and Maureen Jillian (an amateur singer; maiden name, Crowley) Glaister; children: Joseph French, Joshua French, Leo. *Education:* Open University, B.A. (with first-class honors), 1986; University of Sheffield, M.A., 1988.

ADDRESSES: Home—37 Roach Rd., Sheffield, South Yorkshire S11 8UA, England. *Agent*—Bill Hamilton, A. M. Heath and Co. Ltd., 79 St. Martin's Lane, London WC2N 4AA, England.

CAREER: Parsons Cross College, Sheffield, England, teacher of adult education courses, beginning 1982; Sheffield Hallam University, teacher of creative writing. Tutor at Loxley College. Writer-in-residence, Cheltenham Literature Festival, 2001-02.

MEMBER: Royal Society of Literature (fellow).

AWARDS, HONORS: Somerset Maugham Award, and Betty Trask Award, both 1991, both for *Honour Thy Father;* Yorkshire Author of the Year Award, *Yorkshire Post,* 1993, for *Limestone and Clay;* Orange Prize for fiction, 2002, for *Now You See Me.*

WRITINGS:

NOVELS

Honour Thy Father, Secker & Warburg (London, England), 1990, Atheneum (New York, NY), 1991.
Trick or Treat, Secker & Warburg (London, England), 1991, Atheneum (New York, NY), 1992.
Digging to Australia, Secker & Warburg (London, England), 1992, Atheneum (New York, NY), 1993.
Limestone and Clay, Secker & Warburg (London, England), 1993, Atheneum (New York, NY), 1994.
Partial Eclipse, Hamish Hamilton (London, England), 1994.
The Private Parts of Women, Bloomsbury (London, England), 1996.
Easy Peasy, St. Martin's Press (New York, NY), 1997.
Sheer Blue Bliss, Bloomsbury (London, England), 1999.
Now You See Me, Bloomsbury (London, England), 2001.

Contributor of stories to women's magazines.

SIDELIGHTS: Lesley Glaister, according to Lesley McDowell in the *Scotsman,* "is one of those writers credited with creating a world all of her own. It has led to comparisons with authors like Kate Atkinson and Ruth Rendell, where surreal landscape meets read-it-in-one-sitting type narrative. It's a provocative mix that has critics reaching easily for superlatives." Glaister "may be feted as a modern Gothic novelist," Julie Myerson claimed in the *Guardian,* "but she's also a sparkling miniaturist, social comedian and dauntless urban poet" who has also penned "clear, truthful novels, full of tension and bile, honest, embarrassing sex, domestic horror and familial lies. Yet despite the poetry and razzmatazz, they're resolutely low-key pieces, firmly devoid of any grand pretensions." Among Glaister's most popular novels are *Limestone and Clay* and *Now You See Me.*

In *Limestone and Clay* Glaister focuses on the relationship between Nadia, a potter who wants to have a baby, and Nadia's lover, Simon, a teacher of geography

and amateur spelunker. As Mary Scott noted in the *New Statesman,* their relationship "threatens to suffocate them both." When Simon's former lover announces she is pregnant by him, Nadia and Simon must confront the problems they have been avoiding. Nancy Middleton in *Belles Lettres* found that the story "builds gracefully, filling with detail and respect for our most human failings." Scott admitted that "the writing is so strong that it almost sweeps all before it." "Drawn with exceptional clarity," according to a critic for *Publishers Weekly,* "Glaister's complicated, fallible characters linger in the reader's mind."

Now You See Me tells the story of Lamb, a young woman running away from her past. She has been hospitalized, has no family, and no place to live. After moving to London, Lamb cleans houses for a living—using forged references—and begins to live secretly in an elderly client's unused cellar. Lamb's reclusive and delicately balanced life is soon joined by Doggo, an escaped convict hiding from the law. When the elderly client is taken ill and rushed to a hospital, the couple move out of the cellar and into the main house. "Glaister explores the tangle of deceit that the lovers practise on each other to protect their own vulnerability and their agonised need to reveal themselves in order to gain the intimacy that they crave," Katie Owen explained in the London *Times.* In her review of *Now You See Me* for the London *Daily Mail,* Elizabeth Buchan wrote: "With its unflinching detail, its subtle manipulation of emotion and its wary and delicate exploration of trust that can flower between wounded people, it possesses an unsettling resonance." Mark Bostridge in the *Independent* found that "Glaister's greatest talent is her willingness to tell it like it is. Every novelist should learn from this: her subtle punch, the brutal beauty of her writing. And every reader should read her, and prepare to be amazed."

Glaister once told *CA:* "Through my writing I'm interested in exploring the boundaries between such opposite states as love and hate, madness and sanity, danger and safety, laughter and tears, which are often more illusory the closer one looks. My aim is also to peel back the layers that make up characters, to discover and reveal the touching absurdities that lie within."

BIOGRAPHICAL AND CRITICAL SOURCES:

PERIODICALS

Atlantic, June, 1992, Phoebe-Lou Adams, review of *Trick or Treat,* p. 128.

Belles Lettres, fall, 1993, Elaine Romaine, review of *Digging to Australia,* p. 58; fall, 1994, Nancy Middleton, review of *Limestone and Clay,* p. 90.

Booklist, February 15, 1993, Lindsay Throm, review of *Digging to Australia,* p. 1033; March 15, 1994, Alice Joyce, review of *Partial Eclipse,* p. 1326; September 1, 1997, Jennifer Henderson, review of *Easy Peasy,* p. 57.

Book Report, September-October, 1993, Diane Pozar, review of *Digging to Australia,* p. 42.

Daily Mail (London, England), April 27, 2001, Elizabeth Buchan, review of *Now You See Me,* p. 52.

Guardian, May 12, 2001, review of *Now You See Me.*

Independent (London, England), April 29, 2001, Mark Bostridge, review of *Now You See Me,* pp. 31-32.

Irish Times, August 24, 2002, Cathy Dillon, review of *Now You See Me,* p. 60.

Lambda Book Report, May, 1998, Susan Raffo, review of *Easy Peasy,* p. 25.

Library Journal, March 1, 1993, Joanna M. Burkhardt, review of *Digging to Australia,* p. 107; November 1, 1993, Maurice Taylor, review of *Digging to Australia,* p. 176.

New Statesman, August 27, 1993, Mary Scott, review of *Limestone and Clay,* p. 40; September 2, 1994, Wendy Brandmark, review of *Partial Eclipse,* p. 40; April 19, 1996, Carol Birch, review of *The Private Parts of Women,* p. 37; February 5, 1999, Francis Gilbert, review of *Sheer Blue Bliss,* p. 49.

Publishers Weekly, February 8, 1993, review of *Digging to Australia,* p. 73; January 31, 1994, review of *Limestone and Clay,* p. 75; August 4, 1997, review of *Easy Peasy,* p. 67.

Scotsman, May 26, 2001, Lesley McDowell, review of *Now You See Me,* p. 9.

Spectator, September 25, 1993, Cressida Connolly, review of *Limestone and Clay,* p. 31; August 20, 1994, Francis King, review of *Partial Eclipse,* p. 32; June 21, 1997, Kate Hubbard, review of *Easy Peasy,* p. 35.

Times (London, England), May 5, 2001, Katie Owen, review of *Now You See Me;* May 16, 2001, Dominic Bradbury, review of *Now You See Me.*

Times Literary Supplement, October 19, 1990, p. 1130.

ONLINE

Contemporary Writers, http://www.contemporary writers.com/ (November 11, 2003).*

GLENN, Mel 1943-

PERSONAL: Born May 10, 1943, in Zurich, Switzerland (U.S. citizen born abroad, moved to U.S. in 1945, raised in Brooklyn, NY); son of Jacob B. (a physician) and Elizabeth (Hampel) Glenn; married Elyse Friedman (a teacher), September 20, 1970; children: Jonathan, Andrew. *Education:* New York University, A.B., 1964; Yeshiva University, M.S., 1967. *Religion:* Jewish.

ADDRESSES: Home—4288 Bedford Ave., New York, NY 11229. *Office*—Abraham Lincoln High School, Brooklyn, NY 11235. *E-mail*—author114@aol.com.

CAREER: U.S. Peace Corps, Washington, DC, volunteer English teacher in Sierra Leone, 1964-66; English teacher at a public junior high school, New York, NY, 1967-70; Abraham Lincoln High School, New York, NY, English teacher, 1970-2001; currently author and public speaker at schools, libraries, and community groups.

MEMBER: Society of Children's Book Writers and Illustrators, Authors Guild.

AWARDS, HONORS: Best Books for Young Adults citation, American Library Association (ALA), 1982, and Golden Kite Honor Book plaque, Society of Children's Book Writers, both for *Class Dismissed! High School Poems;* Best Books citation, *School Library Journal,* 1986, and Christopher Award, 1987, both for *Class Dismissed II: More High School Poems;* Best Books for Young Adults citation, ALA, 1992, for *My Friend's Got This Problem, Mr. Candler: High School Poems;* Top Ten Best Books for Young Adults citation, ALA, 1997, for *Who Killed Mr. Chippendale? A Mystery in Poems;* Best Books for Young Adults citation, ALA, 2001, for *Split Image.*

WRITINGS:

POETRY

Class Dismissed! High School Poems, illustrated with photographs by Michael J. Bernstein, Clarion (Boston, MA), 1982.

Mel Glenn

Class Dismissed II: More High School Poems, illustrated with photographs by Michael J. Bernstein, Clarion (Boston, MA), 1986.

Back to Class, illustrated with photographs by Michael J. Bernstein, Clarion (Boston, MA), 1989.

My Friend's Got This Problem, Mr. Candler: High School Poems, illustrated with photographs by Michael J. Bernstein, Clarion (Boston, MA), 1991.

Who Killed Mr. Chippendale? A Mystery in Poems, Lodestar (New York, NY), 1996.

The Taking of Room 114: A Hostage Drama in Poems, Lodestar (New York, NY), 1997.

Jump Ball: A Basketball Season in Poems, Lodestar/Dutton (New York, NY), 1997.

Foreign Exchange: A Mystery in Poems, Morrow Junior (New York, NY), 1999.

Split Image: A Story in Poems, Harper Collins (New York, NY), 2000.

FICTION

One Order to Go, Clarion (Boston, MA), 1984.

Play-by-Play, Clarion (Boston, MA), 1986.

Squeeze Play: A Baseball Story, Clarion (Boston, MA), 1989.

WORK IN PROGRESS: "A new book."

SIDELIGHTS: Teacher and writer Mel Glenn is noted especially for books that address the day-to-day concerns of teenagers in a unique manner—through poetry. Written in free verse, using uncomplicated language that makes them accessible to many students who would otherwise steer clear of the genre, Glenn's poems "echo the voices of young adults who are struggling in two separate worlds: the world of adults and the world of children," noted Teri S. Lesesne in *Twentieth-Century Young Adult Writers.* Glenn's verse, Lesesne added, "capture[s] the essence of the adolescent: the emotions which sometimes seem to run out of control, the changing relationships with parents and other adults as the adolescent struggles for independence."

Writing books for young adults was a natural extension of Glenn's interest in teaching. The inspiration for his first book, the poetry collection *Class Dismissed! High School Poems,* was *Spoon River Anthology,* a collection of original verse by poet Edgar Lee Masters. The motivation behind sitting down and actually writing the book was a challenge Glenn gave himself one New Year's Eve. "Another teacher had shown me his unpublished manuscript, and I said to myself that if he could write a book, so could I." Glenn set up a schedule for himself and completed the manuscript in only six months. "The source for the book came easily: I have always prided myself on the fact that I am a good listener, and surrounding me were hundreds of stories—some sad, some happy, some tragic—but all terribly real and poignant. Though styles and fashions may change, there are certain common denominators in being a teenager that connect all generations—the feelings of being alone, different, in love, in conflict with parents. No matter how old we grow there will always be a part of us that will be sixteen years old."

Each of the poems in *Class Dismissed!,* as well as such sequels as 1986's *Class Dismissed II* and 1989's *Back to Class,* is written in the first person using free verse. Each is titled using the name of the fictional author, a teen from Glenn's fictional "class." Each poem is a brief look into the mind of a teen as he or she tries to grapple with a problem that is of momentary uppermost concern. In "Hildy Ross," for example, a young girl writes about her need to cover up the true cause of a bruise on her cheek: she is being beaten by an abusive father. Other adolescent concerns revolve around finding a summer job; the hard work of being an unwed teen parent; frustrations with preoccupied, out-of-touch parents; deciding which colleges to apply to; and even how to finagle the keys to the family car for a date.

While *Voice of Youth Advocates* reviewer Tony Manna questioned whether or not Glenn's verse contains "the kind of universals that we expect good poetry to illuminate" and pondered "whether many of the revelations are in fact poetry rather than the rendering of personal feelings," Candy Bertelson noted in *School Library Journal* that Glenn's works "deal with engaging, very 'real' kids, who are easy to identify with," and should "reach many young people who don't ordinarily read poetry."

Glenn has always taken his subject matter from his direct experiences with young people growing up in Brooklyn. His second book, the young adult novel *One Order to Go,* takes place in a candy store that the author recalled from his own youth: "the old kind where you can get a real malted and an egg cream." The story concerns seventeen-year-old Richie Linder, who hates school and wants to drop out and lead the exciting life of a news correspondent. His strict father will hear nothing of Richie's plans; instead, he fills his son's free time by making him work the counter at his luncheonette. A friendship with Lana finally gives Richie the courage to confront his domineering father with his own aspirations and make plans for an independent future. "I am sure that a large part of [*One Order to Go*] is autobiographical," Glenn once confided to *CA,* "but, in the larger sense, what writing isn't? You bring to your characters a sense of your own personal values and memories."

In *Play-by-Play,* Glenn wrote a story for younger readers. Fourth-grader Jeremy is constantly bested by his own best friend, Lloyd, a natural athlete who uses his talent to assume an air of superiority over those around him, Jeremy included. Through Jeremy's narration the reader watches as a new sport—soccer—and some new teammates—the fourth-grade girls—make both boys more tolerant of others. The two friends are reunited as sixth graders in *Squeeze Play: A Baseball Story,* in which a new coach seems more like a drill sergeant in his management of a school-wide baseball team. "Again, the material was all around me," Glenn once told *CA* of his inspiration. "My son, Jonathan, was actively involved in a local soccer league, and between practices and games on cold Saturday morn-

ings I learned about this 'foreign' sport. As a writer, I tried to pay close attention to the language, characteristics, and social mores of nine-year-olds."

In his 1991 poetry collection, *My Friend's Got This Problem, Mr. Candler,* Glenn presents the day-to-day triumphs and tragedies that make up the life of a high school guidance counselor. *Who Killed Mr. Chippendale? A Mystery in Poems* is a unique whodunit, as students, teachers, and others involved express through free-verse poetry their reactions to the tragic death of a high school English teacher in a random shooting. Several suspects emerge—a fellow teacher who was a former girlfriend, a high schooler who claims she was the murdered man's lover, and an emotionally unstable student whose negative attitude towards Mr. Chippendale and other circumstantial evidence call his alibi strongly into question. "Not only do the poems clue readers into the characters' personalities and sensibilities," said Sharon Korbeck in a *School Library Journal* review, "but they also provide a telling commentary on the attitudes toward violence reflected in our society at large." *Voice of Youth Advocates* reviewer Sally Kotarsky had a somewhat different reaction, however. "The problem with this book is that it tries to be too many things at once," she wrote. "The murder mystery is lost in the large number of poems dealing with immigration views."

The issue of violence in the school system is continued with Glenn's 1997 release, *The Taking of Room 114: A Hostage Drama in Poems.* This time the perpetrator is an emotionally disturbed history teacher, who holds his class at gunpoint on the last day of school. The story unfolds through notes passed under the door, and via the thoughts of the young hostages. More than one reviewer felt the book portrayed a stereotypical student mix: "tramps, nerds, immigrants, underachievers, womanizers, jocks—they're all accounted for," stated Elizabeth Bush in her review for the *Bulletin of the Center for Children's Books. Booklist* reviewer Debbie Carton was another who thought the author dealt in stereotypes, but also called the collection's format and topic "fresh and unusual." Marjorie Lewis of *School Library Journal* likewise pointed to the too-familiar "types" such as the pressured Asian scholar, the gay youth who fears AIDS, the edgy Jewish graduate, and the intrusive reporters. But Lewis also cited the author's "proven ear for the cadence of speech."

In his next story-anthology in verse, Glenn turned his eye to a big-city high school's basketball team. In

Jump Ball: A Basketball Season in Poems, the members of the Tower High School Tigers are enjoying a championship season; however, fate takes a turn when the team bus slides off an icy road. "The author expertly creates dramatic tension with early hints of the tragedy to come," noted a *Kirkus Reviews* contributor. The poems describe the lives of such characters as Garrett James, whose talent can take him all the way to the pros—if he can manage to graduate high school under the pressure of coaches, the media, and fans. With its delineation of dreams and heartbreak, *Jump Ball* is "a richly emotional book that brings readers face-to-face with issues in their own lives," concluded *Booklist* contributor Randy Meyer. Indeed, these young athletes "are not merely characters in a book," said Ted Hipple in *Writers for Young Adults,* "they are teens one might meet in any school in town. This ability to create multidimensional characters who seem to live and breathe off the page is another defining characteristic of Mel Glenn's poetry."

Foreign Exchange: A Mystery in Poems is a free-verse examination of race and class prejudice. When a group of urban teens spends the weekend in an upscale community, tensions run high. And when a murder is discovered, the finger of blame points—all too quickly—at Kwame, an inner-city student who stirs the suspicions of the less-diverse people of Hudson Landing. Similarly, stereotypes and the price of pressure is the theme of Glenn's 2000 collection, *Split Image: A Story in Poems.* The central character here is teenager Laura Li, an immigrant from China who attends Tower High School (from *Jump Ball*). Held up as the "ideal" teen, Laura is secretly unhappy. Torn by the demands of her family and her studies, the girl takes refuge in her school-library job by day, and in bars by night. The varied voices from Laura's life—her teachers, classmates, and family—provide insight into her troubled existence. But at the end of the book, Laura has committed suicide. "Written with raw immediacy," commented GraceAnne DeCandido of *Booklist,* "this [book] will touch teens deep down."

"I write to remember," Glenn was quoted in the *St. James Guide to Young Adult Writers.* "I write to open up the lines of communication, to explain my past to myself and others. On a certain level we are all emotionally fourteen. Good writing can put is in touch with who we were and who we are."

BIOGRAPHICAL AND CRITICAL SOURCES:

BOOKS

Children's Literature Review, Gale (Detroit, MI), 1999, pp. 84-95.

St. James Guide to Young Adult Writers, St. James Press (Detroit, MI), 1999.

Twentieth-Century Young Adult Writers, St. James Press (Detroit, MI), 1994, pp. 248-49.

Writers for Young Adults, edited by Ted Hipple, Scribner (New York, NY), 2000, pp. 67-74.

PERIODICALS

ALAN Review, winter, 1997.

Booklist, June 15, 1982, Stephanie Zvirin, review of *Class Dismissed! High School Poems,* p. 1361; October 1, 1984, Stephanie Zvirin, review of *One Order to Go,* p. 211; May 15, 1986, Carolyn Phelan, review of *Play-by-Play,* p. 1395; December 1, 1986, p. 567; December 1, 1988, Stephanie Zvirin, review of *Back to Class,* p. 634; May 15, 1989, Carolyn Phelan, review of *Squeeze Play: A Baseball Story,* pp. 1648-1649; September 15, 1991, Chris Sherman, review of *My Friend's Got This Problem, Mr. Candler: High School Poems,* p. 134; June 1, 1996, Stephanie Zvirin, review of *Who Killed Mr. Chippendale?: A Mystery in Poems,* p. 1688; March 1, 1997, Debbie Carton, review of *The Taking of Room 114: A Hostage Drama in Poems,* p. 1154; October 15, 1997, Randy Meyer, review of *Jump Ball: A Basketball Season in Poems,* p. 394; September 1, 1998, Sally Estes, review of *Jump Ball,* p. 119; October 1, 1998, review of *Who Killed Mr. Chippendale?,* p. 317; April 15, 1999, Stephanie Zvirin, review of *Foreign Exchange: A Mystery in Poems,* p. 1521; April 1, 2000, GraceAnne DeCandido, review of *Split Image: A Story in Poems,* p. 1447; August, 2000, Gillian Engberg, review of *Split Image,* p. 2133; April 15, 2001, review of *Who Killed Mr. Chippendale?,* p. 1549.

Bulletin of the Center for Children's Books, September, 1982, Zena Sutherland, review of *Class Dismissed!,* p. 9; April, 1986, Zena Sutherland, review of *Play-by-Play,* p. 148; February, 1987, Roger Sutton, review of *Class Dismissed II: More High School Poems,* p. 107; July-August, 1989, Zena

Sutherland, review of *Squeeze Play,* p. 275; July-August, 1996, Deborah Stevenson, review of *Who Killed Mr. Chippendale?,* pp. 372-373; March, 1997, Elizabeth Bush, review of *The Taking of Room 114,* pp. 247-248.

English Journal, February, 1989, Elizabeth Belden and Judith Beckman, review of *Back to Class,* p. 84.

Kirkus Reviews, October 1, 1986, review of *Class Dismissed II,* p. 1522; October 15, 1988, p. 1527; February 15, 1989, review of *Squeeze Play,* p. 292; August 1, 1991, review of *My Friend's Got This Problem, Mr. Candler,* p. 1010; April 1, 1996, review of *Play-by-Play,* p. 545; May 1, 1996, review of *Who Killed Mr. Chippendale?,* pp. 688-689; February 1, 1997, review of *The Taking of Room 114,* pp. 222-223; August 15, 1997, review of *Jump Ball,* p. 1305.

Kliatt Young Adult Paperback Book Guide, July, 2002, Paula Rohrllick, review of *Split Image,* pp. 18-19.

Library Journal, December, 1984, Deborah Locke, review of *One Order to Go,* p. 89.

Publishers Weekly, May 30, 1986, review of *Play-by-Play,* p. 67; July 8, 1996, review of *Who Killed Mr. Chippendale?,* p. 85.

School Library Journal, October, 1982, p. 160; December, 1984, p. 89; August, 1986, Robert Unsworth, review of *Play-by-Play,* p. 92; December, 1986, review of *Class Dismissed II,* p. 567; January, 1989, Kathleen Whalin, review of *Back to Class,* p. 98; May, 1989, Todd Morning, review of *Squeeze Play,* p. 104; September, 1991, Barbara Chatton, review of *My Friend's Got This Problem, Mr. Candler,* p. 288; July, 1996, Sharon Korbeck, review of *Who Killed Mr. Chippendale?,* p. 98; April, 1997, Marjorie Lewis, review of *The Taking of Room 114,* p. 137; November, 1997, Sharon Korbeck, review of *Jump Ball,* p. 128; April 26, 1999, review of *Who Killed Mr. Chippendale?;* June, 1999, Herman Sutter, review of *Foreign Exchange,* p. 1451; June, 2000, Sharon Koreck, review of *Split Image,* p. 165.

Voice of Youth Advocates, August, 1982, James Campbell, review of *Class Dismissed!,* p. 44; February, 1987, Luvada Kuhn, review of *Class Dismissed II,* p. 297; February, 1989, Tony Manna, review of *Back to Class,* pp. 300-301; February, 1992, Diane Tuccillo, review of *My Friend's Got This Problem, Mr. Candler,* p. 394; December, 1996, Sally Kotarsky, review of *Who Killed Mr. Chippendale?,* p. 287.

ONLINE

Mel Glenn Home Page, http://www.melglenn.com/ (November 1, 2003), author biography.

* * *

GOBBELL, John J. 1937-

PERSONAL: Born August 28, 1937, in San Diego, CA; son of Williard M. (a physician) and Dorothy P. (a homemaker) Gobbell; married Janine Govan, July 15, 1960; children: Jennifer Gobbell Cheffer, John J., Jr. *Ethnicity:* "American." *Education:* University of Southern California, B.A., 1960. *Politics:* Republican. *Religion:* Episcopalian. *Hobbies and other interests:* Yacht racing.

ADDRESSES: Home—659 Promontory Dr. E, Newport Beach, CA 92660. *Office*—Gobbell Co., 1001 Dove St., Ste. 190, Newport Beach, CA 92660. *Agent*—Wallace Agency, 177 East 70th St., New York, NY 10021. *E-mail*—jgobbell@pacbell.net.

CAREER: KPMG Peat Marwick (certified public accountants), Los Angeles, CA, consultant, 1967-70; Angeles Corp. (investors), Los Angeles, director of personnel, 1970-73; Boyden Associates, Inc. (executive recruiters), New York, NY, vice president of branch in Newport Beach, CA, 1973-83; Gobbell Co. (executive recruiters), Newport Beach, managing director, 1983—. USC Commerce Associates, president. Orange County Fictionaires (reading group), president, 1996. *Military service:* U.S. Navy, 1960-62, deck officer on a destroyer; became lieutenant.

WRITINGS:

The Brutus Lie (novel), Scribner (New York, NY), 1991.

The Last Lieutenant (novel), St. Martin's Press (New York, NY), 1995.

A Code for Tomorrow, St. Martin's Press (New York, NY), 1999.

When Duty Whispers Low, St. Martin's Press (New York, NY), 2002.

The Neptune Strategy, St. Martin's Press (New York, NY), 2004.

WORK IN PROGRESS: A screenplay adaptation of *The Brutus Lie* titled *Traitor on the Bridge.*

SIDELIGHTS: John J. Gobbell served in the U.S. Navy as a weapons officer aboard destroyers. One of his ships, the U.S.S. *Tingey,* sailed with the Seventh Fleet in the South China Sea. These naval experiences, along with his successful career as a high-level corporate recruiter, inform the themes of his novels.

Gobbell's first novel, *The Brutus Lie,* uses the convention of separated baby twins to tell a cold-war naval thriller. One baby boy is adopted by an American army corporal and taken to America. The other is adopted by a Soviet sergeant and raised in the Soviet Union. In a straight plot narrative, Gobbell pits brother against brother in a technological battle of realistic minisub technology while the two superpowers have their own reasons that the brothers should never unite. *Publishers Weekly* appreciated the technical accuracy of the book, noting, "Readers will be rewarded by a knowledgeable presentation of modern minisub technology and the extended escape and evasion narrative," while former Secretary of the Navy John Lehman wrote, "John Gobbell is the John Le Carré of naval thrillers."

The Last Lieutenant tells the story of the American defeat at Corregidor and the crucial American victory at Midway Island. *Publishers Weekly* noted that the story is based on *South from Corregidor,* the true account of Lt. Commander John H. Morrill II's 1943 escape from Corregidor Island the night it fell to the Japanese.

The novel begins in El Paso, Texas, in 1941 when a Nazi spy infiltrates the Navy by murdering a young sailor named Walter A. Radke and assuming his identity. After becoming a cryptologist, he finds himself on Corregidor holding invaluable secret information on the U.S. plans for the Battle of Midway.

As the island falls to the Japanese, Lt. Todd Ingram is ordered to get the bearers of the codes, Radke and Lt. Epperson, off the island onto a waiting submarine. During the escape, a mortally wounded Epperson tells

Ingram that Radke has disappeared on the island with the codes. Besides protecting the codes, Ingram manages to get seventeen survivors of the battle from the Philippines to Australia on a thirty-six-foot boat. Roland Green wrote in *Booklist,* "The action is continuous, the characterization well above average (even sparked by touches of wit), and the sense of place and time strong. Noteworthy, too, are Gobbell's implicit tribute to the role of the Filipinos in resisting the Japanese and helping Americans escape and the stark realism of his treatment of the fall of Corregidor."

A Code for Tomorrow is a sequel to *The Last Lieutenant.* Lt. Todd Ingram has safely escaped from Corregidor. Although Washington has promised him some easy duty after his Pacific tour, he is sent back to the Pacific onboard a destroyer as executive officer. Gobbell puts Ingram in two of the epic naval battles off Guadalcanal: the Battle of Cape Esperance and the Battle of the Santa Cruz Islands. "The sea action is thoroughly convincing," noted *Kirkus Reviews.* The subplot brings Ingram to Mindanao, in the Philippines, where his girlfriend, Helen Durand, is behind enemy lines with a Philippine resistance group. After being betrayed by a Russian agent he has come to trust, Helen and her Philippine guerilla brigade rescue him from a Japanese base where he had been held and tortured. A *Publishers Weekly* reviewer found the sequel weak, commenting, "Blustering and never notably bright, Gobbell's characters come across as caricatures, especially the Japanese and Russian bad guys."

When Duty Whispers Low continues to follow Ingram, who is again the executive officer aboard the destroyer U.S.S. *Howell.* Gobbell introduces the real-life American technological breakthrough of proximity fuses. This new ordnance was invented in 1943 to assist the U.S. Navy in its fight against Japanese Admiral Isoroku Yamamoto's sea and air attacks to retake Guadalcanal and turn the tide in the Pacific theater.

Since his first novel, Gobbell has been praised for sound research and good storytelling. *Booklist* critic Thomas Gaughan wrote, "The combination of careful research, fascinating back story, and the author's own experience makes this series—and this installment—a real winner. Fans of naval adventure will almost smell the fetid jungle of Tulagi and be deafened by the ship's guns. They will be infuriated by the corrosive careerism of various self-aggrandizing officers."

Gobbell once told *CA:* "My primary motivation for writing is that I finally figured out a way to put my daydreams to work. I am influenced by top-of-the-line thriller and action-adventure authors. My writing process is helter-skelter, undisciplined, and totally unplanned. Scheduling helps, but I am soon distracted and in the process of shooting myself in the foot. I keep trying. I was inspired to write on the subjects I have chosen because I enjoy reading about man, machine, and overcoming enormous circumstances, using wit and intelligence in an extremely limited time."

BIOGRAPHICAL AND CRITICAL SOURCES:

PERIODICALS

Booklist, August 1, 1995, Roland Green, review of *The Last Lieutenant,* p. 1929; June 1, 1999, Budd Arthur, review of *A Code for Tomorrow,* p. 1790; December 15, 2001, Thomas Gaughan, review of *When Duty Whispers Low,* p. 703.

Kirkus Reviews, June 15, 1999, review of *A Code for Tomorrow,* p. 902.

Library Journal, November 15, 2001, Patrick J. Wall, review of *When Duty Whispers Low,* p. 96.

Publishers Weekly, February 15, 1991, Sybil Steinberg, review of *The Brutus Lie,* p. 75; May 29, 1995, review of *The Last Lieutenant,* p. 66; June 21, 1999, review of *A Code for Tomorrow,* p. 57; November 19, 2001, review of *When Duty Whispers Low,* p. 45.

School Library Journal, September 1995, Catherine Noonan, review of *The Last Lieutenant,* p. 232.

ONLINE

John J. Gobbell Home Page, http://www.johnjgobbell.com/ (October 9, 2002).*

* * *

GOLDSTEIN, Malcolm 1925-

PERSONAL: Born August 18, 1925, in Huntington, WV; son of Jack A. (in business) and Lillian (Cohen) Goldstein. *Education:* Princeton University, A.B., 1949, Columbia University, M.A., 1951, Ph.D., 1956. *Hobbies and other interests:* Architectural history, art history.

ADDRESSES: Office—Department of English, Queens College of the City University of New York, Flushing, NY 11367. *Agent*—Oxford University Press, 198 Madison Ave., New York, NY 10016

CAREER: Stanford University, Stanford, CA, instructor, 1953-57, assistant professor of English, 1957-61; Queens College of the City University of New York, Flushing, assistant professor, 1961-65, associate professor, 1965-71, professor of English, beginning 1971, currently professor emeritus. Adjunct professor, Columbia University, 1977-79, 1980. *Military service:* U.S. Army, Signal Corps, 1944-46; became staff sergeant.

MEMBER: PEN, Modern Language Association of America, American Society for Theater Research, Century Association.

AWARDS, HONORS: Guggenheim fellowship, 1967.

WRITINGS:

Pope and the Augustan Stage, Stanford University Press (Stanford, CA), 1958.

The Art of Thornton Wilder, University of Nebraska Press (Lincoln, NE), 1965.

(Editor) Nicholas Rowe, *The Fair Penitent,* University of Nebraska Press (Lincoln, NE), 1968.

The Political Stage: American Drama and Theater of the Great Depression, Oxford University Press (New York, NY), 1974.

George S. Kaufman: His Life, His Theater, Oxford University Press (New York, NY), 1979.

Landscape with Figures: A History of Art Dealing in the United States, Oxford University Press (New York, NY), 2000.

Contributor to *American Drama and Its Critics,* University of Chicago Press (Chicago, IL), 1965.

SIDELIGHTS: Commenting on Malcolm Goldstein's *George S. Kaufman: His Life, His Theater,* a biography of the American playwright, *New York Times* contributor John Russell observed that Goldstein "writes a good plain English, and he tells us everything that we should like to know about George S. Kaufman. . . .

This is a good and painstaking book about a remarkable man and a period in the American theater that came to a full close with his death."

After serving for many years in the English department of the City University of New York, professor emeritus Goldstein turned his efforts to another book, *Landscape with Figures: A History of Art Dealing in the United States.* An anecdotal look at the men and women who influenced the purchase of paintings, *Landscape with Figures* focuses on the New York art scene of the early twentieth century. This proved a sticking point for David Galenson, a reviewer for *Economic History Services.* Given the book's title, Galenson observed, "the book is not actually about art dealing, but rather about dealers . . . . [and] it does not treat the whole United States, but only New York." Galenson singled out what he saw as the lack of "interest in the economics of the art market" as a weakness of Goldstein's book, but a *Times Literary Supplement* contributor saw it differently. William Johnston praised the author's "informative yet entertaining overview of the subject" and felt that the writing is at its best in the portraits of such notable dealers as Sidney Janis, Leo Castelli and Elizabeth Ward. Goldstein "does not neglect the great international [art] houses," Johnston added, "but he is more enthusiastic in discussing the 'rise of modernism.'" To *Wilson Quarterly* reviewer A. J. Hewat, "this history of American art dealing is pleasingly written, attentive to nuance, respectful without being sycophantic, and rife with tales of the titans and oddballs who made art their business."

BIOGRAPHICAL AND CRITICAL SOURCES:

PERIODICALS

New York Times, October 18, 1979, John Russell, review of *George S. Kaufman: His Life, His Theater.*
New York Times Book Review, December 16, 1979.
Times Literary Supplement, November 2, 2001, William Johnston, review of *Landscape with Figures: A History of Art Dealing in the United States,* p. 31.
Wilson Quarterly, winter, 2001, A. J. Hewat, review of *Landscape with Figures,* p. 133.

ONLINE

Economic History Services, http://www.eh.net/ (February, 2001), David W. Galenson, review of *Landscape with Figures.**

GORDEEVA, Ekaterina 1971-

PERSONAL: Born 1971, in USSR (now Russia); daughter of Alexander and Elena Gordeeva; married Sergei Grinkov (a figure skater; died, 1995), April, 1991; married Ilia Kulik (a figure skater), June 10, 2002; children: (first marriage) Daria, (second marriage) Elizaveta.

ADDRESSES: Home—Los Angeles, CA. *Agent*—Author's Mail, Warner Books, 1271 Avenue of the Americas, New York, NY 10020.

CAREER: Figure skater. Narrator for videocassette *Three Cheers for Catherine the Great!,* 2001.

AWARDS, HONORS: First Place award, World Figure Skating Championships, 1986, 1987, 1989, and 1990, for pairs figure skating; Gold Medal, Olympic Games, 1988 and 1994, for pairs figure skating.

WRITINGS:

(With E. M. Swift) *My Sergei: A Love Story,* Warner Books (New York, NY), 1996.
(With Antonina W. Bouis) *A Letter for Daria,* Little, Brown (Boston), 1998.

SIDELIGHTS: Ekaterina Gordeeva is an Olympic champion figure skater who has chronicled her life's darkest hour in two different books. Gordeeva lost her first husband and skating partner, Sergei Grinkov, in 1995 when he collapsed and died on the ice during a practice session. Gordeeva's books *My Sergei: A Love Story* and *A Letter for Daria* both recount her love affair with Grinkov and her despair at his death. Both books were bestsellers, with *My Sergei* topping the lists with more than a million copies sold. In the intervening years Gordeeva has continued to skate as a solo performer and has remarried. As Sally Lodge noted in *Publishers Weekly,* "Ekaterina came back from a great tragedy and is carrying on with her life."

Gordeeva and Grinkov began skating together in 1982 at the ages of eleven and fifteen respectively. Together they won first place at the World Figure Skating Championships four times, as well as winning two Olympic gold medals. After nine years of skating

Ekaterina Gordeeva

together, they married and had a daughter. However, their time together was cut short when Grinkov suffered a fatal heart attack not long after earning the pair's second Olympic gold medal.

With the assistance of E. M. Swift, Gordeeva shares the couple's story in *My Sergei,* a book that met with an enthusiastic reception by fans and critics. A *Publishers Weekly* reviewer called the last chapters "heartrending" and commented, "Their love and their happiness together is deeply moving." Ilene Cooper compared the book to Eric Segal's *Love Story* in her *Booklist* review, and added, "Both are tearjerkers, but this one really happened." As Gordeeva writes in *My Sergei:* "I'd like to live my life over again backward . . . any day I am living now, I'd exchange for a day in the past."

Gordeeva returned to the ice in February, 1996, performing in a *Stars on Ice* show that her skating colleagues had dedicated to Sergei's memory. She retired from competition and with the success of *My Sergei* and her ice show earnings Gordeeva was able to live

in comfort with the couple's daughter, Daria. In 1998 Gordeeva published a children's book called *A Letter for Daria,* in which she speaks to her daughter about Daria's father's death and other family matters. Though it did not match *My Sergei* in sales, Lodge noted in *Publishers Weekly* that *A Letter for Daria* "has enormous human interest" and appeals to the "whole niche of girls out there who are entirely enamored of ice skaters." Another *Publishers Weekly* reviewer concluded of the work: "Gordeeva's sincerity shines through and her life philosophy is one that will inspire many."

Gordeeva's second husband is skater Ilia Kulik. When not performing, the couple live in Los Angeles. Gordeeva's voice can be heard on the Scholastic videocasette *Three Cheers for Catherine the Great!,* a story about an American girl growing up with a Russian grandmother.

BIOGRAPHICAL AND CRITICAL SOURCES:

BOOKS

Gordeeva, Ekaterina. *My Sergei: A Love Story,* Warner (New York, NY), 1997.

PERIODICALS

Booklist, October 1, 1996, p. 290; November 15, 2001, Candace Smith, review of *Three Cheers for Catherine the Great!,* p. 588.
Library Journal, November 15, 1996, p. 67.
Newsweek, December 23, 1996, pp. 58-59.
People, March 25, 1996, pp. 80-87; March 15, 1999, "Ekaterina Gordeeva," p. 274; April 30, 2001, "Twice Blessed," p. 58; January 13, 2003, "Melting the Ice," p. 125.
Publishers Weekly, September 23, 1996, pp. 63-64; May 4, 1998, Sally Lodge, "Skating Star Shines Again As Author," p. 27; May 18, 1998, review of *A Letter for Daria,* p. 81.
School Library Journal, October, 2001, Teresa Bateman, review of *Three Cheers for Catherine the Great!,* p. 82.
Time, January 26, 1998, Steve Lopez, "Life after the Glory," p. 64.*

GORDON, Alison (Ruth) 1943-

PERSONAL: Born January 19, 1943, in New York, NY; daughter of John King (an editor) and Ruth (an editor; maiden name, Anderson) Gordon; married Paul Bennett (an attorney), October 2, 1982. *Education:* Attended Queen's University, Kingston, Ontario, 1960-65. *Politics:* Social Democrat.

ADDRESSES: Home—84 Hogarth Ave., Toronto, Ontario M4K 1K4, Canada.

CAREER: Radio and television broadcaster and writer for Canadian Broadcasting Corp., 1973-78; *Toronto Star,* Toronto, Ontario, Canada, baseball reporter, 1979-86; freelance writer, 1986—.

AWARDS, HONORS: National Magazine Award of Canada humor category runner-up, 1978; National Newspaper Awards (Canada) special award, 1979, for sports writing.

WRITINGS:

"KATE HENRY" SERIES; MYSTERY NOVELS

The Dead Pull Hitter, McClelland & Stewart (Toronto, Ontario, Canada), 1988, St. Martin's Press (New York, NY), 1989.
Safe at Home: A Kate Henry Mystery, McClelland & Stewart (Toronto, Ontario, Canada), 1990, St. Martin's Press (New York, NY), 1991.
Night Game: A Kate Henry Mystery, McClelland & Stewart (Toronto, Ontario, Canada), 1992, St. Martin's Press (New York, NY), 1993.
Striking Out: A Kate Henry Mystery, McClelland & Stewart (Toronto, Ontario, Canada), 1995.
Prairie Hardball, McClelland & Stewart (Toronto, Ontario, Canada), 1997, McClelland & Stewart/ Tundra Books (Plattsburgh, NY), 1998.

OTHER

Foul Balls: Five Years in the American League, McClelland & Stewart (Toronto, Ontario, Canada), 1984, published as *Foul Ball!: Five Years in the American League,* Dodd, Mead (New York, NY), 1985.

Contributor to *Slightly Higher in Canada,* edited by Sean Kelly and Ted Mann, McClelland & Stewart (Toronto, Ontario, Canada), 1978; and *A Toronto Lampoon,* edited by Wayne Grigsby, Eden (Montreal, Quebec, Canada), 1984.

SIDELIGHTS: Alison Gordon is a former sports writer who turned mystery novelist in the late 1980s. Initially working in television and radio, she happened into a career writing about the Toronto Blue Jays for the *Toronto Star* newspaper. Her first book, the nonfiction *Foul Balls: Five Years in the American League,* came out of this experience and relates the ups and downs of a female reporter trying to cover a male-dominated sport. After this, however, Gordon turned to fiction, writing a series of mystery novels featuring female sports reporter and amateur sleuth Kate Henry, who made her fiction debut in 1988.

Henry is introduced to readers in *The Dead Pull Hitter* as a forty-year-old woman reporting on the fictional Toronto Titans for the *Toronto Planet* newspaper. While this is not a great stretch from the reality of Gordon's own life, the murder mysteries obviously are. In this debut, baseball players are being murdered and Henry is assigned to the hot story, thus turning into an investigative journalist for the first time. Critics appreciated the new perspective on the sports mystery subgenre. As a *Publishers Weekly* reviewer noted, "This thoroughly engaging novel . . . provides a colorful inside view of the all-American pastime."

The Dead Pull Hitter was soon followed by *Safe at Home,* in which Gordon combines the story of a serial killer stalking young boys with Henry's experiences in baseball reporting. Henry is also forming a close relationship with police staff sergeant Andy Munro, who is assigned to this case, which involves sex crimes against the victims; and the two stories are tied together by a theme concerning homosexuality when Henry discovers that one of her baseball player friends is gay. Although a *Maclean's* reviewer complained that the mystery was too easily solved, causing a "major weakness" in plotting, Steinberg, in another *Publishers Weekly* review, declared that Gordon "scores another grand slam" with *Safe at Home.*

Night Game and *Striking Out* are the next two Henry mysteries. In the former, a woman sports reporter is murdered, a crime that seems linked to her sexual exploits with numerous baseball players, while in *Striking Out* a baseball strike leads Henry away from sports concerns for a while only to find herself stumbling on another crime when a homeless woman suddenly disappears. Reviewers of these books found both good and bad points about the stories. For example, in a review of *Night Game* a *Publishers Weekly* critic found the author's voice to be "pleasing" yet "derivative," while the solution to the crime was merely "moderately clever." And a *Maclean's* contributor, writing about *Striking Out,* worried that Gordon "tries to cover so many angles—homelessness, anti-abortion demonstrators, race relations—that the observations are superficial." Yet, this critic added, "Still, a good sense of place, deft pacing and the sharp-tongued Kate make the book worth the outing."

Gordon has more recently finished *Prairie Hardball.* This story has Henry going back to her hometown to see her mother, who is being inducted into the Baseball Hall of Fame because she was a player in the All-American Girls Professional League during World War II. Although there is, naturally, a murder in the story involving one of her mother's former teammates, the real interest, according to *Booklist* reviewer Wes Lukowsky, comes with the parts of the novel regarding Henry's relationship with her mother: "[Henry's] amazement as she learns about her mom's poker-playing, beer-drinking, ball-playing youth" makes the novel a pleasure to read, Lukowsky concluded.

Gordon once told *CA:* "It took me a long time to give in to my inevitable vocation. I didn't begin to write professionally until I was in my thirties. The inevitability was genetic. My paternal grandfather, Charles W. Gordon, writing under the pseudonym Ralph Connor, was one of the best-selling authors in the English-speaking world in the early part of this century. My maternal grandfather, Isaac Anderson, was a translator and critic who reviewed mysteries for the *New York Times* for many years during the thirties and forties. My parents met when both were working as editors at Farrar & Rinehart. My brother Charles, also a writer, and I grew up surrounded by books, readers, and a strong reverence for the written word.

"In my teens, my family traveled widely, following my father, who was by then working for the United Nations, and much of my education came in small, international schools in Tokyo, Cairo, and Rome. My politics and world view were very much shaped by that experience, and, when I had a chance at twenty-one to choose my father's nationality (Canadian) or my mother's (American), I chose the former, a decision I have never regretted.

"Before 1979, my field of interest and experience was in current affairs. I worked for various radio and television programs, both on and off the air, while doing magazine writing on the side. One of my great loves is satirical writing, although there are few outlets in Canada.

"In 1979, my love for baseball led, through a series of flukes, to a job as the first full-time female beat writer in the American League, covering the Toronto Blue Jays for the *Toronto Star,* the biggest paper in Canada. I did the job for five years, then wrote *Foul Ball!* and returned to the real world. I think that my strength in that job was that as a woman, as a Canadian, and as one with wide interests outside of sport, I provided an alternative view of the great American pastime, which is, after all, only a game.

"I guess I keep chugging along because I am unable to take myself too seriously. I don't really consider myself a 'real' writer, even though I have been supporting myself as one for a decade. When I was writing for newspapers and magazines, I knew that 'real' writers wrote books. But my first book wasn't 'real' because it was nonfiction. Even my second book, a novel, doesn't make me 'real' because it's only a mystery. I suppose that, if I ever wrote a 'real,' serious work of fiction and won a Nobel Prize, I would still be waiting for someone to find me out and expose me as a fraud. In the meantime, I'm having a lot of fun getting paid for doing what I like best."

BIOGRAPHICAL AND CRITICAL SOURCES:

PERIODICALS

Booklist, March 1, 1993, Wes Lukowski, review of *Night Game,* p. 1159; May 15, 1998, Wes Lukowsky, review of *Prairie Hardball,* p. 1599.
Library Journal, June 1, 1985, Ann Twitchell, review of *Foul Ball!: Five Years in the American League,* p. 139.
Maclean's, March 19, 1980, Jane O'Hara, "From Maggie's Diary to the Boys of Summer," p. 40; October 15, 1990, Diane Turbide, review of *Safe at Home,* p. 85; July 1, 1995, review of *Striking Out,* p. 69.

New York Times, July 21, 1985, Lawrie Mifflin, review of *Foul Ball!,* p. 23.

New York Times Book Review, October 22, 1989, Diane Cole, review of *The Dead Pull Hitter,* p. 22.

People, June 3, 1985, Ralph Novak, review of *Foul Ball!,* p. 20.

Publishers Weekly, July 7, 1989, Sybil Steinberg, review of *The Dead Pull Hitter,* p. 51; April 5, 1991, Sybil Steinberg, review of *Safe at Home,* p. 138; January 11, 1993, review of *Night Game,* p. 56.

School Library Journal, September, 1985, Nancy Choice, review of *Foul Ball!,* p. 156.*

*   *   *

GORDY, Berry, Jr. 1929-

PERSONAL: Born November 28, 1929, in Detroit, MI; son of Berry (a plasterer) and Bertha (an insurance agent) Gordy; married Thelma Coleman, 1953 (divorced, 1959); married Raynoma Liles (divorced, 1962); married Grace Eton, July 17, 1990 (divorced, 1993); children: (first marriage) Hazel Joy, Berry IV, Terry; (second marriage) Kerry, Stefan; (with Margaret Norton) Kennedy; (with Diana Ross) Rhonda Ross. *Education:* Earned G.E.D.

ADDRESSES: Office—Gordy Co., 6255 West Sunset Blvd., Los Angeles, CA 90028-7403.

CAREER: Professional featherweight boxer, 1948-50; 3-D Record Mart, Detroit, MI, owner, 1953-55; Ford Motor Co., Detroit, assembly-line worker, 1955-59; Hitsville, U.S.A. (later Motown Industries, Inc.), Detroit, founder and chair, 1961-88; producer for entertainers, including the Temptations, the Supremes, Marvin Gaye, Smokey Robinson, Diana Ross, Stevie Wonder, and the Jackson Five; songwriter, music publisher, personal manager; Gordy Co. (includes Jobete Music Co., Motown Industries, and Stone Mountain Music), Los Angeles, CA, director, 1988—. Producer of motion pictures, including *Lady Sings the Blues,* Paramount, 1972; *Mahogany* (also director), Paramount, 1975; *Bingo Long Traveling All-Stars and Motor Kings,* Universal, 1976; *Almost Summer,* 1978; *The Wiz,* Universal, 1978; and *The Last Dragon,* TriStar, 1985. *Military service:* U.S. Army, 1951-53; served in Korea.

Berry Gordy, Jr.

MEMBER: Directors Guild of America.

AWARDS, HONORS: Business Achievement Award, Interracial Council for Business Opportunity, 1967; American Music Award for Outstanding Contribution to the Music Industry, 1975; named among five leading entrepreneurs of the nation, Babson College, 1978; Whitney M. Young, Jr. Award, Los Angeles Urban League, 1980; Gordon Grand fellow, Yale University, 1985; inducted into Rock and Roll Hall of Fame, 1988; Black Achievement Award, Brotherhood Crusade, 1988; National Academy of Recording Arts and Sciences Trustee Award, 1991; Black Radio Exclusive Lifetime Achievement Award, 1993; given a star on the Hollywood Walk of Fame, 1996; American Legend Award, and *Essence* magazine "Image Maker" awards, both 1998; inducted into Association for Independent Music Hall of Fame, 2001.

WRITINGS:

To Be Loved: The Music, the Magic, the Memories of Motown (autobiography), Warner Books (New York, NY), 1994.

SONGWRITER

(With others) *I'll Be There,* H. Leonard (Milwaukee, WI), 1997.

(With others) *You've Made Me So Very Happy,* H. Leonard (Milwaukee, WI), 1997.

(With Janie Bradford) *Money (That's What I Want),* H. Leonard (Milwaukee, WI), 1998.

(With Smokey Robinson) *Shop Around,* H. Leonard (Milwaukee, WI), 1998.

Do You Love Me?, H. Leonard (Milwaukee, WI), 2000.

Coauthor of songs, including "Lonely Teardrops," "Reet Peteet," "To Be Loved," "That's Why (I Love You So)," "I'll Be Satisfied," "You Got What It Takes," "I Want You Back," "ABC," and "The Love You Save." Songwriter for films, including *One More Saturday Night,* 1986, *Dirty Dancing,* 1987, *Concrete Angels,* 1987, and *Coming to America,* 1988.

SIDELIGHTS: Berry Gordy, Jr. has been credited with changing the course of twentieth-century pop music with his founding of Hitsville, U.S.A., which would later become Motown Industries. His keen eye for talent and his protective management style boosted the careers of such legendary entertainers as Smokey Robinson, Marvin Gaye, the Temptations, Diana Ross, and the Jackson Five. His business skills built Motown Records from an $800 investment in 1961 into the largest black-owned enterprise in America, selling for $61 million dollars to MCA Incorporated in 1988.

Gordy's rise to success is detailed in his autobiography, *To Be Loved: The Music, the Magic, the Memories of Motown.* Gordy tells of growing up in Detroit, the seventh of eight children born to parents who instilled strong work ethics in their children. After a brief career as a prizefighter and a stint in the Army, Gordy returned to Detroit and, with borrowed money, opened the 3-D Record Mart, which went bankrupt several years later. He then worked for Ford Motor Company as an auto trimmer. To relieve the monotony of assembly-line work, Gordy created tunes in his head. Eventually he left Ford to become a songwriter, quickly selling two of his songs, "Way over There" and "Reet Peteet," the latter which his friend, singer Jackie Wilson, made a hit. Another friend, William "Smokey" Robinson, however, explaining that record company profits were far greater than songwriter royalties, suggested Gordy start his own record company.

In 1961 he founded Hitsville, U.S.A. The fledgling company's first recording was Robinson's hit "Shop Around." Renamed Motown, Gordy's company became a launching pad for the careers of many Detroiters who might otherwise never have been given a chance by major recording companies. The Supremes, led by Diana Ross, the Temptations, and Marvin Gaye were among the local talents Gordy brought to the world. "If not for Berry Gordy, Jr.," a *Rolling Stone* reporter wrote, "most of Motown's greatest artists would not have had music careers in the first place—and popular music, not to mention the business of popular music, would be very different today." Smokey Robinson concurred, telling *Rolling Stone:* "We were fortunate enough and blessed enough that the Lord put Berry Gordy in Detroit. We had somewhere to go to get our music out."

Gordy ran his company as a family business, despite its growth. Many employees were family members, and in an almost fatherly way Gordy guided the careers of Motown artists, even developing a school in which they were taught the finer points of personal grooming and etiquette, as well as business savvy as a means of ensuring personal as well as artistic success. Because of Gordy's active involvement in the lives of his clients, Gordy was sometimes portrayed as a controlling and manipulative manager, extremely protective of his sometimes-resentful money-makers. Writer Milo Miles, in a *New York Times Book Review* assessment of Gordy's autobiography, explained, however, that Gordy's "tightfisted operation" was "perhaps a necessity for a driven black entrepreneur of the era, when there was always someone really trying to snatch away control of money and power."

Motown thrived during the 1960s, and Gordy's discovery of the Jackson Five kept the company financially sound into the seventies. Gordy resigned as president of the company in 1973, however, to pursue his interest in motion picture and television production. Again, his risk-taking paid off; his first effort, *Lady Sings the Blues,* starring Diana Ross as Billie Holiday, was critically acclaimed and garnered Ross an Oscar nomination. Gordy and Ross teamed again in *Mahogany,* with Gordy as director, but, although popular with audiences, the film was panned by critics.

Although Gordy sold Motown Records in 1988 he retained control of Jobete Music Company, the publishing wing of Motown. In 1997 he sold fifty percent of Jobete to EMI Music Publishing, the largest music conglomerate in the world, in what *Black Enterprise* contributor Ann Brown called "one of the most significant music publishing deals of all time." Gordy's take on the deal was $132 million for a catalogue of some 15,000 songs, including the hits "I'll Be There," "Heard It through the Grapevine," and "Ain't No Mountain High Enough." Gordy told *Black Enterprise:* "In the Motown deal, I simply had to remove myself from the record business because it was changing dramatically. But I knew by getting rid of Motown I was still able to preserve the songs and build around it. I bought into the future and it's worked out well."

Gordy's many honors include induction into the Rock and Roll Hall of Fame and an American Legend award. His creative achievements in songwriting, record producing, and crafting a unique niche in U.S. popular music have been well documented and acknowledged by legions of critics. Sylvia Rhone in *Essence* declared that Motown Records is an "institution" that "would shine into the millennium."

BIOGRAPHICAL AND CRITICAL SOURCES:

BOOKS

Benjaminson, Peter, *The Story of Motown,* Grove Press (New York, NY), 1979.
Business Leader Profiles for Students, Gale (Detroit, MI), 2002.
Contemporary Musicians, Volume 6, Gale (Detroit, MI), 1992.
Gordy, Berry, Jr., *To Be Loved: The Music, the Magic, the Memories of Motown,* Warner (New York, NY), 1994.
Gordy, Berry, Sr., *Movin' Up: Pop Gordy Tells His Story,* Harper, 1979.
Posner, Gerald, *Motown: Money, Power, Sex, and Music,* Random House (New York, NY), 2003.
Singleton, Raynoma Gordy, *Berry, Me, and Motown,* Contemporary Books (Chicago, IL), 1990.

PERIODICALS

America's Intelligence Wire, January 14, 2003, "Motown's Demise Chronicled in New Book."

Billboard, September 16, 2000, Jim Bessman, "Gordy Sets Up Fund," p. 12.
Black Enterprise, October, 1997, Ann Brown, "Soul for Sale," p. 22.
Crain's Detroit Business, November 1, 1999, Jeffrey Kosseff, "Berry Gordy, Jr.," p. 14.
Entertainment Weekly, December 2, 1994, pp. 61-62.
Essence, May, 1998, Sylvia Rhone, "The 1998 Essence Awards: Image Makers," p. 98.
Fortune, August 16, 1999, Erik Calonius, "Their Wildest Dreams," p. 142.
New York Review of Books, May 20, 1999, Arthur Kempton, review of *To Be Loved,* p. 68.
New York Times Book Review, February 10, 1991, p. 18; November 27, 1994, p. 26.
Rolling Stone, February 11, 1988, p. 65.

ONLINE

History of Rock, http://www.history-of-rock.com/ (November 10, 2003).*

*   *   *

GRANT, Matthew C.
See MAY, Julian

*   *   *

GREENE, Melissa Fay 1952-

PERSONAL: Born December 30, 1952, in Macon, GA; daughter of Gerald A. (a financial planner) and Rosalyn (a bookkeeper and homemaker; maiden name, Pollock) Greene; married Donald Franklin Samuel (an attorney), April 15, 1979; children: Molly Ilana, Seth, Lee Harry, Lily, Jesse, Helen. *Education:* Oberlin College, B.A. (with high honors), 1975. *Politics:* Democrat. *Religion:* Jewish.

ADDRESSES: Home and office—1708 East Clifton Rd. NE, Atlanta, GA 30307. *Agent*—David Block, 220 Fifth Ave., Suite 1400, New York, NY 10001.

CAREER: Paralegal for General Assistance Legal Services Program, in Savannah, GA, 1975-79, and Rome, GA, 1980-81; writer.

AWARDS, HONORS: Excellence in Journalism Award, Society of Professional Journalists, 1988, for the article "That Old Lonesome High Hollerin' Tenor"; National Book Award finalist, nonfiction, 1991, National Book Critics Circle Award in general nonfiction, Robert F. Kennedy Award, Lillian Smith Award, *Chicago Tribune* Heartland Prize, Georgia Author Award, and Lyndhurst Prize fellowship, all 1992, for *Praying for Sheetrock; Praying for Sheetrock* was also cited as a Notable Book for 1991 by both the American Library Association and the *New York Times;* Southern Book Critics Circle Award, Georgia Author of the Year Award, Georgia Historical Society Book Award, and National Book Award nomination, all for *The Temple Bombing.*

WRITINGS:

Praying for Sheetrock: A Work of Non-Fiction, Addison-Wesley (Reading, MA), 1991.
The Temple Bombing, Addison-Wesley (Reading, MA), 1996.
Last Man Out: The Story of the Springhill Mine Disaster, Harcourt (New York, NY), 2003.

Work represented in anthologies, including *Writing: The Translation of Memory,* edited by Eve Shelnutt, Macmillan, 1990; and *The Confidence Woman: Twenty-six Writers at Work,* edited by Eve Shelnutt, Longstreet Press, 1991. Columnist, *Financial Planning,* 1983-88. Contributor of articles and reviews to magazines and newspapers, including *Los Angeles Times, Chicago Tribune, Washington Post, New York Times, Life, Parenting, Landscape Architecture, Museum News, Atlantic, Southern Exposure, Country Journal, Stagebill,* and *Iowa Review.*

ADAPTATIONS: The Temple Bombing was adapted as a sound recording by Audio Renaissance, 1996; *Praying for Sheetrock* was adapted as a play and produced at Lifeline Theatre, Chicago, IL, 1997.

SIDELIGHTS: Journalist Melissa Fay Greene is a highly respected author of narrative nonfiction books—works that tell factually accurate stories using literary techniques typically employed by fiction authors. Using this method has earned her numerous awards, including two National Book Award nominations for her first two books: *Praying for Sheetrock: A Work of Non-Fiction* and *The Temple Bombing.* Sometimes

considered a southern writer because of her roots in Georgia, though she was largely raised in Ohio, Greene has made it her ongoing concern to write about racism and prejudice, especially racism against African Americans or Jews.

Her first book, *Praying for Sheetrock,* is set in McIntosh County, Georgia, during the 1970s. Although the Civil Rights Act had by this time been signed into law, the community is still sharply divided between blacks and whites; and the local sheriff, Tom Popell, rules the area by manipulating elections and intimidating the citizenry. The conflict of Greene's story arises when shop steward Thurnell Alston decides to oppose Popell, managing to help the local black population with the aid of the Assistance Legal Service Program. In the end, however, the white sheriff is "exonerated on charges of extortion, narcotics trafficking, and counterfeiting," reported a *Contemporary Southern Writers* essayist, while Alston is ironically subjected to a government sting and jailed on drug charges. "By turns inspiring and sad, [Alston's] story is told with dramatic skill," concluded a *Publishers Weekly* reviewer.

After the success of *Praying for Sheetrock,* Greene's publisher suggested she might write a book about the Ku Klux Klan, or perhaps a history about Jews in the American South. Greene, however, felt these topics were too sweeping for her; instead, she decided to focus on a single event and use this as an example of the problems with racism. The result was *The Temple Bombing,* the story of how, on October 12, 1958, the Reform Jewish Temple in Atlanta was bombed with fifty sticks of dynamite. The attack, it was strongly suspected, was the result of white racists who did not like Rabbi Jacob Rothschild's outspoken position in favor of integration. Five arrests were made in the case, but only one man, George Bright, actually went to trial, and he was eventually acquitted. To this day, no one has been found guilty of the crime. As both a Jew and a southerner, Greene was particularly interested in the story; she even managed to interview Bright, though she became convinced that he was not one of the perpetrators. But although Greene never managed to get the "deathbed confession" she sought, "the more significant point," noted Jim Auchmutey in the *Atlanta Journal-Constitution,* "is the way Atlanta rallied around the shaken synagogue." She also wanted to tell the story of Rabbi Rothschild, who had the courage to get involved in the racism issue despite resistance from his conservative congregants, who would have preferred to remain neutral observers.

The *The Temple Bombing,* like its predecessor, received numerous literary awards and earned Greene the title of Georgia Author of the Year. However, some critics did not feel it was as strong a book as *Praying for Sheetrock.* One *Publishers Weekly* reviewer, for example, complained that Greene "opts for a shrill tone where balance would suffice." And *Washington Monthly* critic J. Anthony Lukas said that, although he "found much to admire" in *The Temple Bombing,* he "found it a less fully realized work." On the other hand, a *People* contributor concluded that Greene "delivers a compassionate account of an intolerant era that doesn't devolve into an avenging witch-hunt for the perpetrators."

Although Greene's next book, *Last Man Out: The Story of the Springhill Mine Disaster,* is about a tragedy in Nova Scotia instead of Georgia, the story still has strong connections to the South. The center of the story is a mine disaster that occurred in Springhill, Nova Scotia, on October 23, 1958. Seventy-five miners of the nearly two hundred men in the mine at the time died; of the survivors, nineteen men were trapped underground for over a week before they were rescued. When they were finally saved, they became the subject of a media circus. Some of the heroes of the story who helped keep the others alive during their ordeal were exploited by the governor of Georgia—a segregationist—who separated them into black and white groups, treating each differently despite their equal merits. "The book's most fascinating sections deal with the peculiar nature of heroism," according to *Maclean's* writer John Demont—"the way experienced miners were undone by being buried hundreds of yards underground while other, unlikely leaders came to the fore." A *Publishers Weekly* critic, however, felt that Greene's narrative "comes up short" and that the author has not "effectively captured" the miner subculture. *Library Journal* contributor Sarah Jent had a different view, calling *Last Man Out* "a highly readable account" that will "hold the full attention of readers."

When asked by an *Etude* interviewer—as quoted on the author's Web site—to comment on her choice of writing narrative nonfiction rather than straight nonfiction, Greene replied, "I try to write books which carry historical truth, yet also manage to capture, in the way of great literature, something of human nature, something of landscape, something of the quality of light, some true bit of LIFE. So I would be happy if readers found that my books to some extent inform them and entertain them and touch them."

BIOGRAPHICAL AND CRITICAL SOURCES:

BOOKS

Contemporary Southern Writers, St. James Press (Detroit, MI), 1999.

PERIODICALS

Atlanta Journal-Constitution, May 29, 1996, Jim Auchmutey, "The Sleuth behind *The Temple Bombing*"; April 6, 2003, Teresa K. Weaver, "Unearthing Life's Larger Issues, Greene Exhaustively Researches Mine Collapse in Nova Scotia."
Entertainment Weekly, April 19, 1996, Suzanne Ruta, review of *The Temple Bombing,* p. 73.
Library Journal, April 1, 2003, Sarah Jent, review of *Last Man Out: The Story of the Springhill Mine Disaster,* p. 112.
Maclean's, May 19, 2003, John Demont, "Pits of Sorrow: Two Books Recall the Often Tragic Lives of the Men Who Worked in Nova Scotia's Coal Mines," p. 59.
Newsday, May 19, 1996, Wendy Smith, "Paying for Insight: Talking with Melissa Fay Greene."
People, June 10, 1996, Wayne Kalyn, review of *The Temple Bombing,* p. 40.
Publishers Weekly, August 16, 1991, review of *Praying for Sheetrock,* p. 40; February 12, 1996, review of *The Temple Bombing,* p. 66; June 3, 1996, review of *The Temple Bombing* (sound recording), p. 49; March 17, 2003, review of *Last Man Out,* p. 66.
Washington Monthly, July-August, 1996, J. Anthony Lukas, review of *The Temple Bombing,* p. 50.

ONLINE

Melissa Fay Greene Web Site, http://www.melissafay greene.com/ (February 24, 2004).*

GREENFIELD, Eloise 1929-

PERSONAL: Born May 17, 1929, in Parmele, NC; daughter of Weston W. (a federal government work and truck driver) and Lessie (a clerk-typist and writer; maiden name, Jones) Little; married Robert J. Greenfield (a procurement specialist), April 29, 1950 (divorced); children: Steven, Monica. *Education:* Attended Miner Teachers College (now University of the District of Columbia), 1946-49. *Hobbies and other interests:* Listening to music, playing the piano.

ADDRESSES: Home—Washington, DC. *Office*—Honey Productions, Inc., P.O. Box 29077, Washington, DC 20017. *Agent*—Marie Brown, Marie Brown Associates, 412 West 154th St., New York, NY 10032.

CAREER: U.S. Patent Office, Washington, DC, clerk-typist, 1949-56, supervisory patent assistant, 1956-60; worked as a secretary, case-control technician, and an administrative assistant in Washington, DC, 1964-68. District of Columbia Black Writers' Workshop, co-director of adult fiction, 1971-73, director of children's literature, 1973-74; District of Columbia Commission on the Arts and Humanities, writer-in-residence, 1973, 1985-86. Participant in numerous school and library programs and workshops for children and adults.

AWARDS, HONORS: Carter G. Woodson Book Award, National Council for the Social Studies, 1974, for *Rosa Parks;* Irma Simonton Black Award, Bank Street College of Education, 1974, for *She Come Bringing Me That Little Baby Girl; New York Times* Outstanding Book of the Year citation, 1974, for *Sister;* Jane Addams Children's Book Award, Women's International League for Peace and Freedom, 1976, for *Paul Robeson;* American Library Association Notable Book citations, 1976, for *Me and Neesie,* 1979, for *Honey, I Love, and Other Love Poems,* 1982, for *Daydreamers;* Council on Interracial Books for Children award, 1977, for body of work; Coretta Scott King Award, 1978, for *Africa Dream;* Classroom Choice Book citation, 1978, for *Honey, I Love, and Other Love Poems;* Children's Book of the Year citation, Child Study Book Committee, 1979, for *I Can Do It by Myself;* Notable Trade Book in the Field of Social Studies citations, 1980, for *Childtimes: A Three-Generation Memoir,* 1982, for *Alesia;* New York Public Library recommended list, 1981, for *Alesia;* National Black Child Development Institute award, 1981, for body of work; Mills College award, 1983, for body of work; Washington, DC Mayor's Art Award in Literature, 1983; Coretta Scott King Book Award: Illustration, 1990, for *Nathaniel Talking;* honored at Ninth Annual Celebration of Black Writing, Philadelphia, PA, 1993, for lifetime achievement; Award for Excellence in Poetry for Children, National Council of Teachers of English, 1997.

WRITINGS:

PICTURE BOOKS

Bubbles, illustrated by Eric Marlow, Drum & Spear, 1972, published with illustrations by Pat Cummings as *Good News,* Coward (New York, NY), 1977.

She Come Bringing Me That Little Baby Girl, illustrated by John Steptoe, Lippincott (Philadelphia, PA), 1974.

Me and Neesie, illustrated by Moneta Barnett, Crowell (New York, NY), 1975, reprinted, HarperCollins (New York, NY), 2004.

First Pink Light, illustrated by Barnett, Crowell (New York, NY), 1976, illustrated by Jan Spivy Gilchrist, Writers & Readers, 1991.

Africa Dream, illustrated by Carole Byard, John Day (New York, NY), 1977.

(With mother, Lessie Jones Little) *I Can Do It by Myself,* illustrated by Carole Byard, Crowell (New York, NY), 1978.

Darlene, illustrated by George Ford, Methuen (New York, NY), 1980.

Grandmama's Joy, illustrated by Carole Byard, Collins (New York, NY), 1980.

Daydreamers, with pictures by Tom Feelings, Dial (New York, NY), 1981.

Grandpa's Face, illustrated by Floyd Cooper, Putnam (New York, NY), 1988.

Under the Sunday Tree, illustrated by Amos Ferguson, HarperCollins (New York, NY), 1988.

My Doll, Keshia illustrated by Jan Spivy Gilchrist, Writers & Readers, 1991.

My Daddy and I, illustrated by Jan Spivy Gilchrist, Writers & Readers, 1991.

I Make Music, illustrated by Jan Spivy Gilchrist, Writers & Readers, 1991.

Big Friend, Little Friend, illustrated by Jan Spivy Gilchrist, Writers & Readers, 1991.

Aaron and Gayla's Alphabet Book, illustrated by Jan Spivy Gilchrist, Writers & Readers, 1992.

William and the Good Old Days, illustrated by Jan Spivey Gilchrist, HarperCollins (New York, NY), 1993.

(With Jan Spivey Gilchrist) *Sweet Baby Coming,* HarperFestival (New York, NY), 1994.

On My Horse, illustrations by Jan Spivey Gilchrist, HarperFestival (New York, NY), 1995.

Kia Tanisha, illustrated by Jan Spivy Gilchrist, HarperFestival (New York, NY), 1997.

Kia Tanisha Drives Her Car, illustrated by Jan Spivey Gilchrist, HarperFestival (New York, NY), 1997.

Easter Parade, illustrated by Jan Spivey Gilchrist, Hyperion Books for Children (New York, NY), 1997.

Kia Tanisha, illustrated by Jan Spivey Gilchrist, HarperFestival (New York, NY), 1997.

Angels, illustrated by Jan Spivey Gilchrist, Jump at the Sun (New York, NY), 1998.

Easter Parade, illustrated by Jan Spivy Gilchrist, Hyperion Books for Children (New York, NY), 1998.

Water, Water, illustrated by Jan Spivey Gilchrist, HarperFestival (New York, NY), 1999.

I Can Draw a Weeposaur and Other Dinosaurs (poems), illustrated by Jan Spivey Gilchrist, Greenwillow Books (New York, NY), 2001.

Honey, I Love, illustrated by Jan Spivey Gilchrist, HarperCollins (New York, NY), 2003.

In the Land of Words: New and Selected Poems, illustrated by Jan Spivy Gilchrist, HarperCollins (New York, NY), 2004.

BIOGRAPHIES

Rosa Parks, illustrated by Marlow, Crowell (New York, NY), 1973, illustrated by Gil Ashby, HarperCollins Publishers (New York, NY), 1995.

Paul Robeson, illustrated by George Ford, Crowell (New York, NY), 1975.

Mary McLeod Bethune, illustrated by Jerry Pinkney, Crowell (New York, NY), 1977.

(With Lessie Jones Little) *Childtimes: A Three-Generation Memoir* (autobiography), illustrated by Jerry Pinkney, Crowell (New York, NY), 1979.

(With Alesia Revis) *Alesia,* illustrated by George Ford, with photographs by Sandra Turner Bond, Philomel Books (New York, NY), 1981.

For the Love of the Game: Michael Jordan and Me, illustrated by Jan Spivey Gilchrist, HarperCollins (New York, NY), 1997.

How They Got Over: African Americans and the Call of the Sea, illustrated by Jan Spivy Gilchrist, HarperCollins (New York, NY), 2003.

CONTRIBUTOR TO ANTHOLOGIES

Alma Murray, and Robert Thomas, editors, *The Journey: Scholastic Black Literature,* Scholastic Book Services (New York, NY), 1970.

Karen S. Kleiman, and Mel Cebulash, editors, *Double Action Short Stories,* Scholastic Book Services (New York, NY), 1973.

Love, Scholastic Book Services (New York, NY), 1975.

Encore (textbook), Houghton Mifflin (Boston, MA), 1978.

Daystreaming, Economy Company, 1978.

Forerunners, Economy Company, 1978.

Burning Bright, Open Court, 1979.

Friends Are Like That, Crowell (New York, NY), 1979.

Language Activity Kit: Teachers' Edition, Harcourt (New York, NY), 1979.

Building Reading Skills, McDougal, Littell, 1980.

New Routes to English: Book 5, Collier Books (New York, NY), 1980.

New Routes to English: Advanced Skills One, Collier Books (New York, NY), 1980.

Jumping Up, Lippincott (Philadelphia, PA), 1981.

Emblems, Houghton Mifflin (Boston, MA), 1981.

Listen, Children, Bantam (New York, NY), 1982.

Bonus Book, Gateways, Level K, Houghton Mifflin (Boston, MA), 1983.

New Treasury of Children's Poetry, Doubleday (New York, NY), 1984.

Scott, Foresman Anthology of Children's Literature, Scott, Foresman, 1984.

Pass It On: African American Poetry for Children, selected by Wade Hudson, Scholastic (New York, NY), 1993.

Stic to It, Open Court, 1995.

African American Poets, edited by Michael R. Strickland, Enslow (Springfield, NJ), 1996.

OTHER

Sister (novel), illustrated by Moneta Barnett, Crowell (New York, NY), 1974.

Honey, I Love, and Other Love Poems, illustrated by Diane and Leo Dillon, Crowell (New York, NY), 1978.

Talk about a Family (novel), illustrated by James Calvin, Lippincott (Philadelphia, PA), 1978.
Nathaniel Talking (poems), Writers & Readers, 1988.
Night on Neighborhood Street (poems), illustrated by Jan Spivey Gilchrist, Dial (New York, NY), 1991.
Koya DeLaney and the Good Girl Blues, Scholastic (New York, NY), 1992.
Talk About a Family, HarperCollins (New York, NY), 1993.

Contributor to *World Book Encyclopedia;* author of 1979 bookmark poem for Children's Book Council. Also contributor to magazines and newspapers, including *Black World, Cricket, Ebony, Jr.!, Horn Book, Interracial Books for Children Bulletin, Ms., Negro History Bulletin, Scholastic Scope,* and *Washington Post.*

ADAPTATIONS: *Daydreamers* was dramatized for the Public Broadcasting System (PBS) Reading Rainbow Television Series; *Honey, I Love* was recorded for album and audio cassette with music by Byron Morris and released by Honey Productions, 1982. *Lisa's Daddy and Daughter Day* was adapted as an analog audio cassette by Sundance Publishing.

SIDELIGHTS: Eloise Greenfield is an acclaimed writer of prose and poetry for younger readers whose fiction is admired for presenting strong portraits of loving African American families. Mindful of children's need to understand their cultural antecedents, she has also penned a handful of biographies of African Americans. Greenfield stated that her goal in writing is "to give children words to love, to grow on." The author of more than a dozen prize-winning books for children, Greenfield admits that, since her own childhood, she has loved the sounds and rhythms of words. In her stories and poetry she tries to produce what she calls "word-madness," a creative, joyous response brought on by reading. As she explained in *Horn Book:* "I want to be one of those who can choose and order words that children will want to celebrate. I want to make them shout and laugh and blink back tears and care about themselves." Most of her books have been illustrated by Jan Spivey Gilchrist.

The picture book *First Pink Light,* for example, centers on four-year-old Tyree, who is determined to stay up until dawn to greet his father. *Talk About a Family,* a short novel, shows how a girl named Genny copes with her parents' separation, while *Grandmama's Joy* depicts the relationship between Rhondy and her grandmother, who has taken care of her since her the death of her parents. The author's first collection of children's poems, *Honey, I Love, and Other Love Poems,* describes the experiences of a young black girl and deals with relationships involving family, friends, and schoolmates. Denise Murcko Wilms, commenting in *Twentieth-Century Children's Writers,* observed that Greenfield's works "portray aspects of the black American experience [and] collectively carry a positive message to both the black and the white youngsters who read them." In 2003, to celebrate Greenfield's twenty-five years as an author, HarperCollins republished the poem "Honey, I Love" from the poet's 1978 collection of verse as the stand-alone picture book of the same title.

Greenfield also lists as a priority of her writing the communication of "a true knowledge of Black heritage, including both the African and American experiences." Through her easy-to-read biographies of famous black Americans, such as *Rosa Parks, Paul Robeson,* and *Mary McLeod Bethune,* she has sought to inform young readers about the historical contributions of blacks in this nation. "A true history must be the concern of every Black writer," she stated in *Horn Book.* "It is necessary for Black children to have a true knowledge of their past and present, in order that they may develop an informed sense of direction for their future." In 1997 she added a picture-book portrait of superstar basketball player Michael Jordan to her list of biographies. In *For Love of the Game: Michael Jordan and Me,* Greenfield wrote a lyrical text to encourage children to aspire to reach their dreams. Several reviewers found the text uneven, such as Maeve Visser Knoth, who called the book both "inspirational and full of basketball imagery, but preachy," and a *Publishers Weekly* contributor, who dubbed the tone "melodramatic." *Booklist*'s Susan Dove Lempke, however, described the work as a "teacher's dream" that will "set children soaring." A departure from single-person biographies is Greenfield's collective biography *How They Got Over: African Americans and the Call of the Sea,* in which she profiles seven African-American men and women whose fates were entwined with the sea. They range from eighteenth-century merchant and sailor Paul Cuffe to Commander Michelle Janine Howard, who was appointed in 2000 to work with the U.S. Joint Chiefs of Staff. It also includes shorter descriptions of sea-faring groups, such as the all-black Pea Island Station Lifesavers of North Carolina. The work elicited good reviews. Among its enthusiasts number *Horn Book*'s Betty Carter, who praising its "engaging text," called it a "fine, and unusual collective biography." "Worthwhile reading on an unusual topic" is how *Booklist* reviewer Carolyn Phelan summed up *How They Got Over.*

Greenfield's concern for a personal past as well as a public one has prompted Greenfield to team with her mother for *Childtimes: A Three-Generation Memoir.* The autobiographical work describes the childhood memories of Greenfield, her mother, and her maternal grandmother. According to Rosalie Black Kiah in *Language Arts,* each experience in *Childtimes,* "though set in a different time, is rich in human feeling and strong family love." *Washington Post Book World* contributor Mary Helen Washington wrote: "I recognize the significance of *Childtimes* as a document of black life because . . . it unlocked personal recollections of my own past, which I do not want to lose." Other reviewers praised the work as well. For example, in the *Interracial Books for Children Bulletin,* Geraldine L. Wilson called the book "carefully considered and thoughtful, . . . moving deliberately, constructed with loving care," and M. R. Singer concluded in the *School Library Journal:* "The intimate details of loving and growing up and the honesty with which they are told . . . will involve all readers . . . and broaden their understanding of this country's recent past."

Much of Greenfield's fiction concerns family bonding, a subject the author has found as important as black history. Noting in *Horn Book* that "love is a staple in most Black families," she has written repeatedly of the changing patterns of parental and sibling involvement, stressing the child's ability to cope with novelties both positive and negative. In her Irma Simonton Black Award-winning picture book, *She Come Bringing Me That Little Baby Girl,* for instance, a young character named Kevin must learn to share his parents' love with his new sister. A novel titled *Sister,* which received a *New York Times* Outstanding Book of the Year citation, concerns a girl caught in the family stress following a parent's death. Greenfield explained the point of *Sister* in *Horn Book:* "Sister . . . discovers that she can use her good times as stepping stones, as bridges, to get over the hard times. . . . My hope is that children in trouble will not view themselves as blades of wheat caught in countervailing winds but will seek solutions, even partial or temporary solutions, to their problems."

Unsatisfied with network television's portrayal of black families, which she calls "a funhouse mirror, reflecting misshapen images" in *Horn Book,* Greenfield has long sought to reinforce positive and realistic aspects of black family life. While she told *Language Arts* that she looks back on her own childhood with pleasure, she remains aware of the modern dynamics of family structure. She stated: "Families come in various shapes. There is no one shape that carries with it more legitimacy than any other. . . . In the case of divorce and separation—the problems that parents have—the children can go on and build their own lives regardless of the problems of the parents. Children *have* to go on and build their own lives." Kiah noted that Greenfield does not construct her fiction from personal incidents but rather looks for themes from a more universal background. "She draws from those things she has experienced, observed, heard about, and read about. Then she combines them, changes them and finally develops them into her stories." The resulting work has a wide appeal, according to Betty Valdes in the *Interracial Books for Children Bulletin.* Valdes felt that Greenfield "consistently . . . illuminates key aspects of the Black experience in a way that underlines both its uniqueness and its universality."

The universal nature of her work has been seen in *Grandpa's Face,* in which Greenfield constructs a story about a young girl and her relationship with her grandfather, whom she loves dearly. One day little Tomika sees her grandfather, who frequently acts in community theater productions, rehearsing. His mean countenance frightens her and she worries that she might do something that will cause him to regard her with the same angry look. In her poetry as well as her prose, Greenfield has attempted to involve children in their own worlds. In *Under the Sunday Tree* and *Night on Neighborhood Street,* Greenfield brings her young readers into the happenings around them. *Night on Neighborhood Street* examines the "realistic" life of an urban community, according to a *Tribune Books* reviewer. The volume's seventeen poems show children in typical situations, including attending church, avoiding drug pushers, and playing games with their families. Other books also represent the lives of African-American families, including her 1998 picture book *Easter Parade.* Set during World War II, it shows how young cousins in Washington, DC and Chicago prepare to take part in the Easter parades in their respective communities. Although *Booklist*'s Ilene Cooper noted some "choppiness" in the text, she called the prose "lovely" and the tone warm. Like so many of the author's books, this book is a "testament to family love that sustains and emboldens," to quote Barbara Harrison of *Horn Book.*

As has long been the case, Greenfield's books appeal to young children, so it is no surprise that in the early nineties she and illustrator Gilchrist created a colorful quartet of paper-over-cardboard books for the earliest "readers:" *My Doll, Keshia, My Daddy and I, I Make Music,* and *Big Friend, Little Friend.* While these books celebrate the joy of small accomplishments for young children, *I Can Draw a Weeposaur and Other Dinosaurs* is a collection of "simple, often droll poems" that celebrates their creativity, according to Shelle Rosenfeld of *Booklist.* Joy Fleishhacker suggested in her *School Library Journal* review that this book would be a "fine choice" for art and creative writing classes.

Greenfield has resided in Washington, DC, since childhood and has participated in numerous writing workshops and conferences on literature there. She explained in *Language Arts* that her work with the District of Columbia Black Writers' Workshop convinced her of the need to build a collection of "good black books" for children. "It has been inspiring to me to be a part of this struggle," she affirms. "I would like to have time to write an occasional short story, . . . but I don't feel any urgency about them. It seems that I am always being pushed from inside to do children's books; those are more important." Stating another aim of hers in *Horn Book,* Greenfield claimed: "Through the written word I want to give children a love for the arts that will provoke creative thought and activity. . . . A strong love for the arts can enhance and direct their creativity as well as provide satisfying moments throughout their lives."

BIOGRAPHICAL AND CRITICAL SOURCES:

BOOKS

Children's Literature Review, Volume 4, Gale (Detroit, MI), 1982.
Contemporary Black Biography, Volume 9, Gale (Detroit, MI), 1995.
Greenfield, Eloise, and Lessie Jones Little, *Childtimes: A Three-Generation Memoir,* illustrated by Jerry Pinkney, Crowell (New York, NY), 1979.

St. James Guide to Children's Writers, fifth edition, St. James Press, (Detroit, MI), 1999.
Sims, Rudine, *Shadow and Substance: Afro-American Experience in Contemporary Children's Literature,* National Council of Teachers of English, 1982.
Something About the Author Autobiography Series, Volume 16, Gale (Detroit, MI), 1993.

PERIODICALS

Africa Woman, March-April, 1980.
Black Issues Book Review, November, 1999, review of *Angels,* p. 71, review of *Koya Delaney and the Good Girl Blues,* p. 75.
Bookbird, spring, 1995, Gale W. Sherman, "Hip-Hop Culture Raps into Chlidren's Books," pp. 21-25.
Booklist, September 1, 1980, Judith Goldberger, review of *Grandma's Joy,* p. 44; February 1, 1982, Denise M. Wilms, review of *Alesia,* p. 706; November 15, 1988, Denise M. Wilms, review of *Grandpa's Face,* p. 576; December 15, 1989, Denise Wilms, review of *Nathaniel Talking,* p. 830; August, 1991, Denia Hester, review of *Night on Neighborhood Street,* p. 2156; December 15, 1991, Kathleen T. Horning, review of *First Pink Light,* p. 773, review of *My Doll, Keshia, My Daddy and I, I Make Music, First Pink Light, Big Friend, Little Friend,* pp. 772-773; February 15, 1992, Denia Hester, review of *Koya Delaney and the Good Girl Blues,* p. 1104; September 15, 1993, Quraysh Ali, review of *William and the Good Old Days,* pp. 156-157; February 1, 1995, Hazel Rochman, reviews of *On My Horse* and *Honey, I Love,* pp. 1009-1010; February 15, 1997, Susan Dove Lempke, review of *For the Love of the Game: Michael Jordan and Me* p. 1024; April 1, 1998, Ilene Cooper, review of *Easter Parade,* p. 1320; November 15, 1998, John Peters, review of *Angels,* p. 583; August, 1999, Shelley Townsend-Hudson, review of *Water, Water,* p. 2064; April 1, 2001, Shelle Rosenfeld, review of *I Can Draw a Weeposaur and Other Dinosaurs,* p. 1475; February 15, 2003, Carolyn Phelan, review of *How They Got Over: African Americans and the Call of the Sea,* p. 1080; February 15, 2003, Ilene Cooper, review of *Honey, I Love,* p. 1082.
Bulletin of the Center for Children's Books, March, 1975, Zena Sutherland, review of *She Come Bringing Me That Little Baby Girl,* p. 113; October,

1980, Zena Sutherland, review of *Grandma's Joy,* p. 32; January, 1982, Zena Sutherland, review of *Alesia,* p. 85; December, 1988, Roger Sutton, review of *Under the Sunday Tree,* p. 97; October, 1991, Roger Sutton, review of *Night on Neighborhood Street,* pp. 37-38; March, 1992, Roger Sutton, review of *Koya Delaney and the Good Girl Blues,* pp. 179-180; June, 1998, review of *Easter Parade,* p. 362.

Catholic Library World, April, 1982, review of *Alesia,* p. 401; June, 1998, review of *For the Love of the Game,* p. 60.

Childhood Education, spring, 1992, Phyllis G. Sidorsky, review of *Night on Neighborhood Street,* p. 178.

Children's Book Review Service, February, 1997, review of *For the Love of the Game,* p. 80; April, 1998, review of *Easter Parade,* p. 101.

Children's Bookwatch, February, 1997, review of *For the Love of the Game,* p. 2.

Children's Digest, October-November, 1997, review of *For the Love of the Game,* pp. 14-15; February 15, 2003, Carolyn Phelan, review of *How They Got Over: African Americans and the Call of the Sea,* p. 1080, and Ilene Cooper, review of *Honey, I Love,* p. 1089.

Christian Science Monitor, November 4, 1988, Steven Ratiner, "Poetry Report Card: Grades from A to C," p. B7; February 21, 1990, p. 13; May 1, 1992, p. 10.

Day Care & Early Education, summer, 1994, review of *She Come Bringing Me That Little Baby Girl,* p. 22; fall, 1994, review of *First Pink Light,* p. 36.

Encore, December 6, 1976.

Faces: People, Places, and Cultures, October, 2001, review of *Under the Sunday Tree,* p. 46.

Five Owls, January-February, 1995, Kathie Krieger Cerra, review of *On My Horse,* p. 58; November, 1995, review of *Under the Sunday Tree,* p. 30.

Freedomways, Volume 21, number 1, 1981, Nieda Spinger, "Honest Pictures of Black Life," pp. 67-68; Volume 22, number 2, 1982, Jonetta Rose Barras, "Essence of Poetry," pp. 117-119.

HCA Companion, first quarter, 1984.

Horn Book, December, 1975, Eloise Greenfield, "Something to Shout About," pp. 624-626; April, 1977; December, 1979, Mary M. Burns, review of *Childtimes,* p. 676; March-April, 1989, Hanna B. Zeiger, review of *Grandpa's Face,* p. 197; September-October, 1989, Mary M. Burns, review of *Nathanial Talking,* p. 613; September-October, 1990, Mary M. Burns, review of *Nathaniel Talk-ing,* p. 613; November-December, 1991, Mary M. Burns, review of *Night on Neighborhood Street,* p. 750; January-February, 1992, Maeve Visser Knoth, review of *My Doll, Keshia My Daddy and I, I Make Music, First Pink Light, Big Friend, Little Friend,* p. 59; March-April, 1997, Maeve Visser Knoth, review of *For the Love of the Game,* pp. 209-210; September-October, 1998, Barbara Harrison, review of *Easter Parade,* pp. 607-608; April 1, 2001, Shelle Rosenfeld, review of *I Can Draw a Weeposaur and Other Dinosaurs,* p. 1475; March-April, 2003, Betty Carter, review of *How They Got Over,* p. 224.

Horn Book Guide, spring, 1994, review of *William and the Good Old Days,* p. 34; fall, 1995, reviews of *On My Horse* and *Honey, I Love,* p. 250; fall, 1997, reviews of *Kia Tanisha Drives Her Car* and *Kia Tanisha,* p. 251, review of *For the Love of the Game,* p. 376; fall, 1998, review of *Easter Parade,* p. 319; spring, 1999, review of *Angels,* p. 131; fall, 2001, review of *I Can Draw a Weeposaur and Other Dinosaurs,* p. 405.

Instructor, March, 1990, p. 23; November, 1997, review of *Africa Dream,* p. 14.

Interracial Books for Children Bulletin, Volume 6, numbers 5-6, 1975, review of *Bubbles,* p. 9; Volume 9, number 2, 1978, Beryle Banfield, review of *Honey, I Love and Other Love Poems,* p. 19; Volume 10, number 3, 1979, Eloise Greenfield, "Writing for Children—A Joy and a Responsibility," pp. 3-4; Volume 11, number 5, 1980, Geraldine L. Wilson, review of *Childtimes,* pp. 14-15; Volume 11, number 8, 1980, Beryle Banfield, reviews of *Grandmama's Joy* and *Talk about a Family,* pp. 16-17; Volume 13, numbers 4-5, 1982, Caryl-Robin Dresher, review of *Alesia,* p. 7.

Journal of Negro Education, summer, 1974, Judy Richardson, "Black Children's Books: An Overview," pp. 380-400.

Journal of Reading, April, 1993, Joyce Graham and Susan Murphy, "Growing Up Black: Fiction about Black Adolescents' Experiences," pp. 590-592.

Kirkus Reviews, April 15, 1978, review of *Talk about a Family,* p. 436; September 1, 1988, review of *Under the Sunday Tree,* p. 1322; November 1, 1988, review of *Grandpa's Face,* p. 1604; June 15, 1989, review of *Nathaniel Talking,* p. 916; July 15, 1991, review of *Night on Neighborhood Street,* p. 931; October 15, 1991, review of *My Doll, Keshia My Daddy and I, I Make Music, First*

Pink Light, and *Big Friend, Little Friend,* p. 1353; January 15, 1992, review of *Koya Delaney and the Good Girl Blues,* p. 114; September 1, 1993, review of *William and the Good Old Days,* p. 1144; December 1, 1996, review of *Kia Tanisha Drives Her Car,* p. 1742; February 1, 2001, review of *I Can Draw a Weeposaur and Other Dinosaurs,* p. 183; November 15, 2002, reviews of *Honey, I Love* and *How They Got Over,* pp. 1692-1693; November 15, 2003, review of *In the Land of Words,* p. 1359.

Language Arts, September, 1980, Rosalie Black Kiah, "Profile: Eloise Greenfield," pp. 653-659; December, 1996, review of *On My Horse,* p. 622; December, 1997, Rudine Sims Bishop, "Profile: Eloise Greenfield" pp. 630-634.

Metropolitan Washington, August, 1982.

Negro History Bulletin, April-May, 1975; January-February, 1978, Thelma D. Perry, review of *Africa Dream,* p. 801.

New York Times Book Review, May 5, 1974, Jane Langton, "Five Lives," p. 16; November 3, 1974; March 26, 1989; November 14, 1993, Enola G. Aird, review of *William and the Good Old Days,* p. 55.

Parents Magazine, December, 1991, p. 178.

Publishers Weekly, October 28, 1988, review of *Grandpa's Face,* p. 78; May 19, 1989, review of *Nathaniel Talking,* p. 82; October 11, 1991, review of *My Doll, Keshia, My Daddy and I, I Make Music, First Pink Light,* and *Big Friend, Little Friend,* p. 62; November 15, 1991, review of *First Pink Light,* p. 72; December 20, 1991, review of *Koya Delaney and the Good Girl Blues,* p. 82; August 2, 1993, review of *William and the Good Old Days,* p. 79; January 3, 1994, review of *Sweet Baby Coming,* p. 80; January 16, 1995, review of *Honey, I Love,* p. 456; December 16, 1996, reviews of *Kia Tanisha* and *Kia Tanisha Drives Her Car,* p. 61; December 30, 1996, review of *For the Love of the Game,* p. 66; April 6, 1998, review of *Easter Parade,* p. 77; January 11, 1999, review of *Grandma's Joy,* p. 74; January 25, 1999, review of *For the Love of the Game,* p. 98; January 26, 2004, review of *In the Land of Words: New and Selected Poems,* p. 254.

Reading Teacher, February, 1993, Lee Galda, Donna Diehl, and Lane Ware, review of *Night on Neighborhood Street,* pp. 412-413; December, 1994, review of *Koya DeLaney and the Good Girl Blues,* p. 346; October, 1998, review of *For the Love of the Game,* p. 169.

School Library Journal, April, 1974, Betty Lanier Jenkins, review of *Rosa Parks,* p. 50; May, 1978, Christine McDonnell, review of *Talk about a Family,* pp. 67-68; December, 1979; October, 1980, Betty Valdes, review of *Grandma's Joy,* p. 135; March, 1982, review of *Alesia,* pp. 157-158; October, 1988, Kathleen Whalin, review of *Under the Sunday Tree,* p. 153; November, 1988, Gratia Banta, review of *Grandpa's Face,* p. 88; August, 1989, Kathleen T. Horning, review of *Nathaniel Talking,* p. 146; September, 1991, Eve Larkin, review of *Night on Neighborhood Street,* pp. 245-246; December, 1991, Liza Bliss, review of *My Doll, Keshia, My Daddy and I, I Make Music, First Pink Light, Big Friend, Little Friend,* p. 92; January, 1992, Karen James, review of *First Pink Light,* p. 90; February, 1992, Geeta Pattanaik, review of *My Doll, Keshia, My Daddy and I, I Make Music, First Pink Light, Big Friend, Little Friend,* p. 15; March, 1992, Helen E. Williams, review of *Koya Delaney and the Good Girl Blues,* p. 237; November, 1993, Anna DeWind, review of *William and the Good Old Days,* p. 79; February, 1995, Gale W. Sherman reviews of *On My Horse* and *Honey, I Love,* p. 73; April, 1996, review of *Honey, I Love,* p. 39; March, 1997, Connie C. Rockman, review of *For the Love of the Game,* pp. 174-175; August, 1998, Patricia Pearl, review of *Easter Parade,* p. 139; October 12, 1998, review of *Angels,* p. 79; January, 1999, Susan Scheps, review of *Angels,* pp. 140-141; October, 1999, Kathy Piehl, review of *Water, Water,* p. 137; March, 2001, Joy Fleishhacker, review of *I Can Draw a Weeposaur and Other Dinosaurs,* p. 235; February, 2003, Anna DeWind Walls, review of *Honey, I Love,* p. 131.

Social Education April, 1994, review of *William and the Good Old Days,* p. 249.

Social Studies, January, 2001, review of *Grandma's Joy,* p. 38.

Teacher Librarian, January, 1999, review of *Angels,* p. 42.

Top of the News, winter, 1980.

Tribune Books (Chicago, IL), January 1, 1989, Mary Harris Veeder, review of *Grandpa's Face,* p. 4; February 26, 1989; February 9, 1992, Mary Harris Veeder, review of *Night on Neighborhood Street,* p. 7; March 9, 1997, review of *For the Love of the Game,* p. 7.

Washington Post Book World, May 1, 1977; January 13, 1980; May 10, 1981; November 5, 1989; December 9, 1990; December 1, 1991.

ONLINE

Yale-New Haven Teachers Institute, http://www.yale.edu/ynhti (May 9, 2003), Eleanor Gervasini Willis, "American Women Who Shape the Civil Rights Movement Explored through the Literature of Elise Greenfield."*

* * *

GRUMBACH, Doris (Isaac) 1918-

PERSONAL: Born July 12, 1918, in New York, NY; daughter of Leonard William and Helen Isaac; married Leonard Grumbach (a professor of physiology), October 15, 1941 (divorced, 1972); companion of Sybil Pike; children: Barbara, Jane, Elizabeth, Kathryn. *Education:* Washington Square College, A.B., 1939; Cornell University, M.A., 1940. *Politics:* Liberal. *Religion:* Episcopalian.

ADDRESSES: Home—Sargentville, ME. *Agent*—c/o Tim Seldes, Russell & Volkening, 50 West 29th St., New York, NY 10001.

CAREER: Writer. Metro-Goldwyn-Mayer, New York, NY, title writer, 1940-41; *Mademoiselle,* New York, NY, proofreader and copyeditor, 1941-42; Time Inc., associate editor of *Architectural Forum,* 1942-43; Albany Academy for Girls, Albany, NY, English teacher, 1952-55; College of Saint Rose, Albany, instructor, 1955-58, assistant professor, 1958-60, associate professor, 1960-69, professor of English, 1969-73; *New Republic,* Washington, DC, literary editor, 1973-75; American University, Washington, DC, professor of American literature, 1975-85. Visiting University fellow, Empire State College, 1972-73; adjunct professor of English, University of Maryland, 1974-75. Literary critic; *Morning Edition,* National Public Radio, book reviewer, beginning 1982. Board member for National Book Critics Circle and PEN/Faulkner Award; judge for writing contests. *Military service:* U.S. Navy, Women Accepted for Volunteer Emergency Service, 1941-43.

MEMBER: PEN, American Association of University Professors, Phi Beta Kappa.

Doris Grumbach

AWARDS, HONORS: Lambda Literary Award, Lesbian Biography, 1997, for *Life in a Day;* Whitehead Award for Lifetime Achievement, Publishing Triangle, 2000.

WRITINGS:

NOVELS

The Spoil of the Flowers, Doubleday (New York, NY), 1962.
The Short Throat, the Tender Mouth, Doubleday (New York, NY), 1964.
Chamber Music, Dutton (New York, NY), 1979.
The Missing Person, Putnam (New York, NY), 1981.
The Ladies, Dutton (New York, NY), 1984.
The Magician's Girl, Macmillan (New York, NY), 1987.
The Book of Knowledge: A Novel, Norton (New York, NY), 1995.

NONFICTION

The Company She Kept (biography), Coward (New York, NY), 1967.

Coming into the End Zone (memoir), Norton (New York, NY), 1991.

Extra Innings: A Memoir, Norton (New York, NY), 1993.

Fifty Days of Solitude (memoir), Beacon Press (Boston, MA), 1994.

Life in a Day (nonfiction), Beacon Press (Boston, MA), 1996.

The Presence of Absence: On Prayers and an Epiphany, Beacon Press (Boston, MA), 1998.

The Pleasure of Their Company (memoir), Beacon Press (Boston, MA), 2000.

The author's papers and correspondence are housed at the New York Public Library. Also author of introductions and forewords for books. Contributor to books, including *The Postconcilor Parish,* edited by James O'Gara, Kennedy, 1967, and *Book Reviewing,* edited by Silvia E. Kameran, Writer, Inc. (Boston, MA), 1978. Columnist for *Critic,* 1960-64, and *National Catholic Reporter,* 1968—; author of nonfiction column for *New York Times Book Review,* 1976—, column, "Fine Print," for *Saturday Review,* 1977-78, and fiction column, *Chronicle of Higher Education,* 1979—. Contributing editor, *New Republic,* 1971-73; book reviewer for *MacNeil-Lehrer Newshour,* Public Broadcasting Service (PBS). Contributor of reviews and criticism to periodicals, including the *New York Times Book Review, Chicago Tribune, Commonweal, Los Angeles Times, Nation, Washington Post, Washington Star,* and *New Republic.*

SIDELIGHTS: Doris Grumbach, a biographer and respected literary critic, is the author of several novels with historical, biographical, and autobiographical elements. Early in her career, Grumbach worked as a title writer, copy and associate editor, literary editor, and an English teacher; her career as a novelist did not begin until she was in her early forties, but it continued for three decades. After leaving the hustle and bustle of New York City to settle with her long-time companion, Sybil Pike, in rural Sargentville, Maine, where Pike runs Wayward Books, Grumbach wrote two books of reflections on religion and four volumes of memoirs.

In an essay for *Contemporary Authors Autobiography Series (CAAS),* the author recalled the time when she sought to have her first book published: "The manuscript was in a typing-paper box, wrapped in a shop-ping bag from the A. & P., and taped shut with scotch tape. I left it with the receptionist, remembering too late that I had not put my name and address on the outside of the box. I expected, as one does with an unlabeled suitcase at the airport, never to see it again. Two weeks later I got a phone call from an editor at Doubleday telling me they wished to publish the novel. Two years later they published a second novel." These first two books, *The Spoil of the Flowers,* about student life in a boardinghouse, and *The Short Throat, the Tender Mouth,* about life on a college campus three months before Hitler's march on Poland, "were by a beginner at a time in my life when I no longer should have been a beginner," Grumbach related in *CAAS.* "There are some good things, I believe, in both novels: had I much time ahead of me now, I would rewrite them and resubmit them for publication."

Upon the request of the publisher, Grumbach wrote her third book, *The Company She Kept,* a literary biography of the acerbic novelist Mary McCarthy. This book became the subject of a threatened lawsuit before its publication and of a volatile critical debate after its release. *The Company She Kept* parallels events and characters in McCarthy's novels with those in her life. "The fiction of Mary McCarthy is autobiographical to an extraordinary degree, in the widest sense of autobiography," Grumbach explains in the foreword to the book. "In the case of Mary McCarthy there is only a faint line between what really happened to her, the people she knew and knows, including herself, and the characters in her fictions." To prepare the biography, Grumbach spent a year reading McCarthy's work and criticism of it and interviewed the author extensively at her Paris home. Difficulties with McCarthy arose, Grumbach says, when McCarthy, who suggested she read the galleys of the book to catch any factual errors, protested against some of the information Grumbach had included in the manuscript.

In a *New York Times Book Review* article on her dispute with McCarthy, Grumbach reported that McCarthy voluntarily provided her with intimate biographical details in conversation and in a detailed memorandum. McCarthy's anger over their inclusion therefore came as a surprise, said Grumbach. "I was unprepared for the fury of her response when she saw the galleys . . . and realized that I had used the autobiographical details she had, as she said, given me," commented Grumbach. "She had said, once, that it felt strange to have a book written about one, 'a book that includes you as a person, not just a critical analysis of your writings.' Now she insisted that the *curriculum vitae* had been sent to be 'drawn upon,' not used, although just how this was to be done continues to be a mystery to me. . . . [McCarthy's] feeling was that the tapes and her letters to me had been intended solely for 'your own enlightenment.'"

For all the attendant publicity, however, *The Company She Kept* was not well received by the literary establishment. Stephanie Harrington wrote in *Commonweal:* "To anyone who has read *The Company She Kept* . . . the newspaper stories that followed the book's publication must have seemed too preposterous to be anything but a desperate attempt by the publisher's publicity department to drum up business for a clinker." A *Times Literary Supplement* contributor, who described *The Company She Kept* as "sparkily written and often critically sharp," felt that Grumbach falls short of her stated goal of "weaving one fabric of [the] diverse threads of McCarthy's biography and her fiction." Grumbach, asserted the reviewer, "never fully succeeds in dramatizing the complex interactions that go into such a process; [therefore, *The Company She Kept*] is likely to end up as required reading for gossips." Ellen Moers, writing in the *New York Times Book Review,* did not argue the validity of Grumbach's attempt to find the facts in Mary McCarthy's fiction—the process of "set[ting] out to name names," as Moers called it—but instead claimed that Grumbach misread McCarthy and thus arrived at erroneous conclusions. To Grumbach's statement that "there is only a faint line" between fact and fiction for McCarthy, Moers responded: "This simply cannot be true. The husbands in McCarthy fiction . . . are such dreary mediocrities, her artist colonies and political oases are so bare of talent or distinction, her suites of college girls are so tediously third-rate—only a powerful imagination could have made such nonentities out of the very interesting company that Mary McCarthy actually kept." *Saturday Review* critic Granville Hicks, however, did not find Grumbach's approach in *The Company She Kept* objectionable and approved of her straightforward manner in tackling it. "Although there is nothing novel about finding Miss McCarthy in her books, critics are usually cautious about identifying characters in fiction with real people, and I am grateful for Mrs. Grumbach's refusal to beat around that particular bush."

In the wake of the harsh reviews *The Company She Kept* received, Grumbach tried to deflect some of the

criticism from herself by discussing the circumstances leading to her decision to write the McCarthy biography. Explaining in the *New York Times Book Review* that she was asked to write the book on McCarthy, rather than instigating the project herself, Grumbach stated, "An editor asks, somewhere in the inner room of a dim New York restaurant, would you do a book on Her? And because you do not ordinarily eat and drink such sumptuous lunches in the proximate company of so many successful-looking people, and because you need the money, and because after all, She *is* a good writer (you've *always* thought this) and apparently a *fascinating* woman, you say yes, I will." Commented Harrington: "Mrs. Grumbach's apologia in the *Times* . . . [indicates] that it was foolhardy to expect a serious piece of work in the first place when she only decided to take on Mary McCarthy because an editor asked 'somewhere in the inner room of a dim New York restaurant, would you do a book on Her?'" Recognizing the shortcomings of *The Company She Kept,* Grumbach summarized her difficulties with the book in the *New York Times Book Review:* "The value of the whole experience lies, for me," she said, "in the recognition of how difficult, even well-nigh impossible, it is to write a book that deals with a living person. It does not matter in the least that the living person is willing to assist the writer (beware the Greeks bearing . . .) in conversation or letter; the fact remains, the law being what it is, the subject can give with one hand, take back with the other, and in this process of literary Indian-giving the writer is virtually helpless."

Ten years after publishing *The Company She Kept* and fifteen years after writing her novels, *The Short Throat, the Tender Mouth* and *The Spoil of the Flowers,* Grumbach returned to fiction. Her first novel after the hiatus was *Chamber Music,* written as the memoirs of ninety-year-old Caroline MacLaren, widow of a famous composer and founder of an artists' colony in his memory. Released with a 20,000 copy first printing and a $20,000 promotional campaign, *Chamber Music* won the popular and critical acclaim that eluded Grumbach's earlier books. Writing in the *Atlantic Monthly,* Peter Davison called the book "artful, distinctive, provocative, [and] compassionate." *Chamber Music,* remarked Victoria Glendinning in the *Washington Post Book World,* "is a book of originality and distinction."

Chamber Music is the story of "the chamber of one heart," says narrator Caroline MacLaren in the introduction to her memoirs. The novel's plot revolves around the subjugation of Caroline to her husband Robert and to Robert's music. Their marriage is a cold and barren one and *Chamber Music* charts its course through Robert's incestuous relationship with his mother, his homosexual affair with a student, and, finally, to his agonizing death in the tertiary stage of syphilis. Especially noted for its sensitive handling of its delicate subject matter and for its characterizations, *Chamber Music* was called by the *New York Times*'s John Leonard, "one of those rare novels for adults who listen." The characters in *Chamber Music,* Leonard continued, "are all stringed instruments. The music we hear occurs in the chamber of Caroline's heart. It is quite beautiful." With her third novel, Grumbach "makes us hear the difficult music of grace," wrote Nicholas Delbanco in the *New Republic.*

Although *Chamber Music*'s "revelations of sexuality are meant to shatter," as one *Publishers Weekly* contributor commented, and the passage on Robert's illness gives "a clinical description so simply precise, so elegantly loathsome, that it would do nicely either in a medical text or in a book on style," as Edith Milton observed in the *Yale Review,* it is the contrast between *Chamber Music*'s action and its language that gives the novel its impact. While much of the material in *Chamber Music* is meant to shock, the language is genteel and full of Victorian phrases. "What gives the main part of this book its polish and flavor is the contrast between matter and manner," maintained Glendinning. "Clarity and elegance of style account . . . for the distinction of *Chamber Music,*" wrote Eleanor B. Wymard in *Commonweal,* and other critics offered high praise for Grumbach's writing. For example, a *Washington Post Book World* reviewer claimed the book's language is "as direct and pure as a Hayden quartet," and Abigail McCarthy in *Commonweal* stated that *Chamber Music* has "the classical form, clarity, and brilliance of a composition for strings." Because it is Caroline's story, the novel adopts her voice—a voice that is "slightly stilted, slightly vapid, of the genteel tradition," one *Atlantic* contributor observed. Milton further asserted: "The novel is wonderfully written in [Caroline's] voice to evoke a time gone by, an era vanished. . . . The prose, understated, beautiful in its economies, supports a story of almost uncanny bleakness."

In her short preface to *Chamber Music,* Grumbach states that the novel's characters "are based vaguely upon persons who were once alive" but stresses that the book is fiction. "*Chamber Music* is a thinly, and strangely, fictionalized variation on the life of Marian MacDowell, [composer] Edward MacDowell's widow, who . . . founded an artist's colony in New Hampshire. . . . The names are changed; though not by much considering what else changes with them," wrote Milton. Gail Godwin, writing in the *New York Times Book Review,* suspected that the parallels between the MacDowells and the MacLarens "handicap . . . [Grumbach's] own possibilities for creating a fictional hero who might have come to life more vividly." However, other critics, including Glendinning, found that "the illusion of authenticity is strengthened by the inclusion of real people." "Robert MacLaren himself is given a semihistorical glamour by the parallels between his career and that of . . . Edward MacDowell—the two share teachers, musical styles, even a Boston address, and MacDowell's widow did indeed found an artist's colony in his name," noted Katha Pollitt. "Such details give Caroline's memoirs the piquancy of a historical novel."

Franny Fuller, the protagonist of Grumbach's novel *The Missing Person,* is also patterned after an actual figure. Franny, a 1930s movie star and sex symbol, closely resembles actress Marilyn Monroe. Written as a series of vignettes interweaving the events of Franny's career with an ongoing commentary by a gossip columnist, *The Missing Person* traces the actress's life from her sad beginnings in Utica, New York, through her rise to stardom, and finally to her disappearance from both Hollywood and the public consciousness. "Here, with certain sympathetic changes, is quite visibly another tale about the sad life of Marilyn Monroe," observed the *New York Times*'s Herbert Mitgang. "Missing person," wrote Cynthia Propper Seton in the *Washington Post Book World,* refers to "this sense that one is all facade, that there is no self inside." Franny is supposed to serve as a prototype for all the "missing persons" who are, "above all, missing to themselves," claimed Herbert Gold in the *New York Times Book Review.* "There seems evidence," Abigail McCarthy wrote in *Commonweal,* "that Doris Grumbach may initially have thought of Franny Fuller's story as a feminist statement in that women like Franny whom America 'glorifies and elevates' are sex objects made larger than life. But if so, as often happens in the creative process, she has transcended the aim in the writing. The creatures of the Hollywood process she gives us, men as well as women, are all victims."

Grumbach, in a prefatory note to the novel, comments on the nature of the book. "This novel is a portrait, not of a single life but of many lives melded into one, typical of the women America often glorifies and elevates, and then leaves suspended in their lonely and destructive fame," she says. Still, commented Richard Combs in the *Times Literary Supplement,* "there is no prize for guessing that the novel's heroine is Marilyn Monroe." The close correlation between Marilyn Monroe's life and Franny's life was disturbing to many critics. "The question that poses itself about a book like this is, Why bother? If you must write about Marilyn Monroe then why not do so in fiction or otherwise?," asked James Campbell in the *New Statesman.* "Real names thinly disguised are a bore." Combs believed Grumbach's reliance on the facts of Marilyn Monroe's life hindered her ability to substantiate the point she makes in the preface. "The more the real Hollywood shows through [in the novel], the less satisfying the portrait becomes," Combs maintained. "The author's assumption . . . seems to be that since Hollywood put fantasy on an anonymous, mass-production basis, the results can be freely arranged by the inspired do-it-yourselfer. . . . But in refantasizing the fantasy factory, Mrs. Grumbach allows herself the license of fiction without taking on the responsibility . . . to find revised truth in the revised subject."

"It is hard for [Franny] to have a separate imaginary existence in the mind of the reader," stated McCarthy. "But this flaw, if it is one, is more than compensated for by the writer's evocation of the scene against which Franny moves—tawdry, wonderful Hollywood at its peak." Indeed, Grumbach is praised for her fine writing and for "the adroit structure of the novel," as Gold called it. "There is in this prose a certain leanness, a sparseness that separates most of the characters into a chapter each, surrounded by an implied emptiness. Instead of the usual crowded Hollywood narrative, [*The Missing Person*] has the melancholy air . . . of an underpopulated landscape," stated Combs. Seton commented on Grumbach's ability to capture the tone and feeling of old Hollywood films and newsreels in her writing. "Doris Grumbach's special gift lies in her ability to suit the style and structure of her novels to the world in which she writes," McCarthy said. "*The Missing Person* is itself like a motion picture—a pastiche of scenes centered on the star, complete with flashbacks, close-ups and fade-outs."

About her intentions in writing *The Missing Person,* Grumbach told Wendy Smith of *Publishers Weekly:* "I was interested in seeing what you could do, given a catafalque of fact that I assumed might be known to any literate person who came to the book. I wanted to fantasize about it, to imagine things that probably were not so, and by that process make them true." However, Grumbach was disappointed in her readers, she continued: "I thought you could make that move and people would forget what the catafalque was, but they don't; they superimpose what they know, or think they know, upon what you've written, and they become critical about it."

Grumbach switched her topic from the rise and then demise of a 1930s starlet in *The Missing Person,* to the public ostracism then acceptance of two aristocratic lesbian lovers of the eighteenth century in her novel *The Ladies.* "Grumbach compellingly recreates the lives of two women who so defied convention and so baffled their contemporaries that they became celebrities," lauded Catharine R. Stimpson in the *New York Times Book Review.* The story relates Grumbach's concept of how Eleanor Butler and Sarah Ponsonby, two Irish aristocrats known as "the Ladies of Llangollen," shocked the community with their lesbian relationship but were eventually accepted and visited by such noteworthy individuals as Anna Seward, the Duke of Wellington, and Walter Scott. Stimpson noted that the book "eloquently documents the existence of women who lived as they wished to, instead of as society expected them to."

As Grumbach relates, Lady Eleanor, feeling the lack of love from her parents because she wasn't a boy, becomes the boy in her behavior and dress. Always looking to fulfill her need for acceptance and love, Eleanor falls in love with the orphan, Sarah Ponsonby, who is being sexually harassed by her guardian. Eleanor attempts to rescue Sarah, but the two are caught before they get far. A second attempt prompts the families to allow the couple to leave together, but under the condition that Lady Eleanor is banned from Ireland forever. After a few years of wandering, Eleanor and Sarah settle with a former servant and create their own haven in Wales. Eleanor and Sarah "seemed to each other to be divine survivors, well beyond the confines of social rules, two inhabitants of an ideal society. . . . They had uncovered a lost continent on which they could live, in harmony, quite alone and together," writes Grumbach in *The Ladies.* Eventually, visited by other aristocrats, they become more secure within the outer community; however, problems arise in their relationship as their greed and fame alters their lives.

The Ladies met with good reviews. Stimpson, while recognizing Grumbach's pattern of blurring biography and fiction, praised the book, noting that "*The Ladies* is boldly imagined, [and] subtly crafted." Comparing Grumbach's work with the likes of Virginia Woolf and Charlotte Perkins Gillman, Sandra Gilbert commented in the *Washington Post Book World* that Grumbach has "recounted their story with grace and wit," and she applauded "the sureness with which Grumbach accumulates small details about the lives of her protagonists and the tough but loving irony with which she portrays their idiosyncrasies." She observed, though, that while the protagonists' "road to reposeful Llangollen is strewn with obstacles for the runaway ladies. . . . All ends well once the weary travelers arrive in friendship's vale." Thus Gilbert maintained that "if there is anything problematic about *The Ladies,* it is that all seems to go almost too well" in the novel and "like Grumbach's earlier *Chamber Music,* seems here and there to flirt with the conventions of an increasingly popular new genre: The Happy Lesbian novel."

The title for Grumbach's next novel, the *The Magician's Girl,* is borrowed from Sylvia Plath's poem "The Bee Meeting." In this story Grumbach writes about three women who were college roommates and grew up during the twenties and thirties. In episodic fashion, the stories of Minna, Liz, and Maud are related from their childhood to their sixties, and from their hopes and dreams to their reality. Pretty, shy Minna marries a doctor, has a son, and becomes a history professor. After surviving years in a loveless marriage, at the age of sixty she finally develops a loving relationship with a young man in his twenties. Not long after they meet and she experiences this fulfillment, she is killed in a car accident. Maud, the daughter of a nurse and army sergeant, marries a handsome man whom she eventually rejects, has twins whom she neglects, and spends most of her time writing poetry. Her poetry is good but she destroys it all, except for the copies she sends to Minna in her letters; she commits suicide before realizing the true success of her writings. Liz, the only survivor, lives with her partner in a lesbian relationship, achieving fame as a photographer. Summarizing the book's theme, Anita Brookner in her review for the *Washington Post Book World,* stated that the formulaic stories about these three women demonstrate "the way early beginnings mature into not very much, for despite the achievements that come with age, a sense of disillusion persists." Brookner asserted that Grumbach asks more

questions about women's lives than she answers in her story, including the question, "Is that all?," and surmises that this may be more important than the answers. In conclusion, she praised *The Magician's Girl* as "a beautifully easy read, discreet and beguiling, and attractively low-key. It is an honorable addition to the annals of women's reading."

Several critics faulted Grumbach for too closely describing the lives of Sylvia Plath and Diane Arbus as the characters of Maud and Liz, respectively. Other critics found Grumbach's writing weak in definition and description. The *Times Literary Supplement*'s Marianne Wiggins found events "unlocated in time" and places "without a sense of period." She asserted that it is written "as if the text were a rehearsal for a talent contest"; she considered this especially disconcerting since she regards Grumbach as the "master of the quick sketch" and pointed out that generally "when her narrative shifts to describing the specific, it soars." In contrast, Paula Deitz in the *New York Times Book Review* commended Grumbach's attention to detail in *The Magician's Girl.* She deemed that the characters described "are all rich images, informed with the magic conveyed by the small details that reveal the forming of these lives." Deitz further maintained that "*The Magician's Girl* is most disturbing, and therefore at its best, in its acute awareness of the pains endured unflinchingly by the young." *Christian Science Monitor*'s Merle Rubin summarized: "What is most poignant about this novel is that its special aura of serenity tinged with sadness comes not from the pains and losses the characters endure, although there are many of these, but from the conviction it conveys that life, for all its sorrows, is so rich with possibilities as to make any one life—however long—much too short."

As she turned seventy, Grumbach found herself looking inward and asking important religious and philosophical questions. Because her seventieth birthday "was an occasion of real despair," as she told Smith, Grumbach decided to put pen to paper with a new view in mind—to alleviate her despair. "I thought, well perhaps it would help if I just take notes on this year," she continued; "whatever happens may throw some light on why I'm still here, make some sense out of living so long." What resulted was the first of what would be four autobiographical and reflective volumes: *Coming into the End Zone: A Memoir.* "What is most delightful about *Coming into the End Zone*—[is] the wry, spry, resilient, candid recording of present happenings and suddenly remembered past happenings which fill almost every page with anecdotes and reflections," exclaimed *Washington Post Book World*'s Anthony Thwaite. Grumbach comments on a wide range of topics, including contemporary annoyances such as phrases like "the computer is down," the death of several friends from the complications of acquired immunodeficiency syndrome (AIDS), her dislike of travel, her move to rural Maine, her memories of being fired from the *New Republic,* and Mary McCarthy's last curt comment to her. "The best moments are the passages in which the author seems least to be writing for posterity, merely trying to capture herself on the page, moments when the need to maintain a public persona gives way to the vulnerability of the private person, sometimes even to the young girl still inside this old woman," declared Carol Anshaw in *Tribune Books.* "The book that Ms. Grumbach intended as a confrontation with death winds up being a celebration of life," commented Noel Perrin in the *New York Times Book Review,* adding that "it is a deeply satisfying book." "Grumbach's reflections record—with honesty, fidelity, much important and unimportant detail, and with much grace and informal wit—her feelings of the time. I know no other book like it," wrote Thwaite, who concluded: "This is a book to grow old with even before one is old. The best is yet to be."

Grumbach continues her reminiscences in *Extra Innings: A Memoir.* Reviewers disagreed about how satisfactorily the author presents her experiences. In the *Washington Post Book World,* Diana O'Hehir defined a memoir as a grab bag and, directing her comments to Grumbach, wrote: "I felt yours wasn't enough of a grab bag. Not enough gossip about people. Not enough detail about you, not enough specific detail about relationships, family." However, Kathleen Norris presented the view in the *New York Times Book Review* that the book is "more of a hodgepodge" than *End Zone.* Norris maintained that "for all its recounting of ordinary events, *Extra Innings,* like *End Zone,* is a document still too rare in literary history, an account of a woman who has lived by words. Ms. Grumbach wittily chronicles the absurdities and ambiguities of the modern American writer's life."

She returned to fiction with her 1995 historical novel *The Book of Knowledge.* In it Grumbach introduces four central characters as adolescents the summer before the great stock market crash of 1929, then touches on each of their lives into adulthood, through the Great Depression and World War II. Two of the characters are a brother and sister who become intimate, sexually and emotionally, that summer. The other two are the vacationing son and daughter of a wealthy stockbroker, with whom the brother and sister become friends. All strive for selfhood in various fashions; and the two young men eventually have a homosexual relationship. According to *Tribune Books*'s Nina Mehta, "Grumbach cuts right to sexuality, condemning her main characters to lives stunted by their inability to deal honestly with their sexual feelings." As Julia Markus of the *Los Angeles Times Book Review* remarked, "The stories of [the four] and their families are told and interwoven with great irony, subtlety and beauty." Markus concluded that "with masterful conciseness and with her own unique haunting force, Doris Grumbach has brilliantly delineated the tragedy of an entire generation."

But other reviewers faulted Grumbach for not delving into the interior lives of the foursome. Grumbach makes "a lot of tendentious commentary about puberty and the chasteness of homosexual inclinations," pointed out Mehta, "but what's most disheartening . . . is the book's lack of insight." Mehta further maintained that "by neglecting to ventilate her characters' lives with even a breeze of introspection, Grumbach gives them less personality, less psychological weight, than they deserve." Likewise, Sara Maitland asserted in the *New York Times Book Review:* "Ms. Grumbach prods at her four central characters with a sharp stick, but when they turn over, she withdraws her authorial attention in disgust." Maitland decried that the reader is "never shown the painful workings through of . . . personal choices that we are *told* the characters have to endure."

During the 1990s Grumbach published two works about her spiritual journey: *Life in a Day,* in which she writes about solitude and thanksgiving as she recounts a day at seventy-seven years old, and *The Presence of Absence: On Prayers and an Epiphany.* In the later, which *Cross Currents* reviewer Kenneth Arnold called a "story of spiritual hunger," Grumbach describes a profound religious event that she experienced while in her twenties and her subsequent search for a renewal of that intense experience. After decades of going to church services that only felt sterile, Grumbach has tried solitude and contemplative prayer. "I had discovered how necessary it was (for me) to discard my stale concepts of God and ritual practices in order to approach the pure core of prayer," she explains in *The Presence of Absence.* "A long life in the church had formed me into a half-hearted, secular worshiper. It was a condition I had to cast off." At the time also suffering from the shingles, a painful inflammation of the nerves, and because the pain was so intense as to prevent prayer, she read works by Simone Weil, Thomas Merton, Kathleen Norris, and Thomas Kelly. "Her experiences are set out in graceful prose and with compelling honesty," wrote Notre Dame theology professor Lawrence S. Cunningham in *Commonweal.* And Kathleen Norris, who is herself a writer on spirituality, wrote about the currency of this "brief and forceful" work: "It is an important book for pastors in that Grumbach . . . conveys something that many older people experience but do not articulate—a profound disappointment with the churches to which they have devoted their lives." "One must thank Grumbach for penning an authentic work," Cunningham added. "Anyone who despairs of the church but still clings to prayer will benefit from this woman's struggles and insights."

Grumbach's memoir *The Pleasure of Their Company* ostensibly deals with the author's upcoming eightieth birthday, yet that is only the framework around which she attaches her musings. These include sketches of deceased friends, as well as her former husband and current companion, and reflections on literature, memory, and prayer. Enthusiasts of the work included *Booklist*'s Donna Seaman, who dubbed it "quietly compelling and always satisfying," *Commonweal*'s Lawrence S. Cunningham, who described it as an "elegantly written and very moving memoir," and *Library Journal*'s Carol A. McAllister, who called the author "vibrant and perceptive," and found her observations "meaningful" and ramblings "wise." *Atlanta Journal-Constitution* reviewer Steve Harvey also praised Grumbach's ability to get to the heart of the matter: "[She] has gotten very good at getting under the skin of her own life. She is able in a few words to reveal the heart of the matter, in this case fear of growing old and dying, and yet she approaches it all with such wit, good feeling and candor that we find ourselves delighted, rather than disconcerted by her words." Finally, in the *Lambda Book Report* Karla Jay compared the work favorably to a memoir by Judith Barrington and to exemplars of the genre as a whole: "Memoirs generally tackle thematic issues that reach beyond the immediate life of the author, and these two works are brilliant examples of the genre."

In 2000 Grumbach was awarded the Whitehead Award for Lifetime Achievement by Publishing Triangle, the publishing association of gay men and lesbians in the publishing industry.

BIOGRAPHICAL AND CRITICAL SOURCES:

BOOKS

Contemporary Authors Autobiography Series, Volume 2, Gale (Detroit, MI), 1985.

Contemporary Literary Criticism, Gale (Detroit, MI), Volume 13, 1980, Volume 22, 1982, Volume 64, 1991.

Grumbach, Doris, *Coming into the Endzone,* Norton (New York, NY), 1991.

Grumbach, Doris, *Extra Innings: A Memoir,* Norton (New York, NY), 1993.

Grumbach, Doris, *Fifty Days of Solitude,* Beacon Press (Boston, MA), 1994.

Grumbach, Doris, *Life in a Day,* Beacon Press (Boston, MA), 1996.

Grumbach, Doris, *The Presence of Absence: On Prayers and an Epiphany,* Beacon Press (Boston, MA), 1998.

Grumbach, Doris, *The Pleasure of Their Company,* Beacon Press (Boston, MA), 2000.

PERIODICALS

America, June 2, 1979.

American Spectator, January, 1982.

Atlanta Journal-Constitution, June 4, 2000, Steven Harvey, "The Unexpected 'Pleasure' of Growing Older," review of *The Pleasure of Their Company,* p. L10.

Atlantic Monthly, March, 1979.

Booklist, October 1, 1993; May 1, 2000, Donna Seaman, review of *The Pleasure of Their Company,* p. 1639.

Choice, January, 1999, review of *The Presence of Absence: On Prayers and an Epiphany,* p. 905.

Christian Century, May 19, 1999, Kathleen Norris, review of *The Presence of Absence,* pp. 567-569.

Christian Science Monitor, February 26, 1987, p. 22.

Commonweal, October 6, 1967; June 22, 1979; January 15, 1982; March 26, 1999, Lawrence S. Cunningham, review of *The Presence of Absence,* pp. 25-28; January 12, 2001, Lawrence S. Cunningham, review of *The Pleasure of Their Company,* p. 28.

Cross Currents, spring, 1999, Kenneth Arnold, review of *The Presence of Absence,* 140-143.

Globe and Mail (Toronto, Ontario, Canada), August 4, 2001, review of *The Pleasure of Their Company,* p. D12.

Lambda Book Report, September, 2000, Karla Jay, "Writing beyond the Margins," review of *The Pleasure of Their Company,* p. 18.

Library Journal, March 1, 1979; May 1, 2000, Carol A. McAllister, review of *The Pleasure of Their Company,* p. 112.

Listener, August 9, 1979.

London Review of Books, August 20, 1992.

Los Angeles Times Book Review, July 16, 1995, p. 3.

Ms., April, 1979.

Nation, March 28, 1981, pp. 375-376.

National Review, June 8, 1979.

New Republic, March 10, 1979.

New Statesman, August 17, 1979; August 28, 1981.

Newsweek, March 19, 1979.

New Yorker, April 23, 1979.

New York Times, March 13, 1979; July 20, 1989.

New York Times Book Review, June 11, 1967; March 25, 1979; March 29, 1981, pp. 14-15; September 30, 1984, p. 12; February 1, 1987, p. 22; September 22, 1991, Noel Perrin, "Be Cranky while You Can," review of *Coming into the End Zone;* November 21, 1993, p. 11; October 21, 1993; November 21, 1993, Kathleen Norris, "Not Cranky; Not Grumpy; Not Any of Those Things," review of *Extra Innings: A Memoir;* October 2, 1994, Le Anne Schreiber, "Home Alone," review of *Fifty Days of Solitude;* June 25, 1995, p. 19; August 6, 2000, Leslie Chess Feller, review of *The Pleasure of Their Company,* p. 16.

Observer, August 12, 1979.

Publishers Weekly, January 15, 1979; February 13, 1981; April 24, 2000, review of *The Pleasure of Their Company,* p. 75.

Sewanee Review, January, 1995.

Spectator, August 11, 1979.

Time, April 9, 1979.

Times Literary Supplement, December 7, 1967; November 30, 1979; September 11, 1981; July 12, 1985; June 19, 1987, p. 669.

Tribune Books (Chicago, IL), September 29, 1991; August 13, 1995, p. 6.

Village Voice, August 24, 1987.

Washington Post, June 4, 2000, David Guy, "Look Homeward, Author," p. X08.

Washington Post Book World, March 18, 1979; February 10, 1980; April 5, 1981, pp. 9, 13; September 30, 1984, p. 7; January 4, 1987, pp. 3, 13; September 8, 1991; October 24, 1993, p. 5; October 10, 1996.

Women's Review of Books, December, 1993; December, 1995.

Yale Review, autumn, 1979.*

*   *   *

GWYNN, R(obert) S(amuel) 1948-

PERSONAL: Born May 13, 1948, in Leaksville, NC; son of Dallas Edmund (a sales manager) and Thelma (Howe) Gwynn; married Faye La Prade, June, 1969 (marriage ended, May, 1977); married Donna Kay Skaggs Simon, June 1, 1977; children: (second marriage) William Tyree. *Ethnicity:* "White." *Education:* Davidson College, B.A., 1969; University of Arkansas, M.A., M.F.A., 1973. *Politics:* Democrat. *Religion:* Methodist. *Hobbies and other interests:* Fishing, hunting, cooking.

ADDRESSES: Home—985 Norwood Dr., Beaumont, TX 77706. *Office*—Department of English and Foreign Languages, Lamar University, Beaumont, TX 77710; fax: 409-861-4223. *E-mail*—rsgwynn1@cs.com.

CAREER: Southwest Texas State University, San Marcos, TX, instructor in English, 1973-76; Lamar University, Beaumont, TX, University Professor of English, 1976—. Gives readings from his works throughout the United States.

MEMBER: Associated Writing Programs, Poetry Society of America, Conference of College Teachers of English, South Central Modern Language Association, Texas Association of Creative Writing Teachers, Texas Institute of Letters.

WRITINGS:

Bearing and Distance (poetry chapbook), Cedar Rock (New Braunfels, TX), 1977.

The Narcissiad (poetry chapbook), Cedar Rock (New Braunfels, TX), 1981.

R. S. Gwynn

The Drive-In (poetry), University of Missouri Press (Columbia, MO), 1986.

(With others) *Texas Poets in Concert: A Quartet,* University of North Texas Press (Denton, TX), 1990.

The Area Code of God (poetry chapbook), Aralia, 1994.

No Word of Farewell: Selected Poems, 1970-2000, Story Line, 2001.

If My Song (poetry chapbook), Lisle, 1999.

EDITOR

(And contributor) *Dictionary of Literary Biography,* Volume 105: *American Poets since World War II, Second Series,* Gale (Detroit, MI), 1991.

(And contributor) *Dictionary of Literary Biography,* Volume 120: *American Poets since World War II, Third Series,* Gale (Detroit, MI), 1992.

Drama: A HarperCollins Pocket Anthology, Harper-Collins (New York, NY), 1993, 2nd edition published as *Drama: A Pocket Anthology,* Penguin (New York, NY), 2002.

Fiction: A HarperCollins Pocket Anthology, Harper-Collins (New York, NY), 1993, 2nd edition published as *Fiction: A Longman Pocket Anthology,* Longman (New York, NY), 1997, 3rd edition published as *Fiction: A Pocket Anthology,* Penguin (New York, NY), 2002.

Poetry: A HarperCollins Pocket Anthology, HarperCollins (New York, NY), 1993, 2nd edition (also contributor) published as *Poetry: A Longman Pocket Anthology,* Longman (New York, NY), 1997, 3rd edition published as *Poetry: A Pocket Anthology,* Penguin (New York, NY), 2002.

The Advocates of Poetry: A Reader of American Poet-Critics of the Modern Era, University of Arkansas Press (Fayetteville, AR), 1996.

New Expansive Poetry: Theory, Criticism, History, Story Line, 1999.

(With Dana Gioia) *The Longman Anthology of Short Fiction,* with instructor's manual, Longman (New York, NY), 2001, compact edition, 2001.

Literature: A Pocket Anthology, Penguin (New York, NY), 2002.

(With Dana Gioia) *The Longman Masters of Short Fiction,* with instructor's manual, Longman (New York, NY), 2002.

Contributor to books, including *Miller Williams and the Poetry of the Particular,* edited by Michael Burns, University of Missouri Press (Columbia, MO), 1991; *Rebel Angels: Twenty-five Poets of the New Formalism,* Story Line, 1996; *The Store of Joys,* Blair (Winston-Salem, NC), 1997; *Western Wind: An Introduction to Poetry,* McGraw-Hill (New York, NY), 1999; and *An Exaltation of Forms: Contemporary Poets Celebrate the Diversity of Their Art,* University of Michigan Press (Ann Arbor, MI), 2002. Contributor of more than seventy articles, poems, and reviews to periodicals, including *Sparrow, Tar River Poetry, Sewanee Review, Hudson Review, Poetry Northwest, Hudson Review, River Styx, Ogalala Review, Poetry Miscellany,* and *Texas Monthly.*

WORK IN PROGRESS: Editing *Contemporary American Poetry: A Pocket Anthology,* with April Linder, for Penguin (New York, NY); poetry.

H

HAMILL, Pete 1935-

PERSONAL: Born William Peter Hamill, June 24, 1935, in Brooklyn, NY; son of William and Anne (Devlin) Hamill; married Ramona Negron, February 3, 1962 (divorced, 1970); married Fukiko Aoki, May 23, 1987; children: (first marriage) Adriene, Deirdre. *Education:* Attended Pratt Institute, 1955-56, 1957-58, and Mexico City College (now University of the Americas), 1956-57. *Politics:* Democrat.

ADDRESSES: Home—New York, NY. *Agent*—International Creative Management, 40 West 57th St., New York, NY 10019.

CAREER: Journalist and novelist. Brooklyn Navy Yard, Brooklyn, NY, sheet metal worker, 1951-52; advertising designer, New York, NY, 1957-60; *New York Post,* New York, NY, reporter, 1960-63, political columnist, 1965-67, 1969-74, columnist, 1988-93; editor, 1993; *Saturday Evening Post,* Philadelphia, PA, contributing editor, 1964-65; war correspondent in South Vietnam, 1966; freelance writer, Brooklyn, 1968; former Washington columnist for *Newsday; New York Daily News,* New York, NY, columnist, 1977-79, 2001—, editor, 1997; *Village Voice,* New York, NY, columnist, beginning 1974; *Mexico City News,* editor, 1986-87; *Esquire,* columnist, 1989-91. *Military service:* U.S. Navy, 1952-54.

MEMBER: Writers Guild.

AWARDS, HONORS: Meyer Berger Award, Columbia University Graduate School of Journalism, 1962, for series on slums; Newspaper Reporters Association special award, 1962, for series on police; Society of Silurians Twenty-five-Year Achievement Award, 1989, Peter Kihss Award, 1992.

WRITINGS:

NOVELS

A Killing for Christ, New American Library (New York, NY), 1968.
The Gift, Random House (New York, NY), 1973.
Flesh and Blood, Random House (New York, NY), 1977.
Dirty Laundry, Bantam (New York, NY), 1978.
The Deadly Piece, Bantam (New York, NY), 1979.
The Guns of Heaven, Bantam (New York, NY), 1983.
Loving Women: A Novel of the Fifties, Random House (New York, NY), 1990.
Snow in August, Little, Brown (Boston, MA), 1997.
Forever, Little, Brown (Boston, MA), 2002.

SHORT-STORY COLLECTIONS

The Invisible City: A New York Sketchbook, drawings by Susan Stillman, Random House (New York, NY), 1980.
Tokyo Sketches, Kodansha International (New York, NY), 1993.

Also author of short-story series "Tales of New York," *New York Daily News,* 1982-84.

SCREENPLAYS

Doc (produced by United Artists, 1971), Paperback Library, 1971.

Nightside, American Broadcasting Company (ABC-TV), 1973.

Liberty, National Broadcasting Company (NBC-TV), 1986.

Also author of screenplays, *Badge 373,* 1973, *Report from Engine Co. 82, Death at an Early Age,* and *Neon Empire,* 1987.

RECORDINGS WITH MUSIC; AUTHOR OF SCRIPT

Massacre at My Lai, Flying Dutchman, 1970.

Murder at Kent State University, Flying Dutchman, 1970.

Also author of script for *Snow in August,* read by Tom Merritt, Soundelux.

NONFICTION

Irrational Ravings (collected columns), Putnam (New York, NY), 1971.

Fighters, photographs by George Bennett, Dolphin Books (New York, NY), 1978.

A Drinking Life: A Memoir, Little, Brown (Boston, MA), 1994.

Tools As Art: The Hechinger Collection, foreword by John Hechinger, Abrams (New York, NY), 1995.

Piecework: Writings on Men and Women, Fools and Heroes, Lost Cities, Vanished Friends, Small Pleasures, Large Calamities, and How the Weather Was (collected columns), Little, Brown (Boston, MA), 1996.

Times Square Gym, photographs by John Goodman, EVAN Publishing (New York, NY), 1996.

News Is a Verb: Journalism at the End of the Twentieth Century, Ballantine (New York, NY), 1998.

Why Sinatra Matters, Little, Brown (Boston, MA), 1998.

Diego Rivera, Harry N. Abrams (New York, NY), 1999.

(Editor and author of introduction) *New York Exposed: Photographs from the Daily News,* Harry N. Abrams (New York, NY), 2001.

OTHER

(Author of preface) Paul Sann, *Kill the Dutchman!: The Story of Dutch Schultz,* Da Capo Press (New York, NY), 1971.

(Author of introduction) Harvey Wang, *Harvey Wang's New York,* Norton (New York, NY), 1990.

(Author of afterword) *Tales from the Arabian Nights,* translated by Andrew Lang, illustrations by Edmund Dulac and others, Reader's Digest Association (Pleasantville, NY), 1991.

(Author of introduction) *The Brooklyn Reader: Thirty Writers Celebrate America's Favorite Borough,* edited by Andrea Wyatt Sexton and Alice Leccese Powers, Harmony Books (New York, NY), 1994.

(Author of introduction) Edward Robb Ellis, *A Diary of the Century: Tales from America's Greatest Diarist,* Kodansha International (New York, NY), 1995.

(Author of foreword) William Kornblum, *At Sea in the City: New York from the Water,* Algonquin Press (New York, NY), 2002.

Contributor to books, including *New York: City of Islands,* Monacelli Press, 1998; and *American Perspectives: The Bill of Rights,* Mightywords.com, 2000. Contributor to periodicals, including *Cosmopolitan, Life, New York Times Magazine, Playboy, Reader's Digest,* and *Village Voice.*

ADAPTATIONS: Flesh and Blood and *The Gift* were adapted for television and broadcast by the Columbia Broadcasting System in 1979 and 1980, respectively; a story by Hamill was adapted for television as *Loyalty and Betrayal: The Story of the American Mob,* Fox Broadcasting Company, 1993.

SIDELIGHTS: Pete Hamill learned the craft of writing as a journalist on major metropolitan daily newspapers, and he has been recognized as a preeminent commentator on national news in general and New York City events in particular. *Tikkun* contributor Jack Newfield called Hamill "one of the leading journalists of his generation." Hamill's work as a reporter and columnist is reflected in his fiction, according to many reviewers, who note that among Hamill's talents are his realistic dialogue and settings.

Although best known as a novelist and author of nonfiction books on such varied topics as Diego Rivera and Frank Sinatra, Hamill became something of an institution in New York, where he has written for the *New York Post, Village Voice,* and *New York Daily News. New York Times Book Review* correspondent Andrew O'Hehir claimed that Hamill "embodies the city's finest tradition of popular journalism. His wide-ranging compassion, his commitment to clear and emotional prose and his unabashed love for New York and its people are exemplary." New York historian Kevin Baker told the *Knight Ridder/Tribune News Service:* "He's a wonderful storyteller, in the way of the old-style New York newspaper writers. He's also a newspaperman who sees himself as an advocate for the working class, and there are precious few left."

Perhaps not surprisingly, many of Hamill's novels are set in Manhattan and feature ethnic characters seeking their place in New York City's grand scheme. Assessing Hamill's *Dirty Laundry* in the *Washington Post,* Robert Parker wrote: "Hamill does a lot of things very well. He has a lovely romantic sense of place. . . . Mexico, where much of the action takes place, is vivid and real. . . . Hamill's dialogue is right, especially his ear for New York small talk." *Village Voice* contributor Geoffrey Stokes concurred that one of Hamill's greatest strengths is the realistic voices of his characters. Discussing *The Gift*—a slim novel centering on a neighborhood bar—Stokes declared that Hamill makes "the inarticulate, broken language of late-night drinkers sing for him."

One of Hamill's best-known works is his novel *Flesh and Blood,* which chronicles Irish-American Bobby Fallon's journey from the tough streets of Brooklyn to the arenas of professional boxing. His story is complicated by an erotic entanglement with his mother, who was long ago deserted by Bobby's father. "If you like such fables of the fight game served up tough and sordid with the lyrical strains of 'Danny Boy' to sweeten the anguish of Oedipus, here is a taut, punchy read that makes *Rocky* seem like a fairy tale," commented Eliot Asinof in the *New York Times Book Review.* "Hamill writes through the voice of his hero, sometimes in the first person, sometimes in the second—stark staccato sentences designed to sting, building suspense that is rooted in character, relentlessly knifing through Bobby's ferocity."

Christopher Lehmann-Haupt, writing in the *New York Times,* believed that *Flesh and Blood,* despite some predictable plot devices, "is a powerful story. For one thing, Mr. Hamill's boxing material seems unusually savvy and authentic. . . . The boxing passages are a good deal more sophisticated than they are in most fiction of this sort. For once we can really believe it when . . . [Bobby's trainer] tells his young charge, 'You're not a fighter. You're a bum. An Irish bum. . . . But I can make you a fighter.'"

John Rechy in the *Los Angeles Times* suggested that while Hamill's writing is fine, his stories are somewhat contrived. Discussing *The Invisible City: A New York Sketchbook,* Rechy observed that "such remorseless sweetness coats these doggedly decent vignettes that at times one dislikes oneself for not loving them." As an example, Rechy pointed out the story of an aging actress that features "a fine beginning, splendid writing, [and] an enduring theme." These effects are unfortunately marred, suggested Rechy, when "the happy ending gallops to 'save' her—and trample on the story." But Geoffrey Stokes reacted very differently to the optimism that pervades much of Hamill's fiction. Stokes placed Hamill in the classic tradition of Charles Dickens, writing of Hamill's Christmas story, *The Gift:* "In its stubborn insistence on seeing the best side of tenement life—without hiding the worst—it reminds me of an earlier seasonal classic. As well it might, for in its heightened emotionality and recklessly extravagant language, *The Gift* is our *Christmas Carol.*"

Hamill was the oldest of seven Brooklyn-raised children of Irish immigrant parents. Following in his alcoholic father's footsteps, he started drinking at an early age. Despite this, Hamill's academic record won him entrance to Regis High School, a Manhattan college prep school for Catholic boys. When he was fifteen, he enrolled in Manhattan's Cartoonists and Illustrators School, taking a course in drawing and anatomy. At age sixteen, he quit school to help his struggling family by taking a job at the Brooklyn Navy Yard.

Hamill did a stint in the Navy, then returned stateside, traveling to Mexico City to study art on the G.I. Bill. By then, he'd begun writing short stories. He worked in an advertising agency but soon became frustrated with the work. Hamill landed a job on the *New York Post,* then progressed upward as a journalist, but "I drank in the morning when I worked nights, and at night when I worked days." He became a regular at the Lion's Head bar in Greenwich Village. He married, fathered two children and then divorced. Reportedly, it was actress Shirley MacLaine—whom he met in 1966 while working on screenplays in Hollywood—who helped the writer understand he had a problem with alcohol. He cut down on his drinking, somewhat, for the next ten years, then quit in 1972.

Hamill's autobiography, *A Drinking Life: A Memoir,* received enthusiastic praise from many critics. Tom Walker, writing in the *Denver Post,* commented that "Hamill lets it all out, pulls no punches. It's neither whiney nor preachy. It just tells his story in a straight, this-is-what-happened fashion. The writing is tight, the style graceful. But, most important, when you read it you know he's telling the truth." For those readers who have "toted a heavy drinking habit . . . the book will hit closest to home," maintained Vincent Patrick in the *New York Times Book Review.* However, he added, "you need never have lived the drinking life to savor this brutally honest memoir." Despite *A Drinking Life*'s somewhat downbeat subject matter, Patrick found a good deal of warmth within its pages: Hamill's "fine memoir will evoke an abundance of welcome memories: the *Wonderland of Knowledge* encyclopedia acquired with coupons clipped from the *New York Post,* Mission Bell grape soda, our first street fight, the terrifying sight of the Normandie lying on its side at a Hudson River pier, kegs of beer at a V-E Day block party, the local candy store's seemingly endless racks of comic books."

Snow in August is a novel whose characters, setting, and recurrent motifs are fictionalized versions of the young Pete Hamill readers met in *A Drinking Life.* Eleven-year-old Michael Devlin awakens early on a snowy morning in 1946, his thoughts full of comic-book character Captain Marvel and the power-word "shazam," and plods through the snow to Saturday mass and his role of altar boy. On his way he meets the mysterious Rabbi Judah Hirsch, who later strikes a deal with Michael. Judah will teach the boy Yiddish and spin him remembrances of his life in Prague in return for help in honing his English and lessons in the mysteries of baseball, which the rabbi believes is the key to understanding America.

Religious intolerance, particularly anti-Semitism, in their Irish-Catholic community, is the driving force in *Snow in August,* as Michael witnesses the vicious beating of a Jewish candy-store owner by gang member Frankie McCarthy, and the youthful thugs threaten him, striving to keep him quiet about the crime.

Christopher Lehmann-Haupt noted in the *New York Times:* "In the end [Michael] is pushed to wreak revenge on his tormentors, and Mr. Hamill permits him to act out a juvenile fantasy tantamount to achieving the power of Captain Marvel by speaking the magic word shazam." Lehmann-Haupt concluded, "Although conventional in form, *Snow in August* takes many risks, often approaching the brinks of sentimentality and cuteness without ever going over."

Hamill's novel *Forever* is an extended fable of the history of New York City as seen through the eyes of a supernatural Irish immigrant who is granted immortality so long as he remains on the island of Manhattan. The story commences in the mid-1700s and ends with the attack on the World Trade Centers and its aftermath. Hamill had ostensibly finished writing the book before the Trade Centers were destroyed, but he delayed publication and added to the tale to include this devastating event. Hamill told the *Knight Ridder/ Tribune News Service:* "I knew I had to change the book's ending, but I agonized. Would this be exploiting 9/11? But there was no way to get out of it. I couldn't write a novel about New York's history and leave out the greatest calamity of all. It would be like writing about World War II and leaving out Pearl Harbor. I took another year."

Ambitious in scope and employing magical realism from Celtic and African sources, *Forever* tells of Cormac O'Connor's journey from Ireland to colonial America in search of revenge against his parents' killer. Granted immortality by an African shaman in the wake of a slave uprising, Cormac lives to fight with General George Washington, dine with Boss Tweed, and befriend musicians Duke Ellington and Madonna. Citing *Forever* for its "honorable intentions and its moments of grandeur and elegiac sweetness," *New York Times Book Review* contributor Andrew O'Hehir noted that the novel offers readers "an eye and ear sharply tuned to the street and densely larded chunks of convincing historical detail." In *Entertainment Weekly,* Troy Patterson called *Forever* "a lavish block of Hollywood-worthy wish fulfillment" that "wholeheartedly celebrates human goodness at every turn." Brad Hooper in *Booklist* found the novel to be "remarkably imaginative" and "perfectly enjoyable to read for [Hamill's] great felicity of style . . . as well as his originality of plot."

Hamill's nonfiction includes collections of his newspaper columns, essays on art and art history, and books on artist Diego Rivera and singer Frank Sinatra. The latter, *Why Sinatra Matters,* was one of many retrospectives of the entertainer's life and career published after Sinatra's death. Hamill, however, wrote from experience: he had been friends with Sinatra, so his meditation is interspersed with personal recollections of time they spent together, as well as analyses of the changes in the singer's style and manner over time. A *Publishers Weekly* reviewer called *Why Sinatra Matters* "confident, smart and seamless," concluding that Hamill's book "is a definitive introduction to Sinatra's work." *Booklist* correspondent Brian McCombie likewise praised the book for its "combination biography and cultural analysis," adding that Hamill provides "a heartfelt and intelligent tribute to Ol' Blue Eyes."

In *News Is a Verb* Hamill muses about the changes in the journalism profession that have led to a greater emphasis upon celebrity gossip at the expense of hard reporting. Having himself been fired as editor of the *New York Daily News* before he could have a significant impact on the paper's direction, Hamill speaks to the modern newspaper's inability to meet the needs of an inner-city, immigrant, and resident population with serious concerns about education, the environment, crime, and city services. In *Nieman Reports,* Ying Chan called *News Is a Verb* "a small gem," suggesting that reporters in particular read it to remember "the whys and hows of our crafts, basics of often-forgotten journalistic wisdom that Hamill dispenses throughout the little book: that journalism is about 'helping people' and keeping the country 'functioning as a democracy.'"

BIOGRAPHICAL AND CRITICAL SOURCES:

BOOKS

Contemporary Literary Criticism, Volume 10, Gale (Detroit, MI), 1979.

PERIODICALS

American Journal of Psychiatry, December, 1994, p. 1828.
American Spectator, June, 1991, p. 8.
Atlanta Journal-Constitution, March 10, 1996, p. K12.

Booklist, September 15, 1998, Brian McCombie, review of *Why Sinatra Matters,* p. 184; December 15, 2002, Brad Hooper, review of *Forever,* p. 707.
Chicago Tribune, February 9, 1996, sec. 5, p. 3.
Christian Science Monitor, May 28, 1998, David Holmstrom, "Separating the Wheat from the Tares in News," p. B11.
Commonweal, February 1, 1974; August 15, 1997, p. 26.
Denver Post, April 10, 1995, p. E8.
Entertainment Weekly, January 28, 1994, p. 48; April 22, 1994, p. 51; April 14, 1995, p. 61; January 19, 1996, p. 48; June 19, 1996, p. 48; May 30, 1997, p. 67; January 10, 2003, Troy Patterson, "He Loves N.Y.," p. 72.
Esquire, September, 1989, p. 51.
Forbes, March 11, 1996, p. S20.
Kirkus Reviews, December 15, 1992, p. 1525; November 1, 1993, p. 1365; October 1, 1995, p. 1399.
Knight Ridder/Tribune News Service, January 15, 2003, Celia McGee, "Pete Hamill's Epic New York Novel Tracks City, Time after Time," p. K0745.
Library Journal, April 10, 1989, p. 111; April 1, 1990, p. 154; January, 1993, p. 168; January, 1994, p. 130; December, 1995, p. 120; February 15, 1997, p. 162; February 15, 1998, p. 184; October 15, 1999, Mary Hamel-Schwulst, review of *Diego Rivera,* p. 66.
Los Angeles Times, November 21, 1980; June 25, 1997, p. E6.
Los Angeles Times Book Review, March 14, 1993, p. 6; April 9, 1995, p. 10.
Nation, February 7, 1994, pp. 166-9.
National Catholic Reporter, March 2, 1990, p. 20.
National Review, April 12, 1993, p. 51; February 7, 1994, p. 74.
Newsweek, March 29, 1993, p. 67.
New York, December 4, 1989, p. 162; March 1, 1993, p. 32; May 12, 1997, p. 24.
New York Times, November 18, 1977; October 12, 1979; March 16, 1989, p. C21; March 19, 1993, p. B3; January 10, 1994, P. C18; February 24, 1994, pp. C4, C10; January 7, 1997, p. B1; May 1, 1997, p. C20; May 30, 1997, p. B5; June 14, 1998, Deborah Stead, review of *News Is a Verb: Journalism at the End of the Twentieth Century,* p. B9; November 23, 1998, Christopher Lehmann-Haupt, "Yes, Tough Guys Dance and Sing Blues in the Night," p. E7.
New York Times Book Review, November 11, 1968; November 20, 1977; April 2, 1989, p. 13; January

16, 1994, p. 9; June 5, 1994, p. 24; December 4, 1994, p. 66; March 26, 1995, p. 32; June 11, 1995, p. 58; May 1, 1997, p. C20; May 4, 1997; November 21, 1999, Carolyn T. Hughes, "A Unifying Art," p. 75; January 19, 2003, Andrew O'Hehir, "Not a Bridge-and-Tunnel Guy," p. 6.

Nieman Reports, fall, 1998, Ying Chan, review of *News Is a Verb,* p. 58.

People Weekly, April 10, 1989, p. 36; March 11, 1996, p. 32.

Publishers Weekly, February 17, 1989, p. 64; February 1, 1993, p. 74; November 22, 1993, p. 54; January 10, 1994, p. 38; December 18, 1995, p. 38; March 17, 1997, p. 76; October 6, 1997, p. 38; August 24, 1998, review of *Why Sinatra Matters,* p. 37; December 23, 2002, review of *Forever,* p. 48.

Saturday Review, January 7, 1978.

Tikkun, March-April, 1998, Jack Newfield, "An Interview with Pete Hamill," p. 24.

Time, March 29, 1993, p. 15; January 24, 1994, p. 68; December 9, 1996, p. 25.

Tribune Books (Chicago, IL), April 2, 1989, p. 64; January 23, 1994, pp. 3, 8.

Variety, April 18, 1973.

Village Voice, December 16, 1981.

Washington Post, October 1, 1978; October 13, 1979; November 8, 1980.

Writers Digest, September, 1993, p. 44.

ONLINE

Pete Hamill Web site, http://www.petehamill.com/ (November 10, 2003).*

*   *   *

HAZZARD, Shirley 1931-

PERSONAL: Born January 30, 1931, in Sydney, Australia; daughter of Reginald (a government official) and Catherine (Stein) Hazzard; married Francis Steegmuller (a novelist and biographer), December 22, 1963 (died, October, 1994). *Education:* Educated at Queenwood College, Sydney, Australia.

ADDRESSES: Home—200 East 66th St., New York, NY 10021. *Agent*—McIntosh & Otis, Inc., 475 Fifth Ave., New York, NY 10017.

CAREER: Writer. Worked for British Intelligence in Hong Kong (now China), 1947-48, and for British High Commissioner's Office, Wellington, New Zealand, 1940-50; United Nations, New York, NY, worked in general service category, Technical Assistance to Underdeveloped Countries, 1952-62, served in Italy, 1957. Boyer lecturer, Australia, 1984, 1988.

MEMBER: American Academy and Institute of Arts and Letters.

AWARDS, HONORS: U.S. National Institute of Arts and Letters award in literature, 1966; National Book Award nomination, National Book Foundation, 1971, and National Book Award for fiction, 2003, for *The Great Fire;* Guggenheim fellow, 1974; National Book Critics Circle Award, American Book Award nomination, and PEN/Faulkner Award nomination, all 1981, for *The Transit of Venus.*

WRITINGS:

Cliffs of Fall, and Other Stories, Knopf (New York, NY), 1963.

The Evening of the Holiday (novel), Knopf (New York, NY), 1966.

People in Glass Houses: Portraits from Organization Life (nonfiction), Knopf (New York, NY), 1967.

The Bay of Noon (novel), Atlantic-Little, Brown (Boston, MA), 1970.

Defeat of an Ideal: A Study of the Self-Destruction of the United Nations (nonfiction), Atlantic-Little, Brown (Boston, MA), 1973.

The Transit of Venus (novel), Viking (New York, NY), 1980.

Coming of Age in Australia (lectures), Australian Broadcasting Corp. (Sydney, Australia), 1985.

Countenance of Truth: The United Nations and the Waldheim Case (nonfiction), Viking (New York, NY), 1990.

Greene on Capri: A Memoir, Farrar, Straus & Giroux (New York, NY), 2000.

The Great Fire (novel), Farrar, Straus & Giroux (New York, NY), 2003.

Work appears in anthologies, including several volumes of *Winter's Tales* and *O. Henry Prize Stories.* Contributor to periodicals, including *New Yorker, Ladies' Home Journal,* and *McCall's.*

SIDELIGHTS: Even before the publication of her best-selling novel *The Transit of Venus,* Shirley Hazzard's work met with critical approval. For example, Robie Macauley wrote in the *New York Times Book Review* that Hazzard's *The Bay of Noon* is "one of those rare novels that tries to address itself to the reader's intelligence rather than his nightmares. Its assumptions are fine and modest: That the reader will enjoy a sense of place if that place is drawn for him so perfectly that it seems to breathe, that the reader will understand a story based on the interactions of personality rather than mere violence, that the reader will take pleasure in a style that is consciously elegant and literary." "*People in Glass Houses,*" wrote Laurie Clancy in *Contemporary Novelists,* "is a brilliantly funny and scathing collection of eight interrelated stories concerning an unnamed 'organization' which is transparently the United Nations."

It was with the release of *The Transit of Venus* that Hazzard gained a wider and more diverse readership. Writing in the *Chicago Tribune,* Lynne Sharon Schwartz remarked: "If the literary establishment were given to pageantry, [*The Transit of Venus*] ought to be welcomed with a flourish of trumpets. Last year John Gardner clamored for moral fiction: Here is a book that ventures confidently amid the abiding themes of truth, beauty, goodness, and love, and is informed, moreover, by stringent intelligence and lacerating irony. Hazzard spares no one, not even her reader." Clancy believed that "Hazzard's masterpiece and the basis of her reputation is undoubtedly *The Transit of Venus.* . . . The meticulous—sometimes almost too meticulous—craftsmanship of the novel and the elegance and subtle wit of the style are a delight and almost unique among contemporary Australian fiction writers."

Los Angeles Times critic Doris Grumbach wrote that she was very moved by *The Transit of Venus.* She felt that it "is an impressive, mature novel, full and satisfying, by a novelist whose earlier work—two novels and two collections of stories . . . did not prepare us for this book. Without fear of exaggeration I can say it is the richest fictional experience I have had in a long time, so sumptuous a repast that it may not be to every reader's taste."

Although characterization plays a vital role in all of her writings, Hazzard exhibits particular skill in this area in *The Transit of Venus.* Webster Schott pointed out in the *Washington Post:* "Her purpose is to reveal [the characters] in the act of living and to make their pleasure, anguish and confusion rise out of their personalities as they respond to change. . . . All of *The Transit of Venus* is human movement, and seen from near the highest level art achieves."

John Leonard suggested in the *New York Times* that Hazzard's skill not only lies in her characterizations but in her literary style in general. "Miss Hazzard writes as well as Stendhal," Leonard remarked. "No matter the object—a feeling, a face, a room, the weather—it is stripped of its layers of paint, its clots of words, down to the original wood; oil is applied; grain appears, and a glow. Every epigram and apostrophe is earned. A powerful intelligence is playing with a knife. It is an intelligence that refuses to be deflected by ironies; irony isn't good enough."

The feature that several critics have identified as the underlying factor of Hazzard's skillful characterization and literary style is her sensitivity. Schott wrote: "Her perceptions of gesture, voice, attitude bespeak an omniscient understanding of human personality. The story she tells is, for the most part, so usual as to sound irrelevant. What she brings to it is virtually everything that story alone cannot tell about human lives." Similarly, Schwartz remarked that "*The Transit of Venus* evidences the wisdom of one not only well traveled but well acquainted with truth and falsehood in their numberless guises. Interwoven with the story of Caro's and Grace's lives and loves are a devastating representation of British class structure, with barriers and loopholes clearly marked; an acerbic, satirical view of a governmental bureaucracy that scoops the marrow out of men and leaves them empty bone; a glimpse at underground activists struggling for fundamental political decencies in Latin America, as well as a survey of various modes of contemporary marriage."

BIOGRAPHICAL AND CRITICAL SOURCES:

BOOKS

Contemporary Literary Criticism, Volume 18, Gale (Detroit, MI), 1981.
Contemporary Novelists, 6th edition, St. James Press (Detroit, MI), 1996.

Dictionary of Literary Biography Yearbook: 1982, Gale (Detroit, MI), 1983.

Geering, R. G., *Recent Fiction,* Oxford University Press (Melbourne, Australia), 1974.

PERIODICALS

Australian Literary Studies, October, 1979.

Chicago Tribune, March 9, 1980, Lynne Sharon Schwartz, review of *The Transit of Venus.*

Globe and Mail (Toronto, Ontario, Canada), September 24, 1988.

Listener, October 19, 1967.

Los Angeles Times, March 9, 1980, Doris Grumbach, review of *The Transit of Venus.*

Meanjin, summer, 1970; December, 1970.

National Review, February 27, 1968.

New Statesman, October 20, 1967.

New Yorker, April 13, 1970.

New York Times, February 26, 1980, John Leonard, review of *The Transit of Venus.*

New York Times Book Review, January 9, 1966; November 12, 1967; April 5, 1970, Robie Macauley, review of *The Bay of Noon;* March 16, 1980; May 11, 1980; April 29, 1990.

Publishers Weekly, February 2, 1990, p. 70; March 9, 1990, p. 48.

Saturday Night, June, 1990, p. 59.

Saturday Review, January 8, 1966.

Texas Studies in Literature and Language, Volume 25, number 2, 1983.

Time, January 14, 1966; November 24, 1967.

Times Literary Supplement, July 7, 1966; October 19, 1967; May 7, 1970.

Village Voice, March 3, 1980.

Washington Post, March 9, 1980, Webster Schott, review of *The Transit of Venus.*

Washington Post Book World, April 8, 1990.

*   *   *

HEARNE, Betsy Gould 1942-

PERSONAL: Born October 6, 1942, in Wilsonville, AL; daughter of Kenneth (a doctor) and Elizabeth (Barrett) Gould; married Michael Claffey; children: Joanna Hearne, Elizabeth Claffey. *Education:* Wooster College, B.A., 1964; University of Chicago, M.A., 1968, Ph.D., 1985.

ADDRESSES: Home—Urbana, IL. *Office*—Graduate School of Library and Information Science, 501 East Daniel, Champaign, IL 61820. *Agent*—Philippa Brophy, Sterling Lord Agency, Inc., 660 Madison Ave., New York, NY 10021. *E-mail*—hearne@alexia.lis.uiuc.edu.

CAREER: Wayne County Public Library, Wooster, OH, children's librarian, 1964-65; University of Chicago Laboratory Schools, Chicago, IL, children's librarian, 1967-68; *Booklist,* Chicago, reviewer, 1968-69, children's books editor, 1973-85; *Bulletin of the Center for Children's Books,* children's books editor, 1985-94, consulting editor, 1994—. University of Illinois—Chicago, instructor, 1970-71; University of Chicago, assistant professor, 1985-92; University of Illinois—Urbana-Champaign, assistant professor, 1992-94, associate professor, 1994-99, professor, 1999—. Judge, National Book Awards, 1975, American Book Awards, 1981, *Boston Globe/Horn Book* Awards, 1997. Speaker at colleges, conferences, and libraries.

MEMBER: International Research Society for Children's Literature, International Board on Books for Young People, American Library Association (consultant, Mildred Batchelder Committee, Newbery-Caldecott Award Committee, and Notable Books Committee, 1973-78; chair, Caldecott Award Committee, 2005), Children's Reading Round Table.

AWARDS, HONORS: Agnes Sayer Klein Award for Graduate Study, American Library Association (ALA), 1979; Children's Reading Round Table Award, 1982; Best Books for Young Adults citation, ALA, 1987, for *Love Lines: Poetry in Person;* Carl Sandburg Award, 1988, for *Eli's Ghost;* first place, Chicago Women in Publishing Competition, 1989, for *Beauty and the Beast: Visions and Revisions of an Old Tale;* Parents' Choice Award, 1990, for *Choosing Books for Children: A Commonsense Guide;* Anne Izard Award, 1993, for *Beauties and Beasts;* Choice Book citation, Cooperative Children's Book Center (CCBC), 1996, for *Eliza's Dog;* Jane Addams Children's Book Award, *Boston Globe/Horn Book* Honor Book, *New York Times* Notable Book, Children's Book of the Year, Child Study Children's Book Committee, Notable Book for Children citation, *Smithsonian* magazine, Notable Book selection, ALA, *Booklist* Editors' Choice, Notable Children's Trade Book in the Field of Social Studies, National Council for the Social Studies/

Children's Book Council (NCSS/CBC), Best Book selection, *Working Mother* magazine, and Best Book selection, *New York Family* magazine, all 1998, all for *Seven Brave Women;* Centennial Scholar Award, University of Illinois—Urbana-Champaign, 1998; Notable Children's Trade Book in the Field of Social Studies, NCSS/CBC, 1999, for *Listening for Leroy;* University Scholar Award, University of Illinois—Urbana-Champaign, 2000-03; Children's Choice selection, International Reading Association/CBC, and Choice Book citation, CCBC, both 2001, both for *Who's in the Hall?: A Mystery in Four Chapters;* Parents' Choice Silver Honor Award, and "Outstanding Book" citation, *Horn Book,* both 2003, both for *The Canine Connection: Stories about Dogs and People.*

WRITINGS:

CHILDREN'S BOOKS

South Star, illustrated by Trina Schart Hyman, Atheneum (New York, NY), 1977.

Home, illustrated by Trina Schart Hyman, Atheneum (New York, NY), 1979.

Eli's Ghost, illustrated by Ronald Himler, Simon & Schuster (New York, NY), 1987.

Love Lines: Poetry in Person (poetry for young adults and adults), Simon & Schuster (New York, NY), 1987.

Polaroid and Other Poems of View (poetry for young adults and adults), photographs by Peter Kiar, Macmillan (New York, NY), 1991.

(Editor) *Beauties and Beasts,* illustrated by Joanne Caroselli, Oryx Press (New York, NY), 1993.

Eliza's Dog, illustrated by Erica Thurston, Simon & Schuster (New York, NY), 1996.

Seven Brave Women, illustrated by Bethanne Andersen, Greenwillow (New York, NY), 1997.

Listening for Leroy, Simon & Schuster (New York, NY), 1998.

Who's in the Hall?: A Mystery in Four Chapters, illustrated by Christy Hale, Greenwillow (New York, NY), 2000.

Wishes, Kisses, and Pigs, illustrated by Leslie A. Baker, Simon & Schuster (New York, NY), 2001.

The Canine Connection: Stories about Dogs and People, Simon & Schuster (New York, NY), 2003.

NONFICTION; FOR ADULTS

(Editor, with Marilyn Kaye) *Celebrating Children's Books: Essays on Children's Literature in Honor of Zena Sutherland* (reference), Lothrop, Lee & Shepard (New York, NY), 1981.

Choosing Books for Children: A Commonsense Guide (reference), Delacorte (New York, NY), 1981, 3rd edition, University of Illinois Press (Urbana, IL), 1999.

Beauty and the Beast: A Study of Aesthetic Survival (thesis), University of Chicago (Chicago, IL), 1985, published as *Beauty and the Beast: Visions and Revisions of an Old Tale,* University of Chicago Press (Chicago, IL), 1989.

(Editor, with Zena Sutherland and Roger Sutton) *The Best in Children's Books: The University of Chicago Guide to Children's Literature, 1985-1990,* University of Chicago Press (Chicago, IL), 1991.

(Editor, with Roger Sutton) *Evaluating Children's Books: A Critical Look,* University of Illinois (Urbana, IL), 1993.

(Editor) *The Zena Sutherland Lectures, 1983-1992,* Clarion (New York, NY), 1993.

(Editor, with Janice Del Negro, Christine Jenkins, and Deborah Stevenson) *Story: From Fireplace to Cyberspace,* Graduate School of Library and Information Science (Champaign, IL), 1999.

Also contributor of articles, reviews, and editorials to periodicals such as *Library Quarterly, New York Times Book Review, American Journal of Sociology,* and *Signal.* Recordings include "Evaluating Children's Books," Children's Book Council (New York, NY), 1979, and videorecording, *Sharing Books with Young Children,* American Library Association (Chicago, IL), 1986.

SIDELIGHTS: Since Betsy Gould Hearne began work as a children's librarian in the 1960s, she has made a variety of contributions to children's literature. During her career, Hearne has worked as a critic, editor, scholar, and children's book writer, and she has also earned advanced degrees and developed her talents as a poet. Hearne's commentaries on children's books can be found in *Booklist* and *Bulletin of the Center for Children's Books.* Her books for educators, librarians, and parents include *Choosing Books for Children: A Commonsense Guide* and *Evaluating Children's Books: A Critical Look* (which she edited with Roger Sutton) among others. Indeed, Humphrey Carpenter of the *New York Times Book Review* has described Hearne as "a distinguished cataloger of children's books." Many of Hearne's children's books, such as *South Star, Eli's*

Ghost, Seven Brave Women, and *The Canine Connection: Stories about Dogs and People,* have been well received. Additionally, Hearne's two volumes of poetry have been recommended for mature young adults.

Hearne was born in rural Alabama, the daughter of a country doctor. On her Web site she stated: "I grew up in an Alabama pine forest with no one to play with except a dog, cat, horse, cow, alligator, raccoon, possum, owl, and garter snake. None of them talked much. They were pretty good listeners, though, and I learned from them to listen and also not to be afraid of silence." Hearne's mother taught her to read and write and also entertained her with tales of her ancestors and how they forged lives in a new land. When Hearne was older, the family moved to Tennessee in order to find better schooling, and Hearne grew into a tall, shy young woman who sought solace in literature and music. After earning a college degree, she went to work in the children's department of a public library, and it was there that she found her life's work: evaluating, creating, and relating stories to young audiences. She brought her hands-on experience with youngsters to bear on her own book reviewing and writing, while she also extended the study of children's literature from a scholarly point of view. To quote Mary M. Burns in *Horn Book,* Hearne's efforts result in "a significant contribution to understanding contemporary children's literature."

A *Publishers Weekly* critic described Hearne's first children's book, *South Star,* as "an exciting fantasy." It tells the story of Megan, a young giant girl who has escaped her family's castle, and the Screamer that has frozen the castle and her parents in ice. As Megan flees across a plain from the terrible Screamer, she is befriended and aided by a boy, Randall, who is also on his own. A bear helps the pair find the southern star to follow, and they begin a difficult journey. They finally find a valley populated by Megan's relatives and led by her sister. According to Ethel L. Heins of *Horn Book,* Hearne "successfully creates suspense and casts an atmosphere of primeval magic" in *South Star.*

In *Home,* the sequel to *South Star,* Megan is living with her sister. When Megan dreams that her sister's missing husband is calling for help, she leaves the peaceful valley to find him. While she waits at the seaside for the storms to go away and to train for a trip across the sea, she once again encounters her friend Randall. They journey across the sea to a desert land ruled by lion people, where Megan's brother-in-law is alive in prison. After battling the king of the land, the three return to the valley. "Both Brendan and Megan return home with a new appreciation for the people and places they left" and "better knowledge of themselves," explained Karen M. Klockner of *Horn Book.* Writing in *School Library Journal,* Margaret A. Dorsey commented that this book is "good stuff for growing girls."

Despite its title, according to Elizabeth S. Watson of *Horn Book, Eli's Ghost* "is definitely not scary." The action, set in the southern United States, begins when Eli runs away to a swamp to find his long-lost mother. When Eli falls into the water, his mother arrives just in time to save him. Still, Eli's ghost escapes his body and has some fun with the rescue party that arrives. Furthermore, Eli's ghost is nothing like him. "For Eli Wilson," observed a critic in *Bulletin of the Center for Children's Books,* "life will never be the same." Watson concluded in *Horn Book,* "the humor and suspense will appeal to intermediate readers."

In *Eliza's Dog,* "Hearne shapes a convincing portrait of a feisty, resourceful girl," according to a *Publishers Weekly* reviewer. Eliza, who has always wanted a dog, finds a border collie while on vacation with her parents in Ireland. Although Eliza manages to convince her parents to let her keep the dog, she worries that it will grow too large to fit in its carry-cage for the trip back home from Ireland. In addition, Eliza must learn to deal with her new pet and his many needs. "This book has appeal," wrote a *Kirkus Reviews* critic, "mainly for other dog-obsessed children." Some critics noted that the value of *Eliza's Dog* lies in its realistic depiction of pet care, a job that is sometimes tedious and unpleasant. "The story clearly sends the message that owning a dog entails hard work," pointed out Carol Schene in *School Library Journal. Horn Book* critic Maeve Visser Knoth styled *Eliza's Dog* "a pleasing, well-told story."

In 1979, Hearne went back to graduate school; by 1985, she had completed a dissertation. She published this work, in revised form, in 1989 as *Beauty and the Beast: Visions and Revisions of an Old Tale.* This work traces the beauty and the beast motif from its origins, and takes a look at how it has been revised by various authors, storytellers, and illustrators throughout time for children. "Hearne's conclusions are provocative, illuminating, and stimulating," commented Mary M.

Bush in *Horn Book*. "This book is a fine example of critical analysis of a traditional tale" and "offers a wealth of material for adults to use in fostering critical thinking in children," explained Jane Anne Hannigan in *School Library Journal*. Hearne's related book for children, *Beauties and Beasts,* features twenty-seven beauty and the beast folktales from different cultures and time periods. According to Judy Constantinides of *School Library Journal,* this book "will attract the attention of older primary grade children" and it will be useful to "adults teaching multiculturalism."

Hearne is also the author of two volumes of poetry. *Love Lines: Poetry in Person* includes fifty-nine poems about love, family, and friends that Hearne wrote over the course of twenty-five years. According to *Voice of Youth Advocates* contributor Becki George, the work provides "quickly readable free verse" and "includes many sexual references." However, "None of the book's three sections . . . seems to speak directly to young adult readers," observed Kathleen Whalin of *School Library Journal*. A critic for *Kirkus Reviews* asserted that the volume, "rich in ideas and imagery," "should appeal to anyone mature enough to yearn after love." *Polaroid and Other Poems of View* contains forty-three poems. Many critics enjoyed the black-and-white photos by Peter Kiar, which help introduce each section of poetry. This volume, in the words of Brooke Selby Dillon of *Voice of Youth Advocates,* "will enthrall and delight the mature poetry reader." The "rhythms . . . are capricious and compelling," and the poems are "clearly the work of an artist in control of her medium," related Nancy Vasilakis of *Horn Book*.

Hearne's conviction that the best stories are often the most personal ones led her to write *Seven Brave Women*. This award-winning book for middle readers introduces the former generations of Hearne's family and tells of their adventures, beginning with her great-great-great grandmother, who arrived in America prior to the Revolutionary War. As the book explores each succeeding generation—down to the young narrator, who is still a student—it highlights the courageous acts performed by each woman, even though none of them ever fought in a war or earned headlines in the newspaper. "Although this is about one family of women . . . , children will grasp the universality in these lives," wrote Ilene Cooper in *Booklist*. Writing in *Horn Book*, Mary M. Burns liked the way the women in *Seven Brave Women* "surmount difficulties with grace, imagination, determination, and faith." She

concluded that the work provides "a splendid tribute to women and their history."

Memories of a lonely childhood inform Hearne's novel *Listening for Leroy*. Ten-year-old Alice is growing up in rural Alabama in a home ruled by her strict but principled father. Since she is schooled at home, Alice has no friends her age, but she does find a confidant in Leroy, a hired hand who works for her family. Leroy gives Alice much valuable advice, and when he is run out of town by bigots, she misses him sorely. Even after her family moves to a more populous part of the South, Alice continues to remember Leroy and to wonder what happened to him. A *Publishers Weekly* critic called *Listening to Leroy* a "gentle, reflective coming-of-age novel" that "subtly conveys Alice's revelations about herself, her family, and a prejudiced society." *Booklist*'s Shelle Rosenfeld likewise styled the work "a heartfelt look at the growing pains of an idealistic girl experiencing a less than ideal reality."

Hearne adopts a lighter tone in *Who's in the Hall?: A Mystery in Four Chapters*. In this picture story for younger readers, three sets of children, baby-sitters, and pets in an eight-story apartment building all face the same dilemma: Do they answer the door when a stranger knocks and identifies herself as the janitor? How the children band together to solve the mystery of the unidentified knocker forms the crux of the plot. In *Booklist*, Connie Fletcher concluded: "Suspense in a mundane setting, rhyming games, and tongue twisters make this fun for reading aloud." *School Library Journal* correspondent Marlene Gawron called the book "an excellent blend of good writing and fine illustration," while *Horn Book*'s Joanna Rudge Long found it "a dandy choice for newly independent readers."

Wishes, Kisses, and Pigs brings new life to the old adage, "be careful what you wish for, you just might get it." Quarreling with her brother, Louise Tolliver inadvertently calls him a pig while simultaneously wishing on a star. When her brother disappears, and a strange, white pig with blue eyes appears on the farm, Louise realizes what she has done and seeks to undo it. Complications arise as she tries to formulate a magic spell that will restore her brother before he is chosen to be a menu item at an upcoming picnic. As a reviewer in *Horn Book* put it, the plot's "fairy-tale resolution satisfyingly admits 'how nature's magic and magic's natural.'" In *School Library Journal,* Betsy

Fraser deemed *Wishes, Kisses, and Pigs* "a delightful novel about the dangers of getting what you wish for."

The twelve stories collected in *The Canine Connection: Stories about Dogs and People* explore the interaction between young people and their dogs—with emphasis on the people. The stories range widely in subject matter. In one, a blind and bereft young girl begins to reconnect with the world through the howling of her recently acquired guide dog. In another, a boy and a pit bull band together to protect each other from bullies in a bad neighborhood. Willa, the heroine of "Lab," must help her mother deliver a baby while the family dog, Millie, tends to orphaned kittens. A *Kirkus Reviews* contributor wrote that each story in the collection "chimes to the rhythm . . . best suited for the unique characters involved. Best of all, Hearne writes the concerns and challenges of teens as if each word came from their hearts." In *School Library Journal,* Alison Follos observed: "These stories are well drawn, told with refinement, and enlivened with credible characters." *Booklist* contributor Ellen Mandel concluded that *The Canine Connection* is "a rewarding collection that will stay with readers."

In addition to her steady publishing schedule, Hearne continues to teach courses on children's literature and storytelling at the University of Illinois—Urbana-Champaign. On her Web site she wrote, "The heart of my work is stories, what they tell us and how they are told. Whether stories appear in the oral, print, or electronic traditions, they reflect and shape us." In *Horn Book,* Mary M. Burns commended Hearne for offering works that "lure readers into confronting issues important to intelligent reading of today's literature for children."

BIOGRAPHICAL AND CRITICAL SOURCES:

PERIODICALS

Booklist, April 1, 1996, Lauren Peterson, review of *Eliza's Dog,* p. 1364; June 1, 1997, Ilene Cooper, review of *Seven Brave Women,* p. 1694; November 15, 1998, Shelle Rosenfeld, review of *Listening for Leroy,* p. 587; September 15, 2000, Connie Fletcher, review of *Who's in the Hall?: A Mystery in Four Chapters,* p. 240; March 1, 2001, Michael Cart, review of *Wishes, Kisses, and Pigs,* p. 1278;

April 15, 2003, Ellen Mandel, review of *The Canine Connection: Stories about Dogs and People,* p. 1471.
Bulletin of the Center for Children's Books, March, 1987, review of *Eli's Ghost,* p. 126.
Horn Book, June, 1979, Karen M. Klockner, review of *Home,* p. 301; September-October, 1987, Elizabeth S. Watson, review of *Eli's Ghost,* p. 612; May-June, 1990, Mary M. Bush, review of *Beauty and the Beast: Visions and Revisions of an Old Tale,* pp. 353-354; July-August, 1991, Nancy Vasilakis, review of *Polaroid and Other Poems of View,* p. 471; May-June, 1993, Mary M. Burns, review of *The Zena Sutherland Lectures: 1983-1992,* p. 345; July-August, 1994, Mary M. Burns, review of *Evaluating Children's Books: A Critical Look,* p. 476; September-October, 1996, Maeve Visser Knoth, review of *Eliza's Dog,* p. 596; September-October, 1997, Mary M. Burns, review of *Seven Brave Women,* p. 558; December, 1997, Ethel L. Heins, review of *South Star,* pp. 662-663; November, 2000, Joanna Rudge Long, review of *Who's in the Hall?,* p. 746; May, 2001, review of *Wishes, Kisses, and Pigs,* p. 326; May-June, 2003, Joanna Rudge Long, review of *The Canine Connection,* p. 348.
Kirkus Reviews, August 1, 1987, review of *Love Lines: Poetry in Person,* p. 1157; March 15, 1996, review of *Eliza's Dog,* p. 448; February 15, 2003, review of *The Canine Connection,* p. 307.
Libraries and Culture, summer, 2000, Jennifer Stevens, review of *Story: From Fireplace to Cyberspace,* p. 484.
New York Times Book Review, March 25, 1990, Humphrey Carpenter, review of *Beauty and the Beast,* p. 25.
Publishers Weekly, September 19, 1977, review of *South Star,* p. 146; March 18, 1996, review of *Eliza's Dog,* p. 70; May 19, 1997, review of *Seven Brave Women,* p. 75; October 26, 1998, review of *Listening for Leroy,* p. 66; July 3, 2000, review of *Who's in the Hall?,* p. 70; March 26, 2001, review of *Wishes, Kisses, and Pigs,* p. 93; February 10, 2003, review of *The Canine Connection,* p. 188.
School Library Journal, May, 1979, Margaret A. Dorsey, review of *Home,* p. 62; February, 1988, Kathleen Whalin, review of *Love Lines,* p. 88; February, 1990, Jane Anne Hannigan, review of *Beauty and the Beast,* p. 38; June, 1994, Judy Constantinides, review of *Beauties and Beasts,* p. 55; May, 1996, Carol Schene, review of *Eliza's Dog,* p. 113; August, 2000, Marlene Gawron, review of

Who's in the Hall?, p. 156; April, 2001, Betsy Fraser, review of *Wishes, Kisses, and Pigs,* p. 140; April, 2003, Alison Follos, review of *The Canine Connection,* p. 164.

Voice of Youth Advocates, February, 1988, Becki George, review of *Love Lines,* p. 296; August, 1991, Brooke Selby Dillon, review of *Polaroid and Other Poems of View,* p. 189.

ONLINE

Betsy Hearne Home Page, http://alexia.lis.uiuc.edu/ (June 26, 2003).*

                    *   *   *

HENDERSON, (John) Nicholas 1919-

PERSONAL: Born April 1, 1919, in England; son of Hubert Henderson; married Mary Barber Cawadias, 1951; children: Alexandra (Viscountess Moore). *Education:* Hertford College, Oxford, M.A. *Hobbies and other interests:* Tennis, gardening, dogs.

ADDRESSES: Home—6 Fairholt St., London SW7 1EG, England. *Office*—Hambros Bank Ltd., 41 Bishopsgate, London EC2P 2AA, England. *Agent*—Curtis Brown, 162-168 Regent St., London W1R 5TA, England.

CAREER: British Diplomatic Service, London, England, worked in office of the minister of state in Cairo, Egypt, 1942-43, assistant private secretary to the foreign secretary, 1944-47, member of embassy staff in Washington, DC, 1947-49, and Athens, Greece, 1949-50, assigned to Foreign Office department of the permanent under secretary, 1950-53, member of embassy staff in Vienna, Austria, 1953-56, and Santiago, Chile, 1956-59, assigned to Foreign Office, Northern Department, 1959-62, and to department of the permanent under secretary, 1962-63, head of Northern Department, 1963, private secretary to the secretary of state for foreign affairs, 1963-65, foreign minister in Madrid, Spain, 1965-69, ambassador to Poland, 1969-72, West Germany, 1972-75, France, 1975-79, and the United States, 1979-82. Chair of Channel Tunnel Group; member of boards of directors of Foreign and Colonial Investment Trust, Mercantile

and General Reinsurance Co., and Hambros PLC, all 1982—, Tarmac PLC, 1983—, and Foreign and Colonial Eurotrust Ltd.

MEMBER: Brooks's Club, Garrick Club, Beefsteak Club, Pratt's Club.

AWARDS, HONORS: Order of St. Michael and St. George, Companion, 1965, Knight Commander, 1972, Knight Grand Cross, 1977; honorary fellow of Hertford College, Oxford, 1975.

WRITINGS:

Prince Eugen of Savoy, Weidenfeld & Nicolson, (London, England), 1964, Sterling (New York, NY), 2002.
The Birth of NATO, Weidenfeld & Nicolson, (London, England), 1982.
The Private Office, Weidenfeld & Nicolson, (London, England), 1984.
Inside the Private Office: Memoirs of the Secretary to British Foreign Ministers, Academy Chicago Publishers (Chicago, IL), 1987.
Mandarin: The Diaries of an Ambassador, 1969-1982, Weidenfeld & Nicolson (London, England), 1994.
Old Friends and Modern Instances, Profile Books (London, England), 2000.

Contributor of articles and stories to magazines, including *Horizon, Apollo, Country Life, Economist,* and *History Today.*

SIDELIGHTS: Sir Nicholas Henderson was born into a life of privilege in 1919. He attended Oxford University, served in the armed forces, and then embarked on a political career as a diplomat and ambassador for Britain. He has also served as private secretary to several foreign secretaries, which prompted his book *The Private Office.* In this memoir, Henderson gives an inside look at the Foreign Secretaries' private office. Through anecdotes and entertaining stories, the author helps the reader understand how foreign policy works. George Walden of the *Sunday Telegraph* stated that the book "contains wise thoughts . . . couched in elegant prose and seasoned by diverting tales." Walden also called the memoir "highly entertaining."

Henderson continued writing his memoirs with his 1994 book *Mandarin: The Diaries of an Ambassador, 1969-1982.* Peter Madgewick of *Parlimentary Affairs* felt that this book stands out among political memoirs because instead of a compilation of sketchy notes taken at meetings, it is a collection of "carefully wrought essays reflecting embassy life, diplomacy, entertainment, [and] visiting politicians." Madgewick also noted that it is "an elegant and witty book, a treat for the jaded reader of political memoir."

In 2000, Henderson published a book called *Old Friends and Modern Instances.* Once he retired from the international and travel part of his career, he decided to focus on more personal aspects. Henderson created a collection of stories and recollections about a variety of people he had met throughout his life, including educators, writers and political figures. As he told Selina Hastings of the *Sunday Telegraph,* "[I have] always been interested in how people seek pleasure and spend their spare time." Hastings noted that Henderson "writes with point and elegance," and that the short book "makes a vivid impression of a much longer work." Philip Ziegler of the *Daily Telegraph* felt that Henderson "provides an affectionate and admiring picture of the men and women who inhabited [his] patrician world." Ray Seitz, a critic for the *Times,* called it "a fragrant bouquet of reminiscences."

BIOGRAPHICAL AND CRITICAL SOURCES:

PERIODICALS

Daily Telegraph, November 4, 2000, Philip Ziegler, "Whiggy With It," March 30, 2002, Nicholas Henderson, "The Political Front."
Parlimentary Affairs, April, 1996, Peter Madgewick, review of *Mandarin,* p. 368.
Spectator, November 17, 2001, Douglas Hurd, review of *The Private Office Revisited,* p. 50.
Sunday Telegraph, October 22, 2000, Selina Hastings, "A Diplomatic Corps of Friends"; November 11, 2001, George Walden, "Foreign Affairs Revisited."
Times (London, England), October 25, 1984; November 15, 2000, Ray Seitz, "Nicholas's Friends," p.13.
Times Literary Supplement, May 31, 1985; January 11, 2002, John Ure, review of *The Private Office,* p. 27.*

HIGH, Linda Oatman 1958-

PERSONAL: Born April 28, 1958, in Ephrata, PA; daughter of Robert (a miner and bus driver) and Mary Myrna Millard (an office worker) Haas; married John High (a recycler); children: J. D. High (stepson), Justin Oatman, Kala High (stepdaughter), Zachary High. *Ethnicity:* "Caucasian." *Religion:* Christian. *Hobbies and other interests:* Plays bass guitar in a band.

ADDRESSES: Home and office—1209 Reading Rd., Narvon, PA 17555. *E-mail*—lohigh@supernet.com.

CAREER: Writer. News reporter and feature writer; contributor of a weekly column, "Jake's View," to local newspapers. Formerly a waitress, lifeguard, and secretary.

MEMBER: Society of Children's Book Writers and Illustrators, Pennwriters.

AWARDS, HONORS: John Crane Memorial Scholarship, Highlights Foundation, 1993; work in progress grant, Society of Children's Book Writers and Illustrators, 1994; Notable Book in the Language Arts citation, National Council of Teachers of English, for *Barn Savers;* Blue Ribbon Book citation, *Bulletin of the Center for Children's Books,* best book citation, *Nick Jr.* magazine, 2001, and Best Books of the Year citation, *Parenting* magazine, 2001, all for *Under New York;* Great Lakes Book Award, Lee Bennett Hopkins Poetry Honor Book, and Notable Social Studies Book for Young People, National Council for the Social Studies/Children's Book Council, all 2002, all for *A Humble Life.*

WRITINGS:

Maizie (young adult novel), Holiday House (New York, NY), 1995.
Hound Heaven (young adult novel), Holiday House (New York, NY), 1995.
The Summer of the Great Divide (young adult novel), Holiday House (New York, NY), 1996.
A Stone's Throw from Paradise (young adult novel), William B. Eerdmans (Grand Rapids, MI), 1997.
A Christmas Star (picture book), illustrated by Ronald Himler, Holiday House (New York, NY), 1997.

Linda Oatman High

Beekeepers (picture book), illustrated by Doug Chayka, Boyds Mills Press (Honesdale, PA), 1998.

Barn Savers (picture book), illustrated by Ted Lewin, Boyds Mills Press (Honesdale, PA), 1999.

Under New York (picture book), illustrated by Robert Rayevsky, Holiday House (New York, NY), 2001.

Winter Shoes for Shadow Horse (picture book), illustrated by Ted Lewin, Boyds Mills Press (Honesdale, PA), 2001.

The Last Chimney of Christmas Eve (picture book), illustrated by Kestutis Kasparavicius, Boyds Mills Press (Honesdale, PA), 2001.

A Humble Life: Plain Poems, William B. Eerdmans (Grand Rapids, MI), 2001.

Strum a Song of Angels: Poems about Music, Piano Press (Del Mar, CA), 2002.

The President's Puppy, illustrated by Steve Björkman, Scholastic (New York, NY), 2002.

The Girl on the High-Diving Horse: An Adventure in Atlantic City, illustrated by Ted Lewin, Penguin Putnam (New York, NY), 2003.

Sister Slam and the Poetic Motormouth Road Trip, Bloomsbury (New York, NY), 2004.

City of Snow: The Great Blizzard of 1888, Walker (New York, NY), in press.

The short story "The Shunning of Sadie B. Zook" was included in the anthology *Soul Searching: Thirteen Stories of Faith and Belief,* edited by Lisa Rowe Fraustino, Simon & Schuster (New York, NY), 2002.

SIDELIGHTS: Linda Oatman High's novels for young adults frequently feature spunky heroines whose unwillingness to give up their dreams, even in the face of unpleasant realities, helps ease the passage from childhood to adolescence. In *Maizie,* High's twelve-year-old central character has taken care of her alcoholic father and her four-year-old sister since her mother ran off with a vacuum-cleaner salesman. Maizie and Grace, her little sister, keep their dreams alive by making "wish" books from pictures cut out of magazines. Maizie's most ardent wishes are for a horse and to see her mother again. In pursuit of her dreams, she takes a job at a nursing home to raise money to buy a horse, and writes to her mother.

"The characters [in Maizie] are fresh, and their dialogue is natural, with just a hint of mountain flavor," observed Elizabeth S. Watson in *Horn Book.* Several reviewers noted Maizie's ability to keep her spirits up, even when faced with seemingly insurmountable troubles. This feature of High's narrative "keeps the book from being dreary but makes [Maizie] unrealistically plucky," Susan Dove Lempke wrote in the *Bulletin of the Center for Children's Books,* though she admitted, that "overall, readers will find Maizie both likable and admirable." "Maizie is a character readers will not soon forget," Carrie Eldridge declared in *Voice of Youth Advocates,* adding that High's first effort deserves comparison to Vera Cleaver's classic tale about Mary Call, the strong female protagonist of *Where the Lilies Bloom.*

Like Maizie, Silver Nickles, the main character in *Hound Heaven,* lives in rural poverty on a mountain in the eastern United States. Silver has lived with her grandfather since the death of her parents and little sister in a car crash and only wishes she could have a dog to love, a thing she feels will soothe her aching sadness. "High creates a rich and at times humorous cast of characters around Silver," Jeanne M. McGlinn remarked in *Voice of Youth Advocates.* Others found the plot of *Hound Heaven,* which includes a one-sided schoolboy crush with overtones of stalking and a beauty pageant, strains the story's credibility. But, according to a critic for *Kirkus Reviews,* "this quirky novel is satisfying despite its odd detachment from reality." *Bulletin of the Center for Children's Books* contributor Deborah Stevenson credited the ultimate success of *Hound Heaven* to Silver's first-person narration, which "is touching in its yearning and appealing in its gentle humor."

Also told in the first-person is *The Summer of the Great Divide,* High's third novel for young adults. Set in the turbulent 1960s, this novel finds High's heroine spending the summer on her aunt and uncle's farm while her parents decide whether they should divorce. There, thirteen-year-old Wheezie is confronted by strange and arduous tasks connected with life on a farm, as well as making peace with a mentally-challenged cousin, the onset of puberty, and the ongoing war in Vietnam. *The Summer of the Great Divide* failed to maintain the standard of characterization found in High's earlier novels, some reviewers observed, particularly in the book's secondary characters, who were faulted as sketchy. But readers are likely to sympathize with Wheezie's problems, according to Leone McDermott in *Booklist,* and "the 1960s time frame gives an interesting twist to a familiar theme."

High addresses a slightly younger audience in *The Girl on the High-Diving Horse: An Adventure in Atlantic City.* Set in the summer of 1936, *The Girl on the High-Diving Horse* describes the spectacles of Atlantic City's Steel Pier—boxing kangaroos, surfing dogs, dancing tigers, and of course high-diving horses—through the eyes of eight-year-old Ivy Cordelia. Ivy is thrilled when she becomes friends with the two sisters, Arnette and Sonora, who ride the diving horses. She is allowed to help care for the horses, and at the end of the summer, Arnette takes Ivy on one single high dive before she must return home. "High tells her warm, nostalgic story in musical, well-paced language," Gillian Engberg wrote in *Booklist,* while a *Kirkus Reviews* contributor noted that "the immediacy of the first-person voice and the magnetic force of the scenes are totally engaging."

High has also written several picture books for children, including *A Christmas Star.* During the Depression, a little girl and her family decorate their sleigh and their horse, Star, before they ride to church for the Christmas Eve service. The girl anticipates receiving a new pair of mittens, an orange, and some candy from the church's mitten tree, but when they arrive at the church they discover that the tree and the gifts have all been stolen. However, while the congregation is engrossed in creating their live Nativity scene, the girl catches a glimpse of St. Nicholas returning the presents. This "sensitive, well-paced tale brings the true meaning of Christmas to the fore," a reviewer commented in *Publishers Weekly.*

Other picture books by High focus on the warmer months of the year. "High's spare, poetic descriptions" in *Beekeepers* "make it easy to imagine a dewy spring morning on the farm," a critic declared in a review for *Publishers Weekly.* This book is about a girl and her grandfather, a farmer who raises bees. The two are working together one day to gather honey from the grandfather's hives when the girl must overcome her fear of the bees to deal safely with a swarm all by herself. This "personal triumph, sweet as honey" is "at the heart of the story," Stephanie Zvirin noted in *Booklist.*

High's next picture book, *Barn Savers,* is "one of the few picture books to show rural life outside the farmyard," Carolyn Phelan wrote in *Booklist.* A century-old barn is about to be demolished, and rather than let its boards and beams go to waste, a boy and his father work to take the barn apart piece by piece. For an entire day, the father breaks the barn into single boards, and the son stacks them up. As they work, "the father passes on to his son a belief that the barn is a treasure . . . [that] deserves to be respectfully saved," a critic explained in *Kirkus Reviews.* At the end of the day, the boy takes the barn's old iron weathervane home to display in his room as a souvenir.

Winter Shoes for Shadow Horse is another father-son tale, this time about a blacksmith teaching his son how to shoe a horse. It is a story "about shared love and respect as one generation teaches another," John Peters wrote in *Booklist.* Describing the book as "memorable," *School Library Journal* critic Gay Lynn Van Vleck found *Winter Shoes for Shadow Horse* "remarkably rich in sensual elements."

Under New York is a rarity for High, a book not set in her native farm country. Instead, this book explores the vast slice of life that occurs underground in a big city like New York. Each spread shows a cutaway of the city, with the action above-ground contrasting with what is going on below. "This is a sensational idea for a children's book, as awesome as falling down a rabbit hole, as creepy as looking under a rock," Sam

Swope wrote in the *New York Times Book Review.* Plus, Alicia Eames commented in *School Library Journal,* "tidbits of history and curious facts of present-day life add to the adventure."

High once told *CA:* "I was born and raised in Lancaster County, Pennsylvania, living in the boondocks on Swamp Road. Swamp Road was just a road like any other country road, with no swamp in sight. There were woods and trails and trees and creeks and relatives for neighbors. And there was me, wondering why in the world somebody named it Swamp Road when there was no swamp in sight. That wondering was probably one of the first signs that I'd be a writer. We writers spend lots of time thinking about titles and names and words and why people call things something they're not.

"So there I was, growing up on Swamp Road with two parents, one brother, and an assortment of pets. We had many pets: a nervous Chihuahua named Vester, who trembled whenever we looked his way; a yellow canary named Tweety-Bird, who threw birdseed all over my bedroom; an aquarium full of fish; a strawberry roan pony, Pedro the Burro; a sheep named Lambchop, who thought she was a dog; and Whitey, a fluffy Samoyed dog I loved with all my heart. It was my memory of the love I felt for Whitey which formed the backbone of *Hound Heaven.* In the book, twelve-year-old Silver Nickles longs for a dog to love, to maybe make up for the hurt she's felt since her family died in a car wreck. Silver covers her ceiling with pictures of dogs from the *Sunday News* adoption column, an idea which came to me when my son Justin began clipping pictures of dogs and saving them as a sort of dream dog collection.

"I was a child who believed in everything: angels, fairies, ghosts, UFOs, Santa Claus, the Easter Bunny. Once, I swore I saw Rudolph the Red-Nosed Reindeer through my bedroom window, and it wasn't anywhere near Christmas. Mom said that I had a crazy imagination, and Dad said I ate too many bananas before bed. You need a crazy imagination to write, but you don't necessarily need bananas.

"For first grade, I was lucky enough to attend California School. California School was a one-room school with a hill for sledding and the best spring water ever and a creek out back where I threw my

bologna sandwiches. The teacher said that was why I was so skinny, but he never could explain why California School was on California Road, smack-dab in the center of Pennsylvania.

"My year in first grade—1964—was the last year of California School. The next year, I went to a brand-new school in a nearby town called Churchtown, which of course had lots of churches. The new school had unscratched desks, fresh paint, a cafeteria, a gym, and a black macadam playground with hoops and nets and hopscotch squares. The brand-new school had lots of rooms, but no creek for bologna sandwiches. No hill for sledding. No spring water. No coal stoves in the corners or creaking wooden floors. I thought they should have built another church instead.

"As a child, I had an obsessive fear of death, until I found faith in California Church that day. In *Hound Heaven,* Silver Nickles is dealing with the death of her mama and daddy and baby sister, and faith plays a large part in the novel.

"When I was in the tenth grade, I wrote an essay about the Fireman's Fair in a nearby town. I wrote about the greasy French fries and the hillbilly music and the spinning roulette wheels that steal your money away. I wrote the essay for a creative writing class taught by Mrs. Severs (who we secretly called by her first name, Susie). Mrs. Severs—Susie—loved my essay and hung it on the bulletin board for everybody to see. She raved and raved about my writing and said that I should be a writer. From that moment on, I was. That's all I needed: to hear the words out loud.

"I wasn't officially published until 1984, after my first child was born. I had quit my job as a secretary and wanted to stay home with my baby, while still bringing in some money. Writing fit in my plans perfectly, and I wrote feature articles for local newspapers until 1987, when I decided that I wanted to write from my heart and not my head, as I'd been doing with newspaper reporting.

"In 1987, Justin was four years old, and I was reading a lot of picture books to him, becoming very interested in children's literature in the process. That's when I began writing for magazines, selling some stories to *Highlights for Children, Hopscotch,* and *Children's*

Digest. I loved writing fiction for magazines, but I had a dream. My dream was to write books—picture books, novels, chapter books. So I wrote and I wrote and I wrote, creating and submitting and collecting rejection slips as I acquired three more children: my stepchildren J. D. and Kala, then Zachary.

"There were times when I almost gave up, because it was hard. The writing was hard, the waiting was hard, the competition was tough. I had lots of kids and little time for writing. I almost gave up, but not quite.

"In 1990, right after my son Zachary was born, I wrote a novel called *Maizie,* published by Holiday House in April of 1995. It was my first published book, and *Hound Heaven* was to follow on the fall list of *Holiday House,* then *The Summer of the Great Divide,* in the spring.

"My dream has come true, with a bit of faith, a dash of determination, and lots of hard work. In *Hound Heaven,* Silver Nickles never gives up. She has faith and determination, and she works hard toward her goal. I try to instill all my fictional characters with these very real attributes . . . they can make dreams come true! In giving advice to aspiring writers, I would quote Ben Franklin: 'Never, ever, ever, ever, ever give up.'"

BIOGRAPHICAL AND CRITICAL SOURCES:

PERIODICALS

Booklist, April 15, 1995, Frances Bradburn, review of *Maizie,* p. 1500; June 1, 1996, Leone McDermott, review of *The Summer of the Great Divide,* p. 1718; June 1, 1997, Shelley Townsend-Hudson, review of *A Stone's Throw from Paradise,* p. 1703; September 1, 1997, Hazel Rochman, review of *A Christmas Star,* p. 139; May 15, 1998, Stephanie Zvirin, review of *Beekeepers,* p. 1632; November 1, 1999, Carolyn Phelan, review of *Barn Savers,* p. 524; January 1, 2000, review of *Barn Savers,* p. 824; March 1, 2001, Gillian Engberg, review of *Under New York,* p. 1283; September 1, 2001, John Peters, review of *Winter Shoes for Shadow Horse,* p. 115; September 15, 2001, Ilene Cooper, review of *The Last Chimney of Christmas Eve,* p. 235; December 15, 2001, Susan Dove Lempke,

review of *A Humble Life: Plain Poems,* p. 734; April 15, 2003, Gillian Engberg, review of *The Girl on the High-Diving Horse: An Adventure in Atlantic City,* p. 1478.

Book Report, November-December, 1996, Nancye Starkey, review of *The Summer of the Great Divide,* p. 41; January-February, 1998, Patricia Bender, review of *A Stone's Throw from Paradise,* pp. 32-33.

Bulletin of the Center for Children's Books, April, 1995, Susan Dove Lempke, review of *Maizie,* p. 277; December, 1995, Deborah Stevenson, review of *Hound Heaven,* p. 129; April, 1998, Pat Mathews, review of *Beekeepers,* p. 282.

Childhood Education, spring, 2002, Loline Saras, review of *Winter Shoes for Shadow Horse,* p. 173.

Horn Book, May-June, 1995, Elizabeth S. Watson, review of *Maizie,* p. 332; January-February, 1996, Maeve Visser Knoth, review of *Hound Heaven,* p. 74; July, 2001, review of *Under New York,* p. 439.

Kirkus Reviews, October 15, 1995, review of *Hound Heaven,* p. 1493; February 1, 1998, review of *Beekeepers,* p. 197; August 15, 1999, review of *Barn Savers,* p. 1311; September 1, 2001, review of *A Humble Life,* p. 1290; March 15, 2003, review of *The Girl on the High-Diving Horse,* p. 468.

New York Times Book Review, May 20, 2001, Sam Swope, review of *Under New York,* p. 30.

Publishers Weekly, October 6, 1997, review of *A Christmas Star,* p. 55; February 2, 1998, review of *Beekeepers,* p. 90; February 26, 2001, review of *Under New York,* p. 86; September 24, 2001, review of *The Last Chimney of Christmas Eve,* p. 54; December 3, 2001, review of *A Humble Life,* p. 63; January 13, 2003, review of *The Girl on the High-Diving Horse,* p. 60.

Reading Teacher, November, 1998, review of *A Christmas Star,* p. 280.

School Library Journal, April, 1995, Marie Orlando, review of *Maizie,* p. 132; November, 1995, Carol Schene, review of *Hound Heaven,* p. 100; April, 1996, Beth Tegart, review of *The Summer of the Great Divide,* pp. 134-135; October, 1997, Jane Marino, review of *A Christmas Star,* p. 42; December, 1997, Linda Binder, review of *A Stone's Throw from Paradise,* pp. 124-125; June, 1998, Evelyn Butrico, review of *Beekeepers,* p. 109; May, 2001, Alicia Eames, review of *Under New York,* p. 142; October, 2001, review of *The Last Chimney of Christmas Eve,* p. 65, and Gay Lynn Van Vleck, review of *Winter Shoes for*

Shadow Horse, p. 120; February, 2003, Carol Schene, review of *The Girl on the High-Diving Horse,* pp. 112-113.

Voice of Youth Advocates, October, 1995, Carrie Eldridge, review of *Maizie,* p. 220; February, 1996, Jeanne M. McGlinn, review of *Hound Heaven,* p. 372.

ONLINE

AuthorsDen, http://www.authorsden.com/ (January 22, 2002), Linda Oatman High, "On the Edge of Pennsylvania Dutch Country"; (June 26, 2003), "Linda Oatman High."

Boyds Mills Press Web site, http://www.boydsmills press.com/ (June 26, 2003).

Linda Oatman High Home Page, http://www.lindaoat manhigh.com/ (October 28, 2003).

*   *   *

HILL, Selima 1945-

PERSONAL: Born October 13, 1945, in London, England; daughter of Jas (a painter and writer) and Elisabeth (a painter; maiden name, Robertson) Wood; married Roderic Colin Hill (a painter), July 23, 1968; children: Maisie, Moby, Albert. *Education:* Attended New Hall, Cambridge University, 1965-67, received special degree in English. *Hobbies and other interests:* Swimming, learning Mongolian.

ADDRESSES: Home—Lyme Regis, Dorset, England. *Agent*—c/o Author Mail, Bloodaxe Books Ltd., Highgreen, Tarset, Northumberland NE48 1RP, England.

CAREER: Associated with Morley College of Further Education, 1967-75; Tetric Bookshop, London, England, assistant manager, 1980-85. University of East Anglia, writing fellow, 1991; Royal Festival Hall Dance Festival, writer-in-residence, 1992; South Bank Centre, reader-in-residence, 1998; University of Exeter, fellow, 2003-04. Participant in Greater London Arts program writers in schools; gives readings.

MEMBER: Books against Nuclear Deterrent.

Selima Hill

AWARDS, HONORS: Cholmondeley Award, 1986; Arvon Foundation/*Observer* International Poetry Competition prize, 1988, for *The Accumulation of Small Acts of Kindness*; shortlisted for Forward Prize, Whitbread Poetry Award, and T.S. Eiot Prize, 1997, all for *Violet,*; shortlisted for T. S. Eliot Prize, 2001, for *Bunny;* Whitbread Poetry Award, 2002, for *Bunny.*

WRITINGS:

Saying Hello at the Station (poems), Hogarth Press (Richmond, Surrey, England), 1984.

My Darling Camel, Chatto & Windus (London, England), 1988.

The Accumulation of Small Acts of Kindness, Chatto & Windus (London, England), 1989.

A Little Book of Meat (poems), Bloodaxe Books (Chester Springs, PA), 1993.

Trembling Hearts in the Bodies of Dogs: New and Selected Poems, Bloodaxe Books (Chester Springs, PA), 1994.

My Sister's Horse, Smith/Doorstop Books (Westgate, England), 1996.

Violet, Bloodaxe Books (Chester Springs, PA), 1997.

Bunny (poems), Bloodaxe Books (Chester Springs, PA), 2001.

Portrait of My Lover As a Horse, Bloodaxe Books (Tarset, England), 2002.

Work represented in anthologies, including *Chatto Book of Post-feminist Poetry* and *No Holds Barred: Women's Poetry.* Author of television script for program, "Why Women Write." Contributor of poems and reviews to magazines and newspapers, including *London, Poetry Review, New Statesman, Writing Women, Time Out, Honest Ulsterman, Literary Review, London Review of Books, Observer, Resurgence, Nexus,* and *New Poetry.*

WORK IN PROGRESS: A ninth collection of poetry titled *Suitcase*; editing an anthology of dog poems; a libretto for a multimedia project about bees.

SIDELIGHTS: Selima Hill once told *CA*: "I am interested in learning more old languages and visiting Egypt, black Africa, Easter Island, Peru, Greenland and the Arctic, and the West Indies. Ancient civilizations show us that other ways are possible. I like comparative mythology and religions, especially Buddhism, so-called 'primitive religions,' and Rastafarianism. The last of these is a young black faith, Bible-based but not Christian, rooted in the experience of the black people of Jamaica. I prefer doing workshops and reading other people's work to 'performing' my own, although I value the feedback and the people I meet at poetry readings very much indeed.

"I write because my pen is my friend and will not judge me or tell me to shut up. I write to bear witness, to express my emotion in action, to refract and transform my experience, to explore it by having it in front of me instead of inside of me, to take risks, and to celebrate. Unlike a lot of writers, I write when I am happy as well as when I'm sad. I started writing because I was shy but felt like sharing my thoughts."

BIOGRAPHICAL AND CRITICAL SOURCES:

PERIODICALS

Booklist, March 1, 1994, Whitney Scott, review of *A Little Book of Meat,* p. 1176.

New Statesman & Society, July 15, 1988, Robert Sheppard, "Gravity- Haunted Logos," pp. 41-42.

Times Literary Supplement, June 3, 1988, Fleur Adcock, review of *My Darling Camel,* p. 625; August 4, 1989, Michael O'Neill, review of *The Accumulation of Small Acts of Kindness,* p. 850; November 26, 1993, Ian Sansom, review of *A Little Book of Meat,* p. 15; February 24, 1995, Stephen Knight, review of *Trembling Hearts in the Bodies of Dogs: New and Selected Poems,* p. 23; August 1, 1997, Kevan Johnson, review of *Violet,* p. 26.

ONLINE

Contemporary Writers in the UK, http://www.con temporarywriters.com/ (March 4, 2004), profile of Selima Hill.*

*   *   *

HILLGARTH, J(ocelyn) N(igel) 1929-

PERSONAL: Born September 22, 1929, in London, England; son of Alan Hugh (a naval officer) and Mary (Gardner) Hillgarth; married Nina Pantaleoni (a university administrator), February 25, 1966. *Education:* Queens' College, Cambridge, B.A., 1950; Cambridge University, M.A., 1954, Ph.D., 1957.

ADDRESSES: Office—Pontifical Institute of Mediaeval Studies and Centre for Medieval Studies, University of Toronto, 59 Queen's Park Cr. E, Toronto, Ontario M5S 2CA, Canada.

CAREER: Warburg Institute, London, England, senior research fellow, 1959-62; Institute for Advanced Study, Princeton, NJ, member, 1963-64; Harvard University, Cambridge, MA, assistant professor of history, 1965-70; Boston College, Boston, MA, associate professor, 1970-73, professor of history, 1973-77; University of Toronto, Pontifical Institute of Mediaeval Studies and Centre for Medieval Studies, Toronto, Ontario, Canada, professor of history, 1977—. University of Texas—Austin, visiting lecturer, 1964-65; Hebrew University of Jerusalem, Lady Davis Visiting Professor, 1980.

MEMBER: American Historical Association, Mediaeval Academy of America, Society for Spanish and Portuguese Historical Studies.

AWARDS, HONORS: Guggenheim fellow, 1968-69; fellow, American Council of Learned Societies, 1976-77.

WRITINGS:

(Editor) *The Conversion of Western Europe, 350-750,* Prentice-Hall (Englewood Cliffs, NJ), 1969, revised edition published as *Christianity and Paganism, 350-750: The Conversion of Western Europe,* University of Pennsylvania Press (Philadelphia, PA), 1985.

Ramon Lull and Lullism in Fourteenth-Century France, Clarendon Press, 1971.

The Spanish Kingdoms, 1250-1516, Oxford University Press (New York, NY), Volume 1, 1976, Volume 2, 1978.

(With Miquel Batllori) *Vida de Ramon Llull: Les Fonts escrites i la iconografia coetànies,* Associació de Bibliòfils de Barcelona (Barcelona, Spain), 1982.

(With Giulio Silano) *The Register "Notule Communium" 14 of the Diocese of Barcelona (1345-1348): A Calendar with Selected Documents,* Pontifical Institute of Mediaeval Studies (Toronto, Ontario, Canada), 1983.

(Editor) Mary Hillgarth, *A Private Life: Autobiographical Writings,* privately printed (Majorca, Spain), 1984.

Visigothic Spain, Byzantium, and the Irish, Variorum Reprints (London, England), 1985.

Readers and Books in Majorca, 1229-1550, 1991.

The Liber Communis Curiae of the Diocese of Majorca, 1364-1374, 1992.

The Mirror of Spain, 1500-1700: The Formation of a Myth, University of Michigan Press (Ann Arbor, MI), 2000.

Shorter works include "Who Read Thomas Aquinas?," Pontifical Institute of Mediaeval Studies (Toronto, Ontario, Canada), 1992; author of introduction and notes, *Chronicle/Pere III of Catalonia (Pedro IV of Aragon),* two volumes, by Pedro IV, King of Aragon, translated by Mary Hillgarth, Pontifical Institute of Mediaeval Studies (Toronto, Ontario, Canada), 1980.

Contributor to learned journals, including *Catholic Historical Review, Speculum, Journal of Medieval Studies,* and *American Historical Review.*

BIOGRAPHICAL AND CRITICAL SOURCES:

PERIODICALS

American Historical Review, February, 1980, review of *The Spanish Kingdoms, 1250-1516,* p. 105.

British Book News, February, 1980, review of *The Spanish Kingdoms, 1250-1516,* p. 74.

Catholic Historical Review, January, 1981, review of *The Spanish Kingdoms, 1250-1516,* p. 67; January, 1986, review of *The Register "Notule Communium" 14 of the Diocese of Barcelona (1345-1348): A Calendar with Selected Documents,* p. 70; April, 1991, Jill R. Webster, review of *The Liber Communis Curiae of the Diocese of Majorca, 1364-1374,* p. 302.

Choice, June, 1979, review of *The Spanish Kingdoms, 1250-1516,* p. 588; June, 2001, M. A. Burkholder, review of *The Mirror of Spain, 1500-1700: The Formation of a Myth,* p. 1858.

English Historical Review, July, 1982, review of *The Spanish Kingdoms, 1250-1516,* p. 629.

Historian, August, 1980, review of *The Spanish Kingdoms, 1250-1516,* p. 669.

History: Reviews of New Books, August, 1981, review of *The Spanish Kingdoms, 1250-1516,* p. 219.

History Today, April, 1982, review of *Ramon Lull and Lullism in Fourteenth-Century France,* p. 48.

Journal of Religion, July, 1990, review of *Christianity and Paganism, 350-750: The Conversion of Western Europe,* p. 513.

Journal of Theological Studies, October, 2001, William Horbury, "Altercatio Ecclesiae et Synagogae; Potamii Episcopi Olisponensis: Opera Omnia," p. 909.

Libraries and Culture, winter, 1997, review of *Readers and Books in Majorca, 1229-1550,* p. 133.

Library Journal, April 1, 1979, review of *The Spanish Kingdoms, 1250-1516,* p. 826.

Speculum, October, 1980, review of *The Spanish Kingdoms, 1250-1516,* p. 796; July, 1984, review of *The Register "Notule Communium" 14 of the Diocese of Barcelona (1345-1348),* p. 720; October, 1986, review of *Visigothic Spain, Byzantium, and the Irish,* p. 1024; January, 1992, review of *The Liber Communis Curiae of the Diocese of*

Valerie Hobbs

Majorca, 1364-1374, p. 151; April, 1994, Faith Wallis, review of *Readers and Books in Majorca, 1229-1550*, p. 495.
Times Literary Supplement, June 15, 2001, Henry Kamen, review of *The Mirror of Spain, 1500-1700*, p. 30.*

*   *   *

HIRSCH, William Randolph
    See LINGEMAN, Richard R(oberts)

*   *   *

HOBBS, Valerie 1941-

PERSONAL: Born April 18, 1941, in Metuchen, NJ; daughter of Herbert Trevor Evans and Alise (a painter; maiden name, Hansen) Minney; married Gary Johnson, 1962 (divorced, 1973); married Jack Hobbs (a teacher),

June 18, 1978; children: (first marriage) Juliet. *Education:* University of California, Santa Barbara, B.A., 1968, M.A., 1978. *Politics:* Democrat. *Hobbies and other interests:* Golf, hiking, travel, poker.

ADDRESSES: Home—69 Skyline Cir., Santa Barbara, CA 93109. *Office*—Writing Program, Girvetz 1315, University of California, Santa Barbara, CA 93106. *Agent*—Barbara Markowitz, 117 North Mansfield Ave., Los Angeles, CA 90036. *E-mail*—valhobbs@cox.net.

CAREER: High school English teacher on the Hawaiian island of Oahu, 1971-74; University of California, Santa Barbara, lecturer in writing, 1981-2001, professor emeritus, 2001—; writer. Speaker on writing topics at schools and seminars.

MEMBER: PEN Center West, Society of Children's Book Writers and Illustrators, South Coast Writing Project.

AWARDS, HONORS: Best Young Adult Novels citation, American Library Association, 1995, for *How Far Would You Have Gotten If I Hadn't Called You Back?;* "Flying Starts" citation from *Publishers Weekly*, 1996; PEN/Norma Klein Award for "emerging voice of literary merit in American children's literature," 1999.

WRITINGS:

How Far Would You Have Gotten If I Hadn't Called You Back?, Orchard Books (New York, NY), 1995.
Get It while It's Hot. Or Not, Orchard Books (New York, NY), 1996.
Carolina Crow Girl, Farrar, Straus (New York, NY), 1999.
Charlie's Run, Frances Foster Books (New York, NY), 2000.
Tender, Farrar, Straus (New York, NY), 2001.
Sonny's War, Farrar, Straus (New York, NY), 2002.
Stefan's Story, Farrar, Straus (New York, NY), 2003.
Letting Go of Bobby James, or, How I Found Myself of Steam by Sally Jo Walker, Farrar, Straus (New York, NY), 2004.

Work represented in anthologies, including *California Childhoods*, edited by Gary Soto, 1987. Contributor of stories to magazines, including *Northeast Corridor, Chrysalis, American Fiction, New Renaissance*, and *Kansas Quarterly*.

WORK IN PROGRESS: More novels for young adults.

SIDELIGHTS: Valerie Hobbs did not set out to write novels for young adults, but ever since critics praised her 1995 coming-of-age story *How Far Would You Have Gotten If I Hadn't Called You Back?,* she has been a respected author of fiction for teens. At the rate of approximately one book per year, Hobbs has crafted character-driven tales about young people on the verge of adulthood, forced to make serious decisions about the direction their lives will take. Often the young protagonists are confronted with circumstances beyond their control—the death of a guardian or a boyfriend, parental divorce, or physical disability. How they deal with these challenges forms the core of Hobbs's works. *Horn Book* contributor Jeannine M. Chapman observed that in Hobbs's novels, "the confusion of adolescence is truthfully rendered." A *Publishers Weekly* reviewer likewise credited Hobbs with "a keen understanding of adolescent moods and concerns."

Hobbs keenly recalls the defining moment of her own young adulthood. When she was in high school, her parents relocated the family from New Jersey to California, separating her not only from friends and beloved activities, but also from the urban surroundings in which she had grown up. This experience provides the catalyst for Hobbs's debut novel, *How Far Would You Have Gotten If I Hadn't Called You Back?* The story of a young woman with a love of both racing cars and the men who drive them, the book has drawn praise from critics for its original and sensitive portrait of a teenager struggling to find herself amidst a sea of contradictory influences. The title comes from an expression often used by the author's father; the plot comes from the incidents in her own childhood that probably prompted her father's question.

In *How Far Would You Have Gotten If I Hadn't Called You Back?,* sixteen-year-old Bronwyn Lewis seeks to carve an unconventional life for herself. Growing up in the late 1950s, in a generation where young women her age chose role models like Doris Day and Donna Reed and looked forward to marriage and a future spending hours in the kitchen, Bronwyn prefers to be behind the wheel of a dragster. Like her creator, Hobbs, the fictional Bronwyn has moved from urban New Jersey to rural California at age fifteen. Her interests and hobbies are different than those of the

teens in her new town, and fitting in at her new high school has been almost impossible. The fact that her family is now poor and her out-of-work dad has already attempted suicide makes Bronwyn feel even more withdrawn. Finally, friendship with Lanie, a pretty but poor young woman from the "wild side" of town, allows Bronwyn a way in to a peer group. She falls behind in school, dumps her interest in playing classical piano for rock 'n' roll, and starts dating, drinking, and hanging out with the drag-racing crowd. A sexual fling with the much older racer known as J. C. is interrupted by a budding love affair with the mature and far more suitable Will, but when Will leaves for his first year at West Point, Bronwyn returns to her old ways, with tragic consequences.

Calling Bronwyn "a believable and realistic voice," Joel Shoemaker praised *How Far Would You Have Gotten* in his review in *School Library Journal,* noting that the novel's "themes are subtly evoked and life's lessons are learned the hard way." *Booklist* reviewer Stephanie Zvirin called *How Far Would You Have Gotten* "an enticing coming-of-age story," asserting that Hobbs "manipulates the elements (including the sex) with energy, confidence, and surprise."

How Far Would You Have Gotten was not written with a young adult audience in mind, although the novel was later marketed for YA readers. Instead, Hobbs wanted to write down her personal recollections of her teen years, complete with her bout with personal tragedy and her own growing awareness of her maturing attitudes. "I think it was probably best that I didn't write [the novel] for young adults," Hobbs told Nathalie Op de Beeck in *Publishers Weekly,* "because I didn't know enough to pull punches. I just wanted to say it the way it is, the way people forget that it is. I always see those years as fraught with danger."

Hobbs's second novel, *Get It while It's Hot. Or Not,* focuses on friendships and teen sexual relationships. Megan, Mia, Elaine, and Kit have been fast friends since eighth grade, but as they begin their junior year of high school they find themselves beset with problems. Kit is pregnant and confined to bed, and Megan is being pressured for sex by a boyfriend. Megan's response to her situation is to write a piece on sexual issues for the school newspaper—but the principal bars its publication. According to Marcia Mann in *Voice of Youth Advocates,* readers of *Get It while It's Hot. Or Not* "relate to Megan's struggle to define the boundaries of friendship and her responsibilities to her family and community." Janice M. Del Negro in the *Bulletin of the Center for Children's Books* observed that young adult readers would likely find the "friends, group dynamics and the contemporary themes appealing." And *Horn Book* reviewer Lauren Adams called the novel "well paced and highly readable, taking on serious issues with humor and intelligence."

Both *Carolina Crow Girl* and *Stefan's Story* explore the lives of two unique individuals. Carolina, the heroine of *Carolina Crow Girl,* lives in an old school bus with her single mother and baby sister. When Carolina saves a crow that has been abandoned by its mother, her enthusiasm for the fledgling leads to friendship with Stefan Millington Crouch, a wealthy boy who is confined to a wheelchair. Stefan's family offers Carolina a chance to escape her poverty, but just as she realizes her crow will need its freedom, she rejects the offer and remains with her mother. *Booklist* contributor Lauren Peterson found *Carolina Crow Girl* to be "a deeply moving story with rich, complex characters," and a *Publishers Weekly* critic deemed it "sensitive in its explorations of friendships."

In *Stefan's Story,* Stefan travels by himself to Oregon to attend Carolina's mother's wedding and finds that his feelings for Carolina are deepening from friendship into something more serious. For her part, Carolina is embroiled in a controversy that pits local logging interests against environmentalists and fishermen as preparations are made to cut down an old-growth forest. Hobbs does not settle for easy answers in this novel, as Stefan confronts his disabilities and Carolina sees both sides of the logging dispute. According to Cindy Darling Codell in *School Library Journal,* the author "gives proper balance to the economic pressures of the issue." Writing for *Booklist,* Hazel Rochman commented, "The wonder of this story is the fusion of the small things with exciting action."

Hobbs explores the plight of urban runaways in *Charlie's Run.* Charlie, always a model son, decides to run away from home in protest of his parents' impending separation. He intends his absence to be short, but when he falls in with the volatile Doo, he finds himself in Los Angeles, living on the streets. A *Publishers Weekly* reviewer praised the novel as "an emotionally complex rendition of a familiar story," adding that Hobbs's "cncrgctic, honest storytelling" moves the

story along. Connie Tyrrell Burns in *School Library Journal* likewise admired the "fast-moving plot, complex and appealing characters" in a book she characterized as "a sure winner." A *Horn Book* critic noted that *Charlie's Run* "is a compelling story, convincingly told."

Tender once again addresses the issues of lifestyle change and adjustment to a new household. Olivia Trager is uprooted when her beloved grandmother dies. Forced to move from Manhattan to rural California, Olivia must live with a father who abandoned her at birth. Gradually Olivia's fury gives way to acceptance, particularly after she begins to help her father with his deep-sea diving expeditions. *School Library Journal* correspondent Francisca Goldsmith liked Olivia's strength and personality, adding that the book draws readers in "immediately and inextricably." In her *Booklist* review, Debbie Carton found Hobbs's characters "wonderfully human and fully realized," commending the story for its "loving undertones that will linger."

Hobbs was a college student during the Vietnam War era, and her brother was drafted to serve in the conflict. *Sonny's War* once again draws upon some personal experience as Hobbs crafts a tale of a teenager whose brother is in Southeast Asia while she participates in antiwar protests. Once again Hobbs delves into the morally complex issues surrounding the Vietnam War, as young Cory becomes disillusioned by the actions of a beloved schoolteacher who goes too far during a violent protest. The war's toll on individuals is also portrayed, as Cory's brother returns with wounds both physical and psychological. Miriam Lang Budin noted in *School Library Journal* that the novel reveals "the ambiguities and tensions driving the nation and individual citizens during this difficult time." In her starred review for *Horn Book,* Martha V. Parravano called *Sonny's War* "a convincing, affecting novel," noting that the central character "is as real as real, completely believable in all her teenage vulnerability and sharp-eyed observation."

In an interview with *Authors and Artists for Young Adults (AAYA),* Hobbs said she writes about growing up under pressure because she wants young adults to know that they are not alone in their troubles. "I think I write to share some feelings I've had and some feelings I think a lot of people have, so when they read them there might be a moment of recognition when they say 'I'm not the only one who feels this way,' or 'I'm OK, and I can get through this,'" she said. "I remember the teenage years being very stressful and thinking I was the only one going through certain things. When I talk to teenagers now, they seem to feel that way, too. I think it gives you courage to see that somebody else went through similar situations and made it to the other side. I realize that's a part of why I write—to share common feelings."

For many years Hobbs taught at the University of California, Santa Barbara, while also writing her books. More recently she has cut down on her teaching duties in order to have more time to work on novels. She also enjoys meeting students at seminars and school visits. In her interview, Hobbs told *AAYA:* "We haven't really wanted to think about what teenagers really know and what they really think about. It is a natural tendency to want to protect them from a lot of things, but they are adults now. Everything is so out in the open; there isn't anything that they don't know and don't talk about. To not have it in literature seems hypocritical to say the least."

BIOGRAPHICAL AND CRITICAL SOURCES:

BOOKS

Authors and Artists for Young Adults, Volume 28, Gale (Detroit, MI), 1999.

PERIODICALS

Booklist, October 1, 1995, Stephanie Zvirin, review of *How Far Would You Have Gotten If I Hadn't Called You Back?,* p. 304; February 15, 1999, Lauren Peterson, review of *Carolina Crow Girl,* p. 1070; August, 2001, Debbie Carton, review of *Tender,* p. 2107; November 1, 2002, Hazel Rochman, review of *Sonny's War,* p. 484; September 15, 2003, Hazel Rochman, review of *Stefan's Story.*

Bulletin of the Center for Children's Books, November, 1996, Janice M. Del Negro, review of *Get It While It's Hot. Or Not,* p. 99.

Horn Book, December, 1996, Lauren Adams, review of *Get It While It's Hot. Or Not,* p. 744; March, 2000, review of *Charlie's Run,* p. 195; September,

2001, Jeannine M. Chapman, review of *Tender,* p. 584; November-December, 2002, Martha V. Parravano, review of *Sonny's War,* p. 760.

Publishers Weekly, December 18, 1995, Nathalie Op de Beeck, "Flying Starts: Three Children's Novelists Talk about Their Fall '95 Debuts," pp. 28-30; March 15, 1999, review of *Carolina Crow Girl,* p. 60; February 7, 2000, review of *Charlie's Run,* p. 86; August 27, 2001, review of *Tender,* p. 86.

School Library Journal, October, 1995, Joel Shoemaker, review of *How Far Would You Have Gotten If I Hadn't Called You Back?,* p. 155; March, 2000, Connie Tyrrell Burns, review of *Charlie's Run,* p. 238; September, 2001, Francisca Goldsmith, review of *Tender,* p. 225; November, 2002, Miriam Lang Budin, review of *Sonny's War,* p. 168; August, 2003, Cindy Darling Codell, review of *Stefan's Story,* p. 160.

Voice of Youth Advocates, December, 1995, C. Allen Nichols, review of *How Far Would You Have Gotten If I Hadn't Called You Back?,* p. 302; December, 1996, Marcia Mann, review of *Get It While It's Hot, Or Not,* p. 270.

*   *   *

HOMES, A(my) M(ichael) 1961-

PERSONAL: Born 1961, in Washington, DC; children: one daughter. *Education:* Attended American University; Sarah Lawrence College, B.A., 1985; University of Iowa, M.F.A., 1988.

ADDRESSES: Home—New York, NY. *Agent*—Wylie, Aitken and Stone, 250 West 57th St., Room 2106, New York, NY 10107.

CAREER: Writer. Held position at Columbia University, New York, NY, technical writing program, 1991; member of board of directors of Yaddo, Saratoga Springs, NY, and The Fine Arts Work Center, Provincetown, MA.

MEMBER: PEN.

AWARDS, HONORS: Benjamin Franklin Award; National Endowment for the Arts fellowship; New York Foundation for the Arts Artists fellowship; Center for Scholars and Writers fellowship, New York Public Library; Deutscher jugendliteraturpreis, 1993, for *Jack*; Guggenheim Foundation fellowship, 1998.

WRITINGS:

Jack (novel), Macmillan (New York, NY), 1989.
The Safety of Objects (stories), Norton (New York, NY), 1990.
In a Country of Mothers (novel), Knopf (New York, NY), 1993.
The End of Alice (novel), Scribner (New York, NY), 1996.
Appendix A: An Elaboration on the Novel "The End of Alice," Artspace Books (San Francisco, CA), 1996.
Music for Torching (novel), Rob Weisbach Books (New York, NY), 1999.
Things You Should Know: A Collection of Stories, HarperCollins (New York, NY), 2002.
Los Angeles: People, Places, and the Castle on the Hill, National Geographic (Washington, DC), 2002.

Author of artist's catalogs for Cecily Brown, Rachel Whiteread, Ken Probst, Gergory Crewdson, Carroll Dunham, and Todd Hido. Contributing editor to *Vanity Fair, Mirabella, Bomb,* and *Blind Spot.* Contributor to periodicals, including *Artforum, Harper's, New Yorker, Granta, New York Times,* and *Zoetrope.*

ADAPTATIONS: The Safety of Objects was adapted for film by Rose Troche and released by Metro-Goldwyn-Mayer in 2001.

SIDELIGHTS: A. M. Homes made her literary debut with *Jack,* a novel that follows an adolescent boy's emotionally painful progression into adulthood. Praised for its realistic portrayal of the average American teenager, the story is told from the point of view of the title character, who is in the midst of adjusting to his parents' recent divorce. An excerpt from the book relating the protagonist's anxiety about growing up appeared in Elizabeth Kastor's *Washington Post* article: "I'm stuck between things. I'm stuck between being a kid and being an adult. The things that kids do aren't really a whole lot of fun, but what adults do still seems too hard, and to be honest, boring as hell." Jack's ambivalence is soon intensified when

he learns that his father is homosexual, and the boy subsequently becomes the victim of his classmates' insensitivity. "*Jack* is a story about prejudice and bias," Homes told Kastor. "Jack is this young, white male. He's never been exposed to any kind of prejudice." Both the discovery that his best friend's family is perhaps more dysfunctional than his own and a new friendship with a girl who also has a homosexual father help Jack to ultimately avoid feelings of self-despair. "Homes has given us a good youngster who in the end convincingly grows larger than his circumstances," wrote Crescent Dragonwagon in the *New York Times Book Review.* The reviewer also found that the author "handles the big subjects and adolescent passions subtly, deftly and with an appealing lack of melodrama."

In her next book, a collection of stories titled *The Safety of Objects,* Homes presents a cast of profoundly neurotic characters unable to cope with the tedium of life in middle-class America. Described as "vivid and disturbing" by Margaret Camp in the *Washington Post,* the narratives are concerned with what the reviewer termed "the dark harvest of our postmodern culture: a bunch of lonely, bored, angst-ridden, psycho adults and listless, alienated teenagers brimming with pubescent sexuality." In the story "Adults Alone," for example, a quintessential suburban couple spends ten days reveling in debauchery; they eat and drink to excess, watch pornographic videos, and smoke crack cocaine while the kids stay at their grandmother's house. And in "A Real Doll" a teenage boy has bizarre sexual encounters with his sister's vivified Barbie doll.

Camp assessed the collection as an "enthralling spiral into surrealist Hell," terming the stories "original and stiletto sharp." *Los Angeles Times Book Review* writer Amy Hempel wrote that the author "sustain[s] credibility by getting the details right," especially in "Looking for Johnny," which depicts the abduction of a nine-year-old boy, Erol. The narrative explores the psychological deficiencies of the kidnapper as well as the emotional trauma experienced by Erol when his captor finds him dull and returns the boy to his unsympathetic family. Hempel acknowledged that "there is not a misstep in this difficult story," and she labeled Homes "confident and consistent in her odd departures from life as we know it."

"The imagination that shapes A. M. Homes's fiction is exhilaratingly perverse," wrote *New York Times Book Review* contributor Maggie Paley. Homes's first adult novel, *In a Country of Mothers,* is ostensibly the story of Jody Goodman, a young college-bound woman seeking help from Dr. Claire Roth, a therapist who is old enough to be her mother. As therapy proceeds, however, the focus of the novel seems to move from Jody to Claire. Elaine Kendall explained in the *Los Angeles Times* that "Jody remains virtually unchanged by these meetings" while "Roth's interest in her patient progresses from unusual interest to downright obsession." Claire convinces herself that Jody is the long-lost daughter whom she handed over for adoption many years ago, a conviction based on the coincidence of Jody's date and place of birth. She steps over the threshold that transforms a therapist from an observer and counselor to an active participant in the patient's life. As the doctor's involvement escalates—from including Jody in Roth family outings to spying on the patient in Jody's own neighborhood—Claire is "ultimately . . . driven to the edge of madness," according to Kendall.

Some critics expressed disappointment with Homes's initial entry into adult fiction. *Belles Lettres* reviewer Bettina Berch referred to a novel "about a handful of self-obsessed people who make each other miserable for awhile." A *Kirkus Reviews* critic praised the novel's "snappy dialogue" and "transparently clear style," but decided that the novel's "strong premise has a weak follow-through." Carol Anshaw agreed, commenting in the *Chicago Tribune* that *In the Country of Mothers* fails to fulfill the promise "pulsing behind the type," but credited the author with "a fascinating story of the corruption of trust." Leigh Allison Wilson reported in the *Washington Post Book World,* however, that Homes succeeded in creating "portraits of good people gone terribly wrong, while at the same time offering visions of what might have been, what should have been." Wilson concluded, "A. M. Homes is a very dangerous writer. Danger for a reader of fiction is usually a safe place, the place of voyeurs and bystanders. Homes creates a much scarier place."

In her next novel, *The End of Alice,* Homes "takes us . . . with all the cunning and control of a brilliant lover . . . to places we dare not go alone," wrote Elizabeth Houghton in the *Los Angeles Times Book Review.* A young college woman, home for summer vacation, becomes sexually obsessed with a twelve-year-old boy. She explores her obsession directly, but also by corresponding with a convicted pedophile, sentenced to life in prison for molesting and eventu-

ally murdering a girl named Alice. In her letters, the narrator flirts with the convict, teasing him to revive his memories of Alice and to ponder how such warped events can happen. The memories, like the narrator's responses, grow sexually explicit and graphically pornographic, according to some critics. Jennifer Kornreich suggested in the *Women's Review of Books* that Homes's purpose may have been to achieve "the social . . . [benefit] of shock value" by "confronting people with ugliness . . . [to] force them to think." *Washington Post* reviewer Carolyn See wrote that "to use pornography as a teaching device may be fine for the writer, but the reader may feel put upon." Yet Houghton wrote, "It is easy to understand serious objection to the subject matter. But the writing takes flight from such an original departure point you find yourself transported high up above the noise, leaving judgment grounded." *New York Times Book Review* writer Daphne Merkin reported that the book's "underlying themes are more serious than prurient. *The End of Alice* is concerned with the fluid nature of identity, with the permeable boundaries that divide an overtly deranged consciousness from a smugly socialized one." Kornreich concluded, however, "Ultimately . . . Homes shies away from more questions than she confronts."

Homes returned to the characters she created in "Adults Alone" for her 1999 novel, *Music for Torching.* Paul and Elaine are no more mature than they were in the earlier short story, but their kids are older. The novel begins with them deliberately setting fire to their home after a barbecue accident, and follows each of them through tawdry affairs with neighbors and acquaintances. *Music for Torching* caused David Gates in *Newsweek* to compare Homes to John Cheever, but the critic stated that "Homes shows none of Cheever's nuanced ambivalence about leafy, loony suburbia and the annoyingly provincial, thwartedly poetic souls who live there; for her it's a zoo." L. S. Klepp in *Entertainment Weekly* noted that the novel's "effect is of rapid-fire satire bordering on bedroom farce—a caustic and giddy caricature of hollow, haywire suburbanites." *Review of Contemporary Fiction* writer Trey Strecker concluded that Homes "succeeds in showing that no one is 'normal' when we peer behind their white picket fences."

Three years later, Homes published another collection of short fiction, *Things You Should Know.* Reviewing the volume in *Newsweek,* Susannah Meadows praised "the force of Homes's storytelling," also remarking that, "enthralling and heartbreaking, most of these eleven pieces exemplify the fundamentals of great storytelling." Similarly, James O'Laughlin in *Booklist* noted the "remarkable range of dramas" included in *Things You Should Know,* as well as the "deft compactness" of the author's prose. *Library Journal* contributor Colleen Lougen described Homes's skill in the collection as "hypnotic," noting that it gives "the reader a peek into the exotic thoughts and worlds of people we do not normally meet in literature."

BIOGRAPHICAL AND CRITICAL SOURCES:

BOOKS

Homes, A. M., *Jack,* Macmillan (New York, NY), 1989.

PERIODICALS

Antioch Review, winter, 1994, p. 182.
Belles Lettres, fall, 1993, p. 42.
Booklist, May 15, 1999, Danise Hoover, review of *Music for Torching,* p. 1668; August, 2002, James O'Laughlin, review of *Things You Should Know: A Collection of Stories,* p. 1920.
Chicago Tribune, May 7, 1993.
Detroit Free Press, December 23, 1990.
Economist (US), July 5, 2003, Clare Boylan, review of *Things You Should Know,* p. 76.
Entertainment Weekly, June 11, 1999, L. S. Klepp, "Homes's Town: Following Up on Her Shocking Novel *The End of Alice,* A. M. Homes Takes on Suburban Angst and Marriage in *Music for Torching,* " p. 58.
Kirkus Reviews, March 1, 1993, p. 246; March 15, 1999, review of *Music for Torching,* p. 398; July 1, 2002, review of *Things You Should Know,* p. 905.
Lambda Book Report, July-August, 1999, Elizabeth Brownrigg, review of *Music for Torching,* pp. 14-15.
Library Journal, May 10, 1999, David Gates, review of *Music for Torching,* p. 79; August, 2002, Colleen Lougen, review *Things You Should Know,* p. 148.
London Review of Books, May 9, 1996, pp. 20-21.
Los Angeles Times, July 9, 1993, p. E5.

Los Angeles Times Book Review, October 28, 1990, p. 3; May 26, 1996, pp. 6-7; June 6, 1999, review of *Music for Torching,* p. 11.
New Statesman, January 1, 1999, Phil Whitaker, review of *Jack,* p. 49.
Newsweek, May 10, 1999, David Gates, "Burning Down the House," p. 79; September 2, 2002, Susannah Meadows, "Short Stories That Tell . . . Stories," p. 62.
New York Times Book Review, July 15, 1990, p. 24; May 23, 1993, p. 17; March 24, 1996, p. 14; May 30, 1999, Gary Krist, review of *Music for Torching,* p. 9.
Observer (London, England), December 13, 1998, review of *Jack,* p. 16; January 19, 2003, Zoe Green, review of *Los Angeles: People, Places, and the Castle on the Hill.*
Poets & Writers Magazine, July-August, 1999, Fran Gordon, review of *Music for Torching,* p. 24.
Publishers Weekly, March 15, 1993, p. 67; May 7, 1999, review of *Music for Torching,* p. 59; July 15, 2002, review of *Things You Should Know,* p. 52.
Review of Contemporary Fiction, fall, 1999, Trey Strecker, review of *Music for Torching,* p. 167; spring, 2003, Stacey Gottlieb, review of *Things You Should Know,* p. 149.
Times Literary Supplement, May 10, 1991, p. 20; September 3, 1999, Ali Sith, review of *Music for Torching,* p. 12.
Wall Street Journal, May 7, 1999, Garvirella Stern, review of *Music for Torching,* p. W9E.
Washington Post, September 24, 1990, p. B1; May 10, 1993, p. B2; May 3, 1996, p. D2.
Women's Review of Books, July, 1996, p. 45.

*　　*　　*

HUDSON, Jeffrey
　See CRICHTON, (John) Michael

*　　*　　*

HUNT, Peter (Leonard) 1945-

PERSONAL: Born September 2, 1945, in Rugby, Warwickshire, England; son of Walter Henry (an engineer) and Lillian (McPherson) Hunt; married Angela Sarah Theodora Wilkinson (a researcher), October 24, 1981;

children: Felicity Sarah Eve, Amy Harriet Mary, Abigail Celestine Rose, Chloe Amaryllis Verity. *Ethnicity:* "Anglo-Saxon." *Education:* University of Wales, University College of Wales, Aberystwyth, B.A., 1966; University of Wales, Cardiff, M.A., 1969, Ph.D., 1981.

ADDRESSES: Home—West Sundial Cottage, Downend, Horsley, Stroud, Gloucester GL6 0PF, England. *Office*—School of English Studies, Communication, and Philosophy, University of Wales, P.O. Box 94, Cardiff CF1 3XB, Wales; fax: 44-0-1222-874647. *E-mail*—huntp@cardiff.ac.uk.

CAREER: University of Wales, Cardiff, lecturer in English at Institute of Science and Technology, 1969-88, senior lecturer, 1988-95, reader, 1995-96, professor of English, 1996—. University of Michigan, Ann Arbor, lecturer, 1978; Massachusetts Institute of Technology, Cambridge, visiting professor, 1982, 1983, 1984, 1987, 1990; San Diego State University, San Diego, CA, adjunct professor, 1990; University of Wollongong, visiting fellow, 1991. John Kirkman Communication Consultancy, principal associate, 1981—. Engineering Council, joint examiner, 1978—.

MEMBER: International Research Society of Children's Literature, Institute of Scientific and Technical Communicators (fellow).

AWARDS, HONORS: Award from Society for Technical Communication, 1987; award for distinguished scholarship, International Research Society for the Fantastic in the Arts, 1996.

WRITINGS:

Children's Book Research in Britain: Research in British Institutions of Higher Education on Children's Books and Related Subjects, Wales Institute of Science and Technology, University of Wales (Cardiff, Wales), 1977, revised edition (with Beth Humphries and Sarah Wilkinson), 1982.
Critic into Author: Woodfield Lecture XIII, Woodfield & Stanley (Huddersfield, England), 1990.
Criticism, Theory, and Children's Literature, Basil Blackwell (New York, NY), 1991.

Arthur Ransome, Twayne (Boston, MA), 1991, revised edition published as *Approaching Arthur Ransome,* J. Cape (London, England), 1992.
An Introduction to Children's Literature, Oxford University Press (New York, NY), 1994.
The Wind in the Willows: A Fragmented Arcadia ("Twayne's Masterwork Studies"), Twayne (New York, NY), 1994.
(With Millicent Lenz) *Alternative Worlds in Fantasy Fiction,* Continuum (New York, NY), 2001.

Contributor of numerous articles and reviews to periodicals, including *Times Literary Supplement, Signal, Children's Literature in Education, Advocate,* and *Social Work Today.*

JUVENILE FICTION

The Maps of Time, Julia MacRae (London, England), 1983.
A Step off the Path, Julia MacRae (London, England), 1985.
Backtrack, Julia MacRae (London, England), 1986.
Going Up, Julia MacRae (London, England), 1989.
Fay Cow and the Mystery of the Missing Milk, illustrated by Duncan Smith, Julia MacRae (London, England), 1989.
Sue and the Honey Machine, illustrated by Duncan Smith, Julia MacRae (London, England), 1989.

EDITOR

Further Approaches to Research in Children's Literature, Wales Institute of Science and Technology, University of Wales (Cardiff, Wales), 1977, 2nd edition, 1982.
Richard Jefferies, *Bevis,* Oxford University Press (New York, NY), 1989.
Critical Approaches to Children's Literature, 1989.
Children's Literature: The Development of Criticism, Routledge & Kegan Paul (New York, NY), 1990.
Literature for Children: Contemporary Criticism, Routledge & Kegan Paul (New York, NY), 1992.
Children's Literature: An Illustrated History, Oxford University Press (New York, NY), 1995.
International Companion Encyclopedia of Children's Literature, Routledge & Kegan Paul (New York, NY), 1996, portions published as *Understanding*

Children's Literature: Key Essays from the "International Companion Encyclopedia of Children's Literature," 1999.
Children's Literature: An Anthology, 1801-1902, Blackwell Publishers (Malden, MA), 2001.

SIDELIGHTS: According to Dominic Hibberd in the *Times Literary Supplement,* British educator and author Peter Hunt presents a "fascinating time puzzle" in his *The Maps of Time.* The story follows a curate, four teenagers, and an eleven-year-old boy as they travel through their imaginations back in time, courtesy of magical Victorian maps found in an old bookstore. The worlds in which the characters travel "allow the novelist to enjoy himself," commented Hibberd. "One narrative splits into four (now, then, and two versions of imagined now). . . . Plenty can happen—four times as much, in fact—and there are nice touches of irony and ambiguity. . . . The time machinery is too ingenious, but it does make us think twice—four times—about the art of narrative."

Hunt once told *CA:* "During my sabbatical from 1982 to 1983, I visited nearly one hundred universities and colleges in the United States, Canada, Australia, New Zealand, and India, and lectured at sixty-five of them on children's literature. I believe in the serious (but not solemn) application of the highest and most sophisticated theories to children's literature; I think children are capable of a very sophisticated level of literary appreciation. Contrary to popular thought, I think this appreciation is different in *kind,* rather than degree, from adult appreciation of literature. A new discipline of what might be called 'childist' criticism must be developed to account for it. My writing for children adheres to these principles: that only the best—by which I mean writing that is as sophisticated as any other—will do. The only possible differentiation (if any) is in the *timbre* of the subject matter."

BIOGRAPHICAL AND CRITICAL SOURCES:

BOOKS

St. James Guide to Children's Writers, 5th edition, St. James Press (Detroit, MI), 1999.
Twentieth-Century Children's Writers, St. James Press (Detroit, MI), 1989.

PERIODICALS

Bookbird, February, 1999, review of *Understanding Children's Literature: Key Essays from the "International Companion Encyclopedia of Children's Literature,"* p. 65.
Library Quarterly, January, 1998, review of *International Companion Encyclopedia of Children's Literature,* p. 98.
Times Literary Supplement, February 25, 1983, Dominic Hibberd, review of *The Maps of Time;* November 29, 1985; November 28, 1986; August 10, 2001, Jan Marsh, review of *Children's Literature: An Anthology, 1801-1902,* p. 29.*

* * *

HUTSON, Lorna 1958-

PERSONAL: Born November 27, 1958, in West Berlin, Germany; daughter of John Whiteford (a diplomat) and Doris (a teacher and homemaker; maiden name, Kemp) Hutson. *Education:* Somerville College, Oxford, B.A. (with first class honors), 1979, D.Phil., 1983. *Politics:* Labour. *Religion:* Agnostic.

ADDRESSES: *Office*—Department of English, 322 Wheeler Hall, #1030, University of California, Berkeley, CA 94720-1030. *E-mail*—lhutson@uclink4.berkeley.edu.

CAREER: University of London, Queen Mary and Westfield College, London, England, began as lecturer, became reader in English, beginning 1986; University of Hull, professor of English literature, 1998-2002; University of California—Berkeley, professor of English, 2002—.

AWARDS, HONORS: Fellow at Folger Shakespeare Library and Huntington Library, 1995.

WRITINGS:

Thomas Nashe in Context, Oxford University Press (New York, NY), 1989.

The Usurer's Daughter: Male Friendship and Fictions of Women in Sixteenth-Century England, Routledge & Kegan Paul, 1994.

(Editor) *Feminism and Renaissance Studies,* Oxford University Press (New York, NY), 1999.

(Editor, with Victoria Kahn) *Rhetoric and Law in Early Modern Europe,* Yale University Press (New Haven, CT), 2001.

SIDELIGHTS: Lorna Hutson is the author of *The Usurer's Daughter: Male Friendship and Fictions of Women in Sixteenth-Century England,* in which she argues that Renaissance scholars successfully defined their own intimate friendships with other men, particularly the aristocratic men who were their sponsors, in terms meant to distinguish themselves from homosexuals. According to Alan Bray, writing in *History Today,* Hutson writes that in much of the fiction of the sixteenth century, there are "moments in these stories when the uncertainty in masculine relations is displaced and resolved by a pliant woman. . . . [The stories] are fundamentally concerned . . . with the ambiguities of masculine friendship that the humanists needed to negotiate in their rise to power." *The Usurer's Daughter,* Bray concluded, "brings a new light to the story of how stereotypes of gender have been historically deployed."

In *Feminism and Renaissance Studies,* Hutson gathers together seventeen scholarly essays concerning women's experience of the Renaissance. Among the subjects examined are women painters, the education of women, the decline of the importance of the household, and the persecution of witches. Anne Kelley of *Renaissance Forum* described *Feminism and Renaissance Studies* as an "excellent collection of important essays [which] illuminates the Renaissance period from a feminist viewpoint."

BIOGRAPHICAL AND CRITICAL SOURCES:

PERIODICALS

English: The Journal of the English Association, summer, 1995, Sue Owen, review of *The Usurer's Daughter.*

History Today, February, 1998, Alan Bray, review of *The Usurer's Daughter,* p. 55.

Journal of Women's History, spring, 2001, Kathleen E. Kennedy, review of *Feminism and Renaissance Studies,* p. 222.

Renaissance Forum, Volume 4, number 2, 2000, Anne Kelley, review of *Feminism and Renaissance Studies.*

Renaissance Quarterly, autumn, 1990, Elizabeth Story Donno, review of *Thomas Nashe in Context,* p. 643; spring, 2002, Wayne A. Rebhorn, review of *Rhetoric and Law in Early Modern Europe,* p. 291.*

I-J

ISERSON, Kenneth Victor 1949-

PERSONAL: Born April 8, 1949, in Washington, DC; son of Isadore Irving and Edith (Swedlow) Iserson; married Mary Lou Sherk (a C.P.A.), June 16, 1973. *Education:* University of Maryland, College Park, B.S., 1971; University of Maryland School of Medicine, M.D., 1975; studied surgical practice at Mayo Clinic, 1975; studied emergency medicine at University of Cincinnati College of Medicine, 1976-78; University of Phoenix, M.B.A. (valedictorian), 1986. *Politics:* "Liberal." *Religion:* Jewish.

ADDRESSES: Office—Department of Emergency Medicine, University of Arizona, College of Medicine, Box 245057, 1501 North Campbell Ave., Tucson, AZ 85724. *E-mail*—kvi@u.u.arizona.edu.

CAREER: Cincinnati General Hospital, Cincinnati, OH, emergency medicine residency, 1976-78, chief resident, 1977-78; Community Mercy Hospital, Onamia, MN, general practice, 1976; Division of Emergency Medicine, Texas A&M University College of Medicine, clinical associate professor and chairman, 1980-81; University of Arizona College of Medicine, department of emergency medicine, emergency physician, 1981—, assistant professor, 1981-85, associate professor, 1985-92, professor, 1992—. Senior fellow in Bioethics, University of Chicago, 1990-91; *ER* (television show), ethics advisor, 1994—. Has appeared in many documentaries on death in the U.S., Japan, Canada, Germany, and the United Kingdom. *Military service:* U.S. Air Force, Carswell AFB, Fort Worth, TX, 1978-80, became captain and director of emergency medicine.

Kenneth Victor Iserson

MEMBER: American College of Emergency Physicians (Bioethics Committee), American Medical Association, Emergency Medicine Foundation, European Society for Philosophy of Medicine and Health Care, Society for Academic Emergency Medicine (National Affairs Committee), American Society for Bioethics and Humanities, Southern Arizona Rescue Association (medical director), Disaster Medical Assistance Team

(AZ-1), Wilderness Medical Society, University Medical Center Bioethics Committee (chair), Arizona Bioethics Program (director), Department of Emergency Medicine Promotion and Tenure Committee (chair), Society of Teachers of Emergency Medicine (now SAEM; president, 1982-83), Arizona Medical Association, Authors Guild, American Philosophical Association, Society of Southwestern Authors, Pima County Medical Society, Emergency International, Pan American Medical Development Program (board of directors), Medical Society of the United States and Mexico (vice-president, 2002-04).

AWARDS, HONORS: Diplomate, American Board of Emergency Medicine, 1980; fellow, American College of Emergency Medicine, 1982; senior fellow in bioethics, Center for Clinical Medical Ethics, University of Chicago, 1990-91; Arizona Emergency Medical Services Council, appointed by governor, 1990-91; Arizona Legislative Committee on Advance Directives, appointed by governor, 1991-92; award for best reference books, New York Public Library, 1994, for *Death to Dust: What Happens to Dead Bodies?*

WRITINGS:

(Editor, with A. B. Sanders, D. R. Mathieu, and A. E. Buchanan) *Ethics in Emergency Medicine,* Williams & Wilkins (Baltimore, MD), 1986, 2nd edition, with legal introduction by Alexander Morgan Capron, Galen Press (Tucson, AZ), 1995.
Getting into a Residency: A Guide for Medical Students, Camden House (Columbia, SC), 1988, 6th edition published as *Iserson's Getting into a Residency: A Guide for Medical Students,* Galen Press (Tucson, AZ), 2003.
(Editor) *Wilderness Medical Society: Position Statements, 1989,* The Society (Point Reyes Station, CA), 1989.
Death to Dust: What Happens to Dead Bodies?, Galen Press (Tucson, AZ), 1994, 2nd edition, 2000.
Get into Medical School!: A Guide for the Perplexed, Galen Press (Tucson, AZ), 1997, 2nd edition, 2004.
Non-Standard Medical Electives in the U.S. and Canada, Galen Press (Tucson, AZ), 1997, published as *Non-Standard Medical Electives in the U.S. and Canada, 1998-1999,* 1998.
Grave Words: Notifying Survivors about Sudden, Unexpected Deaths, Galen Press (Tucson, AZ), 1999.

Demon Doctors: Physicians As Serial Killers, Galen Press (Tucson, AZ), 2002.
Dying to Know: A Compendium of the Mortal, Morbid, and Macabre, Galen Press (Tucson, AZ), 2004.

Producer of teaching aids, including educational video and teaching slide set of *The Grave Words: Notifying Survivors about Sudden Unexpected Deaths.*

Also author of over 150 professional journal articles, textbook chapters, and other publications. Reviewer for medical journals, including *Annals of Emergency Medicine, American Journal of Emergency Medicine, American Journal of Diseases in Children, Journal of the American Medical Association, Archives of Internal Medicine, Pediatrics* and *Journal of Clinical Ethics.* Editor for *Journal of Emergency Medicine, Hospital Ethics Committee Forum,* and *Cambridge Quarterly.* Member of editorial board, *Journal of Emergency Medicine,* 1982, and *Cambridge Quarterly of Healthcare Ethics,* 1991.

SIDELIGHTS: Kenneth Victor Iserson wrote *Death to Dust: What Happens to Dead Bodies?* for two reasons. He told *CA* that he hopes not only to inform the public and professional world of post-death procedures that a body may undergo but also to promote organ and tissue donation. "Corpses deteriorate, no matter what," Iserson commented. "There is no reason not to donate organs and tissues, 'the last, best gift a person can leave behind.'" The book itself is laid out in a question and answer format with information ranging from common questions about burial and cremation, funeral costs, and organ donation, to more unusual possibilities, such as cryogenic preservation and scientific study. Iserson also devotes sections of his book to bizarre practices such as head-shrinking and grave-robbing. Not included in the book is a discussion of the afterlife, since, as Iserson told *CA,* he "leaves the spiritual side to others, although the religious rites practiced throughout human history and across cultures comprises a fascinating part of my books and talks." The critical success of *Death to Dust* has led to the author's guest appearances on radio talk shows and speaking engagements at national meetings. "A most curious volume," remarked a critic from *Choice,* adding that the book "should help individuals make more informed choices concerning autopsy, organ donation, and funeral arrangements. The peculiar facts and stories about the dead have a captivating appeal."

Among Iserson's other books are *Ethics in Emergency Medicine* and *Getting into a Residency: A Guide For Medical Students.* Of the first, Iserson told *CA,* "It is still the only book dealing with unique ethical issues faced by emergency physicians, emergency nurses, and ambulance personnel. My unique background in medicine and ethics and the exciting list of case commentators, brings an interesting flavor to this casebook." *Getting into Residency* was the best-selling nonclinical book in medical education in its third edition, according to Iserson, who referred to it as "'The Bible' for medical students seeking a postgraduate position. It gives a step-by-step method for getting through the process intact." Iserson continues to be an active part of the emergency medical system in addition to teaching, speaking, writing articles, and performing various administrative duties and offices; he uses his spare time to write books. The author told *CA* he "firmly believes in the saying, 'It is harder to wear out than to rust out.'" He added that he does not plan on donating his organs and tissues anytime soon (although the card has been signed and next-of-kin notified).

Grave Words: Notifying Survivors about Sudden, Unexpected Deaths was Iverson's next book, which he has also converted to audio-visual teaching aids. Announcing the death of a loved one to next-of-kin is a daunting task that all emergency doctors must face. Despite this unavoidable duty, there has been little written about how to do that. Most training in this area takes place, *JAMA*'s Malinda H. Bell reported, "on the job without benefit of formal instruction." Hence, the generous welcome for Iserson's work, which includes almost every possible scenario that a doctor might have to face, including, wrote Bell, "death as a result of medical error." Bell ended her critique of Iserson's book by suggesting that it become required reading for all resident doctors. Carin E. Reust, for *Journal of Family Practice,* also recommended *Grave Words.* One of the aspects that Reust enjoyed was Iserson's inclusion of real life stories that "keep the reader interested." Also included in the book is a discussion of how to notify the survivors, how to approach the subject of organ donation, how to receive an autopsy permission, and how to handle a discussion of viewing the body. At the end of the book, Iserson includes a question-and-answer section that provides readers with a list of some of the most frequently asked questions. Reust concluded that "the uniqueness of this book lies in the details." Iserson appears to have thought of them all. "Death notification can and should be taught," Reust stated, "and this book provides the framework to do so."

The title of his 2002 book *Demon Doctors: Physicians As Serial Killers* is scary, but so is the possibility, Iserson told *CA.* The book "details many errors in the way we regulate physicians," Iserson said. "What is particularly interesting, however, is that despite their having the knowledge to kill, often without detection, there have been so few physician-serial killers. We must be doing something right with our selection methods for medical school. When they do become killers, they are ruthless, effective, and very scary—as this book demonstrates." Iserson recounts the details of several doctors who have been involved in murder. They include such personalities as H. H. Holmes (whose story was told in the book *Depraved* by Harold Schechter), Harold F. Shipman (who allegedly murdered more than four hundred people), and Linda Burfield Hazzard (known as the Starvation Doctor). Topics also included are the so-called medical experiments practiced by Japanese and German doctors during World War II. *Booklist*'s William Beatty christened this book "true-crime historical paydirt."

BIOGRAPHICAL AND CRITICAL SOURCES:

PERIODICALS

Archives of Pathology & Laboratory Medicine, November, 2001, Joseph Ohr, review of *Iserson's Getting into a Residency,* p. 1517.

Booklist, February 15, 2002, William Beatty, review of *Demon Doctors: Physicians As Serial Killers,* p. 976.

Choice, November, 1994, p.479.

JAMA, The Journal of the American Medical Association, April 12, 2000, Malinda H. Bell, review of *Grave Words: Notifying Survivors about Sudden, Unexpected Deaths,* p. 1888; October 10, 2001, Joseph H. Davis, review of *Death to Dust: What Happens to Dead Bodies,* p. 1767.

Journal of Family Practice, September, 2000, Carin E. Reust, review of *Grave Words,* p. 857.

*   *   *

JACKENDOFF, Ray S.
See JACKENDOFF, Ray (Saul)

JACKENDOFF, Ray (Saul) 1945-
(Ray S. Jackendoff)

PERSONAL: Born January 23, 1945, in Chicago, IL; son of Nathaniel (a professor) and Elaine (a guidance counselor; maiden name, Flanders) Jackendoff; married Hildy Dvorak, 2001; children: Amy, Beth. *Education:* Swarthmore College, B.A., 1965; Massachusetts Institute of Technology, Ph.D., 1969. *Religion:* Jewish.

ADDRESSES: Home—79 Goden St., Belmont, MA 02478-2934. *Office*—Volen Center for Complex Systems, Brandeis University, 415 South St., Waltham, MA 02454. *E-mail*—jackendoff@brandeis.edu.

CAREER: University of California, Los Angeles, lecturer in English, 1969-70; Brandeis University, Waltham, MA, assistant professor, 1971-73, associate professor, 1973-78, professor of linguistics, 1978—. Clarinet soloist with the Boston Pops Orchestra, 1980.

MEMBER: American Academy of Arts and Sciences, Linguistic Society of America, Society for Philosophy and Psychology (president, 1990-91), North East Linguistic Society.

AWARDS, HONORS: Gustave O. Arlt Award from Council of Graduate Schools, 1974, for *Semantic Interpretation in Generative Grammar;* National Endowment for the Humanities fellowship, 1978; Guggenheim fellow, 1993-94; fellow of Wissenschaftskolleg zu Berlin, 1999-2000; Fellow of American Association for the Advancement of Science, elected 1999; Jean Nicod Prize in Cognitive Philosophy, Jean Nicod Institute, 2003.

WRITINGS:

(As Ray S. Jackendoff) *Semantic Interpretation in Generative Grammar,* MIT Press (Cambridge, MA), 1972.
X Syntax: A Study of Phrase Structure, MIT Press (Cambridge, MA), 1977.
(With Fred Lerdahl) *A Generative Theory of Tonal Music,* MIT Press (Cambridge, MA), 1982.

Ray Jackendoff

Semantics and Cognition, MIT Press (Cambridge, MA), 1983.
Consciousness and the Computational Mind, MIT Press (Cambridge, MA), 1987.
Semantic Structures, MIT Press (Cambridge, MA), 1990.
Languages of the Mind: Essays on Mental Representation, MIT Press (Cambridge, MA), 1992.
Patterns in the Mind: Language and Human Nature, Basic Books (New York, NY), 1994.
The Architecture of the Language Faculty, MIT Press (Cambridge, MA), 1997.
(Editor, with Paul Bloom and Karen Wynn) *Language, Logic, and Concepts: Essays in Memory of John Macnamara,* MIT Press (Cambridge, MA), 1999.
Foundations of Language: Brain, Meaning, Grammar, Evolution, Oxford University Press (New York, NY), 2002.

Member of editorial board, *Music Perception, Cognitive Science,* and other professional journals. *A Generative Theory of Tonal Music* has been translated into German.

SIDELIGHTS: Professor of linguistics (and sometime clarinetist) Ray Jackendoff has published a number of works in his field. His 2002 study, *Foundations of Language: Brain, Meaning, Grammar, Evolution,* takes up where the studies of the famed linguist Noam Chomsky left off. Chomsky's view—that the acquisition of language was essentially separate from other human cognitive apparatus—revolutionized the science. Two generations later, Jackendoff theorized that "linguistics is critically important to the study of the mind, and that the basic ideas underlying Chomsky's approach are correct," in the words of a fellow linguist, David Adger. Writing for the *Times Literary Supplement,* Adger continued: "However, Jackendoff is more than willing to compromise about what he sees as the mistakes of theoretical linguistics; his diagnosis is that theoretical linguistics became too obsessed with syntax, thinking it could do everything for us." Indeed, Jackendoff "is not a typical Chomskyan," said Andrew Carstairs-McCarthy in the *American Scientist.* "He is keen to build bridges between research on grammar pure and simple and research that involves modeling or exploring directly what happens in the brain when language is used."

To *Science* reviewer Merrill Garrett, the author "takes a two-pronged approach. Identifying core features of grammatical theory that must be preserved, he seeks to clarify their role in the contemporary scene." Such core theories include mentalism, combinatoriality (grammar rules) and nativism, the latter of which is based on the idea that language arises "from [an] innately specified mental structure," as Garrett wrote. Jackendoff "also identifies flaws in foundational assumptions that he believes must be changed. He wants to recast the architecture of grammatical theory to achieve greater coherence within linguistics and to more effectively embrace psycholinguistics and neurolinguistics." Jackendoff's views, moreover, are not exactly new. Garrett envisioned linguists saying, "Well, this is what I've been saying for years. What's the big deal?" The difference, he said, is that the author articulates the views "in a systematic way that ties the components of formal linguistic theory to the broader issues in human cognition."

Carstairs-McCarthy found *Foundations of Language* accessible to readers with a basic foundation in linguistics. "Readers with no such training but some knowledge of cognitive science or psychology may find it harder going but still rewarding." The reviewer felt Jackendoff's "breadth of knowledge and soundness of judgment, along with just the right amount of adventurousness, make for a book that deserves to be read and reread by anyone seriously interested in the

state of the art of research on language." Adger wondered if Jackendoff's book "will achieve its goal." He thought linguists "will perhaps be unhappy with the diagnosis," and added his view that "Jackendoff's proposals are not worked out in detail, and those of a truly syntactocentric persuasion will probably be irritated at the lack of attention to work in this paradigm over the past ten years." Still, Adger decided that *Foundations of Language* had value in igniting dialogue on the topic: "Maybe we [linguists] could meet at the pub a little more often; and we could do worse than talk about this book when we get there."

BIOGRAPHICAL AND CRITICAL SOURCES:

PERIODICALS

American Scientist, July, 1995, review of *Patterns in the Mind: Language and Human Nature,* p. 378; July-August, 2002, Andrew Carstairs-McCarthy, "Syntax and Semantics," p. 376.

Booklist, December 15, 1993, review of *Patterns in the Mind,* p. 728.

Canadian Philosophical Reviews, February, 1989, review of *Consciousness and the Computational Mind,* p. 53.

Choice, February, 1988, review of *Consciousness and the Computational Mind,* p. 973; March, 1993, review of *Languages of the Mind: Essays on Mental Representation,* p. 1248; July, 1994, review of *Patterns in the Mind,* p. 1743.

Contemporary Psychology, December, 1984, review of *Semantics and Cognition,* p. 949; January, 1989, review of *Consciousness and the Computational Mind,* p. 15; April, 2001, review of *Language, Logic, and Concepts: Essays in Memory of John Macnamara,* p. 200.

Journal of Linguistics, March, 1999, Peter Culicover, review of *The Architecture of the Language Faculty,* p. 137.

Kirkus Reviews, November 15, 1993, review of *Patterns in the Mind,* p. 1439.

Language, December, 1998, Jean Aitchison, review of *The Architecture of the Language Faculty,* p. 850.

Language in Society, September, 1986, review of *Semantics and Cognition,* p. 441.

Library Journal, January, 1994, review of *Patterns in the Mind,* p. 144; February 15, 2002, Marianne Orme, review of *Foundations of Language: Brain, Meaning, Grammar, Evolution,* p. 143.

London Review of Books, June 23, 1994, review of *Patterns in the Mind,* p. 10.

Los Angeles Times Book Review, March 6, 1994, review of *Patterns in the Mind,* p. 3.

Natural History, October, 1994, review of *Patterns in the Mind,* p. 70.

New Scientist, March 16, 2002, Eric Haeberli, "What's That You Said?," p. 53.

Philosophical Review, January, 1985, review of *Semantics and Cognition,* p. 111.

Quarterly Review of Biology, March, 1999, Jeffrey Cynx, review of *The Architecture of the Language Faculty,* p. 117.

Review of Metaphysics, September, 1988, review of *Consciousness and the Computational Mind,* p. 147.

Science, March 25, 1988, review of *Consciousness and the Computational Mind,* p. 1546; June 28, 2002, Merrill Garrett, "New Vines on Old Roots," p. 2341.

Science News, March 30, 2002, review of *Foundations of Language,* p. 207.

SciTech Book News, January, 1988, review of *Consciousness and the Computational Mind,* p. 2; January, 1993, review of *Languages of the Mind,* p. 1.

Times Higher Education Supplement, February 15, 2002, Roy Harris, "Looking in for the Meaning Without," p. 27.

Times Literary Supplement, October 2, 1992, review of *Semantic Structures,* p. 24; June 21, 2002, David Adger, "Time to Talk Things Over?," p. 36.

University Press Book News, June, 1991, review of *Semantic Structures,* p. 27.

Washington Post Book World, July 24, 1994, review of *Patterns in the Mind,* p. 8.

*   *   *

JACKSON, J. P.
See ATKINS, (Arthur) Harold (Foweraker)

*   *   *

JACOBSON, Michael F. 1943-

PERSONAL: Born July 29, 1943, in Chicago, IL; son of Larry and Janet (Siegel) Jacobson. *Education:* University of Chicago, B.A., 1965; graduate study at University of California—San Diego, 1965-67; Massachusetts Institute of Technology, Ph.D., 1969.

ADDRESSES: Office—Center for Science in the Public Interest, 1501 16th St. NW, Washington, DC 20036.

CAREER: Consumer advocate and writer. Research associate, Salk Institute for Biological Studies, 1970-71; Center for the Study of Responsive Law, Washington, DC, technical consultant, 1970-71; Center for Science in the Public Interest, Washington, DC, co-director, 1971-77, executive director, 1977—; Center for the Study of Commercialism, founder, 1990.

WRITINGS:

Eater's Digest: The Consumer's Factbook of Food Additives, 1972, revised and updated as *The Complete Eater's Digest and Nutrition Scoreboard,* Anchor Press/Doubleday (Garden City, NY), 1985.

How Sodium Nitrite Can Affect Your Health, Center for Science in the Public Interest (Washington, DC), 1973.

(With Sandy Kageyama) *Scorecard for Better Eating,* Center for Science in the Public Interest (Washington, DC), 1973.

Nutrition Scoreboard, Avon (New York, NY), 1975.

(Editor, with Catherine Lerza) *Food for People, Not for Profit,* Ballantine (New York, NY), 1975.

Chemical Additives in Booze, Center for Science in the Public Interest (Washington, DC), 1982.

(With George Hacker and Robert Atkins) *The Booze Merchants,* Center for Science in the Public Interest (Washington, DC), 1983.

Salt, the Brand Name Guide to Sodium Content, Workman (New York, NY), 1983.

(With Sarah Fritschner) *The Fast-Food Guide: What's Good, What's Bad, and How to Tell the Difference,* Workman (New York, NY), 1986, revised as *The Completely Revised and Updated Fast-Food Guide: What's Good, What's Bad, and How to Tell the Difference,* 1991.

(With Paula Klevan Zeller) *Eat, Think, and Be Healthy!: Creative Nutrition Activities for Children,* Center for Science in the Public Interest (Washington, DC), 1987.

(With Charles P. Mitchell) *Tainted Booze: The Consumer's Guide to Urethane in Alcoholic Beverages,* Center for Science in the Public Interest (Washington, DC), 1988.

(With Lisa Y. Lefferts and Anne Witte Garland)) *Safe Food: Eating Wisely in a Risky World,* Living Planet Press (Los Angeles, CA), 1991.

(With Laura Hill) *Kitchen Fun for Kids: Healthy Recipes and Nutrition Facts for 7-to-12- Year-Old Cooks,* Henry Holt (New York, NY), 1991.

(With Bruce Maxwell) *What Are We Feeding Our Kids?,* Workman (New York, NY), 1994.

(With Laurie Ann Mazur) *Marketing Madness: A Survival Guide for a Consumer Society,* Westview Press (Boulder, CO), 1995.

Restaurant Confidential: The Shocking Truth about What You're Really Eating when You're Eating Out, Workman (New York, NY), 2002.

Contributor to *Time-Life Science Annual.* Contributor of about three dozen articles to magazines, including *Progressive, Smithsonian, Instructor,* and *Newsday,* and to newspapers.

SIDELIGHTS: Michael F. Jacobson has spent most of his professional career as director of the Center for Science in the Public Interest, a nonprofit organization whose primary goal is to ensure the safety and nutritional quality of the food supply in the United States. Toward this goal, Jacobson has written or co-authored several books.

Kitchen Fun for Kids: Healthy Recipes and Nutrition Facts for 7-to-12-Year-Old Cooks, promotes a better understanding of nutrition on a child's level. The recipes listed in this collection lean toward low-fat and low-sugar recipes that children can put together themselves. Besides providing easy-to-prepare recipes, the book also explains various aspects of food and why the body needs them. For instance, Jacobson defines words such as carbohydrates, protein, vitamins, and minerals. The book also guides children through basic kitchen techniques, such as dicing vegetables and cracking eggs.

Children are not the only audience on which Jacobson is focusing his attention. He most often writes to adults about such topics as salt intake, the consumption of alcohol, and the problems surrounding chemical additives in the food supply. He also writes about food in general, as in his book *Safe Food: Eating Wisely in a Risky World.* In this book, Jacobson argues that consumers need to be aware of the ingredients present in the food that they buy; and he doesn't just mean the additives. He's also referring to the pesticides and other drug residues that agricultural companies use. Jacobson's book presents the risks, but he also offers

suggestions on how to improve the food that people eat, how to prepare food to avoid, or at least decrease, the risk of food-born diseases. Although Virginia N. Hillers, writing for the *Journal of the American Dietetic Association,* thought that Jacobson and his coauthors were possibly over-reacting in their suggestions, she did conclude that people "should be grateful to the authors for presenting the entire gamut of food safety issues in one book." On the other hand, Kirk Johnson, for *East West Natural Health,* referred to *Safe Food* as "a beacon of hope" in the "morass" that has come to define the current agricultural practices in this country. Johnson went on to call *Safe Food* "a practical strategy" for anyone who picks up this book and follows the advice that Jacobson offers.

With the 1995 publication of *Marketing Madness: A Survival Guide for a Consumer Society,* Jacobson moves away from food and focuses on the social effects of what Jonathan Rowe, for the *Washington Monthly,* referred to as the "$150 billion" that the "corporate sector in America" spends on advertising, almost as much money "as the nation spends on higher education." Jacobson points out that it's not just television commercials that bombard the average American citizen everyday but also that teenagers are targeted at school, at shopping malls, and at the movies. The poorer sections of large cities are also a favorite place to put up large billboards that push cigarettes and alcohol. Stories in popular magazines are also often influenced by the magazines' advertisers, who threaten to pull their ads if a particular article makes a negative reference to one of their products. "In a just world," wrote Rowe, Jacobson's book "would find its way into the nation's classrooms," suggesting that *Marketing Madness* should become a part of the school curriculum.

Jacobson took on the restaurant business with his 2002 book *Restaurant Confidential.* Jacobson, who admits that he likes eating out, offers tips on how to do so and stay healthy. He explains how many restaurants offer foods laden with fat, which not only adds calories but also adds cholesterol to one's diet. The book offers a so-called Restaurant Hall of Shame in which Jacobson lists some of the most popular restaurants and their foods that have the highest counts of calories and fat. In an article written for *Chain Leader,* a reviewer stated that Jacobson and his coauthor claim that the restaurant "industry's high-calorie and high-fat fare may be contributing to obesity and other diet-related diseases."

BIOGRAPHICAL AND CRITICAL SOURCES:

PERIODICALS

Chain Leader, July, 2002, review of *Restaurant Confidential,* p. 2.

East West Natural Health, March-April 1992, Kirk Johnson, review of *Safe Food: Eating Wisely in a Risky World,* p. 35.

Environmental Nutrition, April, 1992, review of *Kitchen Fun for Kids,* p. 3.

Journal of the American Dietetic Association, January, 1992, Virginia N. Hillers, review of *Safe Food,* p. 132.

Library Journal, July, 1991, Loraine F. Sweetland, review of *Safe Food,* p. 126; April 1, 1995, Edward Buller, review of *Marketing Madness: A Survival Guide for a Consumer Society,* pp. 105-106.

New York Times, July 10, 1991, Marian Burros, review of *Safe Food,* p. B6.

Publishers Weekly, February 27, 1995, review of *Marketing Madness,* p. 100; January 28, 2002, "How to Bypass the Bypass," review of *Restaurant Confidential,* p. 255; April 15, 2002, review of *Restaurant Confidential,* pp. 57-58.

School Library Journal, October, 1991, Joyce Adams Burner, review of *Kitchen Fun for Kids,* pp. 138-139.

Washington Monthly, June, 1995, Jonathan Rowe, review of *Marketing Madness,* pp. 52-53.*

*   *   *

JENNINGS, Elizabeth (Joan) 1926-2001

PERSONAL: Born July 18, 1926, in Boston, Lincolnshire, England; died, October 26, 2001; daughter of Henry Cecil Jennings (a physician). *Education:* St. Anne's College, Oxford, M.A. (with honors). *Religion:* Roman Catholic. *Hobbies and other interests:* Travel, art, theater, conversation.

CAREER: Oxford City Library, Oxford, England, assistant, 1950-58; Chatto & Windus (publishing firm), London, England, reader, 1958-60; poet and freelance writer, beginning 1961. Guildersleeve Lecturer, Barnard College, Columbia University, 1974.

MEMBER: Society of Authors.

AWARDS, HONORS: Arts Council award, 1953, for *Poems;* Somerset Maugham Award, 1956, for *A Way of Looking;* Arts Council bursary, 1965 and 1968; Richard Hillary Memorial Prize, 1966, for *The Mind Has Mountains;* Arts Council grant, 1972; W. H. Smith award, 1987, for *Collected Poems, 1953-86;* C.B.E.

WRITINGS:

Poems, Fantasy Press (Swinford, England), 1953.

A Way of Looking: Poems, Deutsch (London, England), 1955, Rinehart (New York, NY), 1956.

(Editor, with Dannie Abse and Stephen Spender) *New Poems 1956: A PEN Anthology,* M. Joseph (London, England), 1956.

A Child and the Seashell, Feathered Serpent Press, 1957.

(Editor) *The Batsford Book of Children's Verse,* Batsford (London, England), 1958.

A Sense of the World: Poems, Deutsch (London, England), 1958, Rinehart (New York, NY), 1959.

Let's Have Some Poetry! (nonfiction), Museum Press (London, England), 1960.

Song for a Birth or a Death, and Other Poems, Deutsch (London, England), 1961, Dufour (New York, NY), 1962.

(Editor) *An Anthology of Modern Verse, 1940-1960,* Methuen (London, England), 1961.

Every Changing Shape, Deutsch (London, England), 1961.

Poetry Today, Longmans, Green (London, England), 1961.

(Translator) *The Sonnets of Michelangelo,* Folio Society, 1961, revised edition, Allison & Busby (London, England), 1969, Doubleday (New York, NY), 1970.

(With Lawrence Durrell and R. S. Thomas) *Penguin Modern Poets I,* Penguin (New York, NY), 1962.

Recoveries: Poems, Dufour (New York, NY), 1964.

Frost, Oliver & Boyd (London, England), 1964, Barnes & Noble (New York, NY), 1965.

Christian Poetry, Hawthorn (New York, NY), 1965, published as *Christianity and Poetry,* Burns & Oates (London, England), 1965.

The Mind Has Mountains, St. Martin's Press (New York, NY), 1966.

The Secret Brother and Other Poems for Children, St. Martin's Press (New York, NY), 1966.

Collected Poems, 1967, Dufour (New York, NY), 1967.

The Animals' Arrival, Dufour (New York, NY), 1969.

Lucidities, Macmillan (New York, NY), 1970.

(Editor) *A Choice of Christina Rossetti's Verse,* Faber (London, England), 1970.

Hurt, Poem-of-the-Month Club, 1970.

(With others) *Folio,* Sceptre Press (London, England), 1971.

Relationships, Macmillan (New York, NY), 1972.

Growing-Points: New Poems, Carcanet Press (Manchester, England), 1975.

Seven Men of Vision: An Appreciation (literary criticism), Harper (New York, NY), 1977.

Consequently I Rejoice (poems), Carcanet Press (Manchester, England), 1977.

After the Ark (children's poems), Oxford University Press (New York, NY), 1978.

Winter Wind (poems), Janus Press (Newark, VT), 1979.

A Dream of Spring (poems), Celandine, 1980.

Selected Poems, Carcanet Press (Manchester, England), 1980.

Moments of Grace (poems), Carcanet Press (Manchester, England), 1980.

Italian Light and Other Poems, illustrated by Gerald Woods, Snake River Press (Eastbourne, Sussex, England), 1981.

(Editor) *The Batsford Book of Religious Verse,* Batsford (London, England), 1981.

Celebrations and Elegies (poems), Carcanet New Press (Manchester, England), 1982.

(Editor) *In Praise of Our Lady,* Batsford (London, England), 1982.

Extending the Territory (poems), Carcanet Press (Manchester, England), 1985.

(With others) *Bloodaxe Book of Contemporary Women Poets,* Bloodaxe Books (Highgreen, England), 1985.

In Shakespeare's Company: Poems, Celandine (Shipston-on-Stour, Warwickshire, England), 1985.

(With others) *Poets in Hand: A Puffin Quintet,* Penguin (New York, NY), 1985.

Collected Poems, 1953-1985, Carcanet Press (Manchester, England), 1986.

Tributes (poems), Carcanet (Manchester, England), 1989.

Times and Seasons (poems), Carcanet (Manchester, England), 1993.

Familiar Spirits (poems), Carcanet (Manchester, England), 1995.

(Compiler) *A Poet's Choice,* Carcanet (Manchester, England), 1996.

In the Meantime, Carcanet (Manchester, England), 1996.

A Spell of Words: Selected Poems for Children, Macmillan (London, England), 1997.

Praises, Carcanet (Manchester, England), 1998.

Timely Issues, Carcanet (Manchester, England), 2001.

Contributor of poems and articles to periodicals, including *Agenda, London Magazine, Poetry Review, New Statesman, New Yorker, Scotsman, Spectator, Vogue,* and *Encounter.*

Jennings's manuscripts are in the collections of the Oxford City Library and the University of Washington, Seattle, and Georgetown University Library, Washington, DC.

SIDELIGHTS: Poet Elizabeth Jennings established her literary reputation during the 1950s as part of The Movement, a group of "angry young men" including such writers as Kingsley Amis, Thom Gunn, and Philip Larkin, who used literature as a means of social protest. Jennings "brought the 'sensitive' dimension to the no-nonsense Movement," Alan Brownjohn wrote in the *New Statesman.* "Her work was . . . memorable in its quiet, unstrained way." Since then, Brownjohn noted, Jennings "impressively increased the scope and richness, and the technical variety and command, of her writing."

Jennings published poems in the *Spectator, Poetry Review,* and the *New Statesman* before Oscar Mellor, editor of the Fantasy Press Poetry Series, accepted her first book-length collection. Critical reception for the volume was very positive; it won the Arts Council Prize for a First Book of Poems. Jennings explained in *Contemporary Authors Autobiography Series (CAAS),* "The poems I was writing at this time still showed some influence of W. H. Auden and Robert Graves but there was a clarity, a kind of lyrical innocence which I still find valid today. I never caught Auden's own voice, luckily, but I learned from him something that has proved invaluable to me ever since, even when I have not been able by any means always to follow his example; it is to try to find the precise but unexpected adjective." Her second book, *A Way of Looking,* received mixed reviews, but more important to the poet was the fact that she subsequently won the Somerset Maugham Award for it in 1956. The award requires the winner to spend three months in a foreign country to observe the customs of people in another culture. Jennings chose to go to Italy. "I am quite sure that I owe the happiest and most worthwhile time of my life to this award and I shall always be grateful to Somerset Maugham for his generosity," she wrote in her autobiographical essay.

In 1966, Jennings published *The Mind Has Mountains,* a collection of poems written during her recovery from a mental breakdown. Her book's title is derived from a piece by the British poet, Gerard Manley Hopkins. In *Poetry Review,* Leonard Clark mentioned that he found this work to be "unusual and disturbing. . . . and painful to read" because the author did not dwell in self-pity, but rather accepted her fate with an attitude of resignation. He felt, however, that these poems probably constitute "a state in [her] development."

Jennings's *Collected Poems* appeared a year after *The Mind Has Mountains.* "Her best poems are . . . exploratory of relationships," wrote Margaret Byers in *British Poetry since 1960: A Critical Survey.* Byers noted that in some of the later poems, Jennings is "rediscovering meaning in apparently overused words, finding a linguistic spareness and clarity which render the poems direct and to the heart." Terry Eagleton of *Strand Magazine* praised the poet for her "serious, uncompromising honesty."

Jennings increasingly turned to religious themes in her verse; her "best and natural state is contemplation, and the poems tend to be about the debits and credits of the contemplative attitude," P. N. Furbank pointed out in a *Listener* review of *Recoveries.* "Jennings's God is attractive because one senses that He is the sort of humanist god who reads His horoscope," remarked Will Eaves in a *Times Literary Supplement* review of *Times and Seasons.* In a review of *Moments of Grace* for the *Listener,* Dick Davis found that Jennings's title refers to the "intimations of a peace glimpsed beyond the fret and frustration of daily existence." "The poet herself," Davis added, "seems suspended" between the natural and spiritual worlds.

Andrew Motion of the *New Statesman* observed that "although Jennings has always produced excellently crafted poems, she has also tended to reduce their

lyric force by including ruminatively philosophical material," while a *Books and Bookmen* reviewer of *Selected Poems* praised Jennings's attempt to "balance the mental and emotional demands of the priest and poet." And in the *Spectator,* Emma Fisher asserted that Jennings is "looking earnestly" for moments of grace, "carefully examining pieces of life as if waiting for them to break open in revelations." In addition to the vein of religious feeling that is clearly evident in much of her work, Jennings often wrote about personal relationships and family dynamics, such as in her collection *Familiar Spirits.*

Some of Jennings's poetry was published in the 1985 anthology titled *Bloodaxe Book of Contemporary Women Poets.* The volume includes a variety of her work such as "A Chorus," "A Letter to Peter Levi," "Star Midnight," and "Instinct for Seasons." In an *English Review* article, Gerry Fenge noted that "a key to much of Jennings's work . . . [is] vulnerability, which can at times (but only at times) be overcome by a sort of metaphysical exuberance." He remarked that Jennings's contributions move between "fragility [and] something like a juggler's jauntiness." Yet, as the critic noted, this is not unusual, for "journeys of the self are never straightforward."

Jennings's next book, *Extending the Territory,* is a work that contains many poems referring to her childhood. "She is one of the few living poets one could not do without," said Peter Levi in his *Spectator* review which was cited on the Carcanet Press Web site. Levi commended Jennings's "disarming authenticity and modesty and a certain sense of inward fire." He felt that he had discovered her work anew through *Extending the Territory,* even though he had been a devoted reader of her work for thirty years. Levi remarked: "She conveys a sense of something hidden but powerfully alive in her; she may be the last poet of what used to be called the soul."

Timely Issues, published in 2001 prior to Jennings's death, contains "images of illness, old age, hospitalization and compassion for the aged," according to M. C. Caseley's article in *Stride Magazine* online. Caseley noted the Christian beliefs that underlie much of Jennings's language and the archetypal images from which she borrows. The critic concluded: "This collection . . . finds Jennings exploring themes evident throughout much of her work, but her growing awareness of death and her own calm gaze at mortality make this . . . [an] affecting collection."

BIOGRAPHICAL AND CRITICAL SOURCES:

BOOKS

Contemporary Authors Autobiography Series, Volume 5, Gale (Detroit, MI), 1987.

Contemporary Literary Criticism, Gale (Detroit, MI), Volume 5, 1976, Volume 14, 1980.

Contemporary Poets, 6th edition, St. James Press (Detroit, MI), 1996.

Dictionary of Literary Biography, Volume 27: *Poets of Great Britain and Ireland, 1945-1960,* Gale (Detroit, MI), 1984.

Gramang, Gerlinde, *Elizabeth Jennings: An Appraisal of Her Life As a Poet, Her Approach to Her Work, and a Selection of the Major Themes of Her Poetry,* Edwin Mellen Press (Lewiston, NY), 1995.

Schmidt, Michael, and Grevel Lindop, editors, *British Poetry since 1960,* Carcanet Press (Manchester, England), 1972.

PERIODICALS

Books and Bookmen, December, 1972; February, 1980.

Books for Keeps, July, 1998, review of *A Spell of Words,* p. 7.

English Review, September, 2000, Gerry Fenge, review of *Bloodaxe Book of Contemporary Women Poets,* p. 26.

Listener, July 23, 1964; January 31, 1980.

New Statesman, October 13, 1967; May 30, 1975; November 2, 1979.

Poetry, March, 1977.

Poetry Review, spring, 1967, Leonard Clark, review of *The Mind Has Mountains,* p. 52.

Spectator, December 1, 1979; October 19, 1995, Peter Levi, review of *Extending the Territory.*

Strand Magazine, number 3, 1968, Terry Eagleton, review of *Collected Poems,* p. 69.

TES Primary, September 24, 1999, review of *A Spell of Words,* p. 49.

Times (London, England), January 16, 1986; February 11, 1989.

Times Educational Supplement, January 22, 1999, review of *Praises,* p. 13.

Times Literary Supplement, December 30, 1977; February 1, 1980; July 16, 1982; May 30, 1986; November 28, 1986; May 5, 1989; January 15, 1993, p. 23; May 5, 1995, p. 29.

ONLINE

Carcanet Press, http://www.carcanet.co.uk/ (August 18, 2003).

Stride Magazine, http://www.stridemag.pwp.blue onder.co.uk/ (August 18, 2003), M. C. Caseley, review of *Timely Issues.*

OBITUARIES:

PERIODICALS

Daily Telegraph (London, England), October 30, 2001, p. 1.

Guardian (Manchester, England), October 31, 2001, p. 22.

Independent (London, England), October 31, 2001, p. 6.

Times (London, England), October 31, 2001, p. 19.*

*   *   *

JENNINGS, Maureen

PERSONAL: Born in Birmingham, England; immigrated to Canada; married. *Education:* University of Windsor, B.A.; University of Toronto, M.A.

ADDRESSES: Home—Canada. *Agent*—c/o Author Mail, St. Martin's Press, 175 Fifth Ave., New York, NY 10010. *E-mail*—jenford@sympatico.ca.

CAREER: Psychotherapist, novelist, and playwright. Ryerson Polytechnical Institute, Ontario, Canada, teacher of English, 1964-72; psychotherapist in private practice, beginning 1972.

AWARDS, HONORS: Heritage Toronto Certificate of Commendation, Anthony Award nomination, and Arthur Ellis Award nomination, all 1998, all for *Except the Dying;* Best Novel designation, *Drood Review of Mystery,* 2001, for *Poor Tom Is Cold.*

WRITINGS:

NOVELS; "WILLIAM MURDOCH" SERIES

Except the Dying, St. Martin's Press (New York, NY), 1997.

Under the Dragon's Tail, St. Martin's Press (New York, NY), 1998.

Poor Tom Is Cold, St. Martin's Minotaur (New York, NY) 2001.

Let Loose the Dogs, St. Martin's Press (New York, NY), 2003.

PLAYS

The Black Ace, produced in North York, England, 1990.

No Traveler Returns, produced 1992.

OTHER

The Map of Your Mind: Journey into Creative Expression, McClellan & Stewart (Toronto, Ontario, Canada), 2001.

ADAPTATIONS: Film rights for the "William Murdoch" series were acquired by Shaftesbury Films. The "Murdoch Mysteries" television series premiered on Bravo in 2004.

WORK IN PROGRESS: The fifth novel in the "William Murdoch" series, *Night's Child,* and the novel *Does Your Mother Know?,* both for St. Martin's Press.

SIDELIGHTS: Mystery writer Maureen Jennings chronicles the cases of detective William Murdoch, who serves with the Toronto Police Department at the end of the nineteenth century. In these historical mysteries "Jennings makes us forget we're reading something set more than a century ago; she evokes the past so vividly it almost instantly feels like the present," according to David Pitt in *Booklist.*

Jennings's first novel, *Except the Dying,* is set in Toronto in 1895 and tells of the murder of a young French-Canadian maid who worked for a wealthy family. Investigating the crime is William Murdoch, a detective who has spent the past two years mourning the death of his fiancee. In the course of his work, Murdoch encounters a host of characters—and suspects—including the Rhodes family, who employed the victim, and local prostitutes Alice Black and Ettie Watson. "Everybody is lying or hiding something or both, and the best witnesses are two prostitutes who

don't want to talk to the police," according to Amy Rabinovitz in the *Houston Chronicle.* "At one time or another, the reader can place the guilt on any of the characters."

Except the Dying was well received. More than one critic pointed out that Murdoch's past gives him a depth of character beyond that of many fictional sleuths, while others praised the author's powers of description. "In a bravura piece of writing," reported a writer for *Publishers Weekly,* "Jennings describes the annual newsboys' meeting of scruffy, destitute youngsters, cynical and amoral beyond their years." Rex Klett in his review for *Library Journal* praised the novel's "finely flavored plot, credible characters, and detailed atmosphere." Marilyn Stasio hailed *Except the Dying* in the *New York Times Book Review* as "a first novel enriched by the vividness of its period settings and animated by the lifelike characters caught up in its broad social sweep."

Jennings followed *Except the Dying* with *Under the Dragon's Tail,* another story of murder in nineteenth-century Toronto. The victim, midwife Dolly Shaw, is a contemptible character by any definition: a drunk and a blackmailer. Again, detective Murdoch is on the case, still grieving over the death of his fiancee, and again Jennings explores the stratifications of Canadian society through her portrayals of characters of varying social classes. A critic for *Publishers Weekly* commented that "late-nineteenth-century Toronto comes startlingly alive in Jennings's second gripping tale."

In *Poor Tom Is Cold* Murdoch finds a fellow officer shot dead, apparently a suicide. There is a suicide note and even a woman who claims to be the lover who jilted him. But the more Murdoch investigates, the more it looks like murder. Meanwhile, the children of a wealthy Toronto man seem too intent on keeping their future inheritance out of the hands of their father's new, much-younger wife. A *Publishers Weekly* reviewer called *Poor Tom Is Cold* "a satisfying mystery perfectly wedded to its evocative setting," while Pam Johnson in *School Library Journal* found that "Jennings weaves an intriguing plot through all types of obstacles, and concludes with a great burst of action." Klett concluded in *Booklist* that "contemporary social, religious, and sexual mores frame a strong plot line."

In *Let Loose the Dogs,* Murdoch is reunited with his drunken father, whose violent behavior prompted Murdoch and his sister to run away from home years before. Henry Murdoch is now convicted of murder and sentenced to be hanged. When he insists that he is innocent of the crime, Murdoch interviews with witnesses to see if he can determine the truth for himself. His efforts pit him against a police force and public who are convinced that the right man is behind bars. "Murdoch will do his duty by this old degenerate, but it will cost him," Stasio wrote. "Jennings is too tough and honest a writer to let anyone off her moral hook, even her hero." A critic for *Kirkus Reviews* found the novel to be "the most generously plotted of Murdoch's four cases."

BIOGRAPHICAL AND CRITICAL SOURCES:

PERIODICALS

Booklist, December 1, 2000, David Pitt, review of *Poor Tom Is Cold,* p. 696.
Houston Chronicle, Amy Rabinovitz, "Rookie's Mystery a Chiller," April 5, 1998, p. 25.
Kirkus Reviews, November 1, 2002, review of *Let Loose the Dogs,* p. 1572.
Library Journal, November 1, 1997, Rex Klett, review of *Except the Dying,* p. 120; January 1, 2001, Rex Klett, review of *Poor Tom Is Cold,* p. 161.
New York Times Book Review, December 14, 1997, review of *Except the Dying,* p. 30; January 11, 2003, Marilyn Stasio, review of *Let Loose the Dogs.*
Publishers Weekly, September 22, 1997, review of *Except the Dying,* p. 75; August 24, 1998, review of *Under the Dragon's Tail,* p. 52; November 27, 2000, review of *Poor Tom Is Cold,* p. 57.
School Library Journal, July, 2001, Pam Johnson, review of *Poor Tom Is Cold,* p. 135.

ONLINE

Crime Writers of Canada Web site, http://www.crime writerscanada.com/ (November 14, 2003).
Maureen Jennings Web site, http://www.maureen jennings.com/ (November 14, 2003).
Writers Union of Canada Web site, http://www.writers union.ca/ (November 14, 2003).*

*   *   *

JENSEN, Joan M(aria) 1934-

PERSONAL: Born December 9, 1934, in St. Paul, MN; daughter of Charles J. (an army officer, landscape architect, and salesperson) and Theresa C. (a homemaker; maiden name, Schopp) Tinucci. *Education:*

University of California—Los Angeles, B.A., 1957, M.A., 1959, Ph.D., 1962; New Mexico State University, M.A., 1997.

ADDRESSES: Office—Department of History, P.O. Box 3H, New Mexico State University, Las Cruces, NM 88003. *E-mail*—jjensen@nmsu.edu.

CAREER: U.S. International University, San Diego, CA, 1962-71, began as assistant professor, 1962-67, associate professor of history, 1967-71; New Mexico State University, Las Cruces, assistant professor, 1976-78, associate professor, 1978-82, professor of history, 1982-93, professor emerita, 1994—, director of women's studies program, 1989-92. Visiting assistant professor at Arizona State University, 1974-75; visiting lecturer at University of California—Los Angeles, 1975-76; visiting professor at University of Wisconsin—Madison, 1987; senior Fulbright professor at University of Bremen, 1988, and Lady Shri Ram College, Delhi, India, 1992; lecture tour of India, U.S. Information Agency, 1994.

MEMBER: American Historical Association (Pacific Coast branch: president-elect, 1996), Organization of American Historians (executive board, 1988-91), Western Historical Association, Coordinating Committee of Women in the Historical Profession, Agricultural History Society (vice-president and president, 1991-93), Statue of Liberty-Ellis Island Foundation.

AWARDS, HONORS: Zia Award, New Mexico Presswomen, 1986, and Governor's Award for Historic Preservation, 1987, both for *New Mexico Women: Intercultural Perspectives;* Sierra Prize, Western Association of Women Historians, 1987, and E. Harold Hugo Memorial Book Prize, Old Sturbridge Village Research Library Society, 1988, both for *Loosening the Bonds: Mid-Atlantic Farm Women, 1750-1850.*

WRITINGS:

The Price of Vigilance, Rand McNally (Chicago, IL), 1968.
Military Surveillance of Civilians in America, General Learning Press (Morristown, NJ), 1974.
(Editor) *With These Hands: Women Working on the Land,* Feminist Press/McGraw (Old Westbury, NY), 1981.

Teaching Guide for With These Hands, Feminist Press/ McGraw (Old Westbury, NY), 1981.

(Editor, with Lois Scharf) *Decades of Discontent: The Women's Movement, 1920-1940,* Greenwood Press (Westport, CT), 1982.

(Editor, with Sue Davidson) *A Needle, A Bobbin, A Strike: Women Needleworkers in America,* Temple University Press (Philadelphia, PA), 1984.

(Editor, with Darlis A. Miller) *New Mexico Women: Intercultural Perspectives,* University of New Mexico Press (Albuquerque, NM), 1986.

Loosening the Bonds: Mid-Atlantic Farm Women, 1750-1850, Yale University Press (New Haven, CT), 1986.

(With Gloria Ricci Lothrop) *California Women: A History,* Boyd & Fraser (San Francisco, CA), 1987.

Passage From India: Asian Indian Immigrants in North America, Yale University Press (New Haven, CT), 1988.

Promise to the Land: Essays on Rural Women, University of New Mexico Press (Albuquerque, NM), 1991.

Army Surveillance in America, 1775-1980, Yale University Press (New Haven, CT), 1991.

One Foot on the Rockies: Women and Creativity in the Modern American West, University of New Mexico Press (Albuquerque, NM), 1995.

Contributor to various history journals. Also contributor to history books, including *Labor in the West,* edited by Hugh Lovin, Sunflower University Press, 1987, and *Essays in Twentieth-Century New Mexico History,* edited by Judith Boyce DeMark, University of New Mexico Press (Albuquerque, NM), 1994. Editorial board, *Pacific Historical Review,* 1982-95. Guest coeditor of *Frontiers* and *Agricultural History.*

SIDELIGHTS: Joan M. Jensen, a professor emerita of New Mexico State University, has long had an interest in history and women's studies and her books reflect her predilection for these topics.

With These Hands documents the lives of women who worked America's farmland from the early nineteenth century almost to the present day. Jensen collected letters, diaries, and oral histories, then supplemented the original documents with songs and tales about America's women. The author's careful choice of subject matter and juxtaposition of contrasting perspectives provides the reader with a sense of continuity

that critics found to be sensitive and touching. Carole Bovoso wrote in the *Village Voice:* "I was particularly moved by a Norwegian farm woman's account of the massacre of her family in Minnesota. . . . This is particularly heartbreaking next to . . . a Cheyenne woman's description of her people's doomed last attempt to re-establish their roots in Montana after the battle of Little Bighorn."

Jensen begins her history with the earliest American women farmers, the native Americans and the pioneer women who pushed America's boundaries westward. In *With These Hands* the accounts of enslaved black women are placed next to the letters of white women who lived in isolated parts of the American South. Later in the book, the author includes more recent documents by immigrant farm workers from Puerto Rico and Mexico. Thus the work reflects women's attitudes over the years to such male-dominated issues as agrarian reform, organized protest, and the plight of the migrant worker. Bovoso reflected: "There is so much information here that . . . many books ought to be culled from this one." The critic felt that "the richness, the spirituality inherent in its pages," reflects a universal story and a sense that the pioneer spirit of America's women has not diminished over the years.

In 1984, Jensen and Sue Davidson edited *A Needle, A Bobbin, A Strike: Women Needleworkers in America,* a collection of essays that follow the evolution of needlework labor in the United States during the nineteenth and twentieth centuries. This work documents the intensive labor and long hours involved in the needlework industry, and the accompanying employer exploitation, workers' protests, strikes, and eventual unionization of the sewing trades. The Temple University Press Web site cited a *Library Journal* critic who felt that "The contributors have added new dimensions" that will broaden the reader's understanding of the complex interweaving of cultural, economic and technological factors in the needlework industry.

Loosening the Bonds: Mid-Atlantic Farm Women, 1750-1850 details the lives of poor farm women living in the Philadelphia area during the century before the Civil War. Jensen utilized a wide range of source material for this book: farm almanacs, property inventories, census lists, and the journals of doctors and midwives. She also presents the thoughts and words of the women of that period and examines the Quaker Movement and its effect upon mid-Atlantic culture. *Loosen-*

ing the Bonds was highly regarded by many reviewers and *Yale University Press* called the book "a major contribution to women's history."

Her next work, *Army Surveillance in America, 1775-1980,* is an in-depth look at U.S. military surveillance, from the betrayal of West Point by Benedict Arnold to the government's close scrutiny of Vietnam War protestors and its violent reaction to them.

Jensen turned her attention to women artists in her book, *One Foot on the Rockies: Women and Creativity in the Modern American West.* In this work, she explores the lives and work of painters, writers, craftsmen, photographers and dancers living in the West, including Georgia O'Keeffe, Joseppa Dick (a Pomo basket maker), Ntozake Shange and Isadora Duncan. "A moving critical study. . . . [filled with] concise and compelling portrayals," wrote a reviewer for the *Books Under Review* Web site.

Jensen explained her view of the historian's role in contemporary American society in an interview with Roger Adelson in *The Historian:* "Historians are more important in the United States than they have been in the past because they are expected to provide history in more diverse forms to various audiences. Policymakers want carefully detailed studies of the past to help them understand the complex origins of present politics. Visitors to museums and historic sites want accurate but not-too-complicated versions of the past from public historians. Media producers expect to use our specialized work for their mass-audience productions. We teach students who have far greater differences in experience than the students academic professors taught in the past. Historians may not always produce bestsellers, but their work provides the best, most carefully researched versions of the past that we have."

BIOGRAPHICAL AND CRITICAL SOURCES:

PERIODICALS

American Historical Review, October, 1969.
The Historian, Volume 56, number 2, winter, 1994, p. 245-258.
New York Times Book Review, May 22, 1988.
Village Voice, November 25, 1981.

Virginia Quarterly Review, autumn, 1986.

ONLINE

Books Under Review, http://www.booksunderreview. com (August 19, 2003), review of *One Foot on the Rockies: Women and Creativity in the Modern American West.*
Temple University Press, http://www.temple.edu/ tempress/ (August 16, 2003), reprint of a *Library Journal* review of *A Needle, A Bobbin, A Strike.**

*   *   *

JEWETT, Robert 1933-

PERSONAL: Born December 31, 1933, in Lawrence, MA; son of Walter L. (a clergyman) and Elizabeth (Bailey) Jewett; married Janet Miller (a speech pathologist), June 11, 1956; married Heike Goebel; children: (first marriage) Ellen. *Education:* Nebraska Wesleyan University, B.A., 1955; University of Chicago, B.D., 1958; University of Tuebingen, D.Theol., 1966.

ADDRESSES: Home—Rothenberg im Odenwald, Germany. *Office*—University of Heidelberg, WTS, Kisselgasse 1, D-69117 Heidelberg, Germany. *E-mail*—Robert.Jewett@urz.uni-heidelberg.de; Jewett_Rothenberg@yahoo.com.

CAREER: Theologian, educator, and author. Federated Church, Harvey, IL, minister of education, 1958-60; minister of churches in Dakota City and Homer, NE, 1964-66; Morningside College, Sioux City, IA, instructor, 1965-66, associate professor, 1966-72, professor of religious studies, 1972-80; American Church, Paris, France, theologian-in-residence, 1973; Garrett-Evangelical Theological Seminary, Evanston, IL, professor of new testament interpretation, 1980-87, Harry R. Kendall professor, 1987-96, senior professor, 1996-2000, professor emeritus, 2000—; Joint Garrett/Northwestern Ph.D. program in religious and theological studies, member, coordinating faculty member, 1982-2000.

Visiting lecturer for summer session, Wesley Theological Seminary, 1976, University of Montana, 1978, Iliff School of Theology, 1976-78, Vancouver School of

Theology, 1982-91; guest professor of New Testament, Wissenschaftlich-Theologisches seminar, University of Heidelberg, 2000—.

President, chair, or member of numerous boards and committees, including the Society of Biblical Literature, Social Sciences and New Testament Interpretation, the Pauline Theology Group, *Journal for the Study of the New Testament,* Society of New Testament Studies, Catholic Biblical Association, and American Academy of Religion.

MEMBER: Society of Biblical Literature, Society of New Testament Studies, American Academy of Religion, American Interprofessional Institute, American Association of University Professors, Nebraska Annual Conference of United Methodist Church, Chicago Society of Biblical Research (president, 1993-94), Phi Kappa Phi, Pi Gamma Mu, Blue Key.

AWARDS, HONORS: Blatchford traveling fellowship from Chicago Theological Seminary, 1960-61; Deutscher Akademischer Austauschdienst fellowship, 1961-64; Melcher National Book Award, 1974, for *The Captain America Complex;* honorary D.D., Morningside College, 1995, Kalamazoo College, 1998, Coe College, 1999.

WRITINGS:

Paul's Anthropological Terms: A Study of Their Use in Conflict Settings (monograph), E. J. Brill (Leiden), 1971.

The Captain America Complex: The Dilemma of Zealous Nationalism, Westminster Press (Philadelphia, PA), 1973.

(With John Shelton Lawrence) *The American Monomyth,* introduction by Isaac Asimov, Anchor Press (Garden City, NY), 1977.

A Chronology of Paul's Life, Fortress Press (Philadelphia, PA), 1979.

Jesus against the Rapture: Seven Unexpected Prophecies, Westminster Press (Philadelphia, PA), 1979.

Letter to Pilgrims: A Commentary on the Epistle to the Hebrews, Pilgrim Press (New York, NY), 1981.

Christian Tolerance: Paul's Message to the Modern Church, Westminster Press (Philadelphia, PA), 1982.

(Editor, with D. E. Groh) *The Living Text: Essays in Honor of Ernest W. Saunders,* University Press of America, 1985.

The Thessalonian Correspondence: Pauline Rhetoric and Millenarian Piety, Fortress Press (Philadelphia, PA), 1986.

(Commentary) *Romans,* Graded Press (Nashville, TN), 1988.

Saint Paul at the Movies: The Apostle's Dialogue with American Culture, Westminster/John Knox Press (Louisville, KY), 1993.

Paul the Apostle to America: Cultural Trends and Pauline Scholarship, Westminster/John Knox Press (Louisville, KY), 1994.

(Coeditor) *Common Life in the Early Church: Essays in Honor of Graydon F. Snyder,* Trinity Press International (Philadelphia, PA), 1998.

Saint Paul Returns to the Movies: Triumph over Shame, William B. Eerdmans (Grand Rapids, MI), 1999.

(With John Shelton Lawrence) *The Myth of the American Superhero,* William B. Eerdmans (Grand Rapids, MI), 1999.

(With John Shelton Lawrence) *Captain America in a Time of Jihad,* William B. Eerdmans (Grand Rapids, MI), 2002.

(With John Shelton Lawrence) *Captain America and the Crusade against Evil: The Dilemma of Zealous Nationalism,* William B. Eerdmans (Grand Rapids, MI), 2003.

Also editor of *Christology and Exegesis: New Approaches.* Contributor of more than 130 articles and reviews to numerous publications, including *Christian Advocate, Christian Century, New Testament Studies, Novum Testamentum, Anglican Theological Review, Interpretation: A Journal of Bible and Theology, Sojourners, Christianity and Literature,* and *Journal of Religion.*

Member of editorial board of *Semeia: An Experimental Journal for Biblical Criticism,* 1980-86; member of editorial board of the supplement series of the *Journal for the Study of the New Testament,* Sheffield Academic Press, 1991—; and member of the editorial advisory board of *Jian Dao: A Journal of Bible and Theology,* 1994-2000.

SIDELIGHTS: Robert Jewett is a theologian and author whose books, many of which were written with John Shelton Lawrence, examine American culture through the lens of religion and mythology. In *The Captain America Complex* and *The American Monomyth,* for example, Jewett attempts to explain contemporary American beliefs and behavior in socio-theological terms. In *The Captain America Complex,* Jewett proposes that our actions in the international political arena have been governed by two very different biblical doctrines—"zealous nationalism," which propels us to "seek to redeem the world by the destruction of the wicked," and "prophetic realism," which encompasses "affection and compassion for all humans, skepticism toward claimed superior virtue, and reluctance to draw the sword" in order to "redeem the world for coexistence by impartial justice." In Jewett's view, zealous nationalism has held the upper hand throughout most of our history, even as far back as revolutionary times.

Eric F. Goldman of the *New York Times Book Review,* calling the study "both illuminating and frightening," noted that "Mr. Jewett's presentation is not always felicitous. He can forget the caution of that eminent Prophetic Realist, Reinhold Niebuhr—'Americans are perfectly capable of making fools of themselves without need of any religion at all.' Often he writes as if the predilection for militant ideology in foreign policy comes entirely from Holy Writ, ignoring none-too-holy factors, economic and otherwise, which helped create and sustain the zeal." Nevertheless, concluded Goldman, "*The Captain America Complex* holds its reader. Mr. Jewett's analysis of the nature of the biblical influence on foreign policy attitudes . . . is original in fundamental ways."

An *America* critic basically agreed with Goldman, and wrote: "The book is sound enough sociologically and theologically, but it neglects the structural, economic and political factors that supplement the mythic sources in bringing about and sustaining America's righteous zeal. . . . Still, the book powerfully challenges both scholars and preachers to test concretely the American reality against the best of the Judeo-Christian heritage."

Jewett's *The American Monomyth,* written with Lawrence, explores the American version of the myth of "an Eden-like society helpless in the face of evil but rescued by an outsider, a superhero, who then disappears again." The authors' study focuses on the world of popular entertainment, where a Captain Kirk or a Lone Ranger restores order and goodness by

vanquishing the forces of evil. They trace this myth in its American form back to the time of discovery and colonization in the New World, when America became a symbol of the second chance being granted to Europeans to create a new and better society. A reviewer for *Choice* called *The American Monomyth* "enlightening and frightening," while a *New York Times Book Review* critic noted that the authors' thesis is "sensible" and that they provide "persuasive evidence of its presence in our cultural life." However, the reviewer continued, "the book is written with an uncertain hold on the English language. . . . As a substantive matter, I wish there had been a look at myths of other nations—Robin Hood and the Arthurian legends of England, Japan's Samurai—which look an awful lot like this 'uniquely' American monomyth. Still, this is a useful reminder that a nation's ideas about itself show up in the most unexpected of places."

In *The Myth of the American Superhero,* Jewett and Lawrence revisit the theme of the American monomyth, purporting that the consciousness of the nation still today views the world—and America's place in it—in a mythical manner and argue that the idea of the "superhero" is built upon antidemocratic values. Here the authors trace the violence associated with the superhero abounding in modern media—from Buffalo Bill through the movie *The Matrix.* Rather than focus on one genre of superhero, however, they connect them all by tracing the "mythic similarity" underlying them. "This gives the text an underlying feeling of scope that usually is missing in such works," commented Matthew Kapell in *Extrapolation.*

Kapell was impressed with the authors' insights in their analysis of *The Matrix.* He points out that where most other critics commented on the same religious themes, Jewett and Lawrence (he calls them "nothing if not experts in their field") forego analyzing the "obvious markers of religion" and instead "quietly note that the hero, 'early in his training for world liberation,' must 'ignore a pretty woman in a red dress.' This need to remove oneself from the pleasures of the world is central to [Joseph] Campbell's monomyth, and the application of it here is notable in that so many other critics have missed it."

Fred Edwords pointed out in the *Humanist* that while the role of the myth is clearly obvious in ancient cultures, its role and influence is virtually every bit as predominant and influential in modern culture. "Myths frame social thinking," noted Edwords. "However, some . . . maintain that what we see around us are essentially ancient myths living on in our cinema, literature, and other art forms. [Lawrence and Jewett] beg to differ. Their book is an exploration into what they term the American monomyth and how its unique character manifests itself throughout our culture."

In his review for *Journal of American Culture,* Ray Browne noted that the authors examine present-day cultural dimensions, such as politics, socioeconomics, media, and entertainment, in an effort to comprehend how the superhero of each dimension arrives at that status and what they must do to stay there. "Their fundamental question," wrote Browne, "is: Can democracy coexist with religious heroes?" He remarked that for anyone who wonders or who has an interest in modern-day culture, "this searching and suggestive study is required reading and thinking."

In *Captain America and the Crusade against Evil: The Dilemma of Zealous Nationalism,* Jewett and Lawrence again explore the themes of the superhero, zealous nationalism, and prophetic realism—the latter two having religious roots. Lillian Daniel wrote in the *Christian Century* that the authors "present a compelling argument . . . that American zealous nationalism is expressed less through its often forgotten biblical roots and more by the steady drumbeat of the American entertainment media and their superheroes, who 'reluctantly' step in to rescue passive, incompetent communities." She quotes the authors: "Helpless communities are redeemed by lone savior figures. . . . We are a nation so immersed in Captain America, Superman, Popeye, the Lone Ranger and video games that we are no longer shocked when governments employ nondemocratic means to achieve democratic ends." Daniel explained that, while many people may be concerned that violence in video games and the entertainment industry incites violence in society, the authors have an even more frightening concern: "widespread passivity in the face of force, and the loss of faith in democracy. [They] want to retire Captain America and replace him with responsible, faithful, realistic community." She remarked: "This provocative romp through political history, biblical commentary and pop culture gives the church much food for thought."

BIOGRAPHICAL AND CRITICAL SOURCES:

BOOKS

Jewett, Robert, *The Captain America Complex: The Dilemma of Zealous Nationalism,* Westminster Press (Philadelphia, PA), 1973.

Jewett, Robert, and John Shelton Lawrence, *The American Monomyth,* introduction by Isaac Asimov, Anchor Press (Garden City, NY), 1977.

Jewett, Robert, and John Shelton Lawrence, *The Myth of the American Superhero,* William B. Eerdmans (Grand Rapids, MI), 1999.

Jewett, Robert, and John Shelton Lawrence, *Captain America and the Crusade against Evil: The Dilemma of Zealous Nationalism,* William B. Eerdmans (Grand Rapids, MI), 2003.

PERIODICALS

America, February 16, 1974, review of *The Captain America Complex.*

Choice, October, 1977, review of *The American Monomyth.*

Christian Century, November 14, 1979; August 23, 2002, Lillian Daniel, review of *Captain America and the Crusade against Evil,* pp. 36-39.

Extrapolation (Kent State University, Ohio), summer, 2003, Matthew Kapell, review of *The Myth of the American Superhero,* p. 266.

Humanist, May-June, 2003, Fred Edwords, review of *The Myth of the American Superhero,* pp. 44-45.

Journal of American Culture, March, 2003, Ray Browne, review of *The Myth of the American Superhero,* p. v26.

Library Journal, February 15, 2003, Carolyn Craft, review of *Captain America and the Crusade against Evil,* p. 143.

National Catholic Reporter, April 18, 2003, James Fredericks, review of *Captain America and the Crusade against Evil,* p. 19.

New York Times Book Review, October 21, 1973, Eric F. Goldman, review of *The Captain America Complex: The Dilemma of Zealous Nationalism*; July 31, 1977, review of *The American Monomyth.*

San Francisco Chronicle, June 29, 2003, Don Lattin, review of *Captain America and the Crusade against Evil,* p. E6.

University of Heidelberg, http://theologie.uni-hd.de/
   wts/lampe/jewett.htm/ (November 13, 2003),
   Robert Jewett vita.*

*   *   *

JOHNSON, Alexandra 1949-

PERSONAL: Born November 12, 1949, in San Francisco, CA; married Askold Melnyczuk (a writer), July
30, 1995. *Ethnicity:* "Caucasian." *Education:* University of California, Berkeley, B.A., 1971.

ADDRESSES: Home—11 Chestnut St., Medford, MA
02155; fax: 781-393-0923. *Agent*—Elaine Markson
Literary Agency, Inc., 44 Greenwich Ave., New York,
NY 10011.

CAREER: Christian Science Monitor, Boston, MA,
writer and assistant literary editor, 1976-82; freelance
writer, 1982—. Harvard University, instructor in
creative writing at university extension, 1990-98;
Wellesley College, creative writing teacher. WGBH-
TV, writer, 1986, member of televised book group.

MEMBER: International PEN.

AWARDS, HONORS: Nonfiction award, Jerard Fund
of International PEN, 1990; James Conway Award,
Harvard University, 1994.

WRITINGS:

The Hidden Writer: Diaries and the Creative Life,
   Doubleday (New York, NY), 1997.
*Leaving a Trace: On Keeping a Journal: The Art of
   Transforming a Life into Stories,* Little, Brown
   (Boston, MA), 2001.

Contributor of articles and reviews to magazines and
newspapers, including the *New Yorker, Nation, New
York Times Book Review, Ms.,* and *Boston Globe.*

SIDELIGHTS: Alexandra Johnson once told *CA:* "I
was born in San Francisco into a family of hidden
writers, three generations of diarists. My grandmother
kept a detailed diary recording her work for the Red
Cross in Siberia during World War I. My mother hid
her own diaries and stories in the linen closet. My
aunt, a teacher of film, kept extensive diaries and wrote
novels while raising three children.

"Shortly after moving into my present home in 1993,
my husband and I were given a diary from 1885. It
had belonged to the house's original occupant, a
French and music teacher. The diary had been
preserved by the woman's cousins. When the family
had no more relatives, the diary was passed on to a
neighbor, who then presented it to me, knowing that I
was writing a book on diaries."

Johnson has in fact written two books on the art of
diary- and journal-keeping. *The Hidden Writer:
Diaries and the Creative Life* "assembles seven literary portraits-through-journals into a beguiling biography of the creative process," wrote a contributor to the
Seattle Post-Intelligencer. Through the private writings
of a disparate group of women, from seven-year-old
Marjory Fleming to Virginia Woolf, Alice James, and
May Sarton, Johnson demonstrates how creative writing flows from biography and how closely related life
and work can be. *Library Journal* contributor Jeris
Cassel found *The Hidden Writer* to be an "engrossing
examination of the relationship between diary writing
and creativity."

*Leaving a Trace: On Keeping a Journal: The Art of
Transforming a Life into Stories* uses examples from
famous diaries and journals, as well as advice Johnson
offers in her writing classes, to urge readers to begin a
diary or to continue keeping one even if it seems futile.
According to Stephanie Dickison in *The Writer,*
Johnson "will prove, beyond a shadow of a doubt, that
there is nothing uninteresting about what you have to
say, and that it is all leading to something that you
may not understand now but will." *Library Journal*
contributor Denise S. Sticha described the book as
"beautifully written," and GraceAnne A. DeCandido
in *Booklist* thought it "valuable in all sorts of ways for
anyone looking for the right words." Cleveland *Plain
Dealer* reviewer Karen Sandstrom wrote of *Leaving a
Trace,* "It would be hard to imagine anyone reading

this book and not wanting to run to the store to pick up a pretty new blank book—or at least begin scribbling on the back of grocery receipts and stuffing them into shoe boxes."

BIOGRAPHICAL AND CRITICAL SOURCES:

PERIODICALS

Booklist, January 1, 2001, GraceAnne A. DeCandido, review of *Leaving a Trace: On Keeping a Journal: The Art of Transforming Life into Stories,* p. 901.

Library Journal, April 1, 1997, Jeris Cassel, review of *The Hidden Writer: Diaries and the Creative Life,* p. 92; January 1, 2001, Denise S. Sticha, review of *Leaving a Trace,* p. 126.

New York Times Book Review, October 19, 1997, Nancy Caldwell Sorel, review of *The Hidden Writer,* p. 31.

Plain Dealer (Cleveland, OH), January 10, 2001, Karen Sandstrom, "Good Advice for Diary-Keepers," p. 1E.

Publishers Weekly, April 21, 1997, review of *The Hidden Writer,* p. 57; November 13, 2000, review of *Leaving a Trace,* p. 95.

Seattle Post-Intelligencer, July 3, 1997, "'The Hidden Writer' Looks Deep into the Wellsprings of Creativity," p. C2.

Writer, May, 2002, Stephanie Dickison, review of *Leaving a Trace,* p. 50.*

*   *   *

JOHNSON, Cait 1952-

PERSONAL: Born September 23, 1952, in Andover, MA; daughter of Robert John (an inventor) and Patricia Marie (a craftsperson; maiden name, Lewis) Johnson; married William David Peters, 1974 (divorced, 1980); companion of Stuart Hannan (a special effects designer and musician); children: (first marriage) Reid Johnson. *Ethnicity:* "Anglo." *Education:* St. Mary's College of Maryland, B.A. (cum laude), 1974; Ohio State University, M.F.A., 1979. *Politics:* Liberal Democrat. *Religion:* "Earth-centered spirituality." *Hobbies and other interests:* Singing and performance, fabric arts, sculpting goddess figurines "from anything handy," walking in the woods.

ADDRESSES: Home—R.R.1, Box 382, Clinton Corners, NY 12514; fax: 914-266-4007. *E-mail*—caitjohnson@hotmail.com.

CAREER: Teacher, workshop and ritual facilitator at healing and spiritual centers, 1981—.

AWARDS, HONORS: First prize, Maryland State Poetry Contest, 1970.

WRITINGS:

Tarot for Every Day: Ideas and Activities for Bringing Tarot Wisdom into Your Daily Life, Shawangunk Press, 1994.

(With Maura D. Shaw) *Tarot Games: Forty-five Playful Ways to Explore Tarot Cards Together: A New Vision for the Circle of Community,* HarperSan-Francisco (San Francisco, CA), 1994.

(With Maura D. Shaw) *Celebrating the Great Mother: A Handbook of Earth-Honoring Activities for Parents and Children,* Inner Traditions (New York, NY), 1995.

Cooking Like a Goddess: Bringing Seasonal Magic into the Kitchen, Inner Traditions (Rochester, VT), 1997.

(With Elizabeth Cunningham) *Naked Masks,* 1998.

Witch in the Kitchen: Magical Cooking for All Seasons, Destiny Books (Rochester, VT), 2001.

Earth, Water, Fire, and Air: Essential Ways of Connecting with Spirit, SkyLight Paths (Woodstock, VT), 2003.

WORK IN PROGRESS: Sow at the Fair, a book of poems with illustrations by Ann duBois; *River of Birds,* a novel; *Bone Time,* poems; "Dark Blessing," a performance piece for narrator and six characters; a divination deck for women, with art by Melissa Harris.

SIDELIGHTS: Cait Johnson told *CA:* "My nonfiction has been fueled by involvement with the women's spirituality movement and the compulsion to share what I know about connecting—with the seasons, with the natural world, and with our own inner wisdom. Now, after two books on the Tarot, one on earth-centered activities for parents and children, and one that is as much a recipe for playful, sacred, and connected living as it is a seasonal vegetarian cookbook, my focus is changing. I've carried on a clandestine affair with poetry, fiction, and performance nearly all my life. Now the same spirit of creative play that infuses my nonfiction is urging me to bring those elements more fully into my life and work."

BIOGRAPHICAL AND CRITICAL SOURCES:

PERIODICALS

Publishers Weekly, November 25, 2002, review of *Earth, Water, Fire, and Air: Essential Ways of Connecting with Spirit,* p. 62.*

*   *   *

JUNGREIS, Esther 1936-

PERSONAL: Surname is pronounced *young*-rice; born April 7, 1936, in Szeged, Hungary; immigrated to the United States in 1947, naturalized citizen; daughter of Abraham (a rabbi) and Miriam (Cohen) Jungreis; married Theodore (a rabbi) Jungreis, November 13, 1955; children: Chaya Sora Jungreis Gertzulin, Yisroel, Slova Chana, Osher Anshil. *Education:* Attended Beth Jacob Teacher's Seminary, received teaching diploma, 1955. *Religion:* Jewish.

ADDRESSES: Home—440 Hungry Harbor Rd., North Woodmere, NY 11581. *Office*—Hineni, Inc., 155 East 38th St., New York, NY 10016. *Agent*—Bill Adler, 551 Fifth Ave., New York, NY 10017. *E-mail*— hineni@hineni.org.

CAREER: Writer, lecturer, and broadcaster. *Jewish Press,* Brooklyn, NY, author of weekly column, "The Rebbetzin Viewpoint," 1955—. Founder and president of Hineni, Inc., 1973—. Host of "Hineni," a program on National Jewish Television, 1981—, and on WNYM-Radio, 1982—.

AWARDS, HONORS: Named Woman of the Year by Hadassah, 1975, Knights of Pythias, 1975, Jewish War Veterans, 1976, B'nai B'rith, 1976, Federation of Jewish Women's Organizations, 1978, and Amita Society, 1980; *The Jewish Soul on Fire* was named one of the ten best Jewish books of 1982 by B'nai B'rith.

WRITINGS:

The Jewish Soul on Fire (nonfiction), Morrow (New York, NY), 1982.
The Committed Life: Principles for Good Living from Our Timeless Past, Cliff Street Books (New York, NY), 1998.
The Committed Marriage: A Guide to Finding a Soul Mate and Building a Relationship through Timeless Biblical Wisdom, HarperSanFrancisco (San Francisco, CA), 2002.

SIDELIGHTS: The author of several books on Jewish life and faith, Esther Jungreis is descended from a rabbinic dynasty that traces its lineage back to the days of King David. Before World War II, she reported, there were eighty-five Hungarian rabbis named Jungreis. After the war, only seven remained alive, and she is herself a survivor of the Bergen-Belsen concentration camp. Immigrating to the United States after World War II, she vowed to make her life meaningful and has dedicated herself to fighting the spiritual holocaust she believes is occurring in the United States, a holocaust identified by alienation of American youth, defection of the young to missionary cults, and existence of a drug culture. Jungreis's message is, according to Mark Melady, writing in the Worcester, Massachusetts, *Telegram & Gazette,* a return by Jews to "their spiritual and cultural roots, including the traditional family Sabbath ceremony, and . . . an end to the sectarianism that divides the Jewish community."

To help achieve her goal, Jungreis founded Hineni, Inc., an international movement devoted to awakening the Jewish people to their heritage and inspiring Jewish youth to go back to their roots. Hineni schools have sprung up throughout the United States and, for their classes, Jungreis has written pamphlets on all aspects of Jewish life and thought. These have been distributed on high school and college campuses in the United States and abroad, and have been translated into French, Spanish, and Hebrew. Jungreis's message is also spread via her lectures held weekly at a Manhattan synagogue, meetings that draw over a thousand people. Called by some the Jewish Billy Graham, Jungreis attempts to bring the word of the Torah to people not only through her work at Hineni, but also via weekly broadcasts on the Jewish Television Network. In addition to her teachings, Jungreis has worked strongly in the old tradition of matchmaking, pairing up likely young Jewish men and women for marriage. As quoted by Victor Wishna in the *San Diego Jewish Journal Online,* Jungreis, a Rebbetzin, or rabbi's wife in Yiddish, noted that "This is why it is so important to find a soul mate. . . . Once you find a soul mate, you can establish a home that will change the world."

Jungreis also spreads her word through books such as *The Jewish Soul on Fire, The Committed Life: Principles for Good Living from Our Timeless Past,* and *The Committed Marriage: A Guide to Finding a Soul Mate and Building a Relationship through Timeless Biblical Wisdom.* In the latter title, published in 2002, she serves up "advice on building a strong marriage using religious principles," according to *Library Journal*'s Kay Brodie. Jungreis posits five qualities that people need to develop to this end: creating a positive outlook, making yourself available as both a good friend and neighbor, knowing and understanding the consequences of your actions, and working on having an open and giving heart. Aimed largely at young Jewish people, as are her numerous lectures, *The Committed Marriage* nonetheless provides "practical" advice to readers of all religious persuasions and ages, as Brodie noted. Jana Riess, writing in *Publishers Weekly,* commented that while Jungreis's advice is not much different from that of other relationship experts, "her inclusion of God and religion makes these stories and recommendations unique." In her earlier work *The Committed Life,* Jungreis advises readers on how to build a sense of commitment and responsibility in their lives, using real-life incidents as learning tools. Reviewing that title in *Booklist,* George Cohen felt that though Jungreis "quotes from the Torah and Talmud, . . . her message is universal."

BIOGRAPHICAL AND CRITICAL SOURCES:

PERIODICALS

Booklist, October 15, 1998, George Cohen, review of *The Committed Life: Principles for Good Living from Our Timeless Past,* p. 373.
Jerusalem, October 30, 1997, Netty C. Gross, "Sick of Being Single," p. 32.
Library Journal, April 1, 2003, Kay Brodie, review of *The Committed Marriage: A Guide to Finding a Soul Mate and Building a Relationship through Timeless Biblical Wisdom,* p. 116.

New York Times, April 23, 1997, David Gonzalez, "From Pages of the Torah, a Passion."
Publishers Weekly, April 14, 2003, Jana Riess, review of *The Committed Marriage,* p. 63.
Telegram & Gazette (Worcester, MA), August 14, 2000, Mark Melady, "Author Urges Spiritual Return: Survivor Speaks at Torah Study," p. B1.

ONLINE

Hineni Web site, http://www.hineni.org/ (November, 18, 2003).
Jewish World Review Online, http://www.jewish worldreview.com/ (December 21, 1999), Judy Gruen, review of *The Committed Life.*
San Diego Jewish Journal Online, http://www. sdjewishjournal.com/ (November, 18, 2003), Victor Wishna, "Is Rebbetzin Esther Jungreis the Jewish Billy Graham?"
Shma, http://www.shma.com/june03/Vanessa.htm/ (November 18, 2003), Vanessa L. Ochs, "The Torah of Love."*

*   *   *

JUNKER, Patricia 1952-

PERSONAL: Born August 16, 1952, in OH. *Education:* University of Toledo, B.A. (magna cum laude), 1974; University of Michigan, M.A., 1980.

ADDRESSES: Office—Amon Carter Museum, 3501 Camp Bowie Blvd., Fort Worth, TX 76107-2695. *E-mail*—patricia.junker@cartermuseum.org.

CAREER: Toledo Museum of Art, Toledo, OH, fellow, 1976-77; Smith College, Northampton, MA, intern at art museum, 1978-80, curatorial assistant, 1980-82; University of Rochester, Rochester, NY, curator of American art and chief curator at Memorial Art Gallery, 1982-90; University of Wisconsin—Madison, curator of collections at Elvehjem Museum of Art, 1990-92; Fine Arts Museums of San Francisco, M. H. de Young Museum, San Francisco, CA, assistant curator of American paintings, 1992-94, acting head of American art department, 1994-96, associate curator of American art, 1996-99; Amon Carter Museum, Fort Worth, TX, curator of paintings and sculpture, 1999—.

John Steuart Curry Foundation, member of board of directors, 1992-96; American Decorative Arts Forum, member of board of directors, 1998—.

MEMBER: Midwest Art History Association (member of board of directors, 1992), Upper Midwest Conservation Association (member of board of directors, 1992).

AWARDS, HONORS: National Endowment for the Arts fellowship, 1976-77, internship, 1978-80; scholar of Association of Art Museum Directors at Attingham Summer School, England, 1982; Henry Allen Moe Prize, New York State Historical Association, 1991, for *Winslow Homer in the 1890s*; grant from Henry Luce Foundation.

WRITINGS:

Promoted to Glory: The Apotheosis of George Washington, Museum of Art, Smith College (Northampton, MA), 1980.

The Course of Empire: The Erie Canal and the New York Landscape, 1825-1875, University of Washington Press (Seattle, WA), 1984.

North Country Landscape: Gibson Gallery at the Brainerd Arts Complex, Gallery (Potsdam, NY), 1986.

Winslow Homer in the 1890s: Prout's Neck Observed, Hudson Hills Press (New York, NY), 1990.

(Contributor) *Facing Eden: One Hundred Years of Landscape Art in the San Francisco Bay Area, 1895-1995,* University of California Press (Berkeley, CA), 1995.

John Steuart Curry: Inventing the Middle West, Hudson Hills Press (New York, NY), 1998.

An American Collection: Works from the Amon Carter Museum, Hudson Hills Press (New York, NY), 2001.

Winslow Homer, Artist and Angler, Amon Carter Museum (Forth Worth, TX) and Fine Arts Museums of San Francisco (San Francisco, CA), 2002.

Coauthor of *The Rockefeller Collection of American Art at the Fine Arts Museums of San Francisco,* Abrams (New York, NY). Author of exhibition catalogs. Contributor to periodicals, including *Triptych, Magazine Antiques,* and *Porticus.*

SIDELIGHTS: A long-time museum curator with special expertise in nineteenth-century American art, Patricia Junker has organized numerous art exhibitions and authored many exhibition catalogs and articles for prominent magazines. She has also received prestigious research grants from the Henry Luce Foundation and the National Endowment for the Arts. In 1990 Junker joined the Fine Arts Museums of San Francisco, M. H. de Young Museum, and became associate curator of American Art. In 1999 she was appointed curator of paintings and sculpture at the Amon Carter Museum in Fort Worth, Texas.

In 1998 Junker served as curator of the exhibit "John Steuart Curry: Inventing the Middle West" at the Fine Arts Museums of San Francisco. Junker also was lead author of the exhibit's catalog. Curry was the least known of America's Regionalist triumvirate, which included the artists Thomas Hart Benton and Grant Wood. Curry focused much of his work on rural Kansas, illustrating life on the farm, tornadoes, baptisms, and other aspects of native life.

In an interview on the PBS nightly news show *The NewsHour with Jim Lehrer,* Junker was asked why there had been a resurgence of interest in Curry, who fell into disfavor among arts patrons after he died in 1946 and after abstract expressionism became popular in the American art world. Junker noted that Curry's art depicted both intellectual and cultural issues of the times. "We found that this was an important transforming moment, the period of the thirties and forties." Junker went on to note, "The struggle of man against nature . . . was one of the primary motivations of his art, reminding us that we're vulnerable and that we're always at the mercy of forces greater than human forces."

In 2002 Junker organized a major loan exhibition titled "Winslow Homer: The Art of Fishing." Junker had mounted an earlier 1991 exhibition of Homer's work called "The 1890s: Prout's Neck Observed" and won the 1991 Henry Allen Moe Prize for the outstanding exhibit art catalog of the year. The new exhibit focused on Homer's watercolors of fish and fishing, which was one of the artist's favorite pastimes. In the catalog of the exhibition, titled *Winslow Homer, Artist and Angler,* Junker points to Homer's two Florida black bass paintings as among his most elegant works. "With them he distilled from his Florida angling experience a singularly powerful expression of the joy and miracle of life, a profound sense of death, and the wonder and mystery of nature," wrote Junker.

Reviewing the catalog in London's *Spectator,* John McEwen noted, "This handsome book should be given to all those non-Waltonians who say 'I don't fish because I haven't got the patience,' because it shows that fishing is ultimately about contemplation." McEwen went on to point out that Junker wrote two of the book's seven essays and is "herself a keen angler, and pads out its limited subject with a beginner's guide to fishing lore and brief history of American nineteenth-century fishing art." In a review of the exhibit and catalogue, a contributor to *Library Journal* noted that "no other work has examined his lifelong ardor for the sport in such detail and with such an eye toward clarifying both Homer's creations and the object of his passion."

BIOGRAPHICAL AND CRITICAL SOURCES:

BOOKS

Junker, Patricia, *Winslow Homer, Artist and Angler,* Amon Carter Museum (Forth Worth, TX) and Fine Arts Museums of San Francisco (San Francisco, CA), 2002.

PERIODICALS

Booklist, April 1, 1998, Gilbert Taylor, review of *John Steuart Curry: Inventing the Middle West,* p. 1292.
Library Journal, May 15, 1998, Russell T. Clement, review of *John Steuart Curry,* p. 82; February 15, 2003, review of *Winslow Homer, Artist and Angler,* p. 133.
Spectator (London, England), March 1, 2003, John McEwen, review of *Winslow Homer, Artist and Angler,* p. 55.

ONLINE

Carter Museum, http://www.cartermuseum.org/ (September 27, 1999), "Amon Carter Museum Appoints Patricia Junker As New Curator of Paintings and Sculpture."
Online NewsHour, http://www.pbs.org/newshour/ (August 13, 1998), "Curry's Kansas."
Western Sport Shop, http://www.westernsportshop.com/ (December 31, 2002), "Winslow Homer Casts a Spell."*

K

KAGARLITSKY, Boris 1958-

PERSONAL: Born August 29, 1958, in Moscow, U.S.S.R.; son of Yuly (a literary critic) and Raisa (a translator; maiden name, Pomerantseva) Kagarlitsky; married Irina Gloushtchenko (a translator), July 27, 1985; children: Georgy. *Education:* Attended State Institute of Theatrical Art, 1975-80. *Politics:* Socialist. *Religion:* Jewish.

ADDRESSES: Home—Krasnoarmeyskaya 29, Flat 43, Moscow, Russia 125319. *E-mail*—goboka@online.ru.

CAREER: Writer. Postal employee in Moscow, Russia, 1980-82; caretaker in Moscow, 1983-88; IMA Press News Agency, Moscow, political observer and journalist, 1988-90; Moscow Soviet, deputy, 1990-93; Institute for Comparative Political Studies, Russian Academy of Sciences, Moscow, TNI Global Crisis Project, coordinator.

MEMBER: Soviet Sociological Association.

AWARDS, HONORS: Deutscher Memorial Prize, 1988.

WRITINGS:

The Thinking Reed: Intellectuals and the Soviet State 1917 to the Present, translated by Brian Pearce, Verso (London, England), 1988.
The Dialectic of Hope, S. Covo, 1989.
The Dialectic of Change, translated by Rick Simon, Verso (London, England), 1989.
Farewell Perestroyka, translated by Rick Simon, Verso (London, England), 1990.
The Disintegration of the Monolith, translated by Renfrey Clarke, Verso (London, England), 1992.
Kvadratnye kolesa, translation by Leslie A. Auerback published as *Square Wheels: How Russian Democracy Got Derailed,* Monthly Review Press (New York, NY), 1994.
The Mirage of Modernization, translated by Renfrey Clarke, Monthly Review Press (New York, NY), 1995.
Restavraëtìsiëiìa v Rossii, translation by Renfrey Clarke published as *Restoration in Russia: Why Capitalism Failed,* Verso (London, England), 1995.
(With Roger Burback and Orlando Núñez) *Globalization and Its Discontents: The Rise of Postmodern Socialisms,* Pluto Press (London, England), 1997.
New Realism, New Barbarism: Socialist Theory in the Era of Globalization, translated by Renfrey Clarke, Pluto Press (London, England), 1999.
The Twilight of Globalization: Property, State and Capitalism, translated by Renfrey Clarke, Pluto Press (London, England), 2000.
The Return of Radicalism: Reshaping the Left Institutions, translated by Renfrey Clarke, Pluto Press (London, England), 2000.
Russia under Yeltsin and Putin: Neo-liberal Autocracy, Pluto Press (London, England), 2002.

Editor, *Levy Povorot,* 1979-82.

SIDELIGHTS: Boris Kagarlitsky has focused his writing on the analysis of Russian politics, economy, and social change. He attempts not only to point out the strengths and weaknesses that he discovers but also argues for reforms that he believes are needed. He began his writing career with the publication of *The Thinking Reed: Intellectuals and the Soviet State 1917 to the Present,* a history from the beginning of the Communist presence in Russia (U.S.S.R.) until the beginning of the Soviet Union's collapse in the 1980s. Following this, in 1992, he wrote *The Disintegration of the Monolith.* In this book, Robert Service of *New Statesman & Society* stated, Kagarlitsky "seeks to mark out the ground for a new, unconfused socialist politics in post-Gorbachev Russia." Kagarlitsky, the cofounder of the Party of Labour in Russia, is a proponent of socialism. He is also often referred to as a radical political philosopher. In these roles, he is committed to demanding of his government many benefits, which include full employment, free health care, free education, as well as an extensive range of civil liberties. Service found Kagarlitsky's book, however, to be "clearer in its slogans than in detail," and suggested that Kagarlitsky needs more corroboration of his facts.

In 1990, Kagarlitsky became a member of the Moscow City Council, which only lasted three years, having been disbanded by Boris Yeltsin in 1993. Recounting his experiences on the Council, Kagarlitsky next wrote *Square Wheels: How Russian Democracy Got Derailed,* a book that Robert Weissman, for *Multinational Monitor,* referred to as "a tale equal parts comic and tragic." *Square Wheels,* as its title points out, sadly recalls the inability of the Council to move forward because of the incompetence of many of its members. Precious time was spent in useless projects, Kagarlitsky reports. Street names were changed countless times and the bust of Lenin was moved out of the assembly hall by anti-Lenin members only to be returned by those who still favored the old Soviet leader. Political corruption soon set in and democracy in Russia came to an abrupt halt before it had time to establish itself securely.

In 1995, Kagarlitsky continued the saga of Russian politics in his book *Restoration in Russia: Why Capitalism Failed.* Vincent Barnett, for *Europe-Asia Studies* called this book "an acidic attack on the 'new Russians.'" However, Barnett also found Kagarlitsky's writing quite funny, although the picture that "Kagarlitsky paints is thoroughly bleak." Rather than Russia being restored by a new market economy, Kagarlitsky

concludes that it is being ruled by a group of new elites who are playing scam games on the rest of the population. Barnett enjoyed reading Kagarlitsky's analysis of the times, but he was disappointed that the author did not provide any solutions to the many problems that Russia is facing.

In an interview with a reporter for the *Multinational Monitor,* Kagarlitsky summed up the current status of Russia. "We've come to the point," he says, "where it makes no sense to discuss where somebody wants things to go. We have reached a point where we face a national collapse." He still believes that Russia will survive, as it has in the past. However, there are significantly grand changes that must first occur. He proposes the nationalization of banks and fuel as well as the printing of new money and establishing price controls.

Kagarlitsky has continued his analyses of Russian politics, most recently with *The Return of Radicalism: Reshaping the Left Institutions,* which supports his philosophy of socialism, and *Russia under Yeltsin and Putin: Neo-liberal Autocracy,* an updated history of current politics.

Boris Kagarlitsky told *CA:* "Most of my literary activities have been connected to my political activities. In 1982 I was arrested for editing a *samizdat* (underground) journal, *Levy Povorot,* and I spent thirteen months in prison."

BIOGRAPHICAL AND CRITICAL SOURCES:

PERIODICALS

Capital & Class, autumn, 1998, Jane Wills, review of *Globalization and Its Discontents: The Rise of Postmodern Socialisms,* pp. 161-162.
Europe-Asia Studies, December, 1996, Vincent Barnett, review of *Restoration in Russia: Why Capitalism Failed,* pp. 1417-1418.
Foreign Affairs, summer, 1993, Robert Legvold, review of *The Disintegration of the Monolith,* p. 206.
International Affairs, July 1993, Mike Bowker, review of *The Disintegration of the Monolith,* pp. 607-608; April, 1996, Slavo Radosevic, review of *Restoration in Russia,* p. 405.

Monthly Review, November, 1998, Christopher Rude, review of *Globalization and Its Discontents,* pp. 52-57.

Multinational Monitor, January-February, 1996, Robert Weissman, review of *Square Wheels: How Russian Democracy Got Derailed,* p. 46; October, 1998, "On the Russian Collapse," interview with Boris Kagarlitsky, pp. 15-18.

NACLA Report on the Americas, May-June, 1997, review of *Globalization and Its Discontents,* p. 48.

New Statesman & Society, January 15, 1993, Robert Service, review of *The Disintegration of the Monolith,* p. 41.

Political Geography, January, 1999, Richard Dodgson, review of *Globalization and Its Discontents,* pp. 89-91.

Slavonic and East European Review, July, 1997, Stephen White, review of *Restoration in Russia,* p. 587.

Southern Humanities Review, winter, 1996, Mikhail A. Pozin, review of *The Disintegration of the Monolith,* pp. 80-84.

Times (London, England), February 24, 1990.

Times Higher Education Supplement, January 26, 1996, George Blazyca, review of *Restoration in Russia,* p. 24; March 20, 1998, Mike Cole, review of *Globalization and Its Discontents,* p. 31.

Washington Post Book World, January 29, 1989, p. 11.

ONLINE

Spectrezine, http://www.spectrezine.org/ (August 22, 2002), review of *Russia under Yeltsin and Putin.**

*   *   *

KATZ, Jack 1944-

PERSONAL: Born October 16, 1944, in New York, NY; son of Charles R. (a lawyer) and Rivka (Blacker) Katz. *Education:* Colgate University, B.A., 1966; University of Chicago, J.D., 1969; Northwestern University, Ph.D., 1976.

ADDRESSES: Office—Department of Sociology, University of California—Los Angeles, Los Angeles, CA 90095-1551. *E-mail*—JackKatz@soc.ucla.edu.

CAREER: Yale University, New Haven, CT, research associate in law school, 1974-79; University of California—Los Angeles, assistant professor, 1979-82, associate professor, 1982-89, professor of sociology, 1989—. Consultant for university presses, law and social science journals, and defense in death penalty cases. Visiting professor, University of Paris, Paris, France, 1991-92; visiting professor, EHESS, Paris, 2001. Hans W. Mattick Lecturer, University of Illinois, 1989; Snortum Lecturer, Association of Criminal Justice Research, 1989; Stanley L. Common Lecturer, Union Theological Seminary, 1992; Fortunoff Criminal Justice Speaker, New York University, 1998. Fellow, Center for Advanced Studies in the Behavioral Sciences, 2000-01.

MEMBER: Law and Society Association (trustee, 1984-86).

AWARDS, HONORS: Russell Sage Law and Society fellowship, Yale University, 1973-75; Cooley Award, SSSI, 1989; Pacific Sociological Association annual scholarship award, 1990.

WRITINGS:

Poor People's Lawyers in Transition, Rutgers University Press (New Brunswick, NJ), 1982.

Seductions of Crime: Moral and Sensual Attractions in Doing Evil, Basic Books (New York, NY), 1988.

How Emotions Work, University of Chicago Press (Chicago, IL), 1999.

Contributor of chapters to books, including *Management Fraud,* edited by R. K. Elliott and J. J. Willingham, Petrocelli (New York, NY), 1980; *Criminology in the 1990s,* edited by John E. Conklin, Allyn & Bacon (Boston, MA), 1996; *The Widening Scope of Shame,* edited by Melvin Lansky and Andrew Morrison, Analytic Press (Hillsdale, NJ), 1997; *Social Science, Social Policy and Law,* edited by Austin Sarat, Robert Kagan and Patricia Ewing, Russell Sage (New York, NY), 1999; *Social Dynamics of Crime and Control: New Theories for a World in Transition,* edited by Suzanne Karstedt and Kai-D. Bussmann, Hart Press (Portland, OR), 2000.

Editor, with Robert Emerson, *Field Encounters and Discoveries,* an ethnographic book series for University of Chicago Press. Consulting editor, *American Journal* of Sociology, 1977-79; associate editor, *Symbolic Interaction,* 1995-99; deputy editor, *American Sociological Review,* 2001—. Member of editorial advisory board, *Western Criminology Review, Theoretical Criminology,* and *Ethnography.* Contributor of scholarly papers to numerous periodicals, including *American Journal of Sociology, Social Problems, Law and Society Review, American Bar Foundation Research Journal, Media, Culture & Society,* and *Ethnography.*

SIDELIGHTS: Jack Katz is a sociologist who has done research into aspects of criminal behavior that might reasonably be labeled "evil" or "deviant." Katz's book *Seductions of Crime: Moral and Sensual Attractions in Doing Evil* explores "the social and epistemic dynamics of criminal events," wrote Jeff Ferrell in *Social Justice.* Katz specifically concentrates on criminal events in which the perpetrator deliberately acted with the intent of self-gratification through intimidation or harm to a victim. *New Republic* correspondent Jonathan Rieder noted: "Katz's immense contribution is to force us to dwell on the foreground, on the lived experience, of all manner of fierce malefactors." The critic added that Katz "offers some profound truths about the flight from experience, from culture, and from morality." In the *National Review,* Joseph Sobran declared that the author "has written a fascinating book. He aims not to excuse, but to explain. The criminals he studies are united in the euphoria of violence and other consciously deviant behaviors." Sobran concluded: "*Seductions of Crime* is a keen, imaginative piece of work. It makes nonsense of the idea that we can get rid of crime just by beefing up either the police or the welfare state. It reminds us that criminals are people too, and that this isn't necessarily a compliment."

How Emotions Work examines emotional experiences through the lens of social milieu, or, as Spencer E. Cahill put it in *The American Journal of Sociology,* "the aesthetics of embodied conduct." Examples include road rage on the Los Angeles freeways, Little Leaguers' responses to humiliating strikeouts, families laughing at their reflections in funhouse mirrors, and a toddler whining in day care. Cahill noted that the book "is not only about How Emotions Work, but about how we work. . . . This book is an invitation to change our comfortably worn views of human social experience, and it is an inviting one. Katz . . . will provoke you to rethink what you previously thought about our being, and being together, in the world."

BIOGRAPHICAL AND CRITICAL SOURCES:

PERIODICALS

American Journal of Sociology, November, 1989, Robert J. Bursik, Jr., review of *Seductions of Crime: Moral and Sensual Attractions in Doing Evil,* p. 782; July, 2000, Spencer E. Cahill, review of *How Emotions Work,* p. 257.
Library Journal, October 15, 1999, Lucille M. Boone, review of *How Emotions Work,* p. 257.
National Review, December 9, 1988, Joseph Sobran, review of *Seductions of Crime,* p. 56.
New Republic, November, 19, 1990, Jonathan Rieder, review of *Seductions of Crime,* p. 36.
New York Times Book Review, November 20, 1988, Franklin E. Zimring, review of *Seductions of Crime,* p. 50.
Social Forces, June, 1990, John H. Lindquist, review of *Seductions of Crime,* p. 1329.
Social Justice, fall, 1992, Jeff Ferrell, review of *Seductions of Crime,* p. 110.

ONLINE

Jack Katz Home Page, http://www.sscnet.ucla.edu/soc/faculty/katz/ (September 4, 2002), author's vita.*

*   *   *

KATZ, Welwyn Wilton 1948-

PERSONAL: Born June 7, 1948, in London, Ontario, Canada; daughter of Robert (an electronics manufacturer) and Anne (a nurse; maiden name, Taylor) Wilton; married Albert N. Katz, 1973 (separated, 1989); married Peter Bangarth (an archaeologist); children: Meredith Allison; stepchildren: Aurora Bangarth. *Education:* University of Western Ontario, B.Sc. (mathematics, education), 1970. *Hobbies and other interests:* Playing the flute, sailing, reading myths and legends, finding recipes that incorporate herbs she grows, knitting.

ADDRESSES: Office—346 Blackacres Blvd., London, Ontario N6G 3C9, Canada. *E-mail*—wwiltonkatz@sentex.net.

CAREER: Writer. South Secondary School, London, Ontario, Canada, teacher, assistant head of mathematics, 1970-77. Past refugee coordinator, Amnesty International; treasurer and member of the steering committee, London Children's Literature Round Table; former researcher, Girls' Group Home of London.

MEMBER: Writers' Union of Canada, Canadian Society of Children's Authors, Illustrators and Performers.

AWARDS, HONORS: Book of the Year runner-up, Canadian Library Association, 1985, for *Witchery Hill,* 1986, for *Sun God, Moon Witch,* 1988, for *False Face,* and 1989, for *The Third Magic;* Ruth Schwartz Award finalist, 1987, for *False Face,* and 1988, for *The Third Magic;* International Children's Fiction Prize, Trillium Award finalist, both 1987, Max and Greta Ebel Award, Junior Library Guild (New York, NY) selection, selected one of *School Library Journal's* Best Books, and a Pick of the List from the *American Bookseller,* all 1988, South Carolina Young Adult Book Award finalist, 1990-91, all for *False Face;* Governor-General's Award finalist, 1988, for *False Face,* 1991, for *Whalesinger,* and 1995, for *Out of the Dark;* Governor-General's Award, 1988, for *The Third Magic;* included on Society of School Librarians International Best-Book List, 1990, for *The Third Magic,* and 1991, for *Whalesinger;* Short Grain Award, 1992, for *You Can Take Them Back;* Book of the Year finalist from the Canadian Library Association, 1993, for *Come Like Shadows,* and 1996, for *Out of the Dark;* Vicky Metcalf Award, from Canadian Authors Association, 1994, for entire body of work; Ruth Schwartz Award, 1996, for *Out of the Dark;* Mr. Christie Award finalist, and Blue Heron Award finalist, both 1996, and Red Cedar Award finalist, 1998, all for *Out of the Dark;* Red Cedar Award nominee, 2002, for *Beowulf.*

WRITINGS:

The Prophecy of Tau Ridoo (juvenile), illustrated by Michelle Desbarats, Tree Frog Press (Edmonton, Alberta, Canada), 1982.
Witchery Hill (young adult novel), Atheneum (New York, NY), 1984.
Sun God, Moon Witch (young adult novel), Douglas & McIntyre (Toronto, Ontario, Canada), 1986.
False Face (Junior Literary Guild selection), Douglas & McIntyre (Toronto, Ontario, Canada), 1987, Macmillan (New York, NY), 1988.

The Third Magic, Douglas & McIntyre (Toronto, Ontario, Canada), 1988, Macmillan (New York, NY), 1989.
Whalesinger, Douglas & McIntyre (Toronto, Ontario, Canada), 1990, Macmillan (New York, NY), 1991.
Come Like Shadows, Viking (New York, NY), 1993.
Time Ghost, Simon & Schuster/Margaret K. McElderry (New York, NY), 1995.
Out of the Dark, Groundwood (Toronto, Ontario, Canada), 1996.
(Adapter) *Beowulf,* illustrated by Laszlo Gal, Douglas & McIntyre (Toronto, Ontario, Canada), 1999.

Contributor of short stories to publications, including "You Can Take Them Back" to *Grain* magazine, winter, 1992; "Cat Mundy's Magic" to the *Canadian Children's Annual,* 1988; and "Their Joyous Strain" to the *London Free Press,* December, 1988.

SIDELIGHTS: For Welwyn Wilton Katz, it was the books of J. R. R. Tolkien that changed everything. She once commented, "I found that it was possible, using words alone, to create a whole world, a marvelously complex and unreal world that other people could believe in." Katz has used her interest in myths, legends, and the supernatural to weave stories that incorporate both current problems most teenagers face—insecurity and parental divorce to name just two—and timeless mythological themes that play out the conflict between good and evil. Whether on their home turf or transported to another time or planet, her characters deal with evil outside themselves or within, when the protagonist becomes the unwitting prey of evil powers.

Katz, a fifth-generation Canadian, credits her Scottish and Cornish ancestors with her abiding interest in Celtic myths. Unlike many writers, Katz does not recall writing very much when she was young. One exception was a high school final exam in which she was asked to write for three hours on one of five topics. "I spent two hours trying to decide which of those awful topics I would choose," she once commented, "and the remaining hour 'taking dictation' from some inspired part of my brain, the words simply flowing out of me . . . . It was one of the most exciting experiences I've ever had." But even with the excellent grade she earned and the thrill of this feeling, it took a long time for Katz to try her hand at writing again.

An honors student in mathematics, Katz became a high school teacher, a position she held until she was twenty-eight. She found it difficult to adjust to being in the classroom, though she liked her students and made a good salary. She tried several makeovers—pierced ears, contact lenses, new clothes—but still felt awkward in her chosen profession. Uninspired, Katz worried that her whole life would continue on this steady, dull course and, as she remarked, "it gave me the creeps."

It was at this point that she read Tolkien; the immediate effect was that Katz decided to write an adult fantasy novel. Initially, she devoted evenings and summers to her writing, but found that part-time writing didn't suit her. A year's leave of absence was followed by another, and by then she had finished her first draft, a hefty 750 pages. The ambitious story took place in a different world and had a huge cast of characters, whose complex setting demanded long, detailed exposition. By 1979, she had resigned as a teacher and used another year to rewrite the manuscript.

Katz sent it out to several publishers but none expressed interest. "When there was no one left to send it to, I cried a little—okay, a lot!—and then put the book on my top shelf. There it sits to this day," she commented. But Katz made a very important discovery: she wanted to write. Furthermore, she learned about writing itself from doing the work, honing her technique and style. Among her characters were several children, and Katz thought she might try a children's book next.

Her breakthrough came in 1982, when her first novel, *The Prophecy of Tau Ridoo,* appeared. In it, the five Aubrey siblings find themselves in the strange and threatening world of Tau Ridoo, controlled by the terrifying Red General. He sends his deputies after the children, who become separated from each other. Cooky, a sorceress, comes to their aid and together they manage to defeat the evil General and to be reunited.

Witchery Hill's protagonist is Mike, whose parents have recently divorced. Along with his journalist father, Mike travels to Guernsey (one of the English Channel Islands) for a summer visit with the St. Georges, who are family friends. Mike's friendship with the eldest daughter, Lisa, reveals surprising

turmoil beneath the apparently calm surface of her family life. Diabetic and fiercely attached to her father, Lisa suspects her stepmother is not only a witch, but trying to gain control of the local coven. The job of vanquishing the evil powers set loose on the island and destroying the coven falls to Mike, who must also reconcile himself to a less-than-perfect relationship with his father. A contributor in *Publishers Weekly* lauded Katz for holding the reader in "thrall," concluding that *Witchery Hill* "is a knockout, with each character deftly delineated and a socko finish." John Lord, writing in *Voice of Youth Advocates,* echoed this view, praising Katz's use of the setting, with its Stonehenge-like standing stones and its invitation to adventure in a world of facts interwoven with fantasy. "For the reader who needs action and intrigue," Lord stated, "this book is definitely 'IT.'"

Witchery Hill sprang out of a series of coincidences connected to Katz's chance visit to Guernsey, whose ferry docked in the small town where she dropped off a rental car. A randomly chosen hotel happened to be staffed by a woman with an interest in the island's folklore. Katz found references to witchcraft on the island as late as 1967 and came upon a manual of witchcraft in a bookstore. She decided to set her story on the island and to use a very powerful book of sorcery as the source of the witches' strife.

Historical facts were the inspiration for *Sun God, Moon Witch* as well. Katz read widely on the dowsers (also known as water-witches), who often reported strong electrical shocks when they came into contact with standing stones like those in the stone circles in England. Katz also recalled a family story about a dowser who had discovered a spring on their farm, and she knitted the two together. In *Sun God, Moon Witch,* Thorny McCabe is underwhelmed by the idea of summering with her cousin Patrick in an English village. But she soon discovers that the village is engaged in a controversy over the ancient stone circle of Awen-Ur. Like *Witchery Hill, Sun God, Moon Witch* revolves around the protagonist's struggle to keep evil from taking over the world.

False Face tackles a different kind of ethical dilemma—the appropriate handling of cultural artifacts—as played out against a difficult family drama. Protagonist Laney McIntyre finds an Indian mask in a bog near her London, Ontario, home. The tensions in her house following her parents' recent divorce are symbolized by their different reactions to Laney's find: as a successful antiques dealer, her mother encourages her to profit by it, but her father, a professor, encourages her to donate it to a museum. Meanwhile, the mask itself appears to be emitting corrupting powers that only she and her Indian friend Tom seem able to stop. *Voice of Youth Advocates* reviewer Rosemary Moran pointed out that the novel is "steeped in Canadian lore" and that the characters embodied the difficulties of dealing with different cultures "with enough suspense to keep the reader involved until the climax." A *Publishers Weekly* contributor found that Katz "welds the supernatural element onto the family's conflicts with grace and competence."

Katz describes *The Third Magic* as a kind of predecessor to the King Arthur legend. The novel took her about three years to complete, much of it spent constructing Nwm, an imaginary world, in as much detail as possible. Morgan LeFevre, a fifteen-year-old, has accompanied her father to Tintagel to assist with a television documentary on the King Arthur legend. Centuries before, Morrigan, a sister in the matriarchal society of Nwm, had been sent to Tintagel, fated to become Morgan Le Fay. Because of her resemblance to Morrigan, Morgan is transported to Nwm, confronted by two warring forces of magic. To Margaret Miles of *Voice of Youth Advocates,* Katz tried hard but failed to find a new twist to the Arthurian and Celtic-based fantasies and wrote that Arthurian fans "may be interested in some aspects . . . but are likely to find it rather less magical than the classics of the genre." Although Robert Strang, in reviewing the book for the *Bulletin of the Center for Children's Books,* complained of a plot "convoluted even by genre standards," he found it to be a "unique recasting of a legend."

Katz changed direction a bit with *Whalesinger,* which looks at the relationships between humans, animals, and nature. Set in spectacular Point Reyes National Seashore in northern California, *Whalesinger* features two teenagers with problems, both of whom are involved in a summer marine conservation program. Nick is an angry young man eager to blame the team leader for Nick's older brother's death in a shipboard explosion, and Marty is a learning-disabled, lonely girl who has an empathic bond with a gray whale and her calf. Katz uses the coastline as emblematic of nature's power—the action climaxes in an earthquake; and history—there are references to an accident that occurred centuries before when Sir Francis Drake visited the

area. A critic in *Publishers Weekly* chided Katz for a "veritable bouillabaisse of fishy plot developments," finally determining that she "has gone overboard." *School Library Journal*'s Patricia Manning, however, applauded Katz for her "complex pattern of science, personalities, a lost treasure, and a whale mother with an ailing baby" and pronounced the book "intriguing."

With her interest in the supernatural, it's no surprise that Katz would find herself drawn to *Macbeth,* and making full use of the play's reputation among theater people for being cursed. Teenaged Kinny O'Neill, the protagonist of *Come Like Shadows,* has a summer job with the director of the Stratford, Canada, Shakespeare festival. When she finds the perfect mirror prop, Kinny has no idea that it contains the spirits of the eleventh-century witches that destroyed the real Macbeth. The company travels to perform in Scotland, the witches by now in modern dress and using the apparently helpless Kinny to further their plot to renew their coven. Barbara L. Michasiw wrote of the book in *Quill and Quire* that "*Come Like Shadows* is difficult to reconcile with reality. . . . This is a challenging story that will probably not be comfortably accessible" to all readers. Lucinda Sayder Whitehurst in *School Library Journal* also found the alternating points of view, from Kinny to Macbeth, a little difficult to follow, but felt that it would be "appreciated by drama and Shakespeare enthusiasts." Reviewing the book for *Voice of Youth Advocates,* Mary Jane Santos declared it "an intriguing mystery-fantasy with well developed characters and realistic dialogue."

Again and again, reviewers point to Katz's ability to use landscape and location to great advantage in her work. Her 1995 novel, *Time Ghost,* is set in the polluted world fifty years hence. Along with their friends—brother and sister Josh and Dani—Sara and her brother Karl accompany their grandmother to the North Pole. An argument between Sara and her grandmother catapults Sara and Dani back in time, to the late twentieth century before nature was irrevocably ruined. *Booklist*'s Carolyn Phelan predicted that readers would be drawn to the "flow of action and emotion, the deft descriptions of the natural world, and the sympathetic characters." Susan L. Rogers in *School Library Journal* was impressed with Katz's "absorbing story" that delivers "a serious ecological message," sentiments echoed by a *Publishers Weekly* critic, who also noted the ecological message and found it "stifles neither characters nor the plot."

After a break from myths, Katz returned to the ancient Norse tales for *Out of the Dark,* which *Children's Reader* reviewer Janet Wynne-Edwards termed "satisfying." Thirteen-year-old Ben, his younger brother Keith and their father move from Ottawa to start a new life in Newfoundland, in the town of Ship Cove, where his father grew up. Before her death, Ben's mother told him many of the Viking stories, and in her honor he begins to carve a knarr (a Viking ship), the myths and historical details helping him to deal with his own problems. As Wynne-Edwards wrote, "The young reader is not subjected to an anthropological checklist of artifacts and so may well retain this history." *Booklist* correspondent Susan Dove Lempke described *Out of the Dark* as "a story of quietly rising tension, with . . . appeal for . . . boys who find Vikings so fascinating."

Katz's prose retelling of *Beowulf* brings the story of the ancient hero to a new generation of readers. Told from the point of view of Wiglaf, Beowulf's heir, the tale moves through generations as Wiglaf learns of the wiles of the monster Grendel and then lives to witness Beowulf's slaying of both Grendel and Grendel's mother. *Booklist*'s Carolyn Phelan called Katz's recasting of the classic poem "graceful" and added that, in sum, the work is "a handsome volume."

Despite plots that sometimes strike reviewers as too complex, Katz consistently provides her readers with strong writing, interesting characters, and believable dialogue. She manages to work in her environmental concerns and her own fascination with ancient tales without overloading the story, earning her many awards and an enthusiastic, loyal following. "Katz's books are compelling," declared an essayist for the *St. James Guide to Young Adult Writers.* "She is a strong storyteller . . . and her characters are well drawn. She seems to be in tune with the adolescent psyche and is able to convey the painful confusions of that time of life in a succinct and sympathetic manner. She is harder on the adult characters who, if they are not the actual embodiment of evil, are somewhat remote and slow to understand or respond to the situations around them, almost as if life had deadened their feelings and perceptions." The critic added: "Katz's strongest books, *False Face, Whalesinger,* and to some extent, *Time Ghost,* all display her particular talent for inventive plots. . . . Her love of nature and fascination with the supernatural animates these, as well as all her novels, and her sensitive portrayals of adolescents are particularly compelling. She is always a pleasure to read."

In an interview with Raymond H. Thompson for *Taliesin's Successors: Interviews with Authors of Modern Arthurian Literature,* Katz commented, "Part of the reason I write fantasy is because of the magic. I choose magic because I think it's something that fascinates people, but in any case it fascinates me. I like to use magic to enhance reality. Magic is the thing that's around the corner: we can't see it, but it's there. I'm not sure that I actually believe in magic, but I think that you can use it as a writer. . . . It's always a challenge to write about things that people don't experience, and then try to make them think that they have experienced these things because they've just read about them."

BIOGRAPHICAL AND CRITICAL SOURCES:

BOOKS

Authors and Artists for Young Adults, Volume 19, Gale (Detroit, MI), 1996.
Major Authors and Illustrators for Children and Young Adults, Supplement, Gale (Detroit, MI), 1998.
St. James Guide to Young Adult Writers, 2nd edition, St. James (Detroit, MI), 1999.
Something about the Author, Volume 62, Gale (Detroit, MI), 1990.
Writer's Directory, 15th edition, St. James Press (Detroit, MI), 1999.

PERIODICALS

Booklist, May 1, 1995, p. 1573; October 15, 1996, Susan Dove Lempke, review of *Out of the Dark,* p. 424; December 1, 1999, Carolyn Phelan, review of *Beowulf,* p. 700.
Bulletin of the Center for Children's Books, February, 1989, p. 150.
Canadian Children's Literature, number 47, 1987.
Children's Reader, winter, 1995-96, Janet Wynne-Edwards, review of *Out of the Dark.*
Horn Book Magazine, November-December, 1996, Anne Deifendeifer, review of *Out of the Dark,* p. 737.
Kirkus Reviews, August 1, 1988, p. 1151.
Publishers Weekly, November 2, 1984, p. 77; December 21, 1990, p. 57; July 15, 1996, review of *Out of the Dark,* pp. 74-75; July 29, 1998, p. 234.
Quill and Quire, February, 1993, p. 36.

School Library Journal, May, 1991, p.111; December, 1993, p. 134; May, 1995, p. 108.
Voice of Youth Advocates, April, 1985, p. 48; February, 1989, p. 286; June, 1989, p. 116; October, 1993, p. 228.

ONLINE

Camelot Project, http://www.lib.rochester.edu/camelot/intrvws/katz.htm/ (September 5, 2002), Raymond H. Thompson, interview with Katz from his *Taliesin's Successors: Interviews with Authors of Modern Arthurian Literature* about supernatural elements in her work.
Welwyn Wilton Katz Homepage, http://www.booksbywelwyn.ca/ (May 21, 2002).*

* * *

KATZENBACH, John 1950-

PERSONAL: Born June 23, 1950, in Princeton, NJ; son of Nicholas deB. (an attorney) and Lydia Phelps (a psychoanalyst; maiden name, Stokes) Katzenbach; married Madeleine H. Blais (a journalist and writer), May 10, 1980; children: Nicholas, Justine. *Education:* Bard College, A.B., 1972. *Politics:* "Liberal, and damn proud of it." *Hobbies and other interests:* Fly-fishing.

ADDRESSES: Home—Amherst, MA. *Agent*—John Hawkins & Associates, 71 West 23rd St., New York, N.Y. 10010.

CAREER: Trenton Times, Trenton, NJ, reporter 1973-76; *Miami News,* Miami, FL, reporter, 1976-79; *Miami Herald,* Miami, circuit court reporter, 1981-82, feature writer weekly "Tropic Magazine," 1982-85. Novelist and author of nonfiction books, 1979—.

MEMBER: Authors Guild, Mystery Writers of America, Writers Guild of America, PEN International.

AWARDS, HONORS: Nominated twice for Edgar Award.

WRITINGS:

In the Heat of the Summer, Atheneum (New York, NY), 1982.

First Born, the Death of Arnold Zeleznik, Age Nine: Murder, Madness, and What Came After, Atheneum (New York, NY), 1984.
The Traveler, Putnam (New York, NY), 1987.
Day of Reckoning, Putnam (New York, NY), 1989.
Just Cause, Putnam (New York, NY), 1992.
The Shadow Man, Ballantine (New York, NY), 1995.
State of Mind, Ballantine (New York, NY), 1997.
Hart's War, Ballantine Books (New York, NY), 1999.
The Analyst, Ballantine Books (New York, NY), 2002.

Contributor of articles and book reviews to newspapers and magazines, including *Washington Post Book World, Philadelphia Inquirer Book Review,* and *New York Times Book Review.*

ADAPTATIONS: The motion picture *The Mean Season,* released by Orion in 1985 and starring Kurt Russell and Mariel Hemingway, was based on Katzenbach's novel *In the Heat of the Summer; Just Cause* was made into a film of the same name, starring Sean Connery, Laurence Fishburne, and Kate Capshaw, in 1995; *Hart's War* was made into a film of the same name, starring Bruce Willis and Colin Farrell, released by MGM in 2002.

WORK IN PROGRESS: The Madman's Tale, 2004.

SIDELIGHTS: Former reporter John Katzenbach has become known as a leading author of psychological thrillers. Two of his novels have been nominated for Edgar Awards, and three have been made into Hollywood films. His first novel, *In the Heat of the Summer,* is a mystery thriller wrought with "harrowing, high-tension drama," according to a *New York Times Book Review* critique by Stanley Ellin. The story centers around Miami crime reporter Malcolm Anderson, who covers a brutal murder for his newspaper and then comes into contact with the killer. Promising to strike again, the murderer attempts to justify his assaults on society by relating memories of his horrifying childhood and of his Vietnam War experiences. As the killings mount he makes Anderson his conduit to the public, with a series of rambling telephone monologues that provide the reporter with material for a bonanza of front-page stories and subsequent notoriety. Increasingly, though, Anderson's career interests conflict with his personal commitment to end the reign of terror. Adding to the conflict is Anderson's realization that he too is a potential victim. *New York Times* critic

Christopher Lehmann-Haupt observed that the book "has any number of qualities to recommend it—its realism, its cleverly twisted plot, its rich use of dramatic metaphor, its sensitive development of the dilemma faced by a reporter in telling a news story of which he has become a part." The novel received an Edgar Award nomination and was adapted as a film titled *The Mean Season.*

Katzenbach turned his focus from crime fiction to fact in *First Born, the Death of Arnold Zeleznik, Age Nine: Murder, Madness, and What Came After,* his account of the shocking 1974 murder of a nine-year-old boy. The Carter Zeleznik family of Philadelphia, Katzenbach recalls, had checked into a Miami airport hotel on their way to Costa Rica for Christmas vacation. Zeleznik left his son Arnold to wait in a hotel corridor while he returned a key. In the ninety seconds that the boy was alone, a recently released mental patient in a psychotic frenzy dragged the child into his room, slit his throat, and fled. It was, in the author's words, "a crime of absolutes: complete madness intersecting with total innocence; the barest contact resulting in the most unimaginable of tragedies."

The greater part of *First Born* describes the Zelezniks' dogged legal and bureaucratic battle to win justice in the case. The murder suspect, a thirty-one-year-old Jamaican named Vernal Walford, was quickly captured, and evidence came to light that he believed God had ordered him to kill a child. According to Alan A. Stone in the *New York Times Book Review,* Walford was "later described by a psychiatrist as the craziest person he had ever seen." Walford was ruled incompetent to stand trial and later received an uncontested judicial verdict of not guilty by reason of insanity. Carter Zeleznik, a psychologist, was convinced, however, that the accused understood the moral meaning of his act.

Katzenbach reports that the Zelezniks' real outrage was directed at the Massachusetts state mental health system, which had allowed a raving and violent Walford to walk freely out of a public psychiatric hospital several weeks earlier. Efforts to bring the state agency to account were met with bureaucratic stonewalling, and the family's lawsuit against the Commonwealth of Massachusetts ran aground on legal technicalities. Only after the national television news program *60 Minutes* publicized the Zeleznik case in 1982 did the Massachusetts legislature launch a full investigation,

which determined that the state had indeed been negligent in releasing Walford.

Katzenbach first became involved in the Zeleznik story when he covered the murder case as a reporter for *Miami News.* He subsequently got to know the family intimately in the course of its drawn-out private investigation. The author was unable to get Vernal Walford to tell his own story, however, and as a result, critics observed, the murderer does not figure as a personality in Katzenbach's account. *Washington Post Book World* reviewer Jonathan Yardley noted that the author nevertheless "bends over backward to be fair to everyone involved," and he termed *First Born* "a powerful and provocative book." *Detroit Free Press* critic Joe Swickard commented that Katzenbach "writes with a compelling urgency and toughness, tempered with compassion" in a "fine and worthwhile examination of madness, murder and its aftermath."

In the novel *Day of Reckoning,* the past comes to haunt comfortable yuppies Duncan and Megan Richards, who were members of the radical Phoenix Brigade twenty years earlier. The organization's leader, Tanya, went to prison after a botched bank robbery; released after eighteen years, Tanya is now obsessed with revenge and kidnaps Duncan's and Megan's young son. "Few writers of crime fiction," observed Lorenzo Carcaterra in *People,* "seem to understand the criminal mind as well as Katzenbach." The reviewer went on to praise the novel as "almost frantically fast-paced and extremely well-written." *Just Cause,* the story of a reporter's involvement in uncovering a possible wrongful murder conviction against a black man on death row in Florida, also drew considerable attention. Katzenbach adds a fascinating twist to the plot: after the reporter succeeds in freeing the inmate—winning a Pulitzer Prize to boot—he learns to his horror that he has been duped. A writer for *Publishers Weekly* found *Just Cause* a "riveting, provocative story."

Katzenbach explores a dystopian future in *State of Mind,* a crime story set in a shockingly violent near-future United States. *Booklist* reviewer Mary Frances Wilkens deemed the novel a "frightening and captivating story about family, death, and evil." A writer for *Publishers Weekly* admired the book's intriguing portrait of "an America consumed by rage and chaos" but found Katzenbach's characterization of the killer unconvincing. In *Library Journal,* however, Jo Ann Vicarel praised the book highly and observed that

"Katzenbach is a master at creating believable people caught up in horrific situations." And Charles P. Thobae in the *Houston Chronicle* commended *State of Mind* as a "superb thriller in which the power of the intelligent criminal mind rules violence in the cleverest and most malevolent way imaginable."

The Holocaust figures prominently in *The Shadow Man*. Set in contemporary Miami, the novel follows the efforts of depressed retired police detective Simon Winter to nab the "Shadow Man," a Jew forced by the Nazis to betray other Jews during World War II and now haunting elderly Holocaust survivors in Florida. In the *Times Literary Supplement*, Alex Harrison appreciated Katzenbach's use of thematic contrasts and his exploration of survivor guilt, but felt that the book's "blend of schmaltz and innuendo" was a major flaw. Acknowledging the novel's "interesting premise," a contributor to *Publishers Weekly* nevertheless criticized *The Shadow Man* for flat characterizations and padded plot. *Booklist* critic Emily Melton, however, praised the novel for "solid writing, a plot that's full of menace, and plenty of suspense."

Katzenbach returns to the Nazi era with *Hart's War*, hailed by a *Publishers Weekly* reviewer for its "vivid and unpredictable characters and diabolically imagined suspense." The novel is set in a German POW camp near the end of World War II, where racial tensions among the inmates erupt in a vicious murder. Tommy Hart, a former Harvard Law School student, is assigned to defend the suspect, Lincoln Scott, an antisocial black man who was the target of the murdered officer's racist abuse. *Booklist* contributor Gilbert Taylor described the novel as a mix of *The Great Escape, To Kill a Mockingbird,* and the story of the Tuskegee airmen—a blend Taylor considered less than wholly successful. However, a *Publishers Weekly* contributor hailed *Hart's War* as a "deeply affecting, artfully paced war epic." Jo Ann Vicarel in *Library Journal* expressed similar enthusiasm, praising the novel as a "superb story told with suspense, integrity, and compassion."

In *The Analyst,* a psychopath in New York City threatens to damage one of psychoanalyst Dr. Frederick Stark's relatives in exactly two weeks unless Stark either uncovers "Rumplestiltskin's" identity or commits suicide. "Ticking-clock suspense," commented Connie Fletcher in *Booklist*. A *Publishers Weekly* critic observed that Katzenbach has "potently chronicled a long journey of revenge and redemption" in a novel that stands as "one of his strongest outings." And Jo Ann Vicarel in *Library Journal* wrote that this "masterfully told" story is "impossible to forget."

Katzenbach once told *CA:* "I am often asked why or how I select the subjects for my books. It is simple, really. I enter a state of belief wherein I become persuaded that there is an important moral and psychological truth contained within the circumstances of the plot. (This is true for both fiction and nonfiction.) Then I merely pursue those elements until they are captured on the page, I hope."

Indeed, Katzenbach noted in an interview with *Publishers Weekly* writer Steven M. Zeitchik that his relatively quiet life makes it possible for him to focus on the kinds of stories that have made him a "slimeball pop novelist" in the eyes of the literary elite. Noting that he rather enjoys a "reverse snobbishness" about this categorization, he added that "If you had a really fascinating and adventurous life, you wouldn't have any time to write; you'd be too busy living. I guess if I was getting up in front of a writing class, I'd say, 'Have a normal life.'"

BIOGRAPHICAL AND CRITICAL SOURCES:

PERIODICALS

Booklist, January 1, 1987, review of *The Traveler,* p. 665; March 15, 1995, Emily Melton, review of *The Shadow Man,* p. 1283; May 15, 1997, Mary Frances Wilkens, review of *State of Mind,* p. 1541; November 15, 1998, Gilbert Taylor, review of *Hart's War,* p. 547; November 15, 2001, Connie Fletcher, review of *The Analyst,* p. 524.

Books Magazine, April, 1996, review of *The Shadow Man,* p. 25; spring, 2001, review of *Hart's War,* p. 20.

Christian Science Monitor, April 3, 1987, review of *The Traveler,* p. B7.

Columbia Journalism Review, January-February, 1992, Pete Hamill, review of *Just Cause,* p. 55.

Detroit Free Press, April 14, 1984.

Houston Chronicle, September 28, 1997, Charles P. Thobae, review of *State of Mind,* p. 25.

Kirkus Reviews, October 15, 2001, review of *The Analyst,* p. 1446.

Law Institute Journal, April, 1994, Robert Phillips, review of *Just Cause,* p. 311.

Library Journal, March 1, 1987, Jo Ann Vicarel, review of *The Traveler,* p. 96; March 15, 1989, V. Louise Saylor, review of *Day of Reckoning,* p. 86; January, 1992, A. J. Wright, review of *Just Cause,* p. 175; June 1, 1997, Jo Ann Vicarel, review of *State of Mind,* p. 148; December, 1998, Jo Ann Vicarel, review of *Hart's War,* p. 156; November 1, 2001, Jo Ann Vicarel, review of *The Analyst,* p. 132.

Los Angeles Times, May 21, 1982; February 15, 2002, Alina Tugend, "Telling a POW's Tale," p. F16.

Los Angeles Times Book Review, March 12, 1989, review of *Day of Reckoning,* p. 10; February 1, 1992, review of *Just Cause,* p. 8.

New York Times, May 3, 1982, February 22, 1984; February 17, 1995, Janet Maslin, review of *Just Cause* (film), p. C18.

New York Times Book Review, May 9, 1982, February 26, 1984; March 15, 1987, Todd S. Purdum, "Poetic Rat-a-Tat-Tat," p. 10, and Patrick Anderson, review of *The Traveler,* p. 10; April 9, 1989, Erica Abeel, review of *Day of Reckoning,* p. 11; April 19, 1992, John Hough, Jr., review of *Just Cause,* p. 22; July 30, 1995, Newgate Callendar, review of *The Shadow Man,* p. 22; March 15, 1998, review of *State of Mind,* p. 27; February 17, 2002, Marilyn Stasio, review of *The Analyst,* p. February 17, 2002.

People, May 15, 1989, Lorenzo Carcaterra, review of *Day of Reckoning,* p. 35.

Publishers Weekly, April 23, 1982; January 30, 1987, review of *The Traveler,* p. 371; January 6, 1989, review of *Day of Reckoning,* p. 92; November 15, 1991, review of *Just Cause,* p. 65; March 20, 1995, review of *The Shadow Man,* p. 41; July 7, 1997, review of *State of Mind,* p. 49; January 18, 1999, review of *Hart's War,* p. 323; March 15, 1999, Steven M. Zeitchik, "John Katzenbach: In the Shadow of Battle," p. 31; October 22, 2001, review of *The Analyst,* p. 41.

St. Louis Post-Dispatch, July 10, 2000, Dick Richmond, review of *Hart's War,* p. E3.

San Francisco Chronicle, September 5, 1999, David Lazarus, review of *Hart's War,* p. 6.

School Library Journal, July, 1992, Carolyn E. Gecan, review of *Just Cause,* p. 97.

Time, July 5, 1982.

Times Literary Supplement, June 9, 1995, Alex Harrison, review of *The Shadow Man,* p. 29.

Tribune Books (Chicago, IL), March 1, 1987, review of *The Traveler,* p. 3; March 26, 1989, review of

Day of Reckoning, p. 3; January 26, 1992, review of *Just Cause,* p. 3.

Washington Post, April 12, 1999, Rob Pegoraro, "A POW Lawyer's Emotional Trials," p. C3.

Washington Post Book World, April 4, 1982, February 1, 1984; February 15, 1987, review of *The Traveler,* p. 4; September 30, 1990, review of September 30, 1990, review of *Day of Reckoning,* p. 16; March 1, 1992, review of *Just Cause,* p. 4; May 28, 1995, review of *The Shadow Man,* p. 1; October 19, 1997, review of *State of Mind,* p. 7.

West Coast Review of Books, 1989, review of *Day of Reckoning,* p. 34.

ONLINE

The Mystery Reader, http://www.themysteryreader.com/ (June 28, 2002), review of *Hart's War.*

* * *

KENISON, Katrina 1958-

PERSONAL: Born October 3, 1958, in Philadelphia, PA; daughter of John Burton (a dentist) and Marilyn (an office manager; maiden name, Stancerfield) Kenison; married James Harker, 1980 (divorced, 1985); married Steven Moore Lewers (a publisher), September 12, 1987; children: (second marriage) two sons. *Education:* Graduate of Smith College (cum laude), 1980.

ADDRESSES: Office—Houghton Mifflin Co., 222 Berkeley St., Boston, MA 02166.

CAREER: Houghton Mifflin Co., Boston, MA, editor, 1981-88, 1990; editor of *Best American Short Stories,* published annually, 1991—.

MEMBER: Phi Beta Kappa.

WRITINGS:

(Editor and author of introduction, with Kathleen Hirsch) *Mothers: Twenty Stories of Contemporary Motherhood,* North Point Press (New York, NY), 1996.

(Editor, with John Updike) *The Best American Short Stories of the Century,* Houghton Mifflin (Boston, MA), 2000.

Mitten Strings for God: Reflections for Mothers in a Hurry, Warner Books (New York, NY), 2000.

(Editor) Rolf Gates, *Meditations from the Mat: Daily Reflections on the Path of Yoga,* Anchor Books (New York, NY), 2002.

Author of "A Remembrance," a 150-page biographical essay included in Olive Ann Burns's book of memoirs, *Leaving Cold Sassy,* Ticknor & Fields (New York, NY), 1992.

SIDELIGHTS: As editor of Houghton Mifflin's annual *Best American Short Stories* series, Katrina Kenison has helped to bring outstanding fiction to a wide readership. Every year Kenison works with a distinguished guest editor to identify more than one hundred notable short stories and twenty of the "best" that appear in the annual volume. It is Kenison's job to narrow the list to one hundred entries from the many thousands of stories written and published each year in America. The annual volume is a perennial favorite among book buyers, and inclusion in its pages is considered a high honor. A *Publishers Weekly* reviewer noted that the volumes in the series "thoroughly satisfy fans of quality short fiction."

In *The Best American Short Stories of the Century,* which Kenison edited with John Updike, the task of judging the best stories was monumental. Kenison picked semifinalists from thousands of stories submitted to the publisher's "Best of" series, out of which only fifty-five made Updike's final cut. Reviewers found the volume notable for its diversity: while classics by such writers as Sherwood Anderson, Ernest Hemingway, John Cheever, and Raymond Carver are included, almost half the stories are by women, and the perspectives of black, Jewish, gay, and immigrant writers abound. In Kenison's words, the anthology's stories "are an invaluable record of our century."

Booklist reviewer Brad Hooper noted that the anthology "brims with significance," and a contributor to *Publishers Weekly* observed that "life on this continent may be brutal, but this extraordinary collection offers up dazzling writing that salves wounds, as well as stories full of the pleasures of life."

Kenison mined more specialized material for *Mothers: Twenty Stories of Contemporary Motherhood,* edited with Kathleen Hirsch. The anthology, which a *Publish-*

ers Weekly reviewer considered "well-chosen," presents stories that, in the editors' words, show "the complexities of mothering in America today." The book includes stories by Perri Klass, Barbara Kingsolver, Kate Braverman, Mary Gordon, Sue Miller, and Alice Elliott Dark. In the *Austin American-Statesman,* Rebecca Thatcher observed that the story collection "is an example of the fact that sometimes fiction is the best preparation for reality." Thatcher concluded that the stories "tell a truth that no parenting manual can approximate."

In *Mitten Strings for God: Reflections for Mothers in a Hurry,* Kenison presents a volume of her own personal essays on the themes of family and spirituality. The book sprang from a Christmas note Kenison wrote to her friends one year, in which she expressed ideas about seeking quiet time for reflection and family togetherness. A *Publishers Weekly* reviewer found it a "heartfelt" collection of "richly anecdotal musings" that, though occasionally treacly, nevertheless "resonate with honesty and wisdom." A contributor to the *Christian Science Monitor* wrote: "Ms. Kenison's musings on family life, motherhood, and her own search for balance belong by the bedside, where it can be savored again and again."

Kenison is also editor of Rolf Gates's book *Meditations from the Mat: Daily Reflections on the Path of Yoga.* The book explores the ways a daily practice of yoga can transform the perception of other real-life situations. *Booklist* contributor Jane Tuma found the work "a wonderful book of instructive and encouraging daily meditations" that are "fresh" and "relevant."

BIOGRAPHICAL AND CRITICAL SOURCES:

BOOKS

Kenison, Katrina, and John Updike, editors, *The Best American Short Stories of the Century,* Houghton Mifflin (Boston, MA), 2000.

Kenison, Katrina, and Kathleen Hirsch, editors, *Mothers: Twenty Stories of Contemporary Motherhood,* North Point Press (New York, NY), 1996.

PERIODICALS

Austin American-Statesman, May 12, 1996, Rebecca Thatcher, "Reality of Mothering," review of *Mothers,* p. F8.

Booklist, November 1, 1995, Brad Hooper, review of *The Best American Short Stories 1995,* p. 453; November 15, 1996, Jim O'Laughlin, review of *The Best American Short Stories 1996,* p. 569; September 1, 1998, Brad Hooper, review of *The Best American Short Stories 1998,* p. 56B; April 1, 1999, review of *The Best American Short Stories of the Century,* p. 1384; November 1, 2000, Bonnie Smothers, review of *The Best American Short Stories 2000,* p. 511; October 15, 2001, James O'Laughlin, review of *The Best American Short Stories 2001,* p. 380; September 15, 2002, James O'Laughlin, "State of the Art," review of *The Best American Short Stories 2002,* p. 207; November 1, 2002, Jane Tuma, review of *Meditations from the Mat: Daily Reflections on the Path of Yoga,* p. 464.

Christian Science Monitor, May 9, 1996, "Mothers' Literature Offers New Voices on Child-Rearing," p. 13; December 30, 1996, Carl Wood, review of *The Best American Short Stories 1996,* p. 13; May 24, 2000, "A Mother's Guidebook for the Road Less Traveled," p. 12.

Entertainment Weekly, April 16, 1999, Mark Harris, review of *The Best American Short Stories of the Century,* p. 12.

Family Circle, April 1, 2000, excerpt from *Mitten Strings for God: Reflections for Mothers in a Hurry,* p. 24.

Insight on the News, July 26, 1999, Rex Roberts, review of *The Best American Short Stories of the Century,* p. 36.

Kirkus Reviews, September 1, 2000, review of *The Best American Short Stories 2000,* p. 1303.

Library Journal, February 1, 1994, Eleanor Mitchell, review of *The Best American Short Stories 1993,* p. 114; November 1, 1994, Eleanor Mitchell, review of *The Best American Short Stories 1994,* p. 113; May 1, 1996, Helen Rippier Wheeler, review of *Mothers,* p. 94; October 1, 1996, Adam Mazmanian, review of *The Best American Short Stories 1996,* p. 129; September 1, 1999, Christine DeZelar-Tiedman, review of *The Best American Short Stories 1999,* p. 235.

New York Times Book Review, May 9, 1999, Michael Gorra, review of *The Best American Short Stories of the Century,* p. 8.

Publishers Weekly, September 19, 1994, review of *The Best American Short Stories 1994,* p. 65; September 18, 1995, review of *The Best American Short Stories 1995,* p. 123; April 15, 1996, review of *Mothers,* p. 48; September 8, 1997, review of *The Best American Short Stories 1997,* p. 56; August 24, 1998, review of *The Best American Short Stories 1998,* p. 49; March 8, 1999, review of *The Best American Short Stories of the Century,* p. 47; August 30, 1999, review of *The Best American Short Stories 1999,* p. 47; April 3, 2000, review of *Mitten Strings for God,* p. 74; May 1, 2000, review of *Mitten Strings for God* (audio version), p. 32; August 28, 2000, review of *The Best American Short Stories 2000,* p. 53; September 3, 2001, review of *The Best American Short Stories 2001,* p. 58; September 30, 2002, review of *The Best American Short Stories 2002,* p. 50.

Seattle Times, December 15, 2002, Irene Warner, "Family Ties, Moral Struggles Unite Short-Story Collection," review of *The Best American Short Stories 2002,* p. K11.

ONLINE

New York Times Online, http://www.nytimes.com/ books/ (August 10, 1999), author interview.*

L

LACEY, Robert 1944-

PERSONAL: Born January 3, 1944, in Guildford, Surrey, England; son of Leonard John (a banker) and Vida (Winch) Lacey; married Alexandra Jane Avrach (a graphic designer), April 3, 1971; children: Sasha (son), Scarlett, Bruno. *Education:* Selwyn College, Cambridge, B.A., 1966, diploma of education, 1967, M.A., 1970.

ADDRESSES: Agent—Janklow & Nesbit Associates, 598 Madison Ave., New York, NY 10022-1614. *E-mail*—robert@robertlacey.com.

CAREER: Illustrated London News, London, England, writer, 1968; *Sunday Times,* London, assistant editor of *Sunday Times Magazine,* 1969-73, "Look!" page, editor, 1973-74; writer.

WRITINGS:

Robert, Earl of Essex, Atheneum (New York, NY), 1971, published as *Robert, Earl of Essex: An Elizabethan Icarus,* Weidenfeld & Nicolson (London, England), 1971, reprinted, Phoenix Press (London, England), 2001.

The Life and Times of Henry VIII, Weidenfeld & Nicolson (London, England), 1972, Abbeville Press (New York, NY), 1992.

The Queens of the North Atlantic, Sidgwick & Jackson (London, England), 1973.

Sir Walter Ralegh, Weidenfeld & Nicolson (London, England), 1973, Atheneum (New York, NY), 1973, reprinted, Phoenix Press (London, England), 2000.

Majesty: Elizabeth II and the House of Windsor, Harcourt (New York, NY), 1977, revised golden jubilee edition published as *Monarch: The Life and Reign of Elizabeth II,* Free Press (New York, NY), 2002.

The Kingdom, Hutchinson (London, England), 1981, Avon (New York, NY), 1983.

Princess, Times Books (New York, NY), 1982.

Aristocrats (based on television series of same name; also see below), BBC Publications/Hutchinson (London, England), 1983.

Ford: The Men and the Machine, Little, Brown (Boston, MA), 1986.

God Bless Her!, Century (London, England), 1987.

Little Man: Meyer Lansky and the Gangster Life, Little, Brown (Boston, MA), 1991.

Grace, Putnam (New York, NY), 1994.

Sotheby's: Bidding for Class, Little, Brown (Boston, MA), 1998.

(With Danny Danziger) *The Year 1000: What Life Was Like at the Turn of the Millennium: An Englishman's World,* Little, Brown (Boston, MA), 1999.

Great Tales from English History: Cheddar Man to the Peasants' Revolt, Little, Brown (Boston, MA), 2003.

EDITOR AND CONTRIBUTOR

The French Revolution: A Collection of Contemporary Documents, Grossman, Volume 1: *The Fall of the Bastille,* 1968, Volume 2: *The Terror,* 1968, revised edition published in one volume as *The French Revolution,* Jackdaw (London, England), 1976.

The Rise of Napoleon, Grossman, 1971.

The Pallisers: A Full Guide to the Serial, BBC Publications (London, England), 1971.

The Retreat from Moscow, 1812, Jackdaw (London, England), 1970.

The Peninsular War, Jackdaw (London, England), 1971.

War and Peace: A Full Guide to the Serial, British Broadcasting Corp. (London, England), 1972.

Drake and the "Golden Hinde": A Collection of Contemporary Documents, Jackdaw (London, England), 1975.

Elizabeth II: The Work of the Queen; A Collection of Documents, Jackdaw (London, England), 1977.

Also author of documentary series *Aristocrats,* broadcast on BBC-TV; author of *The Saudi Arabians* (audio cassette), Encyclopedia Americana/CBS News Audio Resource Library (New York, NY), 1982. Contributor to periodicals.

SIDELIGHTS: British historian, journalist, and biographer Robert Lacey specializes in a particular type of "anthropological" biography that analyzes its subject—usually an elite family or a representative individual—in order to illuminate the customs, beliefs, and rituals of an entire segment of society. To get inside his subjects—which have included the British Royal Family, the founding chieftain of Saudi Arabia, and Henry Ford and his automobile company—Lacey has gone to great lengths to gain their trust. For example, he learned Arabic and moved to Saudi Arabia for eighteen months in order to research his history of that country, entitled *The Kingdom.* "I feel it's one of the duties of a biographer to go through a stage of seeing the world exactly as his subject sees or saw it," Lacey once told *CA.* "I just don't understand people who write books which are dismissive of their subjects. I can't imagine myself devoting three or four years to studying something for which I have no respect or interest."

While on the editorial staff of the London *Sunday Times,* Lacey completed two biographies, *Robert, Earl of Essex* and *Sir Walter Ralegh.* On the strength of those critically acclaimed books, he was commissioned to write a history of the reign of Queen Elizabeth II, which he commenced in 1974. Published three years later to coincide with the queen's Silver Jubilee, *Majesty: Elizabeth II and the House of Windsor* became an international bestseller that established Lacey's reputation for accuracy, fairness, thorough scholarship, and a lively prose style.

"If Elizabeth II were not a queen, no one would write a book about her," Lacey observed in *Majesty,* pinpointing one of the primary difficulties he had in enlivening his subject, who was an ordinary woman in extraordinary circumstances. He overcame that obstacle in part by emphasizing the queen's role in the public's imagination and her function as a *tabula rasa* onto which people project their fantasies and opinions of royalty. As the symbol of British nationalism, the queen is almost universally revered in her own country, where people's admiration for her presented Lacey with yet another problem in writing his book. "It was very difficult to get people to say anything uncomplimentary about her," he once remarked to *CA.* "The British royal head of state is almost an icon," he continued. "It is one of her valuable functions to stand for everything that people agree upon, while politicians concentrate on what people disagree about. . . . So one is dealing there with a very precious part of the way the country runs."

Nor had public sentiment dimmed by 2002 When Lacey released *Monarch: The Life and Reign of Elizabeth II* in time to coincide with the queen's golden jubilee. In the intervening years between the first and second books on Her Majesty, the royal family had undergone several divorces and faced the accidental death of the immensely popular Princess Diana, the subject of another Lacey biography. *Monarch* revisits these times of turmoil and examines how Queen Elizabeth II has handled herself in public and private. *Library Journal* contributor Isabel Coates noted Lacey's "mature and thoughtful discussion" of the British royal family, and Elizabeth in particular. While a *Publishers Weekly* reviewer described Lacey's book as "sympathetic" to the queen, the reviewer also felt that the work "offers an incisive analysis of the development of royal media coverage."

In researching his next book, *The Kingdom,* Lacey faced almost the opposite set of circumstances, in which the Arab people would criticize their ruler bluntly on a face-to-face basis but would strenuously avoid putting their complaints in writing. Lacey once explained to *CA* that in Saudi Arabia "there are two sorts of truth: the spoken truth and the written truth. The spoken truth is close to the Western idea of the truth. If you are talking, you can gossip and you can criticize. . . . But when it came to writing, which was my job, writing is like carving out the tablets in marble. This is something which is preserved forever and where you don't have any criticism." Indeed, *The Kingdom* was banned in Saudi Arabia because of its unflattering depictions of the Bedouins and its impartial treatment of Abdul Aziz Ibn Sa'ud, the country's founding ruler. In the West, however, the book was very well received. In his review for the *Chicago Tribune Book World,* Milton Viorst described Laccy's tonc as "fair without being bland, understanding without being apologetic. His sense of balance keeps him to the essentials of the story, preserving him from such labyrinths as international economics and intra-Arab relations. His sure hand makes a forbidding culture intelligible. *The Kingdom* must be ranked as a model work of popular history."

Lacey turned to lighter subjects for his next two publications, *Princess,* a handsome pictorial biography of Diana, Princess of Wales, and *Aristocrats,* a survey of European nobility produced in conjunction with his BBC-TV documentary series of the same name. Neither book received serious critical attention, but both were judged competent treatments of their themes. London *Times* contributor Tim Heald described *Aristocrats* as "an imaginative attempt to make a book out of a TV series." Reviewing *Princess* for the *Times Literary Supplement,* Victoria Glendinning wrote that Lacey "knows more than he has space to write, so within his fairy-story framework every sentence makes its point, and he still finds room for anecdote and dialogue."

Turning to the United States for inspiration for his next project, an examination of four generations of the Ford family and their automotive empire, Lacey, in typical fashion, moved to Michigan in 1984 to conduct research, which included working on an assembly line in a Detroit auto plant. The result of his labor, *Ford: The Men and the Machine,* was published two years later to enthusiastic reviews. Writing in the *New York Times Book Review,* biographer Ted Morgan found that *"Ford* is really two books in one, in which Robert Lacey has indefatigably combed the archives and beguiled 100 birds of various plumage to sing. The first is an Alger-ish account of Henry Ford's triumph. . . . The second book is like a television serial. It is as rich in incident and character as the prime-time soaps and requires no suspension of

disbelief, being true." Morgan concluded that "Robert Lacey has made the transition to the American industrial monarch with no loss of panache." Lacey's "research is prodigious," Ruth Clements noted in her review for the Toronto *Globe and Mail,* "but the impressive accumulation of facts and anecdotes does not in itself account for the book's appeal. It is Lacey's insights into the American psyche—restless, driven, and teeming with unresolved tensions—that give this book its depth and dynamic edge."

Lacey investigated another realm of American mythology—the glamorization of organized crime—in his well-received 1991 biography of the Mafia's accountant Meyer Lansky, on whose life the character of Hyman Roth in the first two *Godfather* movics was based. "Americans cherish their gangsters," Lacey stated in *Little Man: Meyer Lansky and the Gangster Life.* "They delight in the myths of cleverness, power, and wealth which they wreath around these defective outlaws." Evaluating the biography for the *New York Times Book Review,* one critic described *Little Man* as "a useful and informative corrective, an exercise in demythologizing that we do well to take to heart. It does not have the narrative sweep of Lacey's exemplary history of the Ford family and it is longer than need be, but it is sober, balanced and persuasive." Describing Lacey's technique in his review for *Newsweek,* Malcolm Jones, Jr. praised the author for cleverly using "the minutiae of Lansky's existence—what he ate, what he wore, the inscription on his dog's tombstone—not to bring the legend to life but to show that behind the myths there wasn't much life there to start with. Dour and wittily deflating, *Little Man* is a scrupulous, scathing indictment of the gangster life."

Lacey's next project was another doomed royal, Princess Grace of Monaco, who died in an automobile accident at the age of fifty-one. The author told *People* that before he signed to write about the former Grace Kelly he thought she was "insipid" and "rather bland." His research revealed a passionate actress from a high-living family who had affairs with her co-stars and, after marriage, with much younger men. To quote Joanne Kaufman in *People, Grace* "delivers some prime revelations." Brad Hooper in *Booklist* found the book to be "a very respectable biography" in which Lacey makes Princess Grace "real without really diminishing her effect and effectiveness."

One of Lacey's most popular books to date is *Sotheby's: Bidding for Class.* The volume explores the history of the famed auction house from its founding in eighteenth-century England as a rare book dealership to its place in the expanding market for rare items of all sorts. Lacey goes behind the scenes at Sotheby's to learn how its experts evaluate items and then create an atmosphere that will spur bidders to compete at the highest levels. "Robert Lacey tells the story of Sotheby's to match the polish and style of his subject matter," wrote Joan Bridgman in *Contemporary Review.* "As skillfully handled as any popular bestseller, his main narrative is sandwiched between a riveting prologue and an epilogue both detailing the buzz of two major auctions—a compound of cash, greed and folly." A *Publishers Weekly* commentator likewise noted the work "makes a savory read-full of glamour, chicanery, snobbery and sharp practices." *Booklist* contributor Margaret Flanagan concluded that *Sotheby's* offers "charming entrepreneurial and social history."

In an interview with *Publishers Weekly* Lacey said that he aims to write a bestseller each time he takes up his pen and that he enjoys the storytelling aspects of his craft. "It's true, I'm fascinated by elite groups," he said. "My whole life as a grammar-school boy, getting to Cambridge University and working on the London *Sunday Times* has been very aspirational." Indeed, several of the author's works have earned him in excess of one million dollars, and his books have been widely translated and sold in Europe, South America, and Asia. *Publishers Weekly* writer Giles Foden wrote: "Lacey is a fluent writer. On that level, the success of his books is well-deserved. Like Sotheby's punters, Lacey bids for class. And he delivers it—with some sophistication and an appropriate scent of filthy, but delicious, lucre." In the *Library Journal,* Steven J. Mayover concluded that all of Lacey's works "incorporate meticulous historical research, fine storytelling, and a very readable style."

For a previously published interview, see entry in *Contemporary Authors New Revision Series,* Volume 16, 1986, pp. 208-214.

BIOGRAPHICAL AND CRITICAL SOURCES:

BOOKS

Lacey, Robert, *Majesty: Elizabeth II and the House of Windsor,* Harcourt (New York, NY), 2002.

Lacey, Robert, *Little Man: Meyer Lansky and the Gangster Life,* Little, Brown (Boston, MA), 1991.

PERIODICALS

Booklist, August, 1994, Brad Hooper, review of *Grace,* p. 1987; June 1, 1998, Margaret Flanagan, review of *Sotheby's: Bidding for Class,* p. 1683; February 15, 1999, Jay Freeman, review of *The Year 1000: What Life Was Like at the Turn of the First Millennium,* p. 1036.

Chicago Tribune, July 3, 1986, p. 3.

Chicago Tribune Book World, March 7, 1982.

Contemporary Review, December, 1998, Joan Bridgman, review of *Sotheby's,* p. 327.

Detroit Free Press, May 4, 1986.

Globe and Mail (Toronto, Ontario, Canada), August 2, 1986; August 22, 1987; November 30, 1991.

History Today, June, 2002, Robert Lacey, "Story Telling: Robert Lacey, Royal Biographer and Commentator, Describes His Enthusiasm for Joyously Traditional History," p. 62.

Library Journal, May 1, 1998, Steven J. Mayover, review of *Sotheby's,* p. 112; February 15, 1999, Robert James Andrews, review of *The Year 1000,* p. 166; May 1, 2002, Isabel Coates, review of *Monarch: The Life and Reign of Elizabeth II,* p. 112.

Los Angeles Times Book Review, August 3, 1986, p. 4; November 10, 1991, p. 1.

Newsweek, November 11, 1991, p. 71.

New Yorker, September 8, 1986, p. 137; May 20, 2002, Martin Amis, "The Queen's Heart."

New York Times, June 9, 1971; February 23, 1977; June 26, 1986.

New York Times Book Review, July 13, 1986, pp. 1, 36-37; October 20, 1991, p. 29; October 13, 1993, p. 3; July 5, 1998, Carol Vogel, review of *Sotheby's,* p. 17.

People, October 17, 1994, Joanne Kaufman, review of *Grace,* p. 30, and "Amazing Grace: Talking with Robert Lacey," p. 30.

Publishers Weekly, August 1, 1994, review of *Grace,* p. 68; March 23, 1998, review of *Sotheby's,* p. 83; June 8, 1998, Giles Foden, "Robert Lacey: Hooked on Glamour," p. 42; January 18, 1999, review of *The Year 1000,* p. 321; April 22, 2002, review of *Monarch,* p. 60.

Spectator, October 26, 1991, p. 37.

Time, November 4, 1991, p. 93.

Times (London, England), October 20, 1983.

Times Literary Supplement, September 19, 1968, p. 1023; June 25, 1982; February 7, 1992, p. 6.

Washington Monthly, July-August, 1998, Suzannah Lessard, review of *Sotheby's,* p. 42.

Whole Earth, winter, 2000, review of *The Year 1000,* p. 14.

ONLINE

Robert Lacey Web site, http://www.robertlacey.com/ (February 25, 2003).*

*   *   *

LAIRD, Elizabeth (Mary Risk) 1943-

PERSONAL: Born October 21, 1943, in Wellington, New Zealand; daughter of John McLelland (a general secretary) and Florence Marion (a homemaker; maiden name, Thomson) Laird; married David Buchanan Mc-Dowall (a writer), April 19, 1975; children: Angus John, William Alistair Somerled. *Ethnicity:* "Caucasian." *Education:* University of Bristol, B.A. (with honors), 1966; University of Edinburgh, M.Litt., 1972. *Religion:* Church of England.

ADDRESSES: Home—31 Cambrian Rd., Richmond, Surrey TW10 6JQ, England. *E-mail*—lairdmcdowall@ aol.com.

CAREER: Teacher in Ethiopia; full-time writer, 1980—.

MEMBER: Society of Authors, Anglo-Ethiopian Society.

AWARDS, HONORS: Burnley Express Book Award, 1988, for *Red Sky in the Morning;* Children's Book Award for *Kiss the Dust;* Smarties Young Judges Award for *Hiding Out;* Guardian Children's Fiction Prize, 2002, for *Jake's Tower.*

WRITINGS:

English in Education, Oxford University Press (Oxford, England), 1977.

Elizabeth Laird

Welcome: To Great Britain and the U.S.A., Longman (New York, NY), 1983.

Faces of Britain, Longman (New York, NY), 1986.

Faces of the U.S.A., photographs by Darryl Williams, Longman (New York, NY), 1987.

Loving Ben, Delacorte (New York, NY), 1989, published as *Red Sky in the Morning,* Heinemann (London, England), 1989.

Arcadia (historical novel), Macmillan (New York, NY), 1990.

FOR CHILDREN

Anna and the Fighter, illustrated by Gay Galsworthy, Heinemann Educational (London, England), 1977.

The House on the Hill, illustrated by Gay Galsworthy, Heinemann Educational (London, England), 1978.

The Garden, illustrated by Peter Dennis, Heinemann Educational (London, England), 1979.

The Big Green Star, illustrated by Leslie Smith, Collins (London, England), 1982.

The Blanket House, illustrated by Leslie Smith, Collins (London, England), 1982.

The Doctor's Bag, illustrated by Leslie Smith, Collins (London, England), 1982.

(With Abba Aregawi Wolde Gabriel) *The Miracle Child: A Story from Ethiopia,* Holt (New York, NY), 1985.

The Cubby Bears' Birthday Party, illustrated by Carolyn Scrace, Collins (London, England), 1985.

The Cubby Bears Go Camping, illustrated by Carolyn Scrace, Collins (London, England), 1985.

The Cubby Bears Go on the River, illustrated by Carolyn Scrace, Collins (London, England), 1985.

The Cubby Bears Go Shopping, illustrated by Carolyn Scrace, Collins (London, England), 1985.

The Dark Forest, illustrated by John Richardson, Collins (London, England), 1986.

The Long House in Danger, illustrated by John Richardson, Collins (London, England), 1986.

Henry and the Birthday Surprise, illustrated by Mike Hibbert, photographs by Robert Hill, British Broadcasting Corp. (London, England), 1986.

The Road to Bethlehem: A Nativity Story from Ethiopia, foreword by Terry Waite, Holt (New York, NY), 1987.

Prayers for Children, illustrated by Margaret Tempest, Collins (London, England), 1987.

Wet and Dry, Pan Books (London, England), 1987.

Hot and Cold, Pan Books (London, England), 1987.

Light and Dark, Pan Books (London, England), 1987.

Heavy and Light, Pan Books (London, England), 1987.

Happy Birthday! A Book of Birthday Celebrations, illustrated by Satomi Itchekawa, Collins (London, England), 1987, Philomel (New York, NY), 1988.

Hymns for Children, illustrated by Margaret Tempest, Collins (London, England), 1988.

Sid and Sadie, Collins (London, England), 1988.

(With Olivia Madden) *The Inside Outing,* Barron's Educational Services (Woodbury, NY), 1988.

Crackers, Heinemann (Portsmouth, NH), 1989.

Rosy's Garden, illustrated by Satomi Itchekawa, Putnam (London, England), 1990.

The Day the Ducks Went Skating, Tambourine Books (New York, NY), 1990.

The Day Veronica Was Nosy, Tambourine Books (New York, NY), 1990.

The Day Sydney Ran Off, Tambourine Books (New York, NY), 1990.

The Day Patch Stood Guard, Tambourine Books (New York, NY), 1990.

The Pink Ghost of Lamont, Heinemann (Portsmouth, NH), 1991.

Kiss the Dust, Dutton, 1992, Puffin (New York, NY), 1994.

Hiding Out, Heinemann (Portsmouth, NH), 1993.

Secret Friends, Hodder & Stoughton (London, England), 1996.

Jay, Heinemann (Portsmouth, NH), 1997.

Forbidden Ground, Hamish Hamilton (London, England), 1997.

On the Run, Mammoth (Rochester, NY), 1997.

Gabriel's Feather, illustrated by Bettina Patterson, Scholastic (New York, NY), 1998.

A Book of Promises, DK Publishing (New York, NY), 2000.

When the World Began, Oxford University Press (New York, NY), 2000.

Jake's Tower, Macmillan (New York, NY), 2001.

The Garbage King, Macmillan (New York, NY), 2003.

A Little Piece of Ground, Macmillan (New York, NY), 2003.

The Ice Cream Swipe, Oxford University Press (New York, NY), 2003.

Hot Rock Mountain (short stories), Egmont Books (London, England), in press.

Author of ten volumes in the "Wild Things" series, published by Macmillan (New York, NY), 1999-2000, including *Leopard's Trail, Baboon Rock, Elephant Thunder, Rhino Fire, Red Wolf, Zebra Storm, Parrot Rescue, Turtle Reef, Chimp Escape,* and *Lion Pride.* Also writer for television, including *The Toucan 'Tecs* and *Testament.*

SIDELIGHTS: Elizabeth Laird, a linguistics specialist who has written entertaining, educational, and religious books for children, received praise for her two books recounting Ethiopian religious tales. In *The Miracle Child: A Story from Ethiopia* she tells the story of Takla Haymanot, a thirteenth-century Ethiopian saint known for praying on one leg after the other withered away and for performing such miracles as healing the sick and raising the dead. Laird's captions, which accompany the book's reproductions of eighteenth-century paintings by Ethiopian monks, are "informative and explain many of the artistic conventions of Ethiopian paintings in a manner so simple as to be understandable to a child and yet interesting to an adult," according to Vincent Crapanzano of the *New York Times Book Review.* Rosemary L. Bray, an editor of the *New York Times Book Review,* said *The Road to Bethlehem: A Nativity Story from Ethiopia,* which is a retelling of Ethiopian accounts of Jesus Christ's birth and the life of the Holy Family, would be "delightful" for children because of Laird's "graceful" storytelling and insightful captions.

Laird once told *CA:* "I began to write at the age of thirteen when I started the lifelong habit of compulsive diary keeping, but I only began to write for a living when I was married with children of my own. I started by producing English textbooks for speakers of other languages, and moved slowly from there into writing fictional works for children and young teens. Inspiration comes from various sources: personal childhood experiences such as the death of my young brother, my own children's experiences, both happy and unhappy, of their school years, my many years of living and working in Ethiopia, India, Iraq, France, and Lebanon. My historical novel for adults, set in New Zealand and Scotland in the nineteenth century, was based on my own family history. Ethiopia is my special love, ever since my youthful years of working there during the reign of Haile Selassie, and I have recently returned on several occasions in order to travel around that vast and ancient land collecting folk stories and preparing readers for Ethiopian schools."

More recently Laird added: "The older I become, the more I realize that being a writer is not a voluntary condition. I didn't decide to become a writer, I discovered that I was one. This slow revelation, after years of teaching in Britain and abroad, has brought me much joy and many anxieties. The joy comes not only from the satisfactions of the creative process, but also from the freedom that being a writer brings, the ability to choose one's own subjects, to travel in search of inspiration, to meet fellow authors, and receive the responses of readers. The anxieties rise from the insecurity of the writer's life, the erratic income, the uncertain response of reviewers, the fear that inspiration, when the current project is finished, might never come back again.

"I have been exceptionally fortunate to be able to combine travel with writing. My long-term interest in Ethiopia has resulted in *When the World Began,* stories which I collected in the most remote areas of that country from storytellers from all walks of life. *The Garbage King,* too, is set in Addis Ababa, Ethiopia, and enters the world of street children living there. Years spent in the Middle East resulted in *Kiss the Dust,* the story of a Kurdish refugee girl forced to flee from her home in northern Iraq. This was followed by

Forbidden Ground, set in Morocco, and *A Little Piece of Ground,* set in Palestine. Many visits to Africa produced the ten novels in the 'Wild Things' series, in which project I was greatly helped by wildlife experts all over East Africa."

BIOGRAPHICAL AND CRITICAL SOURCES:

PERIODICALS

New York Times Book Review, November 10, 1985, Vincent Crapanzano, review of *The Miracle Child: A Story from Ethiopia;* December 6, 1987, Rosemary L. Bray, review of *The Road to Bethlehem: A Nativity Story from Ethiopia.*
Times Literary Supplement, November 29, 1985.

*   *   *

LANGE, John
    See CRICHTON, (John) Michael

*   *   *

LEE, Sharon 1952-

PERSONAL: Born 1952, in Baltimore, MD; married Steve Miller (a writer), 1980. *Education:* Attended University of Maryland, Baltimore County. *Hobbies and other interests:* Cats.

ADDRESSES: Home—ME. *Agent*—c/o Author Mail, SRM Publications, P.O. Box 179, Unity, ME 04988-0179. *E-mail*—rolanni@mint.net.

CAREER: Science fiction writer. Worked in the secretarial field, c. 1970-76; University of Maryland Professional Schools, administrative aide to dean, School of Social Work, 1976-78; Book Castle (book store), founder and owner, beginning 1978; also worked delivering tractor trailers, selling cider, and as an advertising copy writer.

WRITINGS:

(With husband, Steve Miller) *The Tomorrow Log* (novel), Meisha Merlin Publishing (Decatur, GA), 2003.

Barnburner (mystery), SRM Publications (Winslow, ME), 2003.

The Naming of Kinzel, General Avocations, 1987, SRM Publications (Winslow, ME), 1998.

Agent of Change (see also below), Ballantine (New York, NY), 1988.

Conflict of Honors (see also below), Ballantine (New York, NY), 1988.

Carpe Diem (see also below), Ballantine (New York, NY), 1989.

Gnothi-Kairon (adaptation of *Space Rogue,* a computer game), 1990.

Two Tales of Korval: Adventures in the Liaden Universe, No. 1, SRM Publications (Winslow, ME), 1995.

Variations Three, SRM Publications (Winslow, ME), 1996.

Plan B, Meisha Merlin Publishing (Decatur, GA), 1999.

Partners in Necessity (includes *Agent of Change, Conflict of Honors,* and *Carpe Diem,*) Meisha Merlin Publishing (Decatur, GA), 2000.

Pilots Choice (includes *Local Custom* and *Scout's Progress,*) Meisha Merlin Publishing (Decatur, GA), 2001.

I Dare, Meisha Merlin Publishing (Decatur, GA), 2002.

Balance of Trade, Meisha Merlin Publishing (Decatur, GA), 2004.

Contributor to periodicals, including *Absolute Magnitude, Amazing Stories, Owlflight, A Distant Soil, Fantasy Book, Dragonfields, Pulphouse,* and *Star Triad.* Webmaster of several Web sites, including *Bloo KangaRue* and *Liad.*

WORK IN PROGRESS: *Crystal Soldier,* another "Liaden Universe" novel for Meisha Merlin Publishing, 2005.

SIDELIGHTS: In 1988, with the collaboration of her husband, Steve Miller, science-fiction writer Sharon Lee began her interstellar trilogy involving the Korval clan of Liad. In 1996, two more stories from that fictional setting were published as *Two Tales of Korval: Adventures in the Liaden Universe, No. 1.*

Agent of Change and *Carpe Diem* both involve an interstellar agent. In *Carpe Diem,* Liaden Val Con, the Korval clan leader, and his love, Miri of Terran, crash in a prohibited primitive world while escaping from villains. They attempt to learn the language after reaching inhabitants of this world. Back on Liad, Shan, Val Con's brother, and his sweetheart, Priscilla, mount a search for Val and Miri while others plot to displace Val Con's clan leadership. Eventually the shipwrecked Val Con and Miri return to the clan and defeat the scheme of the Department of the Interior to subvert Val Con. However, as *Analog* reviewer Tom Easton recounted, "the Department remains, its nefarious anti-clan plots intact, and Korval still faces its greatest battles." Easton praised the book, especially for its excellent development of the characters' relationships.

In another Lee-Miller effort, *Conflict of Honors,* a starship crewperson in the same galaxy is on a quest to become a pilot. The stories in *Two Tales of Korval,* noted Easton in another *Analog* review, "are strong on characters, clever, humane, and smooth." The first tale, "To Cut an Edge," describes a young man on an alien world attempting to prove his qualifications to become a Scout. "A Day at the Races," a science-fiction comedy of manners, is also a pleasure to read, according to the reviewer.

Part of the reason Lee and Miller published stories set in the Liaden universe in magazines and chapbooks is that Ballantine dropped the novels in 1990. In 1998, however, the first three books were picked up by Meisha Merlin Publishing of Decatur, Georgia, and eventually issued them together in an omnibus edition in 2000. Sequels to the first three novels also appeared through Meisha Merlin, including *Plan B* in 1999 and *Pilots Choice* in 2001, which was actually composed of two separate novels. Though 2002's *I Dare* is the last novel in the sequence about Val Con, Lee and Miller have started other Liaden novels set in different time periods. Carolyn Cushman, reviewing *Plan B* in *Locus,* praised it as "great adventure, hard to beat for fans of fast-paced space opera," while *Booklist* reviewer Diana Tixier Herald described *I Dare* as "enticing enough to captivate readers new to Lee and Miller's series."

BIOGRAPHICAL AND CRITICAL SOURCES:

BOOKS

Clute, John, and Peter Nicholls, editors, *Encyclopedia of Science Fiction,* St. Martin's Press (New York, NY), 1993.

Reginald, Robert, *Science Fiction & Fantasy Literature, 1975-1991,* Gale (Detroit, MI), 1992.

PERIODICALS

Analog Science Fiction & Fact, April, 1990, pp. 180-181; August 1996, p. 152; October, 1999, Tom Easton, review of *Plan B,* p. 134.
Booklist, December 15, 2001, Diana Tixier Herald, review of *I Dare,* pp. 709-710.
Locus, August, 1999, Carolyn Cushman, review of *Plan B,* p. 31.
Publishers Weekly, November 26, 2001, review of *I Dare,* p. 43.

ONLINE

Bloo KangaRue Web site, http://www.sff.net/people/sharon.lee/ (1998), author profile.
Liaden Universe Web site, http://www.korval.com/liad.htm/ (May 10, 2002), author biography, information, and reviews of author's works.*

*   *   *

LIM, Catherine 1942(?)-

PERSONAL: Born March 23, 1942 (some sources say 1943), in Kedah, Malaysia; immigrated to Singapore, 1970; married, 1964 (divorced, 1980); children: one daughter, one son. *Education:* University of Malaysia, B.A. (honors) in English, 1963; National University of Singapore, M.A. in applied linguistics, 1979, Ph.D., 1987.

ADDRESSES: Home—18 Leedon Heights, #07-05, Farrer Rd., Singapore 1026.

CAREER: Education officer, 1965-78; Institute of Singapore, Singapore, deputy director of curriculum development, 1979-85; Seameo Regional Centre, Singapore, lecturer in sociolinguistics, 1989-90; writer of English instructional texts.

WRITINGS:

SHORT STORIES

Little Ironies: Stories of Singapore, Heinemann Educational Books (Singapore), 1978.

Or Else, the Lightning God and Other Stories, Heinemann Educational Books (Singapore), 1980.
They Do Return, Times Books International (Singapore), 1983.
Three Gifts from the Green Dragon and Other Stories from Chinese Literature (juvenile), Target (Klerksdorp, South Africa), 1986.
The Shadow of a Shadow of a Dream: Love Stories of Singapore, Times Books International (Singapore), 1987.
O Singapore!: Stories in Celebration, Times Books International (Singapore), 1989.
Deadline for Love and Other Stories, Heinemann Asia (Singapore), 1992.
The Woman's Book of Superlatives, Times Books International (Singapore), 1993.
The Best of Catherine Lim, Heinemann Asia (Singapore), 1993.
The Howling Silence: Tales of the Dead and Their Return, Horizon Books (Singapore), 1999.

NOVELS

The Serpent's Tooth, Times Books International (Singapore), 1982.
The Bondmaid, Catherine Lim Publications, 1995, Overlook Press (New York, NY), 1997.
The Teardrop Story Woman, Overlook Press (Woodstock, NY), 1998.
Following the Wrong God Home, Orion (London, England), 2001.
A Leap of Love: A Novella, Horizon Books (Singapore), 2003.

POETRY

Love's Lonely Impulses, Heinemann Asia (Singapore), 1992.

Contributor to books, including *Asian Voices in English,* edited by Mimi Chan and Roy Harris, Hong Kong University Press, 1991; and *Perceiving Other Worlds,* edited by Edwin Thumboo, Times Academic Press (Singapore), 1991.

SIDELIGHTS: Catherine Lim is a highly regarded author in her adopted home of Singapore and is also a literary presence in the United States. In *Contemporary*

Novelists, Susan Ang wrote that "Lim's main themes are the clashes between generations and cultures, the disparity of attitudes and lifestyles found amongst the various income-groups, and the discrepancy between society's ever-improving economic profile and its state of moral poverty." Lim's short story "Father and Son," from *Or Else, the Lightning God and Other Stories,* illustrates these clashes. In "Father and Son," a man alienates and disowns his once-treasured son. Lim also addresses family ties in *Three Gifts from the Green Dragon and Other Stories from Chinese Literature,* a short-story collection intended for children which features Lim's adaptations of traditional Chinese folktales. The stories include the tale of Han Zi and his father and grandfather and another about Yue Guo and his lazy brother. Other stories address economic, class, and gender issues. A reviewer for *Books for Keeps* praised *Three Gifts from the Dragon,* calling it "delightfully compact," suitable "for teaching purposes or simple sheer enjoyment."

Lim's style, as evidenced in *Little Ironies,* is considered deceptively simple, as it describes commonplace occurrences in an understandable manner. *World Literature Today* contributor John Kwan-Terry remarked that "although lacking in subtlety, [the language in *Little Ironies*] avoids pretentiousness and annoying flourishes and sounds very much like someone actually recounting an interesting anecdote."

Lim is also the author of the novels *The Serpent's Tooth* and *The Bondmaid. The Serpent's Tooth* centers on an extended Chinese family in Singapore, particularly the protagonist, Angela, and her mother-in-law. Angela exemplifies the modern, English-speaking Singapore resident with material aims, while her mother-in-law lives the traditional Chinese way of life by maintaining reverence for ancestors and ancient rituals. Lim portrays each extreme as flawed in its own way. As a *Contemporary Novelists* writer noted, in *The Serpent's Tooth,* "what emerges . . . is a sketch of a culture/society comprising morally indifferent and solipsistic individuals. Neither set of values (modern or traditional) is seen as being above reproach."

The Bondmaid tells the story of Han, a little girl who is sold into slavery in 1950s-era Singapore. As she grows to maturity, Han falls in love with her master, a young man with whom she has grown up. Despite her strong will and determination, Han faces bitterness and betrayal as she seeks to fulfill her love. Lim self-published *The Bondmaid* rather than edit some of the sexual and political content in the story, and when the book was finally released by a mainstream publisher, it became a bestseller. Margaret Flanagan in *Booklist* called the work "a heartrending tale of love, exploitation, and betrayal." A *Publishers Weekly* reviewer described it as a "dramatic love story" in which Lim "creates a rich picture of Singaporean life behind the scenes."

Set in 1950s-era Malaysia, *The Teardrop Story Woman* features another ill-fated woman, Mei Kwei, who because of her gender, is rejected by her father and ignored by her mother. Mei Kwei takes solace in her clandestine observations of English lessons at the local Catholic school. As she grows into a beautiful woman despite a disfiguring birthmark, she falls in love with a young French priest who has come to her village. An arranged marriage notwithstanding, Mei Kwei gravitates to the priest because only he sees her as more than a mere possession. *Rocky Mountain News* contributor Joan Hinkemeyer noted that in *The Teardrop Story Woman* Lim "knows her territory and subtly but deftly sketches in the rich variety of human players." The reviewer added: "Lim's spare, controlled prose is . . . rich in evocative physical details and timeless human insight." In an *Eclectica,* Ann Skea concluded that Lim provides "vivid insight into lives lived according to Asian traditions and beliefs. Catherine Lim is a good storyteller, she draws the reader into unfamiliar worlds and provides enough tantalizing and unusual situations in her characters' lives to keep you reading to the end."

Following the Wrong God Home brings up to date Lim's views of Singaporean society. Engaged to the wealthy but self-centered Vincent Chee, intelligent Yin Ling enters a passionate love affair with an American scholar at the national university. Duty calls, however, and Yin Ling goes through with her marriage, only to suffer terribly when her feelings for the American are later rekindled. Calling Lim "Singapore's literary saviour," *Lancet* contributor Robin Gerster added that the author's works "reveal the dramas simmering beneath Singapore's ordered surface." Gerster went on to describe *Following the Wrong God Home* as "an impressive achievement, an intelligently conceived and executed exposure of the relationships between the lawful and the illicit, moral imperatives and social injustice, fake worship and true allegiance."

The Feminist Companion to Literature in English quoted an assertion by *Asiaweek* that Lim is "the best writer in Singapore." Writing in *World Literature Today,* Charles R. Larson remarked that Lim's work is as well-crafted and instructive, as her stories "are haunting tales of a part of the world most of us have only seen obliquely." Lim told an *Angelfire* interviewer that her writings are based on childhood memories and on stories she has been told by others, rather than on written research. "If it needs to be copied onto paper, it probably isn't powerful enough, but if I remember it, it must have that strength, that colour." She added: "Memory to me is the best storehouse for everything."

BIOGRAPHICAL AND CRITICAL SOURCES:

BOOKS

Blain, Virginia, Patricia Clements, and Isobel Grundy, *The Feminist Companion to Literature in English: Women Writers from the Middle Ages to the Present,* Yale University Press (New Haven, CT), 1990.

Brown, Susan Windisch, editor, *Contemporary Novelists,* 6th edition, St. James Press (Detroit, MI), 1996.

Buck, Claire, editor, *The Bloomsbury Guide to Women's Literature,* Prentice Hall General Reference (New York, NY), 1992.

Contemporary Novelists, 7th edition, St. James Press (Detroit, MI), 2001.

Lim, Yi-En, *Women in Bondage: The Stories of Catherine Lim,* Times Books International (Singapore), 1999.

PERIODICALS

Booklist, October 15, 1997, Margaret Flanagan, review of *The Bondmaid,* p. 388; October 15, 1998, GraceAnne A. DeCandido, review of *The Teardrop Story Woman,* p. 404.

Books for Keeps, January, 1986, p. 15.

Independent (London, England), August 9, 1997, Justin Wintle, "House of the Spirits," p. 6.

Lancet, April 20, 2002, Robin Gerster, "Singapore Fling," p. 1443.

Library Journal, July, 1997, Judith Kicinski, review of *The Bondmaid,* p. 126.

New York Times Book Review, February 8, 1998, Kimberly B. Marlowe, review of *The Bondmaid,* p. 18.

Publishers Weekly, August 18, 1997, review of *The Bondmaid,* p. 66; September 22, 1997, Paul Nathan, "Thwarting Censorship," p. 25; October 5, 1998, review of *The Teardrop Story Woman,* p. 79.

Rocky Mountain News, December 27, 1998, Joan Hinkemeyer, "Maylay Girl Finds Life of Her Own," p. 2E.

Sunday Times (London, England), March 11, 2001, Elizabeth Buchan, review of *Following the Wrong God Home,* p. 45.

World Literature Today, winter, 1980, p. 173; summer, 1982, p. 477; summer, 1998, Kathleen Flanagan, review of *The Bondmaid,* p. 691.

ONLINE

Angelfire, http://www.angelfire.com/ (March 25, 2003), Kate Mayberry, interview with Lim.

Eclectica, http://www.eclectica.org/v5n2/skea_lim. html/ (March 25, 2003), Ann Skea, reviews of *The Teardrop Story Woman* and *The Bondmaid.*

National University of Singapore, http://www.scholars. nus.edu.sg/ (March 25, 2003), comprehensive material on Lim and her work.*

*   *   *

LINGEMAN, Richard R(oberts) 1931-
(Niles Chignon; William Randolph Hirsch, a joint pseudonym)

PERSONAL: Born January 2, 1931, in Crawfordsville, IN; son of Byron Newton and Vera (Spencer) Lingeman; married Anthea Nicholson (a graphic designer), April 3, 1965; children: Jennifer Kate. *Education:* Haverford College, B.A., 1953; also studied law at Yale University and did graduate work at Columbia University.

ADDRESSES: Office—*Nation,* 33 Irving Plaza., New York, NY 10003-2332.

CAREER: Monocle (magazine), New York, NY, co-founder and executive editor, beginning 1962; *New York Times Book Review,* New York, NY, associate editor and columnist, 1969-78; *Nation,* New York, NY, executive editor, 1978-95, senior editor, 1995—. Public relations consultant to Peace Corps. *Military service:* U.S. Army, 1953-56.

MEMBER: Authors Guild, Society of American Historians, New York Historical Society.

AWARDS, HONORS: Theodore Dreiser: An American Journey, 1908-1945 named *Chicago Sun-Times* Book of the Year.

WRITINGS:

(Editor, with Victor Navasky) *The Monocle Peep Show,* Bantam (New York, NY), 1965.
(Under pseudonym Niles Chignon) *The Camp Follower's Guide,* Avon (New York, NY), 1965.
(With Marvin Kitman, under joint pseudonym William Randolph Hirsch) *The Red Chinese Air Force Diet, Exercise, and Sex Book,* Stein & Day (New York, NY), 1967.
Drugs from A to Z, McGraw-Hill (New York, NY), 1969, revised edition, 1974.
Don't You Know There's a War On: The American Home Front, 1941-45, Putnam (New York, NY), 1970.
Small Town America: A Narrative History, 1620-the Present, Putnam (New York, NY), 1980.
Theodore Dreiser: At the Gates of the City, 1871-1907, Wiley (New York, NY), 1987.
Theodore Dreiser: An American Journey, 1908-1945, Wiley (New York, NY), 1990.
Sinclair Lewis: Rebel from Main Street, Random House (New York, NY), 2002.
(Editor) Sinclair Lewis, *Sinclair Lewis: Arrowsmith, Elmer Gantry, Dodsworth,* Library of America (New York, NY), 2002.

Contributor to periodicals, including *New York Times Book Review, Der Spiegel, Esquire, Playboy, World, Nation,* and *New Republic.* Editor, *Outsider's Newsletter;* member of editorial board, *Dreiser Studies.*

SIDELIGHTS: "In American folklore," wrote Stephen Darst in *Commonweal,* "the small town is either Eden or Zenith and one of the considerable accomplishments of Richard Lingeman's [*Small Town America: A Narrative History, 1620-the Present*] is that his portrait is balanced, whole and unburdened by either hostility or sentimentality in its pursuit of the reality behind the twin myths." Lingeman's book is both a comprehensive survey and a critical analysis of American small-town life. According to John Leonard of the *New York Times,* the work is "grand social history. It sweeps to generalization and stoops to anecdote. It is full of idealism and flimflam, corn and greed, sod and technology. It takes us from the usual New England theocracy of white churches and green commons to the frontier outposts of the Northwest territories of Ohio, Indiana and Illinois; from the homesteads and prairie junctions of the Great Plains to the mining camps of California and Colorado; from the plantation to the mill town to the trading post to the company store to the tourist trap. Small, it tells us, has seldom been beautiful, although it always wanted to be."

In reviewing *Small Town America,* some critics made special mention of the author's extensive research. Nicholas Lemann suggested that perhaps Lingeman has incorporated too much of what he learned into his book. Lemann wrote in the *New Republic* that the author "has read virtually every word ever written by a sociologist, historian, novelist, or poet on the subject [of small-town life], and done a solid job of putting it all together. The only drawback to his research is that its total reliance on secondary sources makes him a prisoner of what's in the library; when there's a *Babbitt* or a *Middletown* to draw from the book works, and when there isn't it gets bogged down in a mass of the small details of social history, such as the contents of shelves in frontier stores." *New York Times Book Review* critic Evan Connell found the author has done his research "so conscientiously and thoroughly that nobody else will attempt a similar book. Whatever you might conceivably want to know about American small towns is here; . . . everything you might care about is here. Everything and considerably more. The magnitude of Mr. Lingeman's research is not just impressive, it is appalling. The bibliography lists some 300 sources."

Some critics questioned whether all this detail led to an overall understanding of Lingeman's subject. Michael Zuckerman, in a *Nation* article, felt that "for all the pages he devotes to all these aspects of the past, Lingeman never allows his history to intrude importantly on his conceptions of those little communities. His concern is with the residues of the towns in the American mind, not with their realities on the ground. From his first sentence, he deals in 'memory' more than in anything substantial. To his last line, he dwells on 'dreams' more than on anything mundane." *Small Town America* "fairly bursts with interesting material," noted *Washington Post Book World* reviewer Noel Perrin, "but if you really want to *understand* American small towns, you would do better to read something like Truman Capote's *In Cold Blood,* which captures the western-open form, or James Gould Cozzens's novel *By Love Possessed,* which captures the eastern-inward variety. This book documents and describes, but it never captures anything."

Reviewers Robert R. Harris and Walter Clemons, however, found more to praise in the book. According to Harris's *Village Voice* article, "Interspersed throughout and concentrated in two chapters is, in effect, another book, an absorbing and authoritative examination of the creative writers who blew the whistle on small-town hypocrisy—e.g., Sinclair Lewis (*Main Street*), Sherwood Anderson (*Winesburg, Ohio*), Edgar Lee Masters (*Spoon River Anthology*). It is in these sections that Lingeman seems most at home, and where his analysis is most penetrating. It could be argued that he should have written just this second book of literary commentary; he has enough material. But he has seen (rightly, I think) that careful consideration of these novels and poems needs the underpinning history he supplies. He wisely views these creative works as social history." And Clemons, writing about *Small Town America* in *Newsweek,* stated that Lingeman's "most original stroke is his broadening investigation into areas we don't usually consider part of this story. He has a witty chapter on the opening of the Northwest Territory after the American Revolution, when solid towns like Marietta, Ohio— named after Marie Antoinette, considered a patroness of the American cause—sprang up alongside doomed, speculative bubbles like Gallipolis, populated by an untried band of French 'small craftsmen—jewelers, wigmakers, woodcarvers, coachmakers, gilders.'" Clemons concluded that *Small Town America* is a "finely detailed, first-rate social history."

Lingeman is a product of small-town Terre Haute, Indiana. Another notable Terre Haute native—novelist Theodore Dreiser—became the subject of a two-volume biography. Volume one, *Theodore Dreiser: At the Gates of the City, 1871-1907,* explores the youth and career beginnings of Dreiser, who caused a scandal

in the 1900s with the publication of *Sister Carrie.* The novelist came from German stock; his immigrant father worked in dry goods and maintained a strictly Catholic family. Dreiser's mother, Sarah, "was a Mennonite of German ancestry who became a Catholic at her husband's directive," noted *New Republic* reviewer Alfred Kazin. "But (a point nobody before Lingeman has argued) her own sensuousness made her almost too sympathetic to her notoriously wayward daughters." Theodore Dreiser began his career in the newspaper world of 1880s Chicago, a far cry from Terre Haute. "Reporting was the great school then for aspiring novelists," Kazin pointed out, and Dreiser took in the urban atmosphere of Chicago, New York, Pittsburgh, and other large cities. Kazin went on to praise Lingeman for "[catching] Drciscr's doublcness—the suffering submissiveness of his early years in 'the furnace of American capitalism,' his amazing gift for summoning up from below, almost without his will the tidal surge and disaster recurrent in American society."

In volume two, *Theodore Dreiser: An American Journey, 1908-1945,* Lingeman takes up Dreiser at middle age, "not yet rich or famous but a survivor in a world he had come to perceive as a jungle in which the strong and cunning preyed on the weak," as *New Republic*'s Daniel Aaron put it. *Sister Carrie* had been published reluctantly by an editor who feared scandal, and Dreiser's seminal work, *An American Tragedy,* was still years away. "Now," wrote Aaron, "the chronicle picks up speed. Lingeman must cover so much ground, must deal with so many of Dreiser's publishing imbroglios, sexual encounters, trips and travels, political involvement, widening friendships, and metaphysical vagaries that little space remains to pause and reflect." Still, Aaron added, Lingeman "is a trustworthy guide through Dreiser country. . . . He has written the fullest and best informed biography of Dreiser to date and put the untidy life of an unendearing man into perspective without making him any better or worse than he was." Lingeman's "is an undeluded, jargon-free biography," commented Genevieve Stuttaford in *Publishers Weekly,* "which finds much to admire in both the man and his work."

Lingeman explored another American novelist of the early twentieth century with *Sinclair Lewis: Rebel from Main Street.* The author of *Babbitt, Main Street,* and *Elmer Gantry* grew up in Sauk Centre, Minnesota; he subsequently joined the intellectual set in New

York and made a career of skewering small-town American manners and mores. Lewis had, wrote a *Kirkus Reviews* contributor, an "uncanny mimicry of slang, in-depth research into professions and communities, and iconoclastic treatment of business, science, fundamentalism, and marriage." The novelist became the object of controversy for his satiric takes on the American way of life; Lewis was once castigated in print by Archibald MacLeish as among those writers who "[devote] themselves to negativity, thus placing America in spiritual peril," as a *Nation* contributor quoted. But Lewis saw himself as more than a satirist: Those who "love their country," he countered, as quoted in Lingeman's book, and are "willing to report its transient dangers and stupidities, have been as valuable an influence as America has ever known."

A contemporary of Dreiser as well as Ernest Hemingway and Edith Wharton, it was Lewis who became America's first Nobel Prize laureate in literature, a fact made all the more significant by the fact that reviewers of his day often had dismissed the novelist as a lightweight. Lingeman's biography "sets the record straight" on the author who had been the subject of a more "damning" work by Mark Scherer, according to onetime Lewis secretary Barnaby Conrad. Scherer's 1963 *Sinclair Lewis: An American Life* had focused on him as "an unlikable alcoholic who somehow contrived to produce *Main Street* and *Elmer Gantry* in between benders," as *National Review* writer Terry Teachout noted. Conversely, said Conrad in the *Wilson Quarterly*, the Lingeman version "provides a far more empathic picture of the talented, tortured, and ultimately tragic" novelist. Henry Carrigan of *Library Journal* found the book falling prey to "the trap of many literary biographies by reporting minor details," but summed up Lingeman's *Sinclair Lewis* as "an affectionate and engaging portrait of one of our most important novelists."

BIOGRAPHICAL AND CRITICAL SOURCES:

BOOKS

Lingeman, Richard, *Small Town America: A Narrative History, 1620-the Present,* Putnam (New York, NY), 1980.
Lingeman, Richard, *Sinclair Lewis: Rebel from Main Street,* Random House (New York, NY), 2002.

PERIODICALS

American Literature, September, 1991, Jack Wallace, review of *Theodore Dreiser: An American Journey, 1908-1945,* p. 555.
American Scholar, winter, 1988, Thomas Riggio, review of *Theodore Dreiser: At the Gates of the City, 1871-1907,* p. 151.
Atlantic Monthly, August, 1993, review of *Theodore Dreiser: An American Journey, 1908-1945,* p. 98.
Best Sellers, January, 1987, review of *Theodore Dreiser: At the Gates of the City, 1871-1907,* p. 385.
Booklist, September 1, 1986, review of *Theodore Dreiser: At the Gates of the City, 1871-1907,* p. 20; September 15, 1990, review of *Theodore Dreiser: An American Journey, 1908-1945,* p. 134; December 15, 2001, Donna Seaman, review of *Sinclair Lewis: Rebel from Main Street,* p. 699.
Choice, January, 1987, review of *Theodore Dreiser: At the Gates of the City, 1871-1907,* p. 762.
Commonweal, October 9, 1981, Stephen Darst, review of *Small Town America.*
Economist, February 2, 2002, review of *Sinclair Lewis,* p. 88.
English Studies, August, 1989, Edward Margolies, review of *Theodore Dreiser: At the Gates of the City, 1871-1907,* p. 372.
Guardian, November 25, 1990, review of *Theodore Dreiser: An American Journey, 1908-1945,* p. 20.
Hudson Review, spring, 2003, Brooke Allen, review of *Sinclair Lewis,* pp. 191-200.
Kirkus Reviews, August 15, 1986, review of *Theodore Dreiser: At the Gates of the City, 1871-1907,* p. 1273; August 1, 1990, review of *Theodore Dreiser: An American Journey, 1908-1945,* p. 1064; November 15, 2001, review of *Sinclair Lewis,* p. 1597.
Library Journal, August, 1990, Charles Nash, review of *Theodore Dreiser: An American Journey, 1908-1945,* p. 111; January, 2002, Henry Carrigan, review of *Sinclair Lewis,* p. 102.
Modern Fiction Studies, summer, 1988, review of *Theodore Dreiser: At the Gates of the City, 1871-1907,* p. 235.
Nation, August 30-September 6, 1980, Michael Zuckerman, review of *Small Town America;* December 27, 1986, review of *Theodore Dreiser: At the Gates of the City, 1871-1907,* p. 738; March 4, 2002, "Sauk Centre's Finest," p. 37.
National Review, April 10, 1987, review of *Theodore Dreiser: At the Gates of the City, 1871-1907,* p. 50; March 11, 2002, Terry Teachout, "Silly Babbitt," p. 51.

New Republic, August 30, 1980, Nicholas Lemann, review of *Small Town America;* February 23, 1987, Alfred Kazin, review of *Theodore Dreiser: At the Gates of the City, 1871-1907,* p. 31; November 12, 1990, Daniel Aaron, review of *Theodore Dreiser: An American Journey, 1908-1945,* p. 34.

Newsweek, July 28, 1980, Walter Clemons, review of *Small Town America.*

New Yorker, January 14, 1991, John Updike, review of *Theodore Dreiser: An American Journey, 1908-1945,* p. 89; February 4, 2002, John Updike, "No Brakes: A New Biography of Sinclair Lewis," p. 77.

New York Review of Books, June 27, 2002, Elizabeth Hardwick, review of *Sinclair Lewis,* p. 42.

New York Times, June 13, 1980, John Leonard, review of *Small Town America;* October 14, 1987, review of *Theodore Dreiser: At the Gates of the City, 1871-1907,* p. 27; October 10, 1990, review of *Theodore Dreiser: An American Journey, 1908-1945,* p. C20.

New York Times Book Review, July 6, 1980, Evan Connell, review of *Small Town America.*

Publishers Weekly, August 29, 1986, Genevieve Stuttaford, review of *Theodore Dreiser: At the Gates of the City, 1871-1907,* p. 380; August 3, 1990, Genevieve Stuttaford, review of *Theodore Dreiser: An American Journey, 1908-1945,* p. 70; December 10, 2001, review of *Sinclair Lewis,* p. 60.

Saturday Night, January-February, 1991, Douglas Fetherling, review of *Theodore Dreiser: An American Journey, 1908-1945,* p. 51.

Sewanee Review, summer, 1988, Joseph Davis, review of *Theodore Dreiser: At the Gates of the City, 1871-1907,* p. 507.

Smithsonian, May, 1987, Gerald Weales, review of *Theodore Dreiser: At the Gates of the City, 1871-1907,* p. 178.

Times Literary Supplement, December 13, 2002, Michael Greenberg, review of *Sinclair Lewis,* p. 6.

Tribune Books (Chicago, IL), September 28, 1986, review of *Theodore Dreiser: At the Gates of the City, 1871-1907,* p. 7; July 11, 1993, review of *Theodore Dreiser: An American Journey, 1908-1945,* p. 2.

USA Today, December 2, 1986, review of *Theodore Dreiser: At the Gates of the City, 1871-1907,* p. 7D.

Village Voice, September 17-23, 1980, Robert R. Harris, review of *Small Town America.*

Virginia Quarterly Review, spring, 1988, Arthur Casciato, review of *Theodore Dreiser: At the Gates of the City, 1871-1907,* p. 336.

Washington Post Book World, June 13, 1980, Noel Perrin, review of *Small Town America;* September 28, 1986, review of *Theodore Dreiser: At the Gates of the City, 1871-1907,* p. 3; September 30, 1990, review of *Theodore Dreiser: An American Journey, 1908-1945,* p. 3.

Wilson Quarterly, spring, 2002, Barnaby Conrad, review of *Sinclair Lewis,* p. 114.

World Literature Today, winter, 1992, Daniel King, review of *Theodore Dreiser: An American Journey, 1908-1945,* p. 137.

ONLINE

Sinclair Lewis Society, http://www.english.ilstu.edu/ (spring, 1995, and spring, 2003), interviews with Richard Lingeman.*

*   *   *

LOVE, D. Anne 1949-

PERSONAL: Born January 12, 1949, in Selmer, TN; daughter of Oscar W. and Elsie M. (Boleyn) Catlett; married Ronald W. Love, June 8, 1974. *Ethnicity:* "Caucasian." *Education:* Lamar University, B.S., 1972; University of North Texas, M.Ed., 1976, Ph.D., 1984. *Politics:* Independent. *Religion:* Protestant. *Hobbies and other interests:* Jazz music, travel.

ADDRESSES: Home—Austin, TX. *Agent*—Maria Carvainis, Maria Carvainis Agency, Inc., 1350 Avenue of the Americas, New York, NY 10019. *E-mail*—info@dannelove.

CAREER: Writer. School administrator in Richardson, TX, 1974-88; University of North Texas, Denton, professor, 1989-91; Western Hills Area Education Agency, Sioux City, IA, consultant, 1994-96.

MEMBER: Society of Children's Book Writers and Illustrators.

AWARDS, HONORS: Prize for Juvenile Fiction, Friends of American Writers, 1997, for *My Lone Star Summer;* Children's Book Award, Writers League of Texas, 2003, for *The Puppeteer's Apprentice.*

D. Anne Love

WRITINGS:

Bess's Log Cabin Quilt, illustrated by Ronald Himler, Holiday House (New York, NY), 1995.

Dakota Spring, illustrated by Ronald Himler, Holiday House (New York, NY), 1995.

My Lone Star Summer, Holiday House (New York, NY), 1996.

Three against the Tide, Holiday House (New York, NY), 1998.

I Remember the Alamo, Dell Yearling (New York, NY), 1999.

A Year without Rain, Holiday House (New York, NY), 2000.

The Puppeteer's Apprentice, Margaret K. McElderry Books (New York, NY), 2003.

Hypatia: Her Story, illustrated by Pam Papparone, Holiday House (New York, NY), in press.

Contributor to magazines, newspapers, and educational journals.

WORK IN PROGRESS: *The Secret Prince,* for Simon & Schuster.

SIDELIGHTS: A writer of historical fiction for young adults, D. Anne Love writes novels that typically feature strong female protagonists who rise to the occasion when faced with severe challenges. *Bess's Log Cabin Quilt* tells the story of a ten-year-old girl who single-handedly comes to the rescue of her pioneer family. When her father fails to return from his work on the Oregon Trail and her mother falls ill, Bess must handle the incursions of Indians and a money-lender who threatens to seize the family farm. Melissa McPherson, a contributor to *Voice of Youth Advocates,* applauded Love's detailed description of frontier life, going on to claim that "readers of historical fiction will definitely enjoy this."

Dakota Spring, Love's second novel, earned favorable reviews from critics. In this story, Caroline and her brother are left to manage their Dakota farm with the help of just one neighbor after their father breaks his leg. Their straitlaced grandmother arrives shortly to help out, and the children must learn to deal with her cold personality and their shared grief over her daughter's, and their mother's, untimely death. Susan Steinfirst compared *Dakota Spring* to Patricia MacLachlan's classic children's story *Sarah, Plain and Tall* in her review in *Voice of Youth Advocates,* adding that Love's book "should appeal to kids who love these tame wild west sagas." *Booklist* contributor Carolyn Phelan recommended the book strongly, praising Love's "well drawn and intriguing" characters, consistent point of view, and strong sense of place and historical period. "This book will please youngsters looking for good historical fiction," Phelan concluded.

In her first work of contemporary fiction, *My Lone Star Summer,* Love focuses on twelve-year-old Jill, who has visited her grandmother's ranch each summer, enjoying her time spent with B. J., her best friend in Texas. B. J. insists on being called Belinda this year, however, and has started wearing make-up and flirting with boys, leaving little time for Jill. "This is a fairly standard girl-coming-of-age novel for the youngest of YAs," Alice F. Stern remarked in *Voice of Youth Advocates.* Deborah Stevenson of the *Bulletin of the Center for Children's Books* admitted that "the story's a bit formulaic," but praised Love's strong characterizations, adding "the narration is unforced, honest, and touching in its examination of the gains and losses of growing up."

The American Civil War sets the stage for *Three against the Tide,* Love's story of twelve-year-old Susannah, who must care for her younger brothers after her father leaves their South Carolina island home to help in the war effort. As the war worsens and their slaves and neighbors depart, the children struggle to survive on their own, then make a perilous journey down river to Charleston, where they hope to find their father. Charleston offers no shelter, however, after their town home burns to the ground, and the children once again set off in search of their father. Along the way, tomboyish Susannah learns the value of some of the womanly arts she had earlier spurned and finds her unthinking support for the Confederate war effort weakened by encounters with their former slaves, whose quest for freedom Susannah can now understand. This novel is crammed with suspenseful action, reviewers noted, as Susannah and her brothers pass through danger after danger in an attempt to reunite with their father during the last days of the Civil War. Though some critics found the work occasionally marred by sentimentality, the overall recommendation of reviewers was that young-adult fans of historical fiction would enjoy *Three against the Tide.* For Kathleen Squires, writing in *Booklist,* "it's the fast pace, historical detail, and well-drawn heroine that will help readers overlook" the book's flaws. A contributor to *Publishers Weekly* reached a similar conclusion, predicting that despite the book's nostalgic view of "Southern gentility," "readers will revel in the three protagonists' bravery and spirit."

Love turned to a pivotal moment in Texas history for the story of *I Remember the Alamo,* which centers on the McCann family, recent arrivals in Texas from Kentucky. Soon, young Jessie McCann's father and older brother are caught up in the fight that becomes the bloody siege and final rout at the Alamo compound, where Jessie and other women and children find brief refuge. "The strength of the novel . . . lies in its setting and sense of history," observed a contributor to *Horn Book.* The realism of Love's period piece is aided by the appearance of several historical figures, but an important theme of the story is the relationship between the Mexican residents of San Antonio and the recent North American settlers, as symbolized by Jessie's tempestuous friendship with a girl named Angelina. "Her ending is pretty pat after so much blood and tragedy," remarked John Peters in *Booklist,* but readers who enjoy stories about the Alamo "will enjoy her perceptive view of this American turning point." Likewise, a contributor to *Kirkus Reviews* did not find the book without flaws—for this critic it was implausible characterizations—yet nevertheless

concluded: "The pacing is fast, and the historical details captivating."

South Dakota during a year-long drought provides the setting for Love's young-adult novel *A Year without Rain.* Twelve-year-old Rachel has lived alone with her father and her younger brother on a prairie farm since the death of her mother four years earlier. During the summer of the drought, her father sends the children to their mother's sister in Savannah, Georgia, where they reminisce with family and servants who knew their mother, and read through her letters. But when Rachel's father returns to carry them back to their home, he brings news that he plans to marry their teacher, a plan that Rachel intends to foil with disastrous results. All is forgiven in the end, however, and Rachel comes to believe she has her mother's blessing to accept the change in her life that seems inevitable. A contributor to *Horn Book* concluded that "many readers do enjoy this kind of 'touched by an angel' comfort, of course, and they will find the book a pleasing diversion." *School Library Journal* contributor Valerie Diamond called Love's book "simply yet artfully told with characters both realistic and endearing."

In a departure from American settings for Love, *The Puppeteer's Apprentice* takes place in long-ago England and features a heroine so downtrodden that she lacks even a formal name, going by the nickname Mouse. But, like Love's other protagonists, Mouse finds within herself a measure of strength, perseverance, and self-will she had not known she possessed when, brutalized by the manor cook for whom she slaves as a scullery maid, Mouse finally strikes out on her own. At a fair, she becomes mesmerized by the puppet show and begs to be allowed to become the puppet master's apprentice. "Love sketches an eclectic cast and packs in plenty of historical details as she portrays the freedoms and perils of the puppeteer's vagabond life," remarked a contributor to *Publishers Weekly.* Tension builds as Mouse becomes aware of the mysteries surrounding the puppet master's identity and finally earns her own identity, along with a proper name. "This wonderfully written tale holds mystery, suspense, and the realism that comes with a battle fought and won," concluded Kit Vaughan in *School Library Journal.* Reviewers described Mouse as a likable character whose heart, ingenuity, and spunk will win readers' hearts. In addition, many critics found Love writing in top form, offering a tight, suspenseful plot and many realistic period details. A contributor to *Kirkus Reviews* concluded that "colorful, lively, rhythmic language and a strong sense of medieval England make this a great read-aloud."

Love once commented: "I left public school administration in order to devote more time to writing and teaching at the university level. For me, the writing process usually begins with visualizing the last scene and working backward. I am a collector of information and often find that a postcard, brochure, or photograph collected somewhere along the way can spark story ideas. Inspiration flows from my love of history and a strong sense of place."

BIOGRAPHICAL AND CRITICAL SOURCES:

PERIODICALS

Booklist, February 15, 1995, Kay Weisman, review of *Bess's Log Cabin Quilt,* p. 1085; November 15, 1995, Carolyn Phelan, review of *Dakota Spring,* p. 559; May 1, 1996, Susan DeRonne, review of *My Lone Star Summer,* p. 1506; December 1, 1998, Kathleen Squires, review of *Three against the Tide,* p. 667; January 1, 2000, John Peters, review of *I Remember the Alamo,* p. 926; April 1, 2000, GraceAnne A. DeCandido, review of *A Year without Rain,* p. 1477; March 15, 2003, Carolyn Phelan, review of *The Puppeteer's Apprentice,* p. 1327.

Bulletin of the Center for Children's Books, July, 1996, Deborah Stevenson, review of *My Lone Star Summer,* pp. 378-379.

Childhood Education, fall, 2000, Jeanie Burnett, review of *I Remember the Alamo,* p. 45.

Horn Book, March, 2000, review of *I Remember the Alamo,* p. 197; July, 2000, review of *A Year without Rain,* p. 461.

Kirkus Reviews, November 1, 1998, review of *Three against the Tide,* p. 1601; November 15, 1999, review of *I Remember the Alamo,* p. 1812; March 15, 2003, review of *The Puppeteer's Apprentice,* p. 472.

Publishers Weekly, April 17, 1995, review of *Bess's Log Cabin Quilt,* p. 60; December 7, 1998, review of *Three against the Tide,* p. 60; April 10, 2000, review of *A Year without Rain,* p. 99; March 17, 2003, review of *The Puppeteer's Apprentice,* p. 77.

School Library Journal, June, 1995, Lucinda Snyder Whitehurst, review of *Bess's Log Cabin Quilt,* p. 111; November, 1995, Rita Soltan, review of *Dakota Spring,* p. 103; March, 1996, Susan Oliver, review of *My Lone Star Summer,* p. 196; January, 1999, Cindy Darling Codell, review of *Three against the Tide,* p. 128; January, 2000, Coop Renner, review of *I Remember the Alamo,* p. 134; September, 2000, Valerie Diamond, review of *A Year without Rain,* p. 233; May, 2003, Kit Vaughan, review of *The Puppeteer's Apprentice,* p. 156.

Voice of Youth Advocates, October, 1995, Melissa McPherson, review of *Bess's Log Cabin Quilt,* p. 220; April, 1996, Susan Steinfirst, review of *Dakota Spring,* p. 27; October, 1996, Alice F. Stern, review of *My Lone Star Summer,* pp. 211-212.

ONLINE

D. Anne Love, http://www.dannelove.com/ (November 2, 2003).

*   *   *

LOWENTHAL, Cynthia J. 1952-

PERSONAL: Born July 23, 1952, in New York, NY. *Education:* University of Arkansas, B.A., 1974, M.A., 1976; Brandeis University, Ph.D., 1987.

ADDRESSES: Office—Department of English, Tulane University, New Orleans, LA 70118.

CAREER: Tulane University, New Orleans, LA, associate professor of English, beginning 1987.

WRITINGS:

Lady Mary Wortley Montagu and the Eighteenth Century Familiar Letter, University of Georgia Press (Athens, GA), 1994.

Performing Identities on the Restoration Stage, Southern Illinois University Press (Carbondale, IL), 2002.

BIOGRAPHICAL AND CRITICAL SOURCES:

PERIODICALS

Times Literary Supplement, June 20, 2003, Michael Caines, review of *Performing Identities on the Restoration Stage,* p. 35.*

M

MacDONALD, Suse 1940-

PERSONAL: Given name rhymes with "news"; born March 3, 1940, in Evanston, IL; daughter of Stewart Y. (a professor) and Constance R. McMullen; married Stuart G. MacDonald (an architect), July 14, 1962; children: Alison Heath, Ripley Graeme. *Ethnicity:* "White." *Education:* Attended Chatham College, 1958-60; University of Iowa, B.A., 1962; also attended Radcliffe College, Art Institute, and New England School of Art and Design.

ADDRESSES: Home and office—4646 Robbins St., San Diego, CA 92122. *Agent*—Phyllis Wender, 38 East 29th St., New York, NY 10016.

CAREER: United Press International, New York, NY, executive secretary to the picture editor, 1964; Caru Studios, New York, NY, textbook illustrator, 1964-69; MacDonald & Swan Construction, South Londonderry, VT, architectural designer, 1969-76; freelance advertising artist, 1982-85; author and illustrator, 1986—.

MEMBER: Society of Children's Book Writers and Illustrators, Authors Guild, Authors League of America, Graphic Artists' Guild.

AWARDS, HONORS: Editor's Choice citation, *Booklist,* Best Books of the Year citation, *School Library Journal,* and Pick of the Lists citation, American Booksellers Association, all 1986, Golden Kite Award, Society of Children's Book Writers, and Caldecott Honor Award, American Library Association, both 1987, all for *Alphabatics;* Gold Medal for preschool book, National Parenting Publication Awards, for *Nanta's Lion: A Search-and-Find Adventure.*

Suse MacDonald

WRITINGS:

SELF-ILLUSTRATED CHILDREN'S BOOKS

Alphabatics (Junior Literary Guild selection), Bradbury (New York, NY), 1986.

(With Bill Oakes) *Numblers,* Dial (New York, NY), 1988.

(With Bill Oakes) *Puzzlers,* Dial (New York, NY), 1989.

(With Bill Oakes) *Once upon Another,* Dial (New York, NY), 1990.

Space Spinners, Dial (New York, NY), 1991.

Sea Shapes, Harcourt (San Diego, CA), 1994.

Nanta's Lion: A Search-and-Find Adventure, Morrow (New York, NY), 1995.

Peck, Slither and Slide, Harcourt (San Diego, CA), 1997.

Elephants on Board, Harcourt (San Diego, CA), 1999.

Look Whooo's Counting, Scholastic (New York, NY), 2000.

Here-a-Chick, Where-a-Chick?, Scholastic (New York, NY), 2004.

ILLUSTRATOR

Hank de Zutter, *Who Says a Dog Goes Bow-Wow?,* Doubleday (New York, NY), 1993.

Jean Marzollo, *I Love You: A Rebus Poem,* Scholastic (New York, NY), 2000.

Jean Marzollo, *I See a Star,* Scholastic (New York, NY), 2002.

SIDELIGHTS: Suse MacDonald's children's books use bright, imaginative illustrations to illustrate simple stories and concepts for preschoolers. Her first book, *Alphabatics,* is also one of her most successful, having been honored as a runner-up for the prestigious Caldecott Award and numerous other accolades. Aimed at children between two and five years old, it uses two-page spreads to transform letters into images. In *Puzzlers,* which she wrote with Bill Oakes, colorful collages of numbers introduce concepts such as widest, tallest, facing, back-to-back, and so on. A *Publishers Weekly* reviewer praised the illustrations and declared that "the fun-filled presentation . . . will teach children in an encouraging way."

MacDonald and Oakes collaborated again on *Once upon Another,* which features two stories, one reading from front to back, the other from back to front. The stories are retold versions of favorite old fables, "The Tortoise and the Hare" and "The Lion and the Mouse," and the characters are represented by abstract forms created from torn paper. The book is "brilliant in color, conceptions, and design," noted a *Kirkus Reviews*

writer, who also called it "a feast for the eye." Collages were featured again in Hank de Zutter's *Who Says a Dog Goes Bow-wow?,* illustrated by MacDonald. This book presents sixteen animals and tells how the sounds each makes are interpreted in various languages. A *Publishers Weekly* reviewer observed that the book encourages global thinking and praised MacDonald's "expressive menagerie" depicted in "bursts of color."

In *Sea Shapes* MacDonald transforms basic shapes such as diamonds, ovals, and spirals into a variety of sea creatures. A left-hand page shows the transformation of a diamond into multiple fish scales, for instance, and the right-hand page shows the fish in its natural environment. The book also includes a glossary providing information about the creatures and their habitats. According to a *Horn Book* reviewer, "Ocean animals and simple shapes become a very elegant combination" in this book.

MacDonald's book *Nanta's Lion: A Search-and-Find Adventure* features a Masai girl searching for the lion that has been hunting her village's cattle. Nanta is unsuccessful, but attentive readers will find an image of the elusive lion in the book's final spread, built up gradually by the die-cut pages in what a *Publishers Weekly* reviewer deemed a "snazzy surprise ending."

Another animal-oriented book, *Peck, Slither and Slide,* encourages readers to guess which creature is pecking, slithering, or sliding. In comments to *CA,* MacDonald described it as "a playful concept book about animal behavior, action verbs, and visual discovery." The author rounded out the book with notes about the animals' size, habitat, and way of life. MacDonald described *Elephants on Board* as "a playful tale about a dozen elephants' trip to the circus. When their bus breaks down they decide that nearby mammoth construction equipment can get them there on time. A ride is found but not in the way they expect." In *Look Whooo's Counting,* she commented, "the reader joins wise old Owl on a moonlit flight and counts from one to ten by finding the number shapes hidden in the animals she encounters." And, MacDonald wrote, "*Here-a-Chick, Where-a-Chick?* takes young readers on a search for five little chicks. Lifting the flap on each page the reader finds a cat, two mice, three ducks, a cow, and two pigs. The chicks do turn up as a cute surprise on the last page."

MacDonald also illustrated two books by Jean Marzollo. MacDonald told *CA:* "*I Love You: A Rebus*

Poem is a simple poem for the very young reader, featuring commonplace pairings of child-friendly objects. Each item named and the refrain, 'I love you,' are featured as icons in the poem and then are incorporated into a larger picture on the facing page. *I See a Star* is a Christmas pageant story. Each page shows different children dressing for their parts in the play."

MacDonald once told *CA:*"After college I married, and my husband and I settled in New York City. I wanted to get a job using my artistic talents, but several years passed before I landed a position at Caru Studios, where I made illustrations for textbooks. I stayed there for five years.

"Then my husband and I moved back to the family farm in Weston, Vermont, and took over a construction company. We worked together in the construction business for ten years and raised two children. While both kids were young, we spent a lot of time at the farm pond, and I found myself searching, as I had when I was a child, among the reeds and beneath the surface to find out what lived there. I began making drawings and thinking once again about illustrating books.

"When our second child entered first grade, I decided to pursue that interest. I quit my job and went back to school. I drove back and forth between Vermont and Boston for four years, attending classes at Radcliffe, the Art Institute, the New England School of Art and Design, and other schools in the city. I took courses in all sorts of things, including illustration, silk-screening, paper making, sketching, drawing, design, topography, and writing. It is hard to pinpoint the time when I decided that children's book illustration was the field in which I wanted to concentrate my energies. My interests just seemed to lean in that direction.

"Eventually I enrolled in Marion Perry's classes in children's book writing and illustration at Radcliffe. It was then that I really became involved in children's books. After completing my studies, I bought an old house in South Londonderry, Vermont, in partnership with two other artists. We spent six months renovating the building and setting up six artist's studios, one for each of us and three which we rented. I put together a portfolio and began to look for work, in both advertising and the children's book field. My first assignments were paper sculpture for advertising. These kept me going financially as I began to make the rounds of the children's book publishers.

"The idea for *Alphabatics* emerged from the wealth of information which I gathered while taking topography in art school. In that course, we worked exclusively with letter forms, shrinking and expanding them and manipulating their shapes in various ways. I was intrigued by the process and felt there were possibilities in it for a book. It was several years, however, before I put my ideas down on paper. Once I did, the first editor I showed it to bought the idea, and I was on my way.

"Selling that book, which was my first, was very exciting. I love the picture book format and feel it offers challenging opportunities for creative illustration."

BIOGRAPHICAL AND CRITICAL SOURCES:

PERIODICALS

Booklist, May 15, 1993, p. 1693; September 1, 1994, p. 46; April 15, 1995, p. 1506.
Horn Book, January-February, 1990, p. 55; November-December, 1994, review of *Sea Shapes,* p. 722.
Kirkus Reviews, July 15, 1990, review of *Once upon Another,* p. 1005.
Publishers Weekly, August 25, 1989, review of *Puzzlers,* p. 63; August 10, 1990, p. 444; November 1, 1991, p. 80; January 25, 1993, review of *Who Says a Dog Goes Bow-wow?,* p. 86-87; April 24, 1995, review of *Nanta's Lion: A Search-and-Find Adventure,* p. 71; March 31, 1997.
School Arts, April, 1990, p. 61.
School Library Journal, October, 1989, p. 91; November, 1990, p. 96; October, 1991, p. 100; August, 1993, p. 156; November, 1994, p. 84; May, 1995, p. 86.

ONLINE

Go Places with Suse MacDonald, http://www.susemacdonald.com/ (January 24, 2004).

*   *   *

MALCOLM, John
See ANDREWS, John Malcolm

MAUGHAM, W(illiam) Somerset 1874-1965

PERSONAL: Surname is pronounced "Mawm"; born January 25, 1874, in Paris, France; died December 16, 1965, in Nice, France; son of Robert Ormond (a solicitor to the British Embassy) and Edith Mary (Snell) Maugham; married Syrie Barnardo Wellcome, 1915 (divorced, 1927); children: Liza. *Education:* Attended University of Heidelberg, 1891-92; briefly studied accountancy in Kent, England; St. Thomas Hospital, M.R.C.S., L.R.C.P., 1897. *Religion:* Rationalist. *Hobbies and other interests:* Bridge, music, gardening, collecting paintings.

CAREER: Novelist, playwright, editor, and author of short fiction. Narrator for *Quartet* (dramatization of four of his stories), 1949, and *Trio* (film based on three of his stories), 1950, and *Encore* (dramatization based on four of his stories); host of U.S. televised dramatizations of his stories, 1950-51. *Military service:* Served with ambulance unit and as medical officer during World War I; served with British Secret Service in Switzerland; served with British Ministry of Information in Paris during World War II.

MEMBER: Royal Society of Literature (fellow and companion), American Academy of Arts and Letters (honorary member), Garrick Club.

AWARDS, HONORS: Companion of Honour, 1954; C.Litt., 1961; named honorary senator of Heidelberg University, 1961; D.Litt., Oxford University and University of Toulouse; honorary fellow, Library of Congress, Washington, DC; Commander, Legion of Honour.

WRITINGS:

NOVELS

Liza of Lambeth, Doran, Unwin (London, England), 1897, Doran (New York, NY), 1921, reprinted, Penguin Books (New York, NY), 1978.

The Making of a Saint, L. C. Page (Boston, MA), 1898, published as *The Making of a Saint: A Romance of Medieval Italy,* Farrar, Straus (New York, NY), 1966, reprinted, Arno (New York, NY), 1977.

The Hero, Hutchinson (London, England), 1901, reprinted, Arno (New York, NY), 1977.

Mrs. Craddock, Doran, Heinemann (London, England), 1902, Doran (New York, NY), 1920, reprinted, Penguin Books (New York, NY), 1979.

The Merry-Go-Round, Heinemann (London, England), 1905, reprinted, Penguin Books (New York, NY), 1978.

The Bishop's Apron: A Study in the Origins of a Great Family, Chapman & Hall (London, England), 1906, reprinted, Arno (New York, NY), 1977.

The Explorer, Heinemann (London, England), 1907, Baker & Taylor (New York, NY), 1909.

The Magician, Heinemann (London, England), 1908, Duffield (New York, NY), 1909, reprinted, Penguin Books (New York, NY), 1978.

Of Human Bondage, Doran (New York, NY), 1915, reprinted, Penguin Books (New York, NY), 1978.

The Moon and Sixpence, Doran (New York, NY), 1919, reprinted, Dover (New York, NY), 1995.

The Painted Veil, Doran (New York, NY), 1925, reprinted, Penguin Books (New York, NY), 1979.

Cakes and Ale; or, The Skeleton in the Cupboard, Doubleday, Doran (New York, NY), 1930, reprinted, Arno (New York, NY), 1977, published as *Cakes and Ale,* Modern Library (New York, NY), 1950.

The Book-Bag, G. Orioli (Florence, Italy), 1932.

The Narrow Corner, Doubleday, Doran (New York, NY), 1932, reprinted, Pan Books (New York, NY), 1978.

Theatre, Doubleday, Doran (New York, NY), 1937.

Christmas Holiday, Doubleday, Doran (New York, NY), 1939, reprinted, Pan Books (New York, NY), 1978.

Up at the Villa, Doubleday, Doran (New York, NY), 1941, reprinted, Penguin Books (New York, NY), 1978.

The Hour before the Dawn, Doubleday, Doran (New York, NY), 1942, reprinted, Arno (New York, NY), 1977.

The Razor's Edge, Doubleday, Doran (New York, NY), 1944, reprinted, Penguin Books (New York, NY), 1978.

Then and Now, Doubleday (New York, NY), 1946, published as *Fools and Their Folly,* Avon (New York, NY), 1949, reprinted, Pan Books (New York, NY), 1979.

Catalina: A Romance, Doubleday (New York, NY), 1948, reprinted, Pan Books (New York, NY), 1978.

Selected Novels, three volumes, Heinemann (London, England), 1953.

Orientations, Unwin (London, England), 1899.

The Trembling of a Leaf: Little Stories of the South Sea Islands, Doran (New York, NY), 1921, reprinted, Arno (New York, NY), 1977, published as *Sadie Thompson and Other Stories of the South Seas,* Readers Library (London, England), 1928, published as *Rain, and Other Stories,* Grosset (New York, NY), 1932.

The Casuarina Tree: Six Stories, Doran (New York, NY), 1926, reprinted, Arno (New York, NY), 1977, published as *The Letter: Stories of Crime,* Collins (London, England), 1930.

Ashenden; or, The British Agent, Doubleday, Doran (New York, NY), 1928, reprinted, Penguin Books (New York, NY), 1977.

Six Stories Written in the First Person Singular, Doubleday, Doran (New York, NY), 1931, reprinted, Arno (New York, NY), 1977.

Ah King, Doubleday, Doran (New York, NY), 1933, published as *Ah King: Six Stories,* Heinemann (London, England), 1933, reprinted, Arno (New York, NY), 1977.

East and West: The Collected Short Stories, Doubleday, Doran (New York, NY), 1934, published as *Altogether; Being the Collected Stories of W. Somerset Maugham,* Heinemann (London, England), 1934.

Judgment Seat, Centaur (Philadelphia, PA), 1934.

Cosmopolitans, Doubleday, Doran (New York, NY), 1936, reprinted, Arno (New York, NY), 1977, published as *Cosmopolitans: Twenty-nine Short Stories,* Avon (New York, NY), 1943.

The Favorite Short Stories of W. Somerset Maugham, Doubleday, Doran (New York, NY), 1937.

Princess September and the Nightingale (fairy tale; first published in *The Gentleman in the Parlour: A Record of a Journey from Rangoon to Haiphong*), Oxford University Press (London, England), 1939, published as *Princess September,* Harcourt (New York, NY), 1969.

The Mixture As Before, Doubleday, Doran (New York, NY), 1940, reprinted, Arno (New York, NY), 1977.

The Unconquered, House of Books (New York, NY), 1944.

Ah King, and Other Romance Stories of the Tropics (contains selections from *Ah King*), Avon (New York, NY), 1944.

Creatures of Circumstance, Doubleday (New York, NY), 1947, reprinted, Arno (New York, NY), 1977.

Stories of Love and Intrigue from "The Mixture As Before," Avon (New York, NY), 1947.

East of Suez: Great Stories of the Tropics, Avon (New York, NY), 1948.

Here and There, Heinemann (London, England), 1948.

The Complete Short Stories, three volumes, Heinemann (London, England), 1951, Doubleday (New York, NY), 1952, published as *Collected Short Stories,* Pan Books (New York, NY), 1976.

The World Over: Stories of Manifold Places and People, Doubleday (New York, NY), 1952.

Best Short Stories, selected by John Beecroft, Modern Library (New York, NY), 1957.

Favorite Stories, Avon (New York, NY), 1960.

Collected Short Stories, Penguin Books (New York, NY), 1963.

Husbands and Wives: Nine Stories, edited by Richard A. Cordell, Pyramid (New York, NY), 1963.

The Sinners: Six Stories, edited by Richard A. Cordell, Pyramid (New York, NY), 1964.

A Maugham Twelve, selected by Angus Wilson, Heinemann (London, England), 1966.

The Complete Short Stories of W. Somerset Maugham, four volumes, Washington Square Press (New York, NY), 1967.

The Kite, and Other Stories, introduction by Ian Serraillier, Heinemann (London, England) Educational, 1968.

Maugham's Malaysian Stories, edited by Anthony Burgess, Heinemann (London, England), 1969.

Seventeen Lost Stories, edited by Craig V. Showalter, Doubleday (New York, NY), 1969.

A Baker's Dozen: Thirteen Short Stories, Heinemann (London, England), 1969.

Four Short Stories, illustrations by Henri Matisse, Hallmark Editions (Kansas City, MO), 1970.

A Second Baker's Dozen: Thirteen Short Stories, Heinemann (London, England), 1970.

The Hairless Mexican [and] *The Traitor,* Heinemann (London, England) Educational, 1974.

Footprints in the Jungle and Two Other Stories, edited by Rod Sinclair, Heinemann Educational (London, England), 1975.

Sixty-five Short Stories, Octopus Books (London, England), 1976.

A short story, "The Vessel of Wrath," was published by Dell as *The Beachcomber.*

PLAYS

Marriages Are Made in Heaven (produced in Berlin as *Schiffbruechig,* 1902), published in *The Venture Annual of Art and Literature,* edited by Maugham and Laurence Housman, Baillie (London, England), 1903.

A Man of Honour: A Tragedy in Four Acts (produced in Westminster, England, at Imperial Theatre, February 23, 1903), Dramatic Publishing (New York, NY), 1903.

Mademoiselle Zampa, produced in London, 1904.

Penelope: A Comedy in Three Acts (produced in London, 1909), Dramatic Publishing (New York, NY), 1909.

Lady Frederick: A Comedy in Three Acts (first produced in London, 1907; produced in New York, NY, 1908), Heinemann (London, England), 1911, Dramatic Publishing (New York, NY), 1912.

A Trip to Brighton (adaptation of a play by Abel Tarride), produced in London, 1911.

Jack Straw: A Farce in Three Acts (produced in London and New York, 1908), Heinemann (London, England), 1911, Dramatic Publishing (New York, NY), 1912.

The Explorer: A Melodrama in Four Acts (produced in London, 1908), Heinemann (London, England), 1912, Doran (New York, NY), 1920, reprinted, Arno (New York, NY), 1977.

Mrs. Dot: A Farce in Three Acts (produced in London, 1908), Dramatic Publishing (New York, NY), 1912.

Smith: A Comedy in Four Acts (first produced in London, 1909; produced in New York, 1910), Dramatic Publishing (New York, NY), 1913.

Landed Gentry: A Comedy in Four Acts (produced as *Grace* in London, 1910), Dramatic Publishing (New York, NY), 1913.

The Tenth Man: A Tragic Comedy in Three Acts (produced in London, 1910), Dramatic Publishing (New York, NY), 1913.

The Land of Promise: A Comedy in Four Acts (first produced in New York, 1913), Bickers & Son (London, England), 1913.

Love in a Cottage, produced in London, 1918.

The Unknown: A Play in Three Acts (produced in London, 1920), Doran (New York, NY), 1920.

The Circle: A Comedy in Three Acts (produced in New York and London, 1921), Doran (New York, NY), 1921.

Caesar's Wife: A Comedy in Three Acts (produced in London, 1919), Heinemann (London, England), 1922, Doran (New York, NY), 1923.

East of Suez: A Play in Seven Scenes (produced in London, 1922), Doran (New York, NY), 1922, reprinted, Arno (New York, NY), 1977.

Loaves and Fishes: A Comedy in Four Acts (produced in London, 1911), Heinemann (London, England), 1923.

The Unattainable: A Farce in Three Acts (produced in New York and London, 1916), Heinemann (London, England), 1923.

Our Betters: A Comedy in Three Acts (first produced in New York, 1917), Heinemann (London, England), 1923, Doran (New York, NY), 1924.

Home and Beauty: A Farce in Three Acts (produced in New York and London, 1919; produced as *Too Many Husbands* in New York, 1919), Heinemann (London, England), 1923.

The Camel's Back, produced in Worcester, MA, 1923; produced in London, 1924.

The Letter: A Play in Three Acts (based on *The Casuarina Tree*; produced in London, 1927), Doran (New York, NY), 1925, reprinted, Arno (New York, NY), 1977.

The Constant Wife: A Comedy in Three Acts (first produced in New York, 1926), Doran (New York, NY), 1926.

The Sacred Flame: A Play in Three Acts (produced in New York, 1928), Doubleday, Doran (New York, NY), 1928, reprinted, Arno (New York, NY), 1977.

The Bread-Winner: A Comedy in One Act (first produced in London, 1930; produced in New York, 1931), Heinemann (London, England), 1930, published as *The Breadwinner: A Comedy,* Doubleday, Doran (New York, NY), 1931.

Plays, Heinemann (London, England), 1931, reprinted, 1966.

Dramatic Works, six volumes, Heinemann (London, England), 1931-34, published as *Collected Plays,* three volumes, 1952, published as *The Collected Plays of W. Somerset Maugham,* 1961.

For Services Rendered: A Play in Three Acts (produced in London, 1932), Heinemann (London, England), 1932, Doubleday, Doran (New York, NY), 1933, reprinted, Arno (New York, NY), 1977.

Sheppey: A Play in Three Acts (produced in London, 1933), Heinemann (London, England), 1933, Baker, 1949, reprinted, Arno (New York, NY), 1977.

The Mask and the Face (adaptation of a play by Luigi Chiarelli), produced in Boston, 1933.

Six Comedies, Doubleday, Doran (New York, NY), 1937, reprinted, Arno (New York, NY), 1977.

(With Guy Reginald Bolton) *Theatre: A Comedy in Three Acts,* Samuel French, 1942, reprinted, Arno (New York, NY), 1977.

The Noble Spaniard: A Comedy in Three Acts (adapted from Ernest Grenet-Dancourt's "Les Gaites du veuvage"; produced in London, 1909), Evans (London, England), 1953.

The Perfect Gentleman (adaptation of a play by Moliere; produced in London, 1913), published in *Theatre Arts,* November, 1955.

Selected Plays, Penguin Books (New York, NY), 1963.

Three Dramas: The Letter, The Sacred Flame, For Services Rendered, Washington Square Press (New York, NY), 1968.

Three Comedies: The Circle, Our Betters, The Constant Wife, Washington Square Press (New York, NY), 1969.

Also author of *Mrs. Beamish,* 1917; *The Keys to Heaven,* 1917; *Not To-Night, Josephine!* (farce), 1919; *The Road Uphill,* 1924; *The Force of Nature,* 1928.

EDITOR

(With Laurence Housman) *The Venture Annual of Art and Literature,* Baillie (London, England), 1903.

(With Laurence Housman) *The Venture Annual of Art and Literature 1905,* Simpkin Marshall, (London, England), 1904.

Charles Henry Hawtrey, *The Truth at Last,* Little (New York, NY), 1924.

Traveller's Library, Doubleday, Doran (New York, NY), 1933, reissued as *Fifty Modern English Writers,* Doubleday, Doran (New York, NY), 1933.

(With Joseph Frederick Green) *Wisdom of Life: An Anthology of Noble Thoughts,* Watts (New York, NY), 1938.

(With introduction) George Douglas, *The House with the Green Shutters,* Oxford University Press (London, England), 1938.

Tellers of Tales: One Hundred Short Stories from the United States, England, France, Russia and Germany, Doubleday, Doran (New York, NY), 1939, published as *The Greatest Stories of All Times, Tellers of Tales,* Garden City Publishing (Garden City, NY), 1943.

Great Modern Reading: W. Somerset Maugham's Introduction to Modern English and American Literature, Doubleday (New York, NY), 1943.

Charles Dickens, *David Copperfield,* Winston (New York, NY), 1948.

Henry Fielding, *The History of Tom Jones, a Foundling,* Winston (New York, NY), 1948.

Jane Austen, *Pride and Prejudice,* Winston (New York, NY), 1949.

Honore de Balzac, *Old Man Goriot,* Winston (New York, NY), 1949.

Emily Bronte, *Wuthering Heights,* Winston (New York, NY), 1949.

Fyodor Dostoyevski, *The Brothers Karamazov,* Winston (New York, NY), 1949.

Gustave Flaubert, *Madame Bovary,* Winston (New York, NY), 1949.

Herman Melville, *Moby Dick,* Winston (New York, NY), 1949.

Stendhal, *The Red and the Black,* Winston (New York, NY), 1949.

Leo Tolstoy, *War and Peace,* Winston (New York, NY), 1949.

A Choice of Kipling's Prose, Macmillan (New York, NY), 1952, reprinted, Telegraph Books (New York, NY), 1981, published as *Maugham's Choice of Kipling's Best,* Doubleday (New York, NY), 1953.

OTHER

The Artistic Temperament of Stephen Carey (earliest manuscript for novel *Of Human Bondage*), c. 1900.

The Land of the Blessed Virgin: Sketches and Impressions in Andalusia (travel), Heinemann (London, England), 1905, Knopf (New York, NY), 1920.

On a Chinese Screen (travel), Doran (New York, NY), 1922, reprinted, Arno (New York, NY), 1977.

The Gentleman in the Parlour: A Record of a Journey from Rangoon to Haiphong, Doubleday, Doran (New York, NY), 1930, reprinted, Arno (New York, NY), 1977.

The Non-Dramatic Works, twenty-eight volumes, Heinemann (London, England), 1934-1969.

Don Fernando; or, Variations on Some Spanish Themes (travel), Doubleday, Doran (New York, NY), 1935, reprinted, Arno (New York, NY), 1977, revised edition, Heinemann (London, England), 1961.

Works, collected edition, Heinemann (London, England), 1935.

My South Sea Island, privately printed, 1936.

The Summing Up (autobiography), Doubleday, Doran (New York, NY), 1938l, reprinted, Penguin Books (New York, NY), 1978.

Books and You, Doubleday, Doran (New York, NY), 1940, reprinted, Arno (New York, NY), 1977.

France at War, Doubleday, Doran (New York, NY), 1940, reprinted, Arno (New York, NY), 1977.

Strictly Personal, Doubleday, Doran (New York, NY), 1941, reprinted, Arno (New York, NY), 1977.

The W. Somerset Maugham Sampler, edited by Jerome Weidman, Garden City Publishing (Garden City, NY), 1943, published as *The Somerset Maugham Pocket Book,* Pocket Books (New York, NY), 1944.

W. Somerset Maugham's Introduction to Modern English and American Literature, New Home Library (New York, NY), 1943.

Great Novelists and Their Novels: Essays on the Ten Greatest Novels of the World and the Men and Women Who Wrote Them, Winston (New York, NY), 1948, revised edition published as *Ten Novels and Their Authors,* Heinemann (London, England), 1954, published as *The Art of Fiction: An Introduction to Ten Novels and Their Authors,* Doubleday (New York, NY), 1955, published as *The World's Ten Greatest Novels,* Fawcett (New York, NY), 1956, published as *W. Somerset Maugham Selects the World's Ten Greatest Novels,* Fawcett (New York, NY), 1962.

Quartet: Stories by W. Somerset Maugham, Screenplays by R. C. Sheriff, Heinemann (London, England), 1948, Doubleday (New York, NY), 1949.

A Writer's Notebook, Doubleday (New York, NY), 1949, reprinted, Arno (New York, NY), 1977.

The Maugham Reader, introduction by Glenway Wescott, Doubleday (New York, NY), 1950.

Trio: Original Stories by W. Somerset Maugham; Screenplays by W. Somerset Maugham, R. C. Sherriff, and Noel Langley, Doubleday (New York, NY), 1950.

Cakes and Ale, and Other Favorites, Pocket Books (New York, NY), 1951.

Encore: Original Stories by W. Somerset Maugham, Screenplays by T. E. B. Clarke, Arthur Macrae, and Eric Ambler, Doubleday (New York, NY), 1952.

The Vagrant Mood: Six Essays, Heinemann (London, England), 1952, Doubleday (New York, NY), 1953.

The Partial View (contains *The Summing Up* and *A Writer's Notebook*), Heinemann (London, England), 1954.

Mr. Maugham Himself, selected by John Beecroft, Doubleday (New York, NY), 1954.

The Travel Books, Heinemann (London, England), 1955.

The Magician: A Novel, Together with A Fragment of Autobiography, Heinemann (London, England), 1956, published as *The Magician: Together with A Fragment of Autobiography,* Doubleday (New York, NY), 1957.

Points of View (essays), Heinemann (London, England), 1958, Doubleday (New York, NY), 1959.

Purely for My Pleasure, Doubleday (New York, NY), 1962.

Selected Prefaces and Introductions of W. Somerset Maugham, Doubleday (New York, NY), 1963.

Wit and Wisdom of Somerset Maugham, edited by Cecil Hewetson, Duckworth (New York, NY), 1966.

Essays on Literature, New American Library (New York, NY), 1967.

Cakes and Ale, and Twelve Short Stories, edited by Angus Wilson, Doubleday (New York, NY), 1967.

Man from Glasgow and Mackintosh, Heinemann Educational (London, England), 1973.

Selected Works, Heinemann (London, England), 1976.

The Works of Somerset Maugham, forty-seven volumes, Arno (New York, NY), 1977.

A Traveller in Romance: Uncollected Writings, 1901-1964, edited by John Whitehead, C. N. Potter (New York, NY), 1985.

The Great Exotic Novels and Short Stories of Somerset Maugham, Carroll & Graf (New York, NY), 2001.

A Maugham archive is maintained by the Yale University Library.

ADAPTATIONS: The following films were based on Maugham's works: *Smith,* 1917; *The Land of Promise,* Famous Players, 1917, produced as *The Canadian,* Paramount, 1926; *The Divorcee,* based on *Lady Frederick,* Metro Pictures, 1919; *Jack Straw,* Famous Players/Lasky, 1920; *The Circle,* Metro-Goldwyn-Mayer, 1925, produced as *Strictly Unconventional,* Metro-Goldwyn-Mayer, 1930; *Sadie Thompson,* 1928, remade as *Rain,* United Artists, 1932, and as *Miss Sadie Thompson,* Columbia, 1954; *Charming Sinners,* based on *The Constant Wife,* Paramount, 1929; *Our Betters,* RKO, 1933; *Of Human Bondage,* RKO, 1934, remakes by Warner Bros., 1946, and Metro-Goldwyn-Mayer, 1964; *The Painted Veil,* Metro-Goldwyn-Mayer, 1934; *The Tenth Man,* Wardour Films, 1937;

The Beachcomber (based on "The Vessel of Wrath"), Paramount, 1938; *Too Many Husbands,* based on *Not To-Night, Josephine!* Columbia, 1940, remade as *Three for the Show,* Columbia, 1955; *The Letter,* Warner Bros., 1940; *The Moon and Sixpence,* United Artists, 1943; *The Razor's Edge,* Twentieth Century-Fox, 1947, and Columbia, 1984; *Quartet* (film version of *The Facts of Life, The Alien Corn, The Kite,* and *The Colonel's Lady*), J. Arthur Rank, 1949; *Trio,* Paramount, 1951; *Encore* (film version of *The Ant and the Grasshopper, Winter Cruise,* and *Gigolo and Gigolette*), J. Arthur Rank, 1952; *Up at the Villa,* USA Films, 2000. Plays based on Maugham's works: *Rain* (dramatization of *Miss Thompson*), by John B. Colton and Clemence Randolph, produced in New York, 1922, published by Boni & Liveright, 1923, S. French, 1948; *Sadie Thompson,* musical adaptation, produced in New York, 1944; *Before the Party* (dramatization of a short story), by Rodney Ackland, S. French, 1950; *Larger Than Life* (based on the novel *Theatre*), by Guy Bolton, S. French, 1951; *Jane* (dramatization of a short story), by S. N. Behrman, produced in New York, 1952, published by Random House, 1952.

SIDELIGHTS: "Looking back upon my work in my old age," W. Somerset Maugham once wrote, "I am disposed to regard it very modestly and to admit frankly some of its shortcomings. In my youth I had accepted the challenge of writing and literature to idealize them; in my age I see the magnitude of the attempt and wonder at my audacity."

Maugham may have been audacious, but more often people called him cynical, cold, uncharitable. One publisher said, "Willie's been true to himself; he's had a bad word for everybody." His attitude toward humanity was likened by Malcolm Cowley to "the milk of human kindness half-soured." Maugham once commented, "I've always been interested in people, but I don't like them." In *The Summing Up* he wrote: "I have been called cynical. I have been accused of making men out worse than they are. I do not think I have done this. All I have done is to bring into prominence certain traits that many writers shut their eyes to. I think what has chiefly struck me in human beings is their lack of consistency."

Maugham sometimes cynically agreed with his detractors, who saw him as merely an entertainer who became one of the world's richest authors. It was estimated that he earned more than three million dollars from his writings, and his estate came to be valued at about five million dollars. Alan Pryce-Jones wrote: "Of his popular success there can be no question. In the history of literature there is nobody whose work has been more widely sold, translated and devoured—partly because of his real merit as a storyteller, partly because the functional simplicity of his writing made his books unusually accessible." His stories are not difficult to comprehend. He once said that he had "a clear and logical brain, but not a very subtle nor a very powerful one."

Maugham was born in Paris, France, in 1874, the son of a solicitor to the British embassy. However, his father died when he was eight and his mother when he was twelve, and he was raised by his father's brother, a clergyman. When he was thirteen, he was sent to King's School, Cambridge, in England, where he was supposed to prepare for a career as a clergyman. He was more interested in writing, though, and got his uncle's permission to study in Heidelberg, Germany. He ultimately decided to study medicine, and trained for six years in a hospital in London. Although he spent a year-long internship in the London slums, he never went into medical practice. Instead, he moved to Paris, where he worked on his writing and lived in poverty. His first play, *Lady Frederick,* was produced in 1907, and was followed by three others within a year, launching his long and illustrious career as a writer.

The position Maugham established through more than sixty years of writing was no mean accomplishment. He was a storyteller—"the most continuously readable storyteller of our lifetime," said Christopher Morley—one who believed a story should have a beginning, a middle, and an end, carefully delineated characters, a lucid plot, and employ clear, concise language. Maugham was, Walter Allen wrote, "the last survivor of a vanished age, an age which had not divorced, as ours has largely done, the idea of entertainment from the idea of art." The writer, for him, was a purveyor of pleasure, and what he wrote about was more important than how it was presented. He said, "With me the sense is more than the sound, the substance is more than the form, the moral significance is more than the rhetorical adornment. I am not indifferent to the art and music of words, but I habitually treat them as of secondary importance. . . . The fact remains that the four greatest novelists the world has ever known—

Balzac, Dickens, Tolstoi and Dostoyevski—wrote their respective languages very badly. It proves that if you can tell stories, create characters, devise incidents, and have sincerity and passion, it doesn't matter a damn how you write." He added, "I wrote stories because it was a delight to write them."

Of Human Bondage, however, "was written in pain." Its principal character, Philip Carey, sensitive and plagued with a clubfoot, was so like the author, who was afflicted with a stutter, that Maugham was unable to read the book after it was published. Perhaps to avoid similar pain, Maugham chose to write about other people and found material for stories everywhere. He once said, "I am almost inclined to say that I could not spend an hour in anyone's company without getting the material to write at least a readable story about him." "In all my work," he said, "I have tried . . . to touch many classes of readers and many varieties of mind. I can be severely simple and chastely sensuous, classic and grotesque, subtle and passionate, passing with perfect mastery from love to dialectics, from the wail of a somber pessimism to the exaltation and rapture of a triumphant lover. I can even be humorous, too." Coherence was evident in Maugham's ideas, "for the main principles of my philosophy are so simple and so definite, that from my earliest writings to my last there is perfect unity." And always in his travels and sojourns he was an observer, dispassionate and systematic. As he wrote once, "I do not know a better training ground for a writer than to spend some years in the medical profession."

John Brophy called Maugham's writings "extroverted." The resultant artificiality and informality were well suited to certain media in which Maugham had achieved success, notably the stage—at one time he had four plays running simultaneously on London's West End—and the "magazine" story. Maugham had reproached those who favored the mood story characteristic of Anton Chekhov and had defended his own narratives: "Where the critics to my mind err is when they dismiss stories as magazine stories because they are well constructed, dramatic and have a surprise ending."

Of Human Bondage is still regarded as Maugham's best, though he always showed a preference for *Cakes and Ale.* He believed Graham Greene was the best British novelist, and he liked William Faulkner. Though critics attributed influences on Maugham to

such authors as Dickens, Fielding, Defoe, and Trollope, Maugham once said, "I follow no master, and acknowledge none."

"In my twenties," he once wrote, "the critics said I was brutal. In my thirties they said I was flippant, in my forties they said I was cynical, in my fifties they said I was competent, and in my sixties they say I am superficial." By 1959 this compulsive writer was writing, he said, only for himself, and at the time of his death he was reportedly working on an autobiography that was to be published posthumously. A few years before his death he destroyed all of his old notebooks and unfinished manuscripts. Yet he continued to assert that "literature, or pure imaginative creation, was the highest goal toward which man could strive."

Maugham lived in a villa once owned by Leopold II, and replicas of a Moorish symbol surrounded him. He entertained the wealthy, royalty, and great wits and beauties. He observed them all for his stories. He once received over half a million pounds for his collection of paintings. He died in Nice, France, in 1965.

BIOGRAPHICAL AND CRITICAL SOURCES:

BOOKS

Archer, Stanley, *W. Somerset Maugham: A Study of the Short Fiction,* Twayne (New York, NY), 1993.

Brander, L., *Somerset Maugham: A Guide,* Barnes & Noble (New York, NY), 1963.

Breit, Harvey, editor, *The Writer Observed,* World Publishing (New York, NY), 1956.

Brophy, John, *Somerset Maugham,* Longmans, Green (London, England), 1952, revised edition, 1958.

Brown, Ivor, *W. Somerset Maugham,* Barnes (New York, NY), 1970.

Burt, Forrest, *W. Somerset Maugham,* Twayne (Boston, MA), 1986.

Calder, Robert L., *Willie: The Life of W. Somerset Maugham,* Heinemann (London, England), 1989.

Connon, Bryan, *Somerset Maugham and the Maugham Dynasty,* Sinclair-Stevenson (London, England), 1997.

Contemporary Literary Criticism, Gale (Detroit, MI), Volume 1, 1973, Volume 11, 1979, Volume 15, 1980.

Cordell, Richard Albert, *Somerset Maugham: A Biographical and Critical Study,* Indiana University Press (Bloomington, IN), 1961.

Curtis, A. Anthony, *Somerset Maugham,* Macmillan (New York, NY), 1977.

Dictionary of Literary Biography, Gale (Detroit, MI), Volume 10: *Modern British Dramatists, 1940-1945,* 1982, Volume 36: *British Novelists, 1890-1929: Modernists,* 1985, Volume 77: *British Mystery Writers, 1920-1939,* 1989, Volume 195: *British Travel Writers, 1910-1939,* 1998.

Encyclopedia of World Biography, 2nd edition, Gale (Detroit, MI), 1998.

Holden, Philip, *Orienting Masculinity, Orienting Nation: W. Somerset Maugham's Exotic Fiction,* Greenwood Press (Westport, CT), 1996.

International Dictionary of Theatre, Volume 2: *Playwrights,* St. James Press (Detroit, MI), 1993.

MacCarthy, D., *William Somerset Maugham,* Norwood Editions (Norwood, PA), 1977.

Maugham, Robin, *Somerset and All the Maughams,* New American Library, 1966.

Maugham, Robin, *Conversations with Willie: Recollections of W. Somerset Maugham,* Simon & Schuster (New York, NY), 1978.

McIver, C. S., *William Somerset Maugham,* Richard West, 1978.

Menard, W., *The Two Worlds of Somerset Maugham,* Sherbourne, 1965.

Morgan, Ted, *Maugham,* Simon & Schuster (New York, NY), 1980.

Pfeiffer, Karl Graham, *W. Somerset Maugham: A Candid Portrait,* Norton (New York, NY), 1959.

Raphael, Frederic, *Somerset Maugham,* Thames & Hudson (London, England), 1976.

Rogal, Samuel J., *A Companion to the Characters in the Fiction and Drama of W. Somerset Maugham,* Greenwood Press (Westport, CT), 1996.

Rogal, Samuel J., *A William Somerset Maugham Encyclopedia,* Greenwood Press (Westport, CT), 1997.

St. James Guide to Crime and Mystery Writers, 4th edition, St. James Press (Detroit, MI), 1996.

Swinnerton, Frank, *The Saturday Review Gallery,* Simon & Schuster, (New York, NY), 1959.

Whitehead, John, *Maugham: A Reappraisal,* Vision (London, England), 1987.

PERIODICALS

American Scholar, winter, 1993, pp. 98-103.

Armchair Detective, spring, 1996, review of *Ashenden,* p. 225.

Booklist, November 15, 1998, review of *Princess September and the Nightingale,* p. 597.

Chicago Tribune, April 30, 1980; October 19, 1984; May 6, 1987.

Children's Bookwatch, May, 1993, review of *Appointment,* p. 3.

Christian Science Monitor, July 6, 1970.

Connoisseur, April, 1990, pp. 46-48.

Detroit News, February 17, 1985.

English Literature in Translation, March, 1995, review of *The Moon and Sixpence,* p. 329.

Horn Book, spring, 1999, review of *Princess September and the Nightingale,* p. 58.

Library Journal, September 1, 1993, review of *Ashenden,* p. 143; April 15, 2001, review of *Up at the Villa* and *Christmas Holiday,* p. 138.

Listener, October 17, 1968.

Los Angeles Times, October 19, 1984.

Los Angeles Times Book Review, June 2, 1985.

Nation, January 29, 1990, p. 144.

New Advocate, fall, 1993, review of *Appointment,* p. 291.

Newsweek, January 27, 1958.

New York Times, February 18, 1986; February 21, 1986.

New York Times Magazine, January 25, 1959; June 2, 1968.

Playboy, January, 1966.

Publishers Weekly, May 3, 1993, p. 304; November 23, 1998, review of *Princess September and the Nightingale,* p. 69.

Punch, October 16, 1968.

Saturday Review, October 14, 1961; November 5, 1966.

School Library Journal, February, 1999, review of *Princess September and the Nightingale,* p. 87.

Stage, June 4, 1970; June 18, 1970; July 2, 1970; July 23, 1970.

Time, April 20, 1962.

Times (London, England), March 28, 1988.

Times Literary Supplement, April 5, 1985.

Variety, July 8, 1970.

Washington Post, October 8, 1969; October 19, 1984.

Washington Post Book World, August 20, 1995, review of *The Gentleman in the Parlour,* p. 15.

Yale Review, spring, 1987, pp. 428-440.

OBITUARIES:

PERIODICALS

Books Abroad, spring, 1966.

New York Herald Tribune, December 17, 1965.
New York Times, December 16, 1965.
Publishers Weekly, December 27, 1965.
Reporter, December 30, 1965.*

*   *   *

MAY, Julian 1931-
(Bob Cunningham, Lee N. Falconer, John Feilen, Matthew G. Grant, Ian Thorne, Jean Wright Thorne, George Zanderbergen, pseudonyms)

PERSONAL: Born July 10, 1931, in Chicago, IL; daughter of Matthew M. and Julia (Feilen) May; married Thaddeus "Ted" E. Dikty (a writer and publisher), 1953; children: Alan Samuel, David Bernard, Barbara Ellen. *Education:* Attended Rosary College, 1949-52. *Hobbies and other interests:* Electronic music, gardening, fly fishing.

ADDRESSES: Office—P.O. Box 851, Mercer Island, WA 98040. *Agent*—Ralph M. Vicinanza, Ltd., 303 West 18th St., New York, NY 10011.

CAREER: Freelance writer. Booz Allen Hamilton, Chicago, IL, editor, 1953; Consolidated Book Publishers, Chicago, editor, 1954-57; Publication Associates, editor and co-owner, Chicago, 1957-68, Naperville, IL, 1968-74, West Linn, OR, 1974-80, and Mercer Island, WA, 1980-92. Has also worked in art design, art direction, commercial art, and photography.

AWARDS, HONORS: Locus Award for Best Science Fiction Novel, 1982, and Hugo and Nebula Award nominations, all for *The Many-Colored Land.*

WRITINGS:

SCIENCE FICTION; "RAMPART WORLDS" SERIES

Perseus Spur, Del Rey (New York, NY), 1999.
Orion Arm, Del Rey (New York, NY), 2000.
Sagittarius Whorl, Del Rey (New York, NY), 2001.

SCIENCE FICTION; "THE SAGA OF PLIOCENE EXILE" SERIES

The Many-Colored Land, Houghton Mifflin (Boston, MA), 1981.

The Golden Torc, Houghton Mifflin (Boston, MA), 1981.
Brede's Tale (short story), Starmont House (Mercer Island, WA), 1982.
The Nonborn King, Houghton Mifflin (Boston, MA), 1983.
The Adversary, Houghton Mifflin (Boston, MA), 1984.
A Pliocene Companion: A Reader's Guide to "The Many-Colored Land," "The Golden Torc," "The Nonborn King," and "The Adversary," Houghton Mifflin (Boston, MA), 1984.

SCIENCE FICTION; "GALACTIC MILIEU" SERIES

Intervention: A Root Tale to the Galactic Milieu and a Vinculum between It and the Saga of Pliocene Exile, Houghton Mifflin (Boston, MA), 1987, published in two volumes as *The Surveillance* and *The Metaconcert,* Ballantine (New York, NY), 1989.
Jack the Bodiless, Knopf (New York, NY), 1992.
Diamond Mask, Knopf (New York, NY), 1994.
Magnificat, Knopf (New York, NY), 1996.

FANTASY FICTION

(With Marion Zimmer Bradley and Andre Norton) *Black Trillium,* Doubleday (New York, NY), 1990.
Blood Trillium, Bantam Spectra (New York, NY), 1992.
Sky Trillium, Ballantine (New York, NY), 1997.
Conqueror's Moon ("Boreal Moon Tale" Series), Ace (New York, NY), 2004.

JUVENILE NONFICTION

There's Adventure in Atomic Energy, Popular Mechanics Press (Chicago, IL), 1957.
There's Adventure in Chemistry, Popular Mechanics Press (Chicago, IL), 1957.
There's Adventure in Electronics, Popular Mechanics Press (Chicago, IL), 1957.
There's Adventure in Geology, Popular Mechanics Press (Chicago, IL), 1958.
There's Adventure in Rockets, Popular Mechanics Press (Chicago, IL), 1958.
You and the Earth beneath Us, Children's Press (Chicago, IL), 1958.

There's Adventure in Jet Aircraft, Popular Mechanics Press (Chicago, IL), 1959.

There's Adventure in Marine Science, Popular Mechanics Press (Chicago, IL), 1959.

Show Me the World of Astronomy, Pennington Press (Cleveland, OH), 1959.

Show Me the World of Electronics, Pennington Press (Cleveland, OH), 1959.

Show Me the World of Modern Airplanes, Pennington Press (Cleveland, OH), 1959.

Show Me the World of Space Travel, Pennington Press (Cleveland, OH), 1959.

The Real Book about Robots and Thinking Machines, Doubleday (New York, NY), 1961.

There's Adventure in Astronautics, Hawthorn (New York, NY), 1961.

There's Adventure in Automobiles, Hawthorn (New York, NY), 1961.

Motion, Accelerated Instruction Methods, 1962.

(With husband, T. E. Dikty) *Every Boy's Book of American Heroes,* Fell (New York, NY), 1963.

They Turned to Stone, Holiday House (New York, NY), 1965.

Weather, Follett (New York, NY), 1966.

Rockets, Follett (New York, NY), 1967.

They Lived in the Ice Age, Holiday House (New York, NY), 1968.

Astronautics, Follett (New York, NY), 1968.

The Big Island, Follett (New York, NY), 1968.

The First Men, Holiday House (New York, NY), 1968.

Horses: How They Came to Be, Holiday House (New York, NY), 1968.

Alligator Hole, Follett (New York, NY), 1969.

Before the Indians, Holiday House (New York, NY), 1969.

Climate, Follett (New York, NY), 1969.

How We Are Born, Follett (New York, NY), 1969.

Living Things and Their Young, Follett (New York, NY), 1969.

Man and Woman, Follett (New York, NY), 1969.

Moving Hills of Sand, Follett (New York, NY), 1969.

Why the Earth Quakes, Holiday House (New York, NY), 1969.

Do You Have Your Father's Nose?, Creative Educational Society (Mankato, MN), 1970.

Dodos and Dinosaurs Are Extinct, Creative Educational Society (Mankato, MN), 1970.

(With others) *The Ecology of North America,* Creative Educational Society (Mankato, MN), 1970.

The First Living Things, Holiday House (New York, NY), 1970.

How to Build a Body, Creative Educational Society (Mankato, MN), 1970.

Millions of Years of Eggs, Creative Educational Society (Mankato, MN), 1970.

A New Baby Comes, Creative Educational Society (Mankato, MN), 1970.

Tiger Stripes and Zebra Stripes, Creative Educational Society (Mankato, MN), 1970.

Why Birds Migrate, Holiday House (New York, NY), 1970.

Why Plants Are Green Instead of Pink, Creative Educational Society (Mankato, MN), 1970.

Wildlife in the City, Creative Educational Society (Mankato, MN), 1970.

Blue River: The Land beneath the Sea, Holiday House, 1971.

Cactus Fox, Creative Educational Society (Mankato, MN), 1971.

These Islands Are Alive, Hawthorn (New York, NY), 1971.

Why People Are Different Colors, Holiday House (New York, NY), 1971.

The Antarctic: Bottom of the World, Creative Educational Society (Mankato, MN), 1972.

The Arctic: Top of the World, Creative Educational Society (Mankato, MN), 1972.

Cascade Cougar, Creative Educational Society (Mankato, MN), 1972.

The Cloud Book, Creative Educational Society (Mankato, MN), 1972.

Deserts: Hot and Cold, Creative Educational Society (Mankato, MN), 1972.

Eagles of the Valley, Creative Educational Society (Mankato, MN), 1972.

Forests That Change Color, Creative Educational Society (Mankato, MN), 1972.

Giant Condor of California, Creative Educational Society (Mankato, MN), 1972.

Glacier Grizzly, Creative Educational Society (Mankato, MN), 1972.

Islands of the Tiny Deer, Young Scott Books, 1972.

The Land Is Disappearing, Creative Educational Society (Mankato, MN), 1972.

Living Blanket on the Land, Creative Educational Society (Mankato, MN), 1972.

The Mysterious Evergreen Forest, Creative Educational Society (Mankato, MN), 1972.

Plankton: Drifting Life of the Waters, Holiday House (New York, NY), 1972.

The Prairie Has an Endless Sky, Creative Educational Society (Mankato, MN), 1972.

Prairie Pronghorn, Creative Educational Society (Mankato, MN), 1972.

Rainbows, Clouds, and Foggy Dew, Creative Educational Society (Mankato, MN), 1972.

Sea Lion Island, Creative Educational Society (Mankato, MN), 1972.

Sea Otter, Creative Educational Society (Mankato, MN), 1972.

Snowfall!, Creative Educational Society (Mankato, MN), 1972.

What Will the Weather Be?, Creative Educational Society (Mankato, MN), 1972.

Birds We Know, Creative Educational Society (Mankato, MN), 1973.

Fishes We Know, Creative Educational Society (Mankato, MN), 1973.

Insects We Know, Creative Educational Society (Mankato, MN), 1973.

The Life Cycle of a Bullfrog, Creative Educational Society (Mankato, MN), 1973.

The Life Cycle of a Cottontail Rabbit, Creative Educational Society (Mankato, MN), 1973.

The Life Cycle of a Monarch Butterfly, Creative Educational Society (Mankato, MN), 1973.

The Life Cycle of an Opossum, Creative Educational Society (Mankato, MN), 1973.

The Life Cycle of a Polyphemus Moth, Creative Educational Society (Mankato, MN), 1973.

The Life Cycle of a Raccoon, Creative Educational Society (Mankato, MN), 1973.

The Life Cycle of a Red Fox, Creative Educational Society (Mankato, MN), 1973.

The Life Cycle of a Snapping Turtle, Creative Educational Society (Mankato, MN), 1973.

Mammals We Know, Creative Educational Society (Mankato, MN), 1973.

Reptiles We Know, Creative Educational Society (Mankato, MN), 1973.

Wild Turkeys, Holiday House (New York, NY), 1973.

How the Animals Came to North America, Holiday House (New York, NY), 1974.

Cars and Cycles, Bowmar-Noble, 1978.

The Warm-Blooded Dinosaurs, Holiday House (New York, NY), 1978.

JUVENILE BIOGRAPHIES

Captain Cousteau: Undersea Explorer, Creative Educational Society (Mankato, MN), 1972.

Hank Aaron Clinches the Pennant, Crestwood (Mankato, MN), 1972.

Jim Brown Runs with the Ball, Crestwood (Mankato, MN), 1972.

Johnny Unitas and the Long Pass, Crestwood (Mankato, MN), 1972.

Matthew Henson: Co-Discoverer of the North Pole, Creative Educational Society (Mankato, MN), 1972.

Mickey Mantle Slugs It Out, Crestwood (Mankato, MN), 1972.

Sitting Bull: Chief of the Sioux, Creative Educational Society (Mankato, MN), 1972.

Sojourner Truth: Freedom Fighter, Creative Educational Society (Mankato, MN), 1972.

Willie Mays: Most Valuable Player, Crestwood (Mankato, MN), 1972.

Amelia Earhart: Pioneer of Aviation, Creative Educational Society (Mankato, MN), 1973.

Bobby Orr: Star on Ice, Crestwood (Mankato, MN), 1973.

Ernie Banks: Home Run Slugger, Crestwood, 1973 (Mankato, MN).

Fran Tarkenton: Scrambling Quarterback, Crestwood, 1973 (Mankato, MN).

Gale Sayers: Star Running Back, Crestwood (Mankato, MN), 1973.

Hillary and Tenzing: Conquerors of Mount Everest, Creative Educational Society (Mankato, MN), 1973.

Kareem Abdul Jabbar: Cage Superstar, Crestwood (Mankato, MN), 1973.

Quanah: Leader of the Comanche, Creative Educational Society (Mankato, MN), 1973.

Thor Heyerdahl: Modern Viking Adventurer, Creative Educational Society (Mankato, MN), 1973.

Roberto Clemente and the World Series Upset, Crestwood (Mankato, MN), 1973.

Billie Jean King: Tennis Champion, Crestwood (Mankato, MN), 1974.

Bobby Hull: Hockey's Golden Jet, Crestwood (Mankato, MN), 1974.

Lee Trevino: The Golf Explosion, Crestwood (Mankato, MN), 1974.

O. J. Simpson: Juice on the Gridiron, Crestwood (Mankato, MN), 1974.

Roy Campanella: Brave Man of Baseball, Crestwood (Mankato, MN), 1974.

A. J. Foyt: Championship Auto Racer, Crestwood (Mankato, MN), 1975.

Arthur Ashe: Dark Star of Tennis, Crestwood (Mankato, MN), 1975.

Bobby Clarke: Hockey with a Grin, Crestwood (Mankato, MN), 1975.

Chris Evert: Princess of Tennis, Crestwood (Mankato, MN), 1975.

Evel Knievel: Daredevil Stuntman, Crestwood (Mankato, MN), 1975.

Evonne Goolalgong: Smasher from Australia, Crestwood (Mankato, MN), 1975.

Frank Robinson: Slugging toward Glory, Crestwood (Mankato, MN), 1975.

Janet Lynn: Figure Skating Star, Crestwood (Mankato, MN), 1975.

Pele: World Soccer Star, Crestwood (Mankato, MN), 1975.

Joe Namath: High Flying Quarterback, Crestwood (Mankato, MN), 1975.

Muhammad Ali: Boxing Superstar, Crestwood (Mankato, MN), 1975.

Vince Lombardi: The Immortal Coach, Crestwood (Mankato, MN), 1975.

Phil Esposito: The Big Bruin, Crestwood (Mankato, MN), 1975.

SPORTS NONFICTION

The Baltimore Colts, Creative Educational Society (Mankato, MN), 1974.

The Dallas Cowboys, Creative Educational Society (Mankato, MN), 1974.

The Green Bay Packers, Creative Educational Society (Mankato, MN), 1974.

The Kansas City Chiefs, Creative Educational Society (Mankato, MN), 1974.

The Miami Dolphins, Creative Educational Society (Mankato, MN), 1974.

The New York Jets, Creative Educational Society (Mankato, MN), 1974.

The Stanley Cup, Creative Educational Society (Mankato, MN), 1975.

The Super Bowl, Creative Educational Society (Mankato, MN), 1975.

The Indianapolis 500, Creative Educational Society (Mankato, MN), 1975.

The Kentucky Derby, Creative Educational Society (Mankato, MN), 1975.

The Masters Tournament of Golf, Creative Educational Society (Mankato, MN), 1975.

The U. S. Open Golf Championship, Creative Educational Society (Mankato, MN), 1975.

Wimbledon: World Tennis Focus, Creative Educational Society (Mankato, MN), 1975.

The World Series, Creative Educational Society (Mankato, MN), 1975.

The NBA Playoffs: Basketball's Classic, Creative Educational Society (Mankato, MN), 1975.

The Olympic Games, Creative Educational Society (Mankato, MN), 1975.

The PGA Championship, Creative Educational Society (Mankato, MN), 1976.

The Pittsburgh Steelers, Creative Educational Society (Mankato, MN), 1976.

The Winter Olympics, Creative Educational Society (Mankato, MN), 1976.

America's Cup Yacht Race, Creative Educational Society (Mankato, MN), 1976.

Boxing's Heavyweight Championship Fight, Creative Educational Society (Mankato, MN), 1976.

Daytona 500, Creative Educational Society (Mankato, MN), 1976.

Forest Hills and the American Tennis Championship, Creative Educational Society (Mankato, MN), 1976.

The Grand Prix, Creative Educational Society (Mankato, MN), 1976.

The Triple Crown, Creative Educational Society (Mankato, MN), 1976.

The Rose Bowl, Creative Educational Society (Mankato, MN), 1976.

The Washington Redskins, Creative Educational Society (Mankato, MN), 1977.

The Los Angeles Rams, Creative Educational Society (Mankato, MN), 1977.

The Minnesota Vikings, Creative Educational Society (Mankato, MN), 1977.

The New York Giants, Creative Educational Society (Mankato, MN), 1977.

The Oakland Raiders, Creative Educational Society (Mankato, MN), 1977.

The San Francisco 49ers, Creative Educational Society (Mankato, MN), 1977.

The Oakland Raiders: Superbowl Champions, Creative Educational Society (Mankato, MN), 1978.

The Baltimore Colts (different from previous publication of same title), Creative Educational Society (Mankato, MN), 1980.

The Cincinnati Bengals, Creative Educational Society (Mankato, MN), 1980.

The Dallas Cowboys (different from previous publication of same title), Creative Educational Society (Mankato, MN), 1980.

The Denver Broncos, Creative Educational Society (Mankato, MN), 1980.

The Green Bay Packers (different from previous publication of same title), Creative Educational Society (Mankato, MN), 1980.

The Kansas City Chiefs (different from previous publication of same title), Creative Educational Society (Mankato, MN), 1980.

The Miami Dolphins (different from previous publication of same title), Creative Educational Society (Mankato, MN), 1980.

The New York Jets (different from previous publication of same title), Creative Educational Society (Mankato, MN), 1980.

The Pittsburgh Steelers (different from previous publication of same title), Creative Educational Society (Mankato, MN), 1980.

The San Diego Chargers, Creative Educational Society (Mankato, MN), 1980.

NONFICTION; UNDER PSEUDONYM JOHN FEILEN

Air, Follett (New York, NY), 1965.

Deer, Follett (New York, NY), 1967.

Squirrels, Follett (New York, NY), 1967.

Dirt Track Speedsters, Crestwood (Mankato, MN), 1976.

Racing on the Water, Crestwood (Mankato, MN), 1976.

Winter Sports, Crestwood (Mankato, MN), 1976.

Four-Wheel Racing, Crestwood (Mankato, MN), 1978.

Motocross Racing, Crestwood (Mankato, MN), 1978.

NONFICTION; UNDER PSEUDONYM MATTHEW G. GRANT

A Walk in the Mountains, Reilly & Lee, 1971.

Buffalo Bill of the Wild West, Creative Educational Society (Mankato, MN), 1974.

Champlain: Explorer of New France, Creative Educational Society (Mankato, MN), 1974.

Chief Joseph of the Nez Perce, Creative Educational Society (Mankato, MN), 1974.

Clara Barton: Red Cross Pioneer, Creative Educational Society (Mankato, MN), 1974.

Columbus: Discoverer of the New World, Creative Educational Society (Mankato, MN), 1974.

Coronado: Explorer of the Southwest, Creative Educational Society (Mankato, MN), 1974.

Crazy Horse: War Chief of the Oglala, Creative Educational Society (Mankato, MN), 1974.

Daniel Boone in the Wilderness, Creative Educational Society (Mankato, MN), 1974.

Davy Crockett: Frontier Adventurer, Creative Educational Society (Mankato, MN), 1974.

DeSoto: Explorer of the Southeast, Creative Educational Society (Mankato, MN), 1974.

Dolly Madison: First Lady of the Land, Creative Educational Society (Mankato, MN), 1974.

Elizabeth Blackwell: Pioneer Doctor, Creative Educational Society (Mankato, MN), 1974.

Francis Marion: Swamp Fox, Creative Educational Society (Mankato, MN), 1974.

Geronimo: Apache Warrior, Creative Educational Society (Mankato, MN), 1974.

Harriet Tubman: Black Liberator, Creative Educational Society (Mankato, MN), 1974.

Jane Addams: Helper of the Poor, Creative Educational Society (Mankato, MN), 1974.

Jim Bridger: The Mountain Man, Creative Educational Society (Mankato, MN), 1974.

John Paul Jones: Naval Hero, Creative Educational Society (Mankato, MN), 1974.

Leif Ericson: Explorer of Vinland, Creative Educational Society (Mankato, MN), 1974.

Lewis and Clark: Western Trailblazers, Creative Educational Society (Mankato, MN), 1974.

Kit Carson: Trailblazer of the West, Creative Educational Society (Mankato, MN), 1974.

Lafayette: Freedom's General, Creative Educational Society (Mankato, MN), 1974.

Osceola and the Seminole War, Creative Educational Society (Mankato, MN), 1974.

Paul Revere: Patriot and Craftsman, Creative Educational Society (Mankato, MN), 1974.

Pontiac: Indian General and Statesman, Creative Educational Society (Mankato, MN), 1974.

Robert E. Lee: The South's Great General, Creative Educational Society (Mankato, MN), 1974.

Squanto: The Indian Who Saved the Pilgrims, Creative Educational Society (Mankato, MN), 1974.

Sam Houston of Texas, Creative Educational Society (Mankato, MN), 1974.

Susan B. Anthony: Crusader for Women's Rights, Creative Educational Society (Mankato, MN), 1974.

Ulysses S. Grant: General and President, Creative Educational Society (Mankato, MN), 1974.

NONFICTION; UNDER PSEUDONYM IAN THORNE

Meet the Coaches, Creative Educational Society (Mankato, MN), 1975.

Meet the Defensive Linemen, Creative Educational Society (Mankato, MN), 1975.

Meet the Linebackers, Creative Educational Society (Mankato, MN), 1975.

Meet the Quarterbacks, Creative Educational Society (Mankato, MN), 1975.

Meet the Receivers, Creative Educational Society (Mankato, MN), 1975.

Meet the Running Backs, Creative Educational Society (Mankato, MN), 1975.

The Great Centers, Creative Educational Society (Mankato, MN), 1976.

The Great Defenseman, Creative Educational Society (Mankato, MN), 1976.

The Great Goalies, Creative Educational Society (Mankato, MN), 1976.

The Great Wingmen, Creative Educational Society (Mankato, MN), 1976.

King Kong, Creative Educational Society (Mankato, MN), 1976.

Mad Scientists, Crestwood (Mankato, MN), 1977.

Godzilla, Crestwood (Mankato, MN), 1977.

Ancient Astronauts, Crestwood (Mankato, MN), 1977.

Dracula, Crestwood (Mankato, MN), 1977.

Frankenstein, Crestwood (Mankato, MN), 1977.

Monster Tales of Native Americans, Crestwood (Mankato, MN), 1978.

The Bermuda Triangle, Crestwood (Mankato, MN), 1978.

Bigfoot, Crestwood (Mankato, MN), 1978.

The Loch Ness Monster, Crestwood (Mankato, MN), 1978.

UFOs, edited by Howard Schroeder, Crestwood (Mankato, MN), 1978.

NONFICTION; UNDER PSEUDONYM GEORGE ZANDERBERGEN

The Beatles, Crestwood (Mankato, MN), 1976.

Made for Music: Elton John, Stevie Wonder, John Denver, Crestwood (Mankato, MN), 1976.

Laugh It Up: Carol Burnett, Bill Cosby, Mary Tyler Moore, Crestwood (Mankato, MN), 1976.

Nashville Music: Loretta Lynn, Mac Davis, Charley Pride, Crestwood (Mankato, MN), 1976.

Stay Tuned: Henry Winkler, Lee Majors, Valerie Harper, Crestwood (Mankato, MN), 1976.

Sweetly Singing: Cher, Roberta Flack, Olivia Newton John, Crestwood (Mankato, MN), 1976.

NONFICTION; UNDER PSEUDONYM BOB CUNNINGHAM

Ten-Five: Alaska Skip, Crestwood (Mankato, MN), 1977.

Ten-Seven for Good Sam, Crestwood (Mankato, MN), 1977.

Ten-Seventy: Range Fire, Crestwood (Mankato, MN), 1977.

Ten-Thirty-Three: Emergency, Crestwood (Mankato, MN), 1977.

Ten-Two Hundred: Come on Smokey!, Crestwood (Mankato, MN), 1977.

FILM NOVELIZATIONS; UNDER PSEUDONYM IAN THORNE

The Wolf Man, Crestwood House (Mankato, MN), 1977.

The Creature from the Black Lagoon, Crestwood House (Mankato, MN), 1981.

Frankenstein Meets the Wolfman, Crestwood House (Mankato, MN), 1981.

The Blob, Crestwood House (Mankato, MN), 1982.

The Deadly Mantis, Crestwood House (Mankato, MN), 1982.

It Came from Outer Space, Crestwood House (Mankato, MN), 1982.

OTHER

(Under pseudonym Jean Wright Thorne) *Horse and Rider,* Creative Educational Society (Mankato, MN), 1976.

(Under pseudonym Jean Wright Thorne) *Rodeo,* Creative Educational Society (Mankato, MN), 1976.

(Under pseudonym Lee N. Falconer) *A Gazetteer of the Hyborian World of Conan,* Starmont House, 1977.

Editor, "Life in God's Love" series, *Franciscan Herald,* 1963.

ADAPTATIONS: The 1951 novelette *Dune Roller* has been adapted for television and radio.

SIDELIGHTS: "I love action-filled science fiction. I am a fan. I have been accused of being a fan and I admit to it," Julian May told Darrell Schweitzer in

Science Fiction Review. After twenty-five years of earning her living by writing juvenile nonfiction works to order, May returned to her first love, science fiction, in the 1980s with the four-volume "Saga of the Pliocene Exile." This epic series involving time travel, psychic powers, alien conquerors, and human determination has proven popular with readers who enjoy tales of adventure. As the author told Schweitzer: "To me, SF should not be didactic, but rather a literature of entertainment. . . . I [have always] wanted to give the reader books that would be fun."

As a teenager, May was first introduced to the science fiction genre. She briefly became involved in what is known as science fiction "fandom," corresponding with other enthusiasts, editing a science fiction newsletter, and even organizing a convention in her hometown of Chicago. In 1951, her novelette "Dune Roller" was published in *Astounding,* the magazine edited by the legendary John W. Campbell, who had fostered the careers of writers like Isaac Asimov and Robert A. Heinlein. This story brought her to the attention of other editors—leading to the publication of her second story—as well as a young publisher named Ted Dikty, whom she married in 1953.

While "Dune Roller" achieved a wide readership, May left science fiction fandom and writing soon after her marriage. As she explained to Schweitzer, "In the 1950s you couldn't make a living writing science fiction unless you wrote a great volume of work, mostly short pieces for magazines. I am not that sort of writer." Instead, May took a job with a publishing company, where she wrote some 7,000 encyclopedia articles about science and natural history. She discovered a talent for producing nonfiction quickly, and in 1957 she turned freelance, forming an editorial services company with her husband that handled every aspect of book production, from research and writing to printing and binding.

May wrote almost 250 nonfiction books between 1957 and 1982, most of which dealt with science, sports, or biography. While these books gave her the chance to learn about new subjects and hone her writing skills, they provided little room for creativity—even the subjects were assigned by the publishers. As a result, May explained, she had "little emotional involvement in my juvenile books. . . . I did not write my long list of books because of a creative itch, but because I was good at it and it paid the bills." The "itch" to

write science fiction always remained, however, and as her children grew up and the royalties from her nonfiction works accumulated, she began considering a return to science fiction.

A homemade "diamond"-studded space suit May created for a science-fiction convention provided the inspiration that led to her first novel. "At first I had no notion of writing a novel," the author told Schweitzer, "but then as I was writing my other stuff, the damn costume would come creeping back into my subconscious mind and I would wonder what kind of character would wear something like that." May began jotting down notes and collecting research and by 1978 had the outline for a series of novels set in what she called the Galactic Milieu, a future in which humans with extraordinary mental powers such as telepathy and telekinesis have led Earth into a galaxy-wide civilization with several alien races. The author recognized that she might have difficulty marketing a story with such complex concepts, however, and decided to write a more conventional science-fiction story first. This story became the "Saga of the Pliocene Exile," which is comprised of four volumes: *The Many-Colored Land, The Golden Torc, The Nonborn King,* and *The Adversary.*

Set in the early twenty-second century, *The Many-Colored Land* opens upon a near-utopian Earth where the social problems of previous years have been solved with the cooperation of the alien races that form the Galactic Milieu. For those unsatisfied with the new structure of society, however, there exists an intriguing option: a one-way trip to the past, six million years ago, through an invention called the Guderian field. Travellers have been passing through the timegate in Lyon, France, for over seventy years when a unique group of eight individuals makes the same trip. Once in the past, they discover that two related but warring races of aliens, the Tanu and the Firvulag, are already inhabiting this area of Europe, which they call the "Many-Colored Land"; the Tanu's advanced metapsychic powers have allowed them to enslave most of the 100,000 humans who have arrived there. The eight members of "Group Green" are witness to the unique relationships between the races that have developed, with some assimilating into the society and others rebelling. *The Many-Colored Land* is "an enjoyable book," Algis Budrys wrote in the *Magazine of Fantasy Science Fiction,* adding that this "page-turner on an intelligent level" is "a book which signally rewards" science-fiction readers of all stripes. A *Publishers Weekly* critic likewise called the novel "a most enjoyable entertainment that will have readers eagerly turning pages and awaiting the promised sequel."

The Green Group's increasing involvement in and influence on Pliocene society makes up the action of the series' second volume, *The Golden Torc.* Those humans with latent metapsychic abilities or skills otherwise useful to the Tanu have been fitted with collars, called torcs, that can enhance mental skills and stimulate pain or pleasure centers to ensure compliance. They discover some of the secrets of the Tanu, and one human, Aiken Drum, begins insinuating himself into the Tanu royal family, helping them prepare for ritual combat against the Firvulag. The other members of Green Group, originally consigned to labor camps, have managed to escape, kill a Tanu, and secure the cooperation of the Firvulag in searching for their ancient spaceship. Like the first volume, *The Golden Torc* is entertaining "as superhero adventure raised to its highest level," a *Publishers Weekly* critic stated, adding that "May develops her premises seriously and gives her large cast of characters a surprising amount of life." "May seems to be trying to do everything at once," *Booklist* reviewer Roland Green similarly observed of *The Golden Torc*'s many characters, subplots, and themes. "She also seems to succeed most of the time—the book is as powerful and gripping as it is complex."

The third volume of the Pliocene Exile, *The Nonborn King,* relates the sweeping changes that occurred in the wake of a great flood. The human Aiken Drum has assumed kingship of the Tanu and has forged an uneasy peace with the Firvulag. He is beset by enemies from within and without, however, including a previously unknown threat: a band of metapsychics led by Marc Remillard, the leader of an unsuccessful rebellion against the Galactic Milieu who escaped through the timegate almost thirty years before. *The Nonborn King* "maintains the high standard of entertainment established" in previous volumes, a *Publishers Weekly* reviewer asserted, comparing May's skills in creating "richly plotted, extravagant adventures spun from a blend of myth and science" to those of Roger Zelazny. Elton T. Elliott observed that this third volume "marks May's continued growth and maturity as a novelist," as he wrote in *Science Fiction Review.* "There is a surety about her handling of the characters and narrative," he explained, and her writing "is as rich as ever, but more under control."

The saga concludes in *The Adversary,* in which the conflicts are consummated in a spectacular mental battle that could destroy the entire civilization of the Many-Colored Land. "In a rousing climax," Pat Royal commented in *School Library Journal,* the author "brings to a glorious and grand conclusion" her "extraordinarily complex and rich science fantasy." While *Fantasy Review* contributor Susan L. Nickerson found the conclusion somewhat disappointing, noting that "one of the dangers of using time travel as a plot device [is that] sometimes the reader already knows the result," she added that the series is "still a cracking good story."

While the length and "dizzying scope" of this four-volume series makes for "a tough, complex mix of characters, groups and events to manage," Elliott asserted in *Science Fiction Review,* May "handles it admirably." The critic reserved special praise for the author's characterizations, adding that "Marc Remillard is one of the most memorable personalities to ever appear in science fiction. He's complex, utterly ruthless, . . . yet I found him sympathetic." Sue Martin remarked in the *Los Angeles Times Book Review:* "May has a delightful sense of the stately and the wickedly rude that works so well with a cast of decidedly pungent personalities. Her handling of dialogue is smooth and spicy." Assessing the author's "rousing, carousing carnival of a saga," Martin concluded: "Good job, May. The Pliocene will never be the same."

While May's epic has won praise and popularity as an exciting read, several reviewers found more to the Pliocene Saga than just an adventure story. Todd H. Sammons remarked in *Twentieth-Century Science-Fiction Writers* that the series "is Wagnerian in scope: the principals number in the dozens, the chorus in the hundreds, and . . . May uses Freudian concepts or Jungian archetypes (sometimes both) as musical leitmotifs to characterize her human principals, as well as some of the important aliens." The use of these psychological theories was deliberate, May revealed in an interview with Robert A. Collins for *Fantasy Newsletter.* "In my novels, the archetypes, the undercurrents, the different levels of meaning are there. If you're not looking for them, I promise they won't get in the way of the blood and guts and sex and fun. But if you *are* looking, you can find something like six different levels, all deliberately put there. . . . I'm here to entertain us all: the guys looking for a good read as well as the academics who like to find strange things hidden away." Because "The Saga of the Pliocene Exile" contains so much information, May wrote *A Pliocene Companion* in 1984 to help readers enhance their enjoyment of the series. Complete with glossary, characters, maps, chronologies, and genealogies, this work is "a much needed guide," Martin wrote in the *Los Angeles Times Book Review:* "I wish I'd had this when I was sailing through the series."

Since writing the four Pliocene books, May has investigated the origins of the Remillard family's powers and the Galactic Milieu in *Intervention,* which was republished as two books, *The Surveillance* and *The Metaconcert.* Beginning with the explosion of the first atomic bomb in 1945, *Intervention* presents an alternate Earth history which culminates in the telepathic call sent by Denis Remillard and his associates that leads to humanity's first contact with an alien culture. The novel "has the feel of historical fiction," Sammons wrote, "and May uses an array of literary techniques to tell the story—memoirs, straight narration, dramatic dialogue, excerpts from actual speeches or reports, a television script," among other "sources." The development of the new intergalactic society is revealed further in the "Galactic Milieu" trilogy, consisting of *Jack the Bodiless, Diamond Mask* and *Magnificat.* These three works concern events that happen before the Pliocene Era books, explaining the events leading to the rebellion led by Marc Remillard.

Jack the Bodiless begins in the twenty-first century, as humanity's fate as a member of the Galactic Milieu is being decided by five alien races. The birth of Jack Remillard, whose extraordinary metapsychic potential indicates an evolutionary leap for humankind, also poses a problem, for his physical genetic defects are unacceptable under Milieu law. At the same time, a malevolent creature known only as Fury also comes into being, killing off many of the Remillards and jeopardizing Earth's entry into the Milieu. "May combines a compelling vision of humanity's future with the drama and political intrigue" of the Remillards' political involvements, Jackie Cassada remarked in *Library Journal.* While a *Publishers Weekly* reviewer believed May's narrow focus on the Remillard "elites" mars the novel, the critic nonetheless allowed that *Jack the Bodiless* "is engaging and May's prose adequate to it."

In *Diamond Mask,* the story of Earth's fate within the Galactic Milieu continues. As Dorothea, or Dee, Macdonald begins to acknowledge her growing metapsy-

chic powers, she assumes the identity of Diamond Mask and confronts the power of Fury and several renegade Remillards. Working in concert with Jack and Marc Remillard, Dee saves an entire planet from a catastrophic earthquake. A *Kirkus Reviews* critic labeled *Diamond Mask* as "patchy and irritatingly inconclusive," but found that May "handles both the psychic complication and the family interactions with pleasing skill." In *Library Journal,* however, Cassada praised May's book and the development of the trilogy, calling them "rich in intrigue and vibrating with creative energy." In *Metaconcert,* the concluding volume of the trilogy, May details the rebellion of Marc Remillard and reveals the secrets behind the evil entity known as Fury.

May has also ventured into fantasy writing with a series of novels that began with *Black Trillium,* a volume she coauthored with noted writers Marion Zimmer Bradley and Andre Norton, and continued with the solo effort *Blood Trillium.* The series is set on the World of Three Moons, which has been threatened by various sorcerers who can only be defeated by a certain powerful talisman. In *Blood Trillium,* as in the first book, three sisters must fulfill separate quests; unlike *Black Trillium,* May makes the book more positive by changing "its focus from the absolute destruction of evil to the possibility of its ultimate transformation," according to *Library Journal* reviewer Cassada. A *Publishers Weekly* critic noted that May's *Blood Trillium* is "a superior tale, giving life, character, and emotion to the Three Petals of the Living Trillium."

Late in her career, May has finally been able to devote her efforts to her first love, science fiction. She has a positive view of humanity's future, which she hopes to communicate in her works. "I am an optimist," she told Collins. "I don't think we are going to die in a mushroom cloud. I think something great will happen. I don't know if there are flying saucers—if there *are* galactic civilizations they're quite sensible in leaving us alone until we have attained suitable enlightenment. But I *am* an optimist and it shows in my novels. I've been accused of being upbeat. I triumph in being upbeat! I don't know how successful I've been, but it's been a lot of fun."

May once told *CA:* "Voluminous reading, especially in the field of science, eventually led me to science fiction—which remains my first love. My first published novelette, 'Dune Roller,' became a minor classic in the field; but in the early 1950s it was not possible to earn a living writing sf, and so I turned to nonfiction. . . . My avalanche of books for young people includes many science titles, as well as biographies and sports books. I do the book design and art direction for many of my books, as well as write them. Because I am an experienced researcher and a fast writer, I am able to do nonfiction books very quickly.

"Because my juvenile writing has been a job rather than a sideline, I have never been anxious to talk about my work. I have little emotional involvement in my juvenile books, and this tends to disappoint young readers and librarians who have romantic ideas of authorhood. . . . The professional writer is at an economic disadvantage in this country unless he or she produces a Best Seller. Since juvenile books rarely attain such heights, the ambitious writer has no other recourse but to keep on truckin'—which, for better or worse, I have done. The result is manifest."

BIOGRAPHICAL AND CRITICAL SOURCES:

PERIODICALS

Analog, August, 1983, pp. 129-130; February 1, 1996, Roland Green, review of *Magnificat,* p. 920; January 1, 1997, Roland Green, review of *Sky Trillium,* p. 826.

Booklist, March 1, 1982, p. 848; November 1, 1991, p. 475; December 1, 2003, Frieda Murray, review of *Conqueror's Moon,* p. 655.

Book Report, September-October, 1996, Diana Jackson, review of *Magnificat,* p. 41.

Book World, November 10, 1968; November 9, 1969.

Fantasy Newsletter, March, 1983.

Fantasy Review, August, 1984, pp. 16-17.

Kirkus Reviews, February 15, 1994, p. 181.

Kliatt, winter, 1984.

Library Journal, December 1991, p. 202; June 15, 1992, p. 105; March 15, 1994, pp. 103-104; February 15, 1996, Jackie Cassada, review of *Magnificat,* p. 178.

Los Angeles Times Book Review, June 3, 1984, p. 6; December 9, 1984, p. 14.

Magazine of Fantasy and Science Fiction, October, 1981, pp. 29-37.

Publishers Weekly, March 6, 1981, p. 91; December 11, 1981, p. 53; December 24, 1982, p. 51; March 9, 1984, p. 101; December 20, 1991, p. 68; May 25, 1992, pp. 42-43; February 14, 1994, p. 83; February 12, 1996, review of *Magnificat,* p. 63; December 30, 1996, review of *Sky Trillium,* p. 58; December 15, 2003, review of *Conqueror's Moon,* p. 59.

School Library Journal, November, 1984, p. 146.

Science Fiction Review, spring, 1983, p. 25; spring, 1984, p. 36; fall, 1984, pp. 33-36.

Times Literary Supplement, October 16, 1969.

Voice of Youth Advocates, February, 1985, p. 339.

Washington Post Book World, March 28, 1982, p. 22.

Young Reader's Review, May, 1968.

*   *   *

McDONOUGH, Kathryn Susan 1943-
(Kaye McDonough)

PERSONAL: Born August 8, 1943, in Pittsburgh, PA; daughter of Edward Arthur and Lucille Marie (Bechman) McDonough; companion of Gregory Nuncio Corso (a poet); children: Nile Joseph Corso. *Education:* Attended Vassar College, 1961-63, and Boston University, 1964-65; University of California—Berkeley, B.A., 1967; graduate study at Sarah Lawrence College, 1990s.

ADDRESSES: Home—236 Santa Fe Ave., Hamden, CT 06517.

CAREER: Poet and playwright. Greenlight Press, publisher of poetry. Presenter of poetry readings at festivals, universities, and numerous other locations.

AWARDS, HONORS: Finalist for Eugene O'Neill Theater Award, for *Zelda: Frontier Life in America; A Fantasy in Three Parts.*

WRITINGS:

UNDER NAME KAYE MCDONOUGH

Zelda: Frontier Life in America; A Fantasy in Three Parts (play; first produced in New York, NY, at St. Clement's Theater, 1978), edited by Lawrence Ferlinghetti, City Lights Books (San Francisco, CA), 1978.

Work represented in anthologies, including *City Lights Anthology,* 1974; *The Stiffest of the Corpse: An Exquisite Corpse Reader,* 1989; *San Francisco Poets Anthology;* and *California Bicentennial Poets Anthology.* Contributor of poetry to periodicals, including *Ahem, Beatitude, Cafe Society, 7Carmine, Holy Earth Megascene, Manroot, Phoenix, Poetry San Francisco,* and *City Lights Review.*

BIOGRAPHICAL AND CRITICAL SOURCES:

BOOKS

Contemporary Authors Autobiography Series, Volume 29, Gale (Detroit, MI), 1998, pp. 199-221.*

*   *   *

McDONOUGH, Kaye
   See McDONOUGH, Kathryn Susan

*   *   *

MEAD, Alice 1952-

PERSONAL: Born January 11, 1952, in Portchester, NY; daughter of Richard and Jeanne Weber; children: Jeffrey O'Hara, Michael O'Hara. *Education:* Bryn Mawr College, B.A., 1973; Southern Connecticut State University, M.Ed., 1975; University of Southern Maine, B.A. (art education), 1985. *Politics:* Democrat. *Hobbies and other interests:* Flute, gardening, painting, photography, clay.

ADDRESSES: Home—Cape Elizabeth, ME. *Agent*—c/o Author Mail, Farrar, Straus, & Giroux, 19 Union Square W, New York, NY 10003. *E-mail*—amead@maine.rr.com.

CAREER: Has worked as an art teacher in Connecticut and Maine, 1974-92, and as a preschool teacher in Maine, 1980-83. Board member for Project Co-Step for developmentally delayed preschoolers; active in efforts to aid children in Kosovo, Serbia.

MEMBER: Society of Children's Book Writers and Illustrators, New England Children's Book Writers and Illustrators, Kosova Action Network, Maine Writers and Publishers Alliance.

WRITINGS:

Crossing the Starlight Bridge, Bradbury (New York, NY), 1994.
Walking the Edge, A. Whitman (Morton Grove, IL), 1995.
Junebug, Farrar, Straus & Giroux (New York, NY), 1995.
Journey to Kosovo, Loose Cannon Press (Cumberland Center, ME), 1995.
(Editor, with Arnold Neptune) *Giants of the Dawnland: Ancient Wabanaki Tales,* Loose Cannon Press (Cumberland Center, ME), 1996.
Adem's Cross, Farrar, Straus & Giroux (New York, NY), 1996.
Junebug and the Reverend, Farrar, Straus & Giroux (New York, NY), 1997.
Soldier Mom, Farrar, Straus & Giroux (New York, NY), 1999.
Billy and Emma, illustrated by Christy Hale, Farrar, Straus & Giroux (New York, NY), 2000.
Girl of Kosovo, Farrar, Straus & Giroux (New York, NY), 2001.
Junebug in Trouble, Farrar, Straus & Giroux (New York, NY), 2002.
Year of No Rain, Farrar, Straus & Giroux (New York, NY), 2003.
Madame Squidley and Beanie, Farrar, Straus & Giroux (New York, NY), 2004.

WORK IN PROGRESS: Isabella's Above-Ground Pool and *Lindi Meholli: Origin Unknown,* both for Farrar, Straus & Giroux (New York, NY).

SIDELIGHTS: Alice Mead's novels for young adults and middle graders often feature young people coping with dire circumstances, who—with ingenuity, determination, and the aid of helpful adults—make positive, if small, changes in their own lives and the lives of those around them. Mead does not shrink from difficult subjects. She has written about the war in Kosovo, famine and civil war in the Sudan, and the perils of reaching manhood in an inner-city housing project. Mead once told *CA:* "I have always been interested in writing about children who—for some reason—live on the edge of the mainstream society. I feel that authors and artists should travel to these edges, to widen the circle of inclusion through empathy and art."

What Mead's heroes and heroines share is a resiliency of spirit and an ability to find humanity in themselves and others. Junebug, an African-American boy growing up in New Haven, Connecticut, stands up to bullies when they threaten smaller children and nurtures a dream of owning his own boat. Zana Dugolli in *Girl of Kosovo* saves the lives of her Serbian neighbors during an ethnic-inspired riot. *Adem's Cross* features a young teen who comes to understand the meaninglessness of war after being attacked and disfigured. As Susan Dove Lempke observed in *Booklist,* Mead "offers children a glimpse into realistically difficult lives faced with courage, optimism, and conviction."

Mead was born in Portchester, New York, in 1952. On her Web site, she maintains that she began to entertain flights of imagination during a two-year stay in an industrial city in the north of England. The major part of her childhood was spent in America, where she developed an interest in the countries behind the Iron Curtain in Eastern Europe. One summer, when she was twenty, she worked at a camp for inner-city children. Observing their delight in the art supplies she provided helped her to decide to be a teacher. "For many years I was an art teacher working with low-income children," Mead once explained. "In America, wealth abounds yet a large proportion of American children are poor. Everyone tells poor kids to have hopes, to dream—but how do you go about it? We have a society that sees children in very negative ways. I like to celebrate the intensity and steadfastness of kids, their creativity and fresh energy."

When an illness made it impossible for Mead to teach anymore, she stayed home and began writing. Her books reflect her experience with youngsters here and abroad, as well as her beliefs in peaceful cooperation and nonviolence. An early inspiration to write about her adopted state of Maine led to the creation of her first novel, *Crossing the Starlight Bridge.*

Rayanne, the central character in *Crossing the Starlight Bridge,* is a member of the Penobscot tribe of Native Americans. She and her parents have always lived on their island reservation, but now her father, who is unable to find work there, decides to leave. "Mead deftly establishes a child's point of view with simple and unpretentious language," observed Deborah Stevenson in the *Bulletin of the Center for Children's Books,* noting that Rayanne's misery over her father's absence is deepened when she realizes that she and her mother must leave the island, and her pet rabbit, behind. References to traditional Penobscot lore arise in the character of the grandmother, with whom Rayanne

and her mother go to live, "a strong, contemporary, optimistic woman whose warmth and encouragement are restorative," Susan Scheps asserted in *School Library Journal.* A *Kirkus Reviews* critic called *Crossing the Starlight Bridge* "a believable and compelling portrayal of a Native-American family coexisting with white society while retaining its own traditions."

Like Rayanne, Scott, the main character in *Walking the Edge,* looks to something positive outside of himself to give him strength to endure the poverty and unhappiness of his life. Set in Maine and based on real events, *Walking the Edge* describes Scott's involvement in a science project that aims to restock the local bay with clams. The title of the book refers to Scott's penchant for perching on a high cliff overlooking the harbor, even though the footing there is precarious. *School Library Journal* contributor Connie Tyrrell Burns, commenting favorably on Mead's realistic depiction of the turbulent emotions of her adolescent hero, concluded that Scott's "amazement at the delicate and relentless process of life will be shared by readers."

Reeve McClain, known as Junebug, reluctantly approaches his tenth birthday in Mead's novel *Junebug,* knowing that he will then be recruited to join one of the gangs that terrorize his housing project. Junebug develops an idea he hopes will help him realize his dream of learning to sail and captaining his own boat. He collects and cleans fifty glass bottles and seals in each a piece of paper describing his dream, then sets the bottles free on a boat trip around the harbor in New Haven, Connecticut. "The novel is a hopeful one," Maeve Visser Knoth commented in *Horn Book,* "in spite of the vivid portrait of the housing project's grim realities." Elizabeth Bush, on the other hand, writing in the *Bulletin of the Center for Children's Books,* called *Junebug*'s happy ending "soothing but decidedly too easy," though her conclusion echoed that of a critic in *Kirkus Reviews,* who wrote that "readers will be rooting for Junebug and his dreams all the way." Mead once commented to *CA:* "I grew up near the water and have always loved boats. I wanted to be either a sea captain or a lighthouse keeper and live on an island. Writing a book is a lot like putting a message in a bottle and tossing it overboard—you never know who will read it! Or where!"

Junebug proved such a popular character that Mead has built a series around him. In *Junebug and the Reverend,* he moves away from the projects and begins sailing lessons, but still struggles with bullies and with his new duties as an assistant to an elderly emphysema patient. *Junebug in Trouble* finds the hero trying to maintain his friendship with a buddy from the projects while also developing a mature, realistic view of his incarcerated father. In a *Horn Book* review of *Junebug and the Reverend,* Maeve Visser Knoth felt that the themes addressed by Junebug "speak to the life of a young boy faced with many changes." A *Kirkus Reviews* critic called *Junebug in Trouble* "a realistic and touching" tale, concluding that the novel offers "a hopeful, yet hard look at youth growing up in the inner city." In her *Booklist* review of the same novel, Susan Dove Lempke called the novel's hero "a touching character with sensitivity and a loving heart." *School Library Journal* contributor B. Allison Gray concluded that *Junebug in Trouble* "will ring true to many young readers and expose others to the challenges faced by children today."

Mead has set two stories in the war-torn state of Kosovo: *Adem's Cross* and *Girl of Kosovo.* Both novels take a candid approach to describing the lives of children in a war zone—something the author observed first-hand during visits to the former Yugoslavia. In *Adem's Cross,* Kosovo has been taken over by Serbian soldiers bent on "cleansing" the population of Albanians, descendants of the land's ancient conquerors. Twelve-year-old Adem and his family have been waiting for the Serb troops to leave their hometown for four years when Adem's older sister takes the bold stance of participating in a peaceful demonstration against the invaders. She is subsequently killed by Serb soldiers, and Adem, enraged at his family's passivity, rebels by going out alone one night. He is caught by three soldiers who break his hand and carve a Serbian symbol, a Cyrillic cross, into his chest with a knife. He decides to leave Kosovo and is aided in his flight by a Serb and a gypsy, both of whom teach him lessons in practical politics. "Mead preps readers with a quick, efficient sketch of Yugoslavia's recent history before jumping into this disturbing society," observed Marilyn Payne Phillips in *School Library Journal.* Critics noted that Mead does not take sides in the real-life deadly conflict. Instead, she "writes powerfully and eloquently about Adem's attempt to understand why people mistreat each other," Susan Dove Lempke remarked in *Booklist.*

Mead herself once told *CA:* "For the past [several] years, I have been traveling to Eastern Europe. When I was little, I was told that these countries lay behind the Iron Curtain, a place Americans didn't go. Since the collapse of communism, I have traveled there . . . to document the conditions of children's lives. My novel, *Adem's Cross,* is about the cleansing of Albanian children in southern Serbia. I have brought nine teenagers to the United States to study in high schools in Maine. In addition, a group of schools got together and sent a truckload of toys to Kosovo, Serbia."

Girl of Kosovo presents the civil war in Kosovo from the point of view of Zana Dugolli, an Albanian girl who also suffers at the hands of the Kurds. Zana witnesses the murders of her father and brothers and is herself injured in the same attack. As she recuperates slowly, she struggles to remember her father's advice: "Don't let them fill your heart with hate." It is this advice that ultimately guides Zana as she returns to her village and her friendship with a Serbian girl her age. In *Booklist,* Hazel Rochman described *Girl of Kosovo* as a "moving novel," adding: "The power in the story is the personal drama." Describing the story as "powerful and hard-hitting," a *Publishers Weekly* critic remarked that Mead's book "places a human face on the Kosovo crisis."

Continuing to deal with the theme of war, but from a different perspective, Mead's novel *Soldier Mom* deals with a problem inherent when countries go to war: how families continue with their daily lives as their soldier relatives are sent abroad to fight. Eleven-year-old Jasmyn Williams finds her life turned upside down when her mother, an Army Reservist, is called to active duty in the Persian Gulf War. Suddenly Jasmyn faces an onslaught of adult responsibilities—cooking, cleaning, caring for her baby half-brother—while all she wants to do is play basketball for her school team. Jasmyn's mother's boyfriend, Jake, proves inept as a substitute parent, leaving Jasmyn frustrated and overwhelmed. A *Horn Book* reviewer found Jasmyn to be "a realistically prickly heroine" and the book "an entirely convincing and involving picture." A *Publishers Weekly* critic praised Mead's "sharply focused" writing, noting that the "emotions of the heroine are consistently authentic." In *Reading Today,* Lynne T. Burke concluded that *Soldier Mom* "provides insight and confidence that families can survive."

Year of No Rain visits another brutal civil war, this time in the Sudan. In a region laid waste by drought, Stephen Kajok becomes the sole survivor of his family after his father goes away to fight, his two brothers die of disease, and his mother and his sister are kidnapped by rebels. In order to avoid the violence, Stephen and his friend Wol strike out on their own to find a refugee camp. *School Library Journal* contributor Sue Giffard maintained that Mead "gives voice to a vulnerable, often forgotten group of people," while a *Kirkus Reviews* critic called *Year of No Rain* "an artfully told story" in which "Mead puts civil war in human terms through the eyes of one young boy."

Mead lives in a house that overlooks Casco Bay off the coast of Maine. On her Web site the author said, "When I'm stuck writing a story, I can go sit on the rocks and watch the water for a while, something I have enjoyed doing throughout my life."

BIOGRAPHICAL AND CRITICAL SOURCES:

PERIODICALS

Booklist, November 15, 1996, Susan Dove Lempke, review of *Adem's Cross,* pp. 579, 581; September 1, 1998, Susan Dove Lempke, review of *Junebug and the Reverend,* p. 120; September 1, 1999, Chris Sherman, review of *Soldier Mom,* p. 127; March 15, 2001, Hazel Rochman, review of *Girl of Kosovo,* p. 1401; April 15, 2002, Susan Dove Lempke, review of *Junebug in Trouble,* p. 1402; August, 2003, Hazel Rochman, review of *Year of No Rain,* p. 1983.

Bulletin of the Center for Children's Books, June, 1994, Deborah Stevenson, review of *Crossing the Starlight Bridge,* p. 329; December, 1995, Elizabeth Bush, review of *Junebug,* pp. 133-134; December, 1999, Deborah Stevenson, review of *Soldier Mom,* p. 142.

Horn Book, March, 1996, Maeve Visser Knoth, review of *Junebug,* p. 198; September-October, 1998, Maeve Visser Knoth, review of *Junebug and the Reverend,* p. 612; September, 1999, review of *Soldier Mom,* p. 614; May-June, 2002, Roger Sutton, review of *Junebug in Trouble,* p. 334.

Kirkus Reviews, May 1, 1994, review of *Crossing the Starlight Bridge,* p. 634; September 1, 1995, review of *Junebug,* p. 1284; February 1, 2002, review of *Junebug in Trouble,* p. 184; May 1, 2003, review of *Year of No Rain,* p. 680.

New York Times Book Review, January 14, 1996, pp. 23, 66.

Publishers Weekly, December 6, 1999, review of *Soldier Mom,* p. 77; March 19, 2001, review of *Girl of Kosovo,* p. 100; May 19, 2003, review of *Year of No Rain,* p. 74.

Reading Today, February-March, 2002, Lynne T. Burke, review of *Soldier Mom,* p. 32.

School Library Journal, June, 1994, Susan Scheps, review of *Crossing the Starlight Bridge,* pp. 132-133; December, 1995, Connie Burns Tyrrell, review of *Walking the Edge,* p. 106; November, 1996, Marilyn Payne Phillips, review of *Adem's Cross,* p. 109; May, 2000, Susan Hepler, review of *Billy and Emma,* p. 150; March, 2001, Kathleen Isaacs, review of *Girl of Kosovo,* p. 254; March, 2002, B. Allison Gray, review of *Junebug in Trouble,* p. 235; May, 2003, Sue Giffard, review of *Year of No Rain,* p. 157.

ONLINE

Alice Mead Home Page, http://www.alicemead.com/ (July 2, 2003).

*   *   *

MEDINA, Pablo 1948-

PERSONAL: Born 1948, in Cuba; immigrated to United States, 1960.

ADDRESSES: Office—Graduate Writing Program, New School for Social Research, New York, NY 10011.

CAREER: New School for Social Research (later New School University), New York, NY, faculty member in graduate writing program, then director of undergraduate writing program; member, board of directors, Associated Writing Programs; Warren Wilson College, member of M.F.A. faculty.

AWARDS, HONORS: National Endowment for the Arts grant; Woodrow Wilson/Lila Wallace *Reader's Digest* grant.

WRITINGS:

Pork Rind and Cuban Songs, Nuclassics and Science Publishing (Washington, DC), 1975.

Exiled Memories: A Cuban Childhood, University of
Texas Press (Austin, TX), 1990.

Arching into the Afterlife, Bilingual Press (Tempe,
AZ), 1991.

The Marks of Birth, Farrar, Straus (New York, NY),
1994.

The Floating Island, White Pine Press (Buffalo, NY),
1999.

The Return of Felix Nogara (novel), Persea Books,
2000 (New York, NY).

Puntos de apoyo (poetry), Centro Cultral Cubano de
Nueva York (New York, NY), 2002.

Contributor to periodicals, including *Antioch Review,
Pivot,* and *Poetry.*

SIDELIGHTS: In Cuban-born novelist Pablo Medina's
novel *The Return of Felix Nogara,* poet and scholar
Nogara returns to his homeland, the Caribbean island
of Barata, after the death of dictator Nicolas Campion
opens the island up to a more relaxed government. A
United States citizen, but a Baratan exile in Miami
since he was twelve, the middle-aged Nogara struggles
to reconcile thirty-eight years of longing for his home
with the bleak reality he sees after his return. Nogara
has ostensibly returned to the island to find his dying
mother, but under the surface his mission is aimed
toward resurrecting a life of meaning by recovering
the culture, history, and happiness he claimed by right
years ago, before he left Baratan soil.

Local cabbie Martin becomes Nogara's guide to the
run-down cities and unmarked streets of modern
Barata. The frenzied urban and commercial development occurring since Campion's death is matched only
by the decay and dereliction seen elsewhere on the
island. With Martin's help, Nogara eventually finds his
mother, and learns how to function within the new
political and personal reality of Barata. As Nogara's
story unfolds, the history of the island and its people
is revealed. Nogara decides to remain on the island,
where he himself drives a cab until his death. "Medina
paints a vivid and even comedic portrait of the Bara-
tans and their history," observed Kristine Huntley in
Booklist. Barata is a stand-in for Medina's own
homeland of Cuba, and the book functions as a meditation on Cuban life after Castro, a task that "Pablo
Medina has done, with great success, in his second
novel, *The Return of Felix Nogara,*" wrote Bob Shacochis in the *New York Times.* However, "In Medina's

bleak, searing vision, little changes in Barata, which
remains a country of poverty and desolation, where
the future is as fragile as the crumbling edifices of the
past," remarked a *Publishers Weekly* reviewer. Margee
Smith, reviewing the book in *Library Journal,* commented that Medina "crafts a beautifully written tale
that is human, humorous, and full of insight."

"It all sounds a bit gloomy but it is not," Shacochis
commented. "Medina peppers his narrative with the
bawdy irrepressible black humor of Cuba, delivering a
compressed Marquezian history of Barata's brutes and
Caudillos, martyrs and fools, and achieves a comic
gravity that hovers as a backdrop to the existential
challenge of Felix's return."

BIOGRAPHICAL AND CRITICAL SOURCES:

PERIODICALS

Booklist, September 1, 2000, Kristine Huntley, review
of *The Return of Felix Nogara,* p. 66.

Library Journal, August 1, 2000, Margee Smith,
review of *The Return of Felix Nogara,* p. 160.

New York Times, October 22, 2000, Bob Scacochis,
"Return of the Native," review of *The Return of
Felix Nogara,* section 7, p. 21.

New York Times Book Review, August 18, 2002, review
of *The Return of Felix Nogara,* p. 20.

Publishers Weekly, May 9, 1994, review of *The Marks
of Birth,* p. 61; August 21, 2000, review of *The
Return of Felix Nogara,* p. 48.

ONLINE

New York State Writers' Institute Web site, http://www.
albany.edu/writers-inst/ (November 25, 2003),
"Pablo Medina."

Persea Books Web site, http://www.perseabooks.com/
(November 20,2003).*

*   *   *

MOCHIZUKI, Ken 1954-

PERSONAL: Surname pronounced "Moh-chee-*zoo*-
kee"; born May 18, 1954, in Seattle, WA; son of
Eugene (a social worker) and Miyeko (a clerical
worker; maiden name, Nakano) Mochizuki. *Ethnicity:*
"Third-generation American of Japanese descent."
Education: University of Washington—Seattle, B.A.,
1976.

ADDRESSES: Home—25426 213th Ave., SE, #51, Maple Valley, WA 98038. *Agent*—Stimola Literary Studio, 308 Chase Ct., Edgewater, NJ 07020. *E-mail*—kenmoch@aol.com.

CAREER: Journalist and children's book author. Actor in Los Angeles, CA, 1976-81; *International Examiner* (newspaper), Seattle, WA, staff writer, 1985-89; *Northwest Nikkei* (newspaper), Seattle, assistant editor, 1990-97. Gives presentations to schools and other groups.

MEMBER: Society of Children's Book Writers and Illustrators.

AWARDS, HONORS: Parents' Choice Award, Washington State Governor's Writers Award, *Publishers Weekly* Editor's Choice, and American Bookseller Pick of the List, all 1993, all for *Baseball Saved Us;* Notable Children's Trade Book in the Field of Social Studies, National Council for the Social Studies/Children's Book Council (NCSS/CBC), Notable Book for Children, *Smithsonian* magazine, both 1995, and Teachers' Choices selection, International Reading Association (IRA), 1996, all for *Heroes; Parenting* Best Book of the Year designation, Notable Book for Children, *Smithsonian* magazine, both 1997, Notable Children's Trade Book in the Field of Social Studies, NCSS/CBC, Notable Books for a Global Society, IRA, Notable Children's Book in the Language Arts, National Council of Teachers of English, all 1998, and Utah Beehive Award, 1999, all for *Passage to Freedom: The Sugihara Story.*

WRITINGS:

Baseball Saved Us, illustrated by Dom Lee, Lee & Low (New York, NY), 1993.
Heroes (picture book), illustrated by Dom Lee, Lee & Low (New York, NY), 1995.
Passage to Freedom: The Sugihara Story (nonfiction), illustrated by Dom Lee, Lee & Low (New York, NY), 1997.
Beacon Hill Boys, Scholastic (New York, NY), 2002.

Contributor to *A Different Battle: Stories of Asian Pacific American Veterans,* edited by Carina A. del Rosario, University of Washington Press (Seattle, WA), 1999. Some of Mochizuki's works have been translated into Spanish.

ADAPTATIONS: Passage to Freedom: The Sugihara Story was adapted as an audiocassette by Live Oak Media (Pine Plains, NY), 2000; *Baseball Saved Us* was adapted into a stage musical by the Fifth Avenue Theatre and produced in Seattle, WA, 2003.

SIDELIGHTS: Through his award-winning 1993 picture book *Baseball Saved Us,* journalist and children's book author Ken Mochizuki was credited by a *Publishers Weekly* contributor with introducing young readers "to a significant and often-neglected . . . chapter in U.S. history," the imprisonment of Americans of Japanese descent in internment camps during the early 1940s. Mochizuki, whose parents were sent from their home on the West Coast to Idaho's Minidoka camp during World War II, explains the history surrounding his story and attempts to illustrate for children the difficulties caused by living with racism. Ira Berkow wrote in the *New York Times Book Review* that in *Baseball Saved Us,* Mochizuki "captures the confusion, wonder, and terror of a small child in such stunning circumstances with convincing understatement."

Shorty, the book's young Japanese-American narrator, begins the story by remembering how he was ostracized, how other children called him "Jap," and how voices on the radio talked on and on about Pearl Harbor before his family was sent to live in the crowded, dusty camp. Life in the camp was stressful as well as boring, causing tension within families. Shorty's father decides to do something: "One day, my dad looked out at the endless desert and decided then and there to build a baseball field." Everyone's efforts and talents are marshaled and scarce resources are cleverly used: water is channeled to pack down earth for a field, uniforms are sewn from mattress covers, bleachers are constructed, and friends from home are asked to send bats, balls, and gloves. Baseball begins to occupy the minds and time of the camp's captives. For Shorty, baseball becomes a way to excel and battle the racism that follows him even after leaving camp and returning home.

Reviewers recognized the importance of the message in *Baseball Saved Us,* although several voiced concerns regarding the story's presentation. *Horn Book* contributor Ellen Fader maintained that Mochizuki "effectively conveys the narrator's sense of isolation, his confusion about being a target of prejudice, and the importance of baseball in his life." *Bulletin of the Center for Children's Books* writer Roger Sutton, however, thought that while the "political consciousness" reflected in Mochizuki's book rings true, the "children's book vehicle it rides in is dated and sentimental." Hazel Rochman of *Booklist* concluded, nonetheless, that "the baseball action will grab kids—and so will the personal experience of bigotry."

In the 1995 picture book *Heroes*, Mochizuki once again mines his roots as a Japanese American growing up in mid-twentieth-century America by telling the story of Donnie Okada, a young boy who always gets stuck playing the part of the evil enemy when he and his friends play battleground games. The reason? he looks like "them": the Koreans and Japanese that the men of the boys' fathers' generation fought against in World War II and the Korean War. Although Donnie tries to explain that his father and uncles served on the American side in the same wars, his friends do not believe him. It is only after his uncles arrive at his school in full uniform that Donnie's friends begin to understand. Noting that Mochizuki intended *Heroes* as a tribute to the Japanese-American 442nd Regimental Combat Team, a *Kirkus Reviews* contributor praised the book for illustrating "how subtly prejudice was passed on to . . . children" in the postwar years. Comparing the book to *Baseball Saved Us*, a *Publishers Weekly* contributor praised both Mochizuki and illustrator Dom Lee for "adroitly" causing young readers to think about an important social issue by working it into the life of a child, "neither trivializing the issues nor condescending to their audience."

Mochizuki's nonfiction work *Passage to Freedom: The Sugihara Story* was inspired by news articles that circulated in 1994 and focused on a Japanese diplomat stationed in Lithuania during World War II. In 1940, so the news stories explained, Chiune Sugihara issued handwritten visas to hundreds of Polish Jews, allowing them to escape through the USSR into Japan and thus be spared shipment by the Nazis to concentration camps. In his book, Mochizuki adopts the point of view of Sugihara's son, five-year-old Hiroki, and tells the story of the diplomat's courage through youthful eyes. Drawing on his journalist's training, the author met with Hiroki Sugihara in 1995, and was able to obtain a great deal of background information—Sugihara and his family were subsequently interred for over a year in a Soviet detention camp and the diplomat released of his rank—and personal reflec-

tions on the man's childhood experiences during World War II. Scenes of desperate Jewish refugee families huddled at the door of the Japanese embassy and a boy's attempts to understand his parent's fear and agitation are brought to life in a "narrative [that] will grab kids' interest and make them think" according to *Booklist* contributor Hazel Rochman.

Discussing the inspiration for his picture books in an essay posted on the Lee & Low Web site, Mochizuki commented: "The basic theme of . . . *Baseball Saved Us* was the power of positive thinking and believing in oneself. One of the themes implicit in . . . *Heroes* was the definition of a hero as one who knows that actions speak louder than words. . . . *Passage to Freedom* is about the moral choice: Does one do what is considered 'correct' at the time? Or does one do what is 'right' for all time?" Issues of similar import, which *Booklist* contributor Gillian Engberg listed as "racial and cultural identity, prejudice, and family," are woven into the author's first young-adult novel, *Beacon Hill Boys*. Taking place in a Seattle neighborhood during the early 1970s, the novel focuses on a group of teens who are frustrated that the social and political changes sweeping the country in the wake of the civil rights movement are passing Asian Americans by, leaving them to bear the legacy of their traditionalist parents to conform and excel within the "system." Mochizuki's depiction of teenage life in the seventies earned praise from reviewers, with a *Publishers Weekly* critic remarking that "the author's understanding of teen conflicts and the need to forge an individual identity should resonate" with many readers.

"My grandparents were from Japan," Mochizuki once told *CA*, "but my parents, brothers and I grew up and have lived in the U.S.A. all our lives. I have never been to Japan, nor do I speak any Japanese. Yet, I am still sometimes asked, 'Do you speak English?' or . . . 'Where are you from?' I am from Seattle, Washington, and learned my English in an American school like anyone else. When I am asked those kind of questions, I am being judged solely on what I look like. And that is a big reason why I write: to show that people of Asian and Pacific Islander descent in this country are Americans who are a part of everyday American life, and that they have been Americans for a long time.

"I hope to convey to young readers that they should actually get to 'know' others, rather than to 'assume' things about them—that really, all people are basically the same, and that there are only two types of people in this world: good and bad. I also try to communicate to young people a sense of positive thinking and self-esteem—that they should believe in themselves and what they can do, rather than listen to others who tell them what they cannot."

BIOGRAPHICAL AND CRITICAL SOURCES:

BOOKS

Mochizuki, Ken, *Baseball Saved Us,* Lee & Low (New York, NY), 1993.
Something about the Author Autobiography Series, Volume 22, Gale (Detroit, MI), 1996.

PERIODICALS

Booklist, April 15, 1993, Hazel Rochman, review of *Baseball Saved Us,* pp. 1523-1524; May 15, 1997, Hazel Rochman, review of *Passage to Freedom: The Sugihara Story,* p. 86; November 15, 2002, Gillian Engberg, review of *Beacon Hill Boys,* p. 595.
Bulletin of the Center for Children's Books, May, 1993, Roger Sutton, review of *Baseball Saved Us,* p. 290.
Horn Book, July-August, 1993, Ellen Fader, review of *Baseball Saved Us,* pp. 453-454; May-June, 1995, Ellen Fader, review of *Heroes,* p. 327.
Kirkus Reviews, March 1, 1993, p. 303; March 15, 1995, review of *Heroes,* p. 389; November 15, 2002, review of *Beacon Hill Boys,* p. 1689.
New York Times Book Review, April 4, 1993, Ira Berkow, review of *Baseball Saved Us,* p. 26.
Publishers Weekly, March 29, 1993, review of *Baseball Saved Us,* p. 55; March 6, 1995, review of *Heroes,* p. 69; April 21, 1997, review of *Passage to Freedom,* p. 71; November 11, 2002, review of *Beacon Hill Boys,* p. 65.
Reading Teacher, September, 1998, review of *Passage to Freedom,* p. 58.
School Library Journal, June, 1993, Tom S. Hurburt, review of *Baseball Saved Us,* pp. 84-85; July, 1995, John Philbrook, review of *Heroes,* p. 79; June, 2000, Patricia Mahoney Brown, review of *Passage to Freedom,* p. 89; January, 2003, Alison Follos, review of *Beacon Hill Boys,* p. 140.

ONLINE

Children's Literature: Meet Authors and Illustrators, http://www.childrenslit.com/ (December 30, 2003), "Ken Mochizuki."
Lee & Low, http://www.leeandlow.com/ (July 2, 2003), "Book Talk with Ken Mochizuki."
Scholastic, http://www.scholastic.com/ (July 2, 2003), "Ken Mochizuki."

*　　*　　*

MOSIMAN, Billie Sue (Stahl) 1947-
(Naomi Stahl)

PERSONAL: Surname is pronounced *Moe*-sa-man; born June 5, 1947, in Mobile, AL; daughter of Henry Francis (a trapper and carpenter) and Yvonne (a housewife; maiden name, Hyde) Stahl; married Lyle Duane Mosiman (an automotive technician), July 28, 1968; children: Brandon Lee (deceased), Suzanne Jane, Stacey Joy. *Education:* Attended University of Alabama, 1965-67.

ADDRESSES: Agent—Michael V. Carlisle, Carlisle & Company, 6 West 18th St., 12th floor, New York, NY 10011. *E-mail*—bmosiman@quickconnect.net.

CAREER: Louisville General Hospital, Louisville, KY, admitting officer, 1967-68; writer, 1968-72; St. Joseph's Hospital, Tampa, FL, admitting officer, 1972-73; writer, 1973-86; Billie's Book World (bookstore), Livingston, TX, owner, 1986—.

MEMBER: Science Fiction and Fantasy Writers of America.

AWARDS, HONORS: Edgar Allan Poe Award nominee for best original paperback, 1992, for *Night Cruise;* Bram Stoker Award nominee, 1996, for *Widow.*

WRITINGS:

NOVELS

Wireman, Paperjacks, 1984, reprinted, Leisure Books, 1997.

Bloodland, Paperjacks, 1986.

Deadly Affections, Pocket Books, 1988.

Slice, Pocket Books, 1990.

Night Cruise, Jove Books (New York, NY), 1992.

Stiletto, Berkley Books, 1994.

Widow, Berkley Books, 1996.

Pure and Uncut, Headline Books (London, England), 1997.

Final Cut, Five Star (Waterville, ME), 2002 (originally published in England as *Pure and Uncut*).

Bad Trip South, Five Star Press (Waterville, ME), 2003.

(Under pseudonym Naomi Stahl) *Gold Rush Dreams,* Five Star Press (Waterville, ME), 2004.

"RED MOON RISING" SERIES

Red Moon Rising, DAW Books (New York, NY), 2001.

Malachi's Moon, DAW Books (New York, NY), 2002.

Craven Moon, DAW Books (New York, NY), 2003.

OTHER

(Editor, with Martin H. Greenberg) *Death in Dixie,* Rutledge Hill Press (Nashville, TN), 1997.

(Editor, with Martin H. Greenberg) *August Is a Good Time for Killing: And Other Blood-Curdling Stories of Murder in the East,* Rutledge Hill Press (Nashville, TN), 1998.

(Editor, with Martin H. Greenberg) *Blowout in Little Man Flats: And Other Spine-Tingling Stories or Murder in the West,* Rutledge Hill Press (Nashville, TN), 1998.

(Editor, with Martin H. Greenberg) *The Fifth Grave: And Other Terrifying Tales of Homicide in the Heartland,* Rutledge Hill Press (Nashville, TN), 1998.

(Editor, with Martin H. Greenberg) *Never Shake A Family Tree: And Other Heart-Stopping Tales of Murder in New England,* Rutledge Hill Press (Nashville, TN), 1998.

(Editor, with David Drake) *Armageddon,* Baen Books (New York, NY), 2000.

Dark Matter (stories), Wildside Press (Holicong, PA), 2003.

Contributor to *How to Be a Successful Housewife Writer,* edited by Elaine Shimberg, Writers Digest (Cincinnati, OH), 1978. Contributor of more than 150 stories to magazines and anthologies, including *Horror Show, Haunts, Dialog, Fantasy Exchange, Ellery Queen Magazine, Magazine of Fantasy and Science Fiction, Psychos, Blood Muse, Diagnosis Terminal, Warewolves, Prom Night, Fathers and Daughters* and *Invitation to Murder.* Assistant editor of *Touchstone,* 1982-85. Columnist for *Deathrealm Magazine,* 1994-96. Contributor of nonfiction articles to magazines and anthologies, including *Deadly Women, They're Here; Invasion of the Bodysnatchers,* and *Writers Digest Magazine.*

SIDELIGHTS: Billie Sue Mosiman has contributed to the canon of modern vampire fiction with her novels *Red Moon Rising, Malachi's Moon,* and *Craven Moon.* Mosiman laid the basis for her alternative vampire world in *Red Moon Rising,* explaining the existence of a rare blood disease which is usually fatal, but which sometimes transforms its victims into vampires at the time of their apparent death. Among the vampires there exist various clans, each with their own habits and peculiarities. The Predators are aggressive, ready to kill if necessary in order to get access to human blood. Those in the Normal clan try their best to act as they did when they were true humans, but they secretly are dependent on human blood that is supplied to them from blood banks run by Predators. The Craven vampires are weak, sickly beings who beg for blood or simply do without it, hiding away from humankind. In *Red Moon Rising,* the main characters are Ryan, a high school senior, and Dell, a girl who has just changed from human to vampire. The novel "provides a new fascinating twist to the vampire legend," commented Harriet Klausner in *BookBrowser.* Klausner described Mosiman as "excellent at creating characters that appear genuine, even those who are supernatural," thanks to the believable, scientifically plausible character of the underpinnings of her story. Moreover, *Red Moon Rising* provides a coming-of-age story that "deals with choices, morality, and honor," advised Klausner.

In *Malachi's Moon,* the protagonist, Malachi, is the child of a vampire mother and a human father. He is mortal, yet he possesses many of the supernatural powers common to vampires. Balthazar, a dangerous Predator vampire, is convinced that Malachi poses a significant threat to the Predators. Therefore, he sends assassins after Malachi, who in turn flees his home in order to take his family out of danger. Another plot thread involves Charles Upton, a powerful Predator who plots to destroy the Naturals and Cravens in order to dominate the human world. "Well-drawn characters and a complex plot put this a cut above the usual vampire fare," remarked Kristine Huntley in a *Booklist* review of *Malachi's Moon*. Harriet Klausner described *Craven Moon* as "horror the way that it was meant to be written."

Mosiman once told *CA:* "I have been writing in diaries and journals since I was a child, and I decided I wanted to be a professional writer while I was in high school. I traveled after leaving college, married, had my children, and began trying to write for publication about 1975. I have never felt myself fit to work at anything else. I never attended a writing course or had formal instruction. I learned to express myself by writing short stories and then novels, reading widely, and experimenting with idea and form.

"I have always been interested in the abnormal personality and the way it shapes the individual and those surrounding him. I was raised in southern Alabama, where myth, fable, and horror were mixed with reality. The overriding theme of my novels and short stories is one of man drenched in conflict and crisis. Without knowing it, I seemed to have chosen to explore the more extreme emotions and situations: imminent death, destruction, the will to live, the desire to triumph and overcome impossible obstacles. The theme appears whether I am writing horror, fantasy, or mainstream fiction. The macabre, gothic, shadowed past of the South cannot be eradicated from my work without crippling the unique vision I am trying to clarify and understand. It is humankind that I study, and it is my characters' inner worlds that I hope to illuminate."

BIOGRAPHICAL AND CRITICAL SOURCES:

PERIODICALS

Booklist, January 1, 2002, Kristine Huntley, review of *Malachi's Moon*, p. 825.
Bookwatch, June, 1998, review of *Death in Dixie*, p. 8.

ONLINE

The Best Reviews, http://thebestreviews.com/ (April 29, 2002), Harriet Klausner, review of *Malachi's Moon*; (August 13, 2002), Harriet Klausner, review of *Final Cut*; (May 10, 2003), Harriet Klausner, review of *Craven Moon*.
Billie Sue Mosiman Web site, http://www.sff.net/people/bmosiman/ (July 19, 2003).
BookBrowser, http://www.bookbrowser.com/ (April 29, 2002), Harriet Klausner, reviews of *Malachi's Moon* and *Red Moon Rising*.

N

NEIDERMAN, Andrew 1940-
(V. C. Andrews, pseudonym)

PERSONAL: Surname is pronounced "*Ny*-der-man"; born October 26, 1940, in Brooklyn, NY; son of George and Anne (Malisoff) Neiderman; married Diane Wilson, February 8, 1964; children: Melissa Gay, Erik Richard. *Education:* Attended Hunter College, Bronx Campus (now Herbert H. Lehman College of the City University of New York), 1958-60; State University of New York at Albany, B.A., 1962, M.A., 1964. *Politics:* Liberal Democrat. *Religion:* Hebrew.

ADDRESSES: Agent—Robin Rue, Writers House, 21 West 26th St., New York, NY 10010; Bruce Vinokour, CAA, Los Angeles, CA. *E-mail*—Neid1@aol.com.

CAREER: Fallsburgh Central School, Fallsburgh, NY, English teacher, 1964—, audio-visual director; writer. Town historian, Fallsburgh, 1977.

MEMBER: New York State Teachers Association, Sullivan County Teachers Council (president, 1971-72), Fallsburgh Teachers Association (president, 1969).

AWARDS, HONORS: Pin was nominated by Mystery Writers of America as best paperback original of 1981.

WRITINGS:

NOVELS

Sisters, Stein & Day (New York, NY), 1971.
Weekend, St. Martin's Press (New York, NY), 1980.

Andrew Neiderman

Pin, Pocket Books (New York, NY), 1981.
Brainchild, Pocket Books (New York, NY), 1981.
Someone's Watching, Pocket Books (New York, NY), 1983.
Tender Loving Care, Pocket Books (New York, NY), 1984.
Imp, Pocket Books (New York, NY), 1985.
Child's Play, Zebra (New York, NY), 1985.
Night Howl, Pocket Books (New York, NY), 1986.
Love Child, Tor (New York, NY), 1986.
Teacher's Pet, Zebra (New York, NY), 1986.
Sight Unseen, Zebra (New York, NY), 1987.

Playmates, Berkley (New York, NY), 1987.

Reflection, Worldwide Library (London, England), 1987.

Surrogate Child, Berkley (New York, NY), 1988.

Perfect Little Angels, Berkley (New York, NY), 1989.

The Devil's Advocate, Pocket Books (New York, NY), 1990.

Bloodchild, Berkley (New York, NY), 1990.

The Immortals, Pocket Books (New York, NY), 1991.

Sister, Sister, Berkley (New York, NY), 1992.

The Need, Putnam (New York, NY), 1991.

After Life, Berkley (New York, NY), 1993.

The Solomon Organization, Putnam (New York, NY), 1994.

Duplicates, Berkley (New York, NY), 1994.

Angel of Mercy, Putnam (New York, NY), 1995.

The Dark, Pocket Books (New York, NY), 1996.

The Devil's Advocate, 1997.

In Double Jeopardy, Pocket Books (New York, NY), 1997.

Neighborhood Watch, Pocket Books (New York, NY), 2000.

Curse, Pocket Books (New York, NY), 2000.

Amnesia, Pocket Books (New York, NY), 2001.

Dead Time, Pocket Books (New York, NY), 2002.

Under Abduction, Pocket Books (New York, NY), 2002.

The Baby Squad, Pocket Books (New York, NY), 2003.

Deficiency, Pocket Books (New York, NY), 2004.

NOVELS UNDER PSEUDONYM V. C. ANDREWS

(With the original V. C. Andrews) *Garden of Shadows,* Pocket Books (New York, NY), 1987.

Fallen Hearts, Pocket Books (New York, NY), 1988.

Gates of Paradise, Pocket Books (New York, NY), 1989.

Web of Dreams, Pocket Books (New York, NY), 1990.

Dawn, Pocket Books (New York, NY), 1990.

Ruby, Pocket Books (New York, NY), 1991.

Secrets of the Morning, Pocket Books (New York, NY), 1991.

Twilight's Child, Pocket Books (New York, NY), 1992.

Midnight Whispers, Pocket Books (New York, NY), 1992.

Darkest Hour, Pocket Books (New York, NY), 1993.

Pearl in the Mist, Pocket Books (New York, NY), 1994.

All that Glitters, Pocket Books (New York, NY), 1995.

Hidden Jewel, Pocket Books (New York, NY), 1995.

Tarnished Gold, Pocket Books (New York, NY), 1996.

Melody, Pocket Books (New York, NY), 1996.

Also author of *The Sesquicentennial of Fallsburgh Township,* 1976, and of the screenplay for *The Runaways.* Contributor of short stories, poetry, short plays, and articles to periodicals, including *English Record, Interaction, Prairie Schooner, Cimarron Review, Scholastic Magazine's Voice, Media and Methods,* and *Campaign Insight.*

ADAPTATIONS: Pin was adapted for film in 1988; *The Devil's Advocate* was adapted for film in 1998; film rights to *The Dark* have been sold to TriStar; film rights to several novels written under the name V. C. Andrews have been sold to Jaffe/Braunstein Films; *Tender Loving Care* has been opted by Trilobyte for a CD-ROM interactive movie.

SIDELIGHTS: Andrew Neiderman is a prolific writer of horror novels and thrillers. In addition to his own novels, Neiderman has published many bestselling novels under the name of the late author V. C. Andrews.

Neiderman collaborated with Andrews on the novel *Garden of Shadows.* After Andrews died in 1986, Neiderman went on to produce fourteen novels under Andrews's name and based on story outlines developed by her. These novels have proven to be consistent bestsellers. Neiderman explained to Lisa James in the *University of Albany Magazine,* "Writing is very personal, so it takes a great deal of study and attention to be able to write in someone else's voice. . . . I feel successful at it because the V. C. Andrews books are growing in power, they are sold all over the world, and most people don't know where V. C. Andrews stopped and I started. That, to me, is a good testament."

Neiderman's first significant novel is probably *Pin,* wherein an emotionally unbalanced father comforts his rattled children through an imaginary human, Pin, capable of resolving all the children's problems and questions. When the parents die suddenly, the children maintain their illusion of Pin as the guiding adult in their lives. Don D'Ammassa, writing in the *St. James Guide to Horror, Ghost and Gothic Writers,* described *Pin* as a "very fine concept with understated horror."

In the years since *Pin* first appeared in print, Neiderman has issued more than thirty other novels. He quickly followed *Pin* with *Brainchild,* in which a brilliant but undisciplined girl develops the ability to control the wills of fellow humans and animals. A child also serves as the central figure in Neiderman's 1985 novel *Imp,* wherein a spineless mother consigns her hideous child to a series of interconnecting tunnels beneath the family home. From this unlikely location, the child manages, as D'Ammassa reported, "to explore and cause hellish trouble for those he stumbles across." Still another demonic child dominates *Sight Unseen,* in which a telepathic boy undermines the lives of his neighbors, while in *Surrogate Child* a couple replace their late son with an adopted boy who soon exhibits peculiar behavior.

The Need is the story of a brother and sister existing within one human entity. After the vampire brother slays the object of his sister's affections, he finds himself marked for destruction. "The duel of wills that ensues," remarked D'Ammassa, "is the best writing Neiderman has yet produced."

Teacher's Pet concerns a malicious teacher who forces his students to do his evil bidding. In *Perfect Little Angels,* meanwhile, the seemingly gentle behavior exhibited by teenagers in a small town serves to conceal their considerable fierceness. And in *Sister, Sister,* Siamese twins with mutual telepathy use their mental powers to control others.

The Devil's Advocate, made into a film starring Al Pacino, ranks among Neiderman's better-known novels. Here an ambitious young lawyer signs with an impressive law firm only to learn that it serves evil. D'Ammassa explained: "The protagonist is flattered when he is asked to join a prominent law firm, but confused when he discovers that sometimes cases for the defence are prepared even before the crimes are committed. Ultimately he must decide whether or not to sell his soul, quite literally, in order to guarantee himself a prosperous future." Similarly, Neiderman's *The Solomon Organization* concerns a despairing fellow who approaches members of a secret group and then learns that he has consequently jeopardized the well-being of his friends and loved ones. Another of Neiderman's thrillers is *Angel of Mercy,* in which a homicide detective tries to apprehend a fetching private nurse and her retarded twin sister, both of whom are involved in a series of alleged suicides. *The Dark* concerns a group of psychiatric patients whose evil behavior can only be stopped by a priest using the traditional ritual against Satan.

Neiderman once told *CA* that he has been most influenced by Kurt Vonnegut. He added: "Mainly, today, I am concerned with the theme of violence. I am concerned with how we are driven to acts of violence by an imposing society and [an] entrapping environment."

BIOGRAPHICAL AND CRITICAL SOURCES:

BOOKS

St. James Guide to Horror, Ghost and Gothic Writers, St. James Press (Detroit, MI), 1998.

PERIODICALS

Daily Herald (Arlington Heights, IL), October 17, 1997, Dann Gire, "Pacino Stokes the Fire in *Devil's Advocate,*" p. 36.

Kirkus Reviews, January 15, 1992; February 1, 1993; March 15, 1994.

Newsweek, October 27, 1997, Jack Kroll, review of film version of *The Devil's Advocate,* p. 70.

Publishers Weekly, May 29, 1995, Paul Nathan, "Tell Your Own Tale," p. 38; April 15, 1996, "For Andrews Fans," p. 29; May 27, 1996, Paul Nathan, "Shrinking Satan," p. 29; November 10, 1997, p. 71.

Rocky Mountain News (Denver, CO), October 17, 1997, Robert Denerstein, "A Devil of a Time," p. 6D.

Star-Ledger (Newark, NJ), August 24, 1996, "Al Pacino to Play *The Devil's Advocate,*" p. 27.

University at Albany Magazine, spring, 1998, Lisa James, "He's a Soft-Spoken Author of Horror Novels."

Variety, October 13, 1997, review of film version of *The Devil's Advocate,* p. 77.

Washington Post, July 24, 2002, Linton Weeks, "The Plot Thickeners: Brand-Name Authors Hire Writers to Flesh Out Their Bare-Bones Stories," p. C1.

ONLINE

Andrew Neiderman Home Page, http://www.neiderman.com/ (June 6, 2003).

NICHOLLS, C(hristine) S(tephanie) 1943-

PERSONAL: Born January 23, 1943, in Bury, Lancashire, England; daughter of Christopher James (a headmaster) and Olive (a headmistress; maiden name, Kennedy) Metcalfe; married Anthony James Nicholls (a university lecturer), March 12, 1966; children: Alexander, Caroline, Isabel. *Education:* Lady Margaret Hall, Oxford, B.A., 1964, M.A., 1968; St. Antony's College, Oxford, Ph.D., 1968. *Hobbies and other interests:* Reading novels, playing the flute.

ADDRESSES: Home—27 Davenant Rd., Oxford OX2 8BU, England. *Office*—c/o *Dictionary of National Biography*, Clarendon Building, Bodleian Library, Oxford University, Broad St., Oxford OX1 3BG, England. *E-mail*—christine.nicholls@lineone.net.

CAREER: University of London, London, England, Henry Charles Chapman research fellow at Institute of Commonwealth Studies, 1968-69; British Broadcasting Corporation (BBC), freelance media commentator, 1970-74, research assistant, 1975-76; *Dictionary of National Biography*, Oxford University Press, joint editor, 1977-89, editor, 1989-95, "Sutton Pocket Biographies," editor, 1996—. St. Antony's College, Oxford University, associate fellow, 1990—.

WRITINGS:

The Swahili Coast, Allen & Unwin (London, England), 1971.
David Livingstone, Sutton (Stroud, Gloucestershire, England), 1998.
The History of St. Antony's College, Oxford, 1950-2000, Macmillan Press (Oxford, England), 2000.
Elspeth Huxley: A Biography, HarperCollins (New York, NY), 2002.

EDITOR

(With E. T. Williams) *The Dictionary of National Biography, 1961-1970,* Oxford University Press (Oxford, England), 1981.
(With Robert Blake) *The Dictionary of National Biography, 9th Supplement, 1971-1980,* Oxford University Press (Oxford, England), 1986.

(With Robert Blake) *The Dictionary of National Biography, 1981-1985,* Oxford University Press (Oxford, England), 1990.
Power: A Political History of the Twentieth Century, Oxford University Press (Oxford, England), 1990.
(With consultant editor G. H. L. Le May and others) *The Dictionary of National Biography: Missing Persons,* Oxford University Press (New York, NY), 1994.
(With consultant editor Sir Keith Thomas) *The Dictionary of National Biography, 1986-1990: With an Index Covering the Years 1901-1990 in One Alphabetical Series,* Oxford University Press (New York, NY), 1996.
Encyclopedia of Biography, Helicon (Oxford, England), 1996, St. Martin's Press (New York, NY), 1997.

SIDELIGHTS: C. S. Nicholls, British writer, researcher, and editor of the acclaimed *Dictionary of National Biography* (*DNB*), spent part of her youth in Kenya, Africa, and has written biographies of two British citizens who were devoted to Africa, missionary Dr. David Livingstone and writer Elspeth Huxley. Nicholls also wrote *The Swahili Coast* in 1971 and is the author of a book about St. Antony's College, Oxford, where she received her Ph.D.

Nicholls's work first as joint editor and then editor of the *DNB* earned her praise from readers and reviewers. First published in 1901, the classic reference work was updated every ten years until 1981, when, under Nicholls, it began updating every five years, to keep the publication more current and include more individuals. The *DNB* contains biographies of well-known—both famous and infamous—British (and other) citizens who died within the time period covered by each supplement. Those included are from all professions, from royalty and politicians to entertainers and athletes. It begins with the period of early history and continues to the present.

In 1994 Oxford published a special issue of the *DNB, Missing Persons.* It contains biographies of more than one thousand persons, from throughout history to 1985, who were, according the preface, "unjustly omitted" from previous supplements. The *DNB* is noted for its excellent writing—some of the authors are candidates for inclusion themselves—and for its humor and liveliness. It is considered an invaluable reference work for writers, teachers, and other professionals.

P. F. Clarke, in a review of the *DNB: 1981-1985* for the *English Historical Review,* called the five-year updating "a wholly welcome change since it gives us more manageable and up-to-date volumes." In a later review of *Missing Persons,* Clarke described the supplement as "a handsome acknowledgment of the fallibility of British justice in the court of historical reputations, now rectified through an appeal procedure which involved the editors in sifting through over one hundred thousand suggestions." Clarke praised the "fourfold increase in the number of entries for women," who had only a three percent inclusion in the original *DNB.* Some of the missing persons included are Sylvia Plath, Wilfred Owen, Stan Laurel, Bram Stoker, Joseph Merrick ("the Elephant Man"), and Guy Burgess.

The *DNB: 1986-1990* was the last volume for which Nicholls served as editor. Brian Harrison, in the *English Historical Review,* noted that some categories, such as armed services and law, had fewer inclusions, while others, such as first- and second-generation immigrants, had more. There is also a new "secret service" category containing both friends and enemies of Britain. Harrison praised the coverage of scientists and intellectuals, the "trend against inflated entries for monarchs and statesmen," and the "inconsequential but intriguing detail" offered about many of those included.

In addition to the biography of David Livingstone, written for the Sutton "Pocket Biographies" series, which she edited, Nicholls began to write biographies of her own. Robert Pearce, writing in the *History Review,* commented on Nicholls's "shrewd critical judgements," which spice up her biography. He concluded that the book gives enough information and detail to entice readers to learn more about Livingstone.

Elspeth Huxley is Nicholls's first full-length biography. In it, she returns to her love of Africa to write about the journalist, broadcaster, and prolific author who is best known for her memoir *The Flame Trees of Thika,* about her girlhood in Kenya, published in 1959. Huxley was the daughter of British colonists to East Africa, and her mother's journals provide much of the interesting detail in the first part of the biography, according to reviewers. Elspeth married Gervus Huxley, a cousin of Aldous and Julian Huxley, and they had one son, but Elspeth kept working throughout her life. Her permanent home was in England after 1924, but she often returned to Africa to research her books and journalistic pieces and to visit her parents.

Huxley was a liberal who opposed colonialism. As Justin Willis pointed out in a review for the *Times Literary Supplement,* Nicholls shows that "Huxley, as the chronicler of the colonial experience, wrote with extraordinary understanding of both Africans and whites." Huxley served on the Monckton Commission of 1960, which dismantled the white-established Central African Federation. Willis observed, however, that Huxley's writings "are filled with the contradictions of colonialism, as well as its unbearable hubris: a belief in 'civilization' as the mission of whites in Africa combined with a contrary longing for Africa as an unspoilt place of refuge from the complex demands of modern life." A contributor to the *Contemporary Review* stated that Huxley "embodied the transposition from the colonial empire to the self-governing states of modern Africa."

Anne Chisholm, in a review for the *Spectator,* described Nicholls's book as "a thorough, quietly humorous, slightly over-extended biography" that is "full of wonderful stories about people with names like Cockie and Tuppence and Hookie, let alone glimpses of familiar characters like Karen Blixen . . . and Denys Finch Hatton, the Leakeys, Lord Dunsany and Evelyn Waugh." Chisholm also acknowledged that the book is truly about both Elspeth and her mother, Nellie. Kathryn Hughes, in the *New Statesman,* pointed out that Nicholls is "a wonderfully well-informed authority about the externals of the life—the dates, the events, the who and the where of it all" and "sees the landscape as Huxley would have seen it." Yet, Hughes noted, Nicholls is "less good" in "entering into Huxley's interior life," perhaps because there is a lack of good resources, since her mother threw away her letters a week after she read them.

BIOGRAPHICAL AND CRITICAL SOURCES:

PERIODICALS

Albion, spring, 1994, review of *The Dictionary of National Biography: Missing Persons,* p. 113.
American Reference Books Annual, 1994, review of *The Dictionary of National Biography: Missing Persons,* p. 8; 1999, review of *Encyclopedia of Biography,* p. 11.

Booklist, September 1, 1998, review of *Encyclopedia of Biography,* p. 164.

Choice, October, 1993, review of *The Dictionary of National Biography: Missing Persons,* p. 265.

Christian Science Monitor, November 21, 1996, review of *The Dictionary of National Biography, 1986-1990,* p. B2.

Contemporary Review, September, 2002, review of *Elspeth Huxley: A Biography,* p. 187.

Economist, February 13, 1993, review of *The Dictionary of National Biography: Missing Persons,* p. 91.

English Historical Review, October, 1993, P. F. Clarke, review of *The Dictionary of National Biography: 1981-1985,* p. 1089; June, 1994, P. F. Clarke, review of *The Dictionary of National Biography: Missing Persons,* p. 671; April, 1998, Brian Harrison, review of *The Dictionary of National Biography, 1986-1990,* p. 546.

English Literature in Transition, 1880-1920, April, 1994, review of *The Dictionary of National Biography: Missing Persons,* p. 534.

History Review, December, 1999, Robert Pearce, review of *David Livingstone,* p. 48.

History: Reviews of New Books, summer, 1991, review of *Power: A Political History of the Twentieth Century,* p. 188.

History Today, January, 1994, review of *The Dictionary of National Biography: Missing Persons,* p. 50.

Kirkus Reviews, May 1, 2003, review of *Elspeth Huxley,* p. 663.

Libraries & Culture, fall, 1999, review of *Encyclopedia of Biography,* p. 433.

London Review of Books, April 22, 1993, review of *The Dictionary of National Biography: Missing Persons,* p. 13; August 22, 1996, review of *The Dictionary of National Biography, 1986-1990,* p. 21.

New Criterion, October, 2003, "A Return to BEA," pp. 67-72.

New Statesman, May 6, 2002, Kathryn Hughes, "Left of Right," review of *Elspeth Huxley,* p. 50.

New York Times Book Review, October 5, 2003, review of *Elspeth Huxley,* p. 24.

Observer (London, England), November 28, 1993, review of *The Dictionary of National Biography: Missing Persons,* p. 4; July 7, 1996, review of *The Dictionary of National Biography, 1986-1990,* p. 15.

Reference & Research Book News, September, 1993, review of *The Dictionary of National Biography: Missing Persons,* p. 6; February, 1997, review of *The Dictionary of National Biography, 1986-1990,* p. 14; August, 1998, review of *Encyclopedia of Biography,* p. 17.

Rettig on Reference, July, 1998, review of *Encyclopedia of Biography.*

Spectator, July 6, 1996, review of *The Dictionary of National Biography, 1986-1990,* p. 30; June 8, 2002, Anne Chisholm, "A Lifelong Passion for Africa," review of *Elspeth Huxley,* p. 50.

Times Educational Supplement, March 12, 1993, review of *The Dictionary of National Biography: Missing Persons,* p. 10.

Times Literary Supplement, October 2, 1981; November 14, 1986; April 27, 1990; February 5, 1993, review of *Dictionary of National Biography: Missing Persons,* p. 21; August 16, 1996, review of *The Dictionary of National Biography, 1986-1990,* p. 5; November 19, 1996, review of *The Dictionary of National Biography, 1986-1990,* p. 14; May 29, 1998, review of *David Livingstone,* p. 36; August 16, 2002, "Of Mice and Mints," review of *Elspeth Huxley,* pp. 4-5.

Wilson Library Bulletin, September, 1993, review of *The Dictionary of National Biography: Missing Persons,* p. 116.

ONLINE

Oxford University Press Web site, http://www.oup-usa.org/ (March 18, 2003).*

*　　*　　*

NOVA, Craig 1945-

PERSONAL: Born July 5, 1945, in Los Angeles, CA; son of Karl and Elizabeth (Sinclair) Nova; married Christina Barnes, July 2, 1977; children: Abigail, Tate. *Education:* University of California, Berkeley, B.A. (with honors), 1967; Columbia University, M.F.A. (with distinction), 1969.

ADDRESSES: Home—P. O. Box 506, Putney, VT 05346. *Agent*—Peter Watson, Sterling Lord Literistic, Inc., 65 Bleecker St., New York, NY 10012. *E-mail*—nova@sover.net.

CAREER: Writer. Has held jobs as farm hand, truck driver, computer salesman, editor, real estate manager, painter, reporter, proofreader, and gas station attendant.

Craig Nova

AWARDS, HONORS: Harper-Saxton Prize, 1971, for *Turkey Hash;* National Endowment for the Arts fellowships, 1973 and 1975; New York State Council on the Arts fellowship, 1974; Guggenheim fellowship, 1977; American Academy and Institute of Arts and Letters award in literature, 1984; National Endowment for the Arts fellowship, 1985.

WRITINGS:

NOVELS

Turkey Hash, Harper (New York, NY), 1972.
The Geek, Harper (New York, NY), 1975.
Incandescence, Harper (New York, NY), 1979.
The Good Son, Delacorte (New York, NY), 1982.
The Congressman's Daughter, Delacorte (New York, NY), 1986.
Tornado Alley, Delacorte (New York, NY), 1989.
Trombone, Grove Weidenfeld (New York, NY), 1992.
The Book of Dreams, Ticknor & Fields (New York, NY), 1994.
The Universal Donor, Houghton Mifflin (Boston, MA), 1997.

Brook Trout and the Writing Life (memoir), Lyons Press (New York, NY), 1999.
Wetware, Shaye Areheart (New York, NY), 2001.

SIDELIGHTS: Craig Nova's writing career began in the days of the counterculture, but his dark vision of American life knows no particular time period. John Domini wrote in the *New York Times Book Review* that Nova's themes "do not merely live; they burn. . . . Nova has proved that nothing gives off sparks like hard living struck against surfaces even harder: the passing of time and our relentless struggle to make it stop." William O'Rourke in the *Village Voice* described Nova as "one of the finest writers of his generation (post World War II) and, more importantly, one of the few in possession of an entirely unique voice." *Booklist* correspondent Donna Seaman noted that the author "walks a fine line between noir and straight-ahead fiction in his taut, moody, and piercing novels." Perhaps due to their subject matter, Nova's novels have appealed more often to literary readers than the general public. Dorman T. Shindler in the *Denver Post* observed: "Craig Nova . . . is one of those critically acclaimed, consistently great writers who for unknown reasons have failed to grab a wide readership. This is a shame, because in addition to being highly entertaining, his novels have explored a wide range of social interests, from music to fishing, to politics and medical research."

As a young writer in the late 1960s and early 1970s, Nova was influenced by the tenor of the times. His early novels feature surrealistic characters, unusual dialogue, and a sense of social and personal alienation. In *Turkey Hash,* for instance, the central character loses his sanity amidst other social outcasts in urban Los Angeles. In his review of *Turkey Hash,* Martin Levin wrote in the *New York Times Book Review* that the book is filled with "mental defectives, maimed drifters who think with their appetites, geek material, random assassins and their victims—these float in and out of Craig Nova's harsh spotlight. The center of attention is Niles Cabro, an L.A. youth whom the publisher bills as [borderline] psychotic. Tut. Anyone whose idea of fun is to be beaten nearly senseless in an offal orgy is hardly [borderline]." *Saturday Review* contributor Jerry G. Bowles wrote that Nova "is a fine writer. His style is telegraphic and minimal, yet strangely evocative of landscape. His characters appear both real and surreal as they act out strange rituals and plot insane acts. His handling of pace and dialogue is superb, and the writing in general has the feel of a polished hand. Despite its ultimate coldness, [*Turkey Hash*] is a remarkably accomplished first novel."

Nova's second novel, *The Geek,* observes a group of misfits on a Greek island. Once again the central character is a rootless American whose plight worsens as he gradually loses grip on his humanity while working with a traveling carnival. *New York Review of Books* critic Michael Wood felt that "there is something too cryptic about a lot of the novel's transactions, a suggestion of dialogue out of Henry James shifted to a dusty taverna, and . . . the writing keeps reaching for effects that are more than a little lurid. But the blending of emblematic and literal truth . . . is remarkable. The specificity of the island landscape, the clear characters and past history of th e individual islanders . . . all help to pitch *The Geek* somewhere between reality and nightmare." *New York Times Book Review* writer C. D. B. Bryan noted that "there is no point in summarizing this plot; it isn't what happens that makes this book so strong. In fact, I find it difficult to articulate where exactly Craig Nova's genius lies. I know only that it has been a long time—a very long time—since I have come across a novel so gripping, a talent so exciting, so immense and so pure that I am ashamed I have not read him before. This book is so powerful, so alive, it is a wonder that turning its pages doesn't somehow burn one's hands."

In *Incandescence,* Nova again deals with assorted drifters and lowlifes; central among them is a formerly brilliant inventor named Stargell, now barely eking out a living as a New York City cab driver. Under pressure from his loan shark, Stargell seeks a solution to his financial woes but only makes matters worse in a surreal trip through Manhattan's underbelly. *Saturday Review* correspondent Tim O'Brien found the novel's style "brisk and often funny." The critic added: "Stargell's hip cynicism, though grating after a time, produces some very witty lines. And why not? His after all, is an incandescent wit. Studded throughout the book, in counterpoint to the comic aspects, there are several entirely uncomic and even tragic scenes that convey the terrors that can befall a man who can neither understand nor escape his own disintegration."

In *The Good Son* Nova leaves the seedy milieu of his earlier novels to tell the story of an upper-middle-class father and son in conflict. The story is narrated by a number of different characters as the novel progresses, including two parents, the son of the title, two women in the son's life, and a chauffeur. Nevertheless, the narrative flows consistently as the wealthy family patriarch discovers that his son is an independent individual. While *Library Journal* reviewer Carol L. Cardozo called the book "a well-written work," she found, "the Faulknerian obliqueness and unrelieved atmosphere of menace are sometimes overdone." Hermione Lee in the *Observer* wrote that *The Good Son* "reads as though Faulkner had been cloned with the script-writer for 'Dynasty.'" But novelist John Irving, in the *New York Times Book Review,* noted *The Good Son* "is not only Mr. Nova's best novel; it is the richest and most expert novel in my recent reading by any writer now under forty." *Los Angeles Times Book Review* critic Charles Trueheart likewise described the novel as "a dark and affecting exploration of how families inexorably transform love into pain and self-esteem into self-destruction—and somehow survive to endure the wreckage." In the *Kenyon Review,* Dave Smith concluded: "I cannot imagine a reader who would find *The Good Son* anything less than a totally satisfying piece of work. Its prose is as intensely beautiful as a fine poem, and its structure is as precise as a Bach fugue. Yet it is mostly the power with which Nova is able to engage and set free the myth of love that impresses . . . *The Good Son* is a portrait of ourselves, rich and poor, and a good one."

Where *The Good Son* focuses on the relationship between a father and son, *The Congressman's Daughter* examines the relationship between a father and daughter. When her controlling father dies, Alexandra Pearson discovers that she is bound by strict codicils in her father's will. These restrictions limit the scope of her life for the next twenty years, driving her finally into a love affair to escape the husband chosen for her by her late father. "A dry, credible bitterness pervades this latest novel by [Nova]," wrote a *Publishers Weekly* critic. *New York Times* reviewer Christopher Lehmann-Haupt called *The Congressman's Daughter* an "unlikely yet strangely plausible tale" and "a penetrating comment on American life."

In *Tornado Alley* Nova focuses his attention on small-town American life, telling the story of two doomed lovers. The "first two-thirds" of the book, according to Paul Stuewe in *Quill & Quire,* tells "an engrossing tale of mainstream American life, firmly grounded in an understanding of small-town mores and big-time dreams." Stuewe found the novel's violent ending less than credible, however. Andrei Codrescu, writing in the *New York Times Book Review,* praised the realism of the novel's setting. "Its world is painstakingly needlepointed in every detail," Codrescu noted. Nevertheless, the critic considered the plot ultimately unbelievable, although he pointed out "splendid moments that in themselves would have made beautiful small books." A critic for *Publishers Weekly* concluded that *Tornado Alley* is a "riveting American tragedy comparable to that of Dreiser or Cain."

With *Trombone* Nova returns to an examination of a father and son relationship, this time between a minor hoodlum who works as an arsonist for the mob and his teenaged son, "two of the most vivid, appealing and surprising characters to appear in recent American fiction," wrote Jonathan Yardley in the *Washington Post Book World. Trombone* is set in California and Nevada, and Chicago *Tribune Books* writer Bruce Cook wrote that it is written with "an aridity that is altogether consistent with the setting . . . and with [the] characters, who seem as dry and emotionally withered as the landscapes in which they move." Lehmann-Haupt, writing in the *New York Times,* found *Trombone* fascinatingly unpredictable, if not wholly successful: "You get the feeling . . . that with just a few more twists and a good hard shake, its pieces could fall into place to form something completely original," he observed. But *New York Times Book Review* critic George State believed Nova "manages his imagery, his plot and his characters, pathetic or vicious or both, with impressive skill."

Nova writes of Hollywood in *The Book of Dreams,* a work that follows Warren Hodges, a film producer, Marta Brooks, his girlfriend, and Victor Shaw, an ex-con turned blackmailer. When Brooks accidentally kills a man who attacks her, Shaw uses the incident to force her into squeezing money from Hodges. Although Lawrence Thornton in the *New York Times Book Review* felt *The Book of Dreams* to be "a trip down a noirish memory lane" and "far too familiar," a critic for *Publishers Weekly* believed that Nova "deftly interweaves a glitzy Hollywood background with some good noir atmosphere." *Washington Post* reviewer Carolyn See found the book unconvincing and excessively imitative of Hollywood chronicles by other authors, such as F. Scott Fitzgerald and Nathanael West. But Lehmann-Haupt concluded that *The Book of Dreams* is "a powerful if ultimately comic nightmare."

The Universal Donor offers another noir plotline, again set in Southern California. The book opens amidst the Los Angeles riots, as Dr. Terry McKechnie struggles to come to grips with the many grievous gunshot wounds he is expected to treat in the emergency room. Finding himself unraveling, Terry steps back from the abyss when he meets Virginia Lee, a herpetologist who goes through with her loveless wedding even though she has fallen in love with Terry. When Virginia is bitten by a rare poisonous snake, Terry must exert all his powers to save her life, even as the jilted husband seeks revenge. A *Publishers Weekly* reviewer noted that in this story of a desperate love triangle, Nova "does a convincing job of showing that while love may conquer all, the conquest isn't always pretty." *Booklist* correspondent Joanne Wilkinson felt that the nightmarish aspects of the plot "add up to a haunting tale."

Wetware finds Nova in new territory: that of science fiction. Set in the near future, the novel describes a world in which human clones are engineered to perform dirty and demeaning work mindlessly. A rogue clone designer named Hal Briggs, called in to create more intelligent, assassin clones, programs two of his creations—Kay and Jack—with higher human attributes such as the power to love and a feel for music. Kay and Jack escape, and it is only then that Briggs discovers that others have been inserting programming into the two clones as well—with possibly deadly results. *Library Journal* contributor Devon Thomas observed that the novel "hints at a grim civilization in decline" as it offers "a particularly chilling read." A *Kirkus Reviews* critic called the book "a seductive and intelligent novel about love and freedom set in a dreamlike near future." The critic concluded that the work is "odd and oddly moving, with a strange mix of platonic shadow and human detail giving it a lingering power." *Washington Post* reviewer Michael Dirda praised *Wetware* as "a haunting, heart-stoppingly exciting, brilliantly structured novel of suspense, ideas and subtle characterization."

In addition to his fiction, Nova has penned a slight memoir, *Brook Trout and the Writing Life,* that links his profession to his avocation—fishing for fresh-water trout. The author reveals how fishing has sustained him through his bouts of writing and how it has provided ease and pleasure to him throughout his life. In *Booklist,* John Rowen praised the way in which Nova writes about his fishing experiences "in a most genuine, convincing, and never contrived manner." Steve Raymond in *Fly Fisherman* summed up the book in a way that might well describe all of Nova's writing career. Nova, Raymond concluded, "sees things in a unique and personal way and his gift as a writer is an ability to relate them in clear, often memorable prose."

BIOGRAPHICAL AND CRITICAL SOURCES:

BOOKS

Contemporary Literary Criticism, Volume 31, Gale (Detroit, MI), 1985, pp. 296-300.

PERIODICALS

Booklist, June 1, 1997, Norma Seaman, review of *The Universal Donor,* p. 1663; September 1, 1999, John Rowen, review of *Brook Trout and the Writing Life,* p. 61; June 1, 2001, Joanne Wilkinson, review of *The Universal Donor,* p. 1836; December 1, 2001, Donna Seaman, review of *Wetware,* p. 630.
Book World, November 14, 1999, review of *Brook Trout and the Writing Life,* p. 9.
Chicago Tribune Book World, February 25, 1979.
Fly Fisherman, May, 2000, Steve Raymond, review of *Brook Trout and the Writing Life,* p. 20.
Kenyon Review, winter, 1984, Dave Smith, "Myths of Love: New American Fiction," pp. 121-134.
Kirkus Reviews, April 1, 1997, review of *The Universal Donor,* p. 494; August 1, 1999, review of *Brook Trout and the Writing Life,* p. 1205; October 15, 2001, review of *Wetware,* p. 1448.
Library Journal, July, 1982, p. 1346; April 15, 1986, p. 96; September 1, 1999, Will Hepfer, review of *Brook Trout and the Writing Life,* p. 200; November 15, 2001, Devon Thomas, review of *Wetware,* p. 98.
Los Angeles Times, June 16, 1994, p. E6.
New Leader, April 23, 1979, Randall Rothenberg, "Batting in the Dark," p. 20.
New York Review of Books, June 10, 1976, Michael Wood, "Crying for Attention," p. 8.
New York Times, February 21, 1979; April 24, 1986, p. C21; July 23, 1992, p. C21; April 28, 1994, p. C22.

New York Times Book Review, October 29, 1972; December 21, 1973; February 11, 1979; October 3, 1982, John Irving, "Desire, Ambition, and Father," p. 3; May 25, 1986, p. 6; July 23, 1989, pp. 7, 9; July 12, 1992, p. 10; June 5, 1994, p. 41; June 29, 1997, review of *The Universal Donor,* p. 13; December 20, 1998, review of *The Universal Donor,* p. 28.
Observer (London, England), February 6, 1983, p. 33.
Publishers Weekly, February 14, 1986, p. 70; March 17, 1989, p. 77; June 22, 1992, pp. 42-43; March 14, 1994, p. 61; March 31, 1997, review of *The Universal Donor,* p. 59; January 21, 2002, review of *Wetware,* p. 69.
Punch, February 16, 1983, p. 41.
Quill & Quire, December, 1982, p. 30; July, 1989, p. 47.
Saturday Review, September 23, 1972; February 17, 1979, Tim O'Brien, "Falling Star," pp. 53-54.
Tribune Books (Chicago, IL), June 21, 1992, p. 7.
Village Voice, November 3, 1975; summer, 1997, review of *The Universal Donor,* p. 7.
Washington Post, April 7, 1979; April 29, 1994, p. C2.
Washington Post Book World, June 28, 1992, p. 3.

ONLINE

Denver Post Online, http://www.denverpost.com/ (February 3, 2002), Dorman T. Shindler, "Nova Deserves Wider Audience."
Washington Post Online, http://www.washingtonpost.com/ (January 20, 2002), Michael Dirda, review of *Wetware.**

*   *   *

NUTT, Paul C. 1939-

PERSONAL: Born September 14, 1939, in Dowagiac, MI; son of Charles E. and Isabel E. (Brigham) Nutt; married Nancy Davis (a realtor), September 9, 1961; children: Suzanne, Lynn-Nicole, Charles. *Education:* University of Michigan, B.S., M.S., 1963; University of Wisconsin—Madison, Ph.D., 1974.

ADDRESSES: Home—Columbus, OH. *Office*—644 Fisher Hall, Fisher College of Business, Ohio State University, 2100 Neil Ave., Columbus, OH 43210. *E-mail*—nutt.1@osu.edu.

CAREER: Fisher College of Business, Ohio State University, Columbus, professor of management sciences, management and human resources, and public policy and management.

AWARDS, HONORS: Academy of Management, Public and Nonprofit Division, Distinguished Book Award, 1994, for *Strategic Management of Public and Third Sector Organizations: A Handbook for Leaders;* fellow, Decision Sciences Institute, 1999; Academy of Management, Hall of Fame, 2000.

WRITINGS:

Evaluation Concepts and Methods: Shaping Policy for the Health Administrator, revised edition, Luce, 1981.

Making Tough Decisions: Tactics for Improving Managerial Decision Making, Jossey-Bass (San Francisco, CA), 1989.

Managing Planned Change, Macmillan (New York, NY), 1991.

(With Robert W. Backoff) *Strategic Management of Public and Third Sector Organizations: A Handbook for Leaders,* Jossey-Bass (San Francisco, CA), 1992.

Why Decisions Fail: Avoiding the Blunders and Traps That Lead to Decision Debacles, Berrett-Koehler (San Francisco, CA), 2002.

Contributor of nearly a hundred articles to business and management journals. Member of editorial review board, *Academy of Management Review.*

SIDELIGHTS: Professor of management sciences at Ohio State University, Paul C. Nutt is an expert in the field of strategic management and decision making. He has produced more than one hundred articles in business and management journals, as well as several books on the subject of management. Over twenty years of research on organizational decisions went into Nutt's 2002 volume, *Why Decisions Fail: Avoiding the Blunders and Traps That Lead to Decision Debacles.* Out of the more than 400 in his database, Professor

Nutt ultimately chose fifteen failed decisions with disastrous outcomes as case studies to reveal a number of traps he discerned in the decision-making process. According to a *Silicon Valley/San Jose Business Journal* article about the book, "His research demonstrated that failed decisions share three common blunders: managers rush to judgment, misuse their resources, and repeatedly use failure-prone tactics to make decisions." *Library Journal* critic Lawrence Maxted commended Nutt for his "thorough dissection of the debacles and explanation of the decision-making process," as well as for "his clear writing style."

BIOGRAPHICAL AND CRITICAL SOURCES:

PERIODICALS

American Review of Public Administration, September, 1998, John Collins, review of *Strategic Management of Public and Third Sector Organizations,* p. 312.

Choice, September, 1992, S. Newport, review of *Strategic Management of Public and Third Sector Organizations,* p. 176; December, 2002, R. Subramanian, review of *Why Decisions Fail: Avoiding the Blunders and Traps That Lead to Decision Debacles,* p. 672.

Library Journal, August, 2002, Lawrence Maxted, review of *Why Decisions Fail,* p. 113.

Personnel Psychology, spring, 2003, John W. Fleenor, review of *Why Decisions Fail,* p. 235.

Publishers Weekly, January 28, 2002, "It's the Stupidity, Stupid," p. 223.

School Administrator, April, 2003, Perry Berkowitz, review of *Why Decisions Fail,* p. 41.

ONLINE

Paul C. Nutt Home Page, http://fisher.osu.edu/mgtsci/faculty/nutt/ (February 23, 2004).

Silicon Valley/San Jose Business Journal, http://sanjose.bizjournals.com/sanjose/ (April 22, 2003), "Study: Half of All Business Decisions Wrong."*

O

OBSTFELD, Raymond 1952-

(Pike Bishop, Jason Frost, Don Pendleton, Carl Stevens, pseudonyms)

PERSONAL: Born January 22, 1952, in Williamsport, PA; son of Ludwig (a restaurant owner) and Ilse (a restaurant owner) Obstfeld. *Education:* Attended Lycoming College; University of Redlands, B.A.; University of California—Davis, M.A. *Politics:* Democrat.

ADDRESSES: Home—2936 Ballesteros Ln., Tustin, CA 92680. *Office*—Department of English, Orange Coast College, 2701 Fairview, Costa Mesa, CA 92626. *Agent*—Sandra Watt, 7551 Melrose Ave., Los Angeles, CA.

CAREER: Orange Coast College, Costa Mesa, CA, assistant professor of English, 1976—, and head of writing program.

MEMBER: Mystery Writers of America.

WRITINGS:

The Cat with Half a Face (poetry), Advantage Press, 1978.
The Goulden Fleece (mystery novel), Ace Books (New York, NY), 1979.
Dead-End Option (mystery novel), Ace Books (New York, NY), 1980.

Dead Heat (mystery novel), Ace Books (New York, NY), 1981.
Dead Bolt (mystery novel), Ace Books (New York, NY), 1982.
The Remington Factor (suspense novel), Jove (New York, NY), 1985.
The Joker and the Thief (young adult novel), Delacorte (New York, NY), 1993.
Earth Angel, Warner Books (New York, NY), 1995.
(With Patricia Fitzgerald) *Jabberrock! The Ultimate Book of Rock 'n' Roll Quotations,* Holt (New York, NY), 1997.
Kinky Cats, Immortal Amoebas, and Nine-Armed Octopuses: Weird, Wild, and Wonderful Behaviors in the Animal World, HarperPerennial (New York, NY), 1997.
(With Sheila Burgener) *Twang! The Ultimate Book of Country Music Quotations,* Holt (New York, NY), 1997.
Novelist's Essential Guide to Crafting Scenes, Writer's Digest (Cincinnati, OH), 2000.
(With Loretta Obstfeld) *Napoleon Bonaparte,* Greenhaven Press (San Diego, CA), 2001.
Fiction First Aid: Instant Remedies for Novels, Stories, and Scripts, Writer's Digest (Cincinnati, OH), 2001.
(With Loretta Obstfeld) *The Renaissance,* Greenhaven Press (San Diego, CA), 2002.
(With Franz Neumann) *Careers for Your Characters: A Writer's Guide to 101 Professions from Architect to Zoologist,* Writer's Digest (Cincinnati, OH), 2002.

UNDER PSEUDONYM PIKE BISHOP

Diamondback (western novel), Pinnacle Books (New York, NY), 1983.

Judgement at Poison Well (western novel), Pinnacle Books (New York, NY), 1983.

UNDER PSEUDONYM JASON FROST

Warlord (action/suspense novel), Zebra Books (New York, NY), 1983.
Warlord Number Two: Cutthroat (action/suspense novel), Zebra Books (New York, NY), 1984.
Warlord Number Three: Badlands (action/suspense novel), Zebra Books (New York, NY), 1984.
Warlord Number Four: Prisonland (action/suspense novel), Zebra Books (New York, NY), 1985.

UNDER PSEUDONYM DON PENDLETON

Bloodsport (action/adventure novel), Gold Eagle (New York, NY), 1982.
Flesh Wounds (action/adventure novel), Gold Eagle (New York, NY), 1983.
Savannah Swingsaw (action/adventure novel), Gold Eagle (New York, NY), 1985.
Fire Eaters (action/adventure novel), Gold Eagle (New York, NY), 1985.
Copp for Hire (novel), Fine (New York), 1987.
Copp on Fire (novel), Fine (New York, NY), 1988.
Copp in Deep (novel), Fine (New York, NY), 1989.
Copp in the Dark (novel), Fine (New York, NY), 1990.
Copp on Ice (novel), Fine (New York, NY), 1991.
Copp in Shock (novel), Fine (New York, NY), 1992.

UNDER PSEUDONYM CARL STEVENS

The Centaur Conspiracy (action/suspense novel), Gold Eagle (New York, NY), 1983.
The Ride of the Razorback (action/suspense novel), Gold Eagle (New York, NY), 1984.

Author of "The Pilgrim Shadow" (one-act play), first produced in Redlands, CA, at University of Redlands, 1972; "Warlord" (screenplay); "Congregation of the Blue Sonata" (film treatment). Author of "Paper Crimes," a column in *Armchair Detective*. Contributor of stories, articles, and reviews to magazines, including *Fiction, Dogsoldier, Not-So-Private Eye, Journal of Popular Culture, Mystery,* and *Crook's.*

SIDELIGHTS: Raymond Obstfeld writes fiction, and writes about writing fiction. His detective novels, some published under pseudonyms, includes *Earth Angel,* about a woman who goes undercover to make amends to the families of victims murdered by her fiance. Obstfeld also produced a novel for young adults in *The Joker and the Thief.* In this story, two teenagers—affluent Eric and street-smart Griffin—find themselves facing the same conflicts after Eric discovers Griffin hiding out in Eric's family cabin. A *Publishers Weekly* critic deemed this novel "alternately poignant, suspenseful and wryly humorous." In a nonfiction vein, Obstfeld has published two books—*Twang! The Ultimate Book of Country Music Quotations* and *Jabberrock! The Ultimate Book of Rock 'n' Roll Quotations*—that "offer much for browsers but a little less for those in search of a particular quotation," according to *Library Journal*'s Carolyn Mulac.

As head of the writing program of Orange Coast College, Obstfeld set his lessons into text with several books that help writers overcome problems. His *Fiction First Aid: Instant Remedies for Novels, Stories, and Scripts* uses a medical theme to illustrate the causes and cures for several writing problems. Continuing the "first aid" theme, "Physical therapy sections give short writing exercises," as Lisa Cihlar of *Library Journal* put it.

BIOGRAPHICAL AND CRITICAL SOURCES:

PERIODICALS

Booklist, June 1, 1993, review of *The Joker and the Thief,* p. 1816.
Book Report, May, 1993, review of *The Joker and the Thief,* p. 43.
Children's Book Review Service, March, 1993, review of *The Joker and the Thief,* p. 95.
Children's Bookwatch, January, 1995, review of *The Joker and the Thief,* p. 6.
Horn Book Guide, fall, 1993, review of *The Joker and the Thief,* p. 311.
Kirkus Reviews, January 1, 1993, review of *The Joker and the Thief,* p. 66; April 15, 1995, review of *Earth Angel,* p. 502.
Library Journal, November 1, 1997, Carolyn Mulac, review of *Jabberrock! The Ultimate Book of Rock 'n' Roll Quotations* and *Twang! The Ultimate Book*

of Country Music Quotations, p. 70; January, 2002, Lisa Cihlar, review of *Fiction First Aid: Instant Remedies for Novels, Stories, and Scripts,* p. 118.

Los Angeles Times Book Review, April 14, 1985, review of *The Remington Factor,* p. 11.

Publishers Weekly, December 28, 1992, review of *The Joker and the Thief,* p. 74; May 8, 1995, review of *Earth Angel,* p. 289; August 4, 1997, review of *Jabberrock!* and *Twang!,* p. 61.

Rapport, number 4, 1996, review of *Earth Angel,* p. 33.

School Library Journal, March, 1993, review of *The Joker and the Thief,* p. 222.

Voice of Youth Advocates, April, 1993, review of *The Joker and the Thief,* p. 28.*

*   *   *

OSTERBROCK, Donald E. 1924-

PERSONAL: Born July 13, 1924, in Cincinnati, OH; son of William C. (a professor) and Elsie (a homemaker; maiden name, Wettlin) Osterbrock; married Irene L. Hansen, September 19, 1952; children: Carol Ann, William Carl, Laura Jane. *Ethnicity:* "German." *Education:* University of Chicago, Ph.B. and B.S., both 1948, M.S., 1949, Ph.D., 1952. *Religion:* Congregationalist. *Hobbies and other interests:* Reading, drama, hiking, bird watching, travel, conversation.

ADDRESSES: Home—120 Woodside Ave., Santa Cruz, CA 95060-3422. *Office*—Lick Observatory, University of California, Santa Cruz, CA 95064. *E-mail*—Don@ucolick.org.

CAREER: Princeton University, Princeton, NJ, research fellow and instructor, 1952-53; California Institute of Technology, Pasadena, instructor, 1953-55, assistant professor, 1955-58; University of Wisconsin—Madison, assistant professor, 1958-59, associate professor, 1959-61, professor, 1961-73, chairman of department of astronomy, 1969-72; University of California, Santa Cruz, professor of astronomy and astrophysics, 1973-92, professor emeritus, 1993—, director of Lick Observatory, 1973-81. Institute for Advanced Studies, Princeton, research fellow, 1960-61, 1982-83, Ambrose Monell Fellow in Natural Sciences and Otto Neugebauer Fellow in the History of Science, both 1989-90; University of Chicago, visiting professor, 1963-64; University of London, senior post-doctoral fellow, 1968-69; University of Minnesota—Twin Cities, Hill Family Professor, 1977-78; University of São Paulo, lecturer at Advanced Summer School of Astrophysics, 1983; Ohio State University, visiting professor, 1986; Henry Norris Russell Lecturer, American Astronomical Society, 1991; Antoinette de Vancouleurs Lecturer, University of Texas at Austin, 1994. *Military service:* U.S. Army Air Forces, 1943-46.

MEMBER: International Astronomy Union, National Academy of Sciences, American Academy of Arts and Sciences, American Philosophical Society, American Astronomical Society (vice president, 1975-77, president, 1988-90), Royal Astronomical Society (associate), Astronomy Society of the Pacific, Wisconsin Academy of Sciences, Arts, and Letters.

AWARDS, HONORS: Guggenheim fellow, 1960-61, 1982-83; National Science Foundation senior fellow, 1968-69; Professional Achievement Award, University of Chicago Alumni Association, 1982; D.Sc., Ohio State University, 1986, University of Chicago, 1992, and University of Wisconsin—Madison, 1997; named Distinguished Scholar in Physics and Astronomy, University Center (Atlanta, GA), 1990; Catherine Wolfe Bruce Gold Medal, Astronomical Society of the Pacific, 1991; Asteroid 6107 was named Osterbrock in his honor, 1996; Royal Astronomical Society Gold Medal, 1997.

WRITINGS:

(Editor, with C. Robert O'Dell) *Planetary Nebulae,* Springer Verlag (New York, NY), 1968.

Astrophysics of Gaseous Nebulae, W. H. Freeman (San Francisco, CA), 1974.

James E. Keeler, Pioneer American Astrophysicist: And the Early Development of American Astrophysics, Cambridge University Press (Cambridge, England), 1984.

(Editor, with Peter H. Raven) *Origins and Extinctions,* Yale University Press (New Haven, CT), 1988.

(With W. J. Shiloh Unruh) *Eye on the Sky: Lick Observatory's First Century,* University of California Press (Berkeley, CA), 1988.

Astrophysics of Gaseous Nebulae and Active Galactic Nuclei, University Science Books (Mill Valley, CA), 1989.

(Editor, with Joseph S. Miller) *Active Galactic Nuclei,* Kluwer Academic (Boston, MA), 1989.

(Editor) *Stars and Galaxies: Citizens of the Universe,* W. H. Freeman (New York, NY), 1990.

Pauper and Prince: Richey, Hale, and Big American Telescopes, University of Arizona Press (Tucson, AZ), 1993.

Yerkes Observatory, 1892-1950: The Birth, Near Death, and Resurrection of a Scientific Research Institution, University of Chicago Press (Chicago, IL), 1997.

Walter Baade: A Life in Astrophysics, Princeton University Press (Princeton, NJ), 2001.

SIDELIGHTS: Donald E. Osterbrock personally knew the subject of his biography *Walter Baade: A Life in Astrophysics.* Both were astronomers, working together during the 1950s, when Osterbrock—the younger of the two—was just beginning his career. Walter Baade, while not well known to the general public, is a "superstar" among those in his profession, according to Gilbert Taylor in *Booklist.* Baade was known for his exacting standards and extreme accuracy. He started out by observing solar eclipses at the Hamburg Observatory in Germany, but was really interested in cutting-edge projects of the time, such as discovering the size and shape of the Milky Way galaxy. Hoping to become involved with more forward-thinking colleagues, Baade moved to California, where he was associated with the Mount Wilson Observatory. There he established a reputation as an expert on globular clusters of stars. In 1944 he made a tremendous breakthrough by demonstrating that stars can be either ancient or very young. This discovery implied that all components of the universe have an evolutionary history.

Osterbrock's biography of Baade is "painstakingly researched" and "stunningly complete," according to S. Alan Stern in an *Astronomy* review of *Walter Baade.* This "delightfully engaging account" of one man's life also serves as "a welcome addition to the history of twentieth-century astronomy" and is "a wonderful read," concluded Stern. *Library Journal* writer Jack W. Weigel described Osterbrock's book as "a solid biography," and added that the descriptions of Baade's work "are at a moderately technical level; readers with reasonable knowledge of modern astronomy will benefit most from this work."

Osterbrock, whose own specialties lie in the study of interstellar gas and nebulae, once told *CA:* "I am a research astronomer. Most of my books are textbooks, research monographs, or books for the semitechnical, interested reader. I wrote them to communicate my ideas and methods in special fields. I am also an historian of astronomy, especially of American astronomy in the big-telescope era since about 1880 or 1890. I believe that, as an astronomer, I can understand the history of my subject better than most other historians. My familiarity with Lick, Yerkes, Mount Wilson, and Palomar Observatories enables me to understand the scientists who worked there (and in other observatories) earlier. The continuity of the long line of astronomers, from the great figures of the past right down to us today is an endlessly fascinating subject to me."

BIOGRAPHICAL AND CRITICAL SOURCES:

BOOKS

Notable Scientists: From 1900 to the Present, Gale (Detroit, MI), 2001.

PERIODICALS

Astronomy, February, 2002, S. Alan Stern, review of *Walter Baade: A Life in Astrophysics,* p. 93.

Booklist, December 15, 2001, Gilbert Taylor, review of *Walter Baade,* p. 694.

Choice, March, 2002, A. R. Upgren, review of *Walter Baade,* p. 1261.

Library Journal, November 1, 2001, Jack W. Weigel, review of *Walter Baade,* p. 130.

Physics Today, November, 2002, Norriss S. Hetherington, review of *Walter Baade,* p. 69.

ONLINE

University of California Lick Observatory Web site, http://www.ucolick.org/ (February 13, 2004).*

*   *   *

O'TOOLE, Fintan 1958-

PERSONAL: Born 1958, in Ireland.

ADDRESSES: Agent—c/o Author Mail, Granta Books, 1755 Broadway, 5th Floor, New York, NY 10019.

CAREER: Journalist, theater critic, and author.

WRITINGS:

The Politics of Magic: The Work and Times of Tom Murphy, Raven Arts Press (Dublin, Ireland), 1987, updated and expanded edition published as *Tom Murphy: The Politics of Magic,* New Island Books (Dublin, Ireland), 1994.

The Southern Question, Raven Arts Press (Dublin, Ireland), 1987.

No More Heroes: A Radical Guide to Shakespeare, Raven Arts Press (Dublin, Ireland), 1990.

A Mass for Jesse James: A Journey through 1980's Ireland, Raven Arts Press (Dublin, Ireland), 1990.

Black Hole, Green Card: The Disappearance of Ireland, New Island Books (Dublin, Ireland), 1994.

Meanwhile Back at the Ranch: The Politics of Irish Beef, Vintage (New York, NY), 1995.

The Ex-Isle of Erin: Images of a Global Ireland, New Island Books (Dublin, Ireland), 1997.

A Traitor's Kiss: The Life of Richard Brinsley Sheridan, Granta Books (London, England), 1997, published as *A Traitor's Kiss: The Life of Richard Brinsley Sheridan, 1751-1816,* Farrar, Straus & Giroux (New York, NY), 1998.

The Lie of the Land: Irish Identities, foreword by Mike Davis, Verso (New York, NY), 1998.

Shakespeare Is Hard, but So Is Life: A Radical Guide to Shakespearean Tragedy, Granta Books (New York, NY), 2003.

Contributor to Irish periodicals.

SIDELIGHTS: Irish journalist and critic Fintan O'Toole has bridged the worlds of literature and politics during his prolific career. O'Toole's early experiences as a theater critic for Dublin periodicals enabled him to write his first book, *The Politics of Magic: The Work and Times of Tom Murphy.* This is a study of the contemporary Irish playwright named in the title; in the view of *Irish Literary Supplement* contributor Riana O'Dwyer, it is an "important book, the first full-length study of Murphy's work." Murphy, a prolific and often controversial playwright, had allowed O'Toole access to his unpublished material and

agreed to personal interviews. As a result, *The Politics of Magic* is usefully detailed with information and anecdotes about the production histories—including, in some cases, histories of non-production or of terminated productions—of Murphy's plays. O'Toole chronicles the change in the playwright's work from the tragedies of the 1950s and 1960s to the more optimistic plays of later decades. A theater critic with a political frame of mind, O'Toole promotes a vision of theater as a medium for transformation of public perceptions; he views Murphy as having worked with considerable success at creating "beautiful images of transformation at a time when the world seems all too fixed and inescapable." O'Toole also "convincingly," in O'Dwyer's opinion, argues that Murphy was a playwright of more than national scope.

O'Toole wore his theater-critic hat for later books, including *No More Heroes: A Radical Guide to Shakespeare,* and *A Traitor's Kiss: The Life of Richard Brinsley Sheridan.* Other books, however, have focused on the contemporary situation of Irish society and politics. In *The Southern Question,* O'Toole takes up the idea that, as reviewer Richard Pine put it in the *Irish Literary Supplement,* "Ireland since independence has failed 'to create a public realm.'"

In *A Mass for Jesse James: A Journey through 1980's Ireland,* he offers readers a collection of essays. The title essay refers to a parish priest in Ireland who offered an annual mass for the soul of outlaw Jesse James, whose parents had emigrated from Ireland. Reviewer Pine wrote that "O'Toole has always offered a searching view of anything that speaks . . . for the unmediated concept of Ireland, and this collection regards his best journalism to date." O'Toole took up a single, complex Irish political issue at full length in his 1995 book, *Meanwhile Back at the Ranch: The Politics of Irish Beef.* Corruption in the beef industry in that nation, particularly with regard to exports to nations that included Russia and Iraq, was the subject of a two-year government investigation beginning in 1991, and was extensively publicized in Ireland. Reviewing O'Toole's analysis of the issue in the *London Review of Books,* Anne Enright applauded him for working "in the dead space created by [the] separation of the facts from the truth. . . . anatomising the clause, the memo, the precedent and protocol, in the time-honoured interest of nailing the bastards to the wall." Concluded Enright, "This book is salutary reading for all those who think that if you're making money, you're good for the country. It also provides an insight into how the rich feel persecuted." O'Toole, Enright continued, had provided "fascinating" glimpses into "how politicians simply *do* things, how they make their way through the rules."

In 1996 O'Toole put together another collection of journalistic essays titled, *The Ex-Isle of Erin: Images of a Global Ireland.* In fourteen essays that a *Publishers Weekly* critic maintained were "brilliantly written," O'Toole examines the interplay between Irish people on the home island and those who eventually found themselves—or whose descendants found themselves—in other lands. He also looked at his own childhood as an Irish Catholic, debunking some of the conventional wisdom on that subject. The historical transformation of Ireland into a multidimensional, global culture in the twentieth century is perhaps the overarching subject of the essays; and the *Publishers Weekly* critic asserted, "Taken together, these essays are a must-read for any member of our global village, ex-native or ex-emigrant."

BIOGRAPHICAL AND CRITICAL SOURCES:

PERIODICALS

Books in Canada, March, 2003, Keith Garebian, review of *Shakespeare Is Hard, but So Is Life: A Radical Guide to Shakespearean Tragedy,* pp. 24-25.
Irish Literary Supplement, spring, 1989, Riana O'Dwyer, review of *The Politics of Magic: The Work and Times of Tom Murphy,* pp. 14, 30; fall, 1991, article by Richard Pine, p. 36.
London Review of Books, August 3, 1995, Anne Enright, review of *Meanwhile Back at the Ranch: The Politics of Irish Beef,* pp. 26-27.
Publishers Weekly, December 1, 1997, review of *The Ex-Isle of Erin: Images of a Global Ireland,* p. 41.*

*   *   *

OUCHI, William G(eorge) 1943-

PERSONAL: Born June 28, 1943, in Honolulu, HI; son of Sugao (a dentist) and Shizuko (an educator; maiden name, Nakano) Ouchi; married Carol Kagawa (a homemaker), June 19, 1966; children: Sarah Ayako, Jennifer Nakano, Andrew Sugao. *Education:* Williams College, A.B., 1965; Stanford University, M.B.A., 1967; University of Chicago, Ph.D., 1972. *Politics:* Republican. *Religion:* Congregationalist.

ADDRESSES: Office—Anderson Graduate School of Management, University of California—Los Angeles, 405 Hilgard Ave., Los Angeles, CA 90024-1481.

CAREER: University of Chicago, Chicago, IL, instructor in organizational behavior, 1971-72; National Opinion Research Center, Chicago, associate study director, 1971-72; Stanford University, Stanford, CA, assistant professor, 1971-74, associate professor of organizational behavior, 1975-79; University of California—Los Angeles, Los Angeles, professor of management, beginning 1979.

MEMBER: American Sociological Association, Academy of Management.

AWARDS, HONORS: Grand Prix des Meilleurs Livres de Management, University of Paris, 1982, for *Theory Z: How American Business Can Meet the Japanese Challenge;* D.Litt., Williams College, 1983; Woman Warrior Award, Asian-Pacific Women's Network, 1987.

WRITINGS:

Theory Z: How American Business Can Meet the Japanese Challenge, Addison-Wesley (Reading, MA), 1981.
Making Schools Work: A Revolutionary Plan to Get Your Children the Education They Need, Simon & Schuster (New York, NY), 2003.

Contributor to books, including *Information Technology and Organizational Change,* edited by T. L. Whistler, Wadsworth Publishing (Belmont, CA), 1969; *The Organizational Life Cycle,* edited by J. R. Kimberly, R. H. Miles, and others, Jossey-Bass (San Francisco, CA), 1980; *Assessing Organization Design and Performance,* edited by A. H. Van de Ven and W. F. Joyce, Wiley (New York, NY), 1981; *Exploring the New Management,* edited by R. M. Fulmer and T. T. Herbert, Macmillan (New York, NY), 1982; and *Management by Japanese Systems,* Volume II, edited by Sang Lee, Praeger (New York, NY), 1983. Contributor of articles and reviews to management journals.

SIDELIGHTS: In *Theory Z: How American Business Can Meet the Japanese Challenge,* which became a best-seller due to increasing public concern about the role of U.S. business in the world marketplace, William G. Ouchi postulates that the most successful corporations, whether Japanese or American, are those that nurture their human resources. He calls for an end to the adversarial relationship between management and workers that has permeated American business for many years. Ouchi describes an alternative that has enhanced Japanese productivity and profits: an emphasis on long-term goals, in terms of both profits and lifetime careers for workers, coupled with the encouragement of worker participation in management strategy and decision making.

BIOGRAPHICAL AND CRITICAL SOURCES:

PERIODICALS

Los Angeles Times Book Review, May 31, 1981.
New York Times, May 2, 1981; July 26, 1981.
New York Times Book Review, July 5, 1981.
Washington Post Book World, May 17, 1981.*

*   *   *

OWENS, William A. 1905-1990

PERSONAL: Born November 2, 1905, in Pin Hook, TX; died, December 8, 1990, of complications from Alzheimer's disease, in Nyack, NY; buried in Nyack, NY; son of Charles and Jessie Ann (Chennault) Owens; married Ann Slater Wood, December 23, 1946; children: Jessie Ann, David Edward. *Education:* East Texas State Teachers College, earned teaching certificate; Southern Methodist University, B.A., 1932, M.A., 1933; University of Texas, postgraduate study, 1936; State University of Iowa, Ph.D., 1941; Columbia University, postdoctoral study, 1945-46. *Politics:* Independent. *Religion:* Episcopalian.

CAREER: Teacher in Lamar County, TX, schools, 1928-30; Greenville High School, Greenville, TX, teacher, 1934-35; Wesley College, Greenville, TX, instructor in English, 1935-36; Mississippi State College (now Mississippi State University), instructor in English, 1936; Robert E. Lee High School, Goose Creek, TX, teacher of English, 1936-37; The Agricultural and Mechanical College of Texas (now Texas A & M University), College Station, started as instructor, 1937, became associate professor of English, 1941-47, writer in residence, 1976; Columbia University, New York, NY, associate professor and director of summer session, 1947-66, professor of English, 1966-74, dean of summer session, 1969-74, dean emeritus, 1974-81. University of Texas, director of research for folk materials, 1941, and director of the Oral History of Texas Oil Pioneers, 1952-58. Lecturer in the National Humanities Series, Princeton University, 1971-73; visiting professor of English, University of Texas at Austin, summer, 1978. *Military service:* U.S. Army, 1942-45; served in Counter Intelligence Corps; became second lieutenant; received Legion of Merit.

MEMBER: American Association of University Professors, Modern Language Association of America, Texas Institute of Letters, Texas Folklore Society, Phi Beta Kappa.

AWARDS, HONORS: Texas Institute of Letters Award, 1954, for *Walking on Borrowed Land,* 1966, for *This Stubborn Soil,* and 1985, for continuing excellence in Texas letters; Southwest Library Association's award for best nonfiction book, 1974, for *Season of Weathering;* National Endowment for the Humanities fellow, 1974-75.

WRITINGS:

Swing and Turn: Texas Play Party Games, Tardy Publishing (Dallas, TX), 1936.
(Compiler) *Texas Folk Songs,* musical arrangements by Willa Mae Kelly Koehn, Southern Methodist University Press (Dallas, TX), 1950, revised and enlarged edition with musical transcriptions by daughter, Jessie Ann Owens, University of North Texas Press, 1976.
Slave Mutiny: The Revolt on the Schooner Amistad, John Day (New York, NY), 1953, published as *Black Mutiny: The Revolt on the Schooner Amistad,* Pilgrim Press (Philadelphia, PA), 1968.
Walking on Borrowed Land (novel), Bobbs-Merrill (New York, NY), 1954, reprinted, Texas Christian University Press (College Station, TX), 1988.
Fever in the Earth, Putnam (New York, NY), 1958, reprinted, Shearer Publications, 1984.

Pocantico Hills, 1609-1959, Sleepy Hollow Restorations (Tarrytown, NY), 1960.

(Editor) *Energy and Man,* Appleton, 1960.

Look to the River, Atheneum (New York, NY), 1963, reprinted, Texas Christian University Press (College Station, TX), 1988.

This Stubborn Soil (autobiography), Scribner (New York, NY), 1966, published as *This Stubborn Soil: A Frontier Boyhood,* Faber (London, England), 1967.

Three Friends: Roy Bedichek, J. Frank Dobie, Walter Prescott Webb, Doubleday (New York, NY), 1969, reprinted as *Three Friends, Bedichek, Dobie, Webb: A Personal History,* University of Texas Press (Austin, TX), 1975.

(With Mody C. Boatwright) *Tales from the Derrick Floor: A People's History of the Oil Industry,* Doubleday (New York, NY), 1970.

A Season of Weathering (autobiography), Scribner (New York, NY), 1973.

A Fair and Happy Land, Scribner (New York, NY), 1975.

Sing Me a Song, University of Texas Press (Austin, TX), 1983.

Tell Me a Story, Sing Me a Song: A Texas Chronicle, University of Texas Press (Austin, TX), 1983.

Eye-Deep in Hell: A Memoir of the Liberation of the Philippines, 1944-45, Southern Methodist University Press (Dallas, TX), 1989.

Also author, with Michael Frary, of *Impressions of the Big Thicket,* 1973, and *The Letters of Ray Bedichek,* 1985. Contributor to books, including *Writers' Roundtable,* edited by Helen Hull and Michael Drury, Harper (New York, NY), 1959; *And Horns on the Toads,* edited by Mody C. Boatright, Wilson M. Hudson, and Allen Maxwell, Southern Methodist University Press (Dallas, TX), 1959; and *Three Men in Texas,* edited by Ronnie Dugger, University of Texas Press (Austin, TX), 1967. Author of introduction, *The Flush Times of Alabama and Mississippi* by Joseph G. Baldwin, Sagamore Press (New York, NY), 1957, and *Native Son* by Richard Wright, Harper (New York, NY), 1957. Contributor to *Southwest Review, Contemporary Arts in the South and Southwest, Asia and the Americas, Epoch, Ladies Homes Journal, Tomorrow Magazine, New-Story, Southwest Review, Saturday Review, New York Times Book Review, Texas Observer, Du Pont Magazine,* and other periodicals. The Cushing Memorial Library at Texas A & M University holds Owens's personal papers, including his personal correspondence, books, book manuscripts, book reviews, articles, short stories, speeches, photographs, and aluminum disc recordings made by Owens of various folksingers and musicians in the South.

SIDELIGHTS: William A. Owens is especially remembered for his work on the origins of American folk songs. In his book *Texas Folk Songs* Owens gathered some 135 traditional songs from throughout Texas, including ballads, love songs, comic songs, children's songs, and African-American spirituals. Owens dedicated the songs, he wrote in the book, to "those who love to sing them as well as for those who have an interest in the past." In addition to his writings on folk music, Owens also authored *Black Mutiny: The Revolt on the Schooner Amistad,* an account of the historic slave revolt. The book served as a major reference source for a film adaptation in 1997. Owens also wrote an account of the liberation of the Philippines during World War II, based on his own experiences there as an American intelligence officer.

Owens was born in the cotton country of rural Texas in 1905. His father died a few days after his birth. "It was from his mother that he learned the values of hard work and self reliance," a biographer of Owens noted in an essay posted on the Texas A & M University's Cushing Memorial Library Web site. "In addition, he acquired a love of reading and a desire to obtain an education beyond the one-room schoolhouses of Lamar County." He worked odd jobs to pay for his schooling. After obtaining a teaching certificate from the East Texas State Teachers College, Owens went on to earn bachelor's, master's, and doctoral degrees. He taught at high schools and colleges throughout Texas before taking a position with Columbia University, where he stayed for some twenty-five years. Owens also served as the director of research in folk materials and director of the Oral History of Texas Oil Pioneers project for the University of Texas.

BIOGRAPHICAL AND CRITICAL SOURCES:

BOOKS

Lee, James W., editor, *William A. Owens: A Symposium,* Trilobite Press (Denton, TX), 1981.

Owens, William A., *A Season of Weathering* (autobiography), Scribner (New York, NY), 1973.

Owens, William A., *Eye-Deep in Hell: A Memoir of the Liberation of the Philippines, 1944-45,* Southern Methodist University Press (Dallas, TX), 1989.
Owens, William A., *This Stubborn Soil* (autobiography), Scribner (New York, NY), 1966, reprinted, Random House (New York, NY), 1989.

PERIODICALS

American Petroleum Institute Quarterly, spring, 1958, J. Frank Dobie, "What It Felt Like to Be There," pp. 42-43.
Library Journal, February 1, 1998, Michael Rogers, review of *Black Mutiny,* p. 118; April 1, 1998, Nancy Paul, review of audiocassette version of *Black Mutiny,* p. 141A.
Listener, November 30, 1967.
Southwest Review, winter, 1955, Roy Bedichek, "Tension of Jim Crow," pp. 84-86; winter, 1967, Mody

C. Boatright, "Hard Times and Good in Old Pin Hook," pp. 99-101.

ONLINE

Texas A & M University's Cushing Memorial Library Web site, http://library.tamu.edu/cushing/ (December 10, 2002), "Selected Bibliography of William A. Owens" and "Biography."
University of North Texas Press Web site, http://www.unt.edu/ (December 10, 2002).

OBITUARIES:

PERIODICALS

New York Times, December 12, 1990.*

P

PAMUK, Orhan 1952-

PERSONAL: Born 1952, in Turkey; father, a civil engineer and university teacher; married; wife's name Aylin; children: Ruya (daughter). *Education:* Robert College (Istanbul, Turkey), degree (journalism).

ADDRESSES: Agent—c/o Author Mail, Knopf, 1745 Broadway, New York, NY 10019.

CAREER: Writer. University of Iowa, visiting writer fellow, 1985.

AWARDS, HONORS: Nominated for Prix Medici for best foreign novel, 1988, for *Sessiz ev; Independent* Award for foreign fiction, 1990; International IMPAC Dublin Literary Award, 2003, for *My Name Is Red.*

WRITINGS:

(With Dursun Akcam and Celal Ozcan) *Türkiye'den yeni hikayeler,* 12 Antalya Festivali Hikaye Yarismasi, 1976.
Cevdet Bey ve ogullari (novel), Karacan Yayinlari (Istanbul, Turkey), 1982.
Sessiz ev: roman, Can Yayinlari (Istanbul, Turkey), 1983.
Beyaz kale: roman, Can Yayinlari (Istanbul, Turkey), 1985, translation by Victoria Holbrook published as *The White Castle: A Novel,* Carcanet (Manchester, England), 1990, Braziller (New York, NY), 1991.

Kara Kitap (novel), Can Yayinlari (Istanbul, Turkey), 1990, translation by Guneli Gun published as *The Black Book,* Farrar, Straus (New York, NY), 1994.
Gizli yuz (screenplay), Can Yayinlari (Istanbul, Turkey), 1992.
Yeni hayat (novel), Ileti sim (Istanbul, Turkey), 1994, translation by Guneli Gun published as *The New Life,* Farrar, Straus (New York, NY), 1997.
Benim adim kirmizi, Ileti sim (Istanbul, Turkey), 1998.
My Name Is Red, translated from the Turkish by Erdag Goknar, Knopf (New York, NY), 2001.
Kar, Ileti sim (Istanbul, Turkey), 2002.

Contributor to periodicals, including *Times Literary Supplement.*

SIDELIGHTS: Orhan Pamuk is a well-known writer in Turkey who published a number of books at a relatively young age. His first novel, *Cevdet Bey ve ogullari,* was completed when he was twenty-six years old, and he won acclaim for it shortly after publication. Paul Berman, reviewing Pamuk's books in the *New Republic,* called him "a celebrated figure, his country's leading postmodern writer." However, it was only with the publication of *The White Castle,* his fourth book, that Pamuk's writing became accessible to English-language readers.

Cevdet Bey is the story of the lives of Cevdet Bey, a successful Istanbul businessman, and his successors. Savkar Altinel, critiquing Pamuk's work in a *Times Literary Supplement* review, observed that the book is realistic, with a strong plot and characters, and "traces with remorseless clarity the rise of the modern Turkish ruling class and the evolution of Turkish capitalism." This is depicted through the life of Cevdet Bey and his descendants. Bey has earned a fortune in his lifetime. His successors, however, are weak, ineffectual dreamers who, in Altinel's opinion, are partially responsible for Turkey's failure to achieve stature. Bey's achievements are matched, finally, by his grandson who achieves fame as a painter.

Pamuk's second novel, *Sessiz ev,* is written in the modernist tradition, according to Altinel. The setting is a small town near Istanbul, where three siblings are spending a week in their grandmother's house. The story takes place in 1980, a time when Turkey was in the midst of armed political conflicts among various street gangs. The book has five narrators, and they each view the action from different perspectives, marking time through existence and an awareness of their own consciousness. Altinel called it a "beautiful, elegiac book" in which Pamuk explores Turkey's westernization and "the overwhelming, Cartesian awareness of existing as a conscious, thinking being."

John Updike commented in a *New Yorker* review that *The White Castle* was written in "a postmodern atmosphere of fantasy and cleverness." The story begins as a straightforward narrative by the protagonist, a young Italian scholar who is captured by Turkish pirates. He is given as a slave to an eccentric scientist named Hoja who promises him his freedom in return for knowledge. The two men resemble each other physically, and as the plot evolves the reader is led to the realization that their identities have become interchangeable. In Updike's words, "Everything blends and melts into the narrator's misty self." In the end the reader is unsure of the difference between Hoja and his slave. In the *New York Times Book Review,* Jay Parini called the book "a fable of identity, a postmodern tale that explores the murky and recessive byways of Cartesian self-consciousness." Christopher Lehmann-Haupt commented in a *New York Times* review that *The White Castle* was a bridge between two cultures. For him, "the appeal [of the book] resides in the odd marriage of Western rationalism and Eastern religious faith."

Pamuk's next novel is a "complex" work, wrote Altinel. When *The Black Book* was published, western critics found it to be "so dense it will deter all but the most tenacious readers," as Patrick McGrath commented in the *Washington Post Book World,* yet "[h]ere

be marvelous monsters" within the sinuous passageways of this intriguing labyrinth. McGrath was struck by Pamuk's "vision of Istanbul as a city of sinister complexity, a peculiarly Turkish maze with an uneasy, shifting foundation." In the *Times Literary Supplement,* Robert Irwin acknowledged the theme of *The Black Book* as an exploration of "Turkey's shaky cultural identity," the ripples from which spill over into the identity of the individual. On such precarious ground, he wrote, "Pamuk's characters find it very difficult to be themselves."

The Black Book is the story of a young lawyer named Galip. In the book, Galip roams the streets of Istanbul, looking for his wife, Ruya, who has disappeared without giving him any reasons for her absence. Galip searches for clues to his wife's whereabouts in the writings of her half-brother, Jelal, a journalist who has also disappeared, though his newspaper column continues to be published daily. Galip's search never really leads anywhere, and he continues to wander through the streets of Istanbul. According to Altinel, Galip's search for his wife is a symbolic search for reality. Ironically, Ruya's name means "dream," and she always remains elusive. Galip never finds his wife, and he ultimately assumes Jelal's identity and continues his writing. In *Contemporary World Writers,* Pamuk's translator Guneli Gun likened Galip's quest to "the Sufi quest for 'the beloved'. . . . To find God . . . is to become God: to find Oneself, one has to become Another, which makes the self, of course, the ultimate mystery."

The Black Book derives from Pamuk's wide-ranging forays into Sufi mysticism, medieval Turkish verse, western literature, and, according to Gun, "a thousand other sources both from the East, which Pamuk inherits by birthright, and the West, which he has acquired through his own erudition." The author sprinkles gems from this treasury liberally throughout his book. Irwin commented, "as an encyclopedia of esoterica and as a compendium of medieval and modern literary tricks . . . it is quite wonderful."

In Altinel's words, "The book . . . arrives at the Proustian conclusion that reality, which exists in and as time, cannot be captured but only *re*-captured: remembered, reimagined and preserved as literature," and yet, he said, there are doubts about literature's ability to "comprehend all the countless fictions 'reality' consists of." Gun described Pamuk as "a writer for whom the pleasure of the text is the ultimate high. . . . Given a world where man is unable to comprehend reality or solve the mystery, fiction for Orhan Pamuk is not everything, it is the only thing."

The New Life pursues similar themes against a more panoramic backdrop, drawing the reader away from the noisy maze of Istanbul into the wider landscape of the Turkish countryside. Jamie James described the novel in the *Wall Street Journal* as "a telescopic view of a people in whom classical thought, Byzantine glory, and contemporary Islam mingle but do not blend."

In *The New Life,* Osman is a university student who, during a study break in the dark quiet of his room, discovers a book that changes his life. In pursuit of the beautiful Janan, who has also read the book, he meets her boyfriend, Mehmet, and a mysterious group of people who have dedicated their lives completely to this book and its message of a new life. When Janan disappears and it seems that Mehmet may have been murdered, Osman ventures forth on a meandering quest to find the object of his love and the new life promised by the spellbinding book. On one bus trip after another, he experiences what *Washington Post* reviewer Bradford Morrow called a "contemporary Turkey which—like . . . Osman—is poised at the brink of transformation."

Adventures are plentiful. Osman learns that opponents of the "new life" are killing the book's readers wherever they can be found. Highway accidents are frequent. After one such crash, he finds Janan. "Beyond this point . . . nothing is as it seems, no one is as he seems." wrote D. M. Thomas in the *New York Times Book Review.* Traveling together, Osman and Janan meet men who might be Mehmet, but are not. Janan disappears again. It becomes difficult to distinguish the identity of Osman from that of Mehmet. Osman seems to have identified the author of the mysterious book, then he seems to become the author himself. "The plot of Mr. Pamuk's novel," James concluded, ". . . is never more engrossing than when it is utterly improbable."

Tom LeClair wrote in the *Nation:* "When read a second time, *The New Life* reveals elaborate designs: tail-swallowing, double-doubling, mirror settings, webs of minutiae." The novel, like *The Black Book,* left

some critics bemused: the characters never come fully to life; the story is repetitive, the plot obscure; there is too much abstraction and not enough reality; where is the conclusive ending? "That ultimately becomes the novel's strong point," suggested James. "Ambivalence may be the only rational position to take in a land situated at the vortex of East and West."

More postmodern adventures are presented in *My Name Is Red,* a story of mystery, fantasy, and philosophy set in the sixteenth century. A group of famous artists are gathered to illuminate a book that celebrates the Sultan. Such artwork is intended to be in the European style of illuminated manuscripts, but also runs against Islamic "prohibitions on representational art," as Allen Hibbard noted in the *Review of Contemporary Fiction.* Reminiscent of other intellectual mysteries and thrillers, such as Umberto Eco's *The Name of the Rose,* Pamuk's novel "works on three levels," as a contributor for *Publishers Weekly* observed. First, as a murder mystery, the reader is drawn into the plot, attempting to solve the mystery of who killed one of the artists/artisans, Elegant, at work on the illuminated manuscript. The mystery deepens when Enishte Effendi, the man initially commissioned with the art project, is himself killed. On a second level, Pamuk also writes a novel of ideas, in which East meets West in the Ottoman court, and in which Western Renaissance ideas begin to pervade the Islamic worldview and threaten its basic laws. And thirdly, as the *Publishers Weekly* reviewer found, the book functions as a "love story," with Enishte's nephew, Black, attempting to win the hand of the widow Shekure, who is also the murdered Enishte's daughter. To do so, Black must solve the murders.

Told from a myriad of narrative points of view, including that of a coin, a tree, a horse, and even a corpse, *My Name Is Red* is a "nontraditional murder mystery," according to *Library Journal*'s Marc Kloszewski, that also provides "insight into the mores and customs of the time." For the *Publishers Weekly* critic, the novel contains "jeweled prose and alluring digressions." Other critical praise came from a variety of publications. *Booklist*'s Nancy Pearl felt this "intellectual mystery will appeal to fans" of the genre. Hibbard commented positively on the "clever narrative scheme we only wholly grasp on the last page," and the *Spectator*'s Philip Hensher found the novel at once "fabulous, baffling, [and] exciting." Hensher went on to note that Pamuk created a "wonderful novel, dreamy, passionate and august, exotic in the most original and exciting way." A critic for *Kirkus Reviews* added to the praise, calling the book a "rich feast of ideas, images, and lore." Similar commendation came from Richard Eder, writing in the *New York Times Book Review*. Eder dubbed Pamuk a "great" novelist, and found that *My Name Is Red* "is not just a novel of ideas. Eastern or Western, good or bad, ideas precipitate once they sink to human level, unleashing passions and violence." According to Eder, the novel is "chockful of sublimity and sin."

The "chockful" nature of the book, however, was a liability for Sarah Coleman, reviewing the novel in the *San Francisco Chronicle Online*. Coleman thought that "the ingredients [of the novel] are potent, but the balance is off." Coleman further explained, "Like an overenthusiastic master illustrator, Pamuk paints a vivid picture, but loads it with so many details and symbols that the eye has nowhere calm to rest." But for Conor O'Toole, writing in the *Yale Review of Books Online*, Pamuk produced with *My Name Is Red* a "novel unlike any written in English," and one that "should impress and reward every thoughtful reader."

Pamuk's work has been lauded by critics for its depth and innovation. However, Berman felt that it would be a mistake to characterize Pamuk as a purely philosophical novelist. He felt that, although there are connections between the characters and themes of Pamuk's novels, each book has a unique emphasis, and this creates an intrinsic interest in the story. Parini was effusive in his praise of Pamuk and compared him to Jorge Luis Borges and Italo Calvino. Other critics, like Lehmann-Haupt and Altinel, have also linked Pamuk's writing with modernist writers like Franz Kafka because of the imagery and writing style used in *The White Castle*. In conclusion, Berman called Pamuk an "extravagantly talented" writer whose books are entertaining, have fascinating themes, and have a "tendency to excite a certain madly enjoyable spirit of theoretical spritz in the reader." Pamuk explained his art to Sarah A. Smith in a *Guardian Online* interview: "I write modern, some say postmodern, avant-garde-inspired novels, which is a western form, but they carry [a resonance of] suppressed Ottoman culture, Islamic culture."

BIOGRAPHICAL AND CRITICAL SOURCES:

BOOKS

Contemporary World Writers, 2nd edition, St. James Press (Detroit, MI), 1993.

PERIODICALS

Booklist, October 1, 2001, Nancy Pearl, review of *My Name Is Red,* p. 300.

Books, autumn, 2001, review of *My Name Is Red,* p. 21.

Boston Globe, April 17, 1997, p. E5.

Chicago Tribune, April 13, 1997, p. 14.

Christian Science Monitor, April 23, 1997, p. 12; October 11, 2001, review of *My Name Is Red,* p. 19.

Economist, October 27, 2001, review of *My Name Is Red,* p. 80; December 22, 2001, review of *My Name Is Red,* p. 107.

Kirkus Reviews, August 1, 2001, review of *My Name Is Red,* p. 1058.

Library Journal, September 1, 2001, Marc Kloszewski, review of *My Name Is Red,* p. 234.

London Review of Books, October 5, 1995, p. 22.

Los Angeles Times Book Review, June 8, 1997, pp. 11-12; December 2, 2001, review of *My Name Is Red,* p. 11.

Los Angeles Times Books, October 7, 2001, review of *My Name Is Red,* p. 9.

Nation, April 7, 1997, Tom LeClair, review of *The New Life,* pp. 38-39.

New Leader, September, 2001, review of *My Name Is Red,* p. 23.

New Republic, September 9, 1991, pp. 36-39.

New Statesman, August 27, 2001, review of *My Name Is Red,* p. 41.

New Yorker, September 2, 1991, John Updike, review of *The White Castle,* pp. 102, 104-105.

New York Times, April 29, 1991, Christopher Lehmann-Haupt, review of *The White Castle,* p. C15.

New York Times Book Review, May 19, 1991, Jay Parini, review of *The White Castle,* p. 3; January 15, 1995, p. 20; April 6, 1997, D. M. Thomas, review of *The New Life,* pp. 7-8; September 2, 2001, Richard Eder, review of *My Name Is Red,* p. 7; December 2, 2001, review *My Red Is Red,* p. 66; September 8, 2002, review of *My Name Is Red,* p. 28.

New York Times Magazine, May 4, 1997, section 6, p. 33.

Observer (London, England), August 5, 2001, review of *My Name Is Red,* p. 16.

Publishers Weekly, December 19, 1994, pp. 36-37; August 6, 2001, review of *My Name Is Red,* p. 58; November 19, 2001, review of *My Name Is Red,* p. 35.

Quadrant, March, 1999, review of *The New Life*, p. 86.

Review of Contemporary Fiction, fall, 2001, Allen Hibbard, review of *My Name Is Red*, pp. 203-204.

Spectator, August 4, 2001, Philip Hensher, review of *My Name Is Red*, p. 29.

Times Literary Supplement, October 12, 1990, pp. 1087-1088; July 7, 1995, p. 21; September 7, 2001, review of *My Name Is Red*, p. 6.

Tribune Books (Chicago, IL), September 23, 2001, review of *My Red Is Red*, p. 1.

Wall Street Journal, April 4, 1997, Jamie James, review of *The New Life*, p. A7.

Washington Post Book World, February 12, 1995, Patrick McGrath, review of *The Black Book*, pp. 6-7; July 13, 1997, Bradford Morrow, review of *The New Life*, p. 11; September 2, 2001, review of *My Name Is Red*, p. 13.

World, January, 2002, review of *My Name Is Red*, p. 227.

ONLINE

BBC News Online, http://news.bbc.co.uk/ (August 7, 2003), Orhan Pamuk, "Sense of the City: Istanbul."

BookPage, http://www.bookpage.com/ (March 18, 2003), Michael Rose, review of *My Name Is Red*.

Borzoi Reader Online, http://www.randomhouse.com/ (March 18, 2003), "A Conversation with Orhan Pamuk."

Flak Online, http://www.flakmag.com/ (March 18, 2003), Clay Risen, review of *My Name Is Red*.

Guardian Online, http://www.guardian.co.uk/ (December 7, 2002), Sarah A. Smith, "A Private History."

San Francisco Chronicle Online, http://www.sfgate.com/ (December 9, 2001), Sarah Coleman, review of *My Name Is Red*.

Yale Review of Books Online, http://www.yalereviewofbooks.com/ (spring, 2002), Conor O'Toole, review of *My Name Is Red*.*

*   *   *

PARAVISINI-GEBERT, Lizabeth 1953-

PERSONAL: Born March 21, 1953, in Puerto Rico; daughter of Domingo (an accountant) and Virgenmina (a designer; maiden name, Rivera) Paravisini; married Gordon Alan Gebert (an architect), September 24, 1988; children: Gordon Alan III; stepchildren: Carrie Lauren, D'Arcy Allyse. *Education:* University of Puerto Rico, B.A., 1973; New York University, M.A., 1976, M.Phil., 1980, Ph.D., 1982. *Politics:* Democrat. *Religion:* Roman Catholic.

ADDRESSES: Home—63 North Broadway, Nyack, NY 10960. *Office*—Vassar College, Poughkeepsie, NY 12601.

CAREER: Herbert H. Lehman College of the City University of New York, Bronx, NY, associate professor of Puerto Rican studies, 1981-91; Vassar College, Poughkeepsie, NY, associate professor of Caribbean literature and culture, beginning 1991.

WRITINGS:

(Editor, with Carmen Esteves) *Green Cane and Juicy Flotsam: Short Stories by Caribbean Women*, Rutgers University Press (New Brunswick, NJ), 1991.

Luz y sombra, University of Puerto Rico Press (Rio Piedras, PR), 1991.

(With Margarite Fernández Olmos) *El Placer de la palabra*, Planeta (Mexico City, Mexico), 1991.

(With Olga Torres Seda) *Caribbean Women Novelists: An Annotated Bibliography*, Greenwood Press (Westport, CT), 1992.

(With Margarite Fernández Olmos) *Pleasure and the Word: Erotic Writings by Latin American Women*, White Pine Press (Fredonia, NY), 1993.

Phyllis Shand Allfrey: A Caribbean Life, Rutgers University Press (New Brunswick, NJ), 1993.

(Editor, with Margarite Fernández Olmos) *Remaking a Lost Harmony: Stories from the Hispanic Caribbean*, White Pine Press (Fredonia, NY), 1995.

(Editor, with Margarite Fernández Olmos) *Sacred Possessions: Vodou, Santeria, Obeah, and the Caribbean*, Rutgers University Press (New Brunswick, NJ), 1997.

Jamaica Kincaid: A Critical Companion, Greenwood Press (Westport, CT), 1999.

(Editor, with Margarite Fernández Olmos) *Healing Cultures: Art and Religion As Curative Practices in the Caribbean and Its Diaspora*, Palgrave (New York, NY), 2001.

(Editor, with Ivette Romero-Cesareo) *Women at Sea: Travel Writing and the Margins of Caribbean Discourse*, Palgrave (New York, NY), 2001.

(With Margarite Fernández Olmos) *Creole Religions of the Caribbean: An Introduction from Vodou and Santeria to Obeah and Espiritismo*, New York University Press (New York, NY), 2003.

BIOGRAPHICAL AND CRITICAL SOURCES:

PERIODICALS

Library Journal, July, 2003, L. Kriz, review of *Creole Religions of the Caribbean: An Introduction from Vodou and Santeria to Obeah and Espiritismo.**

*   *   *

PARISI, Joseph 1944-

PERSONAL: Born November 18, 1944, in Duluth, MN; son of Joseph C. and Phyllis (a musician; maiden name, Quaranta) Parisi. *Education:* Attended Duns Scotus College, 1962-64; College of St. Thomas (St. Paul, MN), B.A. (with honors), 1966; University of Chicago, M.A., 1967, Ph.D. (with honors), 1973. *Hobbies and other interests:* Music, photography.

ADDRESSES: Home—3440 North Lake Shore Dr., Chicago, IL 60657. *Office—Poetry*, 601 South Morgan St., Chicago, IL 60680.

CAREER: Roosevelt University, Chicago, IL, assistant professor of English, 1969-78; *Poetry,* Chicago, associate editor, 1976-83, editor, 1983-2003; Modern Poetry Association, executive director, 1995-2003; Poetry Foundation, executive director of publications and programs, 2003—. Visiting professor at University of Illinois at Chicago Circle, 1978-79. Guest speaker at numerous universities and conferences, including King's College, Cambridge, Indiana University, Sewanee Writers' Conference, University of Virginia, University of Florida, and University of Michigan

MEMBER: Delta Epsilon Sigma, Cliff Dwellers.

AWARDS, HONORS: Alvin Bentley Award, Duns Scotus College, 1963; fellow, University of Chicago, 1966-69; Guggenheim fellowship, 2000.

WRITINGS:

(Editor) *The Poetry Anthology, 1912-1977: Sixty-five Years of America's Most Distinguished Verse Magazine,* Houghton Mifflin (Boston, MA), 1978, revised with Stephen Young as *The Poetry Anthology, 1912-2002: Ninety Years of America's Most Distinguished Verse Magazine,* Ivan R. Dee (Chicago, IL), 2002.
Poetry: An American Institution, Modern Poetry Association (Chicago, IL), 1980.
(Editor) *Marianne Moore: The Art of a Modernist,* UMI Research Press (Ann Arbor, MI), 1990.
Poets in Person: A Listener's Guide, Poetry Press (Chicago, IL), 1997.
(Editor, with Stephen Young) *Dear Editor: A History of Poetry in Letters: The First Fifty Years, 1912-1962,* W. W. Norton (New York, NY), 2002.

Contributor of articles, photographs, and reviews to magazines, including *TriQuarterly, New Leader, Sewanee Review,* and *Shenandoah,* and to newspapers. Produced fourteen-part audio series in conjunction with his *Poets in Person,* for National Public Radio.

SIDELIGHTS: Long-time editor of *Poetry* magazine and executive director of that magazine's parent organization, the Poetry Foundation, Joseph Parisi has also written widely on poetry and poets. Collaborating with fellow editor Stephen Young, Parisi produced the 2002 commemorative volume, *Dear Editor: A History of Poetry in Letters: The First Fifty Years, 1912-1962.* The book is a historical glance at *Poetry* magazine under its founding editor, Harriet Monroe. Under Monroe's leadership, the magazine was tremendously influential and powerful, helping make the careers of poets such as Ezra Pound, T. S. Eliot, Carl Sandburg, and Marianne Moore, among a host of other twentieth-century greats. "This big volume centers around the epistolary negotiations Monroe conducted during her years at the journal," explained a contributor for *Publishers Weekly.* Included are letters to and from Monroe, including those of William Carlos Williams, Amy Lowell, Sara Teasdale, and Wallace Stevens. The same reviewer felt that the editors "entertainingly flesh out the magazine's history." Here can be read artistic and monetary complaints, humorous asides, advice to young writers, apologies and gossip from both editor and poets. According to *Library Journal*'s Scott Hightower, the "remarkable group of letters" compiled by

Parisi and Young are "smart, valuable, and engaging." Writing in the *Philadelphia Inquirer Online,* David Yezzi found the collection "excellent and often uproarious." *Booklist*'s Donna Seaman had particular praise for Parisi's "expert and marvelously opinionated commentary," and further found the assortment of letters both "intense and humorous." Similarly, David Kirby, writing in the *New York Times Book Review,* commended Parisi's "generous introduction to each grouping of correspondence."

Again working with Young, Parisi also published in 2002 *The Poetry Anthology, 1912-2002: Ninety Years of American's Most Distinguished Verse Magazine,* in celebration of that journal's ninetieth anniversary of publication. In this update of a 1978 work edited by Parisi, the coeditors include works from the brightest names in twentieth-century poetry, such as Eliot, Sandburg, Pound, Williams, Moore, Stevens, H. D., W. H. Auden, Elizabeth Bishop, Sylvia Plath, James Merrill, and others. In all, the editors gather six thousand "sterling poems," according to *Booklist*'s Seaman, out of the twenty-nine thousand published in the nine decades of the journal's publishing history. These verse contributions "cover a grand spectrum of emotions, outlooks, and literary creativity," Seaman further noted. Yezzi, writing in the *Philadelphia Inquirer Online,* praised Parisi's "splendid and thorough introduction." A reviewer for *Publishers Weekly* observed that almost forty percent of the collected poems "come from Parisi's watch" as editor at *Poetry.* However, this same contributor felt that these poems "fail to represent the explosive range and variety of poetry in English from the last quarter century." For Diane Scharper, though, reviewing this "landmark collection" in *Library Journal,* the poems read like a "Who's Who of American verse."

BIOGRAPHICAL AND CRITICAL SOURCES:

PERIODICALS

Booklist, October 15, 2002, Donna Seaman, review of *Dear Editor: A History of Poetry in Letters: The First Fifty Years, 1912-1962,* p. 378; October 15, 2002, Donna Seaman, review of *The Poetry Anthology, 1912-2002: Ninety Years of American's Most Distinguished Verse Magazine,* p. 381.
Chicago, March, 1979.

Library Journal, December, 2002, Scott Hightower, review of *Dear Editor,* p. 126; January, 2003, Diane Scharper, review of *The Poetry Anthology, 1912-2002,* p. 115.
New York Times, September 4, 2003, p. B11.
New York Times Book Review, December 1, 2002, David Kirby, review of *Dear Editor,* p. 17.
Publishers Weekly, September 23, 2002, review of *Dear Editor,* and *The Poetry Anthology, 1912-2002,* p. 68.

ONLINE

Norton Poets Online, http://www.wwnorton.com/ (March 18, 2003).
Philadelphia Inquirer Online, http://www.philly.com/ (February 9, 2003), David Yezzi, review of *The Poetry Anthology, 1912-2002.*
Poetry Online, http://www.poetrymagazine.org/ (May, 2003).
Sydney Morning Herald Online, http://www.smh.com. au/ (January 4, 2003), John Kinsella, review of *Dear Editor.**

*   *   *

PATTERSON, Peter
See TERSON, Peter

*   *   *

PEARY, Dannis 1949-
(Danny Peary)

PERSONAL: Born August 8, 1949, in Philippi, WV; son of Joseph Y. (a professor) and Laura (Chaitan) Peary; married Suzanne Rafer (an editor), June 21, 1980; children: Zoe. *Education:* University of Wisconsin—Madison, B.A., 1971; University of Southern California, M.A. (with honors), 1975.

ADDRESSES: Home—New York, N.Y. *Office*—15 Stuyvesant Oval 9B, New York, N.Y. 10009. *Agent*—Christine Tomasino, Robert L. Rosen Associates, 7 West 51st St., New York, N.Y. 10019.

CAREER: Writer, 1971—. Script reader for Brut Productions, 1975. Sports editor for *Los Angeles Pan-*

orama, 1976. Photo researcher for Workman Publishing, 1977. Writer for syndicated radio program, "The Tim McCarver Show," 1986.

WRITINGS:

UNDER NAME DANNY PEARY

Close-Ups: The Movie Star Book, Workman (New York, NY), 1978.
(Editor, with brother, Gerald Peary) *The American Animated Cartoon: A Critical Anthology,* Dutton (New York, NY), 1980.
Cult Movies: The Classics, the Sleepers, the Weird and the Wonderful, Dell (New York, NY), 1981.
Cult Movies II: 50 More of the Classics, the Sleepers, the Weird, and the Wonderful, Dell (New York, NY), 1983.
(Editor) *Omni's Screen Flights/Screen Fantasies: The Future According to the Science Fiction Cinema,* introduction by Harlan Ellison, Doubleday (New York, NY), 1984.
Guide for the Film Fanatic, Simon & Schuster (New York, NY), 1986.
Cult Movies III: 50 More of the Classics, the Sleepers, the Weird, and the Wonderful, Simon & Schuster (New York, NY), 1988.
(Editor) *Cult Baseball Players: The Greats, the Flakes, the Weird, and the Wonderful,* Simon & Schuster (New York, NY), 1989.
(With Bruce Chadwick) *How to Buy, Trade and Invest in Baseball Cards and Collectibles: Smart Strategies for Starting, Building, and Enjoying Your Collection,* Simon & Schuster (New York, NY), 1989.
Cult Movie Stars, Simon & Schuster (New York, NY), 1991.
Alternate Oscars: One Critic's Defiant Choices for Best Picture, Actor, and Actress from 1927 to the Present, Delta (New York, NY), 1993.
(Editor) *We Played the Game: 65 Players Remember Baseball's Greatest Era, 1947-1964,* Hyperion (New York, NY), 1994.
Super Bowl, the Game of their Lives, Macmillan (New York, NY), 1997.
(With Tim McCarver) *Tim McCarver's Baseball for Brain Surgeons and Other Fans: Understanding and Interpreting the Game So You Can Watch It Like a Pro,* Villard Books (New York, NY), 1998.
(With Tim McCarver) *The Perfect Season: Why 1998 Was Baseball's Greatest Year,* Villard Books (New York, NY), 1999.

(With Harry Sheehy) *Raising a Team Player: Teaching Kids Lasting Values on the Field, on the Court, and on the Bench,* Storey Books (North Adams, MA), 2002.
(With Ralph Kiner) *Baseball Forever: Reflections on 60 Years in the Game,* Triumph Books (Chicago, IL), 2003.
1001 Reasons to Love Baseball, Stewart, Tabori & Chang (New York, NY), 2004.

Contributor to anthologies. Contributor of articles to newspapers and magazines, including *Philadelphia Bulletin, TV Guide* (Canada and America), *Bijou, Focus on Films, Take One, The Velvet Light Trap, Boston Globe, Newsday,* and *Films and Filming.* Contributing editor for *Video Times,* 1985.

SIDELIGHTS: Danny Peary has written and edited, alone and with others, several volumes dealing with film and sports, particularly baseball. Among his earlier works is *The American Animated Cartoon: A Critical Anthology,* a collection he edited of articles by animators and others involved in the animation industry. Selections include Art Babbit's explanation of the drawing techniques used in *Goofy* cartoons, and Richard Thompson's comments on his *Road Runner-versus-Coyote* film shorts and *Bugs Bunny* and *Daffy Duck* cartoons. Winsor McCay, R. Bray, and Vlad Tytla are among the other animators represented. Walt Disney's testimony before the House Un-American Activities Committee is reproduced in *The American Animated Cartoon,* as are John Canemaker's articles about several of the early developers of animation.

According to *Los Angeles Times Book Review* critic Charles Solomon, the book is "valuable for the amount of information compressed in readily accessible form." He adds, "the fact that enough serious criticism exists to fill a book like *The American Animated Cartoon* is indeed a hopeful sign; this medium is finally receiving its due respect and attention."

Another interesting title Peary penned on the subject of film is 1993's *Alternate Oscars: One Critic's Defiant Choices for Best Picture, Actor, and Actress from 1927 to the Present.* While George W. Hunt, discussing the volume in *America,* noted: "I ended up agreeing with [Peary's] choices more often than not," David Thomson in the *New Republic* felt that "Peary's revisionism underlines the arbitrariness of all Oscars, winners and losers."

Later in his career, Peary worked as a writer for former Cardinals catcher Tim McCarver's syndicated radio program. He also collaborated with McCarver on a couple of books about baseball, 1998's *Tim McCarver's Baseball for Brain Surgeons and Other Fans: Understanding and Interpreting the Game So You Can Watch It Like a Pro* and 1999's *The Perfect Season: Why 1998 Was Baseball's Greatest Year.* Of the former, Ray Hoffman in *Business Week* remarked that Peary and McCarver "show how this simple playground game has nuances and imagery extending far beyond that of any other sport," and called the volume "the Gray's Anatomy of baseball." George Robinson, discussing the second Peary-McCarver collaboration in the *New York Times Book Review,* assured readers that "there are moments of tremendous insight." Peary also edited a volume of recollections from some well-known baseball players from the late 1940s through the 1960s—not the superstars, but good, workman-like players like Dick Ellsworth and George Kell. *We Played the Game: 65 Players Remember Baseball's Greatest Era, 1947-1964* met with praise from Wes Lukowsky in *Booklist,* who called it a "wonderful collection." With Harry Sheehy, Peary tackled the issue of sportsmanship for children in 2002's *Raising a Team Player: Teaching Kids Lasting Values on the Field, on the Court, and on the Bench.* Douglas C. Lord, reviewing it in the *Library Journal,* recommended *Raising a Team Player* as a "heartfelt, instructional work."

Peary once told *CA:*"I treat film as a pop culture: part art, part mass entertainment. I write for no specific audience, but my intention is to make the serious film student more of a fan and the fan more of a student. I choose projects that require research because I am very enthusiastic about film and want to learn, as much as I want to enlighten the reader."

BIOGRAPHICAL AND CRITICAL SOURCES:

BOOKS

Science Fiction and Fantasy Literature, 1975-1991, Gale (Detroit, MI), 1992.

PERIODICALS

America, March 25, 1995, George W. Hunt, review of *Alternate Oscars: One Critic's Defiant Choices for Best Picture, Actor, and Actress from 1927 to the Present,* p. 2.

Booklist, April 15, 1994, Wes Lukowsky, review of *We Played the Game: 65 Players Remember Baseball's Greatest Era, 1947-1964,* p. 1500.

Business Week, April 30, 1998, Ray Hoffman, review of *Tim McCarver's Baseball for Brain Surgeons and Other Fans: Understanding and Interpreting the Game So You Can Watch It Like a Pro.*

Library Journal, May 15, 2002, Douglas C. Lord, review of *Raising a Team Player: Teaching Kids Lasting Values on the Field, on the Court, and on the Bench,* pp. 120-121.

Los Angeles Times Book Review, February 11, 1979; October 12, 1980; September 9, 1984.

New Republic, April 12, 1993, David Thomson, review of *Alternate Oscars,* pp. 39-42.

New York Book Review, May 30, 1999, George Robinson, "Baseball Books in Brief; Big Mac, Sammy and the Yanks," p. 16.

Philadelphia Inquirer, November 4, 1983.

Publishers Weekly, February 16, 2004, review of *Baseball Forever: Reflections on 60 Years in the Game,* p. 164.

Seattle Times, January 2, 1987.

Telegram-Post (Bridgeport, CT), October 1, 1983.*

*   *   *

PEARY, Danny
    See PEARY, Dannis

*   *   *

PECK, Dale 1967-

PERSONAL: Born July 13, 1967, in Bay Shore, NY; son of Dale (a plumber) and Eileen (Staplin) Peck. *Education:* Drew University, B.A., 1989.

ADDRESSES: Agent—Irene Skolnick, 121 West 27th St., Suite 601, New York, NY 10001.

CAREER: Novelist. *Out* magazine, former staff member; AIDS Coalition to Unleash Power (ACT UP), member.

AWARDS, HONORS: Guggenheim fellow, 1994.

WRITINGS:

Martin and John: A Novel, Farrar, Straus & Giroux (New York, NY), 1993, published as *Fucking Martin,* Chatto & Windus (London, England), 1993.

The Law of Enclosures, Farrar, Straus & Giroux (New York, NY), 1996.

Now It's Time to Say Goodbye, Farrar, Straus & Giroux (New York, NY), 1998.

What We Lost: Based on a True Story, Houghton Mifflin (Boston, MA), 2003.

SIDELIGHTS: The appearance of *Martin and John: A Novel* catapulted young writer Dale Peck to the forefront of contemporary American gay fiction. Before the publication of his first novel, Peck was a member of ACT UP in New York City, an AIDS activist group known for their controversial tactics—Peck was the man who disrupted an on-air television newscast in 1990. *Martin and John* developed in part out of Peck's own experiences and relationships, and many reviewers of the book discussed its intensely confessional tone, part autobiography, part anti-autobiography. *Los Angeles Times Book Review* critic Richard Eder termed it "a dazzling explosion of voices and stories that hide behind and emerge out of each other. It is a book of theatrical quick changes."

Because of its layers, its hidden corners, its repetitiveness, *Martin and John* resists an easy description of plot. It is narrated by John, a young man who has fled an abusive household. His lover is Martin, who eventually becomes ill with AIDS, and the sequence of events between them takes place primarily in New York City and Kansas. Interspersed into the sparse narrative action are a legion of smaller stories, each one also involving characters named Martin and John. Sometimes Martin is a rich man who showers young John with love, jewelry, and affection; in other instances he is a fellow security guard in Kansas, a teenage runaway found in a barn, or a sadistic New York pimp. John changes character as well, as he recounts an upbringing fraught with conflict and abuse. Most of his recollections involve a widowed father with a drinking problem who savagely beats John when the teenager admits his homosexuality; other vignettes recount his father dressing up in his dead wife's clothes. In some stories the death of John's mother occurred when he was still young, in other instances she

lingers in a nursing home for years or is perfectly healthy, happy, and divorced—but then one of her boyfriends is a man named Martin who seduces the teenage John. "It can be hard to make out, and I had to go back over it a second time," wrote Eder of *Martin and John*'s complicated structure; "and it changed color and shape somewhat when I did. But the darkness, glitteringly backlit or spotlit . . . prevails almost entirely."

In an interview published in *Contemporary Literary Criticism Yearbook,* Peck explained the genesis of *Martin and John:* "There are autobiographical themes in the book but no autobiography. The only 'real life' aspects of the novel are the settings based on places I've lived. . . . There are similarities in the character of the father to my father, there are similarities in the character of John to my own character, and there are similarities in the female characters to my stepmothers. . . . None of them, however, are actually based on real people." Later in the interview, Peck explained how the structure developed: "The novel originally began with a short story—the story 'Transformations' was the first Martin and John story I wrote. Then, when I wrote another story dealing with the same issues, I couldn't think of character names and so I used the [names Martin and John again]. After writing those two stories, I conceived of the whole project of *Martin and John.* I worked on the book for about four years, and when it was finished I had five hundred pages of manuscript from which I cut 300 pages of stories."

Voice Literary Supplement writer Vince Aletti discussed the novel's spiraling effect between Martin and John's real relationship in the traditional narrative and the fantasy episodes that John writes of in the parallel text, comparing it to a puzzle. "Attempting to transform his history into fiction—something healing, revealing, and 'true'—John can only shuffle things around. And no matter how many times he reinvents his story, he keeps coming back to a few ugly, sad facts: abuse, abandonment, lost love, death." Aletti faulted the approach that Peck undertook, suggesting that by "teasing his story every which way—whipping up raw tragedy, offhand comedy, and lots of hallucinated melodrama with a very small constellation of characters—he's playing author in a showy, postmodern way." In the end Martin dies of AIDS, cared for by John until a terrible demise in a bathtub. The reader next finds the surviving John in his room, writing, and waiting for his own illness to develop.

Many critics praised the first-time novelist and his tour-de-force work. *New York Times* reviewer Michiko Kakutani noted that "if this fiercely written novel offers an indelible portrait of gay life during the plague years, it also opens out to become a universal story about love and loss and the redemptive powers of fiction. It is a story about the cycles of pain and grief that spiral through people's lives, and the efforts an artist makes to reorder and transcend that hurt." Kakutani commended the young author's level of compassion and insight, concluding that "his wisdom about human feelings, his talent for translating those feelings into prose and his sophisticated mastery of literary form all speak to a maturity that belies his twenty-five years. In short, a stunning debut." *Times Literary Supplement* reviewer Gregory Woods faulted Peck for "at times sounding as if he had just been given a thesaurus," yet termed the instances "minor faults in a fascinating first novel." In the *Los Angeles Times Book Review*, Eder asserted that "Peck's first novel has a dark brilliance and moments of real beauty, but it is a book that is shocking, hard to accept fully, and hard to ignore. It is impassioned in its identification with the gay condition, yet it rides fiercely athwart any common notion of political correctness."

Peck's novel *The Law of Enclosures,* according to Victoria Stagg Elliott in *Gay and Lesbian Literature,* consists of "two novellas about heterosexual couples. . . . Their stories of marriage gone bad are told in alternating chapters interrupted by an autobiographical interlude about Peck's mother and the three stepmothers he acquired as a result of his father's frequent marrying." John Brenkman in the *Nation* noted: "There is an extraordinary sense of the risk and adventure of writing in every page of this novel." "Peck's talent," wrote Nancy Pearl in *Booklist,* "is undeniable, and readers willing to take on an unconventional novel will find much to admire. It is filled with powerful writing, unforgettable sentences . . . , and perceptions on love and betrayal that are so painfully acute it is hard to believe Peck is only in his late twenties." A critic for *Publishers Weekly* called *The Law of Enclosures* a "lyrical and boldly constructed novel" and "not only an unblinking look at the dark chambers of the human heart, [but] a brave artistic gamble—one that, ultimately, comes up spades."

Now It's Time to Say Goodbye is set in a small Kansas town where Colin Newman and his boyfriend, Justin Time, have decided, after they realize they know 500 fellow New Yorkers who have died of AIDS, to settle. As Vanessa Bush stated in *Booklist,* "The pair brings with them a conceit that their complicated lives of wealth, betrayal, and cruelty are beyond the comprehension of the rural town." "They soon discover, however, that even here human passions and prejudice run deep," noted David W. Henderson in *Library Journal.* When a local girl is abducted and killed, and Justin is attacked, Colin uncovers dark motives and racial antagonisms among the town's social elite. "Peck," wrote the critic for *Publishers Weekly,* "is a powerful stylist, capable of incandescent descriptions of the unforgiving flatlands from which the town emerged." "Peck's novel," concluded Bush, "is a compelling thriller with subtle and informed knowledge of race relations in the U.S."

BIOGRAPHICAL AND CRITICAL SOURCES:

BOOKS

Contemporary Literary Criticism, Volume 81, Gale (Detroit, MI), 1993.

Gay and Lesbian Literature, Volume 2, St. James Press (Detroit, MI), 1998.

PERIODICALS

Advocate, May 26, 1998, p. 78.

Booklist, December 15, 1995, Nancy Pearl, review of *The Law of Enclosures,* p. 686; February 15, 1998, Vanessa Bush, review of *Now It's Time to Say Goodbye,* p. 948.

Boston Phoenix, December, 1995.

Entertainment Weekly, April 16, 1993, p. 49.

Gay Times, February, 1996, pp. 54-56.

JAMA: Journal of the American Medical Association, March 2, 1994, p. 717.

Lambda Book Report, June, 1998, p. 21.

Library Journal, April 15, 1998, David W. Henderson, review of *Now It's Time to Say Goodbye,* p. 115.

Los Angeles Times Book Review, January 24, 1993, Richard Eder, review of *Martin and John: A Novel,* pp. 3, 7.

Nation, January 29, 1996, John Brenkman, review of *The Law of Enclosures,* p. 31.

New Yorker, February 1, 1993, p. 107.

New York Times, February 9, 1993, Michiko Kakutani, review of *Martin and John,* p. C15.

Observer, May 23, 1993, p. 71.

Publishers Weekly, October 16, 1995, review of *The Law of Enclosures,* p. 40; March 16, 1998, review of *Now It's Time to Say Goodbye,* p. 51.

Times Literary Supplement, March 26, 1993, Gregory Woods, review of *Martin and John,* p. 20.

Tribune Books (Chicago, IL), January 16, 1994, p. 8.

Voice Literary Supplement, February, 1993, Vince Aletti, review of *Martin and John,* pp. 5-6.*

*   *   *

PECK, Robert Newton 1928-

PERSONAL: Born February 17, 1928, in VT; son of F. Haven (a farmer) and Lucile (Dornburgh) Peck; married Dorothy Anne Houston (a librarian and painter), 1958 (marriage ended); married Sharon Ann Michael, 1995; children: (first marriage) Christopher Haven, Anne Houston. *Education:* Rollins College, A.B., 1953; Cornell University, law student. *Religion:* Protestant. *Hobbies and other interests:* Playing ragtime piano, sports.

ADDRESSES: Home—500 Sweetwater Club Circle, Longwood, FL 32779.

CAREER: Writer and farmer. Worked variously as a lumberjack, in a paper mill, as a hog butcher, and as a New York City advertising executive. Director of Rollins College Writers Conference, 1978—. Owner of publishing company, Peck Press. Teacher, and speaker at conferences. *Military service:* U.S. Army, Infantry, 1945-47; served with 88th Division in Italy, Germany, and France; received commendation.

AWARDS, HONORS: Best Books for Young Adults citation, American Library Association, Spring Book Festival Award older honor, *Book World,* both 1973, *Media & Methods* Maxi Award (paperback), 1975, and Colorado Children's Book Award, 1977, all for *A Day No Pigs Would Die; New York Times* Outstanding Book citation, 1973, for *Millie's Boy;* Children's Books of the Year citations, Child Study Association of America, 1973, for *Millie's Boy,* 1975, for *Bee Tree and Other Stuff,* 1976, for *Hamilton,* and 1987, for *Soup on Ice;* Books for the Teen Age citations, New York Public Library, 1980 and 1981, for *A Day No Pigs Would Die,* 1980, 1981, and 1982, for *Hang for*

Robert Newton Peck

Treason, and 1980 and 1982, for *Clunie;* Mark Twain Award, Missouri Association of School Librarians, 1981, for *Soup for President;* Notable Children's Trade Book in the Field of Social Studies citations, National Council for Social Studies/Children's Book Council, 1982, for *Justice Lion,* and 1986, for *Spanish Hoof;* Michigan Young Reader's Award, Michigan Council of Teachers, 1984, for *Soup;* Bologna International Children's Book Fair, 1985, for *Spanish Hoof.*

WRITINGS:

FICTION; FOR CHILDREN AND YOUNG ADULTS

A Day No Pigs Would Die, Knopf (New York, NY), 1972.

Millie's Boy, Knopf (New York, NY), 1973.

Soup, illustrated by Charles Gehm, Knopf (New York, NY), 1974.

Bee Tree and Other Stuff (poems), illustrated by Laura Lydecker, Walker (New York, NY), 1975.

Fawn, Little, Brown (Boston, MA), 1975.

Wild Cat, illustrated by Hal Frenck, Holiday House (New York, NY), 1975.

Soup and Me, illustrated by Charles Lilly, Knopf (New York, NY), 1975.

Hamilton, illustrated by Laura Lydecker, Little, Brown (Boston, MA), 1976.

Hang for Treason, Doubleday (Garden City, NY), 1976.

King of Kazoo (musical), illustrated by William Bryan Park, Knopf (New York, NY), 1976.

Rabbits and Redcoats, illustrated by Laura Lydecker, Walker (New York, NY), 1976.

Trig, illustrated by Pamela Johnson, Little, Brown (Boston, MA), 1977.

Last Sunday, illustrated by Ben Stahl, Doubleday (Garden City, NY), 1977.

The King's Iron, Little, Brown (Boston, MA), 1977.

Patooie, illustrated by Ted Lewin, Knopf (New York, NY), 1977.

Soup for President, illustrated by Ted Lewin, Knopf (New York, NY), 1978.

Eagle Fur, Knopf (New York, NY), 1978.

Trig Sees Red, illustrated by Pamela Johnson, Little, Brown (Boston, MA), 1978.

Mr. Little, illustrated by Ben Stahl, Doubleday (Garden City, NY), 1979.

Basket Case, Doubleday (Garden City, NY), 1979.

Hub, illustrated by Ted Lewin, Knopf (New York, NY), 1979.

Clunie, Knopf (New York, NY), 1979.

Soup's Drum, illustrated by Charles Robinson, Knopf (New York, NY), 1980.

Trig Goes Ape, illustrated by Pamela Johnson, Little, Brown (Boston, MA), 1980.

Soup on Wheels, illustrated by Charles Robinson, Knopf (New York, NY), 1981.

Justice Lion, Little, Brown (Boston, MA), 1981.

Kirk's Law, Doubleday (Garden City, NY), 1981.

Trig or Treat, illustrated by Pamela Johnson, Little, Brown (Boston, MA), 1982.

Banjo, illustrated by Andrew Glass, Knopf (New York, NY), 1982.

Soup in the Saddle, illustrated by Charles Robinson, Knopf (New York, NY), 1983.

The Seminole Seed, Pineapple Press (Englewood, FL), 1983.

Soup's Goat, illustrated by Charles Robinson, Knopf (New York, NY), 1984.

Dukes, Pineapple Press (Englewood, FL), 1984.

Soup on Ice, illustrated by Charles Robinson, Knopf (New York, NY), 1985.

Jo Silver, Pineapple Press (Englewood, FL), 1985.

Spanish Hoof, Knopf (New York, NY), 1985.

Soup on Fire, illustrated by Charles Robinson, Delacorte (New York, NY), 1987.

Soup's Uncle, illustrated by Charles Robinson, Delacorte (New York, NY), 1988.

Hallapoosa, Walker (New York, NY), 1988.

The Horse Hunters, Random House (New York, NY), 1988.

Arly, Walker (New York, NY), 1989.

Soup's Hoop, illustrated by Charles Robinson, Delacorte (New York, NY), 1990.

Higbee's Halloween, Walker (New York, NY), 1990.

Little Soup's Hayride, Dell (New York, NY), 1991.

Little Soup's Birthday, Dell (New York, NY), 1991.

Arly's Run, Walker (New York, NY), 1991.

Soup in Love, Delacorte (New York, NY), 1992.

Little Soup's Turkey, illustrated by Charles Robinson, Dell (New York, NY), 1992.

Little Soup's Bunny, Dell (New York, NY), 1993.

Soup Ahoy, illustrated by Charles Robinson, Knopf (New York, NY), 1994.

A Part of the Sky, Knopf (New York, NY), 1994.

Soup 1776, illustrated by Charles Robinson, Knopf (New York, NY), 1995.

Nine Man Tree, Random House (New York, NY), 1998.

Cowboy Ghost, HarperCollins (New York, NY), 1999.

Extra Innings, HarperCollins (New York, NY), 2001.

Horse Thief, HarperCollins (New York, NY), 2002.

Bro, HarperCollins (New York, NY), 2004.

FICTION; FOR ADULTS

The Happy Sadist, Doubleday (Garden City, NY), 1962.

NONFICTION

Path of Hunters: Animal Struggle in a Meadow, illustrated by Betty Fraser, Knopf (New York, NY), 1973.

Secrets of Successful Fiction, Writer's Digest (Cincinnati, OH), 1980.

Fiction Is Folks: How to Create Unforgettable Characters, Writer's Digest (Cincinnati, OH), 1983.

My Vermont, Peck Press (Longwood, FL), 1985.

My Vermont II, Peck Press (Longwood, FL), 1988.

Also author of songs, television commercials, and jingles. Adapter of novels *Soup and Me, Soup for President,* and *Mr. Little* for television's *Afterschool Specials,* American Broadcasting Companies, Inc. (ABC-TV).

ADAPTATIONS: Soup was adapted for television and broadcast by ABC-TV, 1978; *A Day No Pigs Would Die* was adapted for audiocassette and released by Listening Library.

WORK IN PROGRESS: An autobiography, titled *Weeds in Bloom,* scheduled for publication by Random House in 2005.

SIDELIGHTS: The strength of Robert Newton Peck's works stems from their striking depictions of the past. Many of his books bring to life the rural Vermont of his childhood, describing the adventures and encounters with nature that helped shape his life. The six-foot-four-inch tall Peck once described himself as follows: "I wear mule-car boots, a ten-gallon hat, Western shirts and weigh over 200 pounds." Peck went on to observe, "Socially, I'm about as sophisticated as a turnip. . . . I'm an expert skier, a dismal dancer, and I love horses." Sophisticated or not, the author has penned a long list of books for children, many of which reflect his boyhood struggle with the competitiveness of nature and its impending threat of death. Peck, who lives on a five-hundred-acre ranch in Florida, has also written poetry, adult novels, and how-to books for would-be writers.

Educators figure prominently in Peck's fiction, thanks to the influence of his first, much-admired teacher—he still respectfully refers to her as "Miss Kelly." "A lot of my characters are teachers—all of whom are strong, fair, and respected," Peck once explained. Although reading was a skill revered by Peck's family and neighbors when he was a boy, not everyone was privileged enough to learn how to do it. In Peck's own family no one had ever attended school before him, although he was the youngest of seven children. Luckily, he was able to convince his parents to let him join the other students. Miss Kelly kindled the minds of the first-through-sixth grades in what Peck described in an essay for *Something about the Author Autobiography Series* (SAAS) as a "tumble-down, one-room, dirt-road school in rural Vermont." There she taught the children to wash up before handling any of the few, but treasured, books. *Ivanhoe, The Wind in the Willows,* and *Tom Sawyer* were some of the classics Miss Kelly read to her classes, along with biographies of outstanding personalities such as Booker T. Washington, Mark Twain, and Charles Lindbergh.

Peck not only grew up to write many books of his own, he also married a librarian, Dorrie, in 1958. The best man at their wedding was none other than Fred Rogers, the star of the popular *Mister Rogers' Neighborhood* television show for children; Peck had met him in college. Writing about his own children, Christopher Haven and Anne Houston, Peck once stated, "I hope they both grow up to have a tough gut and a gentle heart. Because I don't want to sire a world of macho men or feminist women, but rather a less strident society of ladies and gentlemen."

Peck's writing career began with *A Day No Pigs Would Die.* The book is based on memories of his father, "an illiterate farmer and pig-slaughterer whose earthy wisdom continues to contribute to my understanding of the natural order and old Shaker beliefs deeply rooted in the land and its harvest," Peck once observed. In the story, a young boy comes of age when he must summon the will to kill his pet pig on the family farm in Vermont. The book was met with mixed reviews because of the graphic account of the butchering, but for the most part Peck earned praise for his honest and unsentimental story. *A Part of the Sky* continues the young boy's story as he becomes responsible for his mother, his aunt, and the mortgage payments for the family farm following his father's death. *A Day No Pigs Would Die* marked the beginning of Peck's long writing career in which an *Authors and Artists for Young Adults* essayist noted, "hard work, self-sufficiency, and the importance of education are predominant."

A boy named "Soup" is featured in Peck's *Soup,* and in a number of his following works. "Rob and Soup, though abrim with rascality, respect their beloved Miss Kelly, her Vermont virtue—and her ruler," Peck once remarked. Like Miss Kelly, the character Soup is based on a real person in Peck's life: his closest friend in childhood. Describing the real Soup in his autobiographical essay, Peck expressed his view that "When a boy has a best friend, he's the richest kid on Earth." He went on to note that Soup's "real and righteous name was Luther Wesley Vinson, and he grew up too to become a minister." In *Soup Ahoy,* the thirteenth book of the series, Soup and his pal Rob enter a contest sponsored by Soggymushies cereal and win a visit from radio star Sinker O. Sailor. The book is filled with puns, alliteration, and other forms of word play.

For *Higbee's Halloween* Peck created the humorous "Soup-like" characters of Higbee Higginbottom and Quincy Cobb. Their pranks are typical for boys growing up in the 1930s until the Striker children move to Clod's Corner. After the Strikers use their homemade torture chamber, Higbee comes up with a plan to get revenge during the town's Halloween celebration.

Arly is the story of eleven-year-old Arly Poole, who seems destined to be a vegetable picker and slave to the owner of his hometown of Jailtown, Florida, until a schoolteacher arrives in town. He experiences many heartbreaks, including the death of his father. In *Arly's Run,* Peck continues Arly's harrowing tale. He recounts Arly's unsuccessful attempt as a twelve-year-old to escape Jailtown, his capture by company men and forced labor on a work gang, and his ultimate escape with an elderly picker named Coo Coo.

Peck's *Spanish Hoof* and *The Horse Hunters* are two coming-of-age novels set on ranches. In *Spanish Hoof,* twelve-year-old Harriet, called Harry, lives on a Florida cattle ranch during the Depression with her mother, younger brother, and hired hands. Harry relates the threats to the herd and her family and her decision to sell her pony to save the ranch. "The only problem is the language Harriet uses to tell her story," noted Anne Tyler in the *Washington Post Book World.* "It's dialect in the extreme, and although it may be perfectly authentic, it sounds forced and is often difficult to understand." *The Horse Hunters* likewise is set in Depression-era Florida. The novel features fifteen-year-old Ladd Bodeen, who sets out to prove his manhood to his difficult older brother by going on a wild mustang roundup, an adventure that is danger packed.

Nine Man Tree is the story of "an illiterate, dirt-poor family" who "suffers under the rule of an abusive father," wrote a reviewer in *Publishers Weekly.* The story is set in backwoods Florida in 1931 where a wild boar is terrorizing the swamp, killing anything in its path. The protagonist is Yoolee, whose father is fatally wounded by the boar during the hunt. The boar is finally killed by an elderly Native American man. "The Southern dialect is vigorous, even poetic, and the details shine sharp as a knife blade," continued the reviewer. *Booklist*'s Helen Rosenberg called *Nine Man Tree* "an intriguing story with an unusual setting." Rosenberg noted that Peck's writing "transports readers smoothly to another time and place."

Peck's *Cowboy Ghost* focuses on Titus MacRobinson, the sixteen-year-old son of a Florida rancher. To prove himself to his father, Titus sets out with his older brother, Micah, to lead a cattle drive. Along the way, Titus gains insights into the lives of his brother, his family, and himself. Roger Leslie wrote in *Booklist,* "The strength of the novel emerges from richly drawn characters whose evolution is unpredictable but entirely believable."

"Peck shines as he writes about a Depression-era black baseball team" in *Extra Innings,* lauded Kelly Milner Halls in *Booklist.* Peck tells the story of Tate Stonemason, a recently orphaned young boy left handicapped after a plane crash, whose dream of playing professional baseball has been shattered. Helping him cope with the losses in his life is Aunt Vidalia, the African-American adopted daughter of Tate's great-grandfather. Vidalia relays to Tate the story of a poor African-American baseball team in the South during the Great Depression, who battled racism and hatred in their travels. "The account of the barnstorming team, getting by on a shoestring and finding kindness and hatred in the deep South, is the best part of this book," wrote Todd Morning in *School Library Journal.*

Horse Thief is Peck's entertaining, often humorous, novel about seventeen-year-old Tullis Yoder. Tullis works as a hand at the Big Bubb Stampede Rodeo, hoping to get the chance to one day compete. When the chance arises, Tullis mounts a bull named Gutbuster, only to lose two fingers when he falls from the bull. When the star of the show dies during a bull-riding stunt, the owner decides to close the show and sell the horses to the slaughterhouse. Tullis cannot bear the thought of losing his beloved horses. Adventure ensues as Tullis, his doctor, and her father go on a mission to rescue the thirteen horses. "Witty, unpredictable, and a 'dam' good story that refuses to take itself too seriously, *Horse Thief* will have readers cheering for Tullis, his friends and their herd of thirteen," noted Carol Schene in *School Library Journal.* A *Publishers Weekly* reviewer called *Horse Thief* a "highly entertaining ride," while *Booklist*'s Debbie Carton dubbed it "a convoluted and surprisingly funny odyssey, chock-full of engaging characters."

Among Peck's many other works are three historical novels which arose from his interest in the Colonial and Revolutionary periods in American history. The children in *Hang for Treason, Fawn,* and *Rabbits and Redcoats* are believable because of Peck's view that children are the same regardless of the time period in which they are born.

Although many of his works have been well received by children and young adults, Peck once commented that he "didn't start out to write for any particular age group. If my books turn out to be right for teenagers, as well as adults and/or kids, it just happens that way. I can only write about what I know and I've never been shy about telling people what I know. As a matter of fact, when I told my mother . . . that three of my books were about to be published by a very important publishing house, she thought for a minute, looked up at me and said, 'Son, you always did have a lot to say.'" No matter who reads his books, though, Peck considers it extremely important to motivate young people to read. One motivator is to read a chapter out loud to children, suggested Peck, so they will be eager to find out what happens next. "My richest talent is making a kid smile. And getting him to read and write," Peck pointed out in his autobiographical essay. He even takes the time to answer up to one hundred letters weekly from fans in the United States and abroad.

When asked why he includes so much of himself in his writing, Peck related in his *Fiction Is Folks* that it's "because I've got so much of *me* to give. Like you, I am abrim with likes, dislikes, talents, cumbersome inabilities, joys, triumphs, and failures . . . so why should I even consider wasting such a storehouse?" He went on to say in *SAAS* that "compared to the worth of so many talented authors, my novels aren't really so doggone great. Yet secretly, I truly believe that I am the best teacher of creative writing in the entire galaxy." And most important, he concluded, "Life is fun. It's a hoot and a holler. If you can't revel in America and enjoy all the wonderful Americans you meet, you wouldn't be happy in Heaven or even in Florida." Peck once told *CA* that, after a bout with cancer during the mid-1990s that entailed surgeries and numerous radiation treatments, he is cured and once again appearing onstage "playing concert-level jazz and ragtime piano, and making people laugh."

BIOGRAPHICAL AND CRITICAL SOURCES:

BOOKS

Authors and Artists for Young Adults, Gale (Detroit, MI), Volume 3, 1990, Volume 43, 2002.

Beacham's Guide to Literature for Young Adults, Volume 1, Beacham (Washington, DC), 1990.

Contemporary Literary Criticism, Volume 17, Gale (Detroit, MI), 1981.

Continuum Encyclopedia of Children's Literature, Continuum (New York, NY), 2001.

Encyclopedia of World Biography, 2nd edition, Gale (Detroit, MI), 1998.

Literature and Its Times, Volume 3, Gale (Detroit, MI), 1997.

Peck, Robert Newton, *Fiction Is Folks,* Writer's Digest (Cincinnati, OH), 1983.

St. James Guide to Young Adults Writers, 2nd edition, St. James Press (Detroit, MI), 1999.

Something about the Author Autobiography Series, Volume 1, Gale (Detroit, MI), 1986, pp. 235-247.

Twentieth-Century Children's Writers, 3rd edition, St. James Press (Detroit, MI), 1989.

PERIODICALS

Booklist, February 15, 1989, p. 995; December 15, 1991, p. 759; February 15, 1994, p. 1082; August, 1998, Helen Rosenberg, review of *Nine Man Tree,* p. 2008; June 1, 1999, Roger Leslie, review of *Cowboy Ghost,* p. 1816; February 1, 2001, Kelly Milner Halls, review of *Extra Innings,* p. 1046; May 15, 2002, Debbie Carton, review of *Horse Thief,* p. 1605.

Book Report, March, 1999, review of *Nine Man Tree,* p. 62.

Books for Young People, April 15, 1994, p. 562.

Bulletin of the Center for Children's Books, December, 1998, review of *Nine Man Tree,* p. 142; March, 1999, review of *Cowboy Ghost,* p. 252; March, 2001, review of *Extra Innings,* p. 275.

Children's Book Review Service, April, 1985, p. 100; June, 1989, p. 126; January 1991, p. 58.

Horn Book, August, 1973; October, 1973; April, 1976; December, 1976.

Kirkus Reviews, September 15, 1988, p. 1352; November 15, 1991, p. 1474; July 15, 1994, p. 943; September 1, 1998, review of *Nine Man Tree,* p. 1291; December 15, 1998, review of *Cowboy Ghost,* p. 1802; May 15, 2002, review of *Horse Thief,* p. 739.

Kliatt Young Adult Paperback Book Guide, March, 1998, review of *A Part of the Sky,* p. 14; May, 1999, review of *Cowboy Ghost,* p. 12.

New York Times, January 4, 1973.

New York Times Book Review, May 13, 1973; November 13, 1994, p. 27.

Publishers Weekly, September 16, 1988, p. 66; March 10, 1989, p. 91; October 18, 1993, audiobook review of *A Day No Pigs Would Die,* p. 28; August 22, 1994, review of *A Part of the Sky,* p. 41; August, 17, 1998, review of *Nine Man Tree,* p. 73; November 23, 1998, reviews of *Soup on Wheels, Soup for President, Soup 1776,* and *Soup,* p. 69; January 11, 1999, review of *Cowboy Ghost,* p. 73; January 15, 2001, review of *Extra Innings,* p. 77; June 10, 2002, review of *Horse Thief,* p. 61.

School Library Journal, May, 1985, p. 105; June, 1989, p. 108; October, 1990, p. 118; February, 1992, p. 108; March, 1994, p. 223; October, 1995, p. 139; November, 1998, review of *Nine Man Tree,* p. 126; March, 1999, review of *Cowboy Ghost,* p. 213; March, 2001, Todd Morning, review of *Extra Innings,* p. 255; July, 2002, Carol Schene, review of *Horse Thief,* p. 124.

Voice of Youth Advocates, October, 1985, p. 259; June, 1989, p. 105; August, 1989, p. 160; December, 1990, p. 287; April, 1992, p. 34; August, 2001, review of *Extra Innings,* p. 206.

Washington Post Book World, May 12, 1985, p. 116; May 8, 1994, p. 20.

ONLINE

Children's Literature, http://www.childrenslit.com/ (November 22, 2002), review of *Cowboy Ghost.*

Robert Newton Peck Web site, http://my.athenet.net/~blahnik/rnpeck/ (November 24, 2003).

*   *   *

PENDLETON, Don
    See OBSTFELD, Raymond

*   *   *

PETERSON, Dale 1944-

PERSONAL: Born November 20, 1944, in Corning, NY; son of Paul G. (an engineer) and Hazel (a registered nurse; maiden name, Peterson) Peterson; married Wyn Kelley, June 26, 1979; children: Britt Kelley. *Education:* University of Rochester, B.A., 1967; Stanford University, M.A., 1969, Ph.D., 1977.

ADDRESSES: Home—Stanford, CA. *Office*—261 Hamilton, Suite 211, Palo Alto, CA 94301.

CAREER: Veterans Administration Hospital, Menlo Park, CA, psychiatric nursing attendant, 1969-71; Stanford University, Stanford, CA, instructor in writing, 1977-78; ARS Construction, Palo Alto, CA, carpenter, 1978-79; Rainbow Designs, Palo Alto, CA, carpenter, 1979-80; full-time writer, 1980—.

WRITINGS:

Big Things from Little Computers: A Layperson's Guide to Personal Computing, Prentice-Hall (Englewood Cliffs, NJ), 1982.

Genesis II: Creation and Recreation with Computers, Reston Publishing (Reston, VA), 1983.

(With Don Inman and Ramon Zamora) *Color Computer LOGO,* Wiley (New York, NY), 1985.

The Deluge and the Ark: A Journey into Primate Worlds, Houghton Mifflin (Boston, MA), 1989.

(With Jane Goodall) *Visions of Caliban: On Chimpanzees and People,* Houghton Mifflin (Boston, MA), 1993.

Chimpanzee Travels: On and off the Road in Africa, Addison-Wesley (Reading, MA), 1995.

Storyville USA, University of Georgia Press (Athens, GA), 1999.

Eating Apes, photographs by Karl Ammann, University of California Press (Berkeley, CA), 2003.

EDITOR

A Mad People's History of Madness, University of Pittsburgh Press (Pittsburgh, PA), 1982.

Intelligent Schoolhouse: Readings on Computers and Learning, Reston Publishing (Reston, VA), 1983.

Jane Goodall, *Africa in My Blood: An Autobiography in Letters; The Early Years,* Houghton Mifflin (Boston, MA), 2000.

Jane Goodall, *Beyond Innocence: An Autobiography in Letters; The Later Years,* Houghton Mifflin (Boston, MA), 2001.

Author of "Greetings from Uncle Bert," a monthly column in *Rainbow.* Contributing editor, *Rainbow.*

SIDELIGHTS: Dale Peterson once told *CA:* "I think of myself as a frustrated fiction writer. I wrote some short stories that I thought were pretty good, got tired of receiving rejection slips, then wrote a novel, thinking the publication of that would get stories published. I got tired of receiving rejection slips, so I put together *A Mad People's History of Madness,* thinking that the publication of a nonfiction work would help get the novel published. Meanwhile I supported myself by being a graduate student and then (having graduated) a carpenter.

"*A Mad People's History of Madness* is unique; it is the only history of psychiatry as told by mental patients. It covers five and a half centuries of psychiatry, from 1436 to 1976, is based upon selections from twenty-six mental patient autobiographies, but includes extensive background material on psychiatric history, which I wrote.

"I became interested in mental patient autobiographies during the two years that I worked as a psychiatric nursing assistant. In gathering material for the book, I went through indexes in most major libraries here and in England. I then read the material and selected the pieces I thought were most interesting and representative.

"The leap from a doctorate in literature to psychiatry, thence to carpentry and computers, may seem a little strange, but I believe there is a common thread (excepting carpentry, which was soup-in-the-pot activity). My psychiatry book was really the work of a literature person and humanist looking at psychiatry. Similarly with my book on computers. Generally I write about computers from a 'humanist' perspective—being less concerned about the nuts and bolts and more about the philosophical and human aspects of this technology.

"During the period of carpentry I had been writing children's stories (which I couldn't get published). Then one day I called up Prentice-Hall and told them they needed a book about computers written by someone (me) who knew nothing about the subject. That was my first computer book, *Big Things from Little Computers: A Layperson's Guide to Personal Computing.* My second computer book, *Genesis II: Creation and Recreation with Computers,* is about computers in the visual arts, music, writing, and games. It is a coffee-table book with lots of illustrations, including a color section containing computer-generated art.

"My plan is to earn enough money so that I can afford to take some time off and write fiction."

BIOGRAPHICAL AND CRITICAL SOURCES:

PERIODICALS

Library Journal, May 15, 2003, Beth Clewis Crim, review of *Eating Apes,* pp. 120-121.*

*   *   *

PHILLIPS, Adam

PERSONAL: Male.

ADDRESSES: Home—England. *Agent*—c/o Author Mail, Pantheon Books, 201 East 50th St., New York, NY 10022.

CAREER: Psychoanalyst, literary critic, author, and editor. Charing Cross Hospital, London, England, principal child therapist; Wolverton Gardens Child and Family Consultation Center, London, principal child psychotherapist.

WRITINGS:

Winnicott, Harvard University Press (Cambridge, MA), 1988.

On Kissing, Tickling, and Being Bored: Psychoanalytic Essays on the Unexamined Life, Harvard University Press (Cambridge, MA), 1993.

On Flirtation: Psychoanalytic Essays on the Uncommitted Life, Harvard University Press (Cambridge, MA), 1994.

Terrors and Experts, Harvard University Press (Cambridge, MA), 1996.

Monogamy, Pantheon (New York, NY), 1996.

The Beast in the Nursery: On Curiosity and Other Appetites, Pantheon (New York, NY), 1998.

Darwin's Worms, Basic Books (New York, NY), 2000.

Houdini's Box: The Art of Escape, Pantheon Books (New York, NY) 2001.

Promises, Promises: Essays on Psychoanalysis and Literature, Basic Books (New York, NY), 2001.
Equals (essays), Basic Books (New York, NY), 2002.

EDITOR

Charles Lamb, *Selected Prose,* Penguin (Harmondsworth, Middlesex, England), 1985.

(And author of introduction) Walter Pater, *The Renaissance: Studies in Art and Poetry,* Oxford University Press (Oxford, England), 1986.

(And author of introduction) Edmund Burke, *A Philosophical Enquiry into the Origin of Our Ideas of the Sublime and Beautiful,* Oxford University Press (Oxford, England), 1990.

Michael Eigen, *The Electrified Tightrope* (essays), Jason Aronson (Northvale, NJ), 1993.

(With Hugh Haughton and Geoffrey Summerfield) *John Clare in Context,* Cambridge University Press (Cambridge, England), 1994.

SIDELIGHTS: The prolific and witty Adam Phillips has made his mark as both a psychotherapist writing on that discipline and, earlier, as a literary critic devoted to such British classics as John Clare, Charles Lamb, and Walter Pater. During the 1990s Phillips became known to the educated general public as "the Oliver Sacks of psychoanalysis," in the words of Dwight Garner of *Salon.com,* or "the Will Self of thought," according to Linda Grant in the *New Statesman.*

Phillips's first book on psychotherapy, *Winnicott* (1988), was dubbed an "elegant" study of the British analyst D. W. Winnicott (1896-1971) by Sherry Turkle in the *London Review of Books.* Winnicott, according to *Times Literary Supplement* contributor Peter L. Rudnytsky, was "the most important native-born English psychoanalyst." A specialist in children (as is Phillips), he was best known for his theory of the "good enough mother": the mother who, although by definition imperfect, provides a secure and stable enough bond in the earliest years, thereby allowing the child to grow as an independent person. Rudnytsky found Phillips's study to be "a distinguished addition to the growing body of literature" on Winnicott, and "especially illuminating on Winnicott's life." That reviewer faulted Phillips, however, for accusing Winnicott of a "flight from the erotic" and a "flight into infancy." Nevertheless, Rudnytsky admired "the spirit of

independent thinking that Winnicott himself fostered" in a volume whose author joined "the sensibility of a practitioner with that of a man of letters." For *New Statesman* contributor Daniel Pick, "Phillips's own style nicely replicates something of the gentle charm and the occasionally startling phrase-making to be found in Winnicott's writing. . . . [We] are left, above all, with an image of Winnicott's exceptional good humour."

Phillips next produced *On Kissing, Tickling, and Being Bored: Psychoanalytic Essays on the Unexamined Life* (1993), which Sarah Boxer, in the *New York Times Book Review,* called "poetic." Boxer observed that the general theme of the essays is that of "[the] fear of letting oneself go," and that Phillips values boredom as a stage of preliminary waiting for something unknown: a stage that requires the freedom to let go. *New Statesman* contributor Adrianne Blue labeled the book "brilliant," admiring especially the chapter on obstacles, which, for Phillips, are the screens for unconscious desire. D. J. Enright, in the *London Review of Books,* wrote a respectful essay in which he called *On Kissing, Tickling, and Being Bored* "a peculiarly difficult book to review because it reviews itself as it goes along and is hardly to be described in other than its own words." Enright enjoyed, however, Phillips's "sparkling apophthegms," the effect of which he claimed is "not unlike being hit repeatedly on the head by a small, pointed hammer." Among these apophthegms are descriptions of psychoanalysis as "a circus with many acts," "a story—and a way of telling stories—that makes some people feel better," and "a conversation that enables people to understand what stops them from having the kinds of conversation they want."

Phillips collected more essays, as well as lectures and book reviews, into his 1994 book, *On Flirtation: Psychoanalytic Essays on the Uncommitted Life.* He views flirtation as "the game of taking chances"—a way, in other words, of establishing a "contingent self" which, in contrast to the traditional psychoanalytic view of the self, does not always know what it desires. Fittingly, the collection itself treats briefly a wide number of subjects, including Freud, John Clare, Good and Evil, and, once again, Winnicott. *Los Angeles Times Book Review* contributor Susan Salter Reynolds remarked that this is "not a flirtatious treatment of flirtation." R. H. Balsam, in *Choice,* felt that Phillips's opinions are "extremely interesting" and that his "style dazzles in originality, elegant paradox, and aphorism. He is a master of the arresting opening sentence." Janet Malcolm, in the *New York Times Book Review,* called the collection "interestingly strange" for its "tension between Mr. Phillips's attraction to and revulsion from psychoanalysis, an ambivalence that runs through it like a red thread."

Phillips examines the field of psychoanalysis again in his 1996 book *Terrors and Experts,* a brief collection of six essays. The terrors mentioned in the title are the fears that beset children and adults; and the experts are the therapists. Phillips takes issue with the "mystique of expertise," which he feels many therapists suffered from, and offers a brand of therapy that tries to be interesting—and to make life itself interesting—rather than important or true. For this reason, critic David Herman, in the *New Statesman,* called Phillips himself "an interesting figure" who "has started to put present-day psychoanalysis on the map—who has ditched the old baggage . . . and offers a psychoanalysis which is surprising." Herman felt that the book, at times, needs "some greater ballast . . . solid ground." But he admired Phillips's "striking . . . intellectual confidence" and noted that "few analysts since Freud have written as well as Phillips." Reviewing the slim volume in *Salon.com,* Garner hailed Phillips as "a charming and casually profound essayist," and his books, on the whole, as "wonderful (and wonderfully-titled)." In *Library Journal,* contributor E. James Lieberman applauded Phillips's "provocative, aphoristic style," and added, "This lean book sparkles with ideas, many jewellike." Reviewer Judith Shulevitz of the *New York Times* appreciated Phillips as "a miniaturist, magnifying the apparently trivial or often overlooked," and averred, "In Mr. Phillips's hands, psychoanalysis becomes an instrument of reproducible magic, a poetics you can use at home." And a *Publishers Weekly* contributor gave the nod to *Terrors and Experts* as "lucid" and "comprehensible" to the layperson.

Phillips followed *Terrors and Experts* with another brief volume, *Monogamy,* in which he examines the related questions of the functions of monogamy and of infidelity, beginning by asking what would happen if the human race were commanded not to be monogamous for more than three weeks. Novelist Linda Grant, in the *New Statesman,* responded archly that such an experiment had been tried out in San Francisco's gay community in the 1970s and early 1980s, with the result that later decades of gay men flocked back

toward monogamy as an ideal. Grant called *Monogamy* "the season's sexy must-read," but criticized it for being "intensely irritating, smug, and pleased with itself," and lacking in a felt sense of human life and relationships. Phillips's ideas, Grant believed, are sometimes "genuinely thought-provoking," and sometimes merely showy witticisms. The book is arranged into 121 very short essays, each occupying one page or less; this prompted *Publishers Weekly* to label it an "iconoclastic meditation" and to compare it with Zen koans and some of the writing of Scottish psychiatrist R. D. Laing. "Full of irony and paradox, spiked with psychoanalytic insights, these . . . [essays] titillate but rarely satisfy," the *Publishers Weekly* contributor commented. Melanie Du Bois Custer, reviewing *Monogamy* for the *Washington Post Book World,* compared its disorderly thematic development to that of Shakespeare's sonnets. "Reading this book is like consulting an oracle; its enigmatic, disconnected statements offer stimulation, not advice," Custer said. "If you are not irritated by the gnomic manner, you may be fascinated."

In 1998 Phillips explored psychoanalysis through the lens of childhood in *The Beast in the Nursery: On Curiosity and Other Appetites.* Here, he presents psychoanalysis as a potential tool for restoring people to the sense of curiosity, wonder, and desire—the sense of appetite, according to the title—that a civilized upbringing often destroys. Wrote Stephen Greenblatt in the *New York Times,* "The restoration of a vigorous, wide-ranging interest in life is an admirable goal, and Phillips addresses himself to the task with wit, humane intelligence and a sensitivity to the insights of Shakespeare, Blake, Keats, and Henry James, alongside those of Freud and D. W. Winnicott." *Publishers Weekly* approved of the book as "lively and engaging. . . . well written and accessible," on a subject that is of paramount importance in daily life as well as psychoanalysis.

In *Darwin's Worms,* Phillips argues that two pioneers of biological and social thinking, Charles Darwin and Sigmund Freud, were focused primarily on ideas of death. Phillips examines their theories and life stories to determine how Darwin and Freud dealt with the "implications and consequences" of their theories, wrote a critic on the *Complete Review* Web site. This interest was manifested in Darwin's ideas of the extinction of species central to Darwin's ideas, and "the individual's pursuit of his own happiness and death for Freud," the *Complete Review* critic wrote. "Phillips's ideas may not convince," the *Complete Review* critic concluded, "but they are interesting ideas to entertain, and Phillips presents them fairly well."

In 2002's *Equals,* Phillips offers a collection of essays and reviews centering around the practice of psychoanalysis and the idea of psychoanalysis as a representation of democracy in microcosm. "What could we learn if we took the relationship between therapist and patient as an exercise in democracy? he wonders," related Emily Eakin in *New York Times.* "Could psychoanalysis tell us something about why, in a society formally wedded to the notion of equality, we invest so much energy creating hierarchies of power and prestige?" Further, Nicholas Fearn, writing in the *Spectator,* noted that "the best means yet devised of dealing with the tumult of voices in public life is democracy. So why, asks the psychoanalyst Adam Phillips in his fascinating books, should the same model not be applied to the private life of the mind?" Psychoanalysts such as D. W. Winnicutt and Phillips himself assert that during the psychoanalytic process, the patient and the analyst are both individuals of equal status in the therapeutic relationship. Phillips also argues such points that since therapy is intended to help patients deal with inner conflict, it is a type of democratic process since conflict (and the need to hear all sides of an issue) is "an essential side effect of democracy; everyone has a voice," Eakin wrote. "Despite such promising ammunition and his considerable rhetorical skill, however, Phillips's vision of 'democratic psychoanalysis' never amounts to much more than vague, rose-tinted fantasy," Eakin concluded.

Houdini's Box: The Art of Escape is "a readable and thought-provoking short treatise on the notion of escape," wrote Raj Persaud in the *British Medical Journal.* Phillips "argues that much of our behavior can be properly understood only as reflecting an unconscious desire to run away from something that we want to avoid in our lives," Persaud remarked. Combining detailed case histories with an in-depth analysis of a literal and symbolic master of escape, Harry Houdini, Phillips lays out his theories of escapism and how it manifests itself in the lives of psychiatric patients and those without psychological impairments. The deeply rooted need to escape may be manifested in such behavior as frequent job changes as well as failing to know what one wants until he escapes from it, as was the case with one of Phillips's patients. In addition to what *BookPage* reviewer Alan Prince called "an intellectual autopsy on Houdini," Phillips offers the idea that "our lives are largely shaped by what he calls exits, elsewheres, and avoidances," Prince remarked. "Escape, Phillips suggests, is an end in itself," wrote Gaby Wood for the *Guardian Unlimited,* "and more of a foundation myth for our lives than we might suppose." Notions of escape appear in our literature, our classical mythology, and our philosophy, continually surrounding us with the idea of escape and giving us basic ideas of how to achieve it. Phillips even interprets one of Christendom's fundamental stories, that of Adam and Eve, as a story of escape.

Critics such as Persaud caution against a wholesale acceptance of Phillips's ideas of escape, noting that "it is not always helpful to conclude that everything means something else." A *Publishers Weekly* reviewer observed, "Although Phillips writes elegantly, and is capable of provocative analytic insights, he sometimes lapses into banal aphorisms or puzzling digressions." *Guardian Unlimited* critic Wood found Phillips's approach more straightforward, however. "Though Phillips's territory is complication, he reports back from his travels in the simplest of words," the *Guardian* reviewer observed. "He is perhaps single-handedly continuing the tradition of the world's best essayists, yet there is nothing arch or highfalutin about his writing. I would recommend it to anyone who ever liked to entertain a thought."

BIOGRAPHICAL AND CRITICAL SOURCES:

PERIODICALS

Booklist, July, 2001, Donna Seaman, review of *Houdini's Box: The Art of Escape,* p. 1953.
British Medical Journal, October 13, 2001, Raj Persaud, review of *Houdini's Box,* p. 873.
Choice, May, 1995, p. 1528.
Economist, April 21, 2001, review of *Houdini's Box,* p. 81.
Entertainment Weekly, March 30, 2001, review of *Darwin's Worms,* p. 63; August 3, 2001, review of *Houdini's Box,* p. 63.
Globe and Mail, January 13, 2001, review of *Darwin's Worms,* p. D6.

Kirkus Reviews, May 15, 2001, review of *Houdini's Box,* p. 727.

Library Journal, March 1, 1996, p. 94; February 15, 2001, review of *Promises, Promises: Essays on Psychoanalysis and Literature,* p. 168.

London Review of Books, November 23, 1989, pp. 13-14; March 25, 1993, p. 14; November 11, 1999, review of *Darwin's Worms,* p. 7.

Los Angeles Times Book Review, November 13, 1994, p. 6.

New Statesman, February 24, 1989, p. 46; July 23, 1993, p. 41; November 17, 1995, pp. 39-40; September 20, 1996, pp. 47-48; November 29, 1999, review of *Darwin's Worms,* p. 78; April 16, 2001, review of *Houdini's Box,* p. 56; July 15, 2002, Hugo Barnacle, review of *Equals,* pp. 49-50.

New York Times, June 30, 1996; February 22, 1998; February 18, 2001, review of *Darwin's Worms,* p. 32; October 13, 2002, Emily Eakin, review of *Equals,* section 7, p. 16.

New York Times Book Review, May 16, 1993, p. 19; November 6, 1994, p. 11; May 9, 1999, review of *The Beast in the Nursery: On Curiosity and Other Appetites,* p. 42; August 12, 2001, review of *Houdini's Box,* p. 30.

Observer (London, England), October 31, 1999, review of *Darwin's Worms,* p. 12; January 31, 1999, review of *The Beast in the Nursery,* p. 14; November 23, 2001, review of *Houdini's Box,* p. 5.

Publishers Weekly, February 12, 1996, p. 68; November 4, 1996, p. 58; December 22, 1997, p. 46; June 11, 2001, review of *Houdini's Box,* p. 71.

Readings, September, 2001, review of *Promises, Promises,* p. 33.

Spectator, July 13, 2002, Nicholas Fearn, "The Harmony of Discord," review of *Equals,* pp. 40-41.

Times Educational Supplement, November 5, 1999, review of *Darwin's Worms,* p. 9.

Times Literary Supplement, July 7-13, 1989, p. 751; September 6, 2002, Vincent Deary, "Sunk in Doubt," review of *Equals,* p. 10.

Washington Post Book World, February 9, 1997, p. 6; July 29, 2001, review of *Houdini's Box,* p. 9.

ONLINE

Adequacy, http://www.adequacy.net/ (November 20, 2003), review of *Houdini's Box.*

BookPage, http://www.bookpage.com/ (November 20, 2003), review of *Houdini's Box.*

Complete Review, http://www.complete-review.com/ (November 20, 2003), review of *Darwin's Worms.*

Guardian Unlimited, http://books.guardian.co.uk/ (December 2, 1999), Stephen Moss, review of *Darwin's Worms;* (April 22, 2001), Gaby Wood, review of *Houdini's Box;* (June 30, 2002), Sean O'Hagan, review of *Equals.*

Salon.com, http://www.salon.com/ (June 23, 1998).*

*   *   *

PILKEY, Orrin H. 1934-

PERSONAL: Born September 19, 1934, in New York, NY; son of Orrin H., Sr. and Elizabeth (Street) Pilkey; married Sharlene Greenaa (a researcher), December 31, 1956; children: Charles, Linda, Diane, Keith, Kerry. *Education:* Washington State University, B.S., 1957; Montana State University, M.S., 1959; Florida State University, Ph.D., 1962.

ADDRESSES: Home—3303 Highway 70 E, Hillsborough, NC 27278. *Office*—Department of Geology, Duke University, Old Chemistry Bldg., Durham, NC 27706. *Agent*—Virginia Barber Literary Agency, Inc., 44 Greenwich Ave., New York, NY 10011.

CAREER: University of Georgia, Athens, research associate at Marine Laboratory and assistant professor of geology, 1962-65; Duke University, Durham, NC, assistant professor, 1965-67, associate professor, 1967-75, professor, 1975-83, James B. Duke Professor of Geology, 1983—. University of Puerto Rico—Mayaguez, visiting professor, 1972-73. U.S. Geological Survey, research geologist, 1975-76. Coproducer of *The Beaches Are Moving,* a television documentary special broadcast by Public Broadcasting Service, 1990. *Military service:* U.S. Army; became captain.

MEMBER: International Association of Sedimentologists, American Association of Petroleum Geologists, American Association for the Advancement of Science (fellow), Association of Earth Science Editors, Society for Sedimentary Geology, Geological Society of America, North Carolina Academy of Science (president, 1982), Sigma Xi, Explorers Club.

AWARDS, HONORS: Francis Shepard medal, 1987, for excellence in marine geology; named conservation educator of the year, North Carolina Wildlife Federation, 1991.

WRITINGS:

(With D. J. P. Swift and D. B. Duane) *Shelf Sediment Transport, Process and Pattern,* Dowden, Hutchinson & Ross (Stroudsburg, PA), 1972.
(With father, Orrin H. Pilkey, Sr., and Robb Turner) *How to Live with an Island,* North Carolina Science and Technology Research Center (Research Triangle Park, NC), 1975.
(With Orrin H. Pilkey, Sr. and William J. Neal) *From Currituck to Calabash,* North Carolina Science and Technology Research Center (Research Triangle Park, NC), 1978.
(With W. Kaufman) *The Beaches Are Moving: The Drowning of America's Shoreline,* Doubleday (New York, NY), 1979.
(Coauthor) *Coastal Land Loss,* American Geophysical Union (Washington, DC), 1989.
(Coauthor) *The Corps and the Shore,* Island Press (Washington, DC), 1996.
A Celebration of the World's Great Barrier Islands, illustrated by Mary Edna Fraser, Columbia University Press (New York, NY), 2003.

Contributor of several hundred articles to scholarly journals and other magazines. Editor, *Journal of Sedimentary Petrology,* 1978-83; associate editor, *Marine Geology, Journal of Coastal Research,* and *Geology.*

"LIVING WITH THE SHORE" SERIES

(With R. Morton and William J. Neal) *Living with the Texas Shore,* Duke University Press (Durham, NC), 1983.
(With Sharma Dinesh, H. Wanless, L. J. Doyle, and others) *Living with the East Florida Shore,* Duke University Press (Durham, NC), 1984.
(With William J. Neal and C. Blakeney) *Living with the South Carolina Shore,* Duke University Press (Durham, NC), 1984.
(With L. J. Doyle and others) *Living with the West Florida Shore,* Duke University Press (Durham, NC), 1984.

(With J. R. Kelley, A. R. Kelley, and A. A. Clark) *Living with the Louisiana Shore,* Duke University Press (Durham, NC), 1984.
(With L. R. McCormick, William J. Neal, and Orrin H. Pilkey, Sr.) *Living with Long Island's South Shore,* Duke University Press (Durham, NC), 1984.
(With W. F. Canis, William J. Neal, and Orrin H. Pilkey, Sr.) *Living with the Mississippi-Alabama Shore,* Duke University Press (Durham, NC), 1985.
(With K. F. Nordstrom and others) *Living with the New Jersey Shore,* Duke University Press (Durham, NC), 1986.
(With C. Carter and others) *Living with the Lake Erie Shore,* Duke University Press (Durham, NC), 1987.
(With J. T. Kelley and A. R. Kelley) *Living with the Coast of Maine,* Duke University Press (Durham, NC), 1989.
(With Larry G. Ward, Peter S. Rosen, William J. Neal, and others) *Living with Chesapeake Bay and Virginia's Ocean Shore,* Duke University Press (Durham, NC), 1989.
(Coauthor) *Living by the Rules of the Sea,* Duke University Press (Durham, NC), 1996.
(Coauthor) *Living with the Coast of Alaska,* Duke University Press (Durham, NC), 1997.
(Coauthor) *The North Carolina Shore and Its Barrier Islands: Restless Ribbons of Sand,* Duke University Press (Durham, NC), 1998.

Also editor (with William J. Neal) of *Living with the California Coast, Living with the Connecticut Coast, Living with the Georgia Shore,* and *Living with Puget Sound and Georgia Straight.*

SIDELIGHTS: Orrin H. Pilkey once told *CA:* "My primary motivation is the need for public education concerning the interaction of man and nature at the shoreline."

BIOGRAPHICAL AND CRITICAL SOURCES:

PERIODICALS

Library Journal, July, 2003, Susan E. Brazer, review of *A Celebration of the World's Great Barrier Islands,* p. 118.*

R

RABINOWITZ, Alan 1927-

PERSONAL: Born January 18, 1927, in New York, NY; son of Aaron (in real estate) and Clara (Greenhut) Rabinowitz; married Andrea Wolf (a psychiatric social worker), December 2, 1951; children: Eric W., Peter MacG., Martha L., Katherine W. *Education:* Yale University, A.B., 1948; Harvard University, M.B.A., 1950; Massachusetts Institute of Technology, Ph.D., 1969. *Politics:* Democrat.

ADDRESSES: Home—3400 East Laurelhurst Dr., Seattle, WA 98105.

CAREER: Affiliated with Fred F. French Investing Co., 1950-59; Regional Plan Association, New York, NY, member of staff, 1956-57; Arthur D. Little, Inc., Cambridge, MA, member of staff, 1959-63; Urban Survey Corp., Cambridge, president, 1963-69; Boston Redevelopment Authority, Boston, MA, administrator of program planning and finance, 1969-71; University of Washington, Seattle, professor of urban planning and chairman of department, 1971-86. Fellow, Harvard-M.I.T. Joint Center for Urban Studies, 1969. *Military service:* U.S. Naval Reserve, active duty, 1945-46, 1952-54.

MEMBER: American Institute of Certified Planners.

WRITINGS:

Municipal Bond Finance and Administration, Wiley/ Interscience (New York, NY), 1969.

Industrial Zoning in Seattle, [Seattle], c. 1973.
Development of the Real Estate Investment Industry, 1972-1975, privately printed, 1978.
The Real Estate Gamble: Lessons from 50 Years of Boom and Bust, AMACOM (New York, NY), 1980.
Land Investment and the Predevelopment Process: A Guide for Finance and Real Estate Professionals, Quorum (New York, NY), 1988.
(Coauthor) *Markets for New Construction, 1980-87-95,* NPA Data Services (Washington, DC), 1988.
Social Change Philanthropy in America, Quorum (New York, NY), 1990.
Urban Economics and Land Use in America, M.E. Sharpe (Armonk, NY), 2004.

Contributor to planning journals.*

*   *   *

RAINE, Jerry 1955-

PERSONAL: Born July 5, 1955, in Leeds, Yorkshire, England; son of Peter (a company director) and Margaret (Ward) Raine. *Ethnicity:* "White." *Education:* Attended schools in Surrey, England. *Hobbies and other interests:* Singing and playing guitar, writing songs, jogging.

ADDRESSES: Home—7 Quarry Cottages, London Rd., Seven Oaks, Kent TN13 2JB, England. *Office*—Murder One Bookshop, 71-73 Charing Cross Rd., London WC2 H0AA, England. *Agent*—Pam Smith, 6 Womersley Rd., London N6, England.

CAREER: Murder One Bookshop, London, England, assistant manager, 1988—. Also worked as farmhand and caravan fitter in Australia, gardener, fork-lift driver, factory worker, liquor salesperson, and builder.

AWARDS, HONORS: Fiction prize, *Mail on Sunday,* 1986.

WRITINGS:

Smalltime (crime novel), Dufour (Chester Springs, PA), 1996.
Frankie Bosser Comes Home (crime novel), Gollancz (London, England), 1999.
Small Change (crime novel), Do-Not Press (London, England), 2001.

SIDELIGHTS: Jerry Raine once told *CA:* "My first interest in writing was actually songwriting. When I left school at the age of sixteen, I went to Australia by myself for two years. While working on a farm in the bush I taught myself the guitar and started to write songs. I then started performing a year later in the bars of Sydney. Wanting to further my music career, I returned to England but ended up in a creative writing class. It seemed I had a talent for writing prose, so at the age of twenty-five, I decided to concentrate on that instead of singing, and I didn't perform live again until the age of forty!

"It took a long time for my writing to take off. I wrote a lot of short stories and tried writing novels, but nothing really worked. Then in 1986 I was violently mugged. I decided this would be a good idea for a novel about a man seeking revenge against his mugger. I was heavily into crime novels by this time, my favorites being Elmore Leonard and Charles Willeford, so I wrote *Smalltime* as a crime novel, using the Leonard style of third-person, multiple viewpoint. I found myself an agent, but *Smalltime* was turned down by eight publishers, and I got very disillusioned with the whole publishing process. I withdrew it from the market, parted company with my agent, and put the novel in a drawer for six years.

"I gave up writing prose for awhile, and at the age of thirty-eight got back into my music. Suddenly I started to write some great songs! Thinking the world should hear them, I started performing in London clubs a few years later.

"Meanwhile, a new young publisher called the Do-Not Press heard about *Smalltime* and accepted it straight away. By this time I didn't much care if it was published, but I updated the setting anyway. I thought it would sink without trace when it was published at the end of 1996. Much to my surprise, the book got some good reviews in England and some even better ones in America. My girlfriend said 'You'd better write another one,' so I wrote *Frankie Bosser Comes Home* in about two months. This is a faster moving crime novel, less intense than *Smalltime,* with more humor. It was a lot of fun to write." Bob Cornwell commented on the *Tangled Web UK* Web site, "The observant prose is straightforward, with a nice eye for the casual amorality of life lived on the lower rungs."

In *Small Change,* Raine brings back the protagonist, Chris, from *Smalltime,* and he again sets in motion random events resulting in violence and chaos. Bill Ott observed that *Small Change* "blends the sensibility of 1930s proletarian fiction with the noir mood of a contemporary crime novel."

BIOGRAPHICAL AND CRITICAL SOURCES:

PERIODICALS

Booklist, May 15, 2002, Bill Ott, review of *Small Change,* p. 1580.

ONLINE

Tangled Web UK, http://www.twbooks.co.uk/ (February 5, 2003), Bob Cornwell, review of *Frankie Bosser Comes Home.**

*   *   *

REISS, Kathryn 1957-

PERSONAL: Surname is pronounced "reese"; born December 4, 1957, in Cambridge, MA; daughter of Edmund Alan Reiss and Dorothy Ann (Kauffman) Molnar; married Thomas Strychacz (a professor), October 2, 1981; children: Nicholas, Daniel, Isabel. *Ethnicity:* Caucasian. *Education:* Duke University, B.A. (English and German), 1980; attended

Kathryn Reiss

Rheinische-Friedrich-Wilhelms-Universität (Bonn, Germany), 1980-81; University of Michigan, M.F.A., 1988. *Politics:* Democrat. *Religion:* Presbyterian. *Hobbies and other interests:* Traveling, reading, collecting old series books.

ADDRESSES: Home—Benicia, CA. *Office*—Mills College, English Department, 5000 MacArthur Blvd., Oakland, CA 94613. *Agent*—Marilyn E. Marlow, Curtis Brown, Ltd., 10 Astor Pl., New York, NY 10003. *E-mail*—kreiss@mills.edu.

CAREER: Princeton Language Group, Princeton, NJ, instructor, 1981-82; Stuart Country Day School, Princeton, director of foreign exchange, 1981-82; Princeton Young Women's Christian Association (YWCA), Princeton, instructor, 1981-82, and 1984; Europa at Princeton (a bookshop), Princeton, manager, 1982-83; Princeton Public Library, Princeton, NJ, assistant to children's librarian, 1982-83; Trenton State College, Ewing, NJ, instructor, 1984-86; University of Michigan, Ann Arbor, instructor, 1986-88; Mills College, Oakland, CA, lecturer of English, 1989—. Princeton Arts Council, writer-in-residence, 1986.

MEMBER: Society of Children's Book Writers and Illustrators, Mystery Writers of America, Sisters in Crime, League of University Women.

AWARDS, HONORS: Scholarship, American Field Service, 1975; Fulbright-Hayes Scholar, 1980-81, to study contemporary German short fiction; grant, New Jersey State Council on the Arts, 1983-84; Cowden Memorial Prize for fiction, University of Michigan, 1987; Best Books for Young Adults citation, American Library Association, 1993, for *Time Windows,* and for *The Glass House People;* Black-Eyed Susan Young Reader Medal, state of Maryland; nominations for Edgar Allan Poe award, Mystery Writers of America, for *Pale Phoenix* and *PaperQuake;* award from International School Librarians Association, for *Paint by Magic.*

WRITINGS:

NOVELS

Time Windows, Harcourt (San Diego, CA), 1991.
The Glass House People, Harcourt (San Diego, CA), 1992.
Dreadful Sorry, Harcourt (San Diego, CA), 1993.
Pale Phoenix (sequel to *Time Windows*), Harcourt (San Diego, CA), 1994.
PaperQuake: A Puzzle, Harcourt (San Diego, CA), 1998.
Riddle of the Prairie Bride ("History Mysteries" series), Pleasant Company Publications (Middleton, WI), 2001.
The Strange Case of Baby H ("History Mysteries" series), Pleasant Company Publications (Middleton, WI), 2002.
Paint by Magic: A Time Travel Mystery, Harcourt (San Diego, CA), 2002.
Sweet Miss Honeywell's Revenge: A Ghost Story, Harcourt (San Diego, CA), 2004.

Contributor of short stories to periodicals, including *The Archive, HipMama, Parents,* and *Baby* magazine. Associate editor, *The Archive,* 1979-80.

"GHOST IN THE DOLLHOUSE" SERIES

The Dollhouse of the Dead, Scholastic (New York, NY), 1997.
The Headless Bride, Scholastic (New York, NY), 1997.
Rest in Peace, Scholastic (New York, NY), 1997.

ADAPTATIONS: The Strange Case of Baby H was adapted to audio recording by Recorded Books, 2003.

SIDELIGHTS: Writing young-adult mystery novels and teaching creative writing at Mills College, in California, Kathryn Reiss has earned a reputation as an appealing author for adolescents. In the last decade of the millennium, she published a handful of suspense novels, including her debut *Time Windows* and its sequel *Pale Phoenix,* "The Ghost in the Dollhouse" trio, and several stand-alone novels. A hallmark of these novels is the time-slip element, a premise that has long interested Reiss. "I have a special interest in our various notions of time—memory, perception, history, time travel (as a child I was always looking for ways to travel in time; perhaps my writing is my own version of a time machine!)," she once told *CA.* "I have a special interest in writing for middle-grade and young-adult audiences, and write the sort of books now that I liked when I was the age of my readers— especially favoring books about magic or mystery."

Although as a young girl Reiss wrote "novels," her actual career began in a roundabout way. As a student in high school and college, she took creative writing classes whenever she could, and in 1980, she graduated with a dual degree in English and German. The following year, on a Fulbright-Hayes Scholarship, she attended university in Bonn, Germany, where she began to write her first novel, in English. She once recalled to *CA,* "At one point I was up to my ears in [the German poet Johann Wolfgang] Goethe's works, analyzing them, writing about them, preparing to give an oral report in class (a scary thought!)—and I decided to take a day off from work just to read something light, preferably in English—despite my promise to myself to avoid the English language as much as I possibly could. I had read all of my English novels already, and it was pouring rain outside, so a trip to the bookstore didn't seem so good. I thought to myself: 'This is your chance. You've been saying for years that you want to write a book, right? So, why not start now?' I got a pad of paper and my pen, and sat down and started writing a story. When the rain stopped, I was still engaged in my new story, and I went out to sit on my little balcony (I rented a room in a big, drafty house) and kept on writing far into the night. I continued to write in my free time until I had an entire first draft of a novel. I revised it over several years (taking breaks to get married, to go to graduate school, and to have two children) and so produced my first novel, *Time Windows.*"

Time Windows and its sequel, *Pale Phoenix,* each feature Miranda Brown, who has recently moved to an old house in a small Massachusetts town. In the attic she discovers an old dollhouse, a replica of the larger house, that acts as a time machine, allowing her to see events of the past. This novel garnered good reviews from several critics, including *Kliatt* contributor Gerrie Human, who described it as "a fine mystery, full of suspense." A *Publishers Weekly* reviewer also praised *Time Windows* for being "deft, entertaining, and inventive." A slightly older Miranda deals with the adoption of the mysterious Abby into her family in *Pale Phoenix.* As Miranda discovers, Abby is an unfortunate time traveler from 1680, and Miranda and neighbor Dan try to return her to her own time. Although *Horn Book Guide* reviewer Karen E. Walsh thought the book's premise was "clever" but the denouement "contrived," *New Advocate* reviewer M. Jean Greenlaw likened the work to Natalie Babbitt's *Tuck Everlasting* and predicted that readers would find Reiss's novel "fascinating." "A thoughtful and enjoyable book" is how *Booklist*'s Jeanne Trinner described the sequel.

With their titles reflecting axioms and song lyrics, Reiss's early titles *The Glass House People* and *Dreadful Sorry* deal with almost-ruined lives. The first is a family saga featuring a teenaged brother and sister, who try to unearth the details surrounding the family's present difficult circumstances, in what *Kliatt* reviewer Claire Rosser described as "entertaining throughout." The "page-turner" *Dreadful Sorry,* to quote *Kliatt* critic Barbara Jo McKee, will appeal to teen readers as its protagonist must overcome her fear of the water and a reincarnated girl suggestively named Clementine.

From 1998 to 2002, Reiss published, among other books, another pair of winning titles, *PaperQuake: A Puzzle* and *Paint by Magic: A Time Travel Mystery.* As with several of her other works, these titles use the time-slip element, the first dealing with San Francisco earthquakes in the present and 1906, and the latter a mystery in the present harking to 1924 with a tie to the 1400s. In *PaperQuake,* main character Violet, the third and non-identical sister of triplets, is haunted by a fear of earthquakes and a vision of children fleeing an earthquake. When she, her sisters, and parents go to San Francisco in the aftermath of tremors to clean up a building they own, a letter addressed to Baby V falls from the wall. As similar letters arrive mysteriously, Violet learns of a girl named Verity whom she believes is sending her letters from the past to avert a future disaster. *PaperQuake* caught the attention of reviewers, among them *Horn Book*'s Ann A. Flowers, who dubbed the work "clever and skillfully written." Moreover, Mary Logue of *Hungry Mind Review* maintained that the novel "is a much richer story" than the typical mystery for this age level, with "the most fascinating aspect of this novel . . . [being] the relationship between Violet and her two sisters." Yet the work was not without critics. *Booklist*'s Carolyn Phelan faulted Reiss for relying heavily on coincidence to drive the plot, though she praised the "well-drawn relationships" between Violet and other characters. While "the plot might be overly complicated," Logue conceded, "the twists and turns are a good ride." *PaperQuake* is "an adroit fusion of magic, romance, and adventure," concluded a *Publishers Weekly* critic.

With her 2002 offering *Paint by Magic*, Reiss explores the creative process and "paints an intriguing mystery," punned a *Kirkus Reviews* contributor. The plot revolves around eleven-year-old Connor, who wonders why his mother begins to act strangely all of a sudden. When he finds himself transported back in time, he discovers the truth. While Lisa Prolman, writing in *School Library Journal,* found some of the comparisons of pre-technological times with the present heavy-handed, she also found the plot "unusual and compelling," predicting that readers would hold on until the conclusion. Also noting Reiss's social criticism was *Booklist* reviewer Sally Estes, who deemed the novel both "a compelling mystery" and "a telling look" at modern family life.

Pleasant Company, known for its historical fiction geared to girls in the early and middle grades, included two of Reiss's novels in its "History Mysteries" series, *Riddle of the Prairie Bride* and *The Strange Case of Baby H.* In the former, twelve-year-old Kate investigates the mystery surrounding her father's mail-order bride who arrives at their Kansas prairie home in 1878. While Carol A. Edwards, writing in *School Library Journal,* found *Riddle of the Prairie Bride* lacking in suspense and individual characterizations, other critics offered different opinions. For example, *Horn Book Guide* contributor Frieda F. Bostain found it "well-narrated" and full of "accurate" period details, and *Booklist*'s Denise Wilms likewise dubbed it "formulaic but engrossing." According to critics, Reiss hit her stride with her next novel in the series, *The Strange Case of Baby H,* which harkens back in subject matter

to *PaperQuake.* When an abandoned child appears on her family's doorstep, twelve-year-old Clara Curfman thinks the baby has been kidnapped and decides to find the child's parents. However, being the year 1906, an earthquake of historic proportions rocks Clara's home city of San Francisco, making her job even more dangerous. In a review for *School Library Journal,* Kristen Oravec praised the novel, calling it well-plotted and "full of suspense and action." Oravec also commented on how the author "seamlessly" employed historical details in her tale, a quality that *Booklist*'s Lauren Peterson also noted. The tale of Baby H. is "entertaining recreational reading," Peterson concluded.

Reflecting on the writing process, Reiss once told *CA,* "There are certain stories that simply beg to be told. I feel a kind of urgency to write when I have a good plot in mind. But if I tell the tale verbally, much of the urgency disappears. It has become important for me to keep my plot to myself until I get it down at least in a rough form. If I share a story before it's written, the writing becomes a sort of re-run. Some of the energy is lost."

BIOGRAPHICAL AND CRITICAL SOURCES:

PERIODICALS

Booklist, March 15, 1992, Randy Meyer, review of *The Glass House People,* p. 1350; July, 1993, Candace Smith, review of *Dreadful Sorry,* p. 1959; March 15, 1994, Jeanne Triner, review of *Pale Phoenix,* p. 1344; May 15, 1998, Carolyn Phelan, review of *PaperQuake: A Puzzle,* p. 1627; April 1, 2001, Denise Wilms, review of *Riddle of the Prairie Bride,* p. 1484; April 15, 2002, Sally Estes, review of *Paint by Magic: A Time Travel Mystery,* p. 1418; December 1, 2002, Lauren Peterson, review of *The Strange Case of Baby H,* pp. 666-667.
Book Report, November-December, 1992, Melissa Bibbey, review of *The Glass House People,* pp. 44-45; September-October, 1993, Sylvia Feicht, review of *Dreadful Sorry,* p. 48; September-October, 1994, Rebecca Neuhedel, review of *Pale Phoenix,* p. 44.
Horn Book, July-August, 1998, Ann A. Flowers, review of *PaperQuake,* p. 497.

Horn Book Guide, fall, 1994, Karen E. Walsh, review of *Pale Phoenix,* p. 323; spring, 2002, Frieda F. Bostian, review of *Riddle of the Prairie Bride,* p. 82.

Hungry Mind Review, summer, 1998, Mary Logue, "Far from Clueless: Young Adult Mysteries," review of *PaperQuake,* p. 51.

Kirkus Reviews, May 1, 1993, review of *Dreadful Sorry;* April 15, 1994, review of *Pale Phoenix;* May 1, 2002, review of *Paint by Magic,* p. 666.

Kliatt, July, 1994, Gerrie Human, review of *Time Windows,* p. 11; July, 1996, Claire Rosser, review of *The Glass House People,* p. 15; March, 1997, Barbara Jo McKee, review of *Dreadful Sorry,* p. 20.

New Advocate, fall, 1994, M. Jean Greenlaw, review of *Pale Phoenix,* p. 298.

Publishers Weekly, September 13, 1991, review of *Time Windows,* p. 80; February 24, 1992, review of *The Glass House People,* p. 56; May 10, 1993, review of *Dreadful Sorry,* p. 73; January 26, 1998, review of *PaperQuake,* p. 92.

School Library Journal, October, 1991, Margaret A. Chang, review of *Time Windows,* p. 126; May, 1992, Kathy Fritts, review of *The Glass House People,* p. 134; June, 1993, Sharon Korbeck, review of *Dreadful Sorry,* p. 132; May, 1994, Ruth S. Vose, review of *Pale Phoenix,* p. 132; June, 1998, Steven Engelfried, review of *PaperQuake,* p. 152; May, 2001, Carol A. Edwards, review of *Riddle of the Prairie Bride,* pp. 158-159; May, 2002, Lisa Prolman, review of *Paint by Magic,* pp. 158, 160; November, 2002, Kristen Oravec, review of *The Strange Case of Baby H,* p. 174.

Science Fiction Chronicle, May, 2002, review of *Paint by Magic,* p. 37.

ONLINE

Mills College Home Page, http://www.mills.edu/ (August 7, 2003), "Kathryn Reiss."

*   *   *

RENDELL, Ruth (Barbara) 1930-
(Barbara Vine, a pseudonym)

PERSONAL: Born February 17, 1930, London, England; daughter of Arthur Grasemann (a teacher) and Ebba (a teacher) Kruse; married Donald Rendell, 1950

Ruth Rendell

(divorced, 1975; remarried, 1977); children: Simon. *Education:* Educated in Essex, England. *Hobbies and other interests:* Reading, walking, opera.

ADDRESSES: Home—26 Cornwall Terrace Mews, London NW1 5LL, England. *Agent*—Sterling Lord Agency, 660 Madison Ave., New York, NY 10021.

CAREER: Writer. Express and Independent Newspapers, West Essex, England, reporter and subeditor for the Chigwell *Times,* 1948-52.

AWARDS, HONORS: Edgar Allan Poe Award, Mystery Writers of America, 1974, for story "The Fallen Curtain," 1976, for collection *The Fallen Curtain and Other Stories,* 1984, for story "The New Girlfriend," and 1986, for novel *A Dark-Adapted Eye;* Gold Dagger Award, Crime Writers Association, 1977, for *A Demon in My View,* 1986, for *Live Flesh,* and 1987, for *A Fatal Inversion;* British Arts Council bursary, 1981; British National Book Award, 1981, for *The Lake of Darkness;* Popular Culture Association Award, 1983; Silver Dagger Award, Crime Writers Association, 1984, for *The Tree of Hands; Sunday Times* award for Literary Excellence, 1990.

WRITINGS:

MYSTERY NOVELS

From Doon with Death (also see below), John Long (London, England), 1964, Doubleday (Garden City, NY), 1965.

To Fear a Painted Devil, Doubleday (Garden City, NY), 1965.

Vanity Dies Hard, John Long (London, England), 1966, published as *In Sickness and in Health,* Doubleday (New York, NY), 1966.

A New Lease of Death (also see below), Doubleday (Garden City, NY), 1967, published as *Sins of the Fathers,* Ballantine (New York, NY), 1970.

Wolf to the Slaughter, John Long (London, England), 1967, Doubleday (Garden City, NY), 1968.

The Secret House of Death, John Long (London, England), 1968, Doubleday (Garden City, NY), 1969.

The Best Man to Die (also see below), John Long (London, England), 1969, Doubleday (Garden City, NY), 1970.

A Guilty Thing Surprised, Doubleday (Garden City, NY), 1970.

No More Dying Then, Hutchinson (London, England), 1971, Doubleday (Garden City, NY), 1972.

One Across, Two Down, Doubleday (Garden City, NY), 1971.

Murder Being Once Done, Doubleday (Garden City, NY), 1972.

Some Lie and Some Die, Doubleday (Garden City, NY), 1973.

The Face of Trespass, Doubleday (Garden City, NY), 1974.

Shake Hands Forever, Doubleday (Garden City, NY), 1975.

A Demon in My View, Doubleday (Garden City, NY), 1977.

A Judgment in Stone, Hutchinson (London, England), 1977, Doubleday (Garden City, NY), 1978.

A Sleeping Life, Doubleday (Garden City, NY), 1978.

Make Death Love Me, Doubleday (Garden City, NY), 1979.

The Lake of Darkness, Doubleday (Garden City, NY), 1980.

Put On by Cunning, Hutchinson (London, England), 1981, published as *Death Notes,* Pantheon (New York, NY), 1981.

Master of the Moor, Pantheon (New York, NY), 1982.

The Speaker of Mandarin, Pantheon (New York, NY), 1983.

The Killing Doll, Pantheon (New York, NY), 1984.

The Tree of Hands, Pantheon (New York, NY), 1984.

An Unkindness of Ravens, Pantheon (New York, NY), 1985.

Live Flesh, Pantheon (New York, NY), 1986.

Heartstones, Harper (New York, NY), 1987.

Talking to Strangers, Hutchinson (London, England), 1987, published as *Talking to Strange Men,* Pantheon (New York, NY), 1987.

The Veiled One, Pantheon (New York, NY), 1988.

The Bridesmaid, Mysterious Press (New York, NY), 1989.

Going Wrong, Mysterious Press (New York, NY), 1990.

Kissing the Gunner's Daughter, Mysterious Press (New York, NY), 1992.

The Crocodile Bird, Crown (New York, NY), 1993.

Simisola, Random House (New York, NY), 1995.

Ginger and the Kingsmarkham Chalk Circle, Phoenix (London, England), 1996.

The Keys to the Street, Random House (New York, NY), 1996.

Road Rage, Crown (New York, NY), 1997.

Bloodlines, Wheeler (Rockland, MA), 1997.

Whydunit (Perfectly Criminal 2), Severn House (London, England), 1997.

Thornapple, Travelman (London, England), 1998.

A Sight for Sore Eyes: A Novel, Crown (New York, NY), 1999.

Harm Done: An Inspector Wexford Mystery, Crown (New York, NY), 1999.

Adam and Eve and Pinch Me, Crown (New York, NY), 2001.

The Babes in the Wood, Crown (New York, NY), 2002.

The Rottweiler, Crown (New York, NY), 2003.

STORY COLLECTIONS

The Fallen Curtain and Other Stories, Hutchinson (London, England), 1976, published as *The Fallen Curtain: Eleven Mystery Stories by an Edgar Award-Winning Writer,* Doubleday (Garden City, NY), 1976.

Means of Evil and Other Stories, Hutchinson (London, England), 1979, published as *Five Mystery Stories by an Edgar Award-Winning Writer,* Doubleday (Garden City, NY), 1980.

The Fever Tree and Other Stories, Hutchinson (London, England), 1982, Pantheon (New York, NY), 1983, published as *The Fever Tree and Other Stories of Suspense,* Ballantine (New York, NY), 1984.

The New Girlfriend and Other Stories, Hutchinson (London, England), 1985, published as *The New Girlfriend and Other Stories of Suspense,* Pantheon (New York, NY), 1986.

(Editor) *A Warning to the Curious: The Ghost Stories of M. R. James,* Hutchinson (London, England), 1986.

Collected Short Stories, Hutchinson (London, England), 1987, published as *Collected Stories,* Pantheon (New York, NY), 1988.

Wexford: An Omnibus (contains *From Doon with Death, A New Lease of Death,* and *The Best Man to Die*), Hutchinson (London, England), 1988.

(With Colin Ward) *Undermining the Central Line,* Chatto & Windus (London, England), 1989.

The Copper Peacock and Other Stories, Mysterious Press (New York, NY), 1991.

The Fifth Wexford Omnibus (contains *Means of Evil, An Unkindness of Ravens,* and *The Veiled One*), Hutchinson (London, England), 1991.

(With photographs by Paul Bowden) *Ruth Rendell's Suffolk,* Hutchinson (London, England), 1992.

Blood Lines: Long and Short Stories, Crown (New York, NY), 1996.

(Editor) *The Reason Why: An Anthology of the Murderous Mind,* Crown (New York, NY), 1996.

Piranha to Scurfy and Other Stories, Vintage (New York, NY), 2002.

Contributor of short stories to *Ellery Queen's Mystery Magazine.*

UNDER PSEUDONYM BARBARA VINE

A Dark-Adapted Eye, Viking (New York, NY), 1985.

A Fatal Inversion, Bantam (New York, NY), 1987.

(With others) *Yes, Prime Minister: The Diaries of the Right Honorable James Hacker,* Salem House Publishers, 1988.

The House of Stairs, Harmony Books (New York, NY), 1989.

Gallowglass, Harmony Books (New York, NY), 1990.

King Solomon's Carpet, Harmony Books (New York, NY), 1992.

Anna's Book, Harmony Books (New York, NY), 1993.

No Night Is Too Long, Harmony Books (New York, NY), 1994.

The Brimstone Wedding, Harmony Books (New York, NY), 1996.

The Chimney Sweeper's Boy: A Novel, Harmony Books (New York, NY), 1998.

Grasshopper, Harmony Books (New York, NY), 2000.

The Blood Doctor, Shaye Areheart Books (New York, NY), 2002.

ADAPTATIONS: A Judgment in Stone was filmed as *The Housekeeper,* Rawfilm/Schulz Productions, 1987; several of Rendell's Wexford mysteries have been adapted for British television and subsequently aired on the Arts and Entertainment network's "Masters of Mystery" series.

SIDELIGHTS: Ruth Rendell is a prolific author who, writing under her own name and the pseudonym Barbara Vine, has enthralled both the general public and literary critics with her skillfully written mysteries and suspenseful stories. She has the ability, according to *Dictionary of Literary Biography* contributor Patricia A. Gabilondo, to render tales that could be considered formulaic, into something "always suspenseful and viscerally compelling." In her first novel, the author introduced Chief Inspector Reginald Wexford, a proper Englishman whose town of Kingsmarkham, Sussex, is plagued by many murders. Wexford has been the subject of numerous sequels and has won much praise for his creator for the deft characterizations, clever plots, and surprising endings that mark these books. While the Wexford books are straightforward police procedural novels, the books Rendell publishes under the Vine pseudonym are more gothic, often involving twisted psychology to produce edgy thrillers. Writing in the *Times Literary Supplement,* Francis Wyndham praised the author for her "masterly grasp of plot construction [and] highly developed faculty for social observation." David Lehman of *Newsweek* commented that "few detective writers are as good at pulling such last-second rabbits out of their top hats—the last page making us see everything before it in a strange, new glare."

Rendell's Wexford character is middle-aged, happily married, and the father of two grown daughters. His extensive reading allows him to quote from a wide range of literature during his murder investigations, but despite his erudition, Wexford is not cynical, eccentric, or misanthropic as are many literary detectives. His well-adjusted manner serves as contrast to the many strange mysteries he investigates. Social differences are frequently illuminated in these mysteries, and Rendell has been singled out as particularly skillful at portraying England's social stratification, even in the details of her descriptions of architectural details. Gabilondo mused, "Her meticulous description of setting serves to create atmosphere and, more important, to communicate the intimate relation between the physical and the psychological, especially in terms of the way that landscapes, whether urban or rural, take on the imprints of sociological change and personal conflict."

Wexford is also notable for his philosophical turn of mind and his keen empathy for his fellow man, in whatever the circumstances. His sensitivity makes him quite desirable to the women he encounters, yet Wexford remains determinedly devoted to his wife. Wexford's greatest disdain is for the "inanities of modernity," wrote Gabilondo. "Through Wexford's often ironic eye, Rendell paints a remarkably specific portrait of the changes that have occurred in English life—the encroachment of suburban sprawl, the banal homogenization of consumer culture, the dispossessed youth, the problems with unemployment, and the growing complexities of civil bureaucracies. Able to see both sides of any issue, as well as to grasp the essential poignancy of the human condition, Wexford finds himself often at odds with his official role, for his reliance on intuition and the imagination usually runs counter to the official line, offering a rich resource of dramatic tension," concluded Gabilondo. Wexford's open-mindedness is contrasted with the more narrow vision and rigid morality of his partner, Inspector Michael Burden. Unlike many series characters, Wexford and Burden age and go through many significant changes as the series progresses.

Rendell's early Wexford mysteries dealt frequently with desire and taboo, while in her later books she takes on social issues in a more direct manner. Feminism, ecoterrorism, and other modern concerns are examined, not always in a flattering light. In *A Sleeping Life,* gender-identity conflicts figure prominently in the murder case, while Wexford's daughter becomes involved in a radical feminist group. Rendell actually drew the ire of real-life feminist groups after the publication of *An Unkindness of Ravens,* which features a man-hating group called Action for the Radi-

cal Reform of Intersexual Attitudes (ARRIA). Members of the group vow to carry weapons and refrain from marriage; it even seems that some members advocate the murder of a man as an initiation rite. The author also ruffled feathers with *Kissing the Gunner's Daughter,* which challenges the popular notion that class stratification is much less meaningful in Britain than it has been in the past. Racism is addressed in *Simisola,* another Wexford novel; the problems of urban and suburban sprawl are considered in *Road Rage;* and the subject of wife-beating is approached in *Harm Done.*

Various types of psychological torment are central in Rendell's other books. *A Judgment in Stone* portrays an illiterate woman whose inability to read has led to a life of shame, isolation, and regression. *The Killing Doll* features Dolly Yearman, a schizophrenic whose delusions eventually lead her to murder. *Live Flesh* is told from the point of view of a convicted murderer and rapist, who lives in a strange symbiotic relationship with the police officer he crippled with a gunshot wound. In *The Bridesmaid,* the Pygmalion myth is turned inside out as a beautiful girl is shown to be marred by her mental instability. Despite her flaws, she becomes the object of sexual obsession for Philip; eventually, she brings him to the brink of murder. One of the author's most ambitious novels is *The Keys to the Street,* which uses the concentric circles and paths of London's Regent Park to follow the interconnected threads of human lives, particularly that of a well-to-do man who lives on the streets in the wake of a family tragedy and a young woman struggling to assert her independence. Although it may be the author's "most compassionate and most complex treatment of the human condition," according to Gabilondo, it left "most reviewers disappointed in her failure to bring all the strands together. The effectiveness of the structure, however, lies in this intentional failure to make everything connect. In Rendell's psychological thrillers, those avenues of emotional connection, like the misaligned arcs of Regent's Park, often do not meet, frustrating the hopes and dreams of her characters' lives." A very positive assessment of the book was offered by Emily Melton in *Booklist,* however; she wrote that it is "at once tragic, shocking, satisfying, and hopeful," and added, "Without a doubt, Rendell ranks with today's finest writers, and this book is one of her best. . . . Superbly written and beautifully constructed, the story is unique, powerful, and provocative."

Adam and Eve and Pinch Me is a "gem from the British master," wrote a *Publishers Weekly* reviewer, filled with characters "so vivid they live beyond the frame of the novel." At the center of the plot is Minty Knox, a woman in her thirties who works in a dry-cleaners and is obsessed with germs and cleanliness. Her hygiene phobias, as well as the ghosts she imagines she sees, figure prominently in a plot that is "intricate but brisk," according to the writer, "a literary page-turner, both elegant and accessible." *Booklist* reviewer Connie Fletcher called the book "madly absorbing," and advised, "Rendell's characters are fully drawn, and we become completely caught up in their struggles." Discussing her writing with a *Publishers Weekly* interviewer, Rendell commented, "I do write about obsession, but I don't think I have an obsession for writing. I'm not a compulsive writer. I like to watch obsession in other people, watch the way it makes them behave."

Gabilondo concluded: "Rendell's greatest contribution, in addition to her gifts as a storyteller, has been to track the social and the psychological circulation of that vast system—political, familial, cultural, and genetic—in which people are forced to play out their lives, through a body of work that takes readers not into the cozy drawing rooms of traditional English mystery but into the lives and psyches of men and women in a vividly contemporary Britain."

BIOGRAPHICAL AND CRITICAL SOURCES:

BOOKS

Contemporary Literary Criticism, Gale (Detroit, MI), Volume 28, 1984, Volume 48, 1988, Volume 50, 1988.

Dictionary of Literary Biography, Gale (Detroit, MI), Volume 87: *British Mystery and Thriller Writers since 1940,* 1989, Volume 276: *British Mystery and Thriller Writers since 1960,* 2003.

Mystery and Suspense Writers: The Literature of Crime, Detection, and Espionage, Scribner (New York, NY), 1998.

PERIODICALS

Advertiser (Adelaide, Australia), July 27, 2002, Katharine England, review of *The Blood Doctor,* p. W13.

Antioch Review, winter, 1997, review of *The Keys to the Street,* p. 122.

Belles Lettres, summer, 1993, p. 50; spring, 1994, p. 13.

Booklist, August, 1996, Emily Melton, review of *The Keys to the Street,* p. 1856; August, 1997, Emily Melton, review of *Road Rage,* p. 1848; December 1, 1998, Emily Melton, review of *A Sight for Sore Eyes,* p. 620; April 15, 1999, review of *Kissing the Gunner's Daughter,* p. 1458; August, 1999, review of *A Judgement in Stone,* p. 2025; September 1, 1999, Stephanie Zvirin, review of *Harm Done,* p. 8; November 1, 1999, Karen Harris, review of *A Sight for Sore Eyes,* p. 551; June 1, 2000, Mary McCay, review of *Harm Done,* p. 1922; November 1, 2000, Connie Fletcher, review of *Piranha to Scurfy and Other Stories,* p. 493; November 15, 2001, Connie Fletcher, review of *Adam and Eve and Pinch Me,* p. 524; September 1, 2003, Stephanie Zvirin, review of *The Babes in the Wood,* p. 7.

Chicago Tribune, August 29, 1989; October 31, 1993.

Chicago Tribune Book World, December 19, 1982.

Christian Science Monitor, July 6, 1992, p. 13.

Detroit News, August 12, 1979.

Entertainment Weekly, March 15, 2002, review of *Adam and Eve and Pinch Me,* p. 72.

Europe Intelligence Wire, October 20, 2002, Katie Owen, review of *The Babes in the Wood*; November 2, 2002, Rachel Simhon, review of *The Babes in the Wood.*

Globe and Mail (Toronto, Ontario, Canada), May 31, 1986; September 16, 1989.

Independent (London, England), August 18, 2001, Jane Jakeman, review of *Adam and Eve and Pinch Me,* p. 9; June 15, 2002, Jane Jakeman, "Where Does Ruth Rendell End and 'Barbara Vine' Begin?," p. 30.

Kirkus Reviews, July 15, 2003, review of *The Babes in the Wood,* p. 942.

Library Journal, February 1, 1999, Caroline Mann, review of *A Sight for Sore Eyes,* p. 122; August, 1999, Michael Rogers, review of *Some Lie and Some Die,* p. 149; September 1, 1999, Michael Rogers, review of *Murder Being Once Done,* p. 238; October 1, 1991, p. 144; October 15, 1995; January, 1996, p. 149; September 1, 1999, Francine Fialkoff, review of *Harm Done,* p. 237; October 1, 1999, Sandy Glover, review of *A Sight for Sore Eyes,* p. 150; May 15, 2000, Danna Bell-Russel, review of *Harm Done,* p. 142; June 15, 2000, Michael Rogers, review of *A Judgement in*

Stone, p. 122; December, 2000, Jane la Plante, review of *Piranha to Scurfy and Other Stories*, p. 194; December, 2001, Caroline Mann, review of *Adam and Eve and Pinch Me*, p. 175; October 1, 2003, Caroline Mann, review of *The Babes in the Wood*, p. 122.

Los Angeles Times, June 3, 1992, p. E1.

Los Angeles Times Book Review, August 3, 1980; May 8, 1983; November 21, 1993, p. 12.

Maclean's, May 19, 1986; April 10, 1995, p. 58.

Mademoiselle, February, 1996, p. 94.

New Statesman, September 6, 1996, Carol Birch, review of *The Keys to the Street*, p. 47; October 30, 1998, Francis Gilbert, review of *A Sight for Sore Eyes*.

Newsweek, September 21, 1987.

New York Times, September 9, 1988; February 4, 1990; June 12, 1992, p. C12; April 10, 1995, p. C9.

New York Times Book Review, June 25, 1967; June 23, 1968; August 24, 1969; February 26, 1974; June 2, 1974; December 1, 1974; April 27, 1975; November 23, 1975; February 27, 1977; October 13, 1996, Marilyn Stasio, review of *The Keys to the Street*, p. 29; September 7, 1997, Marilyn Stasio, review of *Road Rage*, p. 34; January 23, 1979; October 14, 1979; February 24, 1980; April 4, 1999, Marilyn Stasio, review of *A Sight for Sore Eyes*, p. 20; November 21, 1999, Marilyn Stasio, review of *Harm Done*, p. 80; March 3, 2002, Marilyn Stasio, review of *Adam and Eve and Pinch Me*, p. 21; August 4, 2002, Marilyn Stasio, review of *The Blood Doctor*, p. 19.

Publishers Weekly, August 16, 1991, p. 49; October 23, 1995; April 22, 1996, p. 61; July 29, 1996, review of *Keys to the Street*, p. 73; July 7, 1997, review of *Road Rage*, p. 53; February 8, 1999, review of *A Sight for Sore Eyes*, p. 197; October 18, 1999, review of *Harm Done*, p.73; November 13, 2000, review of *Piranha to Scurfy and Other Stories*, p. 89; January 28, 2002, review of *Adam and Eve and Pinch Me*, p. 274, interview with Ruth Rendell, p. 275; September 29, 2003, review of *The Babes in the Wood*, p. 46.

Saturday Review, January 30, 1971.

School Library Journal, March, 1997, Judy McAloon, review of *The Keys to the Street*, p. 216.

Seattle Times, February 10, 2002, Adam Woog, review of *Adam and Eve and Pinch Me*, p. J11.

Spectator, November 19, 1994, p. 47; October 4, 2003, Antonia Fraser, "And Now for My Next Trick . . .," review of *The Rottweiler*, p. 55.

Times (London, England), December 11, 1987; October 5, 1995.

Times Literary Supplement, February 23, 1967; December 21, 1967; April 23, 1970; October 1, 1976; June 5, 1981; July 23, 1982; October 7, 1994, p. 30.

Virginian Pilot, July 22, 2001, review of *Grasshopper*, p. E3.

Washington Post, May 19, 1992, p. B2.

Washington Post Book World, September 20, 1981; October 31, 1993.*

* * *

ROBERT, Dana L. 1956-

PERSONAL: Born October 9, 1956, in Lake Charles, LA; daughter of P. Charles (a teacher) and Mary Ellen (a homemaker; maiden name, Spiller) Robert; married Robert Kinloch Massie (a writer; marriage ended); married Marthinus L. Daneel (a missiologist), February 17, 1996; children: (first marriage) Samuel, John. *Education:* Louisiana State University, B.A. (magna cum laude), 1977; Yale University, Ph.D., 1984. *Religion:* United Methodist. *Hobbies and other interests:* Playing the piano, fishing, tatting lace, making Ukrainian Easter eggs.

ADDRESSES: Office—School of Theology, Boston University, 745 Commonwealth Ave., Boston, MA 02215. *E-mail*—drobdan@bu.edu.

CAREER: High school history teacher in Baton Rouge, LA, 1978; Yale University, New Haven, CT, instructor, 1982; Boston University, Boston, MA, assistant professor, 1984-90, associate professor, 1990-97, professor of international mission, 1997—. Zimbabwean Institute for Religious Research and Ecological Conservation, vice president and member of board of trustees. Emmanuel School of Religion, Johnson City, TN, Mission of the Church Lecturer, 1990; Yale University, lecturer, 1992; Gordon-Conwell Theological School, lecturer, 1992; Fuller Theological Seminary, Missiology Lecturer, 1995; Princeton Theological Seminary, Mission Lecturer, 1996. Pew Charitable Trusts, member of executive committee of African Initiatives in Christian Mission in Southern Africa, 1995-98, member of North American Committee, North Atlantic Missiology Project, 1996-98; Boston Theological Institute, chair of International Mission and Ecumenism Committee, 1996.

MEMBER: International Association of Mission Studies, Association of Professors of Mission, American Society of Missiology (member of board of publications, 1985-89), American Society of Church History.

AWARDS, HONORS: Ford Foundation grant, 1996; grant from DeFreitas Charitable Foundation, 1996-2000; *American Women in Mission: A Social History of Their Thought and Practice* was selected as one of fifteen outstanding books in mission studies, *International Bulletin of Missionary Research,* 1997.

WRITINGS:

Arthur Tappan Pierson and Evangelical Movements (in Korean), Yangsuh Publishing (Seoul, Korea), 1988.

American Women in Mission: A Social History of Their Thought and Practice, Mercer University Press (Macon, GA), 1997.

(With Howard Kee, Emily Albu, and others) *Christianity: A Social and Cultural History,* 2nd edition, Prentice-Hall (Englewood Cliffs, NJ), 1997.

Evangelism As the Heart of Mission, General Board of Global Ministries, United Methodist Church (New York, NY), 1998.

Occupy until I Come: A. T. Pierson and the Evangelization of the World, Eerdmans (Grand Rapids, MI), 2003.

Also contributing editor, *International Mission Bibliography,* Scarecrow Press (Metuchen, NJ); editor (with husband, Marthinus L. Daneel), *African Initiatives in Christian Mission,* University of South Africa Press (Pretoria, South Africa). Contributor to books, including *Earthen Vessels: American Evangelicals and Foreign Missions, 1880-1980,* edited by Joel Carpenter and Wilbert Shenk, Eerdmans (Grand Rapids, MI), 1990; *The Good News of the Kingdom: Mission Theology for the Nineties,* edited by Charles Van Engen, Dean Gilliland, and Paul Pierson, Orbis Books (Maryknoll, NY), 1995; and *New Directions in American Religious History,* edited by Harry Stout and Darryl Hart, Oxford University Press (New York, NY), 1997. General editor (with Marthinus L. Daneel) of the series "African Initiatives in Christian Mission," University of South Africa Press (Pretoria, South Africa), beginning 1995. Contributor of articles and reviews to periodicals, including *Missiology, Christian Century,*

Judson Bulletin, Mission Studies, and *Methodist History.* Contributing editor, *International Bulletin of Missionary Research,* beginning 1988; member of international editorial board, *Missionalia,* beginning 1993, and *Religion and Theology/Religie & Teologie,* beginning 1994.

BIOGRAPHICAL AND CRITICAL SOURCES:

PERIODICALS

Library Journal, June 15, 2003, George Westerlund, review of *Occupy until I Come: A. T. Pierson and the Evangelization of the World,* p. 78.*

*   *   *

RODDA, Emily 1948-
(Jennifer Rowe; Mary-Anne Dickinson)

PERSONAL: Born Jennifer Rowe, 1948, in New South Wales, Australia; married; children: one girl, three boys. *Education:* University of Sydney, M.A., 1973. *Hobbies and other interests:* Reading.

ADDRESSES: Home—Sydney, Australia. *Agent*—c/o Author Mail, Omnibus Books, 52 Fullarton Rd., Norwood, South Australia 5067, Australia.

CAREER: Full-time writer, 1994—. Former editor, Angus & Robertson publishers; former editor, *Australian Women's Weekly.*

AWARDS, HONORS: Children's Book of the Year, Children's Book Council of Australia (CBCA), 1985, for *Something Special,* 1987, for *Pigs Might Fly,* 1989, for *The Best-Kept Secret,* 1991, for *Finders Keepers,* and 1994, for *Rowan of Rin;* Bilby Award, Ipswich Festival of Children's Literature, 1995, for *Rowan of Rin;* Dromkeen Medal, Courtney Oldmeadow Children's Literature Foundation, 1995, for contributions to Australian children's literature; Children's Honour Book of the Year, CBCA, 1997, for *Rowan and the Keeper of the Crystal.*

WRITINGS:

FOR CHILDREN

Something Special, illustrated by Noela Young, Angus & Robertson (Sydney, Australia), 1984, Holt (New York, NY), 1989.

Pigs Might Fly, illustrated by Noela Young, Angus & Robertson (Sydney, Australia), 1986, published as *The Pigs Are Flying!,* Greenwillow (New York, NY), 1988.

The Best-Kept Secret, illustrated by Noela Young, Angus & Robertson (North Ryde, Australia), 1988, Holt (New York, NY), 1990.

Finders Keepers, illustrated by Noela Young, Omnibus Books (Norwood, Australia), 1990, Greenwillow (New York, NY), 1991.

Crumbs!, illustrated by Kerry Argent, Omnibus Books (Norwood, Australia), 1990.

The Timekeeper, illustrated by Noela Young, Omnibus Books (Norwood, Australia), 1992, Greenwillow (New York, NY), 1993.

Power and Glory, illustrated by Geoff Kelly, Allen & Unwin (St. Leonards, Australia), 1994, Greenwillow (New York, NY), 1996.

Yay!, illustrated by Craig Smith, Omnibus Books (Norwood, Australia), 1996, Greenwillow (New York, NY), 1997.

Game Plan, illustrated by Craig Smith, Omnibus Books (Norwood, Australia), 1998.

Green Fingers, illustrated by Craig Smith, Omnibus Books (Norwood, Australia), 1998.

Where Do You Hide Two Elephants?, illustrated by Andrew McLean, Omnibus Books (Norwood, Australia), 1998, Gareth Stevens (Milwaukee, WI), 2001.

Fuzz, the Famous Fly, illustrated by Tom Jellett, Omnibus Books (Norwood, Australia), 1999.

The Julia Tapes, Puffin (Ringwood, Australia), 1999.

Bob the Builder and the Elves, illustrated by Craig Smith, ABC Books (Sydney, Australia), 2000, published as *Bob and the House Elves,* illustrated by Tim Archbold, Bloomsbury (London, England), 2001.

Gobbleguts, ABC Books (Sydney, Australia), 2000.

Dog Tales, Omnibus Books (Norwood, Australia), 2001.

Squeak Street, illustrated by Andrew McLean, Working Title Press (Kingswood, Australia), 2002.

The Long Way Home, illustrated by Danny Snell, Working Title Press (Kingswood, Australia), 2002.

Editor of anthology *She's Apples: A Collection of Winning Stories for Young Australians.*

"ROWAN OF RIN" SERIES

Rowan of Rin, Omnibus Books (Norwood, Australia), 1993, Greenwillow (New York, NY), 2001.

Rowan and the Travellers, Omnibus Books (Norwood, Australia), 1994, published as *Rowan and the Travelers,* Greenwillow (New York, NY), 2001.

Rowan and the Keeper of the Crystal, Omnibus Books (Norwood, Australia), 1996, Greenwillow (New York, NY), 2002.

Rowan and the Zebak, Omnibus Books (Norwood, Australia), 1999, Greenwillow (New York, NY), 2002.

Rowan of the Buckshah, Omnibus Books (Norwood, Australia), 2003, published as *Rowan and the Ice Creepers,* Greenwillow (New York, NY), 2004.

"DELTORA QUEST" SERIES

The Forests of Silence, Scholastic Australia (Sydney, Australia), Scholastic (New York, NY), 2000.

The Lake of Tears, Scholastic Australia (Sydney, Australia), 2000, Scholastic (New York, NY), 2001.

City of the Rats, Scholastic Australia (Sydney, Australia), 2000, Scholastic (New York, NY), 2001.

The Shifting Sands, Scholastic Australia (Sydney, Australia), 2000, Scholastic (New York, NY), 2001.

Dread Mountain, Scholastic Australia (Sydney, Australia), 2000, Scholastic (New York, NY), 2001.

The Maze of the Beast, Scholastic Australia (Sydney, Australia), 2000, Scholastic (New York, NY), 2001.

The Valley of the Lost, Scholastic Australia (Sydney, Australia), 2000, Scholastic (New York, NY), 2001.

Return to Del, Scholastic Australia (Sydney, Australia), 2000, Scholastic (New York, NY), 2001.

The Deltora Book of Monsters: By Josef, Palace Librarian in the Reign of King Alton, illustrated by Marc McBride, Scholastic Australia (Sydney, Australia), 2001.

Cavern of the Fear, Scholastic Australia (Sydney, Australia), Scholastic (New York, NY), 2002.

The Isle of Illusion, Scholastic Australia (Sydney, Australia), 2002.

The Shadowlands, Scholastic Australia (Sydney, Australia), 2002.

"FAIRY REALM" SERIES; ORIGINALLY PUBLISHED UNDER NAME MARY-ANNE DICKINSON IN "STORYTELLING CHARMS" SERIES

The Charm Bracelet (also see below), Bantam Books (Sydney, Australia), 1994, HarperCollins (New York, NY), 2003.

The Flower Fairies (also see below), Bantam Books (Sydney, Australia), 1994, HarperCollins (New York, NY), 2003.

The Third Wish (also see below), Bantam Books (Sydney, Australia), 1995, HarperCollins (New York, NY), 2003.

The Last Fairy-Apple Tree (also see below), Bantam Books (Sydney, Australia), 1995, HarperCollins (New York, NY), 2003.

The Magic Key (also see below), Bantam Books (Sydney, Australia), 1995, HarperCollins (New York, NY), 2004.

The Unicorn (also see below), Bantam Books (Sydney, Australia), 1996, HarperCollins (New York, NY), 2004.

The Fairy Realm (contains *The Flower Fairies, The Charm Bracelet, The Third Wish, The Last Fairy-Apple Tree, The Magic Key,* and *The Unicorn*), ABC Books (Sydney, Australia), 2002.

"TEEN POWER INC." SERIES

The Secret of Banyan Bay, Ashton Scholastic (Sydney, Australia), 1994.

The Sorcerer's Apprentice, Ashton Scholastic (Sydney, Australia), 1994.

The Bad Dog Mystery, Ashton Scholastic (Sydney, Australia), 1994.

Beware the Gingerbread House, Ashton Scholastic (Sydney, Australia), 1994.

Cry of the Cat, Ashton Scholastic (Sydney, Australia), 1994.

The Disappearing TV Star, Ashton Scholastic (Sydney, Australia), 1994.

The Ghost of Raven Hill, Ashton Scholastic (Sydney, Australia), 1994.

Green for Danger, Ashton Scholastic (Sydney, Australia), 1994.

Poison Pen, Ashton Scholastic (Sydney, Australia), 1994.

Breaking Point, Ashton Scholastic (Sydney, Australia), 1994.

Nowhere to Run, Ashton Scholastic (Sydney, Australia), 1995.

Crime in the Picture, Ashton Scholastic (Sydney, Australia), 1995.

The Case of Crazy Claude, Ashton Scholastic (Sydney, Australia), 1995.

Fear in Fashion, Ashton Scholastic (Sydney, Australia), 1995.

Dangerous Game, Ashton Scholastic (Sydney, Australia), 1995.

Danger in Rhyme, Ashton Scholastic (Sydney, Australia), 1995.

The Missing Millionaire, Ashton Scholastic (Sydney, Australia), 1995.

Haunted House, Ashton Scholastic (Sydney, Australia), 1995.

Cry Wolf, Ashton Scholastic (Sydney, Australia), 1996.

Photo Finish, Ashton Scholastic (Sydney, Australia), 1996.

Stage Fright, Ashton Scholastic (Sydney, Australia), 1996.

St. Elmo's Fire, Ashton Scholastic (Sydney, Australia), 1996.

Bad Apples, Ashton Scholastic (Sydney, Australia), 1996.

Dirty Tricks, Ashton Scholastic (Sydney, Australia), 1996.

The War of the Work Demons, Ashton Scholastic (Sydney, Australia), 1997.

Hit or Miss, Ashton Scholastic (Sydney, Australia), 1998.

Hot Pursuit, Ashton Scholastic (Sydney, Australia), 1998.

Deep Freeze, Ashton Scholastic (Sydney, Australia), 1999.

The Secret Enemy, Ashton Scholastic (Sydney, Australia), 1999.

Dead End, Ashton Scholastic (Sydney, Australia), 1999.

AS JENNIFER ROWE

The Commonsense International Cookery Book, Angus & Robertson (Sydney, Australia), 1978.

(Editor) *More Poems to Read to Young Australians,* Royal New South Wales Institute for Deaf and Blind Children (North Rocks, Australia), 1980.

Eating Well in Later Life, Angus & Robertson (Sydney, Australia), 1982.

Grim Pickings, Allen & Unwin (Sydney, Australia), 1988.

Murder by the Book, Allen & Unwin (Sydney, Australia), 1989.

Death in Store, Allen & Unwin (Sydney, Australia), 1991, Doubleday (Garden City, NY), 1993.

The Makeover Murders, Allen & Unwin (St. Leonards, Australia), 1992, Doubleday (Garden City, NY), 1993.

Stranglehold, Allen & Unwin (St. Leonards, Australia), 1993, Bantam (New York, NY), 1995.

(Editor) *Love Lies Bleeding: A Crimes for a Summer Christmas Anthology,* Allen & Unwin (St. Leonards, Australia), 1994.

Lamb to the Slaughter, Allen & Unwin (St. Leonards, Australia), 1996, Bantam (New York, NY), 1996.

Deadline, Allen & Unwin (St. Leonards, Australia), 1997, published as *Suspect,* Ballantine (New York, NY), 1999.

Something Wicked, Allen & Unwin (St. Leonards, Australia), Ballantine (New York, NY), 1999.

Angela's Mandrake and Other Feisty Fables, Allen & Unwin (St. Leonards, Australia), 2000, published as *Fairy Tales for Grown-Ups,* Allen & Unwin (St. Leonards, Australia), 2001.

SIDELIGHTS: When she finished her first children's book, Emily Rodda submitted it to a publisher under her grandmother's maiden name rather than use her own birth name of Jennifer Rowe. Little did she know at the time that "Emily Rodda" would become one of Australia's favorite children's authors and a five-time winner of the Children's Book Council of Australia's Children's Book of the Year Award. Rodda has written numerous picture books as well as several series for older readers, most notably the "Rowan of Rin" and "Deltora Quest" books. Her fantasy novels are said to introduce carefully drawn imaginary realms where quests are complicated by riddles, magic, and mixed motives. Rodda also helped launch an adventure/mystery series for young readers for Scholastic Australia, "Teen Power Inc.," to which she has contributed more than two dozen titles. Writing under her real name, Jennifer Rowe, she has produced adult mysteries as well as cookbooks. This prolific output is particularly remarkable because Rodda did not become a full-time writer until 1994. Before that she held a job as a magazine editor, while raising four small children. "I feel very lucky to have a job I love so much," she said on her Web site.

Born in New South Wales, Rodda worked as an editor at both an Australian publishing house and at a woman's magazine before turning her hand to juvenile fiction. She chose her grandmother's maiden name as a pseudonym because at the time of her first publication, her publisher, Angus & Robertson, was also her employer. Rodda's first novel, *Something Special,* was an attempt to document her daughter's growth, and with four children, Rodda had a lot of material at hand for subsequent titles. Aimed at primary graders, *Something Special* tells the story of a little girl, Samantha, who becomes involved in her mother's rummage sale. Set in contemporary times and with a realistic setting, the book nonetheless contains an element of fantasy:

Samantha and her friend, Lizzie, become involved with the spirits of the former owners of the clothing donated for the sale.

At the sale, Sam's friend Lizzie leaves the stall for a while. Sam takes a short nap and is surprised by a quartet of spirits who are admiring their donated clothes. Upon Lizzie's return, these visitors have gone and she suspects they were just a dream of Sam's, but the next day one of them actually returns in the flesh to reclaim a favorite "second skin," a tartan dressing gown he had for years. Ron Morton, writing in *Books for Your Children,* noted: "This is a well written book. . . . Its strength is perhaps its warm, embracing dialogue." Morton concluded that though the "essence" of the story was fantasy, "there is still something quite believable about what happened." A *Books for Keeps* critic called *Something Special* a "thought-provoking and eerie tale" which "catches quite brilliantly the dash, excitement, and movement of the preparations" for the sale. Writing about the U.S. edition, a *Kirkus Reviews* critic commented that the book offers an "unusual story, beautifully structured and simply but gracefully told," while *School Library Journal* contributor Elisabeth LeBris noted that the book "is told in a light tone with lots of dialogue."

With this first book, Rodda won the Australian Children's Book of the Year Award, one of the most prestigious prizes in Australia, which not only helped sales of the initial title, but also had reviewers and readers alike awaiting a second book. Rodda commented in an interview in *Magpies:* "I was astounded and surprised because I hadn't held out the faintest hope of actually winning. . . . As a child I had always wanted to be a writer; now maybe I really was one." Rodda also noted in the interview, however, that "second books are much harder to pull off than first ones."

Rodda's second book, *Pigs Might Fly,* is a lighthearted fantasy that employs mystery and magical travel to another world. Rachel, about age seven, is in bed with a cold and longs for some excitement to break up her boring days. A picture drawn by a sign-painting friend of her father's is meant to cheer Rachel up but leads to much more radical results. The picture shows Rachel riding a unicorn in her pajamas while pigs fly overhead. Soon Rachel finds herself on the unicorn while actual pigs are playing in the sky. Left at the door of a peasant couple who insist on calling her

Grace, Rachel soon discovers that what is transpiring is known locally as a flying pig storm. The peasants think that Rachel has come from "Outside," a rare event that has also initiated the pig storm. Rachel stays in this fabulous land a day and a half, filled with anxiety about how she will get back home, but she eventually does return through the aid of a rhyme discovered at the library. Many reviewers have noted the parallels in the book to *Alice's Adventures in Wonderland* as well as to *The Wizard of Oz,* though Rodda's tale is much shorter and far less complex than either of those two. Howard George, writing in *Reading Time,* commented that Rodda's second novel was "bound to be a great success with young readers" because "only people with a sense of the ridiculous can appreciate unlikely events." George concluded that "this is a finely crafted book" and that "the humour used is never slapstick nor banal." Reviewing the U.S. edition, published as *The Pigs Are Flying!,* Karen P. Smith commented in *School Library Journal* that this is "an engaging fantasy for beginning fans of the genre," while Karen Jameyson called the story a "comfortable swirl of suspense, adventure, and amusing characters" in *Horn Book.* A *Books for Keeps* contributor concluded by stating that *Pigs Might Fly* is a "beautifully unfolded tale from an illuminating, fresh-voiced writer." Award committees reached conclusions similar to reviewers', for this second book also earned a Children's Book of the Year Award from the Children's Book Council of Australia (CBCA).

Rodda stuck with fantasy for her third title, *The Best-Kept Secret,* which features a magical carousel ride. When this carousel comes to town, the residents all find reasons why they should take a ride on it into the future, including young Joanna, who rescues a boy lost in the future. None of the characters who take the magic ride realize that they are at crossroads in their lives; Joanna has just learned she is to become a big sister. Rescuing the young boy in the future, then, is an unconscious acceptance of this new role. Gerald Haigh, reviewing the book in the *Times Educational Supplement,* noted that Rodda's story "is subtle and layered, and pricks at the emotions in all sorts of ways." A *Kirkus Reviews* critic dubbed it a "deceptively simple tale" and a "charmingly original, neatly structured story," while *School Library Journal* contributor Joanne Aswell concluded that *The Best-Kept Secret* is an "amusing, optimistic chapter book fantasy to read alone or aloud."

Rodda's first male protagonist appears in her fourth book, *Finders Keepers,* a longer and more sophisti-

cated juvenile novel. Rodda herself has characterized the book as being special not only for the use of a boy as the central character, but also for the fact that she used "family relationships as a background to the fantasy," as she explained in *Reading Time.* When Patrick takes part in a novel interactive quiz game on his television, he has no idea he will pass through the "Barrier" separating his reality from the "Other Side," but that in fact is exactly what happens. Patrick becomes a Finder of all those things people misplace day to day. His prize is a computer he has been longing for. As Laurie Copping commented in *Reading Time,* the story moves at "a rapid pace, fantasy and reality interchanging so rapidly that sometimes the reader may wonder whether or not they are experiencing the real or the unreal." A *Publishers Weekly* reviewer also noted the "lightning speed" at which Rodda keeps her story going and concluded that the book was "an uncommonly satisfying read."

Patrick reappears in *The Timekeeper,* a sequel to *Finders Keepers,* in which he is once again summoned through the Barrier, this time to prevent the destruction of worlds on both sides. Obstacles make his mission all the harder, and Rodda blends elements of computer technology to create "an action-filled fantasy with warm, believable depictions of family relationships," according to Anne Connor in *School Library Journal.* A *Kirkus Reviews* commentator called *The Timekeeper* an "engaging light fantasy."

Rodda has also used the contemporary world of high tech in other books for young readers, including *Crumbs!* and the picture book *Power and Glory.* The successive competency levels of a video game form the core of the latter title, which Carolyn Phelan dubbed an "unexpected pleasure" in a starred *Booklist* review. John Sigwald, writing in *School Library Journal,* called *Power and Glory* a "big, bold, colorful and cartoony quest for control over electronic nemeses," while a *Kirkus Reviews* contributor noted the "clever analogies" Rodda makes between the witch, goblin, and ogre of the video game and family members of the boy who is playing the game. "Rodda builds up a throbbing rhythm that approximates the intensity of the play," observed a *Publishers Weekly* reviewer of this "rousing" picture book.

Far afield from the techno world of the 1990s are Rodda's series of novels about the adventures of Rowan, two of which have been honored by the

CBCA. The first title in the series, *Rowan of Rin,* tells the magical story of the village of Rin, where the locals awake one morning to discover that their source of water, a nearby river, has slowed to a mere trickle. As the days pass, matters get worse and the stream almost totally dries up. The villagers depend on this stream to water their animals, the "bukshah," and these can no longer get enough water. Something must be done. The villagers agree that someone must travel up the Mountain, an eerie and frightening place, to find out what the problem is. The Wise Woman provides the villagers with a map along with a guiding chant, but it is only the boy who tends the bukshah, Rowan, who can figure out the meaning of the map. Rowan sets out on his quest with six others, braving obstacles, including a dragon, until he reaches the top of the Mountain and is able to restore the stream to life. In the process, Rowan also saves the life of his protector, Strong John.

Horn Book correspondent Karen Jameyson called *Rowan of Rin* a "quest adventure of the highest order" and a "riveting fantasy." Jameyson also noted that Rodda's characters "step off the page as individuals." *Magpies* contributor Joan Zahnleiter commented that the "text is very visual, sparkling with vivid imagery. It would lend itself to an exciting TV production." The "Rowan of Rin" series has become popular worldwide, with Internet chat rooms dedicated to its plots. Throughout the series, Rowan has evolved from a sickly and timid youngster to a careful but courageous lad to whom others look for leadership. In a discussion of *Rowan and the Travelers,* published in Australia as *Rowan and the Travellers,* a *Kirkus Reviews* critic commended Rodda for her novels that "prove . . . that a weak body can hide a hero's heart."

In *Rowan and the Travelers,* it falls to Rowan to save his fellow villagers from a strange curse that causes them to fall asleep where they stand. "Once again Rodda's fantasy world, a folkloric Anytime, becomes a vivid reality for readers," commented Kay Weisman in *Booklist.* In *School Library Journal,* Trish Anderson observed that *Rowan and the Travelers* "proves heroism comes in many sizes." *Rowan and the Keeper of the Crystal,* the third book in the series, finds Rowan in a desperate quest to put together an antidote after his mother is poisoned at the critical moment in which she must choose a new leader for the village. *Horn Book* correspondent Anne St. John felt that the novel "offers an ideal mix of suspenseful plot, unusual characters, and an engaging hero."

The Zebak are the historic enemies of Rowan's people, and in *Rowan and the Zebak,* the young hero must journey to their land to rescue his kidnapped sister. As with the previous titles in the series, Rowan's success depends upon his courage and upon his ability to understand magic and the enigmatic riddles posed to him by the wise woman Sheba. In her *Booklist* review of the title, Weisman declared that "Rowan's adventures are riveting, with plot twists sufficient to keep the outcome in doubt." Writing in *School Library Journal,* Mara Alpert noted that Rowan "is not the flashiest of heroes, but in each story he grows a little more confident."

While the "Rowan of Rin" series is perhaps better known internationally, Rodda is also building an audience for her "Deltora Quest" fantasies, which number a dozen titles. In this series, three friends—Leif, Jasmine, and Barda—face perils both ordinary and fantastic to retrieve a set of seven precious stones that their people have used to ward off enemies in the past. When the stones are restored to the Belt of Deltora, the land will be freed of the Shadow Lord, a force with evil intentions. In the Australian editions of each "Deltora" novel, the belt appears on the spine of the book, with the stones that have been rescued in each previous volume. In his *Magpies* review of books five to eight in the "Deltora Quest" series, Russ Merrin wrote: "The full series is quite simply, a huge achievement. It is vividly written, rich in detail and highly imaginative in its execution. It melds together well, flows cohesively, and reads easily."

Rodda's "Fairy Realm" series, originally published as the "Storytelling Charms" series under the name Mary-Anne Dickinson, is aimed at middle-grade readers having their first taste of fantasy. Jessie, the heroine of these volumes, is an ordinary girl who discovers that her destiny lies equally in the everyday world and in an alternative universe peopled by fairies, elves, trolls, ogres, and other fabulous creatures. In the series debut, *The Charm Bracelet,* Jessie discovers that her grandmother is actually queen of the fairies, and that the two of them must go into the fairy realm to renew its magic and ensure its safety. *Booklist* critic Ellen Mandel suggested that "intergenerational teamwork and a girl's levelheaded thinking combine" in the novel to produce an "exciting fantasy." A *Publishers Weekly* reviewer called *The Charm Bracelet* a "taut, engaging fantasy tale" with "an intriguing plot and appealing characters." According to a *Kirkus Reviews* contributor, "Rodda tells a suspenseful, well-knit tale, enlivened by humor and heroism."

Through the first decade of her writing life, Rodda worked late at night after her children had gone to bed. Now she devotes her days to her craft and enjoys it so much that she says her favorite hobbies are "reading and writing," as she related on her Web site. She has written for nearly every age reader from preschool to retirement, having also penned almost a dozen crime novels for adults under her real name. Rodda said on her Web site: "I am married with four children, and live in the Blue Mountains, west of Sydney. We have a dog called Sunny. And because we live next to the bush, the garden is always full of frogs, lizards, magpies, cockatoos, and kookaburras." In a *Magpies* interview, she described the kind of book she likes to write. "I love things that all tie up and in fact I find things that don't very irritating if they're that type of book," she said. "The kind of book that I regard as an adventure or a fantasy or whatever, I think that deserves a good, neat ending. . . . There' no little clue that doesn't have a meaning. . . . Maybe it's a response to the general messiness of life, but I find it very satisfying."

BIOGRAPHICAL AND CRITICAL SOURCES:

BOOKS

Children's Literature Review, Volume 23, Gale (Detroit, MI), 1994, pp. 207-213.
Helbig, Alethea K. and Agnes Regan Perkins, editors, *Dictionary of Children's Fiction from Australia, Canada, India, New Zealand, and Selected African Countries,* Greenwood Press (Westport, CT), 1992.
Rodda, Emily, *Something Special,* illustrated by Noela Young, Angus & Robertson (Sydney, Australia), 1984, Holt (New York, NY), 1989.

PERIODICALS

Booklist, September 1, 1990, p. 52; April 15, 1996, Carolyn Phelan, review of *Power and Glory,* p. 1441; January, 1997, p. 768; November 15, 2001, Kay Weisman, review of *Rowan and the Travelers,* p. 574; January 1, 2002, Kay Weisman, review of *Rowan and the Keeper of the Crystal,* p. 859;

March 1, 2002, Kay Weisman, review of *Rowan and the Zebak,* p. 1133; January 1, 2003, Ellen Mandel, review of *The Charm Bracelet,* p. 892.
Books for Keeps, September, 1986, review of *Something Special,* p. 23; March, 1989, review of *Pigs Might Fly,* p. 18; January, 1996, p. 10; May, 2001, Annabel Gibb, review of *Bob and the House Elves,* p. 21.
Books for Your Children, spring, 1985, Ron Morton, review of *Something Special,* p. 11.
Horn Book, November-December, 1988, Karen Jameyson, review of *The Pigs Are Flying!,* p. 784; November-December, 1993, Karen Jameyson, "News from Down Under," review of *Rowan of Rin,* pp. 778-780; September, 2001, Anne St. John, review of *Rowan and the Travelers,* pp. 593-594; March-April, 2002, Anne St. John, review of *Rowan and the Keeper of the Crystal,* pp. 217-218.
Kirkus Reviews, November 1, 1989, review of *Something Special,* p. 1597; May 15, 1990, review of *The Best-Kept Secret,* p. 802; October 1, 1993, review of *The Timekeeper,* p. 1278; February 15, 1996, review of *Power and Glory,* p. 299; October 1, 2001, review of *Rowan and the Travelers,* p. 1432; January 1, 2002, review of *Rowan and the Keeper of the Crystal,* p. 50; May 1, 2002, review of *Rowan and the Zebak,* p. 666; January 1, 2003, review of *The Charm Bracelet,* p. 65.
Magpies, July, 1990, "Emily Rodda," pp. 19-21; November, 1993, Joan Zahnleiter, review of *Rowan of Rin,* p. 31; September, 1998, Rayma Turton, review of *Bob the Builder and the Elves,* p. 35; March, 2001, Russ Merrin, "Two Series for Independent Readers," review of *Dread Mountain, The Maze of the Beast, The Valley of the Lost,* and *Return to Del,* p. 35.
Publishers Weekly, October 18, 1991, review of *Finders Keepers,* p. 25; May 6, 1996, review of *Power and Glory,* p. 81; June 9, 1997, p. 46; February 10, 2003, review of *The Charm Bracelet,* p. 188.
Reading Time, number 3, 1987, Howard George, review of *Pigs Might Fly,* p. 66; number 4, 1990, Laurie Copping, review of *Finders Keepers,* p. 25; number 4, 1991, Emily Rodda, "CBCA Acceptance Speech," p. 5.
School Library Journal, September, 1988, Karen P. Smith, review of *The Pigs Are Flying!,* pp. 185-186; January, 1990, Elisabeth LeBris, review of *Something Special,* pp. 106, 108; January, 1991, Joanne Aswell, review of *The Best-Kept Secret,* pp. 79-80; October, 1993, Anne Connor, review of

The Timekeeper, p. 128; May, 1996, John Sigwald, review of *Power and Glory,* p. 97; January, 2002, Trish Anderson, review of *Rowan and the Travelers,* p. 140; May, 2002, Janet Gillen, review of *Rowan and the Keeper of the Crystal,* p. 160; July, 2002, Mara Alpert, review of *Rowan and the Zebak,* p. 124; August, 2003, Debbie Whitbeck, review of *The Charm Bracelet,* p. 140.

Times Educational Supplement, February 17, 1989, Gerald Haigh, "Daredevils," review of *The Best-Kept Secret,* p. B28.

ONLINE

Emily Rodda Home Page, http://www.emilyrodda.com/ (February 20, 2003).

Scholastic Australia, http://www.scholastic.com.au/ (February 20, 2003), "Profile: Emily Rodda."*

*   *   *

ROGASKY, Barbara 1933-

PERSONAL: Born April 9, 1933, in Wilmington, DE; daughter of Charles (a grocer) and Ida (a homemaker; maiden name, Rubin) Rogasky; *Education:* Attended the University of Delaware, 1950-55. *Politics:* "Vacillating Liberal-Left." *Religion:* Jewish. *Hobbies and other interests:* "All-around 'handyperson;' music, especially classical but not only; cars; and a perpetual and pursued curiosity about most things."

ADDRESSES: Office—P.O. Box 34, Thetford, VT 05074. *E-mail*—owl@valley.net.

CAREER: Author and writer. In-house editor, at various levels, for several adult trade publishers; freelance editorial consultant for various publishers, agents, and individuals.

AWARDS, HONORS: Notable Book selection, American Library Association (ALA), 1982, for *Rapunzel;* Best Book for Young Adults selection, ALA, Best Nonfiction for Young Adults selection, *Publishers Weekly,* Best Books of the Year selection, *School Library Journal,* Best Books selection, Young Adult Library Services Association (ALA), Young Adult's

Barbara Rogasky

Choice, International Reading Association, Most Outstanding Book in Secondary Social Studies, Society of School Librarians International, Best Books for the Teenage, New York Public Library, and Present Tense/Joel A. Cavour Award, American Jewish Committee, all 1988, and Children's Book of the Year selection, Bank Street College, Seventy-one Top Books of the Century selection, *Instructor* magazine, and "Top 100 Countdown: Best of the Best Books for Young Adults over Twenty-five Years," *School Library Journal,* all for *Smoke and Ashes: The Story of the Holocaust;* Land of Enchantment Award, New Mexico Library Association, and Sequoia Award, Oklahoma Library Association, both for *The Water of Life: A Tale from the Brothers Grimm;* Notable Book selection, ALA, and Best Books of the Year selection, *School Library Journal,* 1994, both for *Winter Poems;* National Jewish Book Award, 1996, for *The Golem: A Version;* the German edition of *Smoke and Ashes* was presented to the youth of Germany in a special ceremony by President Johannes Rau, Berlin, Germany, 2001; Sydney Taylor Honor Book, Association of Jewish Libraries, 2002, and Best Books for the Teenage, New York Public Library, 2003, both for *Smoke and Ashes* (revised edition).

WRITINGS:

(Reteller) *Rapunzel,* illustrated by Trina Schart Hyman, Holiday House (New York, NY), 1982.

(Reteller) *The Water of Life: A Tale from the Brothers Grimm,* illustrated by Trina Schart Hyman, Holiday House (New York, NY), 1986.

Smoke and Ashes: The Story of the Holocaust, Holiday House (New York, NY), 1988, revised and expanded version, 2002.

(Photographer) Myra Cohn Livingston, *Light and Shadow,* Holiday House (New York, NY), 1992.

(Compiler) *Winter Poems,* illustrated by Trina Schart Hyman, Scholastic (New York, NY), 1994.

The Golem: A Version, illustrated by Trina Schart Hyman, Holiday House (New York, NY), 1996.

(Compiler) *Leaf by Leaf: Autumn Poems,* photographs by Marc Tauss, Scholastic (New York, NY), 2001.

Gilgul, illustrated by Kyrsten Brooker, Holiday House (New York, NY), 2004.

(Compiler) *Spring Poems,* Holiday House (New York, NY), forthcoming.

Dybbuk!: A Version, illustrated by Leonard Everett Fisher, Holiday House (New York, NY), forthcoming.

Contributor of articles to books, including *From Sea to Shining Sea,* compiled by Amy L. Cohn, Scholastic (New York, NY), 1993, and *Young Reader's Companion to American History,* edited by John A. Garraty, Houghton Mifflin (Boston, MA), 1994. *Smoke and Ashes* was translated into German as *Der Holocaust: Ein Buch für junge Leser,* Rowohlt (Berlin, Germany), 1999, and into Dutch and Japanese, 1992.

WORK IN PROGRESS: Research into the history of American immigration for a young-adult book; ongoing search for Eastern-European, Yiddish-flavored tales, myths, and stories to retell.

SIDELIGHTS: Whether in such traditional stories as *Rapunzel* or *Water of Life: A Tale from the Brothers Grimm,* or in collections of verse arranged on seasonal themes, or her acclaimed history of the Holocaust, Barbara Rogasky brings her flair for storytelling to the

fore, claim reviewers. Recalling her early career, Rogasky told *CA:* "I like telling stories, thoroughly enjoy children and teenagers: a combination that led me into this profession. For several years before that, I lived in New York City and worked on staff as an editor in adult trade houses—before I fled to New England. Those years and my freelance work as editor, rewriter, etc., gave me basic helpful tools and insights into the mechanics of writing itself." Although she "always wrote," as she explained to Theresa Gawlas Medoff in an interview for the *University of Delaware Messenger,* she did not think of herself as a writer. "I thought of myself as an editor, as a literate human being, as someone who had a way with words, but not as a writer. I certainly never thought of myself as someone who would write for children."

After working for nearly twenty-five years in the publishing field with such prestigious firms as Macmillan and Harcourt Brace Jovanovich, Rogasky felt she needed to escape New York City. So she moved to rural New England in 1978 and began a career in freelance editing and ghostwriting. Yet it still took a push from someone else to get Rogasky started in writing for children. That someone was Trina Schart Hyman, a Caldecott Medal-winning illustrator, who suggested that she and Rogasky collaborate. "Trina got me started," Rogasky confided to Medoff. "It was very hard to get into publishing then [in the mid-1980s]. It's even harder now. I would never have thought to write *Rapunzel* if Trina hadn't suggested it." With Hyman's clout came Rogasky's entrée into the world of children's books and what eventually turned out to be a four-book collaboration. Rogasky's first two books retell traditional tales by Jacob and Wilhelm Grimm. Though *Rapunzel* is the well-known story of a maiden who uses her extremely long hair to escape captivity in a tower, *The Water of Life* is more obscure, recounting the quest of three princes for magical water to heal their dying father. About the former, *Horn Book*'s Ethel L. Heins noted that Rogasky "slightly prettified the familiar tale and doctored it as if to assure respectability," while a reviewer for the *Bulletin of the Center for Children's Books* dubbed the retelling "adequate" though "undistinguished." That Rogasky honed her skill for the second tale, *The Water of Life,* was evident to several critics, including one for *Kirkus Reviews,* who called it "a graceful, compassionate translation," and another for *Publishers Weekly,* who described it as an "elegant text."

The daughter of Eastern-European Jews, Rogasky has preserved her Jewish heritage in several works. *The*

Golem: A Version, which won the National Jewish Book Award, recounts the traditional and mystical tale of a clay giant fashioned by a rabbi to protect the Jews of Prague, Czechoslovakia (now the Czech Republic), who in the sixteenth century were being persecuted by anti-Semites. Told "with a colloquial warmth and a Yiddish idiom" to quote *Booklist*'s Hazel Rochman, this version of the Golem tale has been expanded to thirteen chapters in order to tell the complete story of the monster from creation to destruction. Although a *Publishers Weekly* reviewer found the combination of horror (prejudice and violence) and humor (misunderstandings and faux pas of the Golem) difficult to accept, others praised the realistic portrayal of life for the Jews in this tumultuous century. Through this tale, Rogasky "lays bare the irrationality and danger of prejudice," a *Kirkus Reviews* contributor remarked. Similarly, two other offerings enlighten readers about other Jewish beliefs as *Gilgul* portrays the conviction that a person may be reincarnated in response to whatever sins that person has committed and uses the seven deadly sins of pride, covetousness, lust, anger, gluttony, envy, and sloth as subject matter, while the forthcoming *Dybbuk!: A Version* features a Jewish tale about preordained love and spirit possession. "My parents were very typical Eastern-European immigrant Jews," Rogasky confided to Medoff. "Though I resisted my Jewishness for many, many years, I came to appreciate what they were and the heritage and culture they reflected."

Although she says that it was not written because of her Jewish heritage, the young-adult title *Smoke and Ashes: The Story of the Holocaust* made Rogasky even more aware of her Eastern-European Jewish heritage. "Knowing the details of the Holocaust taught me how absolute evil can exist in the world, and similar evil continues to exist," she explained to *CA.* She also discovered that fifty members of her family had died in Russia during the Holocaust. In *Smoke and Ashes,* first published in 1988 and expanded and reissued in 2002, Rogasky uses eye-witness accounts, photographs, statistics, and commentary to tell the story of how the Nazis tried to kill the entire Jewish population of Europe. For the later edition, dubbed "readable and evenhanded" by Amy Lilien-Harper of *School Library Journal,* Rogasky added sections about Nazi persecutions of homosexuals, the rescuers of Jews, and a discussion of genocide in other countries. According to a *Kirkus Reviews* contributor, this "clearly written, comprehensive, sensitive, and nuanced" story of the Holocaust is a "monumentally important

history." The first edition of this "stark, powerful and comprehensive" work, to quote Medoff, was translated into several languages, including German, and in 1999, the author attended a ceremony in Berlin that coincided with the launching of the German edition, which earned good reviews in the German media. Because Rogasky believes that young adults need to know about this dark time in history, she often gives presentations on the Holocaust at schools, colleges, and to the general public.

In addition to folktales and Jewish-themed works, Rogasky has compiled several collections of poetry because, as she told *CA,* "I love poetry. The compilations are a joy to do—a wonderful excuse to read all the poetry I can find. And almost any topic lends itself to compilation." Among such topics are the seasonally-themed *Winter Poems, Leaf by Leaf: Autumn Poems,* and *Spring Poems,* each of which contains a selection of poems from a variety of time periods, traditions, and cultures that celebrate that time of year. While some are complete poems, others are snippets from longer works. The anthologies caught the attention of critics. Numbered among their enthusiasts are *School Library Journal* reviewer Shawn Brommer, who called *Leaf by Leaf* a "rich, eclectic collection," and a *Kirkus Reviews* contributor, who praised the "marvelous sense of composition to this attractive volume." A *Publishers Weekly* critic wondered, however, if the gloomy tone and difficult language might be more appropriate for adult readers. Also in picture-book format is the "elegant" anthology *Winter Poems,* to quote a *Publishers Weekly* writer, who likened this exceptional volume to "sun glinting on snow, . . . dazzling." Writing in the *Washington Post Book World,* poet David Barber noted that Rogasky had chosen the twenty-five winter poems with "care and scruple," creating "a mix [that] is well-rounded yet gracefully unassuming" and "all very wintry and agreeably bracing."

After publishing her first children's book at age fifty, Rogasky has found a rewarding second career. Reflecting on the writing process, she told *CA:* "Writing and research are hard work. Accuracy is crucial. But it is work that helps give some sense to being alive, and I enjoy it immensely. Maybe the only thing I enjoy more is my preposterous mutt of a dog, so silly-looking children point and laugh and adults smile." "His name," she says, "and why not, is George."

BIOGRAPHICAL AND CRITICAL SOURCES:

BOOKS

St. James Guide to Young Adult Writers, 2nd edition, St. James Press (Detroit, MI), 1999.

PERIODICALS

Booklist, May 15, 1992, Deborah Abbott, review of *Light and Shadow,* p. 1679; September 15, 1994, Carolyn Phelan, review of *Winter Poems,* pp. 134-135; October 1, 1996, Hazel Rochman, review of *The Golem: A Version,* p. 335; July, 2001, Hazel Rochman, review of *Leaf by Leaf: Autumn Poems,* p. 2002; October 15, 2002, Hazel Rochman, review of *Smoke and Ashes: The Story of the Holocaust* (revised edition), p. 400.

Book Report, January-February, 1997, Mary Hofmann, review of *The Golem,* p. 50.

Bulletin of the Center for Children's Books, July, 1982, review of *Rapunzel,* pp. 206-207; September, 1996, Betsy Hearne, review of *The Golem,* pp. 27-28.

Five Owls, summer, 1988, Susan Stan, review of *Smoke and Ashes,* p. 6.

Horn Book, February, 1983, Ethel L. Heins, review of *Rapunzel,* pp. 38-39; March, 1987, Mary M. Burns, review of *The Water of Life: A Tale from the Brothers Grimm,* pp. 229-230; September, 1988, Margaret A. Bush, review of *Smoke and Ashes,* p. 647; January, 1989, Hazel Rochman, "Booktalking: Going Global," review of *Smoke and Ashes,* pp. 30-35.

Journal of Reading, May, 1989, Susan Murphy and Robert Small, review of *Smoke and Ashes,* pp. 750-754.

Kirkus Reviews, September 15, 1986, review of *The Water of Life,* p. 1449; September 15, 1996, review of *The Golem,* p. 1407; August 1, 2001, review of *Leaf by Leaf,* p. 1131; August 15, 2002, review of *Smoke and Ashes* (revised edition) p. 1234.

Publishers Weekly, July 16, 1982, review of *Rapunzel,* p. 78; August 22, 1986, review of *The Water of Life,* p. 97; May 13, 1988, review of *Smoke and Ashes,* p. 276; April 26, 1991, review of *Smoke and Ashes,* p. 60; October 31, 1994, review of *Winter Poems,* p. 63; October 21, 1996, review of *The Golem,* pp. 84-85; November 15, 1999, review of *Winter Poems,* p. 69; January 10, 2000, review of *Winter Poems,* p. 70; September 3, 2001, review of *Leaf by Leaf,* p. 88.

School Library Journal, November, 1986, Connie C. Rockman, review of *The Water of Life,* p. 83; June, 1988, Jack Forman, review of *Smoke and Ashes,* p. 128; April, 1992, Barbara Chatton, review of *Light and Shadow,* p. 139; October, 1994, Sally R. Dow, review of *Winter Poems,* p. 114; October, 1996, Susan Scheps, review of *The Golem,* p. 126; September, 2001, Shawn Brommer, review of *Leaf by Leaf,* p. 252; October, 2002, Amy Lilien-Harper, review of *Smoke and Ashes* (revised edition), pp. 192-193.

Washington Post Book World, December 4, 1994, David Barber, "The Lure of the Rhyme," review of *Winter Poems,* p. 19.

ONLINE

University of Delaware Messenger, http://www.udel.edu/PR/Messenger/ (Volume 9, number 2, 2000), Theresa Gawlas Medoff, "Children's Author Finds Niche Preserving Jewish Heritage."

*   *   *

ROSS, Stewart 1947-

PERSONAL: Born April 4, 1947, in Aylesbury, England; son of Graham and Marjorie (a physiotherapist) Ross; married; wife's name Lucy (a music administrator), 1978; children: James, Kate, Alex, Eleanor. *Ethnicity:* "Anglo-Saxon." *Education:* Exeter University, B.A., 1969, M.A., 1972; Bristol University, certificate in education, 1970; Rollins College, M.A.T., 1979. *Politics:* Liberal. *Religion:* "Vaguely Christian." *Hobbies and other interests:* Drama, opera, sport.

ADDRESSES: Home—3 Westfield, Blean, Canterbury, Kent CT2 9ER, England.

CAREER: Trinity College, Sri Lanka, teacher, 1965-66; Exeter University, England, assistant tutor, 1970-72; University of Riyadh, Saudi Arabia, lecturer, 1972-74; King's School, Canterbury, England, master/housemaster, 1974-78; Rollins College, Florida,

Stewart Ross

lecturer, 1979-89; full-time writer, 1989—. I.C.E.S. La Roche-sur-Yon, France, lecturer, 1995—; frequent lecturer and broadcaster.

MEMBER: Canterbury Arts Council (vice chairperson), Society of Authors.

AWARDS, HONORS: Best Books citation, American Library Association, 1995, for *Shakespeare and Macbeth: The Story behind the Play;* Pick of the List citation, American Booksellers Association, 1996, for *Witches.*

WRITINGS:

NONFICTION; FOR CHILDREN

Columbus and the Age of Exploration, illustrated by Ken Stott, Bookwright (New York, NY), 1985.

Chaucer and the Middle Ages, illustrated by John James, Wayland (Hove, England), 1985.

A Medieval Serf, illustrated by Alan Langford, Wayland (Hove, England), 1985.

Pepys and the Stuarts, illustrated by Gerry Wood, Wayland (Hove, England), 1985.

A Saxon Farmer, illustrated by Mark Bergin, Wayland (Hove, England), 1985.

A Victorian Factory Worker, illustrated by Alan Langford, Wayland (Hove, England), 1985.

Dickens and the Victorians, illustrated by Gerry Wood, Wayland (Hove, England), 1986.

Spotlight on Medieval Europe, Wayland (Hove, England), 1986.

The Ancient Britons, illustrated by Mark Bergin, Wayland (Hove, England), 1987.

Lloyd George and the First World War, illustrated by Martin Salisbury, Wayland (Hove, England), 1987.

Spotlight on the Stuarts, Wayland (Hove, England), 1987.

Spotlight on the Victorians, Wayland (Hove, England), 1987.

Winston Churchill and the Second World War, illustrated by Richard Scollins, Wayland (Hove, England), 1987.

The Ancient World, Watts (New York, NY), 1990.

Britain between the Wars, Wayland (Hove, England), 1990.

The Home Front, Wayland (Hove, England), 1990.

Elizabethan Life, Batsford (London, England), 1991.

The Nineteen Eighties, Trafalgar Square (London, England), 1991.

Europe, Franklin Watts (New York, NY), 1992.

Racism in the Third Reich, Batsford (London, England), 1992.

Battle of Little Bighorn, D. Bennett (St. Alban's, England), 1993.

Britain at War 1914-1918, Batsford (London, England), 1993.

Gunfight at O.K. Corral, D. Bennett (St. Alban's, England), 1993.

Propaganda, Thomson Learning (New York, NY), 1993.

Wild Bill Hickok and Calamity Jane, D. Bennett (St. Alban's, England), 1993.

World Leaders, Thomson Learning (New York, NY), 1993.

Wounded Knee, D. Bennett (St. Alban's, England), 1993.

Cavaliers and Roundheads, Batsford (London, England), 1994.

Shakespeare and Macbeth: The Story behind the Play, illustrated by Tony Karpinski and Victor Ambrus, Viking (New York, NY), 1994.

Britain since 1930, Evans (London, England), 1995.

Ancient Greece: Greek Theatre, Wayland (Hove, England), 1996.

Ancient Greece: The Original Olympics, Thomson Learning (New York, NY), 1996.

And Then—: A History of the World in 128 Pages, illustrated by John Lobban, Copper Beech (Brookfield, CT), 1996.

Beware the King! The Story of Anne Boleyn and King Henry VIII, Evans (London, England), 1996.

Down with the Romans: The Tragic Tale of Queen Boudicca, Evans (London, England), 1996.

Charlotte Bronte and Jane Eyre, illustrated by Robert Van Nutt, Viking (New York, NY), 1997.

Gods and Giants: Myths of Northern Europe, illustrated by Francis Phillipps, Copper Beech Books (Brookfield, CT), 1997.

Warriors & Witches, illustrated by Francis Phillipps, Copper Beech Books (Brookfield, CT), 1997.

Dragons and Demons: Myths of China, Japan, and India, illustrated by Francis Phillipps, Copper Beech Books (Brookfield, CT), 1998.

Monsters and Magic, illustrated by Francis Phillipps, Copper Beech Books (Brookfield, CT), 1998.

Oxford Children's Book of the 20th Century: A Concise Guide to a Century of Contrast and Change, Oxford University Press (New York, NY), 1998.

Spirits and Sorcerers, illustrated by Francis Phillipps, Copper Beech Books (Brookfield, CT), 1998.

Mark Twain and Huckleberry Finn, illustrated by Ronald Himler, Viking (New York, NY), 1999.

Daily Life, P. Bedrick Books (Lincolnwood, IL), 1999.

The Original Olympics, P. Bedrick Books (Lincolnwood, IL), 1999.

Greek Theatre, P. Bedrick Books (Lincolnwood, IL), 1999.

Vikings, Copper Beech Books (Brookfield, CT), 2000.

The War in Kosovo, Raintree Steck-Vaughn (Austin, TX), 2000.

Assassination in Sarajevo: The Trigger for World War I, Heinemann Library (Chicago, IL), 2001.

The American Revolution, Franklin Watts (New York, NY), 2001.

The Industrial Revolution, Franklin Watts (New York, NY), 2001.

Leaders of World War II, Raintree Steck-Vaughn (Austin, TX), 2001.

The Fall of the Bastille: Revolution in France, Heinemann Library (Chicago, IL), 2001.

Alexander Graham Bell, Raintree Steck-Vaughn (Austin, TX), 2001.

The Story of Anne Frank, Thameside Press (North Mankato, MN), 2001.

The Story of Mother Teresa, Thameside Press (North Mankato, MN), 2001.

The Story of Ludwig van Beethoven, Thameside Press (North Mankato, MN), 2002.

The Star Houses, Barron's (Hauppauge, NY), 2002.

Only a Matter of Time: A Story From Kosovo, Barron's (Hauppauge, NY), 2002.

The Causes of the Cold War, World Almanac Library (Milwaukee, WI), 2002.

The Technology of World War I, Raintree Steck-Vaughn (Austin, TX), 2003.

The Russian Revolution, Raintree Steck-Vaughn (Austin, TX), 2003.

Michael Faraday, Raintree Steck-Vaughn (Austin, TX), 2003.

Leonardo da Vinci, Raintree Steck-Vaughn (Austin, TX), 2003.

Leaders of World War I, Raintree Steck-Vaughn (Austin, TX), 2003.

The French Revolution, Raintree Steck-Vaughn (Austin, TX), 2003.

The Causes of World War I, Raintree Steck-Vaughn (Austin, TX), 2003.

World War I, World Almanac Library (Milwaukee, WI), 2004.

Wolfgang Amadeus Mozart, Raintree (Chicago, IL), 2004.

William Shakespeare, Raintree (Chicago, IL), 2004.

The United Nations, Raintree (Chicago, IL), 2004.

Monarchs, Lucent (San Diego, CA), 2004.

The Collapse of Communism, Heinemann Library (Chicago, IL), 2004.

The Battle of the Somme, Raintree (Chicago, IL), 2004.

"HOW THEY LIVED" SERIES; FOR CHILDREN

A Family in World War II, illustrated by Alan Langford, Wayland (Hove, England), 1985.

A Roman Centurion, illustrated by Alan Langford, Wayland (Hove, England), 1985, Rourke Enterprises, 1987.

An Edwardian Household, illustrated by John James, Wayland (Hove, England), 1986.

A Crusading Knight, illustrated by Mark Bergin, Rourke Enterprises, 1986.

A Soldier in World War I, illustrated by John Haysom, Wayland (Hove, England), 1987.

"POLITICS TODAY" SERIES; FOR CHILDREN

The Alliance Parties, Wayland (Hove, England), 1986.
The Conservative Party, Wayland (Hove, England), 1986.
The House of Commons, Wayland (Hove, England), 1986.
The House of Lords, Wayland (Hove, England), 1986.
The Labour Party, Wayland (Hove, England), 1986.
The Prime Minister, Wayland (Hove, England), 1986.
The Cabinet and Government, Wayland (Hove, England), 1987.
Elections, Wayland (Hove, England), 1987.
The European Parliament and the European Community, Wayland (Hove, England), 1987.
Local Government, Wayland (Hove, England), 1987.
The Monarchy, Wayland (Hove, England), 1987.
Trade Unions and Pressure Groups, Wayland (Hove, England), 1987.

"WITNESS HISTORY" SERIES; FOR CHILDREN

China since 1945, Wayland (Hove, England), 1988, Bookwright (New York, NY), 1989.
Toward European Unity, Wayland (Hove, England), 1989.
The Origins of World War I, Bookwright (New York, NY), 1989.
The Russian Revolution, Bookwright (New York, NY), 1989.
The United Nations, Wayland (Hove, England), 1989, Bookwright (New York, NY), 1990.
War in the Trenches, Wayland (Hove, England), 1990, Bookwright (New York, NY), 1990.
The USSR under Stalin, Bookwright (New York, NY), 1991.

"STARTING HISTORY" SERIES; FOR CHILDREN

Food We Ate, Wayland (Hove, England), 1991.
How We Travelled, Wayland (Hove, England), 1991.
What We Wore, Wayland (Hove, England), 1991.
Where We Lived, Wayland (Hove, England), 1991.
Our Environment, Wayland (Hove, England), 1992.
Our Family, Wayland (Hove, England), 1992.

Our Health, Wayland (Hove, England), 1992.
Our Holidays, Wayland (Hove, England), 1992.
Our Schools, Wayland (Hove, England), 1992.
Shopping, Wayland (Hove, England), 1992.

"FACT OR FICTION" SERIES; FOR CHILDREN

Spies and Traitors, Copper Beech (Brookfield, CT), 1995.
Pirates: The Story of Buccaneers, Brigands, Corsairs, and Their Piracy on the High Seas from the Spanish Main to the China Sea, Copper Beech (Brookfield, CT), 1995.
Cowboys: A Journey down the Long, Lonely Cattle Trail in Search of the Hard-Riding, Gun-Slinging Cowhands of the Old West, Copper Beech (Brookfield, CT), 1995.
Bandits and Outlaws: The Truth about Outlaws, Highwaymen, Smugglers, and Robbers from the Bandit Gangs of Ancient China to the Desperados of Today, Copper Beech (Brookfield, CT), 1995.
Conquerors and Explorers, Copper Beech (Brookfield, CT), 1996.
Secret Societies, Copper Beech (Brookfield, CT), 1996.
Knights, Copper Beech (Brookfield, CT), 1996.
Witches, Copper Beech (Brookfield, CT), 1996.
Beasts, illustrated by Francis Phillipps, Copper Beech Books (Brookfield, CT), 1997.
Monsters of the Deep, illustrated by Francis Phillipps, Copper Beech Books (Brookfield, CT), 1997.

"CAUSES AND CONSEQUENCES" SERIES; FOR CHILDREN

Causes and Consequences of the Arab-Israeli Conflict, Raintree Steck-Vaughn (Austin, TX), 1996.
Causes and Consequences of the Rise of Japan and the Pacific Rim, Raintree Steck-Vaughn (Austin, TX), 1996.
Causes and Consequences of World War II, Raintree Steck-Vaughn (Austin, TX), 1996.
Causes and Consequences of the Great Depression, Raintree Steck-Vaughn (Austin, TX), 1998.
Causes and Consequences of World War I, Raintree Steck-Vaughn (Austin, TX), 1998.

"COMING ALIVE" SERIES; FOR CHILDREN

Long Live Mary, Queen of Scots, illustrated by Sue Shields, Evans Brothers Ltd (London, England), 1998.

Athens Is Saved!: The First Marathon, illustrated by Sue Shields, Evans Brothers Ltd (London, England), 1998.

Find King Alfred!, Evans Brothers Ltd (London, England), 1999.

NONFICTION; FOR ADULTS

Monarchs of Scotland, Facts on File (New York, NY), 1990.

Scottish Castles, illustrated by David Simon, Lochar (Moffat, Scotland), 1990.

Ancient Scotland, Lochar (Moffat, Scotland), 1991.

History in Hiding: The Story of Britain's Secret Passages and Hiding Places, R. Hale (London, England), 1991.

The Stewart Dynasty, Nairn, Thomas & Lochar (Moffat, Scotland), 1993.

FICTION; FOR ADULTS

One Crowded Hour, Warner (New York, NY), 1994.

Beneath Another Sun, Warner (New York, NY), 1994.

OTHER

(Editor) *The First World War,* Wayland (Hove, England), 1989.

(Editor) *The Second World War,* Wayland (Hove, England), 1989.

The Last Clarinet (a libretto), with music by Paul Englishby, Oxford University Press (New York, NY), 1995.

Also author of numerous articles and a play that was performed in 1992.

SIDELIGHTS: In nearly twenty years as a full-time writer, Stewart Ross has published close to 200 books. In an essay for *Something about the Author Autobiography Series (SAAS),* Ross traced his productive career as an author directly back to his childhood love of reading. "I read voraciously. The more I read, the more I wanted to read," he recalled. "This love of books and the words within them made me determined to be a writer." One particular book influenced him toward writing nonfiction in order to provide young readers with interesting glimpses into the past. "My passion for history grew from the seeds planted by an attractive book of stories from the past, brightly colored pictures on one side and the text on the other, most of it myth. That didn't matter at the time: inspiration first, analysis later," he commented in *SAAS.*

Born in Aylesbury, England, in 1947, Ross grew up in the English countryside. When he was not reading, he spent many hours creating daring, imaginative adventures with his brother in the woods and fields near their home. These experiences, too, fueled his desire to become a writer. "My early childhood furnished me with the two things essential to all writers: a love for words and a turbulent imagination. Neither is a gift from on high. We are probably all born with an equal *capacity* to imagine, but we are not given an equal chance to set it free. My upbringing released my imagination, trained it, and encouraged it to develop," he explained in his autobiography. "Nothing feeds the young imagination like a potent cocktail of books, time, and space."

From the age of eight, Ross attended private boarding schools in England. Though he appreciated the high academic standards set forth at the schools and the self-reliance he gained there, he resented being forced to wear a uniform and being subjected to corporal punishment. Only in his last two years was he allowed to concentrate in the subjects he loved: literature and history. Through the work of two enthusiastic teachers, he developed a special fondness for the books of William Shakespeare and Charles Dickens. "My mother says that at the age of seventeen I sat on an Italian beach more engrossed in [Dickens's novel] *Nicholas Nickleby* than the surrounding bikinis," Ross wrote in *SAAS.* "It's a good story, but I don't believe her."

After graduating in 1965, Ross traveled to Sri Lanka as part of the British Voluntary Service Overseas, an organization similar to the American Peace Corps. He spent the next year teaching English "exuberantly and no doubt rather badly," as he admitted in his autobiography, before returning to England by way of India, Ethiopia, Egypt, and Greece. Ross attended college for the next six years, earning bachelor's and master's degrees in history from Exeter University and a teaching certificate from Bristol University. Over the next dozen years, he took teaching positions in Saudi Arabia, England, and Florida. "I discovered early on that you never really know your subject until you have to teach it. To give a course of study you not only have to know the facts, but you have to be able to present them in a memorable and digestible form," Ross noted in *SAAS.* "The hours and hours of reading and research stood me in good stead as a teacher and, later, as a writer. Many of my early books were little more than extensions of my teaching notes."

Ross's writing career got its start in 1984, when he was given the opportunity to write a book for young readers about Christopher Columbus. When the book, *Columbus and the Age of Exploration,* was published the following year, it led to contracts for several more books that explained historical events to students. Before long, Ross, who by this time was married with four children, felt overwhelmed by the demands of teaching, writing, and family. He quit teaching in 1989 in order to become a full-time writer and spend more time with his family, though he continued to work occasionally as a lecturer and broadcaster.

Since then, Ross has produced as many as a dozen books per year about famous people, world events, and historical time periods. In his "superb" *Shakespeare and Macbeth: The Story behind the Play,* for instance, Ross did "a terrific job of making the vitality of Shakespeare accessible" to young readers, according to a writer for *Kirkus Reviews.* The 1994 book describes what London was like during Shakespeare's time, takes readers behind the scenes at the famous Globe Theatre, and explains the pressures the Bard faced while writing his play. Ross contends that Shakespeare wrote and rewrote *Macbeth* in order to please the recently crowned King James—all the while keeping the script secret even from the actors to prevent competing theaters from stealing his ideas. A reviewer for *Publishers Weekly* called the book "intelligent and informative," adding that it "excels at introducing theater as a living art form." Sally Margolis, in a review for *School Library Journal,* stated that "the perpetual grouse by Shakespeare buffs that a book can't give young people the true sense of a stage production is at least partly countered by this dynamic gem."

Ross composes his books in a small, insulated hut in the garden of his family's home. Calling himself "the most fortunate of men" in his *SAAS* essay, he explained that he could hardly wait to make his ten-yard commute each morning and begin writing. "I have no magic formula for those who wish to write. But if you don't love words, stop now and set your sights on something more conventional. Writing is primarily about playing with words, not ideas: expression first, content second," Ross wrote in his autobiography. "If you have a passion for words and wish to write, read, read, and read again. Read critically, omnivorously, all day, every day. Old books, new books—any books: poetry, manuals, novels, essays, newspapers. And as you read, write. Write as much as you can. Get others to read what you have written and listen to what they say. In this way, gradually, you will develop a style of your own, a unique voice."

BIOGRAPHICAL AND CRITICAL SOURCES:

BOOKS

Something about the Author Autobiography Series, Volume 23, Gale (Detroit, MI), 1996.

PERIODICALS

Booklist, June 1, 1989, p. 1726; March 15, 1995, p. 1324; July 1, 1995, p. 1877; December 15, 1995, Hazel Rochman, review of *Arab-Israeli Conflict,* p. 694; March 1, 1999, Susan Dove Lempke, review of *Mark Twain and Huckleberry Finn,* p. 1210; January 1, 2001, Heather Hepler, review of *The Original Olympics,* p. 946; November 15, 2002, Ilene Cooper, review of *The Causes of the Cold War,* p. 599; March 1, 2003, Hazel Rochman, review of *The Causes of World War I,* p. 1154; December 1, 2003, Carolyn Phelan, review of *Leaders of World War I,* p. 663.
Kirkus Reviews, November 15, 1994, p. 1542.
Publishers Weekly, October 31, 1994, p. 63.
School Library Journal, August, 1989, p. 158; July, 1990, p. 93; January, 1995, p. 142; May, 1995, p. 115; January, 1996, p. 136; February, 1996, p. 120; March, 1996, p. 214; June, 1996, pp. 141, 147; December, 1998, Ann W. Moore, review of *Long Live Mary, Queen of Scots,* p. 90; December, 1998, Cynthia M. Sturgis, review of *Athens is Saved! The First Marathon,* p. 90; February, 1999, Cheri Estes, review of *Find King Alfred!,* p. 124; May, 1999, Shawn Brommer, review of *Mark Twain and Huckleberry Finn,* p. 142; August, 2000, Cynthia M. Sturgis, review of *The Original*

Olympics, p. 203; September, 2000, Cynthia M. Sturgis, review of *Greek Theatre,* p. 255; July, 2001, Lana Miles, review of *Assassination in Sarajevo: The Trigger for World War I,* p. 116; March, 2002, Carol Wichman, review of *The American Revolution,* p. 257; December, 2002, Kathleen Isaacs, review of *Only a Matter of Time: A Story From Kosovo,* p. 146; February, 2003, Elizabeth Talbot, review of *The Russian Revolution,* p. 169; May, 2003, Edith Ching, review of *The United Nations,* p. 176; July, 2003, Eldon Younce, review of *The Technology of World War I,* p. 148.

Voice of Youth Advocates, October, 1990, p. 250.

ONLINE

Stewart Ross Home Page, http://www.stewart49.free serve.co.uk/ (March 10, 2004).*

*   *   *

ROWE, Jennifer
    See RODDA, Emily

*   *   *

RUBENSTEIN, Richard E(dward) 1938-

PERSONAL: Born February 24, 1938, in New York, NY; son of Harold S. (in textiles) and Jo (Feldman) Rubenstein; married Elizabeth Marsh, August 26, 1962 (divorced); married Brenda Libman, September 21, 1975; children: (first marriage) Alec Louis, Matthew Robert. *Education:* Harvard University, B.A., 1959, J.D., 1963; Oxford University, M.A.Juris., 1961. *Politics:* "Radical." *Religion:* Jewish.

ADDRESSES: Agent—c/o Author Mail, Harcourt, Inc., 6277 Sea Harbor Dr., Orlando, FL 32887.

CAREER: Steptoe & Johnson (law firm), Washington, DC, attorney, 1963-67; Adlai Stevenson Institute, Chicago, IL, assistant director, 1967-70; Roosevelt University, Chicago, associate professor of political science, beginning 1969; Antioch University, Washington, DC, member of law faculty; also professor of conflict resolution. Malcolm X Community College, Chicago, professorial lecturer, 1969-70; University of Provence, Fulbright visiting professor, 1976-77. Consultant to National Advisory Commission on Causes and Prevention of Violence, 1968-69.

MEMBER: Phi Beta Kappa.

AWARDS, HONORS: Rhodes Scholar at Oxford University, 1959-61.

WRITINGS:

(Editor, with Robert M. Fogelson) *Mass Violence in America,* Arno, 1969.
Rebels in Eden: Mass Political Violence in the United States, Little, Brown (Boston, MA), 1970.
Left Turn: Origins of the Next American Revolution, Little, Brown (Boston, MA), 1973.
(Editor) *Great Courtroom Battles,* Playboy Press (New York, NY), 1973.
The Cunning of History: The Holocaust and the American Future, Harper (New York, NY), 1978.
Reflections on Religion and Public Policy, Paragon House (New York, NY), 1984.
Alchemists of Revolution: Terrorism in the Modern World, Basic Books (New York, NY), 1987.
Group Violence in America, Center for Conflict Analysis and Resolution, George Mason University (Fairfax, VA), 1993.
Frameworks for Interpreting Conflict: A Handbook for Journalists, Institute for Conflict Analysis and Resolution, George Mason University (Fairfax, VA), 1994.
Comrade Valentine, Harcourt (Orlando, FL), 1994.
When Jesus Became God: The Epic Fight over Christ's Divinity in the Last Days of Rome, Harcourt (Orlando, FL), 1999.
Aristotle's Children: How Muslims, Christians, and Jews Rediscovered Ancient Wisdom and Illuminated the Dark Ages, Harcourt (Orlando, FL), 2003.

Contributor to books, including *The Politics of Protest,* edited by Jerome H. Skolnick, Ballantine (New York, NY), 1969; *The Conscience of the City,* edited by Martin Meyerson, George Braziller (New York, NY), 1970; and *The New American Revolution,* edited by R.

Aya and N. Miller, Free Press (New York, NY), 1971. Series editor, with Dan C. McCurry, "American Farmers and the Rise of Agribusiness," Ayer (Salem, NY), 1975.

BIOGRAPHICAL AND CRITICAL SOURCES:

PERIODICALS

Christian Science Monitor, July 3, 1970.
Nation, April 6, 1970.
New York Review of Books, September 24, 1987.
New York Times Book Review, March 12, 1970, June 28, 1987.
Saturday Review, July 11, 1970.
Time, April 20, 1970.
Washington Post, April 24, 1987.*

*   *   *

RUSSELL, P. Craig 1951-

PERSONAL: Born October 30, 1951, in Wellsville, OH; son of Dwight Shontz (a clothing store owner) and Jean (a homemaker and secretary; maiden name, Bushong) Russell. *Education:* University of Cincinnati, B.F.A., 1974. *Politics:* Libertarian. *Hobbies and other interests:* Piano (classical and salon).

ADDRESSES: Home—417 East College, Kent, OH 44240. *Agent*—Mike Friedrich, Star Reach Productions, 2991 Shattuck Ave., Suite 202, Berkeley, CA 94705.

CAREER: Freelance graphic-story artist, 1972—. Kent State University, Kent, OH, instructor in illustration, 1981, 1983.

AWARDS, HONORS: Shazam Award, best new talent, 1974; Eisner Award, for adaptation of *The Ring of the Nibelung;* Eisner Award nomination, for adaptation of *The Magic Flute;* Harvey Award, best graphic album, 1993, for *Fairy Tales of Oscar Wilde,* Volume 1.

WRITINGS:

GRAPHIC FICTION; AND ILLUSTRATOR

The Chimera, Earthart Graphics (San Francisco, CA), 1976.

Night Music 1, Eclipse Enterprises (Forestville, CA), 1979.
(With Don McGregor) *Killraven, Warrior of the Worlds,* Marvel Comics (New York, NY), 1983.
(Adaptor) *Ariane and Bluebeard* (based on the opera by Maurice Maeterlinck and Paul Dukas), Eclipse Books (Forestville, CA), 1989.
(Adaptor) *The Scarlet Letter* (based on the novel by Nathaniel Hawthorne), Berkley Publishing (New York, NY), 1990.
(Adaptor) *The Magic Flute* (based on the opera by Wolfgang Amadeus Mozart), Eclipse Books (Forestville, CA), 1991, reprinted, Nantier Beall Minoustchine (New York, NY), 2003.
(Adaptor) *Opera* (based on works by Gustav Mahler, Richard Wagner, Strauss, and Claude Debussy), Eclipse Books (Forestville, CA), 1990.
(Adaptor) *Fairy Tales of Oscar Wilde,* Nantier Beall Minoustchine (New York, NY), Volume 1, 1992, Volume 2, 1994.

ILLUSTRATOR

Roy Thomas, *Elric—The Dreaming City,* Marvel Comics (New York, NY), 1982.
Roy Thomas, *Elric of Melnibone,* Graphitti Designs, 1986.
Achmed Abdullah, *The Thief of Baghdad,* Donning (Norfolk, VA), 1987.

Adaptor and illustrator of *The Ring of the Nibelung* (based on the opera by Richard Wagner). Contributor to graphic-fiction anthologies, including *Tapping the Vein—Book One,* by Clive Barker, Eclipse Books (Forestville, CA), 1989; *Within Our Reach,* Star*Reach Productions (Hayward, CA), 1991; and *Ray Bradbury Chronicles—Volume 1,* Bantam Spectra (New York, NY), 1992. Also contributor of graphic stories to comic books, including *Voyage to the Moon, War of the Worlds, Killraven,* and *Epic Illustrated,* all Marvel Comics (New York, NY); *Heavy Metal; Imagine; Night Music,* Eclipse Comics (Forestville, CA); and *Robin 3000,* DC Comics (New York, NY). Contributor to magazines, including *National Lampoon.*

Contributor of illustrations to graphic-fiction anthologies, including *Elric: Weird of the White Wolf,* First Comics, 1986. Also contributor of illustrations to comic books, including *Batman* and *Sandman,* both DC Comics (New York, NY), and *Epic Illustrated.*

SIDELIGHTS: "So many stories, so many pictures, so few hours in the day," P. Craig Russell once told *CA.* "I believe the graphic-story art form to be one of the best kept secrets of the day."

"I particularly like doing adaptations. The challenge, like that of the screenplay (from novel to film), is to deconstruct a piece and then to reconstruct it in another form, exploiting the possibilities and meeting the demands of that new form, while remaining true to the spirit of the original.

"It takes a jigsaw puzzle mind combined with a love of imagery to make it work. I can't imagine being in any other field."

BIOGRAPHICAL AND CRITICAL SOURCES:

PERIODICALS

Library Journal, July, 2003, review of *The Magic Flute,* p. 70.*

S

SACKS, Peter
  See SACKS, Peter M.

*   *   *

SACKS, Peter M. 1950-
  (Peter Sacks)

PERSONAL: Born July 15, 1950, in Port Elizabeth, South Africa; immigrated to United States, 1970, naturalized citizen, 1983; son of Samuel (a doctor) and Esther (Gordon) Sacks; married Barbara Kassel (a painter), January 8, 1980. *Education:* Princeton University, A.B. (summa cum laude), 1973; Oxford University, M.Phil., 1976; Yale University, Ph.D., 1980.

ADDRESSES: Home—3519 Newland Rd., Baltimore, MD 21218. *Office*—Department of English, Johns Hopkins University, 34th and Charles Sts., Baltimore, MD 21218.

CAREER: Johns Hopkins University, Baltimore, MD, assistant professor, 1980-86, associate professor of English, beginning 1986—, member of writing seminars department.

AWARDS, HONORS: Christian Gauss Award, Phi Beta Kappa, 1985, for *The English Elegy.*

WRITINGS:

The English Elegy: Studies in the Genre from Spenser to Yeats, Johns Hopkins University Press (Baltimore, MD), 1985.

(Under name Peter Sacks) *In These Mountains* (poetry), Macmillan (New York, NY), 1986.

Promised Lands, Viking (New York, NY), 1990.

Woody Gwyn, Texas Tech University Press (Lubbock, TX), 1995.

Natal Command, University of Chicago Press (Chicago, IL), 1997.

O Wheel (poetry), University of Georgia Press (Athens, GA), 2000.

Necessity (poetry), W. W. Norton (New York, NY), 2003.

Contributor of articles and poems to periodicals, including *Antioch Review, Boulevard, Georgia Review, New Republic, New Yorker, Partisan Review, Tikkun, TriQuarterly,* and *Yale Review.*

SIDELIGHTS: Peter M. Sacks once told *CA:* "I was raised in South Africa. I am now an expatriate, but I am still caught up in that country's history. My work in poetry has usually sought to balance an openness to physical beauty on the one hand against historical suffering on the other.

"In scholarship, I was drawn to the genre of elegy, from the Renaissance to the present. While my chronological focus is now narrowing toward the twentieth century, my interests are widening within the field of poetry at large. Questions of the relationship between individual writers and cultural codes are of particular interest to me.

"Expatriation and the impulse to travel are still uppermost and have led to journeys through such regions as the Amazon, the Andes and Himalayas, Morocco,

Namibia, and southern Mexico. Another strong interest is in writing about painting, primarily on representational painting of the last two centuries."

BIOGRAPHICAL AND CRITICAL SOURCES:

PERIODICALS

Baltimore Sun, July 20, 1986.
Hudson Review, spring, 1987.
Virginia Quarterly Review, autumn, 1986.
Washington Post Book World, May 3, 1987.*

*   *   *

SADLIER, Darlene J(oy) 1950-

PERSONAL: Born October 1, 1950, in Warren, OH; daughter of Robert W. and Margaret L. Sadlier; married James Naremore, January 2, 1984. *Education:* Kent State University, B.A. (summa cum laude), 1971; University of Wisconsin, M.A., 1972, Ph.D., 1977. *Politics:* Liberal Democrat.

ADDRESSES: Home—2304 Rechter Rd., Bloomington, IN 47401-6121. *Office*—Department of Spanish and Portuguese, Indiana University—Bloomington, Bloomington, IN 47405.

CAREER: Indiana University—Bloomington, visiting assistant professor, 1978-79, assistant professor, 1979-85, associate professor, 1985-91, professor of Spanish and Portuguese and adjunct professor of women's studies, 1991—. Kent State University, visiting lecturer, 1977-78.

MEMBER: International Conference Group on Portugal, Associacao Internacional de Lusitanistas, Modern Language Association of America, Asociación de Literatura Femenina Hispánica, Associacao Nacional de Pos-Graduacao e Pesquisa em Letras e Linguistica, Midwest Modern Language Association (president of Luso-Brazilian Division, 1985-86), Faculty Professional Association.

AWARDS, HONORS: Fellowships from National Endowment for the Humanities, 1980 and 1984, Fundacao Calouste Gulbenkian, 1981, Lilly Foundation,

1982-83, West European Center, 1983-85, 1987-90, and Fulbright Foundation, 1985-86, 1988; grants from President's Council on the Humanities, 1982-83, President's Council for International Programs, 1982-83, American Philosophical Society, 1983, West European Center, Indiana University—Bloomington, 1986 and 1988-89, and U.S. Information Agency, 1988 and 1991.

WRITINGS:

Imagery and Theme in the Poetry of Cecília Meireles: A Study of "Mar absoluto," José Porrúa Turanzas (Madrid, Spain), 1983.
Cecília Meireles e Joao Alphonsus, Andre Quince Editor, 1984.
The Question of How: Women Writers and New Portuguese Literature, Greenwood Press (Westport, CT), 1989.
(Editor, translator, and author of introduction) *One Hundred Years after Tomorrow: Brazilian Women's Fiction in the Twentieth Century,* Indiana University Press (Bloomington, IN), 1992.
An Introduction to Fernando Pessoa: Modernism and the Paradoxes of Authorship, University Press of Florida (Gainesville, FL), 1998.
Nelson Pereira dos Santos, University Of Illinois Press (Urbana, IL), 2003.

Contributor of articles, reviews, and translations to periodicals, including *Fiction International, James Joyce Literary Supplement, Luso-Brazilian Review,* and *Latin American Literary Review.* Member of editorial board, *Hispanofila,* beginning 1988.

BIOGRAPHICAL AND CRITICAL SOURCES:

PERIODICALS

Library Journal, June 15, 2003, review of *Nelson Pereira dos Santos,*p. 75.*

*   *   *

SAUERLÄNDER, Willibald 1924-

PERSONAL: Surname cited in some sources as Sauerlaender or Sauerlander; born February 2, 1924, in Waldsee, Württemberg, Germany; married Brigitte Rückoldt; children: George. *Education:* University of Munich, Ph.D., 1953.

ADDRESSES: Office—10 Meiserstraße, Munich 2, Germany.

CAREER: University of Freiburg, Freiburg, West Germany (now Germany), lecturer, 1962-64, professor of art history, 1966-70; Zentral-Institut für Kunstgeschichte, Munich, Germany, director, beginning 1970. Institute of Advanced Study, Princeton, NJ, visiting member, 1961-62, 1973; visiting professor at New York University, 1964-65, Collège de France, Paris, 1981, University of Wisconsin—Madison, 1982, and Harvard University, 1984, 1985.

MEMBER: Comité International d'Histoire de l'Art (vice president), Societé des Antiquaires de France, Societé Française d'Archéologie, Medieval Academy of America, Bayerische Academie der Wissenschaften.

WRITINGS:

Die Kathedrale von Chartres, 1954.
Die Skulptur des Mittelalters, 1963.
(Editor, with George Kauffman) *Walter Friedlander zum 90,* Walter de Gruyter (Hawthorne, NY), 1963.
Die Bronzetur von Nowgorod, R. Piper Verlag (Munich, Germany), 1963.
Von Sens bis Strassburg, Walter de Gruyter (Hawthorne, NY), 1966.
Gotische Skulptur in Frankeich: 1140-1270, Hirmer Verlag (Munich, Germany), 1970, translation by Janet Sondheimer published as *Gothic Sculpture in France, 1140-1270,* Thames & Hudson (London, England), 1972, Harry N. Abrams (New York, NY), 1973.
La Sculpture gothique en France, 1972.
Kunsthistoriker, 1979.
Ein Versuch über die Gesichter Houdons, Deutscher Kunstverlag (Munich, Germany), 2003.

SIDELIGHTS: German art historian Willibald Sauerländer's *Gotische Skulptur in Frankeich: 1140-1270* provides a general, historical introduction to the subject of Gothic sculpture in France, with detailed discussion of hundreds of individual statues. The book contains more than 300 plates, some in color, photographed by Max Hirmer, and more than 100 text illustrations.

BIOGRAPHICAL AND CRITICAL SOURCES:

PERIODICALS

New York Review, July 17, 2003, Andrew Butterfield, review of *Ein Versuch über die Gesichter Houdons,* pp. 7-10.
New York Times Book Review, December 2, 1973.
Times Literary Supplement, April 13, 1973.*

*   *   *

SAWAI, Gloria Ostrem

PERSONAL: Surname is pronounced Sa-*wye*; born in Minneapolis, MN; daughter of Gustav and Ragnhild (Skaret) Ostrem; children: Naomi, Kenji. *Education:* Augsburg College, B.A., 1957; University of Montana, M.F.A., 1977.

ADDRESSES: Home—4403 52A St., Camrose, Alberta T4V 1W2, Canada.

CAREER: Camrose Lutheran College, Camrose, Alberta, Canada, instructor in English, 1958-63; Metropolitan Community College, Minneapolis, MN, instructor in English, 1963-68; University of Calgary, Calgary, Alberta, Canada, instructor in creative writing, 1977-80; Writers' Guild of Alberta, Edmonton, Alberta, Canada, instructor in creative writing, beginning 1982.

MEMBER: Playwrights Canada, Writers Guild of Alberta.

AWARDS, HONORS: Governor-General's Literary Award for fiction, Canada Council for the Arts, 2002, for *A Song for Nettie Johnson.*

WRITINGS:

Neighbour (juvenile play; first produced in Calgary, Alberta, Canada, at Alberta Theater Projects, 1978), Playwrights Canada Press (Toronto, Ontario, Canada), 1981.

The Nose of Edward Wunderlicht (one-act play), first produced in Calgary, Alberta, Canada, at Lunchbox Theater, 1983.

(With Beverly Harris and Fred Stenson) *Three Times Five: Short Stories,* edited by Douglas Barbour, NeWest Press (Edmonton, Alberta, Canada), 1983.

A Song for Nettie Johnson (short stories), Coteau Books (Regina, Saskatchewan, Canada), 2001.

Work represented in anthologies, including *Aurora,* Doubleday (New York, NY), 1978; *Short Stories by Canadian Women,* 1984; *Three by Five,* edited by Douglas Barbour, NeWest Press (Edmonton, Alberta, Canada), 1984; and *Eighty-two: Best Canadian Stories,* Oberon Press (Ottawa, Ontario, Canada). Contributor to magazines, including *Grain* and *Shepherd.*

SIDELIGHTS: Gloria Ostrem Sawai once told *CA:* "Most of my writing has a strong connection to the land. Even titles sometimes refer to the earth. For all kinds of reasons, I think one's relation to the earth is crucial. Although the earth tells of extravagant generosity, renewal, and nurture, it also speaks to me of harshness—birth, violence, indifference, death—the bottom-line realities. The Saskatchewan prairie, where I grew up, provides me with a setting that is severe and barren, a place where the truths of civilization can sometimes be treated. I find this paradox of the destructive yet life-sustaining land interesting and central in my writing.

"Certain religious concepts are also important to me: grace, reconciliation, redemption. I believe that there is redemption for the broken and the flawed of the earth, that redemption comes as a gift from often unexpected sources, that one needs to keep one's eyes open at all times to the many manifestations of this gift so as not to miss it or deny it. This concept is reflected in all my work, especially in the play *Neighbour* and in the short story 'The Ground You Stand On.' Further, I feel reconciliation is the act (or activity) requiring the greatest courage and steadfastness possible. Prospero, in Shakespeare's play *The Tempest,* used his art for the purpose of reconciliation. And although I don't write with a view to some ultimate meaning, I wouldn't mind if someone saw this purpose in my work."

BIOGRAPHICAL AND CRITICAL SOURCES:

PERIODICALS

Books in Canada, January-February, 2003, K. Gordon Neufeld, review of *A Song for Nettie Johnson.**

SCHMID, W. George
    See SCHMID, Wolfram George

*   *   *

SCHMID, Wolfram George 1930-
    (W. George Schmid)

PERSONAL: Born August 5, 1930, in Munich, Germany; son of Wolfram (a model maker) and Maria (a homemaker; maiden name, Zirngibl) Schmid; married Hildegarde Einhauser (a homemaker), August 1, 1953; children: Michael, Henry, Hildegarde, Wilhelmina, Siegfried.

ADDRESSES: Home—4417 Goodfellows Court, Tucker, GA 30084-2701.

CAREER: Practiced architecture and landscape architecture, 1952-64, and forest products engineering and silviculture, 1964-92. North American Plant Protection Council, member; creator of the garden Hosta Hill, 1969.

MEMBER: American Hosta Society (member of national board of directors, beginning 1984; historian, beginning 1989), American Horticultural Society, Hardy Plant Society, Royal Horticultural Society, British Hosta and Hemerocallis Society, Netherlands Hosta Society, Gesellschaft der Stauden, Georgia Perennial Plant Association, Georgia Hosta Society (founder, 1984; president, 1984-86, 1994-96; editor, 1984-88 and 1992-93).

WRITINGS:

The Genus Hosta—Giboshi Zoku, edited by Gilbert S. Daniels, Timber Press (Beaverton, OR), 1991.

(Under name W. George Schmid) *An Encyclopedia of Shade Perennials,* Timber Press (Beaverton, OR), 2002.

Contributor to botany magazines.*

*   *   *

SEGEL, Harold B(ernard) 1930-

PERSONAL: Born September 13, 1930, in Boston, MA; son of Abraham Barney (a publisher) and Florence (Aleshnick) Segel. *Education:* Boston College, B.S., 1951; Harvard University, Ph.D., 1955. *Politics:* Independent. *Religion:* Jewish.

ADDRESSES: Agent—c/o Author Mail, Columbia University Press, 61 West 62nd St., New York, NY 10023.

CAREER: University of Florida, Gainesville, assistant professor of Slavic languages and literatures, 1955-59; Columbia University, New York, NY, assistant professor, 1959-62, associate professor, 1962-69, professor of Slavic literatures, beginning 1969, now professor emeritus. University of Stockholm, visiting professor, 1972.

MEMBER: American Association for the Advancement of Slavic Studies, American Society for Eighteenth-Century Studies, Polish Institute.

AWARDS, HONORS: Fulbright-Hayes and American Council of Learned Societies fellowships.

WRITINGS:

(Compiler, and author of book-length introduction) *The Literature of Eighteenth-Century Russia: A History and Anthology,* two volumes, Dutton (New York, NY), 1967.

(Translator) *The Major Comedies of Alexander Fredro,* Princeton University Press (Princeton, NJ), 1969.

The Trilogy of Alexander Sukhovo Kobylin, Dutton (New York, NY), 1969, 2nd edition, Harwood Academic Publishers (New York, NY), 1995.

The Baroque Poem, Dutton (New York, NY), 1974.

Twentieth-Century Russian Drama: From Gorky to the Present, Columbia University Press, (New York, NY), 1979, updated edition, Johns Hopkins University Press, (Baltimore, MD), 1993.

(Editor and author of introduction) *Polish Romantic Drama: Three Plays in English Translation,* Cornell University Press, (Ithaca, NY), 1977.

(Editor, with John Micgiel and Robert Scott) *Proceedings of the Conference on Poles and Jews—Myth and Reality in the Historical Context,* Columbia University, (New York, NY), 1986.

Turn-of-the-Century Cabaret: Paris, Barcelona, Berlin, Munich, Vienna, Cracow, Moscow, St. Petersburg, Zurich, Columbia University Press, (New York, NY), 1987.

Renaissance Culture in Poland: The Rise of Humanism, 1470-1543, Cornell University Press, (Ithaca, NY), 1989.

(Translator, editor, and author of introduction) *The Vienna Coffeehouse Wits, 1890-1938,* Purdue University Press, (West Lafayette, IN), 1993.

Pinocchio's Progeny: Puppets, Marionettes, Automatons and Robots in Modernist and Avant-Garde Drama, Johns Hopkins University Press (Baltimore, MD), 1995.

(Editor and author of introduction) *Stranger in Our Midst: Images of the Jew in Polish Literature,* Cornell University Press, (Ithaca, NY), 1996.

(Compiler) *Egon Erwin Kisch, the Raging Reporter: A Bio-Anthology,* Purdue University Press, (West Lafayette, IN), 1997.

Body Ascendant: Modernism and the Physical Imperative, Johns Hopkins University Press (Baltimore, MD), 1998.

The Columbia Guide to the Literatures of Eastern Europe since 1945, Columbia University Press, (New York, NY), 2003.

Contributor to *New Leader, Polish Review, Slavic Review,* and other journals.

BIOGRAPHICAL AND CRITICAL SOURCES:

PERIODICALS

Library Journal, May 15, 2003, Paul D'Alessandro, review of *The Columbia Guide to the Literatures of Eastern Europe since 1945,* p. 82.*

*　　　*　　　*

SEWARD, Desmond 1935-

PERSONAL: Born May 22, 1935, in Paris, France; son of William Eric and Eileen (Bennett) Seward. *Ethnicity:* "British." *Education:* St. Catharine's College, Cambridge, B.A. *Religion:* Roman Catholic.

ADDRESSES: Agent—c/o The Andrew Lownie Literary Agency, 17 Sutherland St., London SWIV 4JU, England.

CAREER: Writer.

WRITINGS:

The First Bourbon: Henry IV, King of France and Navarre, Gambit (Boston, MA), 1971.

The Monks of War: The Military Religious Orders, Eyre Methuen (London, England), 1972, Viking Penguin (New York, NY), 1996, published as *The Monks of War: The First Religious Orders,* Archon (Hamden, CT), 1972.

The Bourbon Kings of France, Constable (London, England), 1973, Barnes & Noble (New York, NY), 1976.

Prince of the Renaissance: The Life of Francois I, Constable (London, England), 1973, published as *Prince of the Renaissance: The Golden Life of Francois I,* Macmillan (New York, NY), 1973.

Eleanor of Aquitaine: The Mother Queen, David & Charles (Newton Abbot, England), 1978, published as *Eleanor of Aquitaine,* Times Books (New York, NY), 1979.

The Hundred Years War: The English in France, 1337-1453, Atheneum (New York, NY), 1978.

Monks and Wine, Crown (New York, NY), 1979.

Marie Antoinette, St. Martin's Press (New York, NY), 1981.

Richard III: England's Black Legend, Country Life Books (London, England), 1983, F. Watts (New York, NY), 1984.

(Selector and author of introduction) *Naples: A Traveller's Companion,* Constable (London, England), 1984, Atheneum (New York, NY), 1986.

Napoleon's Family, Viking (New York, NY), 1986.

Italy's Knights of St. George: The Constantinian Order, Gerrards Cross (Buckinghamshire, England), 1986.

Henry V As Warlord, Sidgwick & Jackson (London, England), 1987, published as *Henry V: The Scourge of God,* Viking (New York, NY), 1988.

Napoleon and Hitler: A Comparative Biography, Harrap (London, England), 1988, Viking (New York, NY), 1989.

(With Susan Mountgarret) *Byzantium,* Harrap (London, England), 1989.

(Editor, with Philip Ziegler) *Brook's: A Social History,* Constable (London, England), 1991.

Metternich: The First European, Viking (New York, NY), 1991.

The Dancing Sun: Journeys to the Miracle Shrines (travel), Macmillan (London, England), 1993.

The War of the Roses through the Lives of Five Men and Women of the Fifteenth Century, Viking (New York, NY), 1995.

Sussex (travel), Pimlico County History Guides (London, England), 1995.

Caravaggio: A Passionate Life, Morrow (New York, NY), 1998.

Eugenie: The Empress and Her Empire, Sutton (London, England), 2003.

Contributor to periodicals, including *History Today.*

Seward's books have been translated into at least seven languages.

WORK IN PROGRESS: Portrait of Apulia: Southeastern Italy, with Susan Mountgarret.

SIDELIGHTS: Desmond Seward is one of a small group of historical writers who regards narrative as an essential part of the historical process, looking back to Edward Gibbon, the eighteenth-century English historian best known for his work *The History of the Decline and Fall of the Roman Empire.* Many of Seward's books are concerned with various aspects of England's centuries-old history of conflict with France. Maligned reputations have been attached to several of the key players on both sides of this ongoing antagonism, and Seward's books, which include *The Bourbon Kings of France, Richard III: England's Black Legend,* and *Napoleon and Hitler: A Comparative Biography,* often attempt to shed new light on these leaders and their deeds.

Born in France in 1935, Seward belongs to a Franco-Irish family that have been wine merchants in Bordeaux since the 1860s. He was educated in England by the Benedictine monks of Ampleforth and at St. Catharine's College, Cambridge. He still regards France as his second home. He saw the publication of his first work in 1971 with *The First Bourbon: Henry IV, King of France and Navarre.* Another of his early works is a biography of one of France's sixteenth-century monarchs, *Prince of the Renaissance: The Golden Life of Francois I.* Published in 1973, the work chronicles the life of the ruler who was best remembered as a patron of the arts. Vincent Cronin of the *Washington Post* termed Seward's effort "a sound, brilliantly readable short life."

The Monks of War, published first in 1972, is the book Seward considers his most important work. It is thought to be the first general history of the Templars

Knights Hospitallers, Teutonic Knights, and other related subjects published since the eighteenth century. Additionally, Seward wrote a number of other books on French history—or English history in regard to France—over the next decade. These include *The Bourbon Kings of France,* published in 1976; a biography of Eleanor of Aquitaine; and *The Hundred Years War: The English in France, 1337-1453,* which appeared in an American edition in 1978. In the latter work Seward explains how the acrimonious war over a variety of typical causes—disputed territory, paying tribute, fishing rights—helped England rise from a small nation to a formidable power. Young men went to France during wartime, Seward reveals, not just to fight but to augment personal wealth—helped in part by the French nobility, who rode into battle with their family jewels and willingly paid ransom when captured. A *New Yorker* reviewer praised the work, noting that the author writes of all the major events and persona, "and illuminates them with . . . a most agreeable clarity of style."

Seward skipped ahead to the eighteenth century for his biography of *Marie Antoinette,* published in the United States in 1981. He chronicles the life of this despised French queen—Austrian by birth—who was beheaded by the guillotine during the French Revolution. Marie's profligate spending and haughty attitude have long been seen as the sparks that helped ignite the radical *sans-culottes* and initiate the overthrow of the French monarchy, but Seward sheds a more balanced light on the royal figure. As his biography recounts, Marie Antoinette grew up virtually illiterate, was married at age fourteen to an unkempt and lazy prince, and soon found that spending money was an easy way to relieve boredom. Seward shows her transformation into a more respectable middle age; despite her other flaws, the queen was a good mother, loyal to her friends, and husband Louis XVI eventually grew to respect her. In her last years, Marie Antoinette tried to save the French monarchy through a variety of ruses, but in the end was sentenced by a revolutionary tribunal. Seward, wrote Christopher Hibbert in the *Spectator,* "retells lucidly and sensibly the sad, dramatic story of this woman whose dignified and courageous behaviour towards the end of her life did so much to mitigate the follies of her earlier years."

Seward's 1984 book *Richard III: England's Black Legend* received a fair amount of press, perhaps in part because its publication came just prior to the 500th anniversary of a particularly gruesome event in the history of the English succession. As Seward's biography recounts, King Richard III was the last of the Plantagenet dynasty, a man who usurped the throne after his brother's sudden death. As William Shakespeare would recount in his play about King Richard, the man's grip on power was solidified by the mysterious disappearance of the two nephews who stood between him and the crown of England. The legend of the two princes in the Tower has long been a staple of popular British history and fiction, including Josephine Tey's *The Daughter of Time,* and Seward's text addresses several of these other accounts of Richard's ascension and somewhat barbarous reign. Seward told *CA* that he is "firmly convinced that Richard was every bit as evil as Shakespeare's portrait, though perhaps not hump-backed." *New York Times Book Review* critic Wendy Smith called the biography "a well-written and colorful account of an intriguing period in English history."

In *Napoleon's Family,* published in 1986, Seward presents the untold tale of the French emperor's numerous and involved relatives. Napoleon Bonaparte was actually an Italian, educated in France, who rose to power in the aftermath of the French Revolution. After successfully conquering large parts of Europe, he then installed his family members as rulers and plundered France's treasury to enrich everybody—especially his mother. According to Seward, the rapacious, sexually promiscuous Bonaparte clan were "half-savage squireens, scarcely more than peasants with coats of arms." *Napoleon's Family* also recounts the clotheshorse tendencies of his wife, the Empress Josephine; the story of Louis, his venereal disease-riddled brother; the tale of another brother, the ruler of a small German kingdom who once staged a nude opera at his castle; and the life of a sister, whom Seward describes as "the greatest hussy imaginable." *Napoleon's Family* received unanimously positive reviews: *Book World's* Michael Kernan praised the book's "precision, wit and remarkable clarity," while *Globe and Mail* reviewer David Lancashire termed it "entertaining social history—the story of these social mountaineers hewing their way to the top reads like a nineteenth-century supermarket tabloid."

Seward penned yet another biography of a legendary historical figure from England's past in his 1987 work *Henry V As Warlord,* published in the United States the following year as *Henry V: The Scourge of God.*

The title of the American edition reflects the moniker the ruler gave himself over the course of his nine-year reign in the early fifteenth century. Henry won enormous successes on the battlefield, much of it, as Seward asserts, through the furtherance of more refined weaponry. Invading France in 1415, he reignited the sputtering Hundred Years War and achieved victory at the notorious Battle of Agincourt. A few years later he married a French princess, but the union did little to curb the animosity between the two kingdoms that had resulted from the English army's pillage of the French countryside. Again, Seward's subject matter was previously immortalized in the Shakespearean play that bears his name; the bard's dramatic portrayal helped make Henry V a revered figure in English history. The revisionist *Scourge of God* sets out to show another, less charitable side of Henry V, depicting him, as Seward told *CA,* "as a near psychopath." As *Spectator* reviewer Christopher Allmand noted, Seward's book "reflects some of the latest scholarly research on the king."

Seward's next book appeared on American shores in 1989. *Napoleon and Hitler: A Comparative Biography* gives evidence of the remarkable similarities between the two conquering despots. Both were emigres in their respective domains whose greatest military folly was to invade Russia—a step that eventually led to each leader's downfall. Seward posits that both Napoleon and Adolf Hitler, in their individual quests for control over Europe, were essentially attempting to subdue a powerful English empire. Each possessed an enormous ego, which drove both men to embark on ambitious and deadly military campaigns. Seward also discusses the creation of internal totalitarian machinery within the regimes of both Napoleon and Hitler that had been unknown up until their respective points in history. A reviewer for the *Economist* pointed out that Seward's hypothesis in comparing the two dictators is the book's singular fault—"equating the two men . . . makes the horror of the Holocaust merely relative," the review admonished.

The War of the Roses through the Lives of Five Men and Women of the Fifteenth Century marks Seward's return to the subject of late medieval English history. The 1995 book looks at the internal battle that raged in England, in the years after the death of Henry V, between two opposing royal houses, Lancaster and York, but does so through the intertwined biographies of five key players. One was a courtier whose attempt to save a boy-king from the opposing faction resulted in his own death; another was the mother of a future Tudor king who managed to shape a truce between the two sides. Another key figure in Seward's historical chronicle was the mistress of a king who served as a spy; the earl of Oxford and a future archbishop round out Seward's quintet. An *Economist* reviewer concluded that the work "succeed[s] in bringing medieval England to life," and an *Independent* reviewer maintained that Seward "directs his readers fastidiously and dramatically through the plots, the dynastic marriages, the murders and the exiles . . . and the result is history as compelling as any novel."

In 1998, Seward published the biography of Italian baroque painter Michelangelo da Caravaggio. Though Randy Gener in the *Lamda Book Report* criticized *Carvaggio: A Passionate Life* for concluding that the artist wasn't gay, he conceded that the book "lucidly lays out how Caravaggio's strange, wildly capricious behavior was shaped by a milieu rife with public hangings, terrible plagues, religious vices, . . . and barbarous practices." By contrast, Donna Seaman in *Booklist* felt that "Seward's emphasis on Caravaggio's religious convictions goes much further in explicating the power of his art and the nature of his soul than speculation about his sexuality."

In addition to his many historical works, Seward is also the author of a number of travel books, including the illustrated 1989 travelogue *Byzantium,* authored with Susan Mountgarret, 1995's *Sussex,* and 1993's *The Dancing Sun: Journeys to the Miracle Shrines,* a guidebook to shrines of the Virgin Mary.

BIOGRAPHICAL AND CRITICAL SOURCES:

PERIODICALS

Booklist, November 1, 1998, Donna Seaman, review of *Caravaggio: A Passionate Life,* p. 462; April 15, 2001, Ted Hipple, review of the audiobook version of *Napoleon and Hitler: A Comparative Biography,* p. 1574.
Books and Bookmen, April 1986, p. 18.
Book World, October 10, 1982, p. 12; July 27, 1986, p. 3.
Economist, April 22, 1972; July 11, 1981, p. 91; August 2, 1986, p. 8; June 24, 1989, p. 86; August 26, 1995, p. 73.

Globe and Mail (Toronto, Ontario, Canada), February 14, 1987.

Historian, November 1985, p. 97.

Independent, July 15, 1995, p. 6.

Lamda Book Report, December, 1998, Randy Gener, review of *Caravaggio: A Passionate Life,* p. 24.

Los Angeles Times Book Review, April 22, 1984, p. 8.

New Statesman & Society, April 7, 1995, p. 56.

New Yorker, February 26, 1979, p. 123; August 22, 1986, p. 95.

New York Review of Books, October 7, 1999, Ingrid Rowland, "The Real Caravaggio," p. 11.

New York Times Book Review, August 5, 1984, p. 19.

Observer, September 19, 1993, p. 56; May 21, 1995, p. 16.

Punch, February 16, 1986, p. 56.

Spectator, April 24, 1976, p. 25; August 22, 1981, p. 19; December 12, 1987, p. 35.

Times Educational Supplement, August 11, 1978, p. 18; January 27, 1989, p. B22.

Times Literary Supplement, August 4, 1972, p. 912; December 14, 1973, p. 1546; October 23, 1981, p. 1230; May 13, 1983, p. 484; October 23, 1981, p. 1230; August 4, 1995, p. 12; August 25, 1995, p. 27.

Voice Literary Supplement, September, 1986, p. 4.

Washington Post Book World, November 28, 1973.

*   *   *

SEYMOUR, John 1914-

PERSONAL: Original surname, Turbayne; surname changed to that of stepfather; born June 12, 1914, in England; son of Albert and Christine (an American; maiden name, Owens) Turbayne; married Sally Medworth (an artist and potter); children: Jane, Anne, Kate. *Hobbies and other interests:* Cruising in small open boats, travel, topography.

ADDRESSES: Home—Fachongle Isaf, Pembrokeshire, Wales. *Agent*—David Higham Associates Ltd., 5-8 Lower John St., London W1R 4HA, England.

CAREER: Worked as a farm manager in southwest Africa, skipper of a fishing vessel in southwestern Africa and South Africa, miner in Northern Rhodesia (now Zambia), and government livestock officer in Barotseland (now Zambia); operator of a small farm and freelance writer. *Military service:* British Army, King's African Rifles, 1940-46; served in Ethiopia and Burma.

WRITINGS:

The Hard Way to India, Eyre & Spottiswoode (London, England), 1951.

Round about India, Eyre & Spottiswoode (London, England), 1953, published as *Around India,* John Day (New York, NY), 1954.

One Man's Africa, Eyre & Spottiswoode (London, England), 1955, John Day (New York, NY), 1956.

Boys in the Bundu (juvenile), Harrap (London, England), 1955.

Sailing through England, Eyre & Spottiswoode (London, England), 1956.

The Fat of the Land, Faber (London, England), 1961, reprinted, 1974, Taplinger Publishing (New York, NY), 1962, published as *The Fat of the Land: Family Farming on Five Acres,* Schocken Books (New York, NY), 1975.

On My Own Terms, Faber (London, England), 1963, reprinted, 1980.

Willynilly to the Baltic, William Blackwood (Edinburgh, Scotland), 1965.

Companion Guide to East Anglia, William Collins (London, England), 1970, Scribner (New York, NY), 1975.

(With wife, Sally Seymour) *Farming for Self-Sufficiency: Independence on a Five Acre Farm,* illustrated by S. Seymour, Schocken Books (New York, NY), 1973, published as *Self-Sufficiency: The Science and Art of Producing and Preserving Your Own Food,* Faber (London, England), 1973.

Companion Guide to the Coast of North-East England, William Collins (London, England), 1974.

Companion Guide to the Coast of South-West England, William Collins (London, England), 1975.

The Guide to Self-Sufficiency, Popular Mechanic Books (New York, NY), 1976 published as *The Complete Book of Self-Sufficiency,* Faber (London, England), 1976, revised edition (with Will Sutherland) published as *The Self-Sufficient Life and How to Live It: The Complete Back-to-Basics Guide,* DK Publishing (New York, NY), 2003.

Bring Me My Bow, Turnstone (London, England), 1977.

The Countryside Explained, illustrated by Sally Seymour, Faber (London, England), 1977.

I'm a Stranger Here Myself: The Story of a Welsh Farm, Faber (London, England), 1978.

The Self-Sufficient Gardener, Faber (London, England), 1978, published as *The Self-Sufficient Gardener: A Complete Guide to Growing and Preserving All Your Own Food,* Doubleday (New York, NY), 1979.

Gardener's Delight, Harmony Books (New York, NY), 1979.

The Shepherd, illustrated by Sally Seymour, Sidgwick & Jackson (London, England), 1983.

The Lore of the Land, illustrated by Sally Seymour, Schocken Books (New York, NY), 1983.

The Smallholder, illustrated by Sally Seymour, Sidgwick & Jackson (London, England), 1983.

The Woodlander, illustrated by Sally Seymour, Sidgwick & Jackson (London, England), 1983.

The Forgotten Crafts, Knopf (New York, NY), 1984, revised edition included in *Our Forgotten Arts and Crafts: Skills from Bygone Days,* DK Publishing (New York, NY), 2001.

Forgotten Household Crafts, Knopf (New York, NY), 1987, revised edition included in *Our Forgotten Arts and Crafts: Skills from Bygone Days,* DK Publishing (New York, NY), 2001.

(With Herbert Girardet) *Blueprint for a Green Planet: Your Practical Guide to Restoring the World's Environment,* illustrated by Ian Penney, Prentice Hall (Englewood Cliffs, NJ), 1987.

Our Forgotten Arts and Crafts: Skills from Bygone Days (contains revised editions of *The Forgotten Crafts* and *Forgotten Household Crafts*), DK Publishing (New York, NY), 2001.

Also author of *Getting It Together,* published by Michael Joseph (London, England). Contributor to magazines.

Seymour's books have been translated into Norwegian, Spanish, French, Portuguese, Dutch, German, and Danish.

BIOGRAPHICAL AND CRITICAL SOURCES:

PERIODICALS

Library Journal, May 15, 2003, Ilse Heidmann, review of *The Self-Sufficient Life and How to Live It: The Complete Back-to-Basics Guide,* p. 115.
Times Literary Supplement, June 6, 1980.*

SHAW, Janet 1937-
(Janet Beeler, Janet Beeler Shaw)

PERSONAL: Born September 30, 1937, in Springfield, IL; daughter of Russel Henry (a teacher) and Nadina (a homemaker; maiden name, Boardman) Fowler; married Thomas Beeler, August 22, 1959 (divorced); married Robert C. Shaw (a counselor), September 12, 1978; children: (first marriage) Kristin, Mark, Laura. *Education:* Stephens College, A.A., 1957; Goucher College, B.A., 1959; Cleveland State University, M.A., 1975. *Hobbies and other interests:* Teaching children and adults, reading, gardening, biking, hiking.

ADDRESSES: Home—46 Newcross N, Asheville, NC 28805-9213. *Agent*—Ned Leavitt, William Morris Agency, 1350 Avenue of the America, New York, NY 10019.

CAREER: Novelist. Freelance writer, 1959-80, 1986—. University of Wisconsin—Madison, lecturer, beginning 1980; Edgewood College, Madison, WI, lecturer, 1985. Writer-in-residence, Associated Colleges of the Twin Cities, 1983; visiting writer, Florida State University, 1986. Administrator for South Dakota Arts Board, 1981, Wisconsin Arts Board, 1981-83, Illinois Arts Board, 1985, and National Endowment for the Arts, 1987-88. Member, Dane County Cultural Affairs Commission, 1983-86.

MEMBER: Phi Beta Kappa.

AWARDS, HONORS: Mademoiselle award, 1958, for "A Day for Fishing"; Devins Foundation Award for Poetry, 1978, for *Dowry;* Wisconsin Arts Board fellow, 1981-82; *Seventeen* magazine Poetry Contest award, 1985; Outstanding Literary Achievement citation, Wisconsin Library Association, 1987, for *Taking Leave.*

WRITINGS:

"KIRSTEN" SERIES

Meet Kirsten: An American Girl, 1854 (also see below), illustrated by René Graef, Pleasant Company (Madison, WI), 1986.

Kirsten Learns a Lesson: A School Story, 1854 (also see below), illustrated by René Graef, Pleasant Company (Madison, WI), 1986.

Kirsten's Surprise: A Christmas Story, 1854 (also see below), illustrated by René Graef, Pleasant Company (Madison, WI), 1986.

Happy Birthday, Kirsten! A Springtime Story, 1854 (also see below), illustrated by René Graef, Pleasant Company (Madison, WI), 1986.

Changes for Kirsten: A Winter Story, 1854 (also see below), illustrated by René Graef, Pleasant Company (Madison, WI), 1988.

Kirsten Saves the Day: A Summer Story, 1854 (also see below), illustrated by René Graef, Pleasant Company (Madison, WI), 1988.

Kirsten on the Trail, illustrated by René Graef, Pleasant Company (Middleton, WI), 1999.

Kirsten and the New Girl, illustrated by René Graef, Pleasant Company (Middleton, WI), 2000.

Kirsten's Story Collection (contains *Meet Kirsten, Kirsten Learns a Lesson, Kirsten's Surprise, Happy Birthday, Kirsten!, Changes for Kirsten,* and *Kirsten Saves the Day*), illustrated by René Graef, Pleasant Company (Middleton, WI), 2001.

Kirsten Snowbound!, illustrated by René Graef, Pleasant Company (Middleton, WI), 2001.

Kirsten and the Chippewa, illustrated by René Graef, Pleasant Company (Middleton, WI), 2002.

Kirsten's Promise, illustrated by René Graef, Pleasant Company (Middleton, WI), 2003.

"KAYA" SERIES

Meet Kaya: An American Girl: 1764 (also see below), illustrated by Bill Farnsworth, Pleasant Company (Middleton, WI), 2002.

Kaya's Escape!: A Survival Story: 1764 (also see below), illustrated by Bill Farnsworth, Pleasant Company (Middleton, WI), 2002.

Kaya's Hero: A Story of Giving: 1764 (also see below), illustrated by Bill Farnsworth, Pleasant Company (Middleton, WI), 2002.

Kaya and Lone Dog: A Friendship Story: 1764 (also see below), illustrated by Bill Farnsworth, Pleasant Company (Middleton, WI), 2002.

Kaya Shows the Way: A Sister Story: 1764 (also see below), illustrated by Bill Farnsworth, Pleasant Company (Middleton, WI), 2002.

Changes for Kaya: A Story of Courage: 1764 (also see below), illustrated by Bill Farnsworth, Pleasant Company (Middleton, WI), 2002.

Kaya and the River Girl: 1764, illustrated by Bill Farnsworth, Pleasant Company (Middleton, WI), 2003.

Kaya's Story Collection (contains *Meet Kaya, Kaya's Escape, Kaya's Hero, Kaya and Lone Dog, Kaya Shows the Way,* and *Changes for Kaya*), illustrated by Bill Farnsworth, Pleasant Company (Middleton, WI), 2003.

OTHER

(Under name Janet Beeler) *How to Walk on Water* (poems), Cleveland State University Poetry Forum (Cleveland, OH), 1973.

(Under name Janet Beeler) *Dowry* (poem), University of Missouri Press (Columbia, MO), 1978.

(Under name Janet Beeler Shaw) *Some of the Things I Did Not Do* (short stories), University of Illinois Press (Urbana, IL), 1984.

Taking Leave, Viking (New York, NY), 1987.

Also author of "A Day for Fishing." Short stories represented in anthologies, including *Prize Stories of 1960: The O. Henry Awards,* 1960; *Mademoiselle Prize Stories,* 1975; *The Editors' Choice: New American Stories,* Bantam (New York, NY), 1985; *Family: Stories from the Interior,* Grey Wolf Press (Minneapolis, MN), 1987; *The Norton Anthology of Short Fiction,* Norton (New York, NY), 1988; *Stiller's Pond,* New Rivers Press (St. Paul, MN), 1988; and *Prime Number,* University of Illinois Press (Champaign, IL), 1988. Poetry represented in anthologies, including *Bear Crossings: An Anthology of North American Poets,* 1978; *Poems Out of Wisconsin V,* 1980; and *In the Middle: Ten Midwestern Women Poets,* 1985.

Contributor of stories to periodicals, including *Atlantic, Denver Quarterly, Family Circle, Fiction Journal, Indiana Review, Mademoiselle, McCall's, Milwaukee Journal, Missouri Review, Redbook, Sewanee Review, Shenandoah, Southwest Review,* and *TriQuarterly Review.* Contributor of poetry to *American Poetry Review, Antaeus, Esquire, New Catholic World, New Orleans Review, Open Places, Perspective, Poet Lore,* and *Primavera.*

ADAPTATIONS: Many of Shaw's books in the "Kirsten" series have been adapted for videocassette by Pleasant Company (Middleton, WI).

SIDELIGHTS: In addition to writing many works of short fiction and verse for adult readers, Janet Shaw has established a prolific career penning historical novels focusing on young girls that tie in to the collectible dolls designed and marketed by the Wisconsin-based Pleasant Company. In both the "Kirsten" and "Kaya" books, which contain less than eighty pages and are geared for elementary-grade readers, Shaw introduces plucky and resourceful heroines who deal with the hardship of life in an earlier era and encounter a series of adventures on the way.

As she once explained to *CA,* in the "Kirsten" series of "American Girl" novels, Swedish-born Kirsten and her family experience the loss of their homeland and all that is familiar to them when they immigrate to the United States in 1854. In their new home on the frontier in Minnesota, they create a new life as Americans. The family's strong bonds of love stretch to include their community's new teacher in *Kirsten Learns a Lesson,* a Sioux Indian friend in *Kirsten on the Trail,* and the children and adults they meet in the harsh world they have made home. Taking a great deal of time to research the world of her protagonist, Shaw also works to keep the "Kirsten" books free of sentimentality, preferring to portray the world of the mid-nineteenth-century settlers in a realistic light.

"Kirsten is a resourceful girl with heart," Shaw once commented. "She shows real courage when she saves her father in the blizzard and also makes real mistakes when she thinks she can outsmart the bears. She faces her fears and forms deep bonds of love and friendship—qualities I'd certainly wish for all of us."

Shaw delves even further into America's past in her "Kaya" series, which features a nine-year-old girl of the Nez Perce tribe. The time is 1764, and in the region now divided into the states of Washington, Idaho, and Oregon, Kaya is living among a close family and building her understanding of both her tribe and the natural world around her. In *Meet Kaya: An American Girl: 1764,* the girl and her horse try to win a bareback race, in the process forgetting to care for her younger twin brothers. In *Kaya's Hero: A Story of Giving: 1764,* the girl seeks to win the respect of a highly regarded member of her community. In writing the "Kaya" novels, Shaw benefited from the help of the Nez Perce Tribal Executive Committee, which assisted the author in getting the details of life in the Northwest Territories correct. Reviewing several books in the "Kaya"

series for *School Library Journal,* Carolyn Janssen described Shaw's protagonist as "well developed through her actions and words," while in *Booklist,* Karen Hutt commended the books for being "historically accurate and culturally sensitive . . . a noteworthy result of a unique collaboration."

In an interview for *Kidsreads online,* Shaw described her hopes for the "Kaya" books: "I hope that by looking at the world through Kaya's eyes, . . . readers will learn to understand, appreciate, and respect a rich and intriguing way of life very different from their own. Kaya and her people were strengthened by their powerful sense of community and their relationship with the world around them. They prized justice, independence, bravery, generosity, and spirituality—enduring values we badly need in our lives today."

Shaw, whose short fiction and poetry has been widely anthologized and who published the 1987 adult novel *Taking Leave* as well as several poetry collections, once explained to *CA* that "the skills in writing for children are as much the same as in writing for adults: the story has to have drive and a dramatic question to be resolved; the characters must be believable and empathetic and the source for the conflict within the story; dialogue must be natural. Of course, you must write in shorter sentences, but my husband pointed out to me that I write in short sentences anyway! My pleasure in writing the children's books has been to create stories I'd like my own daughters to read."

BIOGRAPHICAL AND CRITICAL SOURCES:

PERIODICALS

Booklist, January 1, 2003, Karen Hutt, review of *Meet Kaya: An American Girl: 1764* and *Kaya's Escape! A Survival Story: 1764,* p. 893.

Library Journal, April 15, 1987, Maurice Taylor, review of *Taking Leave,* p. 101.

Publishers Weekly, October 31, 1986, review of "Kirsten" series, p. 68; February 13, 1987, review of *Taking Leave,* p. 82; June 24, 2002, review of "Kaya" series, p. 59.

School Library Journal, November, 1986, Elaine Fort Weischedel, review of *Meet Kirsten: An American Girl, 1854,* p. 85; May, 1988, Sylvia S. Marantz, review of *Happy Birthday, Kirsten! A Springtime*

Story, 1854, p. 88; October, 1988, Ruth K. Mac-Donald, review of *Kirsten Saves the Day: A Summer Story, 1854,* p. 148; December, 2002, Carolyn Janssen, review of *Kaya's Escape!* and *Kaya's Hero: A Story of Giving: 1764,* p. 108.

ONLINE

Kidsreads, http://aol.kidsreads.com/ (June 3, 2003), interview with Shaw.

OTHER

Meet Janet Shaw: An American Girls Author (short film), Pleasant Company (Middleton, WI), 1991.*

*   *   *

SHAW, Janet Beeler
     See SHAW, Janet

*   *   *

SHUKMAN, Harold 1931-

PERSONAL: Born March 23, 1931, in London, England; son of David (a tailor) and Masha (Ekinbert) Shukman; married Ann King-Farlow, December 22, 1956 (divorced, 1971); married Barbara King-Farlow (an artist), March 30, 1973; children: (first marriage) David, Henry, Clare; (stepchildren from second marriage) Ghislaine Jacobs, Amelia Jacobs, Adam Jacobs. *Education:* University of Nottingham, B.A. (with first class honors), 1956; Oxford University, D.Phil., 1960. *Politics:* "Mildly reactionary/liberal." *Religion:* "Lapsed psychoanalysand." *Hobbies and other interests:* Silversmithing.

ADDRESSES: Home—11 Cunliffe Close, Oxford, England. *Agent*—A. D. Peters, 10 Buckingham St., London SW1, England.

CAREER: Standard Telephones, London, England, trainee radio engineer, 1947-51; Marconi Telecommunications, Chelmsford, Essex, England, executive, 1956-57; Oxford University, Oxford, England, fellow of St. Antony's College, beginning 1961, lecturer in modern Russian history, beginning 1969; retired. Consultant to British Broadcasting Corp. *Military service:* Royal Air Force, Russian interpreter, 1951-53; became sergeant.

MEMBER: Jewellery and Silver Society of Oxford.

WRITINGS:

Lenin and the Russian Revolution, Putnam (New York, NY), 1967.
(With George Katkov) *Lenin's Path to Power,* Macdonald (London, England), 1971.
(With F. W. Deakin and H. T. Willetts) *A History of World Communism,* Barnes & Noble (New York, NY), 1975.
(Editor) *The Blackwell Encyclopedia of the Russian Revolution,* Basil Blackwell (New York, NY), 1988.
(Editor) *Stalin's Generals,* Grove Press (New York, NY), 1993.
Rasputin, Sutton Publishing (Stroud, England), 1997.
The Russian Revolution, Sutton Publishing (Stroud, England), 1998.
(With Geoffrey Elliott) *Secret Classrooms: An Untold Story of the Cold War,* St. Ermin's (London, England), 2003.

Author of a television script for *The Great War,* a series broadcast by British Broadcasting Corp. Contributor to Slavic studies journals, including *Bulletin of Soviet and East European Jewish Affairs.*

TRANSLATOR

(And editor, with Max Hayward and Michael Glenny) *Three Soviet Plays,* Penguin (New York, NY), 1965.
(With Max Hayward) Valentin Kataev, *Holy Well,* Walker (New York, NY), 1967.
(With others) Yuli Daniel, *This Is Moscow Speaking,* Harvill (London, England), 1968.
Anatoli Rybakov, *Heavy Sand,* Viking (New York, NY), 1981.
Roy Medvedev, *All Stalin's Men,* Doubleday (Garden City, NY), 1984.

Roy Medvedev, *China and the Superpowers,* Basil Blackwell (New York, NY), 1986.

Anatoli Rybakov, *Children of the Arbat,* Little, Brown (Boston, MA), 1988.

Andrei Gromyko, *Memoirs,* Doubleday (Garden City, NY), 1989.

(And editor) Dmitri Volkogonov, *Stalin: Triumph and Tragedy,* Grove Press (New York, NY), 1991.

(And editor) Dmitri Volkogonov, *Lenin: A New Biography,* Free Press (New York, NY), 1994.

(And editor) Dmitri Volkogonov, *Trotsky: The Eternal Revolutionary,* Free Press (New York, NY), 1996.

(And editor) *Autopsy for an Empire: The Seven Leaders Who Built the Soviet Regime,* Free Press (New York, NY), 1998.

SIDELIGHTS: Harold Shukman is a scholar of Russian history, chiefly concerned with the twentieth century. His work includes histories of the Bolshevik revolution, encyclopedias, and especially translations of noted Russian historians and fiction writers. In a *Russian Review* consideration of Shukman's *The Blackwell Encyclopedia of the Russian Revolution,* Donald J. Raleigh praised the work for its "high quality" and noted that it "deserves recognition precisely because it meets the need for a general reference work of high quality on the revolution." Much the same could be said for the rest of Shukman's books, which bear in mind both scholarly aims and general interest.

Shukman has also been recognized for his translations of biographies by the late Colonel-General Dmitri Volkogonov, a Russian military historian who, as a government archivist, had unprecedented access to top-secret documents from the regimes of Lenin, Stalin, and Trotsky. Shukman's translations offer to English-speaking readers "provocative [works] for the specialist as well as many a casual student of world affairs," to quote *New Leader* contributor Anatole Shub. In a *Tribune Books* review of *Trotsky: The Eternal Revolutionary,* Mark Kramer wrote that Shukman "has done an admirable job of preserving the elegance and detail of the original Russian version while eliminating many (though not all) of the repetitive passages and digressions. Some minor mistakes arise, but overall the book makes for splendid reading."

Other critics have expressed gratitude for translations of Volkogonov's writings because the Russian author was able to access new information that shed light on the more gruesome aspects of modern Russian history. Kramer, for instance, concluded that Volkogonov's works are "a major step forward in our understanding of . . . the early years of the Soviet regime. . . . [He] brings to an American audience the finest reassessments of Soviet history we are likely to have for many years to come."

Shukman once told *CA:* "The accident of having Yiddish-speaking Russian parents was responsible for my being propelled into Russian studies in general and aspects of Russian-Jewish history in particular. Otherwise I might have remained in a career with a future—electronics. However, the discovery of the French and Italian languages in 1950-51 coupled with eruption of late adolescent sensuality, diverted me into the vain search for a profession offering culture, luxury, wealth, and ego gratification. An Oxfordian enjoys only one of these all the time, and at most two some of the time."

BIOGRAPHICAL AND CRITICAL SOURCES:

PERIODICALS

American Historical Review, December, 1969, pp. 546-547.

Nation, May 28, 1988, pp. 746-748; March 25, 1996, pp. 31-32.

National Review, December 31, 1994, p. 57.

New Leader, December 19, 1994, article by Anatole Shub, pp. 28-31.

New Republic, March 18, 1996, pp. 41-45.

New Yorker, April 16, 1984, p. 160.

New York Review of Books, June 15, 1967, p. 23; April 4, 1996, pp. 38-41.

New York Times Book Review, April 1, 1990, p. 7; November 13, 1994, pp. 11-12; March 24, 1996, p. 9.

Publishers Weekly, August 22, 1994, p. 45; December 18, 1995, p. 34.

Russian Review, July, 1990, Donald J. Raleigh, review of *The Blackwell Encyclopedia of the Russian Revolution,* pp. 351-352.

Spectator, March 3, 1967, p. 251.

Times Literary Supplement, March 16, 1967; March 14, 2003, M. F. Burnyeat, review of *Secret Classrooms: An Untold Story of the Cold War,* p. 29.

Tribune Books (Chicago, IL), May 19, 1996, Mark Kramer, review of *Trotsky: The Eternal Revolutionary*, pp. 1, 9.

Washington Monthly, December, 1994, pp. 55-56.*

* * *

STAHL, Naomi
   See Mosiman, Billie Sue (Stahl)

* * *

STAMEY, Sara (Lucinda) 1953-

PERSONAL: Born January 23, 1953, in Bellingham, WA; daughter of H. Neil (a machinist) and Helen (a nurse; maiden name, Weihe) Stamey; married Jesse Berst, February, 1976 (divorced, 1979). *Education:* Attended University of Puget Sound, 1971-73; Western Washington University, B.A. (magna cum laude), 1981, graduate study, beginning 1988. *Hobbies and other interests:* Hiking, bicycling, tennis, playing classical piano.

ADDRESSES: Home and office—324 North State St., No. 1, Bellingham, WA 98225. *Agent*—Merilee Heifetz, Writer's House, 21 West 26th St., New York, NY 10010.

CAREER: Nuclear reactor control operator in Hanford, WA, and San Onofre, CA, 1974-78; scuba diving instructor in the Mediterranean, the Virgin Islands, and Honduras, 1982-87; writer, beginning 1987. Teacher of English composition.

MEMBER: Science Fiction Writers of America, Pacific Northwest Writers Conference.

WRITINGS:

Wild Card Run (science fiction novel), Berkley Publishing (New York, NY), 1987.
Win, Lose, Draw (science fiction novel), Berkley Publishing (New York, NY), 1988.
Double Blind (science fiction novel), Berkley Publishing (New York, NY), 1989.

(Editor) Bruce Barbour, *In Our Wildest Dream: An Environmental and Spiritual Adventure,* Xlibris (Philadelphia, PA), 2001.
Islands (novel), Xlibris (Philadelphia, PA), 2001, revised edition, Tarragon Books (Bellingham, WA), 2003.

SIDELIGHTS: Sara Stamey once told *CA:* "My work with nuclear engineers and other scientists stimulated my latent interest in writing science fiction. My travels to teach scuba diving have provided the inspiration for stories and research on such diverse topics as Mayan history, the Vaudun, geology, and lasers.

"My books generally reflect an interest in balance—balancing an active lifestyle with intellectual interests, balancing demands of heart and mind, and balancing technological advance with quality of life. My 'Ruth' science fiction series transforms into fictional conflicts such experiences as my work in the exciting but daunting nuclear industry, my concern about the logging of old-growth timber in the Northwest, and the magic of diving on the beautiful, fragile coral reefs of the Caribbean."

BIOGRAPHICAL AND CRITICAL SOURCES:

PERIODICALS

Locus, May, 2003, Edward Bryant, review of *Islands*, pp. 25, 58.*

* * *

STERNBERG, Robert J(effrey) 1949-

PERSONAL: Born December 8, 1949, in Newark, NJ; son of Joseph and Lillian (Politzer) Sternberg; married; children: Seth, Sara. *Education:* Yale University, B.A. (summa cum laude, with exceptional distinction in psychology), 1972; Stanford University, Ph.D., 1975. *Hobbies and other interests:* Playing with his children, reading (especially science fiction), hiking, investing.

ADDRESSES: Home—105 Spruce Bank Rd., Hamden, CT 06518. *Office*—Department of Psychology, Yale University, Box 11A Yale Station, New Haven, CT 06520. *Agent*—John Brockman, 2307 Broadway, New York, NY 10024.

Robert J. Sternberg

CAREER: Yale University, Department of Psychology, New Haven, CT, assistant professor, 1975-80, associate professor, 1980-83, professor of psychology and education, 1983-86, IBM Professor of Psychology and Education, beginning 1986. Has done research for the Office of Naval Research, the Army Research Institute, the National Institute of Education, and the Venezuelan Ministry for the Development of Intelligence. Member of Educational Testing Service Board of Visitors and of Social Science Research Council on Cognitive Development and Giftedness, both 1984—. Chair of Selection Committee for American Psychological Association Early Career Award in Cognition, 1984. Guest on television program "Today Show."

MEMBER: National Association for Gifted Children, American Association for the Advancement of Science, American Educational Research Association, American Psychological Association (fellow), Society for Mathematical Psychology, Society for Philosophy and Psychology, Society for Research in Child Development, Merrill-Palmer Society, Society of Multivariate Experimental Psychology, Eastern Psychological Association, Sigma Xi, Phi Beta Kappa.

AWARDS, HONORS: Sidney Siegel Memorial Award from Stanford University, 1975; grants from the National Science Foundation, 1976-78, for "The Componential Analysis of Human Intelligence," and from the Spencer Foundation, 1982-84, for "Insight in the Gifted"; Distinguished Scientific Award for an Early Career Contribution to Psychology from the American Psychological Association, 1981; Boyd R. McCandless Young Scientist Award from the American Psychological Association Division of Developmental Psychology, and Cattell Award from the Society of Multivariate Experimental Psychology, both 1982; named by *Science Digest* as one of "America's Top 100 Young Scientists," 1984; included in *Esquire* Register of Outstanding Young Men and Women, 1985; Research Review Award, 1986, and Distinguished Book Award, 1987, both from American Educational Research Association.

WRITINGS:

Barron's How to Prepare for the Miller Analogies Test (MAT), Barron's (Hauppauge, NY), 1974, 3rd and 4th editions published as *Barron's How to Prepare for the MAT Miller Analogies Test,* 1981 and 1986, 8th edition, 2001.

Intelligence, Information Processing, and Analogical Reasoning: The Componential Analysis of Human Abilities, Lawrence Erlbaum (Mahwah, NJ), 1977.

Writing the Psychology Paper, Barron's Educational Series (Hauppauge, NY), 1977.

Beyond IQ: A Triarchic Theory of Human Intelligence, Cambridge University Press (New York, NY), 1985.

Intelligence Applied: Understanding and Increasing Your Intellectual Skills, Harcourt (New York, NY), 1986.

The Psychologist's Companion, 2nd edition, Cambridge University Press (New York, NY), 1988, 4th edition, 2003.

The Triarchic Mind, Viking (New York, NY), 1988.

The Triangle of Love, Basic Books (New York, NY), 1988.

Metaphors of Mind: Conceptions of the Nature of Intelligence, Cambridge University Press (New York, NY), 1990.

Love the Way You Want It: Using Your Head in Matters of the Heart, Bantam (New York, NY), 1991.

In Search of the Human Mind, Harcourt Brace College Publishers (Fort Worth, TX), 1995, 3rd edition, 2000.

(With Todd I. Lubart) *Defying the Crowd: Cultivating Creativity in a Culture of Conformity,* Free Press (New York, NY), 1995.

(With Louise Spear-Swerling) *Off Track: When Poor Readers Become "Learning Disabled,"* Westview Press (Boulder, CO), 1996.

Cognitive Psychology, Harcourt Brace College Publishers (Fort Worth, TX), 1996, 3rd edition, 2003.

(With Wendy M. Williams) *How to Develop Student Creativity,* Association for Supervision and Curriculum Development (Alexandria, VA), 1996.

Successful Intelligence: How Practical and Creative Intelligence Determine Success in Life, Simon & Schuster (New York, NY), 1996.

(With Louise Spear-Swerling) *Teaching for Thinking,* American Psychological Association (Washington, DC), 1996.

Thinking Styles, Cambridge University Press (New York, NY), 1997.

Pathways to Psychology, Harcourt Brace (Fort Worth, TX), 1997, 2nd edition, 2000.

Introduction to Psychology, Harcourt Brace College Publishers (Fort Worth, TX), 1997.

Cupid's Arrow: The Course of Love through Time, Cambridge University Press (New York, NY), 1998.

Love Is a Story: A New Theory of Relationships, Oxford University Press (New York, NY), 1998.

(With Elena L. Grigorenko) *Our Labeled Children: What Every Parent and Teacher Needs to Know about Learning Disabilities,* Perseus Books (Reading, MA), 1999.

(With others) *Practical Intelligence in Everyday Life,* Cambridge University Press (New York, NY), 2000.

(With Anthony V. Azzara and Alexandra Freer) *Cracking the A.P. Psychology,* Random House (New York, NY), 2000.

(With Elena L. Grigorenko) *Teaching for Successful Intelligence: To Increase Student Learning and Achievement,* SkyLight Professional Development (Arlington Heights, IL), 2000.

(With Elena L. Grigorenko) *Dynamic Testing: The Nature and Measurement of Learning Potential,* Cambridge University Press (New York, NY), 2000.

(With Talia Ben-Zeev) *Complex Cognition: The Psychology of Human Thought,* Oxford University Press (New York, NY), 2001.

(With James C. Kaufman and Jean Pretz) *The Creativity Conundrum: A Propulsion Model of Kinds of Creative Contributions,* Psychology Press (New York, NY), 2002.

(With Wendy M. Williams) *Educational Psychology,* Allyn & Bacon (Boston, MA), 2002.

Wisdom, Intelligence, and Creativity Synthesized, Cambridge University Press (New York, NY), 2003.

Psychology, 4th edition, Thomson/Wadsworth (Belmont, CA), 2004.

Psychology 101 1/2: The Unspoken Rules for Success in Academia, American Psychological Association (Washington, DC), 2004.

EDITOR

(With Douglas K. Detterman) *Human Intelligence: Perspectives on Its Theory and Measurement,* Ablex Publishing (Greenwich, CT), 1979.

(And contributor) *Advances in the Psychology of Human Intelligence,* four volumes, Lawrence Erlbaum (Mahwah, NJ), 1982-88.

(With Douglas K. Detterman; and contributor) *How and How Much Can Intelligence Be Increased,* Ablex Publishing (Greenwich, CT), 1982.

(And contributor) *Handbook of Human Intelligence,* Cambridge University Press (New York, NY), 1982.

(And contributor) *Mechanisms of Cognitive Development,* W. H. Freeman (New York, NY), 1984.

(And contributor) *Human Abilities: An Information-Processing Approach,* W. H. Freeman (New York, NY), 1985.

(With Janet E. Davidson; and contributor) *Conceptions of Giftedness,* Cambridge University Press (New York, NY), 1986.

(With Douglas K. Detterman) *What Is Intelligence? Contemporary Viewpoints on Its Nature and Definition,* Ablex Publishing (Greenwich, CT), 1986.

(With Richard K. Wagner) *Practical Intelligence: Nature and Origins of Competence in the Everyday World,* Cambridge University Press (New York, NY), 1986.

(With Ronna F. Dillon) *Cognition and Instruction,* Academic Press (San Diego, CA), 1986.

(With Joan Boykoff Baron) *Teaching Thinking Skills: Theory and Practice,* W. H. Freeman (New York, NY), 1987.

(And contributor) *The Nature of Creativity,* Cambridge University Press (New York, NY), 1988.

(With Michael L. Barnes) *The Psychology of Love,* Yale University Press (New Haven, CT), 1988.

(With Edward Smith) *The Psychology of Human Thought,* Cambridge University Press (New York, NY), 1988.

(With Phillip L. Ackerman and Robert Glaser) *Learning and Individual Differences: Advances in Theory and Research,* W. H. Freeman (New York, NY), 1989.

Wisdom: Its Nature, Origins, and Development, Cambridge University Press (New York, NY), 1990.

(With John Kolligian, Jr.) *Competence Considered,* Yale University Press (New Haven, CT), 1990.

Complex Problem Solving: Principles and Mechanisms, L. Erlbaum Associates (Mahwah, NJ), 1991.

Directors of Development: Influences on the Development of Children's Thinking, L. Erlbaum Associates (Mahwah, NJ), 1991.

(With Cynthia A. Berg) *Intellectual Development,* Cambridge University Press (New York, NY), 1992.

(With Anne E. Beall and Alice H. Eagly) *The Psychology of Gender,* foreword by Ellen Berscheid, Guilford Press (New York, NY), 1993, 2nd edition, 2004.

(With Douglas K. Detterman) *Transfer on Trial: Intelligence, Cognition, and Instruction,* Ablex (Greenwich, CT), 1993.

Encyclopedia of Human Intelligence, Macmillan (New York, NY), 1994.

(With Richard K. Wagner) *Mind in Context: Interactionist Perspectives on Human Intelligence,* Cambridge University Press (New York, NY), 1994.

(With Patricia Ruzgis) *Personality and Intelligence,* Cambridge University Press (New York, NY), 1994.

Thinking and Problem Solving, Academic Press (San Diego, CA), 1994.

(With Janet E. Davidson) *The Nature of Insight,* MIT Press (Cambridge, MA), 1995.

(With Elena L. Grigorenko) *Intelligence, Heredity, and Environment,* Cambridge University Press (New York, NY), 1996.

(With Talia Ben-Zeev) *The Nature of Mathematical Thinking,* L. Erlbaum Associates (Mahwah, NJ), 1996.

Teaching Introductory Psychology: Survival Tips from the Experts, American Psychological Association (Washington, DC), 1997.

(With Mahzad Hojjat) *Satisfaction in Close Relationships,* Guilford Press (New York, NY), 1997.

(With Elena L. Grigorenko and Patricia Ruzgis) *Psychology of Russia: Past, Present, Future,* Nova Science Publishers (Commack, NY), 1997.

Career Paths in Psychology: Where Your Degree Can Take You, American Psychological Association (Washington, DC), 1997.

(With Wendy M. Williams) *Intelligence, Instruction, and Assessment: Theory into Practice,* L. Erlbaum Associates (Mahwah, NJ), 1998.

(With Michel Ferrari) *Self-Awareness: Its Nature and Development,* Guilford Press (New York, NY), 1998.

Handbook of Creativity, Cambridge University Press (New York, NY), 1999.

(With Peter A. Frensch) *The Nature of Cognition,* MIT Press (Cambridge, MA), 1999.

(With Louise Spear-Swerling) *Perspectives on Learning Disabilities: Biological, Cognitive, Contextual,* foreword by Keith E. Stanovich, Westview Press (Boulder, CO), 1999.

(With Richard K. Wagner) *Readings in Cognitive Psychology,* Harcourt Brace College Publishers (Fort Worth, TX), 1999.

(With Joseph A. Horvath) *Tacit Knowledge in Professional Practice: Researcher and Practitioner Perspectives,* L. Erlbaum Associates (Mahwah, NJ), 1999.

Guide To Publishing in Psychology Journals, Cambridge University Press (New York, NY), 2000.

Handbook of Intelligence, Cambridge University Press (New York, NY), 2000.

(With Elena L. Grigorenko) *Environmental Effects on Cognitive Abilities,* L. Erlbaum Associates (Mahwah, NJ), 2001.

(With James C. Kaufman) *The Evolution of Intelligence,* L. Erlbaum Associates (Mahwah, NJ), 2001.

(With Elena L. Grigorenko) *Family Environment and Intellectual Functioning: A Life-Span Perspective,* L. Erlbaum Associates (Mahwah, NJ), 2001.

(With Elena L. Grigorenko) *The General Factor of Intelligence: How General Is It?,* L. Erlbaum Associates (Mahwah, NJ), 2001.

(With Li-fang Zhang) *Perspectives on Thinking, Learning, and Cognitive Styles,* L. Erlbaum Associates (Mahwah, NJ), 2001.

(With Bruce Torff) *Understanding and Teaching the Intuitive Mind: Student and Teacher Learning,* L. Erlbaum Associates (Mahwah, NJ), 2001.

Why Smart People Can Be So Stupid, Yale University Press (New Haven, CT), 2002.

(With Janet E. Davidson) *The Psychology of Problem Solving,* Cambridge University Press (New York, NY), 2003.

(With Elena L. Grigorenko) *The Psychology of Abilities, Competencies, and Expertise,* Cambridge University Press (New York, NY), 2003.

Psychologists Defying the Crowd: Stories of Those Who Battled the Establishment and Won, American Psychological Association (Washington, DC), 2003.

(With Jacques Lautrey and Todd I. Lubart) *Models of Intelligence: International Perspectives,* American Psychological Association (Washington, DC), 2003.

International Handbook of Intelligence, Cambridge University Press (New York, NY), 2003.

The Anatomy of Impact: What Makes the Great Works of Psychology Great, American Psychological Association (Washington, DC), 2003.

Unity in Psychology: Possibility of Pipedream?, American Psychological Association (Washington, DC), 2004.

(With Tina M. Newman) *Students with Both Gifts and Learning Disabilities: Identification, Assessment, and Outcomes,* Kluwer Academic (New York, NY), 2004.

(With Jacqueline P. Leighton) *The Nature of Reasoning,* Cambridge University Press (New York, NY), 2004.

(With John Antonakis and T. Cianciolo) *The Nature of Leadership,* Sage Publications (Thousand Oaks, CA), 2004.

(With David Yun Dai) *Motivation, Emotion, and Cognition: Integrative Perspectives on Intellectual Development and Functioning,* L. Erlbaum (Mahwah, NJ), 2004.

(With Elena L. Grigorenko) *Culture and Competence: Contexts of Life Success,* American Psychological Association (Washington, DC), 2004.

(With Elena L. Grigorenko and Jerome L. Singer) *Creativity: From Potential to Realization,* American Psychological Association (Washington, DC), 2004.

(With Jean Pretz) *Cognition and Intelligence: Identifying the Mechanisms of the Mind,* Cambridge University Press (New York, NY), 2004.

Contributor to more than forty volumes, including *A Model for Intelligence,* edited by H. J. Eysenck; *Classroom Computers and Cognitive Science,* edited by A. C. Wilkinson; *The Development and Assessment of Human Competence,* edited by D. A. Wilkerson and E. W. Gordon; *Current Topics in Human Intelligence,* Volume I, edited by D. K. Detterman; *Arthur Jensen: Consensus and Controversy,* edited by Sohan and Celia Modgil; and *Test Design: Contributions from Psychology, Education, and Psychometrics,* edited by S. E. Embretson. Also contributor of hundreds of articles to numerous science and psychology journals, including *American Scientist, Psychology Today, Behavioral and Brain Sciences, Journal of Experimental Child Psychology,* and *Phi Delta Kappan.*

SIDELIGHTS: An award-winning professor of psychology and education at Yale University, Robert J. Sternberg is renowned for his pioneering work in the study of human intelligence. With the publication of his book *Beyond IQ* in 1985, he established an innovative three-part system for defining and measuring mental ability. The combined impact of his "triarchic theory of human intelligence" and Sternberg's related discoveries advanced the field of cognitive science and called for a re-evaluation of traditional methods, such as standardized tests, used in determining an individual's aptitude or intelligence quotient (IQ). Similarly, Sternberg developed a three-dimensional theory for analyzing human love, which he terms the "love triangle." His diligent research and writings in these areas of human development earned the psychologist widespread professional acclaim and public recognition, and in 1984 *Science Digest* included him among the top one hundred young scientists in the United States.

Sternberg's preoccupation with intelligence dates back to his childhood. Reminiscing about his performance in elementary school, he recalled to Robert J. Trotter in *Psychology Today:* "I really stunk on IQ tests. . . . I had severe test anxiety." A turning point came in the sixth grade when Sternberg had to retake the IQ exam for fifth graders. Experiencing more confidence and less stress in the company of a "bunch of babies" who were a year younger than he, the twelve-year-old outperformed his initial testing. Commenting in a 1985 *Science Digest* article written by Signe Hammer, Sternberg reflected that "the absurdity of that situation helped me get over the test anxiety." Inspired by his breakthrough, the precocious student subsequently fashioned his own "Sternberg Test of Mental Ability," which he administered to classmates as part of a science project; in high school, he examined how various distractions affect individual performance on intelligence tests.

Sternberg continued to study intelligence after completing his secondary education. As a research assistant at the Psychological Corporation in New York and later at the Educational Testing Service in New Jersey, he spent his summers working alongside major designers of formal testing materials. In fact, Sternberg himself devised a system for categorizing the test items that appear on the Miller Analogies Test (MAT) while employed at the Psychological Corporation, which publishes the MAT. Later, as a graduate student at Stanford University, he was prompted by Barron's Educational Publishing Company to write a book on how to prepare for the test. Discouraged by the halt in progressive research on intelligence and yet eager for the opportunity to further his own study in that area, Sternberg agreed and wrote a doctoral dissertation that formed the basis of his first book, the 1974 *Barron's How to Prepare for the Miller Analogies Test (MAT)*.

Throughout the 1970s Sternberg's research focused on the analytical processes involved in taking intelligence tests. Consequently, his work included critical examinations of the kinds of mental exercises typically featured on such tests. Relating Sternberg's observations on his efforts, Trotter wrote, "His research gave a good account of what people did in their heads" to solve the problems "and also seemed to account for individual differences in IQ test performance." Encouraged by the results of these early studies, Sternberg established a "componential" theory of intelligence, in which he associates the various stages of information processing with specific functions of the brain. At that point "I thought I knew what was going on," the psychologist revealed to Trotter, "but that was just a delusion on my part." It became increasingly apparent to Sternberg that there was more to intelligence than just thinking analytically.

Further research and examination of existing theories suggested to the psychologist that there were probably three main aspects or subtheories of intelligence. In addition to the componential aspect, from which he derived his original theory of intelligence, Sternberg formulated two others, which he identified as experiential and contextual (or external). Through their interaction with one another, the psychologist alleges, these subtheories govern and determine the range of cognitive mental ability, thus corroborating Sternberg's triarchic theory of intelligence. Providing Trotter with an example of the individual characteristics dominating each subtheory, Sternberg described three students:

one who excelled in academic or "test smarts" (componential); another who was especially creative and insightful and could formulate original ideas from dissimilar experiences (experiential); and a third whose "street-smart" intelligence enabled her to adapt to, or to manipulate, the environment to her advantage (contextual). In varying degrees each of them possessed "all three of the intellectual abilities" determined by Sternberg, wrote Trotter, "but each was especially good in one aspect." As Hammer pointed out, standard IQ tests ignore such capabilities as insight and adaptability, evaluating only those mental skills used in taking the tests. Sternberg consequently maintains that the results calculated from the intelligence tests say nothing "about why my best student is the one with the relatively low GRE [Graduate Record Examination] scores," or why other students with exceptionally high test ratings "sometimes come to Yale and flop."

Historically, intelligence testing began in France more than eighty years ago. Commissioned by their country's government, psychologists Alfred Binet and Theodosius Simon invented a series of tests initially intended as a means for identifying the special needs of schoolchildren. The Binet-Simon scale—as it was called—subsequently underwent a number of revisions, which were variously implemented not only in schools but in industry and the military as well. Since its inception, this prototype for IQ tests has evolved into what most people generally accept as "a measure of something real—something fixed, innate and inheritable—that was, in fact, intelligence," recorded Hammer, and traditionally intelligence has been collectively interpreted as a strictly academic achievement.

Sternberg redefines the nature of intelligence to include practical knowledge. Insisting that "real life is where intelligence operates" and not the classroom, reported Hammer, the psychologist points out that the true measure of success is not how well one does in school, but how well one does in life. In everyday situations on the job or in person-to-person contact, "people no more go around solving test-like analogies . . . than they go around pressing buttons in response to lights or sounds," Hammer quoted from Sternberg's book *Beyond IQ*. Moreover, what's important and necessary to succeed in the real world generally comes from individual experience rather than a textbook. Described as practical or tacit knowledge, these abilities include such things as "knowing how to prioritize tasks and allocate your time and other resources," Hammer noted, "and how to establish and enhance your reputation in your career, by convincing your boss of the value of your work." In effect, "Sternberg aims to change the way we think about intelligence" by putting it into perspective within the context of real-life situations.

In his groundbreaking *Beyond IQ,* Sternberg expounds on the nature and origin of his triarchic theory of human intelligence. While much of the volume focuses on his early work on the componential aspect of the theory—including research and data on mental skills such as inductive and deductive reasoning, verbal comprehension, and information processing—the overall message in *Beyond IQ* conveys "that a broader view must be taken" to more accurately assess and measure the range of intellectual capabilities, observed Robert Glaser in *Science* magazine. In that respect "Sternberg carries us over the threshold from old to modern thought," but he "separates content and process too much" to achieve a truly integrated theory on the subject, argued Glaser. In Hammer's opinion, however, Sternberg "aims at nothing less than a kind of grand synthesis of ideas that for others are mutually contradictory. . . . And, like the physicist who is comfortable with the knowledge that light is both a particle and a wave," he accepts that intelligence is "a wide array of cognitive and other skills" that are simultaneously unified by their direct interaction with one another. Acknowledging the significance of Sternberg's research, Glaser resolved that *Beyond IQ* serves as a "challenge to further experiment and theory" as well as an indicator of the direction in which scientific study is advancing toward understanding and enhancing intellectual proficiency.

Having established that the range of intelligence is directly influenced by individual skills, Sternberg set to work discovering ways that people could best utilize their practical abilities. In the psychologist's opinion, related Hammer, "most people, including himself, don't work anywhere near their potential." On the other hand, the reviewer added, they "can learn to be smarter." Expanding on that idea, Sternberg wrote *Intelligence Applied: Understanding and Increasing Your Intellectual Skills.* Described by Hammer as a "'how to' version" of Sternberg's triarchic theory of intelligence, the book offers various exercises that serve to hone a person's mental capabilities, to make

the most of what he or she does best. "And that's what I think practical intelligence is about," Sternberg reported to Trotter, "capitalizing on your strengths and minimizing your weaknesses. It's sort of mental self-management," whereby an individual tailors the environment to accommodate his or her particular talents. Claiming that "the ultimate test" is whether our abilities can improve the quality of our lives, Sternberg also intends "to revise intelligence testing to take practical intelligence into account," wrote Hammer. In fact, he has rejoined the Psychological Corporation—now located in Texas—for the purpose of developing the Sternberg Multidimensional Abilities Test, an IQ test based on his triarchic theory of human intelligence.

Sternberg originated a similar theory explaining the intricacies of love. In an article for *Psychology Today,* Robert J. Trotter explained how the psychologist at first concluded "that love, as different as it feels from situation to situation, is actually a common entity." When questions concerning sex were raised, however, Sternberg "had to rethink his position" in order to distinguish between such phenomena as the physical loving of one's lover and the platonic loving of one's child. According to Trotter, the psychologist's "research generated a lot of publicity in 1984 . . . and earned Sternberg the appellation 'love professor.'"

Like his triarchic theory of intelligence, Sternberg's "love triangle" derives from the interaction of three primary components or subtheories. Specifically, the psychologist defines these as emotional, motivational, and cognitive—or more commonly, intimacy, passion, and commitment. Applying some basic principles of mathematics, Sternberg determined that there are eight possible combinations in which the components may occur. From this information he further concluded that there are also eight different kinds of interpersonal relationships: Nonlove, Liking, Infatuation, Empty Love, Romantic Love, Fatuous Love, Companionate Love, and Consummate Love. Only with consummate, or complete, love are all three subtheories present. Conversely, Nonlove represents the absence of all three.

In addition to naming the peculiarities of the different types of love, Sternberg suggests ways to improve or sustain a particular relationship. Foremost among them are a "willingness to change . . . to tolerate each other's imperfections" and "the sharing of values, especially religious values," noted Trotter. Advising people to maintain "realistic expectations for . . . what is going to be important in a relationship," Sternberg further discusses the contradiction that frequently exists between the way we feel and the way we act. He recommends learning how to recognize "just what actions are associated with each component of love" and then conforming our actions to appropriately reflect our feelings. Emphasizing how important it is to understand the various ways in which people express love, Sternberg cautions that in the absence of expression "even the greatest of loves can die."

Sternberg's studies on intelligence have led to other related topics such as creativity. In his book *Defying the Crowd* Sternberg discusses how society stifles creativity, making people fearful to express themselves creatively, and submits that they do not know how because of the oppression of creativity. "The biggest hurdle to being creative . . . is the existence of so much pressure in our society not to be original and different," described Brian McCombie writing for *Booklist.* McCombie went on to describe *Defying the Crowd* as "creativity at its best."

Sternberg returns to his forte, focusing on intelligence and its role in our lives in the book *Successful Intelligence.* McCombie pointed out "memorization does not equal success in life." He continues with the points made by Sternberg in the book, stating "people need to develop and nurture three types of intelligence for personal and professional success— analytical, creative, and practical." Sternberg is swift to note that practical and creative intelligence is truly what shapes success in peoples lives. McCombie surmised that "Sternberg successfully challenges the common notions of what intelligence is and isn't." A reviewer for *Publishers Weekly* gave the book high marks, stating, "This insightful, savvy guide will help readers avoid self-sabotage and translate thought into action."

Thinking Styles addresses how the way in which we think truly predicts our chance at success. Sternberg continues his tirade against the standardized IQ tests in this book, showcasing the effect thinking styles have on society, even down to the social class we are in. Herbert Goldhor with *Library Quarterly* summarized that "style is a way of thinking. It is not an ability, but rather, a preferred way of using the abilities one has." Goldhor went on to note Sternberg as saying that "people . . . overestimate the extent to which others think the way they do." Carol Innerst, with *Insight on the News,* believed this new book is "asserting that IQ is a vastly overblown predictor of success." She remarked that *Thinking Styles* "is churning the waters in the often-bitter tempest over intelligence and thinking." Sternberg contends that our narrow view of teaching and learning is stifling growth and development of the minds of our children in our schools. Quoting Sternberg, Innerst wrote: "We are failing to recognize the variety of thinking and learning styles they [students] bring to the classroom and teaching them in ways that don't fit them well." In Innerst's opinion, Sternberg's work "could redefine scientific ideas on intelligence and how it affects race, culture and social policy."

Intelligence makes us successful, but love makes the world go round, so Sternberg decided to write on love and its effect on our lives. Chogollah Maroufi with *Library Journal* observed that *Cupid's Arrow* "presents diverse views of love in one concise volume without sacrificing scholarship or humanness." A reviewer for *Publishers Weekly* stated "the book in general reads as self-help with a strong scientific twist." The reviewer noted, "Sternberg's statistically derived theory turns love into a set of love phenomena: our need for interpersonal attachment; cognitive tasks adults employ to appraise their love life; trends regarding attraction, relationship satisfaction and how relationships change." The reviewer found the book to be both "interesting and helpful."

Sternberg continues his journey on the "love boat" in pursuit of the true meaning of love and its place in our lives. He felt that *Cupid's Arrow* left too many ends loose. Sternberg states in his next book, *Love Is a Story,* "Even my own theories didn't seem to give me the understanding I was seeking." In this book he addresses such topics as why we are attracted to certain people, and what leads to relationship longevity. *Library Journal*'s Lucille Boone stated, "For each story, case studies are given, dynamics explained, and the benefits and disadvantages of the story discussed." A reviewer for *Publishers Weekly* felt "Sternberg never makes clear what love is and what is to be gained by applying the label of 'love' to the debasement, objectification or terrorization of another, as in various 'asymmetrical stories.'" The same reviewer deemed the book to be for a popular audience due to the "nontechnical writing and the Valentine's Day release date."

Sternberg tackles the issue of learning disabilities in the book *Our Labeled Children.* Mary Ann Hughes of

Library Journal described learning disabled individuals as "those who experience difficulty in one or more academic areas despite displaying average or better IQ." Hughes did not believe this book addressed the issues completely, stating that "parents of learning-disabled children will first want a title geared toward negotiating the current system," while *Our Labeled Children* only addresses idealized solutions.

Practical Intelligence in Everyday Life points out the importance of "street-smarts" over rote intelligence. Linda Gottfredson tired of the redundant theme, stating this latest book "makes the same general claim as do the three previous books on the topic by Sternberg et al." She added that the book is "long on theorizing and short on data."

Competence Considered takes a look at how one's perception of self can have a major impact on one's ability to perform sundry tasks, as well as make or break one's chance at success. This book edited by Sternberg, consists of "fifteen drily academic essays," according to Genevieve Stuttaford in *Publishers Weekly*. She pointed out that the book proves how "fear of failure may lead to arrested development—or to workaholic frenzy." The book notes that many people feel like imposters, or frauds, and it is this feeling that leads to working to live up to the "fraudulent" status in one's mind, or leads to depression from one's feelings of inadequacy. The book is helpful in giving steps to stop the vicious cycle, as well as giving insight into how to develop competency in children through effective parenting.

Sternberg puts a new twist on his obsession with intelligence in the book *Why Smart People Can Be So Stupid.* As the title suggests, this book is more for the general public, in comparison with Sternberg's previous books on the topic of intelligence, which were highly academic. Sternberg is the editor of several papers discussing the topic of how highly intelligent people do remarkably stupid things that ultimately damage their lives. *Washington Post*'s Gregory Mott stated that "stupidness is not the opposite of smartness, but rather the opposite of wisdom—defined as the ability to apply knowledge to achieve the common good." A review on the Yale University Web site stated that "while millions of dollars are spent each year on intelligence research and testing to determine who has the ability to succeed, next to nothing is spent to determine who will make use of their intelligence and

not squander it by behaving stupidly." Not only do the variety of contributors take on different approaches to rebut the question, but they also vary in approaches to prevent one from being "stupid" in the future. Matt Herrington, writing for *Find Law's Book Reviews,* believed there is at least a consensus among the contributors, that "stupidity describes a failure to employ the intellectual capacity available to conform behavior to interests."

BIOGRAPHICAL AND CRITICAL SOURCES:

BOOKS

Gardner, Howard, *Frames of Mind: The Theory of Multiple Intelligences,* Basic Books (New York, NY), 1983.
Sternberg, Robert, *Thinking Styles,* University of Chicago Press (Chicago, IL), 1999.
Sternberg, Robert, *Love Is a Story,* Cahners Business Information (New York, NY), 1997.

PERIODICALS

Administrative Science Quarterly, March, 2000, Jonathan Down, review of *Tacit Knowledge in Professional Practice,* p. 170.
Booklist, February 15, 1995, review of *Encyclopedia of Human Intelligence,* p. 1109; February 15, 1995, Brian McCombie, review of *Defying the Crowd,* p. 1037; October 1, 1996, Brian McCombie, review of *Successful Intelligence,* p.293.
British Medical Journal, January 24, 1998, Stuart W. G. Derbyshire, review of *Intelligence, Heredity, and Environment,* p. 319.
Insight on the News, February 23, 1998, Carol Innerst, review of *Thinking Styles,* pp. 42-43.
Intelligence, October 2001, Linda Gottfredson, review of *Practical Intelligence in Everyday Life,* pp. 363-365.
Library Journal, February 15, 1998, Lucille Boone, review of *Love Is a Story,* p. 162; October 15, 1998, Chogollah Maroufi, review of *Cupid's Arrow,* pp. 86-87; November 1, 1999, Mary Ann Hughes, review of *Our Labeled Children,* p. 112.
Library Quarterly, April, 1999, Herbert Goldhor, review of *Thinking Styles,* p. 290.
New York Times Book Review, June 26, 1988.

Personnel Psychology, spring, 2000, Lynn K. Harland, review of *Tacit Knowledge in Professional Practice,* p. 221.

Psychology Today, April, 1982; June, 1982; August, 1986; September, 1986.

Publishers Weekly, February 16, 1990, Genevieve Stuttaford, review of *Competence Considered,* pp. 65-66; August 19, 1996, review of *Successful Intelligence,* p. 47; December 22, 1997, review of *Love Is a Story,* p. 46; August 10, 1998, review of *Cupid's Arrow,* p. 383.

Quarterly Review of Biology, March, 1999, Friedrich Vogel, review of *Intelligence, Heredity, and Environment,* p. 111.

Science, October, 1985; August 6, 1999, C. R. Gallistel, review of *The Nature of Cognition,* p. 842.

Science Digest, June, 1985.

Teaching Children Mathematics, January, 1998, Swapna Mukhopadhyay, review of *The Nature of Mathematical Thinking,* p. 296.

Washington Post, June 2, 2002, Gregory Mott, review of *Why Smart People Can Be So Stupid.*

ONLINE

Find Law's Book Reviews, http://writ.news.findlaw.com/ (November 25, 2002), Gavin McNett, review of *Why Smart People Can Be So Stupid.*

Salon, http://www.salon.com/ (June 19, 2002), review of *Why Smart People Can Be So Stupid.*

Yale University Press, http://www.yale.edu/yup/ (November 25, 2002), review of *Why Smart People Can Be So Stupid.**

*   *   *

STEVENS, Carl
See OBSTFELD, Raymond

*   *   *

STUMP, Al(vin J.) 1916-1995

PERSONAL: Born October 20, 1916, in Colorado Springs, CO; died, December 21, 1995; married Jo Mosher. *Education:* Attended University of Washington.

CAREER: Freelance writer. *Oregonian,* Portland, OR, sportswriter, 1939-41. *Military service:* U. S. Navy, during World War II.

AWARDS, HONORS: E. P. Dutton Best Magazine Sports Story Award and the Associated Press Best Sports Story of the Year Award, both 1962, both for article "Ty Cobb's Wild Ten-Month Fight to Live."

WRITINGS:

Champions against Odds, Macrae Smith (Philadelphia, PA), 1952.

(With Ty Cobb) *My Life in Baseball: The True Record,* Doubleday (New York, NY), 1961, republished with an introduction by Charles C. Alexander by University of Nebraska Press (Lincoln, NE), 1993.

(With Sam Snead) *The Education of a Golfer,* Simon & Schuster (New York, NY), 1962.

The Champion Breed, Bantam (New York, NY), 1969.

Cobb: A Biography, foreword by Jimmie Reese, Algonquin (Chapel Hill, NC), 1994.

Work appears in anthologies, including *Best Sports Stories 1949, 1950, 1952, 1953, 1958, 1960, 1961, 1962, 1963, 1964, 1967, 1968, 1969, 1970,* and *1971,* Dutton (New York, NY). Contributor of numerous sports articles to periodicals, including *True, Argosy, Sport, Esquire, American Heritage, Saturday Evening Post, Los Angeles Herald-Examiner, Los Angeles Times, Los Angeles Magazine,* and *Golf.*

ADAPTATIONS: A *True* article Stump wrote about Ty Cobb in 1962 was adapted for the motion picture *Cobb,* written and directed by Ron Shelton and released by Warner Bros. in 1994.

SIDELIGHTS: Al Stump was a sports journalist and the author of sports biographies aimed at both adults and children. He is best known for *Cobb: A Biography,* a candid account of the life of Ty Cobb, partially based on the author's experiences working with the former baseball star to compose the autobiography *My Life in Baseball: The True Record,* published in 1961. Richard Sandomir of the *New York Times,* reviewing *Cobb,* called the earlier book "a sanitized account of baseball's greatest hitter and meanest character." Sandomir further stated that in *Cobb,* "Stump has resurrected much of what he excluded from the earlier volume and presented a substantially more rounded picture of Cobb." "Like the Hall of Famer with whom he is always paired," Nate Stone noted in the *Dictionary of Literary Biography,* "Stump had a long career marked by both greatness and controversy. Using his gift for narrative and his insight into the athlete's psyche, Stump helped create myths and then broke them down."

Stump first began writing about sports while attending the University of Washington, where he was the sports editor of the school newspaper. After leaving school, Stump got a job as a sportswriter with the *Oregonian* newspaper, a position he left to serve on an aircraft carrier during World War II. Following the war, Stump began a career as a freelance writer for a number of newspapers and magazines. Stone recounted that Stump "interviewed luminaries such as writer Ernest Hemingway; athlete Jim Thorpe; actors John Wayne, Alan Ladd, and Humphrey Bogart; and gangster Benjamin 'Bugsy' Siegel. Stump covered the Charles Manson murder trial in 1970-1971, reported from Vietnam with Vice President Spiro Agnew, and was evicted from the M-G-M lot by director John Ford. Nevertheless, Stump always considered himself a sportswriter."

In 1959 Stump was asked to collaborate with baseball legend Ty Cobb on the player's autobiography. Cobb, Stone revealed, "had already angered or frightened off six other writers." Stump agreed to the assignment and, during the winter of 1960-61, the two men stayed at Cobb's lodge in Lake Tahoe to write the book. "Cobb needed a wide variety of medications," Stone noted, "to fight his cancer, high blood pressure, heart disease, and diabetes. A heavy drinker, he could neither sort the pills properly nor manage a useful insulin injection; since he had no servants or nurses, despite his multimillion-dollar fortune—their absence was a testament to Cobb's demeanor: he had a short temper and was known to blow up for the most inconsequential actions—Stump took over caretaking details." Cobb passed away in July of 1961, just as Stump was putting the finishing touches on the autobiography.

My Life in Baseball: The True Record was a bestseller, although Stump was to admit in an article for *True* magazine that it whitewashed many incidents in Cobb's career and overlooked the man's personal flaws. Although he had worked with Cobb for some

ten months, Stump did not attend Cobb's funeral because, as Stone quoted him as explaining, "I was fed up with him. I thought he was a monster who had no love for his fellow man."

In 1994 director Ron Shelton filmed the life story of Ty Cobb. The film was based in part on Stump's *True* magazine article of years before and included many of the darker aspects of the baseball star's personality. The renewed interest in Cobb sparked an interest in Stump's own story of having worked with the famous ballplayer. Stump arranged to write a new biography of Cobb, one that told the true story. "This time Stump held nothing back," Stone wrote, "recording a scathing portrayal of a man driven by a competitiveness that went beyond obsession."

In *Cobb,* Stump tells the story of Cobb beginning with his childhood in Georgia and rise to the major league, despite his father's objections to his playing baseball. At age seventeen, Cobb earned a position with Augusta in the South Atlantic League. During his second year in the minors, Cobb suffered the death of his father, who was accidentally shot and killed by Cobb's mother while trying to enter their home through a second-story window. Stump maintained that the loss of his father haunted Cobb for the rest of his life.

The year after his father's death, Cobb moved up to the majors, joining the Detroit Tigers. The hostility Cobb encountered from his teammates, partly because of their prejudice against Southerners, Stump explained, fueled Cobb's natural aggression and caused the player to suffer a nervous breakdown during his first season. After more than a month in a sanitarium, Cobb returned to the field and channeled his rage into his sport, quickly becoming the best player of his time, according to some commentators. Cobb stayed with the Tigers from 1905 until 1926, when he joined the Philadelphia Athletics until his retirement in 1928.

Cobb set records in stealing bases that still stand, including stealing home plate some 35 times. Rival players spread the story that Cobb sharpened the spikes on his athletic shoes to scare any second baseman who tried to tag him out during a feet-first slide, but the rumor has never been proven. Once when he was heckled by a fan who shouted out a lewd remark about his mother, Cobb climbed into the stands and beat the man, earning a suspension that spurred the Tigers into major league baseball's first strike on his behalf. As Gene Lyons wrote in *Entertainment Weekly*, "Cobb was, hands down, the most brilliant player of his era. But he was also almost universally hated by teammates and opponents, and subject to paranoid delusions and fits of ungovernable rage."

Cobb: A Biography received generally positive critical appraisal. A *Publishers Weekly* reviewer predicted it would "stun readers with its brutal candor" and deemed it a "bare-knuckle, shocking biography." Also applauding *Cobb* was *New York Times Book Review* critic Robert Peterson, who wrote: "It is not often that a biographer gets a second chance at a subject. Al Stump has, and he has made the most of it. . . . Ty Cobb was at once despicable, beneficent and a magnificently talented athlete. Al Stump has done an excellent job of plumbing the character of a sports legend." William O. Scheeren, in *Library Journal*, called *Cobb* "the definitive biography of this mercurial man." A writer for *Kirkus Reviews* concluded that "Stump's wonderfully descriptive writing, yeoman historical research, and personal knowledge of Cobb make this an extraordinary achievement in sports biography."

BIOGRAPHICAL AND CRITICAL SOURCES:

BOOKS

Dictionary of Literary Biography, Volume 241: *American Sportswriters and Writers on Sport,* Gale (Detroit, MI), 2001.

PERIODICALS

American Heritage, November, 1994, review of *Cobb: A Biography,* p. 121.

American Libraries, October, 1994, Bill Ott, review of *Cobb,* p. 896.

Booklist, October 15, 1994, Bill Ott, review of *Cobb,* p. 393.

Entertainment Weekly, January 13, 1995, Gene Lyons, review of *Cobb,* p. 56.

Houston Chronicle, December 4, 1994, Richard Sandomir, "The Search for the Real Cobb: Writer Al Stump Gets His Second Swing at the Truth," Sports Section, p. 1.

Kirkus Reviews, August 1, 1994, review of *Cobb,* p 1064.

Library Journal, September 15, 1994, William O. Scheeren, review of *Cobb,* p. 75.

Los Angeles Times, January 26, 1996, Geoff Boucher, "This Raconteur Was Simply the Best of the Best," p. E10.

Movie Maker, March-April, 1995, Tim Rice, review of film *Cobb.*

New York Times, November 30, 1994, Richard Sandomir, review of *Cobb,* pp. B15, B17; December 5, 1994.

New York Times Book Review, November 20, 1994, Robert Peterson, review of *Cobb,* p. 12.

Publishers Weekly, January 13, 1969, p. 95; October 3, 1994, review of *Cobb,* p. 62.

San Francisco Chronicle, January 9, 1995, Lowell Cohn, "Ty's Dirty Laundry: Daughter Angered by Cobb Movie, Book," p. E1.

Sporting News, November 28, 1994, Steve Gietschier, review of *Cobb,* p. 47.

ONLINE

Bibliography Committee of the Society for American Baseball Research Web site, http://sabrbib.home. mindspring.com/ (October 28, 2002), Leverett T. Smith, review of *Cobb.**

T

TAPAHONSO, Luci 1953-

PERSONAL: Surname is pronounced "Top-pa-honso"; born 1953, in Shiprock, NM; daughter of Eugene and Lucille (Deschenne) Tapahonso; married Earl Ortiz (an artist; divorced, 1987); married Bob G. Martin, 1989; children: (first marriage) Lori Tazbah, Misty Dawn, (stepchildren) Robert Derek, Jonathan Allan, Amber Kristine. *Education:* Participated in a training program for investigative journalism at the National Indian Youth Council; University of New Mexico, B.A., 1980, M.A., 1983.

ADDRESSES: Office—P.O. Box 210076, Harvill 430, Tucson, AZ 85721-0076. *E-mail*—tapahonso@ dakotacom.net.

CAREER: Writer and poet. University of New Mexico, Albuquerque, assistant professor of English, 1987-89; University of Kansas, Lawrence, assistant professor, 1990-94, associate professor of English, 1994-99; University of Arizona, Tucson, professor of American Indian Studies and English, 1999—. Served on the board of directors of the Phoenix Indian Center, 1974; member of New Mexico Arts Commission Literature Panel, 1984-86, steering committee of *Returning the Gift Writers Festival,* 1989-92; Kansas Arts Commission Literature Panel, 1990; Phoenix Arts Commission, 1990-92; Telluride Institute Writers Forum Advisory Board, 1992—; commissioner of Kansas Arts Commission, 1992-96; member of editorial review boards of *Blue Mesa Review,* 1988-92, *Frontiers*, 1991-96, and *wicazo sa review.*

MEMBER: Modern Language Association, Poets and Writers, Inc., Association of American Indian and Alaska Native Professors, Habitat for Humanity (member of board of directors, 1990-94), New Mexico Endowment for the Humanities, Spooner Museum of Anthropology (member of advisory board, 1990-92), American Indian Law Resource Center (member of board of directors, 1993—).

AWARDS, HONORS: Southwestern Association Indian Affairs Literature fellowship, 1981; honorable mention, American Book Awards, 1983, for *Seasonal Woman;* Woman of Distinction, American Girl Scouts Council, 1996; Woman of Distinction, National Association of Women in Education, 1998; award for poetry, Mountains and Plains Booksellers, 1998; excellent instructor award, University of New Mexico, 1985; named one of the Top Women of the Navajo Nation, *Maazo* magazine, 1986; New Mexico Eminent Scholar award, New Mexico Commission of Higher Education, 1989; Hall Creative Work fellowship, University of Kansas, 1992; Community Enhancement and Cultural Exchange award, Lawrence Arts Commission, 1993; Outstanding Native American Award, City of Sacramento, 1993; Southwest Book Award, Border Library Association, 1994, for *Sáanii Dahataal: The Women Are Singing;* named an Influential Professor, Lady Jayhawks Faculty Recognition, University of Kansas, 1994; "Storyteller of the Year," Woodcraft Circle of Native American Writers, 1999.

WRITINGS:

One More Shiprock Night: Poems, illustrated by husband, Earl P. Ortiz, Tejas Art Press (San Antonio, TX), 1981.

Luci Tapahonso

Seasonal Woman (poems), drawings by R. C. Gorman, Tooth of Time Books (Santa Fe, NM), 1982.

A Breeze Swept Through (poems), West End Press (Los Angeles, CA), 1987.

Sáanii Dahataal: The Women Are Singing (poems and stories), University of Arizona Press (Tucson, AZ), 1993.

A Song for the Direction of North, Helicon Nine (Kansas City, MO), 1994.

Bah and Her Baby Brother, illustrated by Sam English, Jr., National Organization for Fetal Alcohol Syndrome (Washington, DC), 1994.

(Editor) *Hayoolkaal: Dawn—An Anthology of Navajo Writers,* University of Arizona Press (Tucson, AZ), 1995.

Navajo ABC: A Diné Alphabet Book, illustrated by Eleanor Schick, Macmillan (New York, NY), 1995.

Blue Horses Rush In: Poems and Stories, University of Arizona Press (Tucson, AZ), 1997.

Songs of Shiprock Fair, illustrated by Anthony Chee Emerson, Kiva Publishing (Walnut, CA), 1999.

Also contributor to *Sign Language: Contemporary Southwest Native America,* Aperture (New York, NY), 1989; *A Circle of Nations: Voices and Visions of American Indians,* Beyond Words (Hillsboro, NM), 1993; and *Open Places, City Spaces: Contemporary Writers on the Changing Southwest,* University of Arizona Press (Tucson, AZ), 1994. Contributor of poems, stories, and essays to numerous publications. Contributor to videotape *The Desert Is No Lady: Women Make Movies,* 1996. Member of editorial board, *Blue Mesa Review,* 1988-92, and *Frontiers,* 1991—.

SIDELIGHTS: Writer Luci Tapahonso grew up on a New Mexico farm in a family of Navajo ancestry, and her body of work often evokes the imagery of this part of the country. While a college student she became acquainted with the acclaimed Native American author Leslie Marmon Silko, who encouraged Tapahonso's efforts at creative writing, and her first book of poems was published in 1981. Titled *One More Shiprock Night,* the work draws upon her early childhood and Navajo roots in rural New Mexico. Many of the selections reflect the important role of music in the cultural traditions of the area. Although most of her works use everyday language and speech patterns, Tapahonso sometimes writes poems first in Navajo and then translates them into English. "Hills Brothers Coffee" is one such work, a memory of the iconography of her youth and of a beloved uncle who spoke no English. Tapahonso said in an interview with the *Navajo Times,* that she "[tries] to encourage Indian students to recognize their own wealth as far as their own stories."

Tapahonso's second volume of poetry appeared in 1982 under the title *Seasonal Woman.* It contains such pieces as "Listen," in which a woman is warned about marrying a man who can't sing, for lacking this ability is a metaphor for a lack of interest in the Navajo traditions. A character named Leona Grey shows up in many of the selections, a woman whom Tapahonso described in an interview with *MELUS* writer Joseph

Bruchac III as a composite character. Other poems address issues of violence and racism in the American Southwest.

Having children of her own has also had an impact on Tapahonso's work, and in the interview she questioned the dissonant nature of her childrens' lives as Navajos in contemporary America. Yet she also reflected that she feels comfortable with this new hybrid culture experienced by her children, one that is distinctly different from her own upbringing, noting that when she was in school there were few contemporary Native American writers to study.

In her third collection, 1987's *A Breeze Swept Through,* Tapahonso returns to these themes of her background and contemporary New Mexico. She further explores her interest in the rhythms of common speech in 1993's *Sáanii Dahataal: The Women Are Singing.* The volume incorporated the poet's growing interest in the Navajo tongue, with selections in both this language and English. Many of them center around Tapahonso's New Mexican roots, and the pull she still feels toward it as an adult living several hundred miles away in Kansas.

Sáanii Dahataal put Tapahonso among "such writers as Joy Harjo, Louise Erdrich, and Leslie Marmon Silko as an important female voice in the American Indian literary landscape," according to Gretchen M. Bataille in the *Dictionary of Literary Biography.* "The book demonstrates her versatility and maturity as a writer and brings together the elements of landscape, tradition, and humor that were evident in earlier works." The book contains both poetry and prose selections, and deals with topics including her childhood, relatives, memories, and pets. "This is a loving collection of voices from the hand of one woman," stated Yolanda Montijo in the *Whole Earth Review.*

In one poem, "Navajo Long Walk," Tapahonso recalls Kit Carson's scorched-earth campaign against the Navajo nation. His offensive included slaughtering the Navajos' livestock, destroying their crops and fruit trees, and forcing them to march three hundred miles to a reservation for four years of inadequate food, rampant disease, and death. They were then allowed to return to their homeland. "The poem dwells simultaneously in past and present, jumping time, speaking

grief," advised Linda Hogan in *Parabola.* It reveals a depth of emotion, exquisitely and simply. Although these tales are "simple on the surface," remarked Hogan, they "are enormous and resonant."

Blue Horses Rush In, published in 1997, commemorates the pleasures and sadness of ordinary life in poems and stories. Debbie Bogenschutz in *Library Journal* called the work "poignant." Although the book draws extensively from Tapahonso's Navajo ancestry, "these stories and poems speak to women of all cultures."

The subject of Tapahonso's 1999 children's book, *Songs of Shiprock Fair,* is the oldest fair the Navajo Nation celebrates in Shiprock, New Mexico. The story is told through the expeiences of a young girl and her family. A reviewer for *Horn Book* noted that, although the storyline was a bit weak, the "abundance of sensory detail and a theme of strong family and community bonds" make up for it. Carolyn Stacey of *School Library Journal* wrote that it is a "combination of narrative and poetry" and considered it an "attractive . . . supplement to books on Navajo culture."

BIOGRAPHICAL AND CRITICAL SOURCES:

BOOKS

Bruchac, Joseph, *Survival This Way,* Arizona University Press (Tucson, AZ), 1987.
Crawford, John F. and Annie O. Eysturoy, editors, *This Is about Vision: Interviews with Southwestern Writers,* New Mexico Press (Albuquerque, NM), 1990.
Dictionary of Literary Biography, Volume 175: *Native American Writers of the United States,* Gale (Detroit, MI), 1997.
Farah, Cynthia, editor, *Literature and Landscape: Writers in the Southwest,* Texas Western Press (El Paso, TX), 1988.

PERIODICALS

Booklist, March 1, 1993; December 15, 1995, p. 706; July, 1996, p. 1833.

Chicago Tribune, September 5, 1993, sec. 6, p. 2.
Choice, June, 1986, p. 1508; April, 1988, p. 1254.
Horn Book, January, 2000, review of *Songs of Shiprock Fair,* p. 69.
Library Journal, March 15, 1993, p. 81; August, 1997, p. 88.
MELUS, winter, 1984, pp. 85-91.
New York Times Book Review, October 31, 1993, p. 40.
Parabola, winter, 1993, pp. 96-97.
Publishers Weekly, January 6, 1989, p. 82; July 28, 1997, p. 55.
School Library Journal, April, 2000, Carolyn Stacey, review of *Songs of Shiprock Fair,* p. 116.
Whole Earth Review, winter, 1995, p. 22.*

*　　*　　*

TARN, Nathaniel 1928-

PERSONAL: Born June 30, 1928, in Paris, France; son of Mendel Myer (some sources cite Marcel) and Yvonne Cecile Leah (Suchar) Tarn; married Patricia Renate Cramer, 1956 (marriage ended); married Janet Rodney, 1982; children: (first marriage) Andrea, Marc. *Ethnicity:* "Earth." *Education:* Cambridge University, B.A. (with honors), 1948, M.A., 1952; graduate study at Sorbonne, University of Paris, 1949-51; University of Chicago, M.A., 1952, Ph.D., 1957; additional graduate study at London School of Economics and Political Science.

ADDRESSES: Home—P.O. Box 871, Tesuque, NM 87574. *E-mail*—kandahar@worldnet.att.net.

CAREER: Writer. Anthropologist in Guatemala, Burma, and other countries, 1952-79; Jonathan Cape Ltd. (publisher), London, England, founder and director of Cape Goliard Press and editor of Cape Editions, 1967-69; Rutgers University, New Brunswick, NJ, professor of comparative literature, 1970-84, professor emeritus, 1984—. Lecturer at colleges and universities, including University of Chicago and University of London, 1952-67; visiting professor at State University of New York—Buffalo and Princeton University, 1969-70.

AWARDS, HONORS: Guinness Prize for poetry, 1963; fellow, Wenner Gren Foundation for Anthropological

Research, 1979-81; poetry fellow, Commonwealth of Pennsylvania, 1983; Rockefeller Foundation fellow in Bellagio, Italy, 1988.

WRITINGS:

Old Savage/Young City (poetry), Jonathan Cape (London, England), 1964, Random House (New York, NY), 1965.
(With Richard Murphy and Jon Silkin) *Penguin Modern Poets Number Seven: Richard Murphy, Jon Silkin, Nathaniel Tarn,* Penguin (New York, NY), 1965.
(Translator) Pablo Neruda, *The Heights of Macchu Picchu,* Jonathan Cape (London, England), 1966, Farrar, Straus & Giroux (New York, NY), 1967.
Where Babylon Ends (poetry), Jonathan Cape (London, England), 1967, David Grossman (New York, NY), 1968.
(Editor and co-translator) *Con Cuba: An Anthology of Cuban Poetry of the Last Sixty Years,* David Grossman (New York, NY), 1969.
The Beautiful Contradictions (poetry), Jonathan Cape (London, England), 1969, Random House (New York, NY), 1970.
October (poetry), Trigram Press (London, England), 1969.
(Translator) Victor Segalen, *Stelae,* Unicorn Press (Santa Barbara, CA), 1969.
The Silence (poetry), M'Arte (Milan, Italy), 1970.
(Editor) Pablo Neruda, *Selected Poems,* Jonathan Cape (London, England), 1970, Delacorte (New York, NY), 1972.
A Nowhere for Vallejo (poetry), Random House (New York, NY), 1971.
Lyrics for the Bride of God; Section: The Artemision (poetry; also see below), Tree Books (Berkeley, CA), 1973.
The Persephones, Christopher's Books (Santa Barbara, CA), 1974.
Lyrics for the Bride of God (poetry), New Directions (New York, NY), 1975.
Narrative of This Fall, Black Sparrow Press (Los Angeles, CA), 1975.
The House of Leaves (poetry), Black Sparrow Press (Santa Barbara, CA), 1976.
The Microcosm, Membrane Press (Milwaukee, WI), 1977.
Birdscapes with Seaside, Black Sparrow Press (Santa Barbara, CA), 1978.

(With Janet Rodney) *From Alaska: The Ground of Our Great Admiration of Nature,* Permanent Press (New York, NY), 1978.

(With Janet Rodney) *The Forest: In Part* (poetry), Perishable Press (Mount Horeb, WI), 1978.

(With Janet Rodney) *Atitlán/Alashka,* Brillig (Boulder, CO), 1979.

The Land Songs: Further Annotations from Baja California (poetry), Blue Guitar Books (London, England), 1979.

Weekends in Mexico (poetry), Oxus Press (London, England), 1982.

The Desert Mothers (poetry), Salt-Works Press (Dennis, MA), 1984.

At the Western Gates (poetry), Tooth of Time Press (Santa Fe, NM), 1985.

Palenque: Selected Poems, Oasis Press (London, England), 1986.

Seeing America First (poetry), Coffee House Press (Minneapolis, MN), 1989.

(Translator) Pablo Neruda, *Four Odes, One Song,* Labyrinth Editions (Honolulu, HI), 1990.

Views from the Weaving Mountains: Selected Essays in Poetics and Anthropology, University of New Mexico Press (Albuquerque, NM), 1991.

Flying the Body: Poems, 1991-92, Arundel Press (Los Angeles, CA), 1993.

(Editor) Natasha Tarn, *Multitude of One,* Grenfell Press (New York, NY), 1993.

(With Martin Prechtel) *Scandals in the House of Birds: Shamans and Priests on Lake Atitlán,* Marsilio Publishers (New York, NY), 1998.

The Architextures: 1988-1994, Chax Press (Tucson, AZ), 2000.

Selected Poems, 1950-2000, Wesleyan University Press (Middletown, CT), 2002.

Author and reader of *Nathaniel Tarn Reading His Poems with Comment in the Recording Laboratory, March 23, 1971,* and of *Robin Skelton and Nathaniel Tarn Reading and Discussing Their Poems in the Coolidge Auditorium, March 22, 1971.* Contributor to many anthologies in the United States, including *Talking Poetry,* edited by Lee Bartlett, University of New Mexico Press (Albuquerque, NM), 1987; *American Poetry since 1950,* edited by E. Weinberger, Marsilio (New York, NY), 1996; and *Poems for the Millennium,* edited by J. Rothenberg, University of California Press (Berkeley, CA), 1998; also contributor to anthologies in France, Italy, Russia, China, Mexico, Spain, and the Netherlands. Contributor to periodicals,

including *Poetry New York, First Intensity, Times Literary Supplement, Observer, New York Times, Credences, Grand Street, Temblor,* and *Sagetrieb.* Contributing editor, *Conjunctions, PO&SIE, Courrier du Centre International de Poesie,* and *Modern Poetry in Translation.*

SIDELIGHTS: Nathaniel Tarn's multicultural interests are seen in his early work as an anthropologist and continue in his work as an internationally acclaimed translator, poet, and critic. For his views on "the state of the art of poetry in this complex society," which is, as he once told *CA,* "a most complex business," he recommends the essay "Dr. Jekyll, the Anthropologist, Emerges and Marches into the Notebooks of Mr. Hyde, the Poet" in the literary journal *Conjunctions.* His contribution to *American Poetry,* the essay "Child As Father to the Man," he said, also gives insight into his writings.

Important influences on his poetry among moderns include Ezra Pound, William Carlos Williams, Hugh MacDiarmid, Charles Olson, Robert Duncan, and Jack Spicer. In addition, poets from many countries—André Breton, Guillame Apollinaire, Arthur Rimbaud, Fernando Pessoa, and Rainer Maria Rilke—have shaped his poetic vision. Tarn's characteristic writing style is eclectic, having the inclusiveness and open forms of his masters. His poems refer to the myths, philosophies, political concerns, plant and animal life, and landscapes known to people from many nations and time periods. In *The Beautiful Contradictions,* Tarn states his personal objective: "It is up to me to call into being everything that is." Like Whitman's style, Tarn's style "is a very original mixture of the high and the low, the deliberately elevated and the humorously familiar," observed a *Times Literary Supplement* reviewer. Writing about *Lyrics for the Bride of God* in *Harper's Bookletter,* Hayden Carruth remarked that "Tarn has attempted . . . a poem in the grand modern matter, after Pound's *Cantos* or Williams' *Paterson* and . . . he has largely succeeded." Of the same book, a *Choice* critic noted that in this work, too, Tarn sounds "distinctly like Whitman, a Whitman writing about America in the 1970's. But his style is strikingly different and idiosyncratic, and his poems dazzle with a kaleidoscope of bright images."

A number of critics have responded negatively to Tarn's long sentences and catalogues. As a *Times Literary Supplement* reviewer said of *The Beautiful Contra-*

dictions, "This is the poetry of a man who has come through a tremendous foreign reading list and lived to get it all mixed up for us." Other critics, however, responded more favorably. Of a later book, *The House of Leaves, Times Literary Supplement* contributor D. M. Thomas commented, "There was always a sense of continental ambition in [Tarn's] work, poems that seemed to wish the pages wider. To read his new collection is a little like flying over America: A Whitmanesque grandiloquence . . . , repetition upon repetition, accretion upon accretion. . . . Much of it is beautiful and true."

For a summary of previous stages in Tarn's development as a poet, *American Book Review* contributor Rochelle Ratner recommended *Atitlán/Alashka:* "Each previous book that Tarn published has been such a complete vision in itself that we tend to think it is his *only* vision. *Atitlán* not only shows the scope of Tarn's field, it shows the fusion of his various periods." Theodore Enslin remarked in the same issue of the *American Book Review* that in addition to showing the width of Tarn's range, this collection also shows "how an omnivorous appetite is controlled by a discriminating intelligence, at the same time that the rush of highly colored and charged language fills the landscape with both form and that form's detail." In *At the Western Gates,* Tarn added new resonance to his images while giving "free play to all the senses," observed a *Voice Literary Supplement* reviewer, who concluded, "With a prophetic sense of sure direction, his new poems move beyond their surface splendor into the depths beneath."

Of *At the Western Gates, Artspace* contributor Gene Frumkin commented, "while these poems are shorter and sing more, on the whole, than Tarn's usual pattern of work, the desert does make its appearance; neither positive nor negative in itself, it brings to the poetry a doubleness, an ambiguity which, as it develops, gives us a sure sign of this poet's mastery. Tarn is thoughtful, religiously, and he is a man whose concern lies with the total culture of any place; the songs of his birds and of his whales are the up and down of a cosmos, his encompassing effort to construct lyricism not only as music but as the music of mind's flow through the mystery of nature." Tarn's next book, *The Desert Mothers,* presents longer poems again, but Frumkin believed that the ideas the poems develop are more significant than their length.

Tarn once told *CA* that reviews often overemphasize his style, which he sees "as only one facet of the work

as if there were no other facets. This concerns the 'rambling,' 'long sentences,' 'grandiloquent,' 'omnivorous' aspect. I believe that, if one looks at the books, there is an alternation between this aspect and another which is far tighter and more controlled. Also between lines, spread and compression. Among controlled, short-lined, simple works, I would place *October;* much of *The House of Leaves;* much of *A Nowhere for Vallejo;* and almost all of *At the Western Gates.* The poems in *Seeing America First* are extremely compressed: seventy poems, each one of which has the exact same number of spaces in each line *when typed* so that the poems are perfectly rectangular, justified on each side, looking *like* prose poems, but *not* prose poems. One cannot be less rambling than that!"

Explaining why he works in both shorter and longer forms, Tarn added, "The complexity/simplicity alternation responds to a belief I have that the fundamental contradiction in the poem's role in society is exasperated today more than at any other time in 'modernist/ postmodernist' history. For the craft to progress, the poem has to improve on a long tradition of complexity, difficulty, even obscurity if it is to 'make it new' as Pound prescribed. On the other hand, the whole tradition has of late made it more and more difficult for poetry to find any kind of readership except among other poets. One of the ways of dealing with this is to write (at least) two kinds of poetry so as to give the work as a whole the optimal chance of reaching one or more publics."

Discussing his work in an entry for the *Contemporary Authors Autobiography Series,* Tarn cited "a lifelong interest in religions and symbolic systems—primarily, but not exclusively, Classical, Judaeo-Christian, Mayan and Buddhist—has been a very powerful motivating force. A strong sense of the interrelationships of man and *polis* and a dark view of man's inhumanity to man have also provided the 'matter' of much poetry." Looking back over the years, he remembered: "In childhood and youth a passionate involvement with nature—especially ornithological and vegetal—occasioned many poems. Over the years, this has to some extent given way to an inextinguishable romance with culture in the form of great human works in any medium (the arts, architecture, technology) and a theoretical interest in the interplay between natural and civil ecology and conservation: that some can even discuss these apart from each other seems to me an impossible aberration."

Tarn also discussed his concern about the declining status of the poet and poetry in "our increasingly illiterate culture. At a very banal level, almost all of us poets of my age sense some kind of great difference between the life we used to have and the one we lead now. I dare say I was more fortunate than many in my beginnings, but I treasured the sense of having a publishing house, an editor, the occasional lunch, the pretense that one's vocation was of use to the world." Tarn noted that even as late as the 1960s, there was "extraordinary interest in poetry; the possibility of substantial and extremely well-attended readings; the sense of a potential (probably illusory) for significant political action. . . . All that began to give way—the very day, I believe, when the Vietnam War ended. Only the very smallest number of 'known,' 'famed,' 'noted,' 'awarded' bards now enjoys such luxuries. The world of publishing, sold out to corporatism, is deliquescing beyond all recognition. The culture overproduces 'poets' in the 'creative writing' schools while at the same time underproducing readers throughout the educational system at all levels."

BIOGRAPHICAL AND CRITICAL SOURCES:

BOOKS

Bartlett, Lee, editor, *Talking Poetry: Conversations in the Workshop with Contemporary Poets,* University of New Mexico Press (Albuquerque, NM), 1987.

Bartlett, Lee, *Nathaniel Tarn, A Descriptive Bibliography,* McFarland (Jefferson, NC), 1987.

Bartlett, Lee, *The Sun Is but a Morning Star: Essays on Western American Literature,* University of New Mexico Press (Albuquerque, NM), 1989.

Contemporary Authors Autobiography Series, Volume 16, Gale (Detroit, MI), 1992.

Fisch, Harold, *The Dual Image,* [London, England], 1971.

McQuade, Molly, *An Unsentimental Education: Writers and Chicago,* University of Chicago Press (Chicago, IL), 1995.

Tarn, Nathaniel, *The Beautiful Contradictions,* Jonathan Cape (London, England), 1969, Random House (New York, NY), 1970.

PERIODICALS

American Book Review, Volume 2, number 5, 1980, Rochelle Ratner and Theodore Enslin, review of *Atitlán/Alashka.*

American Poetry Review, Volume 1, number 2, 1984.
Artspace, Volume 5, number 1, 1985-86, article by Gene Frumkin
Boundary 2, Volume 4, number 1, 1975.
Choice, November, 1975, review of *Lyrics for the Bride of God;* April, 1977.
Conjunctions, number 6, 1984.
Credences, number 4, 1977.
Harper's Bookletter, October 13, 1975, Hayden Carruth, review of *Lyrics for the Bride of God.*
Judaism, fall, 1965.
Library Journal, June 15, 1965; April 15, 1971.
New York Times Book Review, September 25, 1966; May 21, 1967; May 7, 1972; September 7, 1975.
Poetry, June, 1968.
Saturday Review, October 9, 1965; December 13, 1968.
Spectator, January 1, 1965.
Sulfur, number 14, 1985/86.
Times (London, England), April 6, 1968; June 7, 1969.
Times Literary Supplement, January 7, 1965; October 12, 1967; August 7, 1969; April 9, 1970, review of *The Beautiful Contradictions;* August 4, 1972; May 20, 1977, D. M. Thomas, review of *The House of Leaves.*
Voice Literary Supplement, February, 1986, review of *At the Western Gates.**

*   *   *

TERSON, Peter 1932-

PERSONAL: Birth name Peter Patterson; known professionally as Peter Terson; born February 24, 1932, in Tyne, England; son of Peter (a joiner) and Jane (a playwright) Patterson; married Sheila Bailey, May 25, 1955; children: Bruce, Neil, Janie. *Education:* Attended Newcastle-upon-Tyne Technical College and Redland Training College, 1952-54.

ADDRESSES: Home—87 Middlebridge St., Romsey, Hampshire, England. *Agent*—Lemon, Unna & Durbridge, 24 Pottery Lane, Holland Park, London W11 4LZ, England.

CAREER: Worked as a drafter; teacher of physical education, 1953-65; playwright, 1965—. Victoria Theater, Stoke-on-Trent, England, resident playwright, 1966-67; National Youth Theater, writer, 1966. *Military service:* Royal Air Force, 1950-52.

AWARDS, HONORS: Arts Council bursary, 1966; John Whitney Award, 1967; award from Writers Guild of Great Britain, 1971; Radio Scriptwriter award, 1972; promising playwright's award from Lord Goodman.

WRITINGS:

STAGE PLAYS

A Night to Make the Angels Weep (first produced in Stoke-on-Trent, England, at Victoria Theater, 1964; produced in London, England, 1971), published in *New English Dramatists Eleven,* Penguin (London, England), 1967.

The Mighty Reservoy (first produced in Stoke-on-Trent, England, at Victoria Theater, 1964; produced in London, England, 1967), published in *New English Dramatists Fourteen,* Penguin (London, England), 1970.

The Rat Run, first produced in Stoke-on-Trent, England, 1965.

All Honour Mr. Todd, first produced in Stoke-on-Trent, England, at Victoria Theater, 1966.

I'm in Charge of These Ruins, first produced in Stoke-on-Trent, England, at Victoria Theater, 1966.

(With others) *Sing an Arful Story,* first produced in Stoke-on-Trent, England, 1966.

Jock-on-the-Go (adaptation of story "Jock-at-a-Venture" by Arnold Bennett), first produced in Stoke-on-Trent, England, 1966.

Holder Dying, first produced in part in Stoke-on-Trent, England, 1966.

Zigger Zagger (first produced in London, England, 1967), published in *Zigger Zagger and Mooney and His Caravans* (also see below), Penguin (Harmondsworth, England), 1970.

(With Joyce Cheeseman) *Clayhanger* (adaptation of a novel by Arnold Bennett), first produced in Stoke-on-Trent, England, 1967.

The Ballad of the Artificial Mash, first produced in Stoke-on-Trent, England, at Victoria Theater, 1967.

The Apprentices (first produced in London, England 1968), Penguin (Harmondsworth, England), 1970.

The Adventures of Gervase Beckett; or, The Man Who Changed Places (first produced in Stoke-on-Trent, England, 1969), Eyre Methuen (London, England), 1973.

Fuzz, first produced in London, England, 1969.

Inside-Outside, first produced in Nottingham, England, 1970.

The Affair at Bennett's Hill, Worcestershire, first produced in Stoke-on-Trent, England, 1970.

Spring-Heeled Jack (first produced in London, England, 1970), published in *Plays and Players,* November, 1970.

The 1861 Whitby Lifeboat Disaster, first produced in Stoke-on-Trent, England, 1970, produced in London, England, 1971.

The Knotty: A Musical Documentary, Methuen (London, England,), 1970.

(With Mike Butler) *The Samaritan* (first produced in Stoke-on-Trent, England, 1971; produced in London, England, 1971), published in *Plays and Players,* July, 1971.

Cadium Firty, first produced in London, England, 1971.

Good Lads at Heart, first produced in London, England, 1971; produced in Brooklyn, NY, at Brooklyn Academy of Music Opera House, 1979.

Slip Road Wedding, first produced in Newcastle-upon-Tyne, England, 1971; produced in London, England, 1971.

Prisoners of the War, first produced in Newcastle-upon-Tyne, England, 1971.

But Fred, Freud Is Dead (first produced in Stoke-on-Trent, England, 1972), published in *Plays and Players,* March, 1972.

Moby Dick, first produced in Stoke-on-Trent, England, 1972.

The Most Cheerful Man, first produced in London, England, 1973.

Geordie's March, first produced in London, England, 1973.

The Trip to Florence, first produced in London, England, 1974.

Lost Yer Tongue?, first produced in Newcastle-upon-Tyne, England, 1974.

Vince Lays the Carpet, and Fred Erects the Tent, first produced in Stoke-on-Trent, England, 1975.

The Ballad of Ben Bagot, published in *Prompt Two,* edited by Alan Durband, Hutchinson (London, England), 1976.

(With Paul Joyce) *Love Us and Leave Us,* first produced in London, England, 1976.

The Bread and Butter Trade, first produced in London, England, 1976.

Twilight Joker, first produced in Brighton, England, 1977; produced in London, England, 1978.

Pinvin Careless and His Lines of Force, produced in Stoke-on-Trent, England, 1977.

Family Ties: Wrong First Time; Never Right, Yet Again (produced in London, England, 1977), published in *Act 2,* edited by David Self and Ray Speakman, Hutchinson (London, England), 1979.

Forest Lodge, produced in Salisbury, England, 1977.

Tolly of the Black Boy, produced in Edinburgh, Scotland, 1977.

Rattling the Railings (produced in London, England, 1978), Samuel French (London, England), 1979.

The Banger, produced in Nottingham, England, 1978.

Cul de Sac, first produced in Chichester, England, 1978; produced in London, England, 1979.

England, My Own, produced in London, England, 1978.

Soldier Boy, produced in London, England, 1978.

VE Night, produced in Chicester, England, 1979.

The Limes, and I Kid You Not, produced in London, England, 1979.

The Pied Piper (musical adaptation of the poem by Robert Browning; produced in Stoke-on Trent, England, 1980), Samuel French (London, England), 1982.

The Ticket, produced in London, England, 1980.

The Night John, produced in London, England, 1980.

We Were All Heroes, produced in Andover, Hampshire, England, 1981.

Aesop's Fables (musical; produced in Stoke-on-Trent, England, 1983), Samuel French (London, England), 1986.

Strippers (produced in Newcastle-upon-Tyne, England, 1984; produced in London, England, 1985), Amber Lane Press (Oxford, England), 1985.

Hotel Dorado, produced in Newcastle-upon-Tyne, England, 1985.

Chestnuts, produced at Bolton Octagen, 1987.

The Weeping Madonna, published in *New Plays 1: Contemporary One-Act Plays,* Oxford University Press (Oxford, England), 1988.

Under the Fish (community play), produced in Bradford on Avon, England, 1990.

Have You Seen This Girl (community play), produced in Southborough, Kent, England, 1991.

Twin Oaks (community play), first produced in Lambersart, France, then Southborough, Kent, England, both 1992.

The Sailor's Horse (community play), produced in Minehead, England, 1997.

(With Jon Hurley) *Labels,* performed at Glewstone Court Hotel, 1998.

Hold Fast (community play), produced in Romsey, Hampshire, England, 1999.

Pigeons Aloft, produced at Ross Festival, 2000.

Mr. Clean, produced at Ross Festival, 2001.

The Big Apple, produced at Ross Festival, 2001.

Campers, performed in Stoke-on-Trent, England, at Edensor High School, 2001.

Also author of *Dobson's Drie Bobs, The Launching of the Esso Northumbria,* and *I Would Prefer Not To* (adaptation of the novella *Bartleby* by Herman Melville).

TELEVISION PLAYS

Mooney and His Caravans (first broadcast in 1966; produced on stage in London, England, 1968), published in *Zigger Zagger and Mooney and His Caravans,* Penguin (Harmondsworth, England), 1970.

The Heroism of Thomas Chadwick, 1967.

The Last Train through the Harecastle Tunnel, 1969.

The Gregorian Chant, 1972.

The Dividing Fence, 1972.

Shakespeare—or Bust, 1973.

Three for the Fancy, 1973.

Dancing in the Dark, 1974.

The Rough and the Smooth, 1975.

(With Paul Joyce) *The Jolly Swagman,* 1976.

The Ballad of Ben Bagot, 1977.

The Reluctant Chosen, 1979.

Put Out to Grass, 1979.

Atlantis, 1983.

Also writer for the *Salvation Army* series.

RADIO PLAYS

The Fishing Party, 1971.

Play Soft, Then Attack, 1978.

The First Flame, 1980.

The Rundle Gibbet, 1981.

The Overnight Man, 1982.

The Romany Trip (documentary), 1983.

The Top Sail at Imberley, 1983.

Madam Main Course, 1983.

Poole Harbour, 1984.

Letters to the Otter, 1985.

When Youth and Pleasure Meet, 1986.

The Mumper, 1988.

Blind down the Thames, 1988.

Stones, Tops, and Tarns, 1989.
Tales My Father Taught Me, 1990.

OTHER

The Offcuts Voyage, Oxford University Press (Oxford, England), 1988.
(Editor) *New Plays 1,* Oxford University Press (Oxford, England), 1988.
(Editor) *New Plays 2,* Oxford University Press (Oxford, England), 1989.
(Editor) *New Plays 3,* Oxford University Press (Oxford, England), 1990.

WORK IN PROGRESS: The Humanitarians, with Dick Parker; *Daphne,* with Doug Braddy and Carol Braddy.

SIDELIGHTS: Peter Terson had already launched a career as a physical education teacher when the birth of his first child revived an interest in writing that had been dormant for years. Finding that he was often up in the middle of the night after caring for his infant son, Terson began work on a novel; he eventually abandoned the project in favor of writing plays, a decision based on his interest in writing dialogue. His first two plays were optioned by the British Broadcasting Corporation but never produced because they were judged to need too much work to adapt them for broadcast. Terson was encouraged by the sales, however, and continued to write in his spare time for the next seven years.

During much of this period Terson lived in the Vale of Evesham, a rural, fruit-growing area in central England. His early plays are set in Evesham and contain a sinister undercurrent: progress and civilization threaten nature and alienate humankind. Terson sent samples of his work to Peter Cheeseman, director of the Victoria Theater in Stoke-on-Trent, an in-the-round theater committed to regionalism. Cheeseman was impressed with Terson's work and *A Night to Make the Angels Weep* was performed at the Victoria in 1964. Other Terson plays set in the Vale of Evesham and sharing the theme of rural tradition opposing the forces of change include *The Mighty Reservoy, Mooney and His Caravans, All Honour Mr. Todd,* and *I'm in Charge of These Ruins.* As a collection the plays constitute a cycle, emphasizing themes in a quiet, dialogue-centered fashion.

Typical of Terson's writing during this period is *Mooney and His Caravans.* The story centers on a married couple, Charley and Mave, who are so determined to escape city life that they are willing to submit themselves to repeated degradation in a rural trailer-park community run like a concentration camp by the evil, cunning Mooney. Humiliated and stripped of all pretense, with Mave carrying Mooney's baby, the couple rediscovers their love for each other and returns to the city.

Terson was named resident playwright of the Victoria Theater in 1966, and was also invited to write a play for the National Youth Theater by its director, Michael Croft. Terson's acceptance of the offer required a major change in his writing style; whereas the productions at the Victoria Theater were small in scale and represented regional, rural interests, the London-based National Youth presented large, showy productions, staged by school children and young adults, and dealt with themes that appealed to urban youth. Terson responded to the challenge with *Zigger Zagger,* a look at almost fanatical adoration of and identification with professional soccer teams as seen through the eyes of Harry Philton, a school dropout seeking his niche in a society in decline. Harry bounces from job to job, falling into unhappy relationships and a dead-end career.

Terson gave up his post as resident playwright at the Victoria Theater in 1967 and began to devote more time to working with the National Youth Theater, evolving the themes he had developed in *Zigger Zagger. The Apprentices* is an elaboration on those themes in a more naturalistic fashion; the hopes and dreams of a working-class youth are stripped away one by one until he finds himself trapped in a colorless, meaningless world with no future.

Terson's ability to tailor a play to fit a particular cast and director has led some observers to classify him as a "primitive" to describe his unsophisticated natural talents and observations of human nature. However, the versatility required to be able to write for both the small, in-the-round Victoria Theater and the National Youth Theater with its large company of amateur players is considerable. In order to fully utilize the potential of the National Youth Theater, Terson would start with a basic outline and, working with cast and director Croft, work out staging details and dialogue.

An example of the success of this technique was observed by *New York Times* critic Richard Eder when *Good Lads at Heart* played in New York in 1979. The play, which examines the life and relationships of eighteen boys in reform school, presented the difficult task of adequately developing each of the characters. Eder wrote: "The play, written by Peter Terson for the group, is descriptive and instructive. Mr. Terson has not created a notable play but he has created a very useful one; and one that beautifully fits the nature and abilities of the performers."

In an essay about Terson in the *Dictionary of Literary Biography,* Gillette Elvgren compared the playwright to such luminaries as Arnold Wesker, John Osborne, and Harold Pinter, who also came from Britain's working class. "But unlike some works of these playwrights," observed Elvgren, "his own plays continue to reflect and draw sustenance from this heritage. Through their language and characters, his dramas depict man's isolation from the land and from his work. . . . Terson imbues his characters with a kind of colloquial relevance (and oftentimes delightful eccentricity) that never loses touch with the sources of work and class from which the writer sprang. Terson's particular and unique strengths as a playwright stem from this ability."

Elvgren commented that the violent climaxes of many of Terson's early plays recalled the youthful work of Anton Chekov, in that it is "somewhat arbitrary and contrived." He mused that television and radio were excellent media for showcasing the strengths of Terson's work, naming *The Last Train through the Harcastle Tunnel, The Fishing Party,* and *The Gregorian Chant* as "humorous, ironic works that do not demand the sustained dramatic intensity of an evening in the theater." He finds these works to be "poetic and mood statements which bring to life the workers who people the rural villages of the Midlands and the industrial back streets of the Northern cities."

Terson has been underrated by many commentators, according to John Elsom in *Contemporary Dramatists.* Referring to the common description of the writer as a "primitive" talent, Elsom surmised that the term was "intended to mean that his technique is artless, his observation fresh and original, and his naturally prolific talent untainted by too much sophistication." Yet the critic decided that "this somewhat backhanded tribute . . . belittles his ability." He theorized that the theater establishment has a difficult time fully accepting Terson's work because it does not include "popular West End comedies" or "middle-class families in the

grip of emotional dilemmas." Instead, he writes about "problems which . . . seem to him more important. He is a highly skilled writer with a particular insight into Northern working-class societies and whose plays have, at best, a richness of imagination and an infectious humour." Elsom concluded: "Terson's plays have a much greater variety and range than is often supposed. . . . His influence in British regional theater has been considerable, and more than any other contemporary dramatist he carries forward the ideas of social drama."

Terson more recently told *CA:* "The most important development in my writing in recent years is working with other people. Since working on community plays, I have found that many people have stories to tell but are unable to do so. I work with them. I hope to get together a group of plays and form a company of local people to put them on in Ross on Wye. Up to now I have written plays with Jon Hurley, a wine specialist; Doug and Carol Braddy, social workers; Didi Lodge, a farmer's wife; and Dick Parker, a retired doctor. All of these add a new dimension (and a new depth) to my work."

BIOGRAPHICAL AND CRITICAL SOURCES:

BOOKS

Contemporary Dramatists, St. James Press (Detroit, MI), 1993.
Dictionary of Literary Biography, Volume 13: *British Dramatists since World War II,* Gale (Detroit, MI), 1982.

PERIODICALS

Drama, winter, 1968.
Evening Sentinel, October 4, 1967, p. 6.
London, June, 1968.
New Statesman, September 29, 1967; March 22, 1968; August 28, 1968; May 15, 1970.
New York Times, March 28, 1979, Richard Eder, review of *Good Lads at Heart.*
Observer, September 3, 1967; May 19, 1968; August 25, 1968.
Plays and Players, September, 1970; October, 1970; November, 1970; March, 1972.

Punch, March 20, 1968; September 2, 1970.
Spectator, September 2, 1967; September 6, 1969.
Stage, August 27, 1970; September 17, 1970; December 3, 1970; August 5, 1971; September 30, 1971.
Times Literary Supplement, April 23, 1970.
Variety, October 6, 1971.

*   *   *

THORNE, Ian
   See MAY, Julian

*   *   *

THORNE, Jean Wright
   See MAY, Julian

*   *   *

TOLKIN, Michael 1950-

PERSONAL: Born October 17, 1950, in New York, NY; son of Mel (a writer) and Edith (a lawyer; maiden name, Leibovitch) Tolkin; married Wendy Mogel (a psychologist). *Education:* Middlebury College, B.A., 1974.

ADDRESSES: Agent—c/o Sterling Lord Literistic, One Madison Ave., New York, NY 10010.

CAREER: Worked variously as a journalist in New York, NY, and as a television story editor in Los Angeles, CA. Screenwriter, novelist, and film director.

WRITINGS:

The Player (novel), Atlantic Monthly Press (New York, NY), 1988, adapted as a screenplay of the same title, Fine Line Features, 1992.
Gleaming the Cube (screenplay), Twentieth Century-Fox, 1989.
(And director) *The Rapture* (screenplay), Fine Line Features, 1991.
(With Henry Bean) *Deep Cover* (screenplay), New Line Cinema, 1992.

Michael Tolkin

Among the Dead, Morrow (New York, NY), 1993.
(With others) *The Burning Season* (teleplay), HBO, 1994.
(And director) *The New Age* (screenplay), New Regency, 1994.
The Player/The Rapture/The New Age: Three Screenplays (screenplay), Grove Press (New York, NY), 1995.
(With Bruce Joel Rubin) *Deep Impact,* DreamWorks, 1998.
(With Michael R. Perry, and director) *20 Billion,* Paramount, 2001.
(With Chap Taylor) *Changing Lanes* (screenplay), Paramount, 2002.
Under Radar (novel), Atlantic Monthly Press (New York, NY), 2002.

SIDELIGHTS: Screenwriter, novelist, and film director Michael Tolkin grew up in Hollywood, California, where his father, Mel, was a television comedy writer, and his mother, Edith, was senior vice president of legal affairs for Paramount Studios. The family lived comfortably. Tolkin told Bernard Weinraub in the *New York Times* that his father's success as a writer led him to believe it was easy to make a living through writing. "And it was a shock for me to find out that it was actually hard to make a living as a writer," he said.

Tolkin is best known as the author of *The Player*. A story of murder set in the author's familiar Hollywood, the book has been critically acclaimed for its unique, darkly comic view of the film industry. Tolkin tells the story of Griffin Mill, an upper-level executive at a major film studio. Mill, power-hungry and aggressive, becomes overwhelmed by the pressure and fast pace of his career and the fear of losing the affluent lifestyle afforded by his job propels him into a paranoiac tailspin. Frustrated by a series of harassing telephone calls from an anonymous screenwriter, the mentally unstable Mill lures his suspect to a parking lot where he strangles him. Janet Maslin, reviewing the novel for the *New York Times Book Review*, commented that Tolkin sees Mill's transformation into a murderer as "a somewhat logical extension of Griffin's executive personality." Maslin found that *The Player* has "everything to do with today's bottomline mentality, carried to a calmly illogical extreme. . . . One needn't share Griffin's scruples to be impressed by his pragmatic style."

Tolkin used his expertise as a film writer—the screenplays *Gleaming the Cube, The Rapture,* and *Deep Cover* are also to his credit—to adapt his novel into a feature-length film that has achieved great critical success at the hand of noted film director Robert Altman. Richard Corliss comments on the film version in *Time*: "A [film] executive will go to A.A. meetings not because he is an alcoholic but because 'that's where all the deals are being made.' Michael Tolkin's script abounds in such cynical wisdom, but it never loses an appreciation for the grace with which these snakes consume their victims." Author Tolkin also took a turn in the director's chair during the filming of his screenplay, *The Rapture,* released in 1991. Tolkin described the film to Matthew Carnahan in *Premiere* as "a sincere exploration of God and faith and . . . the end."

Changing Lanes tells the story of two New Yorkers, Gavin Banek and Doyle Gibson, whose lives intersect when they hit each other in an automobile accident. Banek is a rising young lawyer in a Wall Street firm, and Gipson is an insurance company phone representative and alcoholic who has recently been divorced from his wife. The two men fail to resolve their dispute

about the accident when it occurs, setting off a cycle of vengeance and revenge.

In *Under Radar*, Tolkin depicts the retribution that falls upon a man who commits a senseless murder. Insurance fraud artist Tom Levy takes his ill-gotten earnings and sends his family to Jamaica, but he quickly becomes bored there. He flirts with Debra, but when his four-year-old daughter dances with Debra's husband Barry at a party, he is infuriated, and kills Barry. Naturally, Levy ends up in prison, and spends many years in silence after another prisoner tells him a secret story—a story that affects him so deeply that it turns his hair white. Eventually he remembers the story, and tries to reclaim his family, which has moved on without him. A *Publishers Weekly* reviewer noted that Tom was an extremely unsympathetic character, and that the novel's allegorical, existential tone is "belabored." *New York Times* writer Janet Maslin wrote, "The book's allegorical aspect is as integral as it is cryptic, and none of its story can be taken quite literally." In another *New York Times* article, Charles Taylor commented, "*Under Radar* is [Tolkin's] most explicitly religious work since *The Rapture*. It is also the strangest thing he has ever done, its meanings hanging just out of reach." Taylor also noted, "*Under Radar* leaves us like puzzled pilgrims, struggling with the meaning of the cruel fable that has been so enticingly told."

In an interview in *UnderGroundOnline,* Tolkin said of *Under Radar,* "I wanted to incorporate a number of stories without writing a book of short stories. The more I thought about why these stories were grabbing, the more I wanted to keep the experience of living with the stories as the experience of reading the novel."

BIOGRAPHICAL AND CRITICAL SOURCES:

PERIODICALS

Armchair Detective, spring, 1994, p. 58.
Booklist, April 1, 1993, review of *Among the Dead,* p. 1412; May 15, 2002, Joanne Wilkinson, review of *Under Radar,* p. 1580.
Book World, May 24, 1992, review of *The Player,* p. 12; October 25, 1992, review of *The Player,* p. 14; April 4, 1993, review of *Among the Dead,* p. 4; May 15, 2002, p. 1580.

Guardian, May 23, 1993, review of *Among the Dead,* p. 20.

Kirkus Reviews, February 1, 1993, review of *Among the Dead,* p. 95; April 15, 2002, review of *Under Radar,* p. 523.

Library Journal, March 15, 1993, review of *Among the Dead,* p. 109.

Los Angeles Times Book Review, May 30, 1993, review of *Among the Dead,* p. 2.

National Review, May 11, 1992, John Simon, review of *The Player,* p. 53.

New Statesman and Society, June 4, 1993, Roz Kaveney, review of *Among the Dead,* p. 39; June 4, 1993, p. 39.

Newsweek, April 19, 1993, review of *Among the Dead,* p. 62.

New York Times, April 13, 1993, review of *Among the Dead,* p. C17; May 30, 2002, Janet Maslin, review of *Under Radar,* p. E9; June 16, 2002, Charles Taylor, review of *Under Radar,* p. G19.

New York Times Biographical Service, May, 1992, Bernard Weinraub, "A Writer's View from the Edge of the Playground," author interview, p. 616.

New York Times Book Review, July 24, 1988, p. 10; April 25, 1993, review of *Among the Dead,* p. 14.

Observer (London, England), May 9, 1993, p. 59; March 27, 1994, review of *Among the Dead,* p. 22.

People, March 8, 1993, p. 67; May 24, 1993, Pam Lambert, review of *Among the Dead,* p. 35.

Premiere, September, 1991, pp. 55-56.

Publishers Weekly, March 8, 1993, review of *Among the Dead,* p. 67; July 4, 1994, review of *Among the Dead,* p. 59; April 8, 2002, review of *Under Radar,* p. 201.

Rolling Stone, October 17, 1991, p. 100.

Spectator, May 15, 1993, review of *Among the Dead,* p. 36.

Time, April 13, 1992, Richard Corliss, review of *The Player,* p. 70.

Times Literary Supplement, May 14, 1993, review of *Among the Dead,* p. 22.

Variety, April 8, 2002, Robert Koehler, review of *Changing Lanes,* p. 29.

Washington Post Book World, June 5, 1988, p. 8.

West Coast Review of Books, Art, and Entertainment, April, 1993, review of *Among the Dead,* p. 22.

ONLINE

UnderGroundOnline, http://www.ugo.com/ (August 21, 2002), Dan Epstein, interview with Michael Tolkin.*

TREVELYAN, (Walter) Raleigh 1923-

PERSONAL: Surname is pronounced "Trevillian"; born July 6, 1923, in Port Blair, Andaman Islands, India; son of Walter Raleigh Fetherstonhaugh (a colonel in the Indian Army) and Olive Beatrice (Frost) Trevelyan. *Education:* Attended secondary school at Winchester College, Winchester, England, 1937-42. *Religion:* Church of England. *Hobbies and other interests:* Travel, gardening, collecting, theater.

ADDRESSES: Home—St. Cadix, St. Veep, Lostwithiel, Cornwall PL22 0NG, England; 18 Hertford St., London W1Y 7DB, England. *Agent*—A. M. Heath and Co. Ltd., 79 St. Martin's Lane, London WC2N 4AA, England; Brandt & Brandt Literary Agents, 1501 Broadway, New York, NY 10036.

CAREER: Samuel Montagu (merchant banker), London, England, trainee, 1947-48; William Collins Sons and Co. Ltd. (publisher), London, editor, 1948-58; Hutchinson and Co. Ltd. (publisher), London, editor and director of Arrow Books Ltd. and New Authors Ltd., 1958-61; Penguin Books Ltd. (publisher), Harmondsworth, Middlesex, England, editor, 1961-62; Michael Joseph Ltd. (publisher), London, editorial director, 1962-73; Hamish Hamilton Ltd. (publisher), London, director, 1973-80; Jonathan Cape Ltd. (publisher), London, literary advisor, 1980-86; Bloomsbury (publisher), literary adviser, 1986-88. Member of British Goodwill Mission to Virginia for the Jamestown Festival, 1957. *Military service:* British Army, Infantry, Rifle Brigade, 1942-46; served with military mission to Italian Army in Rome, 1944-46; became captain; mentioned in dispatches.

MEMBER: International PEN (vice chair of English Center), Royal Society of Literature (fellow), Royal Geographical Society (fellow), British-Italian Society, Anglo-Italian Society for the Protection of Animals (chair).

AWARDS, HONORS: John Florio Prize, Translators Association, for *The Outlaws.*

WRITINGS:

The Fortress: A Diary of Anzio and After (Book Society recommendation), William Collins (London, England), 1956, St. Martin's Press (New York, NY), 1957.

A Hermit Disclosed (Book Society choice), Longmans, Green (London, England), 1960, St. Martin's Press (New York, NY), 1961.

(Translator) Giuliano Palladino, *Peace at Alamein*, Hodder & Stoughton (London, England), 1962.

(Editor) *Italian Short Stories/Racconti italiani*, Penguin (Baltimore, MD), 1965.

The Big Tomato, Longmans, Green (London, England), 1966.

(Editor) *Italian Writing Today*, Penguin (Baltimore, MD), 1967.

(Translator from Italian) Luigi Meneghello, *The Outlaws*, Morrow (New York, NY), 1967.

Princes under the Volcano, Morrow (New York, NY), 1972.

The Shadow of Vesuvius, Michael Joseph (London, England), 1976.

A Pre-Raphaelite Circle, Chatto & Windus (London, England), 1978.

Rome '44: The Battle for the Eternal City, Secker & Warburg (London, England), 1981, Viking (New York, NY), 1982.

Shades of the Alhambra, Secker & Warburg (London, England), 1985.

The Golden Oriole: Childhood, Family, and Friends in India, Viking (New York, NY), 1987.

Grand Dukes and Diamonds, Secker & Warburg (London, England), 1991.

(Editor) *A Clear Premonition: The Letters of Lieutenant Timothy Lloyd, 1943-44*, Leo Cooper (London, England), 1994.

The Companion Guide to Sicily, Companion Guides, 1996.

Sir Walter Raleigh, Allen Lane (London, England), 2003.

Contributor of articles and reviews to periodicals, including *Apollo, Connoisseur, New York Times Book Review*, London *Sunday Times, Observer, Listener, Guardian*, and *Times Literary Supplement;* contributor to National Trust publications.

SIDELIGHTS: Raleigh Trevelyan's military histories *The Fortress: A Diary of Anzio and After* and *Rome '44: The Battle for the Eternal City* have both been praised by reviewers. Trevelyan was a twenty-year-old Rifle Brigade subaltern when he took part in the Allied landings at Anzio, Italy, in 1944, and *The Fortress* is the journal that he wrote at that time. A *Times Literary Supplement* contributor called it "a concentrated and brilliantly observed account of the dangers and confusion of infantry warfare" and noted that "the restless immediacy native to the diary form escapes the confines of journalism through the author's self-awareness." In conclusion, the reviewer stated: "The unsentimental humanity of his dealings with his men . . . and the piled-up excitements of the close-quarters action make this one of the most notable memoirs to have emerged from the Second World War." Of *Rome '44*, Norman Lewis wrote in the *New York Times Book Review:* "Raleigh Trevelyan's book is a distinguished addition to the chronicles of war. His writing is of sensitive literary quality."

Trevelyan similarly aroused admiration with *The Golden Oriole: Childhood, Family, and Friends in India*, a wide-ranging look at India under British rule during the 1800s and 1900s, unified by the author's focus on his own family's experiences. Writing in the *New York Times Book Review*, Jan Morris judged it one of the best Anglo-Indian memoirs and "one of the very few that will survive not just as a period piece but as literature." Among Trevelyan's ancestors were a number of administrators, soldiers, and writers who lived and worked in India; using his own memories and details of their lives, writings, and experiences the author "is able to evoke the whole course of the British relationship with India," Morris claimed. The critic applauded Trevelyan's writing skill and unsentimental and often humorous approach, summing up *The Golden Oriole* as a "historical memoir of the profoundest kind."

BIOGRAPHICAL AND CRITICAL SOURCES:

PERIODICALS

New York Times Book Review, February 21, 1982, Norman Lewis, review of *Rome '44: The Battle for the Eternal City*, November 22, 1987, Jan Morris, review of *The Golden Oriole: Childhood, Family, and Friends in India*, pp. 3, 51.

Times Literary Supplement, January 31, 1986, review of *The Fortress: A Diary of Anzio and After;* March 28, 2003, John Bossy, review of *Sir Walter Raleigh*, p. 27.*

*   *   *

TWOMBLY, Robert C(harles) 1940-

PERSONAL: Born November 16, 1940, in Boston, MA; son of L. Stewart (a chemical technician) and Ruth (a secretary; maiden name, Richardson) Twombly; children: Jonathan, David. *Education:* Harvard University, B.A., 1962; University of Wisconsin—Madison, M.A., 1964, Ph.D., 1968. *Politics:* Socialist.

ADDRESSES: Home—17 Old Mill Rd., West Nyack, NY 10994. *Office*—Department of History, City College of the City University of New York, New York, NY 10031.

CAREER: University of Wisconsin—Madison, instructor in history, 1968-69; City College of the City University of New York, New York, NY, assistant professor, 1969-74, associate professor of history, beginning 1974.

MEMBER: Society of American Historians, Institute of Early American History and Culture, Mid-Atlantic Radical Historians Organization.

AWARDS, HONORS: Grants from American Philosophical Society, 1976-77, and National Endowment for the Humanities, 1977.

WRITINGS:

Blacks in White America since 1965, David McKay (New York, NY), 1971.
Frank Lloyd Wright: An Interpretive Biography, Harper (New York, NY), 1973.
Frank Lloyd Wright: His Life and His Architecture, Wiley (New York, NY), 1978.
Louis Sullivan: His Work and His Life, Viking (New York, NY), 1986.
Power and Style: A Critique of Twentieth-Century Architecture in the United States, Hill & Wang (New York, NY), 1996.
(With Narciso G. Menocal) *Louis Sullivan: The Poetry of Architecture,* Norton (New York, NY), 2000.

Contributor of articles and reviews to architecture and history journals and to newspapers. Member of editorial board, *Marxist Perspectives.*

SIDELIGHTS: Robert C. Twombly once told *CA:* "It becomes more important for me to explore the ways in which corporate and state policies affect architectural design. My scholarship is more and more influenced by my politics, so my new work on architecture will actually be an analysis of American political culture. Since architecture is created and purchased by individuals and groups from the dominant classes, it embodies class experiences—ideology, objectives, perspectives. Design history is least of all the history of style or technology, most of all the history of ideas. Although architectural space is consciously composed by clients and designers, most people—including intellectuals—think nothing of it, indeed, take it for granted, even though we all live most of our lives inside buildings. This is but another example of the ways in which people are constantly manipulated by powers over which they have no control. The role of the scholar is to illuminate these phenomena in hopes that people, becoming more aware, will attempt to again more influence over their situations."

BIOGRAPHICAL AND CRITICAL SOURCES:

PERIODICALS

Times Literary Supplement, April 4, 2003, Joseph Rykwert, review of *Louis Sullivan: The Poetry of Architecture,* p. 12.*

*   *   *

TYTELL, John 1939-

PERSONAL: Born May 17, 1939, in Antwerp, Belgium; son of Charles and Lena (Ganopolski) Tytell; married Mary Ellen Gregori (a photographer), May 28, 1967. *Education:* City College (now City College of the City University of New York), B.A., 1961; New York University, M.A., 1963, Ph.D., 1968.

ADDRESSES: Home—69 Perry St., New York, NY 10014. *Office*—Department of English, Queens College of the City University of New York, Flushing, NY 11367.

CAREER: Queens College of the City University of New York, Flushing, NY, lecturer, 1964-69, assistant professor, 1969-74, associate professor, beginning 1974, now professor of English.

MEMBER: Modern Language Association of America, Phi Beta Kappa.

AWARDS, HONORS: National Endowment of the Humanities fellowships, 1974.

WRITINGS:

(Editor, with Harold Jaffe) *The American Experience: A Radical Reader,* Harper (New York, NY), 1970.

(Editor, with Harold Jaffe) *Affinities: A Short Story Anthology,* Crowell (New York, NY), 1970.

Naked Angels: The Lives and Literature of the Beat Generation, McGraw-Hill (New York, NY), 1976.

Ezra Pound: The Solitary Volcano, Anchor Press (New York, NY), 1987.

(Editor and author of foreword) Carl Solomon, *Emergency Messages: An Autobiographical Miscellany,* Paragon House (New York, NY), 1989.

The Living Theatre: Art, Exile, and Outrage, Grove Press (New York, NY), 1995.

Passionate Lives: D. H. Lawrence, F. Scott Fitzgerald, Henry Miller, Dylan Thomas, Sylvia Plath—in Love, Carol Publishing Group (Secaucus, NJ), 1991.

Paradise Outlaws: Remembering the Beats, William Morrow (New York, NY), 1999.

Reading New York, Knopf (New York, NY), 2003.

Contributor to *American Scholar, Partisan Review, Studies in the Novel,* and other professional journals; contributor of poetry to little magazines, including *Fiddlehead* and *Galley Sail Review.*

BIOGRAPHICAL AND CRITICAL SOURCES:

PERIODICALS

Library Journal, June 1, 2003, Rebecca Bollen, review of *Reading New York,* p. 121.*

V

VAN STEENWYK, Elizabeth (Ann) 1928-

PERSONAL: Born July 1, 1928, in Galesburg, IL; daughter of Wilson Andrew and Edith Viola Harler; married Donald H. Van Steenwyk (an executive), June 12, 1949; children: Kedrin (daughter), Matthew, Brett, Gretchen. *Education:* Knox College, B.A., 1950. *Politics:* Republican. *Religion:* Methodist. *Hobbies and other interests:* Hiking and watching sunsets at family walnut ranch, reading.

ADDRESSES: Home and office—885 Chester Ave., San Marino, CA 91108; and Adelaida Cellars, 5805 Adelaida Rd., Paso Robles, CA 93446; fax: 805-239-4671. *E-mail*—wines@adelaida.com.

CAREER: Writer. WGIL-Radio, Galesburg, IL, producer, 1948-51; KTSM-TV, El Paso, TX, producer, 1951-52; Adelaida Cellars, Paso Robles, CA, owner/president and general manager. President of Cardiac League, Guild of Huntington Memorial Hospital. Lecturer and speaker to schools and writers' groups.

MEMBER: International PEN, Society of Children's Book Writers.

AWARDS, HONORS: Silver medal, International Film and Television Festival, 1979, for film adaptation of her book *The Best Horse;* Patriotic Feature of the Year Award, *Highlights for Children* magazine, 1987, for short story "Secrets of the State House"; selection as one of 300 Best Books for Teenagers in 1988, New York Public Library, for *Dwight David Eisenhower,* President; nomination for Bluebonnet Award (Texas), 1989, and Rebecca Caudill Young Readers' Book Award (Illinois), 1991, both for *Three Dog Winter;* Helen Keating Ott Award, Church and Synagogue Library Association, 1990, for outstanding contribution to children's literature.

WRITINGS:

FOR CHILDREN

Dorothy Hamill: Olympic Champion, Harvey House (New York, NY), 1976.
Women in Sports: Figure Skating, Harvey House (New York, NY), 1976.
The Best Horse, Scholastic Book Services (New York, NY), 1977.
Larry Mahan, Grosset (New York, NY), 1977.
Barrel Horse Racer, Walker (New York, NY), 1977.
Women in Sports: Rodeo, Harvey House (New York, NY), 1978.
Mystery at Beach Bay, Creative Education (Mankato, MN), 1978.
Ride to Win, Creative Education (Mankato, MN), 1978.
Cameo of a Champion, McGraw-Hill (New York, NY), 1978.
Fly Like an Eagle, and Other Stories, Walker York, NY), 1978.
Rivals on Ice, Albert Whitman (Chicago, IL), 1978.
Illustrated Skating Dictionary for Young People, Harvey House (New York, NY), 1979.
God, Why Did He Die?, Concordia, 1979.
Presidents at Home, Messner (New York, NY), 1980.
Tracy Austin, Childrens Press (New York, NY), 1980.

Quarter Horse Winner, Albert Whitman (Chicago, IL), 1980.

Stars on Ice, Dodd (New York, NY), 1980.

Illustrated Riding Dictionary for Young People, Harvey House (New York, NY), 1980.

Bucky, Economy, 1981.

The Ghost of Pilgrim Creek, Economy, 1981.

Triangle of Fear, Economy, 1981.

Three Dog Afternoon, Economy, 1981.

Dance with a Stranger, Tempo, 1982.

Southpaw from Sonora Mystery, Childrens Press (New York, NY), 1983.

Ghost in the Gym, Childrens Press (New York, NY), 1983.

Terror on the Rebound, Childrens Press (New York, NY), 1983.

Secrets of the Painted Horse, Childrens Press (New York, NY), 1983.

Lonely Rider, Tempo, 1983.

The Witness Tree, Tempo, 1983.

Behind the Scenes at the Amusement Park, Albert Whitman (Chicago, IL), 1983.

The Face of Love, Dutton (New York, NY), 1983.

Harness Racing, Crestwood, 1983.

Will You Love My Horse Forever?, Dutton (New York, NY), 1984.

Rachel Has a Secret, Willowisp Press (Worthington, OH), 1987.

Sarah's Great Idea, Willowisp Press (Worthington, OH), 1987.

Dwight David Eisenhower, President, Walker York, NY), 1987.

Three Dog Winter, Walker York, NY), 1987.

Lorie for President, Willowisp Press (Worthington, OH), 1988.

Levi Strauss: The Blue Jeans Man, Walker York, NY), 1988.

Can You Keep a Secret?, Willowisp Press (Worthington, OH), 1990.

The California Gold Rush: West with the Forty-Niners, F. Watts (New York, NY), 1991.

Ida B. Wells-Barnett: Woman of Courage, F. Watts (New York, NY), 1992.

Will the Real Me Please Stand Up?, Pages Publishing Group, 1994.

Frederic Remington, F. Watts (New York, NY), 1994.

The California Missions, F. Watts (New York, NY), 1995.

Frontier Fever: The Silly, Superstitious—and Sometimes Sensible—Medicine of the Pioneers, Walker (New York, NY), 1995.

Saddlebag Salesmen, F. Watts (New York, NY), 1995.

Mathew Brady: Civil War Photographer, F. Watts (New York, NY), 1997.

My Name Is York, illustrated by Bill Farnsworth, Rising Moon (Flagstaff, AZ), 1997.

A Traitor among Us, Eerdmans (Grand Rapids, MI), 1997.

Air Shows: From Barnstormers to Blue Angels, F. Watts (New York, NY), 1998.

When Abraham Talked to Trees, illustrated by Bill Farnsworth, Eerdmans (Grand Rapids, MI), 2000.

Let's Go to the Beach: A History of Sun and Fun by the Sea, Holt (New York, NY), 2001.

Maggie in the Morning, Eerdmans (Grand Rapids, MI), 2001.

Seneca Chief, Army General: A Story about Ely Parker, illustrated by Karen Ritz, Carolrhoda Books (Minneapolis, MN), 2001.

OTHER

One Fine Day (radio play), illustrated by Bill Farnsworth, Eerdmans (Grand Rapids, MI), 2003.

Also author of *The Witch Switch, New Girl in Town,* and *Friends Are Like That,* all Willowisp Press. Contributor of more than one hundred fifty articles and stories to periodicals. Developer of a primary reading kit, "TOYS," for Educational Insights.

ADAPTATIONS: *The Best Horse* was filmed by Learning Corp. of America, 1979; *Three Dog Winter* has been optioned by the Public Broadcasting System (PBS) for a ninety-minute television movie.

SIDELIGHTS: Elizabeth Van Steenwyk has written a number of books for young readers on historical subjects. Among her books are *A Traitor among Us,* a novel set in World War II Holland, *When Abraham Talked to the Trees,* an account of Abraham Lincoln's childhood, and *Let's Go to the Beach: A History of Sun and Fun by the Sea.* In addition to her writing, Van Steenwyk also manages her family's vineyards in Paso Robles, California. She claimed in an article posted at the Adelaida Cellars Web site that she got the position because she was "the only family member without a day job."

A Traitor among Us tells of teenaged Pieter Van Dirk, a Dutch boy drawn into working for the Resistance during World War II. While helping a wounded

American soldier hide from the Gestapo, and transmitting secret radio messages, Pieter is under the pressure of knowing that someone in his small village is working for the Nazis and may betray him. Hazel Rochman in *Booklist* praised "the suspense [that] rises to the very last chapter." A critic for *Publishers Weekly* found that "the climax—a furtive, after-curfew bicycle ride in which Pieter flushes out the traitor—is heart-pounding."

When Abraham Talked to the Trees is a biography that focuses on the young Abraham Lincoln's early studies. Aesop's fables, the Bible, and the dictionary were constant companions for the studious boy. Van Steenwyk shows that whatever Lincoln read the evening before was mulled over the next day while he worked in the fields. Lincoln also practiced oratory by standing on a tree stump in the woods and, thanks to his strong memory, delivering sermons he had heard word for word. Writing in *Booklist*, Shelley Townsend-Hudson praised the "simple, anecdotal text, which is filled with gentle humor." A critic for *Publishers Weekly* judged *When Abraham Talked to the Trees* "an amiable portrait of a young Abraham Lincoln as an aspiring scholar and orator."

In *Let's Go to the Beach: A History of Sun and Fun by the Sea,* Van Steenwyk traces the often overlooked history of one of America's favorite pastimes, going to the beach. She chronicles in particular such beach staples as boardwalks, toys, water sports, amusement parks, and swimming attire. Historic photographs, old advertisements for beach products, and illustrations provide a comprehensive look at the development of a popular recreational destination. Van Steenwyk "demonstrates that this smilingly simple setting is an essential part of our collective experience," Karen Simonetti wrote in *Booklist*.

Van Steenwyk once told *CA:* "Why do I write for children? I can sum it up in the words of a child who wrote to me after reading one of my books. She said, 'Happiness must be writing children's books.' I wonder how she knew? Simply, I write for young readers because there are so many more possibilities than limitations."

BIOGRAPHICAL AND CRITICAL SOURCES:

PERIODICALS

Booklist, July, 1995, Mary Harris Veeder, review of *Frontier Fever,* p. 1873; September 1, 1997, Caro-

lyn Phelan, review of *Matthew Brady,* p. 121; August, 1998, Hazel Rochman, review of *A Traitor among Us,* p. 1992; October 1, 2000, Shelley Townsend-Hudson, review of *When Abraham Talked to the Trees,* p. 344; May 1, 2001, Karen Simonetti, review of *Let's Go to the Beach: A History of Sun and Fun by the Sea,* p. 1674; July, 2001, Karen Hutt, review of *Seneca Chief, Army General: A Story about Ely Parker,* p. 2004; January 1, 2002, Michael Cart, review of *Maggie in the Morning,* p. 860.

New York Times Book Review, August 12, 2001, review of *Let's Go to the Beach,* p. 24.

Publishers Weekly, June 22, 1998, review of *A Traitor among Us,* p. 92; February 22, 1999, review of *Three Dog Winter,* p. 97; September 25, 2000, review of *When Abraham Talked to the Trees,* p. 117; July 30, 2001, review of *Let's Go to the Beach,* p. 86; August 5, 2002, review of audiocassette version of *Let's Go to the Beach,* p. 27.

ONLINE

Adelaida Cellars Web site, http://www.adelaida.com/ (November 14, 2002).

Knox College Web site, http://www.knox.edu/knox/ knoxweb/ (September 7, 2002), "Author Elizabeth Van Steenwyk to Speak at Knox, Sept. 20."*

*   *   *

VEDRAL, Joyce L(auretta) 1943-

PERSONAL: Born July 23, 1943, in Bronx, NY; daughter of David (a boxer, wrestler, and mathematician) and Martha (a communications technician; maiden name, Dash) Yellin; married Charles J. Vedral (divorced, April 11, 1976); children: Marthe Simone. *Education:* City College of the City University of New York, B.S., 1970, M.A., 1973; New York University, Ph.D., 1980. *Politics:* Republican. *Religion:* Protestant.

ADDRESSES: Home—P.O. Box A 433, Wantagh, NY 11793-0433. *Office*—Department of English, Pace University—New York, Pace Plaza, New York, NY 10038. *Agent*—Mel Berger, William Morris Agency, 1350 Avenue of the Americas, New York, NY 10019.

CAREER: Pace University—New York, New York, NY, member of faculty, beginning 1980; also worked as a high school teacher.

MEMBER: National Council of Teachers of English, New York City Council of Teachers of English.

WRITINGS:

A Literary Survey of the Bible, edited by Dennis Baker, Logos International (Plainfield, NJ), 1973.

I Dare You! How to Use Psychology to Get What You Want Out of Life, Holt (New York, NY), 1983.

(With Bill Reynolds, Jr.) *Supercut: Nutrition for the Ultimate Physique,* Ballantine (New York, NY), 1985.

(With Gladys Portugues) *Hard Bodies,* Dell (New York, NY), 1985.

Now or Never, Warner Books (New York, NY), 1986.

My Parents Are Driving Me Crazy, Ballantine (New York, NY), 1986.

My Teenager Is Driving Me Crazy, Ballantine (New York, NY), 1987, published as *My Teenager Is Driving Me Crazy: A Guide to Getting You and Your Teen through These Difficult Years,* Adams Media (Avon, MA), 2003.

I Can't Take It Anymore, Ballantine (New York, NY), 1987.

(With Rachel McLish) *Perfect Parts,* Warner Books (New York, NY), 1987.

The Opposite Sex Is Driving Me Crazy, Ballantine (New York, NY), 1988.

The Twelve-Minute Total-Body Workout, Warner Books (New York, NY), 1989.

Boyfriends: Getting Them, Keeping Them, Living without Them, Ballantine (New York, NY), 1990.

(With Cameo Yvette Kneuer) *Cameo Fitness,* Warner Books (New York, NY), 1990.

The Fat-Burning Workout, Warner Books (New York, NY), 1991.

Gut Busters, Warner Books (New York, NY), 1992.

My Teacher Is Driving Me Crazy, Ballantine (New York, NY), 1992.

Get Rid of Him, Warner Books (New York, NY), 1993.

Teens Are Talking: The Question Game for Teens, Ballantine (New York, NY), 1993.

Bottoms Up!: The Total-Body Workout from the Bottom Up; From Cellulite to Sexy—in 24 Workout Hours, Warner Books (New York, NY), 1993.

(With Betty Weider) *Better and Better: Six Weeks to a Great Shape at Any Age!,* Dell (New York, NY), 1993.

(With daughter, Marthe Simone Vedral) *The College Dorm Workout: Fight the Freshman Fifteen in Twenty Minutes a Day without Starving to Death,* Warner Books (New York, NY), 1994.

Definition: Shape without Bulk in 15 Minutes a Day, Warner Books (New York, NY), 1995.

Top Shape: 12 Weeks to Your Ideal Physique, Warner Books (New York, NY), 1995.

Look In, Look Up, Look Out!: Be the Person You Were Meant to Be, Warner Books (New York, NY), 1996.

Eat to Trim: Get It Off and Keep It Off!, Warner Books (New York, NY), 1997.

Weight Training Made Easy: Transform Your Body in Four Simple Steps, Warner Books (New York, NY), 1997.

Bone-Building/Body-Shaping Workout: Strength, Health, Beauty in Just 16 Minutes a Day!, Simon & Schuster (New York, NY), 1998.

The Bathing Suit Workout, Warner Books (New York, NY), 1999.

Contributor to magazines, including *Muscle and Fitness, Shape, Self, Guideposts, Christian Herald,* and *Parent Connections.*

SIDELIGHTS: Joyce L. Vedral once told *CA:* "I write about fitness—physical and mental. All of my books are about empowering: the mind affects the body and the body affects the mind. I approach the problem from both directions, whichever helps first; it doesn't matter. Get in shape first and then your mind will follow, or get your mind in shape, and then your body will follow. In this sense, all roads lead to Rome!

"My book *Get Rid of Him* is a book addressed to women who are in relationships that are draining their energy and are more trouble than they're worth. It is an inspirational book that helps to shine a light on a woman's negative relationship and to build her self-esteem so that she can leave and enjoy and respect her life alone for a while. There are chapters for every situation, from leaving a man who bores you to death to getting out of it if you're staying in it just for the money, the security or the children. The chapter, 'Fifteen Ways to Leave Your Lover' tells you how, and the chapter, 'Oh What a Catch,' warns you when to throw back that 'DOGFISH,' CHAMELEON, CRAB, AND BLOWFISH before you get burned. Not a man-bashing book, the book encourages women to stop blaming men and take responsibility for their own lives.

"My two best-selling bodybuilding books originated with my taking up bodybuilding. *Supercut: Nutrition for the Ultimate Physique* is a bodybuilders diet book, showing professional and amateur bodybuilders how to diet in order to achieve the best possible competitive form. More than 200 low-fat, low-sodium recipes are included. *Hard Bodies* is a book that shows women how to sculpt their bodies through the use of weights into the most sensual possible form.

"My two latest body-shaping books provide a solution for women, *The Fat-Burning Workout,* and men, *Gut Busters,* who want to get in shape but have only fifteen to twenty minutes four to six days a week to spare. Combined, they have sold nearly a million copies. My files are replete with before and after photos of men and women who rejoice that they were able to do it in twelve weeks time!"

BIOGRAPHICAL AND CRITICAL SOURCES:

PERIODICALS

Library Journal, April, 2003, review of *My Teenager Is Driving Me Crazy: A Guide to Getting You and Your Teen through These Difficult Years,* pp. 117-118.*

*   *   *

VERNON, John (Edward) 1943-

PERSONAL: Born June 3, 1943, in Cambridge, MA; son of Elijah James (a printer) and Ruth Doris (Martin) Vernon; married Ann Nancy Frick (a painter), June 29, 1968; children: Charles, Patrick. *Ethnicity:* "Caucasian." *Education:* Boston College, B.A., 1965; University of California—Davis, M.A., 1967, Ph.D., 1969. *Hobbies and other interests:* Mountain climbing.

ADDRESSES: Home—P. O. Box 20620, Estes Park, CO 80511. *Office*—Department of English, State University of New York, Binghamton, NY 13901. *Agent*—Fred Morris, Jed Mattes Agency, 2095 Broadway, #302, New York, NY 10023-2895. *E-mail*—fac026@binghamton.edu.

CAREER: University of Utah, Salt Lake City, assistant professor of English, 1969-71; State University of New York at Binghamton, assistant professor, 1971-75, associate professor, 1975-85, professor, 1985-2002, distinguished professor of English, 2002—; writer.

John Vernon

MEMBER: Sierra Club, National Audubon Society, Center of the American West.

AWARDS, HONORS: Fellowship, National Defense Education Act, 1965-68; faculty research fellowship, State University of New York, 1973; public service fellowship, New York State Council on the Arts, 1973; faculty research fellowship, State University of New York, 1977 and 1980; fellowship, National Endowment for the Arts, 1990-91; *New York Times* notable book listing for *Peter Doyle,* 1991; University Award for Excellence in Research, State University of New York, 1994; fellowship, National Endowment for the Arts, 1996-97; *New York Times,* notable book listing for *A Book of Reasons.*

WRITINGS:

The Garden and the Map: Schizophrenia in Twentieth-Century Literature and Culture, University of Illinois Press (Urbana, IL), 1973.
Ann (poems), Iris Press (Binghamton, NY), 1976.
Poetry and the Body, University of Illinois Press (Urbana, IL), 1979.

Money and Fiction: Literary Realism in the Nineteenth and Early Twentieth Centuries, Cornell University Press (Ithaca, NY), 1984.

La Salle: A Novel, Viking (New York, NY), 1986.

Lindbergh's Son, Viking (New York, NY), 1988.

Peter Doyle, Random House (New York, NY), 1991.

All for Love: Baby Doe and Silver Dollar (novel), Simon & Schuster (New York, NY), 1995.

A Book of Reasons (memoir), Houghton Mifflin (Boston, MA), 1999.

The Last Canyon, Houghton Mifflin (Boston, MA), 2001.

Work represented in anthologies, including *Poetry: Points of Departure,* edited by Henry Taylor, Winthrop Publishers (Cambridge, MA), 1974; *Men of Our Time: An Anthology of Poetry by and about Men,* edited by Fred Moramarco and Al Zolynas, University of Georgia Press (Athens, GA), 1992; *What Have You Lost?,* edited by Naomi Shihab Nye, Greenwillow Books (New York, NY), 1999; and *The Book of Love,* edited by Diane Ackerman and Jeanne Mackin, Norton (New York, NY), 1998.

Contributor to periodicals, including *Harper's, Nation, New York Times Book Review, Paris Review, American Poetry Review, Virginia Quarterly Review, Poetry, Ohio Review, Carolina Review, Epoch, Chicago Review, Western Humanities Review, New American Review,* and *Poetry Northwest.*

WORK IN PROGRESS: A Ghost for Kit Carson; More Than This.

SIDELIGHTS: John Vernon is an English professor and writer who has won particular acclaim for his novels of actual figures from the American West. Among these tales is *All for Love: Baby Doe and Silver Dollar,* which concerns a conniving opportunist who marries an elderly mine owner and becomes a prominent figure in Colorado society, then squanders her fortune, following her husband's death, and falls into poverty before perishing during the Depression. A *Publishers Weekly* reviewer described *All for Love* as "literate and raunchy" and summarized it as "a classically American, true-grit saga of greed, dreams and delusions."

Vernon's next novel, *The Last Canyon,* relates the exploits of a one-armed veteran determined to chart the various canyons of the Green and Colorado rivers after the Civil War. Robert Conroy, writing in *Library Journal,* deemed the novel "well written," and Mary Ellen, in her *Booklist* assessment, noted that "a parallel story of . . . Paiute Indians" provided "extra poignancy." Another reviewer, writing in *Publishers Weekly,* proclaimed *The Last Canyon* "outstanding," and Jonathan Kirsch, in his *Los Angeles Times Book Review* appraisal found the novel "richly imagined." Further praise came from a *Kirkus Reviews* critic, who described the novel as "richly detailed." Less impressed, Dolores Derrickson contended in the *Rocky Mountain News* that *The Last Canyon* "lags." Michael Upchurch, however, lauded the novel, in the *Knight-Ridder/Tribune News Service,* as "a riveting adventure tale," and Verlyn Klinkenborg, writing in the *New York Times Book Review,* noted *The Last Canyon* as "a novel that borrows the exactitude of history."

Vernon's other writings include *A Book of Reasons,* a memoir of his late brother's life of seclusion in an unheated home littered with trash. *Library Journal* reviewer Ronald Ray Ratliff praised *A Book of Reasons* as "extraordinary," and a *Publishers Weekly* critic acknowledged it as "beautiful." Another critic, Bonnie Johnston, wrote in *Booklist* that *A Book of Reasons* serves as "a heartfelt exploration of grieving," and Lisa Jennifer Selzman added in the *Houston Chronicle* that Vernon's memoir is "a powerful story aching to be told." Stanley Trachtenberg, meanwhile, wrote in the *Dallas Morning News* that *A Book of Reasons* is "sometimes anguished, more often anxious."

Vernon once told *CA:* "I began by thinking of myself as a poet but discovered novel writing twenty years ago and do not intend to get sidetracked again. Most of my work is historical in theme or setting, but I don't want to limit myself to that, and I consider myself a literary novelist first. My aspiration is to create works of art that will entertain and instruct a literate audience. I research my books extensively, stitch together fiction and research, crank it up into the imagination, and zap it with a thousand volts. The result is the Frankenstein monster called a novel.

"Two years ago I reduced my teaching commitments and moved to the mountains of Colorado. . . . In Colorado I'm a presence inside a much larger presence—the mountains and gorges of Rocky Mountain National Park—and I find this a conducive spur to the loss of personality necessary for writing fiction."

BIOGRAPHICAL AND CRITICAL SOURCES:

PERIODICALS

Booklist, September 1, 1999, Bonnie Johnston, review of *A Book of Reasons,* p. 58; September 15, 2001, Mary Ellen, review of *The Last Canyon,* p. 197.

Dallas Morning News, October 3, 1999, Stanley Trachtenberg, "Death Spurs Intellectual Odyssey," p. J9.

Houston Chronicle, October 17, 1999, Lisa Jennifer Selzman, review of *A Book of Reasons,* p. 32.

Kirkus Reviews, September 15, 2001, review of *The Last Canyon,* p. 1321.

Knight-Ridder/Tribune News Service, November 7, 2001, Michael Upchurch, review of *The Last Canyon.*

Library Journal, August, 1999, Ronald Ray Ratliff, review of *A Book of Reasons,* p. 108; October 1, 2001, Robert Conroy, review of *The Last Canyon,* p. 144.

Los Angeles Times Book Review, February 17, 2002, Jonathan Kirsch, "West Words," p. 2.

New York Observer, September 27, 1999, Robert Gottlieb, "A Cabinet of Curiosities, Balm for a Mourner's Grief," p. 20.

New York Times Book Review, November 11, 2001, Verlyn Klinkenborg, "A Paradise of Loss," p. 7.

Publishers Weekly, July 24, 1995, review of *All for Love: Baby Doe and Silver Dollar,* p. 46; June 21, 1999, review of *A Book of Reasons,* p. 43; November 1, 1999, review of *A Book of Reasons,* p. 51; August 27, 2001, review of *The Last Canyon,* p. 47.

Rocky Mountain News, October 26, 2001, Dolores Derrickson, "Flat Characters Sink *Canyon,*" p. D29.

*   *   *

VINE, Barbara
See RENDELL, Ruth

*   *   *

von DREHLE, David 1961-

PERSONAL: Born February 6, 1961, in Denver, CO; son of Richard (in business) and Dorothy (a homemaker and administrator; maiden name, Love) von Drehle; married Karen Ball (a journalist), October 7, 1995; children: Henry James, Ella Grace, Adeline Rose, Clara Morgan. *Ethnicity:* "Caucasian." *Education:* University of Denver, B.A., 1983; Oxford University, M. Litt. Hum., 1985. *Religion:* Episcopalian.

ADDRESSES: Home—4625 Reno Rd. NW, Washington, DC 20008. *Office*—Washington Post, 1150 15th St. NW, Washington, DC 20071; fax: 202-496-3883. *Agent*—Esther Newberg, International Creative Management, 40 West 57th St., New York, NY 10019. *E-mail*—vandrehled@washpost.com.

CAREER: Miami Herald, Miami, FL, staff writer, 1983-91; *Washington Post,* Washington, DC, staff writer, 1991-95, assistant managing editor, 1995-99, senior writer, 1999—.

AWARDS, HONORS: Livingston Award, 1989, for national reporting; Silver Gavel Award, American Bar Association, 1989, for coverage of the legal system; Distinguished Writing Award, American Society of Newspaper Editors, 1990; Distinguished Writing Award, American Bar Association, 1996, for *Among the Lowest of the Dead: Inside Death Row.*

WRITINGS:

Among the Lowest of the Dead: Inside Death Row, Times Books (New York, NY), 1995.

Dead Wrong: A Death Row Lawyer Speaks Out against Capital Punishment, University of Wisconsin Press (Madison, WI), 1998.

Triangle: The Fire That Changed America, Atlantic Monthly Press (New York, NY), 2003.

Contributor to books, including *Best Newspaper Writing,* Poynter Institute (St. Petersburg, FL), 1990, 1995; *Best American Sports Writing,* Houghton Mifflin (Boston, MA), 1993; and *Deadlock: The Inside Story of America's Closest Election,* PublicAffairs (New York, NY), 2001.

SIDELIGHTS: David von Drehle told *CA:*"I know only a few things about writing. The best way to communicate most information is to use stories. This worked for the tribal ancestors, and it worked for Homer, and it still works today. Tell a story; for nonfiction writers, tell a factual story. It is impossible to write clearly if you haven't figured out exactly what you are trying to say. By the same token, when your writing turns difficult or muddy, chances are you don't know quite what you want to say. If you are writing a book, choose a subject that you really love. It takes a lot of time and effort to write a good book, and sometimes all you have to keep you going is your belief and passion, so make sure you have it at the start. That's about it.

"The most recent story I told was called *Triangle: The Fire That Changed America,* the most complete account of a dramatic and horrifying turning point in American history. On March 25, 1911, at closing time, a fire broke out in New York's largest blouse factory, in a loft building high above the crowded city streets. A huge crowd watched as more than fifty victims, mostly young immigrant women, plunged from the windows to their deaths. Nearly 100 other victims died out of view of the crowd, many of them behind an illegally locked door.

"The Triangle factory was already well known to New Yorkers. A year earlier, it had been a center of an uprising by garment workers. After the fire, the same alliance of working-class organizers and wealthy progressives that had backed the strike came together again to demand safer facilities. And they forced a surprising reversal: the boss of New York's Tammany Hall machine approved sweeping reforms—paving the way for urban liberalism and the New Deal.

"*Triangle* is a story rich in colorful and important characters, from Tammany boss 'Silent Charlie' Murphy to suffrage leader Alva Smith Vanderbilt Belmont; from the immigrant seamstress Rosie Freedman to the wealthy Shirtwaist Kings Max Blanck and Isaac Harris; from labor firebrand Clara Lemlich to the once-fabled, now forgotten Max D. Steuer, the master trial lawyer who won a controversial acquittal for the owners of the Triangle factory. It recounts a moment when early feminism, progressivism, labor activism, and plain hardball politics came together to force lasting change. From violent picket lines to the horrible inferno itself, culminating in one of New York's most dramatic trials, *Triangle* tells one of America's most powerful and important stories."

W-Z

WALLACE, Daisy
See CUYLER, Margery S(tuyvesant)

* * *

WALZER, Michael (Laban) 1935-

PERSONAL: Born March 3, 1935, in New York, NY; son of Joseph P. and Sally (Hochman) Walzer; married Judith Borodovko, June 17, 1956; children: Sarah, Rebecca. *Education:* Brandeis University, B.A., 1956; Harvard University, Ph.D., 1961. *Religion:* Jewish.

ADDRESSES: Home—103 Linwood Circle, Princeton, NJ 08520-3625. *Office*—School of Social Science, Institute for Advanced Study, Princeton, NJ 08540.

CAREER: Princeton University, Princeton, NJ, assistant professor of politics, 1962-66; Harvard University, Cambridge, MA, associate professor, 1966-68, professor of government, 1968-80; Institute for Advanced Study, Princeton, NJ, professor of social science, 1980—. Hebrew University of Jerusalem, member of board of governors, 1975—; Brandeis University, trustee, 1983-88. United Jewish Appeal, member of faculty advisory cabinet, 1977-81; American Jewish Congress, member of international affairs committee.

MEMBER: Society of Ethical and Legal Philosophy, Conference on the Study of Political Thought.

AWARDS, HONORS: Fulbright fellow at Cambridge University, 1956-57; Harbison Award, Danforth Foundation, 1971.

WRITINGS:

The Revolution of the Saints: A Study in the Origins of Radical Politics, Harvard University Press (Cambridge, MA), 1965.
(Editor, with Philip Green) *The Political Imagination in Literature,* Free Press (New York, NY), 1968.
Obligations: Essays on Disobedience, War, and Citizenship, Harvard University Press (Cambridge, MA), 1970.
Political Action: A Practical Guide to Movement Politics, Quadrangle Press (New York, NY), 1971.
(Editor and author of introduction) *Regicide and Revolution: Speeches at the Trial of Louis XVI,* translated by Marian Rothstein, Columbia University Press (New York, NY), 1974, reprinted, 1993.
Just and Unjust Wars: A Moral Argument with Historical Illustrations, Basic Books (New York, NY), 1977, reprinted, 1992.
Radical Principles: Reflections of an Unreconstructed Democrat, Basic Books (New York, NY), 1980.
Spheres of Justice: A Defense of Pluralism and Equality, Basic Books (New York, NY), 1983.
Exodus and Revolution, Basic Books (New York, NY), 1985.
Interpretation and Social Criticism, Harvard University Press (Cambridge, MA), 1987.
The Company of Critics: Social Criticism and Political Commitment in the Twentieth Century, Basic Books (New York, NY), 1989.
What It Means to Be an American, Marsilio (New York, NY), 1992.
Thick and Thin: Moral Argument at Home and Abroad, University of Notre Dame Press (Notre Dame, IN), 1994.

(Editor, with David Miller) *Pluralism, Justice, and Equality,* Oxford University Press (New York, NY), 1995.

(Editor) *Toward a Global Civil Society,* Berghahn Books (Providence, RI), 1995.

On Toleration, Yale University Press (New Haven, CT), 1997.

(Editor, with Menachem Lorberbaum and Noam J. Zohar) *The Jewish Political Tradition,* Yale University Press (New Haven, CT), Volume 1: *Authority,* 2000, Volume 2: *Membership,* 2003.

Contributor to books, including *Political Theory and Political Education,* Princeton University Press (Princeton, NJ), 1980; *Boundaries: National Autonomy and Its Limits,* Rowan & Littlefield (Totowa, NJ), 1981. Contributor to philosophy and policy journals. Editor, *Dissent,* beginning 1976; contributing editor, *New Republic,* beginning 1976; member of editorial board, *Philosophy and Public Affairs.*

SIDELIGHTS: Michael Walzer "is a political scientist, a social scientist, a political philosopher or a social one, a gently polemical journalist, an ethical putterer," commented Richard Eder in the *Los Angeles Times.* Formerly a professor of government at Harvard University, Walzer later moved to the social science faculty at the Institute for Advanced Study in Princeton. In his numerous books and essays, he tackles such vexing moral issues as the ethics of warfare and the role of the welfare state, speaking always from a socialist perspective and frequently illuminating his theories with examples from history.

In *Spheres of Justice: A Defense of Pluralism and Equality,* Walzer outlines a pluralistic theory of social justice that allows that all people are not created equal—some are born with intelligence, wealth, and talent, while others may be lacking in one of these attributes or even all three. While egalitarians strive for a "simple" equality that aims to keep people as equal as possible in their overall situations, Walzer proposes a "complex" equality that acknowledges individual differences and advocates a different kind of justice.

Rather than restricting the amount of money a person can make, for example, Walzer would instead limit the "spheres" where it has power. "The key to [Walzer's] solution is to worry less about the distribution of money and more about limiting the things that money

can buy," explained Michael J. Sandel in the *New York Times Book Review.* "This is the point of talking about *spheres* of justice. He maintains that different goods occupy different spheres, which are properly governed by different principles—welfare to the needy, honors to the deserving, political power to the persuasive, offices to the qualified, luxuries to those able and willing to pay for them." So long as goods are restricted to their appropriate spheres—or to continue with the example of money, so long as dollars are used to buy material goods rather than political favors or power—then justice prevails.

As a means of determining which goods fit which distributive principles—whether health care, for instance, should be distributed to all as an essential part of life or only to those with the money to pay for medical services—Walzer adopts the concept of community membership. This means that instead of being born with certain inalienable rights, people are born with only those rights considered inalienable by their particular society. For Walzer, "distributive justice must begin with [community] membership," Sandel explained, "because we are all members of political communities before we are bearers of rights. Whether we have a right to a particular good depends on the role that good plays in our communal life and on its importance to us as members."

Writing in the *New York Review of Books,* Ronald Dworkin praised Walzer's "concrete, political analysis. . . . His historical examples are often fascinating, and this, along with his clear prose, makes his book a pleasure to read. The examples are nicely judged to illustrate the characteristic features of each of his spheres of justice." Nonetheless, Dworkin concluded that Walzer's "central argument fails. The ideal of complex equality he defines is not attainable, or even coherent, and the book contains very little that could be helpful in thinking about actual issues of justice." The problem, according to Dworkin, stems from Walzer's assumption that societies such as ours are in agreement about which goods belong to which spheres. Instead, he argued, such issues are constantly debated, analyzed and reevaluated. While acknowledging the contradictions inherent in Walzer's theory, Eder concluded that "Walzer is serious enough. His seriousness is that of Milovan Djilas, who emerged from his years as a social absolutist—and his subsequent years in prison—pale, gentle, and with a vision of utopia that he called, 'The Imperfect Society.'"

Walzer also expounds his theories on social justice in *Exodus and Revolution,* in which he interprets the biblical story of the Israelites' escape from captivity in Egypt as a profound political document. In support of his argument, Walzer cites St. Augustine, Thomas Aquinas, Machiavelii, John Knox, Georg Wilhelm Friedrich Hegel, Karl Marx, contemporary liberation theologists and others as thinkers who have used the book of Exodus to support their positions.

Thinking about Exodus also illuminates "some of the difficulties and dilemmas contained in the promise of liberation," commented *Newsweek* contributor Jim Miller in a review of *Exodus and Revolution,* noting that the most difficult part comes when Moses descends from the mountain to find his people adoring the golden calf. Miller compares the passage in which Moses "asks for faithful volunteers to slay the idolaters" to modern political purges, and suggests that it raises questions about the right and wrong uses for the sword. Walzer himself, stated Miller, "prefers to stress the traditional Jewish image of Moses as a patient teacher" leading his people through the wilderness whose hardships offer "harsh lessons about the unavoidable frustrations, failures and disappointments that are the genuine burden of freedom." In conclusion, Miller declared: "The book captures Walzer at his formidable best: learned, humane, lively."

In *Interpretation and Social Criticism,* Walzer "wants to refute the claim that social criticism requires the radical detachment of critical distance," according to John Patrick Diggins in the *New York Times Book Review.* Diggins cited Walzer's statement that it is wrong to interpret society's standards on the basis of one's personal beliefs, which by definition cannot be extended to others. Among those figures to whom Walzer applies this censure are great philosophers and revolutionaries. "Mr. Walzer singles out Descartes's attempt to arrive at certainty solely by knowing the contents of mind," Diggins declared, adding that "Mr. Walzer reserves his strongest doubts for Sartre and Lenin, ideologues who translated social criticism into class warfare and judged their respective societies against their own, personal standards and prejudices."

Another of Walzer's arguments in *Interpretation and Social Criticism* is that the morality we experience on a daily basis is the route that should be followed for interpretation, a principle which he supports with examples from the ancient prophets of Israel. "The prophet does not claim to be creating a new morality but rather rediscovering a previously accepted and commonly understood one," noted Diggins. Walzer cites the prophet Amos as a perfect example of the social critic who challenges leaders, conventions, and practices of a particular society based on values shared by all. Diggins suggested that Walzer does not go far enough in explaining these shared values: "Mr. Walzer scarcely bothers to explain why equality is preferable to liberty." He also faulted Walzer for not connecting his ideas to his own society: "It is curious that he does not connect his work with American history and culture." Overall, though, Diggins praised *Interpretation and Social Criticism* as "learned, cogent and provocative. It avoids the pretensions of both scientific certainty and grand theory and treats social criticism as the 'educated cousin of common complaint.' It also succeeds brilliantly in making an ancient religion relevant to the contemporary political imagination."

In *The Company of Critics: Social Criticism and Political Commitment in the Twentieth Century,* Walzer continues to question the role of criticism in society. Reviewing the book in the *Times Literary Supplement,* Denis Donoghue quoted Walzer's definition of the three essential duties of social criticism: "The critic exposes the false appearances of his own society; he gives expression to his people's deepest sense of how they ought to live; and he insists that there are other forms of falseness and other, equally legitimate, hopes and aspirations." But then Donoghue challenged these guidelines: "Walzer assumes that 'all of us' have a moral sense, but he doesn't say what it is or how any of us came to have it." Donoghue also charged that *The Company of Critics,* which examines the work of eleven influential philosophers and critics, lacks any guiding theory or principle. "So his book is exactly the sum of its parts; a series of studies, each of them too brief to be entirely just to its occasion."

A comparison of eleven twentieth-century social critics is an interesting idea, commented Peter Halban in a *New Statesman* review of *The Company of Critics,* but it does not follow through on its potential: "This is a coffee-table tally of alienated intellectuals and Walzer has an acute, interesting mind. But while the chapters on each thinker are almost unvaryingly sharp, Walzer's general discussion of the role of the social critic works less well. This may be something to do with his style, which is chatty, elliptical and allusive. It's too easy to read one of his sheeny paragraphs with pleasure only to realise at the end that you're not sure of quite what has been said."

New York Times Book Review contributor J. Peter Euben commended *The Company of Critics* as "richly textured, accessible and always respectful of its readers," further commenting that it "is an example of the sort of connected criticism it commends." According to Euben, Walzer, "a pluralist, a leftist Aristotelian who regards moral principles as embodied in the conventions, customs, beliefs, rituals and institutions of a particular people," when facing the basic questions of social criticism, comes down strongly on the side of those critics he finds most engaged, most a part of the society they analyzc. "That is why Mr. Walzer admires the American writer Randolph Bourne's involvement in the life he criticized; the continuities between the Italian thinker Ignazio Silone's radicalism and his life and opinions before he became radical; George Orwell's love of England, which did nothing to inhibit his opposition to those who tyrannized the working class; Albert Camus's commitment to a morality of love and justice, and Martin Buber's insistence that he must tell the story of the Jewish experience while recognizing that no single correct account of nationalist aspirations is possible." Walzer, on the other hand, continued Euben, faults American political philosopher Herbert Marcuse, French philosopher Michel Paul Foucault and Italian socialist theorist Antonio Gramsci for failing to carry out the true role of a critic: expressing the deepest sense of a people.

Euben cited some weaknesses in the book, including the lack of a clear audience for the subject, indistinct definitions of who "one's own people" really are, and a narrowly focused selection of social critics. "Mr. Walzer says he has chosen 'mainstream' critics; some feminists I know call them 'male-stream' critics," Euben quipped. He suggested that "perhaps we need a third book on criticism from him . . . one that might include chapters on the black lesbian poet Audre Lorde, the American Indian writer Vine Deloria and the Chicano theologian Andres Guerero." Euben also faulted Walzer for not sufficiently delineating his own political theories. "Mr. Walzer's ground is not so much absent as obscured, with unfortunate results." Despite these objections, Euben praised *The Company of Critics*: "This book proves again that Michael Walzer is a writer of rare elegance, intellectual range and moral seriousness."

Expanding on his theme of complex equality presented in *Spheres of Justice,* Walzer claims in *Thick and Thin: Moral Argument at Home and Abroad* that ethical thought operates within two important languages: one complex moral language that operates from a sphere of locally rooted events and conditions—the thick morality or argument—and one simple moral language that applies to everyone and operates from a sphere of universal standards—the thin morality or argument. Walzer argues that moral errors occur when we examine issues from the incorrect sphere of standards, such as when we apply a thin argument to a situation that should be judged by thick morality. Such is the case when we impose our cultural values on a different culture—we are applying our local standards universally onto a culture with different local standards.

Reviews for *Thick and Thin* were mixed. Hailing the book's poetic style, *Commonweal* writer Alan Wolfe asserted: "It is a moving, eloquent, and at times inspiring meditation on the problem of obligation." A *Kirkus Reviews* critic described *Thick and Thin* as a "well-argued, if not always energetic, set of carefully wrought ideas on the state of public moral debate" but stressed that Walzer could expand his awareness of such issues as gender and race. *Library Journal* contributor Leon H. Brody faulted Walzer's writings for its "rambling, anecdotal quality more suitable to . . . [verbal] presentation . . . than to the more stringent requirements for publication" and added that Walzer's arguments are not detailed enough for academics, but too technical for the general reader. Wolfe, on the other hand, although he reported a lack of consistency in part of Walzer's argument, found much to commend in *Thick and Thin*. He summarized: "*Thick and Thin* should be read, not only for its substantive argument, but also for the breadth of its examples and the beauty of its prose. Michael Walzer writes on some of the most explosive issues of the day in a voice that is always calm and thoughtful. Our culture is thicker because of his presence."

BIOGRAPHICAL AND CRITICAL SOURCES:

PERIODICALS

Atlantic Monthly, February, 1978.
Commonweal, October 21, 1994, Alan Wolfe, review of *Thick and Thin: Moral Argument at Home and Abroad,* p. 24.

Kirkus Reviews, April 15, 1994, review of *Thick and Thin,* p. 545.

Library Journal, May 15, 1994, Leon H. Brody, review of *Thick and Thin,* p. 76; June 1, 2003, Paul Kaplan, review of *The Jewish Political Tradition,* Volume 2: *Membership.*

Los Angeles Times, March 27, 1983, Richard Eder, review of *Spheres of Justice: A Defense of Pluralism and Equality;* February 13, 1985; April 5, 1985.

Nation, September 28, 1970; March 25, 1978.

New Statesman, February 24, 1989, Peter Halban, review of *The Company of Critics: Social Criticism and Political Commitment in the Twentieth Century,* p. 40.

Newsweek, January 26, 1981; April 15, 1985, Jim Miller, review of *Exodus and Revolution,* p. 92.

New York Review of Books, October 21, 1971; December 8, 1977; October 23, 1980; April 14, 1983, Ronald Dworkin, review of *Spheres of Justice.*

New York Times, February 4, 1978; August 12, 1980; January 25, 1985.

New York Times Book Review, June 9, 1974; February 5, 1978; December 28, 1980; April 24, 1983, Michael J. Sandel, review of *Spheres of Justice;* January 20, 1985; March 15, 1987, John Patrick Diggins, review of *Interpretation and Social Criticism,* p. 11; January 18, 1989, J. Peter Euben, review of *The Company of Critics,* p. 18.

Times Literary Supplement, July 26, 1974; October 23, 1981; March 3, 1989, Denis Donoghue, review of *The Company of Critics,* p. 217.

Washington Post Book World, January 8, 1978; August 31, 1980.*

*   *   *

WEBER, Katharine 1955-

PERSONAL: Born November 12, 1955, in New York, NY; daughter of Sidney (a film producer) and Andrea (a photographer and bird watcher; maiden name, Warburg) Kaufman; married Nicholas Fox Weber, September 19, 1976; children: Lucy Swift, Charlotte Fox. *Education:* Attended New School for Social Research, 1972-76, and Yale University, 1982-84. *Politics:* "Quite left—a red diaper baby." *Religion:* "Cultural identity, mostly Jewish—religious beliefs, mostly absent."

ADDRESSES: Home—108 Beacon Rd., Bethany, CT 06524. *Office*—210 Prospect St., New Haven, CT 06510. *Agent*—Watkins Loomis, Inc., 133 East 35th St., New York, NY 10016.

CAREER: Harper & Row, New York, NY, editorial assistant, 1975; Richard Meier and Partners Architects, New York, NY, in-house editor, 1975; American Institute of Graphic Arts, New York, NY, assistant to the director, 1976; Josef Albers Foundation, Orange, CT, archivist, 1976-81; *Sunday New Haven Register,* New Haven, CT, weekly columnist, 1985-87; *Publishers Weekly,* weekly fiction reviewer, 1988-92. Fairfield University, guest speaker, 1988-90; Mattatuck Community College, teacher at One Day Writer's Conference, 1992; Connecticut College, visiting writer in residence, 1996-97; Yale University, visiting lecturer, beginning 1997. Administrator of the estate of Kay Swift, 1990-94; Kay Swift Memorial Trust, trustee, beginning 1995; conducted archival research in Warburg family papers in conjunction with Ron Chernow's work for *The Warburgs.* Residents for Rural Roads, founding member, 1980-84.

MEMBER: National Book Critics Circle, Authors Guild, Authors League of America, PEN.

AWARDS, HONORS: Named best columnist of the year, New England Women's Press Association, 1986; Discovery Award, New England Booksellers Association, 1995; included among *Granta*'s best young American novelists, 1996.

WRITINGS:

Objects in Mirror Are Closer Than They Appear (novel), Crown Publishers (New York, NY), 1995.
The Music Lesson, Crown Publishers (New York, NY), 1998.
The Little Women (novel), Farrar, Straus & Giroux (New York, NY), 2003.

Contributor of numerous articles, short stories, and reviews to periodicals, including *New York Times Book Review, New Yorker, Boston Sunday Globe, New Haven Register, Connecticut, Story, Redbook, Journal-Courier,* and *Architectural Digest.*

SIDELIGHTS: Katharine Weber's first novel, *Objects in Mirror Are Closer Than They Appear,* has been greeted enthusiastically by critics. "Tender and funny and sometimes remarkably jolting, this is a first novel of remarkable accomplishment," said a contributor to *Publishers Weekly*. Set in Geneva, Switzerland, the story traces the experiences and thoughts of Harriet Rose, a young American photographer, through a combination journal/letter she sends to her boyfriend, Benedict.

In the novel, events from both the past and present serve to expose the darkness underlying each character's life. Harriet observes Anne Gordon—the friend she is visiting—embark on a self-destructive affair with Victor, her father's friend and fellow Auschwitz survivor, and the relationship causes much concern for Harriet. While wandering the streets of Geneva so that Anne and Victor can continue their daily lunch-time trysts in privacy, Harriet ponders her friend's happiness and gradually succumbs to memories of her own past.

Written in a style that critics found both witty and humorous, as well as dramatic, *Objects in Mirror Are Closer Than They Appear* reminds the reader that the past has a constant influence over the present. Truth can be interpreted on many levels, according to Weber. Harriet's letters and journals may record the events experienced inside a day and interpret her feelings; however, she can never precisely capture the day as it happened—written words can only be impressions and fragments of the complete truth, which is acted on by outside forces and events from the distant past. "Life is nothing but images transformed by reflection, and we rarely understand what we think we see," summarized Sally Eckhoff in the *Voice Literary Supplement*. Harriet's experiences reflect these limits of perception and fragmentation of memory. Elizabeth Benedict wrote in the *New York Times Book Review,* "As her title suggests, Katharine Weber is wise to these issues of artifice, distance and what seems like candor." Despite such weighty thoughts woven through the novel's plot, Weber's novel is never heavy-handed. As Eckhoff observed, Harriet's buoyant character keeps the darkness and danger from oppressing the reader. "Her jokey patter and enthusiastic innocence—that's the book's brightest idea."

Weber once told *CA:* "I have rarely done things in the usual order. I have no high school diploma, having left after eleventh grade to attend the New School when I was sixteen, and I have no college degree, though several years of part-time college at the New School

and Yale. One way of thinking about this as an asset rather than a liability is to consider my education as being an ongoing activity rather than something that has been completed.

"Though I worked as a journalist and critic for several years, my fiction was never published anywhere until a story of mine was selected off the slush pile for publication in the *New Yorker* in January of 1993. That story was to form part of my first novel. I tell this story to encourage all unpublished fiction writers. It can happen."

BIOGRAPHICAL AND CRITICAL SOURCES:

PERIODICALS

Library Journal, June 15, 2003, Eleanor J. Bader, review of *The Little Women,* p. 103.

New York Times Book Review, April 30, 1995, Elizabeth Benedict, review of *Objects in Mirror Are Closer Than They Appear,* p. 20.

Publishers Weekly, February 13, 1995, review of *Objects in Mirror Are Closer Than They Appear,* pp. 62-63.

Voice Literary Supplement, May, 1995, Sally Eckhoff, review of *Objects in Mirror Are Closer Than They Appear,* p.10.*

* * *

WEINSTEIN, James 1926-

PERSONAL: Born July 17, 1926, in New York, NY; son of Joseph and Bobbie (Kaufman) Weinstein; married Anne Farrar (a city planner), June, 1968; children: (prior marriage) Lisa, Joshua David. *Education:* Cornell University, A.B., 1949; Columbia University, M.A., 1957. *Politics:* Socialist.

ADDRESSES: Home—529 Laidley St., San Francisco, CA 94131.

CAREER: Historian and editor. *Military service:* U.S. Navy, 1945-46.

WRITINGS:

The Decline of Socialism in America, 1912-1925, Monthly Review Press (New York, NY), 1967.
The Corporate Ideal in the Liberal State, 1900-1918, Beacon Press (Boston, MA), 1968.
(Editor, with David W. Eakins) *For a New America,* Vintage (New York, NY), 1970.
Ambiguous Legacy: The Left in American Politics, Franklin Watts (New York, NY), 1975.
The Long Detour: The History and Future of the American Left, Perseus (Boulder, CO), 2003.

Contributor to *Nation, Labor History,* and other history and political science journals. Editor, *Studies on the Left,* 1960-67; editor, *Socialist Revolution,* beginning 1970; founding editor, *In These Times* and *Socialist Review.*

BIOGRAPHICAL AND CRITICAL SOURCES:

PERIODICALS

Library Journal, May 15, 2003, Stephen L. Hupp, review of *The Long Detour: The History and Future of the American Left,* p. 106.*

*   *   *

WELSH, Alexander 1933-

PERSONAL: Born April 29, 1933, in Albany, NY; married Katharine C. Tower, 1956; children: three. *Education:* Harvard University, A.B., 1954, A.M., 1957, Ph. D., 1961.

ADDRESSES: Office—Department of English, University of California—Los Angeles, Los Angeles, CA 90024.

CAREER: Yale University, New Haven, CT, instructor, 1960-63, assistant professor, 1963-66, associate professor of English, 1966-67; University of Pittsburgh, Pittsburgh, PA, professor of English, 1967-72; University of California—Los Angeles, professor of English, beginning 1972. *Military service:* U.S. Army, 1954-56.

MEMBER: Modern Language Association of America, Phi Beta Kappa.

AWARDS, HONORS: Guggenheim fellow, 1969-70; National Endowment for the Humanities fellow, 1977.

WRITINGS:

The Hero of the Waverley Novels, Yale University Press (New Haven, CT), 1963, reprinted with new essays on Scott, expanded edition, Princeton University Press (Princeton, NJ), 1992.
(Editor) Sir Walter Scott, *Old Mortality,* Houghton Mifflin (Boston, MA), 1966.
(Editor) *Thackeray: A Collection of Critical Essays,* Prentice-Hall (Englewood Cliffs, NJ), 1968.
The City of Dickens, Oxford University Press (New York, NY), 1971.
Reflections on the Hero As Quixote, Princeton University Press (Princeton, NJ), 1981.
From Copyright to Copperfield: The Identity of Dickens, Harvard University Press (Cambridge, MA), 1987.
Strong Representations: Narrative and Circumstantial Evidence in England, Johns Hopkins University Press (Baltimore, MD), 1992.
Freud's Wishful Dream Book, Princeton University Press (Princeton, NJ), 1994.
Dickens Redressed: The Art of "Bleak House" and "Hard Times," Yale University Press (New Haven, CT), 2000.
Hamlet in His Modern Guises, Princeton University Press (Princeton, NJ), 2001.

Contributor to periodicals, including *New Republic* and *Yale Review.**

*   *   *

WIGGINS, David 1933-

PERSONAL: Born March 8, 1933, in London, England; son of Norman (a barrister at law) and Diana (Priestley) Wiggins; married Jennifer Hornsby, 1979. *Education:* Brasenose College, Oxford, B.A. (with first class honors), 1955, M.A., 1958.

ADDRESSES: Office—University College, Oxford University, Oxford, England.

CAREER: Colonial Office, London, England, assistant principal, 1957-58; Oxford University, Oxford, England, fellow of New College, 1960-67; University of London, Bedford College, professor of philosophy, 1967-80; Oxford University, University College, fellow and praelector in philosophy, beginning 1981. Princeton University, Janie Eliza Proctor visiting fellow, 1958-59, member of visiting faculty, 1980; member of visiting faculty at Stanford University, 1964 and 1965, Harvard University, 1968 and 1972, and All Souls College, Oxford, 1973, 1980; Center for Advanced Study in Behavioral Sciences, Stanford, CA, fellow, 1985-86. Member of Independent Commission on Transport, 1973-74; Transport Users' Consultative Committee for the South East, chair, 1977-79.

MEMBER: British Academy (fellow).

WRITINGS:

Identity and Spatio-Temporal Continuity, Basil Blackwell (Oxford, England), 1967.
Truth, Invention, and the Meaning of Life, British Academy (London, England), 1977.
Sameness and Substance, Basil Blackwell (Oxford, England), 1980.
Essays in the Philosophy of Value, Basil Blackwell (Oxford, England), 1986.
Sameness and Substance Renewed, Cambridge University Press (New York, NY), 2001.

Contributor to philosophy journals.

BIOGRAPHICAL AND CRITICAL SOURCES:

PERIODICALS

Times Literary Supplement, March 28, 2003, Stephen Yablo, review of *Sameness and Substance Renewed,* p. 12.*

*   *   *

WINN, Marie 1936 (?)-

PERSONAL: Born c. 1936 in Prague, Czechoslovakia; immigrated to United States, 1939; daughter of Joseph (a doctor) and Joan (a lawyer and newscaster; maiden name, Taussig) Winn; married Allan Miller (a filmmaker), April, 1961; children: Steven, Michael. *Education:* Attended Radcliffe College, 1954-56; Columbia University, B.S., 1959.

ADDRESSES: Home—194 Riverside Dr., New York, NY. *Agent*—Georges Borchardt, Inc., 136 East 57th St., New York, NY 10022.

CAREER: Freelance writer, translator, and reviewer.

MEMBER: PEN, Authors Guild.

AWARDS, HONORS: Red-Tails in Love was a *New York Times* Notable Book, 1998; *Children without Childhood* was winner of the Grand Prix, International Janusz Korczak Competition, 1985; *Plug-In Drug* was selected as a "notable book" by the American Library Association.

WRITINGS:

FOR CHILDREN

(Editor; with musical arrangements by husband, Allan Miller) *The Fireside Book of Children's Songs,* illustrated by John Alcorn, Simon & Schuster (New York, NY), 1966.
The Fisherman Who Needed a Knife: A Story about Why People Use Money, illustrated by John E. Johnson, Simon & Schuster (New York, NY), 1970.
The Man Who Made Fine Tops: A Story about Why People Do Different Kinds of Work, illustrated by John E. Johnson, Simon & Schuster (New York, NY), 1970.
(Editor and compiler; with musical arrangements by Allan Miller) *What Shall We Do and Allee Galloo!: Playsongs and Singing Games for Young Children,* illustrated by Karla Kuskin, Harper (New York, NY), 1970.
Shiver, Gobble, and Snore, illustrated by Whitney Darrow, Jr., Simon & Schuster (New York, NY), 1971.
The Thief Catcher: A Story about Why People Pay Taxes, illustrated by Whitney Darrow, Jr., Simon & Schuster (New York, NY), 1972.
(Compiler and editor; with musical arrangements by Allan Miller) *The Fireside Book of Fun and Game Songs,* illustrated by Whitney Darrow, Jr., Simon & Schuster (New York, NY), 1974.

The Sick Book: Questions and Answers about Hiccups and Mumps, Sneezes and Bumps, and Other Things That Go Wrong with Us, illustrated by Fred Brenner, Four Winds Press (New York, NY), 1976.

OTHER

(With Mary Ann Porcher) *The Playgroup Book,* Macmillan (New York, NY), 1967, revised edition published as *The Playgroup Book: How to Plan, Organise, and Run Group Activities for Pre-School Children,* Fontana (London, England), 1971.

(Compiler) *The Baby Reader: Fifty-six Selections from World Literature about Babies and Their Mothers, Fathers, Admirers, and Adversaries,* Simon & Schuster (New York, NY), 1973.

(Translator, from the Czech) Zdena Salivarova, *Summer in Prague,* Harper (New York, NY), 1973.

The Plug-In Drug: Television, Children, and the Family, Viking (New York, NY), 1977, revised and updated 25th anniversary edition published as *The Plug-In Drug: Television, Computers, and Family Life,* Penguin (New York, NY), 2002.

Children without Childhood, Pantheon (New York, NY), 1983.

Unplugging the Plug-In Drug, Penguin (New York, NY), 1987.

(Translator, from the Czech) Vaclav Havel, *Temptation,* Grove Press (New York, NY), 1989.

(Author of commentary) Bruce Davidson, *Central Park,* Aperture (New York, NY), 1995.

Red-Tails in Love: A Wildlife Drama in Central Park, Pantheon (New York, NY), 1998.

(Translator) Jiri Weil, *Mendelssohn Is on the Roof,* Northwestern University Press (Evanston, IL), 1998.

Also contributor of articles to *New York Times Magazine, New York Times Book Review, Wall Street Journal,* and *Parade.*

SIDELIGHTS: Author Marie Winn was born in Prague, Czechoslovakia, and came to the United States when she was three years old. Her family settled in a Czech neighborhood in New York City, and continued to speak Czech at home and among their friends, so Winn grew up speaking both English and Czech.

Winn's father, a doctor, provided medical services for the neighborhood, and her mother, who was a lawyer when the family lived in Czechoslovakia, worked for the radio network "Voice of America."

After Winn married and had two sons, she began writing children's books. She once told a writer for *Something about the Author,* "Almost everything I've ever written has in some way centered on children. . . . This is one of my obsessive and natural interests; I even catch myself eavesdropping on kids' conversations."

Her first book, *The Fireside Book of Children's Songs,* was a collection of music for children, and included musical arrangements by her husband, filmmaker Allan Miller. Her second book, written with coauthor Mary Ann Porcher, was *The Playgroup Book,* which showed parents how to plan and organize activities for preschoolers.

Winn was delighted with the success of her books, because it allowed her to work at home, with her children. Although her writing work sometimes required her to travel to do research and give interviews, she was aided by her sons' two grandmothers, who helped her raise them.

While taking care of her sons, Winn noticed that child-drearing practices had changed radically since her own youth. She began considering the nature of this change, and exploring it in her work. Through extensive interviews with parents and children, she determined that children were being raised to be much more precocious and "adultlike" than in previous generations. Winn noted in *Something about the Author,* "The carefree years have disappeared." As a result, Winn noted, adults are no longer as protective of children as they used to be: "Kids' books feature rape, abortion, child-molestation, incest. . . . As adults we should be working to prevent these problems, not to expose our kids to them." In addition, she commented that many children go to R-rated movies, often with their families, despite these movies' depictions of extreme violence and explicit sex. Winn discussed these phenomena in *Children without Childhood.*

In *The Plug-In Drug,* Winn explored the impact of television on children and on family life, noting that this impact is largely negative: television is as addictive and as destructive as heroin. And, she noted, family life that is not dominated by television viewing is richer and more positive for children and parents alike. Rather than discussing the programs children watch on television, she substantiated the negative effects of television viewing, regardless of content, on children's play, imagination, and school work, and detailed its impact on various aspects of child development. In 2002, Winn published a revised and updated version of the book, titled, *The Plug-In Drug: Television, Computers, and Family Life.* It included new chapters on the effects of home computers, VCRs, and video games, as well as of television itself.

Between 1989 and 2001, Winn wrote occasional columns on nature and birdwatching for the Leisure and Arts page of the *Wall Street Journal.* Some of these columns formed the core of her 1998 book, *Red-Tails in Love: A Wildlife Drama in Central Park,* her first book to abandon children as either a subject or an audience. The book's scene is the "ramble," an unknown wilderness in the heart of New York's Central Park. There an odd and amiable band of nature lovers devote themselves to observing and protecting the park's wildlife. When a pair of red-tailed hawks builds a nest atop a Fifth Avenue apartment house across the street from the park, Winn and her fellow "regulars" are transformed into obsessed hawkwatchers. Winn describes the saga of the Fifth Avenue hawks as they struggle to raise a family in their unprecedented nest site, and draws a vivid picture of the humans who fall under their spell. In the *New York Times Book Review,* Patricia T. O'Connor wrote, "Winn infects the reader with her enthusiasm for the park."

BIOGRAPHICAL AND CRITICAL SOURCES:

PERIODICALS

America, March 26, 1977.

Booklist, January 1, 1985, review of *The Plug-In Drug,* p. 603; July, 1985, p. 1571; September 15, 1987, review of *Unplugging the Plug-In Drug,* p. 97; February 1, 1998, Nancy Bent, review of *Red-Tails in Love,* p. 887.

Book Report, September, 1998, review of *Red-Tails in Love: A Wildlife Drama in Central Park,* p. 71.

Books, summer, 1998, review of *Red-Tails in Love,* p. 8.

Childhood Education, December, 1986, review of *Children without Childhood,* p. 136.

Commonweal, August 10, 1984, review of *Children without Childhood,* p. 444.

Journalism Quarterly, spring, 1986, review of *The Plug-In Drug,* revised edition, p. 219; spring, 1988, review of *Unplugging the Plug-In Drug,* p. 221.

Kirkus Reviews, September 1, 1987, review of *Unplugging the Plug-In Drug,* p. 1307; February 1, 1998, review of *Red-Tails in Love,* p. 187.

Kliatt, spring, 1985, review of *The Plug-In Drug,* p. 56; July 1999, review of *Red-Tails in Love,* p. 37.

Library Journal, January, 1986, review of *The Plug-In Drug,* revised edition, p. 66; September 15, 1987, review of *Unplugging the Plug-In Drug,* p. 73; March 1, 1999, review of *Red-Tails in Love,* p. 48; May 1, 2002, Leroy Hommerding, review of *The Plug-In Drug: Television, Computers, and Family Life,* p. 116.

Ms., May, 1985, review of *Children without Childhood,* p. 42.

New Yorker, April 13, 1998, review of *Red-Tails in Love,* p. 77.

New York Review of Books, September 24, 1998, review of *Red-Tails in Love,* p. 41.

New York Times Book Review, April 5, 1998, Patricia O'Conner, review of *Red-Tails in Love,* p. 11; May 31, 1998, review of *Red-Tails in Love,* p. 28; December 6, 1998, review of *Red-Tails in Love,* p. 86; April 4, 1999, review of *Red-Tails in Love,* p. 24.

Publishers Weekly, June 10, 1983; April 20, 1984, review of *Children without Childhood,* p. 86; February 15, 1991, Sybil Steinberg, review of *Mendelssohn Is on the Roof,* p. 75; January 19, 1998, review of *Red-Tails in Love,* p. 363.

Reference and Research Book News, June, 1988, review of *Unplugging the Plug-In Drug,* p. 10.

School Library Journal, August, 1998, p. 199.

Times Educational Supplement, November 2, 1984, review of *Children without Childhood,* p. 20.

Virginia Quarterly Review, autumn 1998, review of *Red-Tails in Love,* p. 142.

Voice of Youth Advocates, February, 1984, review of *Children without Childhood,* p. 352.

Wall Street Journal, April 10, 1998, review of *Red-Tails in Love,* p. W6.

Washington Post, August 15, 1983.

*　　*　　*

WINSTON, Mark L. 1950-

PERSONAL: Born April 7, 1950, in Brooklyn, NY; son of Larry and Ruth Winston; married Susan J. Katz, June 1, 1980; children: Devon. *Education:* Boston University, B.Sc., 1971, M.A., 1975; University of Kansas, Ph.D., 1978, postdoctoral study, 1978-79.

ADDRESSES: Office—Department of Biological Sciences, Simon Fraser University, Burnaby, British Columbia V5A 1S6, Canada. *E-mail*—winston@sfu.ca.

CAREER: Woods Hole Oceanographic Institution, Woods Hole, MA, research assistant in chemotaxis, 1972-73; U.S. Department of Agriculture, research assistant in Gypsy Moth Section, 1973; consultant in Africanized bee management to the ministries of agriculture of Trinidad and Tobago, Guatemala, Mexico, and Panama, 1977-80; Simon Fraser University, Burnaby, British Columbia, Canada, assistant professor, 1980-84, associate professor, 1984-88, professor of biological sciences, 1988—, university research professor, 1990-91. Idaho State University, visiting assistant professor, 1979-80; Hebrew University of Jerusalem, Jerusalem, Isreal, visiting Fulbright professor, 1986-87; Cornell University, Grace Griswold Lecturer, 1991; lecturer at U.S., Canadian, Israeli, Australian, and Mexican colleges and universities. Patented a novel pheromone composition for use in controlling honey bee colonies, 1990. British Columbia Pollination Working Group, organizer, 1984; Wright Institute, member, 1985-91; Pacific National Exhibition, member of Apiculture Committee, 1990-91; Agriculture Canada, member of Apiculture Advisory Committee, 1990-91; public speaker and guest on radio and television programs; consultant to Canadian Broadcasting Co. and Vancouver's Science World. Camp Solomon Schechter, volunteer nature counselor, 1983; Vancouver Committee for Adult Jewish Education, member, 1984; Pioneer House, volunteer, 1991; Burquest Jewish Community Association, member of board of directors, 1992—.

MEMBER: International Union for the Study of Social Insects (president of North American section, 1992-93), International Bee Research Association, International Society of Behavioral Ecology, Canadian Association of Professional Apiculturists (vice president, 1990—; chair of Africanized Bee Response Team, 1990—), Entomological Society of Canada, American Association of Professional Apiculturists, Entomological Society of America, Western Apicultural Society (president, 1992-93), Entomological Society of British Columbia, British Columbia Honey Producers Association (chair of Education Committee, 1981—), Sigma Xi.

AWARDS, HONORS: National Science Foundation fellow, 1978; Student Apiculture Award from Eastern Apicultural Society of North America, 1979; C. G. Hewitt Award from Entomological Society of Canada, 1985; Fulbright fellow in Israel, 1986-87; Hambleton Award from Eastern Apicultural Society, 1992; Outstanding Service to Beekeeping Award from Western Apicultural Society, 1992; Alan Clemson Award from New South Wales Apiarists Association, 1992; Gold Medal in the Natural Science, Science Council of British Columbia, 1992; Nora and Ted Sterling Prize in Controversy, Vancouver, British Columbia, 1998; Killiam Research Fellowship, Canada Council, 2000-2002; grants from U.S. National Science Foundation, NSERC, National Research Council of Canada, Science Council of British Columbia, Okanagan Valley Pollination Association, Knowledge Network of British Columbia, and Government of British Columbia, Wright Institute, and British Columbia Honey Producers Association.

WRITINGS:

The Biology of the Honey Bee, Harvard University Press (Cambridge, MA), 1987.
Killer Bees: The Africanized Honey Bee in the Americas, Harvard University Press (Cambridge, MA), 1992.
Nature Wars: People vs. Pests, Harvard University Press (Cambridge, MA), 1997.
From Where I Sit: Essays on Bees, Beekeeping, and Science, Comstock Publishing (Ithaca, NY), 1998.
Travels in the Genetically Modified Zone, Harvard University Press (Cambridge, MA), 2002.

Creator of the television series *Apiculture: An Introduction to Bees and Beekeeping,* broadcast by Knowledge Network of British Columbia, 1983. Work represented in anthologies, including *Social Insects and the Environment,* edited by G. K. Veeresh, B. Mallik, and C. K. Viraktamath, Oxford Publishing (New Delhi, India), 1990; *The African Honey Bee,* edited by M. Spivak, D. J. C. Fletcher, and M. D. Breed, Westview, 1991; and *The Hive and the Honey Bee,* Dadant and Sons, 1992. Author of a column in *British Columbia Honey Producers Association Newsletter,* 1981—. Editor of "Papers on Pest Management," a series, Simon Fraser University. Contributor of articles and reviews to scientific journals and beekeeping magazines. Associate editor, *Canadian Entomologist,* 1986—.

SIDELIGHTS: Mark L. Winston is a professor of biology at Simon Fraser University in Burnaby, British Columbia, Canada. He is particularly interested in the life history of social insects, notably honeybees, and is the author of several books on bees and their behavior. In an interview in the *Simon Fraser News,* he said, "Bees are fascinating organisms, but they're much more than simply a focus for my job. In many ways, they're a paradigm for understanding the role science should play in society and for exploring the myriad ways humans interact with, understand, and manage nature."

Winston has also written books on bees and biology for the general public. One of these is *Nature Wars: People vs. Pests.* The book covers the age-old war between humans and various pests, including cockroaches, rats, weeds, and bees, but it also considers biotechnology and the use of pesticides, as well as alternative pest controls. Winston notes that people's fear of insects and rodents often drives them to reach for strong chemicals to destroy the pests, but asks readers to adopt a more realistic attitude toward pests, managing only those that make a major economic impact, and recognizing that a few pests are not harmful, and indeed are a necessary part of the ecosystem. In addition, he recommends avoiding the use of pesticide in favor of biological controls, which use a pest's natural enemies to reduce its numbers. In *Bio-Science,* Ronald J. Prokopy wrote, "*Nature Wars* is written in a clear and convincing fashion, and it is readily accessible to lay readers and professionals alike." In *Discover,* Bettyann Holtzmann Kevles commented that the book "leaves room for hope by setting an example of reasonableness." *Quarterly Review of Biology* contributor David Pimentel wrote that the book was "fair and balanced" and that it includes "the salient points that we need to understand about pest control." Marsha Salett wrote in *Conservation Perspectives* that Winston's writing "is so lucid and witty that *Nature Wars* is a 'good read' as well as a thoughtful polemic about the chemical warfare we humans wage against the natural world."

From Where I Sit: Essays on Bees, Beekeeping, and Science is a collection of articles Winston wrote for the beekeeping magazine *Bee Culture,* beginning in 1993. It discusses the relationship between honeybees and scientists, the public, and beekeepers. The first section of the book includes seven essays on bees and beekeeping; the second examines honeybees and the use of pesticides; the third examines political decisions that affect beekeeping; and the fourth considers research on honeybees.

Travels in the Genetically Modified Zone considers the growing debate over genetically modified crops and the food that is made from them. Winston traveled widely, interviewing scientists, activists, farmers, consumers, and government regulators about these crops and foods. He concluded that the widespread public resistance to these foods is not based on science, and has in fact impeded scientific progress in genetic modification that would ultimately benefit humanity. For example, he notes that one company developed "Golden Rice," which has far more Vitamin A than ordinary rice, can be cheaply grown in Asia, where many children become blind because of a deficiency of this vitamin. However, because of hysteria against these foods, Indian activists blocked the use of the rice, stating that it was an attempt by big Western corporations to make Asians dependent on them for a food supply.

BIOGRAPHICAL AND CRITICAL SOURCES:

PERIODICALS

Audubon, March, 1998, review of *Nature Wars: People vs. Pests,* p. 110.

BioScience, November, 1998, Ronald J. Prokopy, review of *Nature Wars,* p. 959.

Booklist, November 1, 1997, Gilbert Taylor, review of *Nature Wars,* p. 442; June 1, 2002, William Beatty, review of *Travels in the Genetically Modified Zone,* p. 1658.

Choice, January, 1999, review of *From Where I Sit: Essays on Bees, Beekeeping, and Science,* p. 911.

Discover, April, 1998, Bettyann Holtzmann Kevles, review of *Nature Wars,* p. 94.

Issues in Science and Technology, spring, 1998, Fred L. Gould, review of *Nature Wars,* p. 86.

Kirkus Reviews, October 15, 1997, review of *Nature Wars,* p. 1573; April 1, 2002, review of *Travels in the Genetically Modified Zone,* p. 480.

Kliatt, January, 1994, p. 38.

Library Journal, November 15, 1997, Teresa Berry, review of *Nature Wars,* p. 74; June 1, 2002, Irwin Weintraub, review of *Travels in the Genetically Modified Zone,* p. 187.

Los Angeles Times, March 11, 1988.

Natural History, November, 1997, review of *Nature Wars,* p. 15.

Nature, December 11, 1997, review of *Nature Wars,* p. 573; October 21, 1999, review of *Nature Wars,* p. 743.

New Scientist, January 17, 1998, review of *Nature Wars,* p. 45.
Publishers Weekly, October 27, 1997, review of *Nature Wars,* p. 62.
Quarterly Review of Biology, March, 1999, David Pimental, review of *Nature Wars,* p. 63.
Times Literary Supplement, January 8, 1999, review of *Nature Wars,* p. 27.
Whole Earth Review, fall, 1999, Kim Flottum, review of *From Where I Sit,* p. 64.

ONLINE

Simon Fraser University Web site, http://www.sfu.ca/ (August 21, 2002), faculty profile of author.*

*   *   *

WOLFE, Barbara (Lea) 1943-

PERSONAL: Born February 15, 1943, in Philadelphia, PA; daughter of Manfred (an owner of a small business) and Edith (a homemaker; maiden name, Hermann) Kingshoff; married Stanley R. Wolfe, March 20, 1965 (divorced, 1978); married Robert Haveman (a professor), July 29, 1981; children: (first marriage) Jennifer Ann, Ari Michael. *Education:* Cornell University, B.A., 1965; University of Pennsylvania, M.A., 1971, Ph.D., 1973.

ADDRESSES: Home—3410 Lake Mendota Dr., Madison, WI 53705. *Office*—7422 Social Science Bldg., University of Wisconsin—Madison, Madison, WI 53706. *E-mail*—bwolfe@wisc.edu.

CAREER: University of Pennsylvania, Philadelphia, instructor in economics, 1970-72; Bryn Mawr College, Bryn Mawr, PA, assistant professor of economics, 1973-76; University of Wisconsin—Madison, research associate at Institute for Research on Poverty, 1976-77, research affiliate, 1977—, director of the institute, 1994—, assistant professor, 1977-81, associate professor, 1981-87, professor of economics and preventive medicine, 1987—, executive chairperson of Center for Health Policy and Program Evaluation, 1985-92. Netherlands Institute for Advanced Study, fellow, 1984-85; National Bureau of Economic Research, research associate, 1987—; La Follette Institute of

Public Affairs, professor, 1990—; Russell Sage Foundation, visiting scholar, 1991-92. International Institute of Public Finance, member of board of management, 1994—. National Academy of Social Insurance, member, 1990—; National Research Council, member of board of International Health, Institute of Medicine, 1992—; National Commission on Childhood Disability, member, 1995—; Social Security Commission, member of technical advisory panel on assumptions and methods; Panel of Economists on Educational Reform, member. Consultant to Federal Reserve Bank of Philadelphia, 1972-76; Wisconsin Clinical Cancer Center, associate member, 1982-89; Wisconsin Consortium for Health Services Research, facilitator, 1988-93; Western Consortium for Public Health, member of national advisory board, 1992-94. Adjunct professor, Australia National University, Canberra, 2002-07.

MEMBER: American Economic Association (member of Committee on the Status of Women in the Economics Profession, 1990-92).

AWARDS, HONORS: Fulbright grant, Netherlands America Commission for Educational Exchange, 1984-85; grants from Ford Foundation, Rockefeller Foundation, Agency for International Development, European Economic Community, U.S. Department of Health and Human Services, National Science Foundation, Veterans Administration, and Sloan Foundation.

WRITINGS:

(With Michael R. Olneck) *Intelligence and Family Size: Another Look,* University of Wisconsin—Madison (Madison, WI), 1977.
(With Jere R. Behrman and John Flecher) *A Monte Carlo Study of Alternative Approaches for Dealing with Randomly Missing Data,* University of Wisconsin—Madison (Madison, WI), 1979.
Earnings Lost and Income Gained: The Equity and Adequacy of Transfers to the Disabled: or, How Well Do the Disabled Fare?, University of Wisconsin—Madison (Madison, WI), 1980.
(With Robert H. Haveman and Jennifer Warlick) *Behavioral Responses to Social Security Retrenchment: Estimates from a Trichotomous Choice Model,* University of Wisconsin—Madison (Madison, WI), 1985.

Health Care Expenditures for the Elderly: Are Prospective Payment Systems and Community Care the Paths to Reduction?, University of Wisconsin—Madison (Madison, WI), 1985.

Health Status and Medical Expenditures: Is There a Link?, University of Wisconsin- -Madison (Madison, WI), 1985.

(Editor, with Hans van de Kar) *The Relevance of Public Finance for Policy-Making,* Wayne State University Press (Detroit, MI), 1987.

(With Robert Haveman) *Succeeding Generations: On the Effects of Investments in Children,* Russell Sage Foundation (New York, NY), 1994.

(With Eric Hanushek and others) *Making Schools Work: Improving Performance and Controlling Costs,* Brookings Institution (Washington, DC), 1994.

(Editor, with Lawrence Wu) *Out of Wedlock: Causes and Consequences of Nonmarital Fertility,* Russell Sage Foundation (New York, NY), 2001.

Contributor to books, including *Poverty and Prosperity in the Twentieth Century,* edited by E. Wolff and D. Papadimitriou, Macmillan (New York, NY), 1993; *Confronting Poverty: Prescriptions for Change,* edited by Sheldon Danziger, Gary Sandefur, and David Weinberg, Harvard University Press (Cambridge, MA), 1994; and *Escape from Poverty: What Makes a Difference for Poor Children?,* edited by P. Lindsay Chase-Lansdale and Jeanne Brooks-Gunn, Cambridge University Press (New York, NY). Contributor of more than sixty articles and reviews to economic and health-care journals. Associate editor, *Journal of Development Economics,* 1982-85; advisory editor, *Social Science and Medicine Journal,* 1983—; coeditor, *Journal of Human Resources,* 1985-91; coeditor of special issue, *Social Justice Research,* 1987.

BIOGRAPHICAL AND CRITICAL SOURCES:

BOOKS

Writers Directory, 16th edition, St. James Press (Detroit), 2001.

PERIODICALS

Industrial and Labor Relations Review, October 1997, pp. 139-140.

International Journal of Comparative Sociology, December 1997, pp. 316-317.
New York Review of Books, April 11, 2002.*

*   *   *

YACOWAR, Maurice 1942-

PERSONAL: Born March 25, 1942, in Prelate, Saskatchewan, Canada; son of Samuel and Sophie (Gitterman) Yacowar; children: Margaret Mia, Sam Jason Eric. *Education:* University of Calgary, B.A., 1962; University of Alberta, M.A., 1965; University of Birmingham, Ph.D., 1968.

ADDRESSES: Office—1901 Varsity Estates Drive NW, Calgary, Alberta, Canada T3B 4T7. *E-mail*—yacowar@shaw.wave.ca.

CAREER: Lethbridge Junior College, Lethbridge, Alberta, Canada, lecturer, 1964-66; Brock University, St. Catherines, Ontario, Canada, assistant professor, 1968-72, associate professor, 1972-78, professor of drama and English, 1978-89, chair of department of drama, 1972-75, dean of humanities, 1980-87; Emily Carr College of Art and Design, Vancouver, British Columbia, Canada, dean of academic affairs, 1989-95; University of Calgary, dean, faculty of fine arts, 1995—. Film reviewer for *St. Catherines Standard,* 1974-89.

WRITINGS:

No Use Shutting the Door (poetry), F. Cogswell (Fredericton, New Brunswick, Canada), 1970.
Hitchcock's British Films, Archon Books (Hambden, CT), 1976.
I Found It at the Movies: Studies in the Art of Ingmar Bergman, Alfred Hitchcock, Howard Hawks, Jean-Luc Godard, and the Genre Film, Revisionist Press (New York, NY), 1976.
Tennessee Williams and Film, Ungar (New York, NY), 1977.
Loser Take All: The Comic Art of Woody Allen, Ungar (New York, NY), 1979, expanded edition, Continuum (New York, NY), 1991.
Method in Madness: The Comic Art of Mel Brooks, St. Martin's Press (New York, NY), 1981, expanded edition, W. H. Allen (Sharon Hill, PA), 1982.

The Films of Paul Morrissey, Cambridge University Press (New York, NY), 1993.

The Bold Testament, Bayeux Arts (Calgary, Alberta, Canada), 1999.

The Sopranos on the Couch: Analyzing Television's Greatest Series, Continuum (New York, NY), 2002, expanded edition, 2003.

SIDELIGHTS: Maurice Yacowar is a professor of drama and English who has written several books on film and television. He is currently dean of the Faculty of Fine Arts at the University of Calgary.

Yacowar became known as a film critic through his studies of Alfred Hitchcock, Tennessee Williams, Mel Brooks, Woody Allen, and Paul Morrissey. He wrote a film review column for the *St. Catherine Standard* and helped launch the first film studies degree program in Canada at Brock University, St. Catherines, Ontario. He was also involved in the transition of the Emily Carr Institute of Art and Design in Vancouver to degree-granting status. Yacowar served on the Ontario Film Review Board from 1986 to 1989, and often spoke and wrote about issues of censorship in films.

In *The Sopranos on the Couch: Analyzing Television's Greatest Series,* Yacowar examines the popular HBO series, which features a Mafia family. He provides background information on the series, and then discusses the show's first three seasons, analyzing why so many viewers find the show compelling, despite the fact that its main character is a criminal and killer. He also discusses the show's themes, similarity to the *Godfather* movies, music, violence, and social stereotypes, among other issues. In *Booklist,* Stephanie Zvirin compared the book favorably to another discussion of the show, Allen Rucker's *The Sopranos: A Family History,* praising its "substance" and thought-provoking analysis.

When Yacowar is not writing or speaking about film, he enjoys collecting and selling Inuit art and international modern graphics.

BIOGRAPHICAL AND CRITICAL SOURCES:

PERIODICALS

Booklist, June 1, 2002, Stephanie Zvirin, review of *The Sopranos on the Couch: Analyzing Television's Greatest Series,* p. 1665.

Films in Review, February, 1994, review of *The Films of Paul Morrissey,* p. 72.

Publishers Weekly, July 1, 2002, review of *The Sopranos on the Couch,* p. 71.

* * *

ZANDERBERGEN, George
See MAY, Julian

* * *

ZEPP, Ira G(ilbert), Jr. 1929-

PERSONAL: Born November 15, 1929, in Madonna, MD; son of Ira Gilbert and Nellie Kathryn (Foard) Zepp; married Mary Dodd, June 21, 1952; children: Alan, Karen, Paul, Jody. *Education:* Western Maryland College, B.A., 1952; Drew University, B.D. (magna cum laude), 1956; attended University of Edinburgh, 1956-57, University of Göttingen, 1957, Harvard University, 1957-58, Institute in Indian Civilization, India, 1967, and Center for Intercultural Documentation, Cuernavaca, Mexico, 1971; St. Mary's Seminary and University, Ph.D., 1971.

ADDRESSES: Home—576 Marshall Dr., Westminster, MD 21157. *Office*—Department of Religion, Western Maryland College, Westminster, MD 21157.

CAREER: Ordained United Methodist minister, 1956; pastor of Methodist churches in Green Village, NJ, and Medford, MA, 1955-60, and Jarrettsville, MD, 1960-63; Western Maryland College, Westminster, dean of chapel and assistant professor, 1963-74, associate professor, 1974-80, professor of religion, beginning 1980. Wesley Theological Seminary, visiting lecturer, beginning 1968. Baltimore Annual Conference of the United Methodist Church, member of board of ministry, beginning 1968, commission on higher education, beginning 1973, and commission on the role and status of women, beginning 1974; St. Mary's Seminary and University, member of administrative advisory board of Ecumenical Institute, 1972. Cohost of *Good Vibrations,* WTOP-TV, 1972. Koinonia Foundation, trustee.

MEMBER: International Bonhöffer Society, National Association of College and University Chaplains, American Academy of Religion, Carl Michalson Society.

AWARDS, HONORS: Fulbright-Hays fellowship in Hinduism, 1967; distinguished teacher award, Western Maryland College, 1973.

WRITINGS:

(Translator, with others) Friederich Gogarten, *The Reality of Faith,* 1959.

(With Kenneth L. Smith) *Search for the Beloved Community: The Thinking of Martin Luther King, Jr.,* Judson Press (Valley Forge, PA), 1974.

(Editor, with Melvin D. Palmer) *Drum Major for a Dream: Poetic Tributes to Martin Luther King, Jr.,* Writer's Workshop (Calcutta, India), 1976.

(Editor) *Rabindranath Tagore: American Interpretations,* Writer's Workshop (Calcutta, India), 1981.

The New Religious Image of Urban America: The Shopping Mall As Ceremonial Center, Christian Classics (Westminster, MD), 1986, revised edition, University Press of Colorado (Boulder, CO), 1997.

The Social Vision of Martin Luther King, Jr., Carlson Publishing (Brooklyn, NY), 1989.

A Muslim Primer: Beginner's Guide to Islam, Wakefield Editions (Westminster, MD), 1992.

Contributor of articles to periodicals, including *Pulpit, Christian Century,* and *Christian Advocate.*

BIOGRAPHICAL AND CRITICAL SOURCES:

PERIODICALS

Los Angeles Times Book Review, August 10, 1987.

New York Review, July 17, 2003, review of *The New Religious Image of Urban America: The Shopping Mall As Ceremonial Center,* pp. 41-43.*